10th E

The New Zealand Bed & Breakfast Book

Book

Homes • Farms • B&B Inns

Compiled by J. & J. Thomas

PELICAN PUBLISHING COMPANY
Gretna 1999

Published in New Zealand and Australia by Moonshine Press
Published by arrangement in the rest of the world by Pelican
  Publishing Company, Inc.

Pelican editions
  First edition, January 1990
  Second edition, January 1991
  Third edition, January 1992
  Fourth edition, January 1993
  Fifth edition, January 1994
  Sixth edition, January 1995
  Seventh edition, January 1996
  Eighth edition, June 1997
  Ninth edition, January 1998
  Tenth edition, February 1999

ISBN: 1-56554-648-2

Prices in this guide are quoted in New Zealand dollars.

*Drawings by Gerald Bull, Dan Mills, and Rema Naish or provided by hosts
Front-cover illustration: Deacons Court, Dunedin
Back-cover illustration: Waimatai, Waikato*

All information in this guidebook has been supplied by the hosts. Information about the homes listed is subject to change without notice. Readers are asked to take this into account when consulting this guide.

Printed in Canada

Published by Pelican Publishing Company, Inc.
1000 Burmaster Street, Gretna, Louisiana 70053

The NZ B&B Book
Schedule of Standards
All properties have been inspected

General

Local tourism and transport information available to guests.
Property appearance neat and tidy, internally and externally.
Absolute cleanliness of the home in all areas used by the guests.
Absolute cleanliness of kitchen, refrigerator and food storage areas.
Roadside identification of property.
Smoke alarms.
Protective clothing and footwear available for farmstay guests.
Hosts accept responsibility to comply with local body bylaws.
Hosts' pets & children must be mentioned in listing.
Host will be present to welcome and farewell guests.

Bedrooms

Each bedroom solely dedicated to guests with -
bed heating
heating
light controlled from the bed
wardrobe space with variety of hangers
drawers
mirror
power point
waste paper basket
drinking glasses
night light or torch for guidance to w.c. if not adjacent to bedroom
opaque blinds or curtains on all windows where appropriate
good quality mattresses in sound condition on a sound base
clean bedding appropriate to the climate, with extra available
clean pillows with additional available

Bathroom & toilet facilities

At least one bathroom adequately ventilated and equipped with -
bath or shower
wash handbasin and mirror
wastebasket in bathroom
lock on bathroom and toilet doors
electric razor point if bedrooms are without a suitable power point
soap, towels, bathmat, facecloths, fresh for each new guest
towels changed or dried daily for guests staying more than one night
Sufficient toilet and bathroom facilities to serve family and guests adequately

Meals

Beverages: water, milk, tea, coffee should be offered.
If fruit juice is offered it must be 100% pure juice, eg "Just Juice"
Breakfast: A generous breakfast must be provided.

New Zealand

Northland

Great Barrier Island

Auckland

Coromandel

Waikato, King Country

Bay of Plenty

Gisborne

Taranaki, Wanganui

Hawkes Bay

Manawatu, Horowhenua

Wellington

Wairarapa

Nelson Golden Bay

Marlborough

West Coast

Canterbury

Chatham Islands

South Canterbury, North Otago

Otago

Southland

Stewart Island

Contents

Tips for easier B&B travel

Ensuite and private bathroom are for your use exclusively,
Guests share bathroom means you may be sharing with other guests,
Family share bathroom means you will be sharing with the family.

In the tariff section of each listing **'continental' breakfast** consists of fruit, cereal, toast, tea/coffee; **'full'** breakfast is the same with an additional cooked course; **'special'** breakfast has something special.

Do not try to travel too far in one day. Take time to enjoy the company of your hosts and other locals.

Telephone ahead to enquire about a B&B. It is a nuisance for you if you arrive to find the accommodation has been taken. And besides hosts need a little time to prepare.

The most suitable time to arrive is late afternoon, and to leave is before 10 in the morning.

If you would like dinner please give your host sufficient notice to prepare.

If you are unsure of anything ask your hosts about it. They will give you a direct answer.

Most of our B&Bs are able to accept credit cards. See our credit card transaction form in the back page.

If you have made your reservations from overseas, check that your dates are correct. You might cross the dateline to come to New Zealand.

Please let your hosts know if you have to cancel. They will have spent time preparing for you.

Make your Cook Strait Ferry reservation in advance.

If you need to use a public phone, use the first one you see. It may be hours before you see another.

Carry a B&B phone card. Most public phones do not take coins. Phone cards can be obtained from any of our hosts.

New Zealand road signs are getting better, but your best directions come from asking a local.

Most listings show hosts accept vouchers. The only vouchers accepted are The New Zealand Bed & Breakfast Book vouchers.

Toll free reservation service

0508 BOOKIN

(0508 266546)

For no cost, no hassle
reservations phone
0508 BOOKIN
toll free.
"Have your Visa or
Mastercard ready"

P.O.Box 41031
Eastbourne
Wellington
New Zealand

Fax : (04) 568 2628
Email: bookin@xtra.co.nz

Members of
**The New Zealand Association
Farm & Home Host Inc.**
maintain the highest standards &
are always delighted to welcome
guests into their homes.

Introduction

The popularity of B&B in New Zealand has doubled each year since we first published *The New Zealand Bed and Breakfast Book.* The reason for this amazing growth is quite simply that the hosts are such wonderful people. The hosts who are listed here are homeowners who want to share their love of the country with travellers. Each listing has been written by the host, and you will discover their warmth and personality is obvious in their writing. Ours is not simply an accommodation guide but an introduction to a uniquely New Zealand holiday experience.

Any holiday is remembered primarily by the people one meets. How many of us have loved a country simply because of one or two especially memorable individuals encountered there? Bed and Breakfast offers the traveller who wants to experience the feel of the real country and get to know the people to do just that. Bed and Breakfast in New Zealand means a warm welcome into someone's home. Most of the places listed are homes, with a sprinkling of private hotels and guesthouses. Remember that Bed and Breakfast hosts cannot offer hotel facilities. Therefore please telephone ahead to book your accommodation and give ample notice if you require dinner. Most of our B&Bs do not have credit card facilities.

Guarantee of Standards
All B&Bs which are newly listed this year have been inspected to ensure that they conform to our required standard. We expect that all B&Bs in *The New Zealand Bed and Breakfast Book* will offer excellent hospitality. Please fill in a comment form for each place you stay at so that our very high standard can be maintained. Some B&Bs belong to *The NZ Association of Farm and Home Hosts, the* national associations, which also inspects the property.

Hosts that display a *KiwiHost* logo have taken part in a special workshop which trains them in communication, customer relations and visitor industry skills. The symbols are shown on each listing.

Tariff
The prices listed will apply until 31st December 1999 unless otherwise stated. Prices are in New Zealand dollars, and include Goods and Sevices Tax. There will be no extra costs to pay unless a surcharge is indicated with vouchers, or you request extra services. Some offer a reduction for children. Unless otherwise stated this applies to age 12 and under.

Breakfast
Breakfast is included in the tariff. Some homes offer a continental breakfast which includes fruit, cereal, toast and tea or coffee. Others offer a full breakfast indicated by (full) in the listing, which includes a cooked course as well. Some offer a special breakfast, indicated by (special) which includes some specialties of the house.

Vouchers

Most hosts have indicated in their listings that they will accept vouchers. The vouchers referred to are *The New Zealand Bed & Breakfast Book* vouchers which can be obtained from your travel agent. *Vouchers accepted* refers only to The Bed & Breakfast Book vouchers.

Self-contained accommodation

Many homes in towns and on farms can offer separate self-contained accommodation. In almost every case linen and food will be provided if required. The tariff will vary depending on your requirements, so check when booking.

Campervans

For those who get to know the country by camping or motor-home, Bed and Breakfast offers wonderful advantages. You will see in many listings the word 'campervans'. These homes have suitable facilities available such as laundry, bathroom, electricity and sometimes meals by arrangement. The charge, usually for up to four people, is modest and is shown in each listing.

Finding your way around

A satisfying part of compiling *The New Zealand Bed and Breakfast Book* is that we have been able to change an irritating aspect of most New Zealand guide books. Usually towns are listed alphabetically so that we hop about the country from such places as Akaroa to Auckland to Blenheim for example. This is infuriating to a reasonably well-travelled native like myself, so I imagine the despair of a visitor unfamiliar with place names and local geography.

New Zealand is long and narrow. It makes more sense to me to travel southwards down the islands listing the homes as we come to them. We have divided New Zealand into geographical regions and have included a map of each region. We have simply listed the homes as they occur on our southward journey. In areas such as Southland where we travel across more than down, the route we have taken should be quite obvious.

Whether you are from overseas or a fellow New Zealander, please take the opportunity to stay with New Zealanders in their homes. Chat with your hosts. Enjoy their company. Each host will be your additional personal travel agent and guide. We wish you an enjoyable holiday and welcome comments from guests. Please write with compliments or suggestions to:

The New Zealand Bed and Breakfast Book
Moonshine Press
PO Box 41-022
Eastbourne
New Zealand

Happy travelling

James Thomas

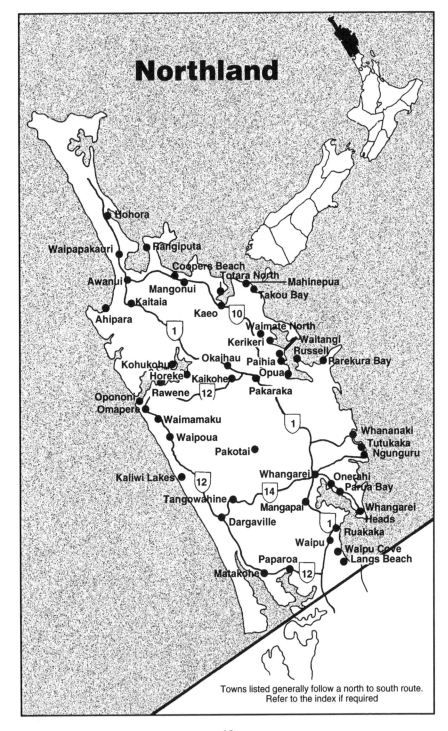

Northland

Towns listed generally follow a north to south route.
Refer to the index if required

Houhora

Homestay
Address: Far North Road, Houhora,
700m North of BP station
opposite Houhora Fire Station.
Name: Bruce & Jacqui Malcolm
Telephone: (09) 409 7884
Fax: (09) 409 7884
Mobile: (025) 926 992
Email: houhora.homestay@xtra.co.nz
Beds: 3 King (or 6 Single), (3 bedrooms)
Bathroom: 2 Ensuite, 1 Private
Tariff: B&B (full) Double $90,
Single $65, Dinner $25. Credit cards. Enquire about seasonal specials.
Nearest Town: Kaitaia - we are 44km north.

We have fled our largest city to live here in paradise. An hour and a half from Kerikeri and the country just gets better.

Why not join us and our cat on the Houhora Harbour. Four wheel drive, and line or deep sea fishing expeditions are all available. Just let us know what to arrange. There are two golf courses, 90 Mile Beach and acres of space. This beautiful country hasn't finished with you until the Far North has cast its spell. The night sky up here can't be beaten, and the sheer power of Cape Reinga or Spirits Bay will stop you in your tracks. Camera essential. We'll supply you with a continental or full breakfast. The bread is homemade, and as much as possible, food on our table comes from our developing 3 1/2 acre garden. Other meals can be supplied as an extra provided by arrangement.

Ahipara – Ninety Mile Beach - Kaitaia

Guest House
Address: "Siesta Luxury Guest Lodge",
P.O. Box 30, Ahipara, Northland
Name: Carole and Alan Harding
Telephone: (09) 409 2011
Fax: (09) 409 2011
Mobile: (025) 965 085
Email: ninetymile@xtra.co.nz
Beds: 2 Queen (2 bedrooms)
Bathroom: 2 Ensuite
Tariff: B&B (full/continental) Double $125, Single $90, Dinner by arrangement. Credit Cards.
Nearest Town: Kaitaia 15 km

We live in a large sunny Mediterranean style home set in private grounds with panoramic views overlooking the sheltered Ahipara Bay and the magnificent Ninety Mile Beach. Each luxurious well-appointed room has a private balcony, comfortable queen-sized bed and ensuite bathroom. Sleep to the sound of the sea and wake up to seaviews from your bed. The most beautiful beaches and hidden treasures are close-by. Horse trekking, 4 WD bike hire or simply walk and discover your own wilderness. Fish, game-fish, surf-cast, scuba dive, surf or swim on our safe local beach. Travel on local air-conditioned buses up Ninety Mile Beach to the Cape.

Home Page: www.ahipara.co.nz/siesta
Directions: *Take the Ahipara road west and drive past Ahipara School, turning left toward Shipwreck Bay. Keep going 1 km until you get to the beach. Opposite, on the left, you will see Tasman Heights. Follow the road up the hill and you will see the "Siesta" signs.*

Ahipara - Ninety Mile Beach. Kaitaia
Self-contained Beach Front Units
Address: "Foreshore Lodge",
Ninety Mile Beach, 269 Foreshore Road,
Ahipara, RD1 Kaitaia.
Name: Maire & Selwyn Parker
Telephone: (09) 409 4860
Fax: (09) 409 4860
Beds: Family Unit: 1 King, 2 Single
(2 bedrooms/lounge, 2 double bedsettees)
Double Unit: 1 Super King, 1 Foldaway Bed.
Bathroom: 1 Private, 1 Ensuite
Tariff: B&B (continental) Double $70-$100 (2 people), seasonal. Single $50.
Price negotiable for longer stays. Children very welcome.
No pets. Credit Cards welcome.
Nearest Town: Kaitaia17km (15 mins)

Foreshore Lodge is situated right on the waters edge in Ahipara Bay, at the sheltered southern end of Ninety Mile Beach facing north. Perfect setting. Our unpolluted water and beach is very safe for fishing, surfing, swimming or walking. Relax and enjoy lovely seaviews from the comfort of your unit or sheltered terrace with BBQ. Golf course 3 km, Take-away's and dairies 2 km, restaurant 500m. All tours to Cape Reinga, Around Reef point over gumfields, 4 WD fishing tours and Quad hire - all from our front door. Our family unit has access for a manual wheelchair inside, and easy walking for everyone across road onto the lovely sandy beach.
Directions: *Take the road to West Coast from Kaitaia to Ahipara 15km. Drive straight past school to the beach along Foreshore Road 2km till you see our sign, Foreshore Lodge. Come relax and enjoy all year round.*

Waipapakauri
Bed & Breakfast
Address: Domain Road,
State Highway One, Waipapakauri.
Name: Waipapakauri Lodge
Telephone: (09) 408 7433
Fax: (09) 408 7433
Beds: 2 Queen, 1 Twin (3 bedrooms)
Bathroom: 1 Ensuite, 1 Guests share

Tariff: B&B (special/full) Double $95, Single $65, dinner $35, Children under 12 half price.
Nearest Town: Kaitaia 12 kms

Ian and Bridget offer style and total relaxation in a beautiful rural setting. Superbly appointed rooms with separate guest lounge, they also welcome you into the main lounge where a cosy four foot log fire awaits you. Situated just five minutes from 90 Mile Beach, a safari along the beach through the river beds bound for Cape Reinga is a must, with full picnic prepared for your enjoyment. We also have thirty three beaches and two oceans within 40 minutes drive which allows a fun day fishing (either coast) also handy golf courses, or why not just relax, lie around the pool, a game of lawn croquet, petanque and enjoy the beautiful surroundings. In the still of the evening Bridget says enjoy her exquisite cuisine around a candle lit table accompanied by a complimentary glass of wine. We look forward to making your stay special.
Your hosts Ian and Bridget
PS: Mr Ties (dog) Miss Daisy and Olly (cats).

14

Awanui, Ninety-Mile-Beach – Kaitaia

Farmstay
Address: Beach Road, Awanui R.D. 1, Northland
Name: Tony & Helen Dunn
Telephone: (09) 406 7494
Beds: 2 Double (2 bedrooms)
Bathroom: 1 Guests share
Tariff: B&B (special) Double $90, Single $45, Children (under 10 yrs) 1/2 price, Dinner $25.
Nearest Town: Awanui 9 kms, Kaitaia 16 km

We have a comfortable, modern home, built for the sun and view, on a hill overlooking the farm, the Aupouri Pine Forest and the Ninety Mile Beach. "Ninety Mile Angoras" is a property of 40 hectares of rolling sand hill country, presently carrying cattle, sheep and goats. Ninety Mile Beach, noted for its fishing, is one minute drive away to the West, while a feast of East Coast Beaches lie within thirty minutes easy drive. All have beautiful golden sands and unpolluted waters. This home is an excellent central point to fully explore the North of New Zealand. Cape tour buses collect and deliver passengers from the farm gate. Mohair products for sale. Horse treks arranged.
Directions: *From Awanui, drive North approximately 6 kms. Turn left at signs to The park Ninety Mile Beach. Our farm is on the right, approximately 3 km after turn off, the last farm before the forestry and beach.*

Rangiputa-Beach – Far North

Name: Leigh & Wayne
Telephone: (09) 406 7997
Fax: (09) 406 7997
Beds: 2 Queen, 2 Single (3 bedrooms)
Bathroom: 1 Ensuite, 1 Guests share
Tariff: B&B (full) Double $70-$80, Single $60, Dinner on request $30pp. Unit as B&B Double $95-$110 Unit as S/C Double $80-$100.
Prices from 1 Oct 1997 to 31 Sept 1998.
Not suitable for children.
Nearest Town: Kaitaia 35 mins, Taipa 25 mins

Relax and enjoy our special place on the Riviera of Doubtless Bay. Rangiputa Beach with beautiful silicone sand and tranquil clear blue water. Safe swimming, good fishing and diving.Our home is modern, clean, warm and glows with natural timber. Lovely sea views from all rooms. Surrounded by a tropical garden.
Cape Reinga tours and others available with pickup and return to our gate. 20 minutes from the Karikari Peninsula turnoff on SH10 signposted. We are a couple in our early-mid 40's and enjoy meeting people, gardening and travel. Wayne is also a keen fisherman and you are welcome to accompany him to try your luck for snapper and others, just minutes off shore. Recent guests comments: "The Fiji of NZ. Wonderful accommodation and great hosts. Thanks for a great holiday". "Great to be back again. We just love being here and look forward to coming again."

Relax – Don't try to drive too far in one day.

Coopers Beach

Homestay
Address: 104 State Highway 10,
Coopers Beach
Name: Mac'n'Mo's
Telephone: (09) 406 0538
Fax: (09) 406 1539
Mobile: 025-286 5180
Beds: 1 Queen, 2 Double,
4 Single (4 bedrooms)
Bathroom: 2 Ensuite,
2 Guests share
Tariff: B&B (continental) Ensuite $75, Double $65,
Single $40, Dinner $25.
NZ B&B Vouchers accepted surcharge $7.50 ensuite.
Nearest Town: Mangonui/Coopers Beach 3 kms

Mac 'n' Mo's has sparkling views over Doubtless Bay with Coopers Beach just across the road and down some steps. Enjoy your breakfast overlooking the bay in our "slice of paradise", you may even see dolphins. We have secure off street parking with a private guest entrance and two into separate en suite units which are $75.00. Refrigerators and tea and coffee making facilities are available for all guests. The tour bus to Cape Reinga stops at our gate, you may like to visit a glow worm grotto, kiwi house, go on a craft or wine trail, swim with the dolphins, visit a Kauri forest, go fishing, diving or just relax on our unpolluted uncrowded beaches. We have several fine restaurants and world famous fish and chips close by. All this can be done from Mac 'n' Mo's. and they will take good care of you. Special winter and long stay rates are available.

Coopers Beach

Guest House+Self-contained Accom.
Address: Doubtless Bay Lodge,
33 Cable Bay Block Rd,
Coopers Beach, Mangonui 0557
Name: Harry and Berwyn Porten
Telephone: (09) 406 1661
Fax: (09) 406 1662
Mobile: (025) 275 2144
Beds: 3 Queen, 2 Single (4 bedrooms)
Bathroom: 4 Ensuite
Tariff: B&B (full) Double $90, Single $55, Children $20, Dinner $25,
Credit Cards. NZ B&B Vouchers accepted $20 surcharge
Nearest Town: Mangonui 3.5 km south.

Our brand new purpose built guest house is 800 metres north of the Coopers Beach shops. We are about an hours drive north of Paihia and 35 minutes south of Kaitaia on State Highway 10. Our children are grown up and off our hands. We are enjoying the sun and the sand, the fishing and the walking. We enjoy the rural and sea views of this lovely place. We have left traffic and hassles of Auckland behind us and invite our guests to do the same! Each room has ensuite and Cable TV (with Sky sport), fridge and tea and coffee facilities. Home style evening meals are provided by arrangement. We also provide a fully furnished self contained cottage with 3 bedrooms which will sleep up to seven people, at $150 per night. Discount for lengthy stays.

Mangonui

Homestay/Farmstay/Seaside Retreat.
Address: Abraham Lincolns Bed and Breakfa
Hihi Road, Mangonui
Name: Neville & Shirley Thomas
Telephone: (09) 406 0090
Mobile: 025-275 8125
Beds: 1 Queen, 2 Double,
1 Single (3 bedrooms)
Bathroom: 1 Guests share, 1 Family share
Tariff: B&B (continental) Double $70, Single $50,
Dinner $20. Self-contained Campervans.
Ask about our off season rates. Pensioners we ofer very low off season rates. NZ
B&B Vouchers accepted
Nearest Town: Mangonui - Kaitaia & Kerikeri 3/4 hour away

Enjoy a completely relaxing stay with wonderful sea views looking across the harbour to Mangonui township. Neville is born and bred in the North and has many interesting and informative stories to share. Neville is also an Abraham Lincoln look alike. Fishing is a great sport in this area and we can organise trips for you or you are welcome to use our dinghy. We also arrange an exciting trip to the cape with our local coach line. Our home is a bird sanctuary and we house many different species. Shirley offers a wonderful and hearty home cooked meal. Neville has an old collection of farm memorabilia on show now. This you must see!! If you are looking for an above average home to stay in then we welcome you to join in the laughter, great food and a very memorable stay. Also experience a spa with bush setting and harbour views.

Mangonui

Homestay B&B
Address: Corner of Beach Road (The Loop) and Grey St west ext,
Mangonui fishing village -
Name: Heaven Dessent, "Frankly Heaven"
Telephone: (09) 406 1068
Beds: 3 Double, 2 Single (3 bedrooms)
Bathroom: 2 Ensuite, 1 Family share
Tariff: B&B (full) Double $65, Single $35, Dinner $20pp, Full breakfast.
NZ B&B Vouchers accepted
Nearest Town: Mangonui - Kerikeri & Kaitaia 3/4 hour away

Welcome to Frankly Heaven's exciting Bed & Breakfast with a difference. Awaken to the panoramic vista of the beautiful "Mill Bay" with its anchorage of sailing and fishing boats, sparkling crystal waters and a necklace of luscious green vegetation upon gently sloping hills. A leisurely stroll to the picturesque Mangonui wharf could see you catching a John Dory or Kingfish - "What a way to spend a day". Our comfortable guest rooms open onto a sunny decking where you can savour our home style country meals that we take particular pride in. We offer our guests a warm and inviting home of old world charm and memorabilia. Dress up in the romantic ballgowns of yesterday. Sing your hearts out around the pianola or enjoy a friendly game of pool. At the end of day indulge yourself in the romance of a candle lit dinner and leave with unforgettable memories to treasure forever.

Mahinepua/Kaeo
Homestay
Address: Waiwurrie,
Mahinepua Bay,
RD 1, Kaeo, Northland
Name: Rodger and Vickie
Telephone: (09) 405 0840
Fax: (09) 405 0854
Beds: 1 Queen (1 bedroom)
Bathroom: 1 Ensuite
Tariff: B&B (full) Double $175,
Single $125, Dinner $35.
Nearest Town: Kaeo (22 kms), Kerikeri (40kms)

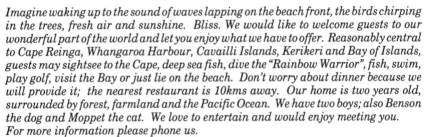

Imagine waking up to the sound of waves lapping on the beach front, the birds chirping in the trees, fresh air and sunshine. Bliss. We would like to welcome guests to our wonderful part of the world and let you enjoy what we have to offer. Reasonably central to Cape Reinga, Whangaroa Harbour, Cavailli Islands, Kerikeri and Bay of Islands, guests may sightsee to the Cape, deep sea fish, dive the "Rainbow Warrior", fish, swim, play golf, visit the Bay or just lie on the beach. Don't worry about dinner because we will provide it; the nearest restaurant is 10kms away. Our home is two years old, surrounded by forest, farmland and the Pacific Ocean. We have two boys; also Benson the dog and Moppet the cat. We love to entertain and would enjoy meeting you. For more information please phone us.

Takou Bay, Kerikeri
2 Self Contained Flats
Address: Te Ra Road, Takou Bay,
Kerikeri RD2
Name: Sandra Thornburgh
Telephone: (09) 407 7617
Beds: 1 Queen, 1 Double,
2 Single (3 bedrooms)
Bathroom: 1 Ensuite, 1 Private
Tariff: B&B (continental) Double $70,
Single $45 NZ B&B Vouchers accepted
Except major holidays.
Nearest Town: Kerikeri

Situated between the Bay of Islands and Matauri Bay, Takou Bay is one of Northland's best kept secrets. Twenty minutes north of Kerikeri off SH10, it is an ideal base to explore all the sights of the Far North right up to Cape Reinga. Or stay close to home and enjoy the quiet, unspoilt beauty of Takou Bay Surf Beach. My house sits a top the hill overlooking the sea, with panoramic views of the beach, river and Cavalli Islands which meet the rolling green hills of Northland. With my sister, I have a 50 acre life style farm carrying goats and horses. Americans by birth, we are Kiwis at heart and love the rural lifestyle. Accommodation consists of two self-contained flats in my warm, two storey house. Both flats offer spectacular seaviews from every window and each have their own kitchen and private bathroom. The upstairs unit has two bedrooms and lounge while the downstairs is a double bedsit with cozy fireplace. Breakfast is provided in the flats to be taken when desired.
Directions: *Please phone or write.*

Te Ngaere Bay, Kaeo

Self-contained Accommodation
Address: Te Ngaere Bay, R.D. 1, Kaeo
Name: Mrs June Sale
Telephone: (09) 405 0523
Fax: (09) 405 0604
Mobile: (025) 903 861
Beds: 2 Single (1 bedroom + 1 combined lounge-kitchen)
Bathroom: 1 Ensuite
Tariff: $60 Dec/March per night inclusive up to 2 people, $20 per extra person;
$50 all other times per night inclusive up to 2 people, $15 per extra person.
Credit cards (VISA/MC/BC). Breakfast not applicable.
NZ B&B Vouchers accepted Doubles only
Nearest Town: Kerikeri, 35km south of Te Ngaere

Our home is situated on the beach at Te Ngaere Bay, a safe and sheltered bay on one of New Zealand's finest stretches of coastline, in the Far North near Matauri Bay. The drive out gives you spectacular views of the beautiful Cavalli Islands and many other secluded bays and islands along the coast. There is much to do in the area: kauri forests to visit, sailing, fishing, big-game fishing, horse riding, coastal walks, swimming, snorkelling and diving are but a few activities, or visit the 'Rainbow Warrior' Memorial at Matauri Bay. We personally run 'Snow Cloud', a skippered charter yacht from Whangaroa, doing day trips and longer. There are excellent licensed restaurants in the area. It is a good central base from which to explore the North, or, you might like to beachcomb or just sit on the beach. "Pickles and Smokey" are our pet cats. Looking forward to having you to stay.
Directions: *Please phone for bookings and details of how to find us. Bookings are essential.*

Kaeo

Homestay, Farmstay
Address: Otangaroa Road, RD2, Kaeo
Name: Jan Tagart and Steve Cottis
Telephone: 09-405 0092
Beds: 1 King, 2 Single (2 bedrooms)
Bathroom: 1 Private.
Tariff: B&B (continental) Double $60, Single $30, Dinner $20.
Children under 12 half price. Credit cards accepted.
Nearest Town: Kaeo is 16km south, Mangonui is 18km north.

Our house is an old kauri villa set in a valley inland from Whangaroa Harbour. We have 70 acres, mostly grazing beef cattle, together with a small vegetable growing business. Taratara Rock, an imposing local landmark, is a stone's throw away. A walk to the top, for the moderately fit, gives bird's eye views of Whangaroa Harbour and the Far North interior. We can provide plenty of country amusements - milk the cow, feed the chooks and pigs, pat the sheep. There are pretty streams and rocks, native bush, birds. Local attractions include boating, beaches, bush walks. We are centrally located for day trips to Cape Reinga, kauri trees and the Bay of Islands. Children are welcome. We have a cot and a fairly childproof house. Our son Sam is three, our daughter Eleanor, 18. We have an outdoor dog called Emma. We request that guests do not smoke inside the house.
Directions: *Please phone for directions*

Waimate North, Kerikeri

Farmstay-Homestay
Address: 'Aspley House', Waimate North,
Kerikeri R.D.3, Bay of Islands
Name: Frank & Joy Atkinson
Telephone: (09) 405 9509
Beds: 1 Double, 2 Single (2 bedrooms)
Bathroom: 1 Ensuite, 1 Private
Tariff: B&B (of your choice) Double $110, Children half price, Dinner $30.
NZ B&B Vouchers accepted Surcharge $25
Nearest Town: Kerikeri 10 mins, Paihia 10 mins, Airport 10 mins

Aspley House with its old-world charm offers a relaxing and comfortable stay and is ideally situated in picturesque rural surrounds of the Atkinson family farms. Two large, well-appointed guestrooms open on to a wide verandah, with views of land-scaped gardens, over-looking a small lake and beyond to rolling farmland where beef cattle graze. Frank and Joy who are both descendants of pioneer families, and well versed in local history, have hosted guests from many countries over the past 17 years, and are themselves well travelled. Family antiques contribute to the atmosphere of this stately, attractive, colonial-styled home. The three-course evening meals feature home-grown fresh produce and New Zealand wines. Summer-time guests can enjoy the inviting kidney-shaped pool. "Aspley House", with its central location is an excellent base from which to explore the many tourist attractions of the Historic Bay of Islands and the far north. We offer quality accommodation. Pets: Jake, a Jack Russell and Mr. Cat.
Directions: *West of SH 10 at Puketona Junction, 3km up Te Ahuahu Road.*

Kerikeri

Bed & Breakfast
Address: 'The Gables',
cnr State Hwy 10 AND Te Ahu-Ahu Rd,
Puketona, Kerikeri
Name: Margaret Dines
Telephone: (09) 407 7923
Fax: (09) 407 7923
Beds: 2 Queens, 2 Singles (3 bedrooms)
Bathroom: 1 Private, 1 Guests share
Tariff: B&B (special) Double $90, Single $70, Dinner $30.
Prices apply to NZ Bed & Breakfast book only
NZ B&B Vouchers accepted $20 surcharge
Nearest Town: Kerikeri

GUESTS are warmly welcome at our country home THE GABLES!
Set in a few acres with a lovely cottage garden and surrounded by picturesque rolling countryside in the heart of The Bay of Islands The Gables is only a short drive to Paihia and Keri Keri. Coaches to Cape Reinga pass the entrance to our property and bookings can be made for you, making this an ideal stopover for those wishing to take in the many attractions this area has to offer. There are three bedrooms, two with queensize beds, one with two singles all delightfully decorated in the Laura Ashley style. Our breakfasts are quite special, enjoy fresh local fruits, home-made breads, muffins, muesli, jams and marmalades. (A cooked breakfast if requested.) We look forward to your visit and sharing this beautiful part of New Zealand with you.
Pets: two dogs an Airedale Emma and a West-Highland white terrier Dougal.
Prices apply to B&B book holders only.
NON SMOKERS PREFERRED.

Kerikeri

Homestay
Address: Matariki Orchard,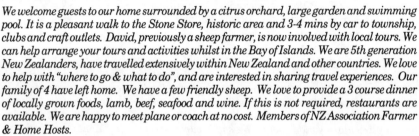
Pa Road, Kerikeri
Name: David & Alison Bridgman
Telephone: (09) 407 7577
Fax: (09) 407 7593
Beds: 1 Queen, 2 Single (2 bedrooms)
Bathroom: 1 Guests share
Tariff: B&B (full) Double $90, Single $50, Children $20, Dinner $25,
Campervans $20, Credit cards. NZ B&B Vouchers accepted surcharge $10
Nearest Town: Kerikeri (4 mins), Paihia (20 mins)

We welcome guests to our home surrounded by a citrus orchard, large garden and swimming pool. It is a pleasant walk to the Stone Store, historic area and 3-4 mins by car to township, clubs and craft outlets. David, previously a sheep farmer, is now involved with local tours. We can help arrange your tours and activities whilst in the Bay of Islands. We are 5th generation New Zealanders, have travelled extensively within New Zealand and other countries. We love to help with "where to go & what to do", and are interested in sharing travel experiences. Our family of 4 have left home. We have a few friendly sheep. We love to provide a 3 course dinner of locally grown foods, lamb, beef, seafood and wine. If this is not required, restaurants are available. We are happy to meet plane or coach at no cost. Members of NZ Association Farmer & Home Hosts.

Directions: *Turn off Highway 10 into Kerikeri township. Turn right at the roundabout into Hobson Rd, continue on at intersection, now Cobham Road, which runs into Inlet Road. Pa Road is first on the left. We are the 3rd house on right. Please phone.*

Okaihau, Kerikeri

Farmstay
Address: Wiroa Road, R.D. 1,
Okaihau
Name: Neville & Shennett Clotworthy
Telephone: (09) 401 9371
Fax: (09) 401 9371
Beds: 1 double, 4 Single (3 bedrooms)
Bathroom: 1 Guests share
Tariff: B&B (full) Double $70, Single $35, Dinner $25.
NZ B&B Vouchers accepted
Nearest Town: Kerikeri 10 minutes, Okaihau 6 minutes.

We have sheep, cattle and horses on our 280 acre farm. Our native bush has resident Kiwis and there are fantastic views of the Bay of Islands area from our home which is 1,000 feet above sea level. Puketi Kauri Forest, historic Hokianga, Kerikeri and Paihia are close by. 7km to the Kerikeri Airport. We are both descended from Northland families that settled in the 1840's and our special interests are travel, tramping, farming, genealogy, Northland history, dog-trialling and equestrian activities. We have an extensive library on Northland history and families.

Directions: *West of State Highway 10. Take Wiroa / Airport Road at the Kerikeri intersection and we are 9km on the right. OR East of State Highway 1. Take the Kerikeri Road, 500 metres South of Okaihau, and we are the 4th house on the left, past the golf course. (8 kms)*

Kerikeri

Farmstay
Address: 'Kilernan', State Highway 10,
Kerikeri, RD2.
Name: Heather & Bruce Manson
Telephone: (09) 407 8582
Fax: (09) 407 8317
Mobile: (025) 790 216
Beds: 1 Queen, 2 Single (2 bedrooms)
Bathroom: 2 Ensuites
Tariff: B&B (full) Double $100, Single $65,
Dinner $30, Not suitable for children. Credit Cards
(VISA/MC). NZ B&B Vouchers accepted with surcharge $30
Nearest Town: Kerikeri 9 km, Airport 10km.

*KILERNAN ORCHARD offers superior accommodation approx. 9km from Kerikeri
and an easy drive - 30 km to Paihia in the Bay of Islands.*
*Set in 45 acres well removed from the highway our brand new home has been specially
designed for guest accommodation. You have the choice of double or twin room with
your own ensuite for complete privacy. Enjoy a full English style breakfast indoors or
on our sunny spacious deck which overlooks stream, pasture and native bush. For your
evening meal we offer the best of local fare including New Zealand wine and preceded
by complimentary sundowners. We share our property with "Monty" our pedigree
boxer and some cattle and our orchard grows mandarins and persimmons which are
picked in May/June. If you are arriving by air we provide pick up from Kerikeri
airport. Directions given at the time of booking which is recommended.*

Kerikeri

Country Homestay
Address: 'Stoneybroke' Edmonds Road,
Kerikeri
Name: Vaughan & Gillian
Telephone: (09) 407 7371
Beds: 1 Double, 2 Single (2 bedrooms)
Bathroom: 1 Guests share
Tariff: B&B (full) Double $70, Single $40, Dinner $25.
NZ B&B Vouchers accepted
Nearest Town: 11 1/2km east of Kerikeri

*Vaughan and Gillian welcome guests to their modern timbered home in its tranquil
rural setting, overlooking Kerikeri inlet. Your hosts are experienced travellers and
enjoy exchanging travel tales and introducing visitors to the varied delights of the
region - historic sites, golf courses, country walks, boat charters and art and craft
galleries abound. Interests include history, travel, gardening and painting. Weary
travellers may prefer to relax in our pleasant garden and read from our extensive book
collection, while sampling life on a typical NZ small holding. We grow macadamia
nuts and almonds and run cattle, but have no household pets. Your accommodation
consists of one double-room with inlet and garden views, one twin-bedded room and
guests own bathroom/toilet. Twin-bedded "sleepout" accommodation is sometimes
available - all smoke free. Dinner is an optional extra featuring home grown vegetables, preserves and homemade bread, accompanied by complimentary wine. Please
telephone in advance.*

Kerikeri

Bed & Breakfast
Address: 'The Ferns' 4 Riverview Rd, Kerikeri
Name: Jim & Penny
Telephone: (09) 407 7567
Beds: 1 Queen, 1 Double, 2 Single (3 bedrooms)
Bathroom: 1 Ensuite, 1 Guests share
Tariff: B&B (full) Double $80-90, Single $45, Credit cards (VISA/BC/MC).
NZ B&B Vouchers accepted $20 Surcharge for ensuite room only.
Nearest Town: Kerikeri township 3km

At 'The Ferns' there is always a warm welcome and friendly service. Conveniently located in Kerikeri, we offer guests, modern two storied comfortable accommodation. The entrance, leads you to the top level - with spacious private guests rooms with quality beds and bathroom facilities on the lower level, all overlooking a spectacular tranquil garden setting. Relax and enjoy complimentary refreshments, served on large sunny decks or in a comfortable fireside TV/lounge. Start your day with a full breakfast of continental and cooked delights served in the dining area or on the balcony, before exploring the Bay of Island's, and Northland's many attractions and activities.
Directions: *From SH10 Kerikeri turn-off, follow the main road, through Kerikeri township, past the Stone Store, over the bridge, straight ahead at Waipapa Roundabout, 2nd street on the right. Off-street parking. Free pick up available from public transport. Phone or call in, "Welcome to the Ferns".*

Kerikeri

Self-contained Accommodation
Address: D'Arcy Lodge, Waipapa Road, (P.O. Box 497), Kerikeri
Name: Yvonne & Neil Burgham
Telephone: (09) 407 8110
Fax: (09) 407 8110
Email:burgham@xtra.co.nz
Mobile: (025) 281 8632
Beds: 2 Queen, 1 Single, (in 2 chalets)
Bathroom: 2 Ensuite
Tariff: B&B (continental) Double $83-$98, Single $60-$78, Extra adult sharing $15, Child $10. Dinner $30. Credit Cards. NZ B&B Vouchers accepted
Nearest Town: Kerikeri 5km

D'Arcy Lodge is situated in a semi-rural location just above Rainbow Falls on the Kerikeri River, but with easy access to Kerikeri and surrounding attractions.
A wish to personally entertain guests has prompted Yvonne and Neil to offer the hospitality of their home, whilst the two chalets also offer both privacy and independence. Their well-appointed chalets are free-standing and self-contained, each with an ensuite and a queen-size bed. The larger one has a small kitchen, a separate bedroom, and its own lounge in which there is a single bed. Ample off-road, car and boat parking is available. Dinner available by prior arrangement.
Directions: *Turn off highway 10 at Waipapa, travel 2km east along Waipapa Road; or through Kerikeri, past the Stone Store, up the hill and left into Waipapa Road.*

Waipapa, Kerikeri
Orchard Stay
Address: Highway 10 Orchard, S.H.10,
Waipapa , Postal: P.O. Box 516 Kerikeri
Name: Nan & Malcolm Laurenson
Telephone: (09) 407 7489
 Fax: (09) 407 7483
Beds: 1 Double, 1 Single (1 bedroom)
Bathroom: 1 Ensuite
Tariff: B&B (full) Double $75, Single $50,
Children under 12 half price, Dinner $25. NZ B&B Vouchers accepted
Nearest Town: Kerikeri 7.3km

We would like to welcome you to our Ranch Style home, on a flat 8 acre Citrus Orchard where access to all areas is easy, whether it is a stroll through the orchard or getting to and from our home and ensuite unit which is adjacent to the house. Meals can be served in your room, beside the swimming pool, or join us in the dining room. You will find our property simple to find, central to sightseeing in the North with genuine friendly attention in a quiet and relaxed atmosphere. A cat lives here as well.
Directions: *Please phone where possible.*

Okaihau
Farmstay
Address: 'Lewood Park',
Mangataraire Road, R.D.1,
Okaihau, Bay of Islands
Name: Ron & Pat Lewis
Telephone: (09) 401 9290/
Private: (09) 401 9941
Fax: (09) 401 9290 **Mobile**: (025) 277 7305
Beds: 2 Double, 1 Single (2 bedrooms)
Bathroom: 1 Guest share
Tariff: B&B (continental) Double $70, Single $40, Dinner $25, Campervans $25,
Credit Cards. NZ B&B Vouchers accepted
Nearest Town: Okaihau 15 mins, Kerikeri 30 mins, Paihia 40 mins.

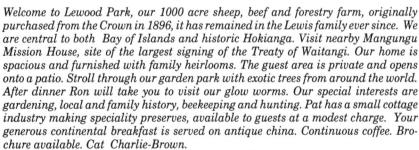

Welcome to Lewood Park, our 1000 acre sheep, beef and forestry farm, originally purchased from the Crown in 1896, it has remained in the Lewis family ever since. We are central to both Bay of Islands and historic Hokianga. Visit nearby Mangungu Mission House, site of the largest signing of the Treaty of Waitangi. Our home is spacious and furnished with family heirlooms. The guest area is private and opens onto a patio. Stroll through our garden park with exotic trees from around the world. After dinner Ron will take you to visit our glow worms. Our special interests are gardening, local and family history, beekeeping and hunting. Pat has a small cottage industry making speciality preserves, available to guests at a modest charge. Your generous continental breakfast is served on antique china. Continuous coffee. Brochure available. Cat Charlie-Brown.
Directions: *Please phone, sign at Mangataraire Road.*

Relax – Don't try to drive too far in one day.

Kerikeri

Homestay
Address: 'Fairway View',
6 Wentworth Terrace, Kerikeri
Name: Betty & Rex Mitchell
Telephone: (09) 407 5001
Fax: (09) 407 5001
Mobile: 025 711306
Beds: 1 Queen, 2 Single (2+ bedrooms)
Bathroom: 1 Ensuite, 1 Family share
Tariff: B&B (special) Double $75, Single $60,
Children $25, Dinner $30, Credit Cards.   NZ B&B Vouchers accepted $10
surcharge 1st September to 1st February
Nearest Town: Kerikeri 300 metres

Guests are assured of warm and generous hospitality. Fairway View, in a quiet cul-de-sac, is definitely Kerikeri's prime central location, with memorable panorama of the local championship golf course (one of New Zealand's best!)
Principal guest accommodation is large and well equipped with ensuite, queen size bed, bed settee, table and chairs, refrigerator, television, wardrobe, baggage rack, laundry and ironing facility, hair dryer, plus an adjoining single bedroom.
A twin room with family share bathroom is also offered. Breakfasts are "never less than special". Local restaurants are within easy walking distance. We also offer dinner, with New Zealand wine, by arrangement to suit all tastes and diets. Extensive use is made of fresh local produce for all meals. Our knowledge of the region enables us to assist guests in planning sight seeing tours. We are a retired couple with varied interests including golf. We have no pets.

Kerikeri

Orchard Stay
Address: Puriri Park Orchard,
SH10, Kerikeri
Name: Puriri Park
Telephone: (09) 407 9818
Fax: (09) 407 9498
Email: puriri @xtra.co.nz
Beds: 1 Double, 1 Single (1 bedroom)
Bathroom: 1 Private
Tariff: B&B (full) Double $75, Single $55,
 Children $10; Dinner $30.
NZ B&B Vouchers accepted
Nearest Town: Kerikeri 8 Kms

Puriri Park has long been known for the warmth of its hospitality to travellers in the Far North. We have a large, rambling house set in beautiful grounds with mature trees and gardens. We have an orchard of export-quality kiwifruit and another of oranges which provide freshly-squeezed juice for breakfast. We have five acres of bird-filled native bush, mostly Totara and Puriri. Guests are welcome to wander around our garden, sit by the lilypond, feed the white fantail pigeons or swim in the large swimming pool. However, if they wish to explore the Far North, we are in an excellent situation for day trips to Cape Reinga and sailing or cruising around the lovely Bay of Islands. Kerikeri itself has a fascinating history and we are only a few minutes from the Stone Store and the Inlet. We can arrange trips for you or pick you up from the airport. Pets: one Persian cat.
sketch and own logo

25

Kerikeri

Self-contained Accommodation
Address: Inlet Road, P.O. Box 230,
Kerikeri
Name: Villa-Maria Petit Hotel
Telephone: (09) 407 9311
Fax: (09) 407 9311
Email: VillaMaria@compuserve.com
Beds: 3 Large Villas with each 2 separate bedrooms,
(Queen and Twins), 1 smaller bungalow, All fully self contained.
Bathroom: 4 Private
Tariff: Double from $130 - $200 Depending Villa. Single from $85 - $150 Depending Villa. Studio Double $120 incl. breakfast. Continental - cooked breakfast $15.
4 adults from $200 - $300 p.n. Depending Villa.
Smoking designated areas. Little angels welcome. Off season rates available.
Nearest Town: Kerikeri 4km

The Villa-Maria Residence - is famous for peace and tranquillity, and personal attention. Four luxurious spacious villas with sea view are set in a subtropical park. Three Mediterranean villas have 2 separate bedrooms, very large lounge, fully equipped kitchen, ironing facilities, tiled bathroom, private indoor garage and terraces. 7000 acres of forest surround the residence and to complete this idyllic picture you can enjoy breathtaking sea views or refresh in our Italian style swimming pool. Your hosts also speak German, French, Italian and Flemish. We advise to book in advance. You will recommend it. Minimum stay 2 nights.
Home Page: http://www.friars.co.nz/hosts/vilamaria.html

Kerikeri

Homestay
Address: "Sunrise Homestay" B&B,
Skudders Road, Skudders Beach, Kerikeri
Name: Judy & Les
Telephone: (09) 407 5447
Fax: (09) 407 5447
Mobile: (025) 774941
Beds: 1 Double, 4 Single (3 bedrooms)
Bathroom: 1 Ensuite, Guests share
Tariff: B&B (full) Double $80, Single $40-$45,
Dinner $30pp, Credit cards.
NZ B&B Vouchers accepted Surcharge 1st Dec to 1st Feb: $10.
Nearest Town: Kerikeri 7Kms.

A warm welcome awaits you at our restful homestay overlooking the Kerikeri Inlet. A magnificent sunrise, we think the best in the world. The Bay of Islands has a wonderful range of things to do and see, we would only be to pleased to help arrange these with you. We are 7 mins from town by car. Laundry facilities available. Tea or coffee available at all times. By prior arrangements Judy and Les offer you meals inc. special diets or you may choose one of our many excellent restaurants. We consider ourselves very lucky to own one of the best locations in Kerikeri, do come and share it with us. Courtesy pick up from town or airport. Please phone or fax for your bookings or leave your number on our answer phone and we will call you. Not suitable for young children. We will endeavour to make your stay in Kerikeri, Bay of Islands an enjoyable as possible. Happy holidays and travelling.
Directions: *Please phone.*

Kerikeri

Homestay
Address: "Ironbark Lodge",
Ironbark Road, Kerikeri
Name: Rangi & Dail
Telephone: (09) 407 9302
Fax: (09) 407 9302
Beds: 2 Queen, 1 Single (3 bedrooms)
Bathroom: 3 Ensuite
Tariff: B&B (full) Double $95, Single $45, Credit Cards (VISA/MC/BC).
NZ B&B Vouchers accepted $20 surcharge Dec 1st to March 31st
Nearest Town: Kerikeri

Your holiday, a special time to have as many adventures as you can, or simply a wonderful opportunity to relax and spoil yourself. Whatever your holiday dream we can help you achieve it. Ironbark Lodge, set in a 20 acre farmlet, close to a Kauri forest, and surrounded by imposing eucalypt trees is the perfect base from which to explore. Each bedroom has a private ensuite. You'll love the comfy beds, and a substantial breakfast will ensure a perfect start to every day. Join us for BBQ evening meals in summer by arrangement ($25pp). Kerikeri restaurants 15 minutes away, Paihia 30 minutes.
Pets: 2 cats, 1 dog. 8 quiet cattle.
A holiday at Ironbark Lodge will never be quite long enough.
Directions: *Ironbark Road, 2km up Pungaere Road off SH10 Waipapa.*

Kerikeri

Homestay
Address: "Glenfalloch", Landing Road,
PO Box 477, Kerikeri
Name: Evalyn & Rick
Telephone: (09) 407 5471
Fax: (09) 407 5471
Beds: 1 Queen, 1 Double, 2 Single (3 bedrooms)
Bathroom: 1 Ensuite, 1 Guests share
Tariff: B&B (full) Double $75-$85, Single $55, Children under 12yrs half price,
Dinner $25p.p., Credit Cards.
NZ B&B Vouchers accepted
Nearest Town: Kerikeri - 2.6km

Evalyn and Rick offer a warm welcome and complimentary refreshments on your arrival at Glenfalloch. We are close to Kerikeri's famous historical Stone Store and adjacent to the beautiful Rainbow Falls Walkway. Venture down our tree lined driveway and our garden paradise is revealed. We are lucky to share this with an abundance of bird life including tuis, kingfisher, pheasant and occasionally wood pigeons. You are welcome to use the lounges, wander about our large garden, or relax on one of the decks. We have a swimming pool and for the energetic a lawn tennis court. On a fine day breakfast can be enjoyed at your leisure on the deck.
Laundry facilities available, smoking outdoors, children welcome.
Directions: *Travel North 0.6km from the Stone Store corner and we are the second drive on left after Dept of Conservation.*

Kerikeri

Bed & Breakfast
Address: "Graleen", Kerikeri Road, RD3, Kerikeri
Name: Graeme & Colleen Wattam
Telephone: (09) 407 9047
Fax: (09) 407 9047
Mobile: (025) 940 845
Beds: 1 Queen, 1 Double, 2 Single (3 bedrooms)
Bathroom: 3 Ensuite
Tariff: B&B Double $70, Single $40, Credit Cards. NZ B&B Vouchers accepted
Nearest Town: Kerikeri 3 mins, Paihia and Waitangi 20 mins.

After extensive travel all over the UK and having experienced and enjoyed the company and hospitality of so many people in their own homes, we decided we would like to do the same in our home town. We designed and built a new home with guest accommodation and comfort in mind. All bedrooms have ensuites and TV with direct access to our lovely sheltered veranda where you may relax and enjoy tea or coffee. We serve a continental breakfast (cooked on request) in our large guest lounge.

Kerikeri is a lovely rural town surrounded by orchards and farms and is centrally situated to all Bay of Islands and Northlands many tourist attractions.

We are only 20 mins from historic Waitangi and Paihia. "Graleen" is only 3 mins from the township, restaurants, RSA Club, bowling club, golf course, and many craft galleries.

Kerikeri

Homestay
Address: Pukanui, Kerikeri Road, Kerikeri
Name: Bill and Elaine Conaghan
Telephone: (09) 407 7003
Fax: (09) 407 7003
Mobile: (025) 771 569
Email: pukanui@igrin.co.nz
Beds: 3 Queen (3 bedrooms)
Bathroom: 3 Ensuites

Tariff: B&B (continental) Double $90-$110, Single $65, Dinner $30 pp.
Not suitable for children. Visa/Bankcard/Mastercard. Off season rates avaialble.
Nearest Town: Kerikeri - 5 minutes stroll

Elaine and Bill invite you to stay in their home set in private park-like grounds and citrus orchard, Kerikeri, with its restaurants, cafe's, craft shops and movie theatre is an ideal location to base your holiday activities in Northland. Our large home offers three spacious guest bedrooms with ensuite and tea and coffee making facilities in a well appointed non-smoking environment. Each has its own patio for breakfast in the sun. Should you wish to "eat in" we are happy to provide an evening meal by prior arrangement. For your enjoyment there is a large inground swimming pool, petanque piste, and lawn for putting practice before visiting the many golf courses in the region. Also of interest are wineries potteries and craft shops. We can also arrange your tours to various points of interest. Pixie the elusive cat also resides here only to appear when hungry. Complimentary airport transfers.

Kerikeri
Bed & Breakfast
Address: "Inlet Manor",
Inlet Road, Kerikeri.
Name: Brian and Diane Henderson.
Telephone: (09) 407 8374 **Fax**: (09) 407 8374
Beds: 1 Queen, 1 Double, 2 single (3 bedrooms)
Bathroom: 1 Guests share, plus extra toilet + hand basin.
Tariff: B&B (full) Double $85, Single $60.
Dinner from $20 pp (on request).   visa/mastercard.
Nearest Town: Kerekeri 2 1/2 kms.

We would like to welcome guests to "Inlet Manor", our English styled home, in its tranquil setting on 8 acres of mixed citrus orchard. Our guest facilities include your own kitchen and lounging area and a large lawn and gardens in which to relax. We have travelled extensively around New Zealand and overseas and enjoy sharing experiences with others. Anna is our friendly Labrador who also enjoys meeting people. Kerikeri is a wonderful area known for its history, scenery, arts and crafts. it is a great base for those seeking to explore the Bay of Islands, Hokianga and Far North. We are happy to pick up guests from our local airport or bus depot if required. Come and enjoy a relaxed atmosphere and quality accommodation.
Directions: *From central Kerikeri, travel down Cobham Rd which runs into Inlet Rd. Look for our sign, left hand side 2 1/2 km from Kerikeri.*

Kerikeri
Homestay, Bed & Breakfast
Address: Blacks Road, Kerikeri
Name: Jane and Tony Holmes
Telephone: (09) 407 7500
Fax: (09) 407 7500
Beds: 1 Queen,
2 Single (2 bedrooms) + 1 Bed settee
in guest lounge.
Bathroom: 1 Private, 1 Family share
Tariff: B&B (continental) Double $70,
Single $45, Dinner $20,
Credit Cards accepted
Nearest Town: Kerikeri (3.5 kms)

Just 3.5 kilometres from town overlooking Kerikeri Inlet you enjoy superb water and country views. Sheep munch next door and we have two pet calves. Bird life is abundant. We warmly welcome guests to our large, comfortable smoke-free bungalow, set amidst delightful shrubs and trees. Relax in the spa, perhaps join us for a bbq at sunset on the deck. Having travelled extensively and lived in many places, we now enjoy sailing and walking. Our yacht is close by. We can show you Kerikeri's bush walks, arrange night kiwi walks and fishing.
Directions: *Turn off Highway 10 towards Kerikeri. At Kerikeri roundabout turn right into Hobson Ave. At 1.1km turn left into Inlet Road. At 3.4km (NB 65km sign left) turn left into Blacks Road. We are half way down hill on left.*

Kerikeri
Homestay
Address: 100 Riverview Road, Kerikeri
Name: Tracy Norris and Robbie Burton
Telephone: (09) 407 6786.
Reservations: 0800 936 786 **Fax**: (09) 407 6786
Mobile: (025) 822 318 **Email**: pescador@xtra.co.nz
Beds: 4 Queen, 2 Double (5 bedrooms)
Bathroom: 4 Ensuites
Tariff: B&B (full) Double $100-$125, Single $80-$100, Dinner $25 pp.
Apartment $145 (does not include meal). Credit Cards:
Visa/Mastercard. NZ B&B Vouchers accepted $30-$50 surcharge
Nearest Town: Kerikeri 3 km

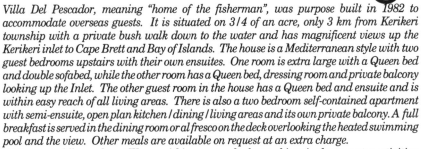

Villa Del Pescador, meaning "home of the fisherman", was purpose built in 1982 to accommodate overseas guests. It is situated on 3/4 of an acre, only 3 km from Kerikeri township with a private bush walk down to the water and has magnificent views up the Kerikeri inlet to Cape Brett and Bay of Islands. The house is a Mediterranean style with two guest bedrooms upstairs with their own ensuites. One room is extra large with a Queen bed and double sofabed, while the other room has a Queen bed, dressing room and private balcony looking up the Inlet. The other guest room in the house has a Queen bed and ensuite and is within easy reach of all living areas. There is also a two bedroom self-contained apartment with semi-ensuite, open plan kitchen / dining / living areas and its own private balcony. A full breakfast is served in the dining room or alfresco on the deck overlooking the heated swimming pool and the view. Other meals are available on request at an extra charge.
We have a toddler and a cat We are within easy reach of many historic places, water activities, arts and crafts shops, wineries and restaurants.
Home Page: www.kerikeri.net/pescador

Bay of Islands, Pakaraka
Farmstay and B&B
Address: Bay of Islands Farmstay
('Highland Farm' on Gate),
Pakaraka State Highway One
(R.D.2, Kaikohe 0400)
Name: Ken & Glenis Mackintosh
Telephone: (09) 404 1040 or (09) 404 0430
Fax: (09) 404 1040 **Mobile**: (025) 989 833
Beds: 1 Double, 4 Single (2 bedrooms)
Bathroom: 2 Ensuite
Tariff: B&B (full) Double $75, Single $50, Children (school age) half price, Cot/
Highchair no charge. Dinner: 3 course $28, including Dinner drinks,
Credit cards (VISA/MC/BC). NZ B&B Vouchers accepted
Nearest Town: Kawakawa, Paihia, Kerikeri, Kaikohe (very central)

Beautiful 51 acre property with historic stone walls, Barbery Hedges, sheep, cattle, pigs. You may enjoy watching and help shift the sheep and cattle, try your hand at shearing. Take farm walks and view the historic Pouerua Mountain, sit on or photograph with "Mr. Angus" our lovable pet steer. Our cats are named "Monkey" and "Governor Grey" you will understand why when you meet them. Summertime: Swim in pool. A cosy home in winter. TV, video, pooltable, hairdrier. We book tours and horse rides. Environmentally safe products. Only 15 minutes drive to Paihia, Kerikeri, Kaikohe. Golf, bowls, beaches, shopping, tours, Ngapha Springs, Kawakawa Vintage Train Rides. A good base, very central. only 1 hour to Whangarei or Kaitaia. Book early or take pot luck! Visa, Mastercard, Bankcard. On SH 1., (10 minutes north Kawakawa) 1km south (Pakaraka Junction). Welcome to the Bay of Islands! Enjoy your holiday. Be our guests!

Pakaraka, Bay of Islands

Farmstay/Homestay
Address: Corner State Highway One
& State Highway 10, Pakaraka, RD 2,
Kaikohe, Bay of Islands
Name: Ten on One Farmstay/Homestay
Jude & Art Hansen
Telephone: (09) 405 9460
Fax: (09) 405 9460 **Mobile**: (025) 886 618
Beds: 2 Queen, 1 Double, (3 bedrooms)

Bathroom: 1 Ensuite, 1 Private, 1 Family Share
Tariff: B&B (full) Double $68, Single $45. Dinners 19.50 pp.
Children not suitable. Credit Cards (VISA/MC/BC).
NZ B&B Vouchers accepted $6.00 surcharge
Nearest Town: Central to Paihia, Kerikeri, Kaikohe, Waitangi, Russell and
Kawa Kawa (18kms)

Ten on One Home / Farmstay, is nestled on 22 acres. Handy to Kauri Forests, Game Fishing, Hot Mud Pools, Russell, Waitangi Treaty House, Hole in the Rock cruises & Golf etc. We also have a swimming pool for your enjoyment. We can recommend and book all local tours. Art is a direct descendent of the first European Family to arrive and settle in New Zealand, and can tell you about the North and many places of interest to visit. Jude loves fishing and can give advise on local fishing trips and fishing spots. Both Jude and I have had many years experience in the tourist business, and our home / farmstay is a New Zealand tourism board Kiwi Host Business, committed to provide excellent service for you. We have assorted farm animals etc to view. Plus Art is a keen model train enthusiast.
Directions: *80 metres North of State Highway One & State Highway 10 intersection at Pakaraka on left hand side (signed TEN ON ONE). Please Phone for bookings. Enjoy your stay with us.*

Waitangi

Bed & Breakfast
Address: 48 Tahuna Road, Waitangi
Name: Laraine & Syd Dyer
Telephone: (09) 402 8551
Fax: (09) 402 8551
Beds: 1 Quen, 2 Single (3 bedrooms)
Bathroom: 1 Family share
Tariff: B&B (continental) Double $65, Single $40, Dinner $20.
NZ B&B Vouchers accepted
Nearest Town: Paihia

Waitangi Bed & Breakfast welcomes you to the North, come share good New Zealand hospitality. Our home has native bush behind so you can enjoy waking to the songs of birds. Waitangi has much to offer you, a beautiful beach, golf course, bush walks and most of all historic places, all within walking distance.
Full breakfast and dinner are available by prior arrangement. We will endeavour to make your stay in our lovely Bay really enjoyable.
Bus pick-ups from Paihia is available.
Pet: We have 1 dog named Bessie.

Paihia

Countrystay
Address: "Puketona Lodge",
Puketona Road, R D 1, Paihia 0252
Name: Heather & Maurice Pickup
Telephone: (09) 402 8152
Fax: (09) 402 8152
Mobile: (025) 770 833
Email: puketona@igrin.co.nz
Beds: 1 King/Twin (2 Single), 1 Double, (2 bedrooms)
Bathroom: 1 Ensuite, 1 Private

Tariff: B&B (full) King/Twin $100, Double $95, Single $75, Dinner $30, Children not suitable, Credit Cards (MC/VISA). 10% discount for 3 nights or longer. NZ B&B Vouchers accepted Not between Dec 20-Jan 7. $20 Surcharge
Nearest Town: Paihia 8 kms

Heather and Maurice invite you to visit us in our modern home, built of native timbers, by Maurice. Originally from England, we also lived in the United States. Our home is situated in quiet countryside with many native birds in our large garden. Our bedrooms are large with private facilities and both open onto the outside deck. We are close to Haruru Falls, Waitangi, beaches and walks. We can book cruises and tours, or drop you off on a walk thru the bush. Breakfast is your choice, cooked or continental featuring home made breads and preserves.Complimentary refreshments are provided on arrival. Evening meals are available on request, including vegetarian meals. We have 2 friendly dogs. Heather has taught ceramics for 30 years, and enjoys showing guests through her studio. We are on the main road from Paihia, 8km from the beach.
Please phone for reservations, and directions. We are a smoke free home.

Central Paihia

Hilltop Bed & Breakfast
Address: 'The Totaras', 6 School Road,
Paihia, Bay of Islands
Name: Frank & Christine Habicht
Telephone: (09) 402 8238
Fax: (09) 402 8238
Beds: Self Contained Studio: 1 Queen, 1 Single
Bathroom: 1 Ensuite
Tariff: B&B (special) Double $150, Single reduction, Dinner $30.
Off season rates. Credit Cards Visa.
Nearest Town: Central Paihia

. . . For the sophisticated traveller . . . luxury with charm and unsurpassed views. Enjoy Paihia's best and central location from a hill top residency. Watch the sunrise from your spacious and well appointed apartment with ensuite and your private sundeck overlooking the harbour, Waitangi, Russell, the islands and the endless horizon. Why not start your day with delicious Austrian pancakes in your scenic conservatory or one of the sundecks. A short track will lead you to the village, wharf (ferry ride to Russell 15 minutes), restaurants and beaches. A leisurely beach stroll will take you to historic Waitangi. Christine has a degree in Hotel Management and Frank is an international photographer. One of his latest books depicts the beauty of the Bay. Australia's "Weekend Away and Holiday Guide" highlighted "The Totaras" amongst their favoured ten Getaways in New Zealand.
Wir sprechen auch Deutsch. Try to book in advance. Minimum stay 2 nights.
PS: Please no smoking inside.

Paihia
Countrystay
Address: Lily Pond Orchard, Puketona Rd,
Paihia, Bay of Islands
Name: Allwyn & Graeme Sutherland
Telephone: (09) 402 7041
Beds: 1 Double, 3 Single (3 bedrooms)
Bathroom: 1 Guests share, Separate toilet.
Tariff: B&B (full) $40 per person.
NZ B&B Vouchers accepted $10 surcharge
Nearest Town: Paihia 7km

Drive in through an avenue of mature liquid amber trees to our comfortable timber home with sloping lawns down to a small lake, refuge for wild duck and home for our black swan and goldfish. Set in 10 acres of park-like grounds the atmosphere is quiet, peaceful and conveniently situated 8 min drive from Paihia.

The guest wing accommodation has views of the fountain and lake with the double and twin rooms having private access from your verandah.

We graze a few sheep and have 500 assorted fruit trees. Freshly squeezed orange juice, fruit and homemade jams are served at breakfast.

We are born N.Zers, have a wide variety of interests, Graeme having won local awards for his traditional Maori beef bone-carving. We have travelled extensively throughout our country and have sailed thousands of miles living aboard our 50ft yacht in the Pacific. We invite you to share the tranquillity of our small piece of paradise in the beautiful Bay of Islands.

Directions: *We can be found on the Paihia – Kerikeri road and the "Lily Pond Orchard" sign is at our gate.*

Central Paihia
Homestay + Self contained Accom.
Address: 5 Sullivan's Road,
Paihia, Bay of Islands
Name: The Cedar Suite, Jo & Peter Nisbet
Telephone: (09) 402 8516 **Fax**: (09) 402 8555
Mobile: (025) 969 281
Beds: 3 Queen, 1 Single (3 bedrooms)
Bathroom: SC studio: 1 Queen with ensuite, SC Apartment: 1 Queen + 1 Single with ensuite. 1 Queen with ensuite
Tariff: B&B (continental) Double $95-$115, Single $85-$107, (Studio + apartment available self-catering $78-$100). Dinner $27pp. Credit cards (MC/VISA) on direct bookings only. NZ B&B Vouchers accepted 1 May to 30 September with surcharge $24 to $44.
Nearest Town: Paihia - 1km to wharf

For a homestay with a difference 'The Cedar Suite' offers you friendliness, atmosphere and fun, while you relax in our modern cedar home amid beautiful mature native bush. Suites are separate, with their own superior ensuite bathroom or shower. Peter has a career background with the New Zealand Symphony Orchestra, and he also very much enjoys cooking. Jo's interests range from photography through fashion to interior design. Both of us enjoy music and gardening, and our use of fresh produce from the Bay makes breakfasts an enticing delight of special homemade creations, which include crunchy muesli, yoghurt and freshly brewed espresso coffee and herb teas. Guests have private parking, TV, quality appointments and particularly comfortable beds; all within easy walking distance of the Bay, Paihia shops and tours. Laundry service available at small extra charge, and in all cases we suggest you book in advance.

Paihia Waterfront

Bed & Breakfast
Address: Te Haumi House, 12 Seaview Road, Paihia
Name: Enid & Ernie Walker
Telephone: (09) 402 8046 **Fax**: (09) 402 8046
Beds: 1 Queen, 2 Single (2 bedrooms)
Bathroom: 1 Guests share
Tariff: B&B (continental) Double $70, Single $45, Children under 12 yrs half price. NZ B&B Vouchers accepted
Nearest Town: Paihia 2km

We have a well established home on the waterfront in Te Haumi Bay with fantastic seaviews of the inner harbour. Location: 3 minutes north of the Opua turn off and 1 minute south of Paihia township and opposite the Beachcomber Motel.
Our interests since retiring, are gardening, floral art and involvement in the Masonic Lodge. We enjoy meeting people from all walks of life and are very proud to share our wonderful area with you and to make your stay as memorable as possible.
Guest pick-up from Paihia is available.
P.S. Please no smoking inside, but outside is fine.

Central Paihia

Self-Contained Accommodation
Address: 'Craicor Accommodation'
49 Kings Road,
Paihia, Bay of Islands
Postal: P.O. Box 15, Paihia
Name: Anne Corbett & Garth Craig
Telephone: (09) 402 7882
Fax: (09) 402 7883
Beds: Garden Room: 1 Super King or
2 Single (1 bedroom) ,
Tree House: 1 Super King (1 bedroom)
Bathroom: 2 Ensuite

Tariff: Accommodation only: Garden Room: Double $80 + $15 for any extra guest (2 maximum), Tree House: Double $95, Optional continental breakfast $7.50 per person, Credit cards.   NZ B&B Vouchers accepted
Nearest Town: We are in Central Paihia.

The perfect spot for those seeking a sunny and quiet central location. Our self contained accommodation offers garden, bush, and sea views from your bed. Your choices are the Garden Room or Tree House. The Garden Room: a self contained attractive unit, garden and sea views, fully equipped kitchen, laundry, ensuite, deck, insect screens, TV, sun all day. Tree House: a self contained deluxe unit nestled into the bush and garden. Deck with sea and bush views, fully equipped kitchen, ensuite, insect screens, TV, sun, peace, solitude. Both units offer safe off street parking. The wharf, restaurants and shopping centre are a five minute stroll down the waterfront. Your hosts have lived in Paihia since 1978, and have a wealth of local knowledge on the B.O.I. area which they will gladly share with you in planning your holiday.
Welcome to Craicor Accommodation.
Home Page: http://nz.com/webnz/bbnz/craicor.htm

Paihia
Self-contained Accommodation
Address: PO Box 126, Paihia (Postal)
29 Bay View Road, Paihia
Name: Iona's Lodge/Malcolm & Mary Sinclair
Telephone: (09) 402 8072 **Fax**: (09) 402 8072
Beds: 2 Double, 1 Single (2 bedrooms)
Bathroom: 2 Ensuite
Tariff: B&B (continental) Double $75-$95, Single $60.
Credit Cards. NZ B&B Vouchers accepted
Nearest Town: In central Paihia

We live in Bay View Road, which is a quiet street with one of the best views in Paihia. We overlook the town and wharf with magnificent sea views across the bay and out to Russell. Centrally situated and within walking distance of all booking offices, Post Office, shops, restaurants and the beach.
One unit is one bedroomed with a double bed and single bed. Upstairs are the bathroom with shower, toilet and washing machine, a lounge area with TV and fold out double sofa and kitchen.
The studio unit has double bed, kitchen, TV and ensuite. Both are well equipped and comfortable. Each unit has their own deck area. There is a gas BBQ and ample parking.
I supply a generous breakfast tray in your fridge for you to enjoy at your leisure. We enjoy welcoming new friends from all over the world.

Paihia, Bay of Islands
Homestay
Address: "Fairlight River Lodge",
107B Yorke Road, Haruru Falls, Paihia,
Bay of Islands.
Name: Anna & Michael
Telephone: (09) 402 8004
Fax: (09) 402 8048
Mobile: (025) 281 9999
Email: fairlight@bay-of-islands.co.nz
Beds: 3 King/3 Double/3 Single, (3 bedrooms)
Bathroom: 2 Ensuite, 1 Guests share.
Tariff: B&B (special) Double/Triple $80-$130, Single $70,
Nearest Town: Paihia 3 mins, Kerikeri 15 mins

Anna, Michael and family welcome you to our RIVERSIDE RETREAT set on the banks of the Waitangi River. A peaceful and tranquil haven surrounded by beautiful native bush, home to over 20 species of birdlife. A "BIRD WATCHER'S PARADISE!"
Single / twin, double / triple rooms / suites with magnificent river, bush and garden views with all day sun. Enjoy spacious grounds with an evening stroll on the rivers edge. Kayakers and bush walkers pass by to nearby "FALLS". Ducks and herons and shags settle in for the night. Sounds of KIWI, owls and fish splashing take over.Anna's special breakfast begins the new day. Onto swimming with DOLPHINS, deep sea FISHING, ISLAND HOPPING or the famous 'Cream Trip", Historical Waitangi / Waimate Treaty houses. Russell, Ninety Mile Beach, MAORI CULTURE, diving ....restaurants / entertainment.We are 3 1/2 hours drive north or a 40 minute flight from Auckland. Please phone for reservations and directions.
Home Page: http://www.bay-of-islands co.nz/accomm/fairlite.htm

Central Paihia

Tourist Lodge: Self-contained Accom. & Private Rooms
(Budget or Superior)
Address: "Helvetia Lodge",
41 School Road, Paihia 0252,
Bay of Islands
Name: Carel Jost and Kees Eitjes
Telephone: (09) 402 7046
FREEPHONE: 0800-688 746 for reservations
Fax: (09) 402 7046 **Mobile**: 025-522 770
Email:helvetia@world-net.co.nz
Beds: 1 Queen, 3 Double, 4 Single (3+ bedrooms + 1 apartment)
Bathroom: 1 Ensuite, 1 Guests share, 1 Family share
Tariff: B&B (continental +) Double $70-90, Single $50-80, Credit Cards
(VISA/MC/AX). NZ B&B Vouchers accepted with seasonal surcharge
Nearest Town: We are in Paihia

Welcome to "Helvetia Lodge" - tranquil setting, clean, comfortable and homely. 5 minutes flat walk to Village, Wharf, Boat Trips, Restaurants and Beach. 2 minutes to Ex-Servicemen's Club. 5 minutes drive to Historic Waitangi. Your breakfast tray is brought to your room or you may choose an outdoor or deck setting. Breakfast is at a variable time to suit your activities, between 7 & 9 am, however earlier breakfast is available, on request. The homestead itself was one of the first houses built in Paihia on the Waterfront, then it was relocated, that's when our story begins. 24 years ago the door opened for the first guest. 18 years ago the homestead was raised to provide more accommodation, whilst still retaining its original character.
We are looking forward to being of service to you. A Courtesy Car is available if required.
Directions: *Easy to find - School Road runs off from Central Paihia Waterfront.*

Central Paihia

Self Contained Accommodation
Address: "Chalet Romantica",
6 Bedggood Close, Paihia
Name: Inge & Edi Amsler
Telephone: (09) 402 8270 **Fax**: (09) 402 8278
Email: CHALET ROMANTICA@xtra.co.nz
Beds: SC Mini-Suite with King-size bed or 2 singles.
Bellavista room with Queen-size bed.
Bathroom: 1 Ensuite, 1 Private
Tariff: Accommodtion only: Bellavista-room: $95 to $130 depending on season.
Mini-suite: $105 to $145 depending on season. Optional Swiss-style breakfast $10.50 pp.
Credit Cards: Visa/Mastercard. NZ B&B Vouchers accepted with seasonal surcharge
Nearest Town: Paihia - 6 mins stroll to town centre

Located on 2 acres, in the heart of Paihia, only a stroll away from all amenities & the beach, CHALET ROMANTICA is the perfect destination for your Bay of Islands holiday. The views are simply stunning! All rooms / suites open onto a sunny, private balcony with amazing vista over the Bay. Beautifully appointed guestrooms with comfortable beds, telephone, TV, radio, fridge, tea / coffee making, bathrooms with hairdryers, are offered to our valuable guests. The Mini-Suite (Honeymoon Suite) is fully self contained with its own kitchen. Guest laundry on site. An indoor heated saltwater swimming pool with exerjets, hot spa and gym are the features of this new, modern Homestead and its unique setting. The famous "SWISS CAFE & GRILL" on the waterfront is part of our set-up, where dining out is to everyone's delight and suits all budgets. CHALET ROMANTICA, a haven for the discerning traveller and adventurers. It is our pleasure to make arrangements and bookings for the great variety of tours and trips available in the Bay of Islands. Wir sprechen deutsch - on parle francais and we speak english.
Home Page: http://nz.com//webnz/bbnz/romantic.htm

Central Paihia
Self-contained Accommodation
Address: 34 Selwyn Road,
Paihia, Bay of Islands
Name: Iris Bartlett
Telephone: (09) 402 8458
Fax: (09) 402 8457 **Mobile**: (021) 684 580
Beds: Paradise Glory: 1 Double,
6 Single / Paradise View: 1 Double, 3 Single + fold out settee.
Bathroom: Private bathroom with comfortable bath, separate shower units.
Tariff: B&B (continental) Double $95, Single $59.
NZ B&B Vouchers accepted $25 surcharge
Nearest Town: Paihia 100 metres (very central)

Welcome to Paradise Glory / Paradise View - 2 fully self contained and separate stand alone units, nestled in virgin native forest with million dollar views over the beautiful Bay of Islands. My husband's family have lived in Paihia since the 1940's. Being early residents, we were able to secure Premium Sites. Paradise Glory - nestled tranquilly on its own, a Romantic Hideaway, an attraction for those wishing to unwind and get away from it all. Balcony at tree top level, gives the best views imaginable while you soak up that warm sun. Paradise View - 1 minute walk to Paihia Village, outdoor gazebo for relaxing. Both units - fully equipped kitchens, microwaves, refrigerators. Laundry has automatic washing machines. Linen, electric blankets, duvets supplied for your comfort. Continental breakfast to have at your leisure. You'll love these idyllic spots with birds singing, golf course, beach for swimming, fishing, bush walks, boating, spectacular ocean views.

Paihia Bay of Islands
Homestay+Self-contained Accom.
Address: 168 Marsden Road, Paihia
Name: Windermeree"
Telephone: (09) 402 7943
Fax: (09) 402 7943
Mobile: (025) 798 367
Beds: 3 queen (3 bedrooms)
Bathroom: 1 Ensuite, 1 Guests share
Tariff: B&B (continental) Double $80/$90,
Single $50. Credit Cards.
NZ B&B Vouchers accepted $12 surcharge
Nearest Town: Paihia

Welcome to historic Paihia and the home hospitality in our large spacious modern home. We have magnificent panoramic views of the Paihia Harbour, islands and historic Russell. We are 10 minutes walk to the centre of Paihia township full of good restaurants and a short ferry ride to Russell. We overlook to Waitangi Reserve and the world famous golf course, a short drive away is Kerikeri famous for its citrus orchards and its arts and crafts. Our residence is directly above a safe swimming beach. The self contained unit has its own terrace for you to enjoy the wonderful views. Bill and Molly enjoy meeting people. They own their own yacht and enjoy sailing. We are happy for you to stay as long as you like. Please no smoking inside, outside OK.
Directions: *Please phone.*

37

Paihia

B&B, also Self Contained
Address: 2 McMurray Road, Paihia
Name: Admiral's view Lodge.
Robyn and Peter Rhodes
Telephone: (09) 402 6236
Beds: 4 double, 6 Single (5 bedrooms)
Bathroom: 4 Private
Tariff: B&B (full/continental) Double $76-$95. Dinner $20. Credit Cards accepted. NZ B&B Vouchers accepted $15 surcharge (March till November)
Nearest Town: Paihia 500 metres

Admiral's View Lodge is in a quiet central location overlooking the Bay with spectacular sea views yet only 100 m walk to beach and a leisurely stroll to town centre, wharf and restaurants. Meals are served on our sunny sheltered deck. We have two bedrooms with private bathrooms, tea & coffee facilities, fridge, TV, own patios, seaviews. One twin/double room fully self contained with private bathroom, own patio. Also a 2-bedroom unit with two double, two single, own bathroom bath/shower, lounge/dining, bay window seat, fridge, toaster, microwave, tea & coffee facilities, seaviews. all units serviced daily to a high standard. Laundry facilities. Off-street parking. Residing in the Bay since 19756 we trust we understand Travellers' needs as we have travelled extensively ourselves and enjoy meeting people. Our interests are gardening, golf, fishing, square dancing. We have two very friendly cats, Cleo and Levi.

Paihia

Bed & Breakfast
Address: 30 Puketiro Place,
Te Haumi, Paihia, Bay of Islands
Name: Glenys and Steven Rossell
Telephone: 09 402 8492
Mobile: 025 277 2239
Beds: 1 Double, 1 Single (1 Bedroom)
Bathroom: 1 Ensuite
Tariff: B&B (continental) Double $70,
Single $35-$45, Children (5-12 years) $20.
NZ B&B Vouchers accepted
Nearest Town: Paihia approx 1 km.

Welcome to our home. Relax and Enjoy.
Your guest room sleeps 3, but to accommodate extra family members it also has a comfortable bed settee. Start your day with breakfast served in your room, to enjoy at your leisure. Tea and coffee always available. For guests without transport we are happy to collect from, or deliver to, Paihia or Opua. For guests with transport, safe off road parking is provided.
We have two children, Dean and Claire and also a cat called Five, so children are most welcome and our home is safe for them to play. We have a variety of interests and are quite well travelled. We look forward to helping to make your stay memorable. Would smokers please refrain from smoking inside.
Directions: *When heading into Paihia from Opua, turn left into Te Haumi Drive. Turn 1st right into Puketiro Place.*

Opua, Paihia

Homestay
Address: 'Rose Cottage',
Oromahoe Road, Opua, Bay of Islands
Name: Pat & Don Jansen
Telephone: (09) 402 8099
Fax: (09) 402 8099
Beds: 1 Double, 1 Twin, (2 bedrooms)
Bathroom: 1 Private (only 1 party taken at a time)
Tariff: B&B (continental) $40 pp. Credit Cards: Mastercard/Visa
NZ B&B Vouchers accepted $10 surcharge Dec-March incl)
Nearest Town: Paihia 5km

Our home is situated on a quiet peaceful site surrounded by native bush and enjoying extensive sea and rural views. Our area features many walking tracks both bush and coastal, boat trips, fishing, sailing or just relaxing on a quiet beach. Private wing sleeps 4 with a private entrance and deck area, fridge, TV, microwave, tea and coffee facilities. Pat is a retired nurse and Don a retired carpenter. Our interests include walking, gardening, reading, sailing, fishing, kauri woodwork and the area in which we live. Russell car ferry 1 km, Russell passenger ferry 5 km. Breakfast includes home-made bread and jams, fresh / cooked fruit, cereals, eggs any fashion, tea, coffee and juice. We enjoy meeting people and look forward to sharing with you our home and the beautiful area in which we live.
Non smokers preferred.
Directions: *Please phone*

Opua, Paihia

Homestay+Self-contained Accom.
Address: 7 Franklin Street, Opua
Name: Margaret Sinclair
Telephone: (09) 402 8285
Fax: (09) 402 8285
Beds: 1 Double, 2 Single (2 bedrooms)
Bathroom: 1 Family share.
Self-cont. Accom: 1 Double,
2 Single, separate toilet & shower.
Tariff: B&B (full) Double $65, Single $40,
Self-cont. Accom: Double $60, $10 each extra guest.
NZ B&B Vouchers accepted
Nearest Town: Paihia

You are welcome to stay in my lovely home above the harbour at Opua sharing the facilities with just myself. Enjoy panoramic views of the water where there is much boating activity - there always seems to be something happening.
You are handy to all the tourist activities of this area and there is a large heated spa pool to relax in on your return from your day's outing. You may like to wander in my garden which is my big interest. Downstairs there is a large 2 roomed fully self-contained unit with separate shower and toilet and a large private deck with the same stunning views. To find my home, take the road to Paihia from Whangarei. Turn right where the sign indicates the Opua-Russell ferry - this is Franklin St. My house is clearly visible on the left, on the seaward side of Franklin Street. I can meet bus arrivals at Paihia.

Opua, Paihia

Homestay+Self-contained Accom.
Address: 17 English Bay Rd,
Opua, Bay of Islands
Name: Frank & Vanessa Leadley
Telephone: (09) 402 7650
Fax: (09) 402-7650
Beds: 1 Double, 2 Single (2 Bedrooms)
Bathroom: 1 Ensuite, 1 Family share

Tariff: B&B (continental) Double $70, Single $50. NZ B&B Vouchers accepted
Nearest Town: Paihia 5 km. Russell ferry 2 mins.

"Seascape" has a tranquil setting on a bush-clad ridge. Enjoy spectacular views over the inner Bay of Islands, stroll 100m. through bush to the coastal walkway, enjoy our beautifully landscaped garden, experience the many activities the Bay offers, or relax on your private deck listening to the sounds of water and birds.
We invite you to share our home, and will welcome you with complimentary afternoon tea on arrival. We are very willing to help you plan your time in NZ. We are keen travellers, and our other interests include music, boating, fishing, gardening, Rotary, and floral art. And we enjoy life to the full!
As well as the Guest Room we have a fully self-contained flat with TV, laundry facilities, own entrance, etc. Look after yourselves at $70.00 per night, or have Bed and Breakfast at $80.00 per night double.
We love it here, and so will you.
Directions: *Phone or fax, or guest pick-up from Paihia. We love it here, so will you.*
Please note new sketch provided

Opua, Paihia

Homestay+Self Contained
Address: 10 Franklin St, Opua
Name: Florence Morrison
Telephone: (09) 402 7488
Fax: (09) 402 7488
Beds: 4 Single (2 bedrooms).
Self Contained flat: Queen bed,
Divan in lounge.
Private Courtyard, BBQ facilities.

Bathroom: 1 Guest share (Separate toilet and shower), plus 1 Family share
Tariff: B&B (continental or full on request) Double $65, Single $40, Dinner $20 pp, Children under 12 half price. Self Contained sunny flat $65, $15 per extra person. NZ B&B Vouchers accepted. Credit cards accepted.
Nearest Town: Paihia 5km.

The front of my home overlooks the beautiful and busy Port of Opua, and the back the tranquil reaches of Kawakawa River, alongside which the Bay of Islands vintage railway travels. Native bush nearby attracts many birds.
You are handy to all tourist attractions, bush and coastal walks. Opua has Boat Charters, yacht club, a restaurant on the water, or just relax on my deck to watch the boats.
I am a local, now retired, with plenty to do, gardening, the local theatre group, family and simply enjoying the Bay. Buses to Cape Reinga pass the door.
Guest pick up from Paihia.
Directions: *Whangarei / Paihia Rd - turn right at Opua (as for Ferry to Russell). No 10 Franklin St will welcome you.*

Russell
Bed & Breakfast/Homestay
Address: 67 Wellington Street
(to the left), Russell
Name: Kay Bosanquet
Telephone: (09) 403 7843
Fax: (09) 403 7843
Mobile: 025 2723 672
Beds: 2 Double, 3 Single (5 bedrooms)
Bathroom: 1 Private, 1 Guests share for one double and one single
(Hair driers and robes)
Tariff: B&B (full) $50 per person.
NZ B&B Vouchers accepted $20 surcharge per person.
Nearest Town: Whangarei 3/4 hour drive. Russell 5 minutes.

My home overlooks Russell Bay with magnificent water and bush views. Born and bred in Northland I take great pride in showing my guests NZ's first capital. I love every type of fishing and frequently escort my guests out game fishing. I am a national doll collector and I love the world coming to stay with me. Meals are usually served on the terrace. I have found my guests like to explore and sample the different fish restaurants that abound in Russell. We have several lovely walks handy, as well as golf, bowls, diving, cruises and yacht charters. I belong to Russell RSA, bowling, gamefishing, yachting clubs, if my guests wish to meet our locals I take them to whichever club interests them. All I ask of my guests is to completely relax and use my home as theirs.
Directions: *By car - take Opua car ferry to Russell, through Russell, on left Wellington St., a no exit road and we are just up the hill on the right - letter box signed. I do have an elevator.*

Russell, Matakaraka Beach
Homestay
Address: Major Bridge Drive,
R.D.1, Russell
Name: Eva Brown
Telephone: (09) 403 7431
Fax: (09) 403 7431
Beds: 1 Double, 1 Single (1 Bedroom)
Bathroom: 1 Private
Tariff: B&B (full) Double $75, Single $50.
Dinner: Pasta and wine $16 per person.
Credit cards. NZ B&B Vouchers accepted $10 surcharge
Nearest Town: Russell, 7 km by car or 20 minutes rowing by our rowboat

Our wooden house is near a quiet beach in a sheltered bay. We recommend walking shoes to our guests because parking is on the top of the hill and our house is by the water. A footpath leads down through a tunnel of native fern, kanuka and manuka. We provide a dinghy free for fishing or crossing to Russell, the historic first capital of New Zealand. Beach walks start at our door. Guests may swim right off our beach or take a sailing trip to the islands. Historic places, Maori pa sites, kauri trees, golf, diving, dolphin watching and kayaking are all nearby. Breakfasts range from fresh fruit, muesli and yoghurt to wholemeal toast with homemade jams, marmalade and bacon and eggs. Please phone ahead as we have only one guest room. We gladly meet guests at the ferry.

Russell

Homestay+Self-Contained Accom.
Address: 2 Robertson Road, Russell (PO Box 203)
Name: 'Te Manaaki' Sharyn & Dudley Smith
Telephone: (09) 403 7200
Fax: (09) 403 7537 **Mobile**: (025) 972 177
Email: triple.b@xtra.co.nz

Beds: Self-Contained Villa: 1 King (1 bedroom)
Homestay Unit: 1 King or 2 Singles (1 bedroom)
Bathroom: 2 Ensuite
Tariff: B&B (full) Villa: Double/Single $150, Homestay: Double/Single $110,
Extra persons $15, Credit Cards. Discounts for extended stays.
NZ B&B Vouchers accepted Vouchers accepted for Homestay unit, $40 surcharge
Nearest Town: Central Russell

We have been welcoming B&B guests to 'Te Manaaki' for over ten years. Our property is centrally situated on an elevated section overlooking the historic town and harbour of Russell - a two minute stroll from the village shops, restaurants, and wharf. Opportunities for Island Cruising and Fishing aboard our charter boat "Triple B".We have two choices of accommodation:An attractively appointed sunny spacious de luxe self-contained Villa with its own private entrance, garden, sundeck and terrace. The Villa enjoys magnificent sea and village views, has a Super-King size bed and tasteful ensuite. Kitchen facilities, TV and BBQ. Breakfast available on request.Our new modern home has a large ground-floor, self contained unit with private ensuite facilities, TV, refrigerator, tea / coffee making. A cosy Bay-Window in which to relax and enjoy the fine Harbour views. Off street parking adjacent to the unit. Breakfast is included in the tariff.
Home Page: http://nz.com/webnz/bbnz/smith.htm

Russell

Farmstay, Self-contained Accom
Address: Wairoro Park, Aucks Road,
PO Box 53, Okiato, Russell
Name: Yan & Beryl Boerop
Telephone: (09) 403 7255
Beds: 3 - 1 bedroom chalets

Bathroom: 3 Private
Tariff: Double $80, Single $80 (Breakfast is not served, all ingredients for a cooked English type breakfast can be supplied as an optional extra - $5).
Credit Cards (Visa/MC). Tariff: from 21 December to 1 March P.O.A.
NZ B&B Vouchers accepted $12 surcharge from 1 March to 21 Dec.
Nearest Town: Russell

Wairoro Park is a 160 acre (64 ha.) coastal estate in central Bay of Islands. Two thirds is native bush, the remainder is pasture. The beach is privately owned and accessible only to our guests.
Our guest accommodation consists of 3 fully detached 1 bedroom chalets situated 60 metres from the beach. The double beds are Queen size. All chalets are tastefully appointed and fully self contained, all have sundecks and have gorgeous sea views. Our artesian water is arguably the purest in the world. In the interest of preservation we have installed heated towel rails in each chalet where your top quality bathtowels are kept permanently dry and are changed twice a week.
Just up from the sandy beach is a shady lawn, tastefully illuminated after dark to enjoy your own romantic barbecue dinner. In addition to the summary below we also have a 6 metre sailing yacht and we might be persuaded to take you out for a day. We encourage our guests to bring their pets and we do not recommend our place to those who are intolerant towards dogs and cats.

Russell - Waipiro Bay

Homestay
Address: 'Gasthaus Waipiro Bay',
P. O. Box 224, Russell
Name: Beate & Thomas Lauterbach
Telephone: (09) 403 7095
Fax: (09) 403 7095
E-Mail: lauterbach@igrin.co.nz
Beds: 2 Queen, 1 Single (2 bedrooms)
Bathroom: 1 Ensuite, 1 Private
Tariff: B&B (special) Double $135/$150, Reduction for singles,
Dinner $45, Credit cards.
Nearest Town: 15km east of Russell on the coastal scenic drive

Dream of a place, an artist's home above a bay, the Pacific Ocean on the horizon, islands to explore, fish to catch, beaches and forests to roam, nature at your doorstep. This world of space and light has inspired artist Thomas Lauterbach to paint strong images of land, sea and the Maori people.
We offer our guests a warm and imaginative home of timber and stone, comfortable bedrooms with spectacular views. Enjoy the spacious private living-room, the open fire place and works of art.
Relax on verandas amidst the beautiful garden or follow a romantic path to the beach. Explore the islands on a local boat - bring home your own fish.
We love to cook gourmet meals with flavours from Italy to the South Pacific.
For a taste of heaven on earth - come and let us spoil you a little.

Russell

Homestay
Address: 'Treetops', 6 Pinetree Lane,
Te Wahapu Rd, Russell, Bay of Islands
Name: John & Vivienne Nathan
Telephone: (09) 403 7475
Fax: (09) 403 7475
Mobile: (025) 272 8881
Beds: 1 King, 1 Double (2 bedrooms)
Bathroom: 1 guests share

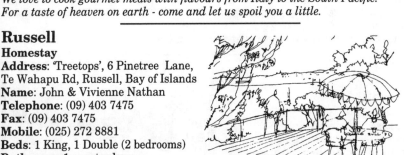

Tariff: B&B (full) Double $85, Single $65, Dinner $30 (incl. wine), Credit cards. NZ B&B Vouchers accepted
Nearest Town: Russell 7km.

Our home is situated at the end of Te Wahapu Peninsula, 2.5km from the Main Russell-Opua Road. We are surrounded by native bush, and Tuis and Fantails are our constant companions. Kiwis are often heard during the night.
Both upstairs bedrooms have beautiful sea views from your bed; one room has colour TV. The guest bathroom is also upstairs. Guests are welcome to sit in the spa pool and watch the sun set over Paihia across the bay.
A track through the bush leads down to the beach where you are welcome to use our dinghy for fishing or a pleasant row out to Torretorre Island for a picnic. Guest barbecue available.
Historic Russell is a mere ten minute drive and offers a unique charm.
Cooked or continental breakfasts are available and you are welcome to join us for dinner. Please phone in advance. Major credit cards accepted.

Russell

Homestay+Self-contained Accom.
Address: 'Inn-The-Pink' B&B,
1 Oneroa Road, Russell
Name: Mary & Kent MacLachlan
Telephone: (09) 403 7347
Fax: (09) 403 7347
Email: mary&kent@xtra.co.nz
Beds: 1 Queen, 4 Single (3 bedrooms)
Bathroom: 1 Ensuite, 1 Private
Tariff: B&B (full/continental) Double $100-$120, Single $60,
No Dinner, Children under 12 half price.
Nearest Town: Central Russell

A warm and friendly welcome awaits you at Inn-the-Pink. Enjoy our unique location with magnificent harbour views overlooking Russell and across the bay to historic Waitangi. Our house sits nestled amongst beautiful gardens, just a few minutes stroll from the picturesque waterfront of downtown Russell. We have two choices of accommodation. Our separate self contained unit has a queen-sized bed, bathroom, fridge, TV, microwave, and coffee/tea making facilities. Relax on your own private deck and enjoy incredible sunsets over the bay. Our smoke-free home has two comfortable twin bedrooms with a private bathroom. Join us for a hearty breakfast which includes fresh orange juice, fresh fruit salad, home-made muesli, yoghurt, muffins and a variety of delicious cooked breakfasts. We are a Kiwi / Canadian couple who enjoy sailing, fishing, gardening and tennis. We spend July & August cruising Lake Ontario.
Home Page: http://www.bay-of-islands.co.nz/inthepnk

Russell

Homestay
Address: 21 Titore Way,
Russell (last house on right)
Name: Michael & Robin Watson
Telephone: (09) 403 7458
Fax: (09) 403 7458
Mobile: 025 765 459
Email: mikerobe@igrin.co.nz
Beds: Guest wing with 2 double bedrooms (one Queen, one 2 Singles), with bathroom and separate toilet.
Bathroom: 1 Private (We cater for one couple only or 4 people in the same party, usually)
Tariff: B&B (full) Double $100, Single $70, Credit Card (VISA).
Nearest Town: Russell 2 minute drive or 10 minute walk

Tokouru, our home is a modern natural timber house with magnificent bush and sea view and large sunny decks, tranquil and relaxing. Bush walks to Russell Village, Flagstaff Hill and a private beach begin at our property.
We are keen cruising yachties with our own 40 foot yacht. The use of a tennis court is available. Historic Russell has many tourist attractions and daily trips.
Predominantly Bed & Breakfast, dinner is supplied only by arrangement. There are excellent local restaurants open nightly or a 10 minutes ferry trip to Paihia can be enjoyed for an evening meal. We have one friendly black Labrador - Ben.

Russell
Historic Guest House + S.C. Cottage
Address: 'Ounuwhao' Matauwhi Bay, Russell
Name: Allan & Marilyn Nicklin
Telephone: (09) 403 7310 **Fax**: (09) 403 8310
Email: ounuwhao@bay-of-islands.co.nz
Beds: 4 Queen, 2 Single (4 bedrooms, 3 with wash-stands in rooms)
Bathroom: 2 Ensuite, 1 Guests share (ie. 2 showers, 2 sep. toilets)
Tariff: B&B (special) Double $95, $120 with ensuite,
Single $60-$100. Children under 12yrs half price (if sharing with adults). Self
contained cottage: 1 Queen, 1 Double, 1 single (2 bedrooms),
full facilities, self catering, suitable for 4 adults or family of 4, $150 per night
(maximum 4 persons). Prices will change from 1.8.99
Nearest Town: 1km from Russell Village

*Welcome to historic Russell; take a step-back into a bygone era and spend some time
with us in our delightful, nostalgic, immaculately restored Victorian Villa (Circa
1894). Enjoy your own large guest lounge; tea/coffee and biscuits always available,
with open fire in the cooler months, and wrap-around verandahs for you to relax and
take-in the warm sea breezes.*
*Each of our four double rooms have traditional wallpapers and paintwork, with
handmade patchwork quilts and fresh flowers to create a lovingly detailed, traditional
romantic interior. Breakfast is served in our farmhouse kitchen around the large kauri
dining table or al-fresco on the verandah if you wish. It is an all homemade affair; from
the freshly baked fruit and nut bread, to the yummy daily special and the jam
conserves. Our self-contained cottage is set in park-like grounds for your privacy and
enjoyment: with two double bedrooms, it is ideal for a family or two couples travelling
together. It has a large lounge overlooking the reserve and out into the bay, a sun-room
and fully self-contained kitchen. Wonderful for people looking for that special place
for peace and time-out. Breakfast is available if required.*
*Complimentary afternoon tea on arrival. Laundry service available. We look forward
to meeting you soon. Our homes are SMOKE-FREE. We are closed June and July. We
are a member of NZ Heritage Inns Group.*

EXPERIENCE OUR HISTORIC B&B. ENJOY A WORLD OF DIFFERENCE.

Home Page: http://nz.com/heritage inns/ounuwhao

Russell
Homestay
Address: 6 Ashby Street, Russell
Name: "Brown Lodge",
Roly and Joan Brown
Telephone: (09) 403 7693
Fax: (09) 403 7683
Beds: 2 Queen, 1 Single (2 Bedrooms)
Bathroom: 2 Ensuite
Tariff: B&B (continental) Cooked breakfast $10 extra, Double $160, Single $150.
Extra person in room $50, Credit Cards (VISA/MC). Rates may change from 1st
November 1999 NZ B&B Vouchers accepted $90 surcharge
Nearest Town: Russell 3 mins walk

*Quite central position with fine sea views over Russell and the Bay. One of the
interesting new homes architecturally designed in keeping with the historic nature of
Russell. An all timber construction featuring New Zealand Kauri, Rimu, Douglas Fir
and Pine. A special place to stay and share an intimate glimpse of a Russell life style.
A look at craftsmanship of today with old world atmosphere combined with modern
private facilities and true home comforts.*

*Friendly and personal attention is assured. Breakfast at our antique Kauri table
amongst Rimu wood panelling, old bricks and over 100 years old re-sited arched
windows. Furnished with antiques, Persian carpets throughout and examples of
Roly's Kauri furniture and cabinetry.*

*Air conditioning and heating for all year round comfort. Two private spacious suites,
each with their own entrance from the main foyer, all have sea views, queen size beds,
one single available, ensuites, TV, fridge and tea / coffee making facilities. Russell
township is easy 3 minute walk to restaurants, shops, wharf. Relax on the front
veranda with peaceful sea views to Waitangi and Paihia.*

*We can advise and book restaurants, boat cruises around the Bay and bus trips to Cape
Reinga etc.*

*Smoke free home, safe off street parking, no wheel chair access. Please phone or fax
ahead to avoid disappointment.*

Home Page: http://nz.com/webnz/bbnz/brownI.htm or http://www.friars.co.nz/hosts/
brown.html

Russell

Homestay
Address: Pomare Rd, Russell
Name: Lesley's
Telephone: (09) 403 7099
Beds: 1 Double, 1 Single (1 bedroom)
Bathroom: 1 Private
Tariff: B&B (special) Double $85,
Single $60, Children half price, Dinner $20pp.
NZ B&B Vouchers accepted $20 surcharge
Nearest Town: Russell 1 Km

My home is in a quiet cul-de-sac and the design inspired by Greece where I once lived. When the weather is fine you can breakfast on the verandah and look out to Matauwhi Bay and Russell Boat Club otherwise relax in the glassed in breezeway with fresh waffles and maple syrup. Or you may like a traditional English breakfast using fresh eggs from our chickens. The guest room has its own entrance and large bathroom featuring an antique bath set in a sun window. Sometimes our guests feel like 'staying at home' for dinner and as a family we enjoy sharing a meal with people from other parts. My two children are comfortable mixing with people from other cultures. Our combined interests include travelling, music, gardening and art (I did the sketch) and our cat Mudge. It is a ten minute walk to Historic Russell. Check out this website http://www.bay.of.islands.co.nz.
Home Page: http://www.bay.of.islands.co.nz.
Directions: *Please phone.*

Russell

Historic Coastal Homestead
Address: Aucks Road, RD 1, Russell
Name: Orongo Bay Homestead
Telephone: (09) 403 7527
Fax: (09) 403 7675
Email: orongo.bay@clear.net.nz
Beds: 2 rooms (Queen),

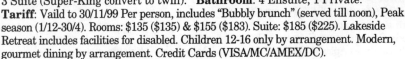

3 Suite (Super-King convert to twin).   **Bathroom**: 4 Ensuite, 1 Private.
Tariff: Vaild to 30/11/99 Per person, includes "Bubbly brunch" (served till noon), Peak season (1/12-30/4). Rooms: $135 ($135) & $155 ($183). Suite: $185 ($225). Lakeside Retreat includes facilities for disabled. Children 12-16 only by arrangement. Modern, gourmet dining by arrangement. Credit Cards (VISA/MC/AMEX/DC).
Nearest Town: Russell

Known as "NZ's First American Consulate", in 17 private acres by bush-clad bay rich in history. Nearby 144 unspoilt islands invite boating pleasure, world-record game fishing, vintage aircraft flights, coastal horse-riding, diving and watersports. Built in the 1860s, now completely restored and classified by Historic Places Trust, looking across the Bay of Islands to Waitangi, New Zealand's birthplace.Rooms have views across spring-fed duck lake and organic orchard to private native bush, or sea views. The Retreat has lake balconies, adjacent to the Finnish sauna and plunge pool. Fluffy robes, hair-dryers, complimentary native plant skin cream, massage by arrangement. Airport transfers by coach or Rolls Royce.A pampering haven with native kauri ceilings, large open fire, organically-grown herbs, cuisine featuring local meat, fish and oysters. Champagnes and fine New Zealand wines from oldest-known private underground cellar. Smoke-free.
Hosts: Christopher Wharehinga Swannell, and writer / broadcaster Michael Hooper (Winner, Guild of Foodwriters' Food & Travel Award 1994 and 1995).
Homepage: http://nz.com/webnz/bbnz/orango.htm

Russell - Okiato

Homestay B&B

Address: Aimeo Cottage,
Okiato Point Road, R.D.1 Russell
Name: Annie & Helmuth Hörmann
Telephone: (09) 403 7494 **Fax**: (09) 403 7494
Mobile: 025-272 2393
Email: aimeo-cottage.nz@xtra.co.nz
Beds: 2 Double, 1 Single (2 Bedrooms)
Bathroom: 2 Private
Tariff: B&B (special) Double $95, Single $75, Children $15, request.
Off season rates, Credit cards.

NZ B&B Vouchers accepted $20 Surcharge : Dec 24 - 15 Mar
Nearest Town: 9km eastw. to Russell

*Aimeo Cottage " a quiet place to relax" Your hosts Annie and Helmuth Hörmann sailed half
way around the world to find this beautiful quiet place in the heart of the Bay of Islands. We
can communicate in English, French, German and some Spanish. Aimeo Cottage is built on
the hill of Okiato Point, a secluded peninsula overlooking the Bay. Only a stone throw from
the site of the country's first Government House and just across the Bay, where the British and
the Maori leaders signed the historic Treaty of Waitangi in 1840. Your accommodation is a
comfortable, private self-contained studio, or a double bed room with private bathroom and
separate entrance. We serve continental or cooked breakfast. Dinner is available on request.
Rates are very moderate. In 10 minutes you are in historic Russell, the site of many historic
buildings, and interesting museum and art galleries. There are bushwalks right from the
door; we provide advice for sightseeing or local tours and you can use our bicycles for free.
Beaches are close by.Ask for off-season rates.*
Home Page: http://www.bay-of-islands.co.nz/aimeo/index.html
Directions: *You find us 200 m behind the car ferry, first road on the left.*

Russell - Te Wahapu

Homestay+Self-contained Accom.
Address: Te Wahapu Road, Russell, R.D. 1
Name: Heino & Brigitte Sass
 'BRISA COTTAGE'
Telephone: (09) 403 7757 **Fax**: (09) 403 7757
Email: brisa@xtra.co.nz
Beds: Self-contained Cottage: 1 Queen (1 bedroom);
Self-contained Aptm: 1 Double (1 bedroom) **Bathroom**: 2 Ensuite
Tariff: B&B (continental) High season (Dec to Easter): Cottage: Double $115, Single
$105. Apartment: Double $95, Single $85. Low Season (after Easter to Dec) Cottage:
$95, Single $85. Apartment: Double $75, Single $65. Extra Person $20 NZ B&B
Vouchers accepted $30/$20 surcharge for Cottage. $25/$10 surcharge for Apartment
Nearest Town: Russell 7 Kms

*BRISA COTTAGE is situated on Te Wahapu Peninsula, tucked away in an idyllic position,
lush native bush, bird life, own beach, views over Orongo Bay. 1 studio-style cottage (separate),
and 1 Apartment (attached to our house) available. Studio and Apartment are new, with
Ensuite, kitchen facilities, cosy and comfortably furnished, TV/Radio. Equipped with firm
slate-bed, Duvet & Patchwork Quilt for a restful sleep.We serve a wholesome breakfast in our
house.We share our 1 acre waterfront property with our friendly dog, cat and some chickens.
Dinghy, fishing gear and BBQ for guest use.A snug hideaway, yet only 10 minutes drive to
historic Russell, which offers several excellent restaurants, craft shops, and an Art Gallery.We
sailed from Germany on our yacht BRISA in the early 70s and believe we found just the right
spot.Come, enjoy this private and tranquil place with us for a while.
Non smokers preferred.*

Parekura Bay, Russell

Self-contained Accommodation
Address: "Carpe Diem", Parekura Bay,
Rawhiti Road, Russell
Name: Martin & Jewel Collett
Telephone: (09) 403 8015
Fax: (09) 403 8015 **Mobile**: (025) 750 814
Beds: 1 Double, 2 Single (2 bedrooms)
Bathroom: 1 Private, 1 Family share
Tariff: B&B (full) Double $75 (share), $95 (private). Single $45 (share), $50 (private). Dinner $35. NZ B&B Vouchers accepted 1st May to 31st October
Nearest Town: Russell

Our house is an upstairs-downstairs, we offer guests our downstairs unit, which is fully self-contained. The view is beautiful. Be part of the Bay of Islands, you relax and enjoy, we will do our best to make your stay memorable. We are situated 20km east of Russell - walk to the beach, walk a track and experience the magic of the Bay of Islands, or just sit and enjoy the view. Historic Russell is always worth a visit, hop a ferry, large or small, across to Paihia, or the vehicular ferry to Opua, from there you can visit the Treaty House at Waitangi - or drive to Kerikeri - take a bus to the Ninety Mile Beach, or a "Quick-Cat" to the hole in the rock - we will arrange for you any activity you may wish to do. - See you soon. -We also rent on a weekly basis, we supply linen, you cook for yourself. - Rates on request - Boat ramp - Mooring when available.

Russell

Guest House
Address: Main Road, Russell
Name: Arcadia Lodge
Telephone: (09) 403 7756
Fax: (09) 403 7657
Email: arcadialodge@xtra.co.nz
Beds: 1 Queen, 5 Double,
2 Suites (Queen) (8 bedrooms)
Bathroom: 3 Guests share, 3 Ensuite

Tariff: B&B special and continental) Double $100, Single $85, Suite $140, Credit Cards (VISA/MC). NZ B&B Vouchers accepted $30 per night/per room
Nearest Town: Russell 0.5km

We are an 1899 rambling two storied Tudor guesthouse with magnificent views across the bay and expansive Olde English gardens. Only a five minute flat walk into Russell village. The romantic bedrooms are beautifully furnished in keeping with the era. There is a choice of double rooms with share bathrooms or Suites comprising bedroom with queensize bed, separate lounge and ensuite bathrooms. The Victorian style lounge and breakfast room is spacious. This is the "heart" of Arcadia, where we host guests to welcome refreshments and informal get togethers. Tours and excursions depart from the local wharf and we are happy to book these and ensure you get the most out of your visit to romantic Russell and the Bay of Islands. We are proud Kiwi Norhlanders and will be honoured to welcome you to the charm and character that has made this lodge a favourite for nearly 100 years!
Peter and Jolene.
Home Page: webmaster@bay-of-islands.co.nz

Russell

Mako Lodge *and Fishing Charters*

Homestay+Self-contained Accom.
Address: "Mako Lodge & Fishing Charters",
Te Wahapu Road, R.D.1, Russell
Name: Graeme & Jean McIntosh
Telephone: (09) 403 7770 or Toll free: 0800 625 669 **Fax**: (09) 403 7770
Mobile: 025 739 787 **Email**: mako.lodge_charters@xtra.co.nz
Beds: Homestay: 1 Double (1 bedroom) Lodge: 1 King, 2 Single, 1 Bedsettee
(double). Studio: 4 Single bunk beds
Bathroom: 1 Private in each
Tariff: B&B (full) Double/Single $95, Dinner $25pp. Lodge: High season $150
Double, addit persons $20, Low season $120 Double, addit persons $20. Studio:
High Season, Double $95 extras $15, Low Season, $75 extras $15. (Breakfasts
and dinners are optional extras). Credit Cards (MC/VISA).
Nearest Town: Russell 7km

Mako Lodge is set in quiet seclusion on the shores of Orongo Bay on the beautiful Te Wahapu Peninsula. We are just 3km on towards Russell from the car ferry.B&B guests amenities include own bathroom, TV, refrigerator, tea / coffee making, verandah, plus garden and water views from your bedroom.Our adjacent luxury lodge can sleep up to 6, has full kitchen facilities, TV, video, laundry and BBQ. Additional accommodation also available in our studio - sleeps 4 singles. You are welcome to amble down the bush path to the waterfront lawn where dinghies are available to explore the sheltered waters of the inner Bay. Perhaps catch your own Flounder or John Dory which we will prepare for your breakfast, or embark on one of our famous light tackle fishing charters on "MAKO" our new 28' fast, modern diesel launch and experience the wonderful fishing and sightseeing of the Bay of Islands.We have a very friendly golden labrador called Tessa. Mako lodge has a 4 star Qualmark rating.
Home Page: htpp://www.bay-of-islands.co.nz/mako

Russell

Homestay
Address: "The Eyrie",
7 Prospect St., Russell
Name: Harold & Susan Williams
Telephone: (09) 403 7306
Fax: (09) 403 7306
Beds: 2 Double (2 bedrooms)
Bathroom: 1 Guests share
Tariff: B&B (special). Double $95, Single $75, Credit Cards.
Nearest Town: Russell - 2 mins to Russell waterfront

Our unforgettable view from "The Eyrie" (eagles nest) which is perched on one of the many hills in Russell, encompasses the township, across the bay to Waitangi where the historic treaty was signed in 1840. Watch the ferries plying the bay to Paihia and yachts sailing in the clear water to the outer islands. Relax in the quiet seclusion of our courtyard garden. We have built our home with the view and sun in mind and our guest bedrooms face the bay and Russell and open onto a verandah surrounding the house. Breakfasts are special with home cooked food awaiting you. Susan drives the local tour bus, giving a commentary on the history of the bay. We both enjoy boating and gardening. We invite you to come and share this lovely spot with us and enjoy our friendly hospitality and we'll make this a stay to remember. Our home is smoke free.

Russell

Homestay
Address: 11 Gould Street, Russell
Name: Danielle & Dino Fossi
Telephone: (09) 403 8299
Fax: (09) 403 8299
Beds: 4 Double,
2 Single (5 bedrooms)
Bathroom: 1 Private,
1 Guests share, 1 Ensuite

La Veduta

Tariff: B&B (continental) Double $95-$130,
Children $25, Dinner $45pp,
Credit Cards (VISA/MC). NZ B&B Vouchers accepted Surcharge $30
Nearest Town: Russell 0.5km

Enjoy our mix of traditional European culture (food) in the midst of the beautiful Bay of Islands, historic heartland of New Zealand. La Veduta is the perfect pied-a-terre for your Northland holiday. Only few minutes walk from the township, sandy beach, bush walks. Relax, or we can arrange a wide range of activities. Deep see fishing, sailing, diving, kayaking etc... Restaurants and ferry are handy. Transport is available for arrivals and departures Kerikeri / Whangarei Airport. We offer our guests a warm welcome and personalised service. By arrangement you may wish to share a 5 course meal with your hosts. English, French, Italian spoken. Large garden and balcony for sunset lovers, TV room, billiard room, laundry.
Home Page: www.KiwihomeCo.NZ/veduta

Russell

Self Contained Accommodation
Address: 4 Russell Heights Road, Russell, Bay of Islands
Name: Eldon and Gill Jackson
Telephone: (09) 403 7109
Fax: (09) 403 7159
Mobile: (025) 276 2870
Email: paws.for.thought@bay-of-islands.co.nz
Beds: 1 Double (1 bedroom)
Bathroom: 1 Private
Tariff: S/C Double $100 ($20 each additional person). Not suitable for children.
Nearest Town: Russell - 10 min walk to village, down hill.

Our self-contained apartment / unit is adjacent to our home with magnificent seaviews and a beautiful garden for you to enjoy, and is located in a quiet no-exit street, just 5 minutes drive from the village and beautiful Long Beach.
The unit has one double bedroom, plus a double sofa / settee in the lounge for extra guests. The fully equipped kitchen adjoins a lounge and dining area, which opens onto a sunny outdoor deck where you can watch the spectacular sunsets that Russell is famous for. Tea and coffee are provided but the unit is self catering. We have lived in Russell for 13 years and would love to share the history and scenic attractions of the region with you. Eldon loves boating and fishing, Gill is a keen gardener. We share our home with a cat and a small friendly dog. Friendly hospitality awaits you.
Home Page: http://www.bay-of-islands.co.nz/paws

51

Russell

Homestay
Address: Pukematu Lodge,
PO Box 145,Russell.
Top of Flagstaff Road Hill,
opp Entrance to Flagstaff Pole.
Name: Kay and Colwyn Shortland
Telephone: 09 403 8500
Fax: 09 403 8500
Mobile: 025 245 7640
Beds: 2 Queen (2 bedrooms each with a Sofa sleeper)
Bathroom: 2 Ensuite
Tariff: B&B (special) Double $195, Single $175. Dinner $50 pp.
Credit cards accepted. Non Smoking
Nearest Town: Russell

Pukematu Lodge named after the hill it sits upon is elevated high above 9 acres of native bush adjacent to the Russell township and Kororareka Bay. You will be amazed with the breath taking views offered in all directions that invite you to gaze upon the natural beauty of this special place.Your private suite is furnished in recycled rimu stylishly decorated with its own bathroom, tea / coffee making facilities, TV, video, sofa, table and chairs complimented with Kay's personal touch.A delicious breakfast will be served in the privacy of your suite of on the deck. Evening meals and picnic hampers are provided by arrangement. An evening BBQ or Hangi is just magical and fresh fish and seafood from the bay speaks for itself.We serve in season home grown organic fruit and vegetables including vegetarian cuisine.We believe a high standard of service and hospitality is paramount and invite you to experience a memorable stay at Pukematu Lodge of Russell.

Russell

Homestay, Self Contained Accommodation
Address: 44 Du Fresne Place,
Russell, Bay of Islands
Name: Villa Helios
Telephone: (09) 403 7229
Fax: (09) 403 7229
Mobile: (025) 581 815
Email: villa.helios@xtra.co.nz
Beds: 2 Queen, 4 Twin (4 bedrooms)
Bathroom: 2 Ensuite, 1 Private
Tariff: B&B (continental) The Villa $225, Island Suite $185, Russell room $135.
Dinner $45. Credit Cards accepted.
Nearest Town: Russell 2 km

Enjoy the bush, coastal and ocean views at the Santorini of the Bay of Islands. We call ourselves VILLA HELIOS because we take our name from the sun and the architecture is Greek. Guest from New York: "the view was the most spectacular I have ever seen". We provide bed and continental breakfast in the guest wing. The ISLAND SUITE has a fully equipped lounge and a queen ensuite bedroom. The RUSSELL ROOM has two large twin beds and ensuite. All accommodation has TV, fridge, stereo etc. The VILLA is a self-contained two storied cottage with extras such as a barbecue and open fireplace. VILLA HELIOS was built in 1996 with guest privacy in mind. We have featured in "NZ House & Garden" and Australia's Channel 9 "Getaway" programme. VILLA HELIOS is at Tapeka Point and just 2 km from Russell over the historic Flagstaff Hill. We have two black poodle dogs.
Home Page: http://babs.com.au/nz/helios.htm

Kohukohu

Homestay/Guest House
Address: Rakautapu Rd,
Kohukohu, Northland
Name: 'Harbour Views Guest House'
Jacky & Bil
Telephone: (09) 405 5815
Fax: (09) 405 5865
Beds: 1 Queen, 2 Single (2 bedrooms/2nd bedroom is twin)
Bathroom: 1 Private (We only take one party at a time)
Tariff: B&B (full/continental) Double $80,
Single $40, Dinner $18.
NZ B&B Vouchers accepted
Nearest Town: Kerikeri, Kaitaia and Kaikohe

Harbour Views Guest House is situated in historic Kohukohu, on the north side of the Hokianga Harbour. Our fully and beautifully restored kauri home is set in two acres of gardens and trees and commands a spectacular view of the upper harbour. Our guest rooms, opening out onto a private and sunny verandah, and with their own luxurious bathroom, are in a private wing of the house, but our guests are encouraged to feel part of the family and to use our living areas. Evening meals are prepared using home grown produce in season. We have lived in this area for twenty years and are interested in and knowledgeable about its history and geography. Kohukohu, once the hub of Northland's kauri timber industry, is now a friendly and charming village. Apart from exploring the village, day trips to the rugged West Coast, Cape Reinga, Bay of Islands and Opononi are all possibilities.
Laundry facilities available.

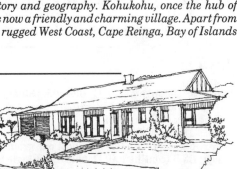

Kaikohe

Farmstay
Address: "Taraire Grove", RD 2,
Kaikohe, State Highway 12
Name: L. A. Sandford
Telephone: (09) 401 0623
Beds: 4 Single
(2 bedrooms: 2 single beds in each room)
Bathroom: 1 Private (Guests only)
Tariff: B&B (full/continental) Double $75, Single $50, School age children half price, under 5yrs $10 each, Dinner $28 (3 course), Campervans $25.
Credit Cards NZ B&B Vouchers accepted
Nearest Town: Kaikohe 5 kms

Spacious 4 bedroom, 2 bathroom home on 42 acre farm with 10 acres in native bush situated on State Highway 12 with name "Taraire Grove" on front gate, 5km from Kaikohe township, five minutes to Ngawha Springs Hot Pools, known for curative and relaxing bathing, two minutes to 18 hole golf course club also squash courts - twenty minutes to Bay of Islands, Paihia and Kerikeri on East Coast, 40 minutes to Opononi on West Coast. One hour to Waipoua Kauri Forest containing the well known huge kauri Tane Mahuta. We have retired and both very much enjoy meeting people. We welcome you to our home and the Bay of Islands and hope you will enjoy your stay.

Hokianga

Guest House
Address: Main Road, Horeke
Name: 'Riverhead Guest House'
(Dick Holdaway)
Telephone: (09) 401 9610
Fax: (09) 401 9610
Beds: 3 Double, 3 Single (4 bedrooms)
Bathroom: 1 Guests share, 1 Family share
Tariff: B&B (full) Double $65-$75, Single $35-$52, School children half price, Dinner $25. Credit Cards. NZ B&B Vouchers accepted
Nearest Town: Kaikohe

Riverhead is a fine 1870's Kauri farmhouse which has been beautifully restored by your hosts, and now offers Victorian elegance and style with 20th century convenience. Dick and Lila are retired folk who will make you welcome and comfortable in true country style sharing with you their wide knowledge of the North. Riverhead overlooks Horeke Village and the head of the Hokianga Harbour, an area rich in history and homeland of the powerful Ngapuhi tribe and the focus of much at NZ's early history with numerous pa sites and quaint old pioneer towns like Kohukohu and Rawene. Its central location makes it a superb base for exploration, within easy reach of Bay of Islands, Whangaroa and Mangonui, Kaitaia and the Ninety Mile Beach, and the Waipoua forest/Opononi area. Marine charters are available on the harbour and horse treks, bushwalks, etc are available locally. The relaxed and hospitable style of the community make a stay in Horeke a memorable experience.

Rawene

Homestay
Address: 'Hokingamai', P.O. Box 105, Gundry Street, Rawene
Name: David & Gillian McGrath
Telephone: (09) 405 7782
Beds: 1 Double, 2 Single (2 bedrooms)
Bathroom: 1 Private (we only host one group at a time)
Tariff: B&B (continental) Double $70, Single $35, Children $25, Dinner on request $20. Credit cards. NZ B&B Vouchers accepted
Nearest Town: Kaikohe 43km

Rawene is NZ's third oldest settlement, and "Hokingamai" is situated on the shores of the Hokianga Harbour. Enjoy glorious harbour views, sunsets, peace and tranquillity. It is a 5 min walk to village, local pub, ferry, restaurant, library etc.
Your hosts have lived and travelled extensively in the South Pacific and Europe, and enjoy meeting people, being of service, and sharing the history of the Hokianga. Our home is sunny, warm and comfortable and it is our pleasure to make your stay enjoyable and memorable.
Laundry facilities available.
We are 1 hour from Bay of Islands and 3/4 hour from Waipoua forest.
Turn left at the Fire Station Rawene, into Gundry Street (B & B sign on corner) drive down to waters edge. Afternoon tea and supper included.
We have a Labrador X dog and a cat (both friendly!)

One of the differences between staying at a hotel and a B&B
is that you don't hug the hotel staff when you leave.

Rawene
Homestay
Address: 'Searell's', Nimmo Street, Rawene
(Postal: PO Box 100, Rawene 0452)
Name: Wally & Nellie Searell
Telephone: (09) 405 7835
Beds: 1 Double, 2 Single (2 Bedrooms)
Bathroom: 1 Private (we only host one group at a time).
Tariff: B&B (full) Double $65, Single $35, Dinner on request $20.
NZ B&B Vouchers accepted
Nearest Town: Kaikohe 43 km east on Highway 12

We are retired couple who enjoy sharing our comfortable home and magnificent panoramic views of Hokianga Harbour and surrounding hills with all who visit. The sunsets are breathtaking. Our 1 acre garden includes many native trees and tropical fruit trees. Fresh fruit can be picked almost every day. Wally is an ex-navalman and member of R.S.A. Our interests are many including gardening, wine making, photography and exploring New Zealand. Rawene is on Highway 12, where the vehicular ferry crosses Hokianga Harbour then it's approx 1 hour to Kaitaia - Waipoua Kauri Forest is 3/4 hour south and Bay of Islands 1 hour east.

Service station, hotel, restaurants, shops, boat hire, ferry and historic Clendon House only 1km. Turn off main road, motor camp sign over hill veer left. At Nimmo St. turn left to top of hill, flat easy parking area, house on right, easy access.

Opononi
Self Contained Accommodation
Address: 62 Fairlie Crescent, Opononi
(PO Box 82, Opononi)
Name: Ruth and Jesse Dawn
Telephone: 09-405 8241
Fax: 09-405 8773
Beds: 2 Queen, 1 Single (2 Bedrooms)
Bathroom: 1 Private
Tariff: B&B (continental) Double $85, Single $45, $20 for each extra person.
Children under 12 years half price. Weekly rate reduced by 15%.
Visa/Mastercard.
Nearest Town: Opononi

Opononi is an enchanting place reminiscent of a Mediterranean village, yet with surprising diversity allows you within minutes to be in the wilderness of subtropical rainforest, climbing soaring desert dunes or alone on a thundering ocean beach - Magical places to discover. We invite you to stay a while in this small community and enjoy our new self contained apartment with magnificent views over the Hokianga harbour. Complete with full kitchen, laundry, phone and fax, you can be totally comfortable for an extended period. Breakfast makings include fresh fruits, real coffee, cereals and farm-fresh eggs to prepare at your leisure. Just a short walk to the beach and pub, you can sit and yarn with the locals or enjoy a meal of the freshest fish possible. Other attractions locally include a rich history and world-class artists and crafts people. Come and see for yourself - we think you'll be enchanted.

Omapere
Bed & Breakfast
Address: Signal Station Road,
Omapere, Hokianga
Name: Alexa & Owen Whaley
Telephone: (09) 405 8641
Fax: (09) 405 8643
Beds: 1 Queen, 3 Single (2 bedrooms)
Bathroom: 1 Ensuite, 1 Family Share
Tariff: B&B (full) Double $70, Single $35, Children half price.
NZ B&B Vouchers accepted
Nearest Town: 60km west of Kaikohe on SH 12; 20km north of Waipoua Forest.

Our 10 year-old home nestles into the hillside overlooking the historic Hokianga Harbour, its unique sandhills and bar-bound harbour entrance - just a short drive up from Omapere village. So we have magnificent views which we feel should be shared. We are a retired couple, our family off our hands, and we are enjoying our escape from city living with tree-planting, gardening, and taming our hilly 5 acres with sheep, goats, chickens and ducks. Two friendly dogs and a marmalade cat help us.
We offer a restful stay for travellers - peaceful surroundings, comfortable sunny rooms with good beds, fresh home-grown produce for breakfast. Restaurants in easy walking distance, as are the ocean and harbour beaches, favourite lookout points and village shops. Kauri forests, bushwalks, spectacular waterfalls are a short drive away.
Directions: *Our name is by the gate and we are exactly 200m west of SH 12 on the Waipoua Forest side of Omapere village.*

Waipoua Forest
Solitaire Historic Homestay
Address: SH12, Waimamaku, South Hokianga
Name: Jenny & Les Read
Telephone: (09) 405 4891
Fax: (09) 4054891
Email: lesjen.read.@clear.net.nz
Beds: 3 Double, 2 Single (4 bedrooms)
Bathroom: 2 Guests share
Tariff: B&B (continental) Double $70, Single $45, Dinner $20pp.
Credit Cards (VISA/MC). NZ B&B Vouchers accepted
Nearest Town: 70 km West of Kaikohe; 6 km North of the Waipoua Forest.

Visit our restored Kauri homestead just north of the enchanting Waipoua Kauri forest. You'll have no trouble finding us, we're adjacent to State Highway 12 in the sheltered Waimamaku Valley. An ideal base to visit the giant Kauri trees, the Hokianga harbour and the West Coast beaches. Solitaire homestay is flanked by two rivers, with 30 acres of farm land abounding with bird life. Peace and tranquillity are guaranteed.
Security doors with fly screens are fitted to all guest rooms. Each bedroom opens out onto a covered verandah. Waimamaku, a place of ancient Maori and European settlement is surrounded by splendid forest and coastal walks. Come and experience the hospitality of the Hokianga region.

Relax – Don't try to drive too far in one day.

Waipoua Forest

Self-contained Accommodation
Address: Waipoua Lodge,
State Highway 12, Waipoua, R.D. 6,
Dargaville
Name: Raewyn & Tony Lancaster
Telephone: (09) 439 0422
Fax: (09) 439 0422 **Mobile**: 025 765 647
Email: Tony@waipoualodge.co.nz
Beds: 3 units: 2 Queen, 1 Super King
Bathroom: Each unit has ensuite facilities.
Tariff: B&B (continental) Double $95-$125 and $115, Single $85. All meals available in our fully licensed restaurant. Credit cards.
NZ B&B Vouchers accepted $25 and $40 Surcharge
Nearest Town: 48km north of Dargaville on the edge of the Waipoua Kauri Forest

Located on State Highway 12, half way between Dargaville and the beautiful Hokianga Harbour, this lovely old homestead at the southern boundary of the mighty Waipoua Forest has been tastefully converted into an award winning licensed restaurant, and offers the ideal base for forest excursions. There are three private accommodation units. Each are peaceful and comfortable with total privacy and overlook the gardens and the native bush where guests can stroll at their leisure. Parking is at the door. A continental breakfast featuring home made bread is provided in your unit - all other meals are available in the restaurant. Your hosts can help you enjoy all that the forest, nearby Kai Iwi Lakes and the ocean beach have to offer, including fishing , night nature walks (with the chance of seeing a kiwi), horse trekking, or just relaxing. We look forward to your company.

Dargaville

Self-contained Accommodation
Address: Awakino Point Lodge, **SH12**
State Highway 14, Dargaville,
Postal: PO Box 168, Dargaville
Telephone: (09) 439 7870 **Fax**: (09) 439 7870
Mobile: 025-519 474

Dargaville — Whangarei
SH12 ← 1.5kms to Dargaville ↓ 1.5kms to Lodge → SH14
Auckland
SH12

Beds: 3 units with 2 Queen, 1 Double, 4 Single (5 bedrooms)
Bathroom: Each unit has its own ensuite facilities. Laundry available.
Tariff: B&B (continental) Double $75, $15 each extra person per suite incl children.
Credit Cards. NZ B&B Vouchers accepted surcharge
Nearest Town: Dargaville 2km

This unique country lodge is situated in a peaceful rural setting on a five acre farmlet surrounded by attractive gardens, orchard and aviary. It's just two minutes drive from the small township of Dargaville less than 2 km along state highway 14. There are two 2 bedroom suites and one 1 bedroom suite. The best features of the New Zealand Motel system and the Bed and Breakfast scheme have been amalgamated to create the best of both worlds. You will enjoy your own private self contained suite with private bathroom combined with friendly personal service and a good breakfast most of which is home produced. Pottery, painting, gardening and making wine from various fruits are just a few of the hobbies pursued, and after twelve years of hosting would say meeting people is yet another hobby. There are plenty of good restaurants in Dargaville reasonably priced but should you wish to have dinner at the lodge please arrange in advance. Credit cards accepted, but cash or travellers cheque would be much preferred. No smoking indoors, please.

57

Dargaville

Farmstay, Bed & Breakfast Inn
Address: 'Kauri House Lodge', Bowen Street, PO Box 382 Dargaville
Name: Doug Blaxall
Telephone: (09) 439 8082 **Fax**: (09) 439 8082
Beds: 2 King, 1 Twin (3 bedrooms)
Bathroom: 3 Ensuites
Tariff: B&B (full) Double $130-$150.
Nearest Town: Dargaville 1.5 kms

We are high on a hill overlooking the town. No highway noise or smells. The only thing to disturb the peace and tranquillity here, are the birds. Our guests enjoy: - Antiques, Kingsize very firm beds with superior line, own ensuites and large fluffy towels. Fly screened windows for your summer comfort. Our home is around 6000 sq. ft. Built by craftsmen early this century, with unique use of native timbers in panelling, ceilings and doors. It took 4 years to build. Billiards room with log fire in winter. Library with thousands of books. Drawing room with unusual Rimu dresser. Fully Kauri panelled dining-room. We are set in 8 acres of grounds and large swimming pool (summer only). Activities nearby include river cruises, horse treks, beaches, lakes, walking tracks and local restaurants. Our farm is separate. Bring good walking shoes to go exploring our beautiful mature native bush with Doug. He also runs our local antique / second-hand shop. Discounts for guests. Outside animals: - Dogs, cats, donkeys, cows. Smoke-free.

Baylys Beach, Dargaville

Self-contained Accomm
Address: Oceanview Bed & Breakfast, 7 Oceanview Terrace, Baylys Beach Dargaville
Name: Paula and John Powell
Telephone: (09) 439 6256
Beds: 1 Double, 1 Single, 1 camp bed (1 Bedroom) **Bathroom**: 1 Ensuite
Tariff: B&B (Continental) Double $70, Single $40, $20 per extra person.
NZ B&B Vouchers accepted **Nearest Town**: 12 kms west of Dargaville off SH12

2 1/2 hours north of Auckland, just of Highway 12 you will find Baylys Beach. Sometimes wild, always wonderful, the west coast is an ideal spot to take time out.
The beach is 200m from our property - go swimming, fishing, surfing, gather shellfish, hike cliff paths or simply stroll the beach to refresh body and soul. Golf, horse-riding and beach tours are available locally. The Kai Iwi Lakes and Waipoua Forest are 1 / 2 and 1 hour away. We enjoy a relaxed lifestyle with our two pre-schoolers and two cats. The children delight in our visitors, however your privacy is assured as your accommodation is independent of our family home. With sea views from the lawn area, the cottage is sunny and comfortable and furnished with TV, radio, refrigerator, tea / coffee facilities and ensuite bathroom with a great shower. Take breakfast at your leisure as this is provided in the cottage for you.
Directions: *Please phone for directions.*

Dargaville
Homestay, Farmstay, Bed & Breakfast,
dinner optional
Address: 'Kauri Ridge', R.D.2, Dargaville
Name: Agnes & Wallace Bennett
Telephone: (09) 439 5163
Beds: 2 Double, 2 Single (3 bedrooms)
Bathroom: 1 Guests share, 1 Family share
Tariff: B&B (continental) Double $60, Single $30, Dinner $20, Campervans
facilities available, $12 per couple - meals available. Credit Cards accepted.
NZ B&B Vouchers accepted
Nearest Town: Dargaville 28km.

Real Country - miles from the hustle and bustle. Young at heart couple invite you to
visit and enjoy our spot of paradise. We own 30 acres of land with Native bush, garden,
orchard, some sheep and cattle and lots of bird life, plus a cat. We can arrange fishing
trips - trout or sea.Handy distance to Whangarei for shopping or visit lovely Kai Iwi
Lakes and Kauri Parks. Several interesting walks or longer tramps in our locality.
Interests include Masonic Lodge, 60's up Movement, and people. There are three
double bedrooms, all upstairs with guest bathroom. Complimentary tea and coffee.
Organically grown vegetables and farm killed meat. No dogs please. Our home is
smoke-free. 50km to Whangarei. 28km to Dargaville. You will be very welcome.
Directions: *Well signposted 12km from Dargaville on Whangarei Road (Large B&B*
sign). Take Tangowahine Valley Road, 15km up Valley Road, turn right into Karaka
Road 1 km turn right into Sommerville Road. 300 yards to our gate.

Matakohe
Farmstay
Address: Tinopai Road, R.D.1,
 Matakohe
Name: "Maramarie" Elinor & Tom Beazley
Telephone: (09) 431 6911
Beds: 1 Double
(1 bedroom - extra beds available for children)
Bathroom: 1 Private
Tariff: B&B (continental) Double $75, Single $40,
 Children half price,
Dinner $15.NZ B&B Vouchers accepted
Nearest Town: Matakohe 4km, Paparoa 10km

"Maramarie" is a secluded kauri homestead 4km from the unique Matakohe Kauri
Museum. A visit to the museum is a great introduction to Northlands Kauri history.
Kauri forests and the west coast with its endless beaches are not far away.
Beautiful farming country and views over the Kaipara Harbour will welcome you to
Matakohe. Our sheep and beef farm is gently rolling and invites you to stretch your
legs. Your room has a verandah overlooking the harbour and the mature garden.
I am Swedish and Tom is a New Zealander. We have three schoolage children. There
are two dogs that help with the stockwork and one lazy cat. Come and visit our family
and relax on our farm. Please phone for reservation and direction. Pick up from
regular bus services to Matakohe available.

Whananaki North, Northland

Homestay+Self-contained Accom.
Address: Rockell's Rd, R.D. 1, Hikurangi (Whananaki)
Name: B & F Scott
Telephone: (09) 433 8242
Beds: 2 Double, 4 Single (3 bedrooms)
Bathroom: 2 Private
Tariff: B&B (continental) Double $70, Single $40, Dinner $20.
Children 1/2 price. NZ B&B Vouchers accepted
Nearest Town: Whangarei 50 Kms

We live on a delightful section of the scenic, sub-tropical Northland East Coast and want to show it off. We are 50km NE of Whangarei, 30km off State Highway 1. Easily accessible yet peaceful, private and beautiful. A sheltered bay is 100 metres from the front door of our new "Triboard" home, with many other beaches within easy reach, offering an excellent selection of recreational pleasures; swimming, snorkelling, surfing, fishing etc. There are scenic, bush and historic walks. Picnics and boat trips can be arranged. Dinghy available. Guests have self-contained accommodation and meals can be shared with our family or served and eaten in the privacy of your own unit. Our wish is that you make this your home away from home. Sample our library or play a game from our collection. One flat is wheel-chair oriented and disabled guests are especially welcome. Please phone ahead so that we can endeavour to make your stay perfect. We have pets. We welcome pets to stay if you choose to bring them.

Ngunguru

Homestay
Address: 'Glengarrjy',
45 Te Maika Road,
Ngunguru, R.D.3. Whangarei
Name: Bet & Noel Glengarry
Telephone: (09) 434 3646
Beds: 2 Single (1 bedroom)
Bathroom: 1 Ensuite
Tariff: B&B (full) Double $65, Single $40.
NZ B&B Vouchers accepted
Nearest Town: Whangarei 25 km

We are a retired couple with a Siamese cat whose cottage style home, set in half acre of tranquil gardens, is situated on the beautiful Tutukaka Coast. The sunny guest room, with ensuite, has its own entrance and tea / coffee making facilities. We grow our own fruit and vegetables and keep hens to provide fresh eggs and home made preserves for your breakfast. There are several excellent restaurants within five minutes drive where you can dine. We are two minutes walk from beautiful beaches and five minutes drive from Tutukaka for diving, Big Game fishing, or sightseeing trips to the world renowned Poor Knights Islands. We aim to make your stay as comfortable and enjoyable as possible and are always happy to help with bookings for dives, cruises etc. **Directions**: *From Whangarei follow Tutukaka Coast Road for 25km. Travel through Ngunguru and turn right into Te Maika Road. Please phone ahead.*

Whangarei - Maungatapere
Farmstay+Self-contained Accom.
Address: Ballater, Box 41,
Maungatapere, Northland
Name: Bill & Rosie Sanderson
Telephone: (09) 434 6514/438 2135
Fax: (09) 430 0278
Mobile: (025) 959 165
Email: ballater@dear.net.nz

Beds: 1 King. 1 Double, 1 Single in main house
Bathroom: 1 Ensuite, 1 Private
Tariff: B&B (full) Double $80-$100, Single $50, Dinner $25,
Credit cards (VISA/MC). NZ B&B Vouchers accepted Surcharge $10.
Nearest Town: Whangarei 10 kms

DISCOVER A SPECIAL PLACE: Enjoy our new, elegantly appointed SELF CONTAINED unit adjacent to our modern home. We have a tranquil country setting of native bush and Avocado trees just 15 minutes from central Whangarei. Enjoy our pool in the summer, astrograss tennis court year round, spa and open fire in winter. We invite you to stroll through the avocados and native bush, or just relax in the Lodge with TV, CD player and a wide selection of books and music. Excellent golf course 5 mins away and we are within easy access of the Bay of Islands, Tutukaka for fishing and diving and many of Northland's glorious beaches.The Lodge has a well equipped kitchen, and Whangarei many good restaurants or join us for dinner by arrangement. We love to serve innovative fresh New Zealand food and good New Zealand wines. Continental or cooked breakfast with fresh juice and fruit, home made muesli, yoghurt, muffins, bread etc. Non smoking.Tariff includes: Use of tennis court, spa and swimming pool, loan of racquets.
Directions: *Please phone.*

Whangarei
Homestay
Address: 477 Whangarei Heads Road,
Waikaraka,R.D.4, Whangarei
Name: Waikaraka Harbour View
  (Marrion & John Beck)
Telephone: (09) 436 2549
Beds: 2 Single (1 bedroom)
Bathroom: 1 Ensuite
Tariff: B&B (continental) Double $60, Single $40.
$5 reduction two nights or more, further $5 May to August. NZ B&B Vouchers accepted
Nearest Town: Whangarei 10 km

Welcome to our self-contained studio built new in 1996 (twin beds, en-suite, tea / coffee facilities, TV, radio, Refrigerator, tables, chairs and adjoining decks). Enjoy the spectacular harbour and landscape views, fishing, beaches, walks, golf, gardens and the many other attractions in the Whangarei area. We retired here in 1990 after 25 years in the area. We enjoy travel, the outdoor life and hope we can help you to find similar enjoyment. With luck, we may help you to witness dolphins or Orcas in the harbour or catch a fish for breakfast. Smoking outdoors or on the decks please.
Directions: *From the "Town Basin" (Whangarei city centre) head east for Onerahi (5 kilometres) - 150 metres past the Onerahi shopping centre, turn left onto the Whangarei Heads Road - 4.77 kilometres to Waikaraka Harbourview B&B. (sign on left).*

Onerahi, Whangarei

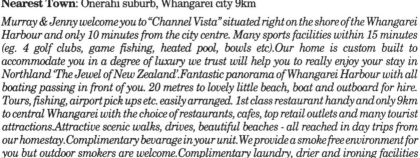

Self-contained Suites
Address: "Channel Vista",
254 Beach Rd.,
Onerahi, Whangarei
Name: Murray & Jenny Tancred
Telephone: (09) 436 5529
Fax: (09) 436 5529
Mobile: (025) 973 083
Beds: 2 Queen (2 fully self-contained suites, own lounge, TV, kitchen),
also 1 Twin, 1 Queen (separate bedrooms in house).
Bathroom: 2 Ensuite + 1 guest share (in house)
Tariff: B&B (full) Double $90-$110, in house bedrooms $70,
1Dinner 2 course $25pp (with wine), Credit Cards-Visa/Mastercard.
Nearest Town: Onerahi suburb, Whangarei city 9km

Murray & Jenny welcome you to "Channel Vista" situated right on the shore of the Whangarei Harbour and only 10 minutes from the city centre. Many sports facilities within 15 minutes (eg. 4 golf clubs, game fishing, heated pool, bowls etc).Our home is custom built to accommodate you in a degree of luxury we trust will help you to really enjoy your stay in Northland 'The Jewel of New Zealand'.Fantastic panorama of Whangarei Harbour with all boating passing in front of you. 20 metres to lovely little beach, boat and outboard for hire. Tours, fishing, airport pick ups etc. easily arranged. 1st class restaurant handy and only 9km to central Whangarei with the choice of restaurants, cafes, top retail outlets and many tourist attractions.Attractive scenic walks, drives, beautiful beaches - all reached in day trips from our homestay.Complimentary bevarage in your unit.We provide a smoke free environment for you but outdoor smokers are welcome.Complimentary laundry, drier and ironing facilities available, also fax.We have a dog and a cat.Phone ahead to ensure your booking, directions and book meal if wanted at this new and popular venue.

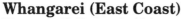

Whangarei (East Coast)

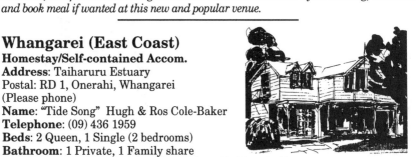

Homestay/Self-contained Accom.
Address: Taiharuru Estuary
Postal: RD 1, Onerahi, Whangarei
(Please phone)
Name: "Tide Song" Hugh & Ros Cole-Baker
Telephone: (09) 436 1959
Beds: 2 Queen, 1 Single (2 bedrooms)
Bathroom: 1 Private, 1 Family share
Tariff: B&B (full) Double $75, Single $40, Children half price,
Dinner $15-$20. Self-catering $60 Double. Credit cards.
Nearest Town: Whangarei 26.7 km

From Whangarei drive east for 25 minutes to our 8 acres on the Taiharuru Estuary. With a bush and seaside setting, there is a small jetty and a variety of small craft including canoes and dinghies. There are also some spectacular walks, with Pacific views and peaks, and a choice of surf beaches 10 to 20 minutes away. Our animals include sheep, dogs and cows (one we milk by hand). We have a farming and teaching background and are interested in sailing, cycling, conservation, gardening, home-cooking, and music. With only one of our four children still living here we enjoy having company and looking after guests. Our accommodation is a separate upstairs flat with its own bathroom, kitchen and TV. If you wish we will provide extra home-cooked meals or there are two restaurants 10 minutes away. We appreciate people not smoking indoors, Looking forward to meeting you.

Whangarei

Homestay/Farmstay
Address: "Gardner Homestead",
Clapham Rd, Whangarei
Name: Margaret Gardner
Telephone: (09) 437 3611
Fax: (09) 437 3611
Beds: 1 Double, 2 Single (2 bedrooms)
Bathroom: 1 Ensuite
Tariff: B&B (full) Double $70,
Children $20, Dinner from $25.
Nearest Town: Whangarei 4km

Enjoy the peace and quiet of the countryside while only five minutes from Whangarei city centre. Our quaint old kauri homestead (the original home of Clapham Clocks) with its large garden and fish ponds lies in thirty acres of bush and paddocks which we share with three very friendly dogs, two cats, and chooks, sheep, cattle and two horses (riding by arrangement). We offer a pleasant walk through our bush down to the Hatea River with its idyllic swimming hole. Reed Park with its kauris is only short walk away. Close by are Parahaki, Abbey Caves and Whangarei Falls. The large upstairs guest suite has an ensuite and a smaller adjacent bedroom with two single beds and has television, radio, microwave, tea & coffee, reading matter and heating. We will be happy to meet you at airport or bus depot.

Whangarei

Homestay
Address: "Koinonia Manor",
260 Ngunguru Road, RD 3, Whangarei
Name: Allan & Adele Kimber
Telephone: (09) 437 5961
Beds: 2 Double, 3 Single (4 bedrooms)
Bathroom: Guests share, Family share
Tariff: B&B (special) Double $70, Single
$40, Children half price, Dinner $20.
Also charming 2 bedroom cottage tariff negotiable.
Nearest Town: Whangarei 8km

Welcome to Koinonia Manor, our lovingly restored historic homestead in Glenbervie built by Lord and Lady Douglas in 1880. Comfortably furnished with antiques and collectables, it is surrounded by cottage gardens and a macadamia nut orchard through which guests can wander. Three kilometres beyond Whangarei Falls, we are situated enroute to beautiful beaches where a playground of coastal adventures abound. Golfing greens and enticements of the town basin are also nearby. Whether you are touring NZ, honeymooning, holidaying or here on business, it is our pleasure to assist you to make your stay memorable. Specialities by arrangement include dining al fresco, relaxing with a barbecue or by intimate candlelight. Guests thoroughly enjoy the charm of yesteryear, warm hospitality, peaceful surroundings, the call of birds and wide verandahs. Bookings by letter are welcome, phoning at mealtimes or evenings is appreciated.

Whangarei
Bed & Breakfast
Address: Graelyn Villa,
166 Kiripaka Road, Whangarei
Name: Grace Green & Linda McGrogan
Telephone: (09) 437 7532
Fax: (09) 437 7533
Beds: 2 Queen,
2 Single (3 bedrooms)
Bathroom: 3 Ensuite
Tariff: B&B (continental) Double $70, Single $55, Children negotiable, Dinner negotiable, Credit Cards (VISA/AMEX/DINERS/MC). NZ B&B Vouchers accepted
Nearest Town: Whangarei (4.5km to city centre)

A very warm welcome awaits you at Graelyn Villa. Beautifully presented in a tranquil garden setting, "Graelyn" is a turn-of-the-century villa that has been lovingly restored to offer comfort and luxury. Mother and daughter team, Grace and Linda, offer you friendly personal service. Breakfast is served on the verandah in summer, or by the cosy pot belly fire on colder days. A hearty cooked breakfast is available for a small extra charge, other meals by arrangement. Our rooms offer superbly comfortable beds, TV, tea and coffee, heaters and electric blankets. We are ideally situated, being only five minutes from the city centre, with a variety of top class restaurants, handy to the spectacular Whangarei Falls, also golf, bush walks, a 20 minute drive to beaches, game fishing and diving on the Tutukaka Coast, local shops nearby. We have a dog and cat, your pets welcome. Smoking on the verandah please.

Whangarei
Self-contained Accommodation
Address: 526 Ngunguru Road,
Glenberrie, Whangarei
Name: Minnie Mora
Telephone: (09) 437 5127
Beds: 2 King/Queen
(2 bedrooms/both with
Danske beds settee)
Bathroom: 2 Ensuite
Tariff: B&B (full) Double $60, Single $35,
Dinner by arrangement $20, Campervans $15.
Nearest Town: Whangarei 10km

Having travelled extensively ourselves we can assure you of friendly hospitality in comfortable surroundings for a memorable stay. Guests have their own entrance, guest lounge with colour television, Sky our home, tea & coffee making facilities, fridge, microwave, cookies and extra little treats. Enjoy full country breakfast in our cosy dining room overlooking our garden.We operate a picturesque three acre country garden teahouse, serving Devonshire Teas, light lunches.Explore our garden charmed full of bulbs iris, daffodils, perennials, succulents shrubs and much more, plants can be purchased.The spacious garden has novelty corners such as gazebo, windmill, statures, archways, water wheel pools, seats to sit, relax in this peaceful area. Stone walls feature of area. Located handy beaches, fishing golf courses and walks, Tutukaka Coast, Whangarei Falls and city centre. Smoking: outdoors only.
Directions: *10km east of Whangarei on Ngunguru Tutukaka Highway. 1 hour to Bay of Islands, 2 hours to Auckland.*

Whangarei
Homestay+Self-contained Accom.
Address: "Taraire Grove", Tatton Road,
RD 9, Whangarei
Name: Jan & Brian Newman
Telephone: (09) 434 7279
Fax: (09) 434 7279
Beds: 1 Queen, 2 Single (2 bedrooms)
Bathroom: 1 Guests share
Tariff: B&B (full) Double $70, Single $40, Dinner $12-$20,
1 Self-contained unit $65-$85. Visa & Master Cards accepted.
NZ B&B Vouchers accepted 1 May to 31 August
Nearest Town: Whangarei 15 mins, Dargaville 30 mins

We welcome you to our charming country residence situated at Maungatapere, and within easy driving distances to East and West coast beaches to enjoy swimming, fishing and picnicking. Sightseeing and good shopping in Whangarei city. We are a semi-retired couple and having travelled overseas using B&Bs, we welcome the opportunity to return hospitality that we have experienced. We have a cat (Joe) and Jack Russell (Max). Our home has lots of decking, a barbecue and spa pool, and overlooks a stream. We are gradually developing the 3 1/2 acres into lawns, gardens and pond. The guest wing is private and has a TV room with tea & coffee making facilities. Our laundry is available for your use. No smoking indoors please. Evening meals - Whangarei has excellent restaurants, or you can choose to relax and dine with us. Ring or fax for reservations and directions.

Whangarei
Homestay
Address: The Wright Place,
2 Memorial Drive,
Riverside, Whangarei
Name: Selwyn and Margaret Wright
Telephone: (09) 438 7441
Fax: (09) 438 7441
Mobile: (025) 245 4177
Email: wright.place@clear.net.nz
Beds: 1 Queen, 1 Double, 2 Single (3 bedrooms)
Bathroom: 1 Ensuite, 1 Family share
Tariff: B&B (full) Double $70-$85, Single $45-$50.
NZ B&B Vouchers accepted $10 surcharge
Nearest Town: Whangarei 2.3km

We invite you to share our centrally situated home overlooking Whangarei City and the Hatea River. We are a twenty five minute stroll to the Town Basin and City Centre. Let us recommend a restaurant or cafe. We are handy to the airport, a golf links and are on the route to Whangarei Harbour, ocean beaches and are within a comfortable drive to the Bay of Islands. Our home has a swimming pool and lovely gardens for your enjoyment. Guests have a choice of cosy detached bedroom with ensuite or guest bedrooms upstairs. A quiet lounge with TV is provided but guests may share family / living room.
We share our home with "Storm" our cat.
We look forward to your company.

Whangarei

Homestay
Address: "City Lights",
40A Vale Road, Riverside,
Whangarei, Norhtland
Name: Kevin and Doug
Telephone: (09) 438 2390
Fax: (09) 438 2390
Mobile: (025) 958 243
Beds: 1 Queen, 2 Single (2 bedrooms)
Bathroom: 1 Guests share
Tariff: B&B (full/continental) Double $70, Single $40.
Nearest Town: Whangarei Post Office 1.2 km

Our comfortable elevated home is only 1.2 km from the town centre and Post Office with views over the Hatea River to the Western Hills with magnificent views over the city. Walking distance to town basin, restaurants, cafes and bars, heated swimming pool. Forum North and Whangarei Area Hospital. We have a lovely walk at the end of our street along the Hatea River and up into Mair Park. An easy drive to many fine beaches and 4 golf courses. Unfortunately our place is not suitable for children. We have to lovable Boxer dogs, Cara and Cass also P4 the cat. We are non smokers but outdoor smokers are welcome. Pick up from downtown and the airport provided. We look forward to meeting you sometime in the future.
Directions: *Please phone ahead to ensure a booking and directions.*

Whangarei Heads

Homestay/Self-contained accommodation
Address: Manaia Gardens, R.D.4, Whangarei
Name: Audrey & Colin Arnold
Telephone: (09) 434 0797
Beds: 1 Queen, 1 Double,
2 Single (3 bedrooms)
Bathroom: 2 Private
Tariff: B&B (special) Double $65
($60 second and subsequent nights),
Single $50, Extra people $15 pp. Self catering: Double $50, Extras $10.
Credit cards (Bank). NZ B&B Vouchers accepted
Nearest Town: Whangarei

A stone's throw from your cabin to the beach, bush behind. Two quaint 60 year old cabins in the garden offer privacy and peace. Around us are beaches, both ocean and harbour, and over 400 hectares of Conservation land. Dinghy, laundry and barbecue, a nearby shop, artists gallery. We have a small farm and a large garden, a lawn mowing sheep and a cat. Breakfast includes home-made bread and free-range eggs. NB: Both cabins have two rooms, own bathroom, TV, microwave, fridge, toaster, tea / coffee, plates and cutlery,linen.
RATA: double bed, kitchenette. POHUTUKAWA; Queen bed, 2 singles.
Directions: *Take the Whangarei Heads Road. We are 31km from the Whangarei Yacht Basin bridge and 1.7km past the Taurikura store. We are the only buildings in the bay. Rock wall in front, red mailbox 2487*

Parua Bay, Whangarei

Homestay/Farmstay/S.C. Studio
Address: Pen-Y-Bryn,
Headland Farm Park,
Parua Bay, R.D.4, Whangarei
Name: Tina & Wayne Butler
Telephone: (09) 436 1941
Fax: (09) 436 1946
Mobile: (025) 976 800
Email: wayne@michaelhill.co.nz
Beds: 1 Double (1 bedroom)
Studio: 1 Queen with ensuite **Bathroom**: 1 Private
Tariff: B&B (full) Double $90-$115, Single $80. Dinner $30,
Credit Cards (VISA/MC/BC).
Nearest Town: Whangarei 15km

ENJOY OUR MILLION DOLLAR VIEWS.
Our spacious modern home and self contained studio are located on a ridge in Headland Farm Park, a unique 300 acre farming / housing concept overlooking Parua Bay and Whangarei Harbour. The Farm runs Deer, Sheep and Cattle, and has a safe swimming beach, orchard and security gates. Adjacent is "The Pines" golf course, which welcomes visitors. We have lovely walks through the Park and a Spa Pool, Dinghy and Kayaks for use. Other activities in the area include horse trekking, fishing, tramping, tennis, harbour and ocean beaches. Enjoy a leisurely breakfast with home made treats.Dinner is by arrangement and served with New Zealand wine. We have a friendly, small house dog, and our varied interests include our garden landscaped with rocks, sports, craft / patchwork, genealogy. We have travelled extensively and lived in the Solomons and the UK. We request NO SMOKING inside. Phone for directions and gate code.

Parua Bay, Whangarei

Farmstay
Address: 'Parua House', Parua Bay,
Whangarei Heads Road, R.D.4, Whangarei
Name: Pat & Peter Heaslip
Telephone: (09) 436 5855
Fax: (09) 436 3419
Email: paruahomestay@clear.net.nz
Beds: 1 Queen, 5 Single (4 bedrooms)
Bathroom: 2 Ensuite, 1 Private
Tariff: B&B (full) Double $80-$90, Single $50, Dinner $25, Children half price.
NZ B&B Vouchers accepted $10 surcharge
Nearest Town: Whangarei 17km

Parua House is a classical colonial house built in 1883, comfortably restored and occupying an elevated site with panoramic views of Parua Bay and the Whangarei Harbour. The property covers 29 hectares of farmland including two protected native reserves which are rich in native trees (including kauri) and birds. Guests are to welcome to explore the farm and bush, milk the Jersey house cow, explore the olive grove and sub-tropical orchard or just relax in the spa-pool or on the verandah. A safe swimming beach adjoins the farm, with a short walk to the fishing jetty. Two marinas and a golf course are nearby. We have travelled extensively and our wide interests include photography, patchwork-quilting and horticulture. The house is attractively appointed with antique furniture and a rare collection of spinning wheels. Home-grown produce is used where possible. Vegetarian food is provided if requested. No smoking inside, but outside is fine. A warm welcome awaits you.
Featured on TV's Ansett NZ Time of Your Life.

Whangarei Heads
Homestay
Address: 'Bantry', Little Munro Bay,
R.D.4, Whangarei
Name: Robin & Karel Lieffering
Telephone: (09) 434 0751
Email: lieffrng@igrin.co.nz
Beds: 1 Queen, 2 bunks (2 bedrooms)
Bathroom: 1 Guests
Tariff: B&B (full) Double $95, Single $50, Children under 12 half price. Dinner $25. Only one party booked at a time. Campervans welcome.
NZ B&B Vouchers accepted $20 surcharge. Same day restrictions Nov - March.
Nearest Town: 28km Whangarei

We are a semi-retired couple (plus cat and dog) in our 50's. Between us we speak English, Dutch, French, German and Japanese and like to laugh. We have travelled extensively and enjoy overseas guests. Our unusual home with rocks being part of the interior walls is at the edge of a safe-swimming beach. We have wonderful views of coastal "mountains", bays and sea. On our doorstep is one of several bush reserves with walking tracks. Photographically a fascinating area. Nearby is a golf course, tennis courts, horse-riding, several beaches and three popular on-shore fishing spots within five minutes walk or you can use our dinghy. Guests have their own entrance and sitting room if they wish to be alone and all rooms have sea views. We prefer guests not to smoke inside. Robin likes to cook and dinner includes good New Zealand wine.
Directions: *Phone for reservations and directions.*

Mangapai, Whangarei
Farmstay
Address: Ngatoka Rd, Mangapai,
R.D.8, Whangarei
Name: Mel & Cathy Clarke
Telephone: (09) 432 2588
 Mobile: (025) 379 976
Email: mel.clarke@clear.net.nz
Beds: 1 Double, 2 Single (2 bedrooms)
Bathroom: 2 Private
Tariff: B&B (full) Double $70, Single $40,
Children half price, Dinner $25, Campervans $15.. Credit cards. NZ B&B Vouchers accepted
Nearest Town: 25km south of Whangarei, 10km from SH1

Our home is an early 1900's kauri villa featuring large rooms with native timber flooring and antique furnishings. We have a small farmlet on which we run a few cattle, pigs, sheep and hens. Relax on the verandah with excellent open rural views and a glimpse of Whangarei Harbour. The extensive gardens are attractively landscaped with a fenced swimming pool and a brick paved courtyard which catches the early morning sun.Because we are in a tranquil rural location, 30 minutes drive from Whangarei, we offer dinner at short notice. Sample fine NZ cuisine e.g. lamb fillets, salmon, kumara and other garden fresh vegetables. Our two school age children have Lily their pet sheep, two cats and Peanut - a Jack Russel terrier. We can take you to see nearby glow-worm caves and recommend a visit to the Matakohe Kauri Museum (3/4 hour) or the Bay of Islands (ninety minutes).
Directions: *Please phone.*

Ruakaka
Farmstay/Self-contained Accomm
Address: Doctor's Hill Road, Ruakaka.
Postal: Dr's Hill Rd., RD 2 Waipu
Name: Vince & Joyce Roberts
Telephone: (09) 432 7842
Mobile: 025 419 585
Beds: 2 Queen, 1 Single (2 bedrooms)
Bathroom: 1 Private, 1 Family share
Tariff: B&B (full) Double $70, Single $40,
Dinner $20 (includes wine), Credit cards. Winter rates & Pensioner discount. NZ
B&B Vouchers accepted
Nearest Town: Ruakaka - approx 2 hrs north of Auckland - 2 hrs south Bay of
Islands.

*Magnificent views, peace and quiet greet you at our home. Your accommodation is a
bedsitter with its own bathroom, kitchenette and fridge, a ranchslider leads onto deck
with views of the entrance to Bream Bay, Mt Mania and surrounding Islands.FREE
bush and scenic drive over our 150 acre dry stock farm can be arranged. Our wetland
area is home to the rare brown bitten. Beautiful beaches, squash courts, golf course,
racetrack where Vince trains our racehorses and good restaurants are a short drive
from our home. Reserve time to see the FREE refinery Video and model at Marsden
Pt, Claphams Clock in Whangarei and the Matakohe Kauri Museum an hours drive
west. As Ex dairy farmers with a grown family of four children, we have enjoyed doing
B&B for the past eight years, other interests include gardening, golf and travel.
As we spend a lot of time outdoors, we suggest you phone in the evening for bookings,
however passing callers are welcome.*

Ruakaka
Homestay/Self-contained Accom.
Address: 15 Camellia Ave, Ruakaka
Name: Belle-vue
Telephone: (09) 432 8977
0Fax: (09) 432 8994
Beds: 1 Queen, 1 Double, 2 Single (3 bedrooms)
Bathroom: 1 Private, 1 Family share
Tariff: Homestay (full) $60 Dbl, $40 Sgl.
Self Contained Unit (continental) $60 Dbl, $50 Sgl.
$20 each extra adult. Credit cards. NZ B&B Vouchers accepted
Nearest Town: Ruakaka (scenic route) 32 kms south of Whangarei

*Our 2 storey home is situated on the ridge 2 minutes drive from the beautiful Ruakaka
surf beach. The 1100 sqft self contained unit on the ground level has its own cooking
facilities, TV and video. Upstairs has 1 Queen (1 bedroom) with shared household
facilities. Both are serviced daily so you may relax and enjoy your stay with us. Your
hosts have many years involvement in the tourist industry welcoming both overseas
and local visitors. Our interests include boating, horse racing, golf, music and your
company. We are handy to Waipu Golf Course, Ruakaka Racecourse (where the Turf
meets the Surf) and the Marsden Point Oil Refinery with video and display model a
must see. We are happy to share with you our wide knowledge of Northland's
attractions to make your stay with us more memorable.*
Directions: *Turn off SH1 at Ruakaka into Marsden Point Road, 1st right into Beach
Road, 1st left into Camellia Ave.*

Waipu Cove
Farmstay+Self-Contained Accom.
Address: Cove Road, Waipu Cove
Name: Andre & Robin La Bonte
Telephone: (09) 432 0645 **Fax**: (09) 432 0645
Beds: 3 Double, 2 Single (3 bedrooms)
Bathroom: 2 Private
Tariff: B&B (continental) Double $80, Single $50, Dinner $20.
NZ B&B Vouchers accepted
Nearest Town: 10km south of Waipu on Cove Rd, 50km south of Whangarei via SH1.

My wife and I are Americans who became residents of New Zealand in 1985. We built a modern home with separate guest accommodation on a 36 acre coastal "lifestyle" farmlet by the edge of the sea. Sleep to the sound of the ocean in either the separate efficiency apartment or in the guest bedrooms, with double or two single beds and private bathroom. No smoking please. Enjoy expansive views of the Pacific Ocean and offshore islands. Fish or explore our 850 ft of shoreline with limestone rock formations and tidepools or just sit and relax under the mature pohutukawa trees that grace the shoreline. The beach at Waipu Cove is a ten minute walk along the shore. We graze cattle, raise fish in our 2.5 acre pond, hand feed wild birds and have flea free cats. Glow worm caves, deep-sea fishing, scuba diving and golf are all available locally.
Directions: *Please phone. Bookings recommended.*

Waipu
Seaside farm stay + Self-contained Accom.
Address: Cove Road, Waipu
Name: The Stone House
Telephone: (09) 432 0432
Email: r-eustace@xtra.co.nz
Beds: 2 Queen, 2 Double,
3 Single (4 bedrooms)
Bathroom: 1 Ensuite, 3 Private
Tariff: B&B (full) Double $80
Single $60,
Children plus Extra Adults $20 pp, Dinner $20
Credit cards accepted. NZ B&B Vouchers accepted $20 surcharge on some rooms.
Nearest Town: 35km south of Whangarei, then 6km from Waipu on Cove Road (Scenic Route)

Relax in a charming self-contained stone cottage by the sea, or if you prefer stay with your hosts Gillian and John in their unique Stone House. We offer a touch of Cornwall complete with cosy log fires in the winterless North! The House and cottage are set in picturesque rock gardens with croquet lawn and sheltered patios. This extends to the green pastures of our farm, a private jetty and lagoon. Use our dinghys or canoes (at no extra charge) to explore an extensive bird sanctuary, sand dunes and unspoilt ocean beach adjoining the property. Fishing including surfcasting, deep sea fishing and boat trips, swimming, horseriding, scenic bush walks, glowworm caves, golf, tennis, talented art / crafts are all at hand. Our specialties include both Kiwi and German cuisine. • Over 3000 beautiful orchids in season • Genuine NZ hospitality • Colour TV, video, coffee / tea facilities • German spoken.

Waipu

Guest House
Address: "Wychwood Lodge", Cove Road,
Langs Beach, RD 2, Waipu
Name: Barry & Jan Dyer
Telephone: (09) 432 0757
Fax: (09) 432 0760 **Mobile**: (025) 277 4440
Beds: 3 King, 1 Double (4 bedrooms)
Bathroom: 3 Ensuite, 1 Private
Tariff: B&B (full) Double $135-$175, Credit Cards (VISA/AMEX/ DINERS).
Nearest Town: Waipu 10 Kms

A very special place. A pastoral and coastal paradise set in 11 acres with native bush, stream and waterfall. We have unsurpassed views across Bream Bay and we are walking distance to two of NZ's most beautiful white sand beaches. All rooms have private bathrooms and balconies. Edwardian style conservatory for breakfast. Two restaurants a few minutes away for dinner. Large guest lounge with log fire. Two golf links nearby. Fishing and diving arranged. Hiking trails and bush walks. Our aim is to give you luxury with friendly informality. Two cats in residence. Our interests include art, design, international travel and we are passionate gardeners. Italian spoken.
Directions: *Less than two hours drive from Auckland, midway to the Bay of Islands. Take Mangawhai turnoff on SH1 past Te Hana. This is the scenic "Coastal Route North" (sealed roads) Wychwood Lodge is 30 mins from here through Mangawhai, alternatively take the Waipu turnoff from SH1, 10 mins to Langs Beach from here through Waipu Cove.*

Waipu Cove

Self-contained Accommodation
Address: Cove Rd., R.D.2,
Waipu Cove, Northland
Name: Waipu Cove Cottages"
Telephone: (09) 432 0851
Fax: (09) 432 0851
Beds: 2 Double,4 Single (2 bedrooms)
Bathroom: 1 Private
Tariff: B&B (continental) Double $80-$120 (Seasonal rates), Children $5, Credit Cards. NZ B&B Vouchers accepted
Nearest Town: 7km south of Waipu on Cove Road (Main Coastal Road).

Waipu Cove cottages are on our 4 acre property, situated in individual settings, directly behind the sand hills of Waipu Cove surf beach. We have direct beach access.
A shallow tidal estuary laps the boundary with a complimentary dinghy available to explore.
Each cottage is fully furnished including baths, separate showers, televisions, microwaves, full stoves, washing machines, heaters, fridge/freezers and gas bbq's.
The original cottage was built in 1937 and enjoys estuary views, claw foot bath and traditional interior. Sea views of the Pacific Ocean and Islands are experienced from the 2 new cottages and wood sarked ceilings compliment a cosy atmosphere. The Waipu area is serviced by shops, take-aways and two restaurants. Local activities include boat fishing excursions, horse trekking, Waipu glow worms caves, golf, private garden visits, Waipu museum, coastal walks, a waterfall, or just seaside rest and relaxation. Truly an idyllic spot for any season. Smoking outside only please.

Waipu Cove
Self-contained Accommodation
Address: 53 St Anne Road,
Waipu Cove, RD 2, Waipu
Name: Flower Haven
Telephone: (09) 432 0421
Mobile: (025) 287 2418
Email: flowerhaven@xtra.co.nz
Beds: 1 Queen, 1 Double (2 bedrooms)
Bathroom: 1 Private
Tariff: B&B (continental) Double $90 (Dec-Feb, Easter & Labour weekend) or $70 (Mar-Nov), Non smokers only. NZ B&B Vouchers accepted. No pets.
Nearest Town: 8km south of Waipu, off Cove Road

Our accommodation is a fully self-contained downstairs two bedroomed flat with separate access, fridge / freezer, stove, microwave, washing machine, radio, TV. One bed is a double innerspring, the other a queen waterbed. Linen, duvets, blankets, and bath towels are provided. The tariff includes continental breakfast which is optional and if not required then reduced charges apply. We enjoy an elevated position with panoramic views of the sweep of Bream Bay and islands and are developing the quarter acre grounds as a garden retreat. We are a 5 minute walk to the shop, sandy surf beach and rocks and are handy to many places of interest such as wild life sanctuary, museum, golf courses, horse riding treks, chartered fishing trips, limestone caves, walking tracks, Marsden Point Oil Refinery visitors centre, with Whangarei 35 minutes and Auckland 1 1/2 hours away.
Directions: *Last house on left of St Anne Road (off Cove Road).*

Langs Beach
Bed & Breakfast
Address: 14 Anderson Place,
Lang Cove B&B, Langs Beach,
Northland
Name: Jim & Kerry Jack
Telephone: (09) 432 0910
Beds: 1 Queen, 1 Double (2 bedrooms)
Bathroom: 1 Ensuite, 1 Guests share
Tariff: B&B (continental) Double $75 & $90,
Accommodation for young children is limited,
Dinner by arrangement.
Nearest Town: 10km to Waipu and SH1, 50km south of Whangarei

Our new home only 1 1/2 hours north of Auckland overlooks Lang Cove with expansive views of Langs Beach (3 minutes walk) and Bream Bay. You will have full use of your own living area with large double room, bathroom, lounge and two decks. A second double room is available to accommodate your family or friends. Accommodation for young children is limited. (Sky TV) Langs Beach is quiet and secluded, the ideal place to relax and enjoy the beach, native bush and unspoiled beauty of the area. For the more adventurous there is an extensive range of local outdoor and sporting activities available. Northland's major tourist attractions including the world famous Bay of Islands are easy day trips from Langs Beach. You are very welcome to join us for dinner. We have a dog (never inside) and a sensible cat. We look forward to welcoming you to Langs Beach.

Waipu
Homestay
Address: Cove Road, Langs Beach, Waipu
Name: Lochalsh
Telephone: 09-432 0053
Fax: 09-432 0053
Email: langs@ihug.co.nz
Beds: 1 King, 2 Single (2 bedrooms)
Bathroom: 2 Ensuite
Tariff: B&B (full) Double $80-$90, Single $65,
Dinner $20. Credit Cards accepted
Nearest Town: 40 mins South of Whangarei,
10 mins South of Waipu

Our great-grandfather, William Maxwell Lang, settled this area in 1853. Our home is the old Lang homestead and it couldn't be closer to this most beautiful of surf beaches looking out over Bream Bay and the Hen and Chicken Islands. The swimming is safe, the fishing is good. Restaurants within 10 minutes drive. As this area and our family are strongly Scottish, we offer either a traditional breakfast or Crofters Breakfast which can include porridge, fresh baps, and oatcakes. For a small charge we will make Scottish teas with girdle scones, jam and cream. The winter has its own charms ...... our King size bedroom has an open fire place for chilly nights. There is a guest lounge and dining area and guest kitchen with fridge/freezer and microwave. Billie and Graham and their cat Ruadh (Rug) would love to share this delightful spot with you.

Kerikeri (Out of sequence)
Homestay, Farmstay, Self-contained cabin
Address: Inlet Road, Kerikeri
Name: Kerikeri "Inlet View"
Telephone: (09) 407 7477
Fax: (09) 407 7478
Mobile: (025) 934 317
Beds: 1 Queen, 2 Double,
2 Single (5 bedrooms). Cabin 1 Double
Bathroom: 2 Ensuite, 1 Guests share
Tariff: B&B (full) Double $65,
Single $45, Dinner $15.
Nearest Town: Kerikeri - 3 mins

Would you like some good old Kiwi hospitality?
Our seven bedroom refurbished home now has superb views, not only of the Inlet, but of Cape Brett and Russell. Our 1100 acre sheep and beef farm borders the Waitangi Forest. Edmonds ruins, beaches and the Great Escape yacht charters are just a few minutes away. Enjoy a full breakfast consisting of free-range chook eggs, our own sausages etc. before exploring the many attractions Kerikeri has to offer.
Wayne the manager may be able to arrange horse treks on our Appaloosa horses.
Note: Not opening till December so please phone first. We may be able to pick you up.
Directions: *At Kerikeri township turn right into Cobham or Hobson Street which turns into Inlet Road. About 8 km on tarseal look out for white B&B sign. For further directions ask the manager (09) 407 5955.*

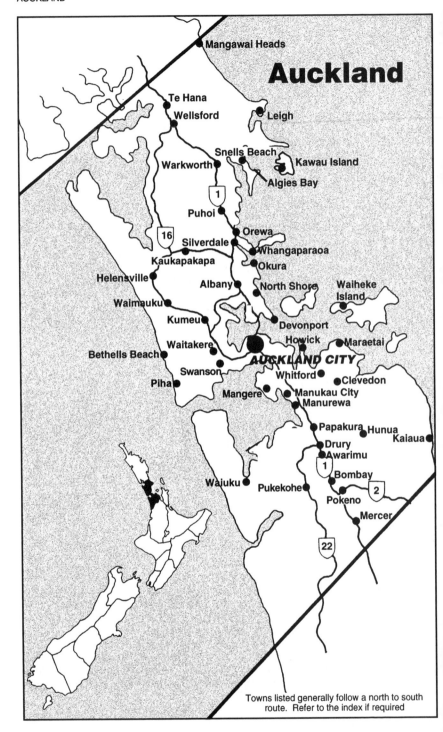

Auckland

Mangawai Heads

Te Hana
Wellsford
Leigh

Snells Beach
Warkworth
Kawau Island
Algies Bay

Puhoi

Orewa
Silverdale
Whangaparaoa
Kaukapakapa
Okura
Helensville
Albany
North Shore
Waiheke Island
Waimauku
Kumeu
Devonport
Waitakere
Howick
Maraetai
Bethells Beach
AUCKLAND CITY
Swanson
Whitford
Clevedon
Piha
Mangere
Manukau City
Manurewa

Papakura Hunua
Drury
Kaiaua
Awarimu
Waiuku
Bombay
Pukekohe
Pokeno
Mercer

Towns listed generally follow a north to south
route. Refer to the index if required

74

AUCKLAND

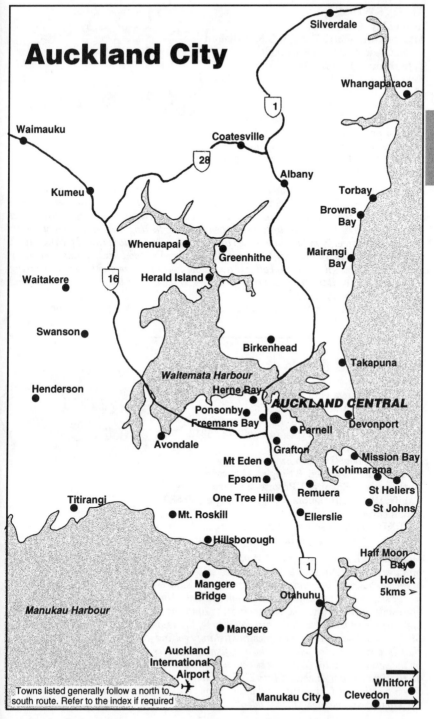

Auckland City

Silverdale

Whangaparaoa

1

Waimauku

Coatesville

28

Albany

Kumeu

Torbay

Browns Bay

Whenuapai

Greenhithe

Mairangi Bay

Waitakere

16

Herald Island

Swanson

Henderson

Birkenhead

Waitemata Harbour

Takapuna

Herne Bay

AUCKLAND CENTRAL

Ponsonby

Freemans Bay

Devonport

Avondale

Parnell

Grafton

Mt Eden

Mission Bay

Kohimarama

Epsom

One Tree Hill

Remuera

St Heliers

Mt. Roskill

St Johns

Ellerslie

Hillsborough

Half Moon Bay

1

Howick 5kms ➢

Mangere Bridge

Otahuhu

Manukau Harbour

Mangere

Auckland International Airport

Whitford

Clevedon

Towns listed generally follow a north to south route. Refer to the index if required

Manukau City

75

Mangawhai

Homestay
Address: Staniforth Road, R.D.5, Wellsford
Name: Jean & Don Goldschmidt
Telephone: (09) 431 5096
Fax: (09) 431 5063
Mobile: (025) 829 736
Email: goldschmidt@xtra.co.nz
Beds: 1 Queen, 1 Twin (2 bedrooms)
Bathroom: 1 Private, 1 Family share
Tariff: B&B (full) Double $85, Dinner $25.
Credit cards NZ B&B Vouchers accepted
Nearest Town: Mangawhai 7 km

High on the hills above Mangawhai on the east coast between Wellsford and Whangarei lies our property. 90 mins north of Auckland makes it a convenient stopover from the airport on the road north. We are on a scenic route which takes in Langs Beach and Waipu. Our delights are the long empty beaches, the fishing, the golf, the walks and the expansive view from the house of sea and islands. Our house is ideal for B&B with the bedrooms in two wings, with a separate sitting room, good heating and charming architectural design. Tea and coffee is available in the private quiet rooms. Sharing our home with visitors gives us great pleasure. Have dinner with us and enjoy good food, good company and fun.
Directions: *13km on Mangawhai Rd from Highway 1. Phone for directions.*

Mangawhai Heads

Guest House
Address: "Mangawhai Lodge",
4 Heather St, Mangawhai Heads
Name: Mangawhai Lodge
Telephone: (09) 431 5311 **Fax**: (09) 431 5312
Mobile: (025) 271 2790
Email: the.lodge@xtra.co.nz
Beds: 3 King, 2 Queen, 8 Single (5 bedrooms)
Bathroom: 2 Ensuite, 1 Private, 2 Guests share
Tariff: B&B (full) Double $85-$130, Single $60-$80.
Credit cards.
NZ B&B Vouchers accepted $25 surcharge. (Not accepted Jan/Feb)
Nearest Town: Mangawhai Heads - 5 minute walk.

Mangawhai Lodge is situated at Mangawhai Heads, a scenic water lovers paradise 90 minutes north of Auckland. This elevated colonial-style lodge offers spectacular views of the harbour, white sandy beaches and outer islands of the Gulf. This makes for an idyllic stop-over or weekend retreat. Rooms furnished in elegant Northland Pacifica style open onto wide verandahs, enhancing the ambience of this gracious house. Being opposite an 18 hole championship golf course, licensed cafe and bowling green makes Mangawhai Lodge ideal for couples and fishing / golfing groups of up to 10 guests. Enjoy the white sandy surf beaches, walkways, fishing charters, golf, crafts and cafes or lounge on the veranda reading the wide selection of magazines, just watching the boats sail by.
Directions: *From Auckland turn R Mangawhai sign (6 km north of Wellsford).*
From North turn L at Waipu and follow scenic coastal route south.
Bookings recommended. Please telephone.

Te Hana, Wellsford

Historic Farmhouse
Address: 'The Retreat', Te Hana, R.D.5, Wellsford
Name: Tony & Colleen Moore
Telephone: (09) 423 8547
Email: theretreat@xtra.co.nz
Beds: 1 Queen, 1 Double, 1 Single (2 bedrooms)
Bathroom: 1 Guests share
Tariff: B&B (full) Double $70, Single $40,
Dinner $20, Credit cards. NZ B&B Vouchers accepted
Nearest Town: Wellsford (6km)

"The Retreat" is a historic kauri homestead built in 1867 for a family with 12 children. The house is set back from the road overlooking farmland, including our eight acres where we graze black and white sheep. The pet sheep enjoy being hand fed. Colleen is a spinner and weaver producing handcrafts from the wool, and the finished articles are available for sale.

We have created an acre of landscaped garden to complement the house, including a large herb garden, croquet lawn, fish pond garden, and walk through perennial borders to the summer house. Fresh vegetables from the garden and fruit from our orchard are on the menu in season. Most of our guests choose to have dinner with us. We have travelled extensively overseas and in New Zealand and are keen to promote our scenic and historic places - especially local ones.

Directions: *"The Retreat" is on the left 6km north of Wellsford on State Highway 1 and 13km south of Kaiwaka. You will see the "Weaving Studio" sign at our entrance.*

Leigh

Homestay
Address: 10 Ferndale Avenue, Leigh
Name: Joan & Ken Helliwell
Telephone: (09) 422 6099
Fax: (09) 422 6099
Beds: 1 Double, 4 Single (2/3 bedrooms.
Guest living room with
TV and tea making equipment)
Bathroom: 1 Guests share
Tariff: B&B (full) Double $65, Single $45,
Dinner $20pp. NZ B&B Vouchers accepted
Nearest Town: Warkworth 23km

Leigh is a seaside fishing village 70-80 minutes drive North of Auckland, situated on the cliffs above the Leigh Cove. It offers facilities for boating, including a ramp and anchorage within the small harbour. The village community has an interdenominational church, a hotel, general store, "take-away" food store, garage and dairy.
Within 5 minutes car travel are sandy swimming beaches, excellent underwater diving, a good surfing beach, tidal flats as well as deep water and rocky shore coastline, coastal and country walks, and the Marine Reserve.
Our home is in the village. We are retired school teachers living in the family home with a large, well laid out garden. We have travelled overseas extensively, enjoying other people's hospitality, and would be glad to offer a warm "Kiwi" welcome to our guests.

Warkworth

Farmstay
Address: 'Blue Hayes Farmstay',
44 Martins Bay Road, 13 km east Warkworth
Name: Rod & Rosalie Miller
Telephone: (09) 425 5612 **Fax**: 09 4255612
Mobile: 025 776 873
Beds: 4 Single (2 bedroom)
Bathroom: 1 Family share, 1 Ensuite
Tariff: B&B (full) Double with ensuite $75, Double share $65, Single $40, Children 1/2 price, Dinner $20, Credit cards. NZ B&B Vouchers accepted
Nearest Town: Warkworth 13 Kms

We live on a 314 acre coastal farm overlooking Kawau Bay, Mahurangi Heads and river in the Hauraki Gulf, approximately 80 km north of Auckland. We farm sheep, poultry, deer and cattle. You are welcome to participate in daily farming activities including hand feeding deer. We live in a private setting with plenty of open space, close to good safe beaches and seaside shopping centre, 13 km from Warkworth on sealed road.
Our family home is 50 years old, comfortable, warm and relaxed with open fireplace, woodstove and beautiful views. Farm walks and natural bush reserves on property with tracks to view N.Z. flora including restored old school.
Rod is a commercial pilot and flying instructor. Scenic flights both local and Hauraki Gulf available. Local area attractions include craft centres, Goat Island Marine Reserve and historic Kawau Island.
Rod and Rosalie welcome you to share their hositality before a 3 course dinner.
Directions: *Please phone.*

Warkworth

B&B+Self-contained Accom.
Address: 'Homewood Cottage',
17 View Rd., Warkworth
Name: 'Homewood Cottage' Ina & Trevor Shaw
Telephone: (09) 425 8667 **Fax**: (09) 425 9610
Beds: 1 Double, 3 Single (2 bedrooms)
Bathroom: 2 Ensuite
Tariff: B&B (continental) Double or Twin $70 plus $20 each extra person. 10% Discount 3 nights or more. NZ B&B Vouchers accepted Double room only
Nearest Town: Warkworth 0.5km - Auckland city 1 hour - SH1

Our individually styled home on the hillside above Warkworth looks over trees to the surrounding hills and the town nestled below. The house is set in a cottage garden lovingly tended for guests tranquillity. This is a peaceful place to relax.

Both rooms are warm, comfortable bed-sitter style rooms, both on ground level with individual parking. The rooms are privately situated as we understand most guests like privacy but do feel free to come in for a chat. Full facilities include all you'd expect; your own entrance, ensuite and toilet, radio, TV, tea / coffee making and a good sized room with a nice place to sit. No cooking facilities but the double room has a kitchen unit. The twin room has an adjoining little bedroom suitable for a family member. The beds are all comfortable with wool blankets, continental quilts and electric blankets. There is a hair drier, small frig and laundry facilities available. Please ask.

Breakfast, listed continental, is substantial and includes a varied selection of fruits, cereals, breads, home-made preserves and goodies. We also provide you with afternoon tea.

Warkworth restaurants are many and varied and we hold menus so you can make a choice. Warkworth, with its tree lined river and old-world shops is one of New Zealand's most charming villages.

Travelling remains one of our loves and walking our favourite way of exploring. We have detailed knowledge of the area to share with you. The golf course is two minutes away, Parry Kauri Park a few minutes and the beaches 10 / 15 minutes. Ina is an artist whose work is selected for Save the Children cards while Trevor has spent a lifetime as a writer and author.

After seven years of hosting, we look forward to guests in our home. We are a smoke free home please.

Directions: *Turn off SH1 at Hill St. Top of Hill St is View Rd.*

Snells Beach, Warkworth

Homestay/Farmstay
Address: 416 Mahurangi East Road,
Snells Beach, Warkworth
Name: Mahurangi Lodge
Alison & Rodney Woodcock
Telephone: (09) 425 5465
Fax: (09) 425 5465
Beds: 3 Double, 1 Twin, 1 Family - sleeps 6 (4 bedrooms)
Bathroom: 1 Ensuite, 1 Guests share, 1 Family share
Tariff: B&B (continental) Double $50-$70, Single $25-$40, Children half price,
Dinner $20 by prior arrangement, Discount for extra nights stay and winter,
Credit Cards Visa/MC/BC. Campervans welcome. BBQ area. NZ B&B Vouchers
accepted $10 surcharge for 1 night stay on long weekends (Public Holidays)
Nearest Town: Warkworth 9km

Welcome to our colonial-style homestay just 1 hour from Auckland (1 1/2 from Airport) on a 30 acre farmlet overlooking Kawau Bay, Great Barrier, Little Barrier, Coromandel and the Mahurangi River. Our upstairs bedrooms are spacious, clean and with superb seaviews in a relaxed friendly smokefree atmosphere, with a Manx cat and native birds around. Your needs are our top priority with some local attractions offering our guests special discounts. A complimentary Kawau Island cruise included in longer stays. Enjoy a welcome 'cuppa' on arrival with everything available anytime you want another. Let us help you maximise your sightseeing of the numerous nearby attractions or further afield. There are several restaurants nearby and in Warkworth. Recommended by Jane King's 'N.Z. Handbook'. At Warkworth traffic lights follow Snells Beach signposts, straight ahead at Roundabout 1 1/2 km right on the hilltop. We have travelled overseas and throughout NZ and love to learn about your area.

Warkworth - Sandspit

Homestay
Address: 38 Kanuka Rd, R.D. 2, Warkworth
Name: Margaret & Ron Everett.
Belvedere Homestay
Telephone: (09) 425 7201 **Fax**: (09) 425 7201
Mobile: (025) 284 4771
Beds: 1 Queen, 1 Double, 2 Single (3 bedrooms)
Bathroom: 1 Ensuite 1 Guest Share
Tariff: B&B (continental) Queen with Ensuite $90. Double & Twin $80, Single $45,
Dinner $30pp. Children's prices on request. NZ B&B Vouchers accepted $15 surcharge
Nearest Town: Warkworth 7km

Set in 11 acres, and overlooking the Spit where the ferries leave for Kawau Island with a 360 degree view from countryside to Kawau and Little Barrier Island. We have farm animals, calves, plus native bush with birds such as swallows, fantails, rosellas, hawks, pheasants. For your relaxing and pleasure, fishing from beach or boat, golf, tennis and town within 7km. Central heating or air conditioning, 3 bedrooms (1 double with ensuite, 1 double, 1 twin with share bathroom). Games room, bar, pool table, darts and a relaxing separate spa pool conservatory with exercise gym plus outside decks for relaxing, a sunken rose garden and barbecue area. $90 with ensuite, $080 double or twin, $45 single, include continental breakfast. (Full breakfast on request) Margaret's flair with cooking is a great way to relax with us over pre-dinner drinks and wine with your 3 course meal $30.00 per person. Childrens prices on request. Warkworth and our house have many attractions, well worth visiting and we look forward to making your stay a memorable one.

Warkworth - Algies Bay
Homestay
Address: 'Ceri', 56 Mera Road, Algies Bay, Warkworth
Name: Ngaire Miller
Telephone: (09) 425 5603
Mobile: (025) 977 941
Beds: 3 Single, 1 Double
(Double and Single bedroom/1 Family room - 2 single)
Bathroom: 1 Private
Tariff: B&B (full) Double $70, Single $40, Dinner $20, Children $15, Packed lunch by arrangement, Vegetarian meals on request. Credit Cards NZ B&B Vouchers accepted
Nearest Town: 10km from Warkworth, 1 hour drive from Auckland. Mahurangi shopping area 2km.

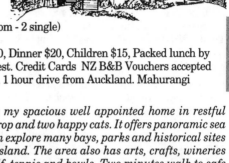

A warm welcome awaits you to share my spacious well appointed home in restful garden surroundings with bush backdrop and two happy cats. It offers panoramic sea views of Kawau Bay. From here you can explore many bays, parks and historical sites including Mansion House on Kawau Island. The area also has arts, crafts, wineries and a selection of restaurants, plus golf, tennis and bowls. Two minutes walk to safe swimming beach, ramp for boating and picnic area. Waken to the sounds of native birds and the smell of fresh home baked bread. TV, fridge, tea and coffee making facilities. Privacy. As a VIC volunteer I am well equipped to assist you maximise your stay in this beautiful area. Come and unwind in this quiet, relaxing smokefree environment. I am a registered nurse and offer therapeutic massages. Only one set of guests accommodated at a time. Telephone or call at Information Centre, Warkworth for directions.

Warkworth
Guest House
Address: 'Kowhai Lodge', 348 Kaipara Flats Rd, R.D.1, Warkworth
Name: Christina & Barrie Ellison
Telephone: (09) 425 9193
Fax: (09) 425 9193
Mobile: (025) 241 3783
Beds: 2 Double, 2 Twin (4 bedrooms)
Bathroom: 1 Guest share, 1 Family share
Tariff: B&B (special) $45pp, Dinner $30pp.
Credit cards. NZ B&B Vouchers accepted $20 surcharge Mon-Thur
Nearest Town: Warkworth 6km

Kowhai Lodge is a beautifully restored 1920's bungalow in a rural location minutes from Warkworth. The bedrooms are furnished in different woods, the doubles are oak or kauri and the twin, rimu or mahogany. Jodie our house dog will make you most welcome as will Chevis our Persian cat. Refreshments are readily available. We take great pride in our special breakfasts. All baking is home-made as are jams and relishes. A hearty meal can be prepared especially for you by prior arrangement, or you can enjoy dinner at one of our local restaurants. We hope your stay with us will be memorable as we do our best to "make you feel special". We welcome you into our home as guests and trust that you will leave as friends. We are a non-smoking household.

Sandspit, Warkworth
Bed & Breakfast
Address: The Saltings Guest House,
Sandspit Rd, R.D.2, Warkworth
Name: Jean Mason
Telephone: (09) 425 9670 **Fax**: (09) 425 9674
Mobile: (021) 675 425
Beds: 2 King, 1 Queen, 1 Double, 4 Single (4 bedrooms)
Bathroom: 3 Ensuite, 1 Private

GUEST HOUSE

Tariff: B&B (full) Double $95-$125, Single $80-$100. Credit Cards. NZ B&B Vouchers
accepted $20 surcharge
Nearest Town: Warkworth 6km.

*Situated on the Sandspit Rd, this is a Bed & Breakfast with a difference. The house
has been renovated to give a French provincial feeling, with the added comfort of Kiwi
hospitality making it ideal for couples who want to get away from it all and enjoy a
clean fresh environment, with plenty of outdoor activities in the area. The Saltings
Guest House sits on six acres of elevated farmland overlooking the beautiful estuaries
of Sandspit and surrounding farmland. Just one hour drive north of Auckland city,
and five minutes from the delightful village of Warkworth, where there are a selection
of restaurants and cafes at your disposal, plus we are within walking distance to the
ferry where many cruises are available, including a visit to Kawau Island and the
historic Mansion House. The four well appointed guest bedrooms are beautifully
decorated with comfort in mind. Myself and friends Tess (Dalmatian dog), Pipi and
Tom (cats) look forward to meeting you, and making your stay a memorable one. Young
adults welcome.*
Home Page: http://nz.com/webnz/bbnz/salting.htm.
Directions: *Please phone for directions.*

Warkworth
Homestay+Self-contained Accom.
Address: 541 Woodcocks Road, Warkworth
Name: Willow Lodgee"
Telephone: (09) 425 7676
Fax: (09) 425 7676
Mobile: (025) 940 885
Beds: 1 Queen, 2 Double,
Single (4 bedrooms)
Bathroom: 2 Ensuite, 1 Private
Tariff: B&B (full) Double $80-$100, Single $60,
Children $20, Dinner $25. NZ B&B Vouchers accepted
Nearest Town: Warkworth 5 kms.

*Your hosts John and Paddy have more than 30 years experience in the hospitality field
and have lived in Warkworth for the past 26 years. Our wealth of local knowledge will
help ensure your stay at Willow Lodge is both memorable and enjoyable. Willow Lodge
boasts tranquil rural views over rolling farmland and is set in two acres of landscaped
gardens. We offer luxury self-contained units which open onto a private courtyard.
Should you prefer, acommodation in the form of a double bedroom with private
bathroom is available within our home. We provide continental or cooked breakfasts
and mouth-watering evening meals by arrangement. We are a comfortable one-hour
scenic drive from downtown Auckland, and therefore well situated for guests arriving
via Auckland Airport.*
P.S. We are more than happy to arrange transport and trips.

Warkworth

Country Homestay, Bed & Breakfast
Address: "Bellgrove",
346 Woodcocks Road, RD 1, Warkworth
Name: John & Julie Bell
Telephone: (09) 425 9770
Fax: (09) 425 9770
Mobile: (025) 989 389
Beds: 1 King, 1 Queen,
2 single (3 bedrooms)
Bathroom: 1 Guests share
Tariff: B&B (full) Double $80, Single $50, Children half price, Dinner $25, Credit
Cards.
Nearest Town: Warkworth 4km

"Bellgrove" is a two-storeyed cedar home set on 3 acres of gardens and paddocks, only 3km on a sealed road from SH1 and 4km from Warkworth. The property is bordered by the Mahurangi stream and adjacent to a native tree reserve. Enjoy the rural and bush views from the extensive decks or swim in our large in-ground pool. Meet the farm animals - our 8 year old daughter Jessica will introduce you to Cecil, our friendly hand-fed ram. We enjoy indoor / outdoor living - Julie excels in fine home cooking - barbecued, rotisserie lamb our specialty. Stay one night or several - there is plenty to see in historic Warkworth and its surrounding area - bushwalking, boating, fishing (only 15 minutes from fabulous beaches), Kawau Island, wineries. Guests accommodation is upstairs and separate from family. All our beds have quality, top of the range mattresses. Children welcome. Non-smoking household. You won't be disappointed at "Bellgrove".

Warkworth

Two Self-contained Accommodations
Address: 105 Ridge Road, Scott's Landing,
RD 2, Warkworth
Name: Island Bay Retreat
Telephone: (09) 425 4269
Fax: (09) 425 4269
Beds: 1 Queen, 2 Singles (2 bedrooms).
Bathroom: 2 Ensuites
Tariff: B&B (continental) Double $95,
Single $75,
NZ B&B Vouchers accepted
Nearest Town: Warkworth 15 mins,
Snell's Beach Shopping Center 8 minutes.

Our new two storey brick home is situated on 2 acres of gardens by the water's edge on the scenic Mahurangi Peninsula. This idyllic spot offers a haven for boating, fishing seashore walks and swimming. Relax and unwind in our cosy and peaceful waterside accommodations. Choose between our large loft apartment with rimu cathedral ceiling or our spacious single level unit. Both are self contained with cooking and dining facilities, ensuites, comfy new beds, TV, BBQ area. With your own separate entrance to each unit you can be assured of complete privacy. Enjoy magnificent sea views from every ranchslider which opens onto your own patio. Share some time with us sightseeing or fishing on our boat (time and weather permitting). Many local attractions and activities such as tennis, golf, horse riding, island cruises, arts and crafts, restaurants, cafes, shopping, are nearby. We Bill and Joyce and our little dog "Toby" enjoy meeting people and look forward to making your stay an unforgetable one.

Warkworth

Farmstay
Address: "Ryme Intrinseca",
121 Perry Road, RD3, Warkworth
Name: Elizabeth & Cam Mitchell
Phone: (09) 425 9448
Fax: (09) 425 9458
Beds: 2 Queen, 2 Single
(3 bedrooms: 1 Queen + 1 Single -
1 room, 1 Queen - 1 room, 1 Single - 1 room)
Bathroom: 1 Guests share
Tariff: B&B (full) Double $80, Single $50, Children half price, Dinner $25.   NZ
B&B Vouchers accepted $10 surcharge
Nearest Town: Warkworth 6 km

Our 110 acre beef and sheep farm is ideally situated for travellers on their way to the Bay of Islands as it is an easy hours drive from Auckland, just 1km off SH1 and 6km south of the attractive rural town of Warkworth. Our spacious cedar and kauri home is set in a secluded valley overlooking native bush and surrounded by gardens and a croquet lawn. Join in farm activities or just relax. We offer comfortable farm house accommodation and the upstairs bedrooms with their extensive farm views open into a large guest sitting room with TV, and tea / coffee making facilities. Evening meals, if requested, feature home-grown produce and NZ wines. Local sightseeing attractions include historic Kawau Island, the Mahurangi Harbour, Regional Parks and many lovely beaches. Our interests include gardening, reading, sailing and caring for our farm and animals including our Jack Russell terrier. We are widely travelled within NZ and overseas and warmly welcome visitors to our home.

Matakana, Warkworth

Homestay+Self-contained Suite+B&B
Address: "Hurstmere House",
Tongue Farm Road, Matakana
Name: Anne & Bob Moir
Telephone: (09) 422 9220
Fax: (09) 422 9220
Mobile: (025) 820 336
Beds: 2 Queen, 2 Single (3 bedrooms/1 S.C. Suite with Queen bed)
Bathroom: 3 Ensuite
Tariff: B&B (full) Double $130, Single $100, Dinner $40pp includes wine & pre-dinner drinks, Self-contained Suite: $150 per couple,
Discount for 2 nights or more, Credit Cards (VISA/MC/American Express).
Nearest Town: Warkworth 10km, Matakana Village 3 minutes

Hurstmere House overlooks picturesque Matakana valley farmland. This gracious two storey homestead is only one hour North of Auckland, 10 minutes from Warkworth, and within coo-ee of the beaches and islands of the golden Kowhai Coast. The charm of the restored old home with rimu timber panelling and staircase blends with the new architecturally designed French Provincial farmhouse kitchen and dining room extensions. Your hosts Anne and Bob offer you genuine North Auckland hospitality and sumptuous dinners with wine and flowers and gourmet or continental style breakfasts. When refreshed you can venture to two golf courses, village crafts markets, walk, fish, play tennis, swim, Heron's Flight vineyard or Morris & James pottery works. Visit nearby Leigh, Goat Island marine reserve, Tawharanui Regional Park, or catch a boat to Mansion House on Kawhau Island. This is heaven on earth - the best of countryside and seaside all rolled into one. Who could ask for anything more?
HomePage:http://www.kiwihome.co.n.z./stay/b-b/auckland/matakana.html#top
Directions: *Please ask when booking.*

84

Puhoi

Farmstay - the gentle way"
Address: 'Our Farm-Park', RD3 Kaukapakapa, Auckland 1250
Name: Peter & Nichola(s) Rodgers
Telephone: (09) 422 0626
Fax: (09) 422 0626
Email: ofp@friends.co.nz
Beds: 1 Queen bedroom, 1 Twin bedroom with child's window-seat bed (2 bedrooms)
Bathroom: 1 Private
Tariff: B&B double $110 (single $85), Dinner $25. All meals available. Children (with parents) under 5 free; 5-12 $10; 13-17 $20. Additional adults $40.
Ask about "Three night family holiday" rates. Credit cards accepted. Prices firm to 1 October 1999. NZ B&B Vouchers accepted $75 value
Nearest Town: Puhoi 4.5km,btwn Orewa & Warkworth; 60km Nth cntrl Akl, International Airport 80km.

Visit Hot Pools, beaches (wild surf or child safe), bush walks, bird sanctuaries, Island trips, marine Reserves, canoeing, snorkelling and diving, fishing, Historic sites, Craft: Auckland shopping, zoo, evening events.
KIA ORA.
Share our 110 acre organic property high in the hills, with beautiful panoramic views, fresh air, clean water. Very comfortable beds. Delicious meals (vegetarian if you ask) based on taste-filled organic fruit and vegetables and adrenaline-free meat. NO-ONE SMOKES HERE.
Farmed with kindness are touchable sheep (lots of spring lambs), beautiful belted Galloway cattle (calves most of year) run in family groupings; safe horses; ducks and poultry run free; milk our cows; make butter, yoghurt, ice-cream and cheeses.....
Sleep off "jet-lag"; share knowledge; learn about organic farming; one-to-one "Conversational English" Lessons with Peter (qualified teacher & psychologist); stress relief; see the unusual home we are building ourselves; share love for Taha Maori; environment; flora and fauna; use our business facilities and base for family contact while anywhere in New Zealand.
Homepage: www.friends.co.nz

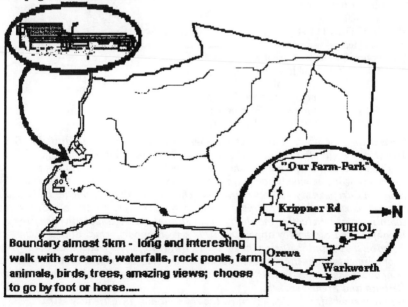

Boundary almost 5km - long and interesting walk with streams, waterfalls, rock pools, farm animals, birds, trees, amazing views; choose to go by foot or horse.....

Orewa

Homestay
Address: 54 Walton Street,
Red Beach, Orewa
Name: Helen and Sonny
Telephone: (09) 426 6963
Beds: 1 Double. 1 Double,
1 Single in detached loft room
Bathroom: 2 Private
Tariff: B&B (continental) Double $60,
Single $35; Dinner $20.
NZ B&B Vouchers accepted
Nearest Town: Orewa 5 km

This is a pleasant place 2km from State Highway 1 and 100 metres from a good beach which we enjoy very much. We have had many guests here, on their way or returning from the North, or simply to enjoy what this area has to offer, the pleasant town of Orewa 5km, Waiwera Thermal Pools 10km, the Whangaparaoa Peninsula with its many Bays, and Auckland 30km. A warm welcome is assured, comfortable beds and a breakfast to suit your taste. There is a resident cat. Approximately 1 hour from airport.

Orewa

Lodge
Address: Moontide Lodge,
19 Ocean View Road,
Orewa - Hatfields Beach
Name: Monika and Jurgen Resch
Telephone: (09) 426 2374
Fax: (09) 426 2398
Mobile: (025) 279 2194
Beds: 4 Queen (4 bedrooms)
Bathroom: 3 Ensuite, 1 Private
Tariff: B&B (full) Double $150-$180,
single $130-$160, Dinner $40
Visa/Mastercard/American Express/Diners Club.
NZ B&B Vouchers accepted $75surcharge
Nearest Town: Orewa (2 minutes by car)

Overlooking the native bush and the sheltered bay of beautiful Hatfields Beach Moontide Lodge offers a high standard of "boutique" accommodation. We are situated on a cliff with access to the beach. Each of our four luxuriously appointed bedrooms features ensuite or private bathroom and breathtaking seaviews. All rooms in European style with writing desk, chairs and table, telephone, TV / video on request, clock / radio, hair dryer, heater and tea / coffee facilities. Enjoy your complimentary tea / coffee and sherry in our elegant guest lounge with open fireplace. Breakfast and dinner (by appointment) is served in our formal dining room or al fresco on the verandah during the summer. We also offer, for a stay exceeding 3 days, a complimentary shuttle service to Auckland Airport. Excursions in our comfortable mini bus to the nearby Tourist attractions can be arranged. Small conference venue. German and French spoken.
We are a smoke-free Lodge. Timmy, the resident dog, is a friendly extra.

Silverdale, Auckland

Farmstay+Bed & Breakfast
Address: 'Mt Pleasant', 468 Pine Valley Road,
Silverdale, Auckland
Name: Bob & Molly Crawford
Telephone: (09) 426 4280
Beds: 1 Double, 2 Single (3 bedrooms)
Bathroom: 1 Guests share
Tariff: B&B (full) Double $90, Single $50,
Children half price, Campervans welcome.
NZ B&B Vouchers accepted with $30 surcharge
Nearest Town: Orewa 8km, 40km north of Auckland

Kia Ora!
Bob and I and our 12 year old son Robert would love to share our 320 acre beef farm and family home with you. Built at the turn of the century, from timber milled out of bush on the property, 'Mt Pleasant' is one of Silverdale's most historic buildings. The unusual design and character of the homestead, furnished throughout with antique colonial furniture, exudes the peace and charm of yester-year. Relax in the garden, by the pool, or feel free to explore the bush.
Robert enjoys being "tour guide", and with his dog and farm bike will escort you around the farm. Our interests include wood turning, gardening, tennis, antiques, local and general history, and having all travelled extensively now enjoy the opportunity to share with others. All nationalities welcome.
Directions: *Please phone for directions.*

Silverdale, Auckland

Bed & Breakfast
Address: 'The Ambers', 146 Pine Valley Road,
Silverdale, Auckland 1462
Name: Diane & Gerard Zwier
Telephone: (09) 426 5354 **Fax**: (09) 426 3287
Email: gzwier@xtra.co.nz
Beds: 2 Double, 2 Twin/Double (4 bedrooms)
Bathroom: 3 Ensuites, 1 Family share

Tariff: B&B (full) Double $110-$120, Single $65-$85, Credit Cards (VISA/MC/DC/AMEX). NZ B&B Vouchers accepted $50 surcharge
Nearest Town: 2 km south of Silverdale on State Highway 1, Auckland City 30 mins, Albany Unviersity 15 mins.

If you think romanticism is dead......think again.
Come and stay at "The Ambers", set on 14 picturesque acres, and enjoy the old world charm and luxury. Share our tranquil country atmosphere and warm hospitality. Relax with complimentary pre-dinner drinks in our elegant guest lounge with French doors into the garden or venture into our woodland area with stream. Both of us have travelled extensively and have interests in Art, Design and Philosophy. We have 3 German shepherd dogs which are very friendly but are restricted from guest areas. Guest rooms are individually decorated. Enjoy our attic suites with sloping ceilings or relax in our European style rooms with wonderfully comfortable beds and finest bed linen. Breakfast on the terrace or in our formal dining room with delicious country style breakfasts. Auckland is only 35 minutes away and we are minutes from beaches, restaurants and shops. Please phone for reservations/directions.
Home Page: www.the-ambers.co.nz

Whangaparaoa Peninsula

Homestay
Address: Cedar Farm, 39 Cedar Tce,
Stanmore Bay, Whangaparaoa
Name: Maureen & Alan Fullerton
Telephone: (09) 424 3133 **Fax**: (09) 424 3134
Mobile: (025) 281 3868
Beds: 1 Queen, 1 Twin, 1 Single (3 bedrooms)
Bathroom: 1 Ensuite, 1 Guests share
Tariff: B&B (continental) Queen $95,
Twin $80, Single $45, Dinner $25pp. Credit cards.
NZ B&B Vouchers accepted $15 surcharge
Nearest Town: Whangaparaoa 1 Km, Orewa 6 Km

We are retired dairy farmers who have travelled widely and now live on a 10 acre lifestyle block, grazing horses. Having guests is one of our great pleasures. Our home has easy flat access and a tranquil setting. Breakfast is served by our courtyard pool, a pleasant relaxing start to the day. For the energetic, swim in our pool or play table tennis or darts in the games room. Whangaparaoa has excellent amenities, restaurants and banks, lovely beaches - golf courses - Shakespeare park for bush walks and bird watching - Gulf Harbour Marina - ferries leave from the Marina for excursions to Tiritiri Matangi Island bird sanctuary - also to Auckland for a day in the city. We will be happy to help you plan activities. We have no pets. Non-smokers preferred. 30 minutes drive north of Auckland Harbour Bridge.
Directions: *Please phone for reservations and directions.*

Whangaparaoa Peninsula

Beachside Bed and Breakfast
Address: 'Matakatia Magic',
58 Matakatia Parade, Whangaparaoa Peninsula
Name: Nola
Telephone: (09) 424 0584
Beds: 5 Double, 2 Single (7 bedrooms)
Bathroom: 2 Guests share
Tariff: B&B (full) Peak Season (Labour weekend to Easter Monday): Beachfront double $120, Double $100, Single $60, children up to five free, $20 extra person.
Off season: Beachfront Double $100, Double $80, Single $50, children up to five free, $20 extra person. Credit Cards accepted. NZ B&B Vouchers accepted $20 surcharge
Nearest Town: Whangaparaoa Penninsula 5 mins. Auckland City 45 mins.

Nola welcomes you to the friendly B&B situated on the beachfront of sheltered Matakatia Bay, with safe swimming, views of Rangitoto Island and the Sky Tower, towards the end of Whangaparaoa Peninsula. The gentle sounds of sea, superb views, create the MAGIC you've been looking for. You are surrounded by the melody of Tui's and other bird life; local bush walks and regional parks. Only five minutes drive from Gulf Harbour village, marine and golf course. In close proximity to hot springs, Tiritiri Bird Sanctuary, fishing and diving day excursions. Our relaxed and tranquil setting, overlooks the America's Cup Race Course. The rooms are clean, with pleasant decor. Whangaparaoa Mall with shops, banks etc. and Hoyts Cinema 5 are within five minutes drive. If you care the big city, downtown Auckland is a 45 minute ferry ride away.
Directions: *Turn onto Whangaparaoa Peninsula. Remain on Whangaparaoa road, until reaching Manly village where the road turns right at the round about, then turn right into Capitol Road, at beach front turn left, the B&B is towards end of the bay.*

Gulf Harbour Whangaparaoa
Apartment Stay
Address: Gulf Harbour,
Whangaparaoa, Hibiscus Coast.
Name: Paul and Jenny Steele
Telephone: (09) 428 1400
Fax: (09) 428 1400
Beds: 1 King/Queen,
1 Double or 2 Single (2 bedrooms)
Bathroom: 2 Ensuites
Tariff: B&B (full) $120-$250 (depending on room and season). Dinner $30 pp.
Nearest Town: Whangaparaoa Town Centre 6.5 kms. Auckland city 50 kms.

A stunning Mediterranean retreat situated above the boat laden canal of Gulf Harbour is truly a GOLFING and AQUATIC paradise. From our comfortably appointed and spacious high-rise apartment there are panoramic views of Sky Tower, the North Shore, Kawau Island and the Gulf Harbour Country Club (venue for the 1998 World Cup of Golf). Play can be arranged mostly at discounted rates. Restaurants within strolling distance or easy driving. New Zealand style dinners cooked by arrangement after first night. We offer a complimentary tour of local highlights including many ferry / cruise options. Safe swimming beaches nearby. Two double ensuite bedrooms ensure privacy. Sauna available. A clean and friendly 14 year old Cocker Spaniel in residence. Airport pick up available.
Please phone for further information and tariff.

Whangaparaoa
Homestay/Self Contained Accommodation/Bed & Breakfast
Address: "Hibiscus Homestay",
895 Whangaparaoa Road, Little Manly,
Whangaparaoa
Name: David and Judy Turnbull
Telephone: 09-424 7507
Fax: 09-424 7507
Mobile: 025-273 9851
Beds: 1 Double (1 bedroom)
Bathroom: 1 Ensuite
Tariff: B&B (continental)
Double $110, Single $75.
Tariff may increase from September 1999.
Nearest Town: Whangaparaoa, 50 kms north of Auckland

Whether kiwis or overseas visitors, we welcome you to join us (and our cat) at our home and spacious grounds overlooking Little Manly beach. Members of our family have lived here since 1925, each generation being captivated by the bay. Whatever the weather, this place is magic. Our interests are sailing, fishing, gardening. Dinghy available for you to try your luck or join fishing / sailing charters at Gulf Harbour Marina. The area offers many interesting activities, cafes, bars, golf courses, excursions to Tiri Island Bird Sanctuary, coach tours, regional park tramping tracks and the clean, safe swimming beaches the Peninsular is reknown for. Self contained with own cooking facilities for long stay (self catering rates available); Continental breakfast for B&B.
Directions: *Phone, fax or write for reservations and directions.*

Kaukapakapa

Bed & Breakfast 1488
Address: "Willowbrook Farm",
Stoney Creek Road, Kaukapakapa
Name: June & Don Lamont
Telephone: (09) 420-5909
Fax: (09) 420-5909
Mobile: (025) 389 675
Beds: 1 Queen, 1 Double
Bathroom: 1 Ensuite, 1 Private
Tariff: B&B (Special) Double $75-$85,
Single $55, Dinner $25 each (by arrangement).
Nearest Town: Helensville or Orewa 12km

Willowbrook is a character 2-storey natural timber farmhouse. It is set in an attractive 50-acre valley on which we run cattle. Your spacious, sunny suite has its own private entranceway and is located on the upper wing of the house. The open plan lounge area is tastefully decorated and very comfortable with excellent views of the farm and garden. This facility also includes a queen size bed, TV, ensuite shower room and tea / coffee making facilities. You can enjoy the gardens and relax on the warm and sheltered verandah. We offer a mouth watering continental breakfast (including freshley baked bread & muffins). Our dog is a golden retriever called 'Barney' who will make you feel welcome. Our home is smoke free.

Directions: *Willowbrook is conveniently located 2.5km along Stoney Creek Road which runs directly off State Highway 16 at Kaukapakapa.*

Members of
**The New Zealand Association
Farm & Home Host Inc.**
maintain the highest standards &
are always delighted to welcome
guests into their homes.

Kaukapakapa

Farmstay+Self-contained Accom.
Address: Kereru Lodge, Arone Farm,
Makarau Road, R.D. 3, Kaukapakapa
Name: Betty Headford
Telephone: (09) 420 5223
Fax: (09) 420 5223
Beds: 1 Queen, 2 Double,
2 Single (3 bedrooms)
Bathroom: 1 Ensuite,
1 Family share, 1 Guests share
Tariff: B&B (full) Double $65, Single $45, Children $15, Dinner $20.
Campervans $25. Self-contained cottage: price on application. Credit cards.
NZ B&B Vouchers accepted
Nearest Town: Kaukapakapa 9 mins

Kereru Lodge

Relax. Be pampered. Come to a quiet rural valley and enjoy the peaceful tranquillity, the large garden and birdsong. The Homestead is large and modern, with plenty of indoor / outdoor living space. Wander in the garden, over the farm and through our native bush. Or you may play pool, petanque and croquet or just sit in the summer house and read. There are several local bush walks and the Kaipara Harbour for fishing, kayaking or watching the Godwits and other migrating birds. Play tennis or go golfing at the many surrounding golf courses. The self contained cottage is large and airy, has two double, two single and 1 set of bunk beds. It is available for weekend or longer stays. The Homestead is B&B or fully catered if required. We have many varied interests and love having a house full of people. We are non smokers. Please phone, fax or write.

Helensville/Parakai

KAIPARA HOUSE

Homestay
Address: Cnr Hwy 16 & Parkhurst Rd,
Parakai/Helensville
Name: John & Diane Barrett
Telephone: (09) 420 7462
Fax: (09) 420 7458
Mobile: (025) 814 617
Beds: 1 Queen, 2 Single
(2 bedrooms) Extra single available
Bathroom: Family share & Ensuite
Tariff: B&B (full) Double $80, Single 45, Children negotiable.
Nearest Town: Helensville 1/2km, Auckland city 35 mins.

Our 105 yr old Villa has been lovingly restored with skill and adorned with yester-years furniture and todays modern lovely rich colours that enhance the enchanting structure of the older homes. We are set on nearly an acre with gardens being seasonal. We offer your Edwardian or Victorian room with morning sun and comfort through our home and the open fire in winter. Breakfast optional, in bed or in front of the old coal-range with home made jams and bottled fruit. We are in our 40's, young at heart, have a scotty dog and two cats and have enjoyed quite some travel throughout New Zealand and abroad. Being on the Northland Tourist Route, we can advise you on local activities, ie visiting antique shops, soaking in hot pools or spa's 2 minutes away, horse-riding, parachuting, Kaipara boat cruises along with the local cafes, restaurants, crafts and historical sights. Now do you see why we choose a conspicuous place to meet people?

Helensville

Bed & Breakfast & Self Contained Accom
Address: 110 Commercial Road,
Helensville
Name: Malolo House
Telephone: (09) 420 7262 **Fax**: (09) 420 7262
Mobile: (025) 280 3008 **Freephone**: 0800 286 060
Email: malolo@xtra.co.nz

Beds: 2 Queen, 3 Double, 6 Single (7 bedrooms)
Bathroom: 2 Ensuite, 1 Private, 2 Guests Share
Tariff: B&B (special) Double $60-$110, Single $40-$80, Children $5, Credit Cards. NZ
B&B Vouchers accepted $0-$30 surcharge.
Nearest Town: Helensville - 50m, Auckland 46km

Our turn-of-the century kauri villa, a former cottage hospital, has been lovingly restored to its former splendour, with old world charm and modern conveniences. In the heart of historic Helensville, steps away from first class restaurants, a boutique brewery, bank, cafes, shops, and pioneer museum, we're listed on the heritage walk. Set amongst gently sloping gardens, we have stunning views of the Kaipara River Valley from our guest lounge and multi-level sundrenced deck, where you can relax in our hot tub / spa after a day visiting vineyards, wild West Coast beaches, Muriwai's Gannet colony, mineral hot springs, river cruises, horse treks, fishing and great golf. Polished kauri floors, tastefully furnished heated guest rooms with incredibly comfortable queen sized beds and feather duvets, and luxurious modern bathrooms all contribute to a fabulous stay. Our spacious guest lounge with library and cosy fire, offers 24 hour tea, coffee, and port. Lavish Kiwi-Canadian breakfasts include freshly ground coffee, home-baked muffins, fresh fruit, and Eggs Kaipara. Our spacious self-contained Studio sleeps 4. Andrea, Michael, Bailey, Clare & Zach.

Helensville

Self Contained Accommodation, Bed & Breakfast
Address: 2191 State Highway 16, Helensville
Name: Dainne and Richard Kidd
Telephone: (09) 420 8007
or toll free 0800 755 433
Fax: (09) 420 7966
Email: kidd.home@xtra.co.nz
Beds: 1 Queen (1 bedroom)
Bathroom: 1 Ensuite
Tariff: B&B (ful) Double $95, Single $60. Not suitable for children. Credit Cards accepted. Discount for two or more nights. NZ B&B Vouchers accepted $25 surcharge
Nearest Town: Helensville and Parakai 4 kms

"Rose Cottage" offers comfort and privacy set within the gardens of the beautifully restored Whenuanui Homestead (Kauri villa circa 1908). Whenuanui is a 320 ha Helensville sheep and beef farm providing magnificent farm walks. We also have thoroughbred horses and farm forestry. The family homestead and gardens have panoramic views over Helensville and the Kaipara Valley. Comfortable and relaxing accommodation includes ensuite, TV, kitchenette with M / wave, fridge and tea / coffee making. Smoking outdoors appreciated.

Whenuanui is located on SH 16 (Northland Tourist Route) 35 minutes north west of Downtown Auckland. It provides an authentic and convenient NZ rural stopover either to or from Northland, or a base to explore the attractions in West Auckland including Kumeu wine trails, fishing / cruises on the Kaipara Harbour, Muriwai gannet colony and thermal pools at Parakai. Other local activities include: horse-riding, 4 wheel motorbike trails, a selection of four golf courses, parachuting and a variety of local restaurants and cafes.

Huapai - Kumeu

Homestay/Farmstay
Address: 45 Trigg Rd, Huapai,
Auckland
Name: Hawkless
Telephone: (09) 412 8862
Fax: (09) 412 8869
Email: hawkless@ww.co.nz
Beds: 2 Queen, 3 Single (3 bedrooms)
Bathroom: 1 Guests share
Tariff: B&B (full) Double $70, Single $50, Children half price, Dinner $20, Credit cards. NZ B&B Vouchers accepted
Nearest Town: Auckland 30 minutes drive.

Foremost Fruits is surrounded by several top NZ wineries on a small orchard specialising in hot house table grapes. You will be warmly welcomed by experienced hosts who provide comfort and relaxation plus swimming and spa pool. Guests have the upstairs to themselves with 2 large bedrooms each with Queensize and one single bed plus another single room. Guests share their bathroom and toilet. Breakfast is of choice with homemade bread and jams. There are top restaurants in the area plus casual and take-aways. We provide details on local attractions which include wineries, beaches, golf, gannet colony, balloon rides, horse riding and canoeing. Smoking permitted outside.
Directions: *From Auckland take Northwestern Motorway to end. Turn left to Kumeu (8k) past Garden Centre over railway line to Trigg Rd (left before 100K sign). No 45 on left.*

Kumeu

Farmstay
Address: Nor-West Greenlands,
303 Riverhead Road, R.D.2, Kumeu
Name: Nor-West Greenlands
Telephone: (09) 412 8167 **Fax**: (09) 412 8167
Mobile: (025) 286 6064
Email: bed@farm-stay.co.nz
Beds: 2 Double, 2 Single (3 bedrooms)
Bathroom: 1 private, 1 Guests share
Tariff: B&B (Full) $55 per person per night, Discount for 2 or more nights or 4 or more guests, Dinner $30; Children negotiable, Credit cards (Mastercard/Visa). NZ B&B Vouchers accepted
Nearest Town: Kumeu 3 1/2 km, Auckland city 26 km south.

Kerry and Kay of Nor-West Greenlands extend a warm welcome to you to join them on their 20 acre farm which is situated 25 minutes north of Auckland midway between the east and west coast beaches. We are the closest working farm to Auckland that offers accommodation, gaining our income from the land by growing flowers and breeding sheep. Our two storied home with private guest bathrooms, and guest lounge, is set in secluded gardens with a swimming pool and bush walks. Our sheep and cattle are tame and can be hand fed. They are part of the family together with Minstrel the Dalmatian dog and three black and white cats. Ranging from summer barbecues to a three course dinner, all meals are available with prior notice. Local attractions; wineries, beaches, gannet colony at Muriwai, surfing, craft shops, orchards, golf, horse-riding, kayaking, parachuting, bush walks, and hot pools.
Home Page: http://homepages.ihug.co.nz/~kk4bb
Directions: *From Auckland city via North Western Motorway on to SH 16, 5 km north, right into Coatsville / Riverhead Highway (H28), Riverhead Road is the second on the left.*

Whenuapai, Auckland
Homestay
Address: "Riverview", 40 Pohutukawa Road,
Whenuapai, Auckland
Name: Carol & John Denton
Telephone: (09) 416 4860
Fax: (09) 416 4861
Beds: 1 Queen, 2 Single (2 bedrooms)
Bathroom: 1 Ensuite, 1 Family share
Tariff: B&B (full) Double $90, Single $55, Children under 12 half price, Not suitable for children under 5, Dinner $25pp. Credit Cards.
NZ B&B Vouchers accepted $20 surcharge
Nearest Town: Henderson 15km, Auckland city 26km

We welcome you to our tranquil home "Riverview", situated right on the waters edge of the Upper Waitemata Harbour. Come and relax on our deck and enjoy uninterrupted views of the water where birdlife is abundant as well as a number of boating activities.
We are a business couple who have travelled extensively. Our interests include boating, fishing, gardening, golf and good conversation. "Riverview" is shared with Gemma our lively German Shorthaired Pointer and contented cat Boots. The Queensized bedroom is complete with its own ensuite, tea and coffee making facilities. We request no smoking indoors. "Riverview" is handy to a number of tourist attractions including Wine Trails, Gannet Colony, Historic Museums, Bush Walks, Horse Riding, Golf Courses. We own and operate our own charter launch "Moondance" and can arrange a personal boat charter for you or cruise on our beautiful Hauraki Gulf where the Americas Cup challenge will take place.
Directions: *Please phone or fax. Transfers available.*

Bethell's Beach, West Auckland
Self-contained Accommodation
Address: 'Turehu Cottage' & 'Te Koinga Cottage'
P O Box 95057, Swanson, Auckland. (Bethells Beach)
Name: Trude Bethell-Paice & John Paice
Telephone: (09) 810 9581 **Fax**: (09) 810 8677
Beds: "Turehu Cottage" 1 Queen, 1 Double Bed/Sofa. "Te Koinga Cottage" 1 Queen, 3 Single & 1 Double Divan
Bathroom: 2 Private
Tariff: "Turehu cottage": $125 + $10 bed/sofa per day, suitable for couple and 1 child or 2 friends. "Te Koinga cottage": 2 people $195 and $15 pp thereafter. Suitable for 2 couples or a family. Meals: Breakfast $15 pp. Dinner $30 pp. Meals by prior arrangement (tariffs inclusive GST). Visa Card Facility. Company workshop days - small functions and weddings quoted on individual basis.
Nearest Town: Swanson 20 minutes, Auckland 30 minutes

Spectacular sunsets and seaviews lends nature to you. As seen in Vogue Australia 98 and LIFE The Observer (Great Britain 98). "Turehu Cottage" has a studio atmosphere with conservatory and views overlooking the beach. Bi-folding doors take you to a brick barbecue, garden and lawn. A bench and table under a pohutukawa tree on the hillside. "Te Koinga Cottage" at 80sq.m this superb home away from home has 2 bi-folding doors onto a 35sq.m deck. Set under a 200 year old pohutukawa. Expansive brick barbecue and garden / pergola area. A fireplace for winter warmth. Sixteen seater table for private functions and weddings. Again fantastic views. For both cottages your beds are made and towels put out, just bring your favourite foods and champagne / wine. John and I are happy to give you ideas for surfing, lake or sea swimming, tramping, golfing, fishing and dining / wineries, (world class selection). Trude is a Marriage Celebrant. Trusting that we have tempted you to telephone us for a chat.
Directions: *Directions given when you book.*

Bethells Valley, West Auckland
Farm/Self-contained Accommodation
Address: Greenmead Farm, 115 Bethells Road,
R.D.1, Henderson, Auckland
Name: Averil & Jonathan Bateman
Telephone: (09) 810 9363 **Fax**: (09) 810 9122
Email: jabat@magic.gen.nz
Beds: 4 Single (2 bedrooms)
Bathroom: 1 Private
Tariff: (accommodation only) Self-contained cottage: Double $70 + $15 for each extra guest; Continental Breakfast $7.50 pp. NZ B&B Vouchers accepted Accommodation only
Nearest Town: Henderson 15 mins, Downtown Auckland 30 mins.

Our property is situated in a rural valley in the Waitakere Ranges, only 30 minutes drive NW of Auckland City. Gardens and orchard surround the homestead and guest cottage including an extensive organic vegetable garden and a herb garden featuring culinary and medicinal plants. Swings for children. We handmilk a house cow, keep cattle, bees, two working dogs, some hens but no cats. Visitors have sole use of the cottage which is fully self contained. There is a well equipped kitchen / dining room, parlour (TV), a bathroom and two bedrooms each with two single beds (linen provided). Usually guests prefer to cater for themselves but breakfast can be provided by prior arrangement. Longer stays welcomed. A network of walking tracks through spectacular scenery link bush, beach and lake. Wine can be sampled at vineyards in Henderson or Kumeu. The cottage offers comfort and privacy in a tranquil setting close to Auckland city.
Home Page: babs.com.au/nz/greenmead.htm
Directions: *Please phone.*

Herald Island, Waitakere City
Homestay
Address: 84 The Terrace, Herald Island, Waitakere City, Auckland
Name: Harbour View Homestay
Telephone: (09) 416 7553
Fax: (09) 416 7553
Mobile: (025) 289 6112
Beds: 1 Queen, 1 Double, 4 Single (4 bedrooms)
Bathroom: 1 Private, 1 Family share
Tariff: B&B (full) Double $80, Single $45, Children under 12 yrs half price, Dinner from $15, Credit Cards. NZ B&B Vouchers accepted
Nearest Town: Glenfield 15kms, Henderson 20kms, Auckland city 26kms.

Your hosts Bev & Les have a two story home with superb accommodation, right on waters edge. Upstairs has 2 bedrooms, 1 Double, 1 Twin, each with its own sundeck overlooking the upper reaches of the Waitemata Harbour. Own lounge, bathroom and tea and coffee making facilities. Downstairs, 1 large Double, 1 Twin share facilities. Very homely, easy access. Within 20 mins radius, wine tasting, horse riding, golf course, bush walks, cinema and vintage car museum. We also have a boat for fishing or a leisurely cruise. Bev serves a hearty home cooked dinner, or lunch if required. Rooms serviced daily and laundry facilities available. We have 1 dog Emma, 1 cat Tiger, both very friendly.
Directions: *Take North-Western (Helensville) Motorway to end. Turn right at traffic lights into Hobsonville Road. 2nd on left Brigham Creek Road. (Liquor store on corner) 1st on right Kauri Road. Continue along until Kingsway Road on right (Herald Island sign). 1st road on left over causeway, The Terrace.*

Swanson, Auckland

Homestay
Address: 1194 Scenic Drive North,
Swanson, Auckland
Name: Janice & Fleur, 'Unser Schön Chalet'
Telephone: (09) 833 4288 **Fax**: (09) 833 4288
Mobile: (025) 786788
Beds: 1 Queen, 1 Twin (2 bedrooms)
Bathroom: 1 Ensuite, 1 Family share
Tariff: B&B (full) Double $95, Single $60,
Children under 12 half price, Dinner $25. Credit cards. NZ B&B Vouchers
accepted $20 surcharge
Nearest Town: Henderson 10 mins, Auckland City 25 mins

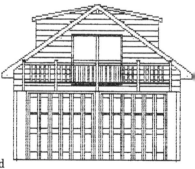

Unser Schön Chalet is situated in the Waitakere Ranges on 17 1/2 acres of native bush and pasture. Our romantic chalet is of Austrian influence and its setting is truly that of peace and tranquillity. Great for honeymooners. We offer you comfy beds, feather duvets, plump pillows and fluffy towels. After a restful night's sleep you will be offered a delicious full breakfast served on your own balcony overlooking the Waitakere Ranges and onto Rangitoto Island, or served with our family. Tea and coffee facilities with plenty of home baking are available any time. Guests are welcome to join in the family barbecue and enjoy our outdoor entertaining area, relax in the spa pool. Our family pet is a large ginger cat, Antony is his name. We request no smoking indoors. Tourist features of the area - scenic drive at the base of the Waitakeres, Western beaches, bush walks, West Auckland vineyards, golf courses, restaurants and cafes. We enjoy having guests and promise them a happy stay.
Directions: *Please phone.*

Henderson

Detached B&B
Address: 295 Swanson Road, Henderson,
Waitakere City, Auckland
Name: Rod & Alma Mackay
Telephone: (09) 833 6018
Fax: (09) 833 6018
Beds: 1 King, 3 Single (2 bedroom)
Bathroom: 1 Ensuite
Tariff: B&B (continental) Double $50,
Single $30, Children $12, under 5 years free,
Campervans $20. NZ B&B Vouchers accepted
Nearest Town: Henderson 3km - 15 min. Downtown Auckland

Rod and I have a new villa type accommodation with high ceilings and colonial furniture with its own terrace above our double garage. The single beds can be arranged as a double if you wish and there are extra folding beds if required. We live in a central area with squash courts, aerobics 10 minutes away. The Waitakare Ranges are right on our doorstep for short walks or all day tramp. It is just 25 mins to West Coast beaches and not far from two golf courses. The Henderson area is well known for its wine trail and restaurants. We are in easy reach of Helensville/Parakai Hot Pools (32km away) and there are many day trips we could book for you or take you on at weekends. Henderson, New Lynn and St Lukes are great for shopping and all close by. Rod and I look forward to seeing you.
Directions: *Please telephone.*

Henderson

Self-Contained Accom
Address: Please phone.
Name: Amethyst Gardens,
Len & Svargo
Telephone: (09) 836-3698
Fax: (09) 836-6410
Mobile: (021) 61-99-52
Email: amfoods@ihug.co.nz
Beds: 1 Queen, 1 Bedroom
Bathroom: 1 Ensuite
Tariff: B&B (continental)
Double $100
Nearest Town: Henderson 1km

Amethyst Gardens is a 2 1/2 acre property adjacent to Henderson, gateway to the vineyard district. The cottage is newly refurbished and fully self contained. It has it's own modern bathroom, kitchen area and a cosy breakfast nook with window seats. A comfortable lounge area and private deck lead onto the cottage garden. The cottage has wonderful views of the Waitakere hills and local vineyards. It is west facing and known for spectacular sunsets. The main garden area is under development with wildflower beds being prepared at the time of writing. We are 3 minutes drive from Henderson, with restaurants, shopping malls and all amenities, and about 20 minutes from central Auckland. We are non-smokers and prefer guests not to smoke in our home. Phone, fax and e-mail facilities are available for those who need to keep in touch. Yours hosts Len and Svargo look forward to meeting you.

Piha

Self Contained Accommodation
Address: 79 Glenesk Road, Piha
Name: Piha Cottage,
Steve and Tracey Skidmore
Telephone: (09) 812 8514
Fax: (09) 812 8514
Beds: 1 Double, 1 Single (1 Bedroom)
Bathroom: 1 Private
Tariff: B&B (continental)
Double high season $85, low season $70.
Extra person over double $15. Children welcome.
Nearest Town: 20 km West of Henderson, Piha is 45 mins drive West from
Auckland

Piha Cottage is a secluded fully self contained cottage in quiet bush surrounds near beach and walking tracks. This open plan home incorporates a compact kitchen, dining area, living area and bed in the open area. A private bathroom is attached. We have one character cat. Children are welcome. Inside the cottage is smoke free. Piha is located 45 minutes west of Auckland on the rugged West Coast, nestled into native forest. The beach is world renown for surfing and is patrolled for swimmers in summer. There is a network of bushwalks to choose from: through lush native forest, along spectacular cliff tops and beaches, beside idyllic streams or to a dramatic water fall. We can provide maps and advise on the tracks which we know intimately.
The cottage is an ideal home to return to after a day in the city or exploring the Waitakere forest or rugged West Coast.
Directions: *Please phone for bookings and directions.*

Okura - North Shore City

Homestay
Address: "Okura B&B",
20 Valerie Crescent Okura RD2 Albany
Name: Judie and Ian
Telephone: (09) 473 0792
Fax: (09) 473 1072
Email: ibgreig@clear.net.nz
Beds: 1 Double, 6 Single (3 bedrooms)
Bathroom: 2 Guests share
Tariff: B&B (full/continental) Double $85, Single $45 NZ B&B Vouchers accepted $20 surcharge
Nearest Town: Browns Bay 8km. Auckland City 23 km.

Situated at the "top" of Auckland's North Shore City, Okura is a small settlement bounded by farmland and the Okura River, a tidal estuary edged with native bush. We offer your own spacious living-room with TV, dining area, coffee and tea making facilities and fridge. There is one double bedroom, one room with two beds, two divans in the lounge area plus a further two single beds in the house guest room with own bathroom, catering for up to eight. (No smoking inside, please). Nearby are the North Shore Stadium, Massey University, RSA, golf courses, beaches, bush and cliff walks, and a wide variety of eating places and shops. Enjoy the ever-changing river view, bird life, peace and quiet of this hideaway so close to the big city, a comfortable place to stay before heading north or south. Okura is one of Auckland's best kept secrets!
Directions: *Directions on request.*

Albany - Coatesville

Farmstay
Address: 'Camperdown',
455 Coatesville/Riverhead Highway,
R.D.3 Albany, Auckland
Name: Chris & David Hempleman
Telephone: (09) 415 9009
Fax: (09) 415 9023
Mobile: 025 727-108

Beds: 1 Queen, 2 Double, 3 Single, 1 Cot (4 bedrooms)
Bathroom: 2 Guests share
Tariff: B&B (full) Double $95, Single $60, Children Neg., Dinner $30, Campervans $35. NZ B&B Vouchers accepted $25 Surcharge
Nearest Town: Albany 7km

We are only 20 minutes from Auckland City. Relax in secluded tranquillity in a park like rural setting, on our 18 acre farmlet running cattle, sheep, and pet lamb. Our large Tudor home opens into lovely cottage gardens native bush and stream, offering the best of hospitality and a friendly relaxed atmosphere. Our guest areas are spacious and well appointed consisting of queen and twins bedrooms, guest bathrooms and delightful sitting room with television and coffee/tea making facilities. Evening meals are available by arrangement. 'Camperdown' is situated in the beautiful Coatesville Valley, just 4km from Highway 1. Nearby activities include orchards, wineries, restaurants, horseriding, river kayaking, hot air ballooning and the Gannet Colony. Guests are also most welcome to play tennis on Camperdown's new tennis court; or have a game of snooker and table tennis in our games room.
Home Page: babs.com.au/nz/camperdown.htm
Directions: *From Auckland city travel north on Highway 1 through Albany - turn left into Coatesville/Riverhead Highway. Transfers are available.*

Free Bottle of Wine
with Dinner at
"The Wine Box Cafe"

AUCKLAND

Albany
Country Home
Address: Albany Country Home, "Birethanti",
57 Ngarahana Ave,Albany
Name: Bruce & Patricia Fordham
Telephone: (09) 413 9580
Fax: (09) 413 9583
Mobile: (025) 745 898
Email: fordham@net.gen.nz
Beds: 1 Queen, 1 Double (2 bedrooms)
Bathroom: 1 Ensuite, 1 Private
Tariff: B&B (special) Double $95-$115,
Single $75-$95. Dinner by arrangement. Credit Cards. NZ B&B Vouchers
accepted $25 surcharge
Nearest Town: Albany - 7 minutes off SH 1

We absolutely guarantee you will enjoy your stay! If you are not absolutely delighted you can renegotiate!

When you arrive to awesome river views you will be greeted to a warm welcome, be offered tea, coffee or juice with freshly baked muffins or slice.
You will sleep in luxurious linen, have plenty of soft fluffy towels and all the little extras that will make your stay special! You will awake to birdsong, the smell of freshly baked bread, you could amble down to the jetty before breakfasting on fresh tropical fruit, your choice of oaty pancakes, French toast and bacon, poached egg with smoked salmon, English or continental breakfast.
"We never think of staying anywhere else " say Barry and Dorothy of Cambridge England (after their third stay).
We are 7 minutes from Albany, North Harbour stadium and university, 19 minutes from Auckland and ideal stopover before heading North. We look forward to sharing our home with you!
Directions: *Turn opposite the "Albany Inn". 7km then turn left into Attwood Road. 1 km left into Ngarahana Avenue. 1km to cul-de-sac, 2nd house on right, down private road. White colonial house.*

99

Albany - Coatesville
Country Stay
Address: 'Hedingham',
446 Coatesville Riverhead Highway,
R.D.3, Albany.
Name: John & Angelika de Vere
Telephone: (09) 415 9292
Fax: (09) 415 7757
Mobile: (025) 864 592
Email: devere@ihug.co.nz
Beds: 1 Queen, 2 Single (2 bedrooms) **Bathroom**: 1 Guests share
Tariff: B&B (full) Double $115, Single $70, Children under 12 half price.
Dinner $35pp. Prior booking essential. **Nearest Town**: Auckland

"Hedingham" is probably New Zealand's only Bio harmonic or environmentally constructed Country Stay Home. This large stately new stone house, with some internal walls of earth and stone, is situated on 22 picturesque acres in the beautiful Coatesville Valley, just 20 minutes north of Auckland City and only 40 minutes from Auckland International Airport.
Enjoy a stay in a tranquil setting, feed our pet sheep and appreciate the myriad of bird life or take a relaxing stroll through the bush by our river, as this grand home offers our guests a real feel of country living. A separate guest wing has two private bedrooms, one double and two singles with an adjacent guest bathroom and separate guest lounge. Your rooms open on to a sunny patio. Nearby activities include helicopter flights, hot air ballooning, horse riding, wineries, gannet colony and guests are welcome to kayak on the small river bordering the estate. Your hosts, John and Angelika, their 3 sons, 2 cats and 2 dogs, offer you a warm welcome and would like to share "the good life" with you. We appreciate guests not smoking inside the house. Angelika is a native German.

Albany
Homestay
Address: 'Fairview Heights'
129 Fairview Ave, Albany, Auckland
Name: Judes and Craig
Telephone: (09) 473 8808 **Fax**: (09) 473 8386
Email: nigelg@kcbbs.gen.nz
Beds: Queen Suites **Bathroom**: Guest Share
Tariff: B&B (full) Double $85-$95, Single $55-$65. Dinner by arrangement.
Nearest Town: Albany 3 minutes, Browns Bay 6 minues. Shuttle bus from airport.

One of Auckland's newest retreats designed for peaceful, homely and spacious accommodation. Just 12 minutes north of the harbour bridge, set in tranquil rural surroundings offering superior short and long stay accommodation. Relax and enjoy expansive country and city views of Auckland and the Sky City Casino. If you are seeking a touch of luxury at affordable prices this is the retreat for you. Everyone enjoys our hideaway and we welcome you to experience it with us. We are within walking distance to the North Harbour Stadium, Massey University and close proximity to East Boast Beaches. Enjoy the nearby sports and entertainment facilities, play golf, or take a helicopter tour directly from our retreat. These tours offer fishing, golfing, vineyard dinners and scenic packages, a once in a lifetime experience.
You may choose to sail the Harbour or take a Scenic Tour. We can arrange this for you.
Whatever activity or pursuit you choose, your hosts Judes and Craig will endeavour to make your stay memorable and offer hospitality plus. We look forward to meeting you. For further information please phone, fax or email.

Greenhithe

Homestay
Address: 'Waiata Tui Lodge',
177 Upper Harbour Drive, Greenhithe,
Auckland
Name: Therese & Ned Jujnovich
Telephone: (09) 413 9270 **Fax**: (09) 413 9270
Beds: 2 Queen, 2 Single (3 bedrooms)
Bathroom: 1 Ensuite, 1 Guest share
Tariff: B&B (special) Double $75, Single $50, Dinner $25, Credit Cards. NZ B&B
Vouchers accepted
Nearest Town: Glenfield 5 km, Auckland city 15 minutes, Albany University 5
minutes.

*You are assured of a warm welcome to Waiata-Tui Lodge. Situated on 9 acres of
pasture and native forest down to the waters edge, it is so peaceful yet only 15 minutes
from Auckland city. Nestled among century old Kauri's our home overlooks the upper
harbour and the more distant Waitakere Ranges.*
*An ideal place to relax, swim in the pool, bird watch or bush walk, yet close enough to
explore the sights of Auckland city, the beaches, the gannet sanctuary and wineries.
Local sightseeing easily arranged, including balloon safaris, fishing trips or horse
riding. Greenhithe is a handy starting-off place for Bay of Islands. Therese is a keen
wine maker and spinner. We have both travelled extensively in New Zealand and
overseas. A smoke-free home.*
Directions: *From Auckland - over the Harbour Bridge - exit left at Upper Harbour
Highway - left at next 2 intersections - turn right at next lights into Upper Harbour
Drive. Travel 2km. 177 is on left at the end of right of way.*

Torbay

Homestay
Address: 23 Auld Street, Torbay,
East Coast Bay's, North Shore,
Auckland
Name: Colleen & Maurie Gray
Telephone: (09) 473 9558
Beds: 1 King, 2 Single (2 bedrooms)
Bathroom: 1 Ensuite (includes bath),
1 Guests share
Tariff: B&B (special)

Double + ensuite $100, Double Guest Share Bathroom $90, Single $65,
Campervans $40 for 2 (includes breakfast and guest bathroom). NZ B&B Vouch-
ers accepted $20 Surcharge
Nearest Town: Browns Bay 3km, Albany 5km, Auckland City 22km

*Our spacious modern home is designed with guests' comfort in mind. We enjoy sharing
the beautiful sea views, luxurious living and rambling garden. We have created a
restful atmosphere and plenty of outdoor living area for the warmer days. Breakfast
is leisurely and special, served 'al fresco' if you choose. A grand-piano graces the large
lounge and we have a huge open-fireplace. We enjoy the outdoors, swimming, sailing,
barbecues and are located within a few minutes walk of a beautiful beach. Torbay
offers safe swimming, coastal walks, and is an easy bus-ride to Auckland City. There
are beachside cafe's & and several restaurants. Dinner by arrangement. Lady, our
Persian cat will love to meet you too! A smoke-free home.*
Directions: *Northbound travellers exit Motorway at Greville Rd, East Coast Bays.
Follow signs to Torbay. Auld Street runs off Beach Rd just before Torbay shops.*

101

Torbay
Bed & Breakfast
Address: 161 Deep Creek Road, Torbay, North Shore City.
Name: Pauline and Geoff Ockleston
Telephone: 09-473 0643
Beds: 1 Queen (1 bedroom)
Bathroom: 1 Private
Tariff: B&B (continental) Double $75 NZ B&B Vouchers accepted $10 surcharge
Nearest Town: Auckland City 20 mins, Browns Bay 5 mins, Takapuna 15 mins.

Torbay is a marine suburb in Auckland's North Shore City. We are one minute's walk from the local village shopping centre, where there are restaurants, take away food outlets, hairdressers, bakeries, Post Office and other shops. We are within walking distance of two of Auckland's most popular beaches, Long Bay and Waiake. There are other cafes and restaurants nearby as well.
Our property has pleasant views over Hauraki Gulf and Waitemata harbour, off road parking is available.

Directions: *Please phone for directions.*

Browns Bay, Auckland
Homestay
Address: 'Amoritz House',
730 East Coast Rd., Browns Bay,
Auckland
Name: Gary & Carol Moffatt
Telephone: (09) 479 6338
Fax: (09) 479 6338
Mobile: 025 806958
Beds: 1 King/Twin, 1 Double (2 bedrooms)
Bathroom: 2 Ensuite
Tariff: B&B (full) Double $90-$110, Single $75-$95,
Dinner by arrangement- $10, $20, $30 pp.
Nearest Town: Browns Bay 1.5km, Downtown Auckland City (south 12 mins by car)

We are a friendly well travelled couple who invite you to stay with us. Spend a peaceful night in our quiet guest bedrooms with garden and rural outlooks, followed by a hearty Kiwi breakfast to prepare you for your day ahead. Each lockable bedroom is provided with electric blankets, heater, fan, clock radio, colour/sky TV. A separate guest entrance leads into a kitchenette with 24hr tea and coffee making facilities, fridge and microwave with a guest lounge beyond. Dinners arranged with prior notice. Breakfast includes fruit juice, cereals, fresh fruit, yoghurts, tea, coffee, toast etc, as well as a cooked breakfast. We have off street parking and a washing machine is available for guest use. Minutes to a variety of restaurants, cafes, beaches, shopping and Auckland City Centre with all its tourist attractions. 2 mins to Northern Motorway. Non-smoking.

Please help us provide the best hospitality in the world.
Fill in a comment form for every place you stay.

Mairangi Bay

Homestay
Address: 12 Marigold Place,
Mairangi Bay, Auckland 10
Name: Anthony & Julie Lewis
Telephone: (09) 479 6392
Beds: 2 Queen (2 bedrooms)
Bathroom: 1 Ensuite, 1 Private
Tariff: B&B (full) Double $80, Single $50. NZ B&B Vouchers accepted surcharge $10
Nearest Town: Browns Bay 4km, Takapuna 8kms, Auckland 13km

We are an English couple who enjoy sharing our home and spending time with travellers to Auckland. Our home has a lovely view to the ocean and Rangitoto Island. We have two guest bedrooms both equipped with Queensize beds and tea and coffee making facilities. There is a comfortable guest lounge complete with Sky TV and stereo should you require privacy. The beach and local shops are an easy ten to fifteen minute stroll away - as well as restaurants and a number of pleasant cafes. You can be sure of a special welcome. We can introduce you to the many local beaches and cliff top walks that Auckland's North Shore has to offer. House rule - No smoking indoors. 2 car garage available.
Directions: *Please phone.*

Takapuna

Homestay
Address: 89 Stanaway St,
Auckland 10
Name: Pat & John Heerdegen
Telephone: (09) 419 0731
Fax: (09) 419 0731
Email: pat&johnh@xtra.co.nz
Beds: 1 Double, 1 Twin
Bathroom: 1 Ensuite, 1 bathroom shower
Tariff: B&B (full) Double $100, Single $65, Dinner $30pp. Credit cards.
NZ B&B Vouchers accepted $20 Surcharge
Nearest Town: Takapuna 8km

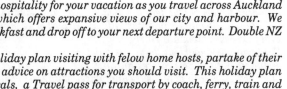

Considering a New Zealand holiday? John will greet you on your arrival at Auckland, with the promise of warm hospitality for your vacation as you travel across Auckland to our North Shore home which offers expansive views of our city and harbour. We provide lunch, dinner, breakfast and drop off to your next departure point. Double NZ $250, Single NZ $150.
Enjoy our home comfort Holiday plan visiting with felow home hosts, partake of their friendship, hospitality and advice on attractions you should visit. This holiday plan includes accomadation, meals, a Travel pass for transport by coach, ferry, train and plane so you may enjoy a hassle free as possible vacation.
Excellent references. No smoking residence.
Homepage: www.visitnz.pl.net

Relax – Don't try to drive too far in one day.

Takapuna

Homestay
Address: 9B Elderwood Lane,
Takapuna
Name: Jim & Val Laidlaw
Telephone: (09) 489 5420
Beds: 3 Single (2 bedrooms)
Bathroom: 1 Ensuite, 1 Family share
Tariff. B&B (continental) Double $75, Single $45, Dinner $15. NZ B&B Vouchers accepted
Nearest Town: Takapuna and Devonport 10 mins, Auckland City 15 mins.

Our house is in a very peaceful and central location with good parking and ready access to shops, buses, ferries and motorways. Main accommodation is downstairs with twin bedroom, bathroom and separate lounge area with TV and radio. Ranch sliders from the lounge lead to a private garden patio, while upstairs is a single bedroom with family share facilities. Tea, coffee and laundry facilities are available to all. We have travelled extensively, both at home and overseas, and offer warm comfortable accommodation with a homely atmosphere. All our family have left home, so you can be assured of a quiet time, with all the attention from us that you ask for. Our interests include Probus, U3A, art, aviation, music, walking and petanque. Our area abounds in restaurants and food halls and we are close to bus routes. We will happily help with any travel arrangements. We request that guests do not smoke in our home.
Directions: *Please phone for directions.*

Devonport

Homestay
Address: "Cheltenham-By-The-Sea",
2 Grove Road, Devonport, Auckland
Name: Joyce & Harry Mossman
Telephone: (09) 445 9437 **Fax**: (09) 445 9437
Beds: 1 Queen, 1 Ensuite, 1 Double, 4 Single (5 bedrooms)
Bathroom: 1 Ensuite, 1 Private, 1 Guests share
Tariff: B&B (continental) Queen/Ensuite $90-$120, Single $65; Children under 12 yrs $15. Transport available by 'Super' Shuttle Bus direct from airport. NZ B&B Vouchers accepted $20 surcharge
Nearest Town: Devonport Auckland

Adjacent to lovely Cheltenham Beach with safe swimming and pleasant walks in unique area. 45 mins from International Airport or 12 mins from downtown Auckland Ferry across Waitemata Harbour.
Contemporary spacious home in quiet area with spacious lawn, shade trees and secluded patio. Several restaurants handy. An escort service by private car for business, sightseeing, pleasure and places of interest is available at reasonable rates. Two minutes walk to bus stops and shops. Short walk to golf course, bowling and croquet clubs, tennis and squash courts.
Our interests are people, travel, family, swimming, camping, fishing and gardening. We have a background of farming, Navy and building.
There is no other marine suburb which offers so much in such a small picturesque area. We have enjoyed 18 years of home hosting, and a warm welcome is assured by your hosts. Reservations are advisable to avoid disappointment. Children are welcome, we have no pets.

104

Devonport
B & B + Self-contained Cottage
Address: 'Karin's Garden Villa',
14 Sinclair St, Devonport, Auckland 9
Name: Karin Loesch
Telephone: (09) 445 8689
Fax: (09) 445 8689

Beds: 2 Double, 3 Single (4 bedrooms)
Bathroom: 1 Ensuite, 1 Private, 1 Guests share
Tariff: B&B (continental) Double $115-$145, Single $75-$95, Children negotiable,
(cot available) NZ B&B Vouchers accepted $45 surcharge
Nearest Town: Auckland - 15 mins by ferry or car.

Tucked away at the end of a quiet cul-de-sac, Karin's Garden Villa offers REAL home comfort with its light cosy rooms, easy relaxed atmosphere and the warmest of welcome from Karin, Tony and her two teenage children, Tina and Stefan. A beautifully restored spacious Victorian villa surrounded by large lawns and old fruit trees. Karin's Garden Villa has also been featured on NZ and Australian television advertising for its relaxed, peaceful setting. Just 5 minutes stroll from tree-lined Cheltenham Beach, sailing, golf, tennis, shops and restaurants and only a short drive or pleasant 10 minute walk past extinct volcanoes to the picturesque Devonport centre with its many attractions. Your comfortable room offers separate private access through French doors, opening onto a wide verandah and cottage garden. And for those visitors wanting ultimate comfort and privacy, there is even a self-contained cottage with balcony and full kitchen facilities to rent (min. 3 days). Sit down to a nutritious breakfast in the sunny dining room with its large bay windows overlooking everflowering purple lavender and native gardens. Guests are welcome to join the family barbecue and relax on our large lawn. We welcome longer stays and can arrange favourable discounts accordingly. Help yourself to tea and German-style coffee and biscuits anytime and feel free to use the kitchen and laundry. Karin comes from Germany, Tony is a native Kiwi, frequently visiting Indonesia. We have seen a lot of the world and enjoy meeting other travellers. Always happy to help you arrange island cruises, rental cars and tours. Children welcome! "See you soon - bis bald - à bientôt"
Directions: *Airport Shuttle Bus to our doorstep or to Downtown Ferry Terminal. Courtesy pick-up from Devonport Wharf. By Car: After crossing Harbour Bridge, take Takapuna-Devonport turnoff. Right at T-junction, follow Lake Road to end, left into Albert, Vauxhall Road and then Sinclair Street.*

Devonport
B&B Inn

Address: Luxury B&B Inn,
46 Tainui Road, Devonport, Auckland
Name: Devonport Villa Inn
Telephone: (09) 445 8397
Fax: (09) 445 9766
Email: dvilla@ihug.co.nz
Beds: 2 King,2 Queen, 2 Single (5 bedrooms)
Bathroom: 5 Private
Tariff: B&B (full) Double $165-$195,
Credit cards (VISA/Amex/MC)
NZ B&B Vouchers accepted $100 surcharge
Nearest Town: Auckland - 15 minutes by car or ferry . Shuttle bus from airport -
24 km

*Devonport Villa Inn, winner of the NZ Tourism Awards for hosted accommodation, is
in the heart of Devonport, 2 minutes walk from Auckland's best kept secret, sandy and
safe Cheltenham Beach. There is something special about every aspect of this exquisite
historic home build in 1903 by a wealthy retired English doctor.*

*Edwardian elegance, spacious individual rooms with king and queen beds, extensive
guest library, rich woollen carpets, restored colonial furniture, outstanding stained
glass windows and the guest lounge with its amazing vaulted ceiling and polished
native timber floor.*

*Choose from the unique upstairs Turret Room, the romantic and sunny Rangitoto
Room with its private balcony, the colonial style Beaconsfield Suite with antique
clawfoot bath and four-poster king bed or the Oxford and Gold rooms.*

*Each cosy room is individually decorated with delightful handmade patchwork quilts,
firm beds, soft woollen blankets, fresh bouquets of flowers from the garden, plump
pillows and crisp white linen.*

*And in the morning you will be cooked a delicious full breakfast, including freshly
squeezed juice, natural yoghurt, nutritious muesli, muffins baked daily, Belgian
waffles, double smoked bacon with eggs and preserves.....join other guests in the dining
room overlooking the garden, or if you like we can serve breakfast in some rooms at a
time to suit. Please ask when booking.*

*Sit in the sunny shell courtyard overlooking the Edwardian style garden with lavender
hedges, old roses and spacious lawns.*

*Enjoy a moonlit stroll along the beach to North Head and dinner at a nearby
restaurant. Devonport Villa is within easy walking distance of the major wedding
reception venues and the historic sights of Devonport.*

Let us help you to make your stay in Devonport relaxing, pleasant and unique.

Fax and E-mail available.

Smoking is not permitted in the house.

Home Page: http://www.DevonportVillaInn.co.nz

Devonport
Self-contained Garden Room B&B + Villa Room

Address: 'The Garden Room',
23 Cheltenham Road, Devonport, Auckland 9
Name: Perrine & Bryan Hall
Telephone: (09) 445 2472 **Fax**: (09) 445 2472
Mobile: (025) 989 643
Email: b.hall@clear.net.nz
Beds: 2 Double, 1 Single (Rollaway) (2 bedrooms)
Bathroom: 1 Ensuite, 1 Private
Tariff: B&B (full) Double $125-$135, Single $110,
Children welcome. NZ B&B Vouchers accepted $75 surcharge
Nearest Town: Auckland 15 mins by car or ferry or take the Airport super
shuttle bus directly to our door.

Nestled at the end of our garden is a private sunny hideaway for guests. The Garden Room has large french doors opening into a tranquil garden of old roses where you may have breakfast in the courtyard or served in the privacy of your room. There is an ensuite, TV, coffee bodum, selection of teas, refrigerator, your own entrance and parking. Grape arbours separate the Garden Room from main villa where one bedroom with private bathroom facilities is offered for guests. Enjoy a swim at Cheltenham Beach a few steps from our door or a walk up North Head before your breakfast of freshly squeezed juices, home-made muesli and yoghurt, tropical and seasonal fruits, plump muffins, croissants, breads and choice of cooked. We are a short stroll from Devonport with its wonderful blend of historic buildings, shops and upmarket cafes. McHughs reception lounge is over the road and Duders nearby. We welcome you warmly to our home and garden.
Directions: *A Super shuttle bus brings you from the airport to our door.*

Devonport
Luxury Accommodation

Address: Hyland House - fine accommodation,
4 Flagstaff Terrace, Devonport, Auckland
Name: Carol and Bruce Hyland
Telephone: (09) 445 9917
Fax: (09) 445 9927
Mobile: (021) 986 221
Email: hyland@voyager.co.nz
Beds: 2 Queen (2 bedroom)
Bathroom: 2 Ensuite
Tariff: B&B (special) Double $180 to $245, Single $160 to $190.
All major credit cards. NZ B&B Vouchers accepted $85-$150 surcharge
Nearest Town: Auckland - 10 minutes by ferry

Hyland house - fine accommodation is an elegant Victorian home on the waterfront in the heart of the seaside village of Devonport, offering the very best in private accommodation for discerning travellers. With two sumptuous suites, guests are assured the ultimate in privacy and personal luxury. The 'Atea Suite' has a huge four poster bed with French Marcella, and fine linen - fresh flowers, chocolates, complimentary port and sherry, a selection of teas and coffee and homemade biscotti. French doors lead to the large ensuite bathroom with antique clawfoot tub, walk-in shower, antique washbasin and toilet, hairdrier, bathrobes and quality toiletries. The 'Atea Suite' has its own sofa and dining area, television, stereo, and telephone. Your gourmet breakfast includes tropical fruits served with homemade yoghurt and passionfruit, plus our own special muesli, and a choice of Eggs Benedict or Smoked Salmon Frittata, served either in your room or al fresco beside the swimming pool. 2 minutes walk to ferry, beach, cafes, shopping.
Home Page: http://nz.com/HeritageInns/HylandHouse

Devonport

Bed & Breakfast
Address: 'Top of the Drive',
15c King Edward Parade,
Devonport, Auckland
Name: Viv & Ray Huckle
Telephone: (09) 445 3362
Beds: 1 King, 1 Queen, 1 Single.
Extra single bed available (3 bedrooms)
Bathroom: 2 Ensuite, 1 Private (1 toilet & vanity),
1 Family share
Tariff: B&B (full) Double $110-$140, Single $70-$100
Nearest Town: Auckland 15 mins by ferry or car

We consider ourselves to be very fortunate to live along Devonport's lovely waterfront, only a delightful 5 minute stroll to our local historic seaside centre with its shops, cinema, wide variety of restaurants and ferry service to down town Auckland. Devonport also offers walks with wonderful views, lovely safe beaches, golf and museums. Our house is newly built. We offer 3 spacious bedsitting rooms with private facilities. Firm comfortable beds (King, Queen, Single), television, tea / coffee and pleasant views. There is also a guest lounge opening onto the garden.
Enjoy a leisurely breakfast in the dining room. We provide fresh fruit, freshly squeezed juice, a selection of cereals and breads, yoghurt, muffins or pastries, and a cooked breakfast to your requirements, with tea and fresh coffee. We have a smoke free home, off street parking, and a friendly pointer who doesn't come into the house.
We look forward to meeting you and making your stay an enjoyable one.

Devonport

Bed & Breakfast
Address: "Amberley Bed & Breakfast",
3 Ewen Alison Ave., Devonport, Auckland 1309
Name: Mary and Michael Burnett
Telephone: (09) 446 0506
Fax: (09) 446 0506
Email: amberley@xtra.co.nz
Beds: 3 Queen, 2 Single (4 bedrooms)
Bathroom: 2 Guests share (one wih double spa bath)
Tariff: B&B (special) Double $90-$120, Single $70-$90.
Credit cards (VISA/MC/AMEX). NZ B&B Vouchers accepted $40 surcharge
Nearest Town: Auckland - 10 min. ferry ride. Door-to-door shuttle bus available from airport.

Nestled at the base of Mt Victoria, our family home is a charming colonial villa within easy walking distance of Devonport's numerous cafés, shops, safe swimming beaches, golf course, and ferry terminal. Spectaclular panoramic views can be enjoyed from the summit of Mt Victoria. Our bedrooms are spacious and charmingly furnished with exceedingly comfortable beds! The guest bathrooms with beautiful stainedglass windows, are not ensuite, but bathrobes are provided. Our large guest lounge has TV, complimentary tea / coffee making facilities, guest frig and homebaking. Early a.m. flight guests are welcome. Laundry facilities are available. A delicious breakfast is served in our spacious diningroom with city views. Relax sitting in the sun in our private bricked courtyard. We have travelled extensively both here and overseas and we look forward to meeting you and making your stay in our beautiful country an enjoyable experience.
Directions: *Turn right at Mt Victoria roundabout, 200 mtrs, first right at Victoria Superette corner. Off-street parking.*

Devonport, Auckland
Bed & Breakfast Inn
Address: 'Villa Cambria Bed & Breakfast Inn ',
71 Vauxhall Road, Devonport, Auckland
Name: Clive & Kate Sinclair
Telephone: (09) 445 7899 **Fax**: (09) 446 0508 **Mobile**: (025) 843 826
Email: villacambria@xtra.co.nz
Beds: 3 Queen, 1 Double, 1 Twin, (5 bedrooms)
Bathroom: 4 Ensuite, 1 Private
Tariff: B&B (full) Double $130-$180, Single $120-$150, Children over 12yrs,
Dinner by arrangement. Credit cards (VISA/MC/AMEX). NZ B&B Vouchers
accepted $75 Surcharge may apply
Nearest Town: Auckland 15 minutes by car or ferry

Villa Cambria is an historic Victorian Villa featuring Nineteenth Century architecture and ambience with amenities styled for todays living. Private and extensive treed grounds attract a variety of birds, and provide a relaxing and private location with quiet nooks, shaded verandahs, sundecks, barbecue and patios.
In our home there are four double bedrooms with ensuite and private bath facilities for our guests, whilst in the garden there is the lovely 'Loft' which is self-contained with its own balcony and extensive views over the surrounding landscape. The villa's guest sitting room looks out onto the garden and the adjacent ante room houses a large collection of books for your enjoyment. The excellent breakfast (try the homemade bread) can be enjoyed on the verandah, patio or in your room, or at the old kauri table with the other guests.
For those who enjoy golf, why not join your host for a round of golf at the Waitemata Golf Course, only 5 minutes walk away. If you enjoy shopping or simply dining out Devonport Village offers gourmet restaurants and sidewalk cafes where you can savour the art studios, museums, antique shops and the delightful harbour walks. It is a 2 minutes walk to Cheltenham Beach. A 20 minute walk will enable you to enjoy the sights from the extinct volcanic peaks of North Head or Mt Victoria, with their unsurpassed views of the city and the harbour.
Having looked after hundreds of visitors from all over the world your hosts Clive and Kate take particular care to make you feel at home. So why not escape and enjoy being in the peace and tranquillity of Devonport only 12 minutes by ferry from the heart of Auckland.
Home Page: http://nz.com/webnz/bbnz/vcambria.htm
Directions: *From Airport: Shuttle Bus door to door service. By car: Travelling north, cross Auckland Harbour Bridge, 1.5km north take Devonport / Takapuna exit from motorway. Follow signs to Devonport along Lake Road. At roundabout turn left into Albert Road. At "T" junction turn left into Vauxhall Road, Villa Cambria is on the corner behind the trees.*

Devonport

Homestay
Address: 'Duck's Crossing Cottage',
58 Seabreeze Road, Devonport, Auckland 9
Name: Peter & Gwenda Mark-Woods
Telephone: (09) 445 8102 **Fax**: (09) 445 8102
Beds: 1 Queen, 1 Double, 2 Single (3 bedrooms)
Bathroom: 1 Ensuite, 2 Private
Tariff: B&B (full) Double $85-$100, Single $65.
Special winter rates, special long stay rates. NZ B&B Vouchers accepted $20
surcharge
Nearest Town: Devonport - 3 mins by car.

Welcome to our charming, modern home built 1994, surrounded by cottage gardens.
Peaceful with attractive decor, spacious and sunny. Two bedrooms open on to
balconies and a third through French doors to the garden. All bedrooms have TV's.
Comfortable warm bedding with patchwork quilts. Delicious home cooking, fresh
garden produce. Tea and coffee facilities. Summer breakfasts available on the
sheltered terrace. Stroll to Narrow Neck Beach alongside the beautiful Waitemata
Golf Course. Swim, sail, walk or explore Devonport Village and sample the many
lovely cafés and restaurants. Hosts are friendly, informative and helpful, well
travelled and enjoy hospitality.
Directions: *From the Airport, take Super Shuttle to our door. If driving take Route*
26, into Seabreeze Road, 1st house on left. Offstreet parking. (Courtesy pick ups to and
from ferry, on request)

Devonport, Auckland

Quality Accommodation
Address: "Badgers of Devonport",
30 Summer Street, Devonport, Auckland
Name: Heather & Badger Miller
Telephone: (09) 445 2099 **Fax**: (09) 445 0231
Mobile: (025) 720 336
Email: Badgers@clear.net.nz
Beds: 4 Double, 2 Single (4 bedrooms)
Bathroom: 3 Ensuite, 1 Private

Tariff: B&B (special) Double $119-$135, Single $95, Dinner $25 (2 course) pp.
Credit Cards Visa/Amex. M/C. NZ B&B Vouchers accepted $30 surcharge
Nearest Town: Auckland 10 mins by ferry or 15 mins by car.

Welcome to our home.
Let us pamper you in our quiet, sunny Villa furnished with antiques, oriental carpets
and memorabilia from our extensive travels. On arrival relax with complimentary
drinks on the verandah. Indulge in chocolates whilst lazing on your Victorian brass
bed or soak in our original antique bath. All bedrooms have en-suites, bathrobes,
toiletries, flowers, TVs and resident teddy bears to cuddle. Enjoy the privacy of your
self-contained guest wing complete with kitchen. Laundry, airport transfers avail-
able. Off-street parking. Sumptuous beakfast for vegetarians and meat lovers. Stroll
to the beach or enjoy Devonports restaurants, cafes, art galleries, shops and museums.
Directions: *From airport take shuttle direct. By car follow Devonport directions*
down Lake Road to Mt Victoria roundabout, turn right, take the 4th right turn into
Calliope Road, Summer Street is 6th road on right. (Courtesy pick up from ferry upon
request.)
Home Page: http://www.friars.co.nz/hosts/badgers.html

Devonport

Bed & Breakfast

Address: 'The Rainbow Villa', 17 Rattray Street, Devonport, Auckland 9
Name: Judy McGrath
Telephone: (09) 445 3597 **Fax**: (09) 445 4597
Beds: 1 King, 1 Queen, 2 Single (3 bedrooms)
Bathroom: 3 Ensuites
Tariff: B&B (full) Double $130-$160, Single $95-$120. Credit Cards (VISA/MC/AMEX).
Nearest Town: Auckland; 15 mins by car or ferry.

I look forward to welcoming you to my home. The Rainbow Villa, a beautiful and historic Victorian villa, built out of kauri in 1885, which I refurbished and restored in December 1996. Your home away from home in charming Devonport is nestled on the lower slopes of scenic Mount Victoria in a quiet cul-de-sac filled with historic homes. Despite the peace and quiet, it is just a two minute stroll from Devonport's main street with its delightful cafes, fine restaurants, unique art and craft shops, a safe swimming beach, peaceful parks and fascinating museums and art galleries, where there is always plenty to see and enjoy. If you are feeling energetic the climb up Mount Victoria produces magnificent 360 degree views of the glorious Waitemata Harbour and the city beyond. Or, if you are looking for more action, then downtown Auckland with its casino, nightclubs, bars and shopping malls is just a 10 minute ferry trip away.

Before setting off to enjoy all that Devonport and Auckland have to offer enjoy a leisurely breakfast in the garden dining room. My breakfasts feature freshly squeezed orange juice, fresh fruit in season, organic muesli, homemade yoghurt, free range eggs, lean bacon, tomatoes, plus all the tea, coffee or herb tea you want. At the end of the day relax in your own room or you can rest in the guest lounge's cosy armchairs, wander outside to the garden chairs where you can soak up the sun or even enjoy a relaxing soak in the hot spa pool to refresh you for your next day's exploration.

The Rainbow Villa has three spacious rooms, each with a private ensuite, comfortable beds, Sky TV and heating. All rooms are lockable and the villa is smoke free. As a sixth generation New Zealander, I have taken great care to preserve the villa's historic appearance and comfortable atmosphere and I am sure you will enjoy staying here as much as I do. Welcome.

Complimentary tea, coffee and sherry are available whenever required and herb teas are also available.

Directions: *Rattray Street is the first on the left going down the hill, past the picture theatre.*

Mt Victoria, Devonport
Self-contained B&B
Address: 'Albertine', 45 Church Street,
Devonport, Auckland 9
Name: Moira & Ross Taylor
Telephone: (09) 445 6443 **Mobile**: (025) 924 420
Beds: 1 Double, 2 Single (foldaways) (1+ bedroom)
Bathroom: 1 Ensuite
Tariff: B&B (full) Double $130, Single $110, Children welcome.
NZ B&B Vouchers accepted $65 surcharge peak season
Nearest Town: Auckland 15 mins by car or ferry.
Airport super shuttle will bring you to our door.

Albertine is a gracious farmhouse built in 1860 on the North Eastern slopes of Mt Victoria. Enjoy lovely views over harbour and suburb and a tranquil garden setting. Open the gate to Flagstaff Lane and take a stroll around Mt Victoria or climb to the summit then down for a swim at nearby Torpedo Bay.
Devonport's artist studios, delicious cafés and restaurants, bar and shops are within easy walking distance as are Duder's and McHugh's reception lounges.
A delicious breakfast of tropical fresh fruit, and juices, homemade muesli, yoghurt and muffins, croissants and breads with a variety of spreads, bacon and free range eggs can be served in your own sitting room or outside on the verandah in the morning sun.
Albertine offers a peaceful and private environment, a romantic old fashioned bedroom and ensuite, your own separate entrance and adjoining sitting room. Tea / fresh coffee / TV available.
A warm welcome awaits you at 'Albertine' from Moira, Ross and family.

Devonport
Bed & Breakfast
Address: 9 Albert Road, Devonport
Name: Devonport Village Inn
Telephone: (09) 445 8668 **Fax**: (09) 445 2668
Mobile: (021) 612 662
Beds: 4 Queen, 4 Single (4 bedrooms)
Bathroom: 2 Ensuite, 1 Guests share
Tariff: B&B (full) Double $95-$130, Single $65-$80, Children $30, Dinner $30, Credit Cards.
Nearest Town: Devonport. Auckland central 10 mins by ferry

Nestled in the nor-western slopes of Mt Victoria, and just above the local seaside township Devonport, often described as one of the most beautiful villages in the world, the Devonport Village Inn is our home and we invite you to share our gracious turn of the century Victorian villa for a friendly and memorable holiday. We offer you a rest in our large, comfortable bedrooms, with crisp clean linens, and in the morning a gourmet breakfast, cooked by either James or Julie, who are both experienced restaurateurs, served either round the old kauri dining table or on the verandah looking over the cottage garden filled with roses. Situated only 5 mins stroll to sandy beaches, golf course, the ferry to Auckland Central, our quaint village, cafés, an amazing museum, art galleries, and cinema. Also available, guest lounge, Sky TV, tea, coffee anytime, courtesy coach, launch charter and skipper.

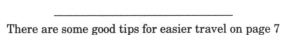

There are some good tips for easier travel on page 7

JEONG·K·PLACE

Devonport
Bed & Breakfast BY·THE·SEA

Address: 'Jeong-K Place Devonport by The Sea'
4 King Edward Parade, Devonport, Auckland
Name: Jeong Sook & Kazuo
Telephone: (09) 445 1358
Fax: (09) 446 1358 **Mobile**: (025) 889 276
Email: jeong-k@ihug.co.nz
Beds: 3 Queen, 2 Single (4 bedrooms)
Bathroom: 4 Ensuite
Tariff: B&B (special) Double $190-$210, Single $170-$180, Dinner $60 to $70pp
3-4 course (prior notice). Not suitable for children. Credit Cards.
Nearest Town: Auckland – 10 minutes by ferry.

"Jeong-K-Place Devonport By The Sea" guest house is located within the heart of Devonport village, specifically with the frontage toward the lovely beach. Enjoy a pleasant swim in this beach or a relaxing stroll along the shore that leads to the historic North Head and Cheltenham Beach. The Ferry Terminal is within a minutes walk. Devonport seaside village offers cafes and restaurants, galleries, museum, historical buildings, antique shops and cinema. 18-hole golf course is 3 minutes drive. The Edwardian villa, originally built circa 1900, features kauri flooring and an extensive balcony and verandah facing the harbour where world-class yachts sail by. This beachfront home has just recently been refurbished and upgraded with a central heating, fire sprinkler system and modern conveniences to provide a smoke-free, warm, cosy and high quality service guest house to today's discerning traveller. Four ensuite guest rooms open individually into the shady garden with its mature trees. Each guest room is tastefully decorated and furnished with furniture's, fixture and fittings to create a comfortable and relaxing atmosphere. Complimentary tea, fresh coffee, sherry, NZ wines are served in the kauri flooring sea view lounge. Our breakfast is freshly prepared with good quality groceries and is served in the elegant dining room that overlooks a tranquil garden and magnificent harbour view. The owners are trained chefs, serving different breakfast each day from a varied cooked menu which includes crabmeat puff, Jeong-k hot spring eggs, waffles and pancakes, okonomiyaki, egg de Nipponese with an abundance of fresh fruits. Dinner is only served by prior arrangement. We also serve Sushi, Sashimi and from our original recipe that are prepared with local products. Come and enjoy your memorable holidays in our friendly, warm and cosy guest house. Look forward to seeing you and we will be glad to be your hosts. Advance booking is recommended.
Home Page: http://homepages.ihug.co.nz/~jeong-k

Devonport, Auckland
Self Contained Apartment B&B
Address: 82B Wairoa Road, Devonport,
Auckland
Name: Ivanhoe - Hosts: Coralie and Philip
Telephone: (09) 445 1900 **Fax**: (09) 446 0039
Mobile: (021) 622 887
Beds: 1 Queen, 1 Single Rollaway (1 bedroom)
Bathroom: 1 Ensuite
Tariff: B&B (continental) Double $120, Single $80, Children $20.
Weekly rates. Visa/Mastercard
Nearest Town: Devonport 5 mins

IVANHOE, our fully furnished private apartment, looks out upon the sparkling waters of the Waitemata harbour off Narrow Neck; the venue for the America's Cup. Situated on the ground floor, this light and airy apartment includes a lounge with TV and private phone; both the bedroom and tiled bathroom are spacious; kitchenette with full cooking facilities.
Complementary continental breakfast available includes: juice, home-made muesli and yoghurt, fruit, toast or muffins, jam and honey.
Within easy access, across the road by the beach is a park, with a golf course, public tennis courts, gym and squash courts all only minutes away.
A 5 minute drive to historic Devonport enables you to enjoy a variety of shops and restaurants. A ferry sails to downtown Auckland every half hour where boat trips depart daily to the many islands in the gulf.
Off-street parking is available. Courtesy pick-up from Devonport Wharf.
We look forward to meeting you and making your stay enjoyable.

Devonport, Auckland
Fully self contained cottage B&B
Address: 3a Cambridge Terrace, Devonport,
Auckland
Name: Devonport Sea Cottage
Telephone: (09) 445 7117
Beds: 1 Queen (1 bedroom)
Bathroom: 1 Ensuite, 1 Private.

Tariff: B&B (full) Double $120, Single $80, Longer stay and winter rates $250-$400 per week. NZ B&B Vouchers accepted $40 surcharge in peak season
Nearest Town: Auckland city 15 mins by car or ferry. Airport Super Shuttle Bus directly to our door.

A unique, restored Arts and Craft style cottage, in our garden and only metres to the sea. Charming and private.
The interior is beautifully appointed with a variety of living spaces including ensuite, dining room and private verandah. Light and airy with a delightful serene atmosphere.
The perfect location in Devonport, ideally situated mid way between lovely Cheltenham Beach historic North Head in one direction and Devonport village and the ferry in the other. Step out of the cottage and cross the road to the park and sea. A short stroll takes you along the water front to Duders or McHughs reception lounges.
Our cottage allows you to do your own thing or we can provide a delicious home cooked breakfast.
We are very suitable for longer stays or a short term. Full Bed & Breakfast service. Tea / coffee and TV provided. John, Michelle and family warmly welcome you.

Waiheke Island
Homestay+Self-contained Accom.
Address: 'Gulf Haven', 49 Great Barrier Road,
Enclosure Bay, Waiheke Island
Name: Alan Ramsbottom & Lois Baucke
Telephone: (09) 372 6629 **Fax**: (09) 3728558
Beds: Homestay: 1 Queen, 1 Double (2 bedrooms). 2 Self-Contained Studio
Apartments: 1 Queen, 1 Super King/Twin option
Bathroom: Homestay: 1 Guests share. Studios: both with ensuites.
Tariff: Dec 1st 98 to Nov 30th 99. Homestay: B&B (continental) Double $80,
Queen $95, Single (double bed) $65. SC Studio Apartments: Double $155.
Continental breakfast option extra. Credit cards (VISA/MC) NZ B&B Vouchers
accepted Homestay only with surcharge $25
Nearest Town: Auckland

*Waiheke Island is different. A unique lifestyle, superb scenery, yet only 35 minutes
from downtown Auckland.*
*Our home and studio apartments sit on a low ridge in 2 acres of garden running down
to the sea. A path takes you via a dramatic deck to secluded rock pools and clear deep
water. Our modern interesting indoor / outdoor home takes advantage of the dramatic
views of the Northern Coast of Waiheke Island with Coromandel Peninsula and Great
Barrier Island beyond.*
*Friendly home hospitality or luxury self-contained studio apartments for two people
with private decks, both offer an exclusive location to relax and unwind. Have
breakfast on the deck, overlooking the sea; savour the Island's cafes and restaurants.
Tea and coffee is always available.*
*Lois and I enjoy the outdoors and Arts and are non-smokers. We have a Burmese cat,
Misty. Regretably Gulf Haven's facilities are not suitable for children. Explore the
Island (we have 2 bicycles) acclaimed for its beaches and fine wines or just relax. We
can arrange tours, kayaking, horseriding, golf etc. We enjoy our Island hideaway and
its mild climate and welcome you to experience it with us.*
Directions: *Shuttle bus from Auckland Airport then passenger ferry from Ferry
Building, Downtown Auckland, approx. every 2 hours. Also vehicular ferry and plane
charter service. We will meet you from the ferry but please phone first.*
Home Page: http://nz.com/webnz/bbnz/haven.htm

Waiheke Island
Homestay B&B and S/C Apartments

Address: "Punga Lodge", 223 Ocean View Rd, Little Oneroa, Waiheke Island
Name: Dyan Sharland & Rob Johnston
Telephone: (09) 372 6675 **Fax**: (09) 372 6675
Beds: Homestay - 3 ensuite Double/Twin, 2 garden ensuite units, 4 S/C apartments.
Bathroom: All with private bathrooms.
Tariff: B&B (continental) Double $95-$115, Single - from $60, Apartments $120-$150. Off season rates available. Children welcome in apartments. Vouchers only for Homestay with a $20 surcharge. VISA/Mastercard accepted.
Nearest Town: Auckland - 35 mins by ferry

Waiheke Island is an island paradise escape. And Punga Lodge provides you with an informal, relaxed atmosphere in a native bush setting just 150 metres from a safe swimming beach and a 12 minute walk to cafes and restaurants in the main town of Oneroa. Our ensuite guest rooms and S/C apartments all open onto sunny decks overlooking the gardens, native bush and birdlife. Complimentary home cooked morning and afternoon teas are our speciality and breakfast includes homemade muffins. We can arrange tours, horseriding, kayaking, scenic flights and fishing outings for you. And we specialise in group bookings - for fun get togethers or conferences (we have separate conference facilities). We take all the hassle out of the planning because we'll do it for you, tailor-made to meet your needs or interests.
Directions: *Ferry from downtown Auckland. Complimentary transfer from Waiheke wharf.*
Home Page: http://homepages.ihug.co.nz/~waiheke/punga.htm

Waiheke Island
Bed & Breakfast

Address: "Blue Horizon", 41 Coromandel Road, Sandy Bay, Waiheke Island
Name: David & Marion Aim
Telephone: (09) 372 5632
Beds: 2 Queen (2 bedrooms)
Bathroom: 1 Ensuite, 1 Family share
Tariff: B&B (continental) Double $70-$85, Single $55-$70, Dinner on request. NZ B&B Vouchers accepted $15 surcharge ensuite
Nearest Town: Auckland

We live above Sandy Bay which is 2-3 mins walk away with spectacular views of the Hauraki Gulf and its many islands, from Rangitoto around to Coromandel Peninsula.
Our home is modest and we are very proud of the new guest wing Marion and I built with help from our neighbours. All the rooms in our home face due north catching the sun all day. After farming while our 4 children were growing up and owning a garden centre, we really enjoy the lifestyle of Waiheke Island with its lovely bush walks, sandy beaches and rock pools to explore. Waiheke caters for adventuring, dining out or just relaxing on one of our decks. The thing most of our guests enjoy about staying with us is our friendliness and the panoramic views from wherever you are in the house. Most days we can see the Americas Cup boats practicing in the distance.
Directions: *Ferry from downtown Auckland. Approx every 2 hrs. Complimentary ferry transfers. We look forward to sharing our beautiful island with you.*

Waiheke
Self Contained Accommodation, B&B
Address: 44 Queens Drive,
Oneroa,
Waiheke Island

Name: Louisa and Cliff Hobson-Corry
Telephone: (09) 372 2200
Fax: (09) 372 2204
Email: givernyinn@ibm.net
Beds: 2 Queen (2 bedrooms)
Bathroom: 1 Ensuite, 1 Private in cottage.
Tariff: B&B (special) Double from $135,
Single from $100, Dinner $65 and up pp.
Children $40 (cotttage only). Credit Cards
accepted.
Nearest Town: Oneroa

*Giverny Inn on Waiheke Island welcomes you to Paradise. Waiheke is a magical island
of wine, olives, lavender, and emerald edged beaches.*

*BACCHUS COTTAGE. You can choose to stay in Bacchus cottage a restored historic
cottage furnished in elegant simplicity. Self service or host service, and a balcony to
sit and enjoy stunning views.*

*VENUS ROOM. A romantic room where you can gaze out to sea views or sit on the
balcony and drink champagne or chilled wine and contemplate. Venus Room is
furnished with antiques, Persian rugs and chandeliers. Both Bacchus Cottage and
Venus Room have fine linens, goosedown comforters, port, chocolates, fresh fruit and
flowers. Oscar our cat welcomes guests also.*
*Stunning walks are nearby, as are restaurants, beaches, golf, vineyards, including the
famous Stoneyridge, scenic flights and fishing.*
*Louisa and Cliff enjoy cooking Waiheke fish for breakfast, and also will provide dinner
from $65 per person. While eating you can gaze at the moon and Oneroa's twinkling
lights.*
Home Page: www.waiheke.co.nz/giverny.htm

Waiheke Island
Self-contained Accommodation
Address: 52 Korora Road, Oneroa,
Waiheke Island
Name: Judy and Keith Johnston
Telephone: (09) 372 9206
Fax: (09) 372 9209
Beds: 1 Queen, 1 Single (in lounge) (1 bedroom)
Bathroom: 1 Ensuite
Tariff: 2 nights (min) $250, thereafter 100 p/n. Credit cards.
Nearest Town: Auckland city 35 mins ferry ride to Downtown Auckland

This cottage is sunny and new. It is nestled in a private coastal garden setting on a north facing peninsula with spectacular close up seaviews. It has a full kitchen, laundry facilities, woodfire and an outdoor eating area. Sky TV, video.
Waiheke Island is a delightful spot noted for its casual lifestyle, beautiful views and many walks and places to explore.
A 1km stroll takes you to the local shopping centre and cafes of Oneroa. The 10 acre peninsula is surrounded by water and there are many lovely walks to enjoy on the property and the nearby locality including a visit to a neighbouring vineyard. The property is not suitable for children.
We have a track to a private beach. A friendly cat called Abba.
Directions: *Bookings advised.*

Auckland Central
Boutique Hotel
Address: 30 Ponsonby Terrace,
Ponsonby, Auckland
Name: The Great Ponsonby Bed & Breakfastt"
Telephone: (09) 376 5989 **Fax**: (09) 376 5527
Email: great.ponsonby@xtra.co.nz
Beds: 5 Queen, 4 Twin or King (9 bedrooms)
Bathroom: 9 Ensuite
Tariff: B&B (full) Double from $125-$140,
Studio from $150-$168, Apartment $210. Credit Cards (MC/VISA/AMEX).
Nearest Town: Auckland City - 5 min by car.

A boutique hotel

The Great Ponsonby Bed & Breakfast is a home away from home for the traveller. In a quiet cul-de-sac, an easy stroll to the heart of Ponsonby's restaurant strip, an immaculately restored Victorian villa offers a welcome retreat from the pressures of the day. The emphasis is on quality. All rooms have en-suites, direct dial phones, irons, sky TV and create an inviting environment with decor which reflects the city's Pacific heritage.
A comfortable sitting room creates the atmosphere of a lodge where guests can pass time talking to other travellers or listen to the CD collection.
We turn out terrific breakfasts; everything from self-service continental to a shearer's special. Here's your chance to step off the travel treadmill.
Smoking on the verandahs. We have a friendly dog and cat.
Home Page: http://www.dmd.co.nz/pons/

Please help us provide the best hospitality in the world.
Fill in a comment form for every place you stay.

Ponsonby
Self-Contained Cottage
Address: 43 Douglas St.,
Auckland 2
Name: Ponsonby Potager
Telephone: (09) 378 7237
Fax: (09) 378 7267
Mobile: 025-272 7310
Email: raywardby@compusereve.com
Beds: 2 Double (2 bedrooms)
Bathroom: 1 Private
Tariff: B&B (full) Double $120, Single $80
Nearest Town: Auckland. You're there! "Downtown" 2 Kms away.

Prepare to be pampered at the "Ponsonby Potager". Enjoy a delicious breakfast served in the garden room, or throw open the french doors and relax on the decks. We respect your privacy but are here to help.

The Potager is divided in two; you have your own entrance, bathroom, lounge and fully equipped kitchen. It is peaceful here but only 3 minutes walk to the shops, cafes and bars of Ponsonby or 5 minutes drive to the casino and city centre.

Your bedrooms have the finest linen, bathrobes, plenty of towels, fresh flowers and TV. Fresh fruit always available. Complimentary laundry service.

Don't forget to pack your favourite CDs and tapes as you have your own entertainment centre as well as fax facilities, a small library of books and videos and Sky TV.

Ponsonby, Auckland Central
Homestay B&B
Address: 35 Clarence Street, Ponsonby,
Auckland City
Name: "Colonial Cottage"
Telephone: (09) 360 2820 **Fax**: 09 360 3436
Beds: 2 Double, 1 Single (3 bedrooms)
Bathroom: 1 Guests share

Tariff: B&B (special) Double from $100, Single from $80, Children by arrangement, Dinner $25. Single party occupancy available. Tariff from $250 depneding on number. Booking essential
Nearest Town: Auckland city centre

Relax in the warm and hospitable ambience of this turn-of-the-century Kauri villa offering olde-worlde charm, warmth, comfort and modern amenities in the heartbeat of the city fringe.

- *Quiet inner-city location*
- *Short walk to Herne Bay, the Ponsonby Cafe Mile and quality restaurants*
- *Handy to public transport including the City Link bus service*
- *Easy distance to City attractions and motorways*
- *Airport shuttle service available door-to-door*
- *Breakfast included, other meals by arrangement, with an emphasis on fresh seasonal produce, organic where possible.*
- *Health foods and special diets readily catered for.*
- *No smoking indoors*
- *Therapeutic massage available in-house, plus Kirlian & Aura photography*

A ready welcome day or night. Please phone first.

Parnell, Auckland City

Guest House, Small Hotel
Address: 36 St. Stephens Avenue, Parnell, Auckland 1
Name: Ascot Parnell
Telephone: (09) 309 9012 **Fax**: (09) 3093-729
Email: AscotParnell@compuserve.com
Beds: 9 Queen/Twin, 2 Single (11 bedrooms, all with phone, private facilities and heating)
Bathroom: 10 Ensuite, 1 Private
Tariff: B&B (full) Double/Twin $128, Single $86, Superior $150-$165. Cooked breakfast included. Parking available. All credit cards accepted.
Nearest Town: Auckland city centre 1 mile, Parnell Village 400m.

The ASCOT PARNELL - an elegant mansion in a subtropical garden - "is one of Auckland's most pleasant and atmospheric inns." (FROMMERS GUIDE NZ).
All 11 charming guestrooms have bathrooms, telephones, heating and electric blankets.
The intimacy of the ASCOT PARNELL makes it possible for the guests to enjoy a friendly service and personal attention. A delightful breakfast is served in a dining room which shows the beauty of this lovely home. Throughout the day tea, coffee and juice is served in the lounge. The airport shuttle stops in front of the house. Bus to all parts of the city every 10 minutes. We will help you to book tours, find reasonable priced rental cars and recommend shops and restaurants. Our house is a peaceful place to stay, very close to the city centre and within walking distance to many tourist attractions such as PARNELL VILLAGE, Auckland Museum and rose gardens. We also speak Flemish / Dutch, French and German.
We advise to book well in advance, you will recommend it.
Your hosts: Bart & Therese Blommaert.
Home Page: http://nz.com/HeritageInns/AscotParnell

Private bathroom is for your use exclusively,
Guests share means you may be sharing with other guests,
Family share means you will be sharing with the family.

Parnell, Auckland

Bed & Breakfast Hotel
Address: 14 Brighton Road,
Parnell, Auckland 1
Name: Fae & David England
Telephone: (09) 309 0290
Fax: (09) 373 5754
Beds: 2 Queen, 4 Double,
12 Single (14 bedrooms)
Bathroom: All ensuites
Tariff: B&B (full) Double/Twin $108-120, Single $78,
Children $25, Credit cards. NZ B&B Vouchers accepted $25 surcharge
Nearest Town: Auckland City centre 2km

Chalet Chevron

Chalet Chevron is a Tudor-style hotel with old-world charm and extensive sea views. Situated in fascinating Parnell, with its historic houses, interesting streets and shops, galleries, and over 30 restaurants. We are close to the Cathedral, Museum, Casino, Parnell Rose Gardens, parks and beaches. We offer warm friendly hospitality and are always pleased to help with tours, hire cars, sightseeing and shopping suggestions. Airport shuttles come to the door. Our comfortable bedrooms have direct dial phones, own bathrooms, electric blankets and heating. You will love staying in Parnell - a special place.

Parnell, Auckland

Bed & Breakfast
Address: 34 Awatea Rd,
Parnell, Auckland
Name: Eleanor Manning
Telephone: (09) 379 4100
Beds: 2 Queen, 1 Double
(3 bedrooms)
Bathroom: 2 Guests share
Tariff: B&B (continental)
Double $90-$120, Dinner $35.
NZ B&B Vouchers accepted
Summer top Price Surcharge on vouchers
Nearest Town: (Centre) Auckland

Peaceful Parnell. Seaviews. Walking distance of Parnell shops and restaurants.
Seaside walks to waterfront via St Stephens Ave and overbridge.
Your hosts are keen to meet people from overseas and fellow Kiwis.
Directions available to places of interest.
Comfortable warm beds and good food.
Dinner on request.
Door to door shuttle.

One of the differences between staying at a hotel and a B&B
is that you don't hug the hotel staff when you leave.

Parnell, Auckland City

Redwood Bed & Breakfast
Address: 11 Judges Bay Rd,
Parnell, Auckland
Name: Sherrie and Alan
Telephone: (09) 373 4903
Fax: (09) 373 4903
Mobile: (025) 758 996
Email: kotuku@wave.co.nz
Beds: 2 Queen, 2 Single (3 bedrooms)
Bathroom: 2 Ensuite, 1 Family share
Tariff: B&B (special) Double $90-$115, Single $65-$85, Children $25, Credit Card (VISA), Off-street parking. NZ B&B Vouchers accepted $30 surcharge (Oct-May)
Nearest Town: Auckland city centre 2km

The Redwood offers a gracious ambience and provides all the modern facilities discerning guests expect. Located in a tranquil bush setting where lovely established trees and shrubs provide a peaceful garden setting. The Redwood is also conveniently adjacent to the Dove-Myer Robinson Park and Auckland's world-famous Rose Gardens.

Our breakfasts are a house speciality! We offer a scrumptious choice of cooked or continental, served in the dining room which has spectacular views of the harbour. Our delightful lounge and verandah are ideal for relaxing.

Conveniently located close to many popular tourist attractions, including the Parnell Village and swimming pools, Auckland Museum, the Domain and Kelly Tarlton's Underwater World. The Redwood is also within easy walking distance of a selection of fine restaurants, and only a one-stop bus ride from the city centre with its shopping and cinemas and live theatres.

Door to door shuttle buses are available and the Airport bus stops close by. We are very happy to advise and assist with on-going travel.

Our attractive bedrooms have comfortable queen or single beds, with electric blankets. Heaters, colour TV, refrigerators, tea and coffee making facilities are standard in all rooms.

Your hosts enjoys most things to do with the great outdoors and its wild life, as well as a great interest in food & wines. We also have a friendly yellow Labrador'. In house beauty therapy and therapeutic massage available.

Having travelled extensively within NZ and overseas, we understand your needs, and aim to provide you with a home away from home. Every effort has been made to ensure that your stay, be it business or pleasure is a pleasant and enjoyable one.

French and German spoken. Office & Fax facilities available.

Home Page: http://www.cyberlink.com.au/bedbreakfast/Redwood

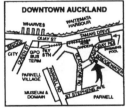

AUCKLAND

Parnell, Auckland City
Bed & Breakfast/Guest House
Address: 43 St Georges Bay Road, Parnell, Auckland 1
Name: St Georges Bay Lodge
Telephone: (09) 303 1050 **Fax**: (09) 303 1055 **Mobile**: (021) 613 501 o
Email: enquiry@stgeorge.co.nz
Beds: 2 King, 1 Queen, 1 Twin, (4 bedrooms)
Bathroom: 2 Ensuite, 1 Private, 1 Guest share
Tariff: B&B (full) Double $145 or $165, Single $125 or $145, Credit Cards (VISA/MC)
Tariffs are reviewed annually at 1st October.
Nearest Town: Auckland city centre 1.5km

St Georges Bay Lodge is an elegant Victorian Villa which has the charm of a by-gone era, with the comfort of modern amenities.

There is no better location for your stay in Auckland City. We are minutes from: picturesque PARNELL VILLAGE, designer boutiques and speciality stores, great cafes, restaurants, and night club life, health centres, swimming pools, gardens, parks, and the Museum in Auckland Domain and Holy Trinity Cathedral. Also within comfortable walking distance: Newmarket and the Central City business district the Casino, yet more restaurants and City night life, the University of Auckland, Waitemata Harbour, watersports, island destinations, ferry tours, and beaches in the City of Sails. At our back door, the Railway Station, buses and the motorway systems.

We have four refined guest rooms, each with central heating, tastefully and comfortably decorated.

Relax in the many open living spaces from the beautiful lounge, to the light and airy conservatory, balcony and verandah.

Start your day with a bountiful and healthy breakfast where every offering is fresh and natural - eggs, fruit, juices, yoghurt, muesli, croissants and muffins.

We are sure you will appreciate the little extras we like to provide, such as speciality teas and coffee, alfresco mornings on the balcony ... and complimentary New Zealand port.

"We look forward to sharing our house with you. We like to offer service with style and are welcoming to all" - Alan and Wendy your hosts.

Continental breakfast consists of fruit, cereal, toast, tea/coffee,
Full breakfast is the same with a cooked course,
Special breakfast has something special.

Parnell
Bed & Breakfast
Address: 41 Birdwood Crescent, Parnell, Auckland
Name: Birdwood House - Barbara Bell-Williams.
Telephone: (09) 306 5900
Fax: (09) 306 5909
Mobile: (025) 777 722
Email: INFO@BIRDWOOD.CO.NZ
Beds: 4 KIng/Twin (4 bedrooms)
Bathroom: 3 Ensuites, 1 Private
Tariff: B&B (Special) Double $130-$150, Single $110-$130.
Not suitable for children. Visa/Mastercard.
Nearest Town: Auckland City 1.5 km

VERY CENTRAL SILVER SERVICE BREAKFAST*
UNIQUELY AUCKLAND THEMED ROOMS

Birdwood House is located adjacent to Auckland's exclusive PARNELL boutiques, 5 minutes by car from Auckland's central CBD, 4 minutes by car or a 10 minute flat stroll from Auckland's trendy fashion centre NEW MARKET, the AUCKLAND HOSPITAL, the DOMAIN, and the MUSEUM, ... we are VERY, VERY CENTRAL. A regular bus service links Parnell, the CBD, Auckland Hospital and New Market. The airport shuttle operates a 24 hour service to our front door (20 minute ride). Motorway access to Auckland's Southern, Western and Northern suburbs is only minutes away.

Enjoy with us our 1914 NEWLY RESTORED, 'Arts and Crafts' Edwardian style character bungalow. We stand majestically in the prestigious suburb of PARNELL, overlooking Auckland city and the sky tower. Our elevated back view takes in the Auckland MUSEUM and the luxurious BOTANICAL GARDENS of the DOMAIN. Parnell village with its range of AWARD winning RESTAURANTS, ART galleries and BOUTIQUE shops is virtually on our doorstep. Birdwood House is located on the Parnell Historic Walk in amongst historic houses / buildings. The NEW MARKET business district is to the south and has a large selection of designer and speciality shops, cinemas and swimming pool and gymnasium. WAITEMATA HARBOUR with its sandy beaches, water sports and Kelly Tarltons Aquarium is close by. We can enhance your stay by arranging tours or by suggesting 'unique' Auckland things to do. At Birdwood House we embody Edwardian quality and hospitality.

A HOME AWAY FROM HOME

Birdwood House's original features include a beautiful KAURI staircase, delightful stained LEADLIGHT windows and a mesmerising inglenook FIREPLACE. Every bedroom in the house is decorated on a sumptuous theme such as the museum room which overlooks the Auckland's museum and the Cathedral room which reflects Parnell's newly renovated Holy Trinity Cathedral.

After a comfortable nights sleep enjoy our healthy SILVER SERVICE GOURMET BREAKFAST with an emphasis on FRESH and in season produce. You can enjoy breakfast in bed if you are feeling decadent. Business facilities are available should you require to hold a meeting we have a separate lounge to accommodate your guests. You may encounter our cat "Chutney" and our small dog "Mandy", but they are confined to a separate living area.

OUR AIM is to make your stay in Auckland memorable and cater for your individual needs. When we first saw this house it beckoned us to enjoy it, we invite you to join us and help us do the same.

Parnell, Auckland
Bed & Breakfast
Address: Amersham House, Corner of Gladstone Road and Canterbury Place, Parnell, Auckland
Name: Jill and Robin Stirling
Telephone: 09-303 0321 **Fax**: 09-303 0621
Email: stirling@xtra.co.nz
Beds: 1 King, 1 Queen, 2 Double, 1 single (4 bedrooms)
Bathroom: 4 Ensuites
Tariff: B&B (full gourmet breakfast) $280, $230, $180, $160
Nearest Town: Downtown Auckland (1 mile), Parnell Village (1/2 mile)

Our guests enjoy Amersham House as much as we do. "Just like home", "Absolutely exceeded all our expectations".

Elegant, Romantic and Relaxing, all our bedrooms are sunny and spacious with Sky TV, phone and office facilities. All en suites are unique and stylish. Perhaps select a room that has an en suite with spa bath and double shower or choose one with a private sauna. They all have great views, original art and top quality beds and linen.

Our "oasis in the city" has a gas heated 10 metre pool surrounded by marble and illuminated palms and orchids as well as an outdoor spa. Indoors, the guest lounge and library has 180 degrees city to harbour views.

Your hosts have travelled extensively and live in a separate part of the home with their two children. You can take our gourmet breakfast with fresh local produce "al fresco" by the garden or pool, privately in our formal dining room, or informally with you New Zealand born hosts.

Amersham House is a short easy walk to the restaurants and boutique shops of Parnell and a little further to the Newmarket malls or to the museum, Winter gardens and parks of the Domain.

Drive to downtown Auckland in 5 minutes or catch the hop-on hop-off tourist bus.

Relax – Don't try to drive too far in one day.

125

Grafton, Auckland City
Homestay
Address: 17A Carlton Gore Road,
Grafton, Auckland 1
Name: George & Janette Welanyk
Telephone: (09) 377 4319 **Fax**: (09) 377 4319
Beds: 1 Twin, 1 Single (2 Bedrooms)
Bathroom: 1 Guests share
Tariff: B&B (full or continental) Twin $75, Single $50.
NZ B&B Vouchers accepted $7.50 Surcharge
Nearest Town: Auckland City centre 1km

From our home it is a ten minute walk to the centre of the city, Newmarket and the Museum. The university, hospital and Parnell Village are nearby.
My wife and I invite you to stay with us, the house was built in 1925, is large and comfortable with excellent facilities.
Facilities for guests include a private sitting room with colour television, tea / coffee making and use of fax.
Your hosts have travelled extensively overseas and welcome visitors.
Private facilities - bathroom and sitting room by arrangement.
We offer a discount for a stay of over 3 nights.
Directions: *From the Airport take the door to door shuttle minibus. Please telephone.*

Grafton
Bed & Breakfast Homestay
Address: Please phone
Name: "Farm Cottage"
Telephone: (09) 366 4669
Fax: (09) 366 4415
Beds: 2 Twin, 1 Single (2-3 bedrooms)
Bathroom: 1 Guests share
Tariff: B&B (continental) $70-$150, Dinner sometimes by arrangement.
Nearest Town: Auckland central 5km

This turn-of-the century colonial cottage which started life as the farmer's dwelling reflects the personality and simplicity from that era. Nestled now in the central inner city environment of Grafton.
Comfortable and reassuringly homely in its style yet a reflection of a quieter time. A warm welcome awaits, created by rich red carpets, open fires and afternoon-sun verandah.
Your accommodation will be an intimate TV lounge for your personal use adjoining little twin room and single room. Guest quarters include cottage's washing machine / drier.
Suitable for one, two or three, plus two in a small upstairs attic. Private entrance for returning from your day's activities or nearby City, Parnell and Newmarket restaurants. Everything's a stroll away, but so is the Link-bus which is faster round these locations.
Continental breakfast, your New Zealand host works too, but traditional home-style fare may be by special arrangement.
Non-smokers please.
Directions: *Motorway exits - Khyber Pass, Gillies Avenue and Grafton.*

Mt. Eden, Auckland City
Bed & Breakfast
Address: "811 Bed & Breakfast"
811 Dominion Road, Mt. Eden, Auckland 4
Name: David Fitchew & Bryan Condon
Telephone: (09) 620 4284 **Fax**: (09) 620 4286
Mobile: 025 289 8863
Beds: 2 Double, 1 Twin (3 bedrooms sharing 2 guest bathrooms).
Bedrooms wiht hot and cold hand basins.
Tariff: B&B (Full) Double $65 Single $45 includes cooked breakfast, home-made
muffins etc. Tea & coffee always available. NZ B&B Vouchers accepted
Nearest Town: Auckland

*Your hosts Bryan and David, Pfeny and their Irish Water Spaniels welcome you to
their turn of the century home. Our home reflects years of collecting and living
overseas. Centrally located on Dominion Road (which is an extension of Queen Street
city centre). The bus stop at the door, only 10 minutes to city and 20 minutes to airport,
shuttle bus from airport. Easy walking to Balmoral shopping area (banks, excellent
restaurants, cinema). All are welcome to 811 B&B.*
*We have operated a bed and breakfast on a farm in Digby County, Nova Scotia,
Canada. The nicest compliment we can receive is when Guests tell us, it's like visiting
friends when they stay with us. Our breakfast gives you a Beaut start to your day in
a layed back atmosphere.*
Directions: *From north-south motorway, Greenlane off ramp, continue on Greenlane,
to Dominion Road. Turn left and we are 7 blocks on your right to 811 (between
Lambeth and Invermay and across from Landscape Road).*

Mt Eden, Auckland City
Small Hotel
Address: 83 Valley Road,
Mt. Eden, Auckland 3
Name: Bavaria B&B Hotel
Telephone: (09) 638 9641
Fax: (09) 638 9665
Beds: 5 King/Queen, 2 Double,
4 Single (11 bedrooms)
Bathroom: 11 Ensuite

Tariff: Delightful Breakfast Buffet, Double $110, Single $78, Children $12.50,
Reduced rates in winter, Major Credit cards accepted. NZ B&B Vouchers ac-
cepted $14 Surcharge/person (1/10-31/4)
Nearest Town: Auckland city centre 2km

*We invite you to stay at Bavaria B&B Hotel, a small professionally run hotel, situated
in the heart of Mt Eden, a quiet century-old suburb only 2km from the city centre.*
*All our 11 non-smoker rooms are furnished with private bathrooms, telephones,
suitcase racks, clock radios, heating and electric blankets.*
*The 80-year-old, completely renovated kauri villa is designed generously, the decor is
fresh and friendly and maintained immaculately.*
*Enjoy sitting in our large sunny lounge and meet other travellers or sunbathe on our
private deck looking on to an exotic small garden.*
*Off-street parking available, city bus stop close-by. All the necessary amenities and
many fine restaurants in walking distance.*
*We speak English and German, offer first-class service and personal attention and are
happy to assist you with your travel plans i.e. recommend tours or inexpensive rental
vehicles.*

Mt Eden, Auckland
Bed & Breakfast Hotel
Address: 22 Pentland Avenue,
Mt Eden, Auckland 3
Name: Pentlands Bed & Breakfast Hotel
Telephone: (09) 638 7031 **Fax**: (09) 638 7031
Mobile: (025) 339 928
Email: hoppy.pentland@xtra.co.nz
Beds: 2 Family, 5 Double, 3 Twin, 5 Single (15 bedrooms)
Bathroom: 4 guests share, 5 toilets.
Tariff: B&B (continental) Double/Twin $79-$89, Single $49.
Additional Adults $25/night, Children $15/night.
Credit Cards (VISA/MC/AMEX). NZ B&B Vouchers accepted $10 surcharge per person
Nearest Town: Auckland

Travellers, holiday makers, business people, families and sporting or cultural groups are all welcome at Pentlands which is located in a quiet cul-de-sac in the heart of Auckland. Pentlands is a stately villa, set in spacious, sunny grounds with elevated views, native trees, a tennis court and picnic tables. The hotel has a large guest lounge with TV (including Sky) and an open fire. It offers ample off-street parking, laundry facilities, guest phone, luggage storage plus internet and fax facilities. 24 hour tea and coffee is included in the tariff. Pentlands is a short walk from buses, supermarket, restaurants, cafes, shops, banks, post office and Eden Park. Your hosts are friendly and helpful and are only too pleased to assist you with car hire, travel and sightseeing arrangements.
Home Page: www.pentlands.co.nz
Directions: *From airport: Shuttle bus to the door. From city terminals: Phone for directions. Driving from south: Exit at Symonds Street from motorway SH1, turn left continue left into Mt Eden Road, right turn into Valley Rd at Mt Eden Village. Third left into Pentland Avenue. Driving from the North: Exit at Gillies Ave; right into Owens Rd; right into mt Eden Rd; left into Valley Rd. Pentland Ave is 3rd on the left.*

Mt Eden Village, Auckland City
B&B Homestay
Address: 536 Mt Eden Rd., Mt Eden, Auckland
Name: "Villa 536" Anna Watson
Telephone: (09) 630 5258 **Fax**: (09) 630 5258
Beds: 2 Queen, 2 Single (3 bedrooms)
Bathroom: 2 Ensuite, 1 Private
Tariff: B&B (special) Double $95-$140, Single $85-$125, Dinner by arrangement, Credit Cards (VISA/MC), Off street parking. NZ B&B Vouchers accepted $30 surcharge Double ensuites only
Nearest Town: Auckland City 3km

Travellers, holiday-makers, business people, special occasion visitors - all are welcome at my charmingly restored, spacious kauri home. Villa 536 is easy to find, close to airport, motorways access and the city, on a city bus route and right beside popular Mt Eden Village with its cafes, winery and speciality shops. The cheerful spacious bedrooms have comfortable beds, electric blankets, fans and clock / radios. Bathrobes, hairdryers, television, telephones and fax are provided. Delicious breakfasts include fresh fruit, yoghurt and home-made muffins. Complimentary teas / coffees / cookies available. Relax in the pleasant lounge, enjoy the view through the treetops to One Tree Hill from the deck and casual living area, chat with me, stroll to the village, or just please yourself! Cinemas, shopping centres, racecourses, parks, antique / collectible shops, Eden Park and the city's major hospitals / tertiary institutions are close. I am well-travelled, enjoy sharing my home and happy to help with holiday plans.

Mt Eden
Homestay
Address: 'Shackleton B&B',
2/128 Shackleton Road, Mt Eden,
Auckland
Name: Janelle and Craig Ritchie
Telephone: (09) 6200 774 or Freephone 0800 270062
Fax: (09) 620 0793 **Mobile**: 021 608 420
Email: craig.ritchie@xtra.co.nz
Beds: 1 Double, 2 Single (2 bedrooms)
Bathroom: 1 Guests share
Tariff: B&B (full) Double $85, Single $65, Children welcome.
NZ B&B Vouchers accepted Surcharge in Summer up to $10
Nearest Town: Auckland City

If having the exclusive use of a guest lounge, generously sized rooms and being close to the central city appeals, then this could be the place for you. Ideal for leisure or business travellers looking for quality accommodation and great hospitality.
Our modern spacious split level architecturally designed townhouse is just 10 minutes drive to the America's Cup village, casino and downtown Auckland. For those that prefer a little privacy or just want to relax in their own company, our guest lounge (which includes TV, table and chairs, tea and coffee) is a must. Alternatively join us in the family room.
Restaurants within walking distance. Dinner by arrangement. Minutes drive to tourist attractions, sports grounds, shopping malls and hospitals. Off street parking or pick up from the Airport by arrangement. Laundry facilities. Close to bus route. Smoke free home. We have a cat. Members of Farm and Homestay Auckland.

Epsom, Auckland City

Homestay
Address: 10 Ngaroma Road, Epsom,
Auckland 3
Name: Janet & Jim Millar
Telephone: (09) 625 7336 **Fax**: (09) 625 7336
Beds: 1 Queen, 1 Double, 2 Single (3 bedrooms)
Bathroom: 1 Ensuite, 2 Private
Email:jmillar@xtra.co.nz
Tariff: B&B (full) Double $75-$90, Single $55-$65, Children $15; Dinner $30.
Credit cards (VISA/Mastercard). NZ B&B Vouchers accepted surcharge $10
Nearest Town: Auckland - 5 km to City centre

Our home, built of heart timber in 1919, is located in the middle of the isthmus, and on the lower slopes of One Tree Hill. We are within easy walking distance to its Domain, Cornwall Park, one of Auckland's loveliest parks with glorious views. Greenwoods Corner Village is at the end of our street and contains wonderful restaurants, P.O., banking facilities and a magnificent china shop with many of Auckland's antique shops nearby. Our upstairs guest bedroom (kingsize bed) has its own en-suite. The downstairs Garden Suite has a double bedroom and a large sun lounge complete with desk, twin beds (enabling us to cater for families), its own bathroom, refrigerator, and a laundry is available. It takes 10 minutes by car to downtown. We have three grown-up married children (one living in Finland), and six grandchildren. We enjoy meeting people and making them feel at home. We've travelled extensively overseas and in N.Z. and we enjoy exchanging experiences. No smoking indoors.

Epsom, Auckland

Homestay
Address: 2/7 Tahuri Rd, Epsom 3, Auckland
Name: Kathy & Roger Hey
Telephone: (09) 520 0154 **Fax:** (09) 520 0184
Mobile: 025 642 652
Email: R.K.Hey@xtra.Co.NZ
Beds: 1 Super King size Double, 2 Single (2 bedrooms)
Bathroom: 1 Guests share
Tariff: B&B (continental) Double $80, Single $50, Children concessions, Dinner $20 by prior arrangement. NZ B&B Vouchers accepted March-Oct
Nearest Town: 4km from central city

In 1993 we built this lovely spacious 4 bedroom house, with ideal features for homestay. All comforts, and bedrooms offer views of One Tree Hill, Mt St John and Mt Hobson. Epsom is a very quiet garden suburb, with parks, restaurants, showgrounds, hospitals, postal facilities, banks and shops around us, one minute from the motorway. The Airport is 15 minutes away on door to door shuttle bus service. Excellent bus service two minutes walk away. We are extensive travellers, both in NZ and overseas, enjoy meeting people, swopping tales and helping guests feel at home. We will collect guests from the railway station, and can suggest a variety of Auckland attractions. Laundry facilities, off-street parking, juice, tea and coffee always available. Family groups welcome. We ask no smoking indoors.
Directions: *Leave Motorway at Market Road, travel west, cross over Great South Road, first left into Dunkerron Ave. Tahuri Road is 2nd left, we're at the end of the cul-de-sac.*

Epsom, Auckland

Luxury Boutique Lodge
Address: 29 Haydn Avenue, Royal Oak, Auckland 3
Name: The Langtons
Telephone: (09) 625 7520 **Fax:** (09) 624 3122
Mobile: 025 285 4493
Email: thelangtons@xtra.co.nz
Beds: 4 King or 8 Single (4 bedrooms)
Bathroom: 4 Ensuite
Tariff: B&B (special) Double/Twin From $185 to $225, Dinner Special $50. Credit Cards (VISA/MC) accepted.
Nearest Town: Auckland City 5kms

Luxury accommodation with personal service and attention to your every need is what George and Sandra Langton offer you in their comfortable smoke free, tudor home. We are sited on the slopes of One Tree Hill bordering 450 acres of parkland with wonderful city views, just 10 minutes from central Auckland.
The upstairs bedrooms are luxuriously appointed with ensuites, superior beds, bedding and furnishings. The main lounges, dining room and conservatory open onto large decks overlooking the swimming pool and garden. Food and wine are our special passion, with Sandra's knowledge of New Zealand wines, and George's experience in the hospitality industry we are able to offer an interesting blend of gourmet delights or even a picnic in the park. Our home is complimented by a collection of New Zealand works of art, and we also have two pets. Situated 10 minutes from the airport, our meet and greet service is available to all guests.
Home Page: www.nzcom/HeritageInns/TheLangtons
or www.dmd.co.nz/thelangtons

Greenlane, Auckland City
Homestay
Address: 'Mary's Place', 22 Maungakiekie Ave,
Greenlane, One Tree Hill, Auckland 5
Name: Mrs M. Heisch
Telephone: (09) 524 4887
Beds: 1 Double, 1 Single (2 bedrooms)
Bathroom: 1 Ensuite, 1 Family share
Tariff: B&B (full) Double $75, Single $45, Dinner $20,
Credit Cards. NZ B&B Vouchers accepted $10 surcharge
Nearest Town: Greenlane, Auckland City - 2km

Our 69 year old home is on the lower slopes of Auckland's lovely Cornwall Park, to which it has walking access immediately across the road. We are close to the Southern Motorway and within a few minutes of Auckland city centre, yet the area is pleasantly secluded while within easy reach of buses and some excellent restaurants. The double guestroom has its own ensuite. Off street parking is available on request. We have a dog and a cat and a large restful garden. We request no smoking indoors. Full or continental breakfast as requested.
Directions: *Exit Motorway at Greenlane West and take the 1st turn to the left after the 2nd set of traffic lights into Maungakiekie Avenue.*

One Tree Hill, Auckland
Homestay+Self-contained Accom.
Address: 39b Konini Road, One Tree Hill, Auckland 5
Name: Ron & Doreen Curreen
Telephone: (09) 579 9531 Doreen (09) 524 4306 **Fax**: (09) 579 9531
Beds: Self cont. 1 King, (1 bedroom), 1 Sofa bed in lounge. Homestay: 1 Queen, 1 Double (2 bedrooms)
Bathroom: 1 Ensuite Homestay: 1Guest share
Tariff: B&B (Continental) King $75, Queen $65, Double $65, Single $45, Children $15, Dinner $25pp. NZ B&B Vouchers accepted, Surcharge, Credit Cards.
Nearest Town: Newmarket

A warm friendly welcome awaits you at 39b.
Situated 15 mintes from the airport and city centre, our large contemporary home in a secluded garden setting on private right of way offers pleasant views and peaceful surroundings. We are close to Ellerslie Racecourse, One Tree Hill Domain, Alexandra Park, Epsom Showgrounds and Ericsson Stadium. Restaurants, antique shops, supermarket and bus service are a short distance away.
Our spacious self contained unit has a large bedroom with king-sized bed, ensuite, lounge with TV, kitchenette, microwave, washing machine and extras.
As an ex-taxi driver Ron can take you on sightseeing tours.
Arrive as a guest - depart as a friend.
Directions: *Take Ellerslie-Pensrose exit on Motorway (1) North, or South to Great South Road. North to traffic lights, left into Rockfield, first right into Konini Road.*

One of the differences between staying at a hotel and a B&B
is that you don't hug the hotel staff when you leave.

One Tree Hill, Auckland City
Homestay
Address: 21 Atarangi Rd, Greenlane, Auckland 5
Name: Clare Ross & Winston Dickey
Telephone: (09) 523 3419, Freephone 0800 254 419
Fax: (09) 524 8506
Email: homestay@xtra.co.nz
Beds: 2 Queen, 2 Single (3 bedrooms)
Bathroom: 1 Guests share, 1 Family share
Tariff: B&B (full) Double $65, Single $40, Dinner $12.50,
Children one. Credit Cards.
NZ B&B Vouchers accepted
Nearest Town: Newmarket - 3km North, Downtown Auckland 6km

Our comfortable non-smoking home has modern facilities and is situated on the lower northern slopes of One Tree Hill and this extinct volcano can be accessed through lovely Cornwall Park at the end of our short street. We have five restaurants within few minutes walk including European, Chinese, Nepalese and McDonalds. Downtown Auckland is 10 minutes away, Airport 20 minutes. Off street parking available. We have one cat. We encourage guests to have the freedom of our home and grounds, with tea, coffee facilities and TV at all times. Ellerslie races, Epsom trotting, NZ Expo, close by.

Directions: *Ex Airport toward Auckland, exit motorway at Queenstown Road, follow route 12, 3.3km, turn right into Greenlane (Route 9). After passing the park turn first right then first left (Atarangi Road)*

Directions: *Exit State Highway 1 motorway at Greenlane, head west - then left at traffic lights, then second right (Atarangi Rd).*

Greenlane, Auckland
Self Contained Accommodation with 2 guest bedrooms
Address: "Wheturangi House",
94 Wheturangi Road,
Greenlane, Auckland
Name: Ruth and Roger Genet
Telephone: (09) 529 4447
Fax: (09) 529 5044
Mobile: (025) 291 2494
Beds: 1 King, 1 Double, 1 Single (2 bedrooms)
Bathroom: 2 Ensuites

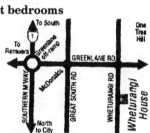

Tariff: B&B (special) Super King $130, Double $100, Single negotiable.
Dinner on request. Children welcome. Credit Cards accepted.
Nearest Town: Auckland 10 minutes Downtown.

* Welcome to a cottage garden setting.
* Fantastic location next to Cornwall Park - an old leafy part of Auckland.
* 15 minutes to beaches, city, airport, night life.
* 5 minutes to One Tree Hill, antique shops, restaurants, theatre, motorway, Greenlane Hospital, Raceway and Expo Centre.
* Delicious breakfasts served in your room or al fresco
* Picnic, BBQ or dinner by arrangement.
* Fresh flowers, coffee and baking.
* Separate guest accommodation includes: 1 Super King ensuite bedroom, 1 Double ensuite bedroom / Single, Guest kitchenette, dining and lounge.
* Extra facilities include fax, laundry, pool table, petanque.
* Special rates on request.
* Your comfort is our pleasure.

133

Remuera
Homestay
Address: 'Lakeside', 18 Darwin Lane,
Remuera, Auckland 5
Name: Tony & Joanna Greenhough
Telephone: (09) 524 6281 **Fax**: (09) 524 6281
Mobile: 025-272 9035
Beds: 1 Queen, 2 Single (2 bedrooms)
Bathroom: 1 Private, 1 Guests share
Tariff: B&B (full) Double $85, Single $60,
Double with private bathroom and lounge $120.
NZ B&B Vouchers accepted Surcharge $15
Nearest Town: Auckland City Centre 5km

Come and enjoy this unique location with its magnificent views to green hills right in the heart of the city, where all rooms overlook the water at the bottom of our peaceful garden. You can walk to local restaurants, or lakeside is only minutes by car from the waterfront beaches and cafés, Parnell/Newmarket with its wider selection of restaurants and excellent shopping, the Museum, and many other visitor attractions.
Our house is interesting and thoroughly comfortable. Guest accommodation is in one wing with large bedrooms, spacious modern bathroom, sittingroom with television and coffee/tea making facility. There is plenty of off-street parking. We look forward to meeting you, and know you will enjoy your stay.
Directions: *Door to door shuttle from the airport; by car take the Greenlane exit from the motorway.*

Remuera, Auckland City
Homestay
Address: 'Woodlands', 18 Waiatarua Rd,
Remuera, Auckland 1005
Name: Judi & Roger Harwood
Telephone: (09) 524 6990 **Fax**: (09) 524 6993
Mobile: (025) 270 6378
Beds: 1 King,1 Double, 1 Single (2 bedrooms),
Bathroom: 1 Ensuite, 1 Private
Tariff: B&B (full) Double $90-110, Single $75, Dinner $45pp, Credit cards (VISA/MC). NZ B&B Vouchers accepted Surcharge $30
Nearest Town: Auckland city centre 10km

Our two guest bedrooms are downstairs overlooking the pool and lush native greenery. The ensuite bedroom is larger and has french windows opening into a private sunny conservatory. The "Pink Room" has a private bathroom. Each room has tea/coffee making facilities, heated towel rails, coloured TV's and electric blankets. Both rooms are very quiet and private. There is safe off-street car parking. Central heating in winter. Our breakfasts are special. Individual platters of seasonal fruits start the day, with homemade jams, yoghurts, choice of teas, or percolated coffee, then a full cooked breakfast of your choice. In the evening, join us for a candlelit Advanced Cordon Bleu dinner. We delight in using good NZ produce, especially seafood. Vegetarians catered for. Bookings essential.
We are close to motorways, shopping centres, Ericsson Stadium, Racecourse, Restaurants, Showgrounds, Hospitals, beaches and Downtown.
No pets, one pet son!
Directions: *Telephone, fax or write.*

134

Remuera
Homestay
Address: 21A Manawa Road, Remuera,
Auckland City
Name: Bruce & Thea Tantrum
Telephone: (09) 524 6812 **Fax**: (09) 524 6812
Mobile: (025) 720 228
Email: cocoon@xtra.co.nz
Beds: 1 Queen, 1 Double, 1 Single (3 bedrooms)
Bathroom: 1 Guests share
Tariff: B&B (full) Double $85, Single $60,
Credit card (VISA). NZ B&B Vouchers accepted $12 Surcharge
Nearest Town: Auckland city centre 6km

Welcome to our spacious contemporary home with its quiet restful setting. The guest area occupies the entire ground floor and includes tea & coffee making facilities and sheltered patio.

Many of Auckland's most popular attractions are nearby, and are easily accessible by private or public transport. We take special pleasure in assisting with planning tour itineraries, as we understand how a little local knowledge really helps make the best use of precious limited travel time.

In addition to enjoying travel and meeting travellers, Thea is interested in fibre arts and crafts and Bruce is an enthusiastic sailor. Our 11 metre yacht is available by prior arrangement for sailing trips.

Casual evening meals can be prepared including NZ wine. We are non smokers and have a cat called Sophie.

Whatever your reasons for visiting Auckland, we would be delighted to share our home and hospitality with you.

Remuera
Bed & Breakfast
Address: 54 Seaview Road, Remuera,
Auckland
Name: Mrs Margaret Brooks & Family
Telephone: (09) 523 3746 **Fax**: (09) 523 3742
Mobile: (025) 744 035
Email: longwood@ihug.co.nz
Beds: 1 Double, 2 Single (2 bedrooms)
Bathroom: 2 Ensuite
Tariff: B&B (full) $70-$120.
Nearest Town: Auckland city centre 3km, 2mins Newmarket,
Parnell or Remuera

We invite you to stay in our beautiful old home. Longwood is a fully restored farmhouse, built in the 1880's, with all the comforts of the 90's. We have two guest rooms, each with ensuite and our spacious home features sunny verandahs overlooking the gardens and pool. Breakfast to suit - healthy or indulgent or a little of both. We are superbly located close to the shops, galleries, theatres and parks of Auckland City, Parnell, Newmarket and Remuera.

We ask no smoking please, our home is not suitable for young children. We have a friendly cat.

Directions: *The airport shuttle will bring you to our door, or phone for easy directions.*

Remuera, Auckland

Boutique Hotel
Address: 39 Market Road, Remuera,
Auckland 5
Name: "Aachen House"
Telephone: (09) 520 2329
Freephone: 0800 AACHEN **Fax**: (09) 524 2898
Email: info@aachenhouse.co.nz
Beds: 3 Californian King, 2 Super King, 2 King/Twin, 2 Twin (9 bedrooms)
Bathroom: 9 Ensuite, 1 Powder Room
Tariff: B&B (full) Suites $220-$295, Super King $195,
King Single/Twin $150-$175. Children 16 years and over. Credit Cards.
Nearest Town: Auckland - 4 km from central city

Enter a timeless world where the qualities of excellence welcome you. Where each step is one into an era where graciousness abounds. Each stay is a further return to a hotel that recognises your appreciation of elegance, and attention to every small detail. This is a grand residence, truly a quality Bed & Breakfast Boutique Hotel for the selective traveller. This immaculately presented residence provides nine spacious guest rooms, each superbly decorated in period style. All rooms feature a luxuriously appointed ensuite bathroom and either Californian king, super king and king twin or twin beds. Guests rooms are complete with direct dial telephones, hairdryer, bathrobes and toiletries while four rooms have direct access to a private balcony. Disabled person facilities are provided in one of the king twin rooms. For the comfort and safety of guests, Aachen House is centrally heated and complies with modern international fire safety standards. Smoking is limited to outdoor areas.

Restaurants, parks, antique shops and public transport are within easy walking distance with major attractions, the airport, city centre and Auckland's renown harbour just ten minutes away by car. Easily located by leaving the main north / south motorway at the Market Road exit and following sign posting 300 metres to Aachen House. Guests arriving from the airport will find taxis or the airport shuttle bus readily available.

Home Page: www.aachenhouse.co.nz

There are some good tips for easier travel on page 7

Auckland
Boutique B&B Hotel
Address: 267 Remuera Road,
Remuera, Auckland
Name: Charlotte Devereux
Telephone: (09) 524 5044
Fax: (09) 524 5080
Mobile: (021) 699 830
Email: the.devereux.hotel@xtra.com.nz
Beds: 10 King/Queen, 1 Double,
1 Single (12 bedrooms)
Bathroom: 10 Ensuite, 1 Guests Share, 2 Family Share.
Tariff: B&B (full) Double $100-$150, Single $85-$135, Children $25.
Credit Cards.
Nearest Town: Auckland, Remuera shops 5 mins walk.

Welcome to 'The Devereux' situated in stylish Remuera, just minutes away from a myriad of Auckland's finest theatres and shopping, galleries and restaurants, parks and cafes, and the stunning Waitemata Harbour.
For business or pleasure 'The Devereux' offers you a boutique Bed & Breakfast with a unique difference!
'The Devereux' situated in an 1890's historic villa is characterised by its distinct, individually decorated rooms. Let 'The Devereux' take you around the world.....!
'The Devereux' emanates pure style and extends creative comforts you'd naturally expect ... Breakfast in the conservatory or 'alfresco' by the fountain. Fully serviced rooms, Les Floralies toiletries, telephone and television all with our unparalleled personal service.
Immerse yourself in an atmosphere and environment bathed in the sense of style unique only to 'The Devereux'.

Remuera
Homestay+Self-contained Accom.
Address: 11B Kitirawa Road, Remuera,
Auckland
Name: Colleen Lea
Telephone: (09) 524 2325
Beds: 1 Queen (1 bedroom)
Bathroom: 1 Ensuite
Tariff: B&B (continental) Double $70, Single $60.
NZ B&B Vouchers accepted
Nearest Town: Downtown Auckland 7 km

Our home, set in one of Auckland most central suburbs, is situated up a short driveway in a quiet treed garden with spacious lawns, which we think, creates a feeling of tranquillity.
We are only minutes from major shopping areas and many good restaurants. Should you feel you would rather go by bus the bus stop is a minutes walk around the corner and will take you to Remuera, Newmarket and Auckland city.
You are assured of a relaxing stay in our "East Wing", modern self-contained accommodation with TV, lying to the sun and an outside deck to enjoy your breakfast on if you so wish.
We will be pleased to direct you to Auckland's major attractions which are many and varied. We wish you to enjoy your stay in our city and our country.
Smoking outside please.
Directions: *The airport shuttle bus will bring you to the door.*

Ellerslie, Auckland

Homestay
Address: 'Taimihinga', 16 Malabar Drive, Ellerslie, Auckland 5
Name: Marjorie Love
Telephone: (09) 579 7796 **Fax**: (09) 579 7796
Beds: 1 Double, 3 Single (3 bedrooms)
Bathroom: 1 Ensuite, 1 Family share
Tariff: B&B (continental) Double $70, Single $50, Dinner $25pp by arrangement,
Full breakfast on request, Credit Cards. NZ B&B Vouchers accepted
Nearest Town: 8km to city centre (12 mins on Motorway), 5 mins to Newmarket
and Remuera

*Taimihinga - softly calling o'er the ocean. Answer the call - enjoy the welcome! A special
pleasure is sharing Auckland's particular attractions with travellers from overseas
and from other parts of New Zealand. My convenient, comfortable, indoor-outdoor
home and garden is situated in Ellerslie in a quiet cul-de-sac with a pleasant northerly
outlook. Ellerslie affords ready access to most places of interest around Auckland.
Parks, racing, sports, gymnasium, cinemas, hospitals, shopping centres and restaurants and motorway are nearby. Family: - 2 daughters, a son, 3 grandchildren - all live
away. Interests: - people, travel, the arts, church (Anglican), Probus club, gardening,
knitting and sewing. The twin and single bedrooms are downstairs and share family
bathroom. Rate is lower - $60 double and $40 single. Rooms have tea and coffee
facilities. Additional amenities - laundry. NO SMOKING PLEASE
Convenient Shuttle Service from Airport.*
Directions: *Please phone, fax or write.*

St Johns, Auckland

Homestay
Address: 47 Norman Lesser Drive, St Johns Park,
Auckland 1005
Name: Jean & Neville Taylor
Telephone: (09) 521 1827 **Fax**: (09) 521 1863
Email: jean.neville.taylor@xtra.co.nz
Beds: 3 Single (2 bedrooms)
Bathroom: 1 Guests share
Tariff: B&B (full) Double $75, Single $40.
Credit cards. NZ B&B Vouchers accepted May to September inclusive only.
Nearest Town: Downtwon Auckland 8 kms

*Relax with tea, coffee or cold drink in our conservatory, comfortable lounge or
courtyard garden on arrival.*
*Our smoke free home with off street parking is warm and comfortable in a quiet
residential area which surrounds Remuera Golf Course. All beds have electric
blankets, cosy duvets and patchwork quilts.*
*Laundry and ironing facilities are available and we have smoke alarms installed in
bedrooms. We are a retired couple who have travelled extensively in Europe, UK, USA
and New Zealand. Choosing to stay in B&B accommodation ourselves we understand
your needs, and can cater for them. Our interests include Travel, Quilting and
Patchwork, Gardening and Probus. There is a range of restaurants nearby. Bus stop
to and from Auckland City at gate. We are handy to Tamaki University Campus,
Adventist and Ascot Hospitals.*
Directions: *Greenlane Exit from Motorway. Shuttle Bus from Auckland Airport.
Phone for directions;*

Mission Bay, Auckland
Homestay
Address: 10 Hawera Rd., Mission Bay, Auckland
Name: Marvyn & Doug Smith
Telephone: (09) 528 3263 **Mobile**: (025) 982 111
Beds: 1 Queen, 1 Single (2 bedrooms)
Bathroom: 1 Ensuite
Tariff: B&B (full) Double $110, Single $90.
Nearest Town: Auckland City 10 minutes by car

Feel at home in our modern architecturally designed house. We have a wonderfully relaxing view of Rangitoto and the Waitemata Harbour. For summer use our swimming pool or winter our cosy fireplace are available for our guests to enjoy. We are situated within walking distance to shops, bus stops and only minutes by car from the beaches and restaurants of Mission Bay, Kohimarama and St Helier's. We can suggest a variety of Auckland based activities. We have a farm on the coast at Waipu Cove (2 hours north of Auckland) which enables us to help you with accommodation there if you are planning to tour Northland. Having travelled extensively both in NZ and overseas we understand and look forward to satisfying your needs. My interest in Ikebana and weaving has brought me into contact with many friends both in Japan and NZ. As Auckland is often arrival or departure point for many visitors, we would like to welcome you to our home.

Mission Bay, Auckland
Bed & Breakfast
Address: "Joyce Residence Bed & Breakfast",
71 Patteson Avenue, Mission Bay, Auckland 5
Name: Adrienne & Lionel Joyce
Telephone: (09) 520 0250 **Fax**: (09) 521 1250
Mobile: (025) 983 060
Email: joyb&b@xtra.co.nz
Beds: 1 Queen, 1 Double (2 bedrooms)
Bathroom: 1 Private
Tariff: B&B (full) Double $125, Single $95.
NZ B&B Vouchers accepted June to October $40 surcharge
Nearest Town: Auckland City 10 mins along scenic Tamaki Dr.10 mins from Nthn & Sthn motorways

Relax in the quiet comfort of our spacious, extensively refurbished, quality home. We serve a delicious breakfast in the sunny dining room or al fresco in the garden courtyard. Refreshments are available on arrival and during stay. Our guest rooms have level access and private sunny sitting rooms with harbour views. These rooms can become a family suite. A cozy fireplace in your own TV lounge, central heating, electric blankets and feather/down duvets ensure your comfort. Swimming pool, telephone, fax, hairdrier, laundry facilities and off street parking are also available. We are a smoke free home. Our house is 1/4 kilometre to Mission Bay beach, movie theatre, restaurants, bars and cafés, Kelly Tarlton's Underwater World and buses to the city and major tourist attractions. We have both travelled extensively and appreciate travellers' needs for assistance with tourist information. Only one party booked at a time. Airport shuttle bus to our door.
Directions: *Phone/fax.*

Mission Bay, Auckland
Homestay
Address: 41 Nihill Crescent,
Mission Bay, Auckland
Name: Jean and Bryan
Telephone: (09) 528 3809
Beds: 1 Queen (1 bedroom)
Bathroom: 1 Private

Tariff: B&B (full) Double $80, single $60, Dinner $25 pp.
Credit Cards accpeted. NZ B&B Vouchers accepted $12 surcharge
Nearest Town: Auckland (10 mins drive)

We warmly welcome you to our modern split level home. The upper level is for your exclusive use featuring sunny north facing patio, double bedroom, fully equipped bathroom and private lounge if preferred. Only 5 minutes walk to Mission Bay beach - cafes and restaurants. The stunning waterfront with its ever changing vista of yachts, marine activities and the unsurpassable islands on the Gulf.
The water front is a walkers' paradise (host to the world famous "Round the Bays Run"). Or should you prefer we are only 10 minutes scenic bus or car ride to downtown Auckland and the ferry terminal, harbour and islands in the Gulf.
We are retired and have enjoyed living and visiting in many parts of the world. We look forward to sharing our special part of Auckland with you.
Airport shuttle bus to our door, please no smoking, please phone for directions.

St Heliers, Auckland
Self-contained Accommodation
Address: 51 Cliff Road, St Heliers,
Auckland
Name: Jill Mathew
Telephone: (09) 575 4052 **Fax**: (09) 575 4051
Beds: 1 King (1 bedroom)
Bathroom: 1 Ensuite
Tariff: B&B (continental) Double/Single $195.
Nearest Town: St Heliers 200 metres, Auckland 8km (5 miles)

For those who would like to enjoy breathtaking views from sheer cliffs high above a succession of some of Auckland's most famous beaches, Mission Bay, St Heliers, Kohimarama, pleasure yachts silently gliding by their windows, cruise ships, ocean liners and harbour ferries leaving and entering the harbour day and night, this may be where you would like to stay for two nights (minimum) or more that four nights (at discount rates).
Just across the road you can make your way down an easy winding track to Ladies Bay, always secluded often deserted, to bathe or fish in the "Sparkling Waters" of the Waitemata Harbour or you may just indulge yourself, rise late enjoy a bountiful continental breakfast while you survey the whole inner harbour, much of the Hauraki Gulf and some of the inner islands from this exclusive guests apartment in a prestage area surrounded by top quality executive homes.

Please help us provide the best hospitality in the world.
Fill in a comment form for every place you stay.

St. Heliers
Bed & Breakfast
Address:
"Seaview Heights",
23A Glover Road,
St. Heliers Bay, Auckland 5
Name: Anthea & John Delugar
Telephone: (09) 575 8159
Fax: (09) 575 8155
Mobile: (025) 854 659
Email: seaview@bitz.co.nz
Beds: 2 King/Queen,
2 Single (3 bedrooms)
Bathroom: 2 Private Ensuites, 2 Family share
Tariff: B&B (full) Room rate Double $120-$220, Single from $95, Credit Cards (VISA/MC/BC).
Nearest Town: Auckland central 15 mins, St. Heliers 2 mins, Airport 35 mins.

TELECOM / TOURISM AUCKLAND "HOSTED ACCOMMODATION" FINALIST 1996 and 1997.

Ich spreche Deutsch / Je parle français / Hablo español / Parlo italiano
Seaview Heights is set high on a hill, 250 metres back from the cliffs at St. Heliers Bay and backs onto a tranquil park, the crater of an extinct volcano. There are extensive sea views from many rooms, overlooking yachts and pleasure boats enjoying Auckland's beautiful Waitemata Harbour. Close to the city, yet very peaceful, with no traffic noise. Only a 2 minute drive or a 5 / 10 minutes stroll past the park, down Cliff Road to the beach, restaurants, cafes at St. Heliers Bay, or to a bird sanctuary nearby with many native birds. The house comprises three levels and has a majestic quality and feeling of grace and space. An impressive spiral staircase leads up to the guest bedrooms on the top floor. The Bay View Suite has a king-size bed, double spa-bath, and balcony - a perfect honeymoon retreat. The Park View suite, also with ensuite bathroom, overlooks the Park and has a balcony with seaviews. Throughout the house fine antiques and Mediterranean decor contribute to the stylish and restful atmosphere.
A delicious breakfast is served in the first floor dining-room overlooking the Bay: muesli; hot home-made muffins; fresh fruit platter and yoghurt. Courtesy car available to drive you to local restaurants in the evening.
John is a lawyer. He is very interested in international affairs. Anthea has worked in Germany, Switzerland and Spain. She is an interpreter of German, French, Spanish and Italian and has been a tour-guide throughout New Zealand. They have a son Andrew, aged 25 and a daughter, Charlotte, aged 22. They all promise you a warm welcome. They have a cat, Tui and a Golden Retriever dog,
Amber. Sorry, our house is smoke-free. Fax and e-mail available.
Homepage:http://nz.com/webnz/bbnz/seaview.
Directions: *From City, take Tamaki Drive to St. Heliers, half-way up Cliff Road, turn into Springcombe, then Glover Rd. OR from Motorway: Green Lane exit; Remuera Rd; St. Johns Rd; then St. Heliers Bay Rd. to seafront, then Cliff Rd, Springcombe, Glover Rd.*

St Heliers

Homestay
Address: "The Totara", 1/17 Glover Road,
St Heliers, Auckland
Name: Peter & Jeanne Maxwell
Telephone: (09) 575 3514 **Fax**: (09) 575 3582
Mobile: (025) 284 0172
Beds: 1 Queen, 1 Twin (2 bedrooms)
Bathroom: 1 Guests Exclusive
Tariff: B&B (full) Double/Twin $120, Single $90,
Tea/Coffee in guest lounge.
Sorry, not suitable for children.
NZ B&B Vouchers accepted $45 surcharge

Nearest Town: St Heliers 500 metres (1/2 mile), Auckland 8km (5 mile)

Stay in our comfortable, modern multi-level home overlooking clean green Glover Park. Enjoy sunny bedrooms, bathrobes, TV, cooked breakfast, guest lounge, exclusive guest bathroom and hairdryer. A 10 minute walk to lovely St Heliers Bay village with its many cafes, restaurants, shopping, banking / postal facilities and a safe sandy beach on the sparkling Waitemata Harbour.
We are away from the hustle yet only 15 minutes from Downtown, Auckland.
We look forward to enjoying your company. Our interests include travel, hosting travellers, golf, walking, rugby, reading and meet Sophie our lucky black cat.
No Smoking indoors.
Directions: *Airport Shuttle to the door. Bookings phone / fax.*

St Heliers, Auckland

Bed & Breakfast
Address: 102 Maskell Street, St Heliers,
Auckland
Name: Jill and Ron McPherson
Telephone: (09) 575 9738 **Fax**: (09) 575 0051
Beds: 1 Queen, 2 single (2 bedrooms)
Bathroom: 1 Private
Tariff: B&B (continental) Double $95, Single $55.
Not suitable for children/pets. NZ B&B Vouchers accepted $20 surcharge
Nearest Town: Auckland city (12 mins drive)

We welcome you to our modern home with off street parking in a smoke free environment. Only one group of guests are accommodated at a time.
Having travelled extensively ourselves both in New Zealand and overseas we are fully aware of tourists' needs.
Only 8 minutes walk to St Heliers Bay beach, shops, restaurants, cafes, banks and post office.
A picturesque 12 minute drive along the Auckland waterfront past Kelly Tarlton's Antarctic Encounter and Underwater World to Downtown Auckland.
Our grown up family have left home and are now living in various parts of the world and are left at home with Tabitha the cat.
Our interests including all sports, gardening and Jill is a keen cross stitch embroiderer.

Mt Roskill, Auckland

Home & Farmstay
Address: 29 Maioro Street, Mt Roskill, Auckland
Name: Helen & Des Doyle
Telephone: (09) 626 4195 **Fax**: (09) 626 3013
Beds: 1 Double, 2 Single (2 bedrooms)
Bathroom: 1 Guest share
Tariff: B&B (full) Double $65, Single $40, Children $15, Dinner $20
Nearest Town: Auckland City Centre 20 minutes.

We invite you to share our home which is very central to most locations in Auckland and is also on a main bus route. We enjoy meeting people from far and near and look forward to making your stay an enjoyable one. A full cooked breakfast is provided and we welcome you to join us for dinner by arrangement. Off street parking is available for guests with their own transport. Non smokers and no pets preferred. We are 20 minutes from Downtown Auckland and 10 minutes from two major shopping centres, St Lukes and Lynmall.
Directions: *Shuttle bus to and from Auckland Airport. Please phone ahead for other directions.*

Titirangi, Auckland

Homestay
Address: "Kaurigrove",
120 Konini Rd,
Titirangi, Auckland 7
Name: Gaby & Peter
Telephone: (09) 817 5608
Mobile: 025-275 0574
Beds: 1 Double, 1 Single (2 bedrooms)
Bathroom: 1 Guests share
Tariff: B&B (special) Double $85, Single $45,
Children negotiable.
Credit cards (VISA/MC).
NZ B&B Vouchers accepted $20 surcharge
Nearest Town: Auckland, 20 minutes to Downtown by car.

Welcome to our home! Situated at Titirangi, the gateway of the Waitakere Ranges and Auckland's historic West Coast with its magnificent beaches and vast native bush areas!
Nearby are other attractions such as the Titirangi Golf course, cafes, restaurants and walking tracks. Gaby and Peter, your hosts of German descent, are keen trampers themselves and are happy to introduce you to the highlights of Auckland and its surrounding areas.
P.S. Non smoking inside residence.

Continental breakfast consists of fruit, cereal, toast, tea/coffee,
Full breakfast is the same with a cooked course,
Special breakfast has something special.

Avondale, Auckland
Christian Community
Address: 31b, Cradock Street, Avondale,
West Auckland. , Postal: P O Box 19404, Avondale
Name: Kodesh Christian Community(Sue or Gayle)
Telephone: (09) 828 5672 Booking essential
Fax: (09) 828 5684
Email: kodesh@xtra.co.nz
Beds: 1 Double , 1Double/single, 2 Single (4 bedrooms)
Bathroom: 2 Guests share + 2 toilets
Tariff: B&B (continental) Double $45, Single $30 Dinner $8. October - December
Double $65, Single $45. NZ B&B Vouchers accepted $5 surcharge for 1 night
stay.
Nearest Town: Auckland 11Kms

Kodesh is an ecumenical (interchurch) Christian community situated in a quiet cul-de-sac in Avondale, West Auckland - 8 minutes by car from downtown and on good bus and train routes.

Most members of the community go out to work each day and are actively involved in various churches and parishes around Auckland. The average number of residents is 25, including families and singles.

Our guest rooms are situated in a large modern home and cooking facilities are available. An evening meal is served in the communal dining room weekdays and guests are welcome, bookings are essential by midday.

The atmosphere is casual and relaxed and guests can amalgamate into the life of the community as much or as little as they desire. Longer term accommodation is available by negotiation.

Hillsborough, Auckland
Self-contained Accommodation
Address: 341A Hillsborough Road, Mt Roskill,
Auckland
Name: "Bird Sanctuary" Jean & Les Bird
Telephone: (09) 624 1932 **Fax**: (09) 624 1964
Mobile: (025) 275 3255
Beds: 1 Queen., 2 Single divans in lounge (1 bedroom)
Bathroom: 1 Ensuite
Tariff: B&B (full) Double $90, Dinner by arrangement.
NZ B&B Vouchers accepted $20 surcharge
Nearest Town: Auckland City Centre 15 minutes

We have a large self-contained apartment with own entrance and ample off street parking. Opening onto a courtyard with heated swimming pool and spa pool. A full equipped kitchen, lounge with own TV, separate bedroom with Queensize bed and ensuite bathroom. Two single divans in lounge. All beds are innerspring with Woolrest sleepers and feather duvets. Laundry facilities and gas barbecue available. We would appreciate NO SMOKING IN APARTMENT. We live in a quiet private situation, but close to all amenities. We would be happy to help you with any travel plans throughout New Zealand. We are 10 minutes from Auckland International and Domestic Airport. Shuttle service available or we would meet with small charge. We and our cocker spaniel Katie will be pleased to welcome you and offer hospitality to NZ and overseas visitors. Please phone for directions.

Hillsborough, Auckland
Homestay+Self-contained Accom.
Address: 11 Saran Place, Hillsborough, Auckland
Name: Wendy & David Rhodes
Telephone: (09) 625 7051 **Fax**: (09) 625 7051
Beds: 1 Queen, 1 Double sofa bed (1 bedroom)
Bathroom: 1 Private
Tariff: B&B (full or continental) Double $95, Single $60, Children $10, under 5 free, Dinner $25. Credit Cards Visa/Mastercard.
NZ B&B Vouchers accepted $20 Surcharge.
Nearest Town: Auckland City Centre 15 mins by car

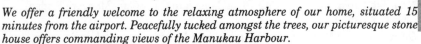

We offer a friendly welcome to the relaxing atmosphere of our home, situated 15 minutes from the airport. Peacefully tucked amongst the trees, our picturesque stone house offers commanding views of the Manukau Harbour.
The self-contained guest wing, with separate entrance and parking, has breathtaking sea views. Facilities consist of bedroom with queen size bed and TV, ensuite, kitchen with mini-oven, microwave, fridge, tea/coffee. The lounge has a double sofa bed.
Join us for homestyle breakfast or we deliver to your table. Within 10 minutes of banks, shopping centres, restaurants and leisure complexes.
We have enjoyed B&B hospitality overseas with our daughters aged 10 and 20. Our retriever and cat complete the family. We can cater for families, cot and highchair available. Separate laundry. Please, no smoking.
Directions: *Door to door shuttle bus from airport. Car hire can be arranged. Please phone for directions.*

Mangere Bridge, Auckland
Homestay
Address: 146 Coronation Rd, Mangere Bridge
Name: Carol O'Connor & Brian Thomas
Telephone: (09) 636 6346 **Fax**: (09) 636 6345
Beds: 1 Double, 2 Single (2 Bedrooms)
Bathroom: 1 Guests share
Tariff: B&B (full) Double $60, Single $40, Children half price, Dinner $15.
NZ B&B Vouchers accepted
Nearest Town: Auckland City 14km, Manukau City 14km

We invite you to share our home which is within 10 mins of Auckland Airport an ideal location for your arrival or departure of New Zealand. We enjoy meeting people from far and near and look forward to making your stay an enjoyable one. A full cooked breakfast is provided and we welcome you to join us for dinner by arrangement. We provide a courtesy car to and from airport, bus and rail depots. Off street parking is available for guests with own transport. If you smoke we ask that you do so outdoors. Although we have a cat we request no pets. Inspection welcomed.
Directions: *Please phone.*

One of the differences between staying at a hotel and a B&B
is that you don't hug the hotel staff when you leave.

Auckland Airport, Mangere Bridge

Homestay
Address: 1 Banbury Place,
Mangere Bridge, Auckland
Name: Gill Whitehead
Telephone: (09) 634 3413 **Fax**: (09) 622 3238
Beds: 1 Queen, 3 Single (3 bedrooms)
Bathroom: 1 Ensuite, 1 Family share
Tariff: B&B (Continental) Twin with ensuite $70, Double $60, Single $40,
Children half price. Dinner by arrangement $15, Credit Cards accepted.
NZ B&B Vouchers accepted $10 surcharge for ensuite
Nearest Town: Auckland City 16km, Manukau City 16km, Mangere Bridge
township 2km.

*Overlooking the Manukau Harbour and only 10 mins from Auckland Airport, I can
offer you a peaceful location for your arrival or departure of New Zealand.*
*I share my home with two teenage daughters a small dog and a cat. We love travel and
meeting new people. Relax with a leisurely stroll or cycle ride along "Kiwi Esplanade"
where spectacular flocks of South Island pied Oyster Catchers can be seen between
December and August or enjoy a game of snooker/pool, darts or table tennis in the
garage , games room / guest lounge.*
*In winter, curl up in front of the fire with a book. In summer laze in the garden and
enjoy the view.*
*BBQ facilities available, restaurant and takeaway bars are close to the airport. Non
smokers and no pets preferred. Off street parking available for guests with own
transport. Otherwise taxi or shuttle bus can be arranged.*
Directions: *Please phone, fax or write.*

Auckland Airport, Mangere

Homestay
Address: 288 Kirkbride Rd., Mangere
Name: May Pepperell
Telephone: (09) 275 6777
Beds: 3 Single plus single fold-away bed (2 bedrooms)
Bathroom: 1 Guests share
Tariff: B&B (continental) Double $60, Single $40, Children negotiable,
Dinner $15. NZ B&B Vouchers accepted
Nearest Town: Papatoetoe 5km

*My clean comfortable home is only five minutes from the airport but not on the flight
path so there is no aircraft noise. Ten minutes from five large shopping centres and
Rainbow's End amusement park. Within walking distance to our local centre,
restaurants and take-away bars. Lakeside Convention Centre is three minutes away,
also Villa Maria Winery. The Aviation Golf Course is situated near the airport and
green fee players are welcome. My interests are golf, travelling, meeting people and
Ladies Probus, and I am involved in voluntary work. An evening meal can be provided
by arrangement. Beds have woollen underlays and electric blankets. There is a sunny
terrace and fenced swimming pool. Courtesy car to/from airport at reasonable hour.
On bus route to city. Vehicles may be left while you are away from $1 per day.*

Private bathroom is for your use exclusively,
Guests share means you may be sharing with other guests,
Family share means you will be sharing with the family.

Auckland Airport, Mangere
Guest House
Address: Airport Pensione B&B, 1 Westney Rd.
cnr Kirkbride Rd, Mangere, Auckland
Name: Airport Pensione Bed & Breakfast
Telephone: (09) 275 0533 **Fax**: (09) 275 0533
Beds: 9 Double, 9 Single (9 bedrooms)
Bathroom: 4 Guests share, 1 Ensuite
Tariff: B&B (continental) Double $65, Single $50, Ensuite Double $80, Extra person $15. Credit cards. NZ B&B Vouchers accepted $15 surcharge for ensuite
Nearest Town: Auckland city (15km north), Manukau city (10km south).

Airport Pensione is the ideal way to spend a night when leaving or arriving in Auckland.
Single, double, twin and family rooms are available, all with private handbasin. A new family ensuite (2 bedrooms sleeping 2-5) is also available.
Having opened only recently, the premises are brand new and tastefully decorated, with central heating and wheelchair facilities.
A spacious dining room and a comfortable TV lounge can accommodate our guests in a friendly and informal atmosphere. Tea and coffee making facilities, guest phone and off street parking are available. Laundry, car storage and poste-restante can all be arranged. Self service continental breakfast is ready also for very early departures. We can also help you book tours and reasonably priced rental cars or campervans. Close to shops, restaurants, take-aways, bus stop and Lakeside Convention Centre.
Directions: *By Car: we are 200 m south of the airport intersection on Kirkbride Rd, opposite the Presbyterian Church. From airport: Freephone at Terminals. Courtesy car can be arranged.*

Otahuhu, Auckland City
Homestay

Address: 70 Mangere Road, Otahuhu, Auckland
Name: Gerard & Jerrine Fecteau
Telephone: (09) 276 9335 **Fax**: (09) 276 9235
Beds: 1 Queen, 1 Double, 2 Single (3 Bedrooms)
Bathroom: 2 Guests share
Tariff: B&B (full) Double $60, Single $40, Children half price, Dinner $20.
Credit cards. NZ B&B Vouchers accepted
Nearest Town: Auckland 10 mins

Gerard and Jerrine offer you Canuck-Kiwi hospitality in their comfortable home in the most central location in Auckland. Otahuhu is half way between central city and Papakura. The motorways and trains are just minutes away and the airport simply 10 minutes down the road. If you begin your Kiwi holiday and want to rest and organize yourselves then #70 is the place or if you want to rest before the long flights "home" - #70 is the rest stop and handy for the early morning flights.
We are also collectors of amazing things and have an interesting variety of many cactus, coins of the world, coloured depression glass tableware, native Canadian art, brass, glass birds and animals and more.
In addition to breakfast you are invited to join us for lunch and dinner by arrangement. Please phone, fax or write for our courtesy van to pick you up at the airport, train, bus depot.

Relax – Don't try to drive too far in one day.

Flat Bush - Manukau City
Homestay
Address: "Tanglewood", 5 Inchinnam Rd,
Flat Bush, Manukau City
Name: Roseanne & Ian Devereux
Telephone: (09) 274 8280 **Fax**: (09) 634 6896
Email: rocklabs@clear.net.nz
Beds: 1 Queen, 1 Double, 2 Single (3 bedrooms)
Bathroom: 1 Ensuite, 1 Guests share
Tariff: B&B (full) Double $70, Single $60, Children $10, Dinner $20,
Campervans $25. Credit Cards: Visa. NZ B&B Vouchers accepted
Nearest Town: Manukau City 6.5km, Howick 5km

*We welcome you to 'Tanglewood'. Our cottage with its 2 acres is in a country setting,
but close to the international airport. The Garden Loft is separate from the house and
overlooks the garden and pond. It has an ensuite, TV, fridge, and table and chairs.
We have accommodation inside the house, with own bathroom.*
*We are 2 minutes from beautiful bush walks, 25 minutes from downtown Auckland,
close to Regional Botanic Gardens, beaches, factory, shops and golf courses. We have
travelled extensively and enjoy meeting people. Delicious home cooked breakfast
including eggs from our free range hens. You can join us for dinner, or by candlelight
by the fire, or served on our terrace on a summer evening. There are several good
restaurants close by. We have a swimming pool, large peaceful gardens, and a friendly
Labrador dog, Daisy. We are non-smoking. Booking is essential.*
Directions: *For directions: please phone*

Half Moon Bay
Homestay
Address: "Endymion Lodge",
21 Endymion Place, Half Moon Bay
Name: Dave & Helen Jeffery
Telephone: (09) 535 8930
Fax: (09) 828 2048
Mobile: (025) 951 038
Email: helenj@xtra.co.nz
Beds: 1 Queen, 1 Single (2 bedrooms)
Bathroom: 2 Private

Tariff: B&B (full) Double $80, Single $50,
Dinner by arrangement $25 - including complimentary pre-dinner drink.
NZ B&B Vouchers accepted
Nearest Town: Howick 10 mins, Pakuranga 10 mins

*Endymion Lodge is situated in a cul-de-sac on a sunny, north facing rise above the Half Moon
Bay marina with views to Rangitoto Island and Bucklands Beach. We are 20km from
Downtown Auckland on the eastern side of Auckland within close distance to several beaches,
golf courses, Howick Colonial Village, theatres and cafes. Join us in our lounge or enjoy the
privacy of your own self contained area comprising bedroom, lounge and kitchenette with
fridge, tea & coffee making facilities. We are a yachting family and would love to take you
sailing or fishing on our glorious Hauraki Gulf. An overnight experience can be arranged if
you wish. We share our home with our cat "BJ". Laundry facilities available. No smoking in
the house.*
Directions: *Shuttle bus to and from airport. Please phone for reservations and directions.*

Manurewa

Homestay
Address: 16 Collie Street, Manurewa, Auckland 1702
Name: Graham & Katrine Paton
Telephone: (09) 267 6847
Mobile: (021) 215 7974
Beds: 1 Double, 3 Single (3 bedrooms)
Bathroom: 1 Ensuite, 1 Guests share
Tariff: B&B (full) Double $70, Single $40, Children half price. Dinner $15. Credit cards NZ B&B Vouchers accepted
Nearest Town: Manukau City, 5 minutes north

Our sunny, spacious home is in Hillpark, a pleasant suburb of Manurewa. We are 15 minutes from Auckland Airport, 20 minutes from Auckland City Centre, by motorway, gateway to the route south and Pacific Coast Highway.
We warmly welcome you to our home, assuring you of a comfortable stay. We have a Tonkinese cat. Beds have electric blankets and fleecy wool underlays.
Within 2 kilometres is the Manukau City Shopping Centre, Rainbow's End Adventure Park, restaurants, Cinema, factory and souvenir shops, Nathan Homestead Community Arts Centre, Regional Botanical Gardens (Ellerslie Flowershow), Totara Park, and bush walks. Golf courses, scenic country drives and beaches are in the area.
Graham is Fund-raising Co-ordinator for the Red Cross, while Katrine is a part-time Primary School teacher. Our interests include painting, pottery, gardening, classical music, Christian interests, photography, reading, woodwork and travel.
Laundry facilities available. We're a smoke-free home.
Directions: *Please phone.*

Manurewa, Auckland

Country Homestay
Address: "Top of the Hill", Fitzpatrick Road, Brookby, RD 1 Manurewa, Auckland
Name: Trevor & Pat Simpson
Telephone: (09) 530 8576 **Fax**: (09) 530 8576
Email: technicolour@xtra.co.nz
Beds: 1 Queen, 5 Single (4 bedrooms)
Bathroom: 4 Ensuite

Tariff: B&B (full) Double $100, Single $65, Dinner $25, Not suitable for children, Credit Cards (VISA/MC).
Nearest Town: Manukau City 15 mins. Auckland city and Airport 25 mins.

A warm Kiwi welcome awaits you at the Top of the Hill. An expansive newly built modern country homestay for the adventurous traveller who likes to get off the beaten track while still being close to Auckland city and airport.
We offer the ultimate in away from home comfort as a result of Trevor's thirty years building experience. Our luxury guest wing with large lounge has breathtaking views overlooking native bush, dairy farms, the beautiful Brookby and Clevedon valleys, to brooding Rangitoto. Wander over the farm, visit our friendly farm animals - take a bush walk at night to see the glow worms. Enjoy taste home cooking, try a summer BBQ under the "Southern Cross".
After living in the area for many years we are keen to share this fantastic spot and our New Zealand way of life.
Directions:
Follow the Pacific Coast Highway signs from Manurewa to Brookby, sign posted "Homestay" from Alfriston School. 149

Howick, Auckland

Homestay
Address: The Fishers, 'Above the Beach',
141 Mellons Bay Road, Howick, Auckland
Name: Max & Marjorie Fisher
Telephone: (09) 534 2245 **Fax**: (09) 534 2245
Email: kea.nz@ibm.net

Beds: 1 Queen, 1 Double, 2 Single (4 bedrooms)
Bathroom: 1 Private (bath & handbasin) + Guests share 1 Sep shower & 1 sep
toilet + 1 Queen has ensuite
Tariff: B&B (continental) Double $75, Single $40, Double with ensuite $90,
Dinner by arrangement, Credit cards (Visa/Bankcard)
NZ B&B Vouchers accepted $10 surcharge
Nearest Town: Howick 1/4 mile

We live 50 yards "Above the Beach" in a comfortable and roomy home with Kauri trees growing through our decks. Looking out to sea views as far as Waiheke Island and Rangitoto. Howick is a quaint village with a historic Selwyn Church, the Howick colonial village, at least ten restaurants, a village pub, and six beaches for swimming and boating within a 2 km radius. It is on the east side of Auckland on the coast 20 kms from Auckland city and 13 kms from Manukau city. The double bedrooms have feather duvets, electric blankets, heaters and individual decks looking onto bush and sea. Tea and coffee making facilities, easy chairs, lounge suite, fridge, TV and radio for your convenience. Our interests are travel, classic cars, genealogy, and walking along our beaches.
Directions: *Shuttle bus to and from the airport. Please phone ahead for more directions. No smoking indoors.*

Howick, Auckland

Homestay
Address: "Cockle Bay Homestay", 81 Pah Road,
Cockle Bay, Howick, Auckland
Name: Jill & Richard Paxman
Telephone: (09) 535 0120 **Fax**: (09) 535 0120
Mobile: (021) 685 638
Email: PaxmanR@xtra.co.nz

Beds: 1 Queen, 2 Single (2 bedrooms)
Bathroom: 1 Ensuite, 1 Private
Tariff: B&B (continental) Double $75-$90, Single $55, Dinner by arrangement
$25pp. Credit Cards. NZ B&B Vouchers accepted
Nearest Town: Howick 3km

A warm welcome awaits you at "Cockle Bay Homestay", situated in a quiet location 3km from historic Howick Village, 25 minutes from Auckland and airport. A five minute bush walk will take you to Cockle Bay beach and historic Windross Restaurant.
Our home is elevated, has extensive sea / rural views with spacious decks to relax on. It is tastefully decorated, and shared with our small friendly well behaved dog. Off street parking is available. We will readily help with any travel arrangements. Breakfast will be served with fresh fruit, croissants, home made muffins, and freshly brewed coffee and tea. The guest rooms are spacious and comfortable. They both have sea views, tea / coffee making facilities, radio, electric blankets and heating. The larger room has two easy chairs to relax on, TV and private balcony. The spacious tiled bathrooms have a shaver / hairdryer power point. Laundry facilities available. Non smokers.
Directions: *Transport to / from the airport can be arranged. Please telephone for directions.*
Home Page: http://home.clear.net.nz/pages/cocklebay.homestay/

Howick, Auckland

Homestay
Address: 33 Kilkenny Drive,
Howick, Auckland
Name: Dorothy and Graham MacKenzie
Telephone: (09) 274 3883
Fax: (09) 273 2222
Mobile: (021) 999 456
Email: graham@impress.co.nz
Beds: 1 Double, 2 Single (2 bedrooms)
Bathroom: 1 Guests share, Separate toilet.
Tariff: B&B (full/continental) Double $75, Single $50,
Family dinner by arrangement. Credit cards.
Nearest Town: Howick

A warm welcome awaits you to our new modern home situated in a quiet restful area of Howick, in the eastern suburbs of Auckland.

Ideally situated close to beaches, rural Auckland, shopping centres, restaurants, easy route to airport and motorways. We are in our early 60's and have travelled widely within New Zealand and overseas. Dorothy enjoys floral art and hospitality. We both enjoy hospitality. Freshly baked bread invites you to enjoy a fully cooked or continental breakfast. Family dinners available by advance arrangements.

Rooms are tastefully decorated. Spacious tiled bathroom with spa bath, shower, toilet and hand basin is for guests use. A separate toilet is for guests. Laundry by arrangement. We will be pleased to assist you to make your stay in Auckland one to be remembered and would welcome you to be our guests but request no smoking, children or pets.

Directions: *Shuttle bus to/from airport. Phone for reservations and details.*

Whitford

Farmstay
Address: Springhill,
Polo Lane, Whitford,
Auckland, (Postal: R.D. Manurewa)
Name: Derek & Judy Stubbs
Telephone: (09) 530 8674
Fax: (09) 530 8274
Beds: 2 Queen, 2 Single (3 bedrooms)
Bathroom: 2 Ensuite
Tariff: B&B (full) Double $75, Single $50, Children $25,
Dinner $25pp by arrangement. NZ B&B Vouchers accepted
Nearest Town: Auckland 30 km, Howick, 12 km

Springhill is a 16 hectare farm situated in Whitford, an attractive rural area approximately 30km south east of Auckland, and 12km from Howick, a village suburb rich in early European settler history. We are only 2km from a beautiful golf course and 10km from Hauraki Gulf beaches. Most of the farm is planted in pine trees. We breed Angora goats and have some sheep, assorted bantams, two cats and two dogs. We have a large comfortable home and spacious garden, BBQs being a specialty during the summer. We enjoy travelling and Derek is a keen sailor.

Our guest accommodation is one double bedroom with ensuite and a large area above the garage, comprising one double room, bathroom and a room with 2 single beds and seating. Ideal for families with children. Both rooms have TV and tea and coffee making facilities. We welcome guests to join us for dinner by arrangement.

Directions: *Left off Whitford Park Road 1km past golf course or please phone.*

Whitford

Bed and Breakfast
Address: 367 Whitford Road, Whitford
Name: Wendy and Ian Blakeney-Williams
Telephone: (09) 530 8981
Fax: (09) 530 8981
Email: wendy39@ibm.net
Beds: 2 Double (2 bedrooms)
Bathroom: 1 Family share, 1 Private toilet
Tariff: B&B (full) Double $95, Single $70, Dinner by arrangement.
Not suitable for children. NZ B&B Vouchers accepted $12 surcharge
Nearest Town: Howick (2km), Auckland City Centre (25 mins)

Wendy and Ian invite you to come and enjoy the ambience of our genuine early colonial grand villa. Relax in beautiful private rose filled garden or laze in front of an open fire. One of Auckland's original homes, built in 1868 by Captain Springs, shifted to its present site and renovated meticulously over the last twenty years. Situated on Whitford Road, two kilometres from both Howick and Whitford and twenty five minutes from Auckland Centre and Airport (transport to and from by arrangement). Our guest accommodation is two double rooms (one with fireplace), separate guest toilet and shared main bathroom. Each bedroom has tea and coffee making facility, bathrobes, electric blankets, TV etc.
Enjoy our breakfast on our rose and Wisteria-clad veranda. We love sharing our beautiful home and warmly welcome all our visitors and guests.
Directions: *Please ring for directions or further information.*

Clevedon

Countrystay, Self contained Accomodation.
Address: 816 North Road,
PO Box 72, Clevedon
Name: A. Hodge
Telephone: (09) 292 8707
Fax: (09) 292 9266
Mobile: (025) 984 102
Email: hodgebb@wave.co.nz
Beds: 1 Twin, 2 Single (3 bedrooms)
Bathroom: 1 guests share
Tariff: B&B (full) Double $70, Single $40, Children half price, Dinner $20;
Campervans welcome. Self-contained 2 bedroom unit, sleeps 5, one ensuite unit sleeps 3, tariff neg. Longer stays welcome.
Credit cards accepted. NZ B&B Vouchers accepted
Nearest Town: 40 km from Auckland, 23 km from Papakura

Relax in a peaceful environment, 35 minutes from Auckland International Airport in a rural community that has a wide range of farming activities. Views from our comfortable home include the lower reaches of the Wairoa River Valley from Clevedon, Waiheke and other small islands in the Hauraki Gulf to the distant Coromandels.
We offer a range of guest accommodation, B&B with own bathroom, 2 self contained motel style units, 1 sleeps 5 with full cooking facilities, 1 sleeps 3 with tea and coffee. Meals, BBQ and games room are available. Activities that are available with hosts or nearby include fishing boat trips, sheep shearing, bush, farm, beach walks, horse riding, dairy and orchard farm visits. We are available by prior arrangement to greet you at plane, train or coach. Kitty, the cat resides somewhere in the garden.
Directions: *Clevedon is 14 km east of Papakura. Our home is on the left on North Road, 9 km from Clevedon.*

Clevedon
Farmstay
Address: 'Willowgrove', Kawakawa Bay Road,
Clevedon, R.D.5, Papakura
Name: Brian & Eileen Wallace
Telephone: (09) 292 8456 **Mobile**: (025) 954 605
Beds: 1 Double, 3 Single (2 bedrooms)
Bathroom: 2 Ensuite
Tariff: B&B (full) Double $85, Single $45, Children half price. Dinner $25.
NZ B&B Vouchers accepted
Nearest Town: Papakura (20km), Manukau City (30km), Howick (30km)

Clevedon is a village in a rural area with craft shops, restaurants and all services. On our property of about 11 acres, we raise beef calves and also have sheep, goats, chickens and ducks. We produce our own vegetables.

The house is set in a delightful garden which has a very restful atmosphere. We have hosted guests from many countries over the past eight years and look forward to meeting you.

We are close enough for visitors to take in any of the Auckland attractions, and golf courses, fishing and swimming beaches are within 15 minutes drive.

The main guest room is a large upstairs room with its own sitting area, and is ensuite. The second room has twin beds and its own bathroom. You may share our family room and lounge or relax in your room.

Directions: *Please phone. If required we can collect from airport or public transport for a small charge.*

Clevedon
Country Home Stay
Address: 'Fairfield', Kawakawa Road,
Clevedon, R.D. 5, Papakura
Name: Christopher & Paddy Carl
Telephone: (09) 292 8852 **Fax**: (09) 292 8852
Beds: 1 Queen (1 bedroom)
Bathroom: 1 Ensuite

Tariff: B&B (full) Double $110, Single $80, Dinner from $40 pp by arrangement.
Nearest Town: Clevedon 10 mins, Papakura 20 mins, Auckland 40 mins

Our Ranch Style house is on a hill, set in 14 acres with extensive rural views and a glimpse of the sea. Mangere airport and Auckland city are 40 minutes away, and there are many lovely beaches nearby leading to the pretty scenic route to the Coromandel. We offer a self-contained bed-sitting room with ensuite and own private courtyard. The room has a television and coffee and tea making facilities. Local activities such as fishing, golf and horse riding can be arranged. We are both well travelled; Paddy is involved in the fashion industry and Chris retired after 35 years as a Naval Officer with the New Zealand Navy. We welcome you to join us in our comfortable spacious home.

Directions: *7kms from the roundabout at Clevedon down the Kawakawa Road or please telephone.*

One of the differences between staying at a hotel and a B&B
is that you don't hug the hotel staff when you leave.

153

Clevedon - Auckland South

Heritage Inn
Address: 'Birchwood', R.D. 3,
Clevedon, Auckland
Name: Birchwood. Ann & Mike Davies
Telephone: (09) 292 8729 **Fax**: (09) 292 8555
Beds: 1 King, 1 Queen (2 bedrooms)
Bathroom: 1 Ensuite, 1 Private
Tariff: B&B (special) King $195, Queen $180.
Credit cards (VISA/MC/AMEX).

"Birchwood"

Nearest Town: Clevedon 5 mins, Manukau 10 mins, Auckland City/International
Airport 20 mins.

*Enjoy the gracious and relaxing atmosphere of this lovingly restored country house
(circa 1887).*
*We have 2 guest rooms offering the ultimate in away from home comfort - fine linens,
fresh flowers, robes and toiletries.*
*Breakfast to suit - healthy or indulgent or a little of both, served in the large farm-house
kitchen or al fresco by the pool.*
*We are located 20 minutes from Auckland Airport / central city, in the picturesque
Clevedon Valley (on Pacific Coast Highway). Minutes from restaurants, golf courses,
polo grounds, Botanical Gardens, beaches and tourist trails. A great central location.
No smoking indoors.*
Come and enjoy Birchwoods 'old-worlde' charm and warm hospitality.
Home Page: http://nz.com/HeritageInns/Birchwood.htm
Directions: *Please phone - bookings advisable.*

Kaiaua, 'Seabird Coast'

Homestay
Address: 'Corovista', 1841B East Coast Road,
Waharau, Kaiaua R.D.3, Pokeno, Auckland
Name: Bob & Julia Bissett
Telephone: (09) 232 2842 **Fax**: (09) 232 2862
Mobile: (025) 245 5269
Beds: 1 Super King/2 Singles, 1 Double (2 bedrooms)
Bathroom: 1 Guests share, 1 Family share
Tariff: B&B (full) Main Bedroom Super King/2 Single: $90,

Single $50. Double Bedroom: $65, Single $40, Dinner (3 course)
$30 pp includes freshly caught fish in season. Packed lunches by arrangement.
Credit Cards NZ B&B Vouchers accepted $25 surcharge
Nearest Town: Thames 53 km, Pukekohe 55 km, Manukau City 72 km

*Our home "COROVISTA", is so named because of its commanding and panoramic views of
the Coromandel Ranges which rise above a foreground of the Hauraki Gulf and sparkling
waters of the Firth of Thames. Surrounded by a delightful garden, the home's elevated position
with its full length deck designed for the view has a private guest wing. The added advantage
of this locality, is its placement upon the recommended scenic route south of Auckland through
Clevedon, and its near proximity to the Hunua Parklands, an internationally recognised bird
sanctuary and thermal hot springs at Miranda, with fishing, tramping and picnicking also
available. We, your hosts, are widely travelled and offer warm hospitality to local and overseas
guests. We retired within easy reach of the city, to a peaceful rural area, and our desire is to
share it with those who travel this beautiful country. We have a small terrier and cat that live
outdoors. Our interests are varied and include golf, arts, crafts, music and the pleasure of a
comfortable smoke free home.*
Directions: *Please phone.*

Kaiaua

Homestay
Address: "Kaiaua Seaside Lodge"
1336 Pacific Coast Highway, Kaiaua
Name: Fran Joseph and Denis Martinovich
Telephone: (09) 232 2696
Fax: (09) 232 2699
Mobile: (025) 274 0534
Beds: 1 Queen, 1 Double,
4 Single (5 bedrooms)
Bathroom: 1 Ensuite, 1 Guests share
Tariff: B&B (special/full) Double $80-$100, Single $50. Dinner by arrangment.
Nearest Town: Thames 30 minutes, Auckland Airport 55 minutes.

Kaiaua Lodge is situated right on the water's edge with panoramic views of the Coromandel across the Firth of Thames. The Seabird Coast is renowned for its birdlife, Miranda thermal pools and nearby Regional Parks.
Kaiaua Lodge is also ideally positioned for visitors who enjoy a leisurely stroll along the seashore or a more active tramp through the Hunua Ranges. Boating and fishing facilities are available and Fran is happy to cook your catch for you. Breakfast includes flounder or snapper, in season. A range of accommodation is available from a large bedroom with ensuite to other bedrooms furnished with double or single beds. There is a separate guest lounge with television and a fridge.
The Lodge is easily found on the Pacific Coast Highway (scenic route), one hour south of Auckland and 3 km north of Kaiaua township, famous for "the best fish n chips in New Zealand".

Papakura

Homestay
Address: "Hunua Gorge Country House"
482 Hunua Road, Papakura
Name: Joy Calway & Richard Massey
Telephone: (09) 299 9922 **Fax**: (09) 299 6932
Mobile: (021) 669922
Email: hunua-lodge@xtra.co.nz
Beds: 1 King suite, 1 Queen room, 1 Twin room, 1 Single, 2 Bunks (5 bedrooms)
Bathroom: 1 Ensuite, 1 Private, 1 Family share (wheelchair)
Tariff: B&B (full) King $120, Queen & Twin $90, Single $80, incl. afternoon tea & full breakfast. 3 Course dinner with NZ wines on request $45.
Credit Cards (VISA/MC).
Nearest Town: Papakura 5 mins, Auckland airport 25 mins,
Auckland city 25 mins.

Welcome to our beautiful wilderness on the doorstep of Auckland City. A great place to start and end your New Zealand holiday. Peace, tranquillity, great food, magic sunsets, wild scenery, leafy greenery, views from all rooms. Large comfortable newly decorated home, verandahs, lawns, garden, bush and rural setting on 50 acres with sheep, ponies and cattle, birdlife ponds and stream. Stay a few days and discover the wonders of Auckland or learn to ride a horse. We can arrange anything from wine or farm tours to horse and trap rides or scenic flights, airport transfer not a problem. We are well travelled 40's interested in food and design, travel and wine, sport and people from all walks of life.
Fresh food, fresh air, comfortable beds, guaranteed.
Please phone

Drury
Bed & Breakfast
Address: Northumberland Lodge,
1810 Great South Road, RD 3 Drury 1750,
South Auckland
Name: Kath and Stan Hansen
Telephone: (09) 236 0888 **Fax**: (09) 236 0888
Beds: 1 Queen, 1 Double, 2 Single
Bathroom: 1 Ensuite, 1 Private
Tariff: B&B (full) Double $110 and $90, Single $55 and $45,
Children 12-15 years half adult rate.
Nearest Town: 15 km south of Papakura via Southern Motorway or Old Great
South Road, and 10km south of Drury Village.

Northumberland Lodge is a large, elegant, five bedroom, two storey home set in seven picturesque acres. Our two spacious guest rooms have different tariffs. Queen size deluxe room has extra single bed, tiled ensuite, TV, sundeck overlooking pool area. Double room has extra 3/4 bed, own bathroom. Swimming pool is surrounded by a huge deck, outdoor tables and seating. Lovely gardens, mature trees and expansive lawns add beauty and charm. We also have our own bush reserve and pond. Ample off street parking. Situated between Bombay and Ramarama on/off ramps from Southern Motorway but on the Old Great South Road. Your hosts are members of New Zealand's oldest European family and are non smokers. Two licensed restaurants in close proximity. Further choices at Drury and Papakura. 15 minutes drive to NZ Bloodstock Centre, 20 minutes to Manukau City, 30 minutes to Auckland City. Closed July, August, September.

Drury
Homestay In The Country
Address: 'Tuhimata Park',
697B Runciman Road, R.D.2, Drury
Name: Pat & Susan Baker
Telephone: (09) 294 8748
Fax: (09) 294 8749
Email: tuhimata@iprolink.co.nz
Beds: 2 Double, 2 single (3 bedrooms)
Bathroom: 1 Ensuite, 1 Guests share
Tariff: B&B (full) Double with Ensuite $110 - Single $70; Other Double $100 -
Single $60: Twin $90 - Single $55: Children - special discount,
Dinner by arrangement $30pp; Campervans $15pp including breakfast.
NZ B&B Vouchers accepted Surcharge $25
Nearest Town: Papakura & Pukekohe 10 mins, Auckland 30 mins,
Airport 20 mins.

An ideal place to start or finish a New Zealand holiday.
A large, comfortable, newly renovated, family home in a setting of giant oak trees and an expansive lawn, in the country but close to the city and only 20 minutes from the Airport. We are also only 3 minutes from the Southern Motorway. Also available are: tennis court, spa pool (hot tub), billiard/pool table, table tennis (ping pong), swimming pool, indoor BBQ, TV (including SKY) in all bedrooms, and lovely wide covered verandahs, large comfortable lounge, and a huge conservatory with an indoor garden. Guests can relax in the spacious setting which overlooks pretty green countryside. Pat and Susan have travelled widely and have entertained overseas visitors for many years. As well as 35 years of dairy farming behind them they have been extensively involved in NZ politics and education. We have a family cat.
Directions: *Please phone for directions.*

Hunua

Homestay
Address: Nairns Road, RD 3,
Papakura, Auckland
Name: Bonami House
Telephone: (09) 292 4191 **Fax**: (09) 292 4291
Beds: 2 Double, 2x1 Single (4 bedrooms)
Bathroom: 1 Private, 2 Guests share
Tariff: B&B (full) Double $80, Single $60, Children $15, Dinner $25.
Nearest Town: Papakura 10 minutes / Clevedon 15 minutes

A large comfortable home set on a elevated position surrounded by 15 green gentle sloping acres.
With decks taking in the views of the Hunua Ranges. Hunua is best known for its many bush walks. The Hunua Falls, the Cossey, Wairoa and Mangatangi dams. Relax in our beautiful garden or just take in the magical views and tranquillity of the property.
Our overseas guests comment to our hospitality which we are proud of as Bonami means friends forever. Hearty cooked dinner on request.
Directions: *Take southern motorway turn off at Ramarama, turn left signposted to Ararimu, continue for 8 minutes turn left at Ararimu Rd, continue until road changes to Gelling Rd, follow road until you come to Nairns Rd which is on the right Bonami House is at end of road and is signposted. On route to Rotorua and Coromandel.*

Ararimu, Auckland

Farmstay
Address: 227 Gelling Road,
Ararimu, RD 3 Papakura
Name: Ken and Jenny Spratt
Telephone: (09) 292 4858
Beds: 1 Queen, 3 Single (2 bedrooms)
Bathroom: 1 Private, 1 Guests share
Tariff: B&B (full) Double $85, Single $55, Dinner from $20 pp.
Children negotiable. Credit cards accepted.
Nearest Town: Pukekohe 15 mins, Papakura 15 mins, Auckland 35 mins,
Airport 25 mins.

We love life on our 30 acre farmlet near the Hunua ranges. The house is ranch-style, large, warm, sunny and welcoming. Ken is a marine engineer, Jenny a riding instructor. Two of our children attend university, one school. We stock eventing horses and ponies with a few other farm pets. If you feel hot, cool off in our private swimming hole in the river. If you feel energetic, the Hunuas provide lovely bush walks and scenery. If you feel lazy, just laze! Riding is usually available at reasonable cost. Join us for a meal, or a barbecue sitting on the spacious deck, enjoying the view. We use organic and home made food when possible. We would love you to join our family as friends but if you want or need a quiet time, there is plenty of space to be alone. No smoking indoors please.
Airport shuttle.
Directions: *Please phone.*

Relax – Don't try to drive too far in one day.

Waiuku

Homestay + Riding School
Address: "Totara Downs", Bald Hill Road, RD 1,
Waiuku, South Auckland
Name: Janet & Christopher deTracy-Gould
Telephone: (09) 235 8505 **Fax**: (09) 235 8504
Beds: 1 Queen, 2 Single (2 bedrooms)
Bathroom: 1 Ensuite, 1 Private
Tariff: B&B (full) with ensuite $100, with private bathroom $90, Single $70,
Children half price, Dinner $25pp. Credit cards.
Nearest Town: Waiuku 5 minutes, Pukekohe 10 minutes

Just 50 minutes drive south from Auckland Airport "Totara Downs" is found on a back country road, in large country house gardens on 10 acres of farm land, offering spectacular rural views.
Our bedrooms offer electric blankets, quality linen, feather duvets and tea/coffee making facilities in each room.
Waiuku offers wild west coast or quiet peninsula beaches, sailing the Manukau Harbour, aboard Scow Jane Gifford, farm or bush walks.
During summer enjoy a game of croquet, or relax beside the pool, in winter around the open fire in the sitting room.
Our Riding school offers sand arena with qualified B.H.S.A.I. instructor, horses/ ponies provided, extra charge. Stables and boxes available.
With our teenage daughter and son plus family cats, Fifi, Turbo and Flora our West Highland terrier we look forward to your company.
No smoking in the house please.
For directions please telephone or fax.

Pukekohe - Auckland

Farmstay
Address: 'Woodside', 195 Ostrich Farm Road,
R.D.1, Pukekohe
Name: Evelyn & Les Atkinson
Telephone: (09) 238 7864
Beds: 5 Single (3 bedrooms)
Bathroom: 1 Guests share
Tariff: B&B (full) Double $70, Single $40, Children half price;
Dinner $17.50 per person. NZ B&B Vouchers accepted
Nearest Town: Pukekohe 6 kms, Auckland 48 kms

Pukekohe is a thriving farm and vegetable growing area situated 48 km south of Auckland. Our 10 acre farm is mostly beef fattening with a few sheep, geese, cats (2), a dog called Buddy, ducks and hens. We are 5 mins away from an excellent golf course and 10 mins to the famous Glenbrook vintage railway. The wild west coast of NZ is a pleasant 20 mins drive. Auckland, our wonderful "City of Sails" is only a 40 mins drive, making it close enough for our visitors to view all of its magnificent attractions. Over the years, Les and I have been fortunate to enjoy travelling throughout NZ and overseas to the UK, Continent and Australia. We love meeting people and can offer warm Kiwi hospitality - we also enjoyed 'farm stays' on our trips abroad. Our guests are very welcome to dine with us, or in their own dining/lounge area.
Directions: *Southern motorway to Drury off-ramp - follow signs to Pukekohe-Waiuku (6 kms). Right turn at Golf Course - first left to Ostrich Road, then left into Ostrich Farm Rd. "Woodside" 2 km down road on right.*

Pukekohe
Homestay
Address: 1 Tremen Place, Pukekohe
Name: Ray & Elaine Golding
Telephone: (09) 238 1664 **Fax**: (09) 238 1664
Beds: 1 King/Queen, 2 Single (2 Bedrooms)
Bathroom: 1 Guests share
Tariff: B&B (full) Double $80, Single $50, Dinner $20.
NZ B&B Vouchers accepted
Nearest Town: Pukekohe

*For the last 7 years we have enjoyed hosting at Clarks Beach and look forward to many
more years at our new address. We have a lovely home on the upper slopes of Pukekohe
Hill with a wonderful garden and views, both rural and urban. The night view is
magical looking out to the Auckland City lights. Pukekohe is one of New Zealand's
greatest vegetable growing areas and we pride ourselves on the onion named 'Pukekohe
Long Keeper' and our potatoes grown almost year round plus acres of cabbage,
cauliflower, squash and lettuce etc. Nearby are golf courses, beaches, the Glenbrook
Vintage Railway and the Grand Prix Track, plus many other attractions. Auckland
is only 45 mins away and the Auckland International Airport is only 35 mins.
Pukekohe has a number of very nice restaurants but you may share a 3 course meal
with us.*
Directions: *10 minutes off the Southern Motorway at the Bombay Service Centre
Complex.*

Pukekohe
Homestay+Self-contained Accom.
Address: "Deveron", Sommerville Rd,
Glenbrook. (Postal: PO Box 146, Patumahoe)
Name: Tony & Sally McWilliams
Telephone: (09) 236 3673
Fax: (09) 236 3631
Email: marcus@ww.co.nz
Beds: Homestay: 1 Queen,
2 Single (2 bedrooms)
Self-contained Accom: 1 Queen, 2 Single
Bathroom: Homestay: 1 Guests share   Self-contained Accom: 1 Private
Tariff: B&B (full) Double $85, Single $60, Self-contained Accom: $125 per night
or weekly by arrangement, Credit Cards.
NZ B&B Vouchers accepted $12 surcharge
Nearest Town: Pukekohe 10 mins

*We welcome you most warmly to "Deveron", our country home which nestles in
beautiful native bush. Location: Franklin County - 45 minutes south of Auckland.
Tranquil, park-like surroundings provide the ultimate in peaceful relaxation. Sunny
comfortable rooms overlook the bush and garden which attract prolific bird life.
Our guests are free to use either their private sitting area (with tea and coffee making
facilities) or join us. We also have a self-contained, fully-furnished apartment with
2 double bedrooms above our barn, where Tony makes woodcrafts. Orcharding and
landscaping are other interests, while Sally is a keen gardener and tramper.
Attractions in the area include west coast beaches, several golf courses, the Glenbrook
Vintage Railway, cruises on the Manukau Harbour on the old scow the "Jane Gifford"
plus garden and farm visits. Airport shuttle available.*
Directions: *Please phone. Non smokers please.*

Pukekohe East - Sth Auckland

Country House
Address: "Holyrood Farm", 308 Runciman Road,
Pukekohe East. Postal: P O Box 48, Bombay,
South Auckland
Name: Marie &Jack Watson
Telephone: (09) 238 2925 **Fax**: (09) 238 1516
Mobile: (025) 315 102
Beds: 1 Queen, 2 Single (2 bedrooms)
Bathroom: 2 Ensuite
Tariff: B&B (full) Double $85, Single $50, Children half price, Dinner $30,
Credit Cards (VISA/MC). NZ B&B Vouchers accepted
Nearest Town: Pukekohe 6km

With over 25 years in the hospitality industry, we welcome guests in our home. Purpose built as a homestay, it is on 12 acres in South Auckland's loveliest countryside. 30 minutes from Auckland City, and 20 minutes from Auckland International Airport. We can meet you (nominal charge). Rental cars and horseriding can be arranged. Many attractions are close at hand, including golf course, Glenbrook Vintage Railway, plant nurseries, and historic scow "Jane Gifford", sailing from Waiuku. Our large house has been designed to provide peace and privacy for guests, our extended family and 2 friendly dogs. Both guest bedrooms feature ensuite bathrooms. We have travelled widely, and welcome overseas guests. No smoking in the house, please.
Directions: *Exit Southern Motorway at Bombay, towards Pukekohe. Right into Runciman Road (3 kilometers). "Holyrood Farm" then 3 kilometres on right.*

Bombay

Country Homestay
Address: "Brookfield Lodge", Great South Road 2114,
RD Bombay, South Auckland
Name: Noreen and Ray Lee
Telephone: (09) 236 0775 **Mobile**: (025) 292 1422
Beds: 1 Double, 2 Single (2 bedrooms)
Bathroom: 1 Guests share.
Tariff: B&B (full) Double $110, Single $70,
Dinner $30 pp by arrangement, Children special rate.
Nearest Town: Pukekohe and Papakura 10 mins.
Auckland 30 mins. Airport 25 mins.

Situated on the North-South Highway a mature tree lined driveway leads to the spacious country home. Secluded in one and a half acres of lovely garden this is perfect for your relaxation and enjoyment and makes an ideal place to start or finish your holiday. We are surrounded by beautiful countryside and close to coastal drives, tourist trails and thermal hot pools.
The twenty acre property with resident cat and Labrador grazes and trains thoroughbred racehorses. This may interest guests.
Attractive bedrooms consist of a double room with patio or a twin bedroom, both with adjacent indoor spa room opening onto a sunny deck.
A three course dinner is available by arrangement and your day begins with a generous breakfast. Filter coffee, tea and homebaking always available. Restaurants nearby. We offer modern elegance, tranquillity and warm hospitality. Airport Pickup - (nominal charge).
Directions: From North. Southern Motorway - Take Pukekohe - Bombay off ramp.
Turn right to Pukekohe. After 50 metres turn left into BP Service Centre. Brookfield
Lodge private access Rd is beside McDonalds carpark 2 mins. From South. 1km from
Beaver Road on left.

Mercer
Farmstay / Self-Contained Acco
Address: 233 Koheroa Road, Mercer
Name: Alan & Dorothy McIntyre
Telephone: (09) 232 6837 **Fax**: (09) 232 6837
Beds: 1 Queen, 1 Double (2 bedrooms)
Bathroom: 1 Private
Tariff: B&B (full) Double $75, Single $40, Children negotiable; Dinner $20,
Campervans welcome. NZ B&B Vouchers accepted
Nearest Town: Pukekohe 24km

*We live on a cattle farm with a modern brick home which has a self-contained unit
attached. We have a large swimming pool. We are 3 km off the main Auckland-
Hamilton highway. Our house site gives wide panoramic views of the countryside from
Bombay to Thames.*
*We are very happy to provide dinner. There are also numerous eating facilities in the
area.*
*The farm provides ample opportunity for taking walks and viewing farm animals plus
turkeys, pheasants, ducks and quail.*
*As we are only 30-40 minutes from Auckland Airport, this is an ideal first or last night
in New Zealand.*
Directions: *Travel State Highway 1 to Mercer, cross railway lines, travel 3 km up
Koheroa Road, house is on left at Kellyville Road junction. Name clearly visible.*

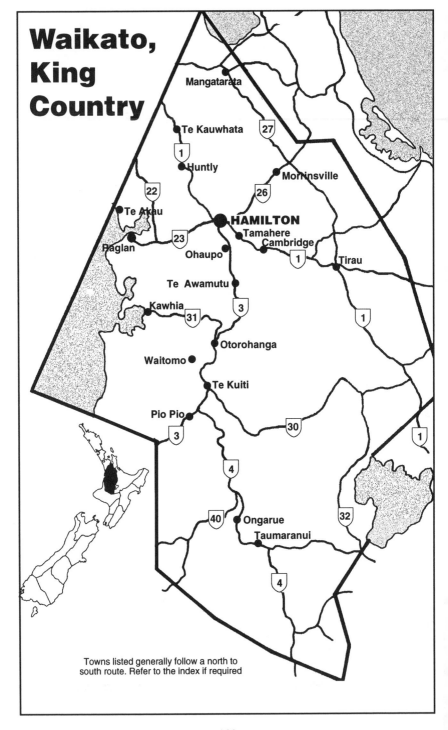

Waikato, King Country

Mangatarata

Te Kauwhata
27

1

Huntly

Morrinsville

22

26

Te Akau

HAMILTON

23

Tamahere
Cambridge

Raglan

Ohaupo

1

Tirau

Te Awamutu

3

Kawhia
31

Otorohanga

1

Waitomo

Te Kuiti

Pio Pio
30

3

1

4

40

Ongarue
32

Taumaranui

4

Towns listed generally follow a north to
south route. Refer to the index if required

Mangatarata

Farmstay
Address: Clark's Country Touch,
209 H/way 27, Mangatarata,
Thames R.D.6
Name: Betty & Murray Clark
Telephone: (07) 867 3070
Mobile: (025) 808 992
Beds: 1 King or 2 Single (1 bedroom)
Bathroom: 1 Family share
Tariff: B&B (continental) Double $65, Single $40, Children discounted.
Dinner $15. Campervans facilities available. NZ B&B Vouchers accepted
Nearest Town: Ngatea 13km to the east, Thames 33km to the east.

Welcome to our beef farm and summer fruit orchard. Our home has lovely views of rolling pastures and bush, and a short walk over the farm gives fabulous views to the Firth of Thames and Coromandel ranges. Our guestroom is sunny and comfortable with TV, tea / coffee / cookies and is opposite the bathroom. We are 2 minutes south of the Hauraki Golf Course / Bowling Club, 8 minutes takes you to Ngatea township and gemstone factory, 15 minutes to Miranda Hot Springs and seabird coast, 25 minutes to Thames and beaches, 50 minutes to Auckland, Hamilton and 90 minutes to Rotorua, Tauranga. We have a friendly dog Becky, who lives outside, and 2 cats, Floyd and Watson! We are aged '50ish', and enjoy sharing our home and local knowledge. Our varied interests include 4 wheel driving, vintage machinery, handcrafts and gardening. We assure you of a very warm welcome. Non-smokers preferred.

Te Kauwhata

Farmstay
Address: "Herons Ridge Farmstay & Stud",
1131 Waikare Road,
RD1, Te Kauwhata
Name: David
Telephone: (07) 826 4646
Fax: (07) 826 4646
Email: herons_ridge@xtra.co.nz
Beds: 2 Queen, 1 Double, 1 Single (3 bedrooms)
Bathroom: 1 Private, 1 Ensuite
Tariff: B&B (Full): Double $80. Studio $120, Single $50, Dinner $25,
Children Discount. NZ B&B Vouchers accepted $12 or $39 surcharge
Nearest Town: Te Kauwhata 7 Kms Auckland 1 hour.

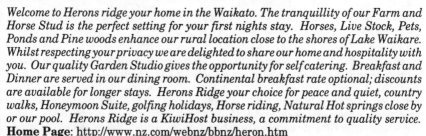

Welcome to Herons ridge your home in the Waikato. The tranquillity of our Farm and Horse Stud is the perfect setting for your first nights stay. Horses, Live Stock, Pets, Ponds and Pine woods enhance our rural location close to the shores of Lake Waikare. Whilst respecting your privacy we are delighted to share our home and hospitality with you. Our quality Garden Studio gives the opportunity for self catering. Breakfast and Dinner are served in our dining room. Continental breakfast rate optional; discounts are available for longer stays. Herons Ridge your choice for peace and quiet, country walks, Honeymoon Suite, golfing holidays, Horse riding, Natural Hot springs close by or our pool. Herons Ridge is a KiwiHost business, a commitment to quality service.
Home Page: http://www.nz.com/webnz/bbnz/heron.htm
Directions: *SH1 Turn off to Te Kauwhata. Pass through town. 6 km along Waerenga Road signpost for Waikare road and Farm Stay. 1 km on right gate number 1131. Welcome*

163

Huntly
Farmstay
Address: "Parnassus Farm & Garden",
Te Ohaki Road, RD 1, Huntly
Name: David & Sharon Payne
Telephone: (07) 828 8781 **Fax**: (07) 828 8781
Beds: 2 Double, 4 Single (3 bedrooms)
Bathroom: 1 Guests share, 1 Family share
Tariff: B&B (full) Double $70,
Single $40, Children under 15 $20,
Dinner by arrangement, Campervans $20.
Credit cards. NZ B&B Vouchers accepted
Nearest Town: 4km west of Huntly

Parnassus offers you all the calm and beauty of the New Zealand countryside only minutes off SH1 and wonderful farmhouse meals using garden fresh produce.
We are a successful farming venture combining dairying, forestry, sheep and beef and have an extensive garden incorporating formal rose beds, woodland area, orchard, berry-fruit courtyard and kitchen gardens. We have both a swimming pool and heated spa. Children enjoy our delightful range of birds and small animals.
The North Waikato has a wide range of amenities and attractions. We are ideally situated for day tripping to Auckland, Raglan, Hamilton, the Coromandel, Waitomo, Rotorua and Taupo.Courtesy pick-up available Huntly rail or bus, Auckland or Hamilton airport transfers at reasonable rate.
Picnic, luncheons and dinners available by arrangement.
Campsites, campervan point available.
We have travelled widely and enjoy the opportunity to return the hospitality we have had bestowed on us.

Morrinsville
Homestay+Farmstay
Address: 'Rose Haven',
2349 State Highway 26,
R.D.2, Morrinsville
Name: Bruce & Adrienne Lornie
Telephone: (07) 889 5393
Fax: (07) 889 5393
Beds: 1 Double, 2 Single (2 Bedrooms)
Bathroom: 1 Ensuite, 1 Private,
Guest share ensuite
Tariff: (full) Double $80, Single $50,
Children under 12 half price, Dinner $25pp. NZ B&B Vouchers accepted.
Nearest Town: Morrinsville 3 Kms

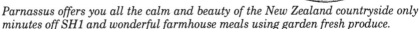

Welcome to Morrinsville, the cream of the dairy heartland. We are a semi-retired farming couple living on 10 acres - 3km to Morrinsville of State Highway 26 and 20 mins to Hamilton. Being so central we are within 1 1 /2 hours of most interest in the Waikato, eg. bush walks, surf beaches, hot pools, Museums and all sporting, cultural activities. Our home is a modern 3 bedroom, dining - plus living, separate lounge, 3 toilets. Guest rooms share ensuite. We have an extensive garden, specializing in roses. We belong to the Waikato and Heritage Rose Society. Adrienne is keen on cooking and loves to entertain. Family: 2 grown up children and 3 grandchildren.
Directions: *From main street - Morrinsville we are 3km towards Hamilton. "Rose Haven", sign is at Gateway.*

Morrinsville
Country Stay
Address: 102 Horrell Road, Morrinsville
Name: Farrand's B&B
Telephone: (07) 889 5843 **Fax**: (07) 889 5843 °¡**Mobile**: (025) 847 688
Beds: 1 Queen, 2 single (2 bedrooms)
Bathroom: 1 Guests share
Tariff: B&B (full/continental) Double $70, Single $35.
Nearest Town: Morrinsville 2 kms NE (1 km from SH 26)

Welcome to Morrinsville, a friendly central Waikato town. We offer a peaceful retreat on 5 acres. Your accommodation is in the form of a cosy, private wing attached to our modern home. We hope you enjoy the new furnishings and bedding which include Queen and King single beds.
If only two guests staying we offer the option of converting the second bedroom into a comfortable lounge.
For those who wish to be totally private, we offer a continental breakfast, including home made muesli in your room.
Honeymoon / Anniversary Suite - total privacy, extras including champagne, nibbles an chocolates, and breakfast in your suite (already set up) $95. Indulge in a little luxury at an affordable price.

Waimai Valley, Te Akau
Farmstay
Address: 'Waimatai',
1015 Waimai Valley,
R.D.2, Ngaruawahia
Name: Jan & Rod McAlpine
Telephone: (07) 825 4753
Fax: (07) 825 4953
Beds: 4 Single (2 bedrooms)
Bathroom: 1 Guests share
Tariff: B&B (full) Double $75, Single $45,
Children half price, Dinner $25.
Credit cards. NZ B&B Vouchers accepted
Nearest Town: Huntly 40km or Ngaruawahia

Our farm which is a 232 hectare sheep and beef unit, is situated in the beautiful Waimai Valley, an easy six kms of metal off the scenic route midway between Raglan and Pukekohe. Built at the turn of the century, the house is the original station homestead, so has the grace and spaciousness of that era, but with modern comforts. Set in mature gardens, with swimming pool, our home offers peace and tranquillity; or as a base to explore the West Coast, visit the nearby thermal baths, go caving, golfing, fishing (tackle available) - it's all there.
We offer a three course dinner (by arrangement) with home-grown produce and NZ wines. Breakfast can be full or continental and we provide lunch.

There are some good tips for easier travel on page 7

Raglan
Farmstay + Self-Contained Acco
Address: 'Matawha', R.D.2, Raglan, No. 61
Name: Peter & Jenny Thomson
Telephone: (07) 825 6709 **Fax**: (07) 825 6715
Beds: 1 Double & 2 Single or 3 Single (1 Bedroom)
Bathroom: 1 Private
Tariff: B&B (special) Double $45, Single $20, Children half price, Dinner $15;
Lunch $10, Campervans $20 (laundry and bathroom facilities available)
Meals $15 per person. NZ B&B Vouchers accepted
Nearest Town: Raglan 30 minutes, Hamilton 1 hour, Auckland 2 1/2

We are a family of four with two boys aged 22 and 19 years. We are fortunate to farm right on the West coast with panoramic views of the Tasman Sea.Our beach is very private with good fishing, hang gliding, surfing and paragliding.Our farm has been in the family for over 100 years and we take great pride in breeding top class Romney sheep, and stud and commercial Hereford cattle. We also do some riding and have a large flower garden. Most of the vegetables and meat are supplied by a large vegetable garden and by the farm. We also have 3 lovely cats.We have excellent scenic drives and bush walks plus of course our own beach. We enjoy having visitors from all over the world and they enjoy participating in all our farm activities. **Directions**: *Take Hamilton—Raglan road (route 23) Travelling approx 30 minutes – through Te Uku, take the Kauroa and Te Mata Bridal Veil Falls (signposted) turning left. Take the first turn to the right at Te mata School - Ruapuke Rd for 9 1/2 kms to the Tutu Rimu Road - turn Left into this road travelling another 1 1/2 kms to the T junction (signposted "Matawha Rd No Exit, Tutu Rimu Rd, Ruapuke Beach Access, Te Mata 11 kms"). Our entrance is at this signpost, and clearly marked on letterbox and cattle-stop. No. 61 on cattlestop.*

Te Mata
Farmstay/Guest House
Address: 334 Houchen Rd, Te Mata,
R.D.1 Raglan
Name: Marcus and Jan-Maree
Telephone: (07) 825 6892 **Fax**: (07) 825 6896
Mobile: (025) 756 276
Beds: 1 Queen, 2 Double, 2 Single (2 bedrooms)
Bathroom: 1 Guests share, 1 Family share
Tariff: B&B (full) Double $75, Single $40, Children $25, Dinner $20, Campervans welcome. Dogs outside, kennel provided. NZ B&B Vouchers accepted
Nearest Town: Raglan - 20 mins.

Our farm is the only one in the world where you can see 3 harbours (Aotea, Raglan and Kawhia) and 4 volcanoes (Mounts Karioi, Pirongia, Taranaki and Ruapehu). At 328 metres above sea level the views are magical.
The farm has 380 acres of rolling pastures and native bush. We have sheep, cattle and pigs grazing and also keep 4 dogs, 10 horses, a turtle and cat, all tame and friendly. We welcome you to ride our beautiful horses around the farm, daylight or moonlight. We also horse trek to the Bridal Veil Falls (55 metres high). For the adventurous we offer fishing and hunting trips (fish, pigs, rabbits, goats and possums).
Join in our daily farm activities or simply relax amongst the tranquil surroundings, soaking up the views from your balcony. This destination is perfect for honey-mooners or families with children. We offer warm country hospitality.
Within a 30 minute drive visit Raglan's cafes, beaches, bushwalks, harbour cruise or swim at Waingaro Hot Springs.

Hamilton
Homestay/Self Contained Accom.
Address: 2 Ruakiwi Road, Hamilton
Name: Richard & Sue Harington
Telephone: (07) 838 2328
Beds: 1 Double, 2 Single (2 bedrooms).
1 Double (self contained accommodation
Bathroom: 1 Ensuite, 1 Private
Tariff: B&B (continental) Double $70,
Single $45.
No Credit Cards. NZ B&B Vouchers accepted
Nearest Town: Hamilton 1km central city

Our spacious, modern home is within 1km from transport terminals and the inner city with its numerous restaurants and cafés. On a fine morning take a stroll through the Hamilton Lake Domain, and breakfast on our roof-top garden and enjoy the views across the city.
We would particularly like to welcome you to our home as we have travelled widely using B&Bs ourselves wherever possible. We know it's a wonderful way to get to know a country, its people and the lifestyle.
Richard belongs to Lions and is a keen woodworker. We both enjoy music, travel, the outdoors and caravaning. We have a cat.
Hamilton is a university city astride the Waikato River and is surrounded by magnificent farming country. We will be happy to show you around or help plan an itinerary.
Laundry facilities are available.
Two single beds convert to one Kingsize. A child's bed is also available.

Hamilton
Homestay
Address: 7 Delamare Road,
Bryant Park, Hamilton
Name: Esther Kelly
Telephone: (07) 849 2070
Beds: 2 Single (1 bedrooms)
Bathroom: 1 Private
Tariff: B&B (continental) Twin $70,
Single $55, Dinner $20.
NZ B&B Vouchers accepted
Nearest Town: Hamilton 3 Kms

I have travelled in many countries and would welcome tourists and would be happy to advise you on travel in New Zealand. I live in the suburb of Bryant Park, close to the Waikato River with its tranquil river walks and I am within walking distance of St Andrews Golf Course. Hamilton is a picturesque city with rose gardens, Museum, Ruakura Animal Research Farm and an agricultural museum called "Farmworld". Hamilton is in the centre of the dairy industry. My interests are cooking, gardening, tramping, boating, trout fishing, playing golf, art and also Mah Jong. I look forward to offering you friendly hospitality.
Directions: *Approaching from Auckland. Leave main highway half way down Te Rapa Straight (4 lane highway entering Hamilton) by turning left at round intersection into Bryant Road. At end of Bryant Road turn left into Sandwich Road. Delamare Road is 2nd street on right.*

167

Hamilton

Farmstay
Address: 'Farndale', R.D.10,
Hamilton
Name: Sylvia & Rod Smith
Telephone: (07) 829 8511
Fax: (07) 829 8511
Beds: 1 Double, 3 Single (3 bedrooms)
Bathroom: 1 Guests share
Tariff: B&B (full) Double $75,
Single $40, Children under 10 half price;
Dinner with NZ wine $25.   NZ B&B Vouchers accepted surcharge $7.50
Nearest Town: Hamilton 12km - good sealed roads all the way.

Our home is roomy and comfortable with good views in every direction. We are situated in beautiful rolling countryside to the west of Hamilton. Local attractions include tramping, horse riding, golf, beach at Raglan (half-hour drive), Waitomo caves (1 hour drive). We farm deer. Our interests include horticulture and animal farming, music, arts and crafts , flying and travel. Laundry facilities available for guests. We have 1 dog and 1 cat.
Directions: *Please phone.*

Hamilton

Homestay
Address: 530 Grey Street,
Hamilton East
Name: Frances & Norman Wills
Telephone: (07) 838 2120
Beds: 1 Twin pr, 2 Single (3 bedrooms)
Bathroom: 1 Private, 1 Guest share
Tariff: B&B (full) Double $65, Single $40, Children under 10 half price.
Credit cards. NZ B&B Vouchers accepted
Nearest Town: Hamilton 1/2km City Centre.

Spacious nicely renovated family home away from traffic noise but only 3 minutes from CPO and central shopping. Secluded offstreet parking.
We have travelled overseas and are accustomed to entertaining visitors – American, Asian and European. We can assist with local and district sightseeing information. Comfort guaranteed.
Directions: *From South, follow Highway one and watch for the sign "Hamilton East" "Grey Street" on right opposite Hamilton Gardens.*
From North, from roundabout at Te Rapa where Highway 1 diverges follow signs to City Centre and continue on south end of main street, turn left on to Victoria Bridge. From Highway 3, turn right at Normandy Avenue roundabout, follow "City Centre" then "Hamilton East" signs to Bridge Street, proceed straight down Bridge Street and across the bridge.
At top of Bridge Street (facing St. Mary's Church) turn left into Grey Street. No. 530 is less than 100m along, down driveway on right - tall trees at entrance.

Hamilton

Homestay
Address: 8 Jennifer Place, Hamilton
Name: Tim & Nan Thorrold
Telephone: (07) 855 6742 **Fax**: (07) 855 0235
Mobile: (025) 948 673
Beds: 1 Double, 2 Single (2 bedrooms)
Bathroom: 1 Guests share
Tariff: B&B (full) Double $70, Single $40, Children half price,
Dinner by arrangement. Credit Cards. NZ B&B Vouchers accepted
Nearest Town: Hamilton. 5 mins from Chartwell Square

Welcome to our warm comfortable home in a quiet street. Close to shopping at Chartwell Square and a variety of restaurants.
Farms and garden visits easily arranged. Have a swim, catch up on your washing or just relax. We look forward to meeting you. We have one cat.

Hamilton

Homestay
Address: 24 Pearson Ave,
Claudelands, Hamilton
Name: Matthews B&B
Telephone: (07) 855 4269
Fax: (07) 855 4269
Mobile: (025) 747 758
Email: mgm@xtra.co.nz
Beds: 3 Single (2 bedrooms)

Bathroom: 1 Guests share, 1 family share
Tariff: B&B (Full) Double $60, Single $40, Children 1/2 price, Dinner $20,
Campervans $20 (up to 4 persons). NZ B&B Vouchers accepted
Nearest Town: Hamilton, 120 km south of Auckland.

We would like to welcome you to our home situated 2 seconds off the city by-pass on Route 9 & 7 through the city in the Five Crossroads area. Adjacent to the showgrounds and only 5 minutes from the inner city, it is a comfortable walk if you wish to shop. Ruakura, the world famous agricultural research station is just two blocks from our home, if farming is your interest. Our home is a 'lived-in' comfortable home, warm in winter and cool in summer with an in-ground swimming pool for your use. Our four children have left home and we enjoy spending time with guests from both NZ and overseas. We have hosted people from many parts of the world and for seven years Maureen taught conversational English to Japanese students. We have travelled extensively and therefore are able to help you plan your holiday.

One of the differences between staying at a hotel and a B&B
is that you don't hug the hotel staff when you leave.

Hamilton

Homestay
Address: 162 Beerescourt Rd,
Hamilton City
Name: John & Glenys Ebbett
Telephone: (07) 849 2005
Fax: (07) 849 8405
Beds: 2 Single (1 bedroom)
Bathroom: 1 Private
Tariff: B&B (full) Double $70 Single $55,
Dinner $20. NZ B&B Vouchers accepted
Nearest Town: Hamilton, 7 minutes drive to city centre.

Having travelled extensively ourselves, we enjoy visitors to our home which was built in 1990 and commands a spectacular view of New Zealand's longest river. You are welcome to share travel anecdotes with us, or just enjoy the privacy of your own bedroom-bathroom-shower-ensuite (own tea making facility). Only minutes from town centre, river walks, swimming complex, St Andrews Golf Course, and excellent restaurants. Auckland International Airport is less than one and a half hours drive. This appeals to many tourists just arriving to or leaving the country. We treat home hosting as a way of reciprocating the pleasure we have had meeting people in other parts of the world, and we have very much enjoyed the 5 years we have been involved. One request - non smokers please. We don't have any animal pets, or young children.

Hamilton

Homestay
Address: 164 Clyde Street, Hamilton
Name: Val Wood
Telephone: (07) 856 0337
Fax: (07) 856 0337
Email: VAL.AND.COLIN.WOOD@xtra.co.nz
Beds: 1 Double, 2 Single (3 bedrooms)
Bathroom: 1 Guests share
Tariff: B&B (continental) Double $65, Single $40, Children $15,
Dinner by arrangement $20. NZ B&B Vouchers accepted
Nearest Town: Central Hamilton 2km.

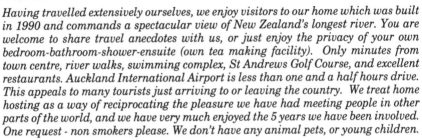

Our home is five minutes drive from the centre of Hamilton and further along Clyde Street is the Waikato University. In daylight hours we are happy to meet you at the Hamilton train or bus station if required. Our guest accommodation has television and tea making facilities and we endeavour to make you feel at home. We encourage people to stay in Hamilton while visiting the tourist areas of the Waikato and Rotorua and return each night to sleep in the same bed without the hassles of packing and unpacking. Hamilton is ideal for this type of holiday as it is within one and a half hours of most places of interest and has many delightful places to visit in the city itself. Our home is a no smoking zone and we have off street parking. We look forward to having you visit us. No Smoking

Continental breakfast consists of fruit, cereal, toast, tea/coffee,
Full breakfast is the same with a cooked course,
Special breakfast has something special.

Hamilton
First Class Manor Accom. & Luxury Cottage
Address: 'Anlaby Manor',
91 Newell Road, R.D.3, Hamilton
Name: Halina & Pryme Footner
Telephone: (07) 856 7264
Fax: (07) 856 5323
Email: AnlabyManor@xtra.co.nz

Beds: Manor: 3 Queen (3 bedrooms) Cottage: 1 Queen, 2 Single (1 bedroom).
Wheelchair facilities in 1 bedroom with ensuite.
Bathroom: Manor: 2 Ensuite, 1 Guests share. Cottage: 1 Own Private.
Tariff: B&B (full) Double $140, Single $100, Children under 14yrs free,
Dinner $40. Credit cards. NZ B&B Vouchers accepted $50 surcharge
Nearest Town: Hamilton 5 minutes. Airport 5 minutes.

Anlaby Manor has been built as a replica Yorkshire stately home after a Sir Edwin Lutyens' design. It features a huge central staircase replicated from that in "Gone With the Wind". A formal English garden of 2.5 acres is planted round a century-old pin oak with neo-Roman statuary, fountains, wishing well, box hedging, old roses and cottage plants. Lead light windows are complemented by antique furniture, heirloom china and English-style oil paintings. A secluded luxury cottage on the property is extremely popular for honeymooners and families or guests may prefer to stay in ensuite bedrooms in the Manor. A continental or cooked breakfast selection is served in the formal dining room. There is a swimming pool, tennis court, sauna and a billiard room. We offer complimentary morning and afternoon teas. Complimentary hors d'oeuvres and pre-dinner wine is served from an outstanding cellar. We both enjoy travel, gardening and meeting our guests. We prefer no smoking.
Brochures available.

Hamilton
Country Retreat
Address: 'The Monastery',
212B Newell Road, R.D.3, Hamilton
Name: Diana & Robert Scott
Telephone: (07) 856 9587
Fax: (07) 856 9512
Beds: 2 Double 4 Single (4 bedrooms)
Bathroom: 2 Ensuite, 1 Guests share
Tariff: B&B (full) Double $130, Single $100, Children half price, Dinner $40.
Credit cards.
Nearest Town: 3km south of Hamilton boundary, Airport 6km

This Historic Home offers the atmosphere and elegance of the Edwardian era. Built in 1907, the private residence later became the Passionist Monastery. Relocated on a peaceful ten acre rural setting near the Waikato River and lovingly restored, it features stained glass windows, pressed steel ceilings, ornately carved panelled doors, verandahs and antiques.
All bedrooms offer comfortable beds, electric blankets, quilts, heaters and attractive garden views. Two peaceful spacious lounges have fireplaces and sunny bay windows. Three course dinners with wine (by arrangement) and special breakfasts are served in our formal dining room. Complimentary pre-dinner drinks, hors d'oeuvres and afternoon teas. Enjoy our large attractive garden, relaxing beach walk, warm hospitality and friendly animals. Robert is a landscape designer. Our interests include gardening, antiques and equestrian pursuits. Central to Hamilton gardens and airport, Mystery Creek and Cambridge. 1 1/2 hr drive to Waitomo Caves, Rotorua and Auckland. No smoking.
Directions: *Please phone.*

171

Hamilton

Homestay
Address: 11 Tamihana Ave,
Hamilton
Name: Des & Marion Slaney
Telephone: (07) 855 3426
Fax: (07) 855 3426 **Mobile**: 025 815 404
Email: slaney.dm@xtra.co.nz
Beds: 1 Double, 1 Single (2 bedrooms)

Bathroom: 1 Guests share
Tariff: B&B (continental) Double $70, Single $40. NZ B&B Vouchers accepted
Nearest Town: Hamilton 1 Km from main street.

Guest accommodation is in spacious studio loft separate from house and overlooking our cottage garden with patio and summer house. Both rooms, double and single, have colour TV, and the upstairs double room has a balcony and a small kitchen with fridge and microwave. We are within walking distance of Hamilton's main street and the Waikato River with its lovely walkways.

With relaxation and privacy in mind we supply a continental breakfast in your studio to have at your leisure. Maps are provided showing Hamilton's main attractions, restaurants etc. For those interested in exploring Hamilton's countryside, you are welcome to our walking and cycling maps.

Directions: *Cross Whitiora Bridge at the northern end of Hamilton's main street, - Victoria Street, turn left off the bridge into Casey Avenue and first again into Tamihana Avenue. We are third house on right. Transfers and pick ups provided. Off street parking available.*

Hamilton

Country B&B
Address: "Twelve Oaks",
Tamahere, Hamilton
Name: Ezra & Craig Campbell
Telephone: (07) 856 2030 **Fax**: (07) 856 2089
Beds: 1 Queen in "Stable Wing", 1 Double or 2 Single in Homestead and Loft.
Bathroom: 1 Ensuite, 1 Private
Tariff: B&B (special) Double $125, Single $95, Children welcome,
Dinne/Picnic Hamper $40 includes wine.
Nearest Town: Hamilton and Cambridge 5-10 minutes. Airport 6 km.

"Twelve Oaks" blends privacy and luxury with tranquillity and charm. Twelve ancient oaks line the driveway to our Homestead. Nestled amongst trees, expansive gardens and walkways on the rise of the historic 1865 Tamahane peace site, we look across leading horse stud countryside, Mt Pirongia to the west, on our eastern boundary a Department of Conservation Reserve, a rare remnant of pre-pioneering forest. Craig enjoys off duty time developing wood lots and gardens. Ezra, a sculptor and designer, has a historic, old studio, visited via a garden stroll. Guests enjoy their own private entrance, charming sitting room, reading room, bathroom and luxurious bedroom with all the comforts of home.. stable doors opening onto delightful courtyard and salt-water pool. Unwind swimming, playing croquet, patting the ponies or the nearby activities of golf, tennis, antique shopping, wineries, museums, galleries, bush walks, mineral spas. Horse stud visits, scenic flights, fishing and jet boating can be arranged or simply relax over a quiet drink by the pool. Discerning travellers will find a little style, a lot of warmth, discreet hospitality, comfort, a good breakfast and sound local knowledge.

Directions: *Please phone / fax for bookings and directions.*

Hamilton
Homestay
Address: 50A Queenwood Avenue,
Chartwell,Hamilton
Name: Judy & Brian Dixon
Telephone: (07) 855 7324
Beds: 2 Single (1 bedroom)
Bathroom: 1 Private
Tariff: B&B (continental) Double $65, Single $45. NZ B&B Vouchers accepted
Nearest Town: Hamilton

*Haere mai - Welcome. Our homestay home is a comfortable smoke free, homely
Lockwood nestled within a quiet garden.*
*Travellers have sole access to their bathroom and bedroom. Our aim is to provide a
warm environment where guests may relax and enjoy themselves.*
*We are within a 100 metres of the popular restaurants Cafe en Q, the Platter Place and
within walking distance of Chartwell Square. Waikato River walks are close by.*
*We have a beach home with guest facilities and magnificent sea views on the East Coast
near Opotiki which is also available if requested. Judy is in Education and Brian is
retired and always willing to make and share in a cuppa and help with maps and
directions. We share our home with a friendly cat named Zapper.*
Directions: *Please phone first. From Auckland turn left at Taupiri and proceed
through Gordonton to Thomas Road on right. Turn left into Hukanui, right at Glenn
Lynn and left into River Road. Queenwood Avenue is first on left. From South follow
River Road North to Queenwood Avenue on right.*

Hamilton
Country Home & Garden Stay
Address: "The Poplars", 402 Matangi Road,
RD 4, Hamilton
Name: Lesley & Peter Ramsay
Telephone: (07) 829 5551
Beds: 1 Double, 2 Single (2 bedrooms)
Bathroom: 1 Guests share
Tariff: B&B (full) Double $90,
Single $65, Children half price, Dinner $25.
Credit Cards accepted.
Nearest Town: 4km south of Hamilton city boundary, airport 12km

*Just fifteen minutes drive from Hamilton, Mystery Creek and Cambridge, the Poplars
offers a relaxed haven of peace and quiet.*
*Feed the donkeys, ducks and geese, take a row on the lake, recline by the solar heated
pool and spa pool, or stroll around the 3 acre garden with its many different rooms.
A garden for all seasons with special emphasis on internationally acclaimed Daffodils
which herald spring followed by over 600 roses. The Poplars has featured on national
TV, in NZ Gardener and Next Magazines. It is a garden of surprises.*
*Each comfortable guest room has tea and coffee making facilities, electric blankets and
TV.*
*Hosts Peter and Lesley offer you the charms of country living along with great Kiwi
hospitality. Seasoned travellers they know the difference a warm welcome can make
especially when shared with their friendly pets.*
A unique and special stay awaits you at The Poplars.
Directions: *Please phone.*

173

Tamahere, Hamilton
Homestay/Farmlet
Address: Pencarrow Road, RD 3, Hamilton
Name: Pat & Roger Williams
Telephone: (07) 856 2499 **Fax**: (07) 856 2499
Email: port.williams@clear.net.nz
Beds: 1 Double, 2 Single
(2 bedrooms/Twin with ensuite & double spa bath)
Bathroom: 1 Ensuite, 1 Guests share
Tariff: B&B (continental) Double $70, Twin $80,
Credit Cards. NZ B&B Vouchers accepted
Nearest Town: Hamilton 6km

P.O.R.T. WILLIAMS is a Mediterranean style villa, on a 5 acre farmlet in the country, on the outskirts of Hamilton. We are conveniently 3km from the Hamilton Airport and 6km from Hamilton, just off State Highway 1.
Our tranquil views are over the Narrows Golf Course, the Waikato River Valley and West to Mt Pirongia and glorious sunsets. The house is placed for maximum sunshine, in a landscaped garden on a ridge, with a farmed gully below, in which 24 sheep and 20 goats graze.
We are a friendly couple and now our family are away, we are happy to share our new home. Having travelled extensively, we understand the importance of hospitality and like meeting people. We are non-smokers and enjoy arts and crafts, many of which are on display. Our 2 dogs live outdoors.
For reservations and directions, please telephone.

Rotokauri, Hamilton
Country Garden Stay, B&B
Address: Please phone for directions
Name: Woodstom Hill
Telephone: (07) 849 9020
Beds: 1 Queen (1 bedroom)
Bathroom: 1 Ensuite
Tariff: B&B (continental deluxe) Double $110, Single $80. Credit Cards accepted.
NZ B&B Vouchers accepted $40 surcharge
Nearest Town: 5 mins (4km) north/west of Hamilton. 1 1/2 hours to Auckland

Set in 3 acres of native and woodland garden, our home overlooks lake Rotokauri, the Hakarimata Ranges and surrounding farmland. Guests are welcome to wander through our garden, soak in the hydrotherapy Jacuzzi spa and enjoy the tranquillity of a country setting. Swimming pool and adjacent spa allow almost year round swimming. The separate guest wing is upstairs and offers magnificent views. Privacy and relaxation are enhanced by your own entrance and balcony. There is a small kitchen with a fridge and microwave. Breakfast is self-serve in your room to have at your leisure. Professional therapeutic massage is available by appointment. We are a "smoke free" home. With our 4 children and 2 cats we look forward to welcoming you.
Directions: *Please phone for reservations and directions.*

Relax – Don't try to drive too far in one day.

Hamilton

Homestay
Address: "Magnolia House",
28B Nixon Street, Hamilton East
Name: Karin and Neil Kitney
Telephone: 07-856 5392
Beds: 4 Single (2 bedrooms)
Bathroom: 1 Guests share

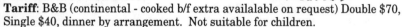

Tariff: B&B (continental - cooked b/f extra availalable on request) Double $70,
Single $40, dinner by arrangement. Not suitable for children.
NZ B&B Vouchers accepted $10 surcharge
Nearest Town: Hamilton (1.5 km to city centre)

*We welcome you to our home at the end of a long drive way (off street parking) only 100
metres from SH1 near Hamilton Gardens. We are surrounded by trees, so it is peaceful.
Located conveniently to Hamilton Gardens, Waikato University and only minutes
from Hamilton East shopping centre and the city centre, bus stop just one block away.
We have travelled widely in New Zealand and overseas and enjoy meeting people and
have many tourist tips to help you explore the local region's places of interest, many of
which are within one and one half hours drive of Hamilton.*
*Karin was born in Germany, speaks German fluently and we have found this helpful
in our travels.*
We thank you for not smoking in our home and look forward to your visit.

Ohaupo, Hamilton

B&B Homestay
Address: 'Ridge House', 15 Main Rd,
Ohaupo 2452
Name: Kay & John Bates
Telephone: (07) 823 6555
Fax: (07) 823 6555

Beds: 1 Double, 2 Single (2 bedrooms)
Bathroom: 1 Guest's (share)
Tariff: B&B (continental) Double $60, Single $35, Dinner $15pp, Full breakfast
$5pp extra. Credit Cards NZ B&B Vouchers accepted
Nearest Town: Hamilton 15km north on SH3 - Te Awamutu 12km south

*A warm friendly welcome awaits you at "Ridge House", offering wonderful views of Mt
Pirongia, the ever-changing Lake Rotomanuka opposite, and beyond, our lush Waikato
pastures. John, a retired New Zealand Railways Locomotive Engineer, enjoys photography, videoing and American Model Railroading; Kay, Homemaking, her Roses and
gardening, sceniking John's model railroad and last but not least, a lovely puss named
'Chessie". Centrally located, we are only minutes to Hamilton International Airport
and Mystery Creek, the site of Fieldays and Farmworld - 15 minutes to central
Hamilton and Cambridge - 30 minutes Waitomo Caves - approx.1 hour Rotorua -
Tauranga, and boast 6 golf courses within a 12km radius! We enjoy travelling and are
members of the Te Rapa Probus Club. COMPLIMENTARY - transport to/from
airport - homebaking and hot drinks (always available). EXTRA - warm muffins with
breakfast. We look forward to sharing with you, our 'Smoke Free' home, our table, and
our lovely countryside. Happy Travelling.   Kay and John.*

Hamilton

Homestay/B&B
Address: "Green Gables of Rukuhia",
35 Rukuhia Road, RD 2, Ohaupo
Name: Earl & Judi McWhirter
Telephone: (07) 843 8511 **Fax**: (07) 843 8514
Beds: 2 Double, 3 Single (3 bedrooms)
Bathroom: 1 Guests share
Tariff: B&B (continental) Double $75, Single $45,
Dinner $20, Special tariff for Field Days, Credit Cards.
Nearest Town: 4km south of Hamilton SH3

Warm, comfortable home surrounded with garden, in a quiet rural setting. Two storeyed house, guest rooms, lounge downstairs; dining, hosts upstairs.
Only 4km south of Hamilton, just off SH3, 5 minutes from airport. Viligrad winery just down the road, Gostiona Restaurant 2 minutes walk. Ideally situated for Field Days. Free pick up / delivery, airport, bus, train terminal just part of friendly service.
With breakfast we include homebaked bread, selection of plunged coffee to suit your taste.
Judi lectures in statistics, University of Waikato. Earl is "retired" school teacher. Both enjoy country music, dancing, outdoors. Earl hires out as a guide on Whanganui River, is a kayak instructor, and masseur. One daughter still lives at home.
We ask that guests do not smoke on the property. Thank you.
We look forward to your company, if we can't provide it, we'll help find someone who can.

Ohaupo/Hamilton

Homestay/Farmstay
Address: RD 1,
235 Kaipahi Road, Ohaupo
Name: Jenny Clarke / Neil Allan
Telephone: (07) 823 6131
Fax: (07) 823 6178
Mobile: (025) 787 885
Beds: 4 Double (4 bedrooms)
Bathroom: 1 Ensuite, 1 Private, 1 Guests share
Tariff: B&B (full) Double $95-$150. Dinner available.
Credit cards accepted. NZ B&B Vouchers accepted
Nearest Town: 15mins to Hamilton, Te Awamutu, Cambridge.

Glendariff is a fine example of one of the earliest pioneer homesteads in the Waikato. The two storied house with its generous rooms and high ceilings, was built in 1877 by a Citizen Malitia Office. The property served as a defensive focal point in those troubled times. It lies close to the Ohaupo Redoubt and was one of a chain of such estates throughout this part of the Waikato. The lookout tower remains, offering panoramic views of the area.
Spacious guest bedrooms with balconies are available, both up and down stairs, with either ensuite or dedicated bathrooms. Comfortable beds, both double and twin are equipped with electric blankets and attractive linen.
Two large drawing rooms, one with formal seating for 25 people. The other with open fire and French doors to verandah, are available for guests.
Breakfast of your choice is included in the tariff. Evening meals are available by prior arrangement.

Cambridge
Bed & Breakfast
Address: 'Park House',
70 Queen St, Cambridge
Name: Bill & Pat Hargreaves
Telephone: (07) 827 6368
Fax: (07) 827 4094
Beds: 1 Queen, 1 Double,
2 Single (3 bedrooms)
Bathroom: 2 Ensuite, 1 Private.
Tariff: B&B (full) Double $120-$130, Single $100,
Credit cards (VISA/MC/Amex). NZ B&B Vouchers accepted $55 surcharge
Nearest Town: Cambridge - 1 block

Step back into a time warp of gracious living at Park House. Built in the 1920's as an Inn, Park House is centrally situated overlooking the tree-lined village green and has been beautifully restored as a private residence. For more than 10 years we have offered this superb setting for guests who appreciate the finer comforts of life. Throughout this large home are antiques, comfortable traditional furniture, patchworks, stained-glass windows all creating an elegant and restful atmosphere for your enjoyment. The lounge features an elaborately carved fireplace, board and battenwork ceiling, fine-art, library, TV and complimentary sherry. The bedrooms, in a separate guest wing, provide every comfort and privacy. In keeping with the Inn of yesteryear, an ample breakfast is served in the Formal Dining Room. A selection of excellent Restaurants, Antique, Craft and Shops are within easy walking distance.

Cambridge
Farmhouse
Address: 'Birches', Maungatautari Rd.,
Pukekura, Postal: PO Box 194, Cambridge
Name: Sheri & Hugh Jellie
Telephone: (07) 827 6556
Fax: (07) 827 3552
Mobile: (025) 882 216
Email: hugh@plade.co.nz
Beds: 1 Queen, 2 Single (2 bedrooms)

Bathroom: 1 Ensuite, 1 Private
Tariff: B&B (full) Double $85, Single $55, Dinner $28 (GST inclusive),
Credit cards. NZ B&B Vouchers accepted $15 Surcharge on double.
Nearest Town: Cambridge 4km

Our 1930s character farmhouse offers comfort from open fires in winter to tennis and swimming pool in summer. The beautiful countryside surrounding our small acreage and rambling cottage garden, is amongst leading horse studs. Hugh, a veterinarian, specialises in dairy cow reproduction. With Lake Karapiro only 2 minutes away we can offer waterskiing or a base for rowing supporters. Picturesque Cambridge, "Town of Trees", and with its many antique shops and restaurants is only 5 minutes away. We are within an hour of Waitomo, Rotorua, Mt Maunganui beach and several top golf courses. We are both extensively travelled and with our one daughter and her pets at home are keen water / snow skiers. Guests have a choice of twin with guest bathroom and spabath, or a quaint garden cottage, queen with ensuite, both with tea making facilities. Dinner by arrangement and we serve countrystyle breakfast in our formal dining room or in the sunshine.
Directions: *Please phone for directions.*

Cambridge

Homestay
Address: 7 Marlowe Drive,Cambridge
Name: Diane and Paul White
Telephone: (07) 823 2142 **Fax**: (07) 823 2143 **Mobile**: (025) 963 224
Beds: 1 Queen, 2 Double (3 bedrooms)
Bathroom: 1 Ensuite, 1 Guests share
Tariff: B&B (special) Double $70-$75, Single $40, Dinner by arrangement,
Children by arrangement. Credit Cards accepted. NZ B&B Vouchers accepted
Nearest Town: Cambridge (5 minutes walk to town centre)

We look forward to welcoming you to our comfortable spacious home beside the river. A pleasant 5 minute stroll will take you into the town centre where you'll find nationally recognised award winning restaurants, local crafts, a myriad of antique outlets, parks and gardens and of course the many hundreds of old majestic trees that give Cambridge its unique identity.
Having spent 5 years hosting guests from New Zealand and overseas at "Riverbank House" in Hawkes Bay we now offer the same level of service and friendly hospitality to our guests here.
All rooms have quality bed linens, TV, ensuite or private bathroom facilities and total privacy.
Both of us are ex Restaurateurs so we guarantee you a lavish breakfast which will set you up for the day.
NO SMOKING PLEASE
Directions: *Cross bridge at south end of the main street (Victoria Street), turn right off bridge, Marlowe Drive is first on right.*

Cambridge

Bed & Breakfast
Address: 58 Hamilton Road and
Cnr of Bryce St. - Also known as SH1 Cambridge
Name: Hansel & Gretel Bed & Breakfast
Telephone: (07) 827 8476 **Fax**: (07) 827 8476
Mobile: 025 537 928
Beds: 1 King/Queen, 1 Double, 2 Single (3 bedrooms)
(only 2 rooms at any one time)
Bathroom: 2 Guests share
Tariff: B&B (continental) Double $75, Single $65,
Credit Cards. NZ B&B Vouchers accepted
Nearest Town: Cambridge - 5 mins walk to centre of town

When you are wanting home comfort and privacy or want to chat you will find it here. Having spent most of our lives on sheep and dairy cow farms we bring country into our town home. In 5 minutes you can walk into Cambridge. We are near restaurants only 5 minutes walk. We have a Cairns terrier dog. There are many horse studs in our area. We have operated motor hotels and enjoy the many and varied people that visit and stay with us. The Waikato region provides visitors easy daily leisurely drives to Waitomo Caves 40 mins - Rotorua 55 mins, Hamilton Fieldays 15 mins - Lake Karapiro 10 mins and a host of other nearby interesting drives and walks. We can arrange visits to horse studs and horse trekking.We have testing golf course but easy walking.
Directions: *SH1 nearby Landmark Large White Anglican Church. Please phone and bookings are recommended.*

Cambridge
Homestay
Address: "Riverlands", 7 Pope Tce, Cambridge
Name: Deborah Evans & Dave Lamb
Telephone: (07) 827 6730 **Mobile**: (025) 578 718
Beds: 1 Queen, 2 Single (2 bedrooms)
Bathroom: 1 Guests share
Tariff: B&B (special) Double $70,
Single $40, Children $15, Dinner $20.
Credit cards. NZ B&B Vouchers accepted Surcharge $10
Nearest Town: Cambridge 1 Km to town centre

We are an energetic young couple, keen to meet new people and offer a warm friendly welcome. Our home is a cosy modern 4 bedroom brick house nestled amongst the trees with the Waikato River flowing nearby with its picturesque bush walks. The town is only a short pleasant walk away with its excellent selection of restaurants, arts and crafts and antique stores. We offer comfortable bedrooms with electric blankets, woollen underlays, heating and tea / coffee making facilities. Breakfasts are hearty with a choice of full or continental and as food and wine are our passion, gourmet dinners are available on request. Laundry facilities, home office, off street parking also available. The local region offers plenty to do with tramping, horse riding, equestrian tours and several golf courses. Lake Karapiro is only minutes away with fishing, boating and we can cater especially for water skiers. We are handy to the Fielddays / Mystery Creek Pavilion and the airport being only 10 mins away with transport to and from if needed. We request no-smoking indoors. We look forward to sharing our home and two cats with you and making your stay an enjoyable one.
Please phone for bookings and directions.

Cambridge
Homestay Bed and Breakfast
Address: 6 Curnow Place, Leamington, Cambridge
Name: "Glenelg" Ken & Shirley Geary
Telephone: (07) 823 0084
Fax: (07) 823 0084
Beds: 1 Queen, 1 Double, 4 Single (4 bedrooms)
Bathroom: 2 Ensuite, 1 Guests share
Tariff: B&B (full) Double $80, Single $50, Children $7.50, Dinner $15,
Credit Cards. NZ B&B Vouchers accepted Surcharge
Nearest Town: Cambridge 2km

Glenelg welcomes you to Cambridge to a new home with quality spacious accommodation - warm quiet and private overlooking beautiful Waikato Farmland, with plenty of off street parking. Dinner meals available on request. A spa bath available for all guests. Beds have electric blankets and woolrests. Therapeutic massage available on request. Lake Karapiro is only 5 minutes away and we can offer accommodation for Rowers and all water sports. Mystery Creek where the NZ National Field Days and many other functions are held is only 15 mins away. Hamilton Airport is 20 mins away. Tours are also available to Waitomo Caves, Rotorua, Tauranga, Mt Maunganui, Auckland, Taupo, Coromandel Peninsula, Cambridge Horse Studs and Farm Tours. Courtesy vehicle available from Hamilton Airport, Cambridge Bus Depot, Hamilton Bus Depot. Small charge for Auckland Airport. Sky TV, laundry facilities available. Non smokers preferred - Smoking area provided.
For a brochure and directions, please phone.

Cambridge

B&B Country Stay
Address: 'Dunfarmin', 55 Gorton Road,
RD 2, Cambridge
Name: Jackie and Bob Clarke
Telephone: (07) 827 7727
Fax: (07) 823 3357 **Mobile**: (025) 862 500
Beds: 1 Queen, 1 Double, 3 Single (3 bedrooms)
Bathroom: 1 Ensuite, 1 Guests share
Tariff: B&B (full) Double $90, Single $50, Dinner $25.
Nearest Town: Cambridge 9 kms.

Welcome to our country home. Dunfarmin is situated 9 kms south of Cambridge just off state highway one, positioned on a commanding knoll, 20 acres sheltered by mature trees which offers the weary traveller peace and tranquillity. The outlook from the spacious home with in-ground swimming pool provides panoramic views of the surrounding Waikato country side. Further amenities include a flootlit tennis court and access to spa bath. Within easy reach of cafes, restaurants, antique and craft shops. Also Lake Karapiro famous for water skiing, rowing and boating. Enjoy your breakfast or other meals by prior arrangement in pleasant surroundings. We delight in meeting people and, having travelled ourselves, we appreciate the needs of the traveller.
Please feel at home with us plus Murdoch the old dog and Possum the cat.
Being non smokers, we appreciate no smoking in the house.

Tirau

Farmstay
Address: 357 Rotorua Road, R D 2,
Tirau 2372
Name: Lin & Joy Cathcart
Telephone: (07) 883 1471
Beds: 1 King, 1 Double, 1 Single (3 bedrooms)
Bathroom: 1 Ensuite, 1 Family share
Tariff: B&B (full) Double $70, Single $40, Dinner $22.
NZ B&B Vouchers accepted $5 surcharge
Nearest Town: Tirau

Our 250 cow dairy farm is an easy 2 1/2 hour drive south from Auckland International Airport. We welcome visitors to our attractive property over which you may wander at leisure, fish our two trout streams or Lin will give you a tour in his "ute". All beds have electric blankets and complimentary tea / coffee are always available. Our family are adult and away from home - however we do have a cat. Hobbies include gardening, golf, patchwork, bridge and travel. By car we are central to Rotorua, Taupo, Waitomo Caves, Tauranga and Hamilton. Our home is "smoke free", and sorry no children under 12 years.
Directions: *Follow SH1 south from Tirau 2 km. Then take SH5 left to Rotorua for 3 km, cross Waihou River Bridge, and 200 metres on left is our gate - name on mailbox.*

Please help us provide the best hospitality in the world.
Fill in a comment form for every place you stay.

Te Awamutu

Farmstay
Address: 'Tregamere',
 2025 Ohaupo Road, Te Awamutu
Name: Ray & Betty Johnson
Telephone: (07) 871 8861
Beds: 1 Double, 5 Single (3 bedrooms)
Bathroom: 1 Ensuite, 1 Guest share
Tariff: B&B (full) Double $80, Single $50, Dinner $20.
Credit cards.   NZ B&B Vouchers accepted
Nearest Town: Te Awamutu 2km

A two hour drive south of Auckland makes Te Awamutu a pleasant stop-over before visiting the famed Waitomo caves. Our home is modern, warm and comfortable set in approx two acres of garden, with a beautiful view west to Mt. Pirongia and easy walks to ponds and bush area. We are middle-aged plus - retired - then decided to go farming again on a 64 acre dry stock farm on the verge of suburbia, and one minute from the Te Awamutu Post Office. Te Awamutu is the Rose Town of New Zealand with a superb rose garden and beautiful park - a pleasure to visit!
Directions: *Very easy to find with a white stone entrance and black railing fence. Situated on State Highway 3, the main road. On the right hand side coming from Hamilton, or first farm on left after leaving Te Awamutu going north.*

Te Awamutu

Farmstay/Guest House
Address: Storey Road, Te Awamutu
Name: Regula Bleskie
Telephone: (07) 871 3301
Beds: 1 Double, 8 Single (5 bedrooms)
Bathroom: 1 Ensuite, 1 Guests share,
1 Family share
Tariff: B&B (full) Double $90, Single $50,
Children $25, Dinner $25, Campervans welcome.
Nearest Town: Te Awamutu 4.5km

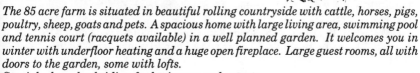

The 85 acre farm is situated in beautiful rolling countryside with cattle, horses, pigs, poultry, sheep, goats and pets. A spacious home with large living area, swimming pool and tennis court (racquets available) in a well planned garden. It welcomes you in winter with underfloor heating and a huge open fireplace. Large guest rooms, all with doors to the garden, some with lofts.
Specials: horsebackriding for beginners and experts
long or short trips only $10.
Gigrides are available too, for children and adults. Blueberry, Raspberry and Persimen picking in season. Access to the milking of 450 dairy cows.
Directions: *100m after signpost Cambridge turn left into Te Rahu Rd, follow 3.5 km - come into Woodstock Rd, follow 1 km - Storey Rd. 1st driveway on your left (it's a long driveway).*

One of the differences between staying at a hotel and a B&B
is that you don't hug the hotel staff when you leave.

Te Awamutu

Farmstay
Address: Leger Farm, 114 St Leger Road,
Te Awamutu
Name: Peter & Beverley Bryant
Telephone: (07) 871 6676 **Fax**: (07) 871 6679
Mobile: (025) 364 419
Beds: 1 Double, 3 Single (3 bedrooms)
Bathroom: 1 Ensuite, 1 Private, 1 Guests share
Tariff: B&B (special/continental) Double $115, Single $60,
Dinner $30. NZ B&B Vouchers accepted $25 surcharge
Nearest Town: Te Awamutu 2km

'Leger Farm' offers country living at its finest.
Panoramic views of the surrounding countryside are seen from every aspect of our home which is built of 'old' red bricks and redwood timber. The stunning architecturally designed home is tastefully decorated and nestled on 40 acres of some of NZ's best grazing land. Garden vistas overlook Mount Pirongia and Kakepuka. Grazing sheep, beef and deer can be seen close by, on our property. All bedrooms offer views, comfortable beds, electric blankets, quilts, flowers, reading material and balconies. We share interests of music, drama, gardening, tramping, travel, antiques, Lions Club and BPW. NZ meals of lamb and venison are our specialty. Leger Farm is located 2km south of Te Awamutu, off SH3. Te Awamutu, renowned world wide for its beautiful rose gardens is centrally situated, 30 mins north of Waitomo, famous 'Black Water' rafting and extensive limestone grotto. One hour to Rotorua thermal area, golf course 1km. Hamilton 30 mns.
Directions: *Please phone or fax for reservations and directions.*

Kawhia

Homestay
Address: Rosamond Tce, Kawhia
Name: "Rosamond House"
Mike Annette&Jessica Warrender
Telephone: (07) 871 0681
Fax: (07) 871 0681
Beds: 1 King (or 2 Single), 2 Double, 2 Single (4 bedrooms)
Bathroom: 1 Guests share
Tariff: B&B (full) Double $65, Single $45, Children half price, Dinner $15.
Nearest Town: Te Awamutu 50 mins and 1 hour 10 mins from Waitomo Caves
SH31

If you are wanting to step back in time, then read on.
Our specialty is hospitality, peace and tranquillity. We want you to enjoy the comfort of our beautiful 96 year old solid kauri villa, which has a million dollar view, overlooking the Kawhia Harbour and township.
Features we can offer you: Swimming pool, sauna, mountain bike riding, kayaking, caving, abseiling.
Other attractions, hot pools, tennis courts, golf course, sports club, walks etc. I also operate Annie's Cafe / Restaurant in the main street. Kawhia which has an "a la carte" menu, come sit and relax over a wine or ale and enjoy the spectacular views of the Kawhia Harbour - open 7 days in summer. Winter hours changeable.
Whether you are touring New Zealand on holiday or just seeking a quiet and peaceful retreat from daily life, we welcome you into our home and cafe.
Directions: *Please phone.*

Otorohanga - Waitomo District
Homestay+ Self-contained Accom
Address: 'Brake's B&B', 147 Main North Road,
(SH3), Otorohanga
Name: Ernest & Ann Brake
Telephone: (07) 873 7734 **Mobile**: (025) 845 419
Beds: 2 Single (1 bedroom)
Bathroom: 1 Family share. Self-contained unit: 1 Queensize, 1 single, plus
rollaway bed.
Tariff: B&B (continental) Double $70, Single $47.50; In self-contained unit:
Double $60, Single $42.50, Third person $17, each extra $12, Children $1 per year
of age minimum $5, Cot available; Breakfast optional and extra (continental $5,
full $8 each). Discounts for 3 or more nights' stay. NZ B&B Vouchers accepted
Nearest Town: Otorohanga 2.5 km, Waitomo Caves 18 km

*We are a retired farming couple with an adult family and have travelled overseas. Our
home is on the northern outskirts of Otorohanga and we enjoy extensive views of the
countryside from our elevated position. The self-contained unit is a quaint little
garden cottage tastefully furnished with walls of natural timber panelling, quiet,
private and comfortable. It has tea/coffee making facilities, toaster, fridge, TV;
laundry facilities available. Evening meals are available at several restaurants in
Otorohanga, while we invite you to enjoy breakfast with us. Otorohanga is an
interesting rural town with its native bird park featuring a Kiwi house and aviary. It
is the nearest town to Waitomo Glow-worm Caves and numerous bush walks, Waitomo
Golf Course and the Waipa River, a good trout fishing stream.*
Directions: *From Otorohanga town centre take the main road (SH3 north and find
us on the left approx 2.5km from town.*

Otorohanga - Waitomo District
Self-contained Accommodation
Address: Crofthill, R.D. 3, Otorohanga
Name: Jim & Jennifer Beveridge
Telephone: (07) 873 8232
Fax: (07) 873 8232
Mobile: (025) 873 8232
Beds: 4 Single (2 Bedrooms - each with 2 beds)
Bathroom: 1 Private
Tariff: B&B (full) Double $80, Single $50, Dinner $25 with pre-dinner drink
available. Credit Cards. NZ B&B Vouchers accepted
Nearest Town: Otorohanga (6kms)

*Crofthill is set in a large rural garden near Otorohanga with panoramic views from
Mt Pirongia to Mt Ruapehu. The modern unit, connected to the house by a walkway,
has 2 large twin bedrooms, shower, separate toilet, sitting room with television, books
etc. and kitchen area with fridge and tea/coffee facilities. You are welcome to relax
there and join us when you wish - perhaps for dinner (with a little notice, please). We
retain an interest in farming through our son who farms in the heart of the King
Country. We are ideally situated for visiting the Kiwi House, Waitomo Caves and other
areas of interest. The Fieldays site is approximately 30-40 minutes away.*
We have a friendly cat by accident, inherited when our daughter went flatting.
Directions: *Turn on to SH31 at the Southern end of Otorohanga (by the BP Service
Station). We are 6 kms from Otorohanga on the left hand side at the top of the first hill.*

Otorohanga, Waitomo District
Rural/Main Road B&B
Address: 'Kiwi Country B&B',
cnr. SH3 & Mangaorongo Rd, North of Otorohanga
(Postal: PO Box 16, Otorohanga)
Name: Edsel & Marg Forde, Sons Rory & Paddy
Telephone: (07) 873 8173
Beds: 2 Double, 1 Single (2 bedrooms)
Bathroom: 1 Guests share, (but we only take one guest at a time so you'll never have to share with stangers.)
Tariff: B&B (continental) One person $38, Two people $70, Three people $100, Four people $130, Five people $150. Children negotiable. Pets negotiable. Cooked breakfast $5 per person extra. NZ B&B Vouchers accepted
Nearest Town: Otorohanga 3km

A warm welcome awaits travellers at our comfortable modern home near NZ's Kiwi town, Otorohanga, closest town to the famous Waitomo Caves. We sampled, and enjoyed, B&B hospitality countless times on our travels of NZ and many parts of the world. Now, we appreciate any chance to offer the same at our home, which is handily located just off the main highway north of Otorohanga, set amongst trees and rolling green paddocks. Otorohanga's Kiwi House Complex is five minutes drive, Waitomo Caves approx 15 mins. Our home is smoke-free but for those who must, both bedrooms and the guest lounge/dining room have their own sunny decks. The lounge offers books, magazines, TV and hot drink making facilities. Our guest bathroom has internal access from both bedrooms so we have ensuite capacity. We offer comprehensive information on our region and NZ, with brochures and based on our own wide personal experience. Cot available. We look forward to meeting you.

Otorohanga - Waitomo
Farmstay+Self-contained Accom.
Address: Meadowland B&B
746 SH 31, R.D.3, Otorohanga
Name: Tony & Jill Webber
Telephone: (07) 873 7729 **Fax**: (07) 873 7719
Beds: 1 Queen, 3 Double, 2 Single plus bunks (5 bedrooms)
Bathroom: 1 Private, 1 Guests share
Tariff: B&B (full) Double $75, Single $50, Children$20. In self contained units: Double $65, Single $45, Extra adult $20, Children $15. Breakfast $5 pp extra (optional). Credit cards. NZ B&B Vouchers accepted
Nearest Town: Otorohanga 8 km

Welcome to Meadowland. Our farm is 8 km north of Otorohanga on State Highway 31. Places to visit in our area include: Kiwi House and bird aviary, Waitomo Caves, black water rafting, abseiling, natural bridge, bush walks, Marakopa Falls etc. We can arrange a visit to a nearby rotary cowshed; or carnation houses next door; or perhaps take you old time dancing or indoor bowling. We have swimming pool, tennis court, magnificent panoramic views of farmland, Pirongia and Kakepuka mountains and weather permitting Mt Ruapehu. Our accommodation is: three double bedrooms in our house with guest shared separate bathroom and toilet; or our self-contained cabin, can sleep up to six, with bunk beds and double bedsettee in one room and double bed in separate room. Own shower / toilet, washing machine, fridge, small stove, microwave, TV, electric blankets, heaters etc., breakfast optional. Non-smokers preferred. We have travelled overseas and enjoy meeting and talking with people.
Directions: *Turn on to SH31 at the South end of Otorohanga (by BP Service Station), we are 8 km from Otorohanga on the right hand side at the top of the second hill.*

Otorohanga
Homestay, Farmstay
Address: 1375 Main North Road,
RD 4, Otorohanga
Name: Mt Heslington Stud
Telephone: (07) 873 1873
Fax: (07) 873 7622
Beds: 1 Double, 4 Single (2 bedrooms)
Bathroom: 1 Guests share
Tariff: B&B (special/full) Double $70,
Single $45, Children $15, Dinner $25 pp (by arrangement).
NZ B&B Vouchers accepted
Nearest Town: 12 kms from Otorohanga, 18 kms from Te Awamutu,

Guests are very welcome in our comfortable home where our aim is your comfort and guests are treated as friends. We are centrally situated on Straight Highway 3, 20 minutes from Te Awamutu, 20 minutes from Waitomo glow worm caves with the picturesque Waitomo golf course past Otorohanga with its wonderful large kiwi house. Our large home is surrounded by dairy farms and on our main highway property we have an Angus cattle stud and thoroughbred race horses. The horses continue to win in New Zealand, Australia and Asia.
We offer a warm welcome and good hospitality, relax around the swimming pool, partake in farm activities, our pool table for evening entertainment.
Warmth in our beds and our home is our criteria.

Waitomo Caves - Waitomo District
Farmstay
Address: Glenview Station, R.D. 8,
Te Kuiti
Name: Cindy & Warren Clayton-Greene
Telephone: (07) 878 7705
Fax: (07) 878 5066
Beds: 2 Double,
1 set of bunks (2 bedrooms).
Bathroom: 1 Ensuite.
Private Lounge with tea and coffee facilities and TV.
Tariff: B&B (full) Double $80, Single $50, Children $25, Dinner (served with beer or wine) $20. NZ B&B Vouchers accepted $20 surcharge
Nearest Town: Waitomo (5 km), Te Kuiti (23 km), Otorohanga (20km

You're invited to stay on a scenic New Zealand sheep and cattle station. A 2,200 acre station with 6000 sheep and 700 beef cattle and other farm animals. The farm is run in the traditional way with horses and dogs. Enjoy the quiet and hospitality of rural life in New Zealand. Relax amongst the beautiful native bush, trout streams and unique limestone formations. Our guests enjoy hiking on the farm, or taking a drive out to the trout streams or relax in the conservatory. We have two school age children, so private lounge is available with tea/coffee facilities and television, or enjoy the evening with the family in the main lounge. We have a large attractive home set in beautiful gardens. You'll find us nestled in the hills above the Waitomo Caves with panoramic views. We are non smokers.
Directions: *5km from Waitomo Caves: carry on past the Waitomo Caves going west towards Marakopa straight ahead at the round-about: we are on the tar seal road. Look on the right for the "Glenview" sign and our name and sign on the mail box. Please phone.*

185

Waitomo Village

Self-contained Accommodation
Address: Waitomo Caves Village
Name: Andree & Peter Dalziel
Telephone: (07) 878 7641 **Fax**: 07 8787466
Beds: 3 King/Queen, 1 Double, 2 Single, (5 Bedrooms)
Bathroom: 5 Ensuite
Tariff: B&B (continental) Double $70, Single $50. NZ B&B Vouchers accepted
Nearest Town: Waitomo Village, 100 metres

Our home is only 100 metres from the Museum of Caves information office in the centre of the village and a few hundred metres from the Glow Worm Caves.

Our detached double and twin rooms with their individual ensuite toilet and shower facilities are of the highest standard.

With a variety of cave adventure trips - Black Water Rafting, Lost World, horse riding, excellent bush walks, a top golf course and a selection of the country's best gardens to visit, all within a short distance - we recommend that you allocate at least two days to spend with us. We will arrange your meals.

If you cannot reach us by phone, just arrive - you will find a place with warm and friendly hospitality.

Waitomo Caves

Farmstay
Address: R.D. 1, Te Kuiti, Please phone
Name: Sue & Bill Kay
Telephone: (07) 878 8762
if no reply (07)878 7702
Fax: (07) 878 8762
Beds: 2 Twin, 1 Single (3 bedrooms)
Bathroom: 1 Guests
Tariff: B&B Double $80, Single $50, Dinner $25, Children negotiable.
NZ B&B Vouchers accepted From 1 April to 31 October with $12 surcharge
Nearest Town: Waitomo Caves Village 7km, Te Kuiti 15km

It would be a pleasure to have you to stay with us in our comfortable large family homestead set amongst extensive garden and mature English trees. Our garden is listed in the book "Gardens to Visit in New Zealand" and "New Zealand Town and Country Gardens". The native bush we look upon attracts beautiful native birds to our garden.

We live on a 2000 acre sheep forestry and beef farm. In our garden we have a swimming pool and hard tennis court. From our house we have a wonderful view of the historic Tumutumu rock, and unique limestone formations. We have 'Tumu Tumu Toobing' operating on our farm, an adventures trip, including cave rafting, awesome cave formations, and famous NZ glow worms. Enquiries and bookings for caving trip phone Waitomo Adventures Ltd on (07) 878 7788, fax (07) 878 6866.

Only six minutes down the road are tourist caves and bush walks. We have both travelled and enjoy meeting overseas visitors and New Zealanders.

Private bathroom is for your use exclusively,
Guests share means you may be sharing with other guests,
Family share means you will be sharing with the family.

Waitomo Caves

Farmstay
Address: Mason's Caves 'Blackdown',
No. 1 R.D., Te Kuiti.
Name: Jill & Derek Mason
Telephone: (07) 878 7622
Fax: (07) 878 7628
Mobile: (025) 778 829
Beds: 4 Single (2 bedrooms)
Bathroom: 1 Ensuite, 1 Family share
Tariff: B&B (continental) Double $80, Single $50, Dinner $25,
Children negotiable. No pets. NZ B&B Vouchers accepted May to October
Nearest Town: Waitomo Caves 12km, Te Kuiti 12km.

*Derek and Jill are happy to invite you to stay at "Blackdown". The property has been
in the family for three generations the daily occupation being sheep and beef cattle
farming. We are located 7 kms from State Highway 3 and 12 kms from the village of
Waitomo. The large homestead, now without family at home, has been developed for
your comfort, heaters in guest rooms, electric blankets, tasteful decor, garden views
from bedrooms and a croquet lawn and petanque for your enjoyment. The large garden
is surrounded by mature trees. Because of its elevation the property offers panoramic
views of the King Country. You are invited to walk the farm for viewing. We are well
travelled and enjoy sharing the experiences of others.*
*An exceptional display of glow worms in caves on the farm can be visited as an extra
in a three hour personally conducted tour.*
Directions: *Please phone / fax.*

Waitomo Caves

Farmstay
Address: 'Forest Hills', Boddies' Rd,
RD 1, Te Kuiti
Name: Jocelyn and Peter Boddie
Telephone: (07) 878 8764
Fax: (07) 878 8764
Beds: 1 Double (1 bedroom)
Bathroom: 1 Private
Tariff: B&B (continental) Double $75,
Single $60, Dinner $25 pp.
Nearest Town: Waitomo Caves 8km,
Te Kuiti 13km

Joss and Peter Boddie invite you to stay,
Enjoy country living down Waitomo way.
In our hilltop residence, Ruapehu the view,
500 hectares of farmland and near the caves too.
Midwife and farmer with interests abounding,
Art, music, gardens in a rural surrounding.
The four kids we had have largely all flown,
Just cats Fred and Presto to call us their own.
A smokefree environment we do highly treasure,
Our large family home now awaits your pleasure.
You're welcome where able to fit in on the farm,
Go for walks, enjoy peace and discover rural charm.
Forget city life, stress, phone and fax,
Enjoy drinks by the fire at days end to relax.

187

Te Kuiti - Waitomo District
Farmstay
Address: 'Tapanui', 1714 Oparure Road, R.D. 5, Te Kuiti
Name: Mark & Sue Perry
Telephone: (07) 877 8549 **Fax**: (07) 877 8541 **Mobile**: (025) 949 873
Email: tapanui@xtra.co.nz
Beds: (Sleepyhead Elite)3 Super-King/twin zipper,1 Single (3 bedrooms)
Bathroom: 1 Ensuite, 1 Guests share, Bathrobes for private bathroom. Toiletries in both bathrooms.
Tariff: B&B (full) Double $110-$140, Single 100-$130, Dinner $30, Not suitable for children. Visa/Mastercard. NZ B&B Vouchers accepted $39-$66 surcharge Double/$30-$57 surcharge Single
Nearest Town: Te Kuiti 20km, Otorohanga 32km, 17km from SH 3.

"A Note From Two Fellow Travellers"
"This is New Zealand at its very best: an extraordinary scenic drive on a sealed road through endless green hills brings you to "Tapanui", not far from Waitomo Caves. You feel genuinely welcome in this magnificent home owned by an active farming couple with wide ranging interests in gardening, fishing and travel."Take part in the farm work or watch their day unfold while you lazily tend to the pet sheep, donkeys, and Charlotte the kune kune pig. Then, enjoy knowledgeable conversation about the farm and about the world."The homestead is wonderful, very large and with tremendous privacy. One separate guest wing includes a spacious bedroom, a super-king bed, a single bed and ensuite. Just out the huge windows are vistas of green, everywhere. And, your own patio!"Other rooms include either comfortable and cosy twin or super-king beds (your choice) with a bathroom. Again, the view is from a story book, the hospitality warm and heartfelt."Everything has been thought of from feather duvets and electric blankets to heated towels rails, fly screens and central heating. The home cooked meals alone are worth the visit."Over 3000 Romney sheep and 700 head of cattle roam the hillsides. Most happily, it all gives you those very special moments that cameras and memories capture. Forever you will treasure your trip to "Tapanui".
"We came as guests and left as friends."Rick Antonson and Janice Sapergia, Vancouver, Canada
Directions: *Please phone, fax or write for reservations and directions. Our home is smoke free.*
Web sites:
http://nz.com/webnz/bbnz/tapa.htm
http://www.friars.co.nz/hosts/tapanui.html
http://www.ginz.com/accomm/tapanui.htm

Te Kuiti - Waitomo District

Homestay
Address: 5 Grey St, Te Kuiti
Name: Pauline Blackmore
Telephone: (07) 878 6686
Beds: 2 Queen, 2 Single (3 bedrooms)
Bathroom: 2 Ensuite, 1 Private
Tariff: B&B (full) Double $60 - $70, Single $40, Children half price,
Credit Cards. NZ B&B Vouchers accepted
Nearest Town: Te Kuiti

I live in a comfortable old bungalow only 50 metres off Highway 3 where you will be greeted with warmth and invited to share a cup of tea or percolated coffee and homemade biscuits. All bedrooms have private toilet facilities and all beds are firm and comfortable with electric blankets, winter or summer duvets and a choice of pillows. There are electric heaters and teamaking facilities in the bedrooms. Fred the ginger cat shares the house with me. The atmosphere is relaxed and guests are welcome to chat or watch TV in the comfortable lounge. Breakfast is timed to suit you and I serve fruit juice, cereals and fruit, followed by the full English breakfast. Tea or coffee or course. Waitomo Caves Village is 18 km north. Attractions there include White and Black water rafting in addition to the Waitomo Glowworm Cave and the Caves Museum.

Te Kuiti - Waitomo District

Homestay
Address: Gadsby Road, Te Kuiti
Name: Margaret & Graeme Churstain
Telephone: (07) 878 8191
Beds: 1 Queen, 3 Single (3 bedrooms)
Unit: 5 Single or 1Double, 3 Single
Bathroom: Ensuite Unit - Guests share upstairs.
Tariff: B&B (continental) Double $60, Single $30, Dinner (with prior notice) $15pp, Campervans facilities available $20pp. NZ B&B Vouchers accepted
Nearest Town: Te Kuiti 3kms - Waitomo District

Our B&B is on a farmlet on Gadsby Road, signposted on S.H.3 at the Northern end of Te Kuiti. We have enjoyed accommodating visitors from all over the world and New Zealand for some years now, offering a relaxed and comfortable homestay. To sit on the deck we guarantee rural views you would find hard to forget, with aerial topdressing and farming activity common scenes from all round views. In one of New Zealand's best sheep and cattle producing areas and boasting the "Shearing Capital of the World" and a statue to match Te Kuiti and surrounding areas offer many leisure activities with the famous Waitomo Caves only 10 minutes away. Warm comfortable beds we can provide with guests share bathroom or if you prefer, a seperate unit is available with private bathroom, ideal for families. Laundry facilities are available at a small charge. Our dog and cat welcome yours.

Continental breakfast consists of fruit, cereal, toast, tea/coffee,
Full breakfast is the same with a cooked course,
Special breakfast has something special.

Members of
The New Zealand Association Farm & Home Host Inc.
maintain the highest standards &
are always delighted to welcome
guests into their homes.

Te Kuiti
Homestay
Address: "Sanaig House",
35 Awakino Road, Te Kuiti
Name: Mike & Sue Wagstaff
Telephone: (07) 878 7128
Fax: (07) 878 7128
Beds: 2 Double, 2 Single (3 bedrooms)
Bathroom: 1 Ensuite, 1 Private with bath
Tariff: B&B (continental) Double $85, Single $65.
Nearest Town: Te Kuiti

Welcome to Sanaig House one of Te Kuiti's gracious homes built in 1903.
Situated on the Awakino Hill, on SH3, overlooking the town and surrounding farmland, our comfortable and spacious home is set in a garden of lovely mature trees. Guest bedrooms are attractive, sunny and either overlook the countryside or have direct access to the garden.
Te Kuiti is close to the famous Waitomo Caves and associated outdoor adventures ..... black water rafting, white water rafting, the Lost World and other caving experiences, horse riding, bush walks, golf, garden visits, hunting and fishing. If notified in advance we are able to arrange trips to hear "The Dawn Chorus" and see the endangered native Kokako in the Mapara Wildlife Reserve.
We look forward to sharing our home and this lovely part of New Zealand with you.
Directions: *Please phone/fax,*

Te Kuiti
Farmstay/B&B
Address: "Panorama Farm",
Carter Road, RD 2, Te Kuiti
Name: Michael & Raema Warriner
Telephone: (07) 878 5104 **Fax**: (07) 878 5104
Beds: 1 Double, 3 Single (2 bedrooms)
Bathroom: 1 Guests share
Tariff: B&B (full) Double $66, Single $35, Children half price, Dinner $20.
Credit Cards. NZ B&B Vouchers accepted
Nearest Town: Te Kuiti 6km

Welcome to Panorama Farm 72 acres of lush pasture producing prime beef and lamb.
Our home is a large renovated house with modern facilities. A verandah shades two
sides providing a panoramic view of bush-clad hills, fertile valleys and distant peaks
with golden dawns and spectacular sunsets.
Situated 6km east of Te Kuiti we provide easy access to many attractions, the famous
Waitomo Glowworm Caves, Lost World, Blackwater rafting and other adventures are
only 25 mins away. Within 2 hours are Rotorua, Taupo, Whakapapa skifields and
Tauranga, Auckland Airport 2 1/4 hours. But why not relax with a farm walk or
garden stroll or just read a good book. Be our guest.
We have lived in this area for 40 years and know and appreciate its points of interest
which we would love to share with you. Phone or fax for directions. Resident cat.

Piopio - Waitomo District
Farmstay
Address: Puke-Kohatu, Aria Road, Piopio, Te Kuiti
Name: Maurice & Jennifer Kearns
Telephone: (07) 877 7801 **Fax**: (07) 877 7801
Beds: 4 Single (2 bedrooms)
Bathroom: 1 Private
Tariff: B&B (full) Double $65, Single $32.50, Children half price, Dinner $20pp.
Credit cards accepted. NZ B&B Vouchers accepted
Nearest Town: Piopio 8 km, Te Kuiti 30 km

We welcome visitors to our modern home on our 163 acre property running dairy cattle
and sheep. The 2 twin rooms have snug beds, feather duvets, electric blankets and
heaters. All rooms have garden outlooks. No steps. We accept only one booking (1-4
persons) per night.Gardening is our special interest and our home is nestled amongst
natural limestone outcrops and mature trees, interspersed with perennial plantings.
A working waterwheel, rock formations and small caves add interest, and contribute
to an atmosphere of peace and tranquillity. Enjoy, too, a walk with us around our
farm Now semi-retired, we enjoy sharing our time and our environment with visitors.
Directions:*Travelling south on SH3, turn left at crossroads in centre of Piopio.*
Proceed for 8 km. We are first home on right after passing the Paekaka Road (which
turns off to right). Name on mailbox.

One of the differences between staying at a hotel and a B&B
is that you don't hug the hotel staff when you leave.

Pio Pio - Waitomo District
Farmstay
Address: Carmel Farm, Main Road, Box 93 Pio Pio
Name: Leo & Barbara Anselmi
Telephone: (07) 877 8130 **Fax**: (07) 877 8130
Beds: 8 Single or 2 King-size & 2 single (5 bedrooms)
Bathroom: Ensuite family unit, 1 Guests share upstairs.
Tariff: B&B (full) Double $100, Single $50, Dinner $25pp (inc wine and pre-dinner drinks). NZ B&B Vouchers accepted
Nearest Town: 18 kms south of Te Kuiti, 7 km south of Junction.

Barbara and Leo Anselmi own and operate a 1200 acre sheep, dairy and cattle farm. The property is on the Main South Road 18km south of Te Kuiti. You will be welcomed into a 3000 square feet modern home set in picturesque gardens in a lovely limestone valley. You will be treated to delicious home cooked meals and the warmth of our friendship. Whether the excitement of mustering mobs of cattle and sheep, viewing the milking of 500 cows, just relaxing as you drive around the rolling hills on the four wheeled farm bike, basking in the pool or wandering through the gardens interest you, no matter what your age you will experience unforgettable memories of breathtaking scenery, a clean green environment. We have many farm pets who all love the attention of our guests including a child's horse to be ridden and a donkey to be fed. As well as farming activities we look over a beautiful 18 hole golf course which welcomes visitors. The property is just minutes from Black Water Rafting and Canoeing activities, The Lost World Cavern and the famous Waitomo Caves. We are only minutes away from breathtaking bush walks, the rare kokako bird and 140km from Rotorua / Taupo.

Directions: *On State Highway 3 to New Plymouth, 6km south of the junction of State Highway 4. We can arrange to pick you up from Otorohanga, Te Kuiti or Waitomo if required.*

Please help us provide the best hospitality in the world.
Fill in a comment form for every place you stay.

Piopio - Waitomo District
Country Homestay
Address: 'Bracken Ridge' Aria Road, Piopio
Name: Rob & Susan Hallam
Telephone: (07) 877 8384
Beds: 4 Single (2 Bedrooms)
Bathroom: 1 Private
Tariff: B&B (full) Double $70, Single $40,
Children half price, Dinner $20pp.
NZ B&B Vouchers accepted
Nearest Town: Te Kuiti 24km, Piopio 1km

Welcome to our large modern, family home which is situated on a 10 acre farmlet. Our elevated site provides panoramic views of the beautiful surrounding countryside. Self-contained private guest facilities are provided on a separate level.

We look forward to your company for a relaxing, enjoyable stay and are happy to share our knowledge of local points of interest such as bush walks, rafting, scenic drives, trout fishing, golf or a stroll over the farm. Waitomo Caves is only 30 minutes away. Visits to sheep, dairy farms and local gardens may be arranged.

We ask guests not to smoke inside our home nor bring pets.

Our interests range from music to boating and we enjoy meeting people from different places.

Directions: *Travelling south on SH 3 turn left at centre of Piopio village and proceed 1 kilometre. Look for our name at gate on right past 100km sign. Please phone ahead.*

Ongarue, Taumarunui
Farmstay
Address: 'Foxley Station', RD Ongarue
Name: Tony & Kitrena Fullerton-Smith
Telephone: (07) 896 6104 **Fax**: (07) 896-6919
Beds: 1 Queen, 2 Single (2 bedrooms)
Bathroom: 1 Private
(only 1 party of guests taken at a time).
Tariff: B&B (continental, Full on request)
Double $85,
Single $50,
Dinner from $25 (with complimentary wine and pre dinner drink).   NZ B&B Vouchers accepted
Nearest Town: 25km north of Taumarunui on SH 40.

'Foxley Station' is a 3500 acre hill country farm situated in the heart of the King Country, running sheep, cattle and deer. The 'Homestead' is set in a lovely country garden with tennis court and swimming pool. We welcome people to observe or participate in our farm life. Go walking through our Native Bush Reserve or just relax. Enjoy home cooked meals or for something special try our 'Game Menu' (trout, duck, venison). Nearby attractions all within one hour of us: Lake Taupo, Wanganui River, Tongariro National Parks, Scenic Flights, Waitomo Caves, Ski Fields, Local Gardens and Golf Course. We are in our early 40's. Our children, Sarah and Andrew are away at University. We invite you to experience our friendly and relaxed farm life and country living. Looking forward to entertaining you in our home.

Directions: *Please phone, fax or write for reservations and directions. Our home is smoke free*

Taumarunui
Farmstay
Address: Eastward Road,
Waituhi, R.D.4, Taumarunui
Name: Yvonne & Eric Walker
Telephone: (07) 896 6041 **Fax**: (07) 896 6040
Beds: 1 Double, 2 Single (2 bedrooms)
Bathroom: 1 Family share
Tariff: B&B (full) Double $60, Single $35, Children half price, Dinner $15,
Campervans accepted. NZ B&B Vouchers accepted
Nearest Town: 25km East of Taumarunui off SH 41.

*Our home is large and comfortable, with a spacious living area, overlooking garden
and swimming pool. It is set in pleasant surroundings in a peaceful valley only 20
minutes from the rural township of Taumarunui.*
*Taumarunui offers Jetboat tours down the Wanganui River, canoeing and trout
fishing, as well as a golf course with an excellent reputation which welcomes visitors.
Our farm is a 45 minute drive from Tongariro National Park where seasonal activities
such as skiing and tramping are available.*
*For those keen on exploring a genuine NZ farm, we have 360 hectares, 60 of which are
in native bush. We farm sheep, cattle, deer and have various other animals such as
pigs, dogs, a cat and also horses suitable for riding.*
Please phone for directions.

Taumarunui
Bed & Breakfast
Address: 'Waimarino Lodge',
P.O. Box 43, Owhango,
Taumarunui, - Please phone for directions
Name: Cristina & Antony Guy
Telephone: (07) 895 4404
Fax: (07) 895-4404 **Email**: Cristina@xtra.co.nz
Beds: 1 Queen, 4 Single (3 bedrooms)
Bathroom: 1 Guests share
Tariff: B&B (special) Queen $90, Single $45, Dinner $35 with aperitif & wine,
Credit Cards. NZ B&B Vouchers accepted $10 surcharge. Same day restriction.
Nearest Town: Taumarunui 20km

*Waimarino Lodge is a big villa set in a beautiful landscaped garden surrounded by
peaceful rolling farmland. We are at the doorstep of Tongario Forest only 25 min drive
from Mt Ruapehu. The house provides the guests with one Queen bedroom, two twins
and a spacious guest bathroom.Downstairs: dining-room, lounge, television room
with billiard table, outside barbeque area.Local attractions include: hunting, fishing,
rafting, tramping, scenic flights, mountain biking with the famous "Traverse 42",
skiing in the winter and we are 20km from Taumarunui where there is a beautiful golf
course.My husband is a New Zealander and I am Italian. Apart from Italian I speak
French as well as English. I have experience in cooking and I love preparing tasty
dishes for our guests. We offer a variety of breakfast: cooked or continental style
including home made bread, muffins, teas, coffee and of course cappuccino!*
Come and experience our warm hospitality. We look forward to meeting you.
Directions: *Please phone, fax or write.*

Taumarunui

Farmstay
Address: Orangi Road, RD 4, Taumarunui
Name: Gayle and Dave Richardson
Telephone: (07) 896 6035
Fax: (07) 896 6035
Beds: 1 Double, 3 Single
(2 bedrooms)
Bathroom: 1 Family Share
Tariff: B&B (full) Double $65,
Single $35,
Children under 12 half price,
Dinner $20 per person,
Campervans welcome $20 max 4 people,
Backpackers welcome.
Nearest Town: 10 km East of Taumarunui on SH 41.

Welcome to Orangi.
Come and relax in our lovely old homestead, with plenty of room for children, while ensuring quiet and privacy for those without.
Our guestrooms are spacious and comfortable, with electric blankets and comfy duvets. Go trout fishing at the backdoor, or just stroll along the riverbank.
Toby and Jana aged 9 and 10 complete our family, they are well mannered and well behaved children, who enjoy company.
Our outside dog and our cats are very friendly.
We love meeting and entertaining people, and look forward to enjoying your company in our spacious home. We hope you will join us for dinner, for a good country meal, or feel free to just come for bed and breakfast. Our laundry is always available for use.

Members of
**The New Zealand Association
Farm & Home Host Inc.**
maintain the highest standards &
are always delighted to welcome
guests into their homes.

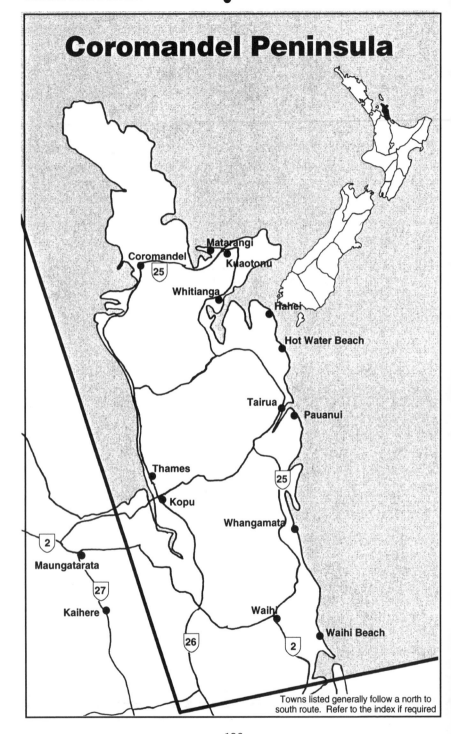

Coromandel Peninsula

Matarangi

Coromandel

25

Kuaotonu

Whitianga

Hahei

Hot Water Beach

Tairua

Pauanui

Thames

Kopu

25

Whangamata

2

Maungatarata

27

Kaihere

Waihi

26

2

Waihi Beach

Towns listed generally follow a north to south route. Refer to the index if required

Thames

Homestay
Address: Please phone
Name: Russell Rutherford
Telephone: (07) 868 7788
Fax: (07) 868 7788
Mobile: (025) 737 993
Email: rrutherford@xtra.co.nz
Beds: 1 Double, 3 Single (2 bedrooms)
Bathroom: 1 Private, 1 Family share
Tariff: B&B (continental) Double $60, Single $35, Children 1/2 price; Dinner $20.
NZ B&B Vouchers accepted
Nearest Town: Thames - 5 mins walk

Glenys and Russell are NZ born and enjoy their comfortable and spacious home overlooking the Firth of Thames. Our interests include, golf, music, gardening, travel and geneology. Our guest accommodation has a private lounge, TV, a selection of books, self service tea and coffee. The garden provides fruit for preserves and breakfast which includes a selection of cereals, muffins, toast, tea and freshly ground coffee. Being an historic goldmining settlement, gold prospecting diggings are of particular interest. Due to its natural beauty the Coromandel has attracted many painters and potters. Their galleries can be visited on a scenic day trip up the coast to Coromandel village, returning back through the beach resorts of Whitianga, Hot Water Beach and Pauanui. The rugged hills and native bush appeal to hikers and nature lovers. Take time to relax in comfort and enjoy Kiwi hospitality. We welcome your visit. Safe off-street parking.

Thames

Farmstay+Self-contained Garden Apartment.
Address: 'Thorold', Kopu, R.D.1, Thames
Name: Helen & Tony Smith
Telephone: (07) 868 8480
Fax: (07) 868 8480
Mobile: 025-941 286
Beds: 1 Queen, 1 Double, 4 Single (4 bedrooms)
Bathroom: 2 Private
Tariff: B&B (continental) Apartment $60pp x 2, $50pp x 4 ($200), Double $120, Single $80, Children $35, Dinner $45 with comp drinks & wine..
NZ B&B Vouchers accepted $40 surcharge
Nearest Town: Thames - 5 Kms

'Thorold' is perfectly situated for visitors to the Coromandel Peninsular - 5 minutes from Thames in a private, peaceful farm setting.
The garden apartment is deluxe, spacious, beautifully appointed and totally private. Two bedrooms - 1 Queen, 1 Twin with bathroom adjoining. Kitchen, sitting room with TV and Billiard table. All rooms open to a large verandah and swimming pool. In our home we have a Double or Twin bedroom with TV and private bathroom.
Only one group of visitors at any one time in apartment or our home.
We have a beef farm at Coromandel and Tony has a Livestock Company based at home and is usually available to enjoy breakfast with our visitors in the dining room.
Our interests include tramping, fishing, building, gardening, trees and forestry. We are 4th generation New Zealanders and can assure you of a memorable stay at Thorold.
Directions: *Please phone.*

Thames Coast
Country Homestay
Address: 29 Eames Crescent, Te Mata Bay, Thames Coast. Please phone for directions.
Name: Helen & Charlie Burgess
Telephone: (07) 868 4754 **Fax**: (07) 868 4757
Mobile: (025) 487 681
Beds: 1 Queen, 1 Double, 2 Single (3 bedrooms)
Bathroom: 1 Guests share + shower room + separate toilet.
Tariff: B&B (full) Double $80, Single $40, Dinner $25.
Nearest Town: Thames 23km, Coromandel 34km

Come and stay with us at Te Mata Bay, any day of the year. You won't be disappointed! Good beds, excellent home cooked meals, great company too! Enjoy the peace, the wonderful sea and mountain views from the balcony which surrounds our large comfortable home. Guests Bedrooms are pleasantly furnished and have sea and mountain views. We have a pianola and pool table for your enjoyment. Also a comfortable lounge with a log fire. Visit our local water garden and square Kauri 15 min drive or Coromandels Driving Creek Railway 35 min away or the famous Hot Water Beach 50 min by car.

Hot bread, croissants, cappucino and fresh perculated coffee along with fresh eggs from our chickens and a large choice of cereals and fruit and offered for breakfast. Complimentary wine with evening meals. Make our day come and stay.
WE ARE A NON SMOKING FAMILY.
Directions: *Please phone for directions.*

Thames
Self-contained Accommodation
Address: 304 Grafton Road, Thames
Name: David & Ferne Tee
Telephone: (07) 868 9971
Fax: (07) 868 3075
Mobile: (025) 220 3780
Beds: 1 Queen, 4 Double, 2 Single (6 bedrooms)
Bathroom: 6 Ensuite
Tariff: B&B (continental) Double $110-$150, Single $90. Visa/Master
Nearest Town: Thames

Grafton cottage is nestled in the foothills of the Coromandel Peninsula overlooking the Historic gold and timber town of Thames.
The tree lined property offers rest and privacy for the romantic weekend away while being central to the many Restaurants, Arts and Crafts centres, Museums and old gold workings. Being just 1 hour from Auckland International Airport, Thames is the ideal base to explore the Peninsula and is away from the hustle and bustle of the city. The Peninsula boasts extensive bush reserves covering rugged mountainous ranges. To the east are world renowned Pacific beaches, while in the west are the calmer waters of the Firth.
Directions: *Turn right at Toyota factory (Bank St) follow to end, turn right into Parawai Road, 4th on left is Grafton Road. Go to the top of road.*

Thames

Farmstay+Self-contained Accom.
Address: 'Wharfedale Farmstay', R.D.1, Thames
Name: Rosemary & Chris Burks
Telephone: (07) 868 8929 **Fax**: (07) 868 8926 **Mobile**: (025) 846 460
Beds: 1 Double, 2 Single (2 bedrooms)
Bathroom: 2 Private
Tariff: B&B (full, special or continental) Double $100-$120, Single $80.
Credit cards accepted.   NZ B&B Vouchers accepted $30-40 surcharge
Nearest Town: Thames. We are situated 8km South East of Thames on S.H. 25A

For 7 years we have enjoyed offering hospitality to guests from around the world and have featured in Air New Zealand "Pacific Way" and Japan's "My Country" magazines.

We cordially invite you to share our idyllic lifestyle set in 9 acres of paddocks and gardens surrounded by lovely native bush.

Meander across the lawn to the riverwalk, picking perhaps peaches or citrus fruits and enjoy in total privacy natures swimming pools whilst kingfisher and rosella swoop overhead.

Our gardens reflect our interests in old roses, no dig organic cultivation. We enjoy wholefoods and home produced meat. Our goat herd allows us to share their lives and milk.

Husband practices medicine and son Christopher has recently returned from university.

We are 75 minutes from Auckland and 10 minutes from Thames. Close proximity to beautiful Coromandel beaches. Wharfedale offers double room or self-contained flat both with private bathrooms.

Cosy log fires and electric blankets in winter and cool shade in summer.

We have no children or indoor animals.

We are non-smoking.

We look forward to meeting you.

Thames

Homestay
Address: Brunton House, 210 Parawai Rd,
Thames
Name: Albert & Yvonne Sturgess
Telephone: (07) 868 5160 **Fax**: (07) 868 5160
Mobile: (025) 832 116
Beds: 1 Queen, 1 Double, 1 Single (2 bedrooms)
Bathroom: 1 Guests share

Tariff: B&B (full) Double $85, Single $50, Dinner $25pp by prior arrangement.
NZ B&B Vouchers accepted $15 surcharge
Nearest Town: Thames 1 mile

We invite you to share the grace and charm of our lovely Victorian home. Built in 1869 it is spacious but also homely, comfortable and smoke-free.
In summer excellent indoor outdoor living, BBQ area, tennis court and swimming pool make this a great place to relax.
In winter with fires and good heating, comfortable beds with electric blankets and fluffy quilts our home is cosy and warm.
Self service tea and coffee always available.
In the evening enjoy the use of our billiard table, read and relax with a book from our comprehensive library, watch TV or sit and chat in the comfortable lounge.
Our interests include travel, steamtrains, embroidery, square dancing, reading, gardening. We have a cat and a dog.
Thames is the gateway to the Coromandel Peninsula for you to explore and enjoy the whole of the Coromandel.
Directions: *Opposite Toyota turn into Banks St, turn right into Parawai Rd. After Brunton Cres look for us on the left.*

Thames

Homestay
Address: 'Huia Lodge',
589 Kauaeranga Valley Rd,
R.D.2, Thames.
Name: Val & Steve Barnes.
Telephone: (07) 868 6557
Fax: (07) 868 6557
Beds: 2 Queen, 1 Single (3 bedrooms).
Bathroom: 2 Ensuite.
Tariff: B&B (full) Double $70, Single $35, Children $15,
Dinner $15 - by arrangement. Credit cards. NZ B&B Vouchers accepted.
Nearest Town: Thames 10 mins, Auckland City 1 hr 40 mins.

Stay with us and enjoy the peace and tranquillity of Kauaeranga Valley, just 10 minutes from the historic town of Thames. Our upstairs unit comprises a double room with an ensuite and a balcony overlooking a garden courtyard. The downstairs unit has a double and single room which share an ensuite. It also enjoys garden views. Both units have tea and coffee facilities. We grow our own fruit and vegetables and enjoy the rural lifestyle with 2 cats on our 4 acre property. We're in our early 50's and have a keen interest in meeting travellers. We'll be happy to suggest outings to suit your interests. These could include a gentle bushwalk in the Valley to examine our native bush and relics of past Kauri logging days, a more energetic tramp over one of the well developed routes or a day out to enjoy the major tourist attractions on the Peninsula.
Directions: *Follow the Kauaeranga Valley sign opposite the BP Petrol Station on the corner of Main Road and Banks Street at the south end of Thames. You'll find our Huia Lodge sign 8 km from the petrol station.*

200

Thames
Country Stay+Self-contained Ac
Address: "Kauaeranga Country",
446 Kauaeranga Valley Rd, Pakaraka, Thames
Name: Lyn and Dave Lee
Telephone: (07) 868 6895 **Fax**: (07) 868 6895
Beds: 1 Queen, 2 Single (2 bedrooms)
Bathroom: 1 Private

Tariff: B&B (continental) Double $90, Single $50, Children $20 by arrangement.
Credit cards. NZ B&B Vouchers accepted May to September
Nearest Town: Thames 6 kms

Our country-stay offers you:
- *A spacious private guest wing.*
- *Peaceful surroundings on the banks of a stream.*
- *Close proximity to bush walks and Dept. of Conservation.*
- *Kayaks for fun in the water.*
- *Safe private swimming in Stoney bottomed stream.*
- *Closeness to beautiful Coromandel beaches.*
- *Only one group of guests at a time.*

Dave and I are a Kiwi couple who have lived most of our lives in Thames, and enjoy gardening, horse riding and local history. Dave has a forge where he shoes our horses and is more than happy to give you a "demo". Arrive as strangers and leave as friends.

Thames
Homestay
Address: 'Mountain Top Bed & Breakfast',
452 Kauaeranga Valley Rd, R.D.2, Thames
Name: Elizabeth McCracken & Allan Berry
Telephone: (07) 868 9662 **Fax**: (07) 868 9662
Beds: 1 Double, 2 Single (2 bedrooms)
Bathroom: 1 Guest share
Tariff: B&B (full) Double $80, Single $45, Children discounted, Dinner $20-$25.
Credit cards. NZ B&B Vouchers accepted between 1 February - 24 December.
Nearest Town: 7km east of Thames

Allan and I grow mandarins, olives and raise coloured sheep on a small organic farm. Our house and dining room overlook river and ranges. The guest wing comprising two bedrooms, decks overlooking the river, shared bathroom, lounge with fridge, TV and extensive library, is well suited to four or spacious for two.
Our families are grown up, leaving us time to entertain and cook for guests from home grown vegetables and lamb.
Coromandel Forest Park, with superb walking tracks, is 15 minutes away. From home we can arrange walks over neighbouring farmland through bush or swimming in forest pools.
In our spare time we garden, raise native trees, teach our grandchildren about the forest, go yachting or entertain our friends here on the lawn, with our Jack Russell Bob and cat Inehitabel. We have both enjoyed meeting people on our travels overseas. Come and let us look after you.

Totara, Thames

Homestay
Address: "Cotswold Cottage"
Maramarahi Road, Totara, Thames
Name: Heather & Bruce Phillips
Telephone: (07) 868 6306 **Fax**: (07) 868-6306
Beds: 2 Double, 1 Twin (3 bedrooms)
Bathroom: 3 Ensuite
Tariff: B&B (special) Double $75-95, Single $50. Dinner (3 course) $35 pp,
Cooked breakfast $5pp, Children $12. Visa, Mastercard.
NZ B&B Vouchers accepted $25 surcharge
Nearest Town: Thames 3km

*"Gracious, comfortable, quiet, genuine old world Kiwi hospitality" say guests at
'Costwold Cottage'. The old villa was shifted from Epsom in Auckland in 1990 and
resited at Totara, overlooking Thames, the Kauaeranga river and valley, where it was
restored and operated as a Restaurant for four years.*

*A separate guest wing was added in 1995, three well appointed rooms to catch the
morning sun and views. A private entrance enables you to come and go as you please.
The lounge, conservatory and terrace offer a choice of places to read, write or relax. TV
& Sky are available. Breakfast is served in the dining / lounge. Fresh fruit salad,
home-made bread, muffins, breakfast bakes, fruit juices, cereals or the more traditional NZ cooked.*

*Evening meals are available on request or being only 5 minutes from Thames to an
assortment of eating houses. Your hosts Heather and Bruce will make you most
welcome.*

Coromandel

Coromandel Homestay
Address: 74, Kowhai Drive,
Te Kouma Bay, Coromandel
Name: Hilary & Vic Matthews
Telephone: (07) 866 8046
Fax: (07) 866 8046
Beds: 2 Double, 1 Single (2 bedrooms)
Bathroom: 1 Ensuite, 1 Private
Tariff: B&B (continental) Double $80, Single $50,
Dinner with wine by prior arrangement $30.
Credit cards NZ B&B Vouchers accepted $15 surcharge.

Nearest Town: Coromandel 11km, Thames 60km, Auckland 2.5 hours. Ferry
service to Auckland. On most days. Docks in Te Kouma Bay.
Transfers by prior arrangement.

*Our modern pole house is situated 740 metres from a safe, sandy beach on the southern
side of the Coromandel Harbour. We have a bush setting and beautiful views. Vic is
a professional furniture designer and maker. Our home is full of beautiful hand made
furniture. Hilary weaves, spins and enjoys gardening and wood turning. We travel
widely and have many interests. We feel that due to open stairs and balconies, the house
is unsuitable for toddlers. We have a pet cat and a smoke free home. Coromandel area
offers beaches, swimming, fishing and walking.*
Directions: *Travel north from Thames (SH 25) for about 60 minutes, down a steep
hill to Coromandel Harbour, turn very sharply left into Te Kouma Road. Drive around
the Harbour's edge, past a big boat ramp for about 3km. Turn left into, Kowhai Drive.
Our house is up the steep hill. There is a large wooden sign on the right giving our
name.*

Coromandel

Homestay/Farmstay
Address: 'Jacaranda' Lodge, 3195 Tiki Rd,
Coromandel
Name: Gary & Gayle Bowler
Telephone: (07) 866 8002 **Fax**: (07) 866 8002
Beds: 3 Queen, 1 Double, 1 Twin (5 Bedrooms)
Bathroom: 2 Ensuite, 2 Guests share
Tariff: B&B (continental) Double $75-$110, Single $45-$60, Dinner $25,
Credit Cards. NZ B&B Vouchers accepted $25 surcharge for ensuites
Nearest Town: Coromandel 3km, Thames 50km, Auckland 2 1/2 hours.
Auckland ferry pick up passes gate.

*Welcome to Jacaranda. A warm, relaxing and spacious home with a special ambience,
enhanced by family antiques, paintings, crafts and needle work. Set on 6 acres of
peaceful farmland, our home features beautifully landscaped gardens. Enjoy our
comfortable large bedrooms and gracious lounge, where you can play the piano, listen
to music or read by the fire. We have ample verandahs, separate TV lounge, and
kitchen facilities for guests. Fortunate enough to have travelled extensively ourselves,
we will be delighted to help you plan your stay in order to take advantage of the
numerous local attractions, including fishing trips. Jacaranda is an excellent base for
your Coromandel holiday. Whenever possible breakfast is served outside overlooking
the rose garden. Home-made bread or muffins are a feature of our special continental
breakfasts as are organically grown vegetables of our dinners. Perfect for small group
bookings. Negotiable off season rates.*
Directions: *On Pacific Coast Highway, (SH25). We look forward to meeting you.*

Coromandel

Guest House
Address: "Karamana",
84 Whangapoua Road,
Coromandel
Name: Richard and Virginia Endean
Telephone: 07-866 7138 **Fax**: 07-866 7477
Mobile: 025-735 707
Email: 10040.707@compuserve.com
Beds: 1 King, 1 Queen, 1 Double, 2 Single (4 bedrooms)
Bathroom: 4 Ensuites
Tariff: B&B (continental) Double $110, single $85, Dinner from $25.
Not suitable for children. Visa, Mastercard
Nearest Town: Coromandel 2km.

*Karamana Homestead, built in 1872, is one of the oldest colonial buildings in Coromandel.
As such the homestead offers guests a unique experience with the opportunity to relax in this
genuinely colonial environment. The house itself is furnished throughout in authentic
Victorian era antiques, and is situated in a quiet and sheltered rural valley near Coromandel
town. Close by are the Coromandel Ranges and harbour and many scenic and tourist
attractions including Driving Creek Railway, craft trails and bush walks. Our guests are
ensured of a high standard of cuisine if required, and our speciality is to ensure that guests
enjoy a total "Coromandel" experience. We also offer fishing and scenic tours in our runabout
and bush walking for the more energetic guests. We offer guests silver service afternoon tea on
arrival, Happy Hour 6pm - 7pm and continental breakfast. Cooked breakfasts also available.*
Directions: *Coast Road from Thames to Coromandel, turn right onto Whangapoua Road
(SH25), go 1 km to right angle bend where you will find Karamana,*

Coromandel
Homestay Bed & Breakfast - "Huntington Lodge"
Address: SH 25. 1745 Tiki Road,
Coromandel
Name: Judy and Bill
Telephone: (07) 866 7499
Fax: (07) 866 7499
Beds: 1 King, 1 Queen, 1 Single (2 bedrooms)
Bathroom: 1 Guests share
Tariff: B&B (continental) Double $70, Single $50, Dinner $30,
Children negotiable. Full breakfast $5 pp extra.
NZ B&B Vouchers accepted $5 surcharge
Nearest Town: Coromandel 1 1/2 km north. 55 km Thames,
Auckland 2 1/2 hours. Ferry pick up passes gate.

We invite you to share our recently renovated comfortable home on 1 1/2 acres of rural land with views of surrounding farm land and bush clad hills.
The bedrooms are warm and inviting, one with a king-size and single bed plus adjoining toilet.
A long shady verandah provides an opportunity to just sit a while or enjoy breakfast (which includes hot, home-made bread) outdoors.
Barbecue available for guests' uses. Dinner is available (by arrangement) with three courses and includes New Zealand wines, home grown produce, our own lamb and local seafood. Guests have the opportunity to talk to our sheep (we have a few), make acquaintance with George our cat, explore the Coromandel Peninsula with is varied tourist attractions, beautiful beaches or just let us pamper you.
We are available by prior arrangement to meet ferry, bus or plane.
Directions: *Easy to find on SH 25 1.5 km south of Coromandel town.*

Coromandel
Self Contained Accommodation B&B
Address: "Country Touch", 39
Whangapoua Road, Coromandel
Name: Colleen and Geoff Innis
Telephone: (07) 866 8310 **Mobile**: (025) 971 196
Beds: 1 Double, 1 Single (2 bedrooms)
Bathroom: 2 Ensuites
Tariff: B&B (full, continental) Double $65, Single $40,
Children negotiable.
NZ B&B Vouchers accepted 1st May - 1st October
Nearest Town: Coromandel 0.5 km

Geoff and I are a retired couple who enjoy meeting people to share local knowledge and invite you to a restful holiday in a country setting of 4 acres with a modern home. Newly established trees and gardens, roses becoming a speciality. you have the independence of two units (sleep 2-4 people) situated slightly apart from our home. One double. One twin with disabled ensuite access, both with fold out sofas, TV, fridge, tea and coffee making facilities. Your choice of continental or cooked breakfast. You have a country touch feeling with just a 10 minute stroll to Coromandel township where you can enjoy our local arts and crafts, restaurants and shops. We can arrange chartered tours or fishing trips. Train rides or anything else you feel you would enjoy.
Directions: *Cost Road from Thames to Coromandel, turn right on Whangapoua Rd, State Highway 25, approximately 300 metres first on left.*

Matarangi Beach
Homestay
Address: 'Pinekatz', 108 Matarangi Drive,
Matarangi Beach, R.D.2, Whitianga
Name: Glenys & Trevor Lewis
Telephone: (07) 866 2103 **Fax**: (07) 866 2103
Email: pinekatz@voyager.co.nz
Beds: 4 Single (2 bedrooms)
Bathroom: 1 Guest share
Tariff: B&B (full) Double $75, Single $45, Dinner $20.
Credit Cards (Visa/MC) NZ B&B Vouchers accepted
Nearest Town: Coromandel 24km, Whitianga 24km

We invite you to share with us the unique unspoilt natural beauty and peaceful tranquillity that is Matarangi Beach. A sun and sea paradise providing an escape from the rigours of today's busy lifestyles. Between its dazzling 5km long ocean beach on one side and the calm sheltered Whangapoua Harbour on the other lies a splendid variety of activities to satisfy all ages. Activities include swimming, diving, snorkelling, boating/fishing (trips by arrangement), tennis, beach and bush walks and a 9 hole golf course designed by Bob Charles (further 9 holes under development). Our family of 4 adults have been replaced by 3 cats who own us. The guest bedrooms are upstairs and are warm and inviting, served by their own bathroom. We look forward to the pleasure of your company and ensuring your stay is a memorable one.
Directions: *24km north of Whitianga or 24km east of Coromandel (1km off SH25).*

Kuaotunu
Bed & Breakfast
Address: The Kaeppeli's, Grays Ave,
Kuaotunu, R.D.2, Whitianga
Name: The Kaeppeli's. Jill and Robert Kaeppeli
Telephone: (07) 866 2445 **Mobile**: (025) 287 3598
Beds: 2 comfortable Kingsize, 4 Single,
1 cot, 1 childs bed
(4 Bedrooms)

Bathroom: 2 Ensuties, 1 Guests share
Tariff: B&B (full) Double $70-$120, Single $43-$70, Children 6-12yrs half price,
Dinner by arrangement $25 NZ B&B Vouchers accepted $10-$50 Surcharge
Nearest Town: 17km north of Whitianga on SH25

We are a Swiss/Kiwi family who have had restaurants in Switzerland for years. We now enjoy sharing with our guests, the peace and tranquillity of Kuaotunu, in our newly built home and garden "suite", on our 5 1/2 hectare property, with its tremendous views out over the bay.
Evening meals by arrangement. Robert is an excellent Swiss Chef who takes pride in preparing our guests meals, using home produce.
Meals can be enjoyed in the guests dining-room or in the garden enjoying the views. Children are welcome and can make acquaintance with our daughter and animals. Kuaotunu has clean, safe, white sandy beaches, is also handy to many other beautiful spots and an ideal starting point for exploring other parts of Coromandel Peninsula or for bush walks, fishing, horse trekking, water-sports, golf, tennis, bike-safaris or just relaxing.
Look forward to welcoming you at "The Kaeppeli's".

205

Kuaotunu

Homestay
Address: "Blue Penguin",
11 Cuvier Crescent, Kuaotunu,
RD 2, Whitianga
Name: Glenda Mawhinney and Barb Meredith
Telephone: (07) 866 2222
Freephone (0800) Penguin
Fax: (07) 866 0228
Email: blue.penguin@xtra.co.nz
Beds: 1 Queen, 2 Double, 2 Single (2 bedrooms)
Bathroom: 1 Guests share
Tariff: B&B (continental) $5 surcharge for full B&B.
Main Guestroom $75 (whether 1 or 2 people), Single $35, Dinner $20, Children
$25. Credit Cards Visa/Mastercard/Bankcard. NZ B&B Vouchers accepted
Nearest Town: From Whitianga, 17km north on State Highway 25

We can offer you the upper level of our architecturally designed home that takes good advantage of spectacular views out to the Mercury Islands and Great Barrier. With just two minutes down to the white, sandy beach, this is a magic spot. A rimu staircase leads you upstairs, the master (or mistress) guest room has a queen sized bed, window seats and a small balcony. A modern bathroom is nestled between this and a large second bedroom which contains two double and two single beds, TV and stereo and is ideal for your children (complete with rainbow on the ceiling and plenty of toys and games) or for your travelling companions. We are two professional women (ex wine industry and theatre nursing) and we also run a Private Beach House Rental business. We enjoy the lifestyle with our Jack Russell, Poodle and Retriever who love to take walks. WELCOME!
Directions: *Phone 0800 Penguin or (07) 866-2222*

Kuaotunu

Homestay
Address: Kuaotunu Bay Lodge
S.H. 25, Kuaotunu, RD 2, Whitianga
Name: Bill and Lorraine Muir
Telephone: (07) 866 4396
Fax: (07) 866 4396
Beds: 2 Queen, 2 Single (3 bedrooms)
Bathroom: 2 Ensuite, 1 Private.
Tariff: (B&B)Double $130-$150, Single $95,
Dinner $35. Credit Cards accepted.
Nearest Town: Whitianga18km South.

Situated on the coast on S.H. 25, 18 km north of Whitianga, our new home has been purpose built for guests, with ensuites, under floor heating and private decks.
Enjoy breakfast in our sunny conservatory or a private dinner on your deck, listening to the waves and watching the sun set over Moehau mountain. The very safe beach is just a short walk through the garden. Ideal for all sea activities, fishing by arrangement or bring your own boat. Close to Matarangi airfield and golf course, a car will pick you up from the airfield - a short flight from Auckland. Whitianga with its restaurants and tourist activities is just a 20 min drive. Close to bush walks, bike safaris and local art and craft. We also have a self contained unit suitable for four people.
Our 10 acre property has a small bush reserve, hens sheep and a friendly dog.

Whitianga - Mercury Bay
Bed & Breakfast
Address: 'Cosy Cat Cottage',
41 South Highway, Whitianga
Name: Gordon Pearce
Telephone: (07) 866 4488
Fax: (07) 866 4488
Beds: 2 Queen, 1 Double, 1 Single
(3 bedrooms/Queens with ensuites)
Bathroom: 2 Ensuite, 1 Private
Tariff: B&B (special) Double $80-$90, Single $50-$60,
Credit cards (Visa/MC). NZ B&B Vouchers accepted $20 Surcharge
Nearest Town: Whitianga 1 km south of Post Office

Welcome to our picturesque two storied cottage, filled with feline memorabilia. Relax with complimentary tea or coffee any time, served on the verandah, in the garden or in the guest lounge which has a library, TV and board games for your use.
Enjoy a good night's rest in comfortable beds. Choose a variety of treats from our breakfast menu - fresh fruit salad, semi-roasted muesli, honey from our own bees, and hot dishes prepared the way you like them. Special diets catered for.
You will probably like to meet our two playful Tonkinese cats or just be amused by the unique feline ambience.
Whitianga enjoys a pleasant climate and relaxed way of life, with magnificent scenery and safe sandy beaches. Our excellent restaurants and other amenities make it an ideal base for your Coromandel Peninsula exploration.
Friendly, helpful service is assured at Cosy Cat Cottage. See you soon!
Home Page: http://nz.com/webnz/bbnz/cosycat.htm.

Whitianga
Homestay
Address: 119 Albert St., Whitianga
Name: Anne's Haven. Anne and Bob
Telephone: (07) 866 5550
Beds: 1 Double, 2 Single (2 bedrooms)
Bathroom: 1 Family share
Tariff: B&B (full) Double $65, Single $35,
Children $20, Dinner $20.
NZ B&B Vouchers accepted $5 surcharge
Nearest Town: Whitianga 400m

A warm welcome awaits you along with a cup of tea or coffee. Relax in our modern spacious home and enjoy the cottage garden. We are ordinary Kiwis who like sharing our home with you. Bob enjoys making and sailing model boats and flying model planes. Anne makes pottery, gardens, line dances and knits. We are in our early 50's. The shower, toilet and bathroom are each separate rooms for easy access. After a good nights sleep in comfortable beds with electric blankets you can enjoy a light and healthy breakfast of fruit and muesli or good hearty bacon and eggs, or both, followed by toast and homemade jams. We are 400 metres from the shopping centre and restaurants, six beautiful beaches within strolling distance, golf course and bush walks nearby. One night or one week let us make your stay a memorable one. Our courtesy car will meet you from the bus or plane.

Whitianga

Homestay
Address: Whitianga Bed & Breakfast
12 Cook Drive, Whitianga
Name: Pat and Bill Carse
Telephone: (07) 866 5547
Fax: (07) 866 5547
Mobile: (025) 383 379
Email: bcarse@ihug.co.nz
Beds: 1 Double, 2 Single (2 bedrooms)
Bathroom: 2 Family share
Tariff: B&B (full) Double $60, Single $45. Credit cards
NZ B&B Vouchers accepted
Nearest Town: Whitianga 500m

We are a retired couple originally from Scotland and have enjoyed home hosting for the past 13 years. Our comfortable modern home is away from busy main street traffic. Guests share the family lounge / TV room. Tea or coffee is available at any time. During the colder months our home is warm throughout. Free pick up from bus station or airfield. We offer a friendly homely atmosphere and a relaxed base from which to explore the many unspoiled features of Mercury Bay. We are always ready to supply local information to make your stay more interesting. Bill is retired from a career in agricultural research. Pat is a legal secretary, and is a volunteer ambulance officer.
Home Page: www.geocities.com/Heartland/Meadows/5845/index.html

Whitianga

Bed & Breakfast
Address: Camellia Lodge - South Highway,
R.D.1 Whitianga
Name: John & Pat Lilley
Telephone: (07) 866 2253
Fax: (07) 866 2253
Mobile: 021-662 538
Beds: 1 Queen, 2 Twin,
2 Double (4 bedrooms)
Bathroom: 2 Ensuite, 2 Guests share
Tariff: B&B (full) Double $80/$95, Single $65,
Children under 12 half price, under 5 free, Dinner $25.
Credit cards. NZ B&B Vouchers accepted sucharge $20
Nearest Town: Whitianga 4km south of Whitianga SH 25

Kia ora. Welcome to our friendly home, surrounded by 73 camellia bushes. Our home is nestled at the rear of a spacious parklike garden, which includes kauri, rimu, totara trees, also we offer for your enjoyment the use of a spa, swimming pool and lots of lovely gardens to relax in.
You may like to have a round of golf or a scenic flight. We would be glad to arrange this for you. You would normally be woken up to the tune of the bellbirds singing in the trees, then you settle into a hearty breakfast which will set you up for the day. We are situated approx 4km south of Whitianga in a quiet rural area, but not to far a bushwalk, swimming, fishing or any of the lovely attraction Whitianga has to offer. We can assure you of a warm friendly welcome and a comfortable stay.
Homepage: http://mercurybay.co.nz.camellia.html

Whitianga

Bed & Breakfast
Address: 252 Cook Drive, Whitianga
Name: Barbara & Trevor Bennett
Telephone: (07) 866 5464
Fax: (07) 866 0446
Beds: 1 Double, 2 Single (1 bedroom)
Bathroom: 1 Private (shared with laundry)
Tariff: B&B (full) Double $70-80, Single $35, Twin $60-70,
Children half price. (Flat: 1 bedroom - 1 double & 2 single beds, own bathroom,
Upstairs: twin bedroom family share bathroom).   NZ B&B Vouchers accepted
Nearest Town: Whitianga 2km.

Whitianga
Bed & Breakfast

Trevor and Barbara welcome you to our home in the holiday mecca of Whitianga situated in semi-tropical Mercury Bay, centrally placed for visiting many Coromandel tourist spots including boating, sightseeing, dolphin watching, fishing, horseriding, tramping and beautiful beaches. We are semi-retired and recently moved to Whitianga because we like it so much. We enjoy meeting people, fishing, swimming, Trevor operates a Coast Guard receiving station and Barbara has lots of hobbies including golf. In the downstairs accommodation you can relax and enjoy TV after a busy day sightseeing or wander 3 minutes to the beach for a refreshing swim or to catch a glimpse of the birds in the bird sanctuary. We have a cat and a dog. As Kiwi hosts we strive to make you welcome and your stay with us a highlight of your holiday. Your satisfaction is our pleasure. No smoking.

Whitianga

Homestay + B&B
Address: Corner Golf Road & State Highway 25,
Whitianga
Name: "A Hi-Way Haven" Joan & Nevin Paton
Telephone: (07) 866 2427
Fax: (07) 866 2424
Beds: 1 Double, 2 Single, 1 Queen,
& 1 large Bedsitting room King,
with Quadraplegic ensuite (4 rooms)
Bathroom: 1 Ensuite, 1 Guests share. Bedsitting King: Quadraplegic ensuite
Tariff: B&B (full,continental) Double & Queen $70, Single $40,
King with quadraplegic ensuite $80. Children under 12 half price,
Credit Cards. NZ B&B Vouchers accepted
Nearest Town: Whitianga (3.2km south of Whitianga)

Looking for peaceful, quiet, comfortable, friendly, homely and affordable accommodation, then we are your answer. We are situated approximately
3.2 km from the beautiful town of Whitianga. A hearty cooked breakfast will keep you going all day. An 18 hole golf course where hire clubs are available set amidst parklike surroundings is adjacent. Only a three minute drive to Whitianga township with many excellent restaurants and your hosts or the Information Centre will be only too happy to arrange all your holiday wishes, which have to be seen to be believed.
Guests own lounge with TV is available as is tea / coffee making facilities and purified cold drinking water. Plenty off street parking and a courtesty car available for meeting buses, planes etc.
We have a friendly dog and cat. We at 'Our World' Hi-Way Haven know that you will come as a visitor and depart as a friend.

Whitianga

Homestay
Address: 48 Centennial Drive,
Whitianga
Name: the Peachey's"
Telephone: (07) 866 5290
Fax: (07) 866 5290
 Mobile: (025) 371 068
Beds: 1 King, 1 Double, 2 Single (2 bedrooms)
Bathroom: 1 Private, 1 Ensuite
Tariff: B&B (Special) King $120, Double $85, Single $60, Dinner $25pp,
Credit Cards Visa, Amex
Nearest Town: Whitianga 4km

Friendly hosts, modern home, bush and sea views. Quiet Location.
Staying with Dale and Yvonne, local identities for over forty years will ensure your time spent in Mercury Bay will be an interesting and memorable experience.
An evening meal can be arranged (seafood if available). Dale enjoys diving and fishing so its a perfect reason for having the day off.
The Peachey's has one double room with a balcony overlooking native bush, with a private bathroom and one twin or king size upstairs with an ensuite. Tea making and laundry available. (Smoke free indoors.)
Dale and Yvonne's home nestles up to a bush reserve, just 4 km north of Whitianga Centre, has a panoramic view overlooking Mercury Bay and Buffalo Beach - just a five minute walk away. Muffin the cat enjoys meeting our guests too.
Stay several nights and discover the magic of the Coromandel Peninsula.

Whitianga - Mercury Bay

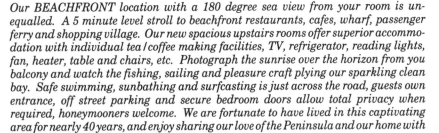

Bed & Breakfast
Address: The Beach House,
38 Buffalo Beach Road, PO Box 162,
Whitianga
Name: Helen & Allan Watson
Telephone: (07) 866 5647 **Fax**: (07) 866 5647
Mobile: (025) 284 7240 or (025) 834 766
Email: swatson@ww.co.nz
Beds: 2 King/Queen, 5 Single (3 bedrooms)
Bathroom: 2 Ensuite, 1 Private
Tariff: B&B (special) Double $70-$150, Single $50-$120. Seasonal rates.
Credit Cards (VISA/MC).
Nearest Town: Whitianga 1km

Our BEACHFRONT location with a 180 degree sea view from your room is un-equalled. A 5 minute level stroll to beachfront restaurants, cafes, wharf, passenger ferry and shopping village. Our new spacious upstairs rooms offer superior accommodation with individual tea / coffee making facilities, TV, refrigerator, reading lights, fan, heater, table and chairs, etc. Photograph the sunrise over the horizon from you balcony and watch the fishing, sailing and pleasure craft plying our sparkling clean bay. Safe swimming, sunbathing and surfcasting is just across the road, guests own entrance, off street parking and secure bedroom doors allow total privacy when required, honeymooners welcome. We are fortunate to have lived in this captivating area for nearly 40 years, and enjoy sharing our love of the Peninsula and our home with our guests.
Courtesy transport to local bus / airfield. Smoke free indoors.

Whitianga

Bed & Breakfast
Address: "Raven-Owl House",
4 Harbour Lights Terrace, RD 2, Whitianga
Name: Rosemary & Jim Grant
Telephone: (07) 866 2957
Fax: (07) 866 2957
Beds: 1 Queen, 2 Single (2 bedrooms)
Bathroom: 1 Guests share + extra toilet
Tariff: B&B (full) Queen $90, Twin $85 , Single $50,
Credit Cards (VISA/MC).NZ B&B Vouchers accepted $10 surcharge
Nearest Town: 5km north of Whitianga town centre

If you are looking for accommodation which conjures up pictures of magical sea and mountain views by day, harbour lights by night, peaceful location, comfortable beds, tasteful breakfast and friendly hospitality then Raven-Owl House would be the ideal place for you to stay.

One guest room has a deck overlooking the Bay and offers the unique comfort of a queen 'Dreambed'. The twin room also has comfortable beds, rural views and doors opening to the garden. Tea and coffee facilities are available.

A full breakfast includes fresh fruit salad and can be served outside (weather permitting). Rosemary and Jim's interests include building, healing modalities, organic gardening and walking. Together with Cassia (Burmese cat) and Katey (King Charles spaniel) we aim to make your stay at our comfortable, smoke free home a memorable experience. Close to beaches and 5 mins drive to town centre.

Whitianga

B&B (homestay)
Address: LynNZ Inn B&B and Cybercafe
25 Arthur Street, Whitianga 2856
Name: "PJ " & "DK" Lynn
Telephone: (07) 866 2880
Mobile: (025) 275 1538
Email: LynNZInn@dk.co.nz
Beds: 1 Private 2 bedroom suite with bath (perfect for families).
1 Queen with pull out sofabed. 1 Double. (2 Bedrooms)
Bathroom: 1 Guests share (one shared solar heated bath in private wing w/spa tub & shower)
Tariff: B&B (special) Queen $ 75, Double $70, Single $60/65
Triple/Quad $20 pp extra, Dinner $20, Children under 12 $10.
Credit Cards: Visa/Mastercard
Nearest Town: Whitianga town centre a short 1.3km north

Our home, vintage 1930s, is newly renovated yet still retains its "old world" charm with polished wood floors and sliding doors with flyscreens throughout. Located one block from the estuary, we have a beautiful view of the surrounding mountains. Upon arrival, relax on our deck to watch a spectacular sunset and listen to our varied CD collection. We also provide a lounge with a 31" screen TV and 300+ videos. PJ's breakfast includes cappuccino, homemade yoghurt, muffins and bread as well as freshly squeezed juices and waffles.. DK's Cybercafe offers complimentary internet access during your stay. We have 3 bicycles, one a racing tandem, which you may use to explore the varied attractions of Mercury Bay. Visit the area's beaches (including the world-renowned Hot Water Beach), hiking trails, Kiwi conservation block, and town centre shops as well as the local potters, knitters and other artisans. Our friendly "Black Magic" Lab answers to "Maggie".

Directions: *Before Whitianga on S/H 25, turn right on Arthur St, cross Sarah Ave.*
Home Page: http://www.wave.co.nz/pages/dklynn/BnB.html

Whitianga

Bed & Breakfast
Address: The White House, 129 Albert Street, Whitianga
Name: Murray and Jessie Thompson
Telephone: (07) 866 5116 **Fax**: (07) 866 5116
Mobile: (025) 341 029
Beds: 1 King/2 Single, 2 Queen, 2 Single (3 bedrooms)
Guest lounge with TV, tea/coffee making facilities.
Bathroom: 1 Ensuite, 1 Guests share
Tariff: B&B (special) Room with Ensuite Double $110/Single $80,
 Shared bathroom Double $100/Single $70,
Credit cards (VISA/MC) NZ B&B Vouchers accepted Surcharge $30.
Nearest Town: Whitianga - 500 metres.

When only the best will do
We are committed to looking after guests in our purpose built home which overlooks the inner harbour where swimming is available at the high tide. On the beach, less than 100 metres away, are a large range of native and migratory seabirds.
Murray has a detailed knowledge of the attractions of the whole area and his particular hobby is gathering food from the sea and preparing it for the table. He has a background in Education, School Consultancy, Life Education Trust and Rotary Club. Jessie is a nurse and has been involved in Hospital Management, Women's Service clubs, Bridge, and Travel.
We believe that Mercury Bay is a special place and has something to offer all visitors. We make a promise that all our guests will enjoy their stay in Whitianga.

Hahei

Bed & Breakfast with Restaurant
Address: THE CHURCH, 87 Beach Road, Hahei
Name: Karen Blair & Richard Agnew
Telephone: (07) 866 3533
Fax: (07) 866 3055
Mobile: 025-596 877
Beds: 7 Queen (7 bedrooms)
Bathroom: 7 Ensuite
Tariff: B&B (full) Double $95-$120,

Single $70, Children by arrangement. Dinner according to menu, Major Credit Cards.
Nearest Town: Whitianga 38km, Tairua 36km

First on the right, entering Hahei, The Church, built in 1913 has been moved and rebuilt to provide a character dining room for our delicious breakfasts and evening meals. Set in native bush and gardens we can accommodate 14 people in cosy wooden cottages, and rooms, all with ensuites, tea and coffee making facilities and fridges. Much of our food is produced on site and our interests include cooking, gardening, fishing, diving and socialising. We emphasise a relaxed homely atmosphere and live here with our 8 year old daughter and dog. Enjoy our warm hospitality, and the beauty of Hahei, Cathedral Cove and Hot Water Beach.   Children accommodated by arrangement. Smoking outside only. Pets are unable to be accommodated.
Directions: *Please telephone for directions.*

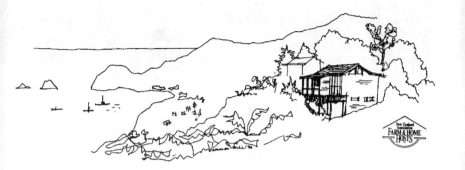

Hahei Beach, Whitianga

Homestay
Address: 'Spellbound Homestay/Bed & Breakfast', 77 Grange Road,
Hahei Beach, R.D.1, Whitianga
Name: Barbara & Alan Lucas
Telephone: (07) 866 3543 **Fax**: (07) 866 3003
Mobile: (025) 720 407
Beds: 3 Queen, 1 Super King/2 Single (4 bedrooms)
Bathroom: 3 Ensuite, 1 Private
Tariff: B&B (Special continental) Double $100-$125, Single $60-$85, Dinner $25,
Children negotiable. Credit cards (VISA/MC/Eftpos.
NZ B&B Vouchers accepted $30-$50 surcharge all year.
Nearest Town: Tairua 36 km, Whitianga 38 km

*Barbara and I live overlooking the sea with panoramic views from the Alderman
Islands to the Mercury Islands.*

*We are five minutes from Hahei Beach and are on the road to Cathedral Cove and its
beaches, a must when visiting this area. Hot Water Beach is just a short distance away
where you can enjoy a warm soak at any time of the year.*

*The area offers bush walks, surf beaches, fishing and spectacular views for photogra-
phy. "The Paradise Coast".*

*Our rooms have sea views with ensuites/private bathrooms, all beds have electric
blankets and insect screens are fitted to most windows.*

We have tea/coffee making facilities and a refrigerator for the use of all guests.

*We can assure you of excellent meals. My wife is a first class cook, at least, I think so.
Weather permitting, our generous continental breakfast is served on our front deck.
We thank you for not smoking in the house. We have no animals.*

*Please give us a telephone call when you wish to come and we can promise you a most
enjoyable stay.*

Directions: *Turn off at Whenuakite (Highway 25). Grange Road is on left by Hahei
Store. We are on left near top of hill. Look for 'Spellbound' signs, follow Service Road.
Street numbers not consecutive.*

Home Page: http://nzcom/webnz/bbnz/spell.htm

Hahei Beach Whitianga

Homestay
Address: "Cedar Lodge", 36 Beach Road,
Hahei, R.D.1, Whitianga
Name: John & Jenny Graham
Telephone: (07) 866 3789
Fax: (07) 866 3978
Beds: 1 Queen, 1 Single (1 bedroom)
Bathroom: 1 Private
Tariff: B&B (full) Double $80, Single $50,
Major Credit Cards. NZ B&B Vouchers accepted $10 surcharge
Nearest Town: Whitianga 38km, Tairua 36km

Come and unwind in our comfortable private upstairs studio apartment and enjoy the sea views and relaxing atmosphere.
Take a 200m stroll to the beautiful beach and experience the magic of Hahei. Scenic boat and fishing trips can be easily arranged with local operators. The Cathedral Cove Walkway is 3 minutes drive from the house, and Hot Water Beach where you can dig your own hot pool in the sand when the tide is low, is nearby. We can recommend the local 9 hole golf course, tennis courts and the various bush walks in the area.
We have an adult family scattered around the world and two friendly cats who live in the family part of our home. We thank you for not smoking indoors.
We enjoy an active retired lifestyle, so please phone ahead for bookings and directions.

Hahei - Cooks Beach

Homestay B&B
Address: Purangi Lodge
Purangi Road, RD 1, Whitianga
Name: Lynne Hammond and Vern Harris
Telephone: (07) 866 3945
Fax: (07) 866 3945
Mobile: (025) 280 9229
Email: lynnvern@xtra.co.nz
Beds: 3 Double, 4 Single (4 bedrooms)
Bathroom: 2 Guests share
Tariff: B&B (full) Double $80, Single $50, Children under 6 free,
6-12 $10, over 12 years of age half price. Dinner by arrangment.
NZ B&B Vouchers accepted $10 surcharge November - March
Nearest Town: Whitianga 28 km. Tairua 27 km.

Purangi Lodge is centrally located in a peaceful rural setting. A five minute drive will take you to Hahei, Cathedral Cove, Hot Water Beach, Cooks Beach or Ferry Landing where a brief ferry ride will deposit you in central Whitianga with its wide choice of quality restaurants.
We offer friendly, caring hospitality in a comfortable upstairs environment with children being most welcome and pets by arrangement. We have plenty of space in which to relax, the Purangi Golf Course is adjacent for the keen golfer, with kayaking, surfing, sailing, bush walking, and mountain bike riding available for the more energetic. Our breakfast fare includes home grown bacon and eggs with delicious home made bread and muesli. Guests share their own lounge with TV (Sky), video, stereo, fridge, tea & coffee making facilities.
Your hosts Lynne, Vern and youngest son Jason enjoy a relaxed family life with a love of sailing and rural living, and together look forward to making your stay memorable.

Hot Water Beach

2 Self-contained units
Address: Auntie Dawns Place
15 Radar Road, Hot Water Beach, R.D.1 Whitianga
Name: Dawn and Joe Nelmes
Telephone: (07) 866 3707
Fax: (07) 866 3701
Beds: Queen + Double, Queen + Single, (2 bedrooms)
Bathroom: 2 Private
Tariff: B&B (continental) Double $70/$80,
Single $40, Children $15.
Credit cards. NZ B&B Vouchers accepted $7 and $8 surcharge
Nearest Town: Whitianga 32km, Tairua 30km

Hot Water Beach is a beautiful surf beach. At low tide hot water bubbles up at a particular place in the sand and you can dig yourself a "hot-pool" to bathe in.
Your hosts "Auntie Dawn" (and Joe) enjoy gardening and relaxing on 1 hectare. Set amongst giant Pohutukawa trees. (And Joe likes making home-brew beer.) We have a small dog. Our home is only 150 metres from the sea. We provide comfortable bedrooms, private bathrooms, private lounges, TVs, cooking and laundry facilities. Juice, tea, coffee, cereal, bread, butter, jam are in units and guests prepare their own breakfast preferred time. Nearest cafe and restaurant 10 mins drive away.
Directions: *Turn right into Radar Road 200m before Hot Water Beach shop. A phone call would be appreciated 07-866 3707.*

COROMANDEL
PENINSULA

Tairua

Bed & Breakfast
Address: The Dunes,
106 Ocean Beach Rd., Tairua
Name: "The Dunes B&B"
Hosts: Tony & Carol
Telephone: (07) 864 7475
Fax: (07) 864 7475
Mobile: (025) 281 3809
Beds: 1 Queen, 1 Double (2 bedrooms)
Bathroom: 2 Ensuite
Tariff: B&B (continental) Double $100, Single $75.
NZ B&B Vouchers accepted $30 surcharge
Nearest Town: Thames 50km

Be lulled to sleep by waves breaking on the beach, wake to a spectacular sunrise over off-shore islands and the smell of home-made bread. Our guest rooms are upstairs and a feature of your stay may be breakfast on the balcony overlooking the sparkling Pacific Ocean. At our backdoor is Tairua's beautiful white sandy beach. Relax with a book on the balcony, engage in the many activities Tairua has to offer or use us as a base for exploring the Coromandel's many attractions, including Hot Water Beach and Cathedral Cove.
We have travelled extensively and enjoy most things to do with the great outdoors. As well as our homestay we run scenic and nature tours which you are welcome to join. Come and enjoy our smokefree home that we share with our children Ayden and Shaan and outside dogs Punta and Tip. Warm hospitality is assured.

215

Tairua

Bed & Breakfast
Address: "Kotuku Lodge",
179 Main Road, Tairua
Name: Dawn & Alan
Telephone: (07) 864 7040
Fax: (07) 864 7040
Email: kotuku@wave.co.nz
Beds: 1 King, 1 Queen,
2 Single (3 bedrooms)
Bathroom: 3 Ensuite
Tariff: B&B (special) Double $90-$105, Single $65-$75, Children $25.
Credit Card VISA. NZ B&B Vouchers accepted $30 surcharge Sept to April
Nearest Town: Thames 45km

Come and unwind in Tairua at Kotuku Lodge which provides all the modern facilities discerning guests expect. Our breakfasts are a house speciality! So start your day with our delicious continental choices served in the dining room with its friendly atmosphere and charming views of the harbour and Paku Mountain. The attractive bedrooms each with their own ensuite and balcony have comfortable King, Queen or single beds, hairdryer, fridge, plus tea and coffee making facilities. The guest TV-Lounge opens onto a paved patio area with a barbecue, swimming pool and a tranquil garden setting which makes it a lovely spot for relaxing at any time of the day.

Tairua is on the beautiful Coromandel Peninsula along the Pacific Coast Highway and has lots of interesting history. Allow time to enjoy nearby CATHEDRAL COVE and HOT WATER BEACH where you can dig your own HOT TUB in the sand beside the sea. There are some outstanding bush walks including walking through a 500m GLOW WORM tunnel to old goldmine workings. For the fishing and diving enthusiasts this is one of the MECCAS of NZ fishing, where you can rockfish, surfcast, dive or snorkel around Paku. Those who want to go out to the off shore islands there are fishing and diving trips available most days as well as charter and hire boats. You can also hire all your fishing and diving equipment. If all of this sounds like hard work you can just relax and swim or surf at the beach...or perhaps enjoy a game of tennis or round of golf on one of the many courses close by.

Top restaurants, reasonably priced are 3-4 minutes level walk away or short drive to others.

We enjoy most things to do with the Great Outdoors and Alan as well as a dedicated fisherman and photographer is also a wood carver.

We have a friendly black labrador.

Having travelled extensively within NZ and overseas, we understand your needs, and aim to provide you with a home away from home with every effort being made to ensure your stay is a pleasant and enjoyable one.
Home Page: http://nz.com/webnz/kotuku/

Tairua

Self-contained Apartment
Address: 18 The Esplanade, Tairua 2853
Name: The Esplanade Holiday Apartment
Telephone: (07) 864 8997 **Fax**: (07) 864 8997
Email: jcharlton@wave.co.nz
Beds: 1 Double, 2 Single (1 bedroom)
Bathroom: 1 Ensuite
Tariff: B&B (by arrangement) Double $50-$95 (seasonal variation),
Credit Cards. NZ B&B Vouchers accepted High season excluded
Nearest Town: Tairua 1km

A quiet relaxing holiday location with unsurpassed natural beauty situated on the waters edge. Sunbathing beach with safe clean swimming on the doorstep. Homely hospitality, or if desired 'just leave you to it'. Private garden area overlooks the harbour activities, ideal for a BBQ or an evening glass of wine. The apartment is modern, fully equipped, and includes washing machine, drier, and garage. Being self contained it is ideal for self catering and offers discerning / private comfort for up to 4 persons. There is a separate double bedroom with comfortable extra sleeping facilities in the lounge. Economical tariff makes this ideal for an impromptu 'get away from it' break. Boat launching location is nearby. Fishing gear is available.
This is our personal paradise, we invite you to share it with us for a while - your stay will be one to remember.
Directions: *A private and discerning self contained apartment in a beautiful water front setting. At the base of Paku Hill.*

Pauanui Beach

Tourist accommodation
Address: 7 Brodie Lane,
(off Dunlop Drive), Pauanui Beach
Name: Pauanui Pacific Holidays:
Hosts Kevin & Kay
Telephone: (07) 864 8933
Fax: (07) 864-8253
Mobile: 025 971 305
Beds: 2 Double, 2 Single (4 bedrooms)
Bathroom: 4 Ensuite

Tariff: B&B (full) Double $100-$115, Single $80-$115, Credit cards accepted.
NZ B&B Vouchers accepted $30 surcharge, but not Public Holiday weekends or
peak season, 20/12-20/2, Easter and Queens Birthday weekend.
Nearest Town: Thames 40 min

Pauanui is on the east coast of the Coromandel Peninsula and one of the most magnificently planned resorts in this area with red chip roads to add to the landscape. Activities are catered for by 9 and 10 hole golf courses, 4 tennis complexes each with 4 courts, mini-putt, restaurants, bistro and internationally known Puka Park Lodge. We are semi-retired dairy and pig farmers (which we still own) from Thames. We shifted to Pauanui in 1991 and built our accommodation complex on the water front. We have 4 units, each with ensuites, TV, fridge and tea / coffee facilities. Games room / lounge, cooking facilities, large BBQ area, sauna, spa and swimming pool. Included in tariff are bikes, canoes and windsurfers. We also cater for fishing trips and scenic tours. Nearest town Thames 40 mins, Hot water beach 1 hr, Tairua 20 mins (5 min by ferry). Auckland 2 hrs. Transport to and from airports arranged. Ask about our free tour of Pauanui.

Pauanui Beach

Bed & Breakfast
Address: Ash-Leigh Cottage,
11 Golden Hills Drive,
Pauanui Beach
Name: Alan & Joan Parker
Telephone: (07) 864 8103 **Fax**: (07) 864 8752
Beds: 2 Single (1 bedroom)
Bathroom: 1 Ensuite
Tariff: B&B (continental) Double $90, Single $70.
Nearest Town: 50km east of Thames

Our home, with off-street parking, is set in a quiet cul-de-sac close to the Tairua Harbour and walking distance to the ocean beach.
Your sunny room has twin beds, a cosy dining area, tea/coffee making facilities, TV,and ensuite. French doors open into the garden.
Breakfast is served in the sunroom or can be delivered to your room.
At Pauanui you can be as active or relaxed as you desire. Play golf, bowls, tennis, go swimming, or tramping or just laze on the golden sands or under the trees. There is a choice of licensed restaurants within a few minutes walk or drive.
Pauanui is an ideal base for exploring the rest of the Coromandel Peninsula.
We, together with Misty, our little dog, look forward to welcoming you to our smoke-free home and making your stay an enjoyable experience.

Whangamata

Homestay
Address: 130 Kiwi Road - Please phone
Name: Fairway
Telephone: (07) 865 7018
Fax: (07) 865 7685
Mobile: (025) 829 943
Beds: 1 Double, 3 Single (2 bedrooms)
Bathroom: 1 Guests share
Tariff: B&B (continental)
Double $95, Single $70,
Dinner by arrangement $25 per person.
Tariff current to September 1999.
Credit cards NZ B&B Vouchers accepted $20 Surcharge
Nearest Town: Waihi 31km south on Highway 25, Thames 55km west

We offer friendly service in the comfortable surroundings of our modern smoke free home. Set beside Whangamata's 9 hole Golf course you are able to walk on to the 8th Fairway and down to the Clubhouse. Alternatively you may wish to walk across the course, down a street to discover our wonderful Surf Beach. Here you can swim or simply stroll along the sand. Whangamata is able to offer the following activities and more, Diving, Fishing, Tramping, Mountain Bike Riding and naturally Surfing. Some of these activities may require prebooking. Snow and I run a Garage and Garage Door business. We enjoy company and with recent changes one of us is always available for our guests. Our beds are comfortable (look for the "Great Bed" remark in our visitors book) with cotton linen, woolrest underlays and electric blankets. Weary travellers can be sure of a great nights sleep.

Whangamata

Guest Lodge
Address: Brenton Lodge, Cnr Brenton Place,
SH 25, Whangamata. , P O Box 216, Whangamata
Name: Jan & Paul Campbell
Telephone: (07) 865 8400 **Fax**: (07) 865 8400
Mobile: (025) 780 134
Beds: 2 Queen (1 bedroom + sofa sleeper)
Bathroom: 2 Ensuite
Tariff: B&B (special) Double $195, Single $175.
Valid until 30 September 1999. Credit cards. Non smoking.
Nearest Town: Whangamata

*Brenton Lodge features new guest chalets, built country style in keeping with the house.
Set in one acre of lovely gardens, with mature trees, aviary and swimming pool.
Panoramic views of Whangamata, with seaviews to Mayor Island, 1.5km to surf beach
and village.
Relax in your separate upstairs guest chalet, which overlooks both the garden and
seaviews. Tastefully furnished country cottage style, with extra touches, crisp white
cotton sheets, fresh flowers, french doors, own balcony, add to the character.
Open plan with its own bathroom, tea/coffee facilities, TV, sofa, table/chairs. Non
smoking.
Delicious special breakfast is served in your chalet.
Hosts have a luxury 6 metre boat available for guest charter.
Experience - fishing, sightseeing with a gourmet lunch.
Escape, and enjoy our peaceful tranquil setting, where the choice of privacy or company
is yours.*

Whangamata

Homestay
Address: 'Tree Tops', 113 Chevron Cres.
Whangamata
Name: Clare & Will Hill
Telephone: (07) 865 8320
Fax: (07) 865 8320
Mobile: (025) 270 4117
Beds: 1 Queen, 2 Single (2 bedrooms)
Bathroom: 1 Ensuite, 1 Private
Tariff: B&B (full) Double $120, Single $80. Dinner $30.
NZ B&B Vouchers accepted $25 Surcharge, same day restriction.

*Our spacious home is set in half an acre of lovely gardens with panoramic views of
ocean and islands. Our guest room upstairs is large, with sitting area, ensuite and has
wonderful views from every window. The downstairs guest room, with private
bathroom, opens into a secluded bush garden with giant tree ferns, a cool and quiet
place to relax on hot summer days. Both rooms have white cotton sheets, white towels,
fresh flowers, and antique furniture.
The area offers beautiful beaches, two golf courses, fishing and bush walks. Shops and
restaurants are close by.
We are retired, have travelled widely and enjoy gardening, music, art, fishing and golf.
We have a cat and a dog. Dinner by prior arrangement. Not suitable for children or
disabled persons.*
Directions: *Please phone for bookings and directions.*

Whangamata

Homestay
Address: Il Casa Moratti, 313 Mary Road,
Whangamata
Name: Bev and George Moratti
Telephone: 07 865 6164 **Fax**: 07 865 6164
Email: moratti@thepeninsula.co.nz
Beds: 1 Double, 2 Single (2 bedrooms)
Bathroom: 1 Guests share
Tariff: B&B (full) Double $95, Single $70, Dinner $25 (by arrangement).
NZ B&B Vouchers accepted $25 surcharge. Credit Cards accepted.
Nearest Town: Whangamata - 1 km to township

Your hosts Bev and George welcome you to their comfortable, clean, modern smoke-free home, only minutes away from our magnificent surf beach. Handy to town, park and surf club. Guests have their own lounge with TV, tea and coffee making facilities, microwave and fridge. We have travelled extensively and enjoy swapping experiences with fellow travellers. Our other interests are gardening, sport, fishing, tramping and conservation. Whangamata has plenty to offer visitors - surfing, swimming, boating, fishing and tramping through beautiful native bush. the area abounds with history of kauri gum digging, gold mining and kauri timber milling. We have one very friendly Boxer dog named Alice. We are registered Kiwi Hosts. Dinner by arrangement.
Directions: *Please phone for bookings and directions.*

Whangamata

Homestay
Address: Waireka Lodge,
108 Waireka Place, Whangamata.
Name: Gail and Dick Wilson
Telephone: 07-865 8859
Fax: 07-865 8859
Beds: 1 Queen, 2 Single (2 bedrooms)
Bathroom: 1 Private

Tariff: B&B (full) Double $95, Single $70,
Dinner by arrangement $25 pp,
Credit Cards accepted.
NZ B&B Vouchers accepted $25 surcharge
Nearest Town: Whangamata 1km.

Whangamata is a pleasant beach side holiday resort on the Coromandel Peninsula, just 2 hours drive south of Auckland International Airport. It features a superb surf beach together with attractive rock and seascapes. The harbour and estuary have much to offer those wanting a more sheltered marine environment. Waireka Lodge is situated on the banks of the Moana-Anu-Anu Estuary. The delightful private garden setting is bordered by a river reserve which features beautiful Pohutakawa and other native trees. We invite you to share our relaxed beach lifestyle in our charming new smoke free home. We can provide, and in some cases share with you, a variety of activities. Others we will arrange: kayaking, petanque, kite flying, fishing, swimming, snorkelling, floral art, golf, bushwalks, tours. Enjoy our quality cuisine, much of the produce coming from our garden. Your party will be our only guests as we limit bookings to one group. We have a cat.

Waihi

Homestay
Address: Westwind Gradens , 22 Roycroft Street, Waihi
Name: Josie & Bob French
Telephone: (07) 863 7208
Beds: 4 Single (2 bedrooms)
Bathroom: 1 Guests share
Tariff: B&B (continental) Double $60, Single $30, Children under 13 years 1/2 price), Dinner $15. 10% Discount for three days or more.
10% Discount May up to Labour weekend/3 nights or more.
Credit Cards. NZ B&B Vouchers accepted
Nearest Town: Waihi (1km from Post Office or Bus Depot)

We welcome you and offer a friendly restful stay at "West Wind Gardens" our modern comfortable home with new beds and electric blankets. Enjoy our lovely 3/4 acre terraced garden which was selected for the New Zealand Open Garden Scheme.
Waihi is the gateway to both the Coromandel Peninsula with its beautiful beaches and the Bay of Plenty the Kiwifruit centre of New Zealand. It is a historic town with a vintage railway running between Waihi and Waikino, a working mine discovered in 1878, worked as an underground mine until 1952, re-opened in 1989 as an open cast mine. Free mine tours available. Beaches 10 minutes away, beautiful native bush walks, golf courses and trout fishing. Enjoy a 3 course home cooked meal or sample our local restaurants. Our interests are gardening, dancing and travel.
Smoking outdoors only.
Directions: *Roycroft St is off the Whangamata Road opposite Eastend Superette.*
Home Page: babs.com.au/nz/westwind.htm

Waihi

"Country House" fine Accommodation
Address: 'The French Provincial Country House',
Golden Valley, Trig Road North, R.D. 1, Waihi
Name: Margaret & Johannes van Duyvenbooden
Telephone: (07) 863 7339 **Fax**: (07) 863 7330
Mobile: (025) 488 845
Beds: 1 Super King, 1 Queen, 1 Double (3 bedrooms)
Bathroom: 1 Luxurious Ensuite,1 Private with 2 person spa bath,1 Guests share
Tariff: B&B (continental special) Super King Ensuite "Bridal Suite" $225, Queen Private 2 person spa bath or double shower $165, Double $130, Credit Card (VISA), Non smoking. Not suitable for children. Tariff current until 30th Sept 1999. Closed during July/August.
Nearest Town: Waihi 5km, Auckland airport 2 hours. Ideal for a day trip to the beautiful Coromandel.

We warmly welcome you to the French Provincial Country House, set in a pretty farming valley, only 5km from Waihi's historic township. A great central location to the Coromandel and Bay of Plenty. Our charming 2 storey smokefree home is spacious and elegant. In summer colourful gardens, large shade trees and swimming pool for your leisure. Our 3 delightful guest bedrooms have individual decor and all modern quality comforts. Privately upstairs a large luxurious "Bridal Suite" where the decor is soft in colour, lavish and romantic. Two private balconies for your use only. A generous breakfast is served in a formal dining area or in the garden room. There's a variety of restaurants, wineries and cafés, beautiful safe beaches, easy bush walks, golf courses, summer gardens, steam train rides. We personally assure your stay will be relaxing and a memorable one. One night in this area is not long enough.
Directions: *Please phone for reservations saves disappointment.*
Home Page: http://wwwFriars.co.nz/hosts/frenchhtml>

Waihi Beach
Spindrift Beachstay & Self-Contained Accommodation
Address: 287 Seaforth Rd, Waihi Beach (cnr Albacore Ave)
Name: Ms Loretta Austin
Telephone: (07) 863 5136 **Fax**: (07) 863 5136
Mobile: (025) 278 1887
Beds: 2 Double, 1 Single (3 bedrooms)
Bathroom: 1 Ensuite, 1 Private
Tariff: B&B (continental) Double $75, Single $50, Dinner $25.
Off-season discount. NZ B&B Vouchers accepted
Nearest Town: 15km east of Waihi, 17km north-east of Katikati

Hear the waves crash on the sand; walk along 3km of untouched dunes; breakfast with the sun dancing on the water; see the sun set over the Coromandel Range. Relax.
My home is a typical New Zealand beach house with a casual, sunny atmosphere. It is situated next to a reserve with direct access through this to the beach. Enjoy the surf or the tranquil harbour bays. Fish off the jetty or arrange line and deep sea fishing in season. Swim in thermal hot pools. The district has lovely walks as well as 9 and 18 hole golf courses. Just 15 minutes away are the historic attractions of Waihi's gold mining boom with ruins situated at various sites along the walkways in the beautiful Karangahake Gorge.
The double rooms have TV and tea / coffee making facilities should you wish for space and privacy.
Directions: *Take the Waihi Beach turn-off from S.H.2 . Continue to the Island View Store and roundabout. Follow the Bowentown sign along Seaforth Road. The third road on the left is Albacore Avenue.*

Waihi Beach
Homestay
Address: 12 Mayor View Tce,
Waihi Beach
Name: Mrs Dulcie Cooper
Telephone: (07) 863 5041
Mobile: 025 277 2381
Beds: 1 King/Queen, 2 Single + 1
Foldaway (2 bedrooms)
Bathroom: 1 Private
Tariff: B&B (full) Double $85, Single $60,
Children under 13 $15, Dinner $20.
NZ B&B Vouchers accepted
Nearest Town: Waihi - distance 10km

Welcome to my home overlooking Waihi Beach a true living leisure treasure. Breathtaking seaviews from three level brick home in beautiful Bay of Plenty set in cottage and tropical gardens. Bathroom is spacious with separate toilet and shower. Also guests lounge, dining room with TV and tea making facilities. Guests will be provided with continental or cooked breakfast as desired. Dinner by arrangement. We have very good eating places at beach or Waihi. There is a short walk to our beach (about 8km of rippling while sand) lovely bush walk, 9 and 18 golf courses, and gardens to visit. We have a large goldmine in our area. There are tours organised. Waihi Beach is truly the centre of a visitors paradise. My interests are tennis, badminton, gardening and providing for you.
Please phone or write for directions.

Waihi Beach

Homestay
Address: 17 The Esplanade,
Waihi Beach
Name: John & Kay Morgan
Telephone: (07) 863 4342
Fax: (07) 863 4342
Mobile: (025) 287 1104
Email: k.morgan@xtra.co.nz
Beds: 1 King/Queen, 1 Double,
1-2 Single (2 bedrooms)
Bathroom: 1 Private
Tariff: B&B (continental) Double $90, $15 per extra persons,
Flat let as self contained unit. Credit Cards.
Nearest Town: Waihi 11km

Waterfront Homestay
Fully self contained two double bedrooms plus single bed. Very suitable for two couples or small family group. Unit on lower floor of family home. Situated on waterfront of beautiful uncrowded ocean beach. Walk from front door directly onto sandy beach. Safe ocean swimming, surfcasting, surfing and coastal walks.
9 hole golf course with club hire in township, 18 hole golf course 11km away.
Restaurant within walking distance of accommodation or use facilities provided with accommodation.
Tariff $90 per couple bed & breakfast, $25 per extra persons.
Hosts John & Kay Morgan

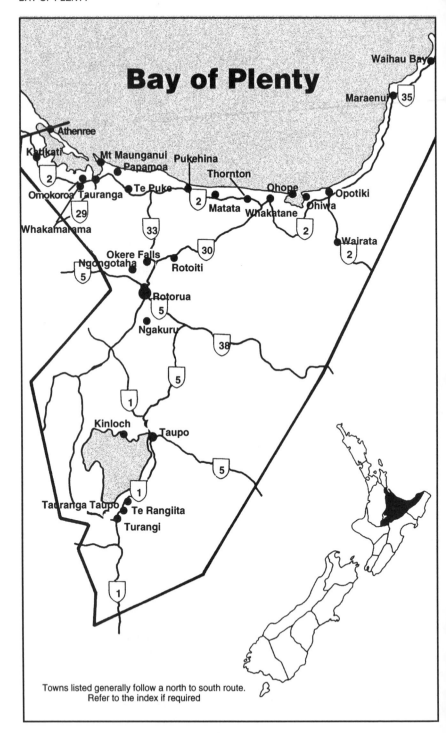

Towns listed generally follow a north to south route.
Refer to the index if required

Athenree
Bed & Breakfast
Address: 25 Ross Ware Drive,
off Waiau Road,Athenree, Bay of Plenty
Name: Chestnut Lodge
Telephone: (07) 549 2495 **Fax**: (07) 549 2495
Beds: 1 Queen, 1 Double, 2 Single (3 bedrooms)
Bathroom: 1 Ensuite, 1 Guests share
Tariff: B&B (continental) Double from $65, Single $40.
Nearest Town: Waihi 12 km, Katikati 12 kms SH2

Welcome to Chestnut Lodge. Nestled at the foot of the Athenree Forest and set in three acres of beautiful gardens and orchard with a fully fenced swimming pool for your enjoyment. Ideally situated as your base to explore both the Bay of Plenty and the Coromandel or as a relaxing stop-over in your touring schedule. Wonderful scenery and peaceful surroundings will ensure your appreciation of the district yet will appeal to beach lovers and ramblers alike with Waihi Beach and numerous stunning walks and tourist attractions only ten minutes away.

Our house design allows guests to choose their own level of privacy with a separate lounge / TV room and entrance. Alternatively join us and our two children in the gardens and pool or try your hand at a barbecue on the deck.

We request no smoking in the house and no pets.

Katikati
Farmstay+Self-Contained Accom.
Address: Jacaranda Cottage,
230 Thompson's Track, RD2, Katikati
Name: Lynlie & Rick Watson
Telephone/Fax: (07) 549 0616.
Mobile: (025) 272 8710
Beds: House: 1 Queen, 2 Single (2 bedrooms) SC Cottage: 1 Double,
1 Single (1 bedroom) + fold-out divan in lounge.
Bathroom: House: 1 Guests share. SC Cottage: 1 Ensuite
Tariff: B&B: (Full) House: Double $65, Single $40, Dinner by arrangement $18,
Children discounted. Campervans $25, Cyclists/backpackers' budget accommodation $15. SC Cottage: Double $70, $25 each extra adult, weekly rate discounted.
Credit cards. NZ B&B Vouchers accepted
Nearest Town: 30 km north of Tauranga, 8 km south of Katikati

A warm welcome awaits you at Jacaranda Cottage, a 5-acre farmlet enjoying magnificent 360 degree views - from sea to mountains, from rolling farmlands and orchards to native forests. We offer you a taste of simple country life - generous hospitality; wholesome farmhouse food; and clean, warm accommodation in either the main house or in the fully-equipped hillside cottage (no smoking inside, please).

Children enjoy the friendly animals on our farmlet and are welcome to help with small farm activities. Swim, horseride, search for glowworms at night. Experience the nearby native forests by tramping to Twin Falls, old Eliza Mine, or the Sentinel Kauri Tree.Visit the unspoilt beaches, hot pools, birdgardens, arts and crafts, winery and good restaurants. See Katikati's many colourful murals depicting scenes from the area's past. Horse treks, guided tramps and local tours available.Good base for Bay of Plenty or Coromandel sightseeing, or simply relax in the tranquil surroundings of Jacaranda Cottage.

Directions: *Thompson's Track is 6 km south of Katikati, on the Tauranga side of the Forta Leza Restaurant. Jacaranda Cottage is 2.3 km up Thompson's Track, on the right.*

Katikati

Self-contained Apartment
Address: Pahoia Road,
R.D. 2, Tauranga
Name: Trevor & Thora Jones
Telephone: (07) 548 0661
Fax: (07) 548 0661
Beds: 1 Queen (1 bedroom)

HARBOURVIEW

1 convertible divan in lounge, 1 cot. Additional beds available in main house.
Bathroom: 1 Private
Tariff: B&B (continental) Double $70, Single $45, Children $15, (includes supply of continental breakfast foods for self-service).
Credit Cards Accepted NZ B&B Vouchers accepted
Nearest Town: 20km south of Katikati, 23km north of Tauranga

We have retired to this pleasant rural region of the Bay of Plenty, with a large home on a horticultural lifestyle property. The modern, self-contained apartment is furnished with all amenities including laundry. For a larger family group, additional beds (and additional guests bathroom) are available in the main house. We look northward across the Tauranga Harbour (water's edge 200 metres away) and westward to the Kaimai Range. Available for guests' use are BBQ, dinghy, grass court and games rooms for billiards, table tennis etc. Attractions in the area include hot pools, beaches, and walking opportunities in the Kaimai Range. We have special interests in gardening, tramping, the bush and mountains. For the less energetic, this is a peaceful place to relax and contemplate the spectacular scenery and listen to the birds.
Directions: *Out on Pahoia peninsula, 3km from State Highway 2. Please phone for bookings and directions.*

Katikati

Farmstay
Address: 'Aberfeldy'
164 Lindemann Road, R.D.1, Katikati
Name: Mary Ann & Rod Calver
Telephone: (07) 549 0363
Fax: (07) 549 0363
)Mobile: 025 909 710
Beds: 1 Double, 3 Single
(2 bedrooms, triple & twin, also private lounge)
Bathroom: 1 Guests share, 1 Family share
Tariff: B&B (full) Double $80, Single $45, Children half price, Dinner $25 3 course, Credit Cards. We have only one party at a time in the guest accomodation. NZ B&B Vouchers accepted
Nearest Town: Katikati 3km

Aberfeldy is on Lindemann Road off State Highway 2, 3kms north of Katikati, the unique murals town. Your hosts have a sheep and cattle farm with a stoney bottomed stream, and 100 year old trees. They also operate a high producing kiwifruit orchard nearby. There are panoramic views of farmland, bushclad hills and the Tauranga Harbour. Mary Ann and Rod have travelled extensively and love people, gardening, horseriding, tramping, music, reading and cooking.Activities can include bush and farm walks, swimming and meeting the various tame animals. A golf course is nearby and we are close to the ocean beach.The comfortable attractive home is set in an extensive garden with the private guest accommodation opening to their own patio. The guests have their own bathroom and sunny lounge with tea and coffee making facilities, TV and video.A warm welcome is assured and we can pick guests up from Katikati at no extra charge.

226

Katikati
Country Homestay+Self-contained
Address: 'Hammond House',
195 Beach Road, Katikati
Name: Jan & John Nicoll
Telephone: (07) 549 1377
Fax: (07) 549 2217
Email: jnicolle@xtra.co.nz
Beds: SC Cottage: 1 Queen, 2 Single.
Bathroom: 1 Private.
Tariff: B&B (full) Double $120, Single $80, Candlelit Dinner by arrangement $35pp.
Nearest Town: Katikati 2 km

"Hammond House" is an elegant and spacious two storey Tudor style home set in 5 acres of trees, cottage gardens and a kiwifruit orchard. We offer guests self-contained accommodation in a two level Tudor style garden cottage a few metres from the main homestead. The cottage has kitchenette, bathroom, a Queen size French bed downstairs and two single beds upstairs all with electric blankets and feather duvets. We provide television, gas heating, fresh fruit from our orchard, guests can read the latest magazines on the balcony and enjoy a glass of port, whilst enjoying the peace and tranquillity. Enjoy a leisurely breakfast in our conservatory. Breakfast may feature fruit juice, fresh fruit and home made yoghurt, cereals, a variety of egg dishes, venison sausages, bacon, tomatoes, mushrooms, home baked bread and freshly ground coffee. Attractions within 15 minutes drive are ocean beaches, beautiful native bush walks, golf, bird gardens, hot mineral springs, a winery and a selection of restaurants. Katikati (the town of murals) is on the main route between Rotorua and Coromandel and two hours from Auckland. We have a Golden Cairn Terrier "Molly" and two Burmese cats - brothers "Eton" and "Harvard". Your hosts will do everything possible to ensure your visit is memorable We look forward to meeting you.

Katikati
Bed & Breakfast/Homestay
Address: Waterford House Bed & Breakfast,
15 Crossley Street, Katikati
Name: Alan & Helen Cook
Telephone: (07) 549 0757

Beds: 1 Queen, 1 Double, 5 Single (2 Twin/1 Single) (5 bedrooms)
Bathroom: 3 Guests share
Tariff: B&B (full) Double $60, Single $40, Children discounted, Dinner $15.
Credit Cards. NZ B&B Vouchers accepted
Nearest Town: Katikati 1km; 37km north of Tauranga on SH2, 26km south of Waihi on SH2

Waterford House provides spacious accommodation with wheelchair access throughout. A large comfortable guest lounge with TV, stereo, radio, fridge / freezer, microwave, and tea / coffee making facilities. Local attractions include historic Twickenham Cafe and Antiques, Morton Estate Winery, Katikati Bird Gardens, Sapphire Springs Hot Pools, Kaimai bush walks, Uretara River walkway, pottery and craft workshops, gardens, and of course Katikati "The Mural Town" and "Best Kept Small Town" with its 20 historic murals. Alan and Helen have travelled extensively in New Zealand and overseas, and have gained first-hand experience on how to cater for their guests. Waterford House is situated in a quiet semi-rural area, one kilometre north of Katikati Post Office, just off SH2, opposite the Uretara Domain.

227

Katikati

Rural Homestay
Address: Cotswold Lodge,
183 Ongare Pt Road, Katikati
Name: Jan & Graham Taylor
Telephone: (07) 549 2110 **Fax**: (07) 549 2110
Beds: 2 Double, 2 Single (3 bedrooms)
Bathroom: 3 Ensuite
Tariff: B&B (full) Double $105, Single $65, Dinner $25pp. Credit card (VISA/MC).
NZ B&B Vouchers accepted $25 Surcharge
Nearest Town: 7km north of Katikati

Welcome to Cotswold Lodge - as the name suggests we originate from the Cotswolds in England. On arrival in New Zealand we fell in love with the colonial architecture and have built our large, comfortable home on those lines complete with facilities for disabled and elderly people. It is set in peaceful gardens with beautiful views to the Kaimai Ranges and just a short stroll to the beach and harbour. Come and stay awhile and unwind from the hurly burly of everyday life. Graham restores antiques from his workshop on the premises while Jan spins, paints and potters in her garden, with the help of her friendly Labrador.

Katikati, the Mural town of New Zealand, is ideally situated to explore the beautiful Bay of Plenty and the Coromandel Peninsula with their varied attractions. We would be happy to arrange tours or transport for you - otherwise just relax and enjoy yourselves.

Katikati

Orchard Stay + Private Suite
Address: Peaceful Panorama Lodge,
901 State Highway 2, R.D.1, Katikati
Name: Heather & Bernie Wills
Telephone: (07) 549 1882
Fax: (07) 549 1882
Email: wills@bopis.co.nz
Beds: 2 Double, 3 Single (3 bedrooms)
Bathroom: 1 Ensuite, 1 Guests share
Tariff: B&B (full/special) Double $75, Single $45. Private Double suite $95
(lounge, bathroom, bedroom) Extra adult in suite $25, Children $20. Dinner $20.
Credit Cards (VISA/MC/AMEX). NZ B&B Vouchers accepted $20 surcharge for
private suite
Nearest Town: Katikati 9km, Auckland 1 1/2 hours, Tauranga 35 minutes.

Peaceful Panorama "Overlooking the Bay". A warm welcome awaits. Large modern colonial home, harbour and ocean views, restful rural setting, pianola, pool, gardens, birds, 10 acres with pet cows, turkeys, hens, kiwifruit and avocado orchard, only minutes to the harbour and ocean beach. Complimentary beverages any time. No smoking or animals indoors. Guests privacy respected.

NEARBY: Tramping, horse-riding, fishing, boating, scenic flights, murals, historic sites, restaurants, ocean beach, gardens and more.INTERESTS: Vintage cars, music, gardening, photography, winemaking, spinning.BREAKFAST: Freshly squeezed juice, selection of cereals, fruit, new laid eggs, pancakes, croissants, muffins, coffee, teas or milo.DINNER: Beef, venison, turkey, lamb or fish. Traditional NZ desserts, special diets if required. Complimentary wine.ROOMS: Double, twin or private suite: with sea views, comfortable beds, wool duvets, electric blankets.Member of B.O.P. Farm Orchard & Home Hosts Network.

Directions: *901 State Highway 2. Yellow letter box. 9km north of Katikati, 16 km south of Waihi.*

Omokoroa, Tauranga

Homestay/Cottage
Address: 'Walnut Cottage'
309 Station Rd,
Omokoroa, R.D. 2, Tauranga
Name: Ken & Betty Curreen
Telephone: (07) 548 0692
Fax: (07) 548 1764
Beds: Cottage: 1 Queen.
House: 1 Double ("Kowhai Suite")
Bathroom: Cottage: 1 Ensuite   House: 1 Ensuite
Tariff: B&B (continental) Double $55-$60, Single $40,
Dinner $15, NZ B&B Vouchers accepted
Nearest Town: 15 minutes north Tauranga on SH2

Walnut Cottage is situated on scenic Plummers Point Peninsular and we overlook beautiful Tauranga Harbour. We are a semi-retired couple who invite our guests to enjoy the tranquillity our "little-corner-of-the-world" has to offer. Both the cottage and Kowhai Suite are clean and comfortable with ensuites, T.V and tea/coffee making facilities. Relaxing mineral hot pools are a 5 minute walk away and a 2 minute stroll takes you to the waters edge where you can enjoy the peace of the estuary or fish from the jetty. Our breakfasts feature freshly squeezed orange juice (in season) homemade jams, muesli, yoghurt and eggs, a good start to see local sights and activities including water gardens, horseriding, golf, bowls and tramping. Our semi-rural retreat is close to Tauranga city, popular for its shopping, fishing trips and sightseeing.
Directions: *Station Rd is opposite Whakamarama Service Station on SH2. We are 3km along Station Rd.*

Omokoroa Peninsula

Homestay
Address: Armadale,
296 Omokoroa Rd.,
R.D.2, Tauranga
Name: Shirley & Graeme Macdonald
Telephone: (07) 548 1944
Fax: (07) 548 1944
Beds: 1 Double, 2 Single (2 bedrooms)
Bathroom: 1 Guests share
Tariff: B&B (full) Double $70, Single $35,
Children 12 & under half price, Dinner $20pp.
Nearest Town: City of Tauranga - 17km

Shirley and Graeme Macdonald welcome guests to our home and property, currently being developed into gardens, home orchard, horticulture and a simple pitch and putt course.
Visitors may take advantage of the wide range of activities offered in the Omokoroa area. These include - safe swimming, hot pools, horse riding, golf, bowls, sophisticated or casual dining, children's playground, and a ferry service to Matakana Island.
There are some excellent open gardens and scenic walks.
We have one friendly cat and a family of fantail pigeons.
Our particular interests include trout and sea fishing, gardening, golf and hosting guests.

Whakamarama

Homestay
Address: 'Highlands',
89 Whakamarama Rd, R.D.6, Tauranga
Name: Shirley & John Whiteman
Telephone: (07) 552 5275
Beds: 1 Queen, 2 Single (2 bedrooms)
Bathroom: 1 Guest share
Tariff: B&B (full) Double $75, Single $45,
Children under 12 half price, Dinner $20.
Credit Cards NZ B&B Vouchers accepted
Nearest Town: Tauranga 14km north on S.H.2 (15 mins)

Our home is situated in a quiet rural area with spectacular views of Mayor Island, Mt Maunganui and Tauranga Harbour.
You are very welcome to dine with us, alternatively there is a selection of good restaurants within 5 mins drive. We offer 2 bedrooms, a lounge and kitchen (with fridge) for your use, all opening to garden, catching morning sun and panoramic views. Laundry facilities available.
We are handy to golf links, bowling green, horse riding, hot pools, bush walks and good boat launching.
Directions: *Highlands is 2km off state highway two on Whakamarama road (no89) which turns right at Whakamarama shops when travelling south. 15 mins from Tauranga. Signposted on main Highway. Please phone if possible.*

Tauranga

Heritage Bed & Breakfast Inn
Address: 'Taiparoro House 1882',
11, 5th Avenue, Tauranga
Name: Kevin & Lois Kelly
Telephone: (07) 577 9607
Fax: (07) 577 9264
Mobile: (025) 223 5675
Email: kl.kelly@clear.net.nz
Beds: 3 Queen, 1 Double, 2 Single (5 bedrooms)
Bathroom: 5 Ensuite
Tariff: B&B (special) Double $140-$190, Single $95-$140, Credit cards.
Nearest Town: Tauranga 100 metres

Enjoy a taste of the past in one of Tauranga's oldest and most beautiful historic homes. Taiparoro's five guest rooms, all have ensuites and telephone, and a lounge/conservatory exclusively for guests. The historic theme is evident with all rooms furnished in keeping with the colonial era. For a special occasion, or just to pamper yourself, stay in the lovely Harbour View Suite and soak in the original claw foot bath.
Breakfast is delightful with fresh fruits, homemade muesli, organic yoghurts, fresh baked croissants, home made bread, brewed coffee plus choose from a selection of cooked meals. An assortment of teas and coffee are available at any time. Go for a stroll, relax in the English Conservatory, in front of the fire, or enjoy the stunning view of Tauranga harbour from the garden. Situated in tranquil surroundings, Taiparoro is only 10 minute stroll to the city centre, excellent restaurants, cafes, bars and quality shopping.
Home Page: http://nz.com.heritageinns/taiparorohouse

Tauranga

Homestay
Address: 'Bolney Gate',
20 Esmeralda Street,
Welcome Bay, Tauranga
Name: Jack & Joyce Ingram
Telephone: (07) 544 3228
Fax: (07) 544 3228
Mobile: (025) 277 5587
Beds: Room 1: Family room, 1 Queen sized double bed,
2 Single beds.Room 2: 2 Single beds.
Bathroom: 1 Family share
Tariff: B&B (continental - special available) Double $60, Single $35,
Children under 10 $15, under 16 $20, Dinner $20,
VISA AND MASTERCARD ACCEPTED. NZ B&B Vouchers accepted
Nearest Town: Tauranga - 6 mins by bus or taxi.

Bolney Gate is interesting and spacious, overlooking a park dotted with a variety of mature trees. The park has activities for both old and young. Practice golf, jogging, jungle gyms, swings & slides, trolley riding, kite flying or just walking.The view is varied from quiet residential homes set on the hills around the park to restful rural views.We have both indoor and outdoor living. An enclosed and secluded pool with an elevated wooden deck at one end as a leisure area for reading, writing, eating out or just sharing.We live in the very heart of the Bay of Plenty and Welcome Bay is just a few minutes drive from downtown Tauranga and Mount Maunganui - 15 to 20 minutes from the horticultural centre of Te Puke or 40 minutes to the delightful small rural town of Katikati, known as the Mural town of New Zealand, offering Kiwi orchards, art in every form, rural and bush walks.We have both travelled widely in N.Z. and many countries of the world and enjoy people from all walks of life. We have Sky TV.

Tauranga

Homestay
Address: Pukemapu Homestead
208 Pukemapu Road, RD 3 Oropi, Tauranga
Name: Jill and John Mitchinson
Telephone: (07) 543 3502
Fax: (07) 543 3512
Mobile: (025) 992 148
Beds: 2 Queen, 2 Single (3 bedrooms)
Bathroom: 1 Ensuite, 1 Guests share
Tariff: B&B (full) Double $90, Single $65, Dinner $25pp,
Credit Cards (MC/VISA).
Nearest Town: Tauranga, 11Kms from C.B.D.

Our home has been custom built to accommodate guests in a degree of luxury during their stay. There are TV's in each room and tea and coffee making facilities available. It has a pleasant country atmosphere but is close to town. We have lovely views over Tauranga city, Mt Maunganui and the rural surrounding area. A few minutes drive to the Greerton shopping centre, Tauranga golf club and heated swimming pool. Fifteen minutes to the heart Tauranga where there is a good variety of shopping and plenty of restaurants to choose from. Also approx 15 mins to Mt Maunganui, one of the most popular beaches in New Zealand. Our speciality is to provide a congenial atmosphere with pleasant surroundings and food.

231

Tauranga
Country Homestay+Self Contained Accom.
Address: 322 Oropi Road,
R.D. 3, Tauranga
Name: 'Baumgarten Lodge',
Henri & Colleen Limacher
Telephone: (07) 543 2799 **Fax**: (07) 543 2799
Beds: 1 King (TV in room), 1 Queen, 2 Single (3 bedrooms)
Bathroom: 1 Guests share.
Tariff: B&B (full) Double $65, Single $40. NZ B&B Vouchers accepted
Nearest Town: Tauranga City Centre 9 minutes.

Baumgarten Country Lodge and Self Contained Accommodation, both clean and comfortable is semi rural, 2km off Highway 29. The lodge is a large spacious single storied home with indoor spa room. Situated on a 5 acre farmlet, nestled amidst our avocado orchard, various fruit trees and gardens. We graze a few calves and have one outdoor dog and a cat called Sammy. Semi-retired we enjoy meeting visitors. Henri, Swiss born speaks German. The outdoor swimming pool and 9 pin bowling ally are features to be enjoyed.
The comfortable detached, self contained and fully furnished accommodation sleeps 5-6 persons. Only minutes from Greerton Village, restaurants, golf club, racecourse, R.S.A and heated pool. Short drive to Mt. Maunganui Beach, plus easy day excursions to Waitomo Caves, Rotorua, volcanic White Island and more. We request no smoking in the house.

Matua, Tauranga
Bed and Breakfast
Address: 210 Levers Road, Matua,
 Tauranga
Name: John & Heather Christiansen
Telephone: (07) 576 6835
Beds: 1 Queen, 2 Single (2 Bedrooms)

Bathroom: 1 Guests share
Tariff: B&B (full) Double $80, Single $50, Credit Cards.
NZ B&B Vouchers accepted $12 surcharge
Nearest Town: Tauranga city centre 6km

Our home is in the pleasant suburb of Matua, enhanced by a garden of New Zealand native trees, shrubs and ferns. The guest wing is quiet and comfortable. Please join us in our lounge, read our books and listen to our music. Our other interests include the performing arts, growing New Zealand native plants, collecting antiques and motor-cycling. Our home is smoke-free. Breakfast - see our special menu when you arrive. We can cater for people with food allergies. We are close to harbour beaches and parks; seven minutes drive to Tauranga city centre and fifteen minutes to Mount Maunganui's ocean beach. We have a broad knowledge of the Bay of Plenty and its attractions. A gift of home grown citrus fruit can be provided, in season, when you depart. Best to call or phone before 9.00am or after 5.30pm. It will be our pleasure to welcome you.

Relax – Don't try to drive too far in one day.

Te Puna, Tauranga
Homestay
Address: 'Taurima', 186 Minden Road,
R.D.6 Te Puna, Tauranga
Name: Ursula Kassin & Judith Simpson
Telephone: (07) 552 5800
Fax: (07) 552 5800
Mobile: 021 703-260
Beds: 1 Queen, 2 Single (2 bedrooms)
Bathroom: 1 Guest private
Tariff: B&B (full) Double $80, Single $45. NZ B&B Vouchers accepted
Nearest Town: Tauranga 15 mins

Your private and personal holiday choice in the Bay of Plenty. Share our home nestled into the hillside with 360 degrees sea, bush and farmland views. This is the ideal stopover for exploring the many natural gifts of the Bay of Plenty. Stride out along our beaches, soak in hot pools, delight in beautiful gardens, visit the thermal wonderland of Rotorua, tempt your taste buds at the wineries and restaurants.
We came to New Zealand 5 years ago from London. Ursula is originally from Vienna, Judith is New Zealand born. Prior to leaving London we spent 2 years working on Menorca (Balearic Islands, Spain). Chocolate the Burmese completes the household. Welcoming, fun loving and ever adaptable, we look forward to meeting you.
Directions: *Please phone.*

Oropi, Tauranga
Homestay/Farmstay
Address: 'Grenofen', Castles Road,
Oropi, R.D.3, Tauranga
Name: Jennie & Norm Reeve
Telephone: (07) 543 3953
Fax: (07) 543 3951
Email: n.reeve@wave.co.nz
Beds: 1 King, 2 Single (2 Bedrooms)
Bathroom: 2 Ensuite
Tariff: B&B (full) Double $90, Single $60, Dinner 3 course incl. wine $30pp, by arrangement. NZ B&B Vouchers accepted $20 surcharge
Nearest Town: Tauranga

We invite you to stay with us in our spacious home overlooking the undulating countryside, with the sea, Tauranga city, and Mount Maunganui in the background. Our property is a sheltered 3 1/2 acres sloping to the north with trees, gardens, lawns and two friendly donkeys. You may choose to relax in total privacy, enjoy the spa or swim in our pool. A short drive takes you to Tauranga racecourse, golf courses, beaches, and historic places, or you may like to sample the excellent shopping facilities available.
Guests may choose double bedroom, with King size bed or twin bedroom, each with ensuite, electric blankets, TV, comfortable chairs and rural views. Tea / coffee making facility with fridge in guest area.
We have travelled extensively and enjoy the company of local and overseas travellers. Our interests include skiing, cycling, golf, gardening, walking and travel. Be sure of a warm welcome.

Tauranga

Homestay
Address: Ohauiti R.D.3, Tauranga
Name: Bernie & Alison Rowe
Telephone: (07) 544 0966
Fax: (07) 544 0916
Mobile: (025) 945 785
Beds: 1 Queen, 1 Double, 2 Single (3 Bedrooms)
Bathroom: 1 Private, 1 Guests share
Tariff: B&B (continental) Double $80, Single $50, Children $25.
NZ B&B Vouchers accepted $12 Surcharge
Nearest Town: Tauranga 8km.

Alison and Bernie welcome you to Tauranga and to our home which is surrounded by beautiful trees, gardens, a tennis court and swimming pool. Tennis racquets available. Guests have own bathroom. Two bedrooms have adjacent private lounge, suitable families.
We are only 10 mins drive from centre of city and a great selection of very good restaurants. Very handy to beautiful golf courses, beaches, diving, deep sea fishing and tramping.
Alison and Bernie enjoy entertaining and meeting new people and are happy for you to stay as long as you like. Please no smoking within the house, outside is fine.
Directions: *Please phone.*

Te Puna, Tauranga
Homestay

Address: 310 Snodgrass Road,
R.D.2, Tauranga
Name: Diana & Alastair Melvin
Telephone: (07) 552 5313
Mobile: 025 589 443
Beds: 2 Double, 2 Single (3 bedrooms)
Bathroom: 1 Ensuite, 1 Guests share
Tariff: B&B (continental) Double $60, Single $35, Children half price.
Dinner $20 (by arrangement).
Nearest Town: Tauranga 10km south Highway 2

We are an outgoing couple with a grown family who live away from home. Our comfortable single storey home is set amongst mature trees. We have a guest wing with all services, including electric blankets and heaters. We are an easy twelve minutes drive from Tauranga, and twenty five minutes from Mt Maunganui beach, in the midst of orchards and lush farmland. A two kilometre drive takes you to a tidal inner-harbour beach with a good boat ramp.
A leisurely continental breakfast is included. A home cooked dinner with complimentary wine is available by prior arrangement. Guests are welcome to see our two acres of fruit trees, glasshouses, and garden. Our home is smoke free. Our interests include gardening, walking, weaving, craftwork. You will be only minutes away from hot pools, golf course, deep sea fishing, diving, superior shopping.
Directions: *Please phone after 5.30pm.*

There are some good tips for easier travel on page 7

Tauranga

Homestay+Self-contained Accom.
Address: The Hollies, Westridge Drive, Bethlehem, Tauranga
Name: Shirley & Michael
Telephone: (07) 577 9678 **Fax**: (07) 579 1678 **Mobile**: (025) 2767 195
Email: hollies@clear.net.nz
Beds: Homestay: 1 Queen, 1 Twin (2 bedrooms) SC: 1 Twin/King with ensuite.
Bathroom: 2 Private, 1 Ensuite
Tariff: B&B (full) Double $110 to $150, Single from $75, Dinner $25pp. Discount for second night and for seven nights. Visa/Mastercard. NZ B&B Vouchers accepted Surcharge $40 to $75
Nearest Town: Tauranga 5km

Relax and enjoy your stay at the Hollies, a five year old two storey country house, with spacious elegant rooms, set in an acre of gardens featuring roses, camellia hedge, and flat stone walls. Smokefree property, not suitable for young children. Guest rooms have fresh flowers, crisp linen, toiletries, hair dryers. Guests have a choice of queen or twin room each with own bathroom overlooking the garden. The luxurious suite with external and internal access, large private balcony with semi rural views, spacious lounge, TV, bedroom king / twin beds, ensuite, kitchenette, for those wanting ultimate comfort and privacy. Ideal for weary travellers, honeymooners and business persons. Amble through our gardens, swim in the pool, play croquet, pentaque or use the guests' lounge with doors opening to the garden, TV and stereo, or simply relax in the tranquil restful atmosphere. Breakfast healthy or indulgent, home-made muffins, muesli and bread, fresh fruit, a selection of tempting cooked dishes. Coffees and teas / herb can be served in the family room or in the garden. Dinner is available by prior arrangement using home grown produce in season, served in the dining room or alfresco outside. Enjoy dining at top award winning restaurants only minutes drive away. Excellent attractions near by such as beaches (for surfers and swimmers), mineral hot pools, winery, 18 hole golf course, historic village, race course, walkways and tennis. Tours can be arranged for jet boating, White Island volcano flights, deep sea fishing. An excellent location for day trips to Auckland, Whakatane, Rotorua, Taupo, Coromandel, Cambridge and Hamilton. Our interests include Jaguar cars, porcelain dolls, gardening, local and overseas travel. Our white tabby cat is called Muffee. Safe off-street parking, laundry facilities. We look forward to meeting you at your home away from home.

Tauranga
Orchard Homestay
Address: "Ripo Moana", 69 Asher Road,
Welcome Bay, RD 5, Tauranga
Name: Rei Preston-Thomas
Telephone: (07) 544 2184
Beds: 2 Single (1 bedroom) S.C. Cottage:
2 Single (1 bedroom)
Bathroom: 1 Private S.C. Cottage: 1 Private
Tariff: B&B (continental) Double $70, Single $40.
NZ B&B Vouchers accepted
Nearest Town: Tauranga 13km

What could be more restful than staying in a cottage overlooking the harbour on an avocado orchard. The cottage is joined to the house by an attractive walkway, and naturally guests are welcome in the house, and usually prefer to come over for breakfast. There is also a double bedroom with private bathroom in the house.
"Ripo-Moana" is a six acre orchard growing avocados and mandarins. It is situated on the edge of the inner harbour with the front lawn extending down to the water.
It offers a very warm welcome, the peace and tranquillity of the countryside, and yet is only twelve minutes drive to downtown Tauranga or Mount Maunganui, and fifty minutes to Rotorua.
Your host has travelled widely and lived and worked in several countries.
Directions: *Approximately 5km along Welcome Bay Road from the Maungatapu roundabout, but it is suggested you ring for detailed instructions.*

Tauranga
Homestay
Address: 34 Tainui Street, Matua,
Tauranga
Name: Peter & Anne Seaton
Telephone: (07) 576 8083
Mobile: 025 915566
Beds: 1 Double, 2 Single (2 bedrooms)
Bathroom: 1 Guests share
Tariff: B&B (continental) Double $75,
Single $40, Children half price, Campervans facilities.
NZ B&B Vouchers accepted
Nearest Town: Tauranga - 8 mins drive

Relax and enjoy our sunny home facilities and private garden in the peaceful suburb of Matua.
Only a 200 metre walk to Fergusson Park to enjoy a spectacular view of estuary and beach. A pleasant 5 minute stroll to Matua Shopping Centre enjoying the modern homes and picturesque gardens enroute. Only 8 minutes drive to Tauranga City centre and 15 minutes drive to Mt Maunganui Ocean beach.
Breakfast may be served indoors or outdoors. Enjoy the hospitality of our spacious lounge with complimentary tea or coffee available at any time. We have enjoyed travelling in New Zealand and overseas and look forward to welcoming you to our home.
Laundry facilities are available. Smokefree inside. Campervans welcome.

Tauranga
Orchard Homestay
Address: 26 Station Road, Omokoroa,
RD 2,Tauranga
Name: Bronwen and Alan Brown
Telephone: (07) 548 1936
Beds: 1 Queen, 2 Single (2 bedrooms)
Bathroom: 2 Private
Tariff: B&B (continental) Double $75-$85, Single $50, Dinner $25,
Children half price. No Credit Cards. NZ B&B Vouchers accepted $10 surcharge
Nearest Town: Tauranga, 15 kms South

*Montrose set among a one acre garden overlooking our avocado orchard, across
farmland to the sea and city lights. The upper storey of our home is solely for guests'
use, has 2 balconies, tea / coffee making facilities and pool table / lounge room. The
bedroom has two single beds and private bathroom. Downstairs we have a bedroom
with Queen bed and private bathroom. Take a stroll in our garden or walk to the local
water gardens. Browse through our New Zealand books, some containing our son's
work - a talented landscape photographer. Relax in the local hot pools. Enjoy home
made bread and home grown fruit and juices. Our interests include bowls, gardening
and our beautiful country. We have two sons and a daughter pursuing careers away
from home.*
*Holly our Cairn Terrier loves visitors. Boris our ginger cat is more shy. We look
forward to your company.*
DIRECTIONS:*Station road is off SH2 opposite Whakamaramara Service Station
200 m on right.*

Tauranga
Bed & Breakfast
Address: Harbinger House,
209 Fraser Street, Tauranga
Name: Helen and Doug Fisher
Telephone: (07) 578 8801
Fax: (07) 578 8801
Email: d-h.fisher@xtra.co.nz
Beds: 2 Queen, 2 Single (3 bedrooms)
Bathroom: 1 Guests share

Tariff: B&B (special) Double $70-$90, Single $55-$75, dinner $25 pp.
Credit Cards accepted. NZ B&B Vouchers accepted $10 surcharge can apply
Nearest Town: Tauranga (2 km to CBD or 30 mins walk)

*Welcome to Harbinger House. Our upstairs has been renovated with your comfort a
top priority. The two queen rooms have vanity units and private balconies. All rooms
have quality furnishings, tea and coffee making facilities and tourist information. A
guest telephone is installed for your use. Laundry facilities are available. Our house
is centrally located being close to the hospital, conference facilities, shops and beaches.
We have a lovely garden which you are welcome to use. Breakfast is a gourmet event
with fresh juice, local fruits where possible, yoghurt, muesli, freshly baked bread and
a cooked dish.*
*Packed picnic lunches are a speciality as is dinner - both by prior arrangement.
Complimentary pick up from airport and bus station. Off street parking. We are a well
travelled couple who enjoy having guests to stay. Helen is a keen cook, loves gardening
and crafts. Our house is smoke free inside.*
Home Page: www.harbinger.co.nz

Tauranga

Homestay, Self Contained Accommodation
Address: 98E Boscabel Drive,
Ohauiti, Tauranga
Name: Lutz and Lydia Heutmann
Telephone: (07) 544 0219 or (07) 578 9113
Fax: (07) 544 0215
Beds: 2 Queen, 1 Double (3 bedrooms)
Bathroom: 3 Ensuite
Tariff: B&B (full) Double $80, Single $60, Dinner $20.
NZ B&B Vouchers accepted
Nearest Town: Tauranga (10 minutes)

We have recently built our dream home in Boscabel, an exclusive rural residential subdivision in Tauranga. Our large home includes two self-contained studio apartments with kitchenettes and one large double ensuite bedroom, all with central video system.The house is set on a landscaped 3/4 acre section with extensive views and a large picturesque pond. Breakfast and dinner and bar-b-que facilities are available by arrangement as Lydia loves cooking and entertaining.

The use of our ozone swimming pool in a tranquil garden setting is available during the summer months. We are located only 10 minutes from the Tauranga city centre and 13 minutes form the Ocean Beach at Mount Maunganui.

We are a recently-retired German couple in our early fifties and would love to welcome Kiwi and overseas visitors to this beautiful part of the Bay of Plenty with its excellent beaches, fishing, four 18-hole golf courses.

Tauranga

Self Contained Accommodation
Address: 6 Wallace Road,
Te Puna, Tauranga
Name: "Selinden Park".
Astrid and Bruce Martin
Telephone: (07) 552 5797
Fax: (07) 552 5790
Mobile: (025) 956 650
Beds: 1 Queen (Single on application) (1 Bedroom)
Bathroom: 1 Ensuite
Tariff: B&B (full) Price for accommodation and dinner on application.
Credit Cards accepted. Laundry facilities available
Nearest Town: Tauranga

Selinden Park is set amidst 2 acres of well maintained park-like grounds, right on the edge of Tauranga harbour. Our guest cottage, surrounded by tropical gardens and with stunning sea views, is fully self contained and includes your own conservatory and deck for outdoor enjoyment.

Facilities available at Selinden park include: sandy beach, hot/cold pool, dinghy and outboard motor, fishing rods, sailing dinghy and canoe.

Day fishing trips, harbour cruises and trout fishing trips can also be arranged.

Within 15 minutes drive you can enjoy 4 golf courses, 2 wineries, surf beach, excellent boutique shopping, deep sea and game fishing, award winning restaurants and white water rafting.Additional meals, picnic lunches and anything else you may need are there for the asking.

Looking for something special? Then Selinden park is the place for you!

Tauranga
Homestay
Address: "Birch Haven", Welcome Bay Road,
RD5, Tauranga
(adjacent Welcome Bay Hotpools)
Name: Judy and George McConnell
Telephone: 07-544 2499
Mobile: 025-414 289
Beds: 1 Super King/Twin, 1 Queen
(2 bedrooms). Campervan for hire.
Bathroom: 1 Guests share
Tariff: B&B (full) Double $80, Single $50, Dinner $25, Children under 12 years
$25. NZ B&B Vouchers accepted $12 surcharge
Nearest Town: Mt Maunganui. Tauranga (15 mins drive).

Have you been travelling or sight-seeing for hours? How about a 'cuppa' once you've settled into our peaceful one-level home on 3 acres amongst lovely trees. In summer perhaps a swim in the pool, a typical New Zealand barbecue or in winter a spa and dinner by the open fire. Sky/TV, music or our company are all evening options but within 15 minutes drive are numerous good restaurants (nearest 1 km) and entertainment. We love walking and can recommend several good walks nearby. We are happy to help you see and do as much or as little as you wish. Travel, good food and wine, gardening, reading and sport interest us and Blackie our cat will join us if he chooses. We offer courtesy pick-up from Tauranga terminals and want to make your stay a happy memory.
No smoking inside please.
Directions: *Please phone if possible.*

Te Puna, Tauranga
Orchard Bed & Breakfast
Address: 63 Snodgrass Road,
RD 2, Te Puna, Tauranga
Name: Maple Lodge'
Telephone: (07) 552 4050
Fax: (07) 552 4050 **Mobile**: (025) 279 4121
Beds: 1 Double, 2 Single (2 bedrooms)
Bathroom: 1 Guests share

Tariff: B&B (continental) Double $70, Single $40.   NZ B&B Vouchers accepted
Nearest Town: Tauranga 10 km South S/H 2.

We invite you to come and experience our character home overlooking a mixed orchard of citrus, avocados and nashis. You can relax beside the pool, ramble through the mature gardens and orchard then relax on the deck and enjoy the sunset.
A short drive takes you to a variety of restaurants and cafes. Harbour beaches are only minutes away as are wonderful garden centres, craft shops, hot pools or the city lights. Breakfast is served using fresh fruit from the orchard or local, with a choice of cereal and toast or croissants.
Gordon works full time on the orchard, is interested in classic cars and plays electric piano.
Robyn is a Natural Therapy Practitioner and has a home clinic specialising in herbal remedies, flower essences and supplements.
Homer our three legged cat joins with us to make your stay a really enjoyable one.
We are smoke free. No children at home.
Directions: *Please phone.*

Tauranga
Homestay
Address: "Bayview Homestead",
Pahoia, Tauranga
Name: Verna and Bill
Telephone: (07) 548 1551
Fax: (07) 548 1551
Beds: 1 Queen, 2 Single (2 bedrooms)
Bathroom: 1 Guests share
Tariff: B&B (special) Double $130, Single $100, Dinner $30.
Credit Cards accepted. Not suitable for children under 12.
Nearest Town: 20 km North of Tauranga

Beauty, peace and tranquillity will be yours while you stay with us. Our three acre property has sweeping lawns, attractive developing gardens and petanque court, with panoramic views of rolling farmland, the Bay of Plenty and the Kaimai Ranges.
Our modern brick house is smoke-free, and guests have their own wing, including formal lounge / dining room with open fire. Retain your privacy or socialise with us - your choice. A billiard room is available.
We offer fine food in a relaxing and friendly environment. Choose a traditional full breakfast or perhaps fresh muffins or pancakes. Enjoy complimentary tea, coffee and home-made cookies. Meals may be taken inside or on the deck.
Located mid-way between Katikati and Tauranga, local attractions include river, coastal and bush walks, tennis, golf, hot pools, restaurants, mural town and historic village. Children over 12 welcome. Fluent French and basic German spoken.
Directions: *Please phone*

Tauranga
Bed & Breakfast
Address: 25 Beach Road, Tauranga.
Name: Beach Road Bed & Breakfast
Telephone: (07) 576 0991
Fax: (07) 576 0922
Mobile: (021) 763 149
Email: Richter.Visser@clear.net.nz
Beds: 2 Double, 2 single (3 bedrooms)
Bathroom: 1 Private, 1 Guests share
Tariff: B&B (continental) Double $95,
Single $75, Children $55.
Credit Cards accepted.
Nearest Town: Tauranga City Centre 10 min.

Our home is situated "on the water edge' with absolutely unsurpassed views of the harbour entrance, Mount Maunganui and Matakane Island. We are on a walking track network that follows the harbours and estuary's waters edge. There are two parks within 100 meters, our local shops are three minutes away and the inner city 25 minutes on foot or 10 minutes by car - we have a 12ft dingy to use for fishing on the harbour and two mountain bikes to explore the city and surrounds with.
Accommodation is offered in two double and a twin room, with separate guest bathroom. A large lounge, living room and oodles of decks to enjoy the magnificent view and sunshine from.
A continental breakfast is included but a cooked breakfast is available at little extra cost.
Angela and I have travelled extensively and enjoy the company of fellow travellers. We look forward to sharing experiences with you.

Tauranga
Homestay Lodge
Address: 20 Williams Road,
Pyes Pa, Tauranga
Name: Reg Turner
Telephone: (07) 543 2000 **Fax:** (07) 543 1999
Mobile: (025) 487 707 **Email:** cassimir@xtra.co.nz
Beds: 6 King, can be split to 12 Single (6 bedrooms)
Bathroom: 4 Ensuite, 2 Guests share
Tariff: B&B (full) Double $300, Single $200, Children welcome $100 per child
Dinner $75. Pets welcome but all must be under control and doctored.
Credit Cards. NZ B&B Vouchers accepted + Surcharge
Nearest Town: Tauranga 15km, Rotorua 32km

A Fairytale Castle fulfilling every imagination. Cassimir Lodge is a hideaway retreat. A grand colonial style landmark built of natural materials atop one of the Bay of Plenty's highest promontories at Pyes Pa near Tauranga. Inside, polished wood, sweeping staircases, elegant furniture and marble tiled bathrooms produce an atmosphere of peace, tranquility and well being. A private home which was expanding, Cassimir today is a transformation created by entrepreneurial visionary Reg Turner who took over the 50 acre property in 1995. He is the dreamer who created Lake Tarawera's Solitaire Lodge. Everyone who comes here agrees that there is a spirit, a presence of uplifting energy which has to be experienced to be believed. At the bottom of the valley, is a small river running through bushlands which are probably as they were before the days of Cook. The deer and goats although exotic to New Zealand, nevertheless fit well in the landscape surrounding the lodge. The stillness and silence is everywhere. Here is a place where frazzled nerves will be calmed and the human spirit revitalised.
Home Page: www.cassimir.co.nz **Directions:** *The Williams Road turn-off to Cassimir is 11.5 kilometres up Pyes Pa Road from the Barkes Corner roundabout - at the inland end of Cameron Road, go a couple of hundred metres up Williams Road, then at the T-intersection turn left into Williams Road South and in less than a minute you're there.*

Mt Maunganui
Homestay+Self-contained Accom.
Address: 'Homestay On The Beach'
85c Oceanbeach Road, Mt Maunganui
Name: Larraine & Bernie Cotter
Telephone: (07) 575 4879 **Fax:** (07) 575 4828
Mobile: (025) 766 799

Beds: 1 Queen, 1 Double, 1 Single (2 bedrooms). Self contained unit.
Double Hydabed in lounge.
Bathroom: 1 Ensuite, 1 Private
Tariff: B&B (continental) Double $100-$110, Single $70, Dinner $25 (BYO).
Dinner by prior arrangement, Children 1/2 price. Credit Cards accepted. Non Smoking. NZ B&B Vouchers accepted May 1st until October 31st. $30 surcharge
Nearest Town: Mt Maunganui 4km, Tauranga 4km

Welcome to our modern home on the beach, with superb seaviews and 25 kms of sand to enjoy leisurely walks. We have one queen sized bedroom with ensuite, one room with double and single bed and bathroom. A guest lounge with kitchenette for tea and coffee facilities, microwave, fridge, TV etc, opening onto a large sundeck to relax and take in the sun and surf. You may choose to rent the self contained unit on its own, sleeping up to 4 guests at $180 per night or $130 per night for 2 guests, including continental breakfast with eggs any style. Close by are golf courses, bowling green and hot mineral pools. A 45 minute walk around the base of the Mount is fantastic. An easy 2 1/2 hour scenic drive from Auckland and one hour from Rotorua. There is off-street parking. Look forward to having you stay.

Mt Maunganui
Bed & Breakfast
Address: 463 Maunganui Rd,
Mt Maunganui
Name: Fitzgerald's Irish Inn
Hosts: Bill + Edna
Telephone: (07) 575 4013
Fax: (07) 575 4013
Mobile: 025 794 555
Beds: 4 Double (4 bedrooms)
Bathroom: 2 Guests share

Cead Mile Failte

Tariff: B&B (full) Double $70-80 (seasonal), Single $55, Dinner $15,
Campervans $25, Credit Cards. NZ B&B Vouchers accepted $25 surcharge
Nearest Town: Tauranga 5 kms

Are you looking for a relaxed, friendly atmosphere? The 'Fitzgerald Irish Inn' offers real hospitality at affordable prices, including warm comfortable rooms with TV's. Billiard and games room with tea and coffee available at all times. We provide supper and a good hearty breakfast (home made muesli or cereal, fruit, toast and marmalade), followed by the favourite bacon and egg. Our Irish Inn is situated close to colourful downtown Phoenix shopping centre, featuring new restaurants and cafes, beautiful harbour and ocean beaches for swimming or strolling, Blake park Sports Centre, golf, RSA, cosmopolitan club, and have you experienced the pleasures of our famous hot salt water pools at the base of Mt Maunganui, which are soooo relaxing after a walk around the base of the Mount or a walk to the top if you so desire. We can help you plan visits to BOP's many places of interest. We are warm and caring hosts ensuring every guest enjoys a memorable stay. Cead mile failte (A hundred thousand welcomes).

Omanu Beach, Mt Maunganui
Homestay
Address: Please phone
Name: Judy & David Hawkins
Telephone: (07) 575 0677
Beds: 2 Single (1 bedroom)
Bathroom: 1 Private
Tariff: B&B (continental) Double $60, Single $35, Dinner $15pp.
NZ B&B Vouchers accepted
Nearest Town: Tauranga/Mt Maunganui - both 5 kms.

We are a retired farming couple who invite you to share our quiet and comfortable home just 60 seconds off one of the country's finest beaches, where you can just relax and enjoy our sea view, or if more energetic there is plenty of good swimming, surfing and walking available or even climb up "The Mount" for a 360 degree view of the Bay. Hot salt water pools (great for tired limbs), the golf course and bowling greens are all just a few minutes away as is the Bayfair Shopping Complex. A twin bedded room with bathroom for guests is available and a home cooked dinner by prior arrangement. Homemade jams and preserves are served for breakfast. An excellent place for visitors to stop and unwind for a day or two between Auckland and Rotorua. We enjoy meeting people and would like to share your travel experiences over supper each evening. A smoke, pet and child free home.
Directions: *Please phone for directions.*

Mount Maunganui

Homestay
Address: 28a Sunbrae Grove, Mt Maunganui
Name: Barbara Marsh
Telephone: (07) 575 5592 **Mobile**: (021) 707 243
Beds: 1 Queen, 2 Single (2 bedrooms)
Bathroom: 1 Guests share
Tariff: B&B (full) Double $95 Single $60, Dinner $25 pp.
Credit cards. NZ B&B Vouchers accepted $15 Surcharge
Nearest Town: Mt Maunganui and Tauranga 9km

We invite you to stay with us and relax, while enjoying stunning ocean views from our lovely home, on the shores of beautiful Mount Maunganui. You may choose to be a Homestay guest or, alternatively, rent the self-contained accommodation (at a separate rate), allowing you to be independent.
Sunbrae Grove is a quiet cul de sac at the end of Oceanbeach Road, and we offer undercover, off-street parking for guests. Dinner is available by prior arrangement please. Laundry facilities.
Your well-travelled hostess shares her smoke-free home with Bella, a very sociable Balinese cat. We are 10 minutes from the hot salt pools at the foot of the Mount itself, and a similar distance from Tauranga. Bayfair Shopping Centre is only minutes away. We welcome your inquiries and look forward to meeting you.
Directions: *Please feel free to phone for directions.*

Mount Maunganui

Homestay and Self-contained apartment
Address: 'Carnoustie', 17B Rita Street,
Mount Maunganui
Name: The Mitchell's
Telephone: (07) 574 4920 **Fax**: (07) 574 4974
Mobile: (025) 886 092
Beds: 2 Double, 2 Single (2 bedrooms)
Bathroom: 1 Ensuite, 1 Private
Tariff: B&B (full) Double $90-$100,
Single $60, Children under 12 half price, Dinner $25 by prior arrangement.
Nearest Town: Mount Maunganui 500m, Tauranga 4km

Welcome to 'Carnoustie'.
Our new double story home is situated only minutes walking distance from the beach, The Mount shops, several restaurants, the hot pools and scenic Mount walk. Park you car in the courtyard and relax. Golf clubs, beach and pool towels are available for your use with our compliments. We have travelled extensively in New Zealand and overseas, staying Bed and Breakfast and have had many enjoyable experiences and understand the traveller's needs. We have a grown up family of four sons and one daughter and eleven lovely grandchildren, six in New Zealand, two in USA and three in UK.
Carnoustie is wheelchair orientated - easy entrance and internal lift. Disabled guests welcome. Transport from bus, plane or railcar can be arranged.
Please feel free to phone, fax or write for reservations. Carnoustie is a smoke free home. Look forward to meeting you - your host Gloria.

Mt. Maunganui

Homestay/Self-contained Accom.
Address: "Fairways",
170 Ocean Beach Rd., Mt. Maunganui
Name: John & Philippa Davies
Telephone: (07) 575 5325 or Bus. (07) 578 5899
Fax: (07) 578 2362 **Mobile**: (025) 277 7363
Beds: 1 Queen, 1 Double (2 bedrooms)
Bathroom: 1 Ensuite, 1 Family Share
Tariff: B&B (full) Double $90, Single $60, Dinner by arrangement including wine
$35pp.
Nearest Town: Mt Maunganui 3 kms

A Golfer's Paradise! Step from our garden onto the 8th Fairway, and enjoy a bonus lesson from John, a former scratch golfer. Work up an appetite with a swim in the surf, a mere 50 meters away, and in winter, relax in our ozone filtered spa! Whatever the weather, enjoy with us our relaxed and comfortable smoke free home, with interesting food, wine, company, music and conversation.

Make us your base while visiting Rotorua, Taupo, Coromandel and Waitomo. Play 6 top golf courses within a 30km radius, or take time to discover the delights of Tauranga city and the local hot salt water pools, mountain walks, and excellent shopping, dining and sporting facilities.

Pippa is a registered nurse enthusiastically involved in a natural health clinic. We both enjoy meeting people, are well travelled, and experienced hosts.

We look forward to welcoming you.

Mount Maunganui

Homestay
Address: "Pembroke House",
12 Santa Fe Key, Royal Palm Beach,
Papamoa, Mt Maunganui
Name: Cathy & Graham Burgess
Telephone: (07) 572 1000
Email: PEMBROKEHOUSE@XTRA.CO.NZ
Beds: 2 Queen, 2 Single (3 bedrooms)
Bathroom: 1 Ensuite, 1 Guests share
Tariff: B&B (full) Double $80, Single $50. Credit cards.
NZ B&B Vouchers accepted $15 surcharge
Nearest Town: Mt Maunganui 9km, Tauranga 9km, Rotorua 50 minutes.

Welcome to our modern smoke-free home, with unrestricted seaview. Cross the road to the ocean beach, where you can enjoy swimming, surfing and beach walks. Near new Palm Beach Shopping Plaza.

One room has queen size bed and ensuite. Two other bedrooms, one queen size and one twin, share a separate guest bathroom. Separate guest lounge with TV and tea making facilities. Laundry available.

Cathy is a primary school teacher and Graham semi-retired - your host. We are widely travelled and both enjoy meeting people. Our home is shared with two precious cats - Twinkle and Crystal. We all look forward to welcoming you.

Directions: *Please phone ahead for reservations and directions.*

Papamoa Beach

Homestay
Address: 'Markbeech Homestay',
274 Dickson Road, Papamoa, BOP.
Name: Joan & Jim Francis
Telephone: (07) 542 0815/0800 168 791
Mobile: (025) 318132
Beds: 1 Double, 3 Single (3 bedrooms)
Bathroom: 1 Guests share
Tariff: B&B (full) Double $65, Single $35, Children half price;
Dinner by arrangement $18. Breakfast full.   NZ B&B Vouchers accepted
Nearest Town: Mount Maunganui or Te Puke 11 km each on SH 2

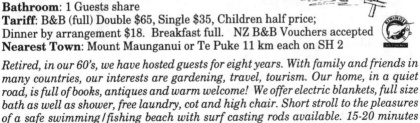

Retired, in our 60's, we have hosted guests for eight years. With family and friends in many countries, our interests are gardening, travel, tourism. Our home, in a quiet road, is full of books, antiques and warm welcome! We offer electric blankets, full size bath as well as shower, free laundry, cot and high chair. Short stroll to the pleasures of a safe swimming / fishing beach with surf casting rods available. 15-20 minutes drive to local tourist attractions all featured on the Pacific Coast Highway route. Children welcome. We will happily meet public transport and take you sightseeing. Good restaurants nearby.
Directions: *From SH2 (Rotorua - Tauranga) turn at Wilsons Garden Centre, signposted 'Papamoa'. Dickson Road fifth turn right (just after the Papamoa Family Tavern).*

Papamoa Beach

Homestay
Address: 8 Taylor Road, Papamoa
Bay of Plenty
Name: Genyth Harwood
Telephone: (07) 542 0279
Mobile: (021) 215 1523
Beds: 1 Double, 2 Single (2 bedrooms)
Bathroom: 1 Ensuite,1 Guests Share, 1 Family share.
Tariff: B&B (full) Double $65, Single $40, Children 1/2 price, under 5 free,
Dinner $15 p.p. NZ B&B Vouchers accepted
Nearest Town: Tauranga 20km

My beachfront home is situated about 50 metres from the waves of the Pacific Ocean, with beautiful views of Mayor & Motiti Islands. Things to do include swimming, fishing, sunbathing, or beach walks plus, endless interesting excursions round the district. We have a two storeyed home with guest accommodation on the lower level serviced by a shower, toilet and laundry facilities. Continental or cooked breakfast is offered and a home cooked dinner if desired - we also enjoy a barbeque in the warmer weather. Resorts such as Mt Maunganui and Rotorua with its thermal attractions are within easy reach.
Directions: *Turn off State Highway 2 (Tauranga to Rotorua) at "Wilsons Garden Centre", proceed about 2 kms to roundabout at Papamoa Domain, take right turn then about 4 kms to Motiti Road on left and left again into Taylor Road.*

Papamoa Beach
Farmstay
Address: 'Bent Hills Farmstays'
1162 Welcoms Bay Rd, R D 7,
Te Puke
Name: Malcolm & Trudie
Telephone: (07) 542 0972
Fax: (07) 542 0972 **Mobile**: (025) 982 354
Beds: 1 Queen, 2 Single (2 bedrooms)
Bathroom: 1 Ensuite, 1 Family share
Tariff: B&B (Full) Double $100, Single $70, Dinner $25.
Children under 12 half price/under 5 free, Cot available.
Nearest Town: 12km Tauranga/Mt Maunganui, 2.5km Papamoa Beach

Situated in a stunning spacious valley Bent Hills Farm is totally private with magnificent rural and coastal views.Our home built house features a range of NZ timbers and unconventional ideas. With 700 sq.ft. of covered decks it is designed for outdoor living to take full advantage of a magical setting.
We are a down to earth couple in our 30's with 3 children and a variety of friendly animals.On farm we offer complimentary horse riding and target shooting.
The farm is situated amongst ancient Maori Pa sites and from the top 360 degree views cover the whole BOP region.
We have extensive gardens featuring 80 varieties of fruits and nuts. Locally there is a bush waterfall, fabulous beach with beachfront bar and restaurant, hot pools, golf and the cities of Tauranga and Mt Maunganui are only 10 mins. away.
We encourage our guests to feel at home and aim to provide the friendliest service.

Paengaroa, Te Puke
Homestay+B&B
Address: 'Hafod', 151 Wilson Road South,
Paengaroa, Te Puke
Postal: P O Box 204, Te Puke
Name: Maureen H Oliver
Telephone: (07) 533 1086 **Fax**: (07) 533 1086
Beds: 4 Single (2 bedrooms)
Bathroom: 2 Ensuite

Tariff: B&B (continental) Double $70, Single $45, Dinner $20, Children half price, Campervans welcome. NZ B&B Vouchers accepted
Nearest Town: Te Puke 10km, Tauranga 25km. Rotorua 40km, Whakatane 40km.

Welcome to the HAFOD.
Two acres of garden, designed on a Welsh theme, compliments this lovely old country home, part of which are turn of the century.
Each bedroom has its own ensuite and the large lounge with piano, library, reading area are available for the use of guests as is the garden room for BBQ.
HAFOD, a Welsh name meaning, peace, retreat, is appropriate for this large rambling home and garden that is used extensively for weddings and open to the public.
Travel, tramping, gardening and local promotions are some of your hosts interests together with the family pets. The Te Puke golf course is only 2 mins away, the beach 10. Rotorua and Whakatane 40 mins.
Pre dinner drinks can be served and your pets are welcome.
Directions: *Travelling south from Te Puke - Whakatane Highway 2, 1st right passed Te Puke Golf Club, 1st drive right.*

Te Puke
Homestay
Address: 'Lindenhof', 58 Dunlop Rd, Te Puke
Name: Henry & Sandra Sutter
Telephone: (07) 573 4592 **Fax**: (07) 573 9392
Beds: 1 Double, 4 Single (3 bedrooms)
Bathroom: 1 Ensuite, 2 Private
Tariff: B&B (full) Double $90, Single $50, Dinner $20.
Credit cards accepted. NZ B&B Vouchers accepted Same day restrictions.
Nearest Town: Te Puke 2km

Lindenhof was built in the kiwifruit boom and is a replica of a mansion. Feature of house is stain glass windows, central stairway and chandelier. House is furnished with period furniture. It is set in semi rural area with landscaped gardens, tennis court and swimming pool. We also offer a spa pool and a full size billiard table. Also available are tours of our area fishing and hunting trips.
We are a multi lingual family. I speak English and Swiss, my husband speaks Swiss, French, German and English.
Hobbies: Doll making, spinning and vintage cars. No smoking in the house.
Directions: *On reaching Te Puke on SH 2 from Tauranga, Dunlop Rd is on your right by the Gas Centre, 'Lindenhof' is at the end of Dunlop Rd. Phone if you need to be picked up.*

Te Puke
Homestay
Address: 'Mi Casa', 706 No.1 Rd,
R.D.2, Te Puke
Name: Peter & Pauline Taylor
Telephone: (07) 573 5284 **Fax**: (07) 573 5284
Mobile: (025) 450 768
Beds: 1 Queen, 4 Single (3 bedrooms)
Bathroom: 1 Guest share, 2 additional toilets available
Tariff: B&B (special) Double $70, Single $40, Dinner $20.
NZ B&B Vouchers accepted
Nearest Town: Te Puke 8km.

Country living, country pace - just what you need for a break.
Arrive to suit yourself, relax in our tranquil interesting garden with swimming pool and spa and an adjacent kiwifruit block guests can wander through.
Situated in the heart of the Bay of Plenty, our area offers a wide variety of leisure activities, or allows you to relax in our lovely surrounds. Mt Maunganui, Tauranga only 30 mins to the North, Rotorua 45 mins to the South.
Our home has two lounges. Guest bathroom has separate toilet and separate shower. Just 8 mins from Te Puke and 15 mins from the golf course. No smoking please. Dinner by arrangement.
Enjoy your own pace and time, without the worry of meals, housework and timetables. Come for a night - come for a week.
Directions: *No.1 Road leaves State Highway 2, south end of Te Puke at Country Lodge. Travel up No.1 Rd 7km to 706 on your right.*

There are some good tips for easier travel on page 7

Te Puke
Farmstay
Address: Paengaroa Te Puke (please phone for directions)
Name: Isabel and Graeme McNaughton
Telephone: 07-533 1196 (after 5 pm)
Beds: 1 Double, 2 Single (2 bedrooms)
Bathroom: 1 Guests share.
Tariff: B&B (continental) Double $70, Single $45, Dinner $20.
NZ B&B Vouchers accepted
Nearest Town: Te Puke 12kms.

We live 2 kms from Paengaroa which is very central in the Bay of Plenty.
A large garden which includes a hard surface tennis court surrounds our home which
is situated on our dairy farm adjacent to our kiwi-fruit orchard.
Our interests are many and varied and include race horses, gardening, we have
recently taken up golf. We have a billiard room.
We have pets, a dog "Jill" and cats, but not in the house.
Directions:
Please phone for directions and booking.

Pukehina Beach
Homestay
Address: 217 Pukehina Parade,
Pukehina Beach, RD9, Te Puke
Name: Alison & Paul Carter
Telephone: (07) 533 3988
Fax: (07) 533 3988 **Mobile**: (025) 276 7305
Email: p.a.carter@xtra.co.nz
Beds: 2 Double (2 bedrooms)
Bathroom: 1 Guests share
Tariff: B&B (continental) Double $90, Single $60, Children half price,
Dinner $25, Campervans $25. Credit cards.
Nearest Town: Te Puke 21k's.

Welcome to our absolute Beachfront home at Pukehina Beach, situated on the Pacific
Ocean. Our two storey home includes two double bedrooms with a bathroom / shower,
toilet, T.V. / Leisure Lounge with Coffee, Tea and Fridge facilities. Extra beds and
laundry facilities available. Your accommodation is situated downstairs, allowing
complete privacy if you so wish. Also, you have your own beach access with a spacious
Sun Deck, overlooking the Ocean and White Island Volcano.
Cast your rod off the beach (rods available), swim, surf, enjoy beach walks or just relax
and enjoy our occasional visits from the friendly dolphins.
We are 13k's from the Te Puke Golf Course and a 30-40 minute drive from Tauranga,
Mount Maunganui, Whakatane and Rotorua.
Pukehina Beach has two Restaurants, but we welcome you to dine with us by prior
arrangement please. Fishing and Diving Charters are also available. We invite you
to enjoy our 'Unique Paradise'.

Continental breakfast consists of fruit, cereal, toast, tea/coffee,
Full breakfast is the same with a cooked course,
Special breakfast has something special.

Pukehina Beach
Beachstay
Address: "Tahamoana", 619 Pukehina Parade,
Pukehina Beach, RD 9, Te Puke
Name: Maureen & Merritt Smith
Telephone: (07) 533 3130 **Fax**: (07) 533 3130
Beds: 1 Double, 2 Single (2 bedrooms)
Bathroom: 1 Private
Tariff: B&B (full) Double $85, Single $60, Children half price,
Dinner $20 by arrangement, Credit Cards (BC/VISA/MC).
NZ B&B Vouchers accepted $15 surcharge
Nearest Town: Te Puke 27km, Tauranga, Rotorua, Whakatane - all 40 min
drive.

Peace and tranquillity in comfortable relaxed surroundings awaits you at "Tahamoana"
on the shores of the beautiful Pacific Ocean. We welcome you to share our home where
dolphins often come in to play while we are breakfasting in the sunshine. We look out
to Motiti, Motunau and Whale Islands and on a clear day can see the volcanic activity
on White Island. We are centrally enough located to use as a peaceful haven after
sightseeing or just come and enjoy a typical "Kiwi" beach holiday. Swimming, surfing,
fishing, gathering shellfish or just relaxing. We have three licensed restaurants nearby,
but are happy to cater for you with wholesome home cooking given prior notice.
Laundry facilities available.
We share our home with our Fox Terrier "Josh".
Directions: *8km off State Highway 2 following signposts to Pukehina Beach.*
Tahamoana Beachstay sign at gate. Please phone if possible to ensure vacancy.

Matata/Pikowai
Farmstay
Address: 'Pohutukawa Farmhouse',
 State Highway 2, R.D 4. Whakatane
Name: Susanne & Jörg Prinz
Telephone: (07) 322 2182 **Fax**: (07) 322 2182
Email: pohutukawa @prinztours.co.nz
Beds: 2 Double, 2 Single (3 bedrooms)
Bathroom: 2 Ensuite, 1 Private

Tariff: B&B (continental) Double $90, Single from $55, Dinner $15/20,
Credit Cards (VISA/Mastercard). NZ B&B Vouchers accepted
Nearest Town: Whakatane 34km, Te Puke 34km

Paradise is the Bay of Plenty!
Pohutukawa Farmhouse is situated in a picturesque location overlooking the Pacific
Ocean with outstanding seaviews to many islands, from Coromandel to the East Cape.
Glance up from the breakfast table and see White Island, New Zealand's most active
volcano 50km off-shore. Sometimes we see dolphins and even whales pass by.
Our farm is the perfect place to relax either in the garden, at the swimming pool or have
a hit on our floodlit tennis court. We offer cosy accommodation and tasty meals with
home-grown meat, fresh fruit and vegetables from our organic farm. We encourage
visitors to stay several days (discounts available) - there is so much to see and do! Many
nearby attractions want to be visited and we are able to organise almost anything for
you. We speak English and German and enjoy making our guests feel welcome in our
lovely home.
Home Page: http://www.prinztours.co.nz/bube.html

Whakatane

Homestay on a Farm
Address: Thornton Road,
i.e. Whakatane - Tauranga Highway
Name: Jim & Kathleen Law
Telephone: (07) 308 7955 **Fax**: (07) 308 7955
Email: Kath.law@xtra.co.nz
Beds: 1 Queen, 2 Single (2 bedrooms)
Bathroom: 1 Guests share
Tariff: B&B (continental) Double $60, Single $35,
Dinner $20; Campervans welcome. Credit Cards (VISA) + Eftpos.
NZ B&B Vouchers accepted
Nearest Town: Whakatane 7km

Whakatane is off the beaten tourist track, yet it is the centre for a wide range of activities. The local golf course is nearby. We can arrange sight-seeing trips, including White Island. Ohope Beach is a short drive away. You may wish to relax in peaceful surroundings or watch the activities in our Red Barn Country Kitchen and Craftshop which promotes over 270 Bay of Plenty artisans. We have lived on this farm for 48 years. Two 50/50 sharemilkers milk over 400 cows. We also grow citrus and feijoas and breed black and coloured and spotted sheep. We have travelled extensively overseas and enjoy meeting people of all ages. As "young oldies" we enjoy bowls, Lions Club, genealogy, organic gardening and ballroom dancing - not necessarily in that order. Vegetarian and special diets catered for. The Kiwihost concept motivates us. A warm welcome awaits. We have one cat.
Directions: *Thornton Road - 9km west of Whakatane P.O. (the old State Highway 2).*
Home Page: http://www.nzhomestay.co.nz/law.html.

Thornton, Whakatane

Farm-Beach Homestay
Address: Postal: P. O. Box 295, Whakatane,
Rural: Thornton Road,
Whakatane
Name: 'T' Tree Lodge Mieke & Max van Batenburg
Telephone: (07) 322 2295 **Mobile**: (025) 221 6542
Email: mmbtnbrk@wave.co.nz
*Dutch, German & French spoken.
Beds: 2 Super King (or 4 singles), 1 Single (3 bedrooms)
Bathroom: 1 Private with shower, 1 Guests share with spa bath.
Facilities: extra guest lounge with piano, TV,
Tariff: B&B (full) Double $65-$90, Single $45-$65. Reduced rates for longer stays. NZ B&B Vouchers accepted $20 surcharge for Double room.
Nearest Town: Whakatane 17 km (west), Matata 8km (east).

Do you wish to "taste" Paradise? Enjoy magnificent sunrises, sunsets, seaviews? On a moonlit night, watch the silvery Pacific from our large wooden deck, go for a walk on our secluded beach only a few minutes away, laze in a hammock with a book, breathing the silence, get pampered with a scrumptious breakfast..... then this is the place for you. We live a few minutes drive from the main Tauranga - Whakatane Road. Our modern cosy smoke free home is built of native and exotic timbers. A warm welcome awaits those who look for a complete rest in tranquil surroundings with only the sounds of the birds, and the symphony of the ocean waves. There are many unique attractions like visiting an active volcano, swimming with dolphins and many more. We have a friendly Labrador and two amiable cats.
Directions: *Please phone for directions.*
Home Page: http://www.freeyellow.com/members3/ttreelodge

Whakatane

Farmstay
Address: Paul Road,
R.D.2, Whakatane
Name: Jill & John Needham
Telephone: (07) 322 8399
Fax: (07) 322 8399
Beds: 1 Queen, 1 King (2 bedrooms) (You will be the only guests)
Bathroom: 1 Ensuite, 1 Private
Tariff: B&B (full) Double $75, Single $40, Dinner $25 with wine.
Nearest Town: Whakatane 18km

We invite you to stay with us on our deer farm where we also grow avocados and hydrangeas for export. Our children have flown the nest and left us a large home which we enjoy sharing. You will be the only guests so you have a luxurious private wing with your own bathroom and deck where you may enjoy the wondrous views. We have a pool room and spa pool or there are thermal pools five minutes away. Your evening meal will be 'Special' - venison, lamb or fresh seafood with organic vegetables (we make superb coffee). Breakfast can be special too. We dive, fish, tramp, ski, golf and travel. A 6 m boat is available for fishing trips. We have a very friendly chocolate Labrador and a Burmese cat. Laundry facilities available.
Directions: *18 kms from Whakatane on State Highway 30. Please phone / fax for bookings.*

Whakatane

Farmstay
Address: 'Rakaunui',
Western Drain Road,
R.D. 3, Whakatane
Name: Lois & Tony Ranson
Telephone: (07) 304 9292
Fax: (07) 304 9292
Mobile: (025) 246 6077
Beds: 1 Queen, 1 Double, 2 single (3 bedrooms)
Bathroom: 1 Private, 1 Family share, 1 Ensuite.
Tariff: B&B (full) Double $70, Single $40, Children half price, Dinner $25, Campervans welcome. Credit cards. NZ B&B Vouchers accepted $10 surcharge
Nearest Town: 12km west of Whakatane

Rakaunui is named after the 80 year old Liriodendron tree which towers over our comfortable 1920's homestead set in the rural Rangataiki Plains within easy distance of coastal beaches, hot water springs and the Rotorua lakes. It is the largest of many big trees under which are seats and swings for visitors to relax in.Lois is a Camellia buff (with over 300 planted in her garden) interested in old roses and antiques. Tony a Civil Engineer also manages the orchard and dry stock and will enjoy sharing his taste of wines with you. Children will enjoy feeding the guinea fowl, doves, hens and sheep.Guests have private bath and shower, heated throughout, tea making facilities in bedrooms, and outdoor spa pool. If dining out is your choice, excellent restaurants in vicinity.Continental or cooked breakfast (breakfast egg courtesy of the household flock).Other attractions: golfing, tour fishing, craft shops, horse treks.
Directions: *1.8km from SH2 between Edgecumbe and Awakeri. Please phone.*

Whakatane

Homestay
Address: "Travellers Rest",
28 Henderson St, Whakatane
Name: "Travellers Rest"
Jeff & Karen Winterson
Telephone: (07) 307 1015
Mobile: (025) 276 6449
Beds: 1 King, 2 Single (2 bedrooms)
Bathroom: 1 Guest Share, Separate Toilet
Tariff: B&B (continental) Double $70, Single $35. Light dinner by arrangement
$15. Campervans welcome, Credit Cards.   NZ B&B Vouchers accepted $10
Surcharge
Nearest Town: Whakatane - Ohope 10 mins.

*Jeff and Karen welcome you to their smokefree brick home, situated on a back section
in a quiet tree lined street overlooking the Whakatane River. Enjoy a swim or scenic
river walk.*
We have some disability aids.Off-street parking available.
Handy to shops, restaurants, hospital.
Short drive to Ohope beach, airport, golf course.
Enjoy a relaxed breakfast overlooking our garden with roses, native trees and shrubs.
All beds have wool underlays, electric blankets, and feather duvets.
We have a friendly dog and cat.
*Interests include church activities, pen and stamp collecting, photography, cottage
gardens, massage, visitors.*
KiwiHost hospitality is assured.

Whakatane

Guest House+Self-contained Acc
Address: "Clifton House",
5 Clifton Road, Whakatane
Name: Ken & June England
Telephone: (07) 307 2145 **Fax**: (07) 307 2145
Beds: 1 King/Queen, 2 Double,
2 Single (3 bedrooms) SC Units: 1 King/Queen,
1 Double, 2 Single (2 units)
Bathroom: 2 Private, 1 Guests share
Tariff: B&B (continental) Double $60-$95, Single $50-$85, $10 each extra person, Credit
Cards (VISA/MC).
Nearest Town: Whakatane

*We have a lovely old stately home 2 minutes walk to the centre of town and just 10 minutes
drive to beautiful Ohope Beach.*
Facilities include:
*• Guests only, large sunny lounge / dining room • Kitchen with fridge, microwave, compli-
mentary tea & coffee available at any time• Electric blankets and heaters in all bedrooms•
Large filtered swimming pool in lovely sheltered garden setting• Off street parking• A non-
smoking environment*
Things to do:
*• Tramping - we have many beautiful bush walks and are only 1/2 hour to breathtaking
Urewera National Park. • Fishing - great choice of trips available • Swimming with dolphins
• Trips to White Island - our very own active volcano • Golf • Horse trekking • Jet boating
Ken is an avid trout and sea fisherman and is happy to arrange, or personally guide fishing
trips. June, as your hostess, is looking forward to welcoming you and making your stay a
happy one.*

Whakatane

Homestay, Private accomodation
Address: 54 Waiewe St, Whakatane
Name: Annette and David Pamment,
BRIAR ROSE
Telephone: (07) 308 0314
Fax: (07) 308 0317 **Mobile**: (025) 942 589
Beds: 1 Queen, 1 Double, 1 Single (2 bedrooms)
Bathroom: 1 Ensuite, 1 Family share

Tariff: B&B (Special, Continental) Double $70, Single $50, Children negotiable,
Dinner $20 by arrangement, Off street parking. NZ B&B Vouchers accepted
Nearest Town: Whakatane - 1 1/2km walking distance. Ohope 5 minutes.

*On the hilltop above the township, Briar Rose and Cottage are nestled in a peaceful
cove of native bush where you can relax on the wagon wheel seat and watch and listen
to the birdlife. You can also enjoy our beautiful Cottage garden specialising in old
fashioned roses. ·*
*Annette and David have a vast knowledge of the region which boasts many attractions.
Active volcano, White Island, Deep sea fishing, boating, diving, Dolphin excursions,
Hunting & Fishing, Jet boating, white water rafting, Golf, Mt Tarawera and
waterfall, Ohope beach sun and surf. Many walking tracks nearby.*
*There is a good selection of cafes, bars, brasseries and restaurants. But alternatively
you can dine with us and enjoy fresh wild game meals or something to your taste. You
will be assured of a warm and friendly atmosphere, you will leave with a basket full
of memories.*

Ohope Beach

Homestay+Self-contained Accom.
Address: "Shiloah", 27 Westend, Ohope Beach
Name: Pat & Brian Tolley
Telephone: (07) 312 4401
Fax: (07) 312 4401
Beds: 1 Twin, 1 Double, 4 Single (3 bedrooms)
Bathroom: 2 Private (total wet areas), 1 Guest share.
Tariff: B&B (full/continental) Double $66-$80, Single $35-$45,
Children half price, Dinner $18-$25, Campervans welcome. Credit cards.
Nearest Town: Whakatane 6 km

*We have retired to Ohope Beach and built a new home in a tranquil setting and hope
to offer hospitality. Disabled guests are welcome in home as we have a lift and two total
wet area bathrooms.*
*Homestay: 1 Double and three single beds with tea / coffee facilities. 1 Twin room, 1
Single room. Tariff: Double $66-$80, Single $35-$45.*
*Self Contained Unit: 1 Twin room, 1 Single with bed settee if required in main room.
Tariff: $25-$35 own bedding, $37-$40 supplied.*
*Access to beach across road. Fishing, swimming, surfing, bush walks, classic car
enthusiasts, well travelled.*
Directions: *On reaching Ohope Beach from Whakatane turn left down Westend
approx. 1km.*

Please help us provide the best hospitality in the world.
Fill in a comment form for every place you stay.

Whale Island and *Volcanic White Island*
as seen from *The Rafters*

Rafter

Ohope Beach

Homestay, Deluxe, self- contained, beachfront suite
Address: 'The Rafters', 261A Pohutukawa Avenue, Ohope Beach
Name: Mavis & Pat Rafter
Telephone: (07) 312 4856 **Fax**: (07)312 4856 **Mobile**: (025) 283 3276
Beds: Suite: King size/Twin beds + Single bed in lounge (2 rms).
Bathroom: Ensuite (bath and shower), hair-drier.
Tariff: B&B (Full, House Speciality) Double $90, Single $75, extra adult $20
(limit 1), Child $10, Infant free. Haute cuisine six course dinner $45 each; 4 course
$35; 3 course $30; 2 course $25; 1 course $20, all served with Premium Cantabilay
wines. Recommended Mains: Roast dinner (Lamb, Beef, Pork, Chicken); Spicy
Persian or Spanish Chicken Casserole; Seafood Platter; Mixed Grill; Porterhouse
Steak; Lamb Medallions; Chinese Stirfry Pork, Beef or Chicken; Vegetarian.
Variety of Soups, Entrees, Desserts. Guests may dine by candle light in suite or
with Hosts. Complimentary pre-dinner drinks with hosts. NZ B&B Vouchers
accepted $30 Surcharge
Nearest Town: Whakatane 8km, Rotorua 80km, Tauranga 90km.

*Panoramic seaviews: White, Whale islands, East Coast. Safe swimming, surfing in
front of suite. Many interesting walks in the vicinity. Golf (clubs r.h. available free),
tennis, bowls, all within minutes. Licensed Chartered Club opposite. Trips to White
Island, fishing (deep-sea and trout), jet boating, diving, swimming with dolphins
arranged. Full cooking facilities, fridge, microwave; laundry, drier; private entrance,
sunken garden, BBQ. Complimentary: tea, coffee, biscuits, fruit, newspaper, personal
laundry service.*
*Mavis, experienced cook, interests: nursing, bowls, art, tramping. Pat, interests: wines,
golf, bowls, music, literature, History, tramping.*
Courtesy car available. House trained dogs, cats, welcome.
*We look forward to your company and we assure you unique hospitality, cuisine and
Cantabilay wines.*
Directions: *On reaching Ohope turn right, proceed 2 km to 261a (beach-side).
Illuminated house*
Number on footpath, name "Rafters" on a brick letterbox, with illuminated B&B sign.

Ohope Beach
Homestay+Self-contained Accom.
Address: "Henton's Bed & Breakfast" 295 Pohutukawa Ave, Ohope Beach
Name: Marion & Graham Henton
Telephone: (07) 312 5095 **Fax**: 07 3125095
Beds: 1 Double (1 bedroom)
Bathroom: 1 Private
Tariff: B&B (continental) Double $70-$90, Single $50-70, Dinner $20pp by arrangement. Credit cards.
Nearest Town: Whakatane 8km

In our guest suite you can be totally private (own entrance, full cooking and laundry facilities) or if you choose, be involved with our family of six, who will give you a warm welcome.
It is spacious and extremely comfortable "Home away from Home". (TV, video, microwave, electric blanket, wool underlay.etc) Private courtyard with outdoor seating. BBQ available. Non smoking inside residence.
Situated 150m from the beach and walking distance to a licensed Chartered Club. (Cafes, craft market, churches, bowling club, golf course and incredible coastal bush walks are all handy.)
We have plenty of parking space and room for your boat. Graham is an enthusiastic fisherman (trout and sea fishing), who will smoke your "catch of the day" for you. Marion plays the guitar and enjoys music. We look forward to welcoming you.
Directions: *On reaching Ohope turn right, proceed 2.5km until you see our sign (on left).*

Ohope Beach
Bed & Breakfast
Address: "Turneys Bed & Breakfast", 28 Pohutukawa Ave,Ohope Beach
Name: Marilyn and Em Turney
Freephone: 0800 266 269
Telephone: 07-312 5040
Fax: 07-312 5040
Mobile: 025-960 894
Email: turneys@ellconweb.net.nz
Beds: 1 King, 1 Double, 2 Single (3 bedrooms)
Bathroom: 2 Ensuites, 1 Private

Tariff: B&B (full) Double $100-$110, Single $50, Dinner $25 (by prior arrangement). Not suitable for children. Off season and extended stays discounted rates. NZ B&B Vouchers accepted $20 surcharge.
Nearest Town: Whakatane 5kms.

Base yourselves with us and stay refreshed and focused for the Eastbay experience.
We are located within a comfortable distance from all the excitement - geysers, erupting White Island, white water rafting, fishing, dolphin swimming, to mention a few. Let us advise and arrange.Our home is multi-level capturing magnificent views.
Treat yourself to the special "Blue Room" which opens on to a private deck overlooking the Pacific Ocean: equipped with fridge, phone, television, continuous tea and coffee and other treats. The "Garden Room" opening onto a patio also with sea views, TV, phone, coffee etc. The Twin Room has its own bathroom.
Served for your pleasure are generous breakfasts plus trimmings including freshly brewed coffee and home-made bread. You are welcome to share our addictions of golf and tennis - gear provided. We have been hosts for many years and promise you wont be disappointed.
Directions: *Upon reaching Ohope, turn right and we are opposite the shops, restaurant and beach.*

Ohiwa Harbour

Farmstay
Address: Wainui Lodge, 181 McCoy Road,
RD 2, Opotiki
Name: Wendy Lynch & Mike Collins
Telephone: (07) 312 5532 **Fax**: (07) 312 5532
Email: wendylyn@wave.co.nz
Beds: 1 Queen, 1 Double, 1 Single (3 bedrooms)
Bathroom: 1 Guest share
Tariff: B&B (full) Double $80, Single $45, Dinner $25pp, Campervans $20/night.
NZ B&B Vouchers accepted
Nearest Town: Whakatane 20km

WAINUI LODGE offers a homely stay in a new passive solar designed house set in 20 hectares of rolling farmland, with views of Ohiwa Harbour. Upstairs are three guest bedrooms, with separate lounge and bathroom. Excellent meals, all organically grown with lots of variety. Farm comprises avocado orchard, flock of coloured sheep for spinning wool and sheepskins, small herd of cows including house cow, free range chooks, boxer dog, cat, native and planted trees. Our interests are: organic farming, gardening, tramping, conservation and Green politics. Trips from here include: fishing, walking, great tramping, swimming with dolphins, White or Whale Islands, or simply doing nothing but looking at the view.
Directions: *10km from Ohope around Wainui Road which skirts Ohiwa Harbour. McCoy Road is third road on right past Oyster Farm. We are well sign-posted. Best to phone after 5pm as we both work part time.*

Haurere Point, Opotiki

Farmstay+Self-contained Accom.
Address: Corals B&B, Morice's Bay,
Highway 35, R.D.1, Opotiki
Name: Coral Parkinson
Telephone: (07) 315 8052/0800-258 575
Fax: (07) 315 8052
Beds: 1 King/Queen, 1 Double, 2 Single (2 bedrooms)
Bathroom: 2 Private
Tariff: B&B (continental) Double $60-$100, Single $40-$50, Children $15, Dinner $30. May to October stay two nights or more and get one free. NZ B&B Vouchers accepted Surcharge on cottage $14-25
Nearest Town: 18km to Opotiki

Signposted on Highway 35, 18 km from Opotiki and halfway between Opape and Torere our stained glass windowed rustic cottage provides the opportunity to drift back to the peace of a bygone era. There are no house rules once settled you may decide, as others have not to venture beyond our small farms boundary. Explore the stoney bed creek, check out the glow worms and the swimming hole, enjoy the bush and bird life. We have a collection of classic English vehicles and memorabilia. Beyond our gate a easy walk takes you to secluded Morices Bay, ramble over the rocks, laze on the sandy beach, explore the caves, surf, safe swimming, fish from the rocks.
Our smaller unit part of our garage complex is fully equipped with full kitchen.
All beds have woollen underlays and feather duvets. We make our own bread and conserves. Free range eggs. Smoking outdoors would be appreciated. Under cover parking.
Directions: *Call, write or fax.*

Wairata, Opotiki

Farmstay
Address: Wairata, Waioeka Gorge, Opotiki
Name: Bob & Mary Redpath
Telephone: (07) 315 7761
Fax: (07) 315 7761
Email: rl.redpath@xtra.co.nz
Beds: 1 Double, 4 Single (2 bedrooms)
Bathroom: 1 Private
Tariff: B&B (full) Double $80, Single $50,
Dinner $20, Children $20.   NZ B&B Vouchers accepted
Nearest Town: 50km south of Opotiki on State Highway 2.

Come and join us in the heart of the scenic Waioeka Gorge on our 1900 hectare hill country farm retreat. We farm cattle, sheep, deer and goats and our valley is surrounded by native bush with a host of activities for you to enjoy. There are numerous tracks to walk, streams to meander alongside, glow worms and a crystal clear river at your doorstep for trout fishing, eeling, swimming or tubing. We can take guests on 4WD farm excursions and there is hunting available for the more adventurous. We serve hearty home baked meals and encourage guests to join the family for meals. Guest accomodation is separate but adjoins the main house, we have a pretty garden, an outside cat and four children two of whom still live with us. We only take one party at a time. We always welcome guests to our home and look forward to meeting you.
Directions: *Please phone.*

Maraenui, East Coast, Opotiki.

Farmstay+Self-contained Accom.
Address: Maraenui Beach,
Motu River (Postal: Oariki Farmhouse,
Box 486, Opotiki)
Name: Chris Stone
Telephone: (07) 325 2678 **Fax**: (07) 325 2678
Beds: 2 King, 1 Double, 2 Single (2 bedrooms)
Bathroom: 1 Ensuite, 1 Private
Tariff: B&B (full) Double $90, Single $45,
School children half price, Dinner $25, Credit Cards.
Self Contained Cottage sleeps 3 $90 night or sleeps up to 5 $130 night.
NZ B&B Vouchers accepted Surcharge $20.
Nearest Town: Opotiki. 40km 25 mins, 2 1/2 hrs from Rotorua, Gisborne and Tauranga. On some maps Maraenui is shown as Houpoto.
Our small subsistence farm is on the beach, in the bush, close to the mighty Motu River. We provide you with comfort, company or solitude and organically grown food, organic wine and fresh fish from the sea whenever possible. Nature provides native birds song, pristine wilderness, boundless sunshine and views of our active volcano "Whakaari" out at sea. Romantic sunsets and a natural paradise. The cottage is set in the orchard; is self contained on two levels with its own private terrace and balcony. The guest room has its own luxury ensuite, pool table and reading area, with huge double bed and wing chairs. Each has sea and garden views. Our dog and the cat love to join you for your walk on the beach. For long stay guests we have 10 activities locally which we can arrange for you. We like to enjoy your conversation as our guests, and prefer non-smokers. Please phone for directions as Oariki Farmhouse is in a very secluded location.

257

Waihau Bay, Opotiki
Homestay+Self-contained Accom.
Address: State Highway 35, Waihau Bay via Opotiki, East Coast
Name: Noelene & Merv Topia
Telephone: (07) 325 3674 **Fax**: (07) 325-3674
Email: n.Topia@clear.net.nz
Beds: 2 Double, 2 Single (3 bedrooms)
Bathroom: 1 Ensuite, 1 Private
Tariff: B&B (continental) Double $75, Single $40, Children half price,
Dinner $25, Campervans welcome. Credit Cards. NZ B&B Vouchers accepted
Nearest Town: 112km to Opotiki

You are invited to share our seaside lifestyle. We have a sunny Lockwood home with magnificent views and wonderful sunsets.
We have a small self contained unit with one twin bedroom and sofa bed in lounge, bathroom with disabled facilities, laundry, kitchen and TV. Our guest room has its own entrance with 1 double bed and ensuite with full disabled facilities.
Our interests are fishing, meeting people, theatre, music and sports.
Come and be as relaxed or as active as you like, we have kayaks and boats and can set you off on a horse trek, jet boat ride or fishing trip. Big game fishing is a feature of Waihau Bay, Dec to March. We have a cat called Wiskey and a wonderful dog called Meg. NZ meals of fish and crayfish (in season) our speciality.
Directions: *Please phone for reservations and directions.*

Ngongotaha, Rotorua

Homestay/Rural B&B
Address: R.D. 2, Rotorua
Name: Roslyn & John Livingstone
Telephone: (07) 357 2368,
Freephone 0800 822 100
Fax: (07) 357 2369
Beds: 1 King, 1 Double (2 bedrooms)
Bathroom: 2 Private
Tariff: B&B (full) Double $70,
Single $45, Credit cards. NZ B&B Vouchers accepted
Nearest Town: Rotorua - 12 minutes to city

We warmly invite you to visit our spacious farmhouse (with panoramic rural, lake and volcanic views), just off Highway 5 (Auckland-Rotorua).
John and I are "originals" in the NZ B&B book. therefore we have fine-tuned our hosting skills for twelve years; and realise the need for rooms with private facilities, TV, tea and coffee making trays, cookie jars, in-room refrigerators, adequate heating / cooling. The breakfast served is as hearty as you require.
Please note:
1. This is a "no smoking" house.
2. Pet cats do come into the house.
3. We provide a FREE PHONE 0800 82 21 00 for ease of booking.

Relax – Don't try to drive too far in one day.

Ngongotaha, Rotorua

Farmstay+Self - Contained Accom.
Address: Jackson Road, Kaharoa (PO Box 22), Ngongotaha, Rotorua
Name: 'Deer Pine Lodge'(John & Betty Insch)
Telephone: (07) 332 3458 **Fax**: (07) 332 3458
Beds: 3 King, 1 Queen, 4 Single (5 bedrooms)
Bathroom: 5 Ensuite
Tariff: B&B (continental) Double $85-$95, Single $65-$70, Extra person $25,
Children 1yr-11yrs half price, Dinner $25 (Children $15). Discount from 3rd night
or longer. Cooked breakfast extra $5 pp. Please inquire about our new winter
rates from $70. Credit Cards Visa/MC NZ B&B Vouchers accepted $20 surcharge
Nearest Town: Rotorua 16km

*Welcome to Deer Pine Lodge. Enjoy the panoramic views of Lake Rotorua, Mt
Tarawera and Mokoia Island. We farm 260 deer, our property surrounded with trees
planted by the New Zealand Forest Research as experimental shelter belts on our
accredited deer farm.*
*The nearby city of Rotorua is fast becoming New Zealand's most popular tourist
destination offering all sorts of entertainment. We have a cat and a Golden Retriever
(Josh), very gentle. Our four children have grown up and left the nest.*
*Our bed / breakfast units are private, own bathroom, TV, radio, fridge, microwave,
electric blankets all beds, coffee / tea making facilities, heaters. Heaters and hair
dryers also in all bathrooms.*
*Our two bedroom fully self contained units, designed by prominent Rotorua architect
Gerald Stock, each having private balcony, carport, sundeck, ensuite, spacious lounge,
kitchen, also laundry facilities, TV, radio, heater etc. Cot and highchair available.
Security arms fitted on all windows, smoke detectors installed in all bedrooms and
lounges, fire extinguisher installed in all kitchens.*
*Holding NZ certificate in food hygiene ensuring high standards of food preparation
and serving - lodge has Qualmark 3 Star rating.*
*Guests are free to do the conducted tour and observe the different species of deer and
get first hand knowledge of all aspects of deer farming after breakfast. If interested
please inform host on arrival. Three course meal of beef, lamb, or venison by prior
arrangement, pre dinner drinks. Hosts John and Betty, originally from Scotland have
travelled extensively overseas and having ten years experience in hosting look forward
to your stay with us. Prefer guests to smoke outside.*
Directions: *Please phone, or write for brochure.*

Rotorua

Farmstay
Address: Please phone
Name: Maureen & John Hunt
Telephone: (07) 348 1352
Beds: 2 Double, 2 Single (4 bedrooms)
Bathroom: 1 Private, 1 Family share
Tariff: B&B (full) Double $75, Single $50, Children under 12 half price, Campervans facilities available. NZ B&B Vouchers accepted Surcharge $7.50
Nearest Town: Rotorua 4 km (10 minutes by car)

Guests will be warmly welcomed to our large, modern home on the city outskirts. Superb views of the lake, city, forest and surrounding countryside. Enjoy our garden and swimming pool. We farm 150 acres running deer, beef and sheep. Scenic farm tours available. Our adult family of five have now sought pastures new allowing us to offer an attractive suite of rooms consisting of one double bedroom, two single bedrooms and a small sunroom. Underfloor heating, innersprung mattresses, plenty of room for cars, campervans and luggage storage. Non-smokers preferred. Be sure and allow a few days stay so you have time to rest as well as enjoy the many nearby world renowned attractions. We enjoy gardening, water-skiing, tramping and travelling and look forward to sharing our home and farm with you.

Ngakuru, Rotorua

Farmstay
Address: 'Te Ana' Farmstay,
Poutakataka Road, Ngakuru,
R.D.1, Rotorua. Please phone
Name: Heather & Brian Oberer
Telephone: (07) 333 2720 **Fax**: (07) 333 2720
Mobile: (025) 828 151
Beds: 2 Queen, 5 Single + Cot (4 bedrooms)
Bathroom: 2 Ensuite, 1 Family share
Tariff: B&B (special) Double from $90, Single $75, Children $25-$35. Dinner $35 adults $15 children. Discount from 3rd night. Visa/Master NZ B&B Vouchers accepted $25 surcharge
Nearest Town: Rotorua 20 miles (NB) Te Ana is 20 miles South of Rotorua.

Bounded by beautiful Lake Ohakuri, "Te Ana", a 569 acre dairy, sheep, and deer farm, offers privacy, peace and tranquillity in a spacious country garden setting with panoramic views of lake, volcanically formed hills and lush farmland. Enjoy farm walks, 4-wheel drive tour, observe milking and calf rearing in season, or use canoe and fishing rod (licence required). Discover the luxuries of farm hospitality - healthy 3 course gourmet meals with an abundance of fresh produce; TV, tea-making facilities, sherry, cookies, fairy down duvets, wool underlays, electric blankets and heaters, fresh flower and reading material in your room. ACCOMMO-DATION a small two roomed cottage with ensuite, sleeps 4; Two homestead bedrooms, one with ensuite, both adjacent to TV lounge. Relax in front of log fire, on full-length verandah or in our sunny garden. IDEAL BASE to enjoy thermal parks and swimming pools, golf courses, trout fishing, lakes, rivers and forests and Rotorua and Taupo attractions.
Directions: *Please phone, fax or correspond.*
Home Page: http://nz.com/web.nz/bb.nz/teana.htm

Rotorua
Homestay
Address: 3 Raukura Place, Rotorua
Name: Ursula & Lindsay Prince
Telephone: (07) 347 0140
or Freephone 0800 223 624
Fax: (07) 347 0107
Beds: 1 Queen with 1 single, 2 Single (2 bedrooms)
Bathroom: 1 Ensuite, 1 Private
Tariff: B&B (special) Double $80, Single $60, (Surcharge $5 for one night only);
Dinner by arrangement $25 with complimentary NZ wine.
Nearest Town: Rotorua city centre 2 kms

We warmly invite you to share our spacious modern home at Rotorua's lakefront; quiet, secluded, 5 minutes drive from downtown. Both spacious guestrooms are well appointed and have private bathrooms. We are an active middle-aged couple who have lived and travelled overseas, take an interest in world affairs and cherish the natural environment.
Home-hosting has been an enjoyable part of our lives since 1988. We hope to give you, too, the feeling of being with friends. Conversations over breakfast which includes home-made specialities are often a highlight for guests and hosts. Use our extensive library and local knowledge to get the most from your stay. We'll be happy to arrange your local bookings. Enjoy the tranquil lake and mountain scene, watch the waterbirds, paddle our Canadian canoe. No smoking please.
Directions: *Lake Road into Bennetts Road, left Koutu Road, first right Karenga Street, right Haumoana Street, Raukura Place on left.*

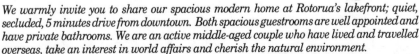

Ngongotaha, Rotorua
B&B Farmstay style
Address: Please phone for directions
Name: Rex & Annie Wells
Telephone: (07) 357 2014
Fax: (07) 357 2014 **Mobile**: (025) 595 157
Beds: 1 King, 1 Queen, 4 Single (2 bedrooms) (billiard room)
Bathroom: 1 Guests share - separate w.c.
Tariff: B&B (special) Double $75, Single $50, Dinner $30, Campervans $30
4 people. Children welcome. 5% discount 3rd night.
NZ B&B Vouchers accepted $15 surcharge
Nearest Town: Ngongotaha 3ks, Rotorua city 8ks.

Would you like to be SPOILT? Then come and stay on our "slice of heaven".
We farm 50 acres having over 200 Red deer. Belted Galloway Cattle Stud. Home is centrally heated, electric blankets, lovely garden and rural views from every room. Garden open to public.Inside spa - wintertime. Full sized billiard table - Rex wanting to learn new shots! Billiard room has open fire, plenty of books, tv to relax in privately. Our familys have grown up - main interests include farm, dogs, antiques, photography, table tennis, travelling anywhere!Having stables operate as Horse Motel.
We use home killed venison, home bottled fruit, jams, relishes from home orchard.
Provide 10 different cereals, yoghurt or cooked breakfast.
Home on one level suitable wheel chairs.Tea / coffee available on request.
Fax facilities available; laundry done - charge.
Campervans welcome - rural views.Annie enjoys showing farm on 4x4 bike.
Agrodome 1km.
Smoke FREE.

Ngongotaha, Rotorua

Homestay
Address: 11 Egmont Road,
Ngongotaha, Rotorua
Name: Joy & Brian Bell
Telephone: (07) 357 2088
Fax: (07) 357 2099 **Mobile**: (025) 804 817
Beds: 1 King, 2 Single (2 bedrooms)
Bathroom: 1 Guests share
Tariff: B&B (special) Double $75, Single $45. Dinner $25,
Credit cards (VISA/MC).   NZ B&B Vouchers accepted Surcharge $7.50
Nearest Town: Rotorua 10km

Our comfortable Lockwood style home sits in a quiet tree lined street close to Lake Rotorua and the Waiteti Trout Stream, no traffic noise or sulphur fumes. We are retired and share our home with our cat Tinkerbell. Our son is overseas, our married daughter lives locally. We are involved in church, community, Probus and Stamp Club. We love entertaining guests from home and overseas. You are assured of a warm welcome, tempting meals, comfortable beds with electric blankets, tea / coffee making facilities. Bath robes available. You are welcome to share dinner with us by prior arrangement. We are non-smokers and would appreciate guests not smoking in the house. Generous, hearty breakfasts include such homemade items as breads, muffins, muesli, preserves and yoghurt, cooked course available. Ample off street parking.
Internet Address: http: / / nz.com / webnz / bbnz / bell.htm
Directions: *Travel north through Ngongotaha, cross railway, take second turning right into Waiteti Road, Egmont Road second on right.*
Home Page: http://nz.com/webnz/bbnz/bell.htm

Rotorua

Homestay
Address: 20 Stanley Drive, Lynmore, Rotorua
Name: Dulcie & Selwyn Collins
Telephone: (07) 345 5778
Beds: 1 Double, 2 Single (2 bedrooms)
Bathroom: 1 Guests share
Tariff: B&B (continental) Double $75, Single $50, Dinner $25.
NZ B&B Vouchers accepted $10 surcharge
Nearest Town: Rotorua

Selwyn and Dulcie are a retired couple with farming and nursing backgrounds. Our new home is gas central heated and our visitors have their own wing with bathroom facilities. Our street is very quiet. Selwyn's interest include Bowls and his Masonic Lodge. His Bowling Club is at the end of the road. I enjoy my golf, establishing new gardens here and trying out new recipes. Give me a little notice and I would enjoy cooking you an evening meal. We have a fabulous outdoor area facing east with barbecue. It is covered over, so wonderful for that quiet read or drink.
We are a 6 minute drive from Rotorua, 1 minute drive from the Redwood Forest with its many walking and bike tracks. Just up the road to the beautiful lakes and fishing, swimming or boating activities. Look forward to meeting you.
Directions: *Tauranga / Whakatane Highway. Turn right into Isles Rd, left into Warwick Drive, right into Stanley Drive.*

Rotorua
Homestay
Address: 9 Henare Place,
Tihi-o-tonga, Rotorua
Name: Brian & Kate Gore
Telephone: (07) 347 9385
Fax: (07) 349 2214
Mobile: (024) 944 270
Email: b.gore@clear.net.nz
Beds: 1 Double, 2 Single (2 bedrooms)
Bathroom: 1 Guests share
Tariff: B&B (full) Double $80, Single $50, Children under 12 years half price,
Dinner $25. NZ B&B Vouchers accepted $15 surcharge
Nearest Town: Rotorua

Greetings and Kia-ora! We are in our early 50's, young at heart, and have been enjoying home hosting for over 15 years. Our modern, spacious home is designed for your needs and is set in Rotorua's quietest suburb, that overlooks the city and surrounding farmlands. We are familiar with all the local attractions and will happily help you plan your time in Rotorua, plus advice on places of interest throughout our lovely country. We know it well!

Breakfast is as you wish. Fresh fruit, cereals, yoghurt, toast or muffins or fully cooked to set you up for your day. Dinner may include Rotorua's speciality - smoked trout or we can suggest suitable restaurants.

Rotorua has much to offer but we like to think we can share so much more to make your New Zealand holiday totally memorable.

Directions: *Please phone*

Rotorua
Homestay
Address: Heather's Homestay,
5A Marguerita Street, Rotorua
Name: Heather Radford
Telephone: (07) 349 4303
Beds: 1 Double, 2 Single (2 bedrooms)
Bathroom: 2 Private
Tariff: B&B (full) Double/Twin $70, Single $40, Children half price.
3 nights or more 10% discount off cash payments only. Credit Cards.
NZ B&B Vouchers accepted
Nearest Town: Rotorua city 2km

Haeremai. Welcome. If you wish to be close to where 'it's all happening' stay with me in my comfortable home in the heart of the thermal area, minutes from the city centre, yet quiet and private.

Walk to Whakarewarewa to see the geysers, mud pools and Maori Arts & Crafts Institute; to the beautiful Redwood Forest; to a traditional Maori Concert and hangi (feast) in the evening; play a round of golf on Arikikapakapa Golf Course just down the road, and take your pick of the many excellent restaurants nearby.

Whether walking or driving you are only minutes away from the weird and wonderful sights that make Rotorua City so unique.

Rotorua born and bred, I am proud of my City and Maori heritage and enjoy sharing what knowledge I have with my guests. I am currently teaching part time at a local College.

Directions: *Just off Fenton Street, turn at Devonwood Manor. First house on right.*

Ngongotaha, Rotorua

Homestay
Address: 'Waiteti Lakeside Lodge',
2 Arnold Street, (off Waiteti Rd), Ngongotaha, Rotorua
Name: Val & Brian Blewett
Telephone: (07) 357 2311 **Fax**: (07) 357 2311
Beds: 4 Queen, 2 Single (5 bedrooms)
Bathroom: 3 Ensuite, 1 Guests share
Tariff: B&B (full) Double $95-$140, Single $85-$125, from 1 October 1998,
Children over 12 welcome, Credit cards (VISA/MC).
NZ B&B Vouchers accepted plus surcharge $25-$70
Nearest Town: Rotorua 10km

The Lodge stands in what has to be the most idyllic location in the region. Waiteti Lakeside Lodge has the advantage of a picturesque trout stream running on its southern boundary and magnificent views across the crystal clear waters of Lake Rotorua with its abundance of wildfowl. Neither traffic noise nor the characteristic Rotorua sulphur fumes intrude on this peaceful setting. You are only 10 km away from Rotorua.

Your hosts Brian & Val built this impressive home with cedar timber and local Hinuera stone. Exposed beams and pine wood panelling features inside and a native rimu stair case leads to the private guest floor. The guest lounge has a TV and video, pool table, fridge, tea and coffee making facilities. Each room has been tastefully decorated, inspired by the tranquil beauty of the lodge's surroundings. The guest suites open to private balconies with panoramic views. Brian is an outdoors man and professional guide, he skippers his own charter boat. With 28 years trout fishing experience he will take guests on the lake or to remote streams by 4 wheel drive. Canadian canoes are also available for guests. Val is a master of homemaking, bringing a warmth and grace to this wonderful place. She serves breakfast in the downstairs conservatory which overlooks the gardens, filled with Rhododendrons and Azaleas, which grow to the waters edge. Brian & Val have gained an unsurpassed reputation for providing excellent accommodation in their unique location.

Directions: *Take Highway 5 from Rotorua, straight on at the Roundabout through Ngongotaha. Drive through the main town centre and you will cross the railway tracks. 2nd turn right in to Waiteti Road. At the end turn right in to Arnold Street. You will see the Alpine Style Lodge on the left hand side.*

Rotorua

Country Stay
Address: 'Paradise Downs',
1080 Paradise Valley Road, R.D. 2 Rotorua
Name: Shirley & Neville Mann
Telephone: (07) 357 5707 **Fax**: (07) 357 5707
Mobile: (025) 790 238
Beds: 2 Queen, 1 Double, 1 Single (3 bedrooms)
Bathroom: 3 Ensuite
Tariff: B&B (full) Double $95-$120, Single $85, Children under 12 $15,
Cot available. Dinner $30. NZ B&B Vouchers accepted $30 surcharge
Nearest Town: Rotorua (8 km)

*We welcome guests to our new spacious home set amongst lovely gardens with rural
views, adjacent to a trout stream, 3km off SH5 on the scenic route to Rotorua.
Enjoy a stroll amongst our sheep, and aviary birds, walk by the stream, or relax and
enjoy the peaceful setting.
We have two pedigree Tibetan terriers.
Our guests rooms have electric blankets and ensuite.
Our home is centrally heated. Enjoy an evening 3 course dinner with us or visit a Maori
Hangi. Rotorua is a tourist mecca. We have fly fishing at our door. 5 mins from
Agrodome, Rainbow springs and Paradise Game Park and can help plan an exciting
few days sightseeing. Our adult family live away from home. Our interests include
gardening, art and building. Being involved in Education, hospitality industry and
travelled we enjoy sharing our home with guests.*
Directions: *Please phone.*

Rotorua

Farmstay & Homestay
Address: 'Peppertree Farm',
25 Cookson Road, R.D. 4, Rotorua
Name: Deane & Elma Balme
Telephone: (07) 345 3718 **Fax**: (07) 345 3718
Beds: 1 Queen, 2 Twin (3 bedrooms)
Bathroom: 1 Ensuite, 1 Private or 1 Guests share (if more than 4 people)
Tariff: B&B (full) Double $90, Single $60, Dinner $25pp, Children under 12 half
price, Campervans $25. Discounts for 3 nights or more.
Credit cards NZ B&B Vouchers accepted Surcharge $12 per person
Nearest Town: Rotorua 10 minutes. Off S.H.30.

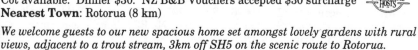

*Just ten minutes from the central city and handy to airport our charming Lockwood
Home, in it's quiet rural tree clad setting overlooking Lake Rotorua, will provide you
with a friendly welcome and homely atmosphere. Upon your arrival you may care to
enjoy a stroll around our small farm where you will see goats, sheep, cows, calves,
horses, working dogs and chickens. Before dinner, you may choose to enjoy your hosts'
hospitality while relaxing on the verandah taking in the spectacular views. There is
an excellent cuisine using fresh garden produce and served with complimentary New
Zealand wine or we can arrange a visit to a Maori Hangi and Concert. Our guest
accommodation consist of two twin bedded rooms and one Queensize room all with
electric blankets and private bathroom facilities. Horse riding and trout fishing can
be arranged. Your hosts are fourth generation New Zealanders with a love of animals
and the land, who wish to share the beauty of their surroundings with you.*
Home Page: peppertree.farm@xtra.co.nz

Owhata, Rotorua

Homestay & Self-contained Accommodation
Address: 13 Glenfield Road, Owhata, Rotorua
Name: Colleen & Isaac (Ike) Walker
Telephone: (07) 345 3882 (after 5pm or leave message)
Fax: (07) 345 3856
Mobile: (025) 289 5003
Email: colleen.walker@clear.net.nz
Beds: S.C.Unit: 1 Double, 2 Single (2 bedrooms/1 Fold Down Sofa in lounge)
Home: 1 Double, 1 Single (1 bedroom)
Bathroom: 1 Private (SC Unit), 1 Ensuite (house)
Tariff: B&B (continental) Double $65, Single $35, Dinner extra, Children half price, Unit: $65 2 persons & $15 extra persons.   NZ B&B Vouchers accepted
Nearest Town: Rotorua - 5km from city centre

Situated in a quiet suburb only 10 minutes drive from Rotorua's city centre, 5 mins from Airport.
The unit is private and fully self contained with one double and one twin bedroom, separate lounge, bathroom, laundry and kitchen.
The house has a comfortable homely atmosphere with one double bed and one single bed available with ensuite. Light breakfast included. Guests have the opportunity of becoming one of the family. Colleen is a tutor at the local Waiariki Polytechnic. Ike has experience in farming and the paper industry. He is a keen fisherman and golfer. They have hosted many visitors and have travelled extensively themselves both within New Zealand and abroad. They enjoy meeting new friends and helping them make the most of their stay in New Zealand by arranging fishing, golfing, sightseeing and cultural experiences if required. Hosts own two small dachshund dogs. To avoid disappointment and to enable the best service to be offered 24 hours notice would be appreciated, especially if meal is required.

Lake Rotorua

Homestay
Address: 'Lake Edge Homestay',
Mokoia Road, Ngongotaha, R.D.2, Rotorua
Name: Jack & Dorothy Cunningham
Telephone: (07) 332 3631
Beds: 3 Queen, 1 Single (2 bedrooms)
Bathroom: 2 Ensuite
Tariff: B&B (full) Double $95, Single $60, Dinner by arrangement.
Credit cards NZ B&B Vouchers accepted
Nearest Town: Ngongotaha 4km

At Lake Edge Homestay, Jack and Dorothy offer you a tranquil setting, relaxed atmosphere in 2 acres of grounds, panoramic views. Satisfying breakfast of your choice. Dinner by arrangement. Vegetarians are catered for. Bedrooms look over Lake Rotorua. One upstairs, one downstairs with sunroom adjoining, all pleasantly spacious. Beds have woollen underlays and electric blankets. Each room has its own private shower, basin and toilet; coffee and tea making facilities, radio and TV. Extensive library of New Zealand books. Interests include: meeting people, trout fishing, pigeon breeding, philately, pet sheep. Non-smokers. Animals: 2 cats and outside dog. Private jetty (dock). We are close to Rotorua's tourist areas: Rainbow Springs Complex, Agrodome. Horse riding, and golf courses nearby. Trout fishing can be arranged. Our home is situated at the end of a no-exit road, in a very peaceful rural area yet only 15 minutes from Tourism Rotorua. 4 kilometres from Ngongotaha township.

Okere-Falls, Rotorua
Countryhome Lake Stay
Address: 'Waitui', Private Bag,
Okere-Falls Post Office, Rotorua
Name: Waituii'
Telephone: (07) 362 4751
Beds: 1 Double, 2 Single (2 bedrooms)
Bathroom: 2 Ensuite
Tariff: B&B (full) Double $80, Single $40, Children under 12yrs half price,
Dinner $25. NZ B&B Vouchers accepted Surcharge $12
Nearest Town: Rotorua 19km (12 miles)

Come and enjoy our warm and comfortable home in a rural setting. We live in a farmland environment because we are retired hill country sheep and cattle farmers. Our home overlooks magnificent Lake Rotoiti and beautiful farmland from three quarters. We are situated 10 minutes from Rotorua airport on Highway 33 towards Tauranga and 20 minutes from Rotorua city. Experience the peace and tranquillity in a countryhome atmosphere on a bush-clad elevated peninsula with superb lake views and alluring native birds amongst our garden. We have a spacious and comfortable traditional style home. The locality offers beautiful bush walks near spectacular Okere-Falls on the Kaituna River, where there is white water rafting, fishing and local store. Telephone bookings are essential.
Directions: *Please phone.*

Ngakuru, Rotorua
Farmstay
Address: 'Lakehill',
1149 Whirinaki Valley Road,
Ngakuru, R.D.1, Rotorua
Name: John & Susan Shaw
Telephone: (07) 333 2829
Fax: (07) 333 2029
Email: johnshaw@voyager.co.nz
Beds: 1 Queen, 3 Single (2 bedrooms,
Triple and Twin)
Bathroom: 1 Ensuite, 1 Private
Tariff: B&B (full) Double $120-$140, Single $90, Dinner $30.
Credit Cards (MC/VISA).
Nearest Town: Ngakuru is 28km south of Rotorua off SH5 or SH30

After seven years of hosting, our enthusiasm for having you to stay at our large comfortable farmhouse remains as strong as ever. We both very much enjoy combining good humour and good conversation with excellent food and wine. Our home interior features New Zealand native timbers, creating a warm and inviting atmosphere. We have several pets, some sheep, cattle, and a commercial chestnut orchard. The farm bounds lake Ohakuri offering excellent views and birdwatching. We are ideally situated between Rotorua and Taupo making a perfect base for central North Island sightseeing including relaxing hot thermal pools only ten minutes away. We challenge you to play a par round on our 4 hole golf course. Success earns a free meal and your name on the Lakehill honours board. Our extensively landscaped grounds also include a mini golf course, grass tennis court and swimming pool. Other interests include Rotary, reading and gardening.

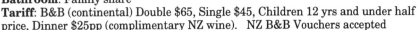

Westbrook, Rotorua
Homestay
Address: 378 Malfroy Rd, Rotorua
Name: Brian & Judy Bain
Telephone: (07) 347 8073
Beds: 4 Single (2 Bedrooms)
Bathroom: Family share
Tariff: B&B (continental) Double $65, Single $45, Children 12 yrs and under half
price, Dinner $25pp (complimentary NZ wine). NZ B&B Vouchers accepted
Nearest Town: Rotorua 3km

*We are retired farmers, of farming stock - live on city outskirts, yet only 3km from city
centre. We live in a warm comfortable Colonial style home with pleasant grounds.
Having been for many years participating in farmstay and currently homestay, our
interests include meeting the people, farming, politics (of a mild nature), current
affairs etc. Brian is a member of Rotorua Host Lions and Judy's interests extend to all
aspects of home making. Both guestrooms are well appointed with comfortable beds
and electric blankets.*
*As well as the friendly welcome at the front door much time can be spent over the meal
table chatting with our guests.*
Our motto is "Home away from home"!
*There is much to do in Rotorua and surrounds and we are happy to assist with your
plans for "Things to do and see"! Transport available to and from "Tourist Centre".
We look forward to your arrival.*

Rotorua
Farmstay
Address: 89 Fryer Road, Off Hamurana Rd, Ngongotaha
Name: Enid & John Brinkler
Telephone: (07) 332 3306
Beds: 1 Queen, 3 Single (2 bedroom)
Bathroom: 1 Private (we only take one party at a time)
Tariff: B&B (full) Double $70, Single $40, Children $20, Dinner $15.
NZ B&B Vouchers accepted
Nearest Town: Rotorua 14km, Ngongotaha 6km

*We invite you to enjoy a little of our 'good life' at our hillside homestay. With
magnificent lake and rural views, our spacious comfortable home is situated in 10
acres.*
*We are in our 50s. John is involved in education and enjoys relaxing in our peaceful
rural environment which we share with 2 cats, 30 sheep, 2 dogs and several chickens.
Our hobbies are fishing, local history, walking, theatre, gardening and travel. We love
to meet fellow travellers.*
*Major tourist attractions are easily accessible from our property. Hamurana Golf
Course, trout fishing and horse-riding are close-by.*
*You will find us 1km up Fryer Road, off Hamurana Road, on the route around Lake
Rotorua. Fryer Road is well sign-posted, 15 to 20 minutes from Rotorua city. Please
telephone in advance of arrival.*

Rotorua
Homestay/Bed & Breakfast
Address: 10 Henare Place,
Tihi-o-tonga, Rotorua
Name: Lorraine & Basil Carter
Telephone: (07) 347 9967
Beds: 1 Queen, 2 Single (2 Bedrooms)
Bathroom: 1 Guests share
Tariff: B&B (continental) Double $60, Single $35, Children half price,
Dinner by arrangement $25. All beds have electric blankets and TV.
NZ B&B Vouchers accepted
Nearest Town: Rotorua

Welcome to our home, "Woodhall" which is located in a quiet suburb of Rotorua. We have extensive and marvellous views of city, lake and geothermal activities. Only 4 km from the city centre and close to golf courses, tourist attractions, forest walks and restaurants. We enjoy travelling ourselves and love to meet and talk with fellow travellers. Basil is a trained masseur and what better than a relaxing therapeutic massage to complete your busy day ($30 / hour). Dine out or have dinner with us, the choice is yours. If you require an evening meal, advance notice is appreciated. We also offer free pick up from airport, bus depot or train. Ours is a non-smoking home and ask that guests not smoke in it. We look forward to meeting you and making your stay an enjoyable one.
Directions: *Please phone.*

Hamurana, Rotorua
Farmstay
Address: 269 Te Waerenga Road,
R.D. 2, Rotorua
Name: Daniel Farmstay
Telephone: (07) 332 3560
Fax: (07) 332 3560 **Mobile**: (025) 775 341
Beds: 1 Queen, 1 Double, 3 Single (3 bedrooms)
Bathroom: 1 Guests share + 1 Private 1/2 bath (toilet and vanity)
Tariff: B&B (full) Double $80, Single $50, Dinner $25, 3 course.
NZ B&B Vouchers accepted Surcharge $10
Nearest Town: 20km north of Rotorua, 12km from Ngongotaha

Come and enjoy the peaceful setting of our deer farm and home with its panoramic views over Rotorua lake and city. Guests are welcome to a farm tour with an opportunity to feed a few friendly hinds. You will be assured of a friendly greeting from our dog who stays outdoors. Our modern home has an upstairs area, which is for the exclusive use of guests, with 2 bedrooms, 1 Triple with balcony (Queen & Single bed), 1 Double, games room and bathroom. Downstairs there is a twin guest room with a private toilet and vanity. Being non-smokers we thank our guests for not smoking inside our home. We are well situated to take advantage of the many renowned tourist attractions, thermal activities, Agrodome, Maori hangi and concert, trout fishing in the area. Rod is a keen trout fisherman. Dianne is a teacher and we wish to extend our hospitality to you.
Directions: *Please phone, fax or write for booking and directions.*

Rotorua

Homestay
Address: 10 Iles Rd, Rotorua
Name: Patricia & Ron Heydon
Telephone: (07) 345 6451 or
Free phone 0800 317 153
Fax: (07) 345 6452 **Mobile**: 025 273 2974
Email: rhvpnz@clear.net.nz
Beds: 1 King, 2 Single or 4 Single beds (2 bedrooms)
Bathroom: 1 Guests share, Family share toilet
Tariff: B&B (continental) Double $60, Single $35, Children under 12yrs half price, Dinner $20 (Vegetarian available with notice).
Credit cards (Visa/MC/BC). NZ B&B Vouchers accepted
Nearest Town: Rotorua - 5km East

We would love to share our home with you in lovely Lynmore, Rotorua, we are easy to find, close to beautiful forest walks in the Redwood Grove and forest, 4 minutes drive from the city, 10 minutes from the airport. Electric blankets, heaters and radios are in each room. The shower, large bathroom (with bath) and toilet are all separate. Relax in our heated spa pool (all year) no charge, cool off in our swimming pool in summer. We are both in our 40's and enjoy meeting people, Patricia belongs to Zonta International, is a nurse, therapeutic massage therapist (tariff on request) whose interests include sailing, windsurfing, walking, jogging, spinning, knitting. Ron is involved with video production, photography, specialising in weddings, conferences, computer graphics,animations, teaching, his hobbies include sailing, windsurfing, sand yachting. We would like to help make your stay in Rotorua a great and memorable experience.

Rotorua

Homestay
Address: 24 Mark Place, Lynmore, Rotorua 3201
Name: Kairuri Lodge: Hosts: Anne & Don Speedy
Telephone: (07) 345 5385 **Fax**: (07) 345 7119 **Mobile**: (025) 929 254
Email: dspeedy@clear.net.nz
Beds: 1 Queen, 1 Twin (2 bedrooms)
Bathroom: Queen with en-suite, Twin with private bathroom
Tariff: B&B (full) Double $110, Single $60, Dinner by arrangement ($30 to $40pp), Credit Cards: Visa, M/C, B/C, JCB. NZ B&B Vouchers accepted $30 surcharge from 1st October to April 30th
Nearest Town: Rotorua 6 km.

Experience Kiwi Hospitality in the smoke-free environment of our spacious home which has panoramic views of Lake Rotorua, the adjoining countryside and Whakarewarewa Forest.
We offer guests a private lounge, use of our spa, off-street parking and modern laundry facilities.
Relax in our private rural retreat, explore the garden with our cat Foxy, or take an evening stroll in the forest to see glow worms and hear the moreporks.
Your experienced hosts welcome opportunities to return hospitality received during their travels by sharing their love of fine food and wine. Anne works part-time, is a creative cook and keen gardener. A semi-retired surveyor, Don enjoys sailing, music, tennis, can provide information on local attractions, and arrange tours with our own tour company for a Maori marae cultural experience, sightseeing, fishing and sailing. Please confirm bookings before arrival, and if you wish to dine with us, Anne appreciates 24 hours notice.

Ngongotaha

Homestay/Self-contained Accommodation
Address: 124 Leonard Road, Ngongotaha (P O Box 14)
Name: Alrae's Lakeview Bed & Breakfast
Telephone: (07) 357 4913 or 0800 RAEMAS
Fax: (07) 357 4913 **Mobile**: 025 275 0113
Email: alraes@xtra.co.nz
Beds: 2 Queen, 1King/Twin (3 bedrooms)
Bathroom: 2 Ensuite, 1 Private
Tariff: B&B (full) Double $85 - $95, Single $60, Unit P.O.A,
Dinner $25 by arrangement. Visa/Mastercard accepted.
NZ B&B Vouchers accepted $30 Surcharge
Nearest Town: Rotorua, 8 Kms

*Welcome to our Homestay / BED & BREAKFAST WITH THE MILLION DOLLAR VIEW
and our two acre lifestyle block with the black sheep and friendly atmosphere where your
comfort is our priority. We are 10 mins from Rotorua city, handy to Skyline Skyrides,
Agrodome, Rainbow and Fairy Springs, Hangi and Maori concert and walking distance to
the Waiteti Stream where you can fly fish and then smoke your catch in our smoker. We can
arrange any other sightseeing you wish to do. Be it Bungy Jumping or White water rafting
or just taking a ramble through some of our beautiful bush in the surrounding lake district.
Breakfast on scrumptious homemade muffins and breads in the conservatory while you enjoy
the stunning 180 degree views of Lake Rotorua, Mounts Tarawera and Ngongotaha and
surrounding countryside. Enjoy the privacy of the studio unit with peaceful lake views, double
bed, single bed and room for a rollaway if needed. Full kitchen, dining / lounge, CTV, gas
heating, electric blankets and private patio with gas BBQ. Bathroom / laundry includes
automatic washing machine, ... or ..... be guests in our comfortable home where you will have
the choice of two bedrooms.*
*Bedroom one has Queen size bed, electric blanket, reading light and ensuite with Jacuzzi (spa
bath), vanity, heated towel rail, toilet, & hairdryer. Bedroom two has twin beds, private
bathroom with shower and full bath, separate toilet, electric blankets, hairdryer and reading
light. Both bedrooms have a pleasant outlook over the garden. There are no traffic noises or
sulphur fumes.*
*The lounge has CTV with teletext, stereo / radio, books and magazines with a relaxing outlook
over the garden and in the conservatory there is tea / coffee making facilities and cookies
(biscuits) available 24 hours for your convenience. If you wish you can enjoy a drink on the
sunny garden patio and listen to the Tuis and Bellbirds. Laundry available. Your hosts have
been hosting for many years and enjoy the wonderful experience of meeting people from all over
the world and our interests include Lions, Masonry, gardening, walking, yachting, trout
fishing, ocean surfcasting and boating. Alf is a retired Commercial Builder and we have
travelled extensively to many places in the world. Our new interest is 11 black sheep.*
Our accommodation is smoke free, but you may smoke outside if you wish.
Directions: *To find the BED & BREAKFAST WITH THE MILLION DOLLAR VIEW
please phone / fax / email / write for reservations and directions.*
We look forward to meeting you.

Rotorua
Bed & Breakfast
Address: 3 Toko Street, Rotorua
Name: Tresco Bed & Breakfast
Telephone: (07) 348 9611
Fax: (07) 348 9611
Beds: 1 Queen, 4 Double,
2 Single (7 bedrooms)
Bathroom: 2 Guests share
Tariff: B&B (full) Double $75, Single $50,
Credit cards (MC/VISA). NZ B&B Vouchers accepted
Nearest Town: Rotorua City Centre (2 blocks)

Owners Gay and Barrie Fenton offer home style Bed and Breakfast hospitality. You will be welcomed into our home as our special guest, with a warm friendly greeting. Star attraction of our thermally heated, non smoking home, is the Hot Mineral pool, which is ideal for travel weary visitors. Our resident chef will start your day with a substantial continental and cooked breakfast. Tea and coffee making facilities are available 24 hours in our cosy TV lounge. We have ample off street parking. Laundry facilities in our thermally heated drying room are available for guests. We are happy to advise on and arrange tours, to ensure you get value for your dollar. We also take pride as Kiwi Hosts in guiding you through New Zealand on a top class Bed and Breakfast trail. With our 2 resident felines: Sybil (of Fawlty Towers) and Mini, we look forward to making our home your home.
Home Page: http://www.leisureplan-live.com

Rotorua
Homestay
Address: Malrex Manor,
29 McDowell Street, Rotorua
Name: Vida Whale
Telephone: (07) 349 0249
Fax: (07) 349 2993 **Mobile**: (025) 772 518
Email: vwmalrex@clear.net.nz
Beds: 2 Queen, 2 Single (3 bedrooms)
Bathroom: 2 Guests share
Tariff: B&B (full) Double $95, Single $60, Dinner by arrangement $20.
Credit Cards Visa, MC, Amex
Nearest Town: Rotorua (Distance: 5 min drive)

A touch of country in the city. Relax and listen to the birds at my spacious quiet home which is surrounded by parkland, overlooking Rotorua. Breakfast in the sunny conservatory while I help you plan your day. Close to two golf courses, Whakarewarewa Thermal area, and only a few minutes drive from the city centre. The house is heated and has electric blankets on all the beds. I can assure you of a peaceful memorable stay. McDowell Street is off both Otonga and Springfield Roads. The house is down the drive beside the park. Please book for dinner, and phone to advise of arrival time on the day. Ample parking. Swimming pool.

Please help us provide the best hospitality in the world.
Fill in a comment form for every place you stay.

Holdens Bay, Rotorua
Lakeside Retreat

Address: 'Studio 21', 21a Holden Ave,
Holdens Bay, Rotorua
Name: Terry Wood & Daphne Frizzell
Telephone: (07) 345 5587 **Fax**: (07) 345 9621
Beds: Large Studio Unit: 1 Queen+ 1 Single (
sitting area, tea making facilities, fridge)
Bathroom: 1 Private (Studio Unit)
Tariff: B&B (full) Double $80, Extra person share Studio Unit $20, Single $50,
Dinner $20pp by arrangement. Stay 3 nights, 4th night is free.
NZ B&B Vouchers accepted $12 surcharge
Nearest Town: Rotorua city centre 10 mins, Airport 3 mins.

Welcome to Studio 21: experience the tranquillity of staying by Lake Rotorua. Waken to birdsong, stroll along the shores of the lake, yet only to 10 minutes from the heart of Rotorua. Your hosts Terry and Daphne love to share their knowledge of camping, fishing, surrounding lakes and bush, local theatre and attractions. Choose from sightseeing or shopping, Maori cultural experience, fishing, tramping, windsurfing, soaking in hot pools, great dining options - or simply relaxing. Our home is spacious, clean and hospitable: even the cats and our Labrador Grace love guests. The large comfortable studio unit has its own private patio and bathroom. You can breakfast in bed, on the deck or by our cosy fire - you choose! Fresh healthy food - our menus are flexible. Dinner, BBQ or spa pool by prior arrangement. Brochures available.

Rotorua
Lakeview Country Homestay + Self-contained Accommodation
Address: 983 Hamurana Rd,
Wilsons Bay, R.D. 2, Rotorua
Name: Carol & Bernie Mason
Telephone: (07) 332 2445 or (07) 362 4087
Fax: (07) 332 2445
Mobile: (025) 467 121
Beds: 1 King, 1 Queen,
2 Single (2 bedrooms)
Bathroom: 1 Guests share
Tariff: B&B (full) Double $80, Single $60, Dinner $25pp.
Discounts for 3 nights or more. NZ B&B Vouchers accepted $15 surcharge
Nearest Town: Rotorua - 15 minutes north of Rotorua, 8 minutes from
Ngongotaha Village

Our home at Wilsons Bay is an ideal spot to relax and enjoy the peaceful surroundings. IMAGINE panoramic views of Lake Rotorua, Mokoia Island, Mt Tarawera, city lights and waking up to a view of Rotorua's steaming thermal area. Enjoy the rural outlook and surrounding farmland, grazing sheep, cattle, pigs, and chickens. There is a cat called Misty, and a very friendly turkey that loves to be stroked.We offer warm friendly Kiwi hospitality, delicious meals (by prior arrangement) prepared by Bernie, my husband a semi-retired chef. Guestrooms are well appointed with lake and countryside views, comfortable beds and electric blankets.We have both travelled extensively and enjoy meeting people. Our interests are gardening, trout fishing and golf.Major tourist attractions, trout streams, horse-riding and golf course are easily accessible from our home. We look forward to meeting you. Smoking designated areas.ARRIVE AS A TOURIST, LEAVE AS OUR FRIEND.
Directions: *Please phone.*

273

Okere Falls, Lake Rotoiti

B&B, Self-contained Accom.
Address: Please phone for directions
Name: Namaste Point
Telephone: (07) 362 4804 **Fax**: (07) 362 4060 **Mobile**: (025) 971 092
Email: namaste.point@xtra.co.nz
Beds: 2 King, 1 Double, 4 Single
Bathroom: 2 Ensuite, 1 Private
Tariff: B&B (Deluxe continental) Double $110, Single $70. Self catered kitchen in units.   Cash & Credit Cards (VISA/MC).
Nearest Town: Rotorua 19km

Our Guests Words .....
"The setting is superb and the bed definitely the best."
"We have been overwhelmed with the beauty of Namaste Point and the hospitality of our hostess."
"Perfect spot for a romantic weekend."
"Just what we needed. The accommodations are first class, the location fantastic."
"The flora, the fauna, the peace and serenity ..... exactly what we were looking for!!"
"Wonderful luxury with perfect privacy. Excellent weekend!"
"You'd be pushed to find a bed and breakfast in New Zealand which offers such top-class facilities in such a picturesque setting as Namaste Point."
A GENUINE KIWI HOSTESS - SECLUSION & PRIVACY - REAL COFFEE - HEATED - SMOKE FREE.
Only 15 minutes drive from Rotorua, our home is on the tip of the Te Akau Peninsula in Lake Rotoiti, surrounded by lake and scenic bush reserve. "Namaste Point" offers modern, first-class self contained accommodation. - A large bedroom with a choice of king or twin beds with electric blankets - view TV and enjoy real brewed coffee in bed - an ensuite bathroom with a hair dryer - a lounge with skylight and two loveseats (convert into single beds), Tibetan floor rugs, TV, stereo, fridge (stocked with delicious breakfast goodies), microwave, oven, coffee perc, kettle, full cutlery and china. - Flowers, fresh fruit, biscuits (cookies), books and magazines. - Private patios with BBQ's, a Jacuzzi spa pool and swimming towels. A paddleboat, dinghy and Coleman Canadian canoe are for our guests use and enjoyment. Our beach is a safe swimming area. Bring your own boat and use our jetty. Use our fly rods to fish in Lake Rotoiti.

We are happy to arrange guided trout fishing trips. Enjoy our rose gardens and scenic bush reserve or relax with friends and family on the large lakefront lawn. Our waterfront is a haven for native birds. Nearby, raft the world famous Okere Falls and enjoy thermal areas, rhododendron gardens, bush walks, two nine hole golf course, and famous fly fishing spots at the Ohau Channel and the Kaituna river trout pools. I have travelled extensively and have chosen this idyllic spot to settle with my pets - Lhasa apsos and a cat. Our accommodation is SMOKE FREE. Telephone booking is essential.

274

Rotorua City
City Homestay
Address: 1126 Whakaue Street, Rotorua
Name: Irvine & Susan Munro
Telephone: (07) 348 8594
Beds: 1 Double, 2 Single (2 bedrooms)
Bathroom: 1 Guests share
Tariff: B&B (full/continental) Double $75, Single $40, Children $10-$20, 10% discount 3 nights or more, Dinner $15-$25. NZ B&B Vouchers accepted
Nearest Town: Rotorua. 200 metres from Tourism Centre.

We welcome guests to a unique situation in Rotorua City adjoining the Lakefront park and close to hospitals. Shops and restaurants and the Novotel Hotel only 100m and, we are also very handy to many tourist attractions, Tourism Centre and Convention Centre only 200m away.
Our home is spacious, comfortable, thermally heated, with an outdoor thermal pool and private gardens with off street parking.
Irvine has had an interest in farming and outdoor sports. Susan's interests are music, sewing, gardening and cooking. Meals may be provided with prior notice and children are welcome there being a children's playground in the adjacent park.
We are happy to transport you to and from the tourism centre and arrange reservations for you.
Rotorua residents for over 50 years.
Directions: *Turn left into Whakaue Street two blocks towards Lake from Tourist Centre. We are 50m from the corner, overlooking the park.*

Lake Rotorua
Homestay/Self-contained Accommodation
Address: Lake Edge, 8 Parkcliff Rd., R.D.4, Rotorua
Name: Paul & Glenda Norman
Telephone: (07) 345 9328
Fax: (07) 345-9328
Mobile: 025 758 750
Beds: 1 King, 2 Single (2 bedrooms)
Bathroom: 1 Ensuite
Tariff: B&B (continental) Double $85, Single $65. Dinner $25pp by arrangement.
Nearest Town: Rotorua. 5 minutes from Rotorua Airport

Lake edge home of professional fishing guide with the most productive rainbow trout fishing at the front doorstep. You can go fishing, charter a cruise with special half day rates for guests or simply enjoy the tranquillity of the lakeside lifestyle and be only 10 minutes from all the attractions of Rotorua.
Your accommodation has a separate entrance, cooking facilities, Sky TV, electric blankets, tea and coffee, own private ensuite and can be as self-contained or catered for as you request.
We can help you arrange sight seeing, golf, rafting and of course trout fishing, or simply relax and join us and our siamese and burmese cats to watch the sun set over Lake Rotorua.
Directions: *From Rotorua City past Airport on Rotorua-Tauranga Highway.*

Ngongotaha, Rotorua
Homestay
Address: "Ngongotaha Lakeside Lodge",
41 Operiana St, Ngongotaha, Rotorua
Name: Ann & Gordon Thompson
Telephone: (07) 357 4020
Fax: (07) 357 4020
Beds: 2 Queen, 2 Single (3 bedrooms)
Bathroom: 3 Ensuite
Tariff: B&B (full) Double $95-$125, Single $80-$100, Dinner $35.
Children over 12 welcome. Credit Cards (VISA/MC).
NZ B&B Vouchers accepted $20-$45 surcharge
Nearest Town: Rotorua 10km

*Our lodge, on the shores of beautiful **Lake Rotorua**, commands panoramic views of the lake and surrounding mountains of New Zealand's central North Island. From our conservatory you can sit and watch local fisherman try their luck for fighting **Rainbow** and wily **Brown trout** at the mouth of the Waiteti Stream. The upper level of this two-storied home is exclusively for guests with three **ensuite bedrooms** and **guest lounge** opening on to the **conservatory** which overlooks the lake. Your room will be serviced daily and a laundry service is available upon request. A full **English breakfast** is served every morning while we help you plan your day using a complimentary map. Canoes, golf clubs and fishing rods are free for guests, plus we'll cook your catch for you.. The guest kitchen provides tea and coffee facilities. Each room has everything you require for a comfortable stay including **T.V, hairdryers, heated towel rails, electric blankets and central heating**. We will arrange Maori Hangi or Concerts, guided fishing tours and horse riding. We have ample off street parking. The city of Rotorua is 10km away - close enough to its many attractions - but far enough away for peace and quiet, and sulphur free! We look forward to hearing from you and hope you join us soon for a wonderful holiday.*
Directions: *Take State Highway 5 to Ngongotaha turn-off. Turn right and continue round the lake. After railway crossing turn right into Wikaraka Road, left into Okona Crescent and left into Operiana Street and the lodge is on the right.*

Members of
**The New Zealand Association
Farm & Home Host Inc.**
maintain the highest standards &
are always delighted to welcome
guests into their homes.

Waikite Valley, Rotorua

Farmstay
Address: "Puaiti", Puaiti Rd.,
R.D.1, Rotorua. Phone for directions.
Name: Barb & Philip Hawken
Telephone: (07) 333 1540
Fax: (07) 333 1501
Mobile: (025) 854 258
Beds: 1 Double, 4 Single (3 bedrooms)
Bathroom: 1 Guests share (Separate bath, shower, toilet)
Tariff: B&B (special) Double $90, Single $70, Children $25-$35, Dinner $30,
Children's dinner $10-$15.
Nearest Town: Rotorua 35 mins.

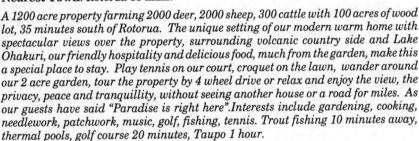

*A 1200 acre property farming 2000 deer, 2000 sheep, 300 cattle with 100 acres of wood
lot, 35 minutes south of Rotorua. The unique setting of our modern warm home with
spectacular views over the property, surrounding volcanic country side and Lake
Ohakuri, our friendly hospitality and delicious food, much from the garden, make this
a special place to stay. Play tennis on our court, croquet on the lawn, wander around
our 2 acre garden, tour the property by 4 wheel drive or relax and enjoy the view, the
privacy, peace and tranquillity, without seeing another house or a road for miles. As
our guests have said "Paradise is right here".Interests include gardening, cooking,
needlework, patchwork, music, golf, fishing, tennis. Trout fishing 10 minutes away,
thermal pools, golf course 20 minutes, Taupo 1 hour.*
Home Page: http://nz.com/webnz/bbnz/puaiti/htm

Rotorua

Homestay
Address: 367 Old Taupo Road, Rotorua
Name: "Thermal Stay"
Wendy & Rod Davenhill
Telephone: (07) 349 1605
Fax: (07)349 1641
Email: davenhill@clear.net.nz
Mobile: (021) 667 122
Beds: 2 King/Queen, 2 Single (3 bedrooms)
Bathroom: 2 Guests share, 1 Family share
Tariff: B&B (full) Double $95, Single $55, Children under 12 half price,
Dinner $25pp. Credit cards. NZ B&B Vouchers accepted $15 surcharge
Nearest Town: Rotorua 3km (1/2 hour walk)

Comfortable, thermally heated two storeyed home, private gardens surround, large thermally heated pool, BBQ. Centrally located, very quiet, no sulphur fumes, off-street parking. Close to two golf courses, shopping centres, city centre and scenic attractions.

Queen bedroom upstairs with adjoining TV lounge and private deck overlooking gardens. Downstairs, a twin bedroom and a twin / king bedroom, large lounge with log fire. We have both travelled and worked in the hospitality industry, Wendy as chef. We enjoy good food, wines, music and conversation.

Privacy or our company - we respect your wishes.

We know that our home and facilities are special and will fill you with a sense of serenity and give you a taste of Rotorua's thermal charm. Let us spoil you and share our loved home and city. No smoking inside. Pets 'Candy', a large, friendly tabby cat - our guests love her!
Directions: *Please phone, fax or write..*

Ngongotaha, Rotorua

Farmstay
Address: 175 Jackson Road, RD2, Rotorua
Name: Clover Downs Estate
Telephone: (07) 332 2366
Fax: (07) 332 2367
Mobile: (025) 712 866
Email: ferris@cloverdowns.co.nz
Beds: 2 King, 1 Queen (3 bedrooms)
Bathroom: 3 Ensuite

Tariff: B&B (special) Double $125-$150, Single $115-$140,
Dinner or BBQ, optional extra, Credit Cards (VISA/MC/DINERS/AMEX).
Nearest Town: 18km north of Rotorua city centre

So country yet so close to town, affordable luxury farm accommodation with total commitment to comfort, quality and high standards, ensuring a memorable stay.

CLOVER DOWNS ESTATE is situated on a secluded 35-acre quality assurance accredited deer and ostrich farm overlooking Lake Rotorua.

Three beautifully appointed spacious bedrooms are each equipped with Sky TV, fridge, tea and coffee facilities and private ensuite complete with toiletries, hairdryer and bathrobes.Take a farm tour on our 4WD bike with Lloyd and the dogs, try a game of pentaque or relax in the hot tub. With extensive overseas and New Zealand travel experience, we can gladly help in arranging bookings for Rotorua attractions and activities as well as assisting you with onward travel plans.

Warm welcome, traditional hospitality and wonderful experience await you at CLOVER DOWNS ESTATE.
Directions: *Please telephone, fax or write for bookings and directions.*

Rotorua

Homestay
Address: 144 Fryer Rd, Hamurana
Phone for reservations & directions
Name: "Panorama" (Chris & Dave)
Telephone: (07) 332 2618
Fax: (07) 332 2618
Email: panorama@wave.co.nz

Beds: King, Superking/Twin, Queen plus single (3 bedrooms)
Bathroom: 2 Ensuite, 1 Private
Tariff: B&B (continental, full optional extra) Double $100-$135, Single $90,
Dinner $30 (complimentary wine). Not suitable for Children under 12 years.
Credit cards. NZ B&B Vouchers accepted $20 surcharge per person
Nearest Town: Rotorua 15km

This is an ideal base to stay whilst visiting Rotorua. Our relaxed lifestyle and country hospitality will ensure your stay with us is memorable. The architecturally designed cedar and brick home takes full advantage of the panoramic views of Lake Rorotua and surrounding countryside. Furnished to a luxury standard, the guest wing with private entrance, has spacious bedrooms and fresh flowers. Be as formal or relaxed as you wish. Enjoy music or a book in front of the open fire or laze in the heated massage spa pool. Play tennis or go for walks to local Hamurana Springs, beside the lake or farm. There are friendly sheep and working dogs waiting for a pat and piece of bread. There are plenty of areas within the landscaped garden where you can escape. Dinner is available. The emphasis on meals is fresh home-grown, home-made, or local produce. Discount for over two nights.

Rotorua

Guest House
Address: "Dudley House",
1024 Rangiuru Street, Rotorua
Name: "Dudley House" B&B
Telephone: (07) 347 9894
Beds: 1 Queen, 1 Double, 1 Twin,
1 Single (4 bedrooms)
Bathroom: 2 Guests share
Tariff: B&B (full) Double $60-$65, Twin $65, Single $40.
Payment by NZ Travellers Cheques or cash. Tea & coffee facilities and transport
to and from local passenger services available free. NZ B&B Vouchers accepted
Nearest Town: Rotorua - 5 mins walk to city centre

"Dudley House" is a typical English Tudor style house built in the 1930's, with rimu doors and trims and matai polished floors. The house is tastefully and warmly decorated, with thermal heating. The dining room is adorned with military and police memorabilia. Non-smoking.
Your hosts are happy to sit and chat about the numerous attractions around Rotorua, some within walking distance. Restaurants, cafes or bars, shops and banks are 5 minutes walk, also a 2 minute walk to lake front and village green.
We welcome your inquiry.

One of the differences between staying at a hotel and a B&B
is that you don't hug the hotel staff when you leave.

Rotorua area Ngakuru

Country Homestay
Address: Salanga, Ngakuru,
 RD 1, Rotorua 3221
Name: Mrs Jo Trent
Telephone: (07) 333 2235
Fax: (07) 333 2235
Beds: 4 Single (2 bedrooms)
Bathroom: 1 Ensuite, 1 Private, Separate toilet
Tariff: B&B (full) Double $85, Single $45, Children over 8,
Dinner $20 by arrangement, Credit Cards.

NZ B&B Vouchers accepted $12 surcharge from 1 Oct to 31 March
Nearest Town: Rotorua 29.8km

*A warm welcome awaits you at Salanga in a tranquil setting on Lake Ohakuri.
Your well travelled and worldwise hosts ex dairy and deer farmers and oriental short-
hair cat offer hearty country cuisine, comfort and conversation.*
*Both guest bedrooms offer twin beds with electric blankets, a choice of blankets or
duvets and either ensuite or private bathrooms. Heaters and fans supplied seasonally.*
*Play carpet bowls inside, petanque outside, flyfish from the garden, amble over
picturesque farmland or visit neighbours cowshed to see milking. Soak in Waikite
Valley Hot Pools (10km) or play golf and squash (10km).*
*Rotorua with its many tourist attractions is just under 30km away. Taupo approxi-
mately 70km.*
Help and advice with itineraries a speciality.
Directions: *Please telephone.*

Rotorua

Country Homestay
Address: 66 State Highway 33, RD 4, Rotorua
Name: M & I Fischer
Telephone: (07) 345 5325 **Fax**: (07) 345 5325
Beds: 3 Queen, 1 Double (4 bedrooms)
Bathroom: 1 Guests share, 1 Family share
Tariff: B&B Double $75, Single $45, Dinner $25, Campervan $25.
Plenty of boat parking. No credit cards.
Nearest Town: Rotorua 12 minutes. Airport 3 minutes.

*Welcome to our newly built high quality country home. On our lifestyle block situated
between Lake Rotorua and Lake Rotoiti, we have cows, sheep, chickens, rabbits and
honey bees.*
*We organically grow vegetables, medicinal herbs and flowers like camomile, lemon
balm, mint and more.*
*In minutes a native bush drive to beautiful Lake Okataina in clear deep trophy trout
fishing lake with beautiful native bush walks. Hells Gate - Rhododendron Gardens
just around the corner, other thermal activities and maori culture, farm shows just
minutes away. We can plan your day and book attractions.*
*Our hobbies are: Trout fishing from boat and fly fishing in close by lakes, fly fishing
in rivers like Rangitaiki Whirinaki, bush walking, shooting and hunting in Kaingaroa
and Whirinaki Forest Park.*
We have considerable experience and can give advice.
*We have travelled the World and lived in the USA, Canada, Indonesia, Mexico and
Germany and speak their languages.*

Rotorua
Homestay and B&B
Address: The Lake House, 6 Cooper Avenue,
Holdens Bay, Rotorua
Name: Susan and Warwick Kay
Telephone: (07) 345 3313
Fax: (07) 345 3310
Email: SusanK@xtra.co.nz
Beds: 2 Queen, 2 Single (3 bedrooms)
Bathroom: 1 Ensuite, 2 Guests share.

Tariff: B&B (full) Double $80-$90, Single $50-$60, Dinner $20 by arrangement,
Children $30 each. Credit Cards NZ B&B Vouchers accepted
Nearest Town: Rotorua 7km. Airport 2 km

Come and enjoy our lovely old holiday home on the shores of Lake Rotorua. Relax on the wide verandah and spend romantic evenings watching the moonlight across the water.Our garden runs on to a white sandy beach great for swimming and boating. Guests are welcome to use our small water craft and windsurfers. A neighbouring playground helps make visits with children a pleasure. Home comforts include tea and coffee anytime, laundry, large lounge with books, music and games. All bedrooms open on to verandah and have wide lake views. We will gladly help with early or late check in / out and information on the cultural, sporting and fun activities available in Rotorua. One retiring cat. Sheltered outdoor area for smokers. Free pick-up and delivery from airport or city.
Directions: *Holdens Bay is down Robinson Avenue off Te Ngae Road (SH30). Cooper Avenue is right off Robinson Avenue.*

Rotorua
Homestay
Address: The Towers Homestay,
373 Malfroy Road, Rotorua
Name: Des and Doreen Towers
Telephone: 07 347 6254
Freephone: 0800 261 040
Beds: 1 Double (1 bedroom)
Bathroom: 1 Private
Tariff: B&B (continental) Double $65, Single $40, Dinner $15-$20 (by arrangement). Credit Cards, NZ B&B Vouchers accepted.
Nearest Town: Rotorua City Centre 3 km.

We are average New Zealanders and our lifestyle enables us to spend time, if required, with our guests. Our home is elevated with views over Rotorua and has a very private garden.
The guest accommodation is downstairs with private facilities, and upstairs you can relax in our spacious lounge.
Our family has grown up and married, giving us time to enjoy visitors to our smoke free home. We offer free pick up from your bus, train or plane, and off street parking is available.
Des has many years experience with a national organisation providing both local and New Zealand touring information to the Rotorua visitor.
His hobbies are Amiga computers and DIY projects. He is also an ex member of Jaycees and Lions. Doreen originally from South Wales enjoys gardening, is an avid reader and enjoys meeting people.
WE LOOK FORWARD TO YOUR VISIT AND GUARANTEE YOU A WARM WELCOME!

Rotorua
Homestay B&B
Address: 155G Okere Road,
Lake Rotoiti, RD4 Rotorua
Name: Laurice and Bill Unwin
Telephone: 07 362 4288 **Fax**: 07 362 4288
Mobile: 025 521 483
Beds: 3 Queen (3 bedrooms)
Bathroom: 2 Ensuites, 1 Private

Tariff: B&B (full) Double $80, Single $50, Dinner $20-$25 pp. Children welcome.
NZ B&B Vouchers accepted $12 surcharge
Nearest Town: Rotorua

We have a lovely home in a beautiful setting beside Lake Rotoiti. Within a short
walking distance there are bush walks, waterfalls, white water rafting, kayaking,
driver and lake fishing.
Our bed and breakfasts are separate from the main living area, are centrally heated
and each has its own ensuite, TV, refrigerator, tea/coffee making.
There are so many different things to do in this region so whatever your interest,
whether thrill seeking, tramping, fishing, boating, golfing, sight seeing, eating or just
relaxing and enjoying yourself - it is all here. Boat mooring available.
Ring, write or fax for information. We are easy to find, just one minute from the
Rotorua-Tauranga highway.
24 hours notice would be appreciated, especially if a meal is required.
Distance please

Rotorua
Country Stay
Address: 351 Dalbeth Road, RD2,
Ngongotaha, Rotorua
Name: Anneke and John Van Der Maat
Telephone: (07) 357 5893
Fax: (07) 357 5893
Mobile: (025) 272 6807
Beds: 4 Queen, 3 Single (5 bedrooms)
Bathroom: 3 Ensuites, 1 Guests share
Tariff: B&B (full) Double $100-$135, Single $75-$110, Dinner $30,
Children negotiable.   NZ B&B Vouchers accepted $30 surcharge + $60 surcharge
for Ensuite.
Nearest Town: Rotorua (12 minutes)

We are only 12 minutes from Rotorua City.
Tourist attractions: Agrodome, Rainbow Springs and gondolas as well as several golf
courses are only minutes away. We welcome you into our "country villa" were we
provide old fashioned hospitality, home cooking and a friendly atmosphere. Our large
villa opens into lovely cottage gardens, with a backdrop of native shrubs and trees
along the Waiteti stream, which runs along our border. The views over lake and city
are magnificent, by day or by night. Our guest areas are spacious and are consisting
of queen bedrooms with ensuites, one for people with special needs. Upstairs we have
cottage style bedrooms with queen and single beds. These rooms share a guest
bathroom and toilet. Evening meals by arrangement. Smoke-free home.
Directions: *From Auckland, travel South on Highway 5. First turn left past*
"Lakeview golf course", or through Ngongotaha, over the railway line. First turn left.

Taupo

Homestay
Address: 23 Rokino Road, Taupo
Name: Colleen & Bob Yeoman
Telephone: (07) 377 0283
Beds: 1 Queen, 3 Single (3 bedrooms, cot + highchair available)
Bathroom: 1 Private, 1 Guests share
Tariff: B&B (full) Double $90, Single $45, Children half price, Dinner $30.
NZ B&B Vouchers accepted $15 surcharge
Nearest Town: Taupo 2kms to Post Office - (20 minute walk). 5 minute walk to Lake.

Welcome to "Yeoman's Homestay" where we warmly invite you to spend a relaxing time in our restful home situated in the bird area of Taupo. Savour the beautiful lake and mountain views from our spacious lounge and sundeck. During winter our log fire burns day and night. Guests attractive bedrooms are superbly comfortable with electric blankets on all beds - always fresh flowers and up to date magazines.
We are retired sheep and cattle farmers, Bob has a great knowledge of New Zealand native trees and is a keen golfer. Colleen's interests are cross-stitch, cooking and CWI. Overseas travel has extensively widened our horizons.
At breakfast we specialise in home-made jams, marmalade and preserved fruit. Bob is in charge of bacon and eggs. Available for guests use are hairdryers, laundry facilities, scrabble board and billiard table. Excellent off-street parking. Guests can be met off public transport.
Directions: *Turn into Huia Street from lake front, take fourth turn on right into Rokino Road.*

Kinloch, Lake Taupo

Country Village B&B
Address: "Twynham at Kinloch",
84 Marina Terrace, Kinloch, Lake Taupo
Name: Elizabeth and Paul Whitelock
Telephone: (07) 378 2862 **Fax**: (07) 378 2868
Mobile: (025) 285 6001
Beds: 1 Double, 2 Single (2 bedrooms)
Bathroom: 1 Guests share
Tariff: B&B (full) Double $115, Single $90,
Dinner $30, Children half price. Visa/Mastercard.
Winter and long stay rates available.
NZ B&B Vouchers accepted $30 surcharge
Nearest Town: Taupo, 15 mins drive.

Nestled within large private gardens in the picturesque lakeside village of Kinloch - Twynham is a haven for fresh air, good coffee and relaxation and unequalled as a base for exploring the delights of Taupo region plus the more strenuous delights of golf (adjacent), fishing (five minute stroll), water sports, snow skiing, bush and mountain walks. Hearty breakfasts, wholesome dinners and warm welcomes assure guests of an enjoyable stay. Guest accommodation is a private wing with bedrooms, large bathroom and elegant lounge. Rooms are furnished for comfort and warmth. Laundry, refreshments and home baking always available. Licensed restaurant nearby. Elizabeth has a wide knowledge of the volcanic and geothermal history of the region, gained over a long career in tourism and industry. Paul is a New Zealand Kennel Club Judge, and dog sports, golf, music and travel are family interests. We have two friendly dogs and pets are welcome. Smoke free environment. We look forward to your company.
Directions: *Please telephone or fax.*

283

Taupo
Farmstay
Address: Reeves Road, Acacia Bay, Taupo
Name: Jay, (Jennefer) & Bruce McLeod
Telephone: (07) 378 7901 **Fax**: (07) 378 7901
Email: temoenga@reap.org.nz
Beds: 1 King, 1 Queen, 1 Twin (3 bedrooms)
Bathroom: 3 Ensuite
Tariff: B&B (full) Double $120-$140, Single $80, Children $30, Dinner $35pp, Lunch $15pp, Credit Cards (VISA/MC). NZ B&B Vouchers accepted $36-$52 surcharge
Nearest Town: Taupo 5km

Jay and Bruce extend a warm welcome to share the unique experience of staying at Te Moenga Farmstay, a working deer, sheep, and cattle farm overlooking the lake and located minutes from central Taupo, boat harbour, three golf courses, and all the major tourist and sporting attractions. From your own private suite to the glorious views of Lake Taupo you will find your accommodation unequalled.
We pride ourselves that we offer complete privacy and perfect comfort.
However if it is your wish more adventurous activities ranging from scenic bush and farm walks through to fishing and all the recreational activities the region offers can be readily arranged.
Te Moenga homestead is spacious, well appointed, and set in large park like surroundings, all suites have their own private lounge, TV etc.
Your hosts have travelled widely and have a detailed knowledge of the region and are able to ensure a memorable experience.
Home Page: http://nz.com/webnz/bbnz/moenga.htm
Directions: *Please phone.*

Taupo

Homestay+Self-contained Accom.
Address: 18 Hawai St., 2 Mile Bay, Taupo
Name: Jeanette & Bryce Jones
Telephone: (07) 377 3242 **Fax**: (07) 377 3242
Beds: 1 Double, 2 Single (2 bedrooms)
Bathroom: 1 Guests share
Tariff: B&B (full) Double $70, Single $45,
Children $20, Dinner $20, Credit Cards.
Cottage Double $45, each extra person $15. NZ B&B Vouchers accepted
Nearest Town: Taupo 3km

Taupo, is great for holidays any season. We invite you to stay in our new home that has panoramic views from lounge and deck. The guest bedrooms are downstairs with a shared bathroom - quiet and comfortable. Home-made muesli, preserves, hot bread and muffins are my breakfast speciality and as I love to cook you are welcome to an evening meal. We are 2 minutes walking distance to the lake where we join up to an excellent walking track. We have travelled extensively and enjoy the stimulation and interest that meeting people from other countries can bring. Bryce is ex RAF Pathfinder WW2. Jeanette's interests include craft, church and voluntary work. Marmite Cottage is beside our house. It is a true Kiwi Bach - complete with 'comfy' mismatched furniture. Self-contained it sleeps 7. Breakfast available on request.

Acacia Bay, Taupo

Homestay

Address: 77A Wakeman Road, Acacia Bay, Taupo
Name: Pariroa Homestay, Joan & Eric Leersnijder
Telephone: (07) 378 3861 **Fax**: (07) 378 3866 **Mobile**: 025 530 370
Beds: 1 Double, 2 Single (2 bedrooms)
Bathroom: 1 Guests share, separate toilet
Tariff: B&B (full) Double $70, Single $45, Children $20,
Credit Cards Visa and Master Card NZ B&B Vouchers accepted
Nearest Town: Taupo 5km

Views Views
Our home is Scandinavian style with a natural wooden interior, situated in a very quiet area of Acacia Bay, and surrounded by native ferns and plants. We have magnificent uninterrupted views of Lake Taupo, Mount Tauhara, and the ranges from the guest bedrooms, living room and sun deck. We are retired farmers who have travelled extensively and enjoy meeting people. Eric, in his younger years, lived in several European countries and was a tea planter in Indonesia before coming to New Zealand in 1952. We are about 5km from Taupo and minutes from the beach. If you enjoy fishing, tramping, mountaineering, playing golf, or relaxing in hot thermal pools, it is all in this area.
Directions: *Vehicular access is the road going down between 95 and 99 Wakeman Road. We are the last house on this short road.*

Private bathroom is for your use exclusively,
Guests share means you may be sharing with other guests,
Family share means you will be sharing with the family.

Taupo
Homestay
Address: 30 Rokino Road, Taupo
Name: Nolan's Homestay
Telephone: (07) 377 0828
Fax: (07) 377-0828
Mobile: (025) 244 9035
Beds: 4 Single (2 bedrooms)
Bathroom: 1 Ensuite, 1 Family share
Tariff: B&B (full) Twin Balcony bedroom with ensuite $85, Single $50,
Dinner $25.   NZ B&B Vouchers accepted
Nearest Town: Taupo 2km, Lake 5 mins

We are located up a tree lined drive onto an elevated section with ample parking, secluded, one level, no steps to overlook the breathtaking views of the mountains, ranges, lake and township. Centrally situated.
We retired from farming where we hosted farmstays from its inception and are widely travelled both in New Zealand and overseas.
Our interests are varied as our activities which include tramping, fishing, horseracing and entertaining. Serving on many voluntary organisations.
Betty loves to cook....dinners are by arrangement.
Remember the Nolan's is not just a Bed & Breakfast but a HOMESTAY!
Directions: *From lakefront going south take Taharepa Road to shopping centre turning left into Rokino Road. Number 30 is on your right up a treelined paved drive.*
99: If possible pls print on different page to C&B Yeoman. Also wish top of page listing if advert on vouchers on same page.

Members of
**The New Zealand Association
Farm & Home Host Inc.**
maintain the highest standards &
are always delighted to welcome
guests into their homes.

Lake Taupo

Homestay
Address: 'Pataka House',
8 Pataka Road, Taupo
Name: Raewyn & Neil Alexander
Telephone: (07) 378 5481
Mobile: 025-473 881
Beds: 1 Queen, 4 Single (3 Bedrooms)
Bathroom: 1 Private, 1 Guest share.
Tariff: B&B (full) Double $90, Single $50, Children half price.
NZ B&B Vouchers accepted $15 surcharge
Nearest Town: Taupo (1km)

Raewyn and Neil extend a warm welcome to Pataka House and we look forward to meeting new people and making new friends. You will find us 100 metres from lake Taupo, opposite Mount Ruapehu and very close to restaurants and shops. our home is on a quiet road up a tree-lined drive way and privately situated. You are provided with a beautiful environment where you may wander around the garden and dell and observe some native birds.

Pataka House is spacious, centrally heated in winter and has a private guest wing of three double bedrooms which are attractively furnished. We are proud of our homestay business which offers guests lounge usage, laundry facilities, swimming pool, barbecue and roomy carpark. Thermal pools are nearby. We also offer a hearty breakfast with home-baked bread, home-preserved fruit, home-made jam and fresh fruit juice or, if you wish, a cooked breakfast.

Directions: *Please phone.*

Taupo

Self-contained Accommodation
Address: Riverway Cottages,
16 Peehi Manini Rd, Waitahanui
R.D.2, Taupo
Name: Joyce & John Johnson
Telephone: (07) 378 8822
Beds: 1 Queen, 1 Double, 1 Single (2 bedrooms)
Bathroom: 1 Private
Tariff: B&B (continental) Double $75, Single $45, Dinner $25pp, Children half price. Free bottle of wine with three night stay B&B booking.
Nearest Town: Taupo 14 kms (10 mins)

Riverway Cottages are situated 100 yds from the famous Waitahanui River, and 200 yds from beautiful Lake Taupo. They are older-type properties, one John and Joyce live in, and the second, comprises lounge with TV, kitchen with fridge, freezer, microwave, and conventional ovens, separate dining room, two double bedrooms and bathroom. There is a deck to relax on in summer, and perhaps enjoy a BBQ with us, with complimentary pre-dinner drinks - as evening dinner is optional. In winter there are gas and electric fires, and electric blankets on all beds, for the comfort of our visitors. We have ample parking space, for visitors driving around beautiful New Zealand. For interested fishermen, John has been a successful Trout Fly Fishing Guide for many years, and can take you to some "magic places", and may be booked by the hour or by the day. Joyce is a keen badminton player. Come and visit Waitahanui. We'd love to meet you.

Directions: *Please phone for directions - and we will pick up if needed.*

Acacia Bay, Taupo
Lakeside Homestay
Address: Paeroa Lakeside Homestay, 21 Te Kopua St., Acacia Bay, Taupo
Name: Paeroa Lakeside Homestay,
Barbara & John Bibby
Telephone: (07) 378 8449
Fax: (07) 378 8449
Mobile: 025 818 829
Beds: 2 King/Queen, 2 Single (3 bedrooms)
Bathrooms: 1 Ensuite, 1 Private (1 Guests share only in peak times)
Tariff: B&B (full or continental) Double $120, Single $85, Dinner $35, Children
under 10 half price. Credit Cards: Visa/Mastercard. NZ B&B Vouchers accepted
$10 pp surcharge
Nearest Town: Taupo 5km

*Your hosts Barbara & John welcome you to their spacious quality Lakefront Homestay at
Acacia Bay, developed on three levels to capture an uninterrupted panoramic view of world
famous Lake Taupo and beyond.*
*You are provided with a warm and welcoming environment with comfort, private facilities,
spacious lounge areas and outdoor living. Enjoy our delightful gardens, with abundant
birdlife leading you to our private beach and boat mooring.*
*We are retired sheep and beef farmers enjoying living in our quiet peaceful and private home
beside the beach, just minutes from the centre of town, 3 golf courses, bushwalks, restaurants,
shops, boating and all major attractions.*
*Amongst your hosts interests are travel, golf, gardening, fishing.Guided trout fishing and
sightseeing experiences are available from Paeroa's hosts John and Barbara - John could
smoke your trout catch for you or maybe cook it for breakfast.A welcome cup of tea or coffee on
arrival if you wish. Tea / coffee facilities in the guest lounge.*

288

Taupo

Country Homestay
Address: 'Te Awanui',
1506 Poihipi Rd, Taupo
Name: Pam & Martin Bull
Telephone: (07) 377 6040
Fax: (07) 377 6023
Mobile: (025) 2425510
Beds: 1 Queen, 2 Single (2 Bedrooms)
Bathroom: 1 Private Bathroom
Tariff: B&B (full) Double $100, Single $50, Children 5 to 12yrs half price,
Dinner $30. Credit cards. NZ B&B Vouchers accepted
Nearest Town: Taupo 15 Kms

Te Awanui is set amongst a country garden with magnificent views of the hills and farmland, which grazes sheep, cattle and horses. We are involved with equestrian horses competing, schooling, breeding and students for lessons. Our home is spacious and comfortable with quality accommodation. We welcome you to have with us a delicious three course dinner with complimentary wine, or if you prefer, only Bed and Breakfast. My husband enjoys playing golf, we also love fishing the beautiful Lake Taupo. We have both travelled extensively and enjoy meeting people from other countries. Taupo is a refreshing, lovely place to stay, it has much to offer. We are able to advise or arrange most activities. We are 15km from Taupo and look forward to meeting you, our directions are simple. 1506 Poihipi Road. Please phone (07) 377-6040 We ask guests not to smoke inside our home.

Acacia Bay, Taupo

Lakestay
Address: 'Kooringa', 32 Ewing Grove,
Acacia Bay, Taupo
Name: Robin & John Mosley
Telephone: (07) 378 8025 **Fax**: (07) 378 6085
Mobile: (025) 272 6343
Email: kooringa@xtra.co.nz
Beds: Guest Wing 1 Queen, 1 Double, 1 Single (2 Bedrooms)
Bathroom: Ensuite
Tariff: B&B (full) Double $90, Single $60,
Credit cards (VISA/MC). NZ B&B Vouchers accepted $10 surcharge per night.
Nearest Town: Taupo 6km

"Kooringa" is situated in sheltered Acacia Bay (2 minutes walk to Lake) surrounded by bush and gardens with magnificent views of Lake Taupo and Mount Tauhara. The guest wing is tastefully furnished with sitting room, TV, tea and coffee making facilities and bathroom. There are 2 bedrooms, one with queen size bed, the other with a double and single bed and your own private deck area. We are a retired professional couple, have travelled extensively with our two sons, lived overseas and now enjoy a relaxed life style in this beautiful area. We are within easy distance of fascinating geothermal activity, famous Huka Falls, bush walks, golf courses, hot pools, restaurants and numerous other attractions. Our interests include gardening, sport, travel, books and hospitality. A generous breakfast with plenty of variety is served in the conservatory overlooking the Lake. We assure you of a warm welcome and comfortable stay.
Directions: *Please phone, fax or Email: kooringa@xtra.co.nz*

Awahuri, Taupo

Semi-Rural Accommodation close to Taupo town.
Address: Awahuri - River's Bend, P O Box 486, Taupo
Name: William & Suzanne Hindmarsh
Telephone: (07) 378 9847 **Fax**: (07) 378 5799
Beds: 2 Double/Twin, 2 Single (4 bedrooms)
Bathroom: 1 Ensuite, 1 Family share
Tariff: B&B Main Room, ensuite: Queen/Twin share $200, Single $150.
Additional person $55, special arrangements for children. Candle-lit dinners by
arrangement $55pp including selected wines and pre-dinner drinks.
Nearest Town: Taupo 1km

*William and Suzanne have lived in Taupo since 1964, in the same secret place beside
the Waikato River. Their extended house blends naturally with a three acre meadow
garden which has three 'lakes', a rock waterfall, and amazing bird life amongst mature
trees, masses of Camellias, Rhododendrons and Roses etc. Their farmlet has superb
river and mountain views, yet it's only two minutes by car from town. For them and
for you, privacy is the keynote, beauty the pleasure.*

*Your specially-designed accommodation invades part of the garden. The Main Room
includes superb queen-size and single beds, Persian rugs and a lovely double bay-
window seat. The ensuite bathroom is off this room, with a single bedroom next door,
for that extra person. The atmosphere is tasteful and beguiling!*

*In the evenings in cooler weather, a large open fire always burns in the house. And
Suzanne's meals are delicious ... perhaps you should experience them for yourselves?!
In the morning, breakfast is served in the dining room at times to suit you.*

*The Hindmarsh's specialise in hosting a single couple, plus children if desired; they
can also cater for another family provided it's in the same party. Their interests vary
from gardens to music, philosophy, classic cars, current affairs, sports and ... cooking!
A grass tennis court lies beside the river, with Rainbow trout lurking in a tempting
manner, ready for smoking in less than 24 hours. All Taupo's facilities are nearby.
Telephone and Facsimile are available for business/forward bookings.*

*Distances: Taupo town 1km. Lake and fishing guides, 1km. Three golf courses, 3km,
including Wairakei International. Arts centres 2km, Snow skiing 100km.*

*William and Suzanne look forward to your company. If you'd like to dine with them,
please advise by morning tea. Remember, if it's a comfortable time you need, with good
food, conversation and care, a special treat awaits!*

Directions: *Please telephone for enquiries and directions.*

Taupo

Homestay
Address: 'Lakeland Homestay',11 Williams Street, Taupo
Name: Lesley & Chris & Pussy cats
Telephone: (07) 378 1952 **Fax**: (07) 378 1912 **Mobile**: (025) 877 971
Beds: 1 Double, 2 Single (2 Bedrooms)
Bathroom: 1 Family share
Tariff: B&B (continental) Double $80, Single $50. Credit cards: MC/Visa. NZ
B&B Vouchers accepted
Nearest Town: Taupo

We invite you to stay in our home five minutes walking from coach terminal and Taupo township. Our street is leafy, small and quiet, our home enjoying views of the lake and mountains. All beds have electric blankets. Taupo is where you can catch a trout, bungy jump, tandem skydive, go jet boating, bush walking, see geothermal activity or just relax in a thermal pool. We enjoy meeting travellers from all countries. Our own interests include golf, fishing and gardening.
Directions: *Travelling from the north turn left into Heu Heu St at the only set of traffic lights, take Heathcote Street on the left and right into Williams St.*
Travelling from the south turn right into Rifle Range Road (at the Firestation) and left into Williams Street after crossing Heu Heu Street.

Taupo

Homestay
Address: 'Tui Glen', 10 Pataka Rd
Name: Robbie & Stan Shearer
Telephone: (07) 378 7007
Fax: (07) 378 2412
Beds: 1 King, 2 Single (2 Bedrooms)
Bathroom: 1 Private, 1 Ensuite
Tariff: B&B (full) Double $80, Single $50,
Dinner with wine and aperitifs by arrangement $35 - $45.
Not suitable for children. NZ B&B Vouchers accepted $15 Surcharge
Nearest Town: Taupo 1 Km to town centre

We welcome you to our comfortable home nestled in a tranquil mature garden. A hundred metres from the lake opposite the snow-capped mountains of National Park we are only a leisurely stroll along the lakefront to town. Our home is comfortably furnished with a hint of old world charm. You will be welcomed as a special guest and leave a friend. Guest bedrooms are attractive and comfortable with matching bathroom facilities. Feel free to use our laundry and barbeque terrace, wander our garden or sample Robbie's gourmet culinary skills. We are a retired couple who enjoy travel, people, good food, golf and hospitality. We were honoured with the New Zealand Travel Association Courtesy Award for the Lodge and restaurant we operated for many years in Taupo. We can advise you how to share our beautiful environment and the numerous local attractions all close by.
Directions: *Please phone - courtesy car available.*

BAY OF PLENTY

Taupo

Farmstay
Address: 'Ben Lomond', 1434 Poihipi Rd,
R.D.1, Taupo
Name: Jack & Mary Weston
Telephone: (07) 377 6033 **Fax**: (07) 377 6033
Mobile: 025-774080
Beds: 1 Double, 2 Single (2 Bedrooms)
Bathroom: 1 Guests share
Tariff: B&B (full) Double $90, Single $45, Children half price. Dinner $25
includes wine, Credit Card. NZ B&B Vouchers accepted
Nearest Town: Taupo 15km west

Ben Lomond is a 500 acre sheep and cattle farm 15km west of Taupo. We have farmed the land for the last 33 years and offer you a pleasant farmstay in our comfortable home. Our interests include equestrian and fishing and we can advise you on the local spots of interest which are wide and varied in the Taupo District. Jack and I have both travelled widely within New Zealand and overseas and enjoy making new friends. Our 3 sons have grown up and virtually left home and we offer you 2 rooms (1 double, 1 twin) and 1 bathroom for guest use only. We have the usual farm animals of which 2 dogs wander in and out. You are welcome to dine with us but please ring and "make a date". We prefer non-smokers.
Directions: *Please phone.*

Taupo

Bed & Breakfast
Address: 115 Shepherd Road, Taupo
Name: Delmont Lodge
Telephone: (07) 378 3304
Fax: (07) 378 3322
Beds: 2 Queen, 2 Single (3 bedrooms)
Bathroom: 2 Ensuite, 1 Private
Tariff: B&B (special) Double $99-$130,
Single $90, Children $15, Dinner $35pp,
Credit cards Visa/MC
Nearest Town: Taupo 3 Kms

A warm welcome awaits you at Delmont Lodge where spoiling, pampering and relaxation abound. Situated adjacent to the Botanical Gardens in half an acre of mature trees, pretty gardens and a large lawn for croquet, this peaceful home commands sweeping views of Lake Taupo and the mountains.
The Lodge features a guest wing with 2 Queen bedded rooms with ensuites and 1 twin bedded room with private bathroom. The living area is very spacious with sunporch and conservatory.
Your host Jenny has been in the hotel business over 20 years, travelled extensively and her experience includes running a Country Inn in America. Afternoon tea / coffee and home baking greet you upon arrival and complimentary drinks are served before dinner. Fresh fruits / juice start your breakfast the perfect way and dinner can be arranged to suit your needs. Excellent restaurants are only minutes away and all tourist activities catered for.

Taupo
Homestay
Address: 28 Greenwich Street, Taupo
Name: Ann & Dan Hennebry
Telephone: (07) 378 9483
Beds: 1 Queen, 1 Single (2 bedrooms)
Bathroom: 1 Guests share
Tariff: B&B (full) Double $80, Single $50, Children half price. Dinner $25,
Credit Cards. NZ B&B Vouchers accepted
Nearest Town: Taupo - 3km from Post Office

*We look forward to meeting you, we enjoy having guests in our spacious home
overlooking farmland and bordering Taupo's Botanical Gardens. We hope you will
join us for dinner (maybe a barbecue in the summer) and complimentary wine in our
pleasant dining room. There are many good restaurants in Taupo should you prefer
that. Breakfast will also be served here at a time to suit you. Our launch "Bonita" is
available if you would like a fishing or sightseeing trip on our beautiful lake - Dan is
an excellent skipper. We have lived in and around Taupo for twenty-five years, so can
help with advice or arrange most activities in the area. You will find our home warm,
comfortable and welcoming.*
Directions: *Please phone.*

Taupo
Country Homestay+Self-contained Cottage
Address: Physical: SH32/Poihipi Rd, Taupo
Postal: South Claragh, RD1, Mangakino
Name: Lesley & Paul Hill "South Claragh"
Telephone: (07) 372 8848 **Fax**: (07) 372 8047
Email: paul.hill@xtra.co.nz
Beds: 1 Queen, 1 Single + extra bed available (2 bedrooms). One party only.
Bathroom: 1 Guest private plus extra W.C.
Tariff: B&B Main guestroom: Single $55, Double $90; Single room with extra bed
available: $45, $30 extra bed. Children half price. Dinner $30.
Bird Cottage: Nightly - $60 Double, $20 each additional person, $10 child.
Weekly - $285 Double, $60 additional person.
Credit Cards. NZ B&B Vouchers accepted
Nearest Town: Taupo 34km

*Welcome to our comfortable, centrally heated farmhouse set in rambling mature
gardens, well situated as a base for exploring the centre of the North Island (tramping,
golf, trout fishing, hunting, skiing, thermal parks and sightseeing). Turn into our
leafy driveway and relax in a hammock under the wisteria, enjoy the rhododendrons
or autumn colours, crack walnuts beside the open fire, play petanque or croquet, join
us for a drink on the terrace, meet our gentle donkeys, coloured sheep and family dog.
The spacious and sunny main guest room has a private deck leading into the garden.
Meals: Delicious farm breakfast. Home-grown produce and excellent cooking mean
that dining is recommended. Bird Cottage is self contained and cosy, perfect for two,
but will sleep 4/5. Linen and firewood provided. Self cater or meals by arrangement.
Your hosts are well travelled, semi-retired professional people with varied interests.
We ask that our guests not smoke indoors.*

Relax – Don't try to drive too far in one day.

Taupo
Bed & Breakfast
Address: "Bramham",
7 Waipahihi Ave, Taupo
Name: John & Julia Bates
Telephone: (07) 378 0064
Fax: (07) 378 0065
Mobile: 025-240 9643
Email: bramham@reap.org.nz
Beds: 1 Double, 3 Single (3 bedrooms)
Bathroom: Private facilities all rooms
Tariff: B&B (full) Double $90-$100, Single $50-$60.
NZ B&B Vouchers accepted Surcharge $21-$30
Nearest Town: Taupo

Bramham is situated some 2 minutes walk from the shores of Lake Taupo and offers tremendous views of the lake and mountains to the south.

John and Julia have spent 24 years in the RNZAF including service on exchange with the USAF in Tucson, Arizona and five years running their dairy farm in South Taranaki.

We offer you a homely peaceful stay with all mod-cons at your call. We take pride in our business and specialize in good hearty breakfasts of your choice ranging from waffles to hot cakes to bacon and eggs, all served with freshly brewed coffee and fruit juice. A continental breakfast is available if you prefer.

We include a pick up service from the bus terminal or Airport and offer sightseeing trips or day excursions by arrangement.

Being non smokers our dogs ask you not to smoke in our home.

Acacia Bay, Taupo

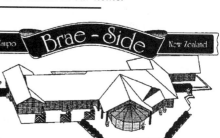

Homestay
Address: "Braeside", 2 Morrell Place,
PO Box 807, Taupo
Name: Doreen and Chris Blyth
Telephone: (07) 378 8774
Fax: (07) 377 6333
Beds: 2 Queen, 1 Single (3 bedrooms)
Bathroom: 3 Ensuite
Tariff: B&B (full) Double $90, Single $50, Children under 12 half price, Dinner $25pp, Credit Cards. NZ B&B Vouchers accepted $25 surcharge
Nearest Town: Taupo 8km

Welcome to our large family home, features include a spa, billiard room, log fire, barbecue area, library, and each guest bedroom with its own TV and ensuite opening out onto a private courtyard takes in the panoramic views of Lake Taupo and the surrounding districts and it's only minutes from the town centre.

Recreation, snow skiing, scenic flying, thermal swimming, fishing, hunting, walking, golf.

We are an aviator family and along with our cats and dogs enjoy meeting people and look forward to your visit.

Directions: *Drop us a line, phone or fax for information and reservations.*

Taupo
Homestay
Address: 55 Grace Crescent, Taupo
Name: Tom & Beverley Catley
Telephone: (07) 378 1403
Fax: (07) 378 1402
Beds: 1 Queen, 1 Double,
2 Single (3 bedrooms)
Bathroom: 1 Private, 1 Family share

Tariff: B&B (full) Double $80-$90, Single $50, Children half price, Dinner by arrangement. Credit Cards. NZ B&B Vouchers accepted
Nearest Town: Taupo 5km, a few minutes walk to the lake

We warmly welcome you to our sunny spacious home. Upstairs we have two double guest bedrooms, one with a Queen bed, the other two singles. The bathroom is shared. At ground level we have a comfortable unit consisting of one double bedroom with private bathroom and lounge with microwave and tea making facilities. You are welcome to use our laundry. The lounge and upstairs bedrooms open onto a pleasant sheltered sundeck and we enjoy extensive rural, mountain and lake views enhanced by beautiful sunsets.
We live in a quiet area away from traffic noise yet handy to tourist attractions. We are one hour by car from Rotorua and for those with aches and pains hot thermal pools are nearby.
Bev's interests include gardening and floral art while Tom enjoys photography and music. We enjoy sharing our home with our guests.

Taupo
Rural Homestay
Address: "Minarapa"
620 Oruanui Road, R.D.1, Taupo
Name: Barbara & Dermot Grainger
Telephone: (07) 378 1931
Fax: (07) 378 1932
Mobile: 025-272 2367
Email: minarapa@voyager.co.nz
Beds: 2 Queen, 2 Single (3 bedrooms)
Bathroom: 2 Ensuite, 1 Family share
Tariff: B&B (full) Double $80-$90, Single $60, Children under 14 half price,
3 course dinner with wine by arrangement $30pp.
Credit cards accepted. NZ B&B Vouchers accepted Surcharge $15
Nearest Town: Taupo 14km - 2km off State Highway 1

We welcome you along our tree-lined drive to enjoy the peace and tranquility of our 11-acre country retreat just 12 minutes from Taupo, 45 minutes from Rotorua and central to Wairakei and all tourist attractions.
Our home is spacious with loads of atmosphere. It has a games room with full-sized billiard table, fridge and TV for guest use and large lounge with feature fireplace. The guestrooms, two with ensuite and balcony, have comfortable beds and individual character. They overlook beautiful park-like grounds where you can relax among mature trees and colourful gardens, play tennis, practise golf or cross the pond and stream to visit our friendly farm animals. Breakfasts, which include homebaking and preserves, may be served indoors or outside on the verandah. We enjoy travel and meeting people. Our interests include gardening, golf, sailing, handcrafts and the arts. Barbara speaks fluent German.
Directions: *Phone for directions.*
Home Page: www.voyager.co.nz/~minarapa/

Taupo
Homestay Farmlet
Address: 466 State Highway 5,
R.D.1, Taupo
Name: "Hereford Lodge" Keith & Lin Roberts
Telephone: (07) 374 8440 **Fax**: (07) 374 8460
Mobile: (025) 959 557
Beds: 1 Queen, 1 Double (2 bedrooms)
Bathroom: 1 Private with separate toilet, Separate laundry
Tariff: B&B (full) Double $80, Single $50, Dinner $30 inc wine.
Nearest Town: Taupo 14km

We welcome you to our 17 acre lifestyle property that has been developed to create a tranquil rural setting 8 minutes north of Taupo, 1/2 hour from Rotorua and only 4 minutes from the renowned Wairakei International Golf Course and other scenic attractions of the area.Our guest wing is private, spacious, and beautifully appointed with your every need catered for.The rooms themselves both open out to a large verandah, overlooking garden and swimming pool (heated in summer).

We are both very keen golfers and would be only too happy to organise your golfing requirements during your stay with us. We also organise trout fishing excursions for you.We are a younger couple with no children living at home, only one cat and 2 dogs and enjoy good food and entertaining.

Directions: *Please phone for directions. Transport is available if required. Nothing will be too much trouble to make your stay in Taupo memorable.*

Taupo
Bed & Breakfast
Address: 70 Blue Ridge Drive
Name: "Ashgrove"
Telephone: (07) 378 9851
Fax: (07) 378 9853
Beds: 1 Double, 2 Single (2 bedrooms)
Bathroom: 1 Guests share
Tariff: B&B (full) Double $90, Single $55.
Nearest Town: Taupo 7km Acacia Bay side

Do you want peace and tranquillity in a glorious setting with easy reach of Taupo's many attractions, then come and share our sunny modern home set in a two acre country garden. Enjoy the magnificent panoramic views of the lake and township while strolling through a garden which is full of surprises and a haven for native birdlife. Our Lockwood home has a spa pool, conservatory, separate guest wing and is smokefree.

We are knowledgable about the region and its attractions, especially the forests, wildlife and gardens. Whatever your interests we can advise on or arrange a wide variety of activities for your enjoyment. Elaine's interests include gardening, floral art, crafts and creative work while Terry's include many sports, tramping, forestry and geography. We both enjoy travelling and meeting people from other countries.

Blue ridge drive is off the eastern end of Mapara Rd.

Directions: *Please phone for availability.*

Blue Ridge Drive is off the eastern end of Mapara Rd.

1642

296

Taupo
Homestay
Address: 25 Puriri Street, Taupo
Name: Rose & Mike Corkin
Telephone: (07) 378 9454
Fax: (07) 378 9459 **Mobile**: (025) 787 286
Email: mikecorkin@xtra.co.nz
Beds: 1 Queen, 2 Single (2 bedrooms)
Bathroom: 1 Guests share
Tariff: B&B (full) Double $75, Single $45,
NZ B&B Vouchers accepted $10 surcharge
Nearest Town: Taupo 2km

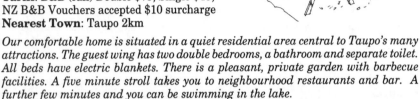

Our comfortable home is situated in a quiet residential area central to Taupo's many attractions. The guest wing has two double bedrooms, a bathroom and separate toilet. All beds have electric blankets. There is a pleasant, private garden with barbecue facilities. A five minute stroll takes you to neighbourhood restaurants and bar. A further few minutes and you can be swimming in the lake.
We enjoy skiing, fishing, back packing, water-skiing and meeting people and will happily assist your participation in these or other activities. Ruapehu's Whakapapa ski field is less than 90 minutes by car. We offer an early breakfast for those keen to be first on the slopes.Bicycles, tennis racquets, some fly fishing gear and golf clubs are available for guest's use. We request no smoking indoors.
We have travelled extensively and lived offshore including Chile "Nuestra Casa Es Tu Casa" (Our home is your home).
Home Page: http://www.reap.org.nz/~mikecorkin/

Taupo
Bed & Breakfast
Address: 77 Gillies Ave, Taupo
Name: Gerry & Kay English
Telephone: (07) 377 2377
Fax: (07) 377 2377
Email: genglish@reap.org.nz
Beds: 4 Double, 12 Single (9 bedrooms)
Bathroom: 9 Ensuite

Tariff: B&B (full) Double $85, Single $65, Children under 12 free,
Credit Cards. NZ B&B Vouchers accepted $15 surcharge on Double
Nearest Town: Taupo 1 1/2kms

Gillies Lodge is situated one and a half kilometres from the shopping area and one kilometre from the lake. We are in a quiet residential spot with a small reserve on one boundary. From the upstairs living space (dining, lounge and bar) we have views of the lake. Our twenty four hour licence allows the bar to be open for your convenience. We enjoy sharing our home with visitors and make every effort to make you feel at home at our place.
Our six children are scattered around the globe.
'Garp' our cat, has not adapted to visitors. He will remain invisible during your stay.
A courtesy car to help you enjoy your stay is available.
A variety of activities are available in Taupo including boating, fishing, kayaking. Eco tours. These can be organised for you prior to your visit, or on arrival.
Inquire at the Information Office or phone for directions.

Taupo

Homestay
Address: Mountain Views,
17b Puriri Street, Taupo
Name: Jack & Bridget
Telephone: (07) 378 6136 **Fax**: (07) 378 6136
Beds: 1 Queen, 2 Single (2 bedrooms)
Bathroom: 1 Guests share
Tariff: B&B (special) Double $70, Single $40, Children 1/2 price under 12 yrs,
Credit cards.
Nearest Town: Taupo 3km

Our new home is situated in the Hilltop area. The house is centrally heated and double-glazed, so it is warm in winter and cool in summer. We have two spacious bedrooms and a guest bathroom with separate toilet upstairs.

We are five minutes walk from two restaurants and shops, and about ten minutes walk from the Lake. We will gladly transport you to and from public transport facilities as required.

We have lived and worked in Taupo for a number of years in hospitality and tourism. We can recommend and book many activities around this area. You may prefer to just relax in our thermal hot pool and gaze at the stars before bedtime. Taupo has lots to offer.

We appreciate guests not smoking in the house.

Taupo

Homestay
Address: 16 Puia Street, Taupo
Name: Tim & Chris Whitman
& Ben our Labrador
Telephone: (07) 377 1565
Mobile: (025) 242 5492
Beds: 1 Queen, 2 Single (2 bedrooms)
Bathroom: 2 Ensuite

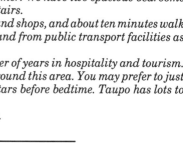

Tariff: B&B (special) Double $80, Single $40, Children under 12 half price,
Credit Cards.
Nearest Town: Taupo - 1.5km town centre

We are a semi retired couple who moved to Taupo Nov '96. We love meeting people and sharing our home. We live 1.6km from the lake in a quiet street overlooking Mt Tauhara. Our greatest joy is walking the shoreline of our fantastic lake. Tim is an avid gardener, his speciality being roses. We enjoy travelling ourselves, when Chris spends much of her time fossicking in antique shops adding to her pottery collection.

We don't supply dinner, but guests are welcome to bring back fast food meals to the house if they aren't sampling one of our numerous restaurants.

For golfers amongst you, we are almost next door to a lovely course, one of many.

Our rooms offer TV, tea & coffee facilities, electric blankets and, for the little people, a cot and highchair. Guests can be met.

Come join us - it's so beautiful here and so much to do.

Please help us provide the best hospitality in the world.
Fill in a comment form for every place you stay.

Taupo
Country Homestay
Address: Richlyn Park,
1 Mark Wynd, Bonshaw Park, Taupo
Name: Lyn and Richard James
Telephone: (07) 378 8023
Fax: (07) 378 8023 **Mobile**: (025) 908 647

Beds: 1 King (ensuite), 2 Queen, 2 Single (4 bedrooms)
Bathroom: 1 Ensuite, 1 Guests share
Tariff: B&B (full) depends on room, time of year and duration of stay: Double $88-$131, Single $52-$85. Dinner $40 pp by arrangement only. Visa/Mastercard.
Nearest Town: Taupo, 6 km to the West

Relax, enjoy the peace and quiet, share our spacious one level homestead, with two toy poodles, two black cats and a lovebird. Make use of our well equipped Gymnasium, outdoor spa pool, petanque and boat / vehicle parking areas.
Stay here, explore the tourist centre of New Zealand, go fishing, skiing, golfing plus many other activities in the area.
We are still developing our eight acres of park and gardens, seven minutes drive east of Taupo, this slice of heaven has peaceful surroundings, meandering paths and magnificent views of mountains, lake and countryside which makes it a perfect place to wind down. Inside our house is a smoke free zone, fitted with smoke alarms for your safety.
Directions: *From Taupo, up Napier Road 6 km, right into Caroline Drive, 2 km to Mark Wynd on left, first drive on left is Richlyn Park.*

Taupo
Homestay
Address: 5 Te Hepera Street, Taupo
Name: Patricia and Russell Jensen
Telephone: 07 378 1888 **Fax**: 07 318 1888
Beds: 1 Queen (1 bedroom)
Bathroom: 1 Private
Tariff: B&B (special/full/continental) Double $95, Single $65, Dinner $35.
Nearest Town: Taupo (1.5 kms on SH1)

Welcome to our sunny home, situated in a quiet cul-de-sac a short walk form the lake and restaurants, within easy reach of all attractions.
Guest accommodation is the upstairs level, featuring a sunny bedroom and adjoining guest lounge, both opening onto private balcony with panoramic views of mountains, lake and town. TV and tea / coffee making facilities are provided in lounge. Guest bathroom includes bath and shower.
We are retired farmers in our 50's who have travelled extensively and love meeting people. Greta our cat shares our home. Guests can enjoy boating and fishing with us by arrangement and we welcome them to relax in our private thermal pool.
You may enjoy a country style evening meal with us by prior arrangement, or breakfast only, if preferred.
We ask smokers to use the balcony or garden - thank you.
Directions: *1st right turn up Shepherd rod or phone. We will collect from terminals.*

Taupo
Homestay
Address: 98 Wakeman Rd., Acacia Bay, Taupo
Name: Bob & Marlene Leece
Telephone: (07) 378 6099
Beds: 1 King, 2 Single (2 bedrooms)
Bathroom: 1 Guests share
Tariff: B&B (continental) Double $80, Single $50. NZ B&B Vouchers accepted
Nearest Town: Taupo 6km

Bob and I (and or two Burmese cats) extend a warm welcome to you, and to our large Lockwood home. We are situated 6km from town with panoramic views of lake and mountains. There are many walks nearby around the shores of the lake, and a very interesting one around the block which contains 150 steps (for the energetic ones). The house has two large rooms, one with 2 single beds, the other with a queen size bed. Guests have their own toilet, bath, shower, but share if both rooms are full. The guests are welcome to use the decks around the house. You are welcome to smoke, but not in our house.
Directions: *Please phone for directions.*

Taupo
Farmstay
Address: 'Brackenhurst',
801 Oruanui Rd., RD 1, Taupo
Name: Margaret and Noel Marson
Telephone: (07) 377 6451
Fax: (07) 377 6451
Beds: 1 Queen 2 Single, 1 Double, 1 single.
Bathroom: 2 Ensuite
Tariff: B&B (full) Double $90, Single $50, Children half price, Dinner $35.
NZ B&B Vouchers accepted $25 surcharge
Nearest Town: Taupo (11 km past Wairakei. 1 km off St Highway 1)

Brackenhurst, set among flower gardens on a hillside overlooking picturesque farm-land, offers a warm welcome, wonderful food, peace and tranquillity.
Enjoy the sounds of Tuis and Bellbirds. Watch the Fantail flit from tree to tree.
Practise your pitch and putt on the hillside green.
A private guest wing in the house or a sperate annex offer the ultimate in away from home comfort - fresh flowers and special touches.
Breakfast to suit, healthy, indulgent, or a little of both. Let us tantalise and spoil you with fine food, New Zealand wines, freshly brewed coffee, and selection of teas.
Guests are welcome to relax by the fire, on the verandah or wander over the farm, viewing the animals. We have a house cat and dog (poodle).
Come and enjoy 'Brackenhurst' and share in our warm hospitality.
Located close to the many 'wonders' of the Taupo area.
RECOMMENDATIONS: Blissfully tranquil - Saret & Manya, South Africa.
Simply the Best - Bob, Elaine, United Kingdom.

Taupo

Homestay
Address: Lakeside Thermal Homestay,
No. 3, 227 Lake Terrace, Taupo
Name: Terri, Bruce, Hayley and Max.
Telephone: (07) 378 1171 (day & eve)
or (07) 378 1202 (day)
Fax: (07) 378 1101
Mobile: (025) 835 827
Beds: 1 Queen, 2 Double Bunks (2 bedrooms)
Bathroom: 1 Guests share
Tariff: B&B (special/full/continental) Double $119, Double Bunks $60 per bunk
(2 bunks in one room). Single $60 or $85, Dinner $25 or $30 (children's dinner
half price), Children $20 p/child. Credit Card: Visa/Mastercard/Bankcard. NZ
B&B Vouchers accepted $30 surcharge
Nearest Town: Taupo 2 km.

*This absolute lakeside location, with natural thermal spa and unobstructed views of the
lake and Mt Ruapehu, places you close to town and a menagerie of activities, i.e. golf,
fishing, skiing, water sports, 4-wheel bike riding, bungy jumping, para gliding etc etc.
You are within walking distance to restaurants with a scenic lakeside walkway out the
front door providing a memorable form of exploration and exercise i.e. thermal steam
rising from the ground, hot water streams, superb sunsets. The homestay motto "your
home while you are with us" introduces your friendly, helpful hosts who can provide a
comfortable, pleasant and interesting stay. They trout fish, tie flies, golf and enjoy
wholesome food and your company. Their small well-behaved dog charms everyone.
Stairs to your cosy room are easy. Children are welcome. We appreciate you not smoking
in our home. Inspections by appointment. We look forward to hearing from you!*
Directions: *Please phone for directions.*

Taupo

Farmstay
Address: 1281 Mapara Road, RD 1, Taupo.
Name: Whitiora Farm Stay
Telephone: (07) 378 6491 **Fax**: (07) 378 6491
Beds: 1 Double, 4 Single (3 bedrooms)
Bathroom: 2 Family share
Tariff: B&B (full) Double $100, Single $50, Dinner $30. Children 5 - 12 years of
age half price. Credit Cards accepted. NZ B&B Vouchers accepted $30 surcharge
Nearest Town: Taupo 12 km.

*3 Course dinner includes wine. Breakfast includes fruit, fresh farm eggs, bacon,
venison sausages, tomatoes, home made bread and conserves, coffee, English or herbal
tea. We have a 461 acre farm 10 km north-west of Taupo, grazing sheep, cattle, deer,
angora goats and thoroughbred horses which we breed, train and race. Judith, a food
professional takes pride in the large garden, including organic vegetables. We enjoy
sharing our large comfortable home, garden and farm, travel extensively, enjoy
meeting people and making new friends.*
*Local attractions include: river, stream and lake trout fishing; golf courses for all
abilities, farm, forest and National Park walks; geothermal and volcanic attractions;
horse / pony riding and trekking; jet boating and white water rafting; snow and water
skiing; bungy jumping; helicopter and float plane rides; shopping.*
We appreciate you not smoking in our home.
Directions: *Please phone.*

Taupo

Homestay
Address: 32 Harvey Street, Taupo
(PO Box 543, Taupo)
Name: Judi & Barry Thomson
Telephone: (07) 378 4558
Fax: (07) 378 4558
E-mail: circus@xtra.co.nz
Beds: 1 Queen, 2 Single (1 bedroom)
Bathroom: 1 Private

Tariff: B&B (continental) Double $95, Single $60, Additional guests same party $40, Cooked breakfast on request, One party only at one time. Credit cards.
Nearest Town: Taupo 3 kms

Your relaxation and comfort are paramount. We, Judi and Barry, love living here and would like to help you enjoy Taupo too.

We have both travelled extensively and enjoy meeting people from other countries. We are happy to offer friendly and comfortable accommodation plus assisting with travel plans and sightseeing. A welcome also from Georgia our Golden Labrador.

Our totally private and peaceful facility includes a thermal spa, central heating plus an open fire and television in the living area. A ranchslider provides easy access to lawn and garden with in-ground pool. Two single beds in the living room if required.

The lake is only a short stroll away and we can recommend three lakeside restaurants for your evening meal. Judi will serve breakfast at a time to suit you.

Ruapehu Skifields are just one and a quarter hours of easy driving and we are very close to three golf courses, fishing and boating, tramping, bush walking and swimming. We request no smoking indoors.

Te Rangiita, Turangi

Homestay
Address: Raukawa Lodge, 265 SH1,
Te Rangiita, RD 2 Turangi,
Postal: PO Box 195, Turangi
Name: John & Sarah Sage
Telephone: (07) 386 7637
Fax: (07) 386 8137
Email: sages@xtra.co.nz
Beds: 1 Queen, 2 Single (2 bedrooms)
Bathroom: 1 Private
Tariff: B&B (full) Double $75, Single $45, Children under 10 half price., Dinner $25pp, Credit card (VISA). NZ B&B Vouchers accepted
Nearest Town: 12km North of Turangi on SH 1

Kia Ora - Our home is halfway between Auckland and Wellington on State Highway One - close to the mountains but closer to the lake with a rural outlook reaching to the Kaimanawa Ranges. We are minutes to the Tauranga-Taupo River for trout fishing, and surrounded by beautiful walking treks. Whatever your interest the Central Plateau can ably cater for all tastes in all seasons.

We accommodate one party at a time and offer comfortable beds with electric blankets and duvets; your own tea making, laundry and toilet facilities; conservatory with wood burner in the games room. We serve simple New Zealand fare with plenty of fresh fruit, vegetables and homemade bread.

We have travelled extensively at home and abroad, are keen golfers, fishers, gardeners - and ... followers of rugby. Our Old English Sheepdog, Sophia, always welcomes new faces.

Directions: *Please phone for directions and availability.*

Tauranga Taupo

Lodge
Address: "Rusty's Retreat"
35 Heu Heu Parade,
Tauranga - Taupo, RD 2 Turangi,
Central North Island
Name: Lynda Gibson and Graham Bell
Telephone: (07) 386 0123
Fax: (07) 386 0122
Mobile: (025) 848 747
Email: rustysretreat@xtra.co.nz
Beds: 3 Queen, 3 Single (4 bedrooms)
Bathroom: 2 Ensuites, 1 Guests share, 1 Family share
Tariff: B&B double $100, Single $60, Dinner from $35, Children half price.
NZ B&B Vouchers accepted - $30 surcharge (double)
Nearest Town: Turangi 11 km, Taupo 38 km

Situated in the central North Island, on the banks of the Tauranga Taupo River and only 200 meters from the lake, Rusty's Retreat is an idyllic escape.
We offer full accommodation or bed and breakfast for your next holiday, sporting adventure or business meeting.
Trout for breakfast, venison for dinner........ it's tough to take.
Stay in our guest rooms which accommodate up to nine people, with ensuite.... step across the road to fish for trout, down the road to swim Lake Taupo, or hit the ski slopes, 45 mins away.... or simply do absolutely nothing and enjoy the hospitality and beautiful surrounds of this district.
Graham is a jeweller and trout fishing guide and Lynda is a communications consultant. We have a seven year old son and two friendly dogs.

Turangi

Homestay
Address: Omori Road, R.D. 1, Turangi
Name: Joy Wardell
Telephone: (07) 386 7386
Beds: 2 Single (1 bedroom)
Bathroom: 1 Private
Tariff: B&B (full) Double $60, Single $40, Dinner $20, Campervans welcome.
Credit Cards. NZ B&B Vouchers accepted
Nearest Town: Turangi 16km

My home is 16 km West of Turangi (off State Highway 41) with magnificent views across Lake Taupo and over the surrounding farmland and bush clad mountains. I share a property with my family whose home is next door to mine and we all enjoy meeting and entertaining people. It gives me much pleasure to cook and serve tasty meals for my numerous guests.
We have a few sheep and there are deer and goats on an adjoining property.
There is a private study with television for the use of guests if required.
You need travel only short distances to the many attractions of this area, e.g. Mountains - Ngauruhoe, Ruapehu and Tongariro, the Tongariro River and of course Lake Taupo itself. Activities such as trout fishing, bush walking, skiing, rafting, jet boating and many more can be enjoyed or if you prefer just relax and enjoy the fresh air and country atmosphere.

Turangi
Homestay & Self-contained Cottage
Address: 3 Poto Street, Turangi
Name: Jack & Betty Anderson
Telephone: (07) 386 8272
Fax: (07) 386 8272
Beds: Home: 1 Queen, 1 Double,
1 Single (2 bedrooms) Cottage: 1 Double, 2 Single (2 bedrooms)
Bathroom: Home: 2 Ensuite Cottage: 1 Private
Tariff: Home or Cottage: B&B (full) Double $80, Single $50, Children price negotiable, Dinner $20pp (by prior arrangement). Cottage: Self-catering: Double $65, Extra adults $20pp, Children half price. Discount 5 + nights.
NZ B&B Vouchers accepted
Nearest Town: Turangi - 35 minutes south of Taupo SH1

Welcome to our relaxed lifestyle beside the Tongariro River, extremely quiet, away from traffic, with bush walks and fishing pools nearby. Maps available. With ensuites for privacy, are two bedrooms: one has a queen bed and one a double and single bed. Electric blankets. Laundry facilities. Off street parking. No smoking inside please. Our self-contained 2 bedroom cottage is adjacent, for travellers preferring independence. Breakfast, leisurely, of your choice. Meals contain fresh vegetables in season. Vegetarians catered for. With both children away, join us in the lounge to share our interest in flying, golfing, skiing and trout fishing. From our central North Island location enjoy trips to Tongariro National Park, Taupo, Rotorua, Napier and Waitomo. Thermal pools are nearby. Scenic flights, guided rafting, horse treks, river and boat fishing arranged. We can meet your bus.

Turangi
Homestay
Address: 155 Taupahi Rd, Turangi
Name: Ika Fishing Lodge
Telephone: (07) 386 5538
Fax: (07) 386-5538
Email: ikalodge@xtra.co.nz
Beds: 2 Queen, 2 Single (3 bedrooms)
Bathroom: 3 Ensuite
Tariff: B&B (full) Double $120, Single $90,

Children half price. Dinner $35. All Credit Cards. NZ B&B Vouchers accepted
Nearest Town: Turangi

Nestled picturesquely beside the Tongariro River (Island Pool), Ika Lodge was originally designed in the 1950's as an exclusive Fishing Lodge. Set in mature gardens, this elegantly refurbished home is protected from road noise by a long driveway bordered by a quiet Reserve - and just 20 seconds' stroll to the river.
The Lodge's comfortable amenities include large guest lounge with an open fire, private dining room ensuite bedrooms. Your hostess Suzanne Simpson is a well-known chef specialising in New Zealand modern cuisine - her dinners are legendary. Special dietary requests are willingly catered for.
Kerry Simpson, your host, is a member of NZFGA and one of the Leading Fishing Guides in the area with over 30 years experience. Join Kerry for a memorable day on Lake Taupo[o trolling or fly fishing in the magnificent rivers on our doorstep - quality tackle and tuition provided.

Turangi
Homestay
Address: "Totara Cottage",
2 Herekiekie Street, Turangi
Name: Anita & Graham Pyatt
Telephone: (07) 386 6032
Fax: (07) 386 6312
Email: grahampyatt@fishnhunt.co.nz
Beds: 2 Singles (1 bedroom)
Bathroom: 1 Ensuite
Tariff: B&B (full) Double $75, Single $50, Dinner $30pp.
Credit Cards (VISA/MC) NZ B&B Vouchers accepted $10 Surcharge
Nearest Town: Turangi 2 kms

We welcome you to "Totara Cottage" in the trout fishing capital of the world situated a few minutes stroll away from the Tongariro River.
Our home is set in relaxing gardens affording extensive views of Lake Taupo and surrounding mountains and farmland.Your accommodation is of a high standard and as our guests you will have your own lounge/bedroom with TV and ensuite facilities.In Summer you may wish to join us for a relaxing evening on the deck or by the fire in winter. We have a friendly cat, dog and budgie.For visiting anglers, Graham, a professional fishing guide can be "booked" to take you to some of those "Special" places on our world famous rivers and lakes.Let us help you to share the magic of our beautiful area which has every outdoor activity imaginable close by. We look forward to meeting you.
Directions: *Please phone.*
Home Page: http://www.fishnhunt.co.nz/trout/pyatt.htm

Turangi
Self-contained Cottage
Address: "Akepiro", 169 Taupahi Road, Turangi
Name: John & Jenny Wilcox
Telephone: (07) 386 7384
Fax: (07) 386 6838
Email: jwilcox@voyager.co.nz
Beds: 1 Queen, 1Double, 2 Single (2 bedrooms)
1 cot and highchair available
Bathroom: 1 Private
Tariff: B&B (continental) Double $65,
Single $40, Extra Adult $25, Children up to 12 $15,
4 adults $100, Continental breakfast on request $5pp.
Nearest Town: Turangi - 54km south of Taupo on SH1

Our cottage is set in half an acre of trees and woodland garden, featuring rhododendrons and a wide variety of native plants. The garden attracts many species of birds and their song mingles with the murmur of the Tongariro River which is just through the garden gate. These idyllic surroundings, far from traffic noise, make a perfect retreat for that restful break. Direct access to the river walkway and fine fishing pools. Excellent and challenging scenic golf course 4 minutes by car (clubs available). Relax in the Tokaanu hot pools just 10 minutes away.
Our home and award-winning garden is adjacent but allowing the cottage every privacy. Come and share this corner of nature's paradise with us and enjoy the many outdoor pursuits and activities the region offers. Fishing guides can be arranged. Continental breakfast is available on request. A warm welcome awaits you at "Akepiro".

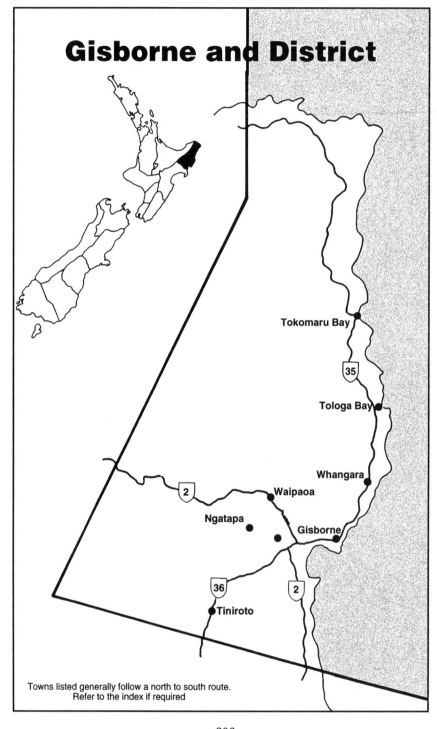

Gisborne and District

Tokomaru Bay

35

Tologa Bay

Whangara

Waipaoa

Ngatapa

Gisborne

36

2

Tiniroto

Towns listed generally follow a north to south route.
Refer to the index if required

Tokomaru Bay

Farmstay
Address: 'Tironui', Mata Road, Tokomaru Bay
Name: David & Caroline Jefferd
Telephone: (06) 864 5619 **Fax**: (06) 864 5620
Beds: 1 Queen, 1 Single (1 bedroom)
Bathroom: 1 Family share
Tariff: B&B (full) Double $60, Single $40, Children half price.
Dinner $25pp, Campervans welcome.   NZ B&B Vouchers accepted
Nearest Town: 11km from Tokomaru Bay, 84km north of Gisborne

We and our two children, live on an 830 hectare sheep and cattle property 11km from the Tokomaru Bay village and beach. Tokomaru Bay is a typical east coast village which is becoming increasingly renowned for its Maori culture and crafts, and for other cottage industries. As well there are the wonderful sandy beaches which are still relatively quiet during our hot summers. Our farm is typical of many hill country farms and where possible we will endeavour to show our visitors farm activities that are of particular interest to them. We have a swimming pool and tennis court which visitors are welcome to use. No smoking inside.
Directions: *Please phone.*

Tolaga Bay

Homestay
Address: 34 Bank Street,
Tolaga Bay

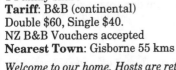

Name: "Puketea" Bob & Del
Telephone: (06) 862 6772
Fax: (06) 862 6772
Beds: 2 Double,
3 Single (3 bedrooms)
Bathroom: 1 Guests share,
1 Family share
Tariff: B&B (continental)
Double $60, Single $40.
NZ B&B Vouchers accepted
Nearest Town: Gisborne 55 kms

Welcome to our home. Hosts are retired farmers. My wife is a keen gardener and I do part time Real Estate. "Puketea" is a spacious comfortable home built in the 20's high Rimu ceilings are a special feature. You will enjoy our lovely gardens. Our home overlooks the golf course with a peep of the sea. Places of interest are the Cashmere Knitting Co, good fishing with charter boat hire, longest wharf in NZ. Walkway to historic Cooks Cove, walkway to lookout on cliff overlooking Bay and countryside. 5 minutes walk to restaurants, take-aways and hotel. A warm country welcom is assured.
Please phone for reservations.

One of the differences between staying at a hotel and a B&B
is that you don't hug the hotel staff when you leave.

Mangatuna, Tolaga Bay
Farmstay/B&B
Address: "Willowflat", Tolaga Bay
Name: June & Allan Hall
Telephone: (06) 862 6341/(06) 862 6848 **Fax**: (06) 862 6371
Mobile: (025) 923 903
Beds: 1 Double (1 bedroom) - Exta beds by arrangement
Bathroom: 2 Family share (sometimes)
Tariff: B&B (full) Double $65, Single $35, Children half price, Dinner $20,
Campervans $10 (2 people), $14 (4 people).
Nearest Town: Tolaga Bay 12km

*"Willowflat" is at Mangatuna on SH35 (the Pacific Coast Highway!) 12km north of
Tolaga Bay, an hour's easy drive north of Gisborne.*
*We have a 1000 acre mixed sheep, cattle and cropping unit including the King Spencer
Reserve. Our home is on a rise in spacious grounds, has a conservatory with spa pool,
and set back 100 yards from the Uawa River where there is a good swimming hole.
Our family at home often consists of a son, his daughter and 1 cat.*
*Within 12km we have 4 beaches (including beautiful Anaura Bay where we own a quiet
beachfront section with 2 power points), scenic reserves, Cooks Cove and Anaura Bay
Walkways, "Half-Mile Wharf" and the "Hole in the Wall". The village of Tolaga Bay
with old English Inn, golf course, bowling green, restaurant, 2 of the 4 beaches, etc.,
is also within this distance.*
Please phone.

Whangara, Gisborne
Farmstay+Self-contained Accom.
Address: Mataurangi Station, Panikau Road, Whangara
Name: Anna & Nick Reed
Telephone: (06) 862 2858 **Fax**: (06) 862 2857
Beds: Cottage: 1 Double, 1 Single (1 bedroom)
House: 1 Double, 1 Single (2 bedrooms)
Bathroom: Cottage: 1 Private/House: 1 Private
Tariff: B&B (continental) Double $70, Single $50, Children reduced rate,
Dinner $25 pp. Minimum charge for cottage $70. Prices valid to 30/6/1999.
NZ B&B Vouchers accepted
Nearest Town: Gisborne 50kms

*Tired of the hustle and bustle of urban life? Get away from it all and experience the
peace and space of rural New Zealand at its very best. Mataurangi is a 600 hectare
hill country sheep and cattle farm. Situated between Gisborne and Tolaga Bay, we are
14 km up Panikau Road off the Pacific Coast Highway (SH35). Stay with us in our
home or enjoy the comfort and seclusion of "The Roost", our well appointed self
contained cottage (full kitchen facilities, BBQ, sundeck and small garden) where,
although you are only 100m from our gate, you will be quite alone without a neighbour
to be seen or heard - nature may intrude but little else.*
*Watch seasonal farm work in progress, take day trips to Gisborne and Tolaga to enjoy
the many offerings of Eastland or just relax.*
Dinner and light lunch available by arrangement.
Directions: *Please telephone for full directions.*

Waipaoa

Farmstay
Address: 'The Willows' Waipaoa, R.D. 1,
Gisborne
Name: Graham & RosemaryJohnson
Telephone: (06) 862 5605
Fax: (06) 862 5601
Mobile: (025) 837 365
Beds: 2 Double, 3 Single (3 bedrooms)
Bathroom: 1 Guests share
Tariff: B&B (full or continental) Double $60, Single $40,
School children 10% discount, Dinner $30. NZ B&B Vouchers accepted
Nearest Town: Gisborne 20km

Our home is probably best described in the American Colonial Style with a panelled entry and dining room of our own oak timber milled from trees of which we have some lovely specimens planted by our forefathers. We enjoy the amenities available in the city and also the country life on our 440 acre property involving deer, cattle, sheep, grapes and cropping.
We enjoy meeting people and look forward to your visit. We welcome you to have dinner with us, or if you prefer only Bed & Breakfast.
We would appreciate if you could ring prior to your arrival.
Directions: *We are situated 20km north of Gisborne on SH2 through to Opotiki and the Bay of Plenty. We have a sign "The Willows" at the end of our driveway above the letter box with the number 1809 close by. A good landmark is the curved Kaiteratahi Bridge and we are 1 km north of that. Our house is white with a black tiled roof situated on a hill overlooking the Waipaoa River.*

Gisborne

Homestay
Address: 159 The Esplanade, Gisborne
Name: Alec & Barbara Thomson
Telephone: (06) 868 9675 **Fax**: (06) 868 9675
Beds: 1 Double, 2 Single (2 bedrooms)
Bathroom: 1 Guests share, 2 Separate toilets
Tariff: B&B (full) Double $70, Single $50, Dinner $20.
(Tariff of 10% discount for any bowlers staying with us when participating in local tournaments). NZ B&B Vouchers accepted
Nearest Town: Gisborne 3-4 mins walk.

Our home is situated overlooking the Waimata River, with river views from each guest room.
We are also a short and pleasant walking distance from the city shopping area, Museum and Art Centre and Lawson Field Theatre, where Gisborne stages many entertaining productions.
Alec and I enjoy meeting people and we look forward to welcoming all who wish to spend time with us.
Off street parking is available.
We are both active members of lawn and indoor bowling clubs.
We also enjoy a game of bridge.

There are some good tips for easier travel on page 7

Gisborne
Homestay
Address: 'Fawnridge',
29 Richardson Ave, Gisborne
Name: Kathlyn & Bryan Thompson
Telephone: (06) 868 8823
Fax: (06) 867 6902
Beds: 1 Queen, 2 Single (2 bedrooms)
Bathroom: 1 Ensuite, 1 Private
Tariff: B&B (continental) Double $95, Single $85,
Dinner $30 by prior arrangement. NZ B&B Vouchers accepted Surcharge $25
Nearest Town: Gisborne 2km

Welcome to Fawnridge set on a private semi rural hill site with sweeping views of Young Nicks Head and City (an easy walk to) but with the tranquillity of country living. We are a working couple with one cat.
Twin bedroom opens onto a private garden deck and each adjoining lounge with TV is exclusively for our guests who are welcome to refreshments at any time.
We are happy to offer a three course meal (venison specialty) by prior arrangement although we can recommend several excellent restaurants nearby.
After your arrival relax in our indoor spa, enjoy the view or take a short walk to view the deer. Brochures on our beautiful area are provided. A must to see is Eastwood Hill Aboretum approx. 20 mins drive.
Our home is smokefree and we request you phone the evening prior to your arrival. Bryan and I look forward to meeting you.

Gisborne
Farmstay
Address: 'Wairakaia' Station,
1952 SH 2, Gisborne RD 2
Name: Sarah & Rodney Faulkner
Telephone: (06) 862 8607
Fax: (06) 862 8607
Beds: 1 Queen,
4 Single (3 bedrooms)
Bathroom: 1 Guests share,
1 Family share, 1 Ensuite.

Tariff: B&B (special) Double $70, Single $40, Children $25, Dinner $30.
Credit cards
Nearest Town: North to Gisborne SH2 25km, south to Wairoa SH2, 75km.

The Wairakaia homestead was built in 1905 on a hill overlooking Poverty Bay. It is surrounded by a large informal garden developed by three generations of the Faulkner family. The 1600 acre sheep, beef and forestry farm offers opportunities for walking with magnificent views from the hilltops.
Rodney is active on the farm, enjoys woodworking and is a member of the Eastwood Hill Trust Board. Sarah spins when time permits. We both enjoy gardening, reading, music and meeting people. We and our family have travelled widely. Our home is ideally situated as a base for exploring the Gisborne district. The attractions include wineries, beaches, Morere Hot Pools, Eastwood Hill Arboretum, Hackfalls Arboretum and many private gardens that can be visited by appointment. We offer you a peaceful and relaxing environment with the very best of local food and wines. Smoke free indoors. 2 cats and a dog are a part of our family.

Gisborne

Farmstay
Address: Hihiroroa Rd, Ngatapa, Gisborne
Name: Sally & Andrew Jefferd
Free phone: 0800 469 4401313
Telephone: (06) 867 1313
Beds: 1 Double (1bedroom)
Bathroom: 1 Ensuite
Tariff: B&B (full) Double $70, Single $40, Dinner $20.
NZ B&B Vouchers accepted
Nearest Town: Gisborne 40 Kms west of Gisborne

We live 5 minutes drive from the famous Eastwood Hill Arboretum. Eastwood Hill is internationally recognized comprising 65 hectares of numerous varieties of trees and shrubs, it is a rewarding experience at any time of the year. We have a 1000 acre hill country property, farming sheep and cattle. We offer our guests separate accommodation with ensuite just a few metres from the main house, giving them the privacy they may desire. We have a tennis court and a swimming pool which the guests are welcome to use. Golf is easily arranged with two courses nearby.
We love meeting people and you can be assured of warm and generous hospitality.
Reservations: Free phone 0800 469 4401313
Directions: *Please phone for directions.*

Gisborne

Bed & Breakfast + Self Contained
Address: Tudor Lodge,
573 Aberdeen Road, Gisborne
Name: Mario & Annie Meier
Telephone: (06) 867 7577 or 0800 62 1234
Fax: (06) 867 7129
Beds: 2 Queen, 1 Twin, 1 Single (4 bedrooms)
Bathroom: 1 Guests share, 2 Separate toilets

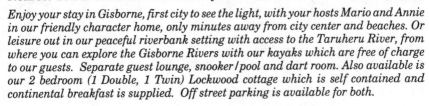

Tariff: House: B&B (full) Queen/Twin $70, Single $50. Cottage: (Continental supplied) $70 - $80. Credit Cards: Visa/Mastercard. NZ B&B Vouchers accepted
Nearest Town: Gisborne 1 Km from city centre and beaches.

Enjoy your stay in Gisborne, first city to see the light, with your hosts Mario and Annie in our friendly character home, only minutes away from city center and beaches. Or leisure out in our peaceful riverbank setting with access to the Taruheru River, from where you can explore the Gisborne Rivers with our kayaks which are free of charge to our guests. Separate guest lounge, snooker/pool and dart room. Also available is our 2 bedroom (1 Double, 1 Twin) Lockwood cottage which is self contained and continental breakfast is supplied. Off street parking is available for both.

Continental breakfast consists of fruit, cereal, toast, tea/coffee,
Full breakfast is the same with a cooked course,
Special breakfast has something special.

Gisborne
Homestay
Address: "Sea View", 68 Salisbury Road, Gisborne
Name: Raewyn & Gary Robinson
Telephone: (06) 867 3879
Fax: (06) 867 5879
Beds: 2 Double, 1 Single (2 bedrooms)
Bathroom: 2 Private
Tariff: B&B (continental) Double $85, Single $50, Children under 12 half price, under 5 free, Dinner $20pp. NZ B&B Vouchers accepted
Nearest Town: Gisborne City 1.3km (2 minutes by car)

We welcome you to our modern beachfront home situated 50 metres from the waters edge, offering safe swimming, surfing and beautiful beaches. Our home is 4 mins by car from the City Centre, 2 golf courses and Tepid Olympic Pool. It is 5 mins walk to the Information Centre and bus depot.
We offer two double bedrooms, one with an extra single bed, TV and kitchenette facilities. All beds have electric blankets. Both bedrooms have their own private bathrooms. A babies cot and highchair are available.
We have both travelled extensively overseas and get great pleasure in meeting people. We look forward to you enjoying our hospitality and home comforts. Our home is smoke free. Dinner can be arranged with prior notice.

Gisborne
Homestay
Address: 111 Wairere Road, Wainui Beach, Gisborne
Name: P &D Rouse
Telephone: (06) 868 8111 or (06) 864 7748
Fax: (06) 868 8162
Mobile: (025) 794 929
Beds: 1 Queen, 2 Double, 2 Single (2 bedrooms)
Bathroom: 1 Ensuite, 1 Private
Tariff: B&B (full) Double $70, Single $45, Children $10, Dinner $20pp, Campervans facilities. NZ B&B Vouchers accepted
Nearest Town: Gisborne 5km

We live 5km out of Gisborne, "worlds first city to see the sun".
We welcome you to our home which is situated right on the beach front at Wainui. The steps from the lawn lead down to the beach, which is renowned for its lovely clean sand, surf, pleasant walking and good swimming.
Gisborne can also offer a host of entertainment including golf on one of NZ's finest golf courses, charter fishing trips, wine trails, Eastwood Hill Arboretum, horse trekking etc. Or you may wish to relax on the beach for the day with light luncheon provided.

Gisborne

Self Contained Accommodation
Address: "All Seasons near the Sea",
4 Roberts Road, Gisborne
Name: Jan Ewart and Marie Burgess
Telephone: (06) 862 7505
Fax: (06) 862 7580
Mobile: (025) 419 424
Email: meb@clear.net.nz
Beds: 1 Queen, 1 Double, 2 Single (3 bedrooms)
Bathroom: 1 Guests share
Tariff: B&B (provisions provided) $150 per night, weekly by arrangement, for review end of 1999).
Nearest Town: Gisborne, 1.5km to Post Office

*THE HOME: **All Seasons near the sea** is a 3 bedroom fully furnished, self contained home ideal for a family holiday or sharing with friends. Amenities include, a deck with outdoor furniture, gas barbecue and a double garage. Inside a cosy Kent woodburning fire, TV/Video and CD player. Complimentary breakfast provisions and a sample of our local products are provided. The nearest store is 5 minutes walk away.*

*THE AREA: **All Seasons near the sea** is 2 minutes walk from Waikanae Beach, and close to golf courses, Olympic Pool, Museum and Art Gallery, restaurants and cafes, shops, rivers, parks and swimming and surfing beaches. Gisborne has many interesting places to visit in close proximity including Eastwood Hill Arboretum, East Coast beaches, marae, gardens, wineries and picnic spots Whatever the season, whatever the reason you are very welcome to stay at All Seasons.*

Gisborne

Farmstay
Address: 457 Pehiri Road, Gisborne
Postal: Private Bag 7122, Gisborne
Name: Sarah and Graeme Eriksen
Telephone: (06) 863 7069 or 0800 467 922
Fax: (06) 863 7006
Beds: 1 Double, 5 Single + trundle (4 bedrooms)
Bathroom: 1 Guests share
Tariff: B&B (full) Double $60, Single $45, Children $15, Dinner $30 pp.
NZ B&B Vouchers accepted
Nearest Town: Gisborne 30 minutes

"Listen to the silence", commented a city visitor in great wonderment. I listened, and heard magpies warbling, sheep baaing and bees buzzing - quite noisy I thought!!
We love to have people to stay and enjoy our rural lifestyle. Your stay with us will be relaxed and emphasis will be on outdoor living. Our home is comfortable and welcoming with a wide verandah for al fresco eating. It is surrounded by a large garden and a tennis court and situated on a 1,000 acre sheep and cattle farm. We are 30 minutes from Gisborne city on an excellent road. We offer trout fishing, golf, a nearby cottage industry, a 30 minute drive to Eastwood Hill Aboretum, and en route to Hackfalls Arboretum, Lake Waikaremoana, Wairoa and Napier/Hastings.
We welcome children who I am certain will get a lot of pleasure from our household pets. Feel free to bring your own pet. Kennel available.

* We also have a separate self-contained lodge accommodating up to ten people. Tariff on request.

Gisborne
Homestay
Address: 'STUDIO 4'
4 Heta Road, Gisborne
Name: Judy and Gavin Smith
Telephone: (06) 868 1571
Fax: (06) 868 1457
Beds: 1 Queen, 2 Single (2 bedrooms)
Bathroom: 1 Private, 1 Family share
Tariff: B&B (continental) Double $70,
Single $50, Dinner $20 pp.
Credit Cards accepted. NZ B&B Vouchers accepted
Nearest Town: Gisborne (8 minutes walk)

Welcome to our American-style character home set amongst old English trees in peaceful surroundings, backing on to Gisborne's most beautiful park and river. We are situated just a very short walk (approximately 8 minutes) to the central shopping area, the Museum and Arts Centre, the 'Wharf' area and most of Gisborne's highly recommended restaurants. Off street parking is available.
Gavin is a well-known local artist and we have a small gallery here, at Studio 4, where original local paintings, prints and cards may be viewed or purchased at your leisure. We have travelled widely ourselves and enjoy meeting and sharing our home with others.
Directions: *Please ring if possible prior to arrival for directions.*

Ngatapa - Gisborne
Homestay
Address: 'Manurere',
1405 Main Ngatapa Road, Ngatapa
Name: John and Joanne Sherratt
Telephone: (06) 863 9852
for Reservations: 0800 469 106
Fax: (06) 863 9842
Email: john.sherratt@xtra.co.nz
Beds: 1 Queen, 1 Single (1 bedroom)
Bathroom: 1 Ensuite

Tariff: B&B (full) Double $70, Single $40, Dinner $20pp.
Credit Cards accepted. NZ B&B Vouchers accepted
Nearest Town: Gisborne (24km)

We have a lovely old villa in a peaceful setting in an old established country garden only 20 minutes away from the city centre and beaches.
We have a tennis court and swimming pool available for use in season. John runs our sheep and beef farm and we enjoy meeting people and regard homestaying as a wonderful way of achieving this by sharing our home and hospitality with others.
Come and enjoy the Ngatapa Valley. Experience our famous 'Eastwood Hill Aboretum" 5 minutes away, and also craft barn, local artists, woodcraft and furniture makers. Reservations by appointment only.

Tiniroto - Gisborne
Farmstay/Self-contained Home
Address: Rongoio Farm Stay, Ruakaka Rd, Tiniroto, Gisborne
Name: Matt & Jude Stock
Telephone: (06) 867 4065
Fax: (06) 863 7018
Email: patstock at clear.net.nz
Beds: 1 King, 1 Queen, 2 Single (3 bedrooms)
Bathroom: 1 Private
Tariff: B&B (full) Double $80, Single $60, Children $10, Dinner $25.
Surcharge $10 for 1 night. NZ B&B Vouchers accepted $12 surcharge
Nearest Town: 60km between Gisborne/Wairoa appox 50 mins

Join us on our 440 hectare hill country sheep and beef property and enjoy all that rural NZ life offers.
Very close to the homestead but secluded by established trees is a three bedroom totally self contained home that sleeps up to six guests. From this cosy home feel the remote peace and tranquillity along with the magnificent views of the trout filled Hangaroa River and waterfall.
At Rangoio we encourage guests to participate in rural activities inc. fishing, wild game shooting, horse and motor bike riding, possum shooting and eeling.
Within our small Tiniroto Community is the Hackfalls Arboretum renowned for its huge selection of Mexican Oak Trees. Guides tours available. Lake Waikaremoana a 1 3/4 hr drive away.
Guests are welcome to enjoy the very best of home cuisine, locally grown cheese and wine. Warm friendly back country hospitality is our specialty.
Directions: *Please phone for bookings along with directions.*
Home Page: http://members.tripod.com/~tony-ford/

Relax – Don't try to drive too far in one day.

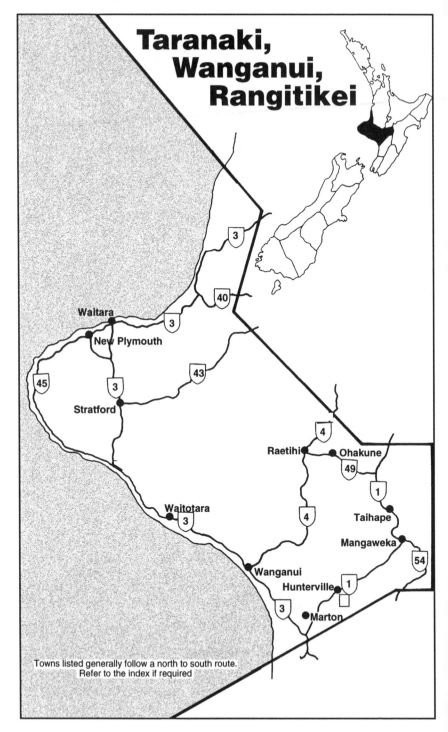

Taranaki, Wanganui, Rangitikei

Towns listed generally follow a north to south route.
Refer to the index if required

Waitara

Farmstay
Address: 31 Tikorangi Road West, 43 R.D. Waitara
Name: John & Anne Megaw
Telephone: (06) 754 6768
Beds: 1 Double, 2 Single (2 bedrooms)
Bathroom: 1 Guests share
Tariff: B&B (full) Double $60, Single $40, Dinner $15. Credit cards.
NZ B&B Vouchers accepted
Nearest Town: Waitara 8 Kms, New Plymouth 20 minutes

Our three bedroomed cosy brick house is situated on a hill with panoramic views of Mt Egmont, the Waitara River Valley farmlands and a glimpse of the sea and is 8 kilometres from Highway 3 turnoff. We live on a dairy farm where we milk 180 cows, and have shade houses for begonias and ferns. Visitors are welcome to participate in any farm activities, or wander to the river or up on the hills if they wish. Taranaki has much to offer scenically with parks and gardens, the mountain and coastline plus numerous walkways. The McKee Energy Field, Waitara Petrolgas, and Motonui Synfuel Plants are all close to Waitara.
Directions: *Travel on Highway 3 to Waitara, turn inland to Tikorangi on Princess St to Ngatimaru Road. Continue to very end of Ngatimaru Road, 8 kms from turnoff Highway 3 and turn right on no exit road. Our house is No. 31.*

New Plymouth

Homestay
Address: 30 Heta Road, Highlands Park,
New Plymouth
Name: Gerry & Beryl Paulin
Telephone: (06) 758 2900
Beds: 1 Double, 2 Single (2 bedrooms)
Bathroom: 1 Guests share

Tariff: B&B (full) Double $60, Single $40, Dinner $20pp.
NZ B&B Vouchers accepted
Nearest Town: New Plymouth City centre 5km

Welcome to our home! We are a cheerful outgoing retired couple with time to look after you. Our comfortable, modern, sunny home in a quiet suburb, has mountain, sea and rural views. We have been hosting with "the Book" since 1988 and have enjoyed meeting people from many countries.
We love to hear about your journeys and your home country while relaxing with a glass of wine and a leisurely dinner. We have travelled extensively overseas and know New Zealand well from Cape Reinga to Stewart Island.
As retired cut flower growers our interests are gardens, horticulture generally and our own garden. Gerry has a special interest in Pukeiti Rhododendron Trust Gardens and he relaxes on the golf course. Beryl enjoys needlework, porcelain painting, flower arranging and cooking. She is also a Kiwi host.
We look forward to sharing our home with you.
Directions: *Please phone*

TARANAKI
WANGANUI
RANGITIKEI

There are some good tips for easier travel on page 7

New Plymouth

Homestay
Address: 'Blacksmith's Rest',
481 Mangorei Road, New Plymouth
Name: Evelyn & Laurie Cockerill
Telephone: (06) 758 6090 **Mobile**: 025-375880
Beds: 2 Queen, 2 Single (2 bedrooms)
Bathroom: 1 Ensuite, 1 Guest share
Tariff: B&B (full) Double $60, Single $40, Dinner $20.
NZ B&B Vouchers accepted
Nearest Town: New Plymouth centre 6km

Welcome to New Plymouth. Our home is situated next to Tupare Gardens which is owned and operated by the Queen Elizabeth II Trust.
From our spacious home you can enjoy glorious sunsets and panoramic views although we are just five minutes drive from New Plymouth City.
Each guest room has a Queen and Single bed with an ensuite in the upstairs bedroom and a separate bathroom downstairs.
We enjoy meeting travellers from far and wide, sharing experieces and having a laugh together in a relaxed atmosphere.
We have a large garden, some sheep and a friendly dog called Bill who lives outside.
We are a retired couple with a grown up family.
There is plenty of off street parking.
Mangorei Road can be easily found when approaching New Plymouth from north or south off SH 3.

New Plymouth

Homestay
Address: Brooklands Bed & Breakfast,
39 Plympton Street, Brooklands, New Plymouth
Name: Neal Spragg
Telephone: (06) 753 2265
Beds: 1 Double, 2 Single (2 bedrooms)
Bathroom: 1 Private
Tariff: B&B (continental) Double $60, Single $35. NZ B&B Vouchers accepted
Nearest Town: New Plymouth centre 2km

My home is located in a peaceful and tranquil setting overlooking a bush clad walkway leading to the renowned Pukekura and Brooklands Parks. The guest wing consists of bathroom and toilet facilities, two bedrooms, one queen size and the other a twin room. I request no smoking in the house.
Being only minutes from central city you may choose to spend time at our museum, art gallery or library or perhaps take in a movie at the cinema complex. Also nearby and worthy of a visit are the sports stadium, aquatic centre, harbour and beaches.
Taranaki offers a unique diversity of attractions and landscapes, the picturesque Mount Egmont, expansive views of the Tasman Sea, beautiful parks, rhododendron gardens, rich dairy farmlands and energy fields.
I enjoy sharing my comfortable home with visitors from abroad and New Zealand travellers. I offer you a warm and friendly welcome and a relaxed stay in New Plymouth.

Relax – Don't try to drive too far in one day.

New Plymouth

Homestay
Address: 11 Tamati Place, Merrilands,
New Plymouth
Name: Evelyn & Ashley Howan
Telephone: (06) 758 8932
Beds: 1 Double, 4 Single (3 bedrooms)
Bathroom: 1 Guests share, 1 Private
Tariff: B&B (continental) Double + Twin $60, Single $35.
Credit cards. NZ B&B Vouchers accepted
Nearest Town: New Plymouth 4km

*We welcome you to New Plymouth, and offer hospitality in a comfortable modern home,
with an unobstructed view of Mount Egmont.*
*We are a newly retired couple who enjoy meeting and entertaining people from all
countries. Our home is located in a quiet cul-de-sac.*
*Guests have their own shower, toilet and bathroom (spa bath). The beds have electric
blankets and innerspring mattresses.*
*Taranaki has a host of things to do and see, being a popular tourist destination.
All Taranaki's main attractions are within easy reach of New Plymouth.*
Evening meals can be enjoyed at your choice of a variety of good restaurants.
No pets please, and we request no smoking in the house.
We will do our best to make your stay enjoyable.

New Plymouth

Farmstay
Address: 1602 Carrington Road, R.D. 1,
New Plymouth
Name: Mountain Dew Farm
Telephone: (06) 753 5123
Fax: (06) 753 5123
Email: m_g.rivers@clear.net.nz
Beds: 2 Queen, 2 Single (2 bedrooms)
Bathroom: 1 Private, 2 Family share

Tariff: B&B (full) Double $75, Single $45, Children N/A, Dinner $20pp.
NZ B&B Vouchers accepted Vouchers not accepted between 20 October-1 December
Nearest Town: New Plymouth 16km.

*If you're looking for a place to spread out and rest or meditate in picturesque, peaceful
surroundings, ours is your place. Our accommodation on our dairy farm is situated
upstairs. From our large home one gets panoramic views south to Mt Taranaki, north
towards the city and Tasman sea, and on a clear day to Mt Ruapehu National Park.
Accommodation includes large sunny lounge, TV and self contained kitchen with
microwave.*
*Near Pukeiti Rhododendron park (10 day Festival held end October yearly), historic
Hurworth cottage, private zoo, 18 hole golf course. Only 15 minute pleasant drive to
New Plymouth city.*
*Come and explore 'the Best in the West'. Walk on a mountain trail and within the hour
paddle in the Tasman Sea. Huggable cats Epo and Jasmine share our home and we
have an ever-friendly cattle dog called Danny. Active, well travelled, outdoor hosts,
non smokers. Adults only please.*
Directions: *Please phone for reservations and directions*

319

New Plymouth
Guest House
Address: 161 Powderham Street,
New Plymouth
Name: Balconies
Telephone: (06) 757 8866
Beds: 3 Queen, 2 Single (3 bedrooms)
Bathroom: 1 Guest share
Tariff: B&B (special) Double $70, Single $50,
Credit cards. NZ B&B Vouchers accepted
Nearest Town: Short walking distance to City centre

Viv and Trevor welcome you to New Plymouth.
'Balconies' is located just 500 metres (5 minute walk) from the New Plymouth shopping centre.. Our warm, comfortable 110 year old character-style manor offers three tastefully decorated guest rooms, large guest bathroom with claw foot bath, separate toilet facilities and spacious guest lounge with tea and coffee making facilities. Heated guest rooms are downstairs, beds are queen-size and have electric blankets. Also within walking distance are the art gallery, library and museum, Heritage Walkway, indoor pool complex and beautiful Pukekura and Brooklands Parks.
After a comfortable nights sleep you will be served a generous fully cooked and / or continental breakfast.
We are also happy to provide courtesy transport and laundry facilities. Ample off-street parking is available.
Join us! We look forward to your company, your comfort and satisfaction are No 1 to us.

New Plymouth
Bed & Breakfast Inn
Address: 'Henwood House',
314 Henwood Road, R.D.2 New Plymouth
Name: Lynne & Graeme Axten
Telephone: (06) 755 1212 **Fax**: (06) 755 1212
Mobile: (025) 248 4051
Email: henwood.house@xtra.co.nz
Beds: 3 Queen, 4 Single (5 Bedrooms)
Bathroom: 3 Ensuite, 1 Guests share

Henwood House - Built 1890 -

Tariff: B&B (full) Double $95-$120, Single $60-$105, Dinner $30, Credit cards (VISA/MC/AMEX). NZ B&B Vouchers accepted $25 surcharge
Nearest Town: 5km north of Bell Block

Henwood House nestles in 2 acres of landscaped grounds. We have extensively restored our homestead to a very high standard with all modern conveniences, yet retaining the romantic charm of the late Victorian era.
Relax in our grand guest lounge with high ceilings, wooden floors, panelling and open fires. Tall French doors open onto wide verandahs which overlook the gardens.
Upstairs are five spacious elegantly furnished bedrooms with quality beds and antique furniture. The Fitzroy Suite features its own fireplace and balcony with views over the countryside to the sea. Guests have their own tea and coffee making facilities. A variety of delicious breakfasts are served in our large country kitchen.
We share our home with our teenage daughter Lauren, Basil a Golden Retriever and Smokey the cat. We ask guests not to smoke indoors.
Directions: *3km up Henwood Road off SH3 from Bell Block, phone for further directions.*

New Plymouth

Homestay
Address: 'Kirkstall', 8 Baring Terrace,
New Plymouth
Name: Lindy MacDiarmid & Ian Hay
Telephone: (06) 758 3222
Fax: (06) 758 3224
Beds: 2 Queen, 1 Twin, 1 Single (4 bedrooms)
Bathroom: 1 Ensuite, 2 Guests share

"Kirkstall"

Tariff: B&B (full) Double $70-$90, Single $50-$70. Dinner by arrangement.
Credit cards. NZ B&B Vouchers accepted plus additional $10 per night
Nearest Town: New Plymouth city 2 mins by car.

.View the mountain, walk to the sea. Enjoy the serenity of a 1920's character home, centrally located only minutes from the main business and shopping area.
Appreciate our lovely views, the warmth of an open fire during winter and the atmosphere of bygone days with a house full of antiques.
The house is set amongst a rambling garden, sloping from street level to the river below with old oak and cherry trees. The garden is open to the public during the Taranaki Rhododendron Festival and close at hand is the well known Tupari Garden.
Within two mintues walk of the house are croquet and bowling clubs with the RSA just around the corner.
Lindy has her own Physiotherapy practise, whilst Ian is involved with tourism.
We enjoy our many rescued animals and look forward to welcoming you to our home which has a non smoking policy.

Omata, New Plymouth

Bed & Breakfast
Address: Rangitui Orchard, Waireka Rd.,
R.D.4, Omata, New Plymouth
Name: Tony & Therese Waghorn
Telephone: (06) 751 2979
Email: twaghorn@taranaki.ac.nz
Beds: 1 Queen, 2 Single (2 bedrooms)
Bathroom: 1 Ensuite, 1 Private
Tariff: B&B (full) Chalet: Double $70, Single $65; House: Double $50, Single $45.
Dinner $25 by arrangement. Credit Cards Mastercard/Visa NZ B&B Vouchers
accepted
Nearest Town: New Plymouth 10 mins

TARANAKI
WANGANUI
RANGITIKEI

Come and stay with us on an established Macadamia nut orchard, only 10 minutes from New Plymouth city. Accommodation consists of a chalet, with ensuite, Queen bed, TV and balcony overlooking bush and sea (separate from the house) and a twin room with guest facilities in our house. We serve continental or cooked breakfasts of your choice (except kippers!) in your room or in our kitchen. Depending on orchard commitments we can offer guests dinner with wine ($25 per head) or perhaps recommend a suitable restaurant. Enjoy bush or orchard walks, and perhaps a swim in our pool, or visit some of the local attractions nearby; e.g. climbing or walking on beautiful Mt. Taranaki; some of the best surf in the world; famous gardens; art gallery and museum; historic Maori sites and excellent golf courses. We have travelled extensively, and enjoy returning some of the wonderful hospitality we have experienced all over the world. "RANGITUI" - Country peace so close to the city!
Directions: *Please telephone for reservations and directions.*

New Plymouth

Homestay/Farmlet
Address: Birdhaven, 26 Pararewa Drive,
New Plymouth
Name: Ann & John Butler
Telephone: (06) 751 0432,
or 0800 306 449 for reservations
Fax: (06) 751 3475
Beds: 1 Queen, 2 Singles (2 bedrooms)
Bathroom: 1 Guests share
Tariff: B&B (special) Double $80, Single $55-$60, Dinner by arrangement.
10% discount 2 or more nights if booked direct with hosts.
Credit cards accepted. NZ B&B Vouchers accepted
Nearest Town: 6.5km to city centre.

We have lived in England, South Africa and New Zealand and enjoy travelling and meeting different people. We would love to welcome you to share the tranquillity and space of our comfortable and recently refurbished home. Relax in the sun room or on one of the patios, overlooking the flight paths of numerous birds as they flit amongst the trees. Stroll down to our duck pond and delight in the native bush and woodland surroundings. Our three acres include horticulture, sheep, and we share our home with Solomon our well-behaved cat. Your comfort and pleasure is important to us; this is reflected in the quality furnishings in the inviting guest rooms and throughout the house, the complimentary refreshments and the special breakfast of fresh seasonal and homemade temptations. We want you to feel at home, to share our appreciation of beautiful Taranaki and our spectacular view of Mt. Egmont. No Smoking.
Directions: *Please phone (we will collect you if required).*

New Plymouth

Farmstay
Address: 248 Junction Road, RD1,
New Plymouth

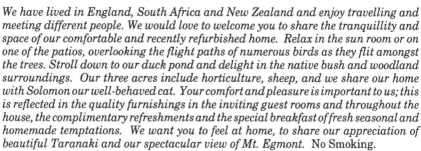

Name: Oak Valley Manor
Telephone: (06) 7581501 **Fax**: (06) 7581052
Mobile: (025) 420 325
Beds: 2 Queen, 1 Single (2 bedrooms)
Bathroom: 2 Ensuite
Tariff: B&B (full) Double $95.00 to $125.00, Single $65, Children half price.
Dinner $25. Credit cards. Pets welcome. NZ B&B Vouchers accepted
Nearest Town: New Plymouth centre 6km.

Your hosts, Pat and Paul, two warm and friendly people with a wealth of experience in the hospitality industry, invite you to a unique romantic bed and breakfast in their beautifully appointed home with views from each room of the Tasman Sea or Mount Egmont. These beautiful views make an impression which will be everlasting.
We have a five acre farmlet with animals for you to enjoy - ostriches, donkeys, deer and several species of wildfowl.
We offer guests the use of our family room, lounge and library and newly developed garden with many exciting features. Only a short distance from the world famous Tupare Gardens, Branch Road Winery and 5 minutes away from Pukekura Park, Brooklands Bowl, Westown Golf Course and New Plymouth's lovely garden facilities. Also several beautiful beaches are close at hand.
We look forward to meeting you and enjoying your company. Guests are asked not to smoke indoors.

New Plymouth
Bed & Breakfast
Address: 75 Morley St., New Plymouth
Name: The Treehouse
Telephone: (06) 757 4288 **Fax**: (06) 757 4288
Mobile: 025 925 859
Beds: 1 King/3 Single (3 bedrooms)
Bathroom: 1 Guests share
Tariff: B&B (full) Double $75, Single $45,
Credit Cards (VISA/MC and Bankcard). NZ B&B Vouchers accepted
Nearest Town: 10 minutes walk to city centre

Marilyn and Noel invite you to New Plymouth. Our home is set among mature trees with views over the city and glimpses of the sea. Just ten minute walk will get you to the city centre, indoor-outdoor aquatic complex, rugby park, museum, library, heritage walkway and also an excellent selection of cafes, bars and restaurants. Our bedrooms which are located downstairs each have doors opening into the garden. Tea and coffee making facilities are available for guests use at their leisure. We have off street parking as well as plenty of parking outside the front gate. Noel is a keen tramper and if required can provide information and arrange transport to and from road ends around Mt Egmont. As we are both non-smokers we would appreciate guests not smoking indoors. Finally we look forward to meeting and accommodating you during your stay in New Plymouth.

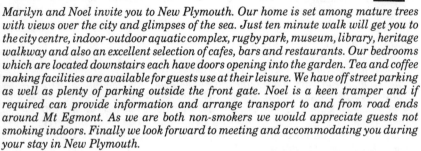

New Plymouth
Heritage Homestay
Address: Hirst Cottage
Name: Daphne
Telephone: (06) 757 9667
Fax: (06) 757 9667
Beds: 2 Queen, (2 bedrooms)
Bathroom: 1 Private, 1 Guest share
Tariff: B&B (full/continental) Queen with private bathroom $75,
Queen Guests share bathroom $ 65, Single $40, Dinner $25pp.
NZ B&B Vouchers accepted $10 surcharge
Nearest Town: New Plymouth , walking distance 5- 10 minutes.

Hirst Cottage is one of New Plymouth's historic homes, built in 1862. It is situated in tranquil parklike surroundings, within walking distance of the city centre. The house has been extensively renovated and offers a comfortable and relaxing stay.
Our facilities include large sunny bedrooms with private bathroom and own sitting room. Full or continental breakfast at a time convenient to you. Complimentary tea, coffee, fruit juice always available.
Our interests are many and varied. Cooking is one of my hobbies and I would look forward to providing you with dinner at the end of the day. Prior notice please.
We share our smoke free environment with our two aged quiet long haired miniature dachshunds, who will also give you a warm welcome to our home.
Directions: *For reservations and detailed directions, please phone. Ample off street parking and easy access.*

TARANAKI WANGANUI RANGITIKEI

Please help us provide the best hospitality in the world.
Fill in a comment form for every place you stay.

New Plymouth
Self-contained Accommodation
Address: Cottage by the sea
66 Lower Turangi Road, Motunui
Name: Nancy & Hugh Mills
Telephone: (06) 754 7915
Fax: (06) 754 4544
Email: nancy.mills@taranaki.ac.nz
Beds: 2 Double (1 bedroom, lounge)
Bathroom: 1 Ensuite
Tariff: B&B (continental) Double $85, Single $65, Each child $20.
Each additional adult $25. Campervans parking only.
Nearest Town: New Plymouth - 25km north of NP, 1k off State Hway 3.

Cottage by the Sea
Go to sleep with the sound of the waves - wake with the birds. This lovely, peaceful cottage is nestled amongst landscaped gardens and lawns.
It offers complete privacy and is self sufficient with one bedroom (double bed), ensuite and fully equipped kitchen. The sofa bed in the lounge can sleep two additional guests. A 2 minute bushwalk takes you down to the beach for a leisurely stroll. Enjoy a fun game of tennis on the grass court, request a private tour of our small commercial flower business, or relax on the veranda looking out to spectacular and ever-changing sea views. Breakfast includes seasonal fruit, and a choice of homemade scones and muffins or cereals . Or, if you wish to provide your own: less $8 adults, $4 child. Ten minutes drive to / from grocery store. Laundry facilities available for small charge. A non-smoking accommodation.
Please ring for bookings and directions.

New Plymouth
Homestay

Address: "The Grange", 44B Victoria Road, New Plymouth
Name: Cathy Thurston and John Smith
Telephone: 06-758 1540 **Fax**: 06-758-1539
Mobile: 025-244 2639 **Email**: cathyt@clear.net.nz
Beds: 1 King, 1 Double, 2 Single.
Bathroom: 2 Ensuites
Tariff: B&B Double $90, Single $60, Dinner $25.
All Credit Cards accepted. NZ B&B Vouchers accepted $20 surcharge
Nearest Town: New Plymouth - 5 minutes walk to city centre.

Come and stay at our brand new architecturally designed award winning home built with your privacy and comfort in mind. Our home is luxuriously appointed and has been designed to take full advantage of the sun.
Each bedroom has its own en-suite, TV, electric blankets, hair dryers and complimentary tea and coffee are provided. One bedroom has a double bed with French doors opening to a covered tiled courtyard. The other bedroom has two single beds convertible to a king-size bed. Our home is centrally heated, security controlled and located adjacent to the well known Pukekura Park and Bowl of Brooklands and is five minutes walk from the city centre. Breakfast is provided with freshly baked bread and espresso coffee, either in the formal dining area, al fresco on the tiled deck, or in the designer kitchen. Cathy and John have travelled extensively overseas and understand and appreciate true hospitality. Non smokers preferred.
Home Page: http://nz.com/webnz/bbnz/grange htm

New Plymouth

Bed & Breakfast Inn
Address: 60 Pendarves street,
Central City, New Plymouth
Name: Alice Jane House
Telephone: (06) 758 1440
Fax: (06) 758 1430
Beds: 2 Queen, 3 Single (3 bedrooms)
Bathroom: 1 Guests share
Tariff: B&B (special/full/continental) Double $75, Single $55.
Visa/Mastercard/Amex.
Nearest Town: New Plymouth (5 mins walk to City Centre)

Warmth and welcome abounds in our tastefully decorated sunny central city 1915 villa, where you can relax and be pampered. Our spacious newly renovated character home offers a charm and ambience of yesteryear. Crisp white linen, large luxurious towels and fresh flowers await you with those extra trimmings that make your stay memorable.

Enjoy the warmth of a fire in winter or just relax in front of the TV in one of our two guest lounges. A cappuccino / espresso machine is available 24 hours as part of our guests facilities.

Gracious breakfast settings of crystal and silver enhance the sumptuous breakfasts served.

Our joys include wood carving, people, laughter and writing. Our family consists of two cats and one dog.

Off-street parking and courtesy car available. Our home is smoke free. Five minutes walk to city centre and all that it offers. Pukekura Park is just around the corner.

New Plymouth

Bed & Breakfast
Address: 'Conifer House',
1148 Devon Road, New Plymouth
Name: Melva and Colin
Telephone: (06) 755 1947
Fax: (06) 755 1947
Beds: 1 Queen, 4 Single (3 bedrooms)
Bathroom: 1 Ensuite, 1 Guests share
Tariff: B&B (full/continental) Double $60,
Single $40, Dinner $18.
Nearest Town: New Plymouth

TARANAKI
WANGANUI
RANGITIKEI

Welcome to our 1920's old-world charm home, situated in 1/2 acre of garden, where you will find a friendly welcome and warm hospitality.

You may enjoy a game of tennis on our court. A swim or spa in our pools, both enclosed in the same building to protect you from all weather.

Our beds are warm and comfortable with electric blankets. We offer you a generous breakfast with a choice of cooked or continental. Tea and coffee making facilities are available to you. Evening meals by arrangement.

We are situated 2 kms from the airport where a courtesy car will collect or deliver you. Golf course and beach are only minutes away. We enjoy meeting people and look forward to welcoming you to our home as will our cat. We ask guests not to smoke indoors.

We are situated 2 kms north of Bell Block on SH 3.

Stratford

Homestay
Address: 'Woodhill' 15 Taylor Road (SH 3),
R.D.23, Stratford
Name: John & Elaine Nicholls
Telephone: (06) 765 5497
Beds: 1 Double, 4 Single (3 bedrooms)
Bathroom: 1 Guests share
Tariff: B&B (full) Double $80, Single $60, Dinner $30,
Credit Cards (VISA/MC). NZ B&B Vouchers accepted
Nearest Town: Stratford - 3km south near Ngaere overhead bridge

Come and enjoy the tranquillity and beauty of the countryside in the heart of Taranaki. Our home is nestled in two acres of old English gardens and is over a hundred years old. Each bedroom opens out onto the gardens and comfortably appointed.

We offer you warmth, hospitality and a haven from the stresses of everyday life. After a generous, leisurely breakfast enjoy a walk in the gardens or a swim in our large outdoor pool. We have an "upper room" suitable for retreats, small seminars and functions, or for just relaxing.

In the evenings guests are invited to enjoy a three course dinner with complimentary wine, or if you prefer there are restaurants in Stratford.

Stratford offers a wide range of activities including a picturesque golf course and all types of mountain sports. For garden enthusiasts there is the Taranaki trail of gardens of which our home is a participant.

Stratford

Farmstay Bed & Breakfast
Address: Stallard Farm, SH 3,
Stratford Nth, 1 km 24 R.D.
Name: Billie Anne & Corb Stallard
Telephone: (06) 765 8324
Fax: (06) 765 8324
Mobile: 025-240 2677
Beds: Comfortable Double, Twin,
Triple and Single rooms,

T.V. Electric blankets. (1 bedroom sleeps 4).
Bathroom: 2 Ensuite, 1 Private, 2 Guests share
Tariff: B&B (full) Double $65, Single $40, Triple $75, 4 Bedroom $80,
Children $15, Cooking facilities, Cot available.
Credit Cards (VISA/MC/AMEX), NZ B&B Vouchers accepted
Nearest Town: Stratford 1 km

Built on the turn of the century, this elegant old house, with its extensive gardens and farm walks, offers genuine "Upstairs Downstairs" B&B. Be private if desired, making use of cooking facilities, or settle in as a home away from home. 1km restaurants, taverns, shops.

The Aga cooker in the main kitchen ensures a warm glow throughout the house in winter, and provides a hearty cooked breakfast, or a light breakfast may be chosen. Complimentary tea and coffee, biscuits etc (continuous self-service). Laundry (small charge). TV in bedrooms, Pooltable, Separate lounge, BBQ. Paddle on the lake. Go tramping or skiing on Mt Egmont 15 mins. Trout fishing. Walkways. Museums. Famous gardens. Helicopter sightseeing. Shopping in Stratford or New Plymouth or just lazing. Family all grown. Cat Fluffy lives outside.

Home Page: www.nz-travelz.com
Directions: *1 km Stratford, north on State Highway 3.*

Egmont National Park

Farm and Homestay
Address: 922 Pembroke Road, P.O. Box 303,
Stratford, Mount Egmont/Taranaki
Name: Anderson's Alpine Residence
Telephone: (06) 765 6620
(if no reply ph/fax (06) 765 6100)
Fax: (06) 765 6100 **Mobile**: (025) 412 372
Email: MOUNTAINHOUSE@XTRA.CO.NZ
Beds: 2 King/Queen, 2 Single (3 bedrooms)
Bathroom: 3 Ensuite
Tariff: B&B (full) Double $95/120, Single $95/120. Credit Cards.
NZ B&B Vouchers accepted Surcharge for $95 room $20 & $120 room $45.
Nearest Town: Stratford 9km

Our Swiss Chalet rests in five acres of native bush. Views of Mount Egmont / Taranaki on our doorstep. The Egmont National Park starts opposite our front gate.   Five kilometres from the Mountain House and its internationally famed restaurant and a further three kilometres to the Stratford Plateau and skifields. The National Park offers family tramps, round-the-mountain trek, summit climbs (guides available) and snow skiing. Trout stream, gardens, museums and scenic drives nearby. Private helicopter for summit scenic flights. We have pet sheep, pig, ducks etc. Kiwi Keith and Swiss Berta Anderson owned mountain lodges for 24 years. Won many tourist and hospitality awards. Keith is noted Taranaki Artist specialising in landscape and mountain scenes.
Directions: *922 Pembroke Road opposite Egmont National Park, nine kilometres west of Stratford - Please phone reservations. If no reply phone or fax (06) 765 6100).*
Home Page: http://wwwmountainhouse.co.nz

Stratford

Country Retreat
Address: "Sarsen House", Te Popo Gardens,
636 Stanley Road, RD 24, Stratford
Name: Bruce & Lorri Ellis
Telephone: (06) 762 8775 **Fax**: (06) 762 8775
Email: tepopo@clear.net.nz
Beds: 1 Queen, 1 King/Twin (2 bedrooms)
Bathroom: 2 Ensuite

Sarsen House

Tariff: B&B (full) Double $90-$110, Single $75, Dinner $30, Credit Cards.
NZ B&B Vouchers accepted $20 surcharge; same day restriction Fri & Sat.
Nearest Town: Stratford 15 km

Sarsen House is set in Te Popo Gardens (34 acres); nestled in the hills 30km east of Mount Taranaki. A peaceful retreat of great beauty in all seasons: stroll in the woodland gardens; explore the unique native-clad gorges and streams; enjoy the abundant birdlife; relax in the comfort of your suite, curled up before your own woodburning fire in colder weather; or venture further afield to enjoy the riches of Taranaki. Our guest wing provides private, quality accommodation in a garden setting. Share the facilities of our formal lounge and dining room, and breakfast in the sun filled conservatory. We would enjoy serving you dinner, however if you wish to self cater, full kitchen facilities are available. We ask guests not to smoke indoors. Our dogs, Sargeant and Pepper are the resident possum hunters.
Directions: *From Midhurst on SH3 travel east on Beaconsfield Road for 5.8km then north on Stanley Road for 6.5km.*
Home Page: http://www.friars.co.nz/hosts/tepopo.html

Stratford

Farmstay
Address: Toko Road, RD 22, Stratford
Name: Heather and Peter Savage
Telephone: (06) 762 2840
Fax: (06) 762 2880
Mobile: (025) 284 3820
Email: savage.toko@xtra.co.nz
Beds: 1 Double (1 bedroom)
Bathroom: 1 Ensuite, 1 Family share
Tariff: B&B (full) Double $80, Single $45, Dinner $15, Children $20.
NZ B&B Vouchers accepted $10 surcharge
Nearest Town: 17 kms from Stratford.

"WOODLEIGH" TOKO TARANAKI
We have a large, modern home and garden. It is extremely private and quiet with a truly magnificent view of Mt Egmont. The guest room has separate bathroom facilities and provides guests with the opportunity to relax in private or join in with family activities. We have a delightful house dog called Brandy, a daughter of 9 and a son of 12, and would welcome children but they would have to share facilities with our children. Our farm is 1150 acres and we run dairy cows, Angus beef cattle and Romney ewes. The farm is approx 15 km east of Stratford, 50 mins by car from New Plymouth and about half an hour from Mt Egmont which has beautiful scenery and bush walks. We offer a quiet, relaxed stay in a rural setting with the opportunity to see and participate in a working farm or maybe even go possum shooting at night!
Directions: *Please phone.*

Waitotara

+ Self-Contained Accommodation
Address: Ashley Park, PO Box 36,
Waitotara, Wanganui
Name: Barry Pearce & Wendy Bowman
Telephone: (06) 346 5917
Fax: (06) 346 5861
Beds: 1 Double,
4 Single (3 bedrooms)
Bathroom: 1 Ensuite, 1 Guests share
Tariff: B&B (full) Double $60-$90,
Single $40; Dinner $25;

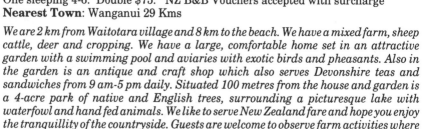

Power points for caravans and campervans with full facilities;
Cabins available; Self-contained unit for 7 people; Two fully equipped motels,
One sleeping 4-6. Double $75. NZ B&B Vouchers accepted with surcharge
Nearest Town: Wanganui 29 Kms

We are 2 km from Waitotara village and 8 km to the beach. We have a mixed farm, sheep cattle, deer and cropping. We have a large, comfortable home set in an attractive garden with a swimming pool and aviaries with exotic birds and pheasants. Also in the garden is an antique and craft shop which also serves Devonshire teas and sandwiches from 9 am-5 pm daily. Situated 100 metres from the house and garden is a 4-acre park of native and English trees, surrounding a picturesque lake with waterfowl and hand fed animals. We like to serve New Zealand fare and hope you enjoy the tranquillity of the countryside. Guests are welcome to observe farm activities where possible and there are scenic drives locally.
Directions: *We are situated 29 km north of Wanganui and 12 km south of Waverley on State Highway 3.*

Wanganui

Homestay
Address: 156 Great North Road,
Wanganui
Name: Janet Dick
Telephone: (06) 345 8951
Beds: 2 Single (1 Bedroom)
Bathroom: 1 Private
Tariff: B&B (continental) Double $60, Single $40, Dinner by special arrangement,
Cooked breakfast on request. NZ B&B Vouchers accepted
Nearest Town: Wanganui 2 Kms

*My home is a eight year old Lockwood set amongst mature trees, two kilometres from
the centre of Wanganui on the main Wanganui / New Plymouth Highway.*
*I have travelled extensively overseas and enjoy meeting and conversing with people
from all countries. I have a small flower growing business and my many interests
include sport, tramping, gardening, bridge and travel.*
*Wanganui has many attractions including excellent golf courses and sporting facili-
ties, the Regional Museum and superb Serjeant Art Gallery and the scenic Wanganui
River which offers something for everyone from sedate paddle steamers cruises to
kayaking the rapids. Or take a day trip by jet boat to see the famous Bridge to Nowhere,
the Drop Scene and the Settlement of Jerusalem. Wanganui also has a good variety of
restaurants, both licensed and BYO.*
I look forward to meeting you.
Directions: *2km up SH 3 from Wanganui towards New Plymouth,*

Wanganui

Farmstay
Address: Operiki, River Road,
641, R.D.6, Wanganui
Name: Trissa & Peter McIntyre
Telephone: (06) 342 8159
Beds: 1 Double,
2 Single (2 bedrooms)
Bathroom: Family share
Tariff: B&B (full) $35 per adult,
Children $15,
Dinner adult $20/children $10, Campervans $15.
NZ B&B Vouchers accepted
Nearest Town: Wanganui 45 Kms

*Farmstay overlooking the Whanganui River - en route to the Bridge to Nowhere - sheep,
cattle and deer farming. Pottery and macadamia nuts and cat. Enjoy a country picnic
or bush walk. Other activities along the river can be arranged: canoeing, jet boat rides,
horse riding, mountain bike riding, Marae visit and farm activities according to
season.*
45km north from Wanganui turn off SH4.

Continental breakfast consists of fruit, cereal, toast, tea/coffee,
Full breakfast is the same with a cooked course,
Special breakfast has something special.

329

Wanganui

Homestay
Address: 50 Riverbank Road
State Highway 4, Wanganui
Name: Peter & Margaret McAra
Telephone: (06) 343 6557 **Fax**: (06) 343 6557 **Mobile**: (025) 507 295
Beds: 1 King, 1 Queen, 1 Double, 3 Single (4 bedrooms)
Bathroom: 2 Ensuite, 1 Guests share
Tariff: B&B (full) Double $95-$115, Single $80-$95,
Special arrangements for families, small groups and stays of more than 2 nights.
NZ B&B Vouchers accepted $30 surcharge
Nearest Town: Wanganui - 3km north on SH4.

Welcome to Arles.
We would like to share our lovely, late 19th Century home with 2 acres of native trees, including New Zealand's most southern Queensland kauri, plus maples, oaks, camellias, rhododendrons, azaleas, kowhai and ferns, citrus grove and numerous other fruit trees including an indoor grape vine. Meet Davy our corgi, and our cat Tiger.
We are situated on State Highway 4 on the road to National Park above the Wanganui River and only 5 minutes from Wanganui City.
The four guest rooms contain 1 King, 1 Queen, 1 Double and 3 single beds. Two rooms have en-suites, the others share a private bathroom. Each contains electric blankets, reading lamps and tea making facilities. Guests are welcome to share the lounge which opens up to an outside verandah and use of a large library. A kitchen is available for guests to use together with laundry facilities.
Our new "Barn" offers spacious, self contained, fully furnished, 2 bedroom accommodation. Enjoy the peace and tranquillity of the Arles' woodlands and gardens. Breakfast is served in the morning sunshine looking out onto the gardens. Outside facilities include a swimming pool, barbeque and children's play area.
Use our home to relax or as a base for a wide range of scenic outdoor and leisure pursuits. Nearby are well established gardens, pottery, arts and crafts. We are close to Mount Ruapehu snowfields, mountain and bushwalks or even a joy ride in the historic paddle steamer on the Wanganui River.
We have six children and six grandchildren. Margaret is a nurse and enjoys flower arranging, needlework, cake decoration and gardening, when she finds time. Peter enjoys tramping, cycling, photography, and family history. No smoking indoors please.
Directions: *Please phone for reservations. Take SH3 to Wanganui. Travel 3km North on Anzac Parade along SH4. Cross white concrete bridge over Mateongaonga Stream and take 2nd driveway on right to Arles.*

330

Wanganui

Homestay
Address: 'Bradgate', 7 Somme Parade,
Wanganui
Name: Frances
Telephone: (06) 345 3634
Fax: (06) 345 3634
Beds: 1 Queen, 1 Double, 2 Single (3 bedrooms)
Bathroom: 1 Guests share
Tariff: B&B (full) Double $70, Single $40, Dinner $25.
Nearest Town: Wanganui town centre 5 mins

*We welcome you to "Bradgate". This gracious superior, 2 storey home built in 1901.
Comfortable furnished, central heating and river-view from all windows, a most
relaxing place for the traveller wanting homestay accommodation. "Bradgate" has a
beautiful entrance hall with carved rimu staircase, which has been restored to reflect
the original character and gracefulness of this house.
I am a qualified chef-caterer, with a grown-up family. 23 years ago my husband and
I came to New Zealand to own and operate Shangri-La Restaurant by Virginia Lake,
Wanganui. After 20 years we retired and decided to welcome guests into our beautiful
old home.
My mother lives next-door, we share her pet dog Bounce.
We are 8 mins walk to town centre and all amenities.
I play golf, enjoy gardening and love meeting people.
If you can't find me at home, check the garden.
Non-smoking home, Dinner by arrangement.*

Wanganui

Guest House
Address: 2 Plymouth Street,
Wanganui
Name: Riverside Inn
Telephone: (06) 347 2529
Fax: (06) 347 2529

Beds: 4 Double, 8 Single (8 bedrooms)
Bathroom: 3 Guests share
Tariff: B&B (continental) Double $70, Single $45,
Campervans parking (No power), Credit Cards (VISA/MC/BC).
Nearest Town: Wanganui - 10 mins walk to main street

*Our homestead, built 1895, has been restored to retain its "old world charm". It is not
a modern hotel, you will share facilities, but you will have the homely atmosphere of
how New Zealand used to be.
Guest rooms are located on the ground floor, a wing which was added when the
original home became a private hospital in 1911. The hospital, named "Braemar",
closed in 1976 after which is was converted to a tourist inn.
We are walking distance to Town Centre, museum, art gallery and cafes. A laundry
and fully equipped self service kitchen are available.
If you choose to stay with us we will give you our personal attention to ensure your visit
is as comfortable as possible.
We request that you do not smoke on the premises and step over "Casper" our cat whose
habit is sleeping on the front door mat.*

TARANAKI
WANGANUI
RANGITIKEI

Wanganui

Homestay
Address: 13 Banks Place, Wanganui
Name: Carnalea Homestay
Telephone: (06) 344 5506
Fax: (06) 344 5506
Mobile: (025) 421 282
Beds: 4 Single (2 bedrooms)
Bathroom: Guests share with one family member
Tariff: B&B (full) Double $70, Single $45.
Nearest Town: Wanganui 7 minutes City Centre

Welcome to Wanganui, "well worth your journey", and to Carnalea where you are assured of a warm, friendly welcome from Elizabeth and the Collie, who lives outside. Our home is modern, very comfortable and set in a quiet cul-de-sac, very central for all Wanganui's many attractions, both sporting and scenic:
* 400 metres to the golf driving range
* less than 10 minutes drive to the other two golf courses
* 7 minutes to City Centre and Cooks Gardens
* 4 minutes to the Stadium
The house is on a back section and there is off-street parking right at the door. A large lounge is available for your comfort and relaxation. The bathroom has a toilet and bath, and there is a separate shower and toilet, shared with other guests and one family member.
Transport is available from airport or travel centre. This is a smoke-free household.
Directions: *Please phone or fax (06) 344 5506*

Raetihi

Farmstay
Address: State Highway 4, P O Box 91, Raetihi
Name: Brian & Pixie Chambers
Telephone: (06) 385 4310
Fax: (06) 385 4331
Beds: 2 Single (1 Bedroom)
Bathroom: 1 Private
Tariff: B&B (full) Double $70, Single $40
Nearest Town: Raetihi

Our four children have left home to pursue their own careers and we now enjoy making new friends and sharing our lives with them. We have a 1600 acre farm on which we run sheep, cattle and deer. There is an outdoor swimming pool, set in idyllic garden surroundings and an indoor spa pool for the cooler season. As we both enjoy gardening, our home is set in gracious, peaceful surroundings, with a panoramic view of mountains and farmland. This is often described by visitors as a "million dollar view". One of the first pleasures you will notice is the crisp, clear, mountain air. We are 30 minutes from the Turoa Ski Resort and scenic mountain drive. There is also a lovely golf course to enjoy nearby. Brian runs his own stock and station business and enjoys taking visitors with him on his trips to buy stock from farmers in the district. Accommodation is twin bedroom, with private shower and toilet.
Directions: *1 km North of Raetihi.*

Raetihi

Farmstay
Address: Pipiriki Road, R.D. 4, Raetihi
Name: Ken & Sonia Robb
Telephone: (06) 385 4581 **Fax**: (06) 385 4581
Beds: 1 Queen, 2 Single (2 bedrooms)
Bathroom: 1 Ensuite, 1 Family share
Tariff: B&B (full) Double $70, Single $40, Children 1/2 price, Dinner $20.
NZ B&B Vouchers accepted
Nearest Town: Raetihi 6km

We welcome you to our 1,000 acres of hill country farm in the quiet, picturesque Mangaeturoa Valley just 10 minutes from Raetihi where Ken runs Romney sheep and Simmental cattle. Our home is set in a spacious garden to which native NZ birds love to visit and offers superb views of the surrounding countryside and Mt Ruapehu. Our interests include travel, flying, photography and gardening. There are many activities available locally throughout the year, skifields, jetboating from Pipiriki on the Wanganui river, scenic tramps or maybe a farm tour with Ken if your time permits. Your accommodation is a double room with very comfortable queen bed and feather duvet and ensuite. Twin room has share facilities with your hosts. A cot is available and there is a spa pool which guests are welcome to use. Dinners are prepared from home grown meat and vegetables served with NZ wine. Cooked or continental breakfast. We are 6 1/2 km from Raetihi on Pipiriki Road.

Raetihi

Homestay
Address: 'The Old Courthouse',
32 George St, Raetihi
Name: David & Judy Squires
Telephone: (06) 385 4399
Fax: (06) 385 4399
Beds: 1 Queen,
3 Single (2 bedrooms)
Bathroom: 1 Guests share
Tariff: B&B (full) Double $70,
Single $40.
NZ B&B Vouchers accepted
Nearest Town: Raetihi 1 km.

The Old Courthouse

Bed & Breakfast

The Old Courthouse provides homely accommodation in a unique historical building which has been developed to include a pottery and art studio. It is sited in a quiet location, ten minutes walk from the town centre. During the Winter Ski Season, the spacious lounge with its log fire and warm timber interior, gives welcoming comfort after a days skiing. Turoa and Whakapapa Ski Fields are accessible within 3/4 - 1 hours drive. In the Summer, Raetihi is ideally situated for excursions throughout the region, from the Hot Pools of Tokaanu, to the Army Museum at Waiouru. The Mount Ruapehu and Whanganui National Park attractions are also readily accessible. These include: Bush Walking, Trout Fishing, Canoeing, Rafting, Mountain Biking and Horse Riding. We invite you to stay at 'The Old Courthouse' and enjoy the attractions of the Ruapehu Region all year round.

Raetihi

Homestay+Self-contained Accom. No kitchen.
Address: Log Lodge, 5 Ranfurly Tce, Raetihi
Name: Jan & Bob Lamb
Telephone: (06) 385 4135
Fax: (06) 385 4135
Email: Lamb.Log-Lodge@Xtra.co.nz
Beds: 2 Double, 5 Single
(large mezzanine) + 1 room.
Bathroom: 2 Private
Tariff: B&B (full) Double $90, Single $48,
Children $35, Credit Cards.
Nearest Town: Raetihi - on edge of town

A unique opportunity to stay in a modern authentic log home sited high on 7 acres on the edge of town. Completely private accommodation with own bathroom. Sleeping on mezzanine floor with room for 6, your own lounge with wood fire, snooker table, TV/ video and stereo and dining area, opening onto large verandah. Your private area is 1500 square feet. Panoramic views across river and farmlands to the Tongariro National Park and Mts. Ruapehu, Ngauruhoe and Tongariro, just 14km away. We are keen skiers and specialize in winter accommodation for those who share our love of skiing. You can be in the snow with your skis on in 30 minutes. We have a pool, solar heated in summer and a secluded spa. Summer visitors have a full range of recreational activities in the national park and we have mountain bikes for hire to explore the many scenic rides in the district.

Ohakune

Homestay/Farmstay
Address: 'Mitredale', Smiths Road,
Ohakune
Name: Audrey & Diane Pritt
Telephone: (06) 385 8016
Fax: (06) 385 8016 **Mobile**: (025) 531 916
Beds: 1 Double, 2 Single (2 bedrooms)
Bathroom: 1 Family share
Tariff: B&B (continental) Double $70, Single $40,
Children 12 and under $20; Dinner $20,
Credit Cards. NZ B&B Vouchers accepted
Nearest Town: Ohakune 6 km, Raetihi 9 km

We are farmers who farm sheep and bull beef in a beautiful peaceful valley with magnificent views of Mt Ruapehu. The Waimarino is an excellent area for holidaying summer or winter. Tongariro National Park offers excellent walks, opportunities for photography and great skiing at Turoa and Whakapapa. The rivers offer good sport for fishermen and an excellent 18-hole golf course 3 km from our door. We are keen members of the Conservation body Ducks Unlimited, and our local Wine Club. We have two Labradors and one large cat. We have two guest-rooms - one with two single beds, the other a double bed. All equipped with electric blankets. The home is heated with a log-fire and open fire - excellent for drying gear after a day's skiing, a comfortable, cosy atmosphere to relax in. We offer dinner with the traditional farmhouse fare or just breakfast - gives you the opportunity to sample our excellent homemade jams. We enjoy sharing our lifestyle with others so come and spend some time on the farm.
Directions: *Take the Raetihi Road at Ohakune Hotel corner/ BP Service Station, travel 4 km to Smiths Road, second side road on the left. We are the last house 2 km at the end of the road.*

Ohakune

Self-contained Accommodation
Address: 'South Fork', 3209
Raetihi-Ohakune Road, Ohakune
Name: Noeline & Trevor Reynolds
Telephone: (06) 385 8412 **Fax**: (06) 385 8425
Beds: 1Queen, 1 Double, 4 Single (3 bedrooms)
Bathroom: 2 Ensuites
Tariff: B&B (continental) Double $90, Single $50, Children $25.
NZ B&B Vouchers accepted Nov to June
Nearest Town: Ohakune

*'South Fork' is sited on 11 acres of quiet park-like grounds with close-up views of Mt
Ruapehu. A good half way stop between Auckland and Wellington.*
*The golf course is adjacent to our
spacious gardens.*
*Activities in our aea include scenic
mountain walks, jet boating, sailing, trout fishing, horse trekking,
white water rafting.*
Directions: *From Waiouru on
S.H.1 turn off to Ohakune. Turn
left at the BP Fuel Station travel
about 5km to a reflectorised hanging sign reading 'South Fork' on
your left. Proceed up the tree lined
drive.*

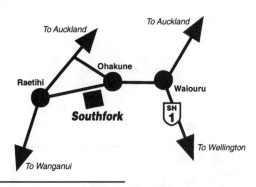

Ohakune

Guest House
Address: Villa Mangawhero,
60B Burns St, Ohakune
Name: Patricia Mountfort
Telephone: (06) 385 8076 **Mobile**: 025-240 2324
Beds: 1 Queen, 1 Double, 5 Single (4 bedrooms)
Bathroom: 1 Ensuite, 2 Guests , 1 Private
Tariff: B&B (full) Double $70*, Single $40*,
Children negotiable, *Tariff different rates ski season. Dinner $20.
No Smoking. Credit cards. NZ B&B Vouchers accepted December to May
Nearest Town: Ohakune 500m approx.

*Situated in Ohakune village Villa Mangawhero, built in 1914, has been extensively
renovated but still retains many original features. Pressed steel ceilings, antique kauri
fire surrounds, rimu tongue and groove wall linings and coloured glass windows and
doors. Guests have exclusive use of two lounges one with TV. Bedsitting rooms have tea
and coffee making facilities and heating.*
*Ohakune halfway between Auckland and Wellington, 17km from Turoa ski field and
42 from Whakapapa offers fishing, tramping, skiing and other outdoor activities plus
sightseeing in national park where some lifts operate all year. Also local shops for
browsing, restaurants and cafes a picture theatre and a disco.*
*Patricia Mountfort an artist has paintings for sale. Her house which is furnished with
antique kauri furniture has featured in February 95 NZ Womens Weekly open home
series under the title of 'Olde World Charm'. Patricia looks forward to sharing this
'charm' with you.*

335

Ohakune

Homestay
Address: 1011 Raetihi Road, Ohakune
Name: Bruce & Nita Wilde & cat 'Shah'
Telephone: (06) 385 8026 Please phone
Beds: 1 Double, 3 Single (3 bedrooms)
Bathroom: 1 Private, 1 Family share

Kohinoor

Tariff: B&B (full) Double $80, Single $45, Children $15, Dinner $20.
Our home is smokefree. NZ B&B Vouchers accepted
Nearest Town: Ohakune 1km

Named 'Kohinoor' (a gem of rare beauty) our home is a warm and cosy place from where you can enjoy the attractions of the Tongariro National Park and the Turoa skifields. 'Kohinoor' is set in 3 acres of tranquil gardens of special note with an exceptional view of Mt Ruapehu across our lake, rural farmland and native bush.
Our interests include gardening, photography, local trout fishing, skiing and alpine walking.
We are just 20 mins drive from Turoa ski resort and 40 minutes from Whakapapa skifields. In the ski season Ohakune has many exciting bars and restaurants. The beautiful Waimarino Golf Course is only 5 minutes away.
One hour's drive gets you to Lake Taupo and the world famous Tongariro trout fishing River.

Directions: *Exactly 1km from Ohakune on the west side of the road to Raetihi.*

Ohakune

Homestay
Address: "Whare Ora", 14 Kaha Street,
Rangataua, Ohakune
Name: Diana & Tiri
Telephone: (06) 385 9385
Fax: (06) 385 9385
Email: whareora@xtra.co.nz
Beds: 2 Queen (2 bedrooms)
Bathroom: 1 Ensuite, 1 Private
Tariff: B&B (full) Double $135-$150,
Children negotiable, Dinner $35pp.
Credit Cards (VISA/MC/Diners/American Express)
NZ B&B Vouchers accepted $61.50 & $75 surcharge
Nearest Town: Ohakune (5km)

Whare Ora can be interpreted as a place of well being, and this is exactly what our home is. The house is set in an established half acre garden with superb views of Mt Ruapehu, and extensive rural views to Mt Taranaki. Whare Ora, originally built in 1910, has been altered and extended into an imaginative contemporary home. The best features of the old house have been retained to blend with the new. One lounge features a large stone open fire and wood panelling and the upstairs lounge includes a library. Guests can choose from an ensuite with a sitting room, or a beautiful attic room with private bathroom. Local attractions include Turoa ski field; trout fishing; mountain and scenic walks; golf; private gardens to visit; a wide range of cafes and a night club. Non smoking. We have two pet cats.
Directions: *From Waiouru travel 21.5km on State Highway, turn right at Rangataua turn off, then 1st left into Kaha Street, Whare Ora is the last house on the right. From Ohakune 4.5km to Rangataua turn off then as above.*

Taihape

Homestay
Address: 'Korirata', 25 Pukeko Street, Taihape
Name: Patricia & Noel Gilbert
Telephone: (06) 388 0315 **Email**: korirata@xtra.co.nz
Beds: 4 Single (2 bedrooms, electric blankets on every bed)
Bathroom: 1 Guests only share
Tariff: B&B (full or continental) Double $65, Single $40, Primary children half
price, Dinner $22, Campervans facilities available,
Credit cards NZ B&B Vouchers accepted
Nearest Town: Taihape - 1/2km from Post Office

A warm welcome to Taihape, where we are situated on top of the hill with panoramic
views of Mt. Ruapehu, the Ruahines and extensive farming country.
Warmth and comfort is a feature in tranquil surroundings for instant relaxation.
The entire section - three-quarters-of-an-acre - has been landscaped with shrubs,
hydroponic and orchid houses, and a large area planted in chrysanthemums.
Dinner and lunch are available on request and almost all types of meals are available.
Meals with hosts using our home grown produce - cooking is a hobby.
Separate toilet and bathroom available for guests. Farm visits, tramping, rafting,
fishing, bunjee jumping and jet boating can be arranged and most are within 1/2 hour.
One hour to Ruapehu (skiing), one hour to Lake Taupo, 2 1/2 hours to Rotorua or
Wellington, 40 minutes to Titoki Point and other well known gardens.
Noel has retired from the farm to horticulture and Pat teaches.
Directions: *Please phone.*

Taihape

Farmstay
Address: Utiku South Road, Utiku, Taihape
Name: Blair & Dot McLeod
Telephone: (06) 388 0439
Beds: 1 Double, 1 Single (2 bedrooms)
Bathroom: 1 Private
Tariff: B&B (full) Double $75, Single $40, Dinner $25.
NZ B&B Vouchers accepted $10 surcharge
Nearest Town: Taihape 11 kms

For a relaxing, peaceful stopover with really beautiful mountain and rural views on a genuine
NZ farm. We are: Conveniently situated between Taupo and Wellington.
Just one kilometre off State Highway 1.
Sheep / cattle farmers of 500 hectares of hill country.
Interested in breeding and training sheepdogs, spinning and woolcraft, gardening, travelling
and meeting people.
We offer: A warm, sunny, cozy, smoke-free home.
Very comfortable, warm beds
A relaxing, tranquil stopover
Delicious meals with home-baking and farm produce
Complimentary morning or afternoon tea
Kiwi hospitality - Dot is a Kiwi Host
You can: Relax and unwind in a very peaceful locality.
Roam the farm and experience farm life (with a packed lunch if required)
Wander in the garden, listen and watch native birds
Sit and absorb the views To help our preparations to make your stay most pleasurable, we
would prefer a letter or phone call in advance. No dogs please.

Taihape

Homestay
Address: 'Papa Pottery and B&B'
24 Huia Street, Taihape
Name: Lindsay & Cathy Baine
Telephone: (06) 388 0318 **Fax**: (06) 388 0318
Beds: 1 Queen, 1 Double, 1 Twin
Bathroom: 1 Guests share
Tariff: B&B (full) Double $65, Single $40,
Children $20, Credit Cards (VISA/MC/BC). NZ B&B Vouchers accepted
Nearest Town: Taihape

We are a young couple who have moved from Wellington to operate a pottery studio. You may enjoy watching pots created during your stay.
Built as a doctors residence, our lovely 1910 two storey home, is situated near the centre of Taihape. Taihape, a small rural township, is an ideal stopover between Auckland and Wellington. It has many attractions to offer; for example, rafting, bungy jumping, trout fishing, jet boating, kayaking, and excellent golf courses are all close at hand. We are also centrally placed for visits to the many famous gardens of the Rangitikei region, and only one hours drive to Turoa Skifields.
We offer you a warm and comfortable stay. Several cafes and restaurants are nearby. Being non-smokers we ask that guests refrain from smoking indoors.
We look forward to having you share our home with ourselves and our family.
Directions: *Huia Street - turn at the Post Office.*

Taihape

Fishingstay/Farmstay/Homestay
Address: Tarata Fishaway, 5251 Mokai Road, RD 3, Taihape
Name: Stephen & Trudi Mattock
Telephone: (06) 388 0354 (Transport available)
Fax: (06) 388 0954
Beds: 1 Queen waterbed, 1 Queen, 4 Single (3 bedrooms)
Bathroom: Guests share 1
Tariff: B&B (continental) $55 per person Children under 12yrs 1/2 price,
Dinner $25, Family concessions available, Approved pets allowed,
Lunch available if requested (extra).
Credit Cards accepted.NZ B&B Vouchers accepted $30 surcharge
Nearest Town: We are 26 scenic Kms from Taihape, only 6km past Mokai Bungy jump
bridge, Rural No. 5251.

We are very lucky to have a piece of New Zealand's natural beauty. Situated in the remote Mokai Valley where the picturesque Rangitikei River meets the rugged Ruahine Ranges. We spend lots of quality time with our daughters down at the river which offers unique fishing opportunities right at our doorstep. Our spacious home offers guests private space to unwind and relax. Whether it be by the pool with a book, milking the house cow and tending to other family pets or you might spend your time just fishing. We offer lay back fishing and rafting experiences or why not check out the amazing night life on Stephens' special spotlight safaris. The energetic person can tramp the Ruahines and the thrill-seekers are well catered for with the nearby tourist attractions. Words cannot express the feeling we have living here but we would love to share it with you.
Directions: *Turn off S/H 1, 6 kms south of Taihape at the Hightime Bungy and Ohotu turn-off. Follow the Bungy signs, we are 6km past Bungy bridge.*

338

Taihape

Homestay
Address: "Harmony",
State Highway One, RD 5, Taihape
Name: Christine and John Tarrant
Telephone: (06) 388 1117
Fax: (06) 388 1117
Beds: 1 Double, 2 single (2 bedrooms)
Bathroom: 1Guests share, separate shower
Tariff: B&B (full) Double $70, Single $40, Children half price.
NZ B&B Vouchers accepted
Nearest Town: Taihape 10 km

Situated on State Highway One 10 km north of Taihape and 20 km south of Waiouru, our farm homestead offers roomy comfort. Now that our children have left home we have two guest bedrooms and separate lounge available with tea / coffee making facilities. The double room also has a single divan bed. Experience country living amongst the real Taihape hills on a 400 hectare farm with stud Romney sheep, Angus cattle, deer and horses - not to mention the resident two cats and dog.

Taihape is the ideal stop over for travellers being halfway between Rotorua and Wellington. The township itself boasts a promising array of cafes and restaurants. It is the gateway to the alpine world of skiing and tramping (Turoa skifield one hour). The local rivers are stocked with fish and river adventures abound - bungy, rafting, kayaking, horse trekking. There are many local gardens open to the public to explore and a golf course 5 km away.

Mangaweka, Rangitikei

Farmstay/Self-contained Accom.
Address: Kawhatau Valley, Mangaweka
Name: Jim & Ruth Rainey
Telephone: (06) 382 5507 **Fax**: (06) 382 5504
Mobile: (025) 549 507
Beds: 2 Single (1 bedroom)
Bathroom: 1 Ensuite
Tariff: B&B (full) Double $80, Single $40, Dinner $20, Baby free.
Nearest Town: Taihape 25km and Mangaweka 15km

Come and enjoy a stay with a typical New Zealand farming family offering fun and conviviality (plus 2500 sheep and cattle, 1 cat, 5 farm dogs, 6 hens, 1 house cow and 4 school-age children!).
Ethanbrae is a 350 hectare hill country farm situated in the beautiful Kawhatau Valley with the homestead being set in a pleasant gardens with magnificent views up the valley.
Accommodation is in a detached room featuring a private verandah with a lovely view. Twin beds with own shower and toilet; tea, coffee and toast-making facilities; homemade biscuits; bread etc supplied and laundry done on request.
Join us on the farm or wander down for a swim in the refreshing Kawhatau River. Jim is also a fishing guide for Rangitikei Anglers and can offer either a half day rafted fishing trip on the beautiful Rangitikei River or streamside guiding. Ideal for district visitors seeking a guided fly fishing experience with minimum commitment.

TARANAKI
WANGANUI
RANGITIKEI

One of the differences between staying at a hotel and a B&B
is that you don't hug the hotel staff when you leave.

Mangaweka

Farmstay/Self-contained Accom.
Address: 'Mairenui Farm Holidays', Ruahine Road, Mangaweka 5456
Name: Sue & David Sweet
Telephone: (06) 382 5564 **Fax**: (06) 382 5885 **Mobile**: (025) 517 545
Email: mairenui.farm.holidays@xtra.co.nz
Beds: 1 Double, 2 Single (2 bedrooms)
Bathroom: 2 Ensuite
Tariff: B&B from $110 - $260, Dinner $35.
Credit Cards: (VISA/MC). NZ B&B Vouchers accepted $30 Surcharge
Nearest Town: Mangaweka 12 km

"Mairenui Farm Holidays" is a farmstay complex comprising two self-contained houses as well as in-house accommodation. Situated on a scenic through route from Mangaweka to Palmerston North, it offers overnight and longer stay accommodation in the spectacular Rangitikei hill country. The 320 hectare property has sheep, cattle, horses, farm dogs, two cats, and Benji, the lovable cockerspaniel.

"The Homestead" has two ensuite bedrooms, (one with a sunken bath) with their own verandahs, tea and coffee making facilities, and homebaked biscuits.

"The Retreat", a three and a half storey architect-designed house set in seven hundred year old native trees, sleeps five in three bedrooms with a shared bathroom. The kitchen amenities are modern, and all linen is provided. Evening meals and breakfasts are available at the Homestead. Tariff - $80 double, $20 each extra person. Breakfasts $10-$12.00.

"The Colonial Villa" is a completely restored hundred year old home which sleeps ten - three doubles, one twin, two singles, with two shared bathrooms. It also has modern kitchen amenities, all linen is provided, and meals can be obtained at the Homestead. Tariff - $25 per person, minimum $60.

On-farm amenities include a concrete tennis court, horse riding, river swimming, farm walks and 4WD farm tours, also petanque and croquet courts. Available locally are river activities, garden visits, four golf courses, an architectural house tour, and scenic flights.

Fine food and wine are provided, with the dinner tariff including a pre-dinner drink and a glass of house wine, and as we have an in-house liquor licence, further drinks may be purchased. A commercial coffee machine ensures perfect espresso, cappucino, or latte!

French and German are spoken.

Directions: *The farm is situated 12 km from Mangaweka and 84 km from Palmerston North on Ruahine Road, three easy hours from Rotorua or Wellington.*

Hunterville

Self-Contained Accommodation

Address: 'Otamaire', R.D. 2, Hunterville
Name: David & Vicky Duncan
Telephone: (06) 322 8027
Fax: (06) 322 8027
Mobile: (025) 447 966
Email: vickymduncan@clear.net.nz
Beds: 1 King, 2 Double, 4 Single (7 bedrooms)
Bathroom: 3 Private
Tariff: Price on application
Nearest Town: Hunterville

We invite you to say at "Otamaire", a lovely 50 year old farm home set in landscaped gardens, 15 minutes off State Highway One. "Otamaire" was until recently our home and is part of an historic sheep and cattle farming business run by four generations of the Duncan family. We have moved to the 100 year old homestead 1 km away so "Otamaire" is available to guests who wish to enjoy privacy of the self-catering option. Large and well appointed the house has a spa bath, dishwasher, automatic washing machine and drier, TV, gas fired AGA cooker, microwave, electric stove, wall panel electric heaters, open fires (wood provided), fully carpeted, linen, towels, duvets, and all other requirements. Daily delivery from Hunterville. Horses and other pets welcome. Stables and grazing available. Well maintained rose gardens, sweeping lawns, mature trees, grass tennis court, swimming in Turakina River or nearby school pool. Garden visits to well known Rangitikei Gardens, eg. Rathmoy, The Ridges, Cross Hills, Westoe and Titoki Point. Lake Namunamu with fishing, row boats and swimming is 30 minute walk away. Otamaire is 30 mins from Rangitikei River for jet boating, rafting, trout fishing and bunji jumping.
Directions: *Phone for brochures, bookings, tariff and directions.*

Hunterville

Farmstay

Address: Vennell's Farmstay, Mangapipi Road, Rewa, R.D.
Name: Phil & Oriel Vennell
Telephone: (06) 328 6780, free phone 0800-220 172 PIN 1837
Fax: (06) 328 6780 **Mobile**: 025-407164
Beds: 1 Queen, 4 Single (3 bedrooms)
Bathroom: 2 Private
Tariff: B&B (full) Double $100 Single $50, Dinner $25. NZ B&B Vouchers accepted $10 pp surcharge
Nearest Town: Hunterville 13 km

VENNELL'S
FARM STAY
HOMESTEAD ACCOMMODATION

TARANAKI WANGANUI RANGITIKEI

We are fifth generation farmers on a 1200 acre sheep and cattle hill country farm. Our spacious home is in a tranquil setting of mature trees and garden with swimming pool. We have a family room with billiard table and cosy living room with a large open fire. Beautiful rural views can be seen from our home and surrounding hills. Enjoy great farm walks or drive to "Stormy Point Lookout" for a view unique in the world. We are situated just off State Highway One near Hunterville on the scenic route to Feilding and in the centre of Rangitikei Private Gardens and golf courses. We are 3 hours drive from Rotorua, 1 1/2 hours from Mt Ruapehu skifields, 2 1/2 hours from Wellington and 30 minutes from Manfield motor sports and Fielddays. Trout fishing, jet boating, bungy jumping can all be enjoyed on the nearby Rangitikei river.
Directions: *Please phone for directions.*

Hunterville

Homestay/Farmstay
Address: Brick 'N Birches,
48 Ongo Road
Telephone: (06) 322 8442
Fax: (06) 322 8442
Mobile: (025) 279 8890
Beds: 1 King, 4 Singles (3 bedrooms)
Bathroom: 3 Ensuite
Tariff: B&B (full) Double $100, Single $60, Dinner by arrangement $25,
Credit Cards. NZ B&B Vouchers accepted $10 surcharge
Nearest Town: Hunterville 2 km

Two minutes from SH1 within Hunterville township, our character two storeyed home set amongst park-like grounds, surrounded by six grazing acres, has been refurbished to provide our visitors with excellent facilities. Spacious airy bedrooms, restful dining and lounge rooms offer a peaceful tranquil atmosphere ensuring enjoyment of a unique rural experience.

Agriculturally interested? Most of New Zealand's diverse land use activities are within thirty minutes driving. In the same driving time, the many Rangitikei River activities, three of New Zealand's finest country golf courses, many bush walks, magnificent country gardens and local historical interests are all available. At 2 1/2 hours from Wellington, 3 hours from Rotorua and 90 minutes from Turoa skifields we are ideally located for your complete leisure enjoyment. We breed Texel sheep on our farm (five minutes away), enjoy golf, gardening, following general sport, current affairs and our family.Pets: Two cats

Directions: *Directions and enquiries - please phone.*

Marton

Farmstay
Address: 'Tataramoa', Howie Road,
R.D. 2, Marton
Name: Janice & Des Gower
Telephone: (06) 327 8778
Beds: 1 Double, 6 Single (4 bedrooms)
Bathroom: 2 Guests share.

Tariff: B&B (continental) $40 per person, Pre-schoolers half price,
Dinner $20 per person BYO, Light snack on request. Picnic table.
NZ B&B Vouchers accepted
Nearest Town: Marton - 9 mins drive (6 miles)

Tataramoa is a 140 year colonial wooden homestead set in peaceful landscaped gardens, surrounded by spacious beautiful mature New Zealand bush filled by many native birds. We have 1000 acres on which we run sheep, cattle and cropping paddocks. There are great opportunities for interesting walks around the flats, hills and valleys. Centre of garden and heritage home visits. Near Palmerston North and Wanganui. A friendly and homely atmosphere with welcome cosy open log fires. Traditional New Zealand farm meal with private lounge if preferred. We really enjoy opening our home to both Kiwis and visitors from all over the world. Ample verandah space for you to relax and unwind.

Directions: *From Marton township turn at Westpac Bank roundabout to Wanganui for 3 miles. Turn right at Fern Flats Road, proceed and turn left to Waimutu Road. Drive until 'Tataramoa" signpost. Farm at end of road through avenue of trees.*

Rangitikei
Historic Home, Farmstay, Guest House, Conference Centre
Address: 'Maungaraupi',
Leedstown Road, R.D. 1, Marton
Name: Kaylene Rose
Telephone: (06) 327 7820
Fax: (06) 327-8619
Beds: 5 Double, 5 Single (8 bedrooms)
Bathroom: 3 Ensuite, 1 Guests share
Tariff: B&B (full) Double $120-$160, Single $90.
Dinner $30. EFTPOS and all credit cards accepted.   NZ B&B Vouchers accepted
$15 surcharge
Nearest Town: Marton or Hunterville. On State Highway One. 10 minutes.

Let Historical Maungaraupi take you back to an era when life was enjoyed in good style.
We invite you to come and experience a unique lifestyle of a 10,000 square foot two storey tudor style home set in five acres of native bush, extensive lawns and lovely gardens. Enjoy the romantic touch of strutting peacocks and abundant native bird life, savour the extensive view of the Ruahine Ranges and rolling farm land, relax in front of one of the open fireplaces, and dine in style at a 16 seat antique five legged Kauri table.
The guest rooms are sunny and attractive with electric blankets on all beds. Three double rooms have ensuite bathrooms, and two have a private balcony.
The atmosphere at Maungaraupi is friendly, relax about the house, take a bush or farm walk, play billiards, tennis or croquet or travel a short distance to play golf, visit well-known gardens, or trout fish, white water raft or jetboat on the scenic Rangitikei River. Mount Ruapehu's Turoa Skifield is 1.5 hours drive away, Wanganui 30 minutes, Palmerston North 40 minutes, and Marton or Hunterville 10 minutes.

Hawkes Bay

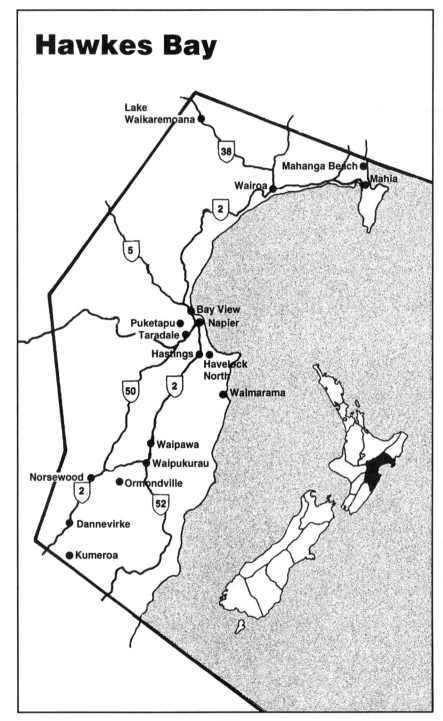

Lake Waikaremoana, Te Urewera National Park

Homestay
Address: 9 Rotten Row,
Tuai village, Highway 38.
Name: Judy Doyle
Telephone: (06) 837 3701
Beds: 1 Queen, 2 Single (2 bedrooms)
Bathroom: 1 Family Share
Tariff: B&B (full) Double $70, Single $40,
Dinner $20. Credit Cards accepted.
NZ B&B Vouchers accepted.
Nearest Town: Wairoa 55kms.

Lake Waikaremoana is a spectacular and unique Native Forest wilderness area on the eastern boundary of Urewera National Park.

This modernised and comfortable bungalow (warm in winter, cool in summer) is located in Tuai Village, built originally as homes for Hydro-Electicity Stations, which still generate electricity, and it adjoins the Whakamarino Lakefront Reserve.

Tuai village nestles 10 minutes east of the awesome natural beauty of Waikaremoana, rich in bird life, and with a chain of lakes abounding with trout.

As we love to share the peace and unspoilt beauty of our surroundings, let us assist you to explore this awesome area.

Arrangements and advice available for fishing, bush walking, boating, canoeing or hunting. Rods etc for guests to hire. Picnic meals, bbq's to your convenience.

Dusky, the cat and I look forward to welcoming you to our relaxed lifestyle in the safe and friendly village of Tuai.

Mahanga Beach, Mahia Peninsula

Farmstay+Self-contained Accommodation.
Address: Postal: "Reo Moana", R D 8,
Mahanga Beach, Nuhaka,
Hawkes Bay
Name: Nicholas & Louise Schick
Telephone: (06) 837 5898 **Fax**: (06) 837 5990
Email: miklos@xtra.co.nz
Beds: 2 Double, 2 Single (4 bedrooms).
Cottage: 2 Double, 2 Single, 2 Bathrooms (sleeps 9).
Bathroom: 2 Private
Tariff: "Reomoana" B&B: (continental) Double $100, Single $60,
Children under 12yrs. half price, Dinner $30.
Cottage Tariff: $75 Double, $15 each extra person. Discount for weekly rental.
NZ B&B Vouchers accepted $40 surcharge for Double only.
Nearest Town: Wairoa 50km, Gisborne 80km

"Reo Moana" - The voice of the sea. Pacific Ocean-front farm at beautiful Mahia Peninsula. Our spacious rustic home with cathedral ceilings, hand carved furniture overlooks the Pacific with breathtaking views. A few steps to bush walks, native bird watching, mustering sheep and cattle. Outside pets, golden labrador and cat. Swimming, surfing, fishing, shell-fishing, horse back riding on miles of white sandy beaches or play golf, visit the Mahia reserve, Morere hot pools and thermal swimming pool. Hunting, fishing excursions possible. The host is fluent in German, Italian and Hungarian. We have both travelled extensively and particularly enjoy meeting overseas visitors. Cottage in avocado orchard: 2 minutes walk to beach ideal for a family holiday beside the sea. Spacious, self contained and simply furnished. Breakfast and dinner not included.   Please telephone/fax for reservations, directions. Nick and Louise Schick, R.D.8, Mahanga Beach, Nuhaka, Hawkes Bay. Ph:06 837 5898 Fax: 06 837 5990.

HAWKES BAY

345

Mahia

Farm/Self-contained Acom.
Address: Tunanui Station, Tunanui Road, RD8, Opoutama-Mahia
Name: Ray & Leslie Thompson
Telephone: (06) 837 5790 **Fax**: (06) 837 5797 **Mobile**: 025-240 2421
Beds: 1 Queen, 1 Double 1 Single (3 bedrooms)
Bathroom: 1 Private
Tariff: Accommodation only: $120 per night. Extra persons $25 each.
Meals by arrangement dinner $20-$40 pp. Continental Breakfast $12 pp.
NZ B&B Vouchers accepted, Two vouchers for 2 people.
Nearest Town: Wairoa 50km

A warm friendly welcome awaits you at Tunanui, a 3200 acre hill country property overlooking the beautiful Mahia Peninsula. Farming sheep and cattle, our family of four, enjoy meeting people.

We offer guests stylish seclusion in our self-contained cottages, providing independence and privacy. A great place to get away from it all and ideal for longer stays. Bookings essential.

The Cottage, 90 years old, is nestled close to native bush, fully restored, furnished with some antique furniture and has all the mod cons. Three bedrooms, open fire in lounge, well-equipped kitchen, tiled bathroom with twin showers. Laundry. Front & back verandah. Barbeque. The Cottage is suitable for a group or family and is the perfect hideaway for a couple.

The Waimare Farmhouse, situated in its own private gardens has panoramic views of farmland, Mahia Peninsula and the sea. Built in 1975, Waimare has recently been redecorated to provide comfortable, stylish accomodation for up to 8 people. It features 4 bedrooms, a lounge with an open fire, a fully-equipped kitchen including a dishwasher, dining room, 2 bathrooms, laundry and garaging. Underfloor heating in some rooms. It is the ideal getaway for a family, study group, or work retreats. Price on application. Minimum stay 2-3 nights.

Guests have access to a fax and each cottage has its own telephone. Phone card needed for toll calls.

On our property, guests can use our grass tennis court, enjoy the garden, take farm walks or visit the historic Kopuawhara Valley. Horses are a family interest and horse-riding, for experienced riders is available by arrangement $25 pp per hour. Or take a dip in a river swimming hole, fly fish for trout in our small catch and release stream. Nearby attractions; beaching, surfing, hot mineral pools at Morere, golf, gardens, caving, fishing, marae visits, Mahia Reserve. Gisborne city "First city in the world to see the sun" and wineries, 1 hours drive.

Eastwoodhill and Hackfalls aboretums and Lake Waikaremoana 1 1/2 hours drive
Directions: *At Opoutama, follow the Mahanga Road for 2km. Turn left into Tunanui Road, we are 4km up the road, on the right.*

Members of
The New Zealand Association
Farm & Home Host Inc.
maintain the highest standards &
are always delighted to welcome
guests into their homes.

Bay View
Beach Homestay
Address: 'Kilbirnie'
84 Le Quesne Road,
Bay View, Napier
Name: Jill & John Grant
Telephone: (06) 836 6929
Beds: 1 firm Queen,
1 soft Double (2 bedrooms)
Bathroom: 1 Ensuite, 1 Spa
Tariff: B&B (full) Double $70,
Single $50, Dinner $20pp,
Not suitable for children. Credit Cards.
NZ B&B Vouchers accepted
Nearest Town: Napier 12km.

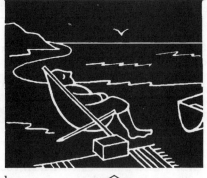

When we moved with our pets to Bayview on an unspoiled fishing beach, people said "it's lovely, you'll like it there". Two years later we still do. Kilbirnie is a few minutes north of Napier airport adjacent to the Taupo turn off and the Pacific Highway via Gisborne. The Pacific Ocean on one side and vineyards on the other give the upstairs rooms panoramic views. The lights of Napier and the moon rising from the sea enchant us as do the sunsets. We invite you to share our local knowledge, fresh imaginative meals, real coffee and juice, tea making facilities and books to read while enjoying these modern peaceful surroundings. We hope to make your stay in Napier memorable.
Directions: *From Taupo first left after intersection Highway Two Franklin Road to Le Quesne, proceed to far end beachfront. From Napier first right after Bayview*

Bay View, Napier
Countrystay and Self Contained
Address: The Grange, 263 Hill Road, Eskdale, Hawkes Bay
Name: Roslyn and Don Bird
Telephone: (06) 836 6666 **Fax**: (06) 836 6456 **Mobile**: (025) 281 5738
Beds: <u>Farmstay</u>: 1 Twin
<u>Self Contained</u>: 1 King or Twin, 1 Double, 2 Singles, (2 bedrooms). (Cot etc)
Bathrooms: <u>Farmstay</u>: 1 Family share plus Private toilet.
<u>Self Contained</u>: 1 Private.
Tariff: <u>Farmstay</u>: B&B (Full), Double $70, Single $50
<u>Self Contained</u>: Double $75, Single $50, $20 extra person
Breakfast provisions $7.50 pp (optional), Dinner $25 pp
Credit Cards accepted.

Nearest Town: Napier 12 Minutes Sth, Bayview 3 minutes.

*In the heart of a thriving wine region overlooking the picturesque Esk Valley, is **The Grange** our modern self contained Lodge built in natural timber. Private, spacious accomodation offering relaxing peaceful surrounds with spectacular rural, coastal and city views. Stay and be treated to farmbaking, tempting snacks and preserves (shortbread and chocolate chippies are "The Grange" favourites). For those staying in our home, our children Rachael 8 1/2, Jeremy 11 and Jarred 12, also enjoy making new friends and sharing their many pets, (bottle fed lambs). We are a fun-loving, active family. Don is involved in the wine industry and Roslyn, Drew (dog) and Sparkie (cat) manage the farmstay and farm, milking Saanan goats (you're welcome to try!) We also have sheep, cows, pigs and chickens. Play petanque, visit wineries, gardens, sea / river rambles, swimming, fishing, tramping, Upland game shooting and Art Deco Napier with its many attractions to explore. Taupo (Kinloch) holiday home also available. Smoking outside.*
Directions: *1km off H5 Eskdale or 2km off H2 at Bay View.*

Taradale, Napier

Homestay
Address: 'Victoria Lodge',
50 Puketapu Road, Taradale
Name: Don & Sheila Copas
Telephone: (06) 844 2182
Beds: 1 Double, 3 Single (3 bedrooms)
Bathroom: 1 Guests share
Tariff: B&B (full) Double $60, Single $30,
Children half price; Dinner $20. NZ B&B Vouchers accepted
Nearest Town: Napier 10 km

Our home is situated in an attractive and interesting one acre garden with sheep in the orchard, a putting green and a swimming pool contributing to its unique rural atmosphere although it is only five minutes walk from the town of Taradale and ten minutes drive from Napier. The climate of Hawkes Bay justifies the title of "Sunny Napier" and the area in and around the city has much to offer of interest and activity, i.e. sailing, fishing, windsurfing, bush walks, wine trail etc. Napier is also well endowed with tourist attractions - museums, aquarium, Marineland and can lay a claim to being the 'Art Deco' centre of the world. We love to entertain and you will be assured of a warm welcome at our comfortable family home from us and our dog and cat.
Directions: *10 km west from Napier. Area maps are available from the Information Centre on Marine Parade or the A.A. Centre in Dickens Street, Napier or phone us for directions.*

Napier

Homestay
Address: 19 Alamein Crescent,
Napier
Name: Pam & Bill McCulloch
Telephone: (06) 843 6744
Fax: (06) 843 6729
Beds: 1 King, 4 Single + Cot (3 bedrooms)
Bathroom: 1 Guests share, 1 Family share
Tariff: B&B (continental) Double $70, Single $35, Dinner $20,
Children under 12 half price. NZ B&B Vouchers accepted
Nearest Town: Napier 3km

We are retired and for the past 8 years have enjoyed home-hosting an ever-increasing circle of friends.
Bill attends Rotary and Probus.
Our rooms have a comfortable King-size bed or single beds, all with electric blankets. Bathroom facilities are shared. Children's toys, cot and high chair available.
Relax in our well-kept garden by the pool or patio, and admire one handsome Cat! Our generous breakfast, served at a time to suit you, may include freshly squeezed juice, local fruit, choice of cereals and yoghurt, home-made preserves, toast, tea or coffee. Dinner available any evening by arrangement, and feel free to relax with us in the lounge.
We have off-street parking for your car. Napier is famous for its Art Deco architecture and surrounding vineyards, has many tourist attractions, plenty of sunshine, shops and restaurants.
Please - no smoking in the house.

Napier

Homestay
Address: 17 Cobden Road, Napier
Name: Kay & Stewart Spence
Telephone: (06) 835 9454 **Fax**: (06) 835 9454
Beds: 2 Queen, 2 Single (2 bedrooms)
Bathroom: 2 Ensuites
Tariff: B&B (full) Double $85, Single $55,
Credit Cards Visa M/C NZ B&B Vouchers accepted $15 Surcharge.
Nearest Town: Napier 1 Km

Our early colonial 1880, two-storeyed home with comfortable and modern facilities is pleasantly situated in a sunny position on Napier Hill. The home is set in attractive grounds spread over almost an acre, in quiet area - just a 10 to 15 minute walk from Napier City Centre.
Two guest rooms include a Queen bed and a single bed and ensuite bathrooms, one suite also includes lounge. All rooms are spacious with lounge chairs and tea making facilities and TV's. Beds have electric blankets and woollen underlays.
We have been welcomed into private homes in New Zealand and overseas and wish to extend a warm welcome to you to share our home in the Art Deco city in sunny Hawkes Bay.
We will be happy to meet you at the Hawkes Bay Airport, Napier Railway Station or City bus depot.
Directions: *Port end Marine Parade, Coote Road, right Thompson Road, left Cobden Road*

Napier

Homestay
Address: 7 Charles Street,
Westshore, Napier
Name: Sheila & Rob Comrie
Telephone: (06) 835 9679
Email: robcom@clear.net.nz
Beds: 1 Double, 2 Single (2 bedrooms)
Bathroom: 1 Guests share
Tariff: B&B (full) Double $65, Single $40, Dinner $20pp.
NZ B&B Vouchers accepted
Nearest Town: Napier 4 Kms

We have retired from farming life and having travelled overseas and enjoyed B & Bs, we would be pleased to share our comfortable modern home with people who enjoy a homely atmosphere. From the house you step out on to a pleasant, safe beach and are only 5 minutes drive from central Napier or the Airport. Hastings, Taradale and Havelock North are all within a 30 minute drive. Accommodation, on the ground floor, consists of lounge, dining room, two double bedrooms, guest bathroom and separate toilet. Kitchen available for tea making. Laundry available. Restaurants handy or dinner by arrangement. We sleep upstairs. All local attractions available including beach walks, windsurfing and sailing almost on the doorstep. Off street parking. Fax available to guests - Toll charges.
Directions: *Please phone. Pick-up from Airport, Station or Bus depot if required.*

Napier

Homestay
Address: 9 Milton Terrace, Napier
Name: Helen & Robert McGregor
Telephone: (06) 835 7434
Mobile: 025-249 2040
Beds: 1 Double (1 bedroom)
Bathroom: 1 Private (bath & shower)
Tariff: B&B (full) Double $75, Single $50.
Credit cards. NZ B&B Vouchers accepted
Nearest Town: Napier 1.3km

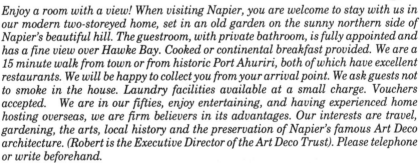

Enjoy a room with a view! When visiting Napier, you are welcome to stay with us in our modern two-storeyed home, set in an old garden on the sunny northern side of Napier's beautiful hill. The guestroom, with private bathroom, is fully appointed and has a fine view over Hawke Bay. Cooked or continental breakfast provided. We are a 15 minute walk from town or from historic Port Ahuriri, both of which have excellent restaurants. We will be happy to collect you from your arrival point. We ask guests not to smoke in the house. Laundry facilities available at a small charge. Vouchers accepted. We are in our fifties, enjoy entertaining, and having experienced home hosting overseas, we are firm believers in its advantages. Our interests are travel, gardening, the arts, local history and the preservation of Napier's famous Art Deco architecture. (Robert is the Executive Director of the Art Deco Trust). Please telephone or write beforehand.

Please help us provide the best hospitality in the world.
Fill in a comment form for every place you stay.

Napier
Homestay
Address: 'Hillcrest', 4 George Street,
Hospital Hill, Napier.
Name: Noel & Nancy Lyons
Telephone: (06) 835 1812
Beds: 1 Double, 2 Single (2 bedrooms)
Bathroom: 1 Guests share
Tariff: B&B (continental) Double $65, Single $40,
Dinner by arrangement $20pp. NZ B&B Vouchers accepted
Nearest Town: 10 mins walk from city centre

A warm welcome awaits you in our comfortable modern, smoke-free home, with panoramic views of Hawke Bay and the hills. All rooms open onto spacious decks where chairs invite you to relax in peace and enjoy the garden. The two guest rooms are downstairs with an adjacent lounge, colour TV and the use of your own telephone. The beds have duvets and electric blankets. Laundry facilities are inclusive. A feature of our home is the beautiful native Rimu timber used throughout. We have travelled extensively and welcome the opportunity of meeting visitors, and sharing our knowledge of this area with you. Our interests are travel, gardening, woodturning, embroidery and live theatre. Off street parking is available. Our holiday home, on the foreshore at Mahia Beach is available for a relaxing holiday.
Directions: *Please phone. Pick-up from Airport, Bus or Train if required.*

Napier
Accommodation

Address: 'Anleigh Heights',
115 Chaucer Road North, Napier
Name: Allan & Anne Tolley
Telephone: (06) 835 1188 **Fax**: (06) 835-1032
Beds: 1 KIng, 1 Queen, 1 Double 4 Poster
Bathroom: 3 Ensuite
Tariff: B&B (special) Double $135-$160. Single $95, Children welcome.
Dinner $45 pp. Credit cards. NZ B&B Vouchers accepted
Nearest Town: Napier 5 mins.

Experience the character and charm of a bygone era. Anleigh Heights offers quality accommodation in Napier's grandest historic home. Situated high on the Napier hill, next to the hospital, our home has commanding views over Hawkes Bay.
We have recreated the cossetted lifestyle of the Edwardian House Party for our guests;
- you are greeted at the door by your hosts or family dog
- your rooms are named not numbered
- tea and coffee is served on a silver tray, in fine china, with tea strainers and silver pots
- open fires, flowers, antique furniture and personal possessions all make you feel as if you're part of the household
- breakfast is a house speciality with a varied menu and is served in the elegant dining room.
For reasons of historic preservation and good health there is no smoking in the house. Off-street parking is available, or we can collect you.

351

Napier City
Bed & Breakfast
Address: Madeira Bed & Breakfast
6 Madeira Road, Napier
Name: Eric & Julie Ball
Telephone: (06) 835 5185
Email: julieball@clear.net.nz
Beds: 1 Queen (1 bedroom)
Bathroom: 1 Family share
Tariff: B&B (full) Double $75, Single $50, Children by arrangement.
NZ B&B Vouchers accepted
Nearest Town: Napier - 3 minute walk

Our home, rebuilt after the 1931 earthquake, commands outstanding views over Hawke Bay and Napier City. As local residents of many years, we can assist you to fill in your days, whether it be sightseeing, wine tasting, golf or dining out, and with parking on site, a 3 minute walk takes you into the city. Your double room has a Queen size bed and ajoining toilet and handbasin. Also tea making facilities. Breakfast may be served on our veranda in the morning sun or in the dining room at a time to suit you. We provide good healthy foods and fresh fruit when available. We have an old, small dog and a cat. Testimony to our popularity can be seen in our visitors book "What a gorgeous place and great hospitality," U.S.A. "The highlight of our trip," England. "We felt most welcome and enjoyed our stay."
Directions: *Please phone.*

Greenmeadows, Napier
Homestay
Address: 7 Forward St, Greenmeadows, Napier
Name: 'Kerry Lodge', Bill & Jenny Hoffman
Telephone: (06) 844 9630 **Fax**: (06) 844 1450
Mobile: (025) 932 874
Beds: 1 King, 1 Queen, 1 Twin (3 bedrooms)
Bathroom: 1 Ensuite (mobility), 1 Guest share
Tariff: B&B (full) Double Ensuite $90, Double $80, Single $50.
Children half price. Credit cards.
NZ B&B Vouchers accepted Surcharge $20 per couple.
Nearest Town: Napier - 8 mins away.

Set in tranquil gardens, close to shops, tourist attractions and wineries. Nestled among trees we invite our guests to share the warmth and comfort of home.
Our large rooms offer independent heating, tea and coffee facilities, colour TV, and electric blankets. We have single, queen and kingsize beds. Full laundry facilities are also available.
For our guest who prefer the ease of mobility suite, we offer full wheelchair access, and a specially designed bathroom for their convenience.
Your day with us will begin with a scrumptious breakfast in our sun filled dining room. Maps and brochures of local attractions are available for you to browse through. After touring the history rich twin cities of Napier and Hastings, relax in our private spa or sparking pool, or view our antique doll collection.
Directions: *Head towards Taradale, turn right into Avenue Rd after Greenmeadows shops, then 1st left into Forward Street.*

Bluff Hill - Napier

Homestay
Address: "Treeways", 1 Lighthouse Road,
Bluff Hill, Napier
Name: Maurie & Cheryl Keeling
Telephone: (06) 835 6567 **Fax**: (06) 835 6567
Email: mckeeling@clear.net.nz
Beds: 1 Double, 2 Singles (2 bedrooms)
Bathroom: 1 Guest share
Tariff: B&B (full) Double $75, Single $50, Dinner $20.
NZ B&B Vouchers accepted
Nearest Town: Napier central city 1km

Peaceful, private, 10 minutes walk to the city centre or Bluff Hill lookout, and set amongst bush and gardens with pleasant views over the sea and northern coastline. A large sunny terrace with tables and chairs, flower garden and lilly pond provide a relaxing atmosphere for people and native birds. Our home with spacious living areas, rimu timber floors and comfortable furnishings is warm and friendly and yours to enjoy. Two double bedrooms, one with double bed, one with Kingsize convertible to two singles have electric blankets, bedside lights, heating and writing desk and chair. Home grown fruits and vegetables are a speciality with meals and we offer complimentary local wine with dinner. We have travelled extensively, enjoy theatre, the outdoors and conversation.
Directions: *Tourist Drive 11 to Bluff Hill Lookout.*

Napier

Homestay
Address: 147 Harold Holt Ave., Napier
Name: Don & Ruth McLeod
Telephone: (06) 843 2521 **Fax**: (06) 843 2520
Email: donmcld@clear.net.nz
Beds: 1 Queen in studio with ensuite. Twin and Single (2 bedrooms)
Bathroom: 1 Ensuite in studio, 1 Family share
Tariff: B&B (full) Queen Ensuite $80, Twin $70, Single $40.
Credit Cards NZ B&B Vouchers accepted
Nearest Town: Napier 5km

Our home is situated on the outskirts of Napier City. It has a rural outlook and is in close proximity to local orchards market gardens and wineries. It is 8 minutes by car to many tourist attractions around the centre of Napier City and 5 minutes by car to Taradale shopping centre.
Our home is designed for outdoor living with an attractive private patio to make the most of the sunny Hawkes Bay climate.
We have enjoyed the comforts and friendliness of Bed & Breakfast homes in New Zealand and overseas and look forward to sharing our home with travellers.
Our interests include travel, gardening including orchid growing and keeping in touch with family and friends in New Zealand and overseas. We both have a background in teaching.
We ask guests not to smoke in the house. We will collect you from airport bus or train if required. Members of NZ Association Farm & Home Hosts Inc.

Relax – Don't try to drive too far in one day.

Napier
Bed & Breakfast
Address: 17A Gallipoli Road, Napier
Name: Jill & Gary Affleck
Telephone: (06) 843 6098
Beds: 1 Double, 2 Single (2 bedrooms)
Bathroom: 1 Guests share
Tariff: B&B (full) Double $70, Single $45.
NZ B&B Vouchers accepted
Nearest Town: Napier 2 kms

Hello fellow travellers - a warm welcome awaits you at our home.
Having travelled extensively ourselves both in New Zealand and overseas we have experienced the friendships that home hosting brings and would love to share our place with you.
Our modern two-storied home is situated overlooking Onekawa Park with its indoor / outdoor swimming pools and tennis courts, and is only a 5 minute drive to central city, Westshore Beach and Taradale. Wineries, orchards, Hastings and Havelock North are all within 20 minutes drive.
The upstairs bedrooms each have TVs and electric blankets and the adjoining guest lounge has tea / coffee making facilities. As longtime residents of Napier we can advise you about sightseeing, dining, sporting activities and local wineries.
Directions: *Please phone or write. We are happy to transport you to and from train, bus or plane if required.*

Indoors.

Taradale, Napier
Homestay
Address: "Garden House", 67 Wharerangi Road, Napier
Name: Dell & Noel Bowkett
Telephone: (06) 844 0685
Fax: (06) 835 9315
Beds: 1 Double,
2 Single (2 bedrooms)
Bathroom: 1 Guests share
Tariff: B&B (continental) Double $60,
Single $45.
NZ B&B Vouchers accepted
Nearest Town: Napier 10 mins drive

A couple in our mid-fifties we are young at heart with a love of life and people.
We very much enjoy sharing our cosy home with travellers and visitors, and be you from within New Zealand or overseas the welcome is the same - warm and genuine. We are delighted to provide pleasant surroundings, hospitality, comfort and commanding rural views with a touch of the city lights. Only ten minutes drive to the city centre or Westshore beach. Just moments from the attractive Mission Hills where the Mission Monastery and restaurant stands majestically with local wineries nestling at its base. An easy trek to the top of Sugar Loaf Mountain lookout is close by giving commanding views of the Heretaunga Plains.
Pet: friendly family Moggie.
Please phone or write beforehand.

Napier

Homestay
Address: "Ourhome",
4 Hospital Terrace, Napier
Name: Nina & Nancy Hamlin
Telephone: (06) 835 7358
Email: OURHOMEHOMESTAY@xtra.co.nz
Beds: 2 Single (1 bedroom) + 1 Double bed-settee available in guest lounge.
Bathroom: 1 Private
Tariff: B&B (continental) Double $75, Single $50.
Credit Cards NZ B&B Vouchers accepted $5 surcharge
Nearest Town: Napier 1km

*Wonderful views of sea and hills from every room (and the private sunny patio) in our
very attractive guest suite. We offer accommodation for up to four in one group, the
bedroom having two single beds, guests' lounge a double bed-settee. Private separate
entry. Tea / coffee making facilities; TV, fridge. Laundry available.
No smoking, please!*
*A three minute drive takes you to the heart of our famous Art Deco city and Marine
Parade, catering for a wide range of interests. Noted Hawkes' Bay wineries (several
offering great food too!), popular craft outlets, Hastings City, Havelock North and
Clifton (the start of tours to the gannets at Cape Kidnappers) are all within a thirty-
minute drive. Off street parking available.*
*We will be happy to collect you from public transport, and look forward to welcoming
you to "Ourhome".*

Napier

Boutique Guest Establishment
Address: The "Large" House,
4 Hadfield Terrace, Napier Hill, Napier
Name: The "Large" House, Judith & John
Telephone: (06) 835 0000
Fax: (06) 835 2244
Mobile: (025) 245 2870
Email: large@xtra.co.nz>
Beds: 1 Super King (1 Twin), 1 King, 1 Queen, (3 bedrooms)
Bathroom: 2 Ensuite, 1 Private
Tariff: B&B (special) Double $155, Single $120, Twin $165, Smoke free inside.
Credit Cards (VISA/MC/AMEX/DINERS).
Nearest Town: A five minute stroll to central Napier City.

*Choose to step back in time ..... to a world of character and courtesy, to where today's needs
blend with the charm of yesteryear.*
*Circa 1858, The "Large" House takes its name from the original owner James Stanibridge
Large Esquire. Share with us one of Napier's earliest landmarks. Discretely nestled in a
picturesque setting of cascading gardens, this historic homestead offers an idyllic private
environment with a backdrop of breathtaking views of bush surrounds and seascape. The
exquisite Grape, Chardonnay and Champagne bedrooms have charming individual features,
sumptuous bed furnishings and classical bathrooms. Relax in elegant comfort in the Guest
Lounge and watch the ships go by. Breakfast on the gracious balcony or in the stunning
conservatory, each with captivating views and the sounds of birdlife, waterfall and waves
breaking on the shore. Romantic retreat, business haven .... perfect for the discerning
traveller. Enjoy your Hawke's Bay experience in The "Large" House.*
Directions: *Kindly telephone for directions.*
Home Page: http://www.friars.co.nz/hosts/largehouse/html

Napier
Bed & Breakfast
Address: "Turangi"
1 Hukarere Road,
Bluff Hill, Napier
Name: Joan & David Donaldson
Telephone: (06) 835 7795
Fax: (06) 835 7096
Mobile: (025) 748 218
Beds: 1 Queen, 2 Single (2 bedrooms)
Bathroom: 1 Ensuite, 1 Private, 1 Family Share
Tariff: B&B (full) Double Suite $90,
Single Suite $70, Treble $115,
Single Room $55. Credit Cards. NZ B&B Vouchers accepted $20 surcharge
Nearest Town: Napier 0.7km

Turangi "From a High Place" a classic two storey 1930's house, our home is set in a Mediterranean garden with lawn and mature trees and has incomparable views of Hawkes Bay and Napier city. Level access off street parking. Private guest suite observes the sunrise over the pacific ocean and the lights of Art Deco Napier, which has been called "Nice of the South Pacific". Elegant suite comprises Queen and Single beds with quality linen, own sitting room, tea making, TV, refrigerator. Ensuite bathroom has separate bath and shower. Also 1 single room. Five minutes walk to Napier by picturesque heritage trail, yet only sound is of birds and sea. Cooked or continental breakfast served in sunny dining room overlooking garden. Comfortable furnished with art and antiques, open fires, garden flowers. Non smoking. Pick up from terminals.
Directions: *Corner of Clyde and Hukarere Roads, past Girls High School.*

Napier
Guest House
Address: 471 Marine Parade,
Napier
Name: Neil and Jeanette
"Blue Water Lodge"
Telephone: 06-835 8929
Fax: 06-835 8929
Mobile: 025-500 192
Email: bobbrown@voyager.co.nz
Beds: 6 Double, 9 Single (9 bedrooms)
Bathroom: 1 Ensuite, 2 Guests share
Tariff: B&B (continental) Double with ensuite $70, Double $60, Single $30,
Children under 14 years $10. All credit cards accepted.
Not open during winter months.
Nearest Town: Napier

Blue Water Lodge is on the beach front opposite the Aquarium car park on Napier's popular Marine Parade.
Close to all local tourist attractions and within walking distance to the city centre, information centre, family restaurants, RSA and Cosmopolitan Club.
Owner operated with 1 dog.

Napier
Self Contained Accommodation
Address: "The Coach-House",
9 Gladstone Road, Napier
Name: Jan Chalmers
Telephone: (06) 835 6126
Beds: 1 Queen, 2 Single (2 bedrooms)
Bathroom: 1 Private
Tariff: B&B (full) Double $100, Single $40. Four people $160.
Dinner $20 (by arrangement). Children school age $25, little chilren free.
NZ B&B Vouchers accepted $30 surcharge
Nearest Town: Napier (5 minutes walk to centre)

The Coach-House built of kauri in the late 1800's, the Coach-house is tastefully renovated and totally self-contained. A lovely Mediterranean style garden on the hill surrounds the Coach-house, and is within sight and sound of the sea. Inside there are two bedrooms (one upstairs) sleeping four people, open plan kitchen / dining / living room. Bathroom adjacent with separate toilet. The fridge will be full of breakfast 'goodies' including "treats". Fresh flowers in the bedrooms. TV, radio and glossy magazines are also included. There are private outdoor living areas including a sunny deck for all fresco dining. Off-street parking and easy access complete the picture. If privacy and relaxation is what you want in an attractive and comfortable home-away-from-home, then the Coach-house is for you. I am also happy to be a 'taxi driver' and do your washing.

Napier
Homestay B&B
Address: No 11,
11 Sealy Road, Napier
Name: Phyllida and Bryan Isles
Telephone: (06) 834 4372
Mobile: (025) 246 3968
Beds: 1 Queen, 1 Twin(2 bedrooms)
Bathroom: 1 Guests share
Tariff: B&B (special) Double $90,
Single $50. NZ B&B Vouchers accepted $20
Nearest Town: Napier 0.5 km

The name says it all!
You will score our home more than 10 for comfort, convenience, and conviviality.
Comfort: Spacious, sunny, quality rooms - each with TV, Tea making facilities, electric blankets, good linen, heater, hairdryer and writing table. Guest toilet and large bathroom just across hall.
Convenience: New hill villa, level access, off street parking, great views. An easy walk to city, cafes, Ahuriri and Napier attractions, dairy, takeaways. Drive or bus to Hawkes Bay's many wineries or gannets.
Conviviality: A warm welcome and all the help you need to make your stay enjoyable. A selection of special breakfasts are offered and while you sit enjoying them and the view, you can plan your day or Bryan will share with you some of Napier's history. We have travelled ourselves and enjoy meeting others.
We look forward to meeting you.
We have a cat and a dog, and please no smoking indoors.
Please telephone or write beforehand.

Napier

B&B
Address: 30 Fitzroy Road, Napier
Name: Hannah House
Telephone: (06) 835 0050
Fax: (06) 835 4455
Mobile: (025) 579 289
Email: Catlover@Clear.net.nz
Beds: 2 Queen, 2 Double (4 bedrooms)
Bathroom: 3 Private, 1 Family Share
Tariff: B&B (full) Double $125-$145,
Single $115, Dinner $30.
Not suitable for children. All major credit cards accepted.
Nearest Town: Napier (5 minutes walk)

An atmosphere of Old World charm and elegance awaits the enthusiastic traveller to one of New Zealand's fine old homes. Hannah house, designed by Louis Hay and built for the Hannah family in 1914, is noted for its distinctive architectural style.

Experience the romantic atmosphere of a bygone era, relax and enjoy the treasures this magnificent home has to offer. A roaring open fire on a cold winters night, or a moonlit garden on a balmy summers evening.

A great place for the individual or small groups, spacious lounges provide privacy, with our main rooms also providing individual ensuites and connected by their own lounge. We also have 2 cats and 2 dogs. Evening meals can be served by prior arrangement, or the large variety of restaurants in the CBD are just a 5 minute walk away. Picnic hampers are also available for either lunch or dinner, by prior arrangement.

Napier

Separate House
Address: Marewa, Napier
Name: Deco Dreams
Telephone: (06) 844 6685
Fax: (06) 844 6685
Mobile: (021) 688 085
Email: vnapier@clear.net.nz
Beds: 1 Double, 2 Single (2 bedrooms)
Bathroom: 1 Private, Only one party at at time.
Tariff: B&B (special/continental) 1 Bedroom $160, 2 Bedrooms $200.
Credit cards: Visa/Mastercard.
Nearest Town: Napier (5 minutes)

Situated in a tree-lined avenue in Napier's Art Deco suburb, this 1930's house is a delightful example of the Art Deco style.

There is a double and a twin bedroom, bathroom with shower over bath, lounge, dining room, fully equipped kitchen and laundry. The house is decorated with 1930's furniture and fittings, and has a private deck with all day sun.

Experience the ambience of life between the wars. Imagine yourself back in those heady days of the great Gatsby, when style and speed ruled, and the tango and charleston were popular. Play 78's on the gramophone, watch 1930's movies on the video and browse through publications of the times.

Napier City centre, with its Art Deco buildings and waterfront attractions, is 5 minutes away. Activities within a 30 minute drive include wineries, gannet safaris, trout fishing, golf, beaches and bush walks.

Directions: Please phone for reservations and directions.

Napier
Self Contained Accommodation B&B
Address: 3 Cameron Terrace, Napier
Name: Inglenook
Telephone: (06) 834 2922
Mobile: (025) 414 992
Beds: 2 Double, 2 Single (twin) (3 bedrooms)
Bathroom: 1 Ensuite, 1 Guests share
Tariff: B&B (special) Double $75, Single $45, Children on application.
No credit cards. NZ B&B Vouchers accepted $10 surcharge
Nearest Town: Napier

Inglenook is situated on the Hill in a peaceful garden setting and offers expansive views of the City Centre across Marine Parade and the sea to Cape Kidnappers. It is only five minutes walk to shops and restaurants.
Inglenook offers privacy and a quiet, restful atmosphere to visitors. It is immaculately presented and serviced, and has quality chattels and linen. Guest suites are self-contained and independent of the owner's living area, with their own separate entrances and keys. Each has its own outdoor living area set in an expanse of cottage garden, overlooked by trees which provide a home to a range of native birds.
A special breakfast including fresh Hawkes Bay fruit or home baking is served to guests each morning at a pre-arranged time, which can be enjoyed outdoors or in guests' rooms as required. Tea and coffee making facilities are available in each suite and a barbecue area is provided.

Napier/Hastings
Homestay/Farmstay
Address: Charlton Road, R.D.2,
Hastings, H.B.
Name: Mr and Mrs B Shaw
Telephone: (06) 875 0177
Fax: (06) 825 0525
Beds: 4 Single (2 bedrooms)
Bathroom: 1 Ensuite, 1 Family share
Tariff: B&B (special) Double $100,
Single $100, Dinner extra.
Campervans welcome.
Nearest Town: Napier - Hastings

Te Awanga is a picturesque coastal village situated fifteen minutes drive from both Napier and Hastings and right next door to the gannets at Cape Kidnappers and one of Hawkes Bay's leading winery restaurants. Charlton Road is the first on your right after passing through Te Awanga and leads to a large and comfortable homestead where you can enjoy space, tranquillity and fine hospitality while receiving every assistance to make your stay in our area as interesting and enjoyable as possible. You will have your own private entrance so can come and go as you please while enjoying the many attractions Hawkes Bay has to offer. For the benefit of those seeking the real New Zealand, ours is a genuine country residence and not a transplant from the city as is sometimes the case. We have a couple of Jack Russell dogs.
Directions: *Please phone Bill or Heather for directions on how to find us and to learn more about what we have to offer.*

Napier/Hastings

Orchard Homestay/SC Accom/own kitchen.
Address: c/- Pakowhai Store, Pakowhai Road,
Napier, Hawkes Bay
Name: Copperfieldss"
Telephone: (06) 876 9710 **Fax**: (06) 876 9710
Beds: 1 Double, 2 Single (2 bedrooms)
Bathroom: 1 Private, 1 Family share (laundry facilities available)
Tariff: B&B (full) Double $75, Single $50, Children under 12yrs half price,
Dinner $25 (3 courses) by arrangement, Credit Card (VISA). Weekly rates
negotiable. NZ B&B Vouchers accepted $5 surcharge
Nearest Town: Midway Napier and Hastings - 10 km to each

Welcome to Hawkes Bay. 'Copperfields' is a small mixed apple orchard on the main road between Napier (famous for its Art Deco buildings) and its 'twin city' of Hastings situated in the rich soil of the Heretaunga Plains. Wineries, craft trails and scenic attractions are readily accessible. We recommend the spectacular view from Te Mata Peak. We are a non smoking married couple with a son overseas and daughter away at university. A friendly cat and dog keep us company at home. Pam is a weaver and interested in craft work generally. Richard makes and restores furniture and is interested in antiques and curiosities. We both like good food and meeting people from other countries and places. We hope to offer you a friendly and comfortable base from which to enjoy your stay in Hawkes Bay. Guests stay in 'Glen Cottage' a self-contained two bedroom dwelling attached to our house. It is the original orchard house and enables guests to be totally private if they wish. A continental breakfast is provided in the cottage for those guests wishing to sleep late. Dogs welcome (conditions apply) and bikes available free for careful riders!.

Puketapu

Homestay
Address: Silverford, Dartmoor Road,
Puketapu, Hawkes Bay.
Name: William and Chris Orme-Wright
Telephone: (06) 844 5600 **Fax**: (06) 844 4423
Email: homestay@iconz.co.nz
Beds: 1 King, 1 Queen, 1 Double (3 bedrooms)
Bathroom: 1 Ensuite, 1 Guests share
Tariff: B&B (full) Double $135-$155, Single $95. Dinner $30 by arrangement.
Credit cards: Visa/Mastercard/Amex
Nearest Town: Napier/Hastings 20 minutes

Situated on the Wine Trail Silverford - one of Hawkes Bay's most gracious Homesteads - is spaciously set in 17 acres of farmland, established trees and gardens. Drive through our half a kilometre long gorgeous Oak lined avenue to the sweeping lawns, bright flower gardens and ponds surrounding our elegant home designed by Natusch at the turn of the century.
We are relaxed and friendly and offer a warm ambience in private, comfortable and tranquil surroundings - a romantic haven with tastefully furnished bedrooms, charming guest sitting room and a courtyard to dream in. Silverford is an idyllic welcoming haven for a private, peaceful and cosy stay whilst at the same time being close to all the amenities and attractions that Hawkes Bay has to offer. Friendly deer, cow, pigeons, ducks and dogs.
Central Heating. Swimming Pool.
We are smokefree and regret the property is unsuitable for children.
Some French and German spoken.

360

Napier/Hastings
Self Contained Accommodation
Address: 524 State Highway 2, Hastings North
Name: Jan and Kerry McKinnie
Telephone: (06) 870 0759 **Mobile**: 025 280 6392
Fax: (06) 870 0528
Beds: 2 Double, 4 Single (3 bedrooms)
Bathroom: 1 Ensuite, 1 guest share.
Tariff: B&B (full) Double $75, Single $45, Dinner by arrangement.
Children price by arrangement. Credit Cards: Visa/Mastercard.
NZ B&B Vouchers accepted.
Nearest Town: Napier 8 kms. Hastings 5 kms.

Set in 1 1/2 acres of tranquil garden bordering the Clive River we offer the friendliness of a homestay combined with the privacy of your own unique cottage, TV, tea and coffee facilities included. We have an in-ground pool and hot spa. As we have our own children we are well equipped to accommodate 'kids on the move' with swings, trampoline etc. We also have a friendly dog. Breakfast is served in the main house or in your unit or in the garden. We have all travelled locally and abroad and look forward to helping you enjoy your Hawkes Bay experience.
Directions: *From Napier take State Highway 2 along the sea front and through Clive village 2 kms south of Clive look for our sign on the right.*

Hastings
Self contained accommodation in Guest House
Address: Musterers' Cottage,
Millstream, R.D.4, Hastings
Name: Maureen Ann Harper
Telephone: (06) 878 9944
Fax: (06) 878 9944
Mobile: 025-548 585
Email: maharper@clear.net.nz
Beds: 1 Double
Bathroom: 1 Ensuite

Tariff: B&B (continental) Double $70, Single $35, Dinner from $15,
3 Course $20, Cooked breakfast extra. Children under 13yrs half price,
Campervans welcome. NZ B&B Vouchers accepted
Nearest Town: 25km south of Hastings on main Highway 2 to Wellington.

Nestled among the beautiful hills of New Zealand's "fruit basket" and premium wine country, my countryside villa is a haven for fresh air, relaxation, and delicious home cooked meals. This sprawling, 20 ha property is adorned with beautiful trees, a quiet stream, and abundant lawns and gardens. Horse trekking is available on site and guests can view one of NZ's few miniature horse herds. I have a few cattle and sheep, and guests are welcome to participate in farm activities that change seasonally. My comfortable home features a large living area, sundeck, cozy fireplace, and nooks to relax or read in. Delicious continental breakfasts served, and my homemade bread (made from local wheat) is addicting! Wholesome and generous dinners can be added to accommodation by arrangement. All guests will enjoy complimentary tea or coffee on arrival, and children and pets are welcome. Pick-up in Hastings can be arranged for a minimal fee.

Hastings

Homestay
Address: 115A Frederick St,
Hastings, Hawkes Bay
Name: Doug & Barbara McConchie
Telephone: (06) 878 4576
Beds: 1 Queen, 2 Single (2 Bedrooms)
Bathroom: 1 Guests share
Tariff: B&B (special) Double $70, Single $40, Children half price, Dinner $20.
Credit Cards. NZ B&B Vouchers accepted
Nearest Town: We live in Hastings city, Napier is 20km north.

We are a retired couple with no children or pets at home.
Our home is modern, attractive and peaceful, being in a back garden setting away from traffic noises. It has a guest wing with ranchslider entry. A short walk takes you to the city centre or to parks. A fifteen minute drive takes you to golf courses or up Te Mata Peak to wonderful views. A gannet sanctuary at Cape Kidnappers is a great trip. Wineries, orchards, gardens or walks abound. A five minute drive takes you to the picturesque village of Havelock North.
We enjoy meeting people and judging by the letters we get, people enjoy being with us. We give you your choice of breakfast. Continental, cooked or special. Long stays discounted. No smoking inside please. Married couples with or without children and single, separate bedroom folk are extremely welcome.
Directions: *Coming from Napier Marine Parade take SH2 via Clive and Karamu Rd to Hastings. At first set of lights turn right into Frederick St. Coming from Napier airport turn off SH2 into SH50, follow signposts to Hastings. Frederick St is 2nd turning on left off Pakawhai Rd. This way 115a is just past 2nd intersection beyond the lights and down a driveway. Turn into first gateway. Coming from Wellington ring for directions. Arriving by bus or train ring and we will meet you.*

Hastings

Homestay/Farmstay
Address: 1984 Maraekakaho Road, R.D.1, Hastings
Name: Bryce Jackson
Telephone: (06) 879 8892 **Fax**: (06) 879 8892
Beds: 1 Double, 2 Single (2 bedrooms)
Bathroom: 1 Ensuite, 1 Family share
Tariff: B&B (full) Double $60, Single $30,
Credit cards. NZ B&B Vouchers accepted
Nearest Town: Hastings 12km, Highway 50 3.5km

Come and stay with me at my quiet rural location south west of Hastings.
I am just 12km from the city centre. My modern home is on an orchard and market garden lifestyle block.
I provide a cooked or continental breakfast. Close by is the Hastings aerodrame offering skydiving, scenic flights and hot air balooning. Only a few minutes away are two excellent golf courses and reputable wineries that welcome visitors.
No smoking inside please. Be welcomed on your arrival with tea or coffee.

One of the differences between staying at a hotel and a B&B
is that you don't hug the hotel staff when you leave.

Hastings

Self-contained Accom. B&B
Address: 79 Carrick Rd, Twyford,
Hastings (Postal) Box 2116, Hastings
Name: Anne & Peter Wilkinson
Telephone: (06) 879 9357 **Fax**: (06) 879 9357
Mobile: (025) 417 807
Email: ph-aawilkinson@clear.net.nz
Beds: 2 Single (1 bedroom)
Bathroom: 1 Private
Tariff: B&B (full) Double $80, Single $60, Dinner $25pp.
NZ B&B Vouchers accepted
Nearest Town: Hastings 8km

We are situated in the country 10 minutes west of Hastings city in a wine growing and orcharding area called Twyford, and our sister city Napier is 20 minutes away. A warm welcome is extended to our visitors.

The Ngaruroro River is very close for good trout fishing during the season, and we are within easy reach of a variety of other rivers and lakes. Guided fishing is offered by Peter. Hawkes Bay offers a wide variety of attractions. Wineries, good restaurants, gardens to visit, jet boating, tramping, Heritage & Art Deco walks, golf courses, Cape Kidnappers gannet colony, hot air ballooning are but a few of them.

Our accommodation is a self contained Lockwood cottage comprising a bedroom with two single beds, bathroom, small kitchen and living room situated in our garden looking towards the Kaweka ranges. Non-smoking accommodation and does not cater for children.

Directions: *Please phone.*

Hastings

Homestay
Address: 'Woodbine Cottage',
1279 Louie Street, Hastings
Name: Ngaire & Jim Shand
Telephone: (06) 876 9388 **Fax**: (06) 876 9666
Mobile: 025 529 522
Email: nshand@xtra.co.nz
Beds: 1 Double, 1 Twin (2 bedrooms).
Bathroom: 1 Guests share.
Tariff: B&B (continental) Double $90, Single $50,
Dinner on request $25 pp, Full breakfast $7.50 pp extra.
Visa/Mastercard/Bank card accepted NZ B&B Vouchers accepted $20 Surcharge
Nearest Town: Hastings 2.5 Kms

Information.
Set in half an acre of cottage garden on Hastings boundary.
Tennis court, Swimming pool.
5 minutes to Havelock North.
5 minutes to Hastings city centre.
2 minutes to Fantasyland.
20 minutes to Napier city.
We enjoy meeting people.
Have travelled extensively.
Tours, sightseeing arranged on request.
Laundry facilities.
No smoking in house.
We look forward to your company!

Hastings
Farm Orchard Homestay
Address: 808 River Road. "Waiwhenua",
RD 9, Hastings, Hawkes Bay
Name: Kirsty and David Hill
Telephone: (06) 874 2435
Fax: (06) 874 2435
Mobile: (025) 245 7964
Email: kirsty.hill@xtra.co.nz
Beds: 2 Double, 3 Single (2 bedrooms)
Bathroom: 1 Guests share, 1 Family shower share.
Tariff: B&B (full/continental) Double $60, Single $30, Dinner $25pp.
Lunch available too. Children accommodation full, meals half price.
Campervans welcome for secluded river section.
NZ B&B vouchers accepted.
Nearest Town: Hastings 50 km

Our farming and horticultural young family of five welcomes you to our large historical Elizabethan homestead set in mature grounds (1200 acres) with magnificent rural views. Situated just off the Napier / Taihape (Gentle Annie) Road, 60 km from Napier, 50 km from Hastings and 100km Taihape. Our home offers a warm friendly family environment catering for individuals or families interested in the outdoor life with no restrictions as to length of stay. Our relaxing outdoor lifestyle includes fishing, sheep, beef and deer farm tours, pip and kiwifruit orchard and garden tours on our property. We also have cats and dogs (home and farm).

Speciality meals of home grown produce provided to all visitors on request. Additional guided tours include hunting and native bush walks, garden tours, golf and general site seeing - all within close proximity.

Directions: *Please phone in advance. Campervans also welcome for our secluded river section.*

Members of
**The New Zealand Association
Farm & Home Host Inc.**
maintain the highest standards &
are always delighted to welcome
guests into their homes.

'PEAK VIEW'

Hastings/Havelock North
Homestay/Farmstay
Address: 'Peak View' Farm, Middle Rd., Havelock North
Name: Dianne & Keith Taylor
Telephone: (06) 877 7408 **Fax**: (06) 877 7410
Beds: 1 Double, 2 Single plus cot & highchair (2 bedrooms)
Bathroom: 1 Family share
Tariff: B&B (full) Double $60, Single $40, Dinner $20pp (2 course $15),
Children half price. Credit Cards (VISA/ MC/BC). NZ B&B Vouchers accepted
Nearest Town: Havelock North 1 km, Hastings 6km

*Our home was built 1900 on 25 acres of horticulture land. Our family being 4th
generation to live here, which is surrounded by big lawns and lovely gardens. We're
looking back over eleven years of "Happy Hosting" with an ever increasing circle of
friends. We enjoy meeting people - our aim is to provide a pleasant and memorable stay.
Interested in caravanning, tramping and bushwalks. Keith enjoys fishing, Dianne
sewing, gardening and genealogy. Dianne is a Kiwi Host, and also has studied and
obtained a certificate in Farm and Homestay Management, consisting of Food and
Safety and Welcome to Tourism plus 10 modules on the business aspects. We offer
comfortable accommodation. Good firm beds all with electric blankets. Dinner with
us be assured of wholesome and generous meals. Afterwards share an evening of
relaxation and friendship or browse through our many New Zealand books. Also can
advise on travel throughout New Zealand from own experiences. Handy to winerys,
tennis and squash courts, indoor and outdoor pools, short drive to Te Mata Peak with
panoramic views. Napier 25 minutes away. No smoking inside please. Be welcomed
with tea or coffee. Laundry facilities available. We are members of N.Z. association
of Farm and Home Hosts. Havelock North is one of the first places in New Zealand
to see the sun.
If you are having trouble finding accommodation in this area phone Dianne - I will
endeavour to do my best for you.*
Home Page: http://nz.com/webnz/bbnz/peakview.htm

Hastings/Havelock North

Homestay

Address: 134 Kopanga Road, Havelock North
Name: Jill & Jock Taylor
Telephone: (06) 877 8797 **Fax**: (06) 877 2335
Beds: 1 Double (1 bedroom) plus one outside unit with 2 beds, shower and toilet.
Bathroom: 1 Guests own
Tariff: B&B Double $75, single $40, Dinner $15 by prior arrangement. Cooked breakfast $5 pp extra. NZ B&B Vouchers accepted $15 surcharge
Nearest Town: Hastings 15 minutes, Havelock North 5 minutes.

Our new wooden home is comfortable and welcomes you. Situated in quiet rural surroundings with extensive views, we are only 5 minutes from Havelock North, Hastings and Napier approximately 15 minutes.
We are gardeners and golfers and what better place to be both than Hawkes Bay, with four excellent golf courses, superb gardens and many reputable wineries. Our family of four have grown and gone but we have two friendly black cats and a small dog. There is a double bed with guests' own bathroom in the house and an outside unit with two single beds, shower, toilet and tea and coffee making facilities.
No smoking please.
Directions: *Please phone.*

Hastings/Havelock North

Homestay/Farmstay

Address: Wharehau, R.D. 11, Hastings
Name: Ros Phillips
Telephone: (06) 877 4111 **Fax**: (06) 877 4111
Beds: 1 Double, 5 Single (4 bedrooms)
Bathroom: 1 guests share
Tariff: B&B (full) Double $60, Single $30, Children half price, Dinner $20.
NZ B&B Vouchers accepted
Nearest Town: Hastings, Havelock North 16 kms

20 minutes from Hastings, Havelock North or Waipawa a welcome awaits. You can enjoy the space and peace of a beautiful Hawkes Bay farm or use the home as a base for the many local attractions.
We have a Hereford and Romney stud. Farm tours are available with fabulous views of Hawkes Bay. There is also 50 acres of native bush and an excellent fishing river, the Tukituki, nearby.
Ros is actively involved in the day to day running of the farm, enjoys gardening and is a keen cook. The farmhouse has three bedrooms and guest bathroom upstairs, and one guestroom downstairs with shared facilities.
Children welcome.

Private bathroom is for your use exclusively,
Guests share means you may be sharing with other guests,
Family share means you will be sharing with the family.

Havelock North

Homestay
Address: 'Overcliff', Waimarama Road,
R.D.12, Havelock North
Name: Joan & Nigel Sutton
Telephone: (06) 877 6852 **Fax**: (06) 877 6852
Beds: 1 Double, 3 Single (3 bedrooms)
Bathroom: 1 Guests share
Tariff: B&B (full) Double $75, Single $50.
Dinner $25 includes wine & pre dinner drinks. NZ B&B Vouchers accepted
Nearest Town: Havelock North 4 Kms

Our comfortable family home is set in ten acres of rolling hill country in the beautiful Tukituki river valley close to Te Mata peak, yet only five minutes from Havelock North, ten minutes from Hastings and fifteen minutes from Napier.
Two golden sandy beaches are about fifteen minutes pleasant drive.
We have a number of friendly animals, Foss, our dog, kunekune pigs, a small flock of sheep, horses, cats and homing pigeons.
We can help you plan your enjoyment of Hawkes Bay's attractions or you can take a stroll with us to the river, meeting and feeding the animals on the way, swim or laze by the pool, play tennis on the grass court, or fish for rainbow trout in the river. Dinner served with local wine is a pleasant time to get to know one another. Enjoy breakfast by the pool on those special Hawkes Bay days.
Being non smokers we would appreciate you not smoking indoors.

Hastings/Havelock North

Homestay
Address: 57c Iona Rd, Havelock North
Name: Colleen & Bruce Hastie
Telephone: (06) 877 4640 **Fax**: (06) 877 4640
Mobile: 025-407 255
Beds: 1 Queen, 2 Single (2 bedrooms)
Bathroom: 2 Private
Tariff: B&B (continental) Double $70, Single $40,
Dinner $20, Credit cards. NZ B&B Vouchers accepted
Nearest Town: Havelock North 1km, Hastings 6km, Napier 20km.

We invite you to join us in our comfortable modern home, which is situated on a rear section where we enjoy peaceful surroundings.
The beautiful picturesque Havelock North village is only 3 minutes away and offers a variety of specialist shops and many excellent restaurants, and an Irish pub in the village. There are interesting walks, good rivers to fish and wonderful picnic spots (we could pack a lunch for you). The area is well known for orchards, wineries and apiaries.
Bedrooms are one upstairs, one down, with their own bathrooms tastefully and comfortably furnished. We also have a separate spa room, which you are welcome to use. Laundry facilities are available.
You will find us a friendly couple who enjoy meeting people, you can be assured of a relaxed atmosphere in our home. We offer a continental or cooked breakfast.
No smoking in house please. Phone or fax for directions. Looking forward to meeting you and have you stay with us.

367

Havelock North
Bed and Breakfast
Address: 'Weldon', 98 Te Mata Road,
P.O. Box 8170, Havelock North
Name: Pracilla Hay
Telephone: (06) 877 7551
Fax: (06) 877 7051 **Mobile**: (021) 214 8469
Beds: Double, Twin, Single (4 bedrooms)
Bathroom: 2 Guests share
Tariff: B&B (special) Double $80, Single $45.
NZ B&B Vouchers accepted $15 surcharge
Nearest Town: Havelock North 1/2 kilometre, Hastings 5km

WELDON was built in 1906 and retains the country elegance of the time. Situated in a quiet, picturesque cottage garden at the end of a lavender lined drive, WELDON offers comfort and quality with old world charm.

Restaurants, cafes and an Irish pub give ambience to our unique beautiful village which is only five minutes walk away.

Havelock North is nestled under the hills of Te Mata Peak and is central to many wineries. The twin cities of Hastings and Napier are close by.

Accommodation at WELDON offers single, twin and double rooms (one has a divan) with open fires, fine bed linen, fluffy towels, fresh flowers, television and tea/coffee making facilities.

The rooms are decorated in the country cottage style. A full breakfast is offered and is served outdoors in warm weather. We have two toy poodles (James and Thomas) to welcome you.

Havelock North
Homestay
Address: "Belvedere", 51 Lucknow Road,
Havelock North
Name: Shirley & Mervyn Pethybridge
Telephone: (06) 877 4551
Beds: 1 Queen, 1 Double, 2 Single (3 bedrooms)
Bathroom: 1 Ensuite, 1 Private
Tariff: B&B (full) Double $70, Single $45, Dinner $20.
Nearest Town: Hastings 5km

Belvedere is a large 2 storeyed Southern style home set in half an acre of well kept lawns and gardens.

The elegant rooms with balconies have views over town and distant ranges. There is an in-ground saline pool and spa for you to relax in.

Our home is a short walk to Havelock North where there are a great variety of shops and restaurants.

Hawkes Bay is a well known tourist resort with so much to fill in your day, visiting local vineyards, orchards, golfing on any of the 5 golf courses. The Gannet Sanctuary or maybe a leisurely drive through to Napier, the Art Deco capital of the world.

We have travelled extensively both in New Zealand and overseas and have enjoyed the hospitality of many homestays and are pleased to be able to offer the same in return. Please phone or write.

Transfer transport available.

There are some good tips for easier travel on page 7

Havelock North

Self Contained Accommodation
Address: Wairunga, 195 Waipoapoa Road,
Maraetotara, Havelock North
Name: John Parker
Telephone: (06) 874 6839
Fax: (06) 874 6815
Email: wairunga@xtra.co.nz
Beds: 4 Queen, 6 Single, 1 Doublebed/settee. (8 bedrooms)
Bathroom: Large cottage: 2 Ensuites, 1 Guests share.
Small cottage: 1 Guests share
Tariff: Large cottage (5 bedrooms) $250. Small cottage (3 bedrooms) $150.
Breakfast provisions supplied, full kitchen facilities in both cottages (perfect for
groups). Eftpos, Visa, Amex, Diners, Mastercard, Farmacard, Bankcard.
Nearest Town: Havelock North 37km, Waimarama 14 km.

*The two self contained cottages are adjacent to the Wairunga homestead which has been
converted into a fully licenced restaurant. Wairunga has its own nine hole golf course,
grass tennis court, squash court, croquet lawn and petanque area, all of which are
available for guests. There are also extensive garden walks and bush walks in the Mohi
Native Forest Reserve nearby. Wairunga is 480 metres above sea level (which makes for
a very comfortable summer climate) and has wonderful views overlooking the Pacific
Ocean and Bare Island. The golf course is set among rolling hills with numerous stands
of native trees, and is considered to be quite challenging.*
*Snacks and meals are available alfresco from dawn to dusk in the beautiful gardens of
the homestead. Hawkes Bay is famous for its natural produce, and our chef has a passion
for food that is clean, simple and retains its natural flavours and goodness. Pets: One
Golden Labrador, Jake. Wairunga is open summers only, usually from "Labour Day"
(late October) until Easter.*

Waimarama Beach

Bed & Breakfast
Address: 68 Harper Road, Waimarama
Name: Murray & Rita Webb
Telephone: (06) 874 6795
Beds: 2 Double (2 bedrooms)
Bathroom: 1 Guests share
Tariff: B&B (full) Double $65, Single $35, Children half price, Dinner $20.
NZ B&B Vouchers accepted
Nearest Town: Hastings 30 mins drive.

*Come and stay a night or three at the lovely Hawkes Bay beach resort of Waimarama,
which has facilities for surfing, diving, fishing trips, horse trekking, bush walks etc.
Our house is situated five minutes walk from the beach with lovely views of the sea,
local park and farmlands. A 9 hole golf course and restaurant is located nearby (15
mins drive).*
*Havelock North is the nearest shopping area, 20 minutes drive away, with Hastings
and Napier 30 and 40 minutes respectively. We have two double bedrooms available
and dinner will be provided if required, also a spa pool for guests' use.*
Laundry facilities also provided. No smoking inside please.
Please phone for reservations - 06-874-6795. Vouchers accepted.
Pets: One cat, two dogs (friendly).

Waipawa

Homestay

Address: Corgarff,
104 Great North Road, Waipawa
Name: Neil & Judy McHardy
Telephone: (06) 857 7828 **Fax**: (06) 857 7055
Beds: 5 Single (3 bedrooms)
Bathroom: 1 Guests share, 1 Family share
Tariff: B&B (full) Double $70, Single $45, Dinner $20.
NZ B&B Vouchers accepted
Nearest Town: 2.5km north of Waipawa

We welcome you to Corgarff, our comfortable and sunny home on the northern outskirts of Waipawa. We are a farming couple, now retired to 13 acres, with a fox terrier, 2 cats, and some Texel sheep; also various black sheep kept for spinning fleeces. Within half an hours drive are 5 safe sandy beaches, 4 golf courses, excellent trout fishing and a choice of many wineries. Our guest wing has a separate entrance, also a private sitting room with TV and terrace. These facilities are suitable for disabled persons. We enjoy meeting people and our interests include books, gardening, music, art and travel, also croquet on the lawn.
Directions: *2.5 km north of Waipawa. An old elm tree drive. Rapid number 1306 on SH2.*

Waipukurau

Farmstay

Address: 'Tukipo Terraces', P O Box 114,
Takapau 4176, Hawkes Bay
Name: Bay & Shona de Lautour
Telephone: (06) 855 6827 Freephone: 0800 301 696
Fax: (06) 855 6808 **Mobile**: (025) 928 908
Beds: 2 Double, 2 Single (2 large, beautifully appointed suites, each opening to garden)
Bathroom: 2 Ensuite
Tariff: Bed & Breakfast: Double $150, Single $90; Dinner $35pp,
Children by arrangement, Lunch Extra, Credit cards (VISA/MC).
NZ B&B Vouchers accepted $65 surcharge.
Nearest Town: Waipukurau 20 km, Takapau Village 8kms

Tukipo Terraces is a unique riverstone and timber home on a sheep, deer and cropping farm in the heart of sunny Hawkes Bay within easy reach of all Hawkes Bay's tourist attractions. Built in 1986 on terraces above the Tukipo trout stream it combines the ambience of an elegant, spacious country home with its homestay facilities designed specifically for the enjoyment and privacy of guests. It has two suites both with double and single bed and sitting area, each independent of the other, opening onto extensive garden with mountain views. Three golf courses, bush walks and river swimming nearby. Pre dinner drinks, delicious three course dinner and finest Hawkes Bay wine shared with hosts in a warm and friendly atmosphere.
Shona and Bay have travelled widely, Shona enjoys golf, gardening and music. Bay, as well as farming, has interests in business, politics and is a private pilot. 'Alice', friendly fox terrier.
Directions: *From south on Highway 2, 30 kms north of Dannevirke turn left onto Highway 50, travel 5 kms, on right just at end of long line of mature pines.*
From north, on Highway 50, 22 kms from Tikokino, first on left over Tukipo stream. 2581 on entrance railings.

Waipukurau

Farmstay
Address: Hinerangi Station, R.D. 1,
Waipukurau
Name: Caroline & Dan von Dadelszen
Telephone: (06) 855 8273
Fax: (06) 855 8278
Beds: 1 Queen, 2 Single (2 bedrooms)
Bathroom: 1 Guests share
Tariff: B&B (continental) Double $90, Single $50, Dinner $25pp.
Campervans welcome. NZ B&B Vouchers accepted $25 Surcharge
Nearest Town: Waipukurau 20km, Takapau 11km

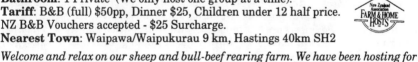

*Hinerangi is an 1800 acre sheep, cattle and deer station set amongst the rolling hills
of Central Hawkes Bay. There are magnificent views to be seen from the Ruahine
ranges to the sea. We are happy to show guests what is happening on the farm while
you are here. Our domestic animals include two small terriers and a cat.*
*Our 7000 sq ft 1920 homestead, designed by architect Louis Hay of Napier Art Deco
fame, has a full sized billiard table and there is a swimming pool and tennis court for
guests to enjoy. Our home is spacious and comfortable with a private entrance for
guests. You are welcome to join us for dinner and an evening by the fire.*
*There are beaches, bush walks and trout fishing streams and golf courses within a
short drive. Hot air ballooning is based nearby. We are 8km off State Highway 2.*
Directions: *Please phone.*

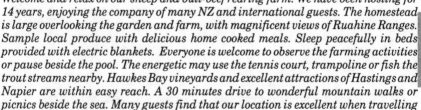

Waipukurau

Farmstay
Address: 'Mynthurst', Lindsay Road,
R.D.3, Waipukurau
Name: David & Annabelle Hamilton
Telephone: (06) 857 8093 **Fax**: (06) 857 8093
Beds: 1 King, 3 Single, 1 Cot (3 bedrooms) Extra space for families.
Bathroom: 1 Private (We only host one group at a time).
Tariff: B&B (full) $50pp, Dinner $25, Children under 12 half price.
NZ B&B Vouchers accepted - $25 Surcharge.
Nearest Town: Waipawa/Waipukurau 9 km, Hastings 40km SH2

*Welcome and relax on our sheep and bull-beef rearing farm. We have been hosting for
14 years, enjoying the company of many NZ and international guests. The homestead
is large overlooking the garden and farm, with magnificent views of Ruahine Ranges.
Sample local produce with delicious home cooked meals. Sleep peacefully in beds
provided with electric blankets. Everyone is welcome to observe the farming activities
or pause beside the pool. The energetic may use the tennis court, trampoline or fish the
trout streams nearby. Hawkes Bay vineyards and excellent attractions of Hastings and
Napier are within easy reach. A 30 minutes drive to wonderful mountain walks or
picnics beside the sea. Many guests find that our location is excellent when travelling
both North and South. Children welcome. Please phone ahead for bookings to avoid
disappointment. We have two friendly cats.*

371

Waipukurau

Homestay/Farmstay

Address: 415 Mangatarata Road, Waipukurau
Name: Donald & Judy Macdonald
Telephone: (06) 858 8275 **Fax**: (06) 858 8270 **Mobile**: (025) 480 769
Beds: 1 Double, 4 Single (3 bedrooms)
Bathroom: 1 Private, 1 Family share
Tariff: B&B (including cooked breakfast) Double $85 & $95, Single $65,
Children under 12yrs half price, Dinner $25.
NZ B&B Vouchers accepted $25 surcharge
Nearest Town: Waipukurau 7km

*Donald and Judy invite you to stay in their 100 year old homestead. Mangatarata is
a large historic home with beautiful views from its sweeping verandahs. The large
garden features mature trees, a lake complete with white swans and other bird life, and
a solar heated swimming pool.*

*Mangatarata was the second sheep station to be established in Hawkes Bay, now 2500
acres farming sheep and cattle. The old thoroughbred stables, original sheds and large
woolshed make an interesting walk. We encourage involvement in the farm.*

*Central Hawkes Bay rivers are becoming internationally known for excellent fishing,
we can assist with local knowledge. Bush or farm walking, beautiful beaches, golf
courses in close proximity.*

*Donald is a flying instructor, flight to wilderness areas or scenic available. Heli
hunting, fishing or tramping with professional guides. Scenic flights in a Tiger Moth
with an open cockpit. Vineyards and wineries within easy driving distance.*

Pets - Rajah the Burmese cat, Mac the two year old Scottish terrier.

Continental breakfast consists of fruit, cereal, toast, tea/coffee,
Full breakfast is the same with a cooked course,
Special breakfast has something special.

Waipukurau
Homestay
Address: "Airlie Mount",
South Service Lane - off Porangahau Road,
PO Box 368, Waipukurau
Name: Aart & Rashida van Saarloos
Telephone: (06) 858 7601 **Fax**: (06) 858 7609
Beds: 1 Queen, 2 Single (2 bedrooms)
Bathroom: 1 Ensuite, 1 Family share
Tariff: B&B (full) Double $90, Single $60, Children 12 & under half price.
Credit cards. NZ B&B Vouchers accepted $20 surcharge
Nearest Town: Waipukurau centre 50 m

Historic fully restored "Airlie Mount", built in the 1870's, is situated in the exact centre of Waipukurau, a few steps away from shops, restaurants and railway station - yet it's an island of tranquillity and surrounded by cottage gardens and native bush. The comfortable (non-smoking) homestead further offers verandahs, billiard room, swimming pool and small croquet lawn. The guest wing, which is very private and large enough for 2 adults and 2 children, has its own bathroom, sitting room, TV and outside courtyard.
Your hosts, Rashida and Aart, have travelled extensively and have two young children, a Labrador and fat cat who all enjoy meeting new guests. We import beautiful Lombok pottery which is available at wholesale prices.
Waipukurau is 1/2 hour drive away from historic Onga Onga, Norsewear and the beaches and vineyards of Hawke's Bay which makes "Airlie Mount" your perfect base to stay and relax.
Directions: *Immediately behind Public Trust Building, Ruataniwha Street.*

Norsewood
Farmstay
Address: Arthur Road, RD, Norsewood
Name: 'The Hermytage'
Hosts: Wayne & Helen Hermansen
Telephone: (06) 374 0735
Fax: (06) 374 0735
Mobile: (025) 248 7988
Beds: 1 Double, 1 Single (1 Bedroom)
Bathroom: 1 Private
Tariff: B&B (full) Double $75, Dinner $15pp BYO if required.
Credit Cards. NZ B&B Vouchers accepted
Nearest Town: Norsewood

Guests will be warmly welcome to our spacious home where you can relax and enjoy the peace of the country and the view of the Ruahine Ranges, or be included in the family and farm activities.
We live on a dairy heifer grazing block and have a Town Supply Dairy farm.
We are only 2km from Norsewood, which is a one hour drive to either Palmerston North or Hastings on SH 2. Our district is steeped in Scandinavian History with a very interesting museum. Tours of Norsewear Woollen Mills can be arranged. The golf course is just around the corner, or you can do a day tramp up the Ranges.
The men run a hay contracting business and you are welcome to watch the harvesting if you wish. Interests include gardening, reading, machinery, travel.
We enjoy people, love entertaining and a good game of cards, especially 500.
No pets, no smoking please.
Directions: *Please phone.*

Ormondville

Self-contained Accommodation
Address: Main Road, Ormandville,
R.D.7 Dannevirke.
Name: Ormondville Railway Station
Telephone: (06) 374 1514
Beds: 1 Double, 2 Single (2 bedrooms)
Bathroom: 1 Private
Tariff: B&B (full) Double $75, Single $70, Dinner $25,
Children discouraged. Credit cards.
Nearest Town: Dannevirke (only6km off SH2 at Norsewood)

Ormondville Station offers a complete railway nostalgia experience in a quiet rural setting. Opened in 1880 it is registered by Historic Places Trust and is winner of the 1997 Rail Heritage Trust restoration award. It is furnished with genuine railway artefacts, and is fronted with a graceful wrought iron veranda. The station precinct includes the goods shed, sidings, and vintage rolling stock restored to a 1950's theme. The main station office, crammed with interesting railway fittings, serves as a "special character" dining room and lounge. You can meet the locals at the "Settlers Arms" hotel opposite. We will provide cycles for touring and suggestions for lunch, walking, fishing and golf. Groups of eight can be accommodated by arrangement.

You can reach Ormondville on the daily "Bay Express" from Wellington. Up to four trains pass on weeknights - a highlight for some. For safety reasons the station is suited to adults rather than children.

Dannevirke

Homestay
Address: 42 Victoria Avenue, Dannevirke
Name: 'Glendane' (Norma & Ian Pedersen)
Telephone: (06) 374 6453
Beds: 1 Double, 3 Single (2 bedrooms)
Bathroom: 1 Private (we take 1 party only at a time)
Tariff: B&B (continental) Double $65, Single $45; Dinner $20 by arrangement.
NZ B&B Vouchers accepted
Nearest Town: 1 km west of Dannevirke

Our lovely modern home is set in one acre of beautiful garden and being on the outskirts of town has a rural view with our Ruahine Ranges in the background. It is very quiet and restful, a great place to break your journey.

You can walk to town in ten minutes or head in the other direction and have a refreshing walk in the country. On returning you are assured of a quiet relaxing evening. Our grown up family have all left home and we have a pet and smoke free home for your enjoyment.

You may enjoy dinner with us or bed and breakfast only if you prefer.

Apart from our interests in gardening and farming we make from pure natural wool our own handspun, handmade woollen goods - jerseys, vests, hats, scarves, etc and these original garments are for sale.

Directions: *Please phone.*

Please help us provide the best hospitality in the world.
Fill in a comment form for every place you stay.

Kumeroa
Country Homestay
Address: "Otawa Lodge", Otawhao Road, Kumeroa, RD 1.
Name: Del & Sue Trew
Telephone: (06) 376 4603
Fax: (06) 376 5042
Beds: 2 Queen, 2 Single (2 bedrooms)
Bathroom: 1 Guests share
Tariff: B&B (special) Double $100, Single $65, Children by arrangement, Dinner on request.
Nearest Town: Dannevirke - 20 mins

Rest ... relax ... rejuvenate in our magnificent home set on 80 acres of beautiful rolling countryside only 10 minutes from Highway 2. Be enchanted by the Edwardian elegance preserved in the wood panelling, stunning leadlights, art nouveau plasterwork and authentic period furniture.

Take a walk through native bush, fish for trout in the nearby Manawatu River, wander past the walnut grove to the stream, listen to the tuis or simply read in our unique octagonal library.

Dine on fresh local produce with a healthy emphasis on fish and vegetarian cuisine. At the end of the day, sleep in luxurious queen sized beds made with pure cotton sheets and enjoy the comfort of complementary bathrobes and toiletries.

We are originally from England, have travelled widely and our interests include antiques, music and the theatre. Joss, our small son, is a delightful host. We request guests not to smoke in the house.

Directions: *Please phone.*

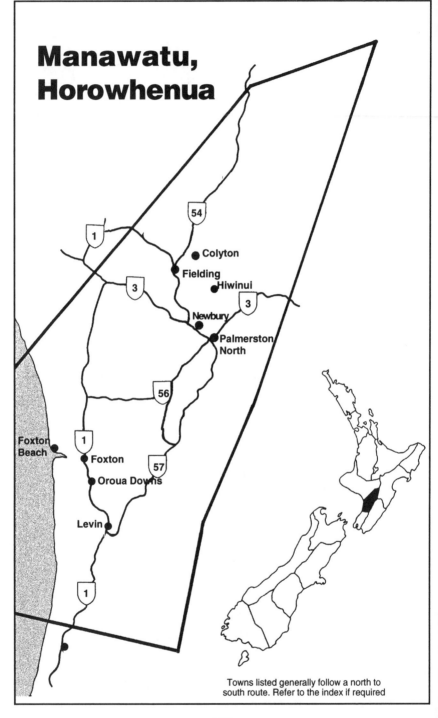

Manawatu, Horowhenua

Towns listed generally follow a north to
south route. Refer to the index if required

Colyton

Farmstay
Address: 'Hiamoe' Waiata, Colyton, Feilding
Name: Toos & John Cousins
Telephone: (06) 328 7713
Fax: (06) 328 7787
Email: johnhiamoe@clear.net.nz.
Beds: 1 Queen, 1 Double,
1 Single (2 bedrooms)
Bathroom: 1 Ensuite with spa bath,
1 Guests share (ensuite)
Tariff: B&B (full) Double $65, Single $40, pre school children free, school age half price, Dinner $15. Credit Cards NZ B&B Vouchers accepted
Nearest Town: Feilding 15 minutes, Palmerston North 25 minutes.

Toos and John, with our 3 young boys, look forward to giving you a warm welcome to "Hiamoe" and during your stay, it is our aim that you experience a home away from home. We are the 3rd generation, farming our sheep, cattle and deer property and live in a 100-year-old colonial home. We have many interests and as Holland is Toos original homeland we are quite accustomed to travel and hosting visitors of all nationalities.
Directions: *Details when booking.*

Feilding

Homestay
Address: 5 Wellington Street, Feilding
Name: Beryl Walker
Telephone: (06) 323 4409
Beds: 1 Double, 2 Single or can be 4 Single (2 bedrooms)
Bathroom: 1 Ensuite, 1 Guests share
Tariff: B&B (full) Ensuite Double $70, Twin $60, Single $40, Children half price. Credit cards. NZ B&B Vouchers accepted
Nearest Town: Feilding 1.3 km from town centre

A comfortable and sunny family home with open fires in winter. Guests should feel free to use all family rooms and facilities as family members. A chance to catch up with your laundry. A choice of breakfast timed to suit your travel arrangements. Cot and highchair available.
Feilding, only 15 minutes from Highway 1 from Sanson if travelling south or through Rongatea, Feilding is the centre of a prosperous farming area with many places of natural beauty within reach. It has easy access to the East Coast and is only 15 minutes from the city of Palmerston North. Manfield Racecourse is situated at Feilding. Feilding has an interesting shopping area and several good restaurants, licensed and unlicensed.
Directions: *For further directions please ring.*

One of the differences between staying at a hotel and a B&B
is that you don't hug the hotel staff when you leave.

Feilding

Farmstay, Self contained accom.
Address: Phone for directions
Name: Robert & Ann Campbell
Telephone: (06) 323 4601 **Fax**: (06) 323 4020
Mobile: (025) 244 7792
Beds: 1 Queen, 1 Double, 3 Single (3 bedrooms)
Bathroom: 1 Private, 1 Guests share
Tariff: B&B (continental) Double $70, Single $40, Dinner $20 pp. Self contained
cottage Sleeps 4, $70 double, $15 per extra person, continental breakfast included.
One cottage with Queen bed + Bed settee (double), Ensuite bathroom, Lounge.
Meals by arrangement. NZ B&B Vouchers accepted
Nearest Town: Feilding 5km. Palmerston North 10km.

A warm welcome to our home and farm.
Our 1900 homestead is surrounded by two large gardens which you are welcome to explore. The farm is one of continual activity, with sheep / lambs, beef (including a Red Poll stud and Highland cows, plus cropping).
Our interests are many, from our grandchildren and family, local government politics, the Lions Clubs, voluntary work, travel and of course, people.
Our guest bedrooms are warm and cozy. Electric blankets provided.
We are centrally located between Feilding and Palmerston North, at Taonui.
Ten minutes from Palmerston North airport, Manfield Auto Course and the Fielddays, two hours from Wellington and three hours to Lake Taupo and the ski fields. We have 4 farm dogs and 2 cats.
For directions please ring, we look forward to meeting you. Non smokers only please.

Feilding

Homestay
Address: 12 Freyberg Street, Feilding
Name: Margaret Hickmott
Telephone: (06) 323 4699
Beds: 1 Queen, 2 Single (2 bedrooms)
Bathroom: 1 Ensuite, 1 Family share
Tariff: B&B (full) Double $70,
Single $40, Dinner $20.
Children half price. Dinner by arrangment.
NZ B&B Vouchers accepted.
Nearest Town: Feilding 1km

Enjoy a break in friendly Feilding, 7 times winner of New Zealand's most beautiful town award. Stay in comfortable home in an attractive garden setting within easy walking distance of town centre, pool complex and parks. Feilding is 15 minutes by car from Palmerston North.
Each well appointed bedroom has garden views and the double room with en suite has its own entrance. Guests are invited to use all family facilities including laundry, and a cot and high chair are available if required. Covered off street parking for your car.
Our interests are music, both classical and easy listening, gardening, cooking, travel and meeting people.
You are assured of a warm welcome and a comfortable stay in a smoke free environment. We look forward to meeting you.
Directions: *For further directions, please phone. Connections with public transport can be arranged if you wish.*

378

Hiwinui

Country Stay
Address: "Puketawa", Colyton Road, RD 5, Feilding
Name: Nelson & Phyllis Whitelock
Telephone: (06) 328 7819
Fax: (06) 328 7919
Beds: 1 Queen, 2 Single (2 bedrooms)
Bathroom: 1 Guests share
Tariff: B&B (full) Double $70, Single $40, Children half price, Dinner $25.
Credit cards accepted (VISA,M/C). NZ B&B Vouchers accepted
Nearest Town: Equal distance to Feilding and Palmerston North (15 mins)

Discover "Puketawa" for yourself and delight in truly tranquil surrounds.
Our comfortable new home, which won a national award in 1996 is situated well back from the road beside 10 acres of native bush. Sheep and beef cattle graze the adjacent family farm. Wander at your leisure through bush and farmland or just relax on the deck overlooking a bush grove which is flood lit at dark. A four wheel drive tour of the property is available. This takes in panoramic views of the Manawatu and beyond. Our interests include our family and grandchildren, camping and tramping around New Zealand, music, floral art, embroidery and of course creating gardens in harmony with the native surroundings. We offer: Warm, friendly hospitality and delicious meals prepared from fresh home grown produce all in a smoke free environment.Situation: Handy to Feilding, Palmerston North, the Manawatu Gorge and beautiful Pohangina Valley.
Directions: *Please phone for details. Pick up service available.*

Newbury, Palmerston North

Homestay/Farmstay/SC accommodation
Address: Rangitikei Line, 5 R.D., Palmerston North
Name: Keith & Margaret Morriss
Telephone: (06) 354 8961 **Fax**: (06) 354 8961
Beds: 2 Queen,1 Single (2 bedrooms).

Self Contained accommodation: 1 Double, 2 Bunks (sleeps 4) - ideal family unit.
Bathroom: Ensuite - guest private
Tariff: B&B (full) Double $70, Single $40, Children half price, Dinner $25.
Self Contained accommodation: Breakfast can be provided.
NZ B&B Vouchers and Credit Cards accepted.
Nearest Town: Palmerston North (5 minutes) on State Highway 3

A friendly welcome awaits you at "Grinton", our 100-year-old home which has recently undergone renovations. - Its namesake in Yorkshire, England, has early family connections. We offer guests a comfortable stay in pleasant garden and country surroundings, yet close to the city. Farming operations consist mainly of beef fattening and calf rearing. Large scale dairying, deer farming, equestrian centre are also in the area.We both enjoy travel and welcome the stimulation of overseas guests, ensuring them a sampling of some of New Zealand's fine food and complimentary wine. We make time to provide enjoyment for our guests. Local scenic drives may include the picturesque Pohangina Valley, The Manawatu Gorge, Massey University, the Esplanade Gardens and International Pacific College. A pleasant day trip in Oct / Nov to the world-renowned Cross-Hills Rhododendron Gardens at Kimbolton, visit Palmerston North's acclaimed Science Museum, National Rugby Museum and Vintage Motorcycle Museum. Our interests include travel, tramping, trout fishing, golf, the Lions Club, music, floral art and dried flowers.

Hokowhitu, Palmerston North

Homestay
Address: "Glenfyne",
413 Albert Street, Hokowhitu,
Palmerston North
Name: Jillian & Alex McRobert
Telephone: (06) 358 1626
Fax: (06) 358 1626
Beds: 1 Double, 2 Single (2 bedrooms)
Bathroom: 1 Guests share (large)
Tariff: B&B (full) Double $70, Single $45,
Children half price. NZ B&B Vouchers accepted
Nearest Town: Palmeston North city centre 3 kms

A warm welcome awaits you in our comfortable home. After many years of staying Bed & Breakfast in Britain, we would now like to return the hospitality shown to us on our travels. We are a retired, non-smoking couple, with varied interests, including meeting people, travel, gardening, cooking and golf. Our home is close to Massey University, College of Education and within walking distance of the Manawatu Golf Club. There are some interesting walkways nearby, and two minutes walk will take you to the Hokowhitu Village. (Post Office, Pharmacy, Bank, Restaurants etc.) In summer, guests can relax in the tranquility of our back garden, enjoy a drink or a barbecue. Jillian is a KiwiHost. Guests are welcome to use our laundry facilities. Tea / coffee always available. We are happy to meet public transport. Covered off-street parking available. Please phone for reservations and directions.

Palmerston North

Bed & Breakfast Hotel
Address: "The Gables",
179 Fitzherbert Avenue Palmerston North
Name: Paul & Monica Stichbury
Telephone: (06) 358 3209 **Fax**: (06) 358 3209
Mobile: (021) 214 2588
Beds: 3 Queen, 1 Twin share, 1 Single (3 bedrooms)
Bathroom: 1 Private, 2 Guests share
Tariff: B&B (continental) Double $80-$110, Single $60-$80, Dinner by arrangement $15. Credit cards NZ B&B Vouchers accepted $20 surcharge
Nearest Town: Palmerston North

Situated 800 metres from the Square and 150 metres from the nearest of many restaurants and cafes, the Gables is a classic English two storeyed 1920's home set in a magnificent mature garden. The main house has been totally restored and a character New England barn style apartment has been built behind the main house. Both have been furnished with antiques and in the country style.
Garaging is available for that special car if requested. The apartment is completely private and is popular with honeymoon couples. We do not usually host small children and smoking is not permitted in the buildings. We offer a discount for repeat business and have special rates for Senior citizens and mature students. The Gables is conveniently located on the main route to Massey University. Monica speaks both Mandarin and Cantonese. We welcome you to experience our hospitality.
Home Page: http://friars.co.nz

Palmerston North

Self-contained Accommodation
Address: "Iti Mara Homestay",
3 Peters Avenue,
Cloverlea, Palmerston North
Name: Dixie & Neil Signal
Telephone: (06) 354 2666
Fax: (06) 354 2666
Beds: 1 Double, 2 Single
(1 bedroom, 1 bedsit)

Iti Mara

Bathroom: 1 Ensuite
Tariff: Unit: Double $70, Single $50, Extra persons $15.00pp, Dinner $20.
Breakfast $5.00pp Full or Continental. NON SMOKING INSIDE.
NZ B&B Vouchers accepted
Nearest Town: Palmerston North 3km from city centre

"Iti Mara" (Little Garden) situated in northwest Palmerston North, on local bus route and easily accessible from all main highways - off road lock up parking.
When our children left home we converted the rooms above the garage into a sunny self-contained flat. This comprises one double bedroom, with ensuite, spacious living area with two divan beds (extra sofa bed available) - laundry downstairs. We rented the house and using the flat as a base travelled the lower North Island 'oddjobbing' - a wonderful way to meet people. Now retired, the flat enables us to still enjoy meeting people. Our guests can be totally independent; join us for meals, or have meals provided in the flat. We are totally flexible - we do appreciate prior notice for dinner.
We enjoy gardening and look forward to sharing our pleasant cottage garden with you. We are able to meet public transport.

Palmerston North

Homestay
Address: 21 Woburn Place,
Palmerston North
Name: Ainslie and Geoff Grey
Telephone: (06) 354 0490
Fax: (06) 354 0490
Beds: 2 Single (1 bedroom)
Bathroom: 1 Guests share
Tariff: B&B (full) Double $75, Single $45, Dinner $20. Children half price.
NZ B&B Vouchers accepted - $15 Surcharge.
Nearest Town: Palmerston North centre 3 kms.

Ainslie and Geoff along with our small dog, enjoy meeting people and sharing our home with visitors from far and near.
Our interests include meeting people, cooking, gardening, travel and walking.
Our home is situated about 5 mins from both the Square and the Airport, with the Railway Station and the Manawatu Sports Stadium Complex being even closer. We are able to provide transport to and from Public Transport. The Massey University campus is about 15-20 mins away.
Our warm, modern home would ideally suit reasonably active guests as the guest bedroom and bathroom are located upstairs and are not suitable for a wheelchair. Guests are most welcome to make use of our laundry facilities.
A welcome is cordially extended to you to come and share our hospitality.

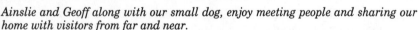

Palmerston North
Homestay
Address: "Karaka House",
473 College Street, Palmerston North
Name: Karaka House, Lynn & David Whitburn
Telephone: (06) 358 8684 **Fax**: (06) 358 8684
Mobile: (025) 245 2765
Beds: 2 Queen, 2 Single (3 bedrooms)
Bathroom: 1 Guests share

Tariff: B&B (full) Double $85, Single $60, Dinner by arrangement.
NZ B&B Vouchers accepted $15 surcharge
Nearest Town: Palmerston North, 1km to City Square

Lynn and David offer you a warm welcome to "Karaka House". We are a friendly couple who enjoy meeting people in the relaxed atmosphere of our home.
Our spacious home is in a tree lined street in Palmerston North's most beautiful suburb of Hokowhitu within easy walk of the city centre restaurants, theatres and shopping, The College of Education, Polytech, Massey and recreation facilities are within easy reach.
The tiled front entrance opens to a wide hall with a rimu staircase leading to the large sunny bedrooms, which have been designed with your comfort in mind and have electric blankets, cotton sheets, duvets, remote TV's and radio.
Tea, coffee, laundry facilities are provided and a large guest lounge is fully equipped for your pleasure. Off street parking is available.
We look forward to meeting you and having you stay with us.
Directions: *Please phone. We are happy to meet public transport.*

Foxton
Farmstay
Address: Karnak Stud, Ridge Road, Foxton
Name: Margaret Barbour
Telephone: (06) 363 7764
Fax: (06) 363 8941
Beds: 1 Double, 2 Single (2 Bedrooms)
Bathroom: 1 Ensuite, 1 Private
Tariff: B&B (Full) Double $80, Single $45,

Dinner $25 each. Children under 5 free (2 folding beds available), Campervans welcome. Dogs welcome.
Horse accommodation: Yard $12, Box $20.
Credit Cards. NZ B&B Vouchers accepted $7 surcharge
Nearest Town: Foxton, 18km to Levin

Welcome to Karnak Stud, a mini farm, full of character and so tranquil - linger awhile. An ideal stopover, 1 1/2 hrs drive from the Interisland Ferry Terminal. Margaret has travelled and enjoys meeting people and making new friends. Our comfortable farmhouse caters for everyone, and includes a large sunny games room with table tennis and darts, toys for the children, and a guests library. Come and walk through our sixteen acres of pasture and woodland. We keep thoroughbred mares and their foals, placid heifers, a farm dog and cat and have a small aviary.
Foxton has a superb beach, horse-drawn tram, doll gallery, river cruises, flax stripper museum, and much more. We are within easy reach of Palmerston North and Levin.
Directions: *Follow Farmstay arrow on State Highway One up Purcell St, over white bridge, we are next on your left.*

Oroua Downs

Farmstay
Address: Omanuka Road,
RD 11, Foxton
Name: Bev & Ian Wilson
Telephone: (06) 329 9859 **Fax**: (06) 329 9859
Mobile: (025) 986 023
Beds: 1 Double, 3 Single (3 bedrooms)
Bathroom: 1 Guests share
Tariff: B&B (full) Double $70, Single $40,
Children half price, Dinner $20pp.
NZ B&B Vouchers accepted
Nearest Town: Foxton 14km, Palmerston North 35km

We would like to welcome you to our comfortable two storey home with 1 double bed downstairs and 3 single beds upstairs. Our home is situated 2 km off State Highway One, amongst Manawatu's dairy farming. We have 5 acres of land, 1 acre of gardens to walk around, listening to the bird life and to relax.

We are situated 1 1/2 hours north of Wellington and 1/2 hours west of Palmerston North. Our region contains a sheepskin tannery, a giftware shop and an antique shop, it also has a childrens play park and wine shop with restaurant. A beach is only 15 mins away. We are self-employed with a wooden toy manufacturing business operating from our property. As we are non-smokers we request no smoking indoors.

We look forward to sharing our home and cat with you and making your stay an enjoyable one.
Directions: *Please phone.*

Levin

Bed & Breakfast Homestay
Address: 'Annandale', 108 Arapaepae Rd.,
Levin (SH 57)
Name: Cheryl & Wayne Strong
Telephone: (06) 368 5476
Beds: 1 Queen, 2 Double (3 bedrooms)
Bathroom: 1 Guests share
Tariff: B&B (full) Queen or Double $80, Single $45
NZ B&B Vouchers accepted $10 surcharge. Closed between May & July
Nearest Town: Levin 3 km

We will make you most welcome at "Annandale".
Our two storeyed old English style home, built in 1917, is set in an acre of trees and gardens, with a further 4 acres of feijoas, marketed from April to July.
We offer our guests a peaceful retreat - whether you are just passing through, or wish to get away from it all for a few days. Horowhenua has a number of attractions, mountains, beaches, golf links and bush walks; or you may choose just to potter around in our orchard and talk to our animals, which include two dogs, cats, kunekune pigs, a sulphur crested cockatoo, chooks, ducks and aviary birds. Levin has a number of reasonably priced restaurants for dinner. We are a no smoking household.
Directions: *We are on State Highway 57, 1km north of the Queen St, Arapaepae Rd (SH57) intersection, on the right hand (eastern) side of the road (sign at gate).*

MANAWATU

Levin

B&B/Homestay/Self Contained Accom
Address: 'The Fantails'
40 MacArthur Street, Levin
Name: Heather & Peter
Telephone: (06) 368 9011 or (06) 368 9279
Fax: (06) 368 9279
Beds: 1 Queen, 2 Double,
2 Single, (4 bedrooms)
Bathroom: 2 Ensuite, 1 Guests share
Tariff: B&B (special) Double $85, Single 55,
Self Contained Cottages $90 - $130,
Dinner $30, Children negotiable. Credit Cards.
NZ B&B Vouchers accepted with $10 surcharge
Nearest Town: Levin, 5 minutes to town centre.

As you enter The Fantails you will feel the tranquility and marvel at the lovely surroundings with its English trees, native bush and bird-life.
Enjoy the English style home with your hosts Heather and Peter, our Homestay will provide you with every comfort and standard you require.All bedrooms have a delightful outlook plus T.V's and videos. Enjoy a fantails special breakfast and garden view. We can offer an evening meal with organic food and N.Z. wines.Levin is situated 1 1/2 hours from Wellington and 1/2 hour from Palmerston North.Levin with its excellent climate and tourist attractions is a great place to spend those extra days. We can provide an appetising picnic basket and assist with planning your stay and onward travel.We also offer self-contained retreat cottages in our one acre of garden. These are wheelchair friendly and smoke free.
Directions: *Please phone for directions.*

Levin
Farmstay
Address: "Lynn Beau Ley", Queen Street East,
R.D. 1, Levin
Name: Beverley & Peter Lynn
Telephone: (06) 368 0310
Fax: (06) 368 0310
Beds: 1 Double, 2 Single (2 bedrooms)
Bathroom: 1 Ensuite, 1 Private
Tariff: B&B (full) Double $65, Single $43,
Dinner by arrangement $20. Credit Cards NZ B&B Vouchers accepted
Nearest Town: Levin - 3.4km east of Levin

10 tranquil rural acres 5 mins from town centre - pastoral retreat. Levin a large horticulture and floriculture centre supplying national and international markets. Activities, tramping / hunting (Tararuas), bush / scenic reserves, golf courses, arts / crafts. Our home is spacious with sunny aspect situated in 1 acre of lawns and gardens. Guest rooms are tastefully decorated - delicious breakfasts. Share a three course dinner with us or visit local restaurants / cafes.
We enjoy meeting and entertaining people, have travelled extensively in New Zealand using Bed & Breakfast accommodation. Beverley has many years experience in the hospitality business. Peter has been involved in Management of Financial Sevices A Jaycee International Senator. Some interests / hobbies handcraft oilpainting gardening hydroponics and Beau our cat.
Members Small Farmers and Black and Coloured Sheep Breeders Assn.
Directions: *Turn east off State Highway 1 at Post Office into Queen Street East we are 3.4km on left. Sign at gate.*

Levin
Farmstay
Address: Buttercup Acres,
55 Florida Road, Ohau, Levin
Name: Ivan and Pat Keating
Telephone: 06-368 0557
Fax: 06-368 0557
Beds: 1 Double, 2 Single (2 bedrooms)
Bathroom: 1 Ensuite, 1 Private
Tariff: B&B (Special) Double $90,
Single $45,Dinner $20.
Credit Cards accepted.
NZ B&B Vouchers accepted $20 surcharge
Nearest Town: Levin, 9 km

Buttercup Acres is a small tranquil rural property situated 9 km SE of Levin at the foothills of the Tararua Ranges. We specialise in breeding Miniature horses and Alpacas. Our home is surrounded by 3 acres of beautiful gardens and a large pond. Guests can feed the animals and explore the garden at their leisure. In the evenings you can relax in the lounge - learn to spin, weave in our weaving studio or view the stars through our telescope. Our model railway layout will fascinate visitors.
The surrounding district offers many interesting walks, beaches, craft shops and gardens.
We have two friendly dogs that live in the weaving studio which is adjacent to the house. We requests guests do not smoke inside. Dinner is available by arrangement and we serve a country style breakfast. Meal times are flexible to suit guests.
Directions: *Levin Information Centre or telephone.*

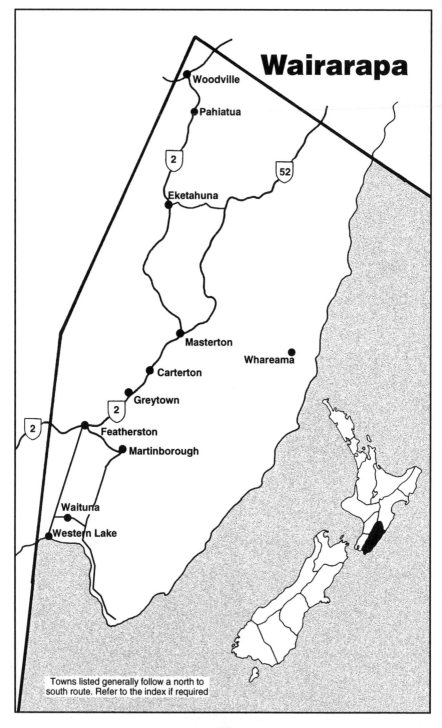

Wairarapa

Woodville
Pahiatua
2
52
Eketahuna
Masterton
Whareama
Carterton
Greytown
2
2
Featherston
Martinborough
Waituna
Western Lake

Towns listed generally follow a north to
south route. Refer to the index if required

Woodville
Farmstay/Self-contained accomm
Address: 370 River Road, Hopelands,
Woodville R.D.1
Name: Chris & Jo Coats
Telephone: (06) 376 4521
Beds: 1 Double, 2 Single (2 bedrooms)
Bathroom: 1 Family share
Tariff: B&B (full) Double $70, Single $35, Children half price; Dinner $20.
NZ B&B Vouchers accepted
Nearest Town: 12 km North East of Woodville off SH 2

We are sheep and cattle farmers on a hill country farm beside the beautiful Manawatu River renowned for its trout fishing. Fishing tackle and day licence extra. The family have fled the nest but return from time to time, seeking quiet from their busy lives. Depending on the time of year, farming activities of possible interest to tourists may be in progress, i.e. mustering, shearing, etc. and you will be very welcome to participate. The self-contained double bed unit has its own toilet and handbasin. Guests share bathroom facilities if requiring a shower.
***Directions**: If approaching via Pahiatua please ring for directions and so avoid Woodville. If travelling between Woodville and Dannevirke - follow the Hopelands Road to cross the high bridge over Manawatu River, turn right heading towards Pahiatua and the fourth house (blue) is where 'Welcome' is on the mat.*

Eketahuna
Farmstay
Address: 'Mount Donald', Newman,
R.D.4, Eketahuna
Name: Jim & Lynne Sutherland
Telephone: (06) 375 8315 **Fax**: (06) 375 8391
Beds: 1 Double, 2 Single (2 bedrooms)
Bathroom: 2 Private
Tariff: B&B (full) Double $90, Single $55, Dinner $25.
Credit cards (Visa, M/C). NZ B&B Vouchers accepted $20 surcharge
Nearest Town: Eketahuna. We are 5km north SH2.

A warm welcome to Mount Donald. Your guest wing is spacious comfortable and private. A large upstairs guest lounge provides lovely country views, help yourself to tea and coffee.
Jim, and Jason our 12 year old son, enjoy showing guests around our 1200 acre sheep and cattle property. Enjoy peaceful country walks, trout fishing, and relax in our large garden. We have lots of sheep and cattle, pet lambs, 2 cats, farm dogs and 2 horses. Our interests include golf at Eketahuna's beautiful 18 hole course, gardening, wildlife, conservation. Mount Bruce Wildlife Centre is 10 minutes drive.
Stop with us before or after Inter-Island Ferry travel. 2 hours from Wellington, 45 minutes from Palmerston North Airport.
***Directions**: We are easy to find, look for our sign on State Highway 2. The Homestead is 68 (2n house on the right) Central Mangaone Road. Mount Donald is written at the entrance.*

Please help us provide the best hospitality in the world.
Fill in a comment form for every place you stay.

Pahiatua

Farmstay
Address: 'Oete', R.D.2, Pahiatua
Name: Pauline, David & Matthew Bolton
Telephone: (06) 376 8082 **Fax**: (06) 376 8081 **Mobile**: (025) 317 267
Beds: 1 King, 1 Double, 1 Single (3 bedrooms)
Bathroom: 1 Ensuite, 1 Guests share
Tariff: B&B (full) Chalet $90, Double $80, Single $60. Dinner $20. Not suitable
for children. NZ B&B Vouchers accepted $30 surcharge for Chalet, $20 for Double
Nearest Town: Pahiatua (13kms)

*Our sheep and cattle property is ten minutes from Pahiatua, off State Highway 2, in
the Wairarapa and our rambling homestead is situated in a large treed garden. Guest
accommodation is sumptuously warm and comfortable and you have the choice of our
separate guest chalet or accommodation in our home. Meals are generous and feature
fresh produce from our farm and garden.*

*As our guests you are free to enjoy a game of tennis on our full sized tennis court, relax
in the swimming pool or enjoy a therapeutic hot spa. Guests are welcome to observe
our daily farming activities, fish for trout in local rivers or enjoy a game of golf at handy
golf course.*

*We share our home with one Burmese cat and our hobbies are gardening, photography
and country crafts. We welcome you to enjoy the very best in country hospitality at
Oete.*

Directions: *Please telephone. Non smokers preferred.*

Relax – Don't try to drive too far in one day.

Masterton

Small Farm Farmstay
Address: 'Tidsfordriv', 4 Cootes Road,
R.D. 8, Matahiwi, Masterton
Name: Glenys Hansen
Telephone: (06) 378 9967
Fax: (06) 378 9957
Beds: 1 Double,
2 Single (2 bedrooms)
Bathroom: 1 Guests share
Tariff: B&B (Full) Double $65,
Single $35, Children half price, Dinner $20,
Campervans $25 . Credit cards. NZ B&B Vouchers accepted
Nearest Town: Masterton 10 km

Divert off the main highway and visit "Tidsfordriv" where a warm welcome awaits you.
A comfortable new home set in park-like surroundings overlooks wetland habitat which attracts many species of wetland birds. Take a walk around the large gardens that have recently been developed and enjoy birdwatching with ease.
Sheep and South Devon cattle graze the fields on this 64 acre farmlet.
Glenys has home-hosted for 11 years and invites you to join her for dinner. Conservation and gardening are her interests.
Many Wairarapa tourist attractions are within a short journey-National Wildlife Centre, gardens, crafts, vineyards to name a few.
Friendly cat and a Labrador dog are the family pets.
Directions: *Please phone for directions. 7km from main Bypass route.*

Lansdowne, Masterton

Homestay
Address: 65 Titoki Street,
Lansdowne, Masterton
Name: Gordon & Doreen McNeilage
Telephone: (06) 377 3817
Beds: 1 Double, 2 Single (2 bedrooms)
Bathroom: 1 Guests share
Tariff: B&B (continental) Double $60, Single $40, Children $20,
NZ B&B Vouchers accepted
Nearest Town: Masterton - 2km north Masterton on SH1 turn right.

We are a family of four, plus one sleepy cat. We are fortunate to live in the beautiful suburb of Lansdowne, about one mile north of the town of Masterton. Our home is nearly fifty years old and we have altered and improved it to give us more living space. It is surrounded by gardens and has an outdoor court area. Masterton has a lovely park, attractive shops and restaurants. It is a very appealing town and we wish to extend warm, friendly hospitality.

Please help us provide the best hospitality in the world.
Fill in a comment form for every place you stay.

Masterton
Small Farmstay + Self-Contained accomodation
Address: Harefield, 147 Upper Plain Road, Masterton
Name: Robert & Marion Ahearn
Telephone: (06) 377 4070
Beds: 1 Double, 1 Single (1 bedroom)
Bathroom: 1 Private / Detached,
fully equipped, self-contained flat, self catering, - 1 Double, 1 Single (1 bedroom)
+ 1 Single & 1 Fold-down Double in Living Room. Cot & Highchair Available.
1 Bathroom. Private.
Tariff: B&B (full) Double $70, Single $45,
Children under 12 half price. Dinner $20,
Campervans $20. Self-contained Flat Double $55, $5 each extra person.
Nearest Town: Masterton 4kms - 1km from Bypass.

*We are farmers whose family have all left home. Eighteen years ago we built our cedar
house on 13 acres, 5 km from the Post Office, 1 km from Bypass Road.*
*Our guest room is away from the kitchen and our bedroom. A cottage garden
surrounds the house and flat, 200 metres back from the road.*
*We look out on to the beautiful Tararua mountains and paddocks with sheep, cattle
and deer. We have been home hosting for some years and have ourselves been guests
in Europe, Australia and New Zealand. Our interests include travel, reading, arts,
tramping, wild life, walking, gardening, Rose Society, Probus Club. We are half an
hour's drive to Martinborough vineyards. If you stay in the flat you can choose to be
self-catering or arrange dinner and breakfast with us. Guests in the house may also
arrange dinner. Complimentary tea and coffee at any time. Excellent restaurants 8
minutes away. Reductions for longer stays. We are half an hour's drive to the National
Wildlife Centre and less than two hour's drive from the Inter-Island Ferry.*
We do not smoke - you may.

Members of
**The New Zealand Association
Farm & Home Host Inc.**
maintain the highest standards &
are always delighted to welcome
guests into their homes.

Masterton
Bed & Breakfast
Address: 'Victoria House',
15 Victoria Street, Masterton
Name: Grant & Jan Beaumont
Telephone: (06) 377 0186 **Fax**: (06) 377 0186
Mobile: (025) 883 461
Beds: 3 Double, 4 Single (6 bedrooms)
Bathroom: 2 Guests share
Tariff: B&B (full) Double $65, Single $39, Not suitable children under 12,
Credit Cards. NZ B&B Vouchers accepted
Nearest Town: 100km north of Wellington on State Highway 2

Welcome to Victoria House. We are forty and have three sons. Our home is a beautiful colonial two storey house built pre 1886. We have renovated the guests' accommodation, keeping the character of the house, while retaining home comforts. (We even stripped light fittings back to the brass and wood).
The guests' bedrooms are like your own room away from home. Furnished colonial style and decorated in soft tonings to create a peaceful atmosphere. All rooms equipped with heaters. Some have handbasins. There are two guests bathrooms, tea, coffee, milo available at all times. There is a comfortable TV lounge where smoking is permitted (No smoking in bedrooms).
Our tariff includes a continental breakfast but cooked can happily be arranged. We aim for quality accommodation that's warm and friendly.
Set in a quiet location we are 2 minutes walk from the town centre and many excellent facilities. No pets.

Whareama, Masterton
Farmstay
Address: 'Alderford', R.D.12, Masterton
Name: Carol & Les Ross
Telephone: (06) 372 3705
Beds: 1 Double (1 Bedroom)
Bathroom: 1 Ensuite
Tariff: B&B (continental - full $5pp extra) Double $70, Single $45, Dinner $25pp
(3 course). NZ B&B Vouchers accepted
Nearest Town: Masterton 40km 1/2 hour, Wellington 2 hours

Les and Carol offer you a warm friendly welcome to "Alderford".
Stay in our tastefully decorated warm cottage room with ensuite, away from the main homestead. Cosy double bed, electric blanket, feather duvet, radio, TV, 2 easy chairs. Also tea, coffee, Milo and homemade biscuits on your arrival. Your breakfast served in you room or in the garden. Picnic lunches available. Dinner served in our dining room with open fire. Homemade country meals with our homemade jam, bottled fruit, fresh veges from garden, free range eggs.
Alderford is a 300 acre sheep, cattle and deer farm. You are very welcome to enjoy the beauty of our farm and our country garden. We are 10 minutes to the beautiful Riversdale Beach with lovely 9 hole golf course, swimming, fishing etc. We are 10 minutes to the well known Tinui pub, craft shop, open gardens and 25 mins to the beauty of Castlepoint Beach. We also arrange canoe trips for your enjoyment.
Our interests include our garden, fishing, cooking and Lions Club activities.
"Alderford" is a 30 min picturesque drive from Masterton.

Masterton

Homestay
Address: 29 Essex St, Masterton
Name: Marion & Rick Long
Telephone: (06) 378 6252 **Fax**: (06) 378 6252
Beds: 1 King, 1 Queen, 2 Single (3 bedrooms)
Bathroom: 1 Ensuite, 1 Guest share
Tariff: B&B (full) Double $95, Single $65,
Credit Cards (VISA/MC)
NZ B&B Vouchers accepted $25 surcharge
Nearest Town: Masterton centre 500m

Essex House was built at the turn of the century and is situated in a quiet tree lined street on Masterton's west Side just a few hundred yards from the centre of town and within walking distance of a fine selection of restaurants. Centrally situated for the many interesting outings available in the wonderful Wairarapa.

Three bedrooms are available for guests; one twin with ensuite (downstairs), one kingsize double amd one queen size double (upstairs) both sharing a guest bathroom. The kingsize room has its own separate sitting room.

There is a large lounge, with an open fireplace, T.V., and tea making facilities set aside exclusively for homestayers. Essex house is centrally heated in winter with a wood stove feeding seven radiators. For Wairarapa sweltering summers relax in the tranquil garden or cool off in the swimming pool. Offstreet parking; Smokefree

Masterton

Guest House
Address: 145 Perry Street, Masterton
Name: "Station Guesthouse"
Gay & Richard Te One
Telephone: (06) 378 9319
Fax: (06) 378 9319
Beds: 2 Double/Twin, 4 Double,
11 Single, 1 Family (12 bedrooms)
Bathroom: 3 Guests share
Tariff: B&B (Continental)
Double/Twin $60,
Single $40, Dinner $20, Credit Cards.
Nearest Town: Masterton 1km

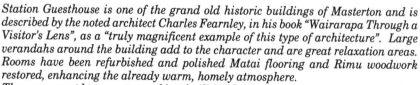

Station Guesthouse is one of the grand old historic buildings of Masterton and is described by the noted architect Charles Fearnley, in his book "Wairarapa Through a Visitor's Lens", as a "truly magnificent example of this type of architecture". Large verandahs around the building add to the character and are great relaxation areas. Rooms have been refurbished and polished Matai flooring and Rimu woodwork restored, enhancing the already warm, homely atmosphere.

There are guest lounges, tea making facilities, log burner and open fire plus outdoor areas and a very friendly black Labrador dog.

We are handy to the railway station, shops and restaurants with the many Wairarapa attractions within short drives.

Smokefree. Offstreet parking.

Masterton

Homestay, Self Contained Accommodation
Address: Ngahape Road, RD 10,
Masterton, Wairarapa
Name: Emily and Noah
Telephone: (06) 372 2772
Fax: (06) 372 2773 **Mobile**: (025) 289 0137
Beds: 2 Queen, 8 Single (3 bedrooms)
Bathroom: 1 Guests share
Tariff: B&B (full) Double $55, Single $30,
Dinner $24. Children half price.
Credit cards accepted. NZ B&B Vouchers accepted
Nearest Town: Masterton (41 km South East of Masterton)

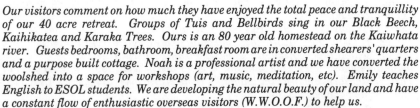

Our visitors comment on how much they have enjoyed the total peace and tranquillity of our 40 acre retreat. Groups of Tuis and Bellbirds sing in our Black Beech, Kaihikatea and Karaka Trees. Ours is an 80 year old homestead on the Kaiwhata river. Guests bedrooms, bathroom, breakfast room are in converted shearers' quarters and a purpose built cottage. Noah is a professional artist and we have converted the woolshed into a space for workshops (art, music, meditation, etc). Emily teaches English to ESOL students. We are developing the natural beauty of our land and have a constant flow of enthusiastic overseas visitors (W.W.O.O.F.) to help us.
Good scenic hill walks with safe water-holes to cool in on your return.
We have two wonderfully natured dogs and a dozen cheeky hens. We would be pleased to pick you up from the bus depot / railway station in Masterton.
You can be self catering or have all your meals with us.
Stays of 2-3 cays are recommended for the complete country experience.
Directions: *Our valley at Ngahape is at the end of a No Exit Rd. From Masterton we drive through Wainuioru. Please phone for reservations and further directions.*

Masterton

Homestay/Private Suites
Address: "Homebush",
Homebush Road, RD 5, Masterton
Name: Rachael and Paul Henry
Telephone: (06) 377 2522
Fax: (06) 377 2522
Mobile: (025) 452 900
Beds: 2 Queen (2 bedrooms)
Bathroom: 2 Ensuite

Tariff: (B&B (continental) Double $110, Single $90. Exclusive (full) Double $150, Single $120. Discounts for 3 nights or more. Visa/Mastercard.
Nearest Town: Masterton 1km from town boundary.

"Homebush" is a unique 1800's Natusch designed Homestead with striking features. Breakfast in the formal wood-panelled dining room and relax in the lovely classic living room. The 2 private suites (purpose built inc. TV, Fridge, Tea / Coffee) are situated next to the main home along with character buildings, in an English village atmosphere. Guests are welcome to enjoy the 5 acre grounds. Relax in the spa, coffee in the Summer House, wander through the gardens. Along with our three daughters we offer very friendly service and are happy to help organise your stay in the Wairarapa. There's something special about the atmosphere at Homebush. Sheds house everything from a Massey Ferguson to a Rolls-Royce. The house holds secrets from the turn of the century and its days as a girl's finishing school.
Directions: *Phone for details, we are easy to find from the centre of Masterton.*

Masterton

Homestay

Address: "Llandaff", Fire No. 155
Upper Plain Road, RD 8, Masterton
Name: Liz Tennet
Telephone: (06) 378 6628
Fax: (06) 378 6612
Beds: 2 Queen, 2 Single (King) (3 bedrooms)
Bathroom: 2 Guests share
Tariff: B&B (full) Double $100, Single $60, Dinner $25,
Children - dollar amount the same as their age.

Nearest Town: Masterton, 5 mins from Masterton Post Office

Llandaff is an historic 1880's Wairarapa homestead providing rural elegance, tranquillity and beauty.

Elegantly restored, the homestead boasts beautiful original New Zealand timbers throughout, including polished floors; old pull-handle toilets; a "coffin" bath; open fire places (also in bedrooms); and a cosy wood burning kitchen stove.

Guests are invited to enjoy the beautiful large garden beneath 100 year old trees, and to wander the farm and feed the animals. There is also bike riding, cricket, croquet, petanque, and cappuccino coffee.

Children are very welcome, and their company is enjoyed by our 10 year old son, and house pets. Llandaff gives peace and tranquillity to the visitor, yet is close enough to a huge range of Wairarapa pursuits - river and sea fishing; canoeing and swimming; bush and farm walks; horse riding; garden visits; wine tasting (35 minutes to Martinborough); antiques; crafts; historic places; and the National Wildlife Centre. Come and enjoy.

Coastal Wairarapa

Farmstay+S.C. Cottage
Address: 'Waimoana Station',
Glenburn Road, R.D.3, Masterton
Name: Lynne & Bill Thompson
Telephone: (06) 372 7732 **Fax**: (06) 372 7782
Beds: Homestead: 1 King, 1Queen, 1 Single (3 bedrooms)
Bathroom: Homestead: 1 Ensuite, 1 Private. Cottage: 1 Private
Tariff: Homestead B&B (full) Double $120, Single $60, Dinner $30.
Cottage Self Contained: Double $80. Cottage B&B: Double $100.
Houses smoke free.
Nearest Town: Masterton and Carterton one hour, Wellington two hours.

Waimoana , a 1000 hectare sheep and beef station, borders the Pacific ocean for three kilometres. Coastal Flats with Ngaio, Karaka and Cabbage trees, rise to hills with areas of native bush. The large homestead is typical of 1920s architecture, with rimu panelling and ornate ceilings. Not suitable for children. Enjoy two acre garden with free ranging hens, guinea fowl, and peacocks. Tennis court and swimming pool in season. Five minute walk to beach. Explore coastline, swimming and rock pools at low tide. Farm walks on tracked hills provide wonderful views. Pre European historic sites on farm. Nearby D.O.C. walkway to seal colony and honeycomb rock.

Waimoana Cottage. Modern, sunny, three bedroom, self contained cottage sited with lawn and garden. Ideal weekend retreat for couples, or suitable for families on holiday. Enjoy homestead garden with childrens play area.

Breakfast by arrangement.

Directions: *Please phone or fax for details, pamphlet and directions.*

Flat Point/Coast

Coastal Farmstay/Self Contained Accommodation
Address: Caledonia Station, RD3, Masterton
Name: Wenda and Paul Kerr
Telephone: (06) 372 7553 **Fax**: (06) 372 7553
Email: wendakerr@xtra.co.nz
Beds: 4 Queen, 2 Single (5 bedrooms)
Bathroom: 1 Ensuite, 2 Private, 1 Guests share.
Tariff: B&B Suites Double $125, Single $90, Children $10.
Cottage Double $150 each extra person $15.
NZ B&B Vouchers accepted $45 surcharge, not on public/school holidays.
Nearest Town: 60 km from Masterton or Carterton.

Come experience the ultimate retreat! We are a young Kiwi / Canadian couple with a 2 year old son, on an 1880 acre sheep and cattle station on the Wairarapa coast, approximately 2 hours from Wellington or Palmerston North. Our self contained luxury accommodation consists of a fully renovated 3 bedroom, 2 bathroom farm cottage and 2 Queen sized suites, newly built in traditional New Zealand style. Each has its own cooking facilities, fireplace, electric blankets and sea view.
Enjoy walking the beach, through our extensive gardens, exploring the farm or just curl up with a book. There is a 3 hour public walk nearby, providing sights such as a seal colony, ship wreck and honeycomb rock. If you enjoy fishing, charters can be arranged. Meals can be arranged with advance notice. Special winter and midweek rates available except for public / school holidays.
Please feel free to contact us for further information and directions.

Carterton

Small Farmstay
Address: 'Longmeadow' Park Road, R.D.2 Carterton
Name: John & Viv Stokes
Telephone: (06) 379 7897 **Fax**: (06) 379 7897
Beds: 1 Double, 2 Single (2 bedrooms)
Bathroom: 1 Guests share
Tariff: B&B (full) Double $65, Single $40, School children half price,
Dinner $20. NZ B&B Vouchers accepted
Nearest Town: Carterton 2km

Welcome to "Longmeadow", which is situated in a quiet rural setting surrounded by picturesque views of the Tararua Ranges and rolling farmland.
Our 25 acre farmlet with sheep, cattle and fowls is just the place to relax, yet only 2km from the town of Carterton.
Come and stay one night or two on your journey through the Wairarapa as Carterton is central to the region's attractions from the Martinborough vineyards to the Mount Bruce Bird Reserve, tramping in the ranges, jetboating etc, etc.
We, together with our youngest son, 18, enjoy meeting people, gardening and just pottering around our place. Our aim is to provide a friendly relaxed atmosphere to make your stay in the area as enjoyable as possible. Evening meal by arrangement. We request no smoking in the house.
Directions: *Please write or phone. Arrangements can be made to collect from public transport.*

Relax – Don't try to drive too far in one day.

Waiohine Gorge - Carterton/Greytown

Farmstay
Address: Waiohine Farm, Waiohine Gorge Road,
Fire No. 21, RD 1, Carterton
Name: Jenni and Trevor Berthold
Telephone: (06) 379 6716
Fax: (06) 379 6716
Mobile: (025) 523 839
Email: waiohine@xtra.co.nz
Beds: 2 Double, 1 Single (2 bedrooms)
Bathroom: 1 Private, 1 Family share
Tariff: B&B (full) Double $80, Single $50, Dinner $20, children half price.
Campervans $20. Credit Cards accepted.
NZ B&B Vouchers accepted $10 surcharge
Nearest Town: Carterton and Greytown both 15 minutes away.

Nestled in the foothills of the Tararua Ranges, alongside the Waiohine River, our 100 acre farm offers tranquillity, comfort and variety. A spacious home with fire, TV room, spa bath and BBQ area. A touch of the past, our double bedroom is charmingly decorated with oak furniture. Port-a-cot available. We are from professional backgrounds, in mid forties and well travelled. Our girls have their own ponies (pony rides can be arranged). The farm runs a Santa-Gertrudis cattle stud, with sheep, horses, dogs, cats, chickens, ducks and a goat! You are welcome to wander through farmland, river flats, native bush, wetlands; enjoy the scenery and native bird life. The river is popular for trout, swimming, rafting and within minutes is the forest park for abseiling, hunting or tramping.
Home Page: http://mysite.xtra.co.nz/~waiohine
Directions: *Only 10 minutes from State Highway 2, between Carterton and Greytown. Please write or phone.*

Greytown

Homestay
Address: 78 Kuratawhiti Street,
Greytown
Name: Marilla & Steve Davis
Telephone: (06) 304 8588
Mobile: (025) 994 394
Beds: 1 King, 1 Queen, 1 Single (2 bedrooms)
Bathroom: 1 Guests share
Tariff: B&B (continental) Double $85, Single $55, Children $20. Credit Cards.
Nearest Town: Masterton 40km/Wellington 80km

From the moment you drive down "The Ambers" tree lined driveway you will begin to experience the old world charm of our large 1920's family home. We have two acres of garden for you to wander in and soak up the country atmosphere. A warm welcome will be extended to you including a joyous greeting from "BJ" our pet corgi.

Our home is ideal for anyone wanting to relax, enjoy life and experience historic Greytown. We are situated just metres from Greytown's renown park which features grand trees, swimming pool and tennis courts.

Your are just minutes away from Greytown's cafes, restaurants, antique shops and ten minutes away from Martinborough's vineyards and golf course.

"The Ambers" offers guests two bedrooms, one with Kingsize and single beds, one with Queensize, a guest bathroom, a spacious guests lounge with open fire, spa pool and sunny verandah.

The tariff is $85 per room per night, including a delicious continental breakfast of muesli, fresh fruit and home-made muffins.

Greytown

Homestay
Address: 40 Kuratawhiti Street, Greytown
Name: Summerfield
Telephone: (06) 304 9942 **Fax**: (06) 304 8165
Beds: 2 Queen, 1 Double, 1 Single (3 bedrooms)
Bathroom: 1 Ensuite, 1 Private, 1 Guests share
Tariff: B&B Double $90, Single $80, Ensuite $100, Double $90
Children $15, under 5 free. NZ B&B Vouchers accepted $20 surcharge
Nearest Town: Greytown

... A touch of country ... ... A place of peace ... Entering the historic tree lined driveway to Summerfield your restorative experience will commence. Set amongst long loved shrubs and trees our pre-1900 homestead with private verandahs exudes a rare, gentle ambience and complements the warm welcome and care enjoyed by our guests. An outdoor spa is available. Facilities are suitable for disabled guests. Our friendly dog and aged cat will also welcome you. Every season brings its special delights as you enjoy the picturesque beauty of the southern Wairarapa. Within short distances you can enjoy gentle bush and river walks or serious tramping, canoeing, tennis, cycling swimming, orchards, berry picking, craft and wine making areas, beautiful gardens, surfing, fishing. We will enjoy sharing your company but will respect your desire for privacy if you wish to 'just be' and relax.
Directions: *Please write or phone.*

One of the differences between staying at a hotel and a B&B
is that you don't hug the hotel staff when you leave.

Greytown

Homestay
Address: 182 West Street, Greytown
Name: Southey Manor
Telephone: (06) 304 9367
Fax: (06) 304 9789
Mobile: (025) 424 035
Beds: 3 Double, 2 Single (4 bedrooms)
Bathroom: 1 Ensuite, 1 Guests share
Tariff: B&B (continental) Double $70-$80.
NZ B&B Vouchers accepted
Nearest Town: Greytown

Spacious relaxed accommodation within easy walking distance of restaurants, cafes and village shops. Double bedroom - ensuite. Twin bedroom, two double bedrooms - share guest bathroom. Group bookings available. Sky, TV, tea / coffee outdoor pool and barbecue facilities provided.
Continental breakfast $70, Double $80 ensuite. Easy to find - follow B&B signs.

Western Lake

Homestay
Address: Tarawai,
Western Lake Road,
RD 3, Featherston
Name: Maria Wallace & Ron Allan
Telephone: (06) 307 7660
Fax: (06) 307 7661
Mobile: 025 962 470
Email: tarawai@xtra.co.nz
Beds: 2 King
(both can convert to singles),
1 Queen (3 bedrooms)
Bathroom: 3 Ensuite
Tariff: B&B (full) $270 per couple,
Single $135, include dinner and breakfast.
Nearest Town: Martinborough or Featherston (approx 32km from either)

We enjoy welcoming people to our home which is situated in the Western Lake area of Palliser Bay. We have 20 hectares of native bush close to Lake Wairarapa, Rimutaka Forest Park, Lake Onoke and Ocean Beach and we love to share our spectacular views of the bay, river, lakes and mountain ranges. The house is designed for space, comfort and warmth and we have large bedrooms, a variety of sitting areas, a sauna and a smoke free environment.
We enjoy cooking and sharing delicious meals of fresh, healthy foods. We have travelled, have wide ranging interests and thoroughly enjoy the company of friends, old and new.
Our region offers many attractions including wetlands, the national wildlife centre, hunting, tramping, duck shooting, trout and sea fishing, bush and beach walks, seal colony, vineyards, beautiful gardens, crafts people and many antique shops.

There are some good tips for easier travel on page 7

Featherston - Waituna

Country Accom+Self-contained Cottage
Address: 'Waituna', East West Access Road,
R.D. 3, Featherston.
Name: Irwin & Kay Luttrell
Telephone: (06) 307 7743 **Fax**: (06) 307 7753
Beds: Homestead: 2 Queen, 2 Single (3 bedrooms). Cottage: 1 Queen, 1Double,
1 set of Bunks + 1 single. Bedsettee in lounge (3 bedrooms)
Bathroom: Homestead: 1 Ensuite, 1 Private. Cottage: 1 Private
Tariff: Homestead: All meals and beverages, Double $260 (full board).
Cottage: B&B Double $120. Self-catering: Double $90. Credit Cards.
NZ B&B Vouchers accepted $50 surcharge for B&B (full) cottage
Nearest Town: Featherston or Martinborough (approx 28 km from either).

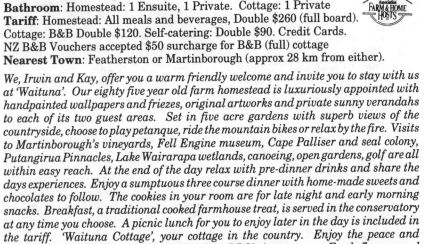

*We, Irwin and Kay, offer you a warm friendly welcome and invite you to stay with us
at 'Waituna'. Our eighty five year old farm homestead is luxuriously appointed with
handpainted wallpapers and friezes, original artworks and private sunny verandahs
to each of its two guest areas. Set in five acre gardens with superb views of the
countryside, choose to play petanque, ride the mountain bikes or relax by the fire. Visits
to Martinborough's vineyards, Fell Engine museum, Cape Palliser and seal colony,
Putangirua Pinnacles, Lake Wairarapa wetlands, canoeing, open gardens, golf are all
within easy reach. At the end of the day relax with pre-dinner drinks and share the
days experiences. Enjoy a sumptuous three course dinner with home-made sweets and
chocolates to follow. The cookies in your room are for late night and early morning
snacks. Breakfast, a traditional cooked farmhouse treat, is served in the conservatory
at any time you choose. A picnic lunch for you to enjoy later in the day is included in
the tariff. 'Waituna Cottage', your cottage in the country. Enjoy the peace and
tranquillity with warm fires in winter, lazy BBQ's in summer. Fresh flowers and
home-made biscuits to welcome you. Self catering or Homestead meals. Relax in the
picturesque homestead gardens.*
Directions: *Please phone us anytime for more information.*

Featherston

Bed & Breakfast
Address: 47 Watt Street,
Featherston,Wairarapa
Name: Woodland Holt Bed & Breakfast
Telephone: (06) 308 9927
Beds: 1 Queen, 2 single (4 bedrooms)
Bathroom: 1 Ensuite, 1 Guests share.
Tariff: B&B (continental) Double $100-$120, Single $60-$65.
Dinner by arrangement.   NZ B&B Vouchers accepted, surcharge applies.
Nearest Town: Featherston (located on edge of town)

Judi Adams and her Burmese cats welcome you.   We enjoy meeting people and providing friendly hospitality.   Interests include travelling (Spanish is spoken), gardening, books, collecting and cross-stitch.   Our home is set in a secluded garden containing native, exotic and rare plants. We offer warm, luxury accommodation with off street parking.   For breakfast enjoy home made treats including home preserved fruit and fresh juice.   During the day explore beautiful Wairarapa or relax in comfort. In the evening dine at a local restaurant or by prior arrangement join me for an evening meal.   Picnic hampers are available (additional charge).   Smoking outdoors only please.
We look forward to your company and making your stay enjoyable.
Directions: *At Featherston, travelling north, turn left (right if southbound) off main road into Wakefield St, turn into Fox St. Follow road around to the right into Watt St. Go straight ahead, Woodland Holt is signposted on your left.   Go up the driveway.*

Martinborough

Country Homestay
Address: 'Shadyvale', Hinakura Road,
R.D.4, Martinborough
Name: Colin & Julie McKinlay
Telephone: (06) 306 9374
Fax: (06) 306 9374
Beds: 2 Double (2 bedrooms)
Bathroom: 1 Ensuite, 1 Private
Tariff: B&B (full) Double $90-$120,
Single $60-$110, Credit Cards (VISA/MC).
Nearest Town: 3km east of Martinborough, and only 1 1/4 hours from central Wellington.

Set amidst an extensive garden and orchard, Shadyvale has breathtaking views to the Tararua ranges across 44 acres of farmland.   Enjoy a peaceful stroll around the property, play petanque, swim or fish in the river, or simply relax around the solar-heated swimming pool. In winter, curl up by the open fire with a good book or join your hosts for a chat in the cosy farmhouse kitchen.   All rooms open onto the spacious verandah, beds have electric blankets, and the woodstove provides central heating throughout the house.   Our farm style breakfast, featuring eggs from our free range hens, is served in the formal dining room or on the verandah, depending on the season. Shadyvale is within walking distance of Martinborough's vineyards and golf course, and we can arrange horse trekking, kayaking, garden visits etc. Martinborough is also renowned for its fine restaurants, and we are happy to make bookings for you.

Martinborough
Homestay/Farmstay/SC Accom/House/Lodge
Address: "Glendoon", RD 4, Martinborough
Name: Glendoon
Telephone: (06) 372 7779 **Fax**: (06) 372 7599
Mobile: (025) 776 968
Beds: 1 Double, 1 Queen and 2 Singles (3 bedrooms)
Bathroom: 2 Private
Tariff: B&B (full) Double $120, Each extra $50, Single $120, Children negotiable.
Nearest Town: 10 mins to Martinborough, 75 mins to Wellington

Enjoy a private, comfortable, self contained, three bedroom, country home in tranquil surroundings, set in oaks. "GLENDOON" is a gentle hill farm, with wildfowl and trout waters, and National Trust native bush. Stroll, picnic, relax in the home or garden, BBQ, feed the doves and chooks, enjoy the books, or simply relax. Glendoon has all amenities, TV, video, laundry, woodburners (farm kitchen and dining room), sitting room open fire, vintage bath, and master bedroom onto the front verandah with ensuite and shower. Glendoon is also available with or without "STONEMEAD COTTAGE," a cozy and comfortable self contained, modern two double bedroomed cottage, in its own private picturesque setting on Glendoon with trees, claw bath, fire, TV, all amenities shower, and front verandah also with lovely valley views.
Both provide breakfast foods and complementary provisions. You do not share. Maps, garaging, and advice available. Both Glendoon and Stonemead welcome you to distinctive country comfort.

Martinborough
Homestay
Address: "Oak House",
45 Kitchener Street,
Martinborough
Name: Polly & Chris Buring
Telephone: (06) 306 9198
Fax: (06) 306 8198
Beds: 1 Queen, 2 Single (2 bedrooms)
Bathroom: 1 Guests share
Tariff: B&B (special) Double $90, Single $45, Children by arrangement, Dinner by arrangement.
Nearest Town: Martinborough 5 mins walk

Oak House

Our characterful seventy year old Californian bungalow offers gracious accommodation only minutes away from Martinborough's renowned vineyards and restaurants. Chris, your host, is a winemaker, and our spacious, cosy guest lounge with ornate ceiling, large bay window and wood burner fire, provides a relaxed setting for sampling Chris's wonderful wines. Breakfast, served in the dining room (or on the verandah when weather permits) features freshly baked croissants, home preserved local fruits and home made conserves. Polly enjoys cooking creatively and dinner, which includes local wild game matched to Chris's wine, is available by arrangement. Our guest wing has its own entrance, bathroom (with large bath and roomy shower) and separate WC and handbasin. Both bedrooms enjoy afternoon sun and garden views.
A stately pin oak provides shade in summer and a backdrop for Polly's rose gardens. Our pets include famous artistic cats, chickens and two kunekune piggies.

Martinborough
Farmstay+S.C. Accommodation
Address: "Tironui", R.D. 1, Martinborough
Name: "Tironui" Farmstay
Telephone: (06) 306 9173
Fax: (06) 306 9173
Email: tironui@xtra.co.nz
Beds: 3 Double, 6 single (5 bedrooms)
Bathroom: 2 Private, 1 Guests share
Tariff: B&B (full) Double $80, Single $40, Children $15, Dinner $20.
Nearest Town: Masterton 60 km

We are a 180 acre beef farm, but also have chooks, pigs, ducks, turkeys, sheep, which in season you may help us feed if you wish to have "hands on" experience.

The Farmhouse sleeps 8. Two double beds available and four single beds. It has two log burning fires (with plenty of firewood), TV, auto washing machine, CD player, full kitchen facilities which include oven and microwave. All linen provided and electric blankets on all beds.

Outside are outdoor table and gas BBQ. In-ground swimming pool, lawn tennis court, volley ball, croquet and pétanque for you to use at your leisure, surrounded with established trees, gardens with many rose bushes.

In the main homestead (200 metres away) we also have one double room and 1 twin room available.

All meals available at a reasonable cost.

Martinborough
Homestay
Address: 87 Dublin Street, Martinborough
Name: Swan House
Telephone: (06) 306 9057
Mobile: (021) 621 673
Beds: 3 Queen, (3 bedrooms)
Bathroom: 3 Ensuite
Tariff: B&B (full) Double $90-$110, Single $45-$50, Children $20-$30, Dinner on request, Credit Cards (VISA/MC), Discount for consecutive nights.
NZ B&B Vouchers accepted Discount for consecutive nights
Nearest Town: Featherston/Greytown 10-15 mins, Masterton 35-40 mins

A warm welcome awaits you at Swan House. Samantha (Sammy) my small very friendly King Charles Spaniel and I enjoy having people to stay. My pleasant home is within walking distance of the 'Square' around which can be found some fine restaurants and our newly refurbished hotel. Our popular vineyards nearby include some charming cafes, golf, squash and tennis facilities are aavailable and the wild Palliser Coast is an easy drive away.

Each of the three large bed sitting rooms have their own entrances and ensuites, all have Queen beds, two of the rooms also have a single bed as well - electric blankets, TV, tea / coffee making facilities. The house is set back from the road on a large well developed section with mature trees providing pleasant surroundings. Ample off street parking available. Private and peaceful.

Martinborough
B&B Homestay, Self Contained Accommodation
Address: Beatson's Harrington, 9A Cologne Street, Martinborough
Name: Karin Beatson and John Cooper
Telephone: (06) 306 8242 **Fax**: (06) 306 8243 **Mobile**: (025) 499 827
Beds: 4 Queen (4 bedrooms)
Bathroom: 4 Ensuites, 1 Family share
Tariff: B&B (special) Double $150, Single $130, Dinner by arrangement.
Not suitable for children. Visa/Mastercard.
Nearest Town: Martinborough

Beatson's is a 1905 villa five minutes walk from Martinborough Square, carefully restored as a boutique Bed and Breakfast with spacious bedrooms and modern ensuites.

One hour's drive form Wellington, the "wine village' is famous for its vineyards, cafes, restaurants, specialist shops and delightful countryside. Visitors come to Martinborough for the good things in life. Beatson's with its friendly, warm and casual atmosphere fits the mood.

The house, with its polished matai floors, is furnished in a comfortable country style, with antique furniture and features work by New Zealand artists.

Overlooking the garden the large open-plan kitchen, dining and living area opens onto the deck and verandah.

Country breakfasts include seasonal local produce, home made breads and preserves and a speciality cooked breakfast.

Guests can breakfast under the trees, on the verandah, in the dining room or in their bedroom, even propped up in bed.

Our original home, Rothesay, a three-bedroomed house suitable for groups and families is also available. It has two double beds and twin beds. The delightful garden has large trees, and good outdoor spaces. This is available as self-contained accommodation.

We have a black curly-coated retriever called Ranui, and visiting neighbours' cats. We request that our guests do not smoke indoors.

Martinborough

Homestay
Address: "Ross Glyn", 1 Grey St, Martinborough
Telephone: (06) 306 9967 **Fax**: (06) 306 8267
Beds: 1 Double, 2 Single (2 bedrooms)
Bathroom: 1 Private, 1 Guests share
Tariff: B&B (full) Double $80, Single $45, Children $25, Dinner $20+. Credit cards.
Nearest Town: Martinborough 5 minutes

Recent retirement has released us to pursue our joint passions of meeting people and developing our 5 acre garden.

Our homestay offers absolute peace and privacy, and yet is only 10 minutes away from the town square, vineyards, picturesque golf course, or trout fishing in the Ruamahunga River.

Guests may enjoy discovering peaceful corners of the garden, - the Summer House to Camellia Walk, Woodland area, enclosed circular Rose Gardens and potager Herb and Vegetable garden, fish spotting beside the Lily Ponds, feeding the Fantail, Pigeons, Doves and Donkeys, playing Petanque or Croquet, all possibilities at Ross Glyn.

Guests are welcome to relax with us and our small dog and cat in our large cosy (woodburner heated) lounge. Each guest room has French doors, providing private access and opening onto a sunny verandah and garden.

Breakfast includes fresh croissants, home made jams, jellies, preserved fruit. Cooked breakfast on request, and dinner by arrangement.

If you have enjoyed B&Bs in New Zealand,

contact

*Pelican Publishing Company, Inc.
to order or learn about our other
bed and breakfast books,
small hotel books, and travel guides.*

**1-800-843-1724
1-888-5-PELICAN
sales@pelicanpub.com**

**Pelican Publishing Company, Inc.
1000 Burmaster Street
Gretna, La. 70053**

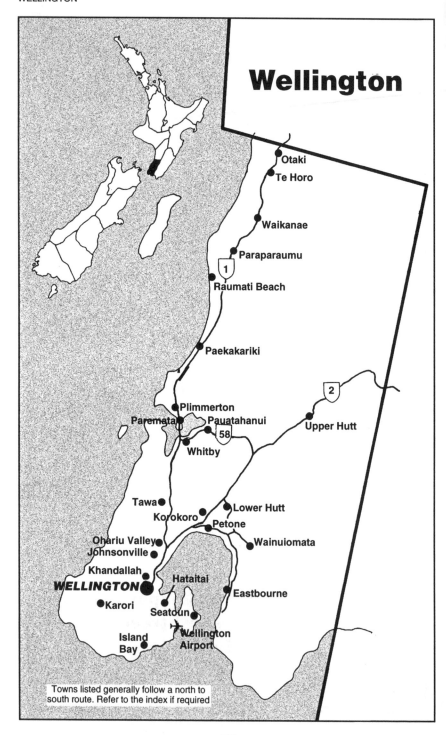

Wellington

Otaki
Te Horo
Waikanae
Paraparaumu
Raumati Beach
Paekakariki
Plimmerton
Paremata
Pauatahanui
Whitby
Upper Hutt
Tawa
Korokoro
Lower Hutt
Petone
Ohariu Valley
Johnsonville
Wainuiomata
Khandallah
Hataitai
WELLINGTON
Karori
Eastbourne
Seatoun
Island Bay
Wellington Airport

Towns listed generally follow a north to south route. Refer to the index if required

Otaki

Country Garden Homestay
Address: Waitohu Lodge,
 294 State Highway 1 North, Otaki
Name: Keith & Mary Oldham
Telephone: (06) 364 5389
Fax: (06) 364 5350
Beds: 1 Queen, 3 Single (3 bedrooms) Guest lounge
Bathroom: 1 Guests share (Private on request, $10 extra)
Tariff: B&B (full) Double/Twin $75, Single $50, Children $25,
Dinner by arrangement $25pp. Discounts available, Credit Cards.
NZ B&B Vouchers accepted $5 Surcharge
Nearest Town: 74km North of Wellington city and 16km South of Levin on State
Highway 1

Welcome to Waitohu Lodge in sunny Otaki. Ideally located as a Te Papa and ferry stopover, we are only 55 mins drive to Wellington city and the Picton ferry. Easy to find we are set well back from the highway in 3/4 acre of trees and gardens, with secure onsite parking. At Waitohu Lodge we offer you warm friendly Kiwi hospitality and top quality accommodation and amenities. We serve wholesome tasty meals, featuring fresh fruit and vegetables from our garden and homemade preserves at breakfast. Guests appreciate their luxury bathroom with spa bath and shower, comfortable rooms with garden views, own private entrance and guest lounge with TV and tea/coffee making facilities. WAITOHU LODGE IS A 'QUALITY AWARD' WINNING HOMESTAY. Retired early, Keith was a Geography teacher and Mary a City Councillor. Our interests include travel, the arts, wine tasting and gardening. We and our Burmese cat Raj look forward to welcoming you into our home. Smoke Free.

Otaki

Country Garden Homestay
Address: 'Glenmore', Rahui Road, Otaki
Name: Jack & Heather Bellaney
Telephone: (06) 364 7319
Beds: 1 King, 2 Single (2 bedrooms)
Bathroom: 1 Guests share
Tariff: B&B (continental) Double/Twin $65, Single $50. Out-of-season discounts.
Cooked breakfast on request. NZ B&B Vouchers accepted
Nearest Town: Levin/Paraparaumu 15 mins, Wellington/Palmerston North 55 mins.

Enjoy 'small town hospitality' in our modern home overlooking Otaki Racecourse and Kapiti Island. Our 5 acre property is in a truly tranquil rural setting incorporating extensive gardens, farmlet, native bush / birds, lagoon and even glow-worms. Sunsets can be quite spectacular. Great start for garden tours. Able to arrange visits to farms, Kapiti Island etc.
Guests' bathroom has spa. Separate lounge available. We request guests don't smoke inside. We enjoy the outdoors, gardening and travel. Lions Club members. Jack is keen on fishing and woodwork.
'Sash' our golden labrador lives outside but loves to welcome visitors.
Within minutes of shops, restaurants, golf course, beach, river and Forest Park. Vintage Car Museum, Tourist Farm Complex, Bird Sanctuary, Outdoor Pursuits Centre all close by.
Guests Comments: Tops in hospitality - Home away from home - Lucky to find you - Magic - Quiet and so relaxing - Like a Botanical Garden.
Directions: *1 1/2km from SH1.*

Te Horo, Otaki

Separate Accommodation

Address: 'Stone Pine Creek', 123 Settlement Road, Te Horo, Otaki RD1
Name: Lorraine & Kerry Hoggard
Telephone: (06) 364 3140
Fax: (06) 364 3468
Beds: 1 Queen (1 bedroom)
Bathroom: 1 Private
Tariff: B&B (special/continental) Double $110. Credit Cards accepted: Visa/Mastercard. NZ B&B vouchers accepted.
Nearest Town: Otaki - 1hr drive from Wellington

Our Italian style farmhouse home and separate accommodation are set in a lavender farm with a backdrop of rolling hills and panoramic seaviews.

You will wake in the gatehouse to views over the lavender and grapes to Kapiti Island. The gatehouse contains a mezzanine sleeping area, ground floor living area and your own bathroom. A special continental breakfast basket will be waiting for you to have, in privacy, at your leisure.

We have a lavender farm in full production and a large garden with a meandering stream. These plus the swimming pool, which is within the walled courtyard, are available to our guests.

We also sell lavender products made from our oil (distilled on the property) and lavender plants.

Our interests include people, books, gardening, music, art, theatre and travel.

We have a few coloured sheep, cows, ducks, cats and two friendly dogs.

Within short distances you may walk in the bush or by the sea, investigate craft places, pick berries, play tennis or golf or just enjoy the peace. We can assure you of a warm welcome and an interesting stay.

Non smokers please.

Directions: *Please write or phone.*

Te Horo

Te Horo Country Homestay
Address: 109 Arcus Road, Te Horo,
Kapiti Coast
Name: Craig Garner
Telephone: 0800 4 Te Horo (483 467)
or (06) 364 3393
Fax: (06) 364 3393 **Mobile**: (025) 306 009
Email: TeHoro.Lodge@xtra.co.nz
Beds: Three luxurious bedrooms (double/twin).
One Master-suite (one queen, one single).
Bathroom: 4 Ensuites
Tariff: B&B (full) Double $150-$165, Single $125, Dinner $40 (by arrangement).
Not suitable for children. Major Credit Cards accepted.
Nearest Town: Otaki, 8km North, Waikanae 7km South,65 km North of Wellington

Let us pamper you in our new purpose built luxurious Country Lodge. Set next to five acres of native bush with a rural outlook, Te Horo Lodge offers a relaxing, tranquil environment.

The three bedrooms downstairs open out to a veranda and expansive lawns. The upstairs "master-suite" has a lounge area with intimate bush views. The decor and furnishings throughout consist of strong vibrant colours.

The feature fireplace anchors our stunning lounge. It is crafted by a local stone artist and is perfect for those cold winter nights. The dining-room has a striking recycled timber table.

The Horo Lodge also offers a "picture perfect" pool area. It includes a secluded in-ground swimming pool and luxury spa pool. The pool area is surrounded by manicured lawns and gardens. It features a gazebo - our summer dining room - an ideal spot to linger over a scrumptious BBQ dinner.

Te Horo Lodge is not suitable for children. For the comfort of our guests the Lodge is smokefree. There are no pets.

A generous cooked country breakfast is provided, including fruit locally grown.

The Kapiti region has some fine restaurants or you are most welcome to dine with me at the Lodge by prior arrangement.

Te Horo Lodge is an ideal escape from the pressures of the city, whether you are looking at just relaxing or exploring this unique part of the countryside. You can even wander around our ten acre property, including a walk through our native bush.

Local attractions include: Golf courses, the "World Class" Southwards Car Museum, Kapiti Cheeses, gardens, nature reserve, bushwalks, arts and crafts and our rugged West Coast beaches.

For the more active try: Fly by Wire, local kayaking, rafting, abseiling or take a tour to Kapiti Island. We will be happy to assist you in planning your local activities.

How to find us: Te Horo Lodge is located just 3 km off State Highway 1, turn across the railway opposite the Te Horo Store, onto School Road, then left into Arcus Road. You'll find us at the end of the road.

Directions: *Please telephone for further directions. I look forward to welcoming you into my home.*

Te Horo

Country Homestay
Address: Shepreth, Te Hapua Rd,
Te Horo, R.D. 1, Otaki
Name: Lorraine & Warren Birch
Telephone: (06) 364 2130
Fax: (06) 364 2134

Beds: 1 Double, 3 Single (2 bedrooms/1 bedroom has double + single bed, other has 2 singles)
Bathroom: 1 Guests share - plus extra toilet.
Tariff: B&B (full) Double $75, Single $45, Dinner $30, Credit cards.
NZ B&B Vouchers accepted
Nearest Town: Waikanae 6km south, Otaki 8km north

Relax in the country, close to the capital. Shepreth is a small farm north of Waikanae just off State Highway 1, and 45 minutes drive north of Wellington. We graze angora goats, cattle and sheep, and have a cat called Gruffyd. Our home is sheltered, sunny and spacious. Among the many places to visit in the area are Southwards Car Museum, Lindale Agricultural Centre, the Nga Manu Bird Sanctuary and local potters. Golf courses, beaches and open gardens are close by.We have a wide range of interests, have travelled in New Zealand and overseas, and enjoy meeting both New Zealanders and people visiting our country.A generous breakfast with plenty of variety is provided. The area has a selection of restaurants available for dinner, or you are welcome to have dinner with us by arrangement. For the comfort of guests our house is smoke-free.We offer friendly, Kiwi country hospitality at Shepreth.
Directions: *Please phone.*

Waikanae

Homestay
Address: 'Waimoana',
63 Kakariki Grove, Waikanae
Name: Ian & Phyllis Stewart
Telephone: (04) 293 7158
Fax: (04) 293 7156
Email: waimoana@nzhomestay.co.nz
Beds: 3 bedrooms, two with 1 Queen and 1 Single bed each, one with two singles and outside entrance.
Bathroom: 3 Ensuite
Tariff: B&B Double $115 or $180, Single $80 or $130. Credit Cards.
Tariffs valid to 30/11/99. NZ B&B Vouchers accepted $43 or $102 Surcharge.
Nearest Town: Waikanae 1km. 58km north of Wellington on State Highway 1

At "Waimoana", the generous use of glass invites the outside inside, without compromising privacy. The decor is restful. Expect fresh flowers, warm fluffy towels and a guests' own balcony to admire the view from the main bedrooms. The living quarters radiate off a glass-roofed atrium containing a swimming pool, an indoor garden and a waterfall. The views are spectacular.Nearby Kapiti Island is a major bird sanctuary. If this interests you, mention it when booking - access is limited. Easier to reach is the Southward Museum, housing a huge collection of vintage cars. Paraparaumu Golf Course is nearby. Or try "Fly-byWire".Day Trips to Wellington are easy, too.
"Waimoana" is not suitable for children and is smoke-free. There are no pets. First-class restaurants are nearby. 45 minutes north of inter-island ferry.
Check in is from 3p.m. on. Check out is 10a.m.Please phone for directions.
Home Page: http://nz.com/webnz/bbnz/waimoana.htm

Waikanae

Homestay
Address: 'Allenby', 12 Te Maku Grove, Waikanae
Name: Quintin & Meg Hogg
Telephone: (04) 293 2428,
Freephone 0800 11 00 82 **Fax**: (04) 293 2428
Beds: 2 Single (1 bedroom)
Bathroom: 1 Ensuite
Tariff: B&B (full) Double $75, Single $45, Dinner $20-$25.
NZ B&B Vouchers accepted $10 Surcharge
Nearest Town: Waikanae 1Km

We offer a warm comfortable self-contained twin bed unit which opens onto a sunny terrace and conservatory. Ensuite, private shower, basin and toilet. Laundry facilities also available. Guests will be provided with continental or cooked breakfast as desired. Tea and coffee making facilities and refrigerator in room. Dinner can be provided given reasonable notice or we can recommend excellent restaurants in Waikanae or nearby Paraparaumu Waikanae has a temperate climate, good beaches, wildlife sanctuaries, bush walks, golf course, arts and crafts, and is close to world famous Southwards Vintage Car Museum and Lindale Farm complex. We are handy to Wellington and the Interisland Ferry Terminal (45 minutes by car). We are keen gardeners and have travelled widely in New Zealand and overseas in Australia, U.S.A., U.K. and Europe. Interests include music, embroidery, trout fishing, and meeting people. We welcome non smokers.
Directions: *Please phone for directions (1km off SH1) or will meet travellers arriving by train or bus.*

Waikanae Beach

Homestay
Address: 115 Tutere St, Waikanae
Name: Pauline & Allan Jones
Telephone: (04) 293 6532
Fax: (04) 293 6543
Mobile: 025 300 785
Beds: 1 Queen, 1 Double, 3 Single (3 bedrooms)
Bathroom: 1 Ensuite, 1 Guests Share
Tariff: B&B (full) Double $75, Single $45,
Children $18, Children under 5 $10, Dinner by arrangement $25, Credit Cards.
Long stays negotiable.
NZ B&B Vouchers accepted
Nearest Town: Waikanae, 4km

Pauline and Allan welcome you to their home. We invite you to sit on our balconies and enjoy the views of the Tasman Sea or Tararua Ranges, walk on the beach, or sleep with the sound of the sea. We have direct access to a sandy swimming beach. Our cedar and brick home is open plan, warm and comfortable. Tea and coffee making facilities are available in each guest room. The main guest bedroom has a separate entrance. We have travelled extensively overseas and look forward to offering warm and friendly hospitality to visitors from home and overseas. Our interests include music and crafts. Children are welcome. Local attractions include Lindale Farm Park, Southwards Vintage Car Museum, a bird sanctuary, and golf course.
Directions: *Please phone. Recommended by Frommers.*

411

Waikanae Beach
Self-contained Accommodation
Address: Konini Cottage, 26 Konini Crescent,
Waikanae Beach
Name: Maggie and Bob Smith
Telephone: (04) 293 6610
Fax: (04) 293 6610
Beds: 1 Double, 2 Single (2 bedrooms)
Bathroom: 1 Private
Tariff: Accomodation only: Double $65
plus $10 each extra person.
Optional breakfast (full) $10 per person
NZ B&B Vouchers accepted
Nearest Town: Waikanae 5 Kms

Imagine a long walk on an endless beach, perhaps a round of golf on the adjoining links, or just lazing on the verandah enjoying the tranquillity of our semi rural setting. This is all possible when you stay in our two bedroom Lockwood cottage, with fully equipped kitchen for self catering, laundry and bathroom facilities and comfortable lounge. As we only take one party of guests at a time all this is for your private use. Whether overseas visitors or fellow Kiwis you will appreciate the spaciousness and quality of our cottage. You can join us in our home for a lingering breakfast or you may choose to have it served in the cottage.
We are a forty something couple with two teenage sons. Bob is a cabinetmaker who restores antiques and makes furniture in his home workshop and Maggie is the inspiration in the landscaping of our large grounds.

Waikanae Beach
Homestay
Address: 36 Fieldway, Waikanae Beach
Name: Jan& Dick Holloway
Telephone: (04) 293 3431
Fax: (04) 293 3431
Beds: 2 Single (1 bedroom)
Bathroom: 1 Private
Tariff: B&B (full) Double $70, Single $40,
Dinner $25pp. NZ B&B Vouchers accepted
Nearest Town: Waikanae 5km.

We are a retired couple who would like to share their comfortable home with guests. The accommodation is a sunny room with private bathroom. Adjoining this is a garden room and paved garden courtyard. Own tea and coffee making facilities. Continental or cooked breakfast, dinner by arrangement or there are several excellent restaurants nearby. Our home that we share with Jessie our gentle dog is only minutes from lovely Waikanae beach that we both enjoy for safe swimming and walking. There are several golf courses nearby and we too enjoy a game of golf, we also enjoy pottering in our garden.
Our district has many attractions including gardens, galleries, Lindale Tourist Farm, Southwards Car Museum and Bird Sanctuaries. Waikanae is approx. 1 hour from Wellington and 10 minutes from Coastlands shopping town at Paraparaumu.
We are non smokers.
Directions: *Please telephone.*

412

Waikanae
Self-contained Accommodation
18 Kea Street, Waikanae
Name: Brian and Sue Wilson
Telephone: (04) 293 5165
Fax: (04) 293 5164
Mobile: 025-578 421
Email: wilbri@freemail.co.nz
Beds: 1 King/Queen,
2 Single (1 bedrooms + mezzanine)
Bathroom: 1 Ensuite
Tariff: B&B (continental) Double $85,
each extra person $30, Single $60, Children $20, under 5 free.
BC/VISA NZ B&B Vouchers accepted $10 surcharge
Nearest Town: Paraparaumu 12 Kms

"Country Patch" is 2 1/2 acres nestled under the bush line of the foothills of Waikanae. It gets panoramic views along the coast to Kapiti Island and beyond.
Comfortable self-contained accommodation for up to 5 people with own kitchen facilities.
Waikanae is the heart of the garden area on the Kapiti Coast and we are 45 mins from Wellington with bush walks, good beaches and excellent restaurants nearby.
We will gladly meet the bus or train and warmly invite you to share our patch of country.
We have two children Kate (13 years) and Simon (11 years) and a friendly golden labrador (Holly). Families welcome . We are strictly smoke free.
Please phone or write.

Paraparaumu
Homestay
Address: 72 Bluegum Road,
Paraparaumu
Name: Vic & Jude Young
Telephone: (04) 297 2773
Beds: 1 Double, 1 Single (2 bedrooms)
Bathroom: 1 Private, 1 Family share
Tariff: B&B (full) Double $70, Single $40,
Dinner $20. Children half price.
NZ B&B Vouchers accepted
Nearest Town: Paraparaumu

Our 1950's beach house has excellent hill, island and sea views, and is situated just two blocks back from Marine Parade and the sea. Shops, cafés and excellent restaurants are a 1 km walk away. Off-street parking is provided and we will meet bus or train. Guests may borrow our bicycles. Jude is, with prior notice, pleased to prepare meals for those on special diets, and packed lunches can be provided for day trips (to Kapiti Island for example). We love walking, food, music, Citroens and meeting travellers from all countries.
Non smokers preferred. We have a cat.
Directions: *Watch for yellow letterbox on seaward corner of Bluegum & Rua Roads.*

Paraparaumu
Self-contained Accommodation
Address: 60A Ratanui Rd,
Otaihanga/Paraparaumu
Name: Marius & Sytske Kruiniger
Telephone: (04) 299 8098 work,
(04) 297 3447 home
Fax: (04) 297 3447
Beds: 1 Queen, 2 Single (2 bedrooms)
Bathroom: Private
Tariff: B&B (continental) Double $65,
Single $50, Extra person $15, Children under 5 $5.
Credit Cards. NZ B&B Vouchers accepted
Nearest Town: Paraparaumu, 55km north of Wellington

Our self-contained lodge offers privacy and tranquillity, with a view of a private small lake, full with wildlife.
It contains a fully equipped kitchen, a cosy lounge with TV, books and some games. We are situated only a few minutes drive from Coastlands Shopping Centre and beaches. Indoor and outdoor attractions, as well as excellent restaurants are within easy reach. Information about these are available in the lodge.
Our rates include supply of continental breakfast for self service. No dogs please and guests are asked not to smoke indoors.
Please phone or fax for bookings and directions.

Paraparaumu
Homestay, Self-Contained Accomodation
Address: 236 State Highway 1,
Paraparaumu North, Pukekohe
Name: Pukekohe
Telephone: (04) 298-9133
Fax: (4) 298-9166
Mobile: (025) 444-296
Email: carvell@paradise.net.nz
Beds: 2 Queen, 1 Single, 2 bedrooms
Bathroom: 2 Private
Tariff: B&B (full) Double $85,
Single $60, Dinner $25pp, Children $15.
NZ B&B Vouchers accepted $15 Surcharge
Nearest Town: Paraparaumu, Waikanae

Pukekohe is a rural homestead with 31/2 acres of garden and trees. The self contained accommodation is situated in a wing of the house. A self contained cottage will be available from January 1999. This cottage is set in native bush and is Japanese in style. Our home is a very comfortable lifestyle property with chickens in the yard, a cat and a dog. We have two children and the property is fully fenced and safe.
Facilities - spa pool, BBQ, exercise gym, meals available. We are 50 minutes from Wellington and very close to all Kapiti tourist attractions, Lindale Tourist Centre, Southwards Car Museum, Nikau Gardens Butterfly House, Kapiti Island Bird Sanctuary, visits can be booked.
Directions: *On State Highway One between Paraparumu and Waikanae - opposite Otahanga and Southwards turn-off.*

Paraparaumu Beach

Homestay
Address: 17 Takahe Drive, Kotuku Park,
Paraparaumu Beach
Name: "Beachstay". Ernie and Rhoda Stevenson
Telephone: (04) 298 7342
Beds: 1 Double, 2 Single (2 bedrooms)
Bathroom: 1 Guests share
Tariff: B&B (continental) Double $70, Single $40, Dinner $25, Chilren $10.
NZ B&B Vouchers accepted
Nearest Town: Paraparaumu (10 mins drive)

Our modern new home is set in peaceful surroundings next to the Waikanae river estuary with access to Paraparaumu beach.
We have panoramic views of the sea, Kapiti Island, small lake in rural setting, hills and distant Mt Kakakapanui.
This is a paradise for outdoor-lovers, bird watchers, and all who enjoy walking or communing with nature.
Paraparaumu is 45 minutes north of Wellington, the centre of the Kapiti Coast, and offers many varied tourist attractions, including trips to Kapiti Island's bird sanctuary.
We are a semi-retired couple who enjoy meeting people and offering warm hospitality. Our interests include bush and mountain walking, love of NZ scenery, painting landscapes, and model railways.
Children are welcome.

Paekakariki

Homestay
Address: 93A Wellington Road, Paekakariki, Kapiti Coast
Name: Frances Cherry
Telephone: (04) 292 8534 **Fax**: (045) 292 7001
Beds: 1 Queen (1 ensuite)
Bathroom: 1 Ensuite
Tariff: B&B (continental) Double $70, Single $45, Dinner $15.
NZ B&B Vouchers accepted
Nearest Town: Paraparaumu (10 mins drive north)

I am a novelist and short story writer and teach writing courses. I love meeting people from overseas and New Zealand. I am interested in politics, human behaviour, and all the arts. My colourful open-plan home is perched on a hilltop and has wonderful views of the sea and Kapiti Island. It takes two minutes to walk to the beach where you can swim or walk for miles along the sand and through Queen Elizabeth Park, where a non-smoking household. Paekakariki, on State Highway One, half an hours drive from Wellington (regular train service) is the home of many well known creative people. It has two cafes, a pub, the famous Fly By Wire, is close to craft shops, restaurants, the world-class Southward Car Museum and Nga Manu Bird Sanctuary.
Directions: *Phone for directions.*

Please help us provide the best hospitality in the world.
Fill in a comment form for every place you stay.

Plimmerton

Homestay
Address: 131 Pope Street, Camborne,
Plimmerton, Wellington
Name: Joan & Denis Sawkins

Telephone: (04) 233 9444 **Fax**: (04) 233 9515 **Mobile**: (025) 461 495
Email: sawkins@xtra.co.nz
Beds: 1 Queen (1 bedroom)
Bathroom: 1 Private
Tariff: B&B (full) Double $90, Single $70, Dinner $30, Cot available.
NZ B&B Vouchers accepted $15 surcharge
Nearest Town: Wellington 20 mins, Porirua 5 mins

We extend a warm welcome to all visitors and offer you:
- *Million dollar views - of coastline, open sea and South Island*
- *Modern, sunny home -open plan with sun and views from every room*
- *Private spacious guest bedroom - with queen size bed*
- *Own bathroom - with shower and bath*
- *Quick access off Highway 1 - just 200 metres*
- *Off street parking - for cars or campervans*
- *Dinner if desired - with prior notice please*
- *Relaxing atmosphere - catch up on your letter writing or laundry*
- *Friendly hosts - who have travelled extensively themselves*
- *Close proximity to beach and railway station - walking distance*
- *Easy connections - to Interisland Ferry and Airport*
- *Local tourist interests - including National Police Museum*
- *Wellington - capital city of New Zealand and Te Papa*

Directions: *Please telephone.*

Plimmerton

Homestay
Address: 57 Pope St, Plimmerton, Wellington
Name: Plimmerton Homestay
Telephone: (04) 233 8329
Beds: 1 King/Queen,1 Single (1 Bedroom)
Bathroom: 1 Family share

Tariff: B&B (full and continental) Double $65, Single $50, Children half price,
Dinner by arrangement, Credit Cards. NZ B&B Vouchers accepted
Nearest Town: Wellington 20 mins, Porirua 5 mins.

Our quiet, comfortable home has beautiful harbour views and glimpses of the South Island. We are easy to find as Pope Street runs off State Highway 1, and guests are welcomed with a cup of tea. Driving time is 20 minutes to the inter-island ferry, 1 minute to the Sea-Cat (Mana).
The large, sunny guest room, in a separate wing, has tea / coffee making facilities and a sitting area. For breakfast we serve fresh fruit and home-made bread. Though we share, the bathroom, toilet and shower are separate rooms.
Cafes, restaurants and beaches for swimming or walking are 1 minute by car. We have travelled and many of our guests have appreciated our suggestions for touring New Zealand, as we have photographs and we know the walking tracks. Our interests are geology, botany, music and walking. There is off-street parking. Guests may smoke on our deck.

Plimmerton
Self-contained Accommodation
Address: 12 Moana Rd, Plimmerton
Name: John & Lauren Hudson
Telephone: (04) 233 1007
Fax: (04) 233 1004
Mobile: (025) 424 409
Email: l&j.hudson@xtra.co.nz
Beds: 1 Queen (1 bedroom)
Bathroom: 1 Private
Tariff: B&B (continental) Double & Single $135.
Visa/MC NZ B&B Vouchers accepted 2 vouchers
Nearest Town: Porirua City 8kms

John and Lauren welcome you to "12 Moana", offering you privacy and sunshine - overlooking Mana Island on the Plimmerton waterfront. Our new, purpose-built accommodation is fully self-contained, including kitchen, allowing you to be independent, yet part of the family. Relax in the garden, swim, walk on the beach - this is a restful and informal environment. We provide continental breakfast for you to enjoy at your own leisure.

Plimmerton is 20 minutes drive from Wellington and Interisland ferry, and five minutes walk from the commuter train service. There are several good local cafes and restaurants, and the Kapiti coast is a nearby place to explore.

We are a busy young family, who have ourselves stayed in many wonderful Bed & Breakfasts in our frequent European travels - we look forward to giving you a friendly, warm welcome. We are you a non-smoking environment.

Plimmerton
Homestay
Address: 82 Moana Road,
Plimmerton, Wellington
Name: Des Shea & Gay Kerr
Telephone: (04) 233 8613 **Fax**: (04) 233 8613
Mobile: (025) 490 161
Beds: 1 Queen (1 bedroom)
Bathroom: Private (Bath and shower)
Tariff: B&B (continental breakfast) Double $60, Single $40, Dinner $20pp,
Nearest Town: Porirua

Right on the sea shore, wonderful walks, boating, fishing, swimming, snorkelling, or just relaxing. The sunsets are spectacular. There are restaurants, shops, tennis courts, strolling distance away.
The famous Karehana Bay is just one bay away.
Our home is modern and comfortable.
Des is a retired accountant, Gay compiles "The New Zealand Camping Guide". We spend much of the year travelling but when there is time enjoy dancing, skiing, swimming, tennis, gardening, reading, music.
We are happy for you to join us for dinner and a drink. (Please let us know in the morning.) We prefer non-smokers.
There is ample parking here.
The third member of our family is 'Dennis" (dog) an SPCA special.
This is a magic spot to enjoy a break. We look forward to meeting you.

Plimmerton

Homestay
Address: 45 Moana Road, Plimmerton
Name: "Southview" John & Robyn
Telephone: (04) 233-9486
Beds: 1 Queen, 1 Bedroom
Bathroom: 1 Ensuite
Tariff: B&B (continental) Double $85, Dinner by arrangement.
NZ B&B Vouchers accepted
Nearest Town: 15 min walk to Plimmerton, Porirua, Wellington, Lower Hutt.

Southview is situated on the waterfront at Karehana Bay, 20 minutes drive from central Wellington, the Interisland ferry terminal and 5 minutes from the new Mana / Picton Sea Cat fast ferry service.
Plimmerton Village a 15 minute walk and the commuter train service, and a short drive north to Kapiti Coast and its many interesting attractions.
Our home is modern, comfortable and quiet with beautiful sea views and sunsets.
Safe swimming beach, and close by Porirua's new aquatic centre. Our combined interests are varied, but most of all we look forward to meeting you.
We are non-smokers.
Not available until November 1998.

Paremata, Wellington

Homestay
Address: 76 Seaview Road,
Paremata, Wellington
Name: Carolyn & Vince O'Sullivan
Telephone: (04) 233 1434
Fax: (04) 233 8794
Beds: 1 Double, 2 Single (2 bedrooms)
Bathroom: 1 Guests share
Tariff: B&B (continental) Double $80,
Single $45,
Children $25. Credit cards.
NZ B&B Vouchers accepted

Nearest Town: Porirua 5 mins, Lower Hutt & Upper Hutt 15 mins, Wellington 20 mins, Paraparaumu 20 mins.

We are two minutes off State Highway one from the Paremata Bridge, an ideal stopover before heading to the South Island or up North.
We have a peaceful, tranquil setting nestled in the trees on the beautiful Pauatahanui Inlet, known for its Wetlands Reserve. Locally there are many interesting walks, including one from the waters edge of our garden around our peninsula. We are handy to safe swimming beaches, water activities, golf courses and good shopping.
We have travelled widely and know NZ well. Our family of three have grown and flown. Guests have the privacy of downstairs including guest bathroom and lounge opening to a private patio.
Enjoy breakfast in our beautiful conservatory while drinking in the glorious views. There are several excellent restaurants nearby. Ours is a "smoke free" house.
Directions: *Please phone, fax or write for bookings and directions.*

Members of
The New Zealand Association Farm & Home Host Inc.
maintain the highest standards &
are always delighted to welcome
guests into their homes.

Pauatahanui
Rural Homestay
Address: 'Braebyre', Flightys Road,
Pauatahanui (R.D.1 Porirua)
Name: Randall & Jenny Shaw
Telephone: (04) 235 9311 **Fax**: (04) 235 9345
Beds: 1 Queen, 1 Double, 2 Single (3 bedrooms)
Bathroom: 1 Ensuite, 1 Guests share
Tariff: B&B (special) Double $90-$110, Single $80-$100, Children $30-$50,
Dinner $35-$40. Credit cards: Visa/MC NZ B&B Vouchers accepted $20-$40
surcharge
Nearest Town: Lower Hutt 15 km, Porirua 12 km

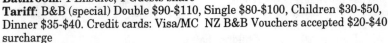

*Are you looking for something special and restful away from city noise yet easily
accessible on major highways? Located closer to the mid-city than many suburbs
"Braebyre" one of Wellington's fine country homes, is nestled in a beautiful rural
environment on a mohair goat farm. Surrounded by four acres of landscaped gardens
you will love the peace and tranquillity. Jenny and Randal have travelled extensively
and have been hosting for many years and enjoy the experience of hearing about guests'
travels and life's adventures. The private guest wing (with separate entrance) provides
superior accommodation with 3 bedrooms, 2 bathrooms (1 ensuite) and recreation
room with table tennis table, log fire and indoor spa pool. Fresh flowers, electric
blankets and duvets ensure your comfort. Evening dinner featuring fine new Zealand
wine and home-grown produce is available on request. The exciting new "Seacat" ferry
to Picton departs close by and we offer a courtesy pickup service.
Our smoke free home welcomes family groups.*
Directions: *Please phone or write.*

Judgeford/Pauatahanui
Homestay
Address: "Kumbelin", Mulherns Road, RD, Porirua
Name: Joan & Paul
Telephone: (04) 235 7610
Fax: (04) 235 7612
Beds: 4 Single (2 bedrooms)
Bathroom: 1 Guests share, 1 Family share
Tariff: B&B Double $60, Single $40,
Dinner by arrangement, Licensed restaurant handy.
Credit cards. NZ B&B Vouchers accepted
Nearest Town: Lower Hutt 15km, Porirua 12km, Upper Hutt 14km, 20 mins to the ferry and Wellington city.

"Kumbelin" is a 5 acre farmlet set in the beautiful Judgeford basin on SH58 and is extensively planted with trees, shrubs and Rhododendrons. A spacious comfortable family home provides total privacy for the guests while the large open plan living areas with woodburner fires ensure guests are made to feel at home. Windbreaks on the boundary ensure the homestead enjoys a pleasant environment all year round. Guests have the option to talk to the sheep, walk down a quiet country road, relax in the peaceful garden setting, play tennis on the floodlit half-sized tennis court come games area or play golf on the excellent 18 hole course over the fence. "Kumbelin" is a quiet rural retreat handy to several cities and places of interest and is ideal as a base to enjoy the many scenic drives the region offers.

Whitby
Bed & Breakfast
Address: 5 Leeward Drive,
Whitby, Wellington
Name: Bella Vista.
Maya Beddie-Geiser and Dennis Hamblin
Telephone: (04) 234 1499
Fax: (04) 234 7250
Beds: 1 Queen, 2 Single (2 bedrooms)
Bathroom: 1 Guests share.
Tariff: B&B (full) Double $70,

Single $35, Dinner $20, School Children half price.
NZ B&B Vouchers accepted
Nearest Town: Porirua 8 kms, Wellington, Hutt Valley and Kapiti Coast 20 mins drive.

The Bella Vista Bed & Breakfast Establishment is looking forward to your visit! Come and enjoy some real Swiss Hospitality. We live 2 minutes away from State Highway one. This is the centre of the Wellington Region - 20 minutes drive to three major points of interests: Wellington, Hutt Valley and Kapiti Coast.
The glorious view over the Pauatahanui Harbour invites you for a stay. You will find comfortable rooms and plenty of privacy. Have a cheese fondue in front of a cozy fireplace! A generous breakfast will energise you for your trip north or a visit to the Capital. We love meeting people from all over the world. Maya speaks German, French and Italian, Dennis speaks English. Our interests are Arts, Photography, Maori History and any alternative Health Remedies.
We are non-smokers and have no children or pets living with us.
Come and enjoy our company!

Upper Hutt
Herritage Inn.
Address: Well Springs,
5 Brentwood Street, Heretaunga
: Neville Blair & Anne Hyde
Telephone: (04) 528 6727
Fax: (04) 528 6725
Mobile: (025) 532 019
Email: john.blair@xtra.co.nz
Beds: 3 Queen, 2 Twin (5 bedrooms)
Bathroom: 2 Guests share
Tariff: B&B (continental) Double $80, Single $58, Dinner by arrangement,
Nearest Town: Upper Hutt

Nestled in the leafy, private suburb of Heretaunga is Wellsprings, a historic English manor. Wellsprings provides a welcome respite to the weary traveller. It was built in 1929 by Chapman Taylor. Enjoy the friendly atmosphere of the shared guest facilities. On-site parking, laundry facilities, guest lounge and a barbecue area make this accommodation ideal whether you're staying one night or one week. Wellsprings is available for functions, day trips, board meetings etc. Located just 20 minutes drive from Wellington, Wellsprings is also within handy reach of a range of leisure pursuits such as golf, horse racing, tennis, swimming, rifle shooting and horse trekking. Be well met, well served and well rested - Wellsprings.

Continental breakfast consists of fruit, cereal, toast, tea/coffee,
Full breakfast is the same with a cooked course,
Special breakfast has something special.

Upper Hutt - Te Marua
Homestay
Address: 108a Plateau Rd,
Te Marua, Upper Hutt
Name: Sheryl & Lloyd Homer
Telephone: (04) 526 7851
Freephone 0800 110 851
Fax: (04) 526 7866 **Mobile**: (025) 501 679
Email: Sheryl.lloyd@clear.net.nz
Beds: 1 Queen, 1 Double (2 bedrooms)
Bathroom: 1 Private
Tariff: B&B (continental) Double $70, Single $40. Dinner $20,
Credit Cards. NZ B&B Vouchers accepted
Nearest Town: Upper Hutt 7.4km

Our home is situated in a tranquil, private bush setting. Guests may choose to relax on one of our large decks and view the native bird life, read books from our extensive library, soak in our outdoor bath or just sit around a cosy fire. For the more energetic there are bush walks, a golf course, mountain bike trails, trout fishing and swimming areas within walking distance and a shooting range and gliding club nearby.
The guest wing has private facilities, a TV, microwave and provision for making tea and coffee.Lloyd is a photographer with over 30 years experience photographing the New Zealand landscape. He would enjoy taking guests on local photographic or tramping tours. Sheryl is a teacher. Travel, entertaining, tramping, skiing, photography and music are some of the interests we enjoy together and look forward to sharing with our guests
- We ask that guests do not smoke indoors. - Dinner available on request.
Directions: *Please phone or fax for bookings and directions.*

Upper Hutt
Farmstay
Address: Whispering Pines, 207 Colletts Road,
RD 1 Mangaroa, Upper Htt
Name: Graham & Ruth Ockwell
Telephone: (04) 526 7785
Fax: (04) 526 7785
Beds: 1 Queen, 3 Single (3 bedrooms)
Bathroom: 1 Ensuite, 1 Guests share
Tariff: B&B (full) Double $80,
Single $40, Dinner $25.
NZ B&B Vouchers accepted $10 surcharge
Nearest Town: Upper Hutt 8km

A country welcome awaits you at Whispering Pines, where the air is fresh and clean, and the views are picturesque. Our spacious Swiss Chalet style home, has a Douglas Fir theme, and is set in 67 acres of elevated farmland.
Backing onto native bush, we share the land with native birds, pedigree Hereford cattle, Angora goats, coloured sheep, hens, geese, turkeys, bees and Jess our collie dog.
Whispering Pines is an ideal stopover on your way to, or from the Wellington Ferry, Airport or while visiting the Trentham races.
Ruth: Co-ordinator for a Budgeting Service, enjoys hobbies of spinning, knitting and sewing.
Graham: A builder, is interested in agriculture, fishing and shooting. Joint interests are, entertaining people, travel, gardening and local Church.
We would appreciate you not smoking in the house.
Please phone or fax to make a booking and receive directions as we are 6km from SH2.

Upper Hutt

Homestay
Address: "Tranquillity", 136 Akatarawa Road,
Birchville, Upper Hutt
Name: Elaine, Alice & Alan
Telephone: (04) 526 6948, Freephone 0800 270 787
Fax: (04) 526 6968 **Mobile**: (025) 405 962
Email: tranquility@xtra.co.nz
Beds: 1 Queen, 2 Single (3 bedrooms)
Bathroom: 1 Ensuite with spa bath, 2 Family share
Tariff: B&B (continental) Queen with ensuite $85, Single $45, Children negotiable, Dinner $20 (2 course) by prior arrangement, Cooked breakfast $5pp extra, Credit Cards welcomed. We will meet you to/from Wellington Airport/Ferry/Rail by prior arrangement at an extra minimal cost.
NZ B&B Vouchers accepted $10 surcharge
Nearest Town: Upper Hutt 3 mins, Lower Hutt 20 mins, Wellington 35 mins, Wairarapa 30 mins.

Executive Timeout / Homestay
Escape from the stress of City Life just approx 40 minutes from Wellington off SH 2.
Close to Upper Hutt - Restaurants, Cinema, Golf, Racecourse, Leisure Centre (swimming), Bush Walks etc. We are near the confluence of the Hutt and Akatarawa Rivers which is noted for its fishing. 15km to Staglands.
Country setting, relax and listen to the New Zealand Tuis and watch the fantails or Wood Pigeons, or just simple relax and read.
Our home is situated on approx 1 acre and is nestled amongst native and planted trees, shrubs with lawn and garden.
Comfortable and warm and friendly hospitality
Good New Zealand style food. Outside barbecue if preferred, weather permits.
We enjoy meeting people of all cultures and invite you to come and stay in our tranquillity settings.
Tea and Coffee facilities available at any time. Laundry facilities.
Pets allowed by prior arrangements.
As we are non smokers we request you do not smoke inside.
TV in room.
Guests lounge.
We have a black cat as a pet.

Directions: *Just off SH2 / motorway - Akatarawa turn off, 1.3km down Akatarawa Road. Approx 200 metres pass Dairy, on the right (White Gate).*

Lower Hutt - Korokoro
Homestay
Address: 'Western Rise' 10 Stanhope Grove,
Korokoro, Lower Hutt
Name: Virginia & Maurice Gibbens
Telephone: (04) 589 1872 **Fax**: (04) 589 1873
Mobile: 025 438 316
Beds: 1 Double, 2 Single (2 bedrooms)
Bathroom: 1 Guests share
Tariff: B&B (special) Double $80, single $50, Dinner $25 NZ B&B Vouchers
accepted $12 surcharge
Nearest Town: Petone 1km, Lower Hutt 5km, Wellington 12km

*Want a restful setting and still in the centre of things? Just off State Highway 2
(highway to the Wairarapa) you can view Wellington's magnificent Harbour. Watch
the planes and boats as you relax over a meal either indoors or out. We have a large
family home which we share with a corgi / fox terrier, Prince and Camelot the cat. We
are in our 50's and do not smoke, therefore request our guests not to smoke indoors. Our
interests include travel, boating and crafts. Maurice works for the New Zealand Police
as a finger print expert and Virginia has always wanted to be involved with home stay
so looks forward to sharing time with you. Laundry Service free for persons staying 2
consecutive nights. We are very handy to all that you wish to see and do. A special
feature, being the many native bush walks in the area. 10-15 mins to Picton Ferry.
Restaurants, many.*
Directions: *Please telephone.*

Lower Hutt
Homestay
Address: 11 Ngaio Crescent,
Woburn, Lower Hutt 6009
Name: Judy & Bob Vine
Telephone: (04) 566 1192 **Fax**: (04) 566-1192
Mobile: (025) 500 682
Email: Bob_Vine@compuserve.com
Beds: 1 Double, 2 Single (2 Bedrooms)
Bathroom: 1 Guests share
Tariff: B&B (full) $40 per person, Dinner $25 by arrangement. Credit cards. NZ
B&B Vouchers accepted $12 surcharge
Nearest Town: Lower Hutt 1km, Wellington 15km

*Our home is situated plumb in the centre of Woburn, a picturesque central city suburb
of Lower Hutt, known for its generous sized houses and beautiful gardens.
We offer a warm welcome to our home, based on many enjoyable experiences with bed
and breakfast hosts in the United Kingdom, Europe and USA and delight in the
opportunity to reciprocate some of the hospitality we have been afforded on our own
overseas jaunts. We are within walking distance of the Lower Hutt downtown; only 15
minutes drive from central Wellington and the Railway Station and Ferry Terminal;
Airport 25 minutes. Our facilities include a separate lounge with TV for the comfort
and enjoyment of our guests should they wish to take some time out to themselves.
Alternatively, we love to entertain and would be delighted to have our guests join us
for some hearty Kiwi style cooking with good New Zealand wine.
Laundry facilities.*
Directions: *Please phone, fax, email or write. Transfer transport available.*

Lower Hutt
B&B

Address: 16 Massey Avenue,
Woburn, Lower Hutt 6009
Name: Dawn & Lawrence Woodley
Telephone: (04) 938 1928
Email: lawrence.w@clear.net.nz
Beds: 2 Single (1 bedroom)
Bathroom: 1 Ensuite
Tariff: B&B (full) $40 per night per person.
Nearest Town: Lower Hutt 1km

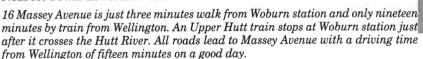

16 Massey Avenue is just three minutes walk from Woburn station and only nineteen minutes by train from Wellington. An Upper Hutt train stops at Woburn station just after it crosses the Hutt River. All roads lead to Massey Avenue with a driving time from Wellington of fifteen minutes on a good day.

From number sixteen a ten minute walk through pleasant streets, or a three minute drive by car finds the city centre conveniently close. A nine hole public golf course and driving range are just two minutes drive away, as is the heated "Huia" swimming pool. A bedroom with comfortable twin beds, TV and adjoining 'own-use' modern bathroom awaits the weary traveller. Breakfast is a choice of continental or cooked. Off-street car parking is available for a single vehicle, or for a modest charge we can arrange to meet the Interisland ferry, train, or airliner. The house is 'smoke free' except for the conservatory which is available to smokers. There are no pets on the premises.

We offer a warm welcome to all travellers, railfans, and members of the world-wide national Model Railroad Association fraternity.

Lower Hutt

Self Contained Accommodation
Address: "Casa Bianca"
10 Damian Grove
Lower Hutt
Name: Casa Bianca
Jo and Dave Comparini
Telephone: (04) 569 7859
Fax: (04) 569 7859
Beds: 1 Kingsize, 1 Single
Bathroom: 1 Private

Tariff: B&B (continental) Double $90, Single $55.
Credit Cards accepted. NZ B&B Vouchers accepted $21 surcharge
Nearest Town: Hutt City

Our comfortable house is situated in the Eastern Hills of Hutt City. The idyllic surroundings make this a great place to enjoy a quiet, peaceful holiday. We are within easy reach of four golf courses, city centre, cinemas, good restaurants and a host of other entertainment. Wellington is 15 minutes by train, or 20 minutes by car on SH1. Our interests include: meeting people, walking and tramping, theatre, sports, travel, and dining out.

We have a self contained apartment with bedroom (double), bathroom, large lounge and fully equipped kitchen. Breakfast provisions provided in apartment. One extra single bed in lounge. Off street parking and use of lock-up garage is available. We aim to provide guests with time to relax at their leisure, and enjoy our special hospitality. We can assist you with your travelling plans. We prefer no smoking in the house.
Directions: *Please phone for directions*

Lower Hutt

Homestay
Address: 'Dungarvin',
  25 Hinau Street, Lower Hutt
Name: Beryl and Trevor Cudby
Telephone: (04) 569 2125
Email: t.b.cudby@clear.net.nz
Beds: 2 Single (1 bedroom)
Bathroom: 1 Private
Tariff: B&B (full) Double $80, Single $50, Dinner $25 (by arrangement). Credit Cards accepted. NZ B&B Vouchers accepted $12 surcharge
Nearest Town: Lower Hutt (2 minutes), Wellington 15 (minutes)

Our 70 year old character cottage has been fully refurbished while retaining its original charm. It is two minutes from the Lower Hutt shops, and fifteen minutes from Wellington city.
We have a secluded property landscaped for quiet living, with ample off-street parking. Our home is centrally heated and has space for you to relax, read, listen to music from our CD collection or watch television. The sunny guest bedroom has windows opening over our well established garden and petanque court which you are welcome to use, and the beds have electric blankets and down duvets. Vegetarians are catered for, and laundry facilities are available.
Our main interests are travel, music, gardening and shows. We also enjoy entertaining and sampling New Zealand wines. We will help you plan local trips and make the most of your stay in this lovely area.
We appreciate our guests not smoking in the house.

Lower Hutt

Homestay
Address: 236 Stratton Street,
  Normandale, Lower Hutt
Name: Black Fir Lodge
Telephone: (04) 586 6466 **Mobile**: (025) 397 614
Email: i.perry@xtra.co.nz
Beds: 1 Queen, 2 Single (2 bedrooms)
Bathroom: 1 Guests Share
Tariff: B&B (full) Double $70, Single $45, Children $30
NZ B&B Vouchers accepted
Nearest Town: Petone 10 minutes, Wellington 20 minutes.

Our modern, spacious, single-storey home is a tranquil haven from the noise and bustle of Wellington, although only 20-30 minutes drive away.
Animals on our 12 hectare property include sheep and chooks, and we share our home with two friendly dogs (a Newfoundland and Labrador) and Splotch the cat.
The guest lounge is an ideal place to relax with a book, or simply enjoy the view of neighbouring Belmont Regional Park. If serious unwinding is required, how about a soak in the bath (and still enjoy the view).The Regional Park is a popular place for walking and mountain biking. We are also handy to the golf courses, museums, cafes and other attractions of Wellington and Lower Hutt.
Our interests include dogs, travel and natural history. Non-smokers please.
Directions: *Take Maungaraki turn-off from SH2. Turn into Stratton St at big sign for St Aidens on the Hill church.*

Petone

Homestay
Address: 1 Bolton Street, Petone
Name: Anne & Reg Cotter
Telephone: (04) 568 6960
Fax: (04) 568 6956
Beds: 1 Double, 2 Single (2 bedrooms)
Bathroom: 1 Family share
Tariff: B&B (full) Double $60, Single $30,
Children half price, Dinner $15 per person.
Credit cards. NZ B&B Vouchers accepted
Nearest Town: Lower Hutt 5 km, Wellington 8 km

TAIKO

We have an older type home by the beach which we have modernised. It has three bedrooms, a large lounge, dining room, kitchen, bathroom with shower and bath. We are two minutes from the museum on the beach, two minutes from the shops and the bus route into the city. A restaurant is nearby. We offer one double bed in one room, two single beds in another room with room for an extra bed or a child's cot which is available. Children are very welcome. Laundry facilities available. We are ten minutes by road to the Picton ferry. Off street parking available. Reg is a keen amateur ornithologist and he goes to the Chatham Islands with an expedition trying to find the nesting place of the Taiko - a rare sea bird which is on the endangered list. We are keen to show any folk interested in birds the local places of interest. Member of the genealogy society.

Petone

Homestay
Address: Pipi Cottage,
23 Patrick Street, Petone
Name: Gary & Tui Lewis
Telephone: (04) 568 5159
Mobile: (021) 656 828
Beds: 1 Queen, 1 Single (2 bedrooms)
Bathroom: 1 Private, 1 Family share
Tariff: B&B (special) Double $80,
Single $50, Dinner $25. NZ B&B Vouchers accepted
Nearest Town: Wellington 8km, Lower Hutt 5km

Kia Ora
We believe there can't be many places in the world where you can stroll along the beach looking out over a beautiful harbour to a city humming with activity, Wellington, a magnificent city.
If you're passing through, using the ferries we're only 10 minutes away. Perhaps you'd care to stay awhile?
Our warm and inviting two storey cottage is in a quiet historic street just off Petone's foreshore.
Breakfast time is a treat with loads of fresh brewed coffee, croissants, pancakes, fruit, yoghurt, musterers eggs and home made goodies being just some of the fare offered.
Whatever your reason for visiting our capital or its surrounds we look forward to meeting you and making your stay a warm, friendly one.
We are a non smoking home.

Korokoro, Petone

Homestay
Address: 100 Korokoro Road,
Korokoro, Petone
Name: Bridget & Jim Austin
Telephone: (04) 589 1678 **Fax**: (04) 589 1678
Email: jaustin@clear.net.nz
Beds: 1 Double, 1 Twin (2 bedrooms)
Bathroom: 1 Guests share

Tariff: B&B (continental) Double $75, Single $45, Dinner with wine $30.
Credit cardsNZ B&B Vouchers accepted
Nearest Town: Petone 3km, Lower Hutt 7km, Wellington 12km

Our house and one acre garden has a rural setting being one in a block of large sections originally offered for ballot in 1901. We are conveniently placed, being only 12-15 minutes from central Wellington and Ferry and 10 minutes from Lower Hutt and just 1.7km up the hill off SH2.

Originally from England (40 years ago) we enjoy travelling and meeting people. Bridget trained as a teacher and still works part-time. Jim's background is in mechanical engineering and is now a desultory woodworker, "fix-it" man, and indispensable gardener's mate to Bridget who is a keen gardener and also a weaver and feltmaker.

We live in an as environmentally friendly way as possible, definitely a non-smoking house, with spacious bedrooms. We enjoy all visual and performing arts, classical music, and books.

Wainuiomata

Homestay
Address: 22 Kaponga Street, Wainuiomata
Name: Kaponga House
Telephone: (04) 564 3495 (after 5pm)
Fax: (04) 564 3495
Beds: 1 Queen (1 bedroom)
Bathroom: 1 Private
Tariff: B&B (continental) Double $70, Single $45.
 NZ B&B Vouchers accepted
Nearest Town: Lower Hutt 6 kms

Wainuiomata Wonderland (just 20 minutes by car from Wellington City). Hilary and Neville invite you to experience the peace and tranquillity of our lovely bush setting. We love entertaining and enjoy a relaxed lifestyle. With this in mind we have made our ground floor available to homestay guests. The apartment includes one double bedroom with private bathroom, lounge/living room with TV, tea/coffee making facilities and a fridge. Extra bedding in the form of a divan is available in the lounge, if needed.

We have neither children nor pets at home and we are smokefree.

Attractions close by include the Rimutaka Forest Park, seal colony and an 18 hole golf course.

We enjoy gardening, golf, tennis, and making new friends, and we look forward to welcoming you to our home.

Mahina Bay, Eastbourne

Homestay
Address: 27 Marine Drive,
Mahina Bay, Eastbourne
Name: Janete & Jim Thomas
Telephone: (04) 562 8990 **Fax**: (04) 562 7667
Beds: 1 Queen, 1 Single (2 adjoining bedrooms)
Bathroom: 1 Private
Tariff: B&B (full) Double $90, Single $70.
NZ B&B Vouchers accepted
Nearest Town: Wellington City 20 minutes

Welcome to our home which we have restored and now has the atmosphere of an old European farmhouse. We live right beside the water, so all rooms have wonderful views of Wellington Harbour and the city beyond. Your room is large and attractive and the queen bed is very comfortable.

We would love you to join us for a pre-dinner drink and four excellent restaurants are only 4 minutes drive away. Breakfast can be as healthy or as wicked as you fancy from muesli, fresh fruit, and herb tea to croissants and loads of freshly brewed coffee.

Jim and I enjoy music, books, theatre, anything old and our city. We enjoy the company of our daughter Elizabeth and Elliott our Golden Retriever dog.

Eastbourne is a pretty seaside village 20-30 minutes from Wellington city and the Interisland ferry.

We will have achieved our aim if you leave us feeling refreshed and 'special'. Non smokers preferred.

Directions: *Please phone, write or fax.*

York Bay, Eastbourne
Homestay
Address: Bush House,
12 Waitohu Road,
York Bay, Eastbourne
Name: Belinda Cattermole
Telephone: (04) 568 5250
Fax: (04) 568 5250
Beds: 1 Double, 1 Single (2 bedrooms)
Bathroom: 1 Private, 1 Family share
Tariff: B&B (full) Double $90, Single $60,
Dinner $35. NZ B&B Vouchers accepted $15 surcharge
Nearest Town: Wellington City 20 minutes

Come and enjoy the peace and tranquillity of the Eastern Bays. You will be hosted in a beautifully restored 1920's settler cottage nestled amongst native bush and looking seawards to the Kaikoura mountains of the South Island. My love of cordon-bleu cooking and the pleasures of the table are satisfied through the use of my country kitchen and dining room. Other attractions: - Outdoor spa and a Devon Rex cat. Eastbourne is a small seaside village across the harbour from Wellington city with several craft shops, restaurants, a range of other attractions and a good beach. Wellington - 20 minutes: Lower Hutt - 10 minutes: Eastbourne - 5 minutes by car. Non-smokers preferred.

York Bay, Eastbourne

Homestay
Address: 15 Marine Dr., York Bay, Eastbourne
Name: Barry & Bev
Telephone: (04) 568 7104 **Fax**: (04) 568 7104 **Mobile**: (021) 2146960
Beds: 2 Single (1 bedroom)
Bathroom: 1 Private
Tariff: B&B (continental) Double $70, Single $50, 1 adult + 1 child (under 10) $60, Dinner $30 only by previous arrangement.
Credit Card NZ B&B Vouchers accepted
Nearest Town: Lower Hutt 10 mins

A breath of fresh air, 20 mins from Wellington City. Quiet, relaxed, nestled between native bush and the beach. Wake to the dawn chorus. Steps to the house allow a spectacular panorama of Hutt Valley, Wellington City, harbour and the Kaikouras. Cosy woodburner for the winter. Garage parking for 1 car. Laundry and drying facilities available. Tourist attractions: Harbour ferry from Days Bay to City centre. Bus transport to Lower Hutt and Wellington leaves from our front gate. Golf course. Indoor & outdoor swimming pools. Restaurants. All within a few minutes drive. Interests: Dog Shows, Obedience & Agility, we have 2 Belgian Shepherd puppies, which we show and work, NZ wines, our Children and Grandchildren. Barry a Retired Sales Consultant is now a professional Dog Trainer and Bev formerly a School Dental Nurse, is now a Counsellor and kennel maid. Specials: Vegetarian food only, Special diets catered for (vegan, dairy free) Transport can be arranged. Non smokers preferred.

Days Bay, Eastbourne

Self-contained Accommodation
Address: 7 Huia Rd (off Moana Road), Days Bay, Eastbourne
Name: Robyn & Roger Cooper
Telephone: (04) 562 7692
Fax: (04) 562 7690
Email: r.cooper@gns.cri.nz
Beds: 1 Double (1 bedroom).
(1 Double + 1 Single divan in lounge)
Bathroom: 1 Private
Tariff: B&B (continental) Double $85, Single $65, Extra adult $20, Children $15.
Credit Cards. Laundry and drying facilities by arrangement.
NZ B&B Vouchers accepted
Nearest Town: Wellington City 20 minutes, Eastbourne Village 3 minutes

Welcome to our home nestled high in the bush above Wellington harbour - a secluded peaceful retreat. Take our private cable car, with seating for two, for a stately scenic two-minute ride up the hillside to the front door or walk up through the beech trees and native bush. The warm attractive guest accommodation is fully self-contained with bedroom, lounge, kitchenette, bathroom and separate downstairs entrance. Wake to the sounds of the bellbird; breakfast on your private garden patio (provisions supplied in apartment); relax indoors with a variety of books, puzzles and games, TV and radio. We are a three minute walk to a picturesque swimming beach, sailboat hire, tennis courts, bush walks, interesting restaurants, bus routes and the ferry to central Wellington (20 minute ride). We look forward to meeting you and making your stay an enjoyable one. Our interests include geology, music, writing, orchid-growing, travel. We request no smoking indoors.

431

Lowry Bay, Eastbourne

Homestay
Address: 35 Cheviot Rd, Lowry Bay, Eastbourne
Name: Forde & Pam Clarke
Telephone: (04) 568 4407 **Fax**: (04) 568 4407
Mobile: (025) 283 3895
Email: forde.clarke@xtra.co.nz
Beds: 1 King, 2 Single (2 bedrooms)
Bathroom: 1 Guests share
Tariff: B&B (full) Double $95, Single $70, Children half price, Credit Cards. Laundry and drying facilities. NZ B&B Vouchers accepted
Nearest Town: Lower Hutt 10 minutes, Wellington City 20 minutes

Enjoy your stay in our sunny, warm, friendly family home in sheltered Lowry Bay. Centrally heated and attractively decorated our bedrooms have their own tea and coffee facilities and windows overlooking gardens and our sealed tennis court. You may enjoy a sail on our 28 foot yacht, which is berthed in a local marina, a 5 minutes stroll to the beach or a bush walk (which could take 15 minutes to a full day!). Within a ten minute drive we have heated swimming pools, golf courses, Hutt City and the village of Eastbourne with specialty shops, art galleries and restaurants.

We are 20 to 30 minutes from the Inter-island ferries and the airport. There is an excellent bus service to Eastbourne, Hutt City and Wellington and a ferry service from Days Bay to Somes Island and Wellington. We enjoy travelling (both in NZ and internationally), sailing, skiing, tennis and gardening. We are strictly non-smoking. With our two daughters, Isabella (15) and Kirsty (9) and our cat, we live in one of the nicest places in New Zealand. We will love sharing it with you.

Directions: *From State Highway 2 follow signs for Seaview then Eastbourne.*

Wellington. Seatoun

Homestay
Address: 10 Monro Street, Seatoun, Wellington 6003
Name: Frances Drewell
Telephone: (04) 388 6719
Fax: (04) 388 6719 **Mobile**: 025-241 4089
Beds: 1 Double, 2 Single (2 bedrooms)
Bathroom: 1 Guests share
Tariff: B&B (continental) Double $80, Single $50, Children $20, Dinner $20, Full breakfast on request,
Credit Cards. NZ B&B Vouchers accepted all year
Nearest Town: Wellington 9km

Handy to Wellington Airport our modern home is located in a quiet seaside village. A unique 'Fairy Shop' is a must to visit. Enjoy a NZ style dinner or dine at the local Village Inn or nearby restaurants. A warm welcome awaits those who want a home away from home which includes Doodo a very independent cat. Interests mainly in travel and sport and I play golf regularly. Laundry facilities available.

Directions: *Entering Wellington from the North or off the Interisland Ferry follow the signs to the Airport and following the signs to Seatoun. Monro Street is the second street on the left after the shops. From the Airport take the first turn right and then as above. One minute walk to bus stop. Travel around Wellington 'The City of a Thousand Views' on a $5 DAYTRIPPER TICKET. Discover New Zealand History by visiting 'TePapa' Wellington's new unique Museum.*

Wellington, Mt Victoria

Homestay
Address:"Villa Alexandra" 16 Roxburgh Street, Mount Victoria, Wellington
Name: Sheridan & Warwick Bishop
Telephone: (04) 802 5850 **Fax**: (04) 802 5851 **Mobile**: (025) 420 165
Email: 100245.2124@compuserve.com
Beds: 1 Queen, (1 bedroom)
Bathroom: 1 Private
Tariff: B&B (full) Double $95, Single $70, Dinner $25.
Credit Cards. NZ B&B Vouchers accepted $20 surcharge
Nearest Town: Wellington Civic Centre 1km, a 10 minute walk.

Our beautiful villa was built in 1906 and has been redecorated in the 90's so we can offer the best of both eras. We are just a short walk from Courtenay Place, the centre of Wellington's restaurant and theatre district. Within a ten to fifteen minute stroll there are over 50 restaurants of all ethnic persuasions, the new museum of New Zealand - "Te Papa", the Civic Centre, the CBD, many movie and live theatres, the Botanical Gardens, the shops and the excitement of New Zealand's capital city. The Airport, the Railway Station and the Inter Island Ferry terminal are all within a 10-minute drive.

We have gas and electric heating so the house is always warm. The Queen room is upstairs and has electric blankets, a feather duvet and a private bathroom alongside. You are welcome to make use of our laundry. We particularly look forward to chatting over meals with a bottle of wine. We know our country well and delight in meeting fellow travellers either from overseas or around New Zealand.

Sherry enjoys gardening, cooking and sewing while Warwick is interested in painting, photography, and computing. We both enjoy travel, films and shows. We request that guests not smoke in the house. Secure off street parking available.

Home Page: http://www.nzhomestay.co.nz/bishop
Directions: *Please Phone, Fax, Write or E-mail to make a booking or seek directions.*

Wellington , Karori

Homestay
Address: 83 Campbell Street,
Karori, Wellington
Name: Murray & Elaine Campbell
Telephone: (04) 476 6110
Fax: (04) 476-6593 **Mobile**: 025-535 080
Email: ctool@ihug.co.nz
Beds: 1 Queen, 3 Single (3 bedrooms)
Bathroom: 2 Private, 1 Guests share
Tariff: B&B (continental) Double $80, Single $45, Dinner $20pp, Children half
price, NZ B&B Vouchers welcomed. Credit cards.
Nearest Town: Wellington (10 minutes from city.)

*Welcome to our place, your home away from home. We accommodate families / groups, long
stay and business people. Our three guest rooms are 1:large queen, 2:twin (2 beds), 3:one single.
Upstairs the queen and twin bedrooms share the Guest Shower, Toilet, and bathroom while
downstairs the single room has its own toilet and bath. We have an old cat and a very well
behaved young Border Collie dog; enjoy sailing, skiing, boatbuilding, travel and running our
garden tool making business from home. Feel free to join us for pre-dinner drinks, dine with
us, or make use of our laundry / drying facilities, large garden and patio. Whilst very handy
to bus stops, whenever possible we will provide transport to ensure you enjoy your stay in our
wonderful city.*
Directions: *Telephone and we will meet you at the ferry / train / bus / air terminals. Driving
down State Highway 1 via the Motorway take the Hawkestone Exit and follow signs to Karori.
From Interisland Ferry terminal take exit to the city and pick up Karori signs. Look out for
our Bed & Breakfast sign on the lamp post at the bottom of the drive and park at the top.*

Wellington, Tawa

Homestay
Address: 17 Mascot Street, Tawa, Wellington
Name: Alf & Jeannette Levick
Telephone: (04) 232 5989
Fax: (04) 232 5987 **Mobile**: (025) 283 1256
Beds: 1 Queen, 1 Single (2 bedrooms)
Bathroom: Family share
Tariff: B&B (full) Double $60, Single $30. Dinner $20pp.
NZ B&B Vouchers accepted
Nearest Town: Wellington 15km.

*Our home is in a quiet street in the suburb of Tawa. 15 kilometres (15 minutes drive
or train) from the central city. We are nestled on the side of the valley with views over
farmland. Two bedrooms available for guests, one with a queen sized bed and the other
with a single bed, both with electric blankets, and electric heater in each room. We live
in a comfortable family home with a wood burner fire, separate bath and shower and
two toilets. You are welcome to use our laundry facilities and swimming pool. We know
New Zealand well and enjoy having people share our home. Freshly ground coffee a
speciality, breakfast of your choice, continental or full cooked meal. Enjoy a New
Zealand style dinner with us in the evening.*
*Jeannette's interests are: Ikebana, embroidery, knitting, dressmaking, tennis, learn-
ing to play golf and the piano, tennis, Japanese language and gardening.*
*Alf's interests are: Lions International, amateur radio, woodwork, Toastmasters and
- being allowed to help in the garden!!*
Directions: *Please phone.*

Wellington, Khandallah

Homestay
Address: 10A Izard Road, Khandallah, Wellington
Name: Genevieve & Peter Young
Telephone: (04) 479 5036 or Peter(work) (04) 477 4444
Beds: 5 Single (3 bedrooms)
Bathroom: 1 Guests share. Pool table
Tariff: B&B (full) Double $70, Single $40; Dinner by arrangement $20.
NZ B&B Vouchers accepted
Nearest Town: Khandallah, 10 mins bus ride to Wellington

We are a couple who enjoy relaxing and meeting people and our particular interests are travel, sport, food, wine, and the Arts. We have a small tabby cat called Amy. Our family of 3 girls have left home, and while we both work, we are able to take time off to show guests our beautiful harbour city. Khandallah is a hillside suburb handy to all the attractions of the capital, with a village atmosphere and a ten minute bus or train ride to town. Very close to the ferry terminal.
We look forward to making your stay an enjoyable one.
Directions: *Please phone and we will arrange to pick you up.*

Wellington, Ngaio

Homestay+Self-contained Accom.
Address: 56 Fox Street, Ngaio, Wellington
Name: Brian & Jennifer Timmings
Telephone: (04) 479 5325 **Fax**: (04) 479 4325 **Mobile**: (025) 276 9437
Email: jennifer.timmings@clear.net.nz
Beds: 2 Double, 2 Single (4 bedrooms). 2 Self contained units - one with double bed, one with twin beds, kitchen/lounge and laundry facilities.
Bathroom: 3 Ensuite, 1 Private
Tariff: B&B (continental) Double $85 Ensuite, Single $60, Children by arrangement, Dinner $20. SC Accom: Double $95, extra person $25pp (can sleep 4), Credit Cards (VISA/MC). NZ B&B Vouchers accepted $16 surcharge for ensuites, $20 surcharge for Unit
Nearest Town: Wellington city 7 km

We love our city of Wellington with its beautiful harbour, dramatic hills and spectacular scenery, and we would enjoy having you as our guests and sharing your "Wellington Experience" with us. We live 10 minutes from Wellington Railway Station and Ferry Terminal, in the suburb of Ngaio, surrounded by bush and hills. (We could meet/deliver guests from any central point.)We have an open plan home, but guests using the ensuite double room would have their own privacy with French doors opening onto a deck and sunny quiet garden.The two fully furnished units are separate from the house giving guests their own space and independence; perfect for corporate stays, extended vacations, sabbatical visitors, honeymooners or job relocations. Dinner is optional. In the evening guests may like to relax in our music room as we are a music oriented family. We also enjoy art and the outdoors.Off-street parking is available (also handy to good train service to city). Non smokers only, thank you.Hospitality guaranteed.
Directions: *Please phone, preferably before 11am or after 3pm, or fax or write or Email.*
Home Page: http://www.kiwihome.co.nz/timmings

Please help us provide the best hospitality in the world.
Fill in a comment form for every place you stay.

Wellington, Ohariu Valley

Farmstay
Address: Mill Cottage, Papanui Station,
Boom Rock Road, Ohariu Valley, Wellington
Name: Cliff & Bev Inglis
Telephone: (04) 478 8926
Email: Ohariu Valley, Johnsonville
Beds: 1 Double, 1 Twin (2 Bedrooms)
Bathroom: 1 Guests share
Tariff: B&B (full) Double $76, Single $38, Children under 12 half price,
Dinner $28.NZ B&B Vouchers accepted
Nearest Town: Johnsonville 10 minutes

Bev and Cliff invite you to experience a stay on a coastal high country sheep and cattle station Wellington's only farm stay only 25 minutes drive from central Wellington. Arrangements can be made for pick-up and drop off. Entering the Ohariu Valley opens the gateway to some of the most rugged coastline in the North Island and the ever-changing waters of Cook Strait with mountain views of the North and South Islands Wellington's highest point, Colonial Knob, 1500ft is at the north end of Papanui and at the south end is Boom Rock with its vast collection of sealife, great fishing, seals during winter months and bird life all year around. A tour of Papanui with us at no charge is to experience the magic viewed daily will make your stay with us unforgettable. Available to our guests, walks, cycling, mini golf, horse riding, BBQ on our private beach, during your stay our home is your home.
Home Page: Wellington
Directions: *Phone for directions - (04) 478 8926/24 hours.*

Wellington, Island Bay

Self-Contained Accommodation
Address: 326 The Esplanade,
Island Bay, Wellington
Name: The Lighthouse
Telephone: (04) 472 4177
Fax: (04) 472 4177 **Mobile**: (025) 425 555
Email: bruce@sportwork.co.nz
Beds: 1 or 2 Double (1 or 2 bedrooms)
Bathroom: 1 Private

Tariff: B&B (special) Double $180 Friday and Saturday, $150 Sunday - Thursday.
Nearest Town: Wellington - Central Wellington 10 mins

The Lighthouse Nestled in Island Bay 10 minutes from the airport or from Wellington City the recently constructed lighthouse has already achieved landmark status. The fishing boats in the bay, the view of the South Island, the ships steaming out of Wellington harbour, the rocky coast, and the Island with its wheeling seagulls provide the perfect setting for a day or two away. Just a few hundred metres around the corner from buses, shops and a top restaurant the Lighthouse balances modern living with a splendid coastal outlook. There are three floors comprising: Kitchen and bathroom; bedroom / sitting room; top floor of studio with bed-settee and balcony. The bed settees each take two. Whether winter or summer, on holiday, business or passing through, this is a unique accommodation opportunity not to be missed. Walk the beach, explore the rocks or walk to the seal colony. Bed and special breakfast rate is $180 or $150 per night for two people. Bookings to (04) 4724177, (025) 425555 or The Lighthouse, PO Box 11-275 Wellington.

Wellington, Johnsonville

Homestay
Address: 12 Nethergreen Crescent, Johnsonville, Wellington
Name: 'Antrim Villa Wellington', Dympna & Terry Brbich
Telephone: (04) 478 3444 **Fax**: (04) 478 3448
Mobile: (025) 840 850 **Email**: antrimvilla@xtra.co.nz

Beds: 1 King, 1 Queen,1 Double,1 Single (4 bedrooms)
Bathroom: 2 full ensuites with spa baths, 2 Guests share (with spa)
Tariff: B&B (full buffet style) Double $105-$145, Single $95-$130, Children welcome rates/negotiable. Campervans $50, Dinner $40 pp (BYO).
Credit cards accepted. NZ B&B Vouchers accepted Subject to seasonal surcharge
Nearest Town: Wellington 7kms, Johnsonville 1km.

"NOT A FIVE STAR HOTEL, BUT A FIVE STAR HOME"

*Discover affordable luxury just 10 minutes to Wellington centre, 7 minutes to interislander ferry, 1km from Johnsonville suburb, intercity coach stop or 20mins from airport. Courtesy transfers / safe off road parking.Imagine a majestically positioned quality five star retreat enjoying all day sunshine while offering a picturesque rural outlook so close to Wellington. Enjoy a family atmosphere or the quiet ambience of the formal lounge. A magic place to relax while enjoying complimentary drinks after a days travel. We happily arrange *sightseeing / picnic tours *onward travel *rental cars / accommodation.Bedrooms provide peaceful, tranquil valley views; are elegantly decorated with superior furnishings; TV / video, fridge / microwave, herbal teas / filter coffee facilities. Indulge yourself in luxuriously appointed bathrooms all mod / cons, toiletries, even bathrobes.Whether you enjoy an amble around our unique city, horse trekking, scenic coastal walks, golf, superb dining; staying at "Antrim Villa Wellington" guarantees a most enjoyable experience. "Your home away from home". CALL SOON for easy directions and a warm welcome.*
Home Page: http://www.nzcentrepoint.co.nz/antrimvilla/ Or http://www.nzcentre.com/antimvilla

Wellington City, Mt Victoria

Bed & Breakfast
Address: Dunrobin House,
89 Austin Street (Cnr Derby St),
Mt Victoria, Wellington City
Name: Carol & John Sutherland
Telephone: (04) 385 0335 **Fax**: (04) 385-0336 **Mobile**: (025) 525 952
Beds: 3 Queen, 1 Single (3 bedrooms, room with luxury ensuite has large dressing room with single bed)
Bathroom: 1 Ensuite, 2 Private
Tariff: B&B (special) Double $115-$145, Single $95-$120.
Credit cards (VISA/MC).
Nearest Town: Wellington Central 500 m

Dunrobin House is an elegant, romantic two-story Victorian Villa which is centrally situated in sunny, quiet Mt Victoria, a 3-10 minute easy walk to the city's cafes / excellent restaurants, Te Papa Museum of NZ, theatres, art galleries, convention centres, shopping and waterfront. An excellent location to explore our lovely City. Enjoy the luxury of our three spacious guest rooms which have comfortable beds, fluffy duvets, feather pillows, cotton bed linen, fresh flowers and lovely city views from 2 of the rooms. Relax in our sunny courtyards or elegant lounge with complimentary coffee / tea or Port. Enjoy a gourmet breakfast of orange juice, fresh seasonal fruit, home-made muesli, yoghurt, freshly baked muffins and a choice of specialty cooked dishes. Freshly brewed coffee (expresso / cappuccino) and a selection of teas. We are pleased to help you plan your stay in a city we both enjoy and would love to share with you. Parking available.

Wellington, City
Serviced Apartment
Address: "Talavera"
7 Talavera Terrace, Wellington 6001
Name: Bobbie Littlejohn
Telephone: (04) 471 0555 **Fax**: (04) 471 0551
Beds: 1 Queen, 2 Single (2 bedrooms)
Bathroom: 1 Private
Tariff: B&B (full) Double $140, Single $120, Addditional Guest $30. Seasonal Rates may apply. Not suitable children. Credit cards (VISA/MC).
Nearest Town: Wellington city centre 3 minutes walk

NO SHARE ACCOMMODATION to ensure privacy. 'Talavera' an inner city 100 year old villa, in a quiet cul-de-sac offers guests their own private apartment. The bedrooms are light and airy, with firm new beds, quality duvets, blankets and cotton linen. The bathroom has a deep, claw foot bath and shower over. A heated towel rail, wall heater, thick towels and a variety of toiletries for guests' enjoyment. The spacious living room provides comfortable seating, TV, radio, current magazines, binoculars, good heating, plus a built in refrigerator with tea / coffee making facilities. A door leads from here to an open verandah with seating overlooking our garden with fine views of the city, harbour and the Tararua Ranges beyond.

Always beautiful at night, a myriad of lights. The historic CABLE CAR stops at Talavera, a 3 minutes walk from the house. Everything is close to hand when you stay at 'Talavera'. A ten minute stroll will take you to the beautiful Botanic Gardens, Parliament, Victoria University with the popular Museum of New Zealand (Te Papa) only a little further away, Wellington today is the cafe city!

Friendly breakfasts are shared downstairs with David and Bobbie, in their home on an antique table with silver and fresh flowers. Daily squeezed orange juice, home baked muesli, fresh fruit platter, followed by omelettes, with delicious croissants / brioches and espresso coffee - a speciality! One resident black cat named 'Hoover'.

Parking available.

WE REQUEST NO SMOKING.

Directions: *For directions please phone Bobbie.*

438

Wellington, Thorndon

Bed & Breakfast
Address: Holdsworth, 292 Tinakori Road, Thorndon, Wellington
Name: Miriam Pennington
Telephone: (04) 473 4986 **Fax**: 04 473 9566 **Mobile**: 025 512 502
Email: mkp@voyager.co.nz
Beds: 1 Double, 1 Queen (2 bedrooms)
Bathroom: 1 Ensuite, 1 Private
Tariff: B&B (Full) Double $125-$160, Single $95-$125.
Credit Cards (Visa/MC/BC).
Nearest Town: Wellington CBD 500m

Holdsworth is an 1890's Heritage listed house situated in the heart of Tinakori Road, Thorndon, Wellington's most historic area.

Tinakori Road is bound by Botanic Gardens at one end, Katherine Mansfield birthplace at the other end and provides a unique collection of houses (including the Prime Minister's residence), shops, galleries, restaurants and cafes.

Public transport is only 3 minutes away and a 5 minute walk takes you to Parliament Buildings, into the city then on to the waterfront. For those wanting it there are more strenuous walks along the town belt or through the Botanic Gardens to catch some wonderful views of the city. Both the Interisland Ferry Terminal and Railway Station are very close.

Holdsworth offers luxuriously decorated spacious rooms with a warm welcoming atmosphere. The queen bedroom has an attractively appointed ensuite and guests have their own elegant sitting room with open fire for their relaxation. Complimentary tea, coffee, port are available.

Enjoy a gourmet breakfast of freshly squeezed fruit juice, seasonal fruits, a variety of delicious muffins and breads with homemade preserves and a range of specialty cooked breakfasts.

Off street parking is available. I request that guests do not smoke indoors.

Wellington, Tawa
Homestay
Address: 3 Kiwi Place,
Tawa, Wellington
Name: Joy & Bill Chaplin
Telephone: (04) 232 5547
Fax: (04) 232 5547
Email: chapta@xtra.co.nz
Beds: 1 Double, 1 Single (2 bedrooms)
Bathroom: 1 Guests share
Tariff: B&B (full) Double $60,
Single $30, Dinner $20pp,
Campervans (Sml/Med) facilities.
NZ B&B Vouchers accepted
Nearest Town: Wellington 15 kms

Guests are most welcome at No. 3, which is situated in a quiet street 7 minutes by car and rail from Porirua City and 15 minutes from Wellington and the Interisland Ferry Terminal.
Our rooms are warm and comfortable.
Tea / coffee making facilities and TV available also an extra bedroom downstairs with single bed or cot if required at reduced rate of $15. Spa, telephone / fax, laundry facilities and off-street parking also available.
The house is wheelchair friendly and suitable for elderly and young alike with areas indoors and out for relaxing.
Tawa is close to beaches, ten-pin bowling, roller skating rink, 1/2 size Olympic Swimming Pool and fine walks.
Our house is "smokefree"
Dinner and "pick-up" by arrangement.

Wellington, Khandallah
Homestay
Address: 22 Lohia Street, Khandallah, Wellington
Name: Ted & Sue Clothier
Telephone: (04) 479 1180 **Fax**: (04) 479 2717
Beds: 1 Twin with electric blankets (1 bedroom)
Bathroom: 1 Ensuite
Tariff: B&B (full) Double $100, Single $70, Dinner $30 by arrangement.
Credit Cards
Nearest Town: Wellington 7km

This is a lovely, sunny, warm open plan home with glorious harbour and city views. We enjoy sharing our home with guests.
We are situated in a quiet easily accessible street just ten minutes from the city and five minutes from the ferry. We are five minutes from the Khandallah Village and the local 'Posties Whistle" which is the nearest thing to an English pub out of England. Excellent food, wine and bar service.
We are a non smoking household. Another family member is an aristocratic white cat called Dali.
Dinner by arrangement.
Directions: *Please phone or fax.*

Wellington , Seatoun

Homestay
Address: "Edge Water Homestay",
459 Karaka Bay Road, Karaka Bay,
Seatoun, Wellington
Name: Stella & Colin Lovering
Telephone: (04) 388 4446
Fax: (04) 388 4446 **Mobile**: (021) 613 357
Beds: 2 Queen, 2 Single (3 bedrooms)
Bathroom: 2 Ensuite, 1 Guests share
Tariff: B&B (full) Double $90-$130, Single $70
Dinner from $35. Lunch $20. Credit Cards.
Nearest Town: Seatoun, Wellington

Edge Water Homestay is situated on the sea front at Karaka Bay, Seatoun. Seatoun is a quiet historic seaside village where waterfront houses were originally built as convalescent and holiday homes. Edge Water offers attractive, spacious rooms with a warm and welcoming atmosphere. Complimentary tea, coffee, chocolates and ports are available and guests can relax and take in the expansive seaside views. Enjoy gourmet breakfast of freshly squeezed orange juice, local fruits, homemade breads and preserves and a range of cooked breakfasts a speciality. Lunches and dinners are prepared by Stella, ex Wellington restaurateur (Marbles Restaurant), using fresh vegetables and meats and sometimes shellfish and seafoods caught in Karaka Bay. Swimming, fishing, snorkelling, cycling and walking are all available.
We have a small scruffy dog. Edge Water is 10 mins from the City and 5 mins. from the Airport. Bus stop is outside the front door. Off street parking available.

Wellington, Hataitai

Homestay
Address: "Top o' T'ill", 2 Waitoa Road,
Hataitai, Wellington 6003
Name: Dennis & Cathryn Riley
Telephone: (04) 386 2718
Fax: (04) 386 2719 **Mobile**: (025) 495 410
Beds: 1 Double, 1 Twin, 1 Single (3 bedrooms)
Bathroom: 1 Ensuite, 1 Guests share
Tariff: B&B (full) Double (ensuite) $80, Twin $75, Single $50.
NZ B&B & TAN Vouchers accepted. Credit Cards (MC/VISA)
Nearest Town: Wellington 3.2km

Our comfortable 1919, two storey home in the suburb of Hataitai (breath of the ocean), offers you a peek at Evans Bay and the eastern hills; to the west, our village and Mount Victoria. The house has been in our family for nearly 60 years and reflects the character of its time.
We enjoy the beauty of our harbour city, including its range of superb restaurants. Arts, sports venues and CBD are 5-10 minutes drive away.
We have travelled widely overseas and in New Zealand, and share interests in the arts, historic places, conservation and meeting people.
An enclosed spa pool in our back garden is one aspect of hospitality we can offer you along with other comforts. Pre-arranged transport transfers are available.
Our home is smokefree inside, and not suitable for children under 14 years.
Directions: *Please phone, write or fax.*

Wellington , Oriental Bay
Bed & Breakfast
Address: No 11, 11 Hay Street,
Oriental Bay, Wellington City
Name: Virginia Barton-Chapple
Telephone: (04) 801 9290 **Fax**: (04) 801 9295
Beds: 1 King convertible to twin (1 bedroom)
Bathroom: 1 Share
Tariff: B&B (special) Double $85, Single $65. Credit Cards.
Nearest Town: Wellington City 2 minutes drive

Oriental Bay is perhaps the finest location in Wellington. Take the opportunity to stay in this inner city area which is within strolling distance of any of the attractions that Wellington has to offer.
No 11 has an intimate view of the city and Virginia has extensive knowledge of what's going on, and where to go. You may be so captivated by the location that you wish only to promenade along the Parade. Or in summer to swim or take a harbour cruise.
The accommodation is in a comfortable room for two, with the bathroom adjacent. Electric blankets and tea and coffee facilities are available.
Breakfast will be an occasion ..... the freshest in season ingredients will be used.
Smoking outside would be appreciated.
Cat in residence.

Wellington, Thorndon
Self Contained B & B
Address: 8 Parliament Street,
Thorndon, Wellington
Name: Eight Parliament Street
Fax: (04) 479 6705
Mobile: (025) 280 6739
Email: grasenack@xtra.co.nz
Beds: 3 Queen (3 bedrooms)
Bathroom: 1 Ensuite, 1 Guests share
Tariff: B&B (full) Double $118-$140, Single $95-$118. Children over 12 years only. Visa/Mastercard.
Nearest Town: Wellington 5 minutes walk to City

From the outside a house in the traditional Thorndon character. From the inside a stylish artistic home. Eight Parliament located in a quiet street in Wellington's historical part of town, Thorndon is in walking distance to attractions like Parliament Buildings, Botanical Gardens, shops and restaurants.
The house features three bedrooms (one ensuite) with contemporary interior and changing artwork (available for sale). A courtyard offers outdoor relaxation and privacy. There is a modern kitchen/dining area for entertainment and a cup of espresso after a long day of sightseeing. Eight Parliament Street is a serviced self contained B&B where guests are treated with a breakfast of their choice served inside or al fresco in the courtyard.Eight Parliament caters for the traveller and busy executive alike who prefer personal ambience.Smoking is possible in the courtyard only. Laundry service available. Please phone prior to arrival. German spoken.
Home Page: http://www.webnz.co.nz/8parliament

Wellington, Newtown

Homestay
Address: Newtown Homestay,
85 Rintoul Street, Wellington.
Name: Keith and Gail
Telephone: (04) 389 0416
Beds: 1 Queen, 3 single (3 bedrooms)
Bathroom: 1 Guests share
Tariff: B&B (full) Double $79-$89, Single $49-$55.
Nearest Town: Wellington 2km

Newtown Homestay is a quiet spacious refurbished Victorian villa centrally situated 10 minutes from both the CBD and airport with pleasant views over picturesque Newtown. It is only a quick ride to Courtenay Place cafes, theatres, and Te Papa New Zealand national museum, via trolley buses regularly passing our gate. A short stroll takes you to village shops, restaurants, public and private hospitals yet we offer a quiet secure haven from the busy city. Complimentary tea and coffee making facilities are available in the TV lounge which guests can access at any time. All our bedrooms have electric blankets and heaters. We offer a smoke free house however, there is a delightful private back garden for those who wish to smoke. We are a mature couple with previous guest house experience and offer you unobtrusive but friendly hospitality. Our children have long since left home and we have no pets.

Wellington, Palmer Head

Homestay
Address: "Birkhall House"
14 Birkhall Grove,
Palmer Head, Wellington 6003.
Name: Jocelyn Scown
Telephone: 04-388 2881 **Fax**: 04-388 2833
Mobile: 025-762 870
Beds: 1 King, 1 Double (2 bedrooms)
Bathroom: 1 Guests share

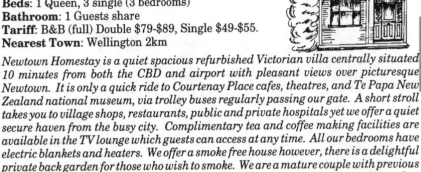

Tariff: B&B (continental/full on request) Double $85, Single $65,
Dinner $35 on request with wine, Credit Cards accepted.
NZ B&B Vouchers accepted $10 surcharge
Nearest Town: Wellington 10 minutes by car

Relax in my lovely sunny home and enjoy the finest views in Wellington. Palmer Head is a new suburb situated on a hill with views from the South Island to Wellington Harbour. I am only 5 minutes drive from Wellington Airport and 10 mins drive to Wellington City with all its many attractions, including the world acclaimed Te Papa Museum.
Enjoy a continental breakfast (cooked on request) on the deck, and with notice I am also happy to serve dinner with the finest NZ wines. For those who have energy to burn, there are several walk tracks nearby, and for the sports minded I overlook the golf course.
I would be delighted to have you as my guest and have no objection to house trained dogs and kids. (Babys cot, pushchair and carseat available on request)
Complimentary: Tea, Coffee, Juice and biscuits.
Smokefree inside, Centrally heated, laundry facilities available.
Directions: *Please phone, fax or write for directions.*

443

GERALD BULL '91

ABSOLUTELY
POSITIVELY
WELLINGTON

Wellington , Island Bay
Island Bay Homestay
Address: 52 High Street, Island Bay, Wellington 6002
Name: Theresa & Jack Stokes
Telephone: (04) 383 5169, Toll free 0800 33 53 83 **Fax**: (04) 383 5169
Email: tandj@actrix.gen.nz
Beds: 2 Double or Double 1 & Twin 1 (2 bedrooms)
Bathroom: 2 Private
Tariff: B&B (full) Double/Twin $70, Single $45. NZ B&B Vouchers accepted
Nearest Town: Island Bay, Wellington 10 mins drive

A modern, ten year old Lockwood house standing in a very private three acre section with probably the finest view in Wellington. Overlooking Island Bay harbour with its fishing boats - the entrance to Port Nicholson (Wellington's harbour) - the Cook Strait with its ferries and cargo vessels on the move day and night. Ten minutes drive to town centre. Ten minutes walk to the bus terminus. Not suitable for children under 14. We have a small dog and a Moggy.
Directions: *From State Highway 1 or 2 take the Aotea Quay turnoff. (From the ferry take city exit). Follow the main road which bears slightly to the left to a T junction (Oriental Parade). Turn right and in to Kent Terrace - get in the right hand lane before going round the Basin Reserve (cricket ground) and in to Adelaide Road. Straight up the hill, leaving Athletic Park (large stand) on your left and the road becomes The Parade. Keep going straight until you reach the sea and then turn SHARP right in to Beach Street. Left and left again in to High Street and straight up the private road at the end. Plenty of parking.*
From Wellington Airport take the rear exit (past the cargo warehouse) and turn right. Follow the coast road for ten minutes and Beach Street is on the right.
For the Navigator, we live at: Lat. S.41.20.54/Long. E174.45.54

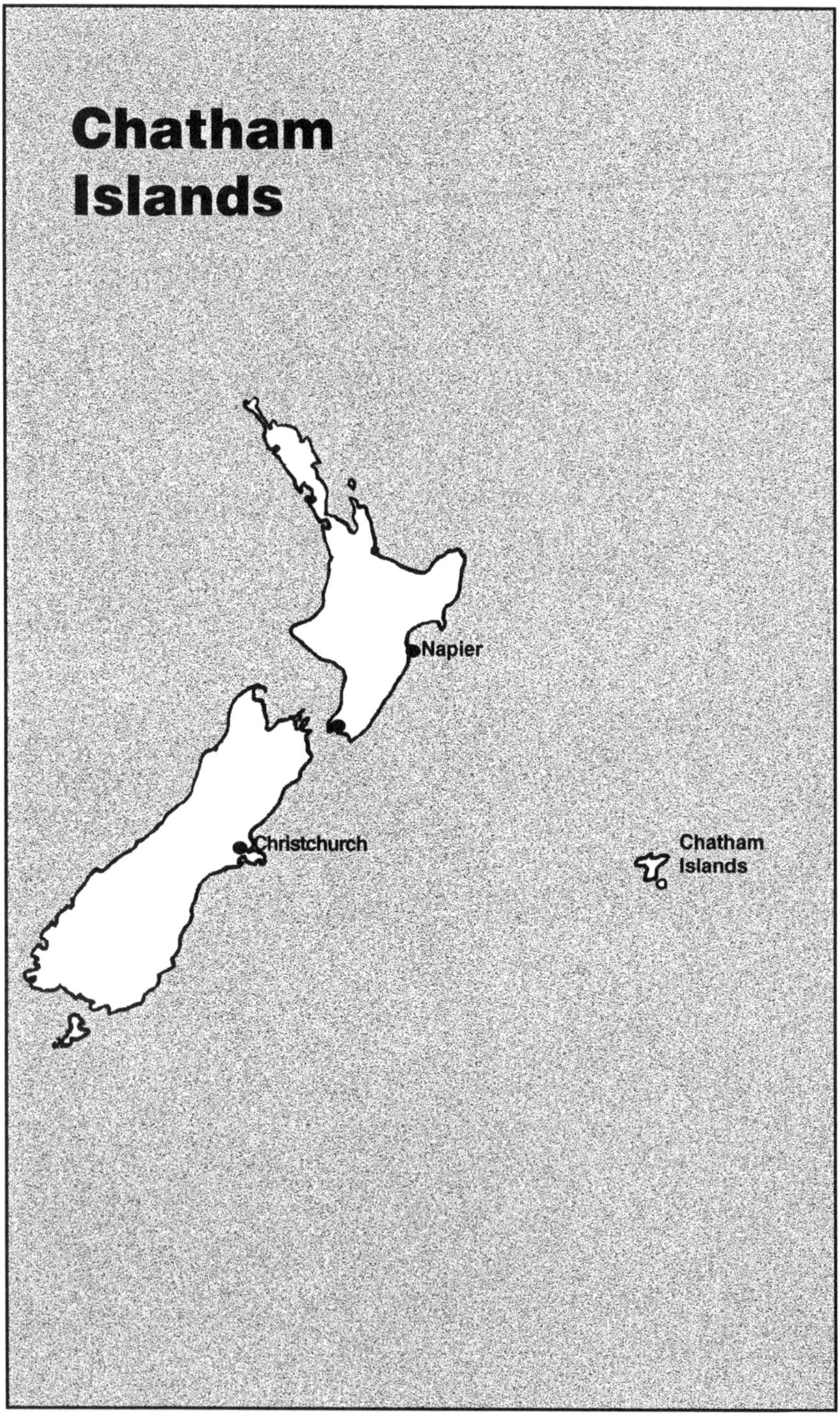

Chatham
Islands

Napier

Christchurch

Chatham
Islands

Chatham Islands

Farmstay
Address: Te Matarae, Chatham Islands
Name: Smith
Telephone: (03) 305 0144 **Fax**: (03) 305-0144
Beds: 2 Queen, 2 Single (3 bedrooms)
Bathroom: 2 Ensuite, 1 Family share
Tariff: B&B (continental) Double $85, Single $73, Dinner $17
Nearest Town: Waitangi (Chatham Islands)

Relax in our natural wood home which is situated in eighty acres of bush on lagoon edge with mown walkways throughout. The lagoon is ideal for swimming and has nice sandy beaches. Flounder, whitebait, eels and cockles may also be caught seventy-five yards from house. Farm activities and kayaks available. Farm is eleven hundred acres and includes four other bush reserves.

Guests may meal with family or in separate dining room. Bedrooms are separated from main house by covered swimming pool and home gym area.

We are a non smoking household; so request guests to refrain from doing so in our home.

Most meal ingredients are home produced.

Air travel exit points are Christchurch and Wellington. Rental car with guide available.

Free pick up and deliver to airport.

The Chatham Islands situated 800km east of Mainland New Zealand, are Islands of Mystery. A place where volcanic cones rise from the mist and sea. Due to isolation and recent history of colonisation, many plants and animals are unique.

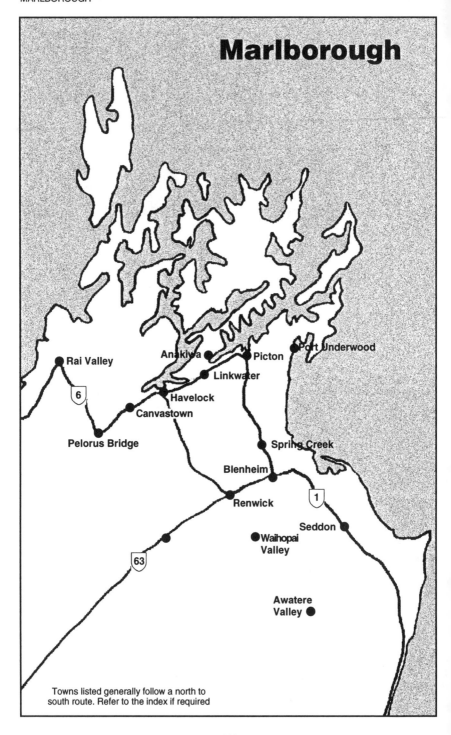

Marlborough

Rai Valley

6

Anakiwa   Picton   Port Underwood

Linkwater

Havelock

Canvastown

Pelorus Bridge

Spring Creek

Blenheim

Renwick

1

Seddon

63

Waihopai Valley

Awatere Valley

Towns listed generally follow a north to
south route. Refer to the index if required

Picton

Bed & Breakfast Homestay
Address: 'The Gables', 20 Waikawa Road, Picton
Name: Annette and Peter Gardiner
Telephone: (03) 573 6772 **Fax**: (03) 573 8860
Mobile: (025) 220 5786
Email: gables@mlb.planet.gen.nz
Beds: 2 Queen, 1 Double, 2 Single (3 bedrooms)
Bathroom: 2 Ensuite, 1 Private
Tariff: B&B (special) Double $90-$115, Single $70.
Not suitable for very young children.
Credit cards: Visa/Mastercard.
NZ B&B Vouchers accepted June - August
Nearest Town: Picton 1 block

A warm welcome awaits you at "THE GABLES" in Picton, your destination in the Marlborough district, well known for the Queen Charlotte Walkway, kayaking, eco tours, sailing, fishing activities and wineries.

"THE GABLES", built in 1924 and purchased by Annette and Peter especially to share with guests, is situated within 1 block of the town centre and the beautiful harbour foreshore. Award-winning restaurants and cafes are all within easy walking distance, most within 2 blocks. Ferry, bus, train and other facilities are within 5 minutes walk of "THE GABLES".

Our guest rooms are upstairs, and have been named to recognise the previous families who have owned "THE GABLES".

The large "Townshend" room (previous Mayor of Picton) has tea and coffee making facilities, small pink tiled fireplace, an ensuite bathroom and firm queen size bed.

The large "Thomson" room has a firm queen size bed and two single beds, private bathroom across the hallway, and tea and coffee making facilities.

The "Findlater" room is comfortable with a double size bed and ensuite bathroom, tea & coffee making facilities.

Breakfasts are special at "THE GABLES" - after fruit juice, fruit platters, cereal, home-made muesli, you will be offered a choice of our legendary bluecod and smoked salmon crepes, banana pancakes with maple syrup, or traditional bacon and eggs. Delicious home made muffins are baked fresh every morning, to be enjoyed with freshly brewed coffee or a selection of teas. The lounge, with open fire, TV, piano, reading material, tea and coffee making facilities, is where we enjoy a pre-dinner drink with our guests. You are likely to be met by our very friendly black spaniel, Blackie, or Penelope the cat. Off street parking. Smoking area on front porch.

Tariff:
Townshend Room: $115 Double
Thomson Room: $115 Double or Twin, extra person $25
Findlater Room: $90 Double, $70 Single
Home Page: http:/nz.com/webnz/bbnz/gables.htm

449

Picton, Whatamango Bay
Homestay+SC Apartments
Address: 424 Port Underwood Rd,
Whatamango Bay, Queen Charlotte Sound,
PO Box 261, Picton
Name: 'Seaview', Pam & John Anders
Telephone: (03) 573 7783 **Fax**: (03) 573 7783
Beds: Apartments: 2 Double Homestay: 2 Single (1 bedroom)
Bathroom: Apartments: 2 Private Homestay: 1 Private
Tariff: B&B (full) Double $70, Single $40, Dinner $25,
Self-contained apartment: Double $60. Credit cards NZ B&B Vouchers accepted
Nearest Town: Picton 9km

'Seaview' is set in peaceful surroundings only 10 minutes by road from Ferry Terminal.
Our apartments are quiet, clean, comfortable and private with extensive views over
Queen Charlotte Sound, forest and distant mountains to the north.
Walk in our large garden which abounds with native birds, hike the forest trail behind
our home, or take the 1km walk to the historic Maori storage pits. You may see Dolphins
in the bay. Take our small boat and try your luck fishing or relax and watch the
shipping pass by.
Join us in the morning when a full breakfast is served including our own free range
eggs.
Directions: *Follow the Port Underwood Road from Waikawa for 4km. Sign at bottom*
of drive. 'Seaview' No. 424.
Dinner by arrangement.

Anakiwa, Picton

Homestay-S.C. Apartment
Address: 'Crafters', Anakiwa Road,
Queen Charlotte Sound, R.D. 1, Picton
Name: Ross & Leslie Close
Telephone: (03) 574 2547
Fax: (03) 574 2547
Beds: 2 Single (1 bedroom)
Bathroom: 1 Private
Tariff: B&B (NZ style) Double $75, Single $45, Dinner $25.
Credit cards. NZ B&B Vouchers accepted
Nearest Town: Picton 22 Kms, Havelock 18 Kms

Our home at the head of Queen Charlotte Sound has a magnificent 25 mile long sea
view and is in a tranquil and peaceful area, noted for its bush walks and variety of bird
life. It is only a short walk to New Zealand's Cobham Outward Bound School, and the
start of the Queen Charlotte Walkway, a wonderful scenic route from Anakiwa to Ship
Cove.
Our warm and comfortable guest area has one bedroom with twin beds, a sunny lounge
with TV and a large double sofa bed if required, a fully equipped kitchen and private
bathroom.
Ross is a woodturner and Leslie is a potter and both are happy to demonstrate their
skills and their Gallery is open every day. Other interests we enjoy are sea fishing in
our motor launch and walking our Jack Russell terrier.
Transport to and from local departure points can be provided by arrangement.
Directions: *Please phone.*

Waikawa Bay, Picton

Homestay
Address: Please Telephone
Name: Yvonne & Gary Roberts
Telephone: (03) 573 8965 **Fax**: (03) 573 8965
Beds: 4 Single (2 bedrooms)
Bathroom: 1 Guests share
Tariff: B&B (full) Double $75, Single $50, Dinner $30.
NZ B&B Vouchers accepted $10 Surcharge
Nearest Town: 3km from Picton

Our home is a warm, roomy colonial sort of cottage in a quiet leafy area of Waikawa Bay about 3km from Picton.

We are a young middle-aged non smoking couple recently escaped from big city corporate life and fond of fine food and wines, good conversation, and a classic motor launch. We can be enthusiastic about books, serious music and the outdoors. Yvonne is much preoccupied by patchwork and quilting followed closely by gardening and rambling. Gary cooks, is interested in things nautical and cricket from a distance - he may one day write a book.

We enjoy introducing like minded people to our version of Marlborough. Close by are sheltered waterways, a skifield, vineyards with boutique restaurants and a unique back country.

To plan for some style in the care and feeding of our guests, we prefer reservations in advance.

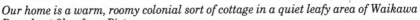

Linkwater, Picton

Lodge with Licenced Restaurant
Address: Linkwater Lodge,
Queen Charlotte Scenic Drive, R.D.1, Picton
Name: John Smart
Telephone: (03) 574 2507 **Fax**: (03) 574 2517
Beds: 2 Queen, 2 Twin (4 bedrooms)
Bathroom: 2 Guests share

Tariff: B&B (continental) Double $75, Single $45, Children half price, Dinner - meal in restaurant, Campervans $25 (no electrical power), Credit cards (VISA/ MC). NZ B&B Vouchers accepted $7.50 Surcharge
Nearest Town: Havelock 12km, Picton 22km

Linkwater Lodge is approximately 30 minutes (22 kilometres) drive from Picton Ferry Terminal along beautiful Queen Charlotte Drive. This old homestead, built of native timbers in 1926, is surrounded by farmlands and is centrally located in the Marlborough Sounds. Guests can walk from the Lodge to historic Cullensville Goldfields (1888). All Sounds' attractions, including the Queen Charlotte Walkway, are only a short drive. Upstairs rooms provide comfortable beds and peaceful farmland views. A small restaurant serves home-cooked food ranging from tasty soups and sandwiches to tender steaks and succulent seafood. Nearby Havelock is the green-lipped mussel capital of the world. Marlborough tap beer and wines are served at a magnificent bar milled from a walnut tree standing 90 years on the farm. Enjoy the goldfields atmosphere and learn about this exciting district from friendly locals.

Your host, John, is a former outback worker and university professor, now glasswasher and philosopher.

451

Picton

Historic Homestay
Address: 'House of Glenora', 22 Broadway, Picton
Name: Birgite & Neale Armstrong
Telephone: (03) 573 6966 **Fax**: (03) 573 7735
Beds: 3 Queen, 6 Single (6 bedrooms)
Bathroom: 2 Ensuite, 1 Private, 1 1/2 Guests share
Tariff: B&B (continental) Double $85-$105, Triple $95,
Twin $75, Single $50, Children not suitable.
Credit cards. Vouchers accepted Surcharge Double $20
Nearest Town: 50 m Post Office Picton

House of Glenora, built for the South Island's first magistrate in 1860, renovated and converted in B&B with GALLERY, showing weaving from our INTERNATIONAL WEAVING SCHOOL, and a selection of local crafts. Ground floor central heating / air conditioning. Wide, sunny verandahs, guests' own ground floor lounge and dining room with log burning stove, and sunny kitchen. Furnished throughout in a mix of antique and contemporary art pieces.
Enjoy our Scandinavian style breakfast plus wonderful view of the Sounds and Picton Harbour. Guests are welcome to look at the Weaving Studio. Tuition from beginners to experts, available by appointment. Mature, well cared for garden. Off street parking. One (double) bedroom has ground floor, private access. All have complimentary tea and coffee making facilities. First floor rooms with spectacular harbour views. House of Glenora offers a creative and comfortable environment, within easy walking distance of Picton's restaurants and Ferry.
Laundry facilities. No smoking. Courtesy car.
WINNER MARLBOROUGH TOURISM AWARD.

Ngakuta Bay, Picton

Homestay
Address: 'Ngakuta Bay Homestay and Pottery',
Ngakuta Bay, Queen Charlotte Sounds, R.D.1,
Ngakuta Bay,Picton
Name: John Hadfield & Heather Dixon
Telephone: (03) 573 8853 **Fax**: (03) 573 8353
Mobile: (025) 277 9597
Beds: 1 Queen with ensuite, French doors to verandah. 2 Single (3 bedrooms)
Bathroom: 1 Ensuite, 1 Guests share
Tariff: B&B (continental) Double $90, Single $50.
Dinner $25pp on request.
Credit Cards (BC/VISA). NZ B&B Vouchers accepted surcharge
Nearest Town: Picton 11km

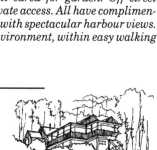

Ngakuta Bay Homestay and Pottery is 11km from Picton and 21km from Havelock, on the scenic Queen Charlotte Drive, with access to beautiful bays, beaches and recreational areas. The Homestay and Pottery is built in NZ Larch and set in 1/2 an acre of bush with large verandahs and magnificent views over Ngakuta Bay. Sky TV. From this setting guests can go fishing, mountain bike riding, bush walking. We can arrange Kayaking, Dolphin watching or we can set you in the right direction for a day in the out and beyond. John and Heather are experienced yachts persons and from time to time we take guests sailing or power boating in the Queen Charlotte Sounds (time and weather permitting) or alternatively you can just vege out in this splendid atmosphere soaking up the Marlborough climate and the sounds beauty.
John is an established potter and ceramic artist and guests are invited to try their hand at making or decorating pottery.

Picton

Homestay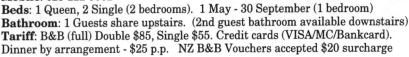
Address: 'Retreat Inn',
20 Lincoln Street, Picton
Name: Alison & Geoff
Telephone: (03) 573 8160
Answer phone: (03) 573 7799
Fax: (03) 573 7799
Mobile: 025-222 5062
Beds: 1 Queen, 2 Single (2 bedrooms). 1 May - 30 September (1 bedroom)
Bathroom: 1 Guests share upstairs. (2nd guest bathroom available downstairs)
Tariff: B&B (full) Double $85, Single $55. Credit cards (VISA/MC/Bankcard).
Dinner by arrangement - $25 p.p. NZ B&B Vouchers accepted $20 surcharge
1 May - 30 Sept.
Nearest Town: A 3 minute drive to Picton's main street.

We welcome you and offer a friendly, peaceful stay at 'RETREAT INN' - our little patch
of privacy on a quiet wooded hillside, mere minutes to the village and restaurants,
walks and waterways, fishing and boating.
In our home, your cosy bedrooms are upstairs - all beds have new firm mattresses with
electric blankets. The wood fire in our family living room - (which our cat Sandie also
enjoys) - makes for warm conversation on cooler evenings, while our outdoor patio
areas beckon those who just want to unwind.
'RETREAT INN' breakfasts are special - fruit juice, fruit platters, choice of cereals -
with homemade muesli and yoghurt, fresh jams and croissants, teas and freshly
brewed coffee. Cooked course also available. We will happily provide transport for
buses, ferries, trains. Laundry facilities available. Secure off-street parking. Sorry,
no smoking in the house. We look forward to seeing you. Safe travelling.
Directions: *For directions, please phone.*

Picton

Bed & Breakfast
Address: 'The Bungalow',
21 Leicester St., Picton
Name: Christine & Mike Lake
Telephone: (03) 573 7858
Beds: 2 Double, 1 Single (2 bedrooms)
Bathroom: 1 Guests share
Tariff: B&B (full) Double $60,
Single $35, Children welcome.
Credit cards. NZ B&B Vouchers accepted
Nearest Town: Picton 1km.

The Bungalow is an early 20th century character house set in relaxing tree-studded
grounds. We invite you to share our hospitality in the quiet peaceful atmosphere which
our spacious rooms and tranquil setting provides. We have a lounge set aside for guest
use where you will find books, jigsaws and board-games in addition to TV and video.
In the mornings you may linger as long as you desire over your breakfast served in front
of an open fire in the colder months. We are situated one kilometre from Picton town
centre, just a short stroll away from the domain and several spectacular bush and
scenic walks. We will provide a courtesy car to and from the Ferry Terminal and town
if required. Our young sons are happy to share their toys with your children and we
will gladly child mind if parents wish.

Picton

Self-contained Apartment
Address: 'Grandvue', 19 Otago Street, Picton
Name: Russell & Rosalie Mathews
Telephone: (03) 573 8553
Fax: (03) 573 8556
Email: grandvue-mathews@clear.net.nz
Beds: 1 Queen
Bathroom: 1 Ensuite
Tariff: B&B (full) Double $75, Single $55,
Children $15, Dinner optional extra.
Vouchers accepted $7.50 surcharge
Nearest Town: Picton 2mins walk

Nestled on the hills overlooking Picton, Grandvue offers sweeping panoramic views of the township and port looking out onto Queen Charlotte Sound. Situated at the end of a cul-de-sac, Grandvue is a quiet haven with a secluded garden, only five minutes walk from the main shopping area of Picton with its assortment of restaurants, and only ten minutes walk from the Inter-Island Ferry Terminal. Grandvue offers accommodation in a comfortable and warm self-contained apartment with its own kitchen and ensuite. A television and video is also available as is access to a private barbeque area. Feast on panoramic views from our conservatory upstairs while enjoying a delicious continental or cooked breakfast. If required a portable cot and high chair are also available. Your hosts, Russell and Rosalie will provide courtesy transport to and from the Ferry Terminal, Railway Station or Airport.

The Grove, Picton

B&B Self Contained Accommodation
Address: Tanglewood, Queen Charlotte Drive, The Grove, R.D.1, Picton
Name: Tanglewood
Telephone: (03) 574 2080 **Fax**: (03) 574 2044
Email: tangles@voyager.co.nz
Beds: 1 Super King, 2 Single (2 bedrooms)
Bathroom: 2 Ensuite
Tariff: B&B (full) Double $80, Single $55, Dinner $25pp,
Credit Cards (VISA/MC), Not suitable for children.
Nearest Town: Picton 16km, Havelock 16km

Snuggled amongst native ferns - yet only 4 minutes stroll to swimming beach and jetty, Tanglewood has a private and separate guest wing. There is a guest lounge, also kitchenette where evening meals may be self catered.
Use us as a stopping-off spot to kayak round the bays, take a fishing rip or enjoy local bush walks, including queen Charlotte Walkway.
Sample some of New Zealand's best wines on the wine trail, visit local arts and crafts. Take a trip to watch or swim with the dolphins and observe some rare and endangered birds.
Relax on the verandah and listen to the sounds of birds and our stream. Our super king or twin beds are of unsurpassed comfort.
We both share interests in craft including Paper Tole and patchwork quilting. Our two cats help us in the garden. We look forward to making you feel welcome.

Picton

Homestay
Address: 21 Otago Street, Picton
Name: Panorama View
Telephone: (03) 573 6362
Fax: (03) 573 6362
Beds: 1 Double, 2 Single (2 bedrooms)
Bathroom: 1 Ensuite, 1 Private
Tariff: B&B (full) Double $75, Single $50.
NZ B&B Vouchers accepted
Nearest Town: Picton 2 minutes

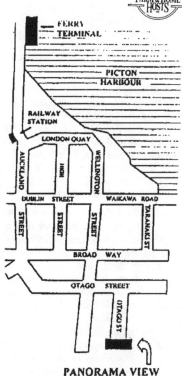

We would like to invite you in our sunny-spacious home in Picton, The Diamond of the South Island, where we have a breathtaking view over the city and the harbour, with a 5 minutes walk to the foreshore, shops, boating facilities, mini-golf, Ferry terminal, restaurants etc.
You might like to join us for a 'cuppa' on the balcony and watch the ferry and activities on the water.
The bedrooms have coffee and tea facilities, radio / clock, colour TV, fridge, electric blankets etc.
A warm welcome awaits you at "Panorama View" including a generous breakfast.
We are looking forwards to meeting you.
Courtesy car available.
Your Hosts Colin and Din

455

Queen Charlotte Sounds - Picton

Homestay+Self-contained Accom.
Address: 'Tirimoana House', Anakiwa Road,
Picton R.D.1, Queen Charlotte Sounds, Marlborough
Name: Peter & Robyn Churchill
Telephone: (03) 574 2627
Fax: (03) 574 2647 **Mobile**: (025) 393 649
Beds: Homestay: 1 King, 1 Queen,
1 Twin (2 bedrooms)
SC Unit: 1 Double, 3 Single
Bathroom: Homestay: 1 Guests share (incl spa bath and sep shower)
SC Unit: Private bathroom, kitchen, laundry
Tariff: B&B (full) Double $75, Single $50, Dinner $25pp.
Self-contained Unit: $60 Double, $10 each extra person.
Nearest Town: Picton 22km, Havelock 18km

'SOUNDS MAGIC'
Come and share a slice of Heaven: Set in beautiful grounds of native and exotic plants at the head of Queen Charlotte Sound, enjoy panoramic views of the Sounds and surrounding bush clad hills from all rooms, terraces and swimming pool. Our large waterfront home overlooks Okiwa Bay, the Cobham Outward Bound School and the start / finish of the beautiful Queen Charlotte Walkway. For your enjoyment we offer hospitality, orthopaedic beds, extensive sun decks, fernery spa pool, barbeque on marble terrace, good food, dawn chorus, billiard table, underfloor heating, convivial glass, log fire, interesting conversation and friendly cat 'Merp". We respect your wish to laze, gaze and watch the swans go by but will happily encourage you to share our interests of fishing in our launch, boating, golf, bush walks, music. We can arrange kayaking, wine trails, mountain biking, etc. Courtesy car available by arrangement.
Directions: *Please phone.*

Picton

Bed & Breakfast
Address: Echo Lodge, 5 Rutland Street, Picton
Name: Lyn & Eddie Thoroughgood
Telephone: (03) 573 6367 **Fax**: (03) 573 6387
Beds: 1 Double, 3 Single (3 bedrooms)
Bathroom: 2 Ensuite, 1 Private
Tariff: B&B (special) Double $75, Single $40.
Credit Cards accepted.
Nearest Town: Picton 800 m

Lyn and Eddie welcome you to our older style home named after the ship in our harbour "Echo". We invite you to share a cup of tea, coffee, wine or juice on arrival. The atmosphere at Echo Lodge is friendly and relaxed. Enjoy our lovely spacious lounge with its Turkish carpets and cozy log fire for cold winter nights. Through the arch way to our dining room, where you will be served our special breakfast. The smell of hot baked bread, special pancakes, muffins, omelets, percolated coffee, home made jams, yoghurt, fruit, muesli awaits you. You may like to have breakfast on our patio.
The "Quarter Deck" and "The Bridge" have ensuite bathrooms, comfortable firm beds and tea / coffee making facilities. The Fo'c'sle, single with private facilities.
We are 5 mins walk from shops, restaurants, busses, ferries. With a courtesy car available. We're happy to help you with your travel arrangements. Come stay with us. you will not regret it. A warm Picton welcome awaits you.
Directions: *800m up Waikawa Road from round about in town. Rutland Street on your right.*

Kenepuru Sound

Farmstay
Address: "The Nikaus", Waitaria Bay, RD 2, Picton
Name: The Nikaus Country Garden & Farmstay
Telephone: (03) 573 4432 **Fax**: (03) 573 4432
Mobile: (025) 544 712
Beds: 1 Double, 2 Single (2 bedrooms)
Bathroom: 1 Guests share
Tariff: B&B (full) Double $70, Single $40, Children 12 & under half price,
Dinner $20, Credit Cards.
NZ B&B Vouchers accepted all year round
Nearest Town: Blenheim 110km, Havelock 80km, Picton 80km

*The Nikaus is a Sounds sheep & cattle farm situated in Waitaria Bay Kenepuru
Sound, 2 hours drive from Blenheim or Picton.*
*We offer friendly personal service in our comfortable spacious home. The large gardens
(in AA Garden Book) contain many rhododendrons, roses, camellias, lilies and
prennials, with big sloping lawns and views out to sea. A swimming pool is available
for guests use. We have 3 children (2 away and 1 at boarding school). A non-smoking
household with interests in farming, boating, fishing and gardening.*
*We have 2 dogs Sam (corgie) and Micky (foxy x). Other animals include the farm dogs,
donkeys, pet wild pigs, "Miss Piggy", turkeys, hens and peacocks.*
*Good hearty country meals, home grown produce and home made ice cream a
speciality, thanks to "Muggles" our friendly house cow.*
*We are happy to arrange local fishing trips, launch charters and water taxis for
visitors.*
Directions: *Please phone.*

Mahau Sound, Picton

Homestay
Address: "Kairangi", Moetapu Bay,
Mahau Sound, RD 2, Picton
Name: Pauline & Gary Graham
Telephone: (03) 574 2548
Freephone: 0800 16 99 14
Fax: (03) 574 2580
Email: soundswise@xtra.co.nz
Beds: 2 Twin, 1 set of bunks (3 bedrooms)
Bathroom: 1 Guests share

Tariff: B&B (continental) Double $55, Single $30, Children under 12 half price,
Dinner $25, Credit Cards. NZ B&B Vouchers accepted
Nearest Town: Havelock 22km, Picton 32km

*We are located just moments off the Queen Charlotte Scenic Drive, within an hour of
Picton. Our home is situated to make the most of majestic views of the Inner Sounds
(Pelorus and Mahau) and yet enjoy the concealment and quietness of the surrounding
bush, where numerous native birds make their homes. All rooms have their own access
to decks - where meals can be taken - and you can enjoy the panoramic views. Guests
can also relax in our recreation room. We have a large, friendly dog.*
*Our interests include sailing (boats and instruction can be made available if required),
gardening, meeting people, overseas travel and if you're looking for a quiet, peaceful,
idyllic retreat - this is it.*
*Transport can be provided to, and/or from the Anakiwa end of the Queen Charlotte
Walkway, vehicles can be left with us, undercover, for safe-keeping. Our home is
smoke-free. Please phone (fax) for directions.*

Picton

Homestay/B&B
Address: "Palm Haven", 5 Newgate St, Picton
Name: Peter & Damian (Dae) Robertson
Telephone: (03) 573 5644
Fax: (03) 573 5645
Mobile: (025) 275 0860
Beds: 2 Queen, 3 Single (3 bedrooms)
Bathroom: 1 Ensuite, 1 Guests share
Tariff: B&B (continental) Double $60,
Single $35, Children under 12yrs $20, Dinner $25.
NZ B&B Vouchers accepted $15 surcharge for ensuite
Nearest Town: Picton 500m

"Palm Haven" is set in a large garden featuring paths, seating and birdlife, all in one quiet cul-de-sac. We have three guest rooms: one en-suite queen; one twin; one with queen and single beds. Latter rooms share guest-only bathroom and separate toilet. Families can be very suitably accommodated and we enjoy children. We provide cot and highchair. We also welcome single travellers at a single rate.

Our laundry and evening child-minding services are populaar - so are our breakfast muffins! An easy 5-minute walk takes guests to town and our lovely foreshore. And while there's plenty to do in Picton itself, "Palm Haven" provides a great homebase while guests explore the whole of the top of the South.

We are keen outdoor bowlers and dabble also in fishing, writing and machine quilting. Our elderly cats, Puffin and Bijou, are people-friendly and sleep outside at night.

Members of
The New Zealand Association
Farm & Home Host Inc.
maintain the highest standards &
are always delighted to welcome
guests into their homes.

Picton

Homestay
Address: The White House,
114 High Street, Picton
Name: The White House
Telephone: (03) 573 6767 **Fax**: (03) 573 8871
Beds: 2 Double, 3 Single (4 bedrooms)
Bathroom: 1 Guests share
Tariff: B&B (Continental) Double $55, Single $35. Full cooked breakfast extra.
Not suitable for children.
Nearest Town: Picton (opposite the Police Station)

The White House at 14 High Street (Picton's main street) offers affordable luxury - just ask any previous guest - in a friendly, quiet, warm home environment. It nestles on a sunny 1/4 acre, surrounded by mature trees and gardens, and is just a 2 minute walk to Picton's fabulous cafes and restaurants for your evening meal.

Located conveniently in the middle of town, this delightful 70 year old home is filled with Gwen's porcelain doll collection and numerous 'old worlde' touches. It has been immaculately maintained throughout with all refurbishments reflecting the era in which it was built.

Guest bedrooms are upstairs, all of which have quality beds to ensure a good nights sleep. Also on the same floor is the guest lounge which affords panoramic views over Picton to the harbour and hills beyond. However, if they prefer, guests are most welcome to share the downstairs lounge with their host.

Gwen's long association with the hospitality industry has made her aware that some of the things people miss when travelling is being able to pop into the kitchen and make a pot of tea or a cup of coffee when they like. White House guests are invited to do just that. The laundry facilities are also available for guests.

We look forward to making our guests' Picton visit an enjoyable and memorable one. And while The White House is a non-smoking residence, guests are most welcome to smoke on the front verandah or the back deck areas. We regret our house is unsuitable for children.

Picton
Self-Contained Accommodation
Address: 'Bridgend Cottage', 36 York Street, Picton
Name: Steve & Mila Burke
Telephone: (03) 573 6734 **Fax**: (03) 573 8323
Email: STEVEJB@VOYAGER.CO.NZ
Beds: 1 King, 1 Double, 2 Single - Paraplegic unit (3 bedrooms)
Bathroom: 2 Ensuite. All beds with 'Slumbertime' mattresses
Tariff: B&B (special) Double $80, Single $50, Children $20, Dinner $25, Credit cards Visa/Mastercard. Ask us to quote special rates for families & small groups. NZ B&B Vouchers accepted Surcharge $10
Nearest Town: Picton

We welcome you to Picton and our property, which is situated within easy walking distance of all activities in Picton. The accommodation is self contained and warm including colour TV, tea / coffee making facilities, a lavish breakfast that caters for all tastes and diets and sets you up for the day. Breakfast arranged for early inter-island ferry passengers.
Dinner is a gourmet meal with wine featuring specialities of our region.
Safe and secure off street parking, sun deck, transport provided from buses, train or inter-island ferry.
Our hobbies are walking, gardening, gourmet cooking, and reading. Mila enjoys sewing, embroidery and art. Steve is interested in all sport. He has worked in the Travel / Industry and we can assist you with onward travel if required. We also speak French.

Laundry facilities available.
We are a non smoking household, you are most welcome to smoke on the deck or verandah.

"We enjoy making new friends."

460

Moenui Bay, Havelock, Pelorus Sound
Bed & Breakfast/Homestay
Address: Moenui Bay, Queen Charlotte Drive,
R.D.1 Picton (Near Havelock)
Name: "The Devonshires"
Telephone: (03) 574 2930 **Fax**: (03) 574 2930
Mobile: 025-463 118
Email: devs.1@clear.net.nz
Beds: 1 Queen, 2 Twin (2 bedrooms)
Bathroom: 1 Guests share, 1 Private
Tariff: B&B (full) Queen $80, Twin $70, Single $45, Children not suitable, except
by arrangement. Dinner $20-$25 each. Special winter rates. Credit cards.
NZ B&B Vouchers accepted $20 surcharge ensures exclusive use of guest facilities
Nearest Town: Blenheim 32km, Picton 32km

*The Devonshires invite you to share with them the peaceful sounds of forest, bird and
sea. Visit Moenui Bay, just ten minutes from Havelock along the scenic Queen
Charlotte Drive and forty minutes from the Ferry. Enjoy warm hospitality and sample
Marlborough's harvest from orchard, farm, vineyard and sea.*
*Brian, an educator, American Football buff and keen fisherman, has a good working
knowledge of South Island wines. Susan enjoys painting, gardening, craftwork and
practising her culinary skills. Your guest bathroom is adjacent to the well appointed
bedrooms. Enjoy spacious living areas with expansive sea views. Guests can choose to
enjoy the garden and listen to the birds or use our home as a base for exploring
Marlborough. Our meals, served with pride, feature home-baking and preserves,
herbs, fresh seafood, fruit, local cheeses and flavoursome egg dishes.*
*Please - no smoking in the house. Longer visits welcomed. Water and vineyard tours
arranged. P.S. Lucy and Mindy are the resident cats.*

Port Underwood Sound
Homestay Lodge
Address: 'Ocean Ridge', Ocean Bay,
Private Bag, Blenheim
Name: Ken & Sara Roush
Telephone: (03) 579 9474 **Fax**: (03) 579 9474
Beds: 1 Queen, 1 Double, 2 Single (3 bedrooms)
Bathroom: 3 Ensuite
Tariff: B&B (continental) Double $85/$110, Single $60/$80.
Dinner by arrangement $25pp. Not suitable for children.
Credit Cards MC/Bankcard/Visa NZ B&B Vouchers accepted $15-$40 surcharge
Nearest Town: 35km (45 mins)Nth of Blenheim, 35km (60 min)Sth of Picton via
Port Underwood Rd.

*Fifty acres of solitude from Cliff tops to shore line with magnificent views of Port
Underwood Sound, Pacific Ocean, snow-capped mountains and rocky coastline, a
perfect place to break your journey for several days. Sara and Ken invite you to share
this beautiful, peaceful area with them, their cats, and friendly dog. For the active
there is fishing, diving and beach combing nearby, and several steep, rugged nature
tracks to the water's edge on the property. A hot spa pool is available for those wishing
to relax. You might see orcas, dolphins or seals playfully swimming in the waters just
below our home, watch Ken and Sara create their unique pewter sculptures and
jewellery, or at night, star gaze with Ken and his telescope.*
*The separate guest area has three large bedrooms (each with its own bathroom) and
a kitchen, dining, lounge area for the exclusive use of our guests. All rooms have water
views.*

Blenheim
Farmstay
Address: 'Rhododendron Lodge', State Highway 1,
St Andrews, R.D.4, Blenheim
Name: Charlie & Audrey Chambers
Telephone: (03) 578 1145
Fax: (03) 578 1145
Beds: 2 Queen, 2 Single (2 bedrooms + 1 Suite)
Bathroom: 1 Ensuite, 1 Private
Tariff: B&B (full) Double $70, Single $50, Suite $90.
10% discount 3 days or more. NZ B&B Vouchers accepted Suite $10 surcharge
Nearest Town: Blenheim 1.5km

Welcome to previous guests and new ones. We have retired to an attractive small farm in Blenheim, where we provide quality accommodation in our spacious home. Excellent beds with Woolrest underlays and electric blankets. Bacon, eggs and tomatoes all produced on our farm make a delicious breakfast.

Our executive suite has a "Bechstein" piano in it. A private courtyard with tree ferns and gardens surrounds a large swimming pool. Extensive lawns and gardens with rhododendrons, roses and many trees.

We are close to Blenheim's gourmet restaurants and have available a selection of their menus. Marlborough has much to offer - beautiful parks, wine trails, scenic Marlborough Sounds and walkways.

Visitors travelling by train or bus will be collected in Blenheim. Laundry available and courtesy phone call for next homestay. Purified water available for guests.

Directions: *1.5 km south from town centre on SH 1. Large sign at gate. We are 20 minutes from Picton ferry - "Happy Holidays".*

Blenheim

Homestay
Address: "Hillsview" - Please phone
Name: Adrienne & Rex Handley
Telephone: (03) 578 9562
Fax: (03) 578 9562
Beds: 1 King, 1 Double,
5 Single (4 bedrooms) -
1 double, 2 twin (1 converts Kingsize) 1 single
Bathroom: 2 Private
Tariff: B&B (Full) Kingsize $75, Double/Twin $70,
Single $40, (Tariff less 10% if prebooked by night before), Dinner by arrangement.
NZ B&B Vouchers accepted
Nearest Town: Blenheim 3km from Town Centre

Welcome to our warm and spacious 1970's era home situated in a quiet southern suburb with its mature trees, flowering shrubs, sundeck, outdoor pool, ample off road parking and no pets. Two renovated private bathrooms (one per party) serve the four heated guest rooms. All beds have quality mattresses, electric blankets and wool overlays. Your hosts are a non smoking married couple with a grown up family and enjoy sharing mutual travel experiences. Rex, a retired airline pilot, has interests in all aspects of aviation from models to home builts and gliding - also builds miniature steam locomotives. Adrienne enjoys cooking, spinning and woolcraft hobbies. We offer our vintage model A Ford soft top tourer for hood down rides or to be photographed in, and sightseeing flights around Marlborough can also be arranged. Comments from our guest book suggest our home has a warm and friendly atmosphere. We invite you to sample this along with our caring personal attention and complimentary beverages.

Blenheim
Homestay
Address: 'Mirfield', 722 Severne Street,
Blenheim
Name: Pam & Charles Hamilton
Telephone: (03) 578 8220 **Freephone**: 0800 395 720
Fax: (03) 578 8220
Beds: 2 Queen, 1 Double, 2 Single (4 bedrooms)
Bathroom: 2 Private, 1 Family share
Tariff: B&B (continental, cooked breakfast $5 extra pp) Double $60,
Single $35, Children half price up to 12 yerars, Dinner (by arrangement) $17.50.
NZ B&B Vouchers accepted
Nearest Town: Blenheim Town Centre: 3km

Welcome to Marlborough and our spacious family home that offers two private TV lounges, comfortable beds and homely hospitality. If you haven't tried B&B before - try us, as we cater for individuals, couples or small groups. We enjoy meeting people having hosted for ten years, and will be sensitive to your needs. Our interests include commercial flower growing, sports, hand knits, and we offer organically grown produce for your enjoyment. "Mirfield" is handy to wineries, Rainbow Skifield and the Sounds with its walkways and sea activities. It is a stopping place for those using the ferries, airport, or en route elsewhere. Our rates should entice you to stay longer. By arrangement, transport could be provided to and from departure points.
Make your destination Marlborough and stay with us.
Directions: *Highway 6 from Blenheim to Nelson. Turn first left after the Shell Service Station. Opposite the last street light.*

Blenheim
Farmstay
Address: Maxwell Pass, PO Box 269,
Blenheim
Name: Jean & John Leslie
Telephone: (03) 578 1941
Fax: (03) 578 1941
Beds: 1 Double,
3 Single (3 bedrooms)
Bathroom: 1 Private, 1 Family share
Tariff: B&B (full) Double $75, Single
$40, Dinner by arrangement.
Credit cards NZ B&B Vouchers accepted
Nearest Town: Blenheim 8 km

We live 8 km from Blenheim on a 750 acre hill country property running beef cattle. Our home is two-storeyed in a quiet valley with spacious grounds and lots of native birds. All beds have woollen overlays and electric blankets. Laundry available. Now that our family are all married we enjoy spending time with guests. Marlborough is a major grape growing area with several wineries plus horticulture, agriculture and livestock farming from high country to the coast. Marlborough Sounds is nearby either by sea or road. Trout fishing is also close at hand and there is a skifield 1 1/2 hours drive. Blenheim has a golf course, croquet green and hard and grass tennis court as well as beautiful gardens. Horse trekking 5 mins drive.
Directions: *Please phone.*

Blenheim
Country Homestay
Address: 'Green Gables' SH1, St. Andrews, R.D.4, Blenheim
Name: Raelene & Bill Rainbird
Telephone: (03) 577 9205 **Fax**: (03) 577 9206
Email: linknz@voyager.co.nz
Beds: 1 Queen, 3 Double (2 bedrooms)
Bathroom: 2 Ensuite
Tariff: B&B (full) Double $85, Single $50, Dinner $25, Campervans welcome, 10% discount 3 days or more. NZ B&B Vouchers accepted $15 Surcharge
Nearest Town: 2km from Blenheim town

Enjoy your stay at our exceptionally spacious two storey home located in rural Blenheim. Only 2km from the town centre, Green Gables is set in a beautiful, one acre landscaped garden.

Guest accommodation comprises of two large double bedrooms, both with ensuite bathrooms. The Blue room has a Queen-size bed and a double bed, the Apricot room has two double beds. Both rooms are fully equipped with electric blankets, radio clocks, hair driers and room heating and have glass doors that open onto private balconies affording panoramic views of Blenheim. An adjoining guest lounge has a small library and television set, tea making facilities are available, and you are invited to use our laundry facilities.

For breakfast choose either a full, country-style, cooked breakfast or a light continental breakfast or if you prefer a delectable combination of both, served with delicious home made jams and preserves.

Dinner is available by arrangement and features traditional New Zealand cuisine served with a complimentary drink.

We are horticulturists and grow fresh vegetables and flowers in our green houses.

Green Gables backs onto the picturesque Opawa River. In season this gentle river offers trout fishing, eeling and whitebaiting. A small rowing boat is available for your use at no extra charge.

An additional courtesy, we would be pleased to help you with the on-booking of your bed and breakfast accommodation. Let us phone ahead for you and you'll make valuable savings on your phone card.

Directions: *On SH1, 2km south of Blenheim town, gate number 859A. 20 minutes from Picton ferry. Green Gables sign at drive entrance.*

Blenheim
Vineyard Homestay+Self-contained Accommodation
Address: Thainstone, Giffords Road.,
R.D. 3, Blenheim
Name: Jim & Vivienne Murray
Telephone: (03) 572 8823
Fax: (03) 572 8623
Mobile: (025) 283 1484
Email: thainsto@voyager.co.nz
Beds: 1 King, 1 Queen, 1 Double, 1 Single (3 bedrooms).
Self contained house: 1 Queen, 2 Single (2 bedrooms)
Bathroom: 1 Ensuite, 1 Guests share; Self contained house: 1 bathroom
Tariff: B&B (full) Double $95, Single $55, Dinner $25. Accommodation only in
self-contained house $90-150 (2 to 4 people), Credit Cards (VISA/MC/BC/American Express). NZ B&B Vouchers accepted $20 surcharge, same day restriction.
Nearest Town: 12km north west of Blenheim off Rapaura Rd, a Picton-Nelson
through route.

*We have a very large comfortable home set in our own vineyard and surrounded by
neighbouring vineyards and orchards. We have our own wine labels, Thainstone Sauvignon
Blanc and Chardonnay and our winery on Rapaura Road. We are central to most other
Marlborough wineries, only a few minutes from the airport, and 30 minutes from the ferry.
Our home has a guest wing that includes three spacious bedrooms, a lounge, dining room, 2
bathrooms and also tea / coffee making facilities. The self-contained house, set back from our
home with its own driveway, is fully equipped with a modern kitchen, bathroom, two
bedrooms and lounge. We have a swimming pool in our BBQ area. We are widely travelled
and have many interests including woodworking, tramping, card playing and trout fishing.
Our family have left home and we have no pets, but enjoy bird watching and the outdoor life.
Our evening meals, by prior arrangement, are served with Marlborough wines.*

Blenheim
Homestay+Self-contained Accom.
Address: Chardonnay Lodge,
Rapaura, R.D.3, Blenheim
Name: Lorraine & Alan Hopkins
Telephone: (03) 570 5194
Fax: (03) 570 5194
Beds: 3 Queen, 5 Single (4 bedrooms)
Bathroom: 1 Ensuite. 1 Private
Tariff: B&B (continental) Double $85, Single $65, Children welcome, Credit cards
(VISA/MC). Two Self-contained units with Queen & Single beds $89, Double $15
per extra person. NZ B&B Vouchers accepted &20 surcharge
Nearest Town: Blenheim 5 mins

*Our excellent accommodation is set in lovely park-like grounds in a country locality
featuring a large heated swimming pool, spa and a full-sized all weather tennis court.
Almost on our doorstep are Marlborough's famous wineries, vineyards and superb
restaurants. A very popular destination for visitors from around the world. We
provide "In House" accommodation with own ensuites OR self-contained units. You
can cook your own meals or breakfast is available at a small extra cost. All beds have
electric blankets. A high standard is maintained. We are a "fishing and golfing"
couple, have lived beside the sea in the "Sounds" for 19 years, have travelled extensively
and enjoy people. We are situated on Rapaura Road (turn off at Spring Creek), 5
minutes from Blenheim and 20 minutes from Picton.
We are happy to provide our courtesy vehicle for airport and ferry pick ups.*

Blenheim

Country Retreat
Address: 'The Sentinel', Wrekin Road, R.D.2,
Fairhall, Blenheim
Name: Neil & Lyn Berry
Telephone: (03) 572 9143 **Fax**: (03) 572 9143
Beds: 2 Queen, 2 Single (2 Bedrooms)
Bathroom: 2 Ensuite

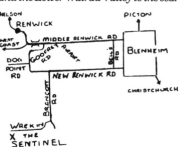

Tariff: B&B (special) Double $90, Single $65. Dinner $30pp,
Credit Cards. NZ B&B Vouchers accepted Surcharge $20
Nearest Town: Blenheim 15km

Your hosts Neil and Lyn and their Labrador "Rusty" welcome you to "The Sentinel", a 35 acre (14ha) property situated 15km west of Blenheim, in the Brancott Valley beside Marlborough's famous wine trail. We overlook vineyards in the area and the Lower Wairau Valley to the sea.

Our two upstairs guest bedrooms, each containing a double and a single bed, have their own private ensuites. A farm style breakfast is provided. Dinner is additional by arrangement. Meals may be taken on the terrace, with the hosts or in the guest lounge. Our interests are winemaking, pottery, sports, fishing, painting. We can help you plan, wine trail visit, golf, skiing, tours of Marlborough, to name just a few. Transport can be provided to and from Blenheim and the airport.

Directions: *See Marlborough's Wine Trail map.*

Blenheim

Homestay+Self-contained Accom.
Address: 60 Beaver Road, Blenheim,
Marlborough
Name: Beaver Bed & Breakfastt'
Telephone: (03) 578 8401 **Fax**: (03) 578 8401
Mobile: (021) 626 151
Email: jhopkins@voyager.co.nz
Beds: 1 Queen (1bedroom)
Bathroom: 1 Ensuite

Tariff: B&B (continental - self serve) Double $70, Single $50.
Credit cards. NZ B&B Vouchers accepted
Nearest Town: Blenheim 1 Km

Our self-contained unit can accommodate one couple and is a modern addition to our 90 year old home.
Features include your own entrance, queen size bed, mini kitchen, bathroom - large bath, shower and a separate toilet. Use of our laundry can be made upon request. Two cats and a bird live with us in a quiet street. We have off-street parking.
We are within ten minutes walk from central Blenheim and many excellent restaurants. We have a broad local knowledge and are happy to assist you in exploring Marlborough.
Please phone before 8 am or after 4.30 pm during the working week. If no response, Jennie can be contacted via her cell phone or fax us anytime.
Home Page: http://marlborough.co.nz/beaver

466

Blenheim

Farmstay Retreat
Address: 'Charmwood',
415 Murrays Rd,
R.D.3, Blenheim
Name: Bill & Ann Betts
Telephone: (03) 570 5409
Fax: (03) 570 5110
Beds: 2 Queen, 2 Single (3 bedrooms)
Bathroom: 1 Ensuite, 2 Private
Tariff: B&B (full) Double $95-$110, Single $60.
Credit cards. NZ B&B Vouchers accepted
Nearest Town: Blenheim 5 mins, Picton ferry 20 mins, Airport 10 mins.

Charmwood is comfortably furnished with country charm and touch of luxury and surrounded by large trees and garden areas overlooking paddocks containing stud cattle and sheep. Stroll with our two corgis through the home orchard and aviary area, enjoy game of tennis or swim in pool.
Start the day with our special country fare breakfast where we would be happy to help with your itinerary. Close to ferry and airport and conveniently placed at start of wine, craft, garden trails also handy to excellent restaurants and golf courses, trout fishing streams. We are ideally sited to enjoy the boating trips, fishing, visiting green mussel or salmon farms in Marlborough Sounds or taking outback safari.
We have enjoyed overseas travel to many countries, have extensive interests and members of Lions service club, non-smokers and welcome guests to our home.

Blenheim

Homestay
Address: 'Wycoller', 106a Maxwell Road,
Blenheim, Marlborough
Name: Valerie & Terry McCormick
Telephone: (03) 578 8522
Beds: 1 Double, 1 Twin (2 bedrooms)
Bathroom: 1 Ensuite, 1 Private
Tariff: B&B (full/continental) Double $90,
Twin $80, Single $60.
Nearest Town: Blenheim 10 minutes walk.

Set amongst tall trees and an expanse of fragrant garden, "Wycoller" has been architecturally designed to blend into its surroundings.Less than an 10 minute stroll into town, Wycoller enjoys the best of both worlds - old fashioned tranquillity and modern convenience. We have a separate guest wing, including tea / coffee making facilities. Relax totally in your own spacious guest wing, or join us to "chat" .... as you wish. Your own private patio is there for you to enjoy the garden. Soak up the atmosphere of Wycoller. A short walk away, the town centre offers a diversity of restaurants and excellent cuisine. We are a retired couple, with four grown children, all who have travelled extensively. We enjoy meeting people from all walks of life and would like to extend our warmest hospitality. Modern elegance, tranquillity and exceptional location all give Wycoller a special feel. We welcome you to our home. Please phone first.

Blenheim

Homestay
Address: 'Philmar Lodge',
6 Gaylee Place, Blenheim
Name: Lex & Wynnis
Telephone: (03) 577 7788
Fax: (03) 577 7788

Beds: 3 Queen, 2 Single (3 bedrooms)
Bathroom: 1 Ensuite, 1 Guests share
Tariff: B&B (continental) Double $65, Single $40, Children half price.
Dinner $20. Bedroom with ensuite $75.
Nearest Town: Blenheim 2 Kms

Welcome. Our modern home is just 2km from the town centre and has three guest bedrooms, with Queen or Single beds. Guests share bathroom and toilet facilities, one bedroom with ensuite. The TV and tea/coffee area open to a large balcony where you are welcome to smoke as we don't encourage smoking indoors. But to sit with us in our very large formal lounge would be our pleasure.
Both members of the Lions organisation. Our other interests include woodturning and all handcrafts. We are also keen TV sports persons.
Blenheim is an ideal base from which to visit Nelson, whale watch, wine trails and many other places of interest. Originally from the far South with many years of hosting we enjoy meeting people from most parts of the world. We have 2 cats, Snookie and Cuddles share our home.
Just phone from airport, train or bus to be picked up.

Blenheim

Vineyard Homestay
Address: 'Stonehaven', 445A Rapaura Road,
R.D.3, Blenheim
Name: David & Jocelyn Wilson
Telephone: (03) 572 9730
Fax: (03) 572 9730
Mobile: 025-222 1656
Email: dgwilson@voyager.co.nz
Beds: 1 King, 1 Queen, 1 Single (3 bedrooms)
Bathroom: 1 Ensuite, 2 Private
Tariff: B&B (full) Double $105-$120, Single $80. Dinner $40pp by arrangement (with selected wines) .
Nearest Town: 12km from Blenheim. 4km from airport. Transport available.

Our recently built stone and cedar home is surrounded by gardens and 17 acres of Sauvignon Blanc vines. Closeby are some of NZ's most outstanding wineries which we can arrange for you to visit. We have the space, comfort, and privacy to make your stay relaxing and memorable.
We like to serve an interesting breakfast in the 'Pavilion' overlooking the pool with its spacious surrounds for summer relaxing.
In winter you many enjoy the comfort of an open fire and a good book.
Our special interests include travel, books, music, gardening and good food. We are skiing enthusiasts and in winter can introduce you to Marlborough's Rainbow Ski-area. Closer to home we can teach you to play P'etanque on the lawn or arrange golf, tennis, fishing or voyages of discovery in Marlborough's Sounds.
Blenheim has a number of excellent restaurants or, if you prefer you may dine with us. We have a friendly Burmese cat, and are non-smokers.

Blenheim

Vineyard Homestay
Address: 'Black Birch Lodge',
Jeffries Rd, R.D.3, Blenheim
Name: Black Birch Lodge
Telephone: (03) 572 8876
Fax: (03) 572 8806
Email: barnsley@ihug.co.nz
Beds: 2 Queen, 3 Single (3 bedrooms)   *Black Birch Lodge*
Bathroom: 2 Ensuite
Tariff: B&B (full) Double $90-$105, Single $70, Children under 15 half price,
Dinner by arrangement $30 (3 course), Credit Cards (VISA/MC).
NZ B&B Vouchers accepted Surcharge applies
Nearest Town: Blenheim 10 mins, Renwick 5 mins

Black Birch Lodge is ideally situated for exploring the Marlborough wine trail. Just off Rapaura Road, Black Birch is within ten minutes drive of most of Marlborough's wineries some of which are within easy walking distance.
Your hosts David and Margaret Barnsley have been involved in the local wine industry since 1981, both as grape growers and David as editor of "Winepress". They can help you plan your wine trail itinerary or if preferred David offers personally conducted winery tours. In the evening you will return to your ensuite bedroom overlooking our Pinot Noir vineyard. We offer two separate guest lounges; an extensive library; Sky television; tennis court; swimming pool; petanque and barbecue areas. Mountain bikes are available. Our breakfasts feature freshly baked bread, local preserves, conserves, honey and fruit. Cooked breakfasts available on request. Reduced tariffs for more than two night stays.
Directions: *Please phone, write or fax.*

Blenheim

Homestay
Address: 28 Elisha Drive,
Blenheim
Name: Brian & Kathy Baxter
Telephone: (03) 578 3753
Fax: (03) 578 3796

Beds: 1 Double, 2 Single (2 bedrooms)
Bathroom: 1 Private
Tariff: B&B (full) Double $85-$95, Single $60, Dinner $25pp.

Our modern comfortable home is in a quiet cul-de-sac with magnificent views over Blenheim and across Cook Strait to the North Island.
Guests are able to enjoy their privacy as all the top level of our home is solely allocated to them, including a sheltered deck with outstanding views. A perfect spot to relax and enjoy a coffee or a local wine.
Brian is a well known New Zealand artist with home studio/gallery for viewing original paintings i.e. New Zealand landscapes (including local scenes), flowers etc. Our landscaped colourful gardens which have been selected for "Garden Marlborough" tours include special deciduous trees, roses, rhododendrons, camellias, perennials etc. Walks up the Wither Hills behind our home are great exercise and also offer spectacular views.
We can arrange tours to wineries, gardens, ski field etc. for our guests.
Our interests are: music, fishing, ski-ing, travel, gardens and meeting people.

Blenheim
Vineyard Stay
Address: De Gyffarde Vineyard,
Giffords Road, Rapaura, Blenheim
Name: Rod & Di Lofthouse
Telephone: (03) 572 8189
Fax: (03) 572 8178
Mobile: (021) 362 777
Email: lofthous@voyager.co.nz
Beds: 1 Queen and second bedroom available
Bathroom: 1 Ensuite + separate toilet
Tariff: B&B (continental) Double $95-$110, Single (with ensuite) $75.
Credit Cards (Visa, M/C) accepted.
Nearest Town: 15km west of Blenheim

De Gyffarde Vineyard in the heart of Marlborough's world renowned wine region is the setting for our pine built home, a few minutes walk from the Wairau river. Sheltered raised decks and paved patios lead to the gardens and solar heated pool. Guest bedroom with views over the vineyard has a Queen size bed and en-suite. Second bedroom (own toilet, share ensuite) is available for two singles. Complimentary welcome platter and De Gyffarde wines served to guests on arrival.

Your hosts Rod & Di Lofthouse, originally from England, have both been involved in the film and TV industry for many years and have travelled extensively and enjoy sailing, skiing, and riding.

Wine trails can be arranged for you and vineyard restaurants are close by for lunch and dinner. Together with their golden retriever, Brix, and burmese cat, Sizi, Rod and Di look forward to meeting new friends in their smoke-free home.

Blenheim
Homestay
Address: "Creekside" Homestay,
436 Rapaura Rd., R.D.3, Blenheim
Name: Libby Fulton & Ken Prain
Telephone: (03) 570 5372
Fax: (03) 570 5650
Email: Ken.creekside@xtra.co.nz
Beds: 2 Queen, 2 Single (2 bedrooms)
Bathroom: 2 Ensuite
Tariff: B&B (continental) Twin $110, Single $85,
Credit Cards welcome (VISA/MC/BC).
Nearest Town: Blenheim 10 mins

"Creekside" Homestay is superbly located on the banks of Spring Creek in the heart of the grape growing area of Blenheim. Our house and attached self-contained units are new and modern.

The outlook from the house and units is beautifully rural and private down to trees and the creek. We have a 500 tree Olive Grove in the making and will shortly be planting grapes.

Your rooms are particularly comfortable with queen size beds, underfloor heating, ensuite bathrooms and individual coffee and tea making facilities.

We are ideally situated in a rural location close to Blenheim 10 mins, the airport 10 mins, and Picton 20 mins. Vineyard restaurants are close by for lunches and dinner. We are also located adjacent to 6 grass tennis courts for those who want to play tennis. We have a very friendly small dog called VITA who loves chasing tennis balls. Please phone, fax or email for bookings and directions.

Blenheim
Vineyard B&B+Self-contained
Address: 'Four Winds'
26 Rowberrys Road
Name: Ross and Mary Spicer
Telephone: (03) 578 8881 **Fax**: (03) 578 8574
Email: fourwind@voyager.co.nz
Beds: 1 Double, 3 Single (2 bedrooms)
Bathroom: 1 Private
Tariff: Single $40. Double/Twin $60. Self-contained: sleeping up to 5: Families
or up to 3 adults $80 - extra adults $15. Continental Breakfast $5pp.
Nearest Town: Blenheim 2 1/2km

*We are a married couple with family left home and would like to share our lovely
country surroundings with you.*
You look out onto our small vineyard, and can wander through the garden.
Our hobbies include viticulture, photography and videography.
*Our guest accommodation is a spacious, self-contained unit with 2 bedrooms sleeping
up to 5. WE WELCOME FAMILIES.*
*Breakfast is continental, with cooked available on request. Dinner by arrangement, or
recommend local restaurants. Meals can be served in the unit, or join us at the main
house. We are happy to transport to and from airport, station etc.*
Directions: *We are 2 1/2km from the railway station. Down Dillons Point Rd 2km,
turn into Rowberrys Rd on left. We are on left before Swamp Rd. Phone to book if
possible.*

Blenheim
Farmstay
Address: "Windmill Farm",
908B Main Rd,
Riverlands, Blenheim
Name: Millie Amos
Telephone: (03) 577 7853
Fax: (03) 577 7853
Beds: 1 Double,
2 Single (2 bedrooms)
Bathroom: 1 Ensuite, 1 Private
Tariff: B&B (continental)
Double $75, Single $50. Credit cards.
Nearest Town: Blenheim 5km

WINDMILL FARM

MARLBOROUGH

*Only 5km south of Blenheim on SH1, you will find Windmill Farm, a spacious and
modern home in close proximity to the golf driving
range and to Montana Winery. Comfortably appointed
spacious twin bedroom with private ensuite and one
double bedroom with private bathroom and spa.*
*We have travelled to many countries overseas and aim
to make our guests feel welcome and relaxed.*
*We are non smokers who enjoy gardens, travel and
meeting people.*
We welcome you to our home. Please phone first.

Blenheim

Bed & Breakfast/Homestay
Address: "Grove Bank", 362c SH 1,
Grovetown, Blenheim, Marlborough.
Name: Pauline & Peter Pickering
Telephone: 0800 422 632 (0800 4 B and B)
Fax: (03) 578 8407
Email: pickeringg@chchpoly.ac.nz
Beds: 4 Queen, 2 Single (4 bedrooms).
Plus Family Unit 3 bedrooms,
1 ensuite (sleeps up to 6)
Bathroom: 3 Ensuite, 1 Private
Tariff: B&B (full and continental) Double $75,
Single $45, Dinner $25pp.
3 nights or off season 20% discount.
Family Unit: $30 pp. Credit cards.
NZ B&B Vouchers accepted $5 surcharge
Nearest Town: 1 1/2km from Blenheim town centre

Pauline and Peter invite you to stay at our 8 acre olive grove and vineyard, which is located conveniently on SH1 on the northern boundary of Blenheim. We offer 4 double bedrooms with ensuites plus bedroom and bathroom appliances. Our home is designed especially with homestay guests in mind. Spacious guest lounges (with televisions) opening onto large balconies, offer panoramic views of the plains ranges and river. After a day of sightseeing and enjoying the delights of the "Gourmet Province", cool off in the swimming pool, relax in the spa, take a stroll in Pauline's gardens the olive grove / vineyard.
Some courtesy transport is available for evening wining and dining. We offer continental and cooked breakfast and meals as requested. A former restaurateur and butcher, Peter's breakfasts are legendary. Evening meals may consist of meats and fresh grown vegetables or fish caught by Peter from the Marlborough Sounds, rivers and lakes.
If you feel like dining out, Marlborough's finest Italian Restaurant (best pasta in the world - "Cuisine"), the Whitehaven winery and cafe and local bar and bistro are within 5 minutes walking distance. We are happy to share our extensive local knowledge and contacts which will enable you to personalise and optimise your stay in the "Gourmet Province".

Directions: *North of Blenheim on SH1 turn left into entrance 100 metres past Grove Road bridge. Travelling south 18 mins / 28 kms from Picton turn right into entrance 100 metres before Grove Road bridge.*

472

Blenheim

Homestay
Address: "Opawa Lodge"
143A Budge Street, Blenheim
Name: Brian & Cindy Pratt
Telephone: (03) 577 9989 **Fax**: (03) 577 9949
Mobile: (025) 411 214
Email: b.pratt@xtra.co.nz
Beds: 1 Queen, 1 Double, 2 Single (3 bedrooms)
Bathroom: 1 Ensuite, 1 Guests share
Tariff: B&B (full) Double $90-$115, Single $80, Dinner by arrangement $30,
Campervans facilities, Credit Cards (VISA/MC).
Nearest Town: Blenheim C.P.O. 2 kms

Our home overlooks of the Opawa River with stunning rural views of Marlborough.
Enjoy breakfast in your private conservatory, with gardens rolling down to the river
where you can try your hand at trout fishing or rowing our boat, maybe just feed the
ducks. This tranquil setting offers a superb opportunity for relaxation. Opawa Lodge
offers outstanding comfortable accommodation with close proximity to the town with
its excellent restaurants. However dinner is available by arrangement. The guest
lounge has tea and coffee facilities and television, there is also a swimming pool for
your enjoyment. Blenheim is ideally situated to visit the world renown Marlborough
Sounds, Vineyards and Rainbow Skifield. Courtesy transport can be provided from
airport or ferry, we would be delighted to help with your itinerary.
Brian and Cindy's interests included travel, gardening, music and a 1935 vintage
sports car. We and our golden retriever "Fenton" look forward to making your stay
memorable.
Home Page: http://marlborough.co.nz/opawa/

Blenheim

Homestay
Address: Uno Più, 75 Murphy's Road, Blenheim
Name: Gino & Heather Rocco
Telephone: (03) 578 2235 **Fax**: (03) 578 2235
Mobile: (025) 241 4493
Email: unopiu@iname.com

Beds: 2 King, 2 Single (3 bedrooms)
Bathroom: 2 Ensuite, 1 Private
Tariff: B&B (special) Double $100, Single $65, Extra person $30pp, Dinner
$35pp, Credit Cards.
NZ B&B Vouchers accepted $30 surcharge.
Nearest Town: Blenheim 3km from town centre

Come and enjoy the comfort and relaxation of Uno Piu' where you will experience
Italian hospitality in the heart of the Marlborough wine region. Gino is Italian and
Heather a N.Zer. Uno Piu' is set in 4 acres on the north west boundary of Blenheim
near a number of wineries. Our gracious, character home, surrounded by a country
garden where roses feature, has a swimming pool, sauna and spa. The bedrooms have
quality linen and spacious bathrooms. A baby grand piano and open fire are in the
guest lounge, and in winter our home is centrally heated. Breakfast includes an Italian
platter, crepes, maple syrup, fruit and cream served with Italian coffee or a choice of
teas. Dinner is by arrangement, fresh home made pasta is a speciality. We enjoy
welcoming guests and have interests in wine, food, opera, sea fishing and gardens. We
have a friendly collie and 2 cats.
Home Page: http://www.geocities.com/TheTropics/Shores/3129

Blenheim
Bed & Breakfast
Address: Henry Maxwell's B&B,
28 Henry Street, Blenheim
Name: Ken and Christy
Telephone: (03) 578 8086
Fax: (03) 578 8089
Email: b&b@mlb.planet.gen.nz
Beds: 2 Queen, 1 Double, 2 Single (4 bedrooms)
Bathroom: 2 Ensuite, 1 Guests share
Tariff: B&B (full) Double/Twin $70-$90, Single $45.
Credit Cards accepted. NZ B&B Vouchers accepted, $20 surcharge on $90 rate only.
Nearest Town: Blenheim, 1 block from town.

A gracious residence, centrally located adjacent to Maxwell Rd within a short walk to all town amenities, affording spacious quiet bedrooms with your own TV and comfortable chairs. Complimentary hot and cold drinks are available at any time. A downstairs formal sitting room provides comfort and elegance where you may meet other guests or friends. A traditional or lifestyle breakfast is served in the dining room. The residence is set in a large, semi-formal garden complete with spa. Off-street parking is available and the bikes are at your disposal.
Your hosts look forward to offering you a warm and friendly welcome. Ken and Christy have a wide range of interests, are well-travelled ultralight enthusiasts and offer their services to liaise with cultural and recreational services to assist the traveller to maximise their stay in this fantastic corner of the planet.
Air and Rail pickups may be arranged.

Blenheim
Vineyard Stay
Address: "Stoneburn",
555A Matthews Lane, Blenheim.
Name: Neville and Tessa
Telephone: (03) 572 8463
Fax: (03) 572 9463
Mobile: (025) 248 0579
Beds: 3 Queen, 2 Single (3 bedrooms)
Bathroom: 3 Ensuites
Tariff: B&B (Continental) Double $110, Single $80, Dinner by arrangement.
Nearest Town: 9km from Blenheim, 4km from airport.

'Stoneburn', a twenty acre vineyard, situated in the very heart of Marlborough's premium grape growing area, offers you the ultimate in country living.
Enjoy all day sun, and panoramic views of the hills and mountains that form a 290 degree arc. Two minutes walk from our gate, and you are in the famous Cloudy Bay tasting room; just around the corner you can lunch at Alan Scott's or Cairnbrae Vineyards, and there's lots more. 'Stoneburn' is a modern home in a great location. Whatever your interests we can put you in touch with the right places and people. We enjoy good wine and conversation, music and books, the beauty of the great outdoors and its activities. We have 3 family cats.
Stoneburn is a place for non-smokers to relax, take time out, enjoy the ambient atmosphere and most of all discover the hidden secrets of Marlborough.
Directions: *Please phone, write or fax. Pick up service available from airport.*

Blenheim
Bed and Breakfast
Address: "The Old St Mary's Convent",
Giffords Creek Lane, Rapaura, Blenheim
Name: Mieke and Wilfried Holtrop
Telephone: 03 570 5700 **Fax**: 03 570 5700
Email: oldstmary@xtra.co.nz
Beds: 4 Queen (4 bedrooms, incl. 1 suite with wheelchair access).
Bathroom: 4 Ensuites
Tariff: B&B (Special/Full) Double $160-$220. Credit Cards accepted.
Nearest Town: Blenheim - approx 10 mins

In the heart of Marlborough's wine growing area lies The Old St Mary's Convent, designed by Thomas Turnbull and built in 1901 for the Sisters of Mercy. It is a haven for the discerning traveller, where luxury accommodation and an intimate retreat may be found.

Old St Mary's Convent is situated on an estate of 20 acres and surrounded on all sides by the vineyards and olive groves Marlborough is famous for. Spring Creek with its abundant bird life and trout meanders lazily through the property. Each of the guest rooms has its own ensuite bathroom. The rooms are very spacious and airy with easy access onto the balcony.

Continental or cooked breakfast is served in the large formal dining room or on the verandah. The library with its ornate Kauri fire place is for the exclusive use of guests. Your hosts speak German, Dutch and a little French.

Homepage: http://www.nz.com/travel/old.st.marys

475

Blenheim

Homestay
Address: Maxwell House,
82 Maxwell Road, Blenheim
Name: Gary and Jeanette Tee
Telephone: (03) 577 7545
Beds: 1 Queen, 2 single (2 bedrooms)
Bathroom: 2 Ensuites
Tariff: B&B (full) Double $115, Single $90.
Credit Cards accepted. NZ B&B Vouchers accepted $25 surcharge
Nearest Town: Blenheim (800 metres)

Welcome to Marlborough. Make your stay memorable by staying at Maxwell House, a grand old Victorian residence. Built in the 1880's, our home has been elegantly restored and is classified with the Historic Places Trust.
Our large guest rooms are individually appointed with ensuite, lounge area and television. Breakfast will be a memorable experience. Served either in your room, on the verandah or around our original 1880's kauri table. Make breakfast as formal or informal as you desire. An assortment of teas and coffee are available at any time.
Set on a large established property with ample parking, Maxwell House is an easy ten minute walk to the town centre with its many fine restaurants, bars and cafes.
Your hosts, Gary and Jeanette, love travel. Having travelled extensively throughout the world we will enjoy sharing your experiences with ours.
We have a non smoking home. Inspection invited.
Directions: *Please phone or write.*

Renwick - Blenheim

Vineyard Stay+Self-contained Accommodation
Address: LeGrys Vineyard, Conders Bend Road,
Renwick, Marlborough
Name: John & Jennifer Joslin
Telephone: (03) 572 9490
Fax: (03) 572 9491
Mobile: (025) 313 208
Email: legrys@voyager.co.nz
Beds: 1 Queen (1 bedroom) Self-contained:1 Queen, 2 Single (2 bedrooms)
Bathroom: 1 Private. Self-contained: 1 bathroom, lounge, cooking & dining facilities
Tariff: B&B (full) Double $120, Self-contained: $170 for two guests, $35 pp each extra person. Continental breakfast inc. Champagne breakfast available to order. Visa/MC.
Nearest Town: Blenheim. 12 kms. Picton 25 mins

LeGrys vineyard "Homestay" and "Water-fall Lodge" separate-secluded, self-contained accommodation, offer you the chance to stay on a vineyard in either a unique cottage or home both built of Mud-blocks. The two bedroom Lodge offers peace, tranquillity and seclusion beside a trickling stream admid the vines. House and Lodge both offer rustic charm with complementary furnishings, warm comfortable beds, luxury bathroom, gas BBQ available. Lodge is a one group situation and is ideal for honeymooners, champagne breakfast available to order. Stunning views - Richmond ranges and vineyard. We are ideally situated for winery visits, many with restaurants. River walks, trout fishing, country gardens, olive-groves, Sounds cruising, and the delightful town of Blenheim only 10 mins drive. "LeGrys" own label wines are available with complimentary tastings and snacks on arrival to welcome you. John and Jennifer cruised the world in their yacht, enjoy meeting people and look forward to making your stay memorable. We have a springer spaniel called Pippin who is part of our family.
Home Page: http://nz.com/webnz/bbnz/legrys.htm

Renwick

Homestay
Address: "Devonia", 2A Nelson Place,
Renwick, Marlborough
Name: Maurie & Marg Beuth
Telephone: (03) 572 9593
Beds: 1 Queen, 2 Single (2 bedrooms)
Bathroom: 1 Private, 1 Guests share
Tariff: B&B (full) Double $75-$85, Single $55. Credit cards.
Nearest Town: Blenheim 10km

Our colonial style home is set in 1/2 acre of lovely private grounds, in the very heart of vineyard country. We overlook orchards and out to the Richmond Range.
In summer, relax under the trees with complimentary tea, coffee or a house wine - or by a glowing fire in winter.
Visit our quaint local English country pub or dine at one of the many vineyard or village restaurants.
We are within "stroll and taste" distance of a number of prestigious vineyards.
Our interests are many and varied. In early married life we farmed and later chartered our 37' sloop. We have four adult children - all now flown the nest.
For a number of years we have been well known in the hospitality industry and are suitably equipped to meet all your needs.
A warm welcome definitely awaits you at "Devonia"
10km from Blenheim, on Highway 6 to Nelson and West Coast.

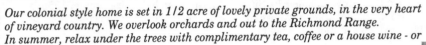

Renwick

Garden Homestay
Name: "Broomfield"
Telephone: (03) 572 8162
Mobile: (025) 266 1769
Beds: 1 King (1 bedroom)
Bathroom: 1 Ensuite
Tariff: B&B (full) Double $120.
Nearest Town: Blenheim 12 Kms

Broomfield is our two storeyed rammed earth house set beside a nectarine orchard in the heart of Renwick wine country.
The house decor is very country as befits its earthy origins. We have a spacious upstairs bedroom for you with excellent bedding, a sitting area, and TV. The bedroom overlooks our charmingly laid out gardens with an interesting potager. Our garden is very much a feature of our home and guests are most welcome to wander through. The house is warmed throughout by radiators from a wood and coal range.
We are 15 mins from Blenheim and 5 mins from the airport. Around us within 5-10 mins are 16 wineries (8 with restaurants) plus country gardens, an olive grove, a pottery and wonderful fruit orchards. Transport around the wineries can be (for the hirage) by horse and cart. Breakfast is of your choice, either cooked or continental.
We look forward to meeting you. Please phone if possible.
Directions: *Off High Street Renwick into Inkerman Street, 1st house on L past old hotel on corner. Signposted.*

477

Blenheim - Waihopai Valley

High Country Farmstay & S.C. Cottage
Address: "Netherwood",
Waihopai Valley Road,
6 RD Blenheim 7321
Name: Nola & Bruce Dick
Telephone: (03) 572 4044
Fax: (03) 572 4044
Beds: 1 Queen, 2 Single (2 bedrooms)

Bathroom: 1 Private (as we take only one booking per night)
Tariff: B&B (full) Double $70, Single $55, Children half price, Dinner $25pp,
Lunch available. Campervans $25. Credit Cards. NZ B&B Vouchers accepted
Nearest Town: Blenheim 50km

*An idyllic setting in which to relax on our 3000 acre sheep and beef property in the
beautiful Waihopai Valley. Only 1 hour drive to Picton, 45 minutes to Blenheim on
sealed road. Closer to wine trail.*
*Congenial non-smoking hosts. You are welcome to smoke outdoors or on the veran-
dahs. Country-style meals, complimentary pre-dinner drinks. Grown up family away
from home, we have an indoor cat.*
*On farm experiences - animals and farm activities, the garden, swimming, walking
and tramping. Farm or wine tasting tours by arrangement.*
*Guest annexe has woollen underlays and electric blankets on the beds, heaters in the
rooms. Also available - self contained cottage, enquiries welcome.*
Directions: *From Blenheim follow SH6 to West Coast Road, then SH63 for 3km. Turn
left at Grove Mill Winery into Waihopai Valley Road. Continue on this sealed road
40km to Netherwood - Gate No. 1114. Please phone ahead as booking necessary.*

Awatere Valley, Blenheim

Farmstay
Address: "Duntroon", Awatere Valley Road,
Private Bag, Blenheim
Name: Trish & Robert Oswald
Telephone: (03) 575 7374 **Fax**: (03) 575 7374
Beds: 1 Double, 6 Single (4 bedrooms)
Bathroom: 1 Guests share, 1 Family share
Tariff: B&B (full) Double $90, Single $65, Children under 15 half price,
Lunch $15, Dinner $30 (three course), Credit Cards.
Nearest Town: Blenheim 63km, Oak Tree Cottage 42km

*We welcome you to our character villa built in 1917, set in lovely established grounds
with pool and tennis court. Our home has been renovated and centrally heated, the
bedrooms are spacious with comfortable beds, electric blankets and guest shared
bathroom. Laundry available. Lunch and dinner by arrangement.*
*"Duntroon" a 3500 acre property has been in the Oswald family for three generations,
and carried 4500 Merino sheep and 300 Angus cattle. It is located in the high country
of the picturesque Awatere Valley.*
*We have three sons, all away from home at present, our family also includes cat and
Labrador, our interests include clay target shooting, boating, tennis, skiing, sewing,
fishing. We enjoy meeting people and invite you to share high country life with us for
a night or longer. Farm tours by arrangement. Over the summer the Awatere Valley
Road is open through Molesworth Station to Hanmer Springs. Some of the Awatere
Valley road is gravel, but it is very lovely and well worth the drive.*
Home Page: oswald@xtra.co.nz
Directions: *Please phone ahead as bookings are necessary.*

Pelorus Bridge
Guest House/Self Contained Accom
Address: Lord Lionel, SH6 Pelorus,
RD2 Ra Valley Marlborough
Name: Lionel & Monika Neilands
Telephone: (03) 574 2770 **Fax**: (03) 574 2770
Beds: 1 King/Queen, 3 Double, 2 Single (6 bedrooms)
Bathroom: 2 Guests share or 1 Private
Tariff: B&B (full) Double $65-$85, Single $50, Children 1/2 price,
Major Credit cards accepted. NZ B&B Vouchers accepted Surcharge $5-$20
Nearest Town: Blenheim or Nelson 45 mins away. 5 minutes from Canvastown, 10 mins from Rai Valley.

We wish to invite you to our beautiful Fraemos Lodge. It is the ultimate in peace and tranquillity. Enjoy breakfast by the river. A fishing paradise in the heart of the Pelorus River Country with excellent fishing for Rainbow, brown trout and some salmon. We are situated 45 minutes from Nelson and Blenheim on State Highway 6 in the midst of 1 1/2 acre of untouched natural South Island native forest with prolific bird life. We are 1 1/2 km from Pelorus Bridge Scenic Reserve, which is one of the finest reserves in New Zealand. There are plenty of nearby options, such as excellent walking tracks, tea-rooms, gold panning at Canvastown and French Pass and launch trips from Havelock. As we have our own private dwelling, the guests have the run of the house with excellent cooking facilities. Ideal for small conferences, business meetings, tour fishing, walking groups and newly weds. Entire house available. Budget accommodation available. Bitte kommen Sie uns besuchen. Overseas visitors please phone / fax 64 3 5742770.
Directions: *1.5km the Blenheim side of Pelorus bridge on the left before Browns creek bridge*

Rai Valley
2 Self-contained Chalets
Address: Bulford Lodge,
Bulford Road, RD 2, Rai Valley
Name: Iris & Helmut
Telephone: (03) 571 6049 **Fax**: (03) 571 6049
Mobile: 025- 2414 498
Beds: 1 King, 2 Queen, 1 Double, 4 Single (3 bedrooms).
Bathroom: 2 Private
Tariff: Double $75-$100, Single $65. Breakfast (continental) $8 pp extra.
Dinner $30 by arrangement. NZ B&B Vouchers accepted $31 surcharge
Nearest Town: Halfway between Blenheim and Nelson 76km

Bulford Lodge offers a unique combination of European style accommodation with warm hospitality of their 125 acre property. Guests will enjoy the comfort of their own chalet with kitchen and bathroom. Chalet 2 has its own dishwasher.
The chalet nestled amongst the trees on the hills overlooks the lush pastureland of Rai Valley. Bulford Lodge is ideally situated to take advantage of all recreational and cultural activities of Marlborough and Nelson.
Walking, fishing and hunting in nearby Mount Richmond Forest Park and Rai River. Boat and fishing tours in the Marlborough Sounds.
Explore the historic Maungatapu track and Wakamarina goldfields. Alternatively you may relax on the terrace and enjoy the flower garden or choose to walk around the property and listen to the birds. Homemade bread a speciality. Foot reflexology massage available on request. Wir freuen uns auf Ihren Besuch.
Iris and Helmut speak English, German and French.

479

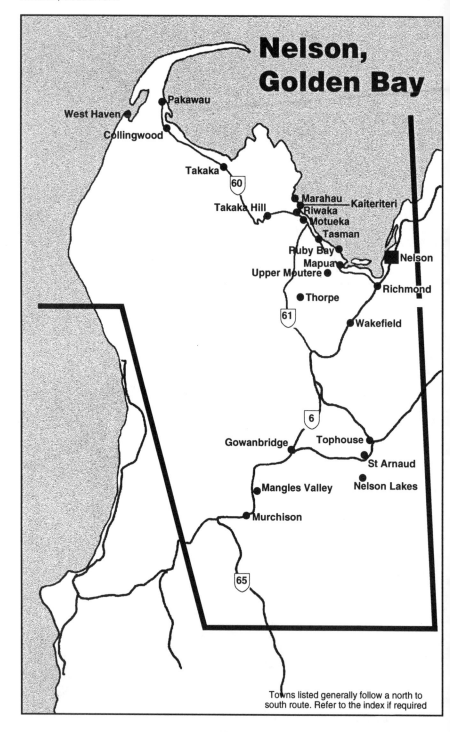

Nelson, Golden Bay

Pakawau
West Haven
Collingwood
Takaka
60
Marahau — Kaiteriteri
Takaka Hill Riwaka
Motueka
Tasman
Ruby Bay
Mapua Nelson
Upper Moutere
Richmond
Thorpe
61
Wakefield
6
Gowanbridge Tophouse
St Arnaud
Mangles Valley Nelson Lakes
Murchison
65

Towns listed generally follow a north to south route. Refer to the index if required

Nelson

Homestay/B&B
Address: Please Telephone
Name: Dorothy & Bob Brown
Telephone: (03) 548 4751
Beds: 2 Single (1 bedroom)
Bathroom: 1 Private
Tariff: B&B (continental) Double $65,
Single $45. NZ B&B Vouchers accepted
Nearest Town: Nelson (2 mins)

We are retired and would like to welcome you to our comfortable, modern home which is in a garden setting on the banks of the Maitai River and opposite the Queens Gardens, just five minutes' walk to the city centre, shops and restaurants, art gallery, cinema and covered heated swimming pool and spa. Central yet quiet. Off-street parking. The guest accommodation is spacious and sunny, consisting of a large bedroom with twin beds, your own sitting room to relax in, with colour TV, fridge, tea and coffee making facilities, and of course your own bathroom. Why not spend a few days exploring the wonderful scenic Nelson region? We will pick you up (and deliver!) to airport or bus. We just love meeting people and making new friends. We are non smokers.

Directions: *Please phone.*

Nelson

Heritage Inn
Address: 'California House Inn'
29 Collingwood Street, Nelson
Name: Neil and Shelley Johnstone
Telephone: (03) 548 4173
Fax: (03) 548 4173
Email: calhouse@tasman.net
Beds: 3 Queen, 1 Double, 1 Twin,
1 Triple (4 bedrooms)
Bathroom: 4 Ensuite

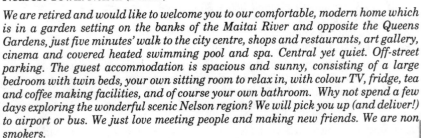

1893

Tariff: B&B (Special) Double $150-$185, Single $125-$140.
Credit cards (MC, Visa) NZ B&B Vouchers accepted $90 surcharge
Nearest Town: Nelson - 3 blocks from town centre.

CALIFORNIA HOUSE is set back from the street in a quiet residential area yet is handily located within 5 minutes walk from the town centre. This beautifully preserved example of Victorian architecture built in 1893 is classified by the NZ Historic Places Trust and features wide, sunny verandahs overlooking established gardens, English oak panelling, art nouveau stained glass windows, open fires and spacious rooms.

Our guest accommodation includes sitting room and library with games and morning/afternoon tea facilities and 4 individually decorated guest rooms, each with ensuite bathroom. The house is furnished throughout with colonial oak furniture, antiques, Persian rugs, memorabilia and fresh flowers from the garden.

Guests enjoy leisurely home-baked Californian breakfasts in our sunny dining room. These may include Finnish pancakes with strawberries, asparagus frittata, baked French toast, ham and sour cream omelette and fresh juices, muffins, coffee and teas. No smoking inside the house please.

Home Page: http://nz.com/travel/cal.house.inn

Tahunanui, Nelson

Homestay
Address: 'Bagust Retreat',
201 Annesbrook Drive, Nelson
Name: Junie Bagust
Telephone: (03) 548 5868
Mobile: 025 263 1280
Beds: 1 Queen, 1 Queen Postupaedic,
1 Single (2 bedrooms)
Bathroom: 2 Ensuite
Tariff: B&B (continental) Double $60 & $65,
Single $50, Children $12,
NZ B&B Vouchers accepted
Nearest Town: Tahunanui, Nelson 4 km

Drive up our private drive from Highway 6 to our peaceful home in a quiet sunny bush setting with views. Each delightful bedsit has its own separate entrance with some covered parking, ensuite, TV, fridge, electric blankets, hair dryer, heating, table and chairs, tea and toast facilities, microwave, also homemade extras. Telephone available.

Our ancestors came to Nelson in 1842 and we feel very proud of our city and district with its many tourist attractions. We have toured extensively throughout N.Z. Also overseas and we delight to return the hospitality we have received from both our overseas and NZ friends. We extend a warm welcome to anyone visiting our city.

Near Tahuna beach, golf course and airport we are only 4 kilometres to the city centre on a main bus route. Our nicest compliment is that all our guests want to return. Reasonably priced restaurants near. Look for the lime green letterbox!!

Nelson

Homestay
Address: Harbour View Homestay, 11 Fifeshire Crescent, Nelson
Name: Judy Black
Telephone: (03) 548 8567 **Fax**: (03) 548 8667
Beds: 2 Queen, 2 Single (3 bedrooms)
Bathroom: 2 Ensuite, 1 Private
Tariff: B&B (full or continental) Double $110, Single $60-$80, Children by arrangement. Credit cards (VISA/MC).
NZ B&B Vouchers accepted $35 surcharge for double
Nearest Town: Midway between Tahunanui Beach and Nelson City via the waterfront.

Our home is above the harbour entrance with huge windows and decks to capture the spectacular views of beautiful Tasman Bay, Haulashore Island, Tahunanui Beach, and across the sea to Abel Tasman National Park and mountains. You can observe from the decks, dining-room, or BBQ, ships and pleasure craft cruising by as they enter and leave the harbour.

If you can tear yourself away from our magnificent view, within walking distance along the waterfront there are excellent cafes and restaurants. A few more minutes will take you to our popular swimming beach or city centre for shopping.

We want our guests to completely relax therefore all our bedrooms have private bathrooms, electric blankets and central heating in winter. We thank you for not smoking inside, outside is fine. Judy, your host, offers you a warm welcome and a memorable stay.

Directions: *We would be happy to meet you at the airport or bus or if directions are required please phone.*

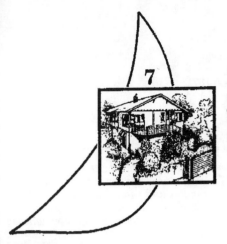

NELSON WATERFRONT

SPINNAKER HOMESTAY

Margaret & George

Nelson Central

Homestay
Address: 'Spinnaker Homestay', 7 Victoria Road, Nelson
Name: George & Margaret Collins
Telephone: (03) 548 8669 **Fax**: (03) 548 8663 **Mobile**: (025) 487 603
Beds: Queen, Twin & Single accommodation available.
Bathroom: Guest rooms have private bathrooms.
Tariff: B&B (full) Double $85, Single $60. NZ B&B Vouchers accepted $15 surcharge.
Meals: Home-style meals available by arrangement.
Nearest Town: Nelson city centre 2.5 kms, Tahunanui Beach 2kms.

Spinnaker Homestay offers all that is best in warm Kiwi hospitality. Margaret and George have a friendly, informal private home - a very comfortable and peaceful, convenient environment. It has extensive views of harbour, Tasman Bay and mountain ranges.

The colourful waterfront area is just a few steps away; the centre of Nelson City is a few minutes drive or a pleasant flat walk; beautiful Tahunanui Beach is within an easy distance; and the airport is about 10 minutes away. This is an ideal stepping off point for your Nelson-Golden Bay experience.

We are a hospitable couple, keen trampers and much travelled. We enjoy exchanging "travellers tales" with congenial company.

Complimentary pick-up and delivery of guests for airport and other local terminals.

THIS IS A SMOKE FREE ZONE.
000000000000000

ASK ABOUT MARGARET'S "SPINNAKER KNITS"
Hand knitted garments for adults and children are available from stock or to order at knitter to buyer prices.

Directions: *WE'RE EASY TO FIND!*
Victoria Road is easy to find. It is about half-way between the City and Tahunanui, on the waterfront drive South of the City. You'll see the Boatshed Cafe on Wakefield Quay. Victoria Road is almost directly opposite. Spinnaker Homestay is just four houses up on the left ... look for our sign.

Nelson

Homestay
Address: 4 Seaton Street, Atawhai, Nelson
Name: Mike Cooper & Lennane Kent
Telephone: (03) 545 1671 **Fax**: (03) 545 1671
Beds: 1 Double, 2 Single (2 bedrooms)
Bathroom: 1 Guests share
Tariff: B&B (full) Double $60, Single $40, Three persons $90, Dinner $25pp,
Credit Cards. NZ B&B Vouchers accepted
Nearest Town: 6km from Nelson close to main Picton & Blenheim Road

*Our home is set in a quiet suburb with views of Nelson Haven, Boulder Bank, Tasman
Bay and the mountains beyond. Breakfast with this view is an ideal way to start a
holiday. Our interests include our guests' comfort and enjoyment, travel, distance
running (veterans' class), education, and training our new Schnauser dog.*
*Families with children or adults with disabilities are welcome on the understanding
that the house has not been modified for special needs.*
*Guest accommodation is virtually self contained with its own entrance, small lounge /
library with TV, microwave oven, tea and coffee making facilities. Laundry facilities
available. Guests are welcome to use the conservatory, verandah or garden for their
enjoyment. You may join us for an evening or be as independent as you wish.*
Ours is a non-smoking household.
Directions: *We can give you simple directions or meet you in town or at the airport.*

Nelson

Inner-city Bed & Breakfast
Address: 'Borogove',
27 Grove St, Nelson
Name: Bill & Judy Hiener
Telephone: (03) 548 9442
Beds: 2 Queen, 1 Single (3 Bedrooms)
Bathroom: 3 Ensuite
Tariff: B&B (cooked) Double $85, Single $60.
NZ B&B Vouchers accepted May to Sep $16.50 surcharge
Nearest Town: Central Nelson

*Borogove is under 5 minutes' stroll from the Information Centre, Post Office, shops
and restaurants. Set within a secluded and fragrant English garden, our elegant 1907
Edwardian villa is of authentic New Zealand design, with the characteristic high
ceilings, glowing rimu woodwork and spaciousness of that era. Period furnishings and
antiques contribute to its unique charm. Each self-contained bedroom is delightfully
decorated and has its own ensuite bathroom. Relaxing arm-chairs, tea / coffee, heaters,
electric blankets, reading lights, TV and writing table ensure your comfort. A generous
cooked breakfast is served in our Victorian Dining room, warmed by an open fire in
winter. Nelsonians for many years, we are familiar with its many attractions and we
look forward to welcoming you to our heritage home. Arrangements made for Abel
Tasman bus collection from our door. Off-street parking available. No smokers
please.*

Nelson

Guest House+Self-contained Acc
Address: 'Beachside Villas', 71 Golf Road,
Tahunanui, Nelson 7001
Name: Andrea & Gerhard Merschdorf
Telephone: (03) 548 5041
Fax: (03) 548 5078
Email: beachside@clear.net.nz
Beds: 1 Super King/Twin,
5 King, 1 Twin (7 bedrooms)
Bathroom: 7 Ensuite
Tariff: B&B (continental) Double $85-$140, Single $75-$110. Dinner $20. All major
credit cards accepted. NZ B&B Vouchers accepted surcharge $16.50-$66
Nearest Town: Nelson 4km to city centre

*Opened in 1997 BEACHSIDE VILLAS combines Mediterranean ambience with high
modern standards. Each room / suite is individually decorated and equipped with Sky-TV,
phone and kitchen or tea and coffee making facilities. Our honeymoon-suite also features a
double bath and - like all the upstairs rooms - a sunny and spacious balcony with panoramic
views of the Mt. Arthur mountain range. All rooms are smokefree and serviced daily.
In walking-distance from the beach and local restaurants and only a one hour drive from three
National Parks.
BEACHSIDE VILLAS is the perfect place to enjoy and explore the Nelson area. Our beautiful
gardens and the swimming pool also invite you to just relax and have a break.
Have a delicious breakfast at your room, alfresco on the balcony / verandah or at the dining
room with your hosts and their two children (8 and 11 yrs). On request we serve homemade
German-and Swiss style bread.
Wir freuen uns auf Ihren Besuch*
Home Page: http://home.clear.net.nz/pages/beachside

Tahunanui, Nelson

Homestay
Address: 'Treetops', 156 Moana Avenue,
Tahunanui, Nelson
Name: Jim & Jill Mills
Telephone: (03) 548 5831 **Fax**: (03) 548 5831
Beds: 1 Double, 2 Single (2 bedrooms)
Bathroom: 1 Guests share

Rooms with a View

Tariff: B&B (full) Double $80, Single $55, Dinner by arrangement $25. NZ B&B
Vouchers accepted
Nearest Town: Nelson 3 Kms

*We warmly welcome visitors to our hillside home above Tahunanui Beach. Panoramic
views from the house and deck of Tasman Bay and the Mount Arthur Range are part
of our life, as are the frequent magnificent sunsets. Alternatively we have a secluded
patio with herb garden for sitting and relaxing.
Downstairs, between the modern, comfortable guest rooms, is a sitting room with TV,
books, writing area, tea / coffee facilities and a deck if you wish to be on your own. Our
house is a few minutes drive from the airport, beautiful beach, city centre, many
excellent restaurants, golf course and tennis courts.
Having travelled extensively ourselves, we love to meet visitors from all parts. Our
interests include sailing, gardening, walking, tennis, golf, cooking, fly and sea fishing,
and we can usually arrange these and other activities for our guests.*
Directions: *Please ring for directions or we can pick you up from the city or airport.*

Nelson

Self-contained Homestay Units
Address: 'Arapiki', 21 Arapiki Road, Stoke, Nelson
Name: Kay & Geoff Gudsell
Telephone: (03) 547 3741 **Fax**: (03) 547 3742
Mobile: (025) 517 131
Email: arapiki@nelson.planet.org.nz
Beds: 1 Queen, 1 Double, 1 Single (2 bedrooms)
Bathroom: 2 Private

Arapiki

Tariff: Unit: 1 Single $60, Double $75; Unit 2: Single $50, Double $65 (ask about reductions for longer stays), Continental Breakfast $5, Dinner $20 pp.
NZ B&B Vouchers accepted $15 surcharge for Unit 1. Same day restriction.
Nearest Town: Stoke Shopping Centre 1km, Nelson/Richmond 7km

The two units in our large home offer you comfort and privacy and are also very suitable for longer stays. You need at least two days to enjoy the attractive Nelson area and we can help with information and advice. Unit 1 which is larger is in a pleasant and private garden setting with seating available for your use. It has an Electric Stove, Microwave, TV, Auto Washing Machine and Phone available. 2 beds in private 'Sunroom' could sleep additional family members. Unit 2 has a balcony setting with seating to enjoy sea and mountain views. It has TV, Microwave, and Phone available. We have 2 cats and an elderly Labrador dog. Offstreet parking is provided.
We are very centrally located in the Nelson area. Meals are by arrangement. Quiet, Friendly and Comfortable. Both units are 'SMOKEFREE'.
Home Page: www.ts.co.nz/brochures/arapiki

Stoke, Nelson

Homestay
Address: 'Tarata Homestay'
5 Tarata St, Stoke, Nelson
Name: Mercia and John Hoskin
Telephone: (03) 547 3426
Freephone 0800 107 308
Fax: (03) 547 3640
Mobile: (025) 378 308
Beds: 1 Double, 2 Single (2 bedrooms)
Bathroom: 1 Guests share

Tarata Homestay

Tariff: B&B (continental) Double $65, Single $45. NZ B&B Vouchers accepted
Nearest Town: Nelson or Richmond 6 km

In a quiet cul-de-sac away from the busy main road, surrounded by gardens and mature trees, our home captures the best of the Nelson sun. Centrally located between Nelson and Richmond Tarata Homestay makes an ideal base for exploring the Tasman Bay area. Let us help you plan your sightseeing and activities, or for that evening meal assist you in selecting one of Nelson's fine restaurants.
Ample off street parking is provided and guests have their own entrance to the house. Guests also have their own comfortable lounge with TV and tea/coffee making facilities. Our continental breakfast includes a popular home made muesli, fruit in season, freshly brewed coffee and a selection of teas.
Our interests include travel, yachting, social dancing and gardening, and regular exercise is guaranteed by our friendly Labrador dog who loves a long walk.
Complimentary pick-up/delivery to transport services available. We request no smoking indoors.

Nelson Central

Homestay
Address: Jubilee House, 107 Quebec Road, Nelson
Name: Jubilee House. Sheridan & Patsy Parris
Telephone: (03) 548 8511 **Fax**: (03) 548-8511 **Mobile**: (025) 487 767
Beds: 2 Double, 2 Single (4 bedrooms)
Bathroom: 1 Guests share
Tariff: B&B (special) Double $80, Single $50, Children 12+. Dinner $25. Credit cards Visa, Mastercard, Bankcard. NZ B&B Vouchers accepted $10 surcharge
Nearest Town: Nelson 2km

We offer probably the best views you will experience in any homestay in New Zealand, one hundred and twenty five metres high, almost a 360 degree view, of the environs. You are encouraged to come upstairs to view the panorama from our lounge, and soak in the scenery, Tasman Bay, mountains, harbour entrance, and all of Nelson city the other side, three minutes by car, twelve walking. Even our bedrooms have splendid views.

It's been our privilege to host many folk, from all over the world, we want you feeling at home when you visit us.

Breakfasts are SPECIAL, a choice of home-made muesli, yoghurt, preserves, in season fruit, waffles with maple syrup fruit, and bacon to make your mouth water. No matter what you choose our breakfasts will give you the start needed to explore our region. Our home is smoke free. Complimentary pick-up from airport and bus depot.
Directions: *Please phone or fax for bookings and directions.*

Nelson

Homestay
Address: 23 Brougham St, Nelson
Name: Leanne & Lenard Dillimore
Telephone: (03) 545 6494
Fax: (03) 545 6494
Mobile: (025) 248 2798
Beds: 2 Queen (2 bedrooms)
Bathroom: 1 Ensuite, 1 Guests share
Tariff: B&B (full) Double $100,
Single $85,
Children $20. Credit cards.
NZ B&B Vouchers accepted $25 surcharge
Nearest Town: Nelson 4 blocks.

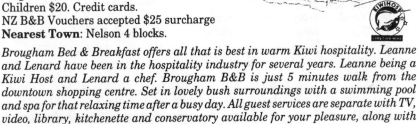

Brougham Bed & Breakfast offers all that is best in warm Kiwi hospitality. Leanne and Lenard have been in the hospitality industry for several years. Leanne being a Kiwi Host and Lenard a chef. Brougham B&B is just 5 minutes walk from the downtown shopping centre. Set in lovely bush surroundings with a swimming pool and spa for that relaxing time after a busy day. All guest services are separate with TV, video, library, kitchenette and conservatory available for your pleasure, along with phone and fax facilities.

Leanne, Lenard, young family (twins) and two delightful cats would love to share their home with you. Non smokers preferred.

Nelson

Homestay
Address: "Wainui Villa",
5 Wainui Street, Nelson
Name: Carolynn & Kevin Hannah
Telephone: (03) 545 7062
Mobile: (025) 589 229
Beds: 1 Queen (1 bedroom)
Bathroom: 1 Ensuite
Tariff: B&B (special) Double $85, Single $60,
Credit Cards. NZ B&B Vouchers accepted $25 surcharge
Nearest Town: Nelson centre 500m

Wainui Villa

Our home is a recently restored villa (c 1904) combining the charm and character of the past with modern comforts, only minutes walk from the city centre.

Your warm, sunny guestroom is spacious and attractively decorated. It includes your own entrance, ensuite, comfortable bed, TV/video, complimentary tea, coffee, juice, plus many more homely touches to make your stay memorable. Our luxurious spa pool is also available for your relaxation. Breakfast, served at your leisure, may include homemade muffins or bread and other treats.

Your hosts have over ten years experience in the hospitality industry and along with Darrell (4) you can be assured of friendly, personal attention. Feel free to join us and our friendly Labrador, Paddy, or relax in your room or cosy guest lounge with an inviting fire in winter and a wisteria covered verandah in summer.

Off street parking is provided. Our home is smokefree. Mr Frisky is resident cat.

Nelson

Homestay/Bed & Breakfast
Address: "Walmer", 7 Richardson St,Nelson
Name: Bob & Janet Hart
Telephone: (03) 548 3858
Fax: (03) 548 3857
Beds: 1 Queen, 1 Single (2 bedrooms)
Bathroom: 1 Private
Tariff: B&B (full) Double $110,
Single $80,
Not suitable for children under 12.
Credit Cards: Visa, MC, BC.
 NZ B&B Vouchers accepted $35 surcharge
Nearest Town: Nelson city centre 2.4km, Tahunanui Beach 1.4km

"Walmer" is a spacious, sunny, colonial house superbly situated opposite the harbour entrance, close to the sea, beach and city. Three seaside restaurants are within easy walking distance.

You have your own lounge and sunroom with stunning and immediate views of the harbour and Tasman Bay. Harbour views with ships and yachts are also gained from the main bedroom. There is also a private bathroom, kitchenette and single bedroom. A private and relaxing stay is assured as we cater for single party bookings only. Two Labrador dogs complete the household. A full, cooked, New Zealand breakfast is offered. Our home is an excellent base for exploring Nelson's three national parks including Abel Tasman National Park with its beautiful beaches. There are also arts and crafts trails and wine trails.

"Walmer" is easy to find and has off-street parking. Smokefree.

Nelson

Bed & Breakfast
Address: "Muritai Manor",
48 Main Road, Wakapuaka, Nelson
Name: Jan & Stan Holt
Telephone: (03) 545 1189 Reservations
Freephone: 0800 260 662 **Fax**: (03) 545 0740
Mobile: (025) 370 622
Email: muritai.manor@xtra.co.nz
Beds: 1 super King/Twin, 2 Queen, 1 Double (4 bedrooms)
Bathroom: 4 Ensuite
Tariff: B&B (full) Double $130-$145, Single $95- $110, Children half price,
Dinner $45, Credit Cards (MC/VISA/Amex).
NZ B&B Vouchers accepted $85 surcharge
Nearest Town: 6km north of Nelson on State Highway 6, five mins by car to
Nelson city centre.

Built in 1903, recently restored and renovated, relax in an elegant country atmosphere, with superb views of Nelson Haven and the Western Ranges across Tasman Bay.Our home combines colonial charm with modern facilities and timeless decor. Relax in the hot spa or in the lounge by a cosy fire in winter. Cool down on summer evenings by dipping in the swimming pool, or enjoying the sunset from the verandahs.Breakfast can be tailor made to your needs. a full cooked breakfast, freshly squeezed juices, homemade preserves, yoghurt, fruit, muesli, with gresh ground coffee and selection of teas. A good start to days of sightseeing, sailing, tramping, kayaking or just relaxing!We are a non-smoking home with one twelve year old daughter and two friendly dogs. We also have a self-contained sleepout suitable for family use.
Directions: *Muritai Manor is 6 kms north of Nelson city on State Highway 6 towards Blenheim, 1/2 km beyong Clifton Terrace School on right.*
Home Page: http://nz.com/webnz/bbnz/muritai.htm

Nelson

Guest House, Bed & Breakfast
Address: 8 Ardilea Ave, Stoke, Nelson
Name: R & C Maguire
Telephone: (03) 547 6754
Fax: (03) 547 6735
Beds: 1 King, 2 Queen, 2 Single (3 bedrooms)
Bathroom: 1 Ensuite, 1 Guests share
Tariff: B&B (full) Double $110-$150, Single $95, No children. Credit Cards.
Nearest Town: Nelson 8km, Richmond 3km, Stoke 1km.

Hosts Carolyn and Ray Maguire have created a warm friendly atmosphere where guests have freedom to come and go as they please, enjoy the privacy provided or company.All rooms are tastefully decorated with King, Queen or Single beds, electric blankets and heating for winter. The bathrooms are very luxurious.
Guests have a private dinning room with tea and coffee facilities available, also a very comfortable lounge which is home away from home, this opens out to a half acre garden which is complemented by a lovely swimming pool to relax and enjoy the tranquil surroundings.
If its peace and quite in the ultimate of luxury you are looking for then look no further you won't be disappointed.
Central to wineries and craft shops, activities arranged.
Directions: *Travelling on Main Road Stoke look for Robinsons complex and Kensington Rest Home drive straight through car park coming onto Ardilea Ave, or phone.*

Nelson
B & B
Address: 'Sussex House', 238 Bridge Street, Nelson
Name: Carol Palmer
Telephone: (03) 548 9972 **Fax**: (03) 548 9972 **Mobile**: (025) 784 846
Email: carolmp@xtra.co.nz
Beds: 3 Queen, 3 Single (4 bedrooms)
Bathroom: 2 Ensuite, 1 Guests share
Tariff: B&B (full) Double with ensuite $100, Double $90, Single $65, Twin $80-$90, Credit cards. NZ B&B Vouchers accepted $30 surcharge
Nearest Town: Nelson city centre 1/2 km

A fine character home that is friendly, relaxing, and centrally situated on the banks of the peaceful Maitai River. That's "Sussex House", our charming guest house which is only 2 / 3 minutes from the centre of Nelson, great restaurants, the Suter Art Gallery, the beautiful Queen's Gardens, Botanical Hill (the centre of New Zealand) and many good walks, river and bush.

The house features four sunny bedrooms that have access to the verandahs overlooking the river.

Enjoy our private swimming pool, winter spa or just relax and make the most of the secluded garden and the tranquil surroundings. In the winter sip your coffee by the big fire after dinner.

Travelling musicians can enjoy the use of musical instruments including 6 & 12 string guitars, fiddles, mandolins, banjolin, piano and an upright double bass. Breakfast includes a selection of seasonal fruit and berries, fresh homemade bread, muffins, jams and preserves with a cooked breakfast available on request.

Vegetarians and / or guests on special diets are catered for individually. This is a non-smoking house.

Your host, Carol Palmer

Nelson

Homestay
Address: 106 Brooklands Road,
Atawhai, Nelson
Name: Lorraine & Barry Signal
Telephone: (03) 545 1423
Beds: 1 Double, 2 Single (2 bedrooms)
Bathroom: 1 Guests share
Tariff: B&B (full) Double $85, Single $55,
Dinner $25. Credit Cards accepted.
NZ B&B Vouchers accepted $15 surcharge
Nearest Town: Nelson 3km

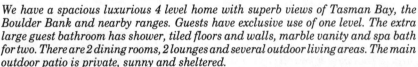

We have a spacious luxurious 4 level home with superb views of Tasman Bay, the Boulder Bank and nearby ranges. Guests have exclusive use of one level. The extra large guest bathroom has shower, tiled floors and walls, marble vanity and spa bath for two. There are 2 dining rooms, 2 lounges and several outdoor living areas. The main outdoor patio is private, sunny and sheltered.

Lorraine has a keen interest in crafts and makes porcelain dolls and teddy bears. Her other interests include gardening, walking and cooking. We both enjoy sports, running and the outdoors. We have no family left at home except a friendly persian cat. We are close to all the attractions of Nelson and the surrounding areas including its beaches, wine and craft trails, national parks, rivers, lakes, mountains and skifields. We enjoy meeting people and making new friends. We are non smokers. Courtesy transport available.

Nelson

Bed & Breakfast
Address: Collingwood House,
174 Collingwood Street, Nelson
Name: Emmy & Lane van Wessel
Telephone: (03) 548 4481
Fax: (03) 548 4481
Beds: 2x2 King/Queen, 3 Double,
2 Single (4 bedrooms)
Bathroom: 3 Ensuite, 1 Private

Tariff: B&B (full) Double $85, Single $70, Credit Cards.
NZ B&B Vouchers accepted Off-peak season
Nearest Town: Nelson 3 mins walk to city centre.

Our centrally located Bed & Breakfast is a character family home. Having lived in many parts of the world we know how to make a guest at ease. Spacious bedrooms have excellent beds, comfortable chairs, duvets, woolrests, fresh flowers, TV, coffee & tea compliments. We'll welcome you with refreshments. Breakfast at Collingwood house is a real feature. A hearty continental of cereals, yoghurt, fruits, or traditional breakfast farm fresh eggs, bacon, tomatoes, fine teas and freshly ground coffee.

Our house is located three minutes walk to many fine restaurants, Queens Garden and Nelson Cathedral. We have no pets. No smoking please. We have two boys aged 13 and 10. They are involved in classical music.

Nelson

Homestay
Address: 122 Milton Street, Nelson
Name: Judith Wilson
Telephone: (03) 548 0483
Fax: (03) 548 0483
Beds: 1 Queen (1 bedroom)
Bathroom: 1 Family share
Tariff: B&B (special) Double $75,
Single $50,
Credit Cards.
NZ B&B Vouchers accepted
Nearest Town: Nelson 1km

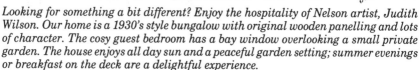

Looking for something a bit different? Enjoy the hospitality of Nelson artist, Judith Wilson. Our home is a 1930's style bungalow with original wooden panelling and lots of character. The cosy guest bedroom has a bay window overlooking a small private garden. The house enjoys all day sun and a peaceful garden setting; summer evenings or breakfast on the deck are a delightful experience.

After 27 years of living in California, I can provide true specialty breakfasts. Try a Spanish omelette with my home-cooked bagels and a bowl of raspberries, or blueberry pancakes with fresh peaches and cream. I'm happy to share my own artwork, and my unique collection of over 400 dolls from around the world.

The house is in a quiet area within walking distance of town, river, botanical hill, art gallery and Japanese gardens. Bookings preferred.

Smoke-free house.

Nelson Central

Bed and Breakfast
Address: 70 Tasman Street, Nelson
Name: Sunflower Cottage,
Marion and Chris Burton
Telephone: (03) 548 1588
Email: sunflower@netaccess.co.nz
Beds: 1 Queen, 2 Single (2 bedrooms)
Bathroom: 2 Ensuites
Tariff: B&B (continental) Double $75, single $50, Dinner $25.
NZ B&B Vouchers accepted $5 surcharge
Nearest Town: Nelson, five minutes walk

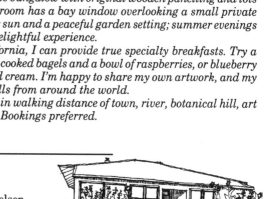

We would like to welcome you to Nelson, giving you a relaxing stay in our sunny home on the banks of the Maitai River. Our freshly decorated large bedrooms, with fully tiled ensuite bathrooms, are serviced daily with fresh flowers, complimentary basket of fruit, homemade bread and jams. Both rooms contain TV, microwave, fridge, tea / coffee making facilities, and toaster. Our continental breakfast is self-service.

Queen's Gardens and the Suter Art Gallery are nearby. We overlook the Botanical Hill, where you can take a shady walk to the Centre of New Zealand, to experience wonderful views over Tasman Bay and Nelson township.

We enjoy meeting people and making new friends, as does our friendly Border Collie. Our hobbies are gardening in our cottage garden, cooking, travelling, sailing and the Internet. We are happy to collect you from the airport of bus depot. We are non-smokers and appreciate no smoking inside.

Home Page: http://webnz.co.nz/sunflowercottage

Nelson

Guest House
Address: 24 Richardson Street, Nelson
Name: Te Puna Wai Lodge
Telephone: (03) 548 7621
Fax: (03) 546 7261
Mobile: (025) 242 3519
Beds: 1 Queen,
1 Double (2 bedrooms)
Bathroom: 2 Ensuites
Tariff: B&B (continental) Double $125-$145,
Single $115-$125. Children by arrangement.
Credit Cards accepted.
NZ B&B Vouchers accepted
Nearest Town: Nelson 1.5km

"Tis distance lends enchantment to the view and robes the mountains in its azure hue".
Alexander Pope.

This elegant early Victorian villa, once home of noted New Zealand photographer William Tyree, is set in the magnificent Port Hills, commanding unsurpassed sea and mountain views. The house provides a well designed living area, sunny verandahs and secluded gardens.
You will be warmly greeted by Ko Ko, a black standard poodle and her two Burmese cat companions.
The two luxurious double units, decorated with antique furniture and Oriental rugs, have private en-suites incorporating Indian marble tiling and underfloor heating.
Directions: *From the city centre, head South on the waterfront for approximately 1.5km. Richardson Street is located left up into the Port Hills. We provide complimentary pick up/drop off transfer from Nelson Airport and the city coach terminal.*

Nelson

Bed & Breakfast
Address: The Baywick Inn,
51 Domett Street, Nelson
Name: Janet Southwick and Tim Bayley
Telephone: (03) 545 6514
Fax: (03) 545 6514
Mobile: (025) 545 823
Email: baywicks@iconz.co.nz
Beds: 2 Queen, 1 Single (2 bedrooms)
Bathroom: 2 Ensuite.
Tariff: B&B (full) double $120, Single $90. Dinner by arrangement.
Not suitable for children. Visa/Mastercard. Winter & Business rates available.
Nearest Town: Nelson - 5 minutes stroll to down town.

Overlooking the Maitai River and Brook Stream, the Baywick Inn is an elegantly restored 1885 Victorian 2 story villa. Here a warm New Zealand-Canadian welcome awaits you as you're greeted by their lively wire haired fox terrier, who will want to join you (but isn't allowed to) for afternoon tea or cappuccino served in the Brookside garden.
Guest rooms are luxuriously appointed with comfortable beds, down duvets, antique furnishings, ensuites (one with the original 'claw' foot tub and a shower) and with a sunroom or an open air deck. Relax in the sitting room with its cozy fireplace and enjoy a conversation with Tim about his classic MG's or wine cellaring systems. Janet, a cook by profession, makes breakfasts to order, healthy or indulgent, cooked or continental, but always a treat served in the sunny dinning room. Private off street parking is provided. Non smoking.

Richmond, Nelson

Homestay
Address: 46 Rochfort Drive, Richmond, Nelson
Name: Jean & Jack Anderson
Telephone: (03) 544 2175 **Fax**: (03) 544 2175
Beds: 1 Double, 2 Single (2 bedrooms)
Bathroom: 1 Guest share
Tariff: B&B (full) Double $55, Single $30, Children half price, Dinner $12.50,
Credit Cards. NZ B&B Vouchers accepted
Nearest Town: Richmond 1/2km, Nelson 11km

*We are a couple who like meeting people. We live in a modern comfortable home just
minutes from the Richmond Shopping area. Near by are lovely gardens, many crafts,
such as Pottery, Glass Blowing, Dried Flowers, Weaving and Wood Turning. Beaches
at Tahuna and Rabbit Island are only 10 minutes away by car. A two minute walk will
take you to a bus to go to Nelson city. We are situated in an area which is very central
for travellers going South or North or into the lovely Golden Bay and Tasman areas.
We are happy to meet planes or buses and trust that we can make your stay enjoyable.
Enjoy Kiwi hospitality in Richmond. A phone call or letter would be appreciated before
arrival.*
Directions: *At round-about on Queen Street Richmond, continue on Queen Street
toward the hills, first turn right, Washbourn Drive, first turn left, Farnham Drive,
second turn right, Rochfort Drive.*

Richmond, Nelson

B&B+Self-contained Accom.
Address: 'Bayview', 37 Kihilla Road,
Richmond, Nelson
Name: Ray & Janice O'Loughlin
Telephone: (03) 544 6541
Fax: (03) 544 6541
Email: bayview@ts.co.nz
Beds: 1 Super King, 2 Queen (3 bedrooms)
Bathroom: 1 Ensuite, 1 Guests share
Tariff: B&B (full or continental) Double $85-$100, Single $65, Dinner $25 pp,
Credit Cards: Visa/Mastercard. NZ B&B Vouchers accepted $15 surcharge
Nearest Town: Richmond 1 km. Nelson 10 km

*Bayview is a modern, spacious home built on the hills above Richmond township, with
spectacular views of Tasman Bay and mountain ranges.*
*We offer rooms that are quiet, private and immaculately furnished with your complete
comfort in mind. A large guest bathroom has shower and spa bath. The lounge opens
onto a sheltered deck where you can relax, enjoy a drink or sit and chat.*
*The self-contained suite with private entrance, off-street parking, kitchen, bathroom/
laundry, lounge area and Queen bed offers privacy and all home comforts.*
*We have two miniature Schnauzer dogs, a variety of birds in a large aviary, tend our
colourful garden and enjoy meeting people from new Zealand and overseas.*
*By car Bayview is 15 minutes from Nelson, 2 minutes from Richmond and award-
winning restaurants, close to National parks, beaches, vineyards and crafts.*
Be assured of warm, friendly hospitality and a happy stay in our smokefree home.
Home Page: http://nz.com/webnz/bbnz/bayview.htm

Richmond

Homestay
Address: 3 George Kidd St, Richmond, Nelson
Name: Lesley & Tony Marshall
Telephone: (03) 544 7741
Fax: (03) 544 7741
Email: t-I-marshall@clear.net.nz
Beds: 2 Queen (2 bedrooms)
Bathroom: 1 Guests share
Tariff: B&B (full) Double $85, Single $65,
Dinner $25.
NZ B&B Vouchers accepted $15 surcharge
Nearest Town: Richmond 1km, Nelson 12km

Our large modern home is located in a quiet area on the Richmond foothils with views across the plains to the mountains.
We offer guests a warm, friendly, relaxed atmosphere. Our sunny, spacious guest bedrooms, which open onto a deck area, have comfortable quality furnishings to make your stay enjoyable.
Our special breakfast includes fruit juice, seasonal fresh fruit platter, croissants, home preserves, yoghurt, a selection of cereals, vegetable omelettes, home made jams, and freshly brewed coffee or tea.
Join us for dinner in the evening, by prior arrangement, and relax with us in the lounge over coffee.
We are 20 minutes from Nelson City and central to all the attractions of our region. laundry facilities available. A non-smoking house. We prefer a phone call prior to arrival.
Directions: *Please phone.*

Richmond
Country Homestay B&B
Address: 87 Main Rd, Hope, Nelson
Name: Alison & Murray Nicholls
Telephone: (03) 544 8026 **Fax**: (03) 544 8026
Beds: 1 Queen, 1 Double, 2 Single (3 bedrooms)
Bathroom: 1 Guests share, 1 Family share
Tariff: B&B (full or continental) Double $65, Single $40, Dinner by arrangement $12.50pp. NZ B&B Vouchers accepted
Nearest Town: Richmond 2km, Nelson 17km

Our home is situated on a kiwifruit and apple orchard, on State Highway 6 2km south of Richmond. A lengthy driveway ensures quiet surroundings in a lovely garden setting.
Guests may enjoy a stroll through the orchard, or swim in our pool.
We are centrally situated placing Nelson's many attractions within easy reach. We will happily provide information about these and make arrangements as required.
Complimentary tea or coffee is available to guests upon arrival.
Full or continental breakfast is included, and dinner is provided by arrangement.
A phone call before arrival would be appreciated.
Ours is a non smoking home.

Richmond
Exclusive Bed & Breakfast
Address: "Althorpe", 13 Dorset St,
Richmond, Nelson
Name: Bob & Jenny
Telephone: (03) 544 8117/0800 258467
(0800 Althorpe) **Fax**: (03) 544 8117
Email: rworley@voyager.co.nz
Beds: 1 Double, 2 Single/King
(2 bedrooms)
Bathroom: 1 Ensuite, 1 Private
Tariff: B&B (full) Double $110-$120, Single $90-$100, Dinner $30. Credit cards. NZ B&B Vouchers accepted $30 Surcharge
Nearest Town: Richmond - 5 mins walk

althorpe
THE BED & BREAKFAST ESTABLISHMENT

Call us out of this world if you will. But with just two intimate guest rooms, ALTHORPE provides warm old fashioned fuss and care that defines the art of hospitality.
An ensuite serves our double bedroom while a private bathroom is provided for the twin/king suite. Guests are afforded the quiet luxury of two relaxing lounge rooms while outside spacious gardens with their own swimming pool invite a casual stroll or a dip in summer.
Among the services that have our guests reluctant to leave us you'll find a delightful, tasty gourmet breakfast. By arrangement guests may also enjoy an evening dinner complemented by a vintage wine from the cellar.
And it all comes within walls and grounds that carry the echoes of bygone colonial years. At the end of the day's journey you deserve nothing but a little pampering, personal attention and all the comforts of home.
Directions: *Please phone for details. Smoking outside please.*

Richmond, Nelson

Farmstay
Address: Redwood Vly Rd,
Richmond R.D. 1, Nelson
Name: Cecelia Miller
Telephone: (03) 544 0801
Fax: (03) 544 0801
Beds: 1 King/Queen,
3 Single (3 bedrooms)

Bathroom: 1 Ensuite, 1 Guests share
Tariff: B&B (full) Double $85, Single $55, Children same, Dinner $25,
Campervans welcome.
Credit cards. NZ B&B Vouchers accepted same day restriction
Nearest Town: Richmond 10km, Nelson 28km

*Experience the warm hospitality of our good food and well presented gardens and
lawns. The farm is set on 38 acre with Hereford cattle and breeding ewes. You are
welcome to enjoy a conducted tour of the property. All bedrooms are very well appointed
with panoramic views of rolling hills and open green tree studded valley.*
*Within the Nelson region there is a large variety of activities including fishing, skiing,
boating, trekking, tramping, golf, conducted wine trails, pottery trails, glass blowing.
You are welcome to enjoy a dinner (3 course) including fresh garden vegetables and
fruit of your choice.*
Relax with a game of snooker / pool in the large games room.
Your welcome and comfortable stay is assured.
Directions: *Please phone or write.*

Richmond, Nelson

Homestay B&B
Address: 39 Washbourn Drive,
Richmond, Nelson
Name: Mike & Noelene's Place
Telephone: (03) 544 7279
Fax: (03) 544 7279
Email: n.smith@xtra.co.nz
Beds: 1 Queen, 4 Single (3 bedrooms)
Bathroom: 1 Ensuite, 1 Guests share, 1 Family share
Tariff: B&B (full) Double $80-$95, Single $50, Dinner $25, Credit Cards.
NZ B&B Vouchers accepted $15 surcharge
Nearest Town: Richmond 1/2km, Nelson 10km

*Join us in our lovely family home overlooking the sea, hills and the lovely borough of
Richmond. Our three guest rooms (1 ensuite) are warm and cosy, with a private guest
lounge if desired. We would be happy for you to join us for dinner or unwind over a
typical kiwi barbecue in our sheltered courtyard. We are close to beaches, potteries and
wineries and would be happy to help you with recommendations. Trout fishing rivers,
lakes, golden Bay and Abel Tasman National Park are but a short drive away.*
*Please phone for easy directions. If required transport to and from airport / bus depot
etc is available. Smoking outside please. Laundry facilities are available and a lock
up garage for your vehicle.*

497

Richmond, Nelson

Homestay
Address: "Hunterville", 30 Hunter Avenue,
Richmond, Nelson
Name: Cecile & Alan Strang
Telephone: (03) 544 5852
Fax: (03) 544 5852
Beds: 1 King Extra Large, 3 Single (2 Bedrooms)
Bathroom: 1 Private, 1 Family share
Tariff: B&B (special) Double $70, Single $50, Dinner $20.
Credit cards NZ B&B Vouchers accepted
Nearest Town: 2 Blocks up Queen Street, off Main Road.

When you are travelling south or the Able Tasman Park Area, don't stop in busy Nelson City, but come a little further to Richmond where you will be welcomed with tea or coffee or pre-dinner drinks. Having recently travelled several months on a budget in Europe, we appreciate the needs of travellers. Our guest rooms are spacious, sunny, and have views over Tasman Bay, and our Laundry is available. Our special breakfast caters for all tastes with homemade muesli, fresh fruit, and muffins or a cooked selection. Join us for dinner and share our enjoyment of good food, wine and travellers tales, or we will recommend the regions best restaurants close by. Our interests are music, bridge, bowls and you will be surrounded by books. We look forward to sharing with you our private garden, our friendly Dalmation, "Co,Co", ample parking, and our beautiful countryside by the sea.

Richmond, Nelson

Boutique Accommodation
Address: Kershaw House,
10 Wensley Road, Richmond,
Nelson 7002
Name: Deidre and Ashley Marshall
Telephone: (03) 544 0957
Fax: (03) 544 0950
Mobile: 025-389 347
Beds: 1 King, 2 Queen, 1 Single (4 bedrooms)
Bathroom: 3 Ensuite
Tariff: B&B (full) Double $145-$165, Single $125, Credit Cards (VISA/MC).
Nearest Town: Richmond 5 mins walk, Nelson 13km

We invite you to experience the genuine warmth of Kiwi hospitality in our elegant (1929) home.
You are welcome to enjoy our comfortable, character residence which is both restful and relaxing, and yet only 3 minutes walk to the Richmond shopping centre and its excellent restaurants.
"Gateway to the Nelson Region", the Abel Tasman National Park, Golden Bay and Nelson Lakes, Richmond is but a short drive to many of areas renowned attractions. Off-street parking is available and for our guests' comfort we are a "smoke free" home. We enjoy meeting people and will make every endeavour to ensure that your stay with us is both enjoyable and memorable.
The resident dog is Henry (a mini Dachshund).
Directions: *Please phone or fax for reservations or directions. A courtesy car is available.*

Richmond, Nelson
Guest House
Address: Surrey Road, Richmond,
Nelson (1/4 hr drive south of Nelson)
Name: Antiquarian Guest House
Telephone: (03) 544 0253 or 544 0723
Fax: (03) 544 0253 **Mobile**: (025) 417 504
Beds: 1 King, 1 Queen, 1 Twin (3 bedrooms)
Bathroom: 1 Ensuite, 1 Guest share
Tariff: B&B (full) Double $95,
Single $75, Credit Cards.
NZ B&B Vouchers accepted
$25.50 surcharge on Double, $16.50 on Single.
Nearest Town: 11km south of Nelson

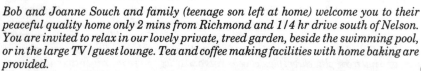

Bob and Joanne Souch and family (teenage son left at home) welcome you to their peaceful quality home only 2 mins from Richmond and 1/4 hr drive south of Nelson. You are invited to relax in our lovely private, treed garden, beside the swimming pool, or in the large TV/guest lounge. Tea and coffee making facilities with home baking are provided.

Breakfast includes local seasonal fruits, freshly baked bread and muesli, coffee, tea etc, and we are happy to cook you an English breakfast, if desired. Our family cat is called Zoe.

Richmond is an excellent base for exploring the Nelson region close to Abel Tasman Park, Golden Bay, Nelson Lakes and Rainbow Skifield.

We are also owners of a local antique shop and know the area well. You are assured of a warm welcome and a discount is offered to guests staying 3 nights or more. We thank you for not smoking inside.

Wakefield, Nelson
Homestay, Self Contained Accommodation
Address: 'Serenity Gardens',
72A Eighty-Eight Valley Road, Wakefield, Nelson
Name: Barbara and Graham
Telephone: 03 541 8895 **Fax**: 03 541 8895
Beds: 1 Double, 1 Single (1 bedroom) + 1 additional bed available
Bathroom: 1 Ensuite
Tariff: B&B (continental) Double $80, Single $50, Dinner $25. No pets.
Nearest Town: Richmond, 14 km on SH6

* We offer a self contained unit situated on four acres in a tranquil valley with complete privacy and quietness (2 minutes drive off Nelson-West Coast SH6).

* Bordering idyllic stream setting with mature trees. Extensive gardens in process of development, including over 250 rose bushes.

* Homestay unit adjoins main homestead with modern kitchen, microwave, TV and video with comfortable dining area and ample off-road parking.

* Positioning ideally centrally located for exploring Nelson - Golden Bay - Nelson Lakes areas.

* Assistance gladly given with local sightseeing. We have both travelled extensively.

* Guests welcome to share evening meal with us. Farmstyle meals using our own organically grown fresh vegetables. Complimentary tea/coffee and home-made baking upon arrival.

* We appreciate your support for our smoke-free home. Smoke alarms for your protection.
Directions: *Please phone for details.*

Thorpe, Nelson

Accommodation
Address: Rerenga Farm, Thorpe,
Dovedale-Woodstock Road, Nelson
Name: Robert & Joan Panzer
Telephone: (03) 543 3825
Fax: (03) 543-3640
Email: Tailored@ts.co.nz
Beds: 1 Double (1 bedroom).
Bathroom: Ensuite
Tariff: B&B (special) Double $85, Single $65, Dinner $25.
Nearest Town: Upper Moutere 25 mins.

We regard our guests as visiting friends; not as commercial clients.
Thorpe is halfway between Nelson and Motueka, with plenty of nearby options for tramping (Abel Tasman and Kahurangi National Parks); fishing (Motueka River 3 minutes away); or the local crafts and vineyards. We offer a peaceful, rural retreat with the sunny Nelson climate, view of Mt Arthur, good food, and international hosts. Our 85 year old homestead surrounded by rolling hills, forests and situated along the Dove River, is in the middle of 20 acres of planted fruit and nut trees, plus sheep, pigs, chooks, cats and a dog. You can arrive at our door by foot crossing over our own swingbridge or by driving over a vehicle bridge. Robert is from the Netherlands and Joan from the United States. We have two small children who are real "Kiwi's".
E-mail and fax facilities available for you to use.
Note: We also operate Tailored Travel: Personal custom tours (6 max) tailored to specific requirements and dates.
Home Page: http://webnz.com/nzct

Wakefield, Nelson

Bed & Breakfast + Self-Contained Accommodation
Address: Pigeon Valley Road,
RD 2, Wakefield
Name: Peter & Alison Warren
Telephone: (03) 541 8500/(0800 347 208)
Fax: (03) 541 8500
Email: pigeon@iconz.co.nz
Beds: 1 Queen, 2 Single (2 bedrooms)
Bathroom: 2 Ensuite

Pigeon
Valley
Lodge

Tariff: B&B (full) Double $140, Single $120, Dinner $30, Credit Cards.
Nearest Town: Wakefield, Richmond 10 mins

Imagine waking to the sound of native birdsong. After a day on the road, perhaps the thought of a refreshing dip in our swimming pool appeals.
At Pigeon Valley Lodge you will be our special guests (single party booking). Our contemporary lodge with warm timber interior offers all facilities for your relaxation and comfort, in a secluded hillside setting. Both bedrooms have ensuite bathrooms with lovely rural views.
A brief stroll leads you to our historic homestead, where we provide country style hospitality, including a gourmet breakfast and optional dinner. Our family includes four children and two friendly dogs.
Just 2km from Wakefield, the lodge is within easy reach of wineries, arts and craft studios, National Parks and skifields. Totaradale Golf Course is a minute away and we have golf clubs. If you would like to go fly fishing, your in-house guide, Peter, is on hand.
Home Page: http://webnz.co.nz/pigeon

Mapua, Nelson

Bed & Breakfast
Address: "Village Bed & Breakfast",
10 Higgs Road, Mapua, Nelson
Name: Heather
Telephone: (03) 540 2665 **Fax**: (03) 540 2665
Beds: 1 Double, 2 Single (2 bedrooms)
Bathroom: 1 Guests share
Tariff: B&B (full) Double $80-$90, Single $50-$60.
Nearest Town: Richmond (15 mins), Motueka (15 mins)

Our architecturally designed home in Mapua has rural views from estuary to mountain range. Trees and shrubs surround the house and from the decks the tuis, bellbirds and fantails will delight as they feed and sing. The swimming pool area at back is a restful place for a quiet drink or with a good book.
Breakfasts are at a leisurely pace and include fresh local produce from fruit to seafood. This can be enjoyed in the cosy dining area or outdoors by the pool.
Mapua Village is situated off State Highway 60 halfway between Nelson and Kaiteriteri, and has a unique mix of food, wineries, gardens, potteries, and arts and crafts within a few minutes of our home which we would be happy to share with you. In winter our cat can be found in the open plan living area in front of the fire. No smoking in the house.

NELSON GOLDEN BAY

Mapua, Nelson

Country Accommodation
Address: "Atholwood Country Accommodation",
Bronte Rd East, R.D.1, Upper Moutere, Nelson
Name: Robyn & Grahame Williams
Telephone: (03) 540 2925
Fax: (03) 540 2925 **Mobile**: (025) 310 309
Beds: 2 Queen, 1 Single (2 bedrooms)
Bathroom: 2 Ensuite
Tariff: B&B (full) Double $120-$135, Single $100-$120. Dinner by arrangement.
Credit cards.
Nearest Town: Nelson (25 mins) and Motueka (20 mins)

Our home is set well back from the road, within two acres of landscaped gardens. Bordered by the Waimea Inlet, abundant with birdlife, you can enjoy peace and total privacy. Within the gardens are a swimming pool, spa, croquet lawn, secret garden paths and a Gazebo for your pleasure.
The interior decor of natural rimu adds to the casual and country atmosphere. Two well appointed guest rooms, each with adjoining ensuites have extensive views. The upstairs guest wing has a separate lounge with tea and coffee making facilities.
Breakfast at "Atholwood" is arranged to suit your timetable and is wholesome and filling, taking advantage of local fresh fruit and produce. Evening meals and lunches are available by prior arrangement, and local restaurants are close and excellent.
At "Atholwood" you can be assured of our personal attention in a relaxed and informal atmosphere.

Mapua Village, Nelson

Coastal Village Accommodation
Address: "Hartridge", 103 Aranui Road,
Mapua Village, Nelson
Name: Sue & Dennis Brillard
Telephone: (03) 540 2079 **Fax**: (03) 540 2079
Beds: 1 Super King/Twin, 1 Queen (2 bedrooms)
Bathroom: 2 Ensuite
Tariff: B&B (special) Double $125, Single $95,
Dinner by arrangement $25, Credit Cards (MC/VISA).
NZ B&B Vouchers accepted $50 surcharge double,
$35 surcharge single

Nearest Town: Motueka/Richmond 20km (15 mins), Nelson 34km(30 mins).

Set on a rise in mature grounds with huge English beech trees and large circular rose garden, Hartridge is listed with Historic Places Trust and offers friendly hospitality, peace, tranquillity and 1915 ambience. New upstairs guest accommodation is stylish and private. The two spacious guest rooms are sunny, light, and airy with large firm beds, comfortable seating and ensuite bathrooms. Breakfast here is a special event and may include fresh raspberries, strawberries, home-made bread, free-range eggs and hot-smoked fish. It is served at an antique mahogany table using grandmother's tableware, or outside on the sunny verandah. There is a large comfortable guest lounge, friendly dog and vintage Morgan. Within walking distance are beach walks, swimming, award winning cafes / bars. National Parks Kahurangi, Nelson Lakes and Able Tasman provide swimming, hiking, sea-kayaking and scenic beauty whilst golf, trout fishing, wineries, arts / crafts are nearby. Smoke free house, private parking.

Upper Moutere, Motueka

Quality Accommodation
Address: Harakeke RD 2, Upper Moutere
Name: "The Maples",
Maya Mosimann & Ruedi Kappeli
Telephone: (03) 543 2008 **Fax**: (03) 543 2008
Beds: 3 King (3 bedrooms)
Bathroom: 1 Guests share, 1 Family share.
Tariff: B&B (special) Double $85-$95, Single $55, Dinner $25, Children under 12
half price.
Nearest Town: 14 km south of Motueka, 6km north of Upper Moutere

Peaceful, rural retreat in the sunny Moutere Valley.
Built as one of the first farm houses in the region, The Maples has been tastefully restored combining traditional features with modern comfort. This interior designers home offers beautifully decorated bedrooms with comfortable beds and a luxurious rimu bathroom.
Relax on the verandah or play badminton in our delightful parklike garden. Our delicious breakfasts include home-made Swiss fruit muesli, breads, croissants and jams. You will love our real fresh ground coffee / cappuccino.
Guests may also enjoy an evening dinner with produce from our own garden complemented by a New Zealand wine.
We have a friendly tabby cat, and the inside of our home is smoke free.
We are the ideal base for visiting Abel Tasman and Kahurangi National Parks and many local wineries.
Directions: *You find us 12km south from Motueka airport on the Moutere Hwy. 6km north from Upper Moutere township. Wir sprechen auch Deutsch.*

502

Tasman
Farmstay
Address: Permin Road Tasman R.D.1, Upper Moutere
Name: "Aporo Orchard" Marian & Mike Day
Telephone: (03) 526 6858 **Fax**: (03) 526 6258 **Mobile**: 025 240 3757
Beds: 1 Queen, 1 King/Twin (2 bedrooms)
Bathroom: 2 Ensuite
Tariff: B&B (full) Double $120, Single $95, Dinner by arrangement $35. Credit
Cards: Master Card/Visa. NZ B&B Vouchers accepted $50 surcharge
Nearest Town: Motueka 11km, Nelson 40km

Our comfortable secluded home, with grape and hop clad verandahs, is set in a colourful garden which attracts many birds and is enthusiastically maintained by Marian. It overlooks our apple orchard, with magnificent views of Tasman Bay to D'Urville Island and the Kahurangi ranges to the west. Guests can enjoy the swimming pool, relax in the garden, compete on the petanque court or croquet lawn, stroll through the orchard to the beach (5 mins) or woodland walk. Or simply enjoy a complimentary glass of our own grape wine or cider.

We are centrally situated in the heart of Nelson's fruit growing region, only 200 m off Coastal Highway 60 between Nelson / Motueka enabling travellers to explore the best of the Nelson Province, Golden Bay, Abel Tasman and Kahurangi National parks. Beautiful safe swimming beaches and walks are nearby, as are two golf courses, award winning wineries, trout fishing rivers, art and craft trails and great restaurants in nearby Mapua on the water's edge.

The Nelson region, arguably NZ's sunniest spot, offers a wealth of activities to warrant a 2-3 days stay. An ideal area to relax away from the pleasures of long driving days.

We offer two spacious well appointed, purpose built double bedrooms each with TV, refrigerator, coffee / tea making facilities, home made biscuits, fresh fruit and flowers.

Delicious home baked breakfast is served in our farmhouse kitchen or sunny deck outside. Picnic lunches and 3 course diners are available by arrangement featuring fresh, seasonal local produce, organically home grown vegetables and local wine.

Cat and farm dog.

503

Tasman, Motueka
Holiday & Health Retreat
Address: "Kina Colada", Kina Peninsula, RD 1, Tasman/Upper Moutere
Name: Dr Hans & Susanne Brutscher
Telephone: (03) 526 6700 **Fax**: (03) 526 6770
Beds: 3 King, 3 Single (3 bedrooms)
Bathroom: 3 Ensuite
Tariff: B&B (special) Double $160/suite, $125/apartment, Single $95-$130, extra person $50, 3 Course Dinner $30, Credit Cards (VISA/MC).
Nearest Town: Motueka 7km, Nelson 40km

Kina Colada - a healthy cocktail for body and soul! Our Mediterranean home offers more than just charming suites with excellent sea and mountain views plus scrumptious breakfasts! Spend all or part of your holidays amid uniquely beautiful surroundings on our 8 ha property adjoining estuary and Tasman Bay, directly above Kina Beach.

Located on lovely and tranquil Kina Peninsula with its own golf course we are in the centre of many activities. Our area offers something exciting to every seeker! After a good night's sleep in our great European beds let your eyes do the walking from Abel Tasman to Kahurangi National Park, Rainbow Skifield, Richmond Ranges to the Marlborough Sounds. Nearby you find famous beaches with a variety of watersports, excellent fishing, inviting vineyards, arts and crafts.

Is your understanding of the true 'dolce vita" more like total relaxation? Perfect - enjoy quiet days on the peninsula! After a yummy breakfast with homemade goodies take the 5 minutes private bushwalk down to the beach, watch the large variety of birds, enjoy long walks. Our stunning pool invites you to float for ages! Shape up in the fitness room or relax in the sauna with a book and your favourite music from our library!

The cosy suites are equipped with stylish ensuites, tea making facilities, fridge, TV, phone and private balcony. Meals can be served by prior arrangement in the Mediterranean courtyard, the charming guest lounge with fireplace or ... by the pool in romantic setting.

For recharging your batteries we recommend the traditional German "Cure" spa treatments in our in-house clinic; enjoy the lasting effects of Moor-mud, loampacks, medical baths, oxygen therapy, Kneipp-water-treatments and massages. Prices $9-$25.

We welcome children above 10 years; exceptions during off-seasons can be arranged. During the last 14 years we have been working with tourists and patients in a German Spa Resort, and we enjoy to spoil you with our experience!

Our children are 10 and 20 years; a friendly family dog lives with us. Tariff includes great breakfast, tea and coffees, a "blue hour" drink (try the Pina Colada!), sauna and pick-up service from Motueka or Nelson airport. Special winter tariff available!

Tasman/Motueka
Boutique Accommodation/Self Contained Accommodation
Address: 58 Kina Peninsula Road,
RD 1, Tasman
Name: Baycrest Accommodation
Telephone: (03) 526 6233
Fax: (03) 526 6133
Email: baycrest@xtra.co.nz
Beds: 1 Queen, 2 Twin, 1 Single (3 bedrooms)
Bathroom: 1 Private, 1 Guests share.
Self Contained Accommodation - 2 single beds.
Tariff: B&B (full) Double $90-$130, Single $50-$70. Dinner by arrangement.
Visa/Mastercard. Not suitable for children under 12.
Nearest Town: Motueka 7km, Nelson 40 km

SUPERIOR ACCOMMODATION AT AFFORDABLE PRICES.
BAYCREST, with its outstanding location offers panoramic views towards the Abel Tasman National Park, the surrounding mountain ranges as well as Nelson, Richmond and the Motueka areas. BAYCREST is set on twelve acres of private land. The house is modern and spacious, which allows a magnificent view from every room. We have a separate lounge with library and sundeck for our guests with coffee and tea making facilities. There is a large swimming pool for you to relax by.For those guests wishing to go overnight tramping in one of Nelson's National parks, we provide lock up luggage storage.
We are close to some of New Zealand's best trout fishing rivers and are only a stone's throw away from beach and golf course. For guests wishing total independence, why not book into our self contained unit with full kitchen facilities.
SMOKEFREE INDOORS.

Motueka Valley
Country Homestay
Address: "The Kahurangi Brown Trout"
Westbank road, Pokororo, Motueka, R.D. 1
Name: Heather Lindsay & David Davies
Telephone: (03) 526 8736 **Fax**: (03) 526 8736
Email: katselig@xtra.co.nz
Beds: 2 King, 2 Single (2 bedrooms)
Bathroom: 2 Ensuite
Tariff: B&B (continental) Double $75, Single $55, Children under 12 half price, Dinner $25. NZ B&B Vouchers accepted
Nearest Town: Motueka (26km), Nelson (66km)

Comfortable country homestead situated on the banks of the beautiful Motueka River. On the doorstep of Kahurangi National Park, and within easy reach of Abel Tasman and Nelson Lakes National Parks. A multitude of recreation is at hand from lovely swimming holes, hiking, fishing (world-class brown trout territory), kayaking, rafting, horse-trekking, wine-trailing, or simply relaxing - we will be happy to facilitate. Large gardens overlooking pond and river. Private track through farm to spectacular views overlooking Motueka River, Mt Arthur, and out to sea.
Evening meals available by arrangement featuring organically home grown vegetables, fruit, local products, and NZ wines. Vegetarians or omnivores equally welcome! Smoking outdoors only.
There are one small dog and one cat in the household, and cattle, goats and ducks.
Directions: *2nd house downstream from Pearse River- Motueka River confluence. Approx. halfway (26km) between Motueka and Tapawera on the west bank of the Motueka River.*

Motueka Valley
Country Homestay
Address: "Doone Cottage", Motueka Valley Highway, R.D.1, Motueka
Name: Glen & Stan Davenport
Telephone: (03) 526 8740 **Fax**: (03) 526 8740 **Mobile**: (021) 707 055
Email: doone-cottage@xtra.co.nz
Beds: 1 King/Twin, 1 Double, 1 Single (2 bedrooms).
Garden Chalet: 1 Double, 1 Single
Bathroom: 3 Ensuite
Tariff: B&B (full) Double $110-$135, Single $80-$95, Dinner by arrangement,
Not suitable for children, Credit cards.
NZ B&B Vouchers accepted $25-$30 surcharge per person.
Nearest Town: Motueka (28 km), Nelson (64 km)

Homely hospitality, peace and tranquillity, trout fishing, beautiful garden and bush setting, native birds, household pets, goats, sheep, chickens, ducks and donkeys, weaving studio - all abound at Doone Cottage. A lovely 100 year old home, comfortably furnished cottage style in an attractive 4 acre setting of garden, native trees and ferns, lawns and shrubs, which have a beautiful outlook across the Motueka Valley to the Mt Arthur range. King, double and twin accommodation available each with own private verandah. Home cooked meals, home made bread, fresh garden vegetables, free range eggs etc. NZ wines are served with dinner.

Your hostess spins wool from the raw fleece and has her own weaving studio where you can see the finished garments, blankets, wallhangings, rugs etc.

There is much to interest the tourist and fisherman. The Motueka River is at the gate, with several others closeby, providing the opportunity to fish some of the best brown trout rivers in the South Island. Fishing licences and a local guide are available. Advance bookings are advisable. Wilderness trips can be arranged. Excellent day trips include 3 national parks, Abel Tasman, Nelson Lakes and Kahurangi, Kaiteriteri beaches, Golden Bay and Nelson.

This is one of New Zealand's main fruit producing regions where the sun shines over 2,400 hours annually. The region is rich in crafts of all descriptions.

We are very fortunate to live in this beautiful corner of New Zealand and have enjoyed sharing our family home and surroundings with visitors from all over the world for many years.

Home Page: http:/nz.com/webnz/bbnz/doone.htm
Directions: *From Motueka we are 28K on Motueka Valley H'way (old SH 61) heading south. From the south turn left off H'way 6 at Kohatu Hotel Motupiko, we are 28K from this junction on Motueka Valley H'way (old SH 61).*

R. Nank

Motueka

Boutique Accommodation
Address: Weka Road, Mariri, RD 2, Upper Moutere, Nelson
Name: Wairepo House
Telephone: (03) 526 6865 **Fax**: (03) 526 6101 **Mobile**: 025 357 902
Email: wairepo@xtra.co.nz
Beds: 4 Super King, 2 Single (4 bedrooms), Top suite sleeps 2-4.
Bathroom: 2 Ensuite, 1 Private
Tariff: B&B (special/full) Double $165-$210, Single $145-$165, valid to 1st Nov
99, Dinner $45pp by special arrangement only, Children under 12yrs half price,
Children under 5 no charge, each extra person $45, cot provided.
Credit Cards (VISA & M/C).
Nearest Town: Motueka 6km

*Wairepo House is a charming and tastefully decorated modern homestead enhanced
by a spacious garden setting, offering a hospitable welcome with a superb standard of
comfort and delicious food. Relax in privacy in the tranquil setting or be pampered in
one of our executive suites.*

*Upstairs suite comprises 2 bedrooms, double spa overlooking native fernery, kitchen-
ette, private lounge with library, open fire, with balconies, with views to Tasman Bay
mountain ranges beyond the estuary.*

*Middle suite has own private marble tile bathroom, private sun lounge with views of
garden and estuary. French doors open from bedroom to sundeck where alfresco
breakfast can be served at time of guest choosing.*

*Third well appointed suite set in garden has own private lounge, spa bath, kitchenette
with doors opening to garden and pool area.*

*Cobbled paths lead through established garden which attracts many native birds, to
tennis court beyond. Adjacent are 40 hectares of apple and pear orchard, 7,000 paeonie
tubers which flower from October - December.*

*We are only minutes from some of Nelson's beautiful beaches for swimming, walking
and windsurfing. 2 hours from Picton ferry.*

*Centrally placed to visit Abel Tasman and Kahuangi National Park, kayaking, wine
and craft trails. Excellent trout fishing with guides available.*

Directions: *On State Highway 60 Coastal Route to Motueka 40kms from Nelson, first
stone entrance right Weka Rd, 3kms from Tasman Township.*
Home Page: http://nz.com/webnz/bbnz/wairepo.htm

Motueka Valley
Farmstead & Self-contained Accommodation
Address: 'Mountain View Cottage',
Waiwhero Road, R.D.1, Motueka
Name: Veronica & Alan Hall
Telephone: (03) 526 8857
Beds: Cottage: 1 Double (1 bedroom),
Homestead: 1 Twin (1 bedroom)
Bathroom: 1 Private, 1 Ensuite
Tariff: B&B Double $65-$75, Single $45,
Dinner $20pp.
Credit cards. NZ B&B Vouchers accepted
Nearest Town: Motueka 18km

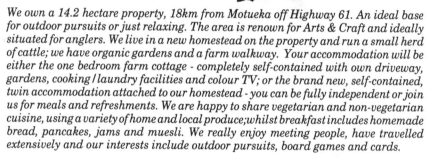

We own a 14.2 hectare property, 18km from Motueka off Highway 61. An ideal base for outdoor pursuits or just relaxing. The area is renown for Arts & Craft and ideally situated for anglers. We live in a new homestead on the property and run a small herd of cattle; we have organic gardens and a farm walkway. Your accommodation will be either the one bedroom farm cottage - completely self-contained with own driveway, gardens, cooking/laundry facilities and colour TV; or the brand new, self-contained, twin accommodation attached to our homestead - you can be fully independent or join us for meals and refreshments. We are happy to share vegetarian and non-vegetarian cuisine, using a variety of home and local produce;whilst breakfast includes homemade bread, pancakes, jams and muesli. We really enjoy meeting people, have travelled extensively and our interests include outdoor pursuits, board games and cards.

Motueka
Homestay B&B
Address: 15 North St, Motueka
Name: The Blue House
Telephone: (03) 528 6296
Beds: 1 Double, 2 Single (2 bedrooms)
Bathroom: 1 Guest share, 1 Family share
Tariff: B&B (full) Double $60, Single $40, Children under 5 free, 5-12 $10, over 12 adult price, Dinner $15. Credit cards. NZ B&B Vouchers accepted
Nearest Town: Motueka 2km

Our house, shared with one cat, is located on the beach in a quiet locality, with safe swimming, beautiful walks and an estuary which is a bird-watchers paradise, all within minutes of our gate. Secure off-street parking. Guest accommodation is an annexe comprising lounge, bathroom, two bedrooms and a private courtyard. Tea/coffee making facilities. Breakfast is shared with us in our house. No smoking inside. There are heaps of things to do in this area close to two national parks, catering for all interests. Explore this beautiful place by car, foot, kayak, horse-back etc or quietly enjoy the magic of golden beaches, sea and a myriad birds while we provide a comfortable friendly base for you. We have travelled widely ourselves and thoroughly enjoy meeting people from near or far away.
Directions: *At the southern roundabout in High St, turn into Wharf Road, continue straight into Everett St, at the end turn left into North St.*

Relax – Don't try to drive too far in one day.

Motueka

An Artist's Home.
Address: 240 Thorp Street, Motueka
Name: Copper Beech Gallery.
John and Carol Gatenby
Telephone: (03) 528 7456 **Fax**: (03) 528 7456
Beds: 1 Queen, 2 Single (2 bedrooms)
Bathroom: 2 Ensuite
Tariff: B&B (Special) Double $130, Single $90,
Credit Cards (MC/BC/VISA). NZ B&B Vouchers accepted $55 double surcharge,
$20 single surcharge, May-Oct
Nearest Town: Motueka 1km

EXPERIENCE elements in harmony.
TREAT yourself to a stay at the home of John R. Gatenby one of New Zealand's leading sea and landscape artists.ENJOY the welcoming ambience of John and Carols smokefree contemporary home and two acre garden with its hidden treasures. Both were designed with art and B&B in mind and overlook a bird and waterfowl sanctuary.BROWSE through the interior gallery which separates the living areas from the guest accommodation.RELAX in the privacy and comfort of your guest rooms, personalised with Carols artistic and whimsical touches.REFLECT on the stunning vistas to distant horizons. This is a generous home of light, space and tranquillity.....truly an artists home.INDULGE in Carols breakfasts......a culinary and visual delight. PAMPER yourself with complimentary beverages and refreshments from the guest fridge.Tea / Coffee making and full laundry facilities. On site gallery - painting tuition available.John, Carol and outdoor Abbi - a golden labrador
- take pleasure in the art of hospitality.

Motueka

Bed & Breakfast
Address: 259 Riwaka-
Kaiteriteri Rd,
R.D. 2, Motueka, Nelson
Name: "Seaview B&B"
Jackie & Tig McNab
Telephone: (03) 528 9341
Fax: (03) 528 9341
Beds: 1 Queen, 1 Double,
1 Single (2 bedrooms)
Bathroom: 1 Guests share
Tariff: B&B (continental) Double $75,
Single $50.
Nearest Town: Motueka 9km

Ideally located Jackie and Tig's coastal property is just 5 minutes to Kaiteriteri beach and handy to the Abel Tasman National Park. Set against a large area of private native bush with abundant bird life, we offer panoramic views of Tasman Bay with breathtaking sunrises and sunsets not to be missed. A secluded beach is a short stroll from the guest rooms which are situated at ground level. At your convenience a leisurely continental breakfast is served in the house dining room immediately above. With a lifetime of farming experience in this district we can provide a unique insight into local history and opportunities to explore the region. We offer you Kiwi hospitality and clean, comfortable accommodation. Bar and restaurant 4 mins. BBQ available.
Directions: *9 kms north of Motueka on Riwaka-Kaiteriteri Road. "Seaview B&B" sign on left at entrance.*

Motueka

Bed & Breakfast
Address: "Rosewood",
48 Woodlands Avenue, Motueka
Name: Barbara & Jerry Leary
Telephone: (03) 528 6750
Email: Barbara.Leary.Rosewood@xtra.co.nz
Beds: 1 Double, 2 Single (2 bedrooms)
Bathroom: 1 Ensuite, 1 Family share
Tariff: B&B (full) Double $75, Single $40, Children half price.
Credit Cards accepted.
Nearest Town: Motueka - 5 minute walk

*Hi, welcome to Rosewood, where our home is your home, a home away from home.
We are situated in private, peaceful surroundings 1km from the centre of Motueka.
Our rooms are tastefully decorated to meet your needs with a double bedroom upstairs
with small ensuite and one twin downstairs. The upstairs lounge and bedroom offer
magnificent views of the surrounding bush-covered mountains and is always warm
and cosy. Our interests include gardening, travel, music, golfing, fishing, hunting or
just enjoying a friendly chat with our guests over a cuppa or a complimentary glass of
sherry. Jasper our cat will be around to welcome you.*
*Motueka District has a myriad of attractions to offer. Beautiful Kaiteriteri, magnifi-
cent Abel Tasman National park, arts and crafts, some of the best wines in New
Zealand, a picturesque golf course, canoeing, trout fishing, hunting, boating, kayaking
and beautiful swimming beaches. Come indulge yourself.*
Directions: *Take second turning on right after the Clock Tower.*

Motueka

Self Contained Accommodation
Address: 430 High Street, Motueka
Name: Ashley Troubadour.
Coral and John Horton
Telephone: (03) 528 7318
Fax: (03) 528 7318
Beds: 2 Queen, 2 Double,
2 Single bunks (4 bedrooms)
Bathroom: 2 Ensuite, 2 Guests share
Tariff: B&B (continental) Double $70, Single $52, Ensuites Self Contained $75-
$85, Children $10. Mastercard/Visa NZ B&B Vouchers accepted
share bathroom facilities only
Nearest Town: Motueka (Town Centre 1km)

*Ashley Troubadour used to be a nunnery! Nowadays, it is used as a base into the
Kahurangi and Able Tasman National Parks or to Golden Bay. We provide friendly
hospitality and a personal service in a smokefree atmosphere. Also we are more than
happy to share our homegrown fruit and veges with our guests 'free' of charge. We have
full laundry facilities available for guests use. Ample off-street parking. Should you
be walking in one of the parks, we make sure you have a memorable day providing
suitable information and arranging bookings if required. Our rooms with ensuite are
near new, have a sunny verandah overlooking a lovely garden. They contain queensize
beds, TV, and coffee and tea making facilities. "It is all in MOT". "We have the Lot".
Restaurants, winebars, banks, good shopping, friendly people and "Ashley Troubadour". Going into the Able Tasman?? Stay in MOT and be right on the doorstep for an
early start.*

Motueka

Homestay
Address: Tri-angle Inn,
142 Thorp Street, Motueka
Name: Lesley and Daniel Jackson
Telephone: 03-528 7756
Mobile: 025-484 778
Email: Daniel.hdt@xtra.co.nz
Beds: 2 King, 4 Single (3 bedrooms)
Bathroom: 2 Ensuite

Tariff: B&B (special, continental) Double $95, Single $50.
Not suitable for small children.
Nearest Town: 1km from Motueka

We offer comfort at affordable prices and aim to help guests in having a wonderful holiday experience in Motueka. Our rooms are large and comfortable, each suite has its own private entrance and ensuite. Delicious, wholesome breakfasts can be enjoyed in guest rooms, outside on the sunny decks or in the large farm-house kitchen.
Our family are 'outdoors' people, who have tried and enjoyed the multitude of recreation facilities on offer in the area - kayaking, rafting, horse and llama trekking and of course we are in world famous Brown trout territory.
We are on the doorstep of the Kaharangi, Nelson Lakes and Abel Tasman National parks and very close to some beautiful beaches where we walk our two dogs.
At the end of the day sit and relax and watch the sun go down over the magnificent Mt Arthur Range.
Regrettably not suitable for small children. No smoking.

Motueka

Bed & Breakfast
Address: Bracken Hill B&B,
265 Riwaka Kaiteriteri Road, RD 2,
Motueka, Nelson
Name: Bracken Hill B&B.
Grace and Tom Turner
Telephone: (03) 528 9629 **Fax**: (03) 528 9629
Beds: 1 Queen, 1 Twin (2 bedrooms)
Bathroom: 2 Guests share.
Tariff: B&B (continental) Double $85-$90, Single $60.
Visa/Mastercard.   NZ B&B Vouchers accepted $25 surcharge
Nearest Town: Motueka 10 kms

We welcome you to enjoy and experience our modern home with marvellous views over Tasman Bay from D'Urville Island to Nelson and St Arnaud Range. The guest TV lounge and dining room (with tea / coffee making facilities) and two bedrooms have native bush, lagoon, and sea views. In the evening when the moon shines on the sea you would think you are half-way to heaven!! We are a few minutes from Tapu Bay, Stephens Bay, beautiful Kaiteriteri Beach and close to Kaharangi and Abel Tasman National Park. We would share with you our extensive knowledge of the Nelson, Golden Bay area, which has a diverse range of attractions to experience. From the guest lounge a large sun deck leads you to a natural rock garden for your relaxation and enjoyment, BBQ available. Our home is non smoking. We have a friendly Labrador Jake, who will greet you on arrival.
Directions: *2.65 kms from Cook Corner on Riwaka Kaiteriteri Road.*

Motueka

Homestay
Address: 184 Thorp Street, Motueka
Name: Ian and Rebecca Williams
Telephone: (03) 528 9385
Fax: (03) 528 9385
Mobile: (025) 480 466
Beds: 1 Queen, 1 Double, 2 Single (2 bedrooms)
Bathroom: 1 Ensuite, 1 Family share
Tariff: B&B (full) Double $60, Single $40, Children $15,
Dinner by arrangement.
Nearest Town: 50 km West of Nelson City.

Children are welcome to our home set on a two acre block with plenty of room to roam or spend time in the swimming pool. We have Major, the friendly family cat. We are 1.4 km to shopping centre and 1.2 km to a 18 hole golf course.
We have two bedrooms for guests, one upstairs has one queen size and one single bed with own ensuite and lounge. Downstairs one double and one single bed, guests share bathroom with us.
Motueka is the stop over place for visitors to explore Abel Tasman and Kahurangi National Parks, Golden Bay and Kaiteriteri golden sands beach is 10 km away.
Local attractions include Alpine and coastal walks, trout and sea fishing, boating and many interesting crafts and wine trails. Guided tours can be arranged. Motueka has New Zealand's best climate.
No Smoking inside please.

Riwaka, Motueka

Homestay
Address: 'Bridge House', 274 Main Road,
Riwaka, R.D.3, Motueka
Name: Alwynne & Joe Farrow
Telephone: (03) 528 6217 **Fax**: (03) 528 6217
Email: JoeFarrow@xtra.co.nz
Beds: 1 Double, 3 Single (3 bedrooms)
Bathroom: 1 Guests share, 1 Family share
Tariff: B&B (full) Double $70, Single $40, Children 50%,
Credit Cards. NZ B&B Vouchers accepted
Nearest Town: 3km north of Motueka

We welcome guests to share our comfortable home situated on State Highway 60, midway between Nelson and Takaka, with easy access to Kahurangi and Abel Tasman National Parks. We are centrally located for wineries, local artists and crafts people, just 10km from Kaiteriteri Beach and adjacent to the Motueka River - a popular whitebait and trout fishing venue. Our own interests include music, embroidery, tramping, gardening, woodworking and woodturning and we enjoy sharing these interests with others. We recommend evening dining out at any of the excellent licensed restaurants nearby. Our home is a non-smoking zone, but smokers may use the covered verandah off the lounge. We have no children at home and we have no animals.
Directions: *3km north of Motueka township, first house on right across the Motueka River Bridge on State Highway 60. (Watch for following traffic as you slow to turn in!)*

Riwaka Valley, Motueka

Self-contained Accommodation
Address: Riwaka Valley, R.D. 3, Motueka
Name: Lois & Kim Woods
Telephone: (03) 528 9267 **Fax**: (03) 528 9267
Beds: 2 Double, 2 Single (4 bedrooms)
Bathroom: 1 Private, 1 Guests share
Tariff: B&B (full) Double $70, Single $35, Campervans welcome
Nearest Town: Motueka 15km

We offer accommodation in a modern self-contained self service flat and in our own home where we have set aside the upstairs area as semi-private for guests. Kaiweka Farm is situated in the north branch of the Riwaka Valley adjacent to the scenic reserve at the Riwaka River source. We are close to the Abel Tasman National Park, Kaiteriteri Beach and beautiful walks.

The homestead and flat are situated in a large garden with BBQ area overlooking farmland and native bush. We run sheep, goats, and cattle and run an engineering business from the farm. Hobbies include weaving, spinning, gardening, yachting, boating, camping and walking. Our flat contains 2 rooms, sleeps 4, fully equipped with fridge, TV, microwave oven, electric blankets; - linen and towels supplied. $60 two people. A gas BBQ available.

Directions: *From Motueka follow Highway 60 to bottom of the Takaka Hill. Turn left at sign "Riwaka Valley" and continue on "North branch" towards "source of the Riwaka River". Kaiweka Farm is 7 km from Highway 60 and our sign is on the right of road.*

Kaiteriteri Beach, Nelson Bays

Homestay
Address: Bayview Terrace,
Kaiteriteri Heights
Name: Bayview Bed & Breakfast.
Aileen and Tim Rich
Telephone: (03) 527 8090
Fax: (03) 527 8090 **Mobile**: (025) 545 835
Beds: 1 Twin, 1 King (2 bedrooms)
Bathroom: 2 Private
Tariff: B&B (special) Double $120, Single $90, Dinner by arrangement.
Credit cards accepted.
Nearest Town: Motueka (10 mins by car) Nelson 60kms

Come and enjoy our hospitality at one of the sunniest and most beautiful areas of New Zealand.

Bayview is a new, architect-designed home with extensive terraces overlooking the sparkling blue waters and golden-sand beaches at the edge of the Abel Tasman National Park. Your beautifully decorated room has extensive views from inside and your private terrace. Each room has a comfortable area for sitting and relaxing, ensuite, fridge, tea/coffee making facilities, and all other conveniences such as laundry, hair dryers, phones, TV etc are available.

Cooked or special breakfast, featuring home made delights is served at your convenience on your terrace. A beautiful beach is only minutes walk away, you can walk to catch the boat to the Abel Tasman National Park. There are 3 restaurants within 5 minutes drive. Packed lunch, barbecue, or dinner by arrangement. Private boat trips, fishing, local history or gold panning trips with Tim are also available.

513

Marahau - adjacent to Abel Tasman National Park
Homestay+Self-contained Accom.
Address: 'Abel Tasman Stables'
Marahau Valley Road, R.D. 2 Motueka
Name: George Bloomfield
Telephone: (03) 527 8181 **Fax**: (03) 527 8181
Email: abel.tasman.stables.accom@xtra.co.nz
Beds: Homestay: 1 Queen, 2 Single (2 bedrooms) SC Cottage: 1 Double,
2 Single (2 bedrooms). SC Studio Units: 1 Double in each unit.
Bathroom: Homestay: 1 Ensuite, 1 Family share SC Cottage: 1 Private.
Studio Units: Ensuite
Tariff: Homestay B&B: Double &75 to $85, Single $55 includes continental breakfast.
Self contained cottage: $80 two persons, $10 each additional person. Continental
breakfast $7 per person. Studio Units: $85 Continental breakfast $7 per person. Cooked
breakfast $5 extra. Dinner $25 by arrangement. Credit Cards Visa/Mastercard. NZ
B&B Vouchers accepted $10 surcharge Dec-Apr.
Nearest Town: Motueka 18 Kms

Abel Tasman Stables accommodation situated alongside the very beautiful and popular Abel Tasman National Park offers a variety of accommodation, friendly NZ hospitality in extensive garden setting only five minutes walk to beach and Abel Tasman coastal track. The house situated on elevated site gives magnificent views of Tasman Bay and Marahau valley. Activities available in Marahau include sea kayaking, boat trips, swimming with seals, tramping or walking in the national park, fishing and gathering shellfish. Meals available at the licensed Park Cafe at the start of the coastal track or by arrangement with host.
Directions: *From Motueka travel north 18km following signs to Abel Tasman National Park Marahau. Marahau Valley Road is well signposted. The homestay property is up the first drive on the left.*

Marahau, Abel Tasman National Park
Self-contained Accommodation
Address: Beach Rd, Marahau, RD2 Motueka
Name: Robert Palzer
Telephone: (03) 527 8232 **Fax**: (03) 527-8211
Email: o.v.ch@xtra.co.nz
Beds: 8 Double (8 bedrooms)
Bathroom: 8 Ensuite
Tariff: B&B (full) Double $109-$119, Children $17. Accommodation only: $88-$98.
Credit cards accepted. NZ B&B Vouchers accepted, surcharge for Chalet with B&B:
$34.00, Chalet only: $13.00 - Studio with B&B: $24.00 - Studio only: no surcharge.
Nearest Town: 15km north of Motueka on SH60. Signposted to: Abel Tasman National
Park-Marahau.

Your hosts Robert and Constanca Palzer welcome you to the OCEAN VIEW CHALETS - right at the entrance to that beautiful ABEL TASMAN NATIONAL PARK. Located on a 20 ha coastal farm, slightly elevated you will find the natural timber Chalets, fully self-contained, with excellent panoramic views towards Tasman Bay, Fisherman Island, Marlborough Sounds, Durville Island and onto rural farm land. Each Chalet has a kitchen, ensuite bathroom, spacious living area, bedroom with view, balcony, TV phone, radio / clock. We offer also two double studio bedrooms with panoramic views, ensuite bathroom, coffee / tea making, phone, balcony. We will serve you a delicious and healthy breakfast (continental or traditional cooked) at our sunny main building or alternatively you can provide your own breakfast. Within walking distance you will find: Park Cafe-Restaurant, sea kayaking, horse trekking, water taxi, swim with seals and Marahau beach. We are looking forward to welcoming you at sunny Marahau.
Home Page: http://abel.tasman.chalets.webnz.com/

Takaka Hill - Motueka
Farmstay+Self-Contained Accom.
Address: Kairuru State Highway 60, Takaka Hill, Motueka
Name: David & Wendy Henderson
Telephone: (03) 528 8091/Freephone 0800-524 787
Fax: (03) 528 8091 **Mobile**: (025) 337 457
Email: kairuru@xtra.co.nz
Beds: Homestead: 1 Dble,1 Twn(2 bdrms):Kea Cttge:1 Dble,1 Twn,1 Attic(2 bdrms)Pipit Cttge:1Qun,1Twn(2bdrm)
Bathroom: Homestead: 1 Private. Cottages: Each has private bathroom.
Tariff: B&B (Full) Double $100, Extra person $20, Children under 5 free; Dinner $25 adult, with complimentary wine / beer, Children $10; Reduction for long stays and off season. Selfcatering: $80- 2 people - $10 extra person.
Credit cards (VISA/MC). NZ B&B Vouchers accepted $15 Surcharge
Nearest Town: Motueka 17km

Kairuru is a working hill country sheep and cattle farm of 4000 acres, nestled high on the unique Marble Mountain. Guests accommodation is offered in two fully equipped two bedroom cottages. Both cottages have wonderful sea views overlooking the Abel Tasman National Park. We are ideally situated to explore both Golden Bay and the Abel Tasman National Park. The wooden cottages - exclusively yours, are modern and comfortable with sittingroom, telephone, TV, electric blankets, kitchen and laundry. A good selection for breakfast is supplied and made by yourselves. Peaceful and relaxing, your accommodation is completely private yet close to our home for dinner and socialising. Our home is set in an established attractive garden with swimming pool and many native birds. You are welcome to join in on farming activities or to stroll around the farm.

We look forward to your company and we will do our very best to ensure your stay is enjoyable.

Directions: *From Motueka take the road to Takaka (State Highway 60). Kairuru is 17km from Motueka on the right hand side of the road.*
Home Page: http://webnz.com/kairuru

Patons Rock, Takaka

Farmstay
Address: Patons Rock Road, Takaka
Name: Patondale
Telephone: (03) 525 8262/
Toll Free: 0800 306 697
Fax: (03) 525 8262
Beds: 1 Double, 2 Single (2 bedrooms)
Bathroom: 1 Private (we take one party at a time).
Tariff: B&B (full) Double $100, Single $70, Children $20, Dinner $20.
Nearest Town: Takaka 10km, Collingwood 17km

A BAY BEAUTY.

IMAGINE! Waking to the sounds of the waves breaking on the beach below, enjoy a leisurely stroll along our long sandy beach and then taste a "real farmers" breakfast with us using farm fresh produce. We are CENTRALLY situated for all Golden Bay attractions.

Our architecturally designed home nestled above Patons Rock beach offers "SIMPLY MAGIC" 360 degree views and is well appointed for your comfort.

Our 200 acre Dairyfarm allows you the chance to see a modern dairying operation in action. We have interests in travel, gardening and local government and are non smokers.

David, Vicki and Hayden INVITE YOU to be our guest at "Patondale" where we offer genuine Kiwi hospitality, peace and tranquillity.

Directions: *Turn off at Patons Rock sign on SH60, 10km from Takaka township enroute to Collingwood. E.S. No 197*

Takaka

Self-contained Accommodation
Address: 'Amanzi', Rangihaeata Road, R.D.2, Takaka
Name: Barbara & John Dunn
Telephone: (03) 525 9615
Fax: (03) 525 9678
Mobile: (025) 247-0378
Beds: 2 Single, Divan bed in living area (1 bedroom)
Bathroom: 1 Private
Tariff: B&B (full) Double $75, Single $45, $70 stays 3 nights or more.
Credit cards accepted. NZ B&B Vouchers accepted
Nearest Town: Takaka 6 kms

Our two-acre property is situated above the Takaka Estuary where we are privileged to enjoy one of the most spectacular views in Golden Bay. We enjoy travel but love to return here to our cat, our garden and our seaside lifestyle. For our guests we have a self-contained wing-bedroom, bathroom and living room with a well-equipped kitchen area. This gives the option of preparing light meals as an alternative to going out each night to one of Takaka's wide range of eating places, and allows a self-catering option (Discount tariff). We aim to provide a comfortable base for guests while they explore Golden Bay: beautiful wild beaches, walking tracks, limestone caves, boat trips, restaurants in remote places, art and craft trails. Weary guests can sit on the deck and gaze at the view! Breakfast full or continental as requested. No smoking inside, please.
Directions: *Please phone.*

Takaka 1, Golden Bay
Self-contained Cottage
Address: 'Rocklands Cottage',
c/o Robin Robilliard, "Rocklands",
R.D. Takaka 1, Golden Bay, Nelson
Name: Robin Robilliard
Telephone: (03) 525 9051
Fax: (03) 525 9065
Beds: 2 Queen,
1 Single (2 bedrooms)
Bathroom: 1 Ensuite
Tariff: Self-contained cottage: $80 a night.
Continental breakfast $10 per person, only if requested.
Nearest Town: Takaka 10km, Pohara Beach with store,
restaurant and cafe 1km.

Five-year old Cottage built in charming, pioneer style, in a totally private and secluded native-bush setting, with own grass clearing, native bird songs and view over Golden Bay. Fully furnished, chintzy style, including TV, electric blankets, linen. Popular with honeymooners and romantics of all ages. The cottage is on a sheep farm, 300m out of sight of homestead, 4 minutes drive from the golf course end of Pohara Beach. What guests say: "A honeymoon paradise","a fantastic place","a superb balance of relaxation and adventure in New Zealand's best kept secret","we don't want to leave","you go the extra mile to give us tourist information". N.B.If this is not sought, guests are left totally in peace. Takaka township 5 miles. General store, superb restaurant and a cafe/bar 1 km at Pohara Beach.

Takaka
Bed & Breakfast and Self contained accommodation
Address: "Rose Cottage", Hamama Rd, R.D.1,
Takaka, Golden Bay
Name: Phil & Margaret Baker
Telephone: (03) 525 9048
Beds: 1 King/Queen,
2 Single (2 bedrooms)
Bathroom: 1 Guests share
Tariff: B&B (continental)
Double $70, Single $45.
Self contained Double $75-$95,
$15 extra person.
Credit Cards.
Nearest Town: Takaka 5km

Rose Cottage, much loved home of Phil and Margaret is situated in the beautiful Takaka Valley 103km from Nelson and 5km before Takaka township. Set on 2 1/2 acres amongst mature totara trees with bush and mountain views, the perfect place from which to explore this peaceful area of New Zealand. The two room Bed & breakfast was refurbished last year, the furniture being made by Phil in his craft workshop. The three self contained units which are separate from Rose Cottage have full kitchens, quality furnishings and private sun decks.
The 12 metre indoor solar heated swimming pool is available to all guests.
Phil and Margaret have travelled extensively on photographic and mountaineering expeditions around the world, other interests include natural history, gardening, arts & crafts, and helping to make their guests stay a memorable one.

Takaka, Golden Bay

Homestay
Address: 177 Commercial Street Takaka
Name: "Haven House"
Telephone: (03) 525 9554 **Fax**: (03) 525 8720
Beds: 1 Queen, 3 Single (2 bedrooms)
Bathroom: 1 Guests share, 1 Family share
Tariff: B&B (full/continental) Double $70-$85 , Single $50, Triple $95,
(off season May to October Double $60, Single $40), Dinner $15pp on request.
Credit Cards. NZ B&B Vouchers accepted
Nearest Town: Takaka - 400m from township

Haven House, centrally located, situated 10 minutes walk from shops / cafes and all amenities, has been our home and 'haven' for many years. My grown family are now away enjoying life elsewhere. We have always loved travelling and meeting new people and have decided to share with you the tranquillity and comforts of our home for your pleasure. The guest lounge (TV) and dining room overlooks the established secluded garden. A barbeque area, (crockery etc supplied) is available. Enjoy grapefuit from our trees and other 'home' goodies for your breakfast. Complimentary afternoon teas in the garden. (Winter time in front of a cosy fire. Bedrooms have electric heating, beds electric blankets. Golden Bay enjoys moderate winter temperatures.)

A courtesy vehicle pick up service to aerodrome and bus depot is available. Day tours by arrangement. Notification and bookings for accommodation recommended.

My aim is personal service and hospitality, endeavouring to make your stay a memorable one. Looking forward to meeting you.
Your Host
Pam Peacock

Takaka

Homestay
Address: "Halcyon Homestay",
Rangihaeata Rd, PO Box 21, Takaka
Name: Bev & Jock Harrison
Telephone: (03) 525 8125
Fax: (03) 525 8127
Beds: 1 Queen, 1 Single (2 bedrooms)
Bathroom: 1 Private
(we take one party at a time)
Tariff: B&B (full/continental) Double $70,
Single $45, Children half price.
Credit Cards NZ B&B Vouchers accepted
Nearest Town: Takaka 5 kms

Sited on ten acres just 5km from Takaka township, Halcyon homestay overlooks Golden Bay and the Takaka estuary with its myriads of birds. Here we enjoy a relaxed, rural lifestyle with a couple of cats, a few ducks, sheep and resident pukeko.

The guest accommodation has quality beds (one queen size and one extra length single with a choice of feather or fibre pillows), a private bathroom and a sitting room with television and tea / coffee making facilities.

Our interests include tramping, weaving and photography and gardening. We have a good knowledge of the Bay and we are happy to offer advice on what to see and how to get there.

Directions: *Rangihaeata Road, emergency No. 44. Phone for detailed directions.*

Pohara, Takaka
Bed & Breakfast
Address:
Name: Bay Vista House
Telephone: (03) 525 9772 **Fax**: (03) 525 9772
Beds: 2 Queen, 1 King (3 bedrooms)
Bathroom: 3 Ensuite
Tariff: B&B (continental) Double from $130, Singles from $90, Suite available from $180. Dinner by prior request
(Local cuisine prominent) $36, Credit Cards (Visa/Mastercard).
NZ B&B Vouchers accepted 2 vouchers for rooms, 3 vouchers for Suite.
Nearest Town: Takaka 10km

Bay Vista House is easy to locate. Situated up on an elevated section above Pohara Beach and Camping ground. This new accommodation has spectacular views out to Collingwood and across to Farewell Spit. A native bush reserve to the right of the house gives you wonderful bird life and a chance to meander through the lush undergrowth. A spa pool set in the garden is available for our guests to use.
If you have boating or fishing on your mind Tarakohe is just around the corner. Golf course and Tennis Court is only a minute away by car.
These new bedrooms are spacious with TV and armchairs, each room has its own ensuite and spectacular views making outdoor living a must on this particular site. Tea and coffee is available at all time in the guest separate entrance area.
A suite is available with your own lounge, TV and private outdoor area, tea / coffee facilities. We are happy to do honeymoon packages or local scenic travel arrangements. Laundry is also available to our guests.
We regret that this accommodation is not suitable for children under 12.

Directions: *We are seven minutes from Takaka following Abel Tasman Drive to Pohara. We are sign posted at the corner of Marina Restaurant & Bar Pohara. Come and enjoy all the beauty that Golden Bay has to offer.*

Please help us provide the best hospitality in the world.
Fill in a comment form for every place you stay.

Takaka, Golden Bay

Homestay
Address: Croxfords Homestay Dodson Road,
RD 1 Takaka, Golden Bay
Name: Pam and John Croxford
Telephone: (03) 525 7177 **Fax**: (03) 525 7177
Email: croxfords@xtra.co.nz
Beds: 2 Double, 2 Single (3 bedrooms)
Bathroom: 1 Ensuite, 1 Guests share
Tariff: B&B (full) Double $70, Single $50. Dinner $20.
Children under 5 free of charge.
Visa/Mastercard/Bankcard. NZ B&B Vouchers accepted
Nearest Town: Takaka 2 km

Pam and John would like to welcome you to our spacious modern home in a peaceful rural setting overlooking the Kahurangi National Park.Golden Bay offers many activities and crafts; we enjoy assisting visitors make the most of their time here. We are close to the beautiful beaches of the Bay, and our two magnificent National Parks, Kahurangi and Abel Tasman. Pam loves cooking, using fruit and vegetables from our garden. She enjoys catering for special diets, our substantial breakfasts include home-made bread, muesli, yoghurt, marmalade and jams. In summer we often have evening barbecues.Our library has many New Zealand books available for browsing in the peaceful guests' lounge. We have no children at home, nor pets, but we do have an alpaca! We ask guests not to smoke inside.We also operate Kahurangi Guided Walks specialising in walks for all ages and levels of fitness.
Directions: *Turn left at the 1st or 2nd junction (both Dodson Rd) after Paynes Ford bridge, 2 km before Takaka*

Takaka

Homestay
Address: Central Takaka Road,
RD 1, Takaka
Name: Baytime Manor
Telephone: (03) 525 8551
Beds: 1 Queen (1 bedroom)
Bathroom: 1 Private

Tariff: B&B (full) Double $105 (November 1 - April 3).
Double $80 (May 1 - October 31). NZ B&B Vouchers accepted $34 surcharge Nov 1 - Apr 30. $20 surcharge May 1 - Oct 31)
Nearest Town: Takaka (2.5 kms)

We look forward to welcoming you to our home and helping you switch to 'baytime'! Our beautiful 1880's homestead has been lovingly renovated and we offer our upper living area being a large comfortable double room and private bathroom. Baytime Manor is set in a lovely developing garden which includes a huge variety of fruit trees which we hope you will enjoy. A swim in the pool or a game of Petanque on the lawn are great ways to end the day. We are close to Takaka township and are centrally located to many of Golden Bay's pleasures including stunning scenery, great walks, arts and crafts, fishing, golden sand beaches and freshwater swimming holes. Joe, Dee, Sarah (aged 6 years), Kobe the dog (occasionally) and Darmah the cat will be happy to help you discover the best the Bay has to offer and make your stay special. Sorry but there's no smoking in the Manor.
Directions: *After crossing Paynes Ford bridge on your way into Takaka, turn right at the 1st junction by the Community Hospital on to Central Takaka Road & we are 200 metres up on the left.*

Takaka, Golden Bay
Beachfront Bed & Breakfast
Address: "Beach House",
Patons Rock Beach, Takaka, Golden Bay
Name: Lesley & Murray McIver, & Iain (aged 12 yrs)
Telephone: 03-525 8133
Mobile: 025-302 729
Beds: 1 Super King or 2 Single (1 bedroom)
Bathroom: 1 Ensuite
Tariff: B&B (full) Double $100, Single $80.
Surcharge $20 may apply Dec, Jan.
Nearest Town: Takaka 11 km, Collingwood 18 km.

Patons Rock is a north facing beach within the beautiful sheltered waters of Golden Bay. Great for swimming, walking, fishing, beach combing or just sitting in the sun on your own terrace. Your room is well appointed, right on the beach, with space to relax and have the kind of holiday you would usually have to travel overseas for. Sit in bed and watch the tide come and go, or the moon reflecting on the water - this is truly a magic place. We offer peace and privacy in quality surroundings. We enjoy a wide variety of interests including gardening, embroidery and handcrafts, kayaking, walking, fishing, and share our home with our three beautiful cats.
Lesley and Murray both enjoy cooking and will provide a full and varied breakfast menu.
Guests are welcome to smoke outside. We are happy to collect you from the airport or bus station.

Takaka
Homestay
Address: 9 Waitapu Rd, Takaka,
Golden Bay
Name: Cate's Bed & Breakfast
Telephone: (03) 525 8888 (evening) or
(03) 525 9419 (work)
Beds: 2 Queen (2 Bedrooms)
Bathroom: 2 Ensuite
Tariff: B&B (special) Double $120, Single $80,
Children $40, Credit Cards.
Nearest Town: Takaka 1km (10-15 min walk)

I'd like to welcome you to Golden Bay, and my old Villa home, which I have recently renovated, keeping in style with the house. Originally built in 1912 and used as a Parsonage, the rooms are spacious, with their own open fire places and ensuites, to add to your comfort.
Why not relax on the verandah, sipping on a glass of wine, served with New Zealand made cheeses, pate and crackers, or enjoy my homemade treats with tea or coffee. A very private and tranquil place to be.
Having travelled a great deal myself, breakfast is a great start to any day and I offer a healthy one at that, consisting of home-made granola, fresh fruit, omlettes, potatoes, muffins, juice, tea or coffee. The choice is yours.
Picnic baskets are available upon request.
Within walking distance to shops, restaurants and cafes.

Takaka and Collingwood

Homestay, Self Contained Accommodation
Address: Tukurua RD 2, Takaka
Name: Golden Bay Lodge and Garden.
Ray and Mary Nelson
Telephone: (03) 525 9275
Fax: (03) 525 9275
Beds: 3 Queen, 2 Single (4 bedrooms)
Bathroom: 3 Private
Tariff: B&B (full) Double $120, Single $80, Dinner $25 by arrangement,
Children $35. No pets.
Nearest Town: Collingwood 10 km, Takaka 18 km.

*We have recently purchased "Elliotts Garden" and are pleased to welcome you to
"Golden Bay Lodge and Garden".*

*We offer you 10 acres of piece and tranquillity with the best views of Golden Bay taking
in Fairwell Spit to Separation Point and Durville Island.*

*Quality self contained and B&B accommodation is available with panoramic views
from well appointed and comfortable cliff top units, twenty metres from the beach
front.Walk down the pathway to the sandy beach and enjoy all that Golden Bay has
to offer or spend time strolling among acres of magnificent rhododendrons, azaleas
and camellias in the company of Tuis and other native birds. 100 old fashion roses
have recently been added to the garden.*

*We are handy to all of Golden Bay's many attractions and are happy to help with any
tourist information you may require.*

*We look forward to your visit, where we are sure your expectations will be exceeded.
Non smokers preferred.*

Collingwood (Village)

Homestay
Address: Collingwood Homestead,
Elizabeth Street, Collingwood, Golden Bay
Name: Adrian & Maggie Veenvliet
Telephone: (03) 524 8079 **Fax**: (03) 524 8979
Beds: 2 King, 1 Queen, 2 Single (4 bedrooms)
Bathroom: 3 Ensuite, 1 Private
Tariff: B&B (special) Double $125-$150, Single $95-$125, Dinner $35 includes
pre-dinner drink & wine, Credit Cards (VISA/Mastercard/Bankcard).
Nearest Town: Collingwood (we are in the village)

Welcome to Collingwood Homestead.

*At the top of our drive you will find our "Slice of Paradise". Our beautifully renovated
colonial style home is situated in an unbeatable location, overlooking the Aorere River
Estuary and mountain range. Enjoy the ever-changing views from an easy chair!
Enjoy the romance and elegance, with good food, candle light, an open fire, antiques
and flowers everywhere. We aim to recapture the gracious lifestyle that most people
have forgotten. So come and stay and let us pamper you.*

We regret our home is not suitable for children.

Collingwood

Bed & Breakfast
Address: Hakea Hill House, Para Para, Collingwood, Golden Bay
Postal: P O Box 35, Collingwood, Golden Bay
Name: Vic & Liza Eastman
Telephone: (03) 524 8487. From USA: 011-64-3-524 8487 **Fax**: (03) 524 8487
Email: vic.eastman@clear.net.nz
Beds: 2 Double, 6 Singles (3 bedrooms).
Bathroom: 1 Guests share
Tariff: B&B (special) Double $100, Single $75, Children $35 each.
Nearest Town: Takaka 20Kms /Collingwood 10 Kms

Hakea Hill House, built above an estuary behind Para Para Beach, has views that encompass Para Para Peak and the Wakamarama Ranges to the South, Farewell Spit to D'Urville Island beyond Separation Point over Golden Bay, and to Mount Taranaki on the North Island. The house is modern and spacious with a hint of Southwest and New Mexico style. Two guest rooms have large balconies. Both American and New Zealand electric outlets are installed. Television and tea or coffee in guest rooms and telephone and Fax and modem access are available at all times. Vic is a practising physician specialising in Family Practice and Emergency Medicine. His hobbies include astronomy; guests are welcome to explore the magnificent Southern skies with Questar 3.5 and Odyssey 17.5 inch telescopes weather permitting. Liza, besides homemaker, community activist, and expert cook, is interested in sailing, horse riding, machine quilting and wearable art. We have three adult children, five computers, two outdoor dogs, and thirty five hectares of hills and trails. Golden Bay is well worth the effort of a visit. The best weather is late summer and autumn. One may fly from Wellington for the weekend with Takaka Valley Air Services (Telephone 0800 501 901) or drive from Nelson (two hours) to explore Farewell Spit, Kaihoka Lakes, Aorere gold fields, limestone caves, Waikoropupu Springs, Settlers' Museums, pottery and craft outlets, wild West Coast or serene Bay beaches, mudflats and estuaries, scenic light plane flights, pony trekking, golf, Bay and estuary sailing, canoeing, river rafting, fishing, scalloping and whitebaiting in season, bush walks.
No smoking in the house please.
Directions: *Reservations are necessary. Please telephone in person for reservations and detailed directions.*

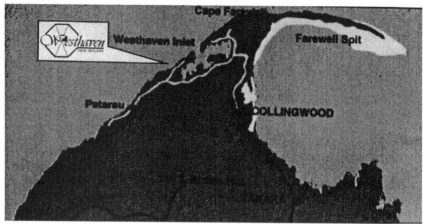

Westhaven

Retreat
Address: Te Hapu Road, Collingwood
Name: Westhaven Retreat
Telephone: (03) 524 8354 **Fax**: (03) 524 8354 **Mobile**: (025) 220 3941
Email: Westhaven.Retreat@xtra.co.nz
Beds: 3 King, 1 Queen, 4 Single (5 bedrooms)
Bathroom: 2 Ensuite, 1 Guests share, 1 Family share
Tariff: B&B (full) Double $118, Single $35-$85, Dinner by arrangement.
Credit Cards.
Nearest Town: Collingwood 30km

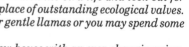

Westhaven Retreat invites you to take a break and relax on our Peninsula. Overlooking the Tasman Sea and the complete Westhaven Inlet, which is the second largest estuary in the South Island. There are 800 acres of unspoiled wilderness for you to explore to leave you breathless. Take a stroll on the beach, swim, fish or discover beautiful rock formations, caves, palm groves and rainforests. Watch the bird life and look out for seals and dolphins. Westhaven is a very special place of outstanding ecological valves. Enjoy a guided eco-tour in total comfort with our gentle llamas or you may spend some quality time with them.

It is a place of complete relaxation in a brand new house with an ever-changing view. Tranquillity and peace with a variety of delicious meals make you forget the stress of daily life.

Bruno and Monika will do their utmost to make you feel at home. For friendly and old fashioned European hospitality you have come to the right place.

Directions: *Please phone, fax or email for reservations. Pick up can be arranged.*

Pakawau Beach, Collingwood

Homestay+Self-contained Accom.
Address: Pakawau Beach, Collingwood R.D. Golden Bay
Name: Val & Graham Williams
Telephone: (03) 524 8168
Beds: 1 Double, 1 Single (1 bedroom)
Bathroom: 1 Family share, Spa available.
Tariff: B&B (full) Double $75, Single $60, Dinner $20.
NZ B&B Vouchers accepted All year.
Nearest Town: Collingwood 12km

We are the northern most bed and breakfast accommodation in the South Island, 9km from Farewell Spit. We are on the beachfront with views from Separation Point to Farewell Spit with a safe swimming beach only metres from our front door. We offer self contained accommodation with a base rate of $70 per night.

We are keen gardeners and grow most of our vegetables. Local seafoods available eg. whitebait, scallops, cockles. We have lived here for fourteen years and can advise or guide you to the 'Beauties of the Bay'.

The Farewell Spit Safari and Westhaven Mail Scenic Run will pick you up from our gate. We are handy to Wharariki Beach, Kaihoke Lakes, Te Anaroa Caves, Heaphy Track and Pupu Springs. A licensed cafe and tennis court are within walking distance. We are non smokers who enjoy walking, biking and swimming. Our two children have left home but not our cats. We look forward to meeting people and sharing our lifestyle.

Nelson Lakes

Country Stay
Address: Korere/Tophouse Road, Kikiwa, Nelson
Name: Kikiwa Homestead
Telephone: (03) 521 1020 **Fax**: (03) 521 1021
Beds: 1 Queen, 2 Twin (3 bedrooms)
Bathroom: 3 Ensuites
Tariff: B&B (full) Double $140, single $90,
Dinner $35.
Credit Cards: Eftpos/Diners/Amex
Nearest Town: Nelson70km, Blenheim 100km,
Murchison 50km, St Arnaud 20km

Nestled in the lovely Kikiwa Valley and surrounded by rivers, mountains and farm land, this 1914 homestead glows with native timbers milled on the property. Kikiwa is ideally situated close to the many activities and magnificent scenery of the Nelson Lakes: boating, fishing, tramping, horse trekking, alpine flora / fauna, gold panning tours, climbing, kayaking, skiing, hunting, white water rafting. A short ride in any direction will have you fishing in the rivers and lakes for which NZ South Island has become famous.

Enjoy relaxing on our verandahs and soaking in the peace and tranquility of Kikiwa. We have planted lavender for commercial oil production (13,000 plants) and we are anticipating a visual feast in summer. Kikiwa is fully licensed, smoke free, not suitable for children. Our aim is to make your stay everything you could wish for with friendly hospitality, fresh country cuisine and top quality accommodation.
KIWI HOST. FARM AND HOME HOSTS

Tophouse
Historic, Farmstay and Self Contained cottages
Address: Tophouse, R.D.2, Nelson
Name: Melody & Mike Nicholls
Telephone: Freephone/fax 0800 Tophouse (867468) **Fax**: (03) 521 1848
Beds: 4 Cottages: 1 Double, 2/3 Singles (2 Bedrooms). Homestay: 1 Queen, 1 Double, 6 Single (4 Bedrooms).
Bathroom: Cottages: Private. Homestay: 3 Guests share
Tariff: B&B (continental) $35/Adult, Dinner $20, Children double age plus $10. Cottages $80/2 Adults plus $10/Extra, $8/Child. Credit cards.
Nearest Town: Blenheim 98 km, Murchison 57 km, Nelson 72 km, St Arnaud 9 km.

We, Melody and Mike Nicholls, with our young sons and two cats, invite you to share our unique home with its huge open fires, lovely setting and homely atmosphere.
Tophouse, a cob (mud) building, dating from the 1880's when it was a hotel, and reopened in 1989 as a Farm Guest House, has that 'good old days' feel about it.
Situated on 300 ha (730 acres) of picturesque high country farm running cattle, with much native bush and an abundance of bird life, a popular holiday spot for its peace and beauty, bush walks, fishing, and in the winter serves the two local ski fields. Tophouse is only 9 km from St Arnaud, gateway to Nelson Lakes National Park.
A typical farmhouse dinner is taken with the family and since the fire's going, 'real' toast for breakfast.
Cottages are 2 bedroom, fully self contained, with great views of the surrounding mountains.

Directions: *Just off State Highway 63 between Blenheim and Murchison and 9 km from St Arnaud is Tophouse, that's us! The area took its name from the building. If travelling from Nelson, leave State Highway 6 at Belgrove and travel towards St Arnaud, we're signposted from the main road and looking forward to your visit.*

St Arnaud

Homestay
Address: St Arnaud Homestays,
C/- Counter Post, St Arnaud, Nelson
Name: Colin & Jill Clarke
Telephone: (03) 521 1028 **Fax**: (03) 521 1028
Email: c-clarke@st-arnaud.co.nz
Beds: 3 Queen, 2 Single (3 bedrooms)
Bathroom: 2 Ensuite, 1 Private
Tariff: B&B (full) Double $85-$105, Single $65.
Dinner $25 (by prior arrangement). Credit cards.
Nearest Town: Blenheim and Nelson each about 1 hour travelling.

Our beautiful timbered home, warm and private, is set amidst native forest with a 3 minute walk to Lake Rotoiti (one of NZ's most beautiful and unspoiled lakes), Nelson Lakes National Park. The home affords lovely views of surrounding forests and mountains. Native birds abound. We offer superior accommodation and varied cuisine. Game meats (Colin is the hunter) may be served with quality NZ wines. Vegetarians also catered for. Guests may simply relax in comfort, enjoy the Park, or select one of Colin's highly acclaimed eco-activities and adventures. Colin operates St Arnaud Eco-Activities and Adventures. As a former ecologist, well versed in natural history, he has an extensive local knowledge. His 4WD alpine flora and fauna tours provide unparalleled access to the mountain summits, for any age or ability. A range of guided activities include nature walks, treks, historical and scenic 4WD tours (e.g. Molesworth), and gold prospecting. We warmly welcome you to our lifestyle hideaway.
Home Page: http://www.ts.co.nz./~c-clarke
Directions: *At St Arnaud, turn off at Black Valley Stream Bridge, into Bridge Street. We are at the first intersection.*

Mangles Valley, Murchison

Farmstay+Self-contained Accom.
Address: 'Green Hills Farm',
Mangles Valley, Murchison
Name: Margaret & Henry Rouse
Telephone: (03) 523 9067
Beds: 4 Single (2 bedrooms)
Bathroom: 1 Private (Cottage), 1 Family share (separate shower)
Tariff: B&B (continental) Double $80, Single $50, Dinner $20pp.
NZ B&B Vouchers accepted $10 Surcharge
Nearest Town: 5kms North Murchison SH6. 7kms up Mangles Valley on sealed road.

We welcome you to our hill country sheep and beef farm set in the beautiful Mangles Valley. We have hosted overseas and New Zealand visitors for many years and all have appreciated the beauty and relaxed atmosphere.
There is excellent trout fishing, and gold-panning in the Mangles River below the house. We are within close proximity of a nine-hole golf course (clubs available), horse trekking, white water rafting and kayaking. We are surrounded by native bush, beautiful rivers and peaceful bush walks.
We are still actively farming, have travelled overseas several times, love meeting people and welcoming them to our home and lovely garden. We are involved in community affairs - Lions, W.D.F.F. and S.P.E.L.D. teaching.
Breakfast includes home-made muesli, fresh fruits from the garden, local honey, home-made marmalade and farm eggs if wanted.. All vegetables home grown.
A very comfortable self-contained cottage (can sleep 4) is also available - includes colour TV, wood-burner. This is ideal for a longer stay.
Directions: *Please phone.*

Gowanbridge, Murchison

Homestay
Address: Dizzy's Corner,
Gowanbridge, R.D.3, Murchison
Name: Heather Davis & Gordon Trotter
Telephone: (03) 523 9678
Fax: (03) 523 9678
Email: dizzycorner@xtra.co.nz
Beds: 1 Queen, 1 Double, 1 Single (3 bedrooms)
Bathroom: 1 Guests share
Tariff: B&B (full) Double $100, Single $50, Children negotiable, Dinner $30pp,
Campervans welcome. NZ B&B Vouchers accepted $30 surcharge (double)
Nearest Town: Murchison, 30km south on SH6

We invite you to share the quiet beauty of our 40 acre farmlet which has magnificent native bush and the Buller river as its boundaries.

Gowanbridge was the end of the now defunct Nelson line and our home, converted from a railway's goods shed is solid, warm and comfortable. Guests bedrooms, bathroom and separate lounge are upstairs. No smoking indoors please. Delicious breakfasts and evening meals are prepared from fresh local food, some home grown.

Semi retired, we enjoy golf and fishing. Gordon's interests include car racing and yachting; Heather's gardening and cooking. As well as sheep we have friendly ducks, pet goat and Jess, our bearded collie. Along the woodland track beside the river, native birds abound.

Excellent trout fishing (guides available), bushwalking, rafting, kayaking, goldpanning, horse trekking and hunting are some of the local outdoor activities available. Nelson Lakes National Park is closeby.

Directions: *Please phone.*

Murchison

Farmstay
Address: 'Awapiriti', Highway 65,
Maruia Valley,
Private Bag, Murchison
Name: Irene & David Free
Telephone: (03) 523 9466
Fax: (03) 523 9777
Beds: 1 Double, 2 Single (2 bedrooms)
Bathroom: 2 Ensuite
Tariff: B&B (continental/full) Double $95,
Single $70, Dinner $25pp.
Nearest Town: Murchison 17km

At Awapiriti, we farm elk, deer, bison, cattle and sheep. Set in a bush-clad valley the homestead is complimented by extensive lawns and gardens with native birds and peacocks adding a special touch. Guests are welcome to take a casual bush or farm walk and visit the glow-worms after dark. The beautiful Maruia River which bounds the farm offers fishing and swimming. The guest bedrooms are sunny and attractively decorated in colonial style with fluffy duvets, electric blankets and ensuites for comfort. Dinner is by arrangement (3 course) and may consist of goodies like wildpork, venison, lamb or chicken. Our vegetables are freshly picked and organically grown. Great care is taken to provide healthy country meals with a flair. Breakfast is full or continental with fresh fruit and home-made bread. This is a lovely informal time to further friendships already made. Conveniently placed we are 3 hours approximately from the Cook Strait ferry, Christchurch or Hokitika. A cheerful wood fire will await you on cold days. Awapiriti is a haven for adults unsuitable for children. Please phone ahead.

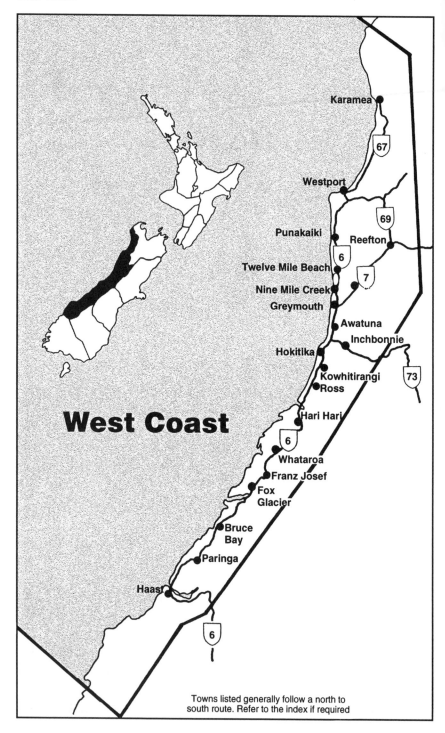

Karamea

67

Westport

69

Punakaiki   Reefton

6

Twelve Mile Beach   7

Nine Mile Creek
Greymouth

Awatuna
Inchbonnie

Hokitika

Kowhitirangi   73
Ross

Hari Hari

6

Whataroa

Franz Josef

Fox
Glacier

Bruce
Bay

Paringa

Haast

6

West Coast

Towns listed generally follow a north to
south route. Refer to the index if required

Karamea

Farmstay
Address: "Beachfront Farmstay",
Karamea, RD 1, Westport
Name: Dianne & Russell Anderson
Telephone: (03) 782 6762
Fax: (03) 782 6762
Mobile: (025) 222 1755
Email: farmstay@xtra.co.nz
Beds: 1 Double, 3 Single (3 bedrooms)
Bathroom: 1 Family share, 1 Ensuite
Tariff: B&B (full) Double $75, Single $45,
Children $15, Dinner $20pp,
Credit cards. No smoking inside.
NZ B&B Vouchers accepted
Nearest Town: 84km north of Westport on H67.

We welcome you to our comfortable family farmhouse situated 16km south of Karamea. We milk 330 Friesian cows and also pick and dry sphagnum moss. Our runoff which is 8km away in an isolated valley runs into the Kahurangi National Park, a delightful place for a couple of hours walk. Our home is 2 mins walk from the beach. Our interests include fishing, boating, spinning, gardening, and I am learning Japanese. Karamea is surrounded by the Kahurangi National Park with spectacular limestone caves, rivers, native bush, beaches and scenic walking tracks including the Heaphy and Wangapeka tracks.
So come as far north as you can on the West Coast and relax for a couple of days with some home cooking (shortbread a specialty) and farm grown meat and vegetables. Children welcome (portacot & highchair).
Directions: *3km north of Little Wanganui on H67.*

Westport - Buller District

Homestay
Address: 'Wynyard' Fairdown Beach,
PO Box 127, Westport, Buller District
Name: Dinty Stephens
Telephone: (03) 789 9860
Fax: (03) 789 9820
Beds: 1 Double, 2 Single (2 bedrooms)
Bathroom: 1 Guests share,
1 separate shower room.
Tariff: B&B (continental) Double $70,
Single $50, Children $25, Dinner $20.
Credit Cards. NZ B&B Vouchers accepted Surcharge $5
Nearest Town: Westport 11 kms. Phone for directions.

Forget pollution and noise. Watch the breakers roll, enjoy the peace of native bush – or how about just lazing? Come and enjoy the hospitality and scenery of the West Coast. Westport, where friendly people live, has much to offer - jet boating, caving, white and black water rafting. You tell us where your interest lies and we will try to help. "Wynyard" is designed so that those with disabilities, paraplegics or simply needing a quiet rest can enjoy this peaceful environment. Should you need a special diet, we at "Wynyard" can help – comfortable, warm, and friendly hospitality assured. It is advisable to make a reservation. Please phone before 9 am or in the evening.

Westport
Rural Bed & Breakfast
Address: SH6 Buller Gorge Road.
Riverview Lodge.
Name: Noeline Biddulph
Telephone: (03) 789 6037
Free phone 0800 184 656
Fax: (03) 789 6037
Beds: 3 Queen, 1 Single (4 bedrooms)
Bathroom: 3 Ensuite, 1 Guests share
Tariff: B&B (Full) Double $110-$125,
Single $85-$95, Children under 14 $15,
Dinner (3 course) $30pp, Credit Cards (VISA/MC).
Nearest Town: Westport 7km

Our lodge is a peaceful retreat overlooking the Buller River, 10 min from Westport on the main road from Picton to the West Coast. It is set on 35 acres farming deer and sheep. The suites are private tastefuly decorated, luxuriously appointed with ensuites. Large verandahs for outside meals if required. All amid the glory of a large flower garden and lawns. Activities close by include jet boating, horse trekking, underworld rafting, golf course, visit the seals.
We also have a good selection of restaurants and cafes close by. We serve breakfast continental or full in your suite or our dinning room. Lunch and dinner by arrangement. Laundry facilities available. We have one small dog, very friendly. Smoking outside only.

Westport
Guest House+SC Accommodation + Campervan Points
Address: "Marg's Travellers Rest",
56 Russell St., Westport
Name: Margaret Anne Broderick
Telephone: (03) 789 8627
Free Phone 0800 737 863 (REST ME)
Fax: (03) 789 8396
Beds: 4 Double, 2 Twin (6 bedrooms)
Bathroom: 3 Guests share
Tariff: B&B (continental) Double $70, Single $58,
Campervans $18, 2 persons, Credit Cards (MC/VISA).
Nearest Town: Nelson 230km, Greymouth 103km

"Marg's Travellers Rest" is a fully renovated Gentleman's Club offering you comfortable, warm homely accommodation. It is situated in the centre of town 100 yds from central shopping area, hotels and restaurants. The bed and breakfast is adjacent to but separate from our Hostel which as self contained units with bunk beds. Also available are campervan points. Relax and enjoy our under cover, all weather garden area.
Westport's natural surroundings have much to offer in the way of walkways, seal colony, beach walks, fishing, cave tours, coal town, museum. For the adventurer there is white water rafting, underworld rafting, jet boating, 4 wheel ATV's, horse trekking, mounting biking, kayaking or coal mining tours. An information and booking service available. Off street parking. Self catering kitchen for main meal if you wish. Pick up from bus or airport by arrangement. Inspection welcome. We look forward to meeting you.
Directions: *Turn right at Post Office. Turn left into Russell St.*

Westport

"Steeples" Homestay
Address: Lighthouse Road, RD 2,
Cape Foulwind
Name: Pauline & Bruce Cargill
Telephone: (03) 789 7876
Mobile: (025) 291 7665
Beds: 1 Queen, 2 Single (2 bedrooms)
Bathroom: 1 Private, 1 Family share
Tariff: B&B (full) Double $70, Single $40,
Children $15, Children under 5 free.
Nearest Town: Westport 11kms

We are in a peaceful rural area with beautiful views of the Tasman Sea and coastline, surrounded by beaches great for swimming, surfing, diving, fishing, walking. We are 3 mins walk from the end of the very popular Cape Foulwind Seal Colony Walkway.

Tourist attractions in our area are white water rafting, jetboating, horse-riding, underworld rafting, golf links, scenic bush walks and Coal Town Museum. We are 5km from Tauranga Bay and the very popular Bayhouse Restaurant Café overlooking the sea.

Guests have full use of laundry, kitchen, BBQ, outdoor living facilities and off street parking. Westport is a historic town with a good selection of restaurants, cafés and bars, also 500 metres from our home is a friendly country tavern.

We are keen gardeners, enjoy all sports, and whitebaiting. We hope to be able to offer our guests an evening meal of whitebait at $15 a head, depending how good the season was.

Westport

Rural Homestay and Detached Self Contained Accommodation
Address: "Chrystal Lodge", Crn Craddock Drive & Derby Street,
PO Box 128, Westport.
Name: Ann and Bill Blythe
Telephone: 03 789 8617
Fax: 03 789 8617
Reservations: Freephone 0800 259 953
Email: chrystal@clear.net.nz
Beds: Homestay: 1 Double, 2 Single (2 bedrooms).
Units (2): 1 Queen and double settee. 3 Single and double settee
Bathroom: Homestay: 1 Guests share (spa bath, separate toilet). Units: 2 ensuite.
Tariff: Homestay: B&B (special continental) - full $3.00 extra. Double $65, Single $40.
Units: Double $65, Single $50, Extra adults $10. Children half price. Breakfast optional
$7.50. Discounts after 2 nights and off season rates. Credit Cards: Visa, Mastercard,
Bankcard. NZ B&B Vouchers accepted $10 surcharge for units.
Nearest Town: Wesport Town centre 2 km.

We are a friendly semi-retired couple enjoying the extra time we have to provide hospitality and promote our unique region with its many attractions. Our modern home built on 20 acres is beside the beach used for fishing, surfing and swimming in a quiet setting near race course and sporting venues. We are midway between two whitebaiting rivers with nets available during the season. All guest beds have electric blankets. The near new units are fully equipped with stove, microwave, fridge/freezer and heating. Phone, barbecue and video available on request. Free bicycles and pony. Guest laundry. Household guests are free to help themselves to drinks and biscuits any time and relax in our sunny lounge, conservatory and outdoor verandah. Continental breakfast includes home-made bread, croissants, bagels and fresh yoghurt. We have a very shy cat. Smoking outside please.

Directions: *Turn right at Post Office and continue down Brougham Street, turn left at Derby Street until at end of street.*

Westport
Bed and Breakfast
Address: 'Havenlee', 76 Queen Street,
Westport.
Name: Ian and Jan Stevenson
Telephone: (03) 789 8543 (after 3 pm)
or 0800 673 619 PIN1950
Beds: 1 Double, 2 Single (2 bedrooms)

Bathroom: 1 Private, 1 Guests share, Plus separate shower room.
Tariff: B&B (continental) Double $80, Single $40, Children half price.
Credit Cards accepted.
Nearest Town: Nelson - north 3 hours. Greymouth - south 1 1/4 hours.
Chirstchurch - east 4 1/2 hours.

Ian and Jan welcome you to Havenlee. We are both born and bred West coasters and would love to share our modern spacious home with you. We live in a tranquil area of town amongst an array of native and exotic trees and shrubs yet being only 300 metres from our town centre. Our area boasts some of the most beautiful scenery in the world as well as some of the most thrilling adventure trips. Westport has an interesting history, from the early gold and coal mining eras through to our present time. A visit to the Coal Town Museum is very worthwhile.
We can offer our guests full laundry facilities, continental breakfast, restaurant and cafe recommendations (within close walking distance of our home), lots of local knowledge in a friendly, relaxed, smokefree environment. We also have a cat.
Directions: *Turn right at Wakefield Street, left at Queen Street (first house)*

Reefton
Dinner Bed & Breakfast
Address: 78 Sheil St, Reefton,
West Coast
Name: Marie & Ray Armstong
Telephone: (03) 732 8383
Freephone: 0800 302 725
Fax: (03) 732 8383
Beds: 1 King, 1 Queen, 2 Single (3 bedrooms)
Bathroom: 2 Ensuite, 1 Private, 1 Guests share

*Q*UARTZ
*L*ODGE

Tariff: B&B (special/full/continental) Double from $70, Single from $35,
Children half price. Dinner from $20. All credit cards. Off peak tariff: Double $60.
Nearest Town: Reefton - 1 hr from Greymouth, 1 hr from Westport

*Marie and Ray invite you to experience "Quartz Lodge" nestled within Victoria Forest Park and in the heart of the West Coast quartz gold / coal mining country. We consider ourselves very lucky to own a lovely large modern two storeyed centrally heated lodge with sun all day and the "Best View In Town" from huge picture windows in every room, a fantastic location only one block from the town centre close to all activities yet quite tranquil. * Spacious sunny guests only lounge / dining / TV room * Guests own entrance * Luxurious beds * Self-service tea, coffee, biscuits * Original paintings and crafts * Marie's breakfast and dinners have become famous and are always available * Latest newspapers * Laundry facilities Our central location makes us an ideal stopover as we are: 3 1/2 hours from Christchurch and Franz Josef Glacier 2 1/2 hours from Nelson 4 hours from Picton Ferry and Kaikoura 1 hour from Greymouth and Westport We are always open and looking forward to meeting you.*

Reefton

Bed & Breakfast/Self-contained Accommodation

Address: "Reef Cottage Bed & Breakfast Inn",
51-55 Broadway, Reefton
Name: Susan & Ronnie Standfield
Telephone: (03) 732 8440
FREEPHONE: 0800 770 440
Fax: (03) 732 8440 **Mobile**: 025-226 4013
Email: rstandfield@clear.net.nz
Beds: 1 King/twin, 1 Queen, 1 Double, 1 Single (4 bedrooms)
Bathroom: 1 Ensuite, 1 Private, 1 Guests share
Tariff: B&B (special) Double $70-$95, Single $40-$75,Children half price.
Dinner $10-$35, Credit cards. As self contained cottage - tariff negotiable (seasonal). NZ B&B Vouchers accepted $10 surcharge
Nearest Town: Reefton - We are situated in central Reefton.

The ideal stopover between attractions
Reef Cottage takes its name from the discovery of Gold Bearing 'Reefs' last century. Built from local native Rimu in 1887, this colonial cottage was transformed into a quality bed and breakfast in 1995 adding ensuite, bathroom / laundry and full kitchen in harmony with the existing style. French doors open from the lounge on to a private courtyard and riverbed garden backed by wooded hills. An enchanting cottage, featuring high ceilings, Rimu panelling, antique furnishings and a superb breakfast combining to produce fine hospitality, the hallmark of the Reef Cottage experience. Susan, Ronnie and family live next door close enough to provide personal attention yet separate to ensure guests total privacy. Cafes and restaurants and shops within 2 mins walk. Full disabled facilities: Single party bookings.

Punakaiki

Homestay/Guest House

Address: No. 3 Hartmount Place Extension.
"The Rocks", PO Box 16, Punakaiki
Name: Kevin and Peg Piper
Telephone: (03) 731 1141 **Fax**: (03) 73 1142
Freephone: (0800) 272 164
Email: therocks@minidata.co.nz
Beds: 1 Queen, 4 Single (3 bedrooms)
Bathroom: 1 Ensuite, 1 Private, 1 Family Share
Tariff: B&B (continental/full if needed) Double $92, Single $60, Dinner $25 pp.
NZ B&B Vouchers accepted $22 surcharge
Nearest Town: Punakaiki - halfway between Greymouth and Westport.

We are a semi-retired couple who welcome you to share our home and surrounds. We have recently built "The Rocks Homestay" in a unique wilderness setting at the edge of the bush overlooking the Tasman Sea at Punakaiki.
Our guests have electric blankets, heaters, heated towel rails, phone and TV facilities. We offer home cooking, fresh vegetables and NZ wine. Visitors enjoy exclusive views of the Pancake Rocks and Paparoa National Park. We enjoy taking our guests on complimentary eco-tours of superb rainforest limestone landscapes and beaches while sharing our interests in photography and the outdoors. We can arrange a wide variety of other activities. Visitors can refer to our extensive library of New Zealand books. Smoke-free.
Directions: *Turn off SH 6 (Hartmount Place) at the Blue Bed sign 3.5 km North of Punakaiki Visitor's Centre - drive 500 metres towards the coast.*

Twelve Mile Beach

Self-contained Accom.
Address: 'Tasman Beach' Bed & Breakfast,
Twelve Mile Beach, 1R.D., Runanga, Westland
Name: Tasman Beach
Telephone: (03) 731 1886 **Fax**: (03) 731 1886
Beds: Cottage : 1 Double, 1 Single (2 bedrooms).
Cottage 2: 1 Queen, 1 Double, 1 Single (2 bedrooms).
Bathroom: Both cottages private facilities
Tariff: B&B (continental) Double $50-$85.
NZ B&B Vouchers accepted
Nearest Town: Greymouth 21km

Two self-contained beach cottages in a stunning location, giving garden access to the rocky shoreline plus a wondrous backdrop of bush clad slopes and views of Mt. Cook. Sea views from bedrooms. Bountiful soft mountain water. Organic vegetable garden for guests wishing to self cater. Your stay will be full of discoveries perhaps of gold and greenstone. The Cottages are well placed for visitors to walk in the National park. Breakfast supplied - evening meal - self cater or enjoy the restaurant 5 mins away. Families children and pets enjoyed and welcome here.
Directions: *23 kms north of Greymouth. 22 km south of Punakaiki.*

Nine Mile Creek, Greymouth

Homestay
Address: 'The Breakers' Nine Mile Creek,
Greymouth, Highway 6, Coast Road, Westland
Name: Dot & Bill Dee and Barbara & Frank Ash
Telephone: (03) 762 7743 **Fax**: (03) 762 7733
Email: breakers@minidata.co.nz
Beds: 1 Queen Suite, 1 Double, 1 Twin,
(1 Double + 1 Single), 3 Bedrooms
Bathroom: 3 Ensuites
Tariff: B&B (full) Double from $95, Single from $75,
Dinner $27.50 by prior arrangement.
Visa/Mastercard NZ B&B Vouchers accepted $20 surcharge October-April
Nearest Town: 14 kms north of Greymouth on SH6

Stunning. Is the only way to describe the ocean views from our two acre, landscaped beach front property. Lie in bed and listen to the surf and then next morning pull the drapes and watch the ocean for ever changing. After a good breakfast use our private access and walk along the beach fossicking for greenstone (Jade), pretty stones and shells. You'll probably want to stay another night and enjoy our home cooked dinner and Kiwi hospitality, which is the second thing that our guests write glowingly about in our comments book. Being just 14kms north of Greymouth and 35 kms south of the Pancake Rocks, we are central to all north Westland's tourist attractions and we would be happy to offer advice on what to see and do. We don't have any pets, but "Henry" a tame Weka and other native birds share our property. "The Breakers" is non smoking indoors.
Home Page: www.minidata.co.nz/breakers

Greymouth

Homestay
Address: 'Ardwyn House' 48 Chapel Street, Greymouth
Name: Mary Owen
Telephone: (03) 768 6107 **Fax**: (03) 768 5177
Mobile: (025) 376 027
Beds: 2 Queen, 3 Single (3 bedrooms)
Bathroom: 1 Guests share
Tariff: B&B Double $70, Single $45, Children half price, Credit cards (Visa/BC) NZ B&B Vouchers accepted
Nearest Town: Greymouth 3 mins walk

Ardwyn House is three minutes walk from the town centre in a quiet garden setting of two acres offering sea, river and town views.
The house was built in the 1920s and is a fine example of an imposing residence with fine woodwork and leadlight windows, whilst being a comfortable and friendly home shared with two small elderly dogs.
We are ideally situated for travellers touring the west coast as Greymouth is central and a popular stopover with a good choice of restaurants.
We offer a courtesy car service to and from local travel centres and also provide off-street parking.

Greymouth

Bed Breakfast Rural Homestay
Address: 'Oak Lodge', Coal Creek, Greymouth
Name: Zelda Anderson
Telephone: (03) 768 6832 **Fax**: (03) 768 4362
Beds: 2 Double, 1 Single (3 bedrooms)
Bathroom: 3 Ensuite
Tariff: B&B (full) Double $95-$130, Single $90, Credit cards (VISA/MC). 10% Discount on two night stay only on direct bookings. Winter rates from May until September applicable. NZ B&B Vouchers accepted $50 surcharge
Nearest Town: Greymouth. Centre of the West coast and natureally amazing. Deserves two nights.

OAK Lodge is set in rural surroundings 3km North from Greymouth, State Highway 6 and is centrally situated to visit Shantytown, Punakiki, The Paparoa National Park with good fishing rivers and lakes nearby.
Antique furniture and many interesting curio's will fascinate you in what was an old farmhouse built in 1901. While the gardens are an outdoor treat, especially in early spring when the rhododendrons, azaleas and bulbs are in full bloom.
We have lived in Greymouth much of our lives and can share our knowledge of the area particularly the lovely bushwalks. The 20 acre hobby farm supports sheep and Scottish Belted Galloway cows.
Delicious breakfasts of your choice are offered at your leisure. Percolated coffee and herbal teas. Try the freshly baked bread. There are a choice of excellent restaurants in Greymouth. On the premises are a spa, sauna, swimming pool, and tennis court available for guests.

natu*really* amazing!
THE GREYMOUTH DISTRICT

Greymouth
Homestay
Address: 20 Stanton Crescent,
Greymouth
Name: Bev & Graham Piner
Telephone: (03) 768 5397
Fax: (03) 768 5397
Beds: 4 Single (2 Bedrooms)
Bathroom: 1 Guests share
Tariff: B&B (special) Double $79 ($75 two nights or more), Single $55,
Children up to 12 half price, Dinner $25. NZ B&B Vouchers accepted
Nearest Town: Greymouth 3 Kms

Guests no smoking in our home please.
One family consists of ourselves plus adult son at home and 2 friendly cats.
We offer a very comfortable home complete in lovely bush surroundings with wonderful view of sea and mountains.
Our interests are travelling, meeting people, gardening, antiques and curios, decorating, cooking. Graham is a gold miner who loves fishing in his spare time.
We can include visits to a working gold mine. Sightseeing trips arranged also guided fishing trips plus you can have your catch beautifully cooked and presented for a special treat. If you like comfy beds with pretty linen, thick fluffy bathrobes and great food come and stay with us. Can meet bus or Tranz Alpine.
We look forward to meeting you.
Directions: *Please phone.*

Greymouth
Lodge
Address: 58 Herd Street, Dunollie
(12km north of Greymouth and
2km off Highway 6)
Name: Graeme
Telephone: (03) 762 7077
Fax: (03) 762 7077
Email: kereru.lodge@xtra.co.nz
Beds: 2 Queen, 1 King,
1 Twin (4 bedrooms)
Bathroom: 1 Ensuite, 3 Private or Share

Tariff: B&B (continental) Double $65-$110, Children negotiable, Dinner $20-$25.
All Credit Cards. NZ B&B Vouchers accepted $5-$35 surcharge depending on
room requirements
Nearest Town: Greymouth

KERERU LODGE is located at the head of a quiet, sleepy valley, surrounded by native bush and birds. This is the centre of Westland. You can use KERERU LODGE to "take a holiday from your holiday" and try some of the lesser demanding activities in the area like easy walks of 1-2 hours, lazy canoeing, black-water rafting, dolphin and seal watching, bird watching -or our favourite - putting your feet up and relaxing. If you're into collecting high-adrenalin rushes then use KERERU as a base for New Zealand's least known, but arguably its best, adventure area. 2-4 day tramps, horse trekking, wild deer and pig hunting, fantastic fishing, white-water rafting, jet-boating - it's all here. Good music. Large traditional baths. Great traditional food. Cottage gardens. Peaceful streams. Large beds. Warm fires. Good coffee. This is KERERU LODGE - A haven for the discerning Traveller and Adventurer.

Greymouth
Homestay
Address: 20 Weenink Rd,
Karoro, Greymouth
Name: Glen & Allison Palmer
Telephone: (03) 768 0706 **Fax**: (03) 768 0599
Mobile: (025) 380 479
Email: maryglen@minidata.co.nz
Beds: 1 Queen, 1 King/Twin, 3 Singles (3 bedrooms)
Bathroom: 2 Ensuites, 1 Host Share
Tariff: B&B (continental) Double $65-$80, Single $40-$50. Dinner $17.50 pp.
Children welcome. Credit Cards accepted. NZ B&B Vouchers accepted $10
Surcharge Downstairs - Dec-April
Nearest Town: Greymouth - 2.5km south of town (off the main road)

A warm welcome awaits you at our home which is situated in the bush and overlooking the Tasman Sea. From the two downstairs rooms (which have ensuites) you can step out onto our large deck and relax in the beauty and quietness and in the evening enjoy many beautiful sunsets. Our family is now grown up, so our only resident family is a very friendly dog "Lady". For over 30 years now we have enjoyed having guests in our home and endeavour to offer a relaxed and pleasant stay. Alison enjoys gardening, hospitality being a grandma and playing bridge. Glen enjoys restoring furniture, large jigsaws and reading. If there are guests who like playing cards or games we would be willing starters. We also have Cable / Sky TV plus some videos of the West coast that are available to guests. We are happy to collect guests from the Trans Alpine train or buses. We can take those without transport to the beautiful attractions of our area (for a moderate cost). We look forward to serving our guests and making their stay a "home away from home".
Home Page: www.minidata.co.nz/maryglen
Directions: *2.5km south of Greymouth, off Main Road.*

Greymouth
Homestay
Address: 'Shakespeare House',
43 Shakespeare Street, Greymouth
Name: Ian Wooster and Margaret Smith
Telephone: (03) 768 4646
Fax: (03) 768 4646
Mobile: 025-220 3525
Beds: 1 King/Twin, 1 Single (2 bedrooms)
Bathroom: 1 Private
Tariff: B&B (full) Double $85, Single $65, Credit Cards.
NZ B&B Vouchers accepted surcharge $15
Nearest Town: 1.3 km from Greymouth business area.

Shakespeare House is a turn of the century villa, providing guests with relaxed, homely accommodation Special touches will make for lasting memories of your West Coast stay. At Shakespeare House you will be the sole guests on any given night, which means a comfortable room with an excellent bed, a private TV lounge / sunroom and full private bathroom. Guest robes, fresh flowers, chocolates, cooked or continental breakfasts..... Centrally located, we offer an excellent base from which to experience several national parks, the internationally acclaimed Glaciers and Punakaiki rock formations, as well as the wide range of recreational activities our region offers. We also operate an environmental programme - Walks and Drives - with trips from 2 hours to a full day, using our air-conditioned 4WD vehicle (House guest discount applies). We are happy to meet public transport and assist with itinerary suggestions. Close to restaurants. A smoke free house. Inspection invited. A polite 9 year old and friendly cat is a bonus.

539

Greymouth
B&B

Address: "Rosewood",
20 High Street, Greymouth
Name: Graham and Glenda Weavers
Telephone: 0800 185 748
or (03) 768 4674 **Fax**: (03) 768 4694
Email: rosewoodnz@xtra.co.nz
Beds: 3 Queen, 3 Single (5 bedrooms)
Bathroom: 3 Ensuite, 1 Guests share
Tariff: B&B (full) Double $85 - $100
Single from $50, Children $10, Credit Cards.
NZ B&B Vouchers accepted $25 surcharge
Nearest Town: Greymouth P.O. 1km

Rosewood B&B is one of Greymouth's finest old homes built in the 1920's and recently lovingly restored. We are situated within a few minutes walk of the shops, restaurants and Dixon Park. Our rooms are spacious and beautifully decorated, with telephones, excellent beds and new bathrooms. Tea, coffee and biscuits are available any time in our cosy guest lounge. We also offer laundry service, Cable / Sky TV, free Email access and complimentary pick up and drop off to your transport. Secure off street parking. No smoking in the house please.
We endeavour to provide for our guests the peace, warmth and comfort needed for an enjoyable stay.

Members of
The New Zealand Association
Farm & Home Host Inc.
maintain the highest standards &
are always delighted to welcome
guests into their homes.

Greymouth
Homestay
Address: 345 Main South Road,
Greymouth
Name: Paroa Homestay (formerly Pam's
Homestay)
Telephone: (03) 762 6769
Fax: (030) 762 6765

Beds: 2 Super Kingsize, 1 Single (3 bedrooms)
Bathroom: 1 Guests share, 1 bedroom with basin
Tariff: B&B (cooked or continental) Double $79,(2 or more nights $75),
Single $55, Children under 12yrs half price.
NZ B&B Vouchers accepted $10 surcharge (continental only)
Nearest Town: Greymouth 6 kms

A warm welcome awaits you at our modern, spacious, well appointed home, centrally situated six minutes from Greymouth and Shantytown. Take a 3 minute walk to the beach or enjoy the wonderful seaviews and brilliant sunsets from the twin terraces of our home overlooking the Tasman Sea. Established shrubs and Pohutukawa trees surround our home enhancing its lovely setting. Guest facilities include off street parking and lovely lounge. TV, Bath robes and hairdryers in bedrooms for your convenience. Within 6km are excellent dining establishments for evening meals. My interests are meeting people, baking, cooking, gardening, antiques and walking Ruby our friendly dog (who lives outside).
Being Westcoast born my local knowledge and contacts are an asset to guests in offering assistance regarding itinerary arrangements. Bush walks, fishing tours, visits to a working Goldmine can be arranged. Bookings not always essential, but recommended to ensure availability. Smoking outside. Looking forward to meeting you.

Greymouth
Rural Homestay
Address: "Chapel Hill",
Rutherglen Road,
Marsden, Greymouth
Name: Lynette and Bill
Telephone: (03) 762 6821
Fax: (03) 762 6470
Beds: 1 Double, 4 single (3 bedrooms)
Bathroom: 1Ensuite, 1 Guest Share
Tariff: B&B (continental) Double $80, Single $45, Children under 12 half price.
Dinner $25 by prior arrangement NZ B&B Vouchers accepted.
Nearest Town: Greymouth 17km, Hokitika 40 km

Bill and I invite you to share our comfortable, peaceful home built with the history of our area in mind - old church doors, windows, recycled staircases, furniture, and filled with old relics of the past. A home of interest! Would you believe all of this is nestled in amongst our West Coast rain forest - tuis, bellbirds, pigeons, wekas and native trees. We are both much travelled - Bill the carpenter, Lynette the teacher and have four adult children. Passionate organic gardeners we are!
Staying with us you have the best of both worlds, 30 minutes to Hokitika, 15 minutes to Greymouth, 4 minutes to Shantytown. Come visit the Woods Creek Track, Punakaiki, Glaciers, Shantytown and beautiful Arthurs Pass. We promise you a wonderfully, peaceful time!
Directions: *From Greymouth or Hokitika. Turn at the Paroa turnoff to Shantytown. continue 4 km past the Shantytown Gates. Sign posted "Chapel Hill" on the left.*

Inchbonnie

Self-Contained Accom. Farmstay
Address: 'Whispering Pines', Inchbonnie,
R.D.1, Kumara, Westland 7871
Name: Russell & Jean Adams
Telephone: (03) 738 0153 **Fax**: (03) 738 0353
Beds: 1 Double, 4 Single (2 bedrooms)
Bathroom: 1 Private
Tariff: B&B (full) Double $80, Single $60, Children under 12 $15,
Dinner by arrangement $25 adults. Campervan facilities $25,
Credit Cards (VISA/MC). NZ B&B Vouchers accepted
Nearest Town: Arthurs Pass apprx 30 km (East) Hokitika or Greymouth approx
70km (West)

An opportunity to stay in an authentic sawmiller's cottage built in the 1930's restored and refurbished in the 1970's. The cottage 1km from the homestead is simply furnished in 70's style, comfortable and clean with all "mod cons" except TV and phone. The original rough sawn exterior cladding and interior hand planed window and door frames have been retained keeping the original charm. This is a great place to relax and "catch up" - with reading, letters, fishing in nearby lakes and rivers, bird watching or walking in clear country air. Inchbonnie is a small farming community - no shops - so fill up with petrol etc. before arriving. We farm sheep, beef and deer. Russell being the farmer, while Jean cares for inside the "garden gate" and also handspins, handknits garments to sell. Our two cats share the garden and sometimes the house. A true West Coast welcome awaits all our guests.
Directions: *Turn over Taramakau River at Stillwater-Greymouth sign near Jacksons (S.H. 73) onto Lake Brunner Road, continue straight on to Mitchells Road. We are on the left. "Whispering Pines" at gate. Approx. 8.5 km from S.H. 73.*

Hokitika

Homestay
Address: 'Rossendale',
234 Gibson Quay, Hokitika
Name: Vi & Arthur Haworth
Telephone: (03) 755 6620
Fax: (03) 755 6620
Beds: 1 Queen, 2 Single (2 bedrooms)
Bathroom: 1 Guests share.
Tariff: B&B (Full) Double $75, Single $50, Dinner $20,
Children under 12 half price.   NZ B&B Vouchers accepted
Nearest Town: Hokitika

We are a semi retired couple with a grown up family who are now married. We have travelled extensively both within NZ and overseas and enjoy meeting people from other countries, also fellow New Zealanders. We offer hospitality in a spacious home situated at the edge of town on the banks of the Hokitika River and are 1 km from the centre of town with full view of the Southern Alps and with off street parking. We have two guest bedrooms, one double with H & C, and one twin. All beds have electric blankets and wool rests. Guests have their own bathroom. We offer a full cooked breakfast or a continental, whichever you prefer. Dinner by arrangement. Our hobbies are gardening, fishing, bush walks, gold panning and meeting people. Hokitika is within easy reach of all 'West Coast' main attractions, from the beaches to the Alps, together with pleasant bush walks, and scenic drives. We will meet the plane or bus.

542

Hokitika
Bed & Breakfast
Address: 'Teichelmanns Bed & Breakfast Inn',
20 Hamilton Street, Hokitika
Name: Lorraine Johnston & Norm Duncan
Telephone: (03) 755 8232, Reservations:
Freephone 0800 743742 **Fax**: (03) 755 8239
Email: teichel@xtra.co.nz
Beds: 3 King/Twin, 2 Double, 2 Single/Twin (7 bedrooms)
Bathroom: 4 Ensuite, 3 Guests share
Tariff: B&B King/Twin $105-$115, Double/Twin $75-$95, Single $60-$85, Credit
Cards. NZ B&B Vouchers accepted $10-$20 surcharge
Nearest Town: Located adjacent to Hokitika business area.

At Teichelmann's we pride ourselves in offering friendly, informal hospitality with the comforts of a warm character home, and the opportunity to relax after an eventful day. Teichelmann's is a large home giving our guests the freedom to come and go as they please. Our comfortable guests lounge enables you to interact with others if desired. Teichelmann's has been recently refurbished including new beds, quality furnishings and modern bathroom facilities.

Moments away by foot from our central, yet quiet location, is a comprehensive range of services, shopping, museum, excellent restaurants, beach and river. We will be pleased to assist you in getting the most from your stay, including local attractions, excellent day trips to National Parks including the Glaciers, Punakaiki Pancake Rocks, and the dramatic Arthurs Pass. We have a non smoking environment and are suitable for children 10 years old and over.

Home Page: http://nz.com/webnz/bbnz/teichel.htm
Directions: *Turn left at Town Clock into Sewell Street, then take first street to right into Hamilton Street.*

Hokitika

Homestay
Address: 70 Tudor Street, Hokitika
Name: Brian & Berna McCarthy
Telephone: (03) 755 7599
Beds: 1 Double, 2 Single (2 bedrooms)
Bathroom: 1 Guests share
Tariff: B&B (continental) Double $75, Single $50, Dinner $25.
NZ B&B Vouchers accepted Off season
Nearest Town: Hokitika 1km from town centre

We are both fourth generation West Coasters who have retired to Hokitika from South Westland and have been home hosting for 12 years. We enjoy meeting people, are proud of our region and are only too keen to tell you of it's attractions. Our interests are Rugby, Lions, gold prospecting, West Coast history, we both play golf and lawn bowls as well as fishing for whitebait in season. Guest's comments returned all say "Hospitality excellent".
The glow worm dell is only 5 minutes walk away.
Hokitika has three green stone shops where you can watch the artifacts being made, a paua jewellery, a gold room, museum, excellent craft shops, and a glass blowing studio.
Directions: *When travelling from North take the first turn on your left. Our two storied brick home is the third house on the left. Travelling from South take the last turn on your right (Tudor Street) third house on your left. Turn off SH6 at airport sign from either direction.*

Hokitika

Homestay/Country Living
Address: 'Harris Creek'
Kowhitirangi R.D.1, Hokitika
Name: Carol & Sid Singer
Telephone: (03) 755 7935
Fax: (03) 755 7935
Beds: 2 Double, 1 Single (2 bedrooms)
Bathroom: 1 Private, 1 Guests share.
Spa Bath. Separate Toilet.
Tariff: Start of season tariff: B&B (special) Double $80, Single $50.
NZ B&B Vouchers accepted
Nearest Town: Hokitika 18km (15 mins) East to Kowhitirangi

SO YOU THINK YOU'RE READY FOR THE COAST?!
Here's a hint of what YOU could experience while staying with Sid and Carol......
•Fly fishing at the front gate (you catch -we cook-you feast!)
•Incredible Turquoise water of the Hokitika Gorge (including a slightly scary swingbridge!)
•Famous NZ Lamb in the front paddocks
•Mountains, Lakes, Rivers or the Ocean, depending on which direction you turn!
•Country peace and quiet in a modernised home
•Cows, a duck or two, the occasional Pukeko and a lazy Apricot Poodle!
We enjoy and welcome visitors form all walks of life. Our 4 girls have travelled overseas, 2 now reside in America. Building is Sid's trade, enjoys woodturning, whitebaiting, tramping and other outside activities. Carol enjoys crafts, voluntary community work, books, also a good movie. Both delight in their loving family. Offering home-made treats and breads, electric blankets, woolrests, feather quilted beds, realaxing spa bath plus peaceful surroundings. Appreciate smoking outside.
Directions: *Please phone or fax for reservations and fuller directions to expereince our rural charm and lush green valley. "A Warm Welcome Awaits You".*

544

Awatuna, Hokitika
Farmstay/Homestay
Address: 'Gold and Green', Awatuna,
SH6, R.D.2 Kumara, Westland
Name: Helen & John Hadland
Telephone: (03) 755 7070 **Fax**: (03) 755-7070
Beds: 1 Queen, 1 Double, 2 Single (3 Bedrooms)
Bathroom: 1 Guests share, 1 Family share
Tariff: B&B (special continental) Double $75, Single $55, Children half price.
NZ B&B Vouchers accepted $15 surcharge
Nearest Town: Hokitika SH 6 (8 mins south), Greymouth SH6 (25mins)

Welcome to our comfortable, modern, rural, family home perched high above the road on a bushclad terrace overlooking the driftwood strewn coast of the Tasman Sea with fantastic sea views.

Explore the native bush of our 160 acre farm, with sheep and cattle. Feed the pigs and goats and enjoy our farm dogs. Perhaps stroll the beach.

John and I have in the past fostered scores of children but now welcome the opportunity to share genuine West Coast hospitality.

John's work is in conservation enjoying fishing and gold-panning while my interests are centred around the home and gardens.

We offer FREE evening guided trips to nearby glowworm dells and their historic abandoned mines and day trips, fishing or goldpanning should they stay a day or two. Large covered spa and outdoor swimming pool. Children welcome.

Directions: *15km north of Hokitika on SH6 or 7km south of Kumara Junction roundabout. Look for the Gold and Green signs.*

Members of
**The New Zealand Association
Farm & Home Host Inc.**
maintain the highest standards &
are always delighted to welcome
guests into their homes.

Hokitika

Homestay
Address: 24 Whitcombe Terrace, Hokitika
Name: Terrace View Homestays
Telephone: (03) 755 7357 **Fax**: (03) 755 8760
Mobile: (025) 371 254
Email: c.ward@minidata.co.nz
Beds: 1 Queen, 2 Single (2 bedrooms)
Bathroom: 1 Guests share
Tariff: B&B (full) Double $75, Single $55. Dinner $25pp. Credit cards. NZ B&B Vouchers accepted
Nearest Town: Hokitika 1 Km (to town centre)

Our spacious, warm home offers guests privacy and comfort in 2 ground floor bedrooms. Beautiful views of Mounts Cook and Tasman, Hokitika, the Tasman Sea and spectacular sunsets can be viewed from our upstairs lounge.
Also: complimentary night tour to the glow-worms and replica ship is offered.
Chris, a Property Consultant runs his own business and is keen on golf and fishing. Dianne a Reading teacher enjoys handcrafts, ceramic dolls and cooking.
We are centrally situated to the Coast's many attractions and can assist you in making the most of your time. We have lived in several NZ locations and have a good knowledge of local and national features.
Directions: *You are invited to meet us by turning into Tudor Street from the main highway; take the next turn left into Bonar Drive, which will take you up the hill. When you reach the top, turn left into Whitcombe Terrace.*

Hokitika

Boutique Lodge
Address: "Villa Polenza", Brickfield Road, Hokitika
Name: Russell & Trina Diedrichs
Telephone: (03) 755 7801
Freephone 0800 241 801
Fax: (03) 755 7901
Mobile: (025) 477 123
Email: c.diedrichs@xtra.co.nz
Beds: 2 Queen, 2 Single (3 bedrooms)

Bathroom: 2 Ensuite, 1 Private
Tariff: B&B (full) Double $140-$160, Single $90. Credit cards.
NZ B&B Vouchers accepted Surcharge Double $66-$84, Single $21
Nearest Town: Hokitika 4 mins

Our home is new, modern Italian, situated high on the top terrace overlooking Hokitika with each bedroom providing breathtaking views of Mts Cook and Tasman to the south, and to the west, the wonderful sea sunsets. The area is very quiet except for the birdlife in the adjacent native bush.
The bedrooms, all with underfloor water heating have large french doors opening to a patio while all beds have feather / down duvets.
We have one daughter at home, a Persian cat called Oscar and a German roller canary with a voice surpassed only by Pavaroti.
Continental or cooked breakfast is available with freshly squeezed orange juice, home-made bread and espresso coffee. Dinner is by arrangment. Our house is smoke-free and not suitable for children under 13.
Home Page: http://www.friars.co.nz/hosts/polenza.html
Directions: *For reservations and directions, please phone.*

Hokitika
Rural Homestay
Address: Golf Links Road,
Southside or Box 38, Hokitika.
Name: Elaine and John Fuller.
Kowhaioak Homestay
Telephone: (03) 755 7933 **Fax**: (03) 755 7933
Beds: 1 Double, 5 Single (3 bedrooms)
Bathroom: 1 Ensuite, 1 Guests share
Tariff: B&B (full) Double $80, Single $60, Children 12 and under half price,
Dinner $20pp by prior arrangment. Credit Cards.
NZ B&B Vouchers accepted $10 Surcharge
Nearest Town: Hokitika 2km

Welcome to our warm and comfortable home in a rural setting on 3 acres 2km from Hokitika.
We are semi retired dairy farmers looking forward to a new challenge. Elaine born in Wales
and enjoys handcrafts and meeting people. John enjoys hunting, fishing, pool and people.
We have a pool table and squash court for your use. Just 1.5km to the Golf Course or a day
trip down to the glaciers or up to the Pancake Rocks at Punakaikai. Our home is a unique and
interesting design. An open fireplace is framed by two walls of local stone. A gentle sloped rimu
stairway leads up to the bedrooms.
A cot and highchair are available. We will meet the plane or bus. Thank you for not smoking
in our home. Pets: 2 house cats.
Directions: *Turn at large Blue B&B sign off State Highway 6 south of Hokitika Bridge onto*
Golf Links Road. Second house on right set back off the road. Sign at gate. Welsh flag by house.

Hokitika
Country Lodge+Self-contained Cottage
Address: Chesterfield Rd, S/Hway 6, Kapitea Creek,
RD 2, Westland.
Name: Kapitea Ridge Country Lodge & Cottage
Telephone: (03) 755 6805 **Freephone**: 0800 186 805
Fax: (03) 755 6895 **Mobile**: (025) 223 4905
Beds: Country Inn: 1 King, 3 Queen, 4 Single (6 bedrooms).
Cottage: 1 Queen, 2 Single, 1 Sofabed (2 bedrooms)
Bathroom: Country Inn: 6 ensuites. Cottage: 1 private
Tariff: Country Inn: B&B (special) Room Rate $110-$165, Single by arrangement.
Cottage: S.C. Double $85, Extra person $15. Dinner $40 pp. Credit Cards.
NZ B&B Vouchers accepted with Surcharge
Nearest Town: Hokitika 17km, Greymouth 23km

Hospitality and comfort Within Nature.
Experience superior contemporary rural accommodation in our architecturally designed
lodge, completed 1998, situated on our authentically farmed coastal property. A spacious
retreat with commanding views of surf, sunsets, wild storms and distant mountains.
Breakfast and evening summertime dining in conservatory. Garden spa. Country fare,
dinner is by prior arrangement. Enjoy country living in laid back luxury suitable for children
over 12 years. Kapitea cottage is our self contained accommodation designated especially for
families and folks seeking an independent stay. Charming interior decor, full facility kitchen.
French doors lead to a covered deck and developing cottage garden. Gas BBQ. Single and
party bookings. Surrounding area offers, native birds / bush, sheep and cattle. Gumboots and
gold pans, pentaque, clay bird shooting, walking distance to beach. Golf. Jade and Gold
Artisans, Historic Gold fields, fishing lakes and rivers within 20 minutes drive.
Home Page: www.nz.travel.co.nz/brochure rack/West Coast/Kapitea.html
Directions: *On s/Hway 6, 17km north of Hokitika, 5km south of Kumara junction.*
Signposted 'Lodge 2 km' at Chesterfield Road.

Kowhitirangi, Hokitika
Farmstay
Address: Hokitika Gorge Farm Stay,
Whitcombe Valley Road, Kowhitirangi, RD 1,
Hokitika, West Coast
Name: Barry & Sally Paterson
Telephone: (03) 755 7242 **Fax**: (03) 755 8081
Mobile: 025 228 1199
Beds: 1 King, 2 Single (2 bedrooms)
Bathroom: Family share
Tariff: B&B (special) Double $85, Single $55, Dinner $25pp.

Nearest Town: Hokitika 28km (25 mins)

*Come and stay on our third generation dairy farm and experience 350 Jersey cows
being milked. Farm tours are also offered.*
*The farm is set in against the southern Alps and only walking distance from the scenic
Hokitika Gorge.*
Ideal day's travelling from Christchurch, Arthurs Pass, Haast, Nelson, etc.
*The area offers picturesque views, numerous bush walks, trout fishing, hunting,
abundance of bird life and true tranquillity for those who just want to rest for a while.*
Our home is modern, specious and homely
We offer delicious fresh home cooked meals, comfortable beds and superb company.
You are welcome to stay a while and fit into our daily farm routine.
Families are welcome.
Directions: *We are 28 kms inland from Hokitika. Please follow all the signs to
Kokatahi, then proceed to follow all the signs to the Hokitika Gorge. We are the last
house down Whitcombe Valley road (farm supply number 220).*

Hokitika
Homestay
Address: Alpine Vista Homestay,
38 Bonar Drive, Hokitika
Name: Rayleine and Jon Olson
Telephone: (03) 755 8732 **Fax**: (03) 755 8732
Email: jolson@minidata.co.nz
Beds: 1 Queen, 2 Single (2 bedrooms)
Bathroom: 1 Ensuite
Tariff: B&B (full) Double $85, Single $50, Children $25. Credit Cards accepted.
NZ B&B Vouchers accepted $15 surcharge
Nearest Town: Hokitika, town centre: 1 km

*We look forward to meeting you and welcoming you to our comfortable home situated
on a terrace overlooking Hokitika, affording us unsurpassed views of Mount Cook,
Southern Alps, Tasman Sea and brilliant sunsets.*
*There is a private entrance to the guest rooms which include one queen size bedroom
with ensuite and a small sitting area containing a settee, table, chairs and TV (Sky).*
Adjoining this is a twin bedded room so it is especially suitable for one or two couples.
There are tea and coffee making facilities and guests are welcomed with home baking.
Credit cards accepted, off street parking and laundry provided.
*We have travelled widely and invite guests to share a drink with us in the evening as
we enjoy listening to your experiences. Jon is a fourth generation West Coaster with
an abundant knowledge of the area. Interests include gardening, reading, boating,
bowls, spinning, patch working, travel.*
Home Page: http://www.minidata.co.nz/wdc/nztour/alpine v.htm

Hokitika

Semi Rural Homestay-close to Hokitika Town.
Address: 'Prospect House', Blue Spur, RD2, Hokitika
Name: Danielle & Lindsay Smith
Telephone: (03) 755 8043 **Fax**: (03) 755 6787
Mobile: (025) 221 2779
Email: prospect@minidata.co.nz
Beds: 1 King, 1 Queen, 1 Double, 1 Single (3 Bedrooms)
Bathroom: 2 Ensuites, 1 Private
Tariff: B&B (full) Double $90-$105, Single $60-$70,
Dinner by arrangement, Children half price, Credit Cards.
NZ B&B Vouchers accepted with surcharge depending on requirments.
Nearest Town: Hokitika 4km

Prospect House is situated on the outskirts of Hokitika on an ancient river terrace property of some 10 acres.

This lovely colonial style family home commands sweeping views of the Southern Alps, has beautiful gardens and trees and is owned by a caring, friendly family. Our guest books are full of accolades as to the space and luxurious comfort of our home, the friendliness of the host family as well as the fine food and wines that we provide thus ensuring a truly relaxing stopover. All say that they wish they had arranged their trip so that they could stay longer.

This spacious home features native rimu timbers, central heating, separate gym, large deck and BBQ facilities, piped music throughout, Sky TV and full office facilities too. The main suite contains a King size double bed and full ensuite plus tea and coffee making facilities as well.

Adjoining this is a separate bedroom with a double and single bed.

The second suite has a Queen size bed and ensuite.

We enjoy catering by arrangement for our guests and provide full 3 course meals. Breakfast can be either continental or a full cooked breakfast.

Our interests vary from the garden to music, current affairs, sport flying and yes .... catering for guests.

We can arrange scenic flights for you to the Glaciers or to the historic goldtown port of Okarito or to other interesting destinations. We can also assist to arrange other adventures for you.

We have three dogs, a Westie, a Scotty and a Lab. We also have two cats.

Directions: *To find us, if travelling from North turn left into Hampden Street, continue on for 3KM without turning again.*

Ross

Homestay+Self-contained Accom.
Address: Bellbird Bush, 4 Sale Street, Ross, Westland
Name: Peter & Vicky Bennett
Telephone: (03) 755 4058 **Fax**: (03) 755 4064 **Mobile**: (025) 314 819
Beds: 1 Queen + bed settee, 2 Single (2 bedrooms)
Bathroom: 1 Private, 1 Family share
Tariff: B&B (continental) Double $70, Single $40, Children under 12 $15.
Nearest Town: 30km south of Hokitika on SH6

Welcome to our comfortable and secluded home overlooking the historic gold town of Ross, site of the largest gold nugget ever discovered in NZ. Located at the base of the pine forested Mont D'Or (Mountain of Gold) with beautiful views of the Tasman Sea and Alps our home, set in 5 acres, enjoys a quiet privacy but within easy walking distance of the town's goldfield, walkways and historic sites. We offer the choice of a self-contained unit (new) or accommodation in our home. Coming from rural Welsh and Welsh border background we consider ourselves very fortunate to live in such a beautiful and rugged part of NZ and we are very keen to share our West Coast hospitality with you.
Directions: *If travelling south turn / left (right if northbound) off SH6 at Goldfields Garage / City Hotel intersection and go straight ahead 400m turning right into driveway at road end.*

Ross

Self Contained Accommodation
Address: Dahlia Cottage,
47 Aylmer Street, Ross, Westland
Name: Dianne and Bill Johnston
Telephone: 03 755 4160 **Fax**: 03 755 4160
Beds: 1 Queen, 3 Single (3 bedrooms)
Bathroom: 1 Private
Tariff: B&B (Full/Continental)
Double $65, Single $40, Dinner $20, Children under 12 years half price.
NZ B&B Vouchers accepted
Nearest Town: Hokitika 20 mins

Dianne and Bill welcome you to Dahlia Cottage. We are situated on the main North South Highway 2nd house on your right travelling from North. We are 20 minutes from Hokitika and only 1 1/2 hours drive from the Glaciers. Our home is surrounded with Dahlias in the summer which we show nationally. We offer a cosy quiet self contained cottage with TV next door to our home with private parking.
We have electric blankets on all beds.
Ross is a very pretty place with the native bush surrounds with Tasman Sea and Totara River well known for its whitebait. You can fish for whitebait in season. You can also enjoy at your leisure sea and river fishing, hunting, gold panning and bush walks.
A traditional West Coast welcome awaits you at Dahlia Cottage.
Our interests are gardening, showing Dahlia's, meeting people, farming, fishing, hunting and craft work.

Private bathroom is for your use exclusively,
Guests share means you may be sharing with other guests,
Family share means you will be sharing with the family.

Hari Hari

Country Lodge/Farmstay
Address: State Highway 6,
Hari Hari, South Westland
Name: Wapiti Park Homestead
Telephone: (03) 753 3074   International 64 3 753 3074 **Fax**: (03) 753 3074
Beds: 2 King, 2 Queen, 1 Double, 3 Single (5 bedrooms)
Bathroom: 3 Ensuite, 2 Private (5 bathrooms)
Tariff: B&B (continental) Double $110-$165, Single $90-$125, Dinner $30. Credit
cards (VISA/MC). NZ B&B Vouchers accepted Surcharge: King/Ensuite $75,
Queen/Ensuite $55, Queen/Twin Private $35.
Nearest Town: Hari Hari 1/2km north. Hokitika 75km north.

"Our favourite place, true hospitality"
"The highlight of our tour this year - it was fantastic"
"Loved it all - from feeding the Wapiti to enjoying the bountiful dinners and breakfast!
Your enthusiasm for your farm and guests was contagious"
"What a wonderful way to end our stay in NZ!"

*Hosts Bev & Grant Muir invite you to join past guests and discover the unique
experience of staying at Wapiti Park Homestead, South Westlands premier hosted
establishment for the discerning traveller.*
*Set in tranquil surroundings, our modern colonial style homestead overlooks the deer
farm which specialises in breeding Rocky Mountain Elk (wapiti). Join Grant on the
6pm farm tour and learn about and feed the wapiti or feel free to wander out to view
and hand feed the other deer; and ducks and swans on the lake.*
*Our accommodation, described by many as luxurious, features large spacious rooms
with attractive individual decor and firm superior comfort King, Queen and Twin
beds; two lounges and a trophy/games room with pool table.*
*Delicious meals promote traditional country fare, cater for a wide variety of tastes and
our memorable dinners are three courses, complimented by NZ wines. Special diets/
menus can be provided for by prior request.*
*Our location on SH6 makes us an ideal midway stopover between Picton-Christchurch
and Wanaka/Queenstown areas, or to spoil yourself with an extended stay. Wake to
the enchanting call of the bellbird and tui; partake of a leisurely breakfast, enjoy the
"Special of the Day" and then relax in the warm, friendly, informal atmosphere of this
country retreat that allows you to enjoy as much peace and quiet as you wish. You can
then explore the region renowned for its scenic beauty, glaciers, white heron sanctuary,
gold fields, walks and national parks at your own pace.*
*WE ALSO OFFER GUIDED TROUT AND SALMON FISHING AND HUNTING and
can arrange other activities such as, horse treks, kayaking and nature tours.*
*A warm welcome and traditional hospitality await you at Wapiti Park. Your hosts look
forward to making your stay a special holiday highlight.*
No smoking indoors. Advance booking recommended. Unsuitable for children.
Reservations Free Phone: 0800 Wapiti
Home Page: http://nz.com/webnz/bbnz/wapiti.htm

Hari Hari

Homestay and Self Contained Accommodation
Address: Carrickfergus B&B, Haddock Road,
Off Robertson Road, RD 1, Hari Hari,
South Westland
Name: Catherine Healy and Lindsay Grenfell
Telephone: 03 753 3124
Fax: 03 753 3124
Beds: Homestay: 1 Queen, 1 Double, 1 Single (2 bedroom)
2 Units: 1 Double, 1 Sofasleeper (Double)
Bathroom: Homestay: 1 Guests share
Units: Private.
Tariff: B&B (continental) Double $85, Single $50,
Dinner $25 pp (by arrangement) with convivial glass.
Nearest Town: Hari Hari 50 minutes from Hokitika, sign on SH6 Turn into
Robertson Road for 5km)

Our modern home and new studio units are north facing, set in landscaped grounds which adjoin our 32 acre sheep and cattle farmlet affording extensive mountain and rural views. You are welcome to stroll around our property which enjoys native trees and birds.

You may choose to enjoy the peace and privacy of our units with equipped mini kitchen and we will bring a hearty breakfast to be eaten at your leisure, or you are welcome to join us in our home. It is our endeavour to make your stay comfortable, as will our placid Basset Hound - Fillip, who is at present unemployed.

Renowned La Fontaine River is closeby for trout and local lakes afford salmon and trout. Hari Hari coastal walkways to Doughboy lookout is worth time-out as is Wilberg walking track (glow worms).

Lake Ianthe, White Herons at Whataroa and the glaciers are within close proximity. We look forward to meeting you.

Members of
**The New Zealand Association
Farm & Home Host Inc.**
maintain the highest standards &
are always delighted to welcome
guests into their homes.

Whataroa, South Westland

Farmhouse
Address: 'Matai Lodge' Whataroa, South Westland
Name: Jim & Glenice Purcell
Telephone: (03) 753 4156 **Fax**: (03) 753 4156
Beds: 2 Queen, 2 Single(3 bedrooms)
Bathroom: 2 Private
Tariff: B&B (full) Double $120, Single $70 person, Dinner $25
Nearest Town: Franz Josef 20 mins (south), Hokitika 1 hour 30 mins (north) SH6.

You are warmly welcomed to share with us our tranquil rural retreat 5 mins from the main highway, on a 400 acre farm of sheep, cows, horse and sheep dog, only 20 mins from the Franz Josef Glacier.

Our spacious modern home has been designed for farmstay guests, with large lounge and dining area downstairs, looking out over farmland to the spectacular views of the Southern Alps and the world Heritage Park.

Upstairs our guests have their own suite of two bedrooms one Queensize and one twin with lounge, conservatory and private bathroom, or downstairs Queensize room with ensuite.

Enjoy delicious three course home cooked dinners, including complimentary NZ wines, in a relaxed atmosphere where we can share interesting and entertaining conversations.

As we have travelled overseas and enjoyed meeting people, we find this an ideal way to extend that pleasure, and our motto is; "A Stranger is a Friend we have yet to meet".

I speak Japanese and have taught felting spinning and weaving in Japan, Jim and I play golf and tennis, there is a very picturesque golf course nearby.

Now our family has left home we look forward to sharing our home and knowledge of this beautiful scenic area with our guests.

Activities in the area: Horseriding, Kayaking (Okarito Lagoon) 15 mins drive; Fishing salmon and trout Lake Mapourika and Waitangi river can be arranged; Golf course (clubs available); White heron bird Sanctuary by jet boat, from November to February; Gold panning in natural riverbed and bush valley.

Driving Time:
Christchurch - Whataroa 5 hours
Queenstown - Whataroa 6 hours
Greymouth - Whataroa 2 hours
Nelson - Whataroa 6 hours

Whataroa, South Westland

Bed & Breakfast /Farmstay

Address: Sleepy Hollow, State Highway 6, Whataroa, South Westland
Name: Carolyn and Colin Dodunski
Telephone: FREEPHONE: 0800 575 243 **Fax**: (03) 753 4079
Email: hollow@xtra.co.nz
Beds: 3 Queen, 1 Single. Self contained accommodation: 1 Queen, 1 Single +
sofabed/portacot available.
Bathroom: Homestead: 1 Guests share S.C. Unit: 1 Ensuite
Tariff: B&B (continental) Double $80-$90, Single $50. Credit Cards: Visa/MC/
Amex//Diners. NZ B&B Vouchers accepted $10-$20 surcharge
Nearest Town: Franz Josef 20 mins south, Hokitika 1 1/2 hours north

Heading to the glaciers? Stay a night or two at Sleepy Hollow, your Ideal base in glacier country. We are just 20 minutes drive North of the Franz Josef Glacier!! Here you can relax, away from the sometimes hectic pace of travel and take time to unwind whilst admiring the breathtaking scenery of dramatic mountain views (even from your room!).

The 3 year old homestead accommodation is on the top floor with guest share bathroom. Each beautifully decorated bedroom has queen sized beds and big fluffy towels, tea / coffee facilities, heater, electric blankets and television, enabling you to relax in privacy if you wish, or feel free to pop downstairs for a chat, but be warned! the jolly and relaxing atmosphere at Sleepy Hollow is contagious.

The self contained unit is a real little gem and excellent for guests with children, with your own bathroom, lounge, dining & kitchen area, microwave, electric frypan and television, this is your own little home away from home. Telephone, fax, email and laundry are available.

Our 400 acre dairy farm milks 200 friesian cows, we have 3 horses and some sheep. Mint Sauce our pet sheep loves being fed a slice or two of bread and is eagerly awaiting your arrival. We have one house cat, Angus the friendly fox terrier (who lives outside!!) and 2 farm dogs Waite and Buff. A short bush walk takes you to the farm lane where you can view and feed our peacocks, pheasants, ducks etc in the bird enclosure or take a leisurely stroll over the farm.

The area has lots to offer with breathtaking views of the glacier to be had via a helicopter or fixed wing ski-plane flight both of which we would be happy to provide details or make your reservations for you.

At Okarito (20 mins drive) you can kayak on the Lagoon, and take some excellent walks, view beautiful sunsets on the beach. Whataroa has a population of around 300 people, there is a 9 hole golf course, excellent fishing and tours to New Zealand's only White Heron Colony, Gold prospecting is available on the Whataroa riverbed.

Casual evening meals are available at the local tearooms in Whataroa.

Nearest banks are Hokitika and Wanaka. Credit cards are welcome here.

We look forward to sharing our little slice of paradise and some laughter with you!!

Distances: Picton-Whataroa: 6 hours. Hokitika-Whataroa: 1.5 hours. Whataroa-Wanaka: 4.5 hours. Whataroa-Queenstown: 6 hours. Christchurch - Whataroa: 5 hours

Home Page: http://nz.com/webnz/bbnz/sleepyh.htm
Directions: *Sleepy Hollow is very easy to find, we are on State Highway 6, 1km north of Whataroa village.*

Franz Josef
Boutique Country Stay
Address: Waiho Stables Country Stay, Docherty Creek, Franz Josef Glacier
Name: Alex and Suzy Miller
Telephone: (03) 752 0747 **Fax**: & Ph (03) 752 0786
Beds: 2 Queen, 1 Double, 2 Single (3 bedrooms)
Bathroom: 2 Ensuite, 1 Host share
Tariff: B&B (special) From 1st Oct Double $135-$150, Single $120-$135, Extra person $75-$85, Children by arrangement. A la carte vegetarian meals $15-$45, BYO. Credit cards. Min. two nights' stay Nov - Mar. NZ B&B Vouchers accepted (two double + $25 surcharge)
Nearest Town: Franz Josef village 6km

The South-West World Heritage Area is a vast reservoir of wilderness. Its 2.6 million hectares, including four national parks, contain towering peaks, majestic glaciers, temperate forests and rugged coastlines. Air and water could scarcely be purer anywhere on earth.

In the heart of the World Heritage Area at Franz Josef Glacier, guests at Waiho Stables Country Stay can sojourn on the edge of wilderness. Ten horses graze the 20 hectare property, which has created wetland areas and is traversed by a private airstrip. Here, guests sleep soundly, intoxicated by the pure air and the pleasant pursuits of the day, and they can be as indolent or as active as they wish.

Numerous activities compete for attention, from ski-plane flights with snow landings, to golf, guided fishing and hunting, from glacier heli-hikes and coastal wilderness excursions to kayaking and horse riding. There is spring heli-skiing over 5000 ha of snow neves, there are craft shops, jet boating and sky diving, and endless kilometres of walking tracks both coastal and alpine.

Alex Miller is a former mountaineer and park ranger, now flying a Mount Cook ski plane, and Suzy studied painting at university, and is an amateur naturalist. Alex and Suzy do their utmost to enhance the wilderness experience with some of the trappings of civilisation.

Two stylish rooms for a select number of guests open onto expansive courtyards boldly landscaped with enormous boulders. Teas and plunger coffee, fruit and chocolate bowl, hairdryer, toiletries, bathrobes, telephone and books on the New Zealand environment are 'essential accoutrements' of wilderness here.

At breakfast, which is flexitime, a resplendent panorama of the Alps may be viewed while sampling an array of fruits and mueslis, omelettes, muffins and bagels, with juice, designer drinks and espresso coffee. Delicious ethnic vegetarian meals may be served in the rooms or al fresco under sun umbrellas, and guests also dine at Franz Josef Village.

The vastness of wilderness, plus a thin veneer of civilisation, combine at Waiho Stables Country Stay, to provide a respite from schedules and a tonic for the senses.
Homepage: http://www.waiho.co.nz

Fox Glacier
Farm Bed & Breakfast
Address: 'The Homestead',
Cook Flat Road, Fox Glacier
(Postal: P.O. Box 25, Fox Glacier)
Name: Noeleen & Kevin Williams
Telephone: (03) 751 0835
Fax: (03) 751 0805
Beds: 2 Queen,
2 Single (3 bedrooms)
Bathroom: 2 Ensuite, 1 Private
Tariff: B&B (continental, full $3.00 pp extra).
Queen $90-$100,
Twin $85-$95, Single $70-$78. Travellers cheques accepted.
Nearest Town: Fox Glacier 1/2 km, Hokitika SH6 (North) 160 km.

Kevin, Noeleen and Chancy our friendly Corgi welcome you to our 2,800 acre beef-cattle and sheep farm (guests welcome to stroll through house paddocks). Beautiful bush-clad mountains surround on three sides, and we enjoy a view of Mt Cook.

Our spacious home, built by Kevin's Grandparents in the mid 1890's, has fine examples of leadlight windows. A guest lounge, with open fire for late autumn nights, is provided in our smoke-free home. Firm, comfortable beds have Woolrests and electric blankets. Hairdryers provided. Breakfast includes muesli, home-made yoghurt, marmalades and preserves, with cooked if required.

We feel our home has the best of both worlds, having no immediate neighbours, yet within walking distance of village and tourist facilities (Glacier, walks, helicopters, restaurants), 6 km to Ice, 4 km to world famous Lake Matheson with its mirror reflection.

Directions: *On Cook Flat Rd (road to Lake Matheson), 5th house on right, before Church.*

Members of
**The New Zealand Association
Farm & Home Host Inc.**
maintain the highest standards &
are always delighted to welcome
guests into their homes.

Fox Glacier
Homestay
Address: Roaring Billy Lodge,
PO Box 16, Fox Glacier
Name: Billy & Kathy's Place
Telephone: (03) 751 0815
Fax: (03) 751 0815
Email: billy@xtra.co.nz
Beds: 1 Double, 3 Single (2 bedrooms)
Bathroom: 1 Guests share, robes available
Tariff: B&B (special, cooked) Double $75-$85, Single $60-$69. (from 1st Oct).
Nearest Town: 2 minute walk to Fox Glacier. Hokitika (North) 2 hours (160 km)
SH6

Guest wanted no experience needed!
We invite you to our home, formally a single story farm workers house. Renovated into what is now a very warm, sunny, comfortable two story home with good examples of native timbers. Relax in our panoramic farm valley and mountain view lounge. Try our legendary cooked breakfast and then wear yourself out on the glacier and surrounding walks. Fortunately we're only two minutes walk from the action in the town centre and can make any bookings needed. Use our local knowledge to discover Fox Glacier and surrounding areas.
A Guided evening bush walk is complimentary and is full of interesting information about the forest and animals. We provide Alpine, Rainforest, Hunting and Fishing day trips.
If you visit us in April you might be lucky enough to hear the stags roaring. They're the clue to our name. We have one cat and hunting dog! Kiwihost.

Fox Glacier
Lodge/Self Contained Accommodation
Address: Fox Glacier Lodge,
Main Highway 6, Fox Glacier (PO box 22)
Name: Fran and Laurie Buckton
Telephone: (03) 751 0888
Reserv. freephone 0800 369 800
Fax: (03) 751 0888
Beds: 5 Queen (5 bedrooms)
Bathroom: 5 Ensuites

Tariff: B&B (continental) Double $110-$140. Special winter rates. Not suitable for children. Credit cards: Vsa/Mastercard/Eftpos
Nearest Town: Hokitika 2 hours North, Wanaka 3 hours South.

Fox Glacier Lodge is nestled in a pristine forest setting with mountain backdrop, yet is right in the heart of Fox Glacier village itself. The recently completed solid timber lodge is clean, warm and welcoming.
Bathrooms are private ensuite. Two have private double spa baths.
The country kitchen is fully equipped and well stocked with supplies for self-serve continental breakfasts. Also available: coin laundry.
"Glow-worm forest walk" is right here: a short stroll after dark to the grotto where glow-worms live amongst ferns and mosses. Walk to the Glacier, around Lake Matheson, or enjoy the magnificent views of Mt Cook and Tasman. Also available: Heli-hikes, kayaking, bird watching, scenic flights, fishing, hunting, biking, information. Lodge is smoke free. Reservations recommended.
Directions: *On the southern fringe of Fox Village (opposite BP) you'll see our home / office. The lodge is beyond, hidden from view.*

Bruce Bay

Farmstay
Address: Mulvaney Farm Stay,
Condons Road, Bruce Bay, South Westland
Name: Peter & Malai Millar
Telephone: (03) 751 0865 **Fax**: (03) 751 0865
Email: mulvaney@xtra.co.nz
Beds: 1 Double, 1 Twin (2 bedrooms)
Bathroom: Family share
Tariff: B&B (full/continental) Double $75, Single $50, Children $20, Dinner $20
pp. No smoking inside.
Nearest Town: Fox Glacier

Welcome to Mulvaney Farmstays! The Mulvaneys were Irish and my great grandfather settled in this valley 130 years ago. Our home was built in the 1920's by my great uncle for his wife to be, but she never arrived. So he lived there by himself until 1971 raising Hereford cattle. We have lived here with our children (who are all away at school) for 19 years. Our home has been fully renovated into a comfortable home. We offer an evening meal - Malai your hostess offers you European or Thai dinners (with bookings).
We are close to the sea, lakes and rivers which are ideal for fishing, walking or just relaxing. We are only 30 minutes from Fox Glacier and can arrange helicopter flights and glacier walks, or you can just relax with us enjoying our surrounding scenery. We have two cats and you shall be heartily greeted by our friendly dog Monty!
Directions: *1km off SH6 on Condons Rd. Well sign posted.*

Paringa

Farmstay
Address: State Highway 6, Paringa,
South Westland
Name: Glynis and Tony Condon
Telephone: (03) 751 0895 **Fax**: (03) 751 0001
Beds: 1 Double, 4 Single (3 bedrooms)
Bathroom: 1 Family Share
Tariff: B&B (full) Double $70, Single $35, Dinner $20, Children $10.
No Credit Cards. NZ B&B Vouchers accepted
Nearest Town: Fox Glacier (45 mins north), Haast (45 mins south)

We run a 4th generation working beef farm, with a few sheep. We enjoy meeting people. Our interests include hunting, jet boating, fishing, spinning, knitting and reading. Our farm is nestled beneath the bush-clad foothills of the Southern Alps, close to Lake Paringa and the Paringa river.
We have three adult children, one living in New Zealand, the other two overseas. We have travelled to America, England, Scotland, some parts of Europe, Kenya and Australia.
We live only three quarters of an hour from Fox Glacier, four hours from Queenstown and we are quite happy to arrange helicopter flights etc. at Fox Glacier.
We are Kiwi Hosts and belong to the NZ Association Farm & Home Hosts and Tourist Industries Association.
We have two house cats and a small dog.
Directions: *70 kms south of Fox Glacier, 50 kms north of Haast on State Highway 6. 4 kms from South Westland Salmon Farm Cafe.*

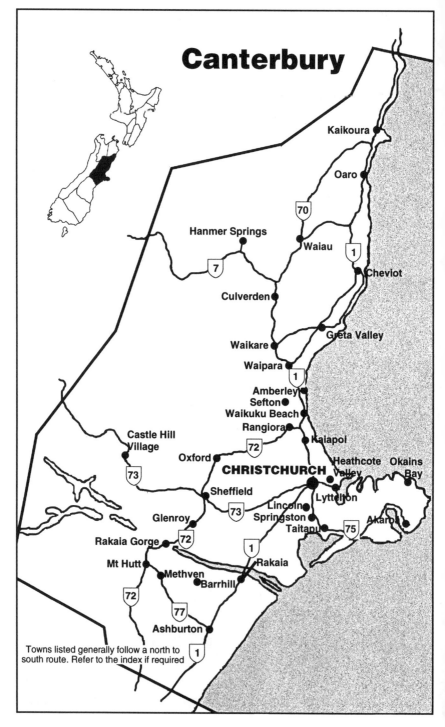

Canterbury

Kaikoura

Oaro

70

Hanmer Springs

Waiau

7

1

Cheviot

Culverden

Greta Valley

Waikare

Waipara

1

Amberley
Sefton
Waikuku Beach
Rangiora

Kaiapoi

Castle Hill
Village

Oxford

72

CHRISTCHURCH

Heathcote
Valley

Okains
Bay

73

Sheffield

Lyttelton

Glenroy

73

Lincoln
Springston
Taitapu

Akaroa

75

Rakaia Gorge

72

1

Mt Hutt

Methven

Barrhill

Rakaia

72

77

Ashburton

Towns listed generally follow a north to
south route. Refer to the index if required

1

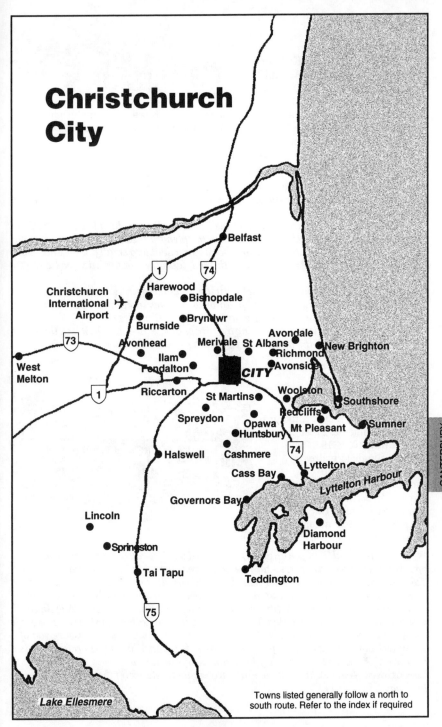

Christchurch City

Christchurch International Airport

West Melton

Belfast

Harewood

Bishopdale

Brynwr

Burnside

Avonhead

Merivale

St Albans

Avondale

New Brighton

Richmond

Ilam

Fendalton

Avonside

CITY

Riccarton

St Martins

Woolston

Southshore

Spreydon

Redcliffs

Opawa

Mt Pleasant

Sumner

Huntsbury

Halswell

Cashmere

Lyttelton

Cass Bay

Lyttelton Harbour

Governors Bay

Lincoln

Diamond Harbour

Springston

Tai Tapu

Teddington

Lake Ellesmere

Towns listed generally follow a north to south route. Refer to the index if required

Kaikoura

Homestay
Address: 'Bay-View',
296 Scarborough Street, Kaikoura
Name: Bob & Margaret Woodill
Telephone: (03) 319 5480
Beds: 2 Double, 2 Single (3 bedrooms)
Bathroom: 1 Ensuite, 1 bathroom Guests share, 1 shower + toilet Guests share.
Tariff: B&B (full) Double $65, Single $40, Children half price, Dinner $20.
NZ B&B Vouchers accepted
Nearest Town: Blenheim - State Highway 130 km north

We are a retired couple with four children and seven grandchildren. We have many interests, golf, lawn bowls, woodwork, cake icing, stretch sewing.and ceramics. We are keen gardeners and for many years grew tomatoes and cucumbers under glass. We also make our own bread.

Our home on an acre of garden high on the Kaikoura Peninsula, a few minutes from the town centre, very peaceful and private with splendid views of the mountains and sea. The accommodation attached to our home has a double, a small double and a twin bedroom. We have a guest lounge and bathroom, laundry and facilities for tea / coffee making.

We have a swimming pool. District activities include golfing, nature walks, bird watching, museum, fishing, sea trips to view whales, dolphins, seals, sea birds, limestone caves and many more. We have a friendly Burmese cat.

We offer transport for visitors travelling by train or bus. Scarborough Street, the access to the Peninsula, is off the main highway on the south side of the town.

Oaro, Kaikoura

Country Homestay
Address: Oaro, R.D.2, Kaikoura
Name: Kathleen & Peter King
Telephone: (03) 319 5494
Beds: 2 Single (1 bedroom)
Bathroom: 1 Private
Tariff: B&B (full) Double $65,
Single $40, Children half price;
Dinner $15, Credit Cards.
NZ B&B Vouchers accepted
Nearest Town: 22 km south of Kaikoura

We are semi-retired living on 48 acres having sold our hill-country property some years ago. We have three daughters - all live away from home - and seven grandchildren. Two cats share our home with us. This is a mild climate and we are experimenting in a small way growing citrus and subtropical fruits, predominantly feijoas. Oaro is close to the sea and we have a fine view north along the Kaikoura coast. A walk south along the coast is always popular. The 20 minute drive to Kaikoura takes you alongside our scenic rocky coast. We enjoy sharing our home with visitors and assure you of a warm welcome. We are happy for you to join us for dinner but if you prefer there is a restaurant 2 km north where they have takeaways as well as meals.
Directions: *We are 22 km south of Kaikoura, a short distance off the main north-south highway.*

Kaikoura

Bed & Breakfast
Address: 'Bevron',
196 Esplanade, Kaikoura
Name: Bev & Ron Barr
Telephone: (03) 319 5432
Beds: 2 Double, 3 Single
(3 bedrooms)
Bathroom: 1 Guests share,
1 Family share
Tariff: B&B (full) Double $65, Single $40,
Children under 12 half price. NZ B&B Vouchers accepted
Nearest Town: 130 km south of Blenheim, 183 km north of Christchurch.

We are a friendly, active retired couple who enjoy meeting new people and sharing the delights of our wonderful two storeyed home on the Kaikoura beachfront. The view from our balcony is breathtaking, giving an unobstructed panorama of the sea and mountains.
We offer two very comfortable guest rooms (each with double and twin beds) and one single room. We have a private guest TV lounge, games room, off street parking, and a spacious private garden. There is a safe swimming beach opposite the house with children's playing area, BBQ and swimming pool. Kaikoura is well endowed with tourist attractions and we are able to offer local advice to help make the most of your stay. We are willing to make Whale Watch bookings for you prior to your arrival. Our home is centrally located, being a short walk to restaurants, galleries and many scenic attractions.

Kaikoura

Bed & Breakfast Inn
Address: The Old Convent ,
Cnr Mt Fyffe & Mill Road, Kaikoura
Name: Marc & Wendy Launay
Telephone: (03) 319 6603 **Fax**: (03) 319 6603
Mobile: (021) 353 954
Email: o.convent@xtra.co.nz
Beds: 3 Queen, 7 Double,5 Twin,
2 Single (17 bedrooms/4 rooms suitable for family,
Double/Twin with bathroom)
Bathroom: 14 Ensuite, 2 Private Facilities
Tariff: B&B Queen $125, Family Unit $170,
Double/Twin Ensuite $100, Single $65, Dinner $40,
Credit Cards Visa and M/C.
NZ B&B Vouchers accepted $40-$65 surcharge on rooms with ensuite
Nearest Town: Kaikoura town centre - 3.6km.

THE OLD CONVENT
B & B   KAIKOURA

Experience the atmosphere in our beautifully preserved homestead built in 1911.Owned by French Architect Marc and his New Zealand wife Wendy you will find personal service, charm, French Cuisine and a relaxed setting amongst a quiet and peaceful environment.Kaikoura has some of the most incredible marine and land attractions in the world, and we will assist you to visit these wonderful experiences.In the morning enjoy home baked Breads and Croissants, home made yoghurt and muesli and our French Brioche with freshly brewed coffees.In the evening meet Marc in the kitchen where his passion for French cooking will overwhelm you. William is 8 years old and loves other children, Jack the Labrador, Midget the horse and Pussy the cat, are all very friendly.Laundry facilities are available at a minimal charge. Coffee, tea, biscuits, bicycles and courtesy car complimentary.
Directions: *At the North edge of town turn west off SH 1 and travel down Mill Road .*
Home Page: http://nz.com/webnz/bbnz/convent.htm

Kaikoura
B&B
Address: 'The Gums',
Schoolhouse Road, Kaikoura
Name: Ian & Alison Boyd
Telephone: (03) 319 5736, Freephone 0800-226164
Fax: (03) 319 5732 **Email**: The.Gums@xtra.co.nz
Beds: 3 Queen, 1 Single (3 Bedrooms)
Bathroom: 3 Ensuites/Spa Bath
Tariff: B&B (continental) Double $85, Single $55, triple $115
Credit cards (VISA/MC). NZ B&B Vouchers accepted $10 surcharge
Nearest Town: Kaikoura 5km

You will enjoy a relaxed and peaceful stay in a beautiful rural setting near the magnificent Kaikoura mountains. Relax on our deck and enjoy Alison's colourful garden which completes the panoramic view. Our land was bought by Ian's Irish Great, Great Uncle in 1883 and he milked cows here. Each ensuite bedroom has quality queen beds, TV, fridge, settee, and coffee / tea facilities. You have your own private entrance and you can come and go as you please. We offer laundry facilities, off street parking, courtesy car from bus / train, bookings for local tourist attractions, restaurants and farm tours can be arranged. Ian's brother Murray, has Donegal House, an Irish garden bar and restaurant, which is within walking distance. There will also be a new self contained unit available from December 98. Ian is a retired teacher and Alison a Librarian. Our hobbies are tennis, golf, designing and building houses, gardening, handcrafts, spinning and we like to travel. No smoking indoors please. We look forward to your company.

Directions: *Driving north, 4km from Kaikoura on SH 1, turn left, 1.5km along Schoolhouse Road.*

Home Page: http://www.whalewatch.co.nz/Gums.htm

Kaikoura
Farmstay
Address: 'The Kahutara',
Dairy Farm Road, Kaikoura
Name: John & Nikki Smith
Telephone: (03) 319 5580
Fax: (03) 319-5580
Beds: 1 Queen, 4 Single (3 Bedrooms)
Bathroom: 1 Luxury Ensuite,
1 Private, 1 Guest share
Tariff: B&B (full) Double $95, Single $55, Dinner $30pp wine served.
NZ B&B Vouchers accepted $20 surcharge
Nearest Town: 20km from Kaikoura township on inland Waiau route - 183km north of Christchurch, 130km south of Blenheim.

The Kahutara is a haven in the hills. Situated 20km from Kaikoura on Highway 70. Our comfortable country home is nestled among the hills in a tranquil garden setting. We operate a 2000 acre beef cattle and sheep farm with a small thoroughbred stud. The Kahutara river runs through our property with the nearby Lake Rotoroa providing a sanctuary for the unique cormorant colony. Enjoy quality homestead accommodation and experience country hospitality. Guests can take a pleasant walk to explore the surrounding valleys, including the bridle path used as the early mail route over the hills to avoid the rocky coastline; or enjoy lawn croquet. Our well appointed guest rooms include one single room and one twin room with private bathroom; and one Queen bedroom with Luxury Ensuite. We are 40 minutes to the popular Mt Lyford Skifield. We can book you on a Whale Watch, swim with the dolphins. Our three daughters are living away from home.

Directions: *Please phone or fax.*

564

Kaikoura

Self-contained B&B
Address: 'Churchill Park Lodge',
34 Churchill St, Kaikoura
Name: Moira & Stan Paul
Telephone: (03) 319 5526
Fax: (03) 319 5526
Email: churchill.park@xtra.co.nz
Beds: 2 Double, 1 Single (2 bedrooms)
Bathroom: 2 Ensuite

Tariff: B&B (continental) Double $80, Single $55,
Credit Cards (VISA/MC). NZ B&B Vouchers accepted $15 surcharge
Nearest Town: Blenheim 130kms

We are a middle age couple and have a modern 2 storey home centrally situated in one of Kaikoura's most popular and picturesque locations. We offer 2 luxury upstairs guest rooms with their own private entrance and facilities. Each room is serviced daily and is tastefully decorated for your comfort with ensuite, settee, dining suite, crockery, tea and percolated coffee making facilities, fridge, heater and electric blankets.

We place your breakfast in your room to enjoy at your leisure. Relax on your own balcony and soak up the sun and spectacular views across Churchill Park to snow capped mountains, coastline and sea.

Take a 5 minute walk through the Park to the beach and Town Centre where an excellent selection of shops and cafe / restaurants are available.

Our home is non smoking, and we guarantee to make you welcome and your stay in Kaikoura most enjoyable.

Home Page: www.canterburypages.co.nz/churchillpark

Kaikoura (on the Peninsula)

Homestay+Self-contained Accom.
Address: "Austin Heights",
19 Austin Street, Kaikoura
Name: Margaret & Kevin Knowles
Telephone: (03) 319 5836
Fax: (03) 319 6836
Beds: 1 Queen, 1 Double, 2 Single (3 bedrooms)
Bathroom: 1 Ensuite, 1 Family share
Tariff: B&B (full) Queen Ensuite $ 75, Double $65, Single $40,
Children half price. NZ B&B Vouchers accepted $5 - $15 Surcharge
Nearest Town: 130km south of Blenheim, 183km north of Christchurch

We are friendly semi-retired grandparents having lived in Kaikoura for 23 yrs and enjoy lawn bowls, tramping, walks, gardening and patchwork. We look forward to welcoming you into our comfortable modern home set on half an acre of gardens and lawns on the Kaikoura Peninsula, just a few minutes from shops and restaurants. We offer peaceful private comfortable surroundings, sea and mountain views, tea and coffee making facilities and a delicious breakfast. Our accommodation consists of a queen with own private facilities, a double and two singles with private lounge and family share bathroom. We are happy to make bookings for the many tourist attractions and offer transport for guests to and from terminals. Austin St is the second turn left off Scarborough St, which is off the main highway on the south side of town. We have a friendly Persian cat and are a non smoking household.

Kaikoura
B&B Lodge
Address: "Carrickfin Lodge", Mill Road, Kaikoura
Name: Roger Boyd
Telephone: (03) 319 5165, Freephone 0800 265 963 **Fax**: (03) 319 5162
Beds: 5 Queen, 5 Single (6 bedrooms)
Bathroom: 6 Ensuite, 1 Family share
Tariff: B&B (continental) Double $80, Single $50, Credit Cards. This property is
not suitable for children.
NZ B&B Vouchers accepted $20 surcharge
Nearest Town: Kaikoura 3km

WELCOME TO KAIKOURA (Kai = Food, Koura = Crayfish)
My name is Roger and I'm the fourth generation "BOYD" to own and farm "Carrickfin".
It is an ancient Irish name from where my Great Grandfather originated. He bought
and settled this land in 1867 for 100 Gold Sovereigns.
The Lodge is a Colonial home built on 100 acres adjoining the Kaikoura township. It
is a large and spacious place with an open fire, and guest bar, two outdoor areas with
seating and barbecue facilities. It was built well back from the road amidst two acres
of lawn and shrubs to give complete privacy.
There are breathtaking views from all rooms, looking directly at the "Seaward
Kaikouras" a spectacular mountain range which rises to 8500ft.
These mountains are home to a unique variety of wild life including the giant weta,
rare ghekos, keas, falcons, deer, pig and most native birds. This is also the habitat of
the Hutton Shearwaters, an artic petrel which returns ever year from the Northern
Hemisphere and nests in burrows high in these mountains.
As well as fattening cattle I am a professional Woolclasser, and have worked in
Shearing Sheds throughout the South Island High Country.
In keeping with Irish hospitality, Complimentary drinks with local cheese is served in
the evening.
I am 3kms from Whale Watch, Dolphin Encounter and some of the best Seafood
Restaurants in the South Island.

Directions: *At North End of town, turn West off SH1 into Mill Road, drive 1km and*
I'm there on the left.

Kaikoura

Farmstay
Address: "Okarahia Downs",
Private Bag, Kaikoura
Name: Richard & Hillary Watherston
Telephone: (03) 319 5187 **Fax**: (03) 319 5187
Mobile: (025) 338 051
Beds: 1 Queen, 1 Double, 2 Single (2 bedrooms)
Bathroom: 1 Ensuite, 1 Family share
Tariff: B&B (full) Double $60-$80, Single $40, Children under 15 half price.
Nearest Town: Kaikoura 25 mins.

Okarahia Downs is a 4500 acre sheep, cattle and deer farm running from the coast to very steep hills with large native bush gullies which allow excellent bush walks.
We are situated on State Highway 1, 1/2 hour north of Cheviot and 25 mins south of Kaikoura.
Our home is a large comfortable recently renovated homestead.
We offer a guest room with Queen bed and ensuite, and also tea/coffee making facilities. Extra beds are available with shared facilities. Children very welcome.
We run commercial farm tours, jet boating, fishing and hunting trips are available by arrangement. Meals available.

Kaikoura

Farmstay+Self-contained Accom.
Address: "Clematis Grove",
Blue Duck Valley, RD 1, Kaikoura
Name: Ken & Margaret Hamilton
Telephone: (03) 319 5264 **Fax**: 3195278
Mobile: (025) 242 1959

Beds: 1 King, 1 Double, 2 Single (2 bedrooms)
Bathroom: 1 Guests share
Tariff: B&B (continental) Double $75, extra adults $30 each, Single $55,
Children half price, Dinner $25pp.Winter rates apply.
Credit cards. NZ B&B Vouchers accepted $10 surcharge
Nearest Town: Kaikoura

Clematis Grove B&B and Farmstay
Your hosts Ken & Margaret Hamilton welcome you to stay in our modern self contained unit situated in a lovely bush clad valley 23km north of Kaikoura just 3km off SH1 and from the sea.
Our unit is of a high standard incorporating one double bedroom and one twin room, the kitchen has a electric stove, microwave and fridge. The lounge and dining area are modern and comfortable.Also available for guests a large lounge upstairs with great views.Enjoy the bush and birdlife. Shearing demonstration can be arranged, also farm trips with incredible views of sea and mountains. Also transport from and to K.K. charges for these by arrangement with your hosts. Continental breakfast supplied, you can have this in your unit or with us. Full breakfast and other meals by arrangement or you can prepare these yourself. You may arrive as a stranger but its our intention that you leave as a friend.

Kaikoura
Licenced Rest & accommodation
Address: Donegal House,
Schoolhouse Road, Kaikoura
Name: Mimi and Murray Boyd
Telephone: 03 319 5083
Fax: 03 31905083
Beds: 2 Double, 2 Single (3 bedrooms)
Bathroom: 2 Ensuite, 1 Private
Tariff: B&B (full/continental) Double $85,
Single $45, Dinner $18 (main),
Children half price. Credit Cards, Eftpos.
NZ B&B Vouchers accepted
Nearest Town: Kaikoura 5.5 km Transit sign on main road.

"One Hundred Thousand Welcomes" - "Donegal House", the little Irish Pub in the country, brimming with warmth and hospitality, open fires and accordion music. Set on an historical dairy farm which has been farmed by the Boyd family since their arrival from Donegal, Ireland in 1865, "Donegal House" offers, accommodation, full bar facilities and a public licensed restaurant. The a-la-carte menu, specialising in Kaikoura's famous crayfish and seafood, plus locally farmed beef.
NZ beers and Guinness are on tap along with a good selection of Marlborough wines. Two spring fed lakes, home to Chinook salmon, Mute and Black Swans, Blue Teal, Paradise and Mallard ducks, are feature in the extensive lawns and gardens which surround "Donegal House". the towering Kaikoura Mountains make a perfect backdrop to this unique setting.
"Even if you're not Irish - this is the place for you!" A home away from home!

Kaikoura
Guest House/Inn
Address: 53 Deal Street, Kaikoura
Name: Nikau - the inn with the view
Telephone: (03) 319 6973
Fax: (03) 319 6973
E-mail: nikau@kaikoura.co.nz
Beds: 3 Double, 2 Twin,
1 Triple/Quad (6 bedrooms)
Bathroom: 5 Ensuites, 1 Private

Tariff: B&B (continental) Double $65-$85, Single $60. Credit Cards accepted.
Nearest Town: Blenheim 1hour 45mins North

It is big, it is blue and what a view. Sea and mountains fill the windows. Nikau has bedrooms with balconies, bathrooms, arm chairs. Privacy guaranteed. There's books, magazines, tea, coffee, a writing place (with view), a big lounge.
Nikau is just a few minutes walk to Information, restaurants and shops. Freshly baked bread, muffins, fruit, tea and real coffee is served at a giant rimu table (once the local Council's).
Nikau is restful, the garden colourful, cottage-like. Nikau is run by Judith, a journalist, born just south of Kaikoura. Her travel photos fill the stairway. Many are of Bhutan where she lived and worked for 2 years.
Nikau is easy going, leisurely. There's a kitchen for guests to use if they wish.
Home Page: http://www.kaikoura.co.nz
Directions: *Easy to find, just off SH1, near the hospital, south side of town centre.*

Kaikoura
Homestay B&B

Address: Thistledhu,
Cnr Rakanui and Bullens Road, Peketa,
RD 2, Kaikoura
Name: Robyn and George
Telephone: (03) 319 6960
Fax: (03) 319 6960
Beds: 2 Queen, 2 Single (3 bedrooms)
Bathroom: 1 Ensuite, 1 Family Share
Tariff: B&B (full) $60-$70, Single $50,
NZ B&B Vouchers accepted
Nearest Town: Kaikoura, 8kms North on S.H.1

Located 8 km south of Kaikoura on SH1 at Peketa. Enjoy a wee touch of Kiwi and Scottish hospitality at our house, surrounded by hills, mountains, bird song and the sounds of the sea. A warm welcome, comfortable bed and cooked Scottish breakfast awaits you.

Just a 10 min drive to Kaikoura to see the whales, dolphins, seals and various other places of interest, for skiers and snowboarders Mt Lyford an hour away. Golf course and airport also close by.

We share our property with our dogs Nina and Molly, two black cats and four hens. We are non smokers.

Waiau
Farmstay/Homestay

Address: Mason Hills,
Inland Kaikoura Rd,
Waiau R.D., North Canterbury
Name: Averil & Robert Leckey
Telephone: (03) 315 6611
Fax: (03) 315 6611
Email: mason-hills@xtra.co.nz
Beds: 1 Queen, 2 Single (2 bedrooms)
Bathroom: 1 Ensuite, 1 Private
Tariff: B&B (full) Double $90, Single $50, Dinner $25,
Campervans parking (No power), Credit Cards.
NZ B&B Vouchers accepted $20 surcharge
Nearest Town: Kaikoura 1 hour, Hanmer Springs 1 hour, Christchurch 1 hour & 45 mins.

Welcome to Mason Hills, a hill country beef and sheep farm. We are situated on the inland route from Kaikoura to Hanmer Springs. Our lovely character homestead looks directly at Mount Lyford ski area which is only 8km away.

We can offer a four wheel drive adventure as an extra. See the Coast from Kaikoura to Banks Peninsula and the Southern Alps spreading away into the distance. Visit the unique "potholes" and stand on top of the "Battery". See sheep and cattle grazing in picturesque surroundings. Or you can stroll along the Mason river, visit native bush or relax on our verandah and listen to the bellbirds.

We are centrally situated to visit the Whales at Kaikoura or swim at Hanmer's hot springs. A home cooked meal is available in the evenings and we would welcome you company by the open fire. We share our home with 2 cats and a friendly Labrador.
Home Page: http://www.destination-nzcom/masonhills/

Hanmer Springs

Homestay
Address: Champagne Flat Hanmer Springs
Name: Chris & Virginia Parsons
Telephone: (03) 315 7413
Fax: (03) 315 7412
Beds: 1 Queen,1 Double, 1 Single (3 Bedrooms)
Bathroom: 1 Guests share
Tariff: B&B (full) Double $45pp, Single $50pp,
Children half price, Dinner $25pp. Credit cards.
NZ B&B Vouchers accepted Surcharge $20.
Nearest Town: Hanmer Springs 6km

Champagne Flat is a small farmlet situated just 6 kilometres from the tiny township of Hanmer Springs. Its history is closely tied in with the building of the Ferry Bridge in 1887 and we are only 2 minutes from this historic construction which is now used for bungy jumping. Our home is a modern two-storeyed farm house with its own facilities for guests. Each guest room has its own outstanding views - wake up to a spectacular view of the snow-capped mountains and the braided Waiau River. You will have warm, spacious surroundings and share our enjoyment of the peace and tranquillity of the Hanmer Valley. We are a friendly, outgoing couple - husband a school principal, wife a 'retired' social worker dabbling in art, gardening and Red Cross. We specialise in scrumptious full English breakfasts and you may join us for dinner if you wish. Participate in local activities - thermal pools, trout fishing, forest walks, golf, skiing, jet-boating.
Directions: *1 1/2 hours easy drive north from Christchurch. SH 7 Hanmer turn off. 4 hours south from the Picton Ferry via Kaikoura inland.*

Hanmer Springs

B&B + Luxury Suites
Address: "Glenalvon Lodge",
29 Amuri Avenue, Hanmer Springs
Name: Anna & Theo Van de Wiel
Telephone: (03) 315 7475 Free Booking
Phone: 0800 GLENALVON **Fax**: (03) 315 7361
Email: VDWIEL@XTRA.CO.NZ
Beds: 6 Queen, 7 Double, 6 Single (11 bedrooms)
Bathroom: 10 Ensuites, 1 Private.
Tariff: B&B (continental) Double $80, Suites $79-$125 breakfast optional extra.
Single from $60, Dinner $25pp, All credit cards accepted. NZ B&B Vouchers
accepted $10-$15 surcharge
Nearest Town: Town Centre

Glenalvon is a historic colonial style building on a beautiful tree-lined avenue in the heart of Hanmer. It is situated opposite the famous thermal pools and only a few minutes from restaurants and shops.The main house has 3 bedrooms, 2 ensuites and one private bathroom, a lovely lounge and dining room, solely for guests. We are non-smoking. Eight suites have been added on. All with ensuites, mini kitchen and TVs. Our executive / honeymoon suite is particularly pretty and includes a spabath. Each suite has been decorated with great care and taste.We are retired chefs and our interests are music, art and crafts, cooking, gardening, travelling and meeting interesting people. Our village has many outdoor activities available. We are happy to arrange these for you.We speak Dutch and German. We like you to feel at home away from home and hope you enjoy your stay with us.
Home Page: http://nz.com/infocus

Cheltenham House

Hanmer Springs
Bed & Breakfast
Address: 13 Cheltenham Street, Hanmer Springs
Name: Len & Maree Earl
Telephone: (03) 315 7545 **Fax**: (03) 315 7645
Email: cheltenham@xtra.co.nz
Beds: 4 Queen, 2 Single (4 bedrooms)
Bathroom: 3 Ensuite, 1 Private
Tariff: B&B (special) Double $130-$140, Single $100,
Credit Cards (VISA/MC/BC).
NZ B&B Vouchers accepted $60 surcharge
Nearest Town: Located in centre of Hanmer Springs

Cheltenham House

Built in the 1930's for the daughter of Duncan Rutherford, an early settler in Hanmer, Cheltenham House has recently been refurbished to share with guests. Situated on a quiet side street, it is within two minutes stroll to the Thermal Pools, restaurants and shops.

All suites are north facing and tastefully furnished to create a relaxed, private atmosphere. Each is equipped with a television, tea and coffee making facilities and superior quality Queen size beds with woollen underlays and duvets. Breakfast which includes homemade muesli, yoghurt, fruit, local smoked salmon and eggs, and the traditional cooked breakfast, is served in the privacy of your suite at your leisure.

Three of the spacious bedrooms have ensuites. The fourth suite has a private bathroom which caters for people with disabilities.

The billiard room with its full size table, open fire and upright grand piano provides an ideal environment to relax and socialise. For our guests' comfort, our house is centrally heated. Guests are welcome to smoke in our extensive garden.

Hanmer Springs is an alpine resort providing an extensive range of activities, for the most adventurous to the most relaxed tourist.

Along with our daughter Emma, son Anthony and our gentle Labrador and sociable Siamese cat, we love to meet people and share our gracious home with them.

Home Page: http://www.cheltenham.co.nz

Members of
**The New Zealand Association
Farm & Home Host Inc.**
maintain the highest standards &
are always delighted to welcome
guests into their homes.

"Merlins"
country homestay
Old Fashioned Hospitality
Modern Comfort Lovely Food
HOSTS
ALEX & SALLY ALEXANDER

Tariff: B&B Full Special (menu) Breakfast: Double $100 - $110 Single $85
QUOTES:
"What a gem...Setting stunning... The lamb dinner was spectacular as well as the salmon for breakfast" *I. Roper, Vienna, Virginia. U.S.A.*
"The reality exceeded by far what we had hoped to find" *Dr C Menke, Schwabish Hall, Germany.*
"Perhaps Pa Larkin has it right - 'Perfick, just perfick'!" AND THE FOLLOWING YEAR: "We came back to check! Arguably the best evening meal in NZ. Still perfick!" *R&J Goldson, Cropston Leics. Britain*
".... may we tell you that NOWHERE in Australia or NZ did we have finer accommodation or more delicious food". *M&J Robey, Ross-on-Wye. Britain.*
"We have lovely memories of your beautiful home in Hanmer Springs...warm hospitality.....and delicious cuisine". *Ida Phillips and Marie Bartholomew, Lewes, Sussex, Britain.*

Full Details Opposite -

Hanmer Springs
Homestay
Address: "Merlins", Rippingale Road,
Hanmer Springs

Name: Alex & Sally Alexander
Telephone/Fax: (03) 315 7428
Bookings: **Freephone** 0800 342 313.
Overseas Callers:
Phone/Fax: 0064 3 315 7428
Beds: 1 King, 1 Super King/Twin
(2 bedrooms)
Bathrooms: 2 Ensuites
(1 with Spa bath)

BREAKFAST AT MERLINS
Start with Fruit Juice
Fresh Fruit Salad, Yoghurt & Cereals
or Hot Porridge & Cream
followed by Hot Dish Choice
served with our Home Baked Meatloaf
1. Smoked Salmon & Scrambled eggs
2. Fillet of Sole
3. Full English Breakfast
4. Various Savoury Omelettes
5. Sweet Souffle Omelette
6. Crepes with Honey & Lemon
7. French Toast, Bacon & Banana
Sally's Preserves
Toast, Coffee or Tea

Tariff: B&B (full/special)
Double $100-$110, Single $85
Quality **Menu** Dinners by Arrangement
$30-$37.5 0pp BYO
Gourmet Suppers $17.50 pp.
Credit Cards (VISA/MC).
NZ B&B Vouchers accepted, Surcharge $20-$25 on Doubles.

Nearest Town: Town centre 1½ km

A Warm Welcome and Modern Comfort await at "MERLINS", a fine, new, centrally heated, one storey home, on two acres in a quiet country lane. The spacious, comfortable GUEST ROOMS are very private, have large beautifully fitted ENSUITES, cosy armchairs, electric blankets, television, books, own tea & coffee facilities and majestic mountain, forest and rural views. With easy access and excellent parking, "MERLINS" is across from a beautiful GOLF COURSE, surrounded by fields of grazing sheep and cattle and horses, yet ONLY 1½ KM to the VILLAGE and its renowned THERMAL SPA Complex.

Our memorable COUNTRY HOUSE BREAKFASTS, noted for the VARIETY of substantial and delicious HOT DISH choices, are served in the conservatory with magnificent views of the alpine landscape.

DINNER AT "MERLINS" (ESSENTIAL TO BOOK BY 10 a.m.). Now retired, we created Hanmer's "Garden House" Restaurant, (1978-1983), renowned for SALLY'S IMAGINATIVE COUNTRY COOKING. Local and international clientele included two Governors General. Enjoy in the cosy private dining room, a DELECTABLE DINNER, cooked SPECIALLY FOR YOU. Bring your own wine. Choose from our MENU, the best of NEW ZEALAND foods: Smoked Salmon, Pates, filled Crepes, Seafoods, homemade Soups & Consommés, Prime Tenderloin Fillet Beef, Racks of Baby Lamb, Venison, Ocean Farmed Salmon, Duckling, Vegetarian Dishes, tempting Desserts and Specialist Cheeses.

Alternatively, we offer a delicious GOURMET SUPPER with dessert, served in your room. Relax in the sitting room, where we have a fine collection of records. We have many interests, and our extensive local knowledge can help with Forests Walks, Golf, Horse Trekking, Fishing, Hunting, Scenic and Kaikoura Whale Watch Flights. Non-smoking but those who haven't given up YET, may use our covered verandah.

Directions: *At the cross road junction before the village (look for our sign on sign post) take ARGELINS ROAD (Centre branch). Go past the Country & Golf Club on the left. RIPPINGALE ROAD (no exit) is first on left. We are 800 metres down, at the end of the road, on the right.*

573

Culverden
Farmstay
Address: 'Ballindalloch', Culverden,
North Canterbury
Name: Diane & Dougal Norrie
Telephone: (03) 315 8220
Fax: (03) 315 8220
Mobile: (025) 373 184
Beds: 1 Queen, 2 Single (2 bedrooms)
Bathroom: 1 Guests share
Tariff: B&B (full) Double $105, Single $55, Children under 14 $30. Dinner $30pp.
NZ B&B Vouchers accepted
Nearest Town: Culverden - 3km south of Culverden

Welcome to "Ballindalloch" a 2000 acre (800 hectare) dairy and sheep irrigated property 3km south of Culverden. We milk 1060 cows in 2 floating rotary dairy sheds (parlours) a concept unique to New Zealand. We farm 3000 Corriedale sheep as well as a Corriedale stud. Our German daughter-in-law has recently introduced emus to our farming scene. Our newly refurbished ranch style home is set amongst lawns and gardens with a swimming pool. Panoramic views of the hills and mountains surround us. The house is centrally heated in winter; as well as a log fire.
Culverden is situated between 2 excellent fishing rivers; has a golf course; nearby is the Amuri salmon farm and Mt Lyford ski village. Being 100km from Christchurch; Half an hour to Hanmer Springs thermal pools and 1 1/2 hours to Kaikouras whale watch.We have travelled extensively overseas and appreciate relaxing in a homely atmosphere. This we extend to all guests. Complementary farm tour. Please ring or fax for reservations. Non smoking household. One family cat Thomas.

Culverden, North Canterbury

Farmstay
Address: "Pahau Pastures",
St. Leonards Road, Culverden,
North Canterbury
Name: David & Di Bethell
Telephone: (03) 315 8023 **Fax**: (03) 315 8023
Mobile: (025) 362 530
Beds: 1 Double, 4 Single (3 bedrooms)
Bathroom: 1 Ensuite, 1 Private
Tariff: B&B (full) Double $110, Single $55, Children under 12 half price,
Dinner $35. NZ B&B Vouchers accepted. Credit Cards.
Nearest Town: Culverden 4.5km, 100kms to Christchurch.

Pahau Pastures is a sheep and cattle property of 3500 acres, with border-dyke irrigation, and has been in our family for 120 years. Our large rambling historic kauri homestead has been restored, as has our garden with mature trees, sweeping lawns, stunning views, and acres of daffodils which are a feature late September. Now areas are planted in roses, paeonies, perennials, irises, lavender and rhododendron. Tour the farm or relax on our huge verandah or by a warming fire in winter. Dinner is by arrangement, with local wine complimentary. Local activities available are hot thermal pools, bungy jumping, fishing, ski-ing, golf, jet boating, Maori rock art, whale watching, bush walks and local wineries. We have a Labrador and a cat, and you are welcome to smoke outdoors. We have travelled a lot and enjoy meeting new people.
Directions: *Please ring for details.*

Gore Bay, Cheviot
Homestay
Address: 'Saltburn', Gore Bay,
Cheviot RD3, Canterbury
Name: Dorothy & Les Jefferson
Telephone: (03) 319 8686
Beds: 1 Double, 2 Single
(2 bedrooms, electric blankets)
Bathroom: 1 Private, 1 Family share

SALTBURN

Tariff: B&B (full) Double $70, Single $40, Children half price;
Dinner by arrangement $20. NZ B&B Vouchers accepted.
Nearest Town: Cheviot 9 km

Originally from England, my husband and I have retired to the house we have built overlooking the bay in this attractive area.
We have travelled extensively, both in New Zealand and overseas, and thoroughly enjoy meeting people from other countries. At home we are keen gardeners and appreciate the mild climate we experience here.
We also enjoy tramping and there are many walking tracks, delightful views and a safe surfing and swimming beach. We have a small dog.
Native birds abound and a seal colony lies along the coast to the north, while a walkway follows the coastline southward through natural bush to the Hurunui River mouth, an excellent fishing spot.
Cheviot, the nearest shopping area is 1 hour 30 mins drive north of Christchurch on State Highway One and 1 hours drive south from Kaikoura.

Waikari
Historic home & Farmstay
Address: 'Waituna', Waikari,
North Canterbury
Name: David & Joanna Cameron
Telephone: (03) 314 4575
(Best before 8.30am or after 5pm) **Fax**: (03) 314-4575
Beds: 1 King/Twin, 1 Queen, 3 Single (4 Bedrooms)
Bathroom: 1 Guests share plus extra loo and handbasin
Tariff: B&B (continental) Double $100, Single $50, Dinner includes wine $35pp
by arrangement. Credit cards. From 30/9/99: Double $110, Single $55,
Dinner $40 pp NZ B&B Vouchers accepted $30 surcharge per double
Nearest Town: Waikari 5km, 76km north of Christchurch, under 1' hour from
Christchurch airport.

'Waituna' is a sheep and cattle farm situated 2.5km off Highway 7, halfway between Christchurch and Hanmer Springs. The homestead, one of the largest and oldest in this area, is listed with the Historic Places Trust, the original part, built of limestone in 1879 and the last addition with extensive use of kauri, was completed in 1905. Nearby are well known wineries, golf courses, horse treks and good fishing rivers, while in Hanmer (45 mins) there are thermal pools, forest walks, skiing, bungy jumping, jet boating etc. We enjoy all sports, meeting people and travelling, being drawn mainly to the United Kingdom and Ireland, where we lived until 1972. (David is English and Jo a New Zealander.) We have a big dog called "Othello". We look forward to welcoming you to our gracious old home.
Directions: *Please phone, fax or write for bookings and directions.*

Waipara

Country Inn
Address: 161 Church Road, Waipara
Name: The Old Glenmark Vicarage
Telephone: (03) 314 6775
Fax: (03) 314 6775
Beds: 2 queen, 1 Single (2 bedrooms)
Bathroom: 2 Ensuite
Tariff: B&B (special) Double $165-$185, Single $135,
Credit Cards (VISA/MC/AMEX).
Nearest Town: 15km north of Amberley.

The Old Glenmark Vicarage - in the heart of the Waipara wine region, just 40 mins north from Christchurch airport, and enroute to Kaikoura, Blenheim, Hanmer Springs the West Coast and Nelson. Come and experience the history, warm relaxed hospitality, the peaceful rural setting. This rambling kauri villa, circa 1906, features colourful country-style bedrooms, spacious ensuites, fresh flowers, hand-crafted beds. Laze on wide verandahs amongst old roses and wisteria, or the shade of the beautiful oaks, enjoy vistas of vineyards and rolling hills. Have a leisurely lunch at one of our local wineries, take a country walk. Cafe, wine bar, country pubs all close by. On cool evenings enjoy the open fire in our well stocked cosy library. And in the morning enjoy breakfast in our wonderful farmhouse kitchen. Home baked breads and muffins, fresh fruits, cooked choice. We have donkeys, sheep, cats and Stanley.
We are smoke-free indoors and unsuitable for children.

Waipara

Cottage Bed & Breakfast
Address: Winery Cottage,
9 Johnson Street,
Waipara, North Canterbury
Name: Julian Ball
Telephone: (03) 314 6909
Fax: (03) 314 6909
Beds: 2 Queen (2 bedrooms)
Bathroom: 2 Ensuite
Tariff: B&B (full) Double $110, Credit Cards.
NZ B&B Vouchers accepted $30 surcharge
Nearest Town: 12km north Amberley, 70km north Christchurch, 75km Hanmer Springs.

Situated on the northern edge of Aipara village, Winery Cottage offers you the ideal location to experience the many attractions that make our area unique.
Base yourself in a cosy cottage with warm, spacious bedrooms and your very own modern ensuite bathroom. In the morning take a relaxed hearty breakfast with freshly baked breads, home-made muesli, fruit juice, hot porridge and filling cooked breakfast.
Evening meal available upon request.
Within walking distance, the Weka Pass Railway will take you on a steam train excursion. Through the hills to Frog rock - a spectacular limestone outcrop. Colmonel Horse Treks provides wagon rides through the vineyards, Glenmarr church and nearby wineries.
Smoke Free. Not suitable for children.

Amberley

Homestay/Farmstay
Address: Bredon Downs, Amberley RD 1,
North Canterbury
Name: Bob & Veronica Lucy
Telephone: (03) 314 9356 **Fax**: (03) 314 8994
E-mail: lucy.lucy@xtra.co.nz
Mobile: (025) 224 4061
Beds: 1 Double, 3 Single (3 bedrooms)
Bathroom: 1 Guests share
Tariff: B&B (full) Double $90, Single $50, Dinner $25,
Credit Cards (VISA/MC). NZ B&B Vouchers accepted $15 surcharge for "doubles".
Nearest Town: 1km South of Amberley township

Our old farmhouse is off the road and surrounded by an English style garden with swimming pool and lawn tennis court. We breed ostriches and we are only too pleased to show these to anyone interested. Bob and I have lived abroad and travelled extensively and very much look forward to the company of local and overseas visitors and to entertaining them in our home.
Bredon Downs is on SH1 and conveniently on the way to or from the inter-island ferry - just 48km north of Christchurch, and will appeal to those who prefer seeking country accommodation rather than the hustle and bustle of a city. The well known Waipara Wine Trail starts just north of Amberley, offering a wide selection of tasting and excellent lunches. The beach is only 2km away and there is an attractive Golf Course. We share our lives with 3 geriatric donkeys, a friendly Newfoundland dog, an ancient Labrador and Rupert the cat.

Waikuku Beach

Homestay
Address: 74 Waikuku Beach Road,
Waikuku Beach
Name: Graeme & Pauline Barr
Telephone: (03) 312 2292
Fax: (03) 312 2235
Mobile: 03 3122292
Beds: 1 Double, 2 Single (2 bedrooms)
Bathroom: 1 Private, 1 Family share
Tariff: B&B (continental) Double $60, Single $40, Children half price.
Mastercard/Visa, Credit cards. NZ B&B Vouchers accepted
Nearest Town: Rangiora 10 mins, Christchurch 30 mins.

Nestled amongst pine trees in a rural atmosphere at a quiet beach settlement, and not far from the main highway, we are just 30 minutes drive north of Christchurch city and International Airport.
We offer a friendly bed and breakfast service with off-street parking in our modern two storeyed comfortable accommodation. Guests can relax on spacious decks or in a comfortable fireside lounge.
Tea and coffee-making facilities are available at all times.
Enjoy a continental breakfast before exploring the nearby beach, bird life (sanctuary), lavender fields and potteries. Mt Grey and Mt Thomas, with their numerous walking tracks, are a short drive away. We are keen trampers (trekkers) and have first hand experience of many of the well-known tracks in the South Island.
We have a friendly Labrador dog which lives outside.
Our home is smoke-free, peaceful and warm.

Oxford

Homestay + Self-Contained Acco
Address: 137 High Street, Oxford
Name: Norton & Helen Dunn
Telephone: (03) 312 4167
Beds: 3 Double bedrooms,(one brm has guest shower, toilet, sitting room, kitchen facilities, verandah ent)
Bathroom: Other bathrooms are handy
Tariff: B&B (full) Self-contained unit Double $70, Single $40, Homestay B&B (full) Double $60, Single $35, Dinner $20 by arrangement, Children 5-13yrs $12, under 5 no charge.
Nearest Town: Walking distance to the shops, 55 km from Christchurch

Our house is 80 years old and has a spacious garden – warm and sunny. We are a contented married couple with a family of three grown-up sons. We retired from Dunedin to live in Oxford – a charming, restful town and a friendly community. Oxford offers scenic walks, horse treks, homecrafts, pottery and home spun hand-knitted garments, bowls, tennis, squash, restaurant, golf and bridge club handy.
Directions: *High Street is off the Main Road – left – sign outside the gate.*

Oxford

Bed & Breakfast
Address: 'Glenariff', 136 High St, Oxford
Name: Beth Minns
Telephone: (03) 312 4678
Beds: 1 Double, 2 Single (2 bedrooms)
Bathroom: 1 Guests share
Tariff: B&B (full) Double $60, Single $30, Children half price.
Dinner $20 by arrangement. NZ B&B Vouchers accepted
Nearest Town: Oxford - town centre 500m

Your hosts John and Beth came to Oxford leaving the hustle and bustle of the city to sample the 'good-life' in the country. Along the way acquiring sheep, hens plus a handsome goat named 'Walter'. We would like you to share our hospitality and enjoy a taste of country life. A leisurely breakfast, candle-light dinner or a Devonshire Tea served on the verandah.
'Glenariff' is a 2 storey character home (circa 1886) operated as a Devonshire Tea Rooms, set in 1 1/4 acres of lawns with mature trees and a paddock for Walter and friends. Oxford caters for most sports including tennis, squash and bowls with golf, fishing, horse riding, and jet boating close by.
There are walks and tramps to suit all levels of interest and fitness.
We enjoy meeting people and as Beth's forte is cooking we guarantee you'll leave well fed and rested.

Continental breakfast consists of fruit, cereal, toast, tea/coffee,
Full breakfast is the same with a cooked course,
Special breakfast has something special.

Oxford
Farmstay+B&B
Address: 345 Woodside Rd, Coopers Creek, Oxford, North Canterbury
Name: Don and Anne Manera
Telephone: (03) 312 4964
Beds: 1 Double, 1 Twin, 1 Single (3 bedrooms)
Bathroom: Family share
Tariff: B&B (continental) $35 per person, Children $20,
Dinner $20pp. NZ B&B Vouchers accepted
Nearest Town: Oxford 3km, Rangiora 25km

Welcome to Twin Bridge Farm our home set amidst tranquil situated on rolling farm land with views of the Southern Alps. Our farm of 86 acres has sheep, cattle, 3 farm dogs. A short walk to a pond has wild life in different seasons. Oxford area featues many walks casual or for more experienced trampers through forest reserve, native bush and birds. 2 local rivers for fishing, jetboating, golf course, horseriding tuition trecking hourly or day within 10 min. Approx. 45 minutes away to ski fields in the Southern Alps.

1 double, 1 twin and 1 single bedrooms, shared bathroom with hosts. Large combine dining-lounge room with featured open fire, Evening meal consists of local meat and produce.

We are 3.7km west of Oxford Township watch for sign. 45 minutes from Christchurch. Bed & Breakfast $35 per person. Dinner $20 per person. Ph. 03-312-4964. No smoking.

Oxford
Homestay/Bed and Breakfast
Address: 74 Bush Road, Oxford
Name: Hielan' House,
Shirley and John Farrell
Telephone: (03) 312 4382
Mobile: 025 359 435
Fax: (03) 312 4382
Freephone for bookings: 0800 279 382
Email: meg29@ihug.co.nz

Beds: Apartment with 1 Queen, 1 Twin, bedsettee in lounge
Bathroom: Private
Tariff: B&B (full/special) $90 double, $50 single, children negotiable,
Dinner $20pp. Visa, Mastercard, NZ B&B Vouchers accepted (Surcharge $10 on double)
Nearest Town: Oxford 1 1/2km, ChCh Airport 40 minutes.

Our two storied home on 6 acres (inground swimming pool), has lovely surroundings, with rural views to the Mountains. As we homestay one party at a time; the new guest apartment is ideal for couples, or families; includes lounge, electric blankets / electric heating, TV, tea / coffee making facilities and separate entrance.

The warmest of welcomes with all the trimmings, from ourselves, three friendly dogs and cat. Generous menu breakfasts with excellent choices, dinners with homegrown meat and produce. BBQ area. The golf course, jetboating, superb fishing and bush walks and Darfield Railway Station for the TransAlpine Express, all within easy reach. Relax in the heart of the country at a gateway to the West Coast, North Canterbury, yet Christchurch Airport only 40 mins away. Non smoking, but there's a big ashtray outside.

Directions: *Turn into Bay Road (off Main Street) first left into Bush Road. Our signposted entrance is on left, 740 metres along road. A phone call would be appreciated.*

Christchurch City
Private Hotel
Address: 52 Armagh Street, Christchurch
Name: Windsor Private Hotel
Telephone: (03) 366 1503 or 366 2707
Fax: (03) 366 9796
Email: reservations@windsorhotel.co.nz
Beds: 40 bedrooms
Bathroom: Guests share
Tariff: B&B (full) Double $90, Single $60, Children under 12 years $15.
Credit cards/Eftpos. Quote this book for 10% discount.
NZ B&B Vouchers accepted 1st April to 30th September
Nearest Town: Christchurch City

"The Windsor", originally named Warwick House, was built at the turn of the century. Situated in the quiet northwest situation of Cranmer Square, we are centrally located on the tourist tram route and within easy walking distance of the Art Centre, museum, gardens, theatre, convention centre, Casino and Cathedral Square (our city centre), with its banks, buses, shopping arcades and excellent restaurants.Guests are greeted on arrival and shown around our charming colonial style home. Our nicely furnished bedrooms all with a small posie of flowers, and an original water colour by local artist Denise McCulloch, lend charm to the warm and cosy bedrooms which are all individually heated. The shared bathroom facilities are all conveniently appointed for guests comfort with bathrobes provided on request. The dining room where our generous morning menu includes juice, fresh fruit and cereals, followed by a choice of bacon and eggs, sausages, tomatoes, toast and marmalade. The lounge where we serve tea, coffee and biscuits each evening at 9.00 pm is where everyone gathers to watch television and have a chat. There are 24 hour tea, coffee and laundry facilities along with off-street parking for the motorist. For the comfort and convenience of our guests we encourage non-smoking.
Home Page: www.windsorhotel.co.nz

Christchurch - Bryndwr
Homestay
Address: 'Allisford', 1/61 Aorangi Road
(off Ilam Rd), Bryndwr, Christchurch
Name: Allison Crawford
Telephone: (03) 351 7742
Mobile: (025) 229 2486
Beds: 2 Single (1 bedroom)
Bathroom: share with Allison
Tariff: B&B (special, continental)
Double $60-$70, Single $40. NZ B&B Vouchers accepted
Nearest Town: Christchurch city centre 10 mins by bus or car. Airport 10 mins

A warm welcome awaits you in my comfortable home which I enjoy sharing with guests. My hobbies are gardening, walking, travel, some clubs, and meeting people. I am easily reached from North, South and West Highways or drive down memorial Avenue from the Airport turn left into Ilam Road, past Aqualand and you are in Aorangi Road. Golf courses are close by and Race courses are an easy drive away. Beds have electric blankets, there are heaters in your bedroom and bathroom, laundry and ironing facilities are available. You are assured of no waiting for the bathroom and are welcome to make tea or coffee any time. Excellent licensed restaurants are ten minutes pleasant walk or you are welcome to bring home take-aways. The bus stop is three minutes walk away and passes the Gardens, Arts Centre and Tourist Information Centre on the way to the City Centre.
Directions: *Please phone. If I am out, the answer phone will direct you.*

Christchurch - Woolston
Homestay
Address: "Treeview", 6 Lomond Place,
Woolston, Christchurch
Name: Kathy & Laurence Carr
Telephone: (03) 384 2352
Beds: 1 Double, 2 Single (2 bedrooms)
Bathroom: 1 Guests share
Tariff: B&B (continental) Double $60, Single $40, Children half price,
Dinner $20. Credit cards NZ B&B Vouchers accepted
Nearest Town: Christchurch 10 minutes

Welcome to "Kathy's Place", 10 mins drive from City. We offer Friendly Kiwi hospitality. Enjoyed many years of hosting. Smoke Free home, no stairs. Guests Carport. Guests delighted at the quiet relaxed atmosphere. Lounge and dining room have Cathedral Ceilings and Log fire for warmth, are away from guest bedrooms.
Remarks:- Comfortable beds, generous breakfasts, central position. 10 mins drive to Beaches, Brighton Pier, Tower Bungy, Sumner, Port Hills, Para Gliding, Lancaster Park, 5 mins walk to buses, Restaurant.
Directions: *From Cathedral Square take Gloucester Street to Roundabout at Linwood Avenue, turn Right, pass Eastgate Mall to traffic lights end of Avenue of trees. Right into Hargood Street, First Left into Clydesdale Street, first Left Lomond Place. Cul-de-sac, no 6 on right. Alternative:- Ferry Road Woolston to traffic lights Hargood Street. 4th street on right is Clydesdale. First Left is Lomond Place.*
Courtesy Transport from Railway or Coach Depot. Super Shuttle from Airport. Please phone (03) 384 2352.

Christchurch - St Martins

Homestay & Self-contained accommodation
Address: "KLEYNBOS",
59 Ngaio Street, St Martins,
Christchurch
Name: Hans van den Bos & Gerda de Kleyne
Telephone: (03) 332 2896 **Fax**: (03) 332 2896 **Mobile**: 025-223 4144
Email: Lucien.dol@xtra.co.nz
Beds: 1 Queen, 1 Double, 1 Single (2 bedrooms)
Bathroom: 1 Ensuite, 1 Guests share
Tariff: B&B (continental) Double $65-$80, Single $40-$55, Triple $95, Studio
Room $75 (only $55 when fully self catering). Credit Cards accepted. NZ B&B
Vouchers accepted (No charge, or $10 surcharge for ensuite bathroom or studio
room).
Nearest Town: City Centre only 4km, Railway Station 6km, Airport 15km.

*Away from the "hustle and bustle". close to the city centre, meet warm character
ambience and VERY IMPORTANT a comfortable bed!!!*
*Even though you are enjoying travelling it is rather wearing on your body and mind.
We want to be a place you enjoy to settle in for a few days.*
*Hans and Gerda host because we enjoy meeting you. Hospitality and personal
attention are priority.*
*We are relatively small and very flexible. Our homestay accommodation can be used
as B&B, self-contained B&B, or for self catering. So we can provide you with any
degree of privacy and independence you desire.*
*Your large ensuite room has impressive rimu beams and floor. The studioroom is
artistic with full kitchen facilities including microwave and TV. They are excellent
value for money.*
Your hostess works in mental health, our children are 6 and 9 years.
*We have enjoyed the privilege to live in New-Zealand for over 10 years and having
guests is to us a little like having family come to stay.*
We look forward to meeting you.
Home Page: http://www.nzhomestay.hn.pl.net/chch/chch1.htm
Directions: *From airport (15km) and railway station (6km) take shuttle or taxi. From
city (4km) take bus.*

	Gamblins rd.	Brougham st-sh 73	inner city centre
59 Ngaio st. ←			
Wilsons rd	Waltham rd	Waltham rd-sh 74	Barbadoes st-sh74
S ←---			
		Brougham st-sh74	

Christchurch - Spreydon

Self-contained Accommodation
Address: 105 Lyttelton Street, Christchurch
Name: Bev & Kerry Bloomfield
Telephone: (03) 332 5360 **Fax**: (03) 332 5362
Beds: 1 Queen, 2 Single (2 bedrooms)
Bathroom: 1 Private
Tariff: B&B (continental) Double $70,
$10 each extra person. Children welcome, Campervans welcome.
Credit Cards. NZ B&B Vouchers accepted

If you wish peace and quiet in the city, we have a modern two bedroom self-contained apartment which is situated on a back section.
It is separated from our house by a carport into which you can put your car. The apartment has a private phone, TV, fridge/freezer, stove, microwave, washing machine and your own front lawn. We also have a cot and highchair available and a swing and slide for children to play on.
We are also close to the Railway Station, Princess Margaret and Public Hospital, Addington Raceway, Addington Entertainment Cenre, Indoor swimming pool and the Pioneer Sports Stadium and a 5 min drive from the centre of the city.
We provide a comprehensive continental style breakfast. This is prepared and placed in your apartment so you can breakfast at leisure. If your prefer you may do your own catering (discount tariff).

Christchurch - Lyttelton

Homestay+Self-contained Accom.
Address: Randolph House 49 Sumner Road,
Lyttelton, Christchurch
Name: Judy & Jonathan Elworthy
Telephone: (03) 328 8877 **Fax**: (03) 328 8779
Mobile: (025) 356 309
Email: randolph@es.co.nz
Beds: 2 Double, 2 Single (3 bedrooms)
Bathroom: 1 Ensuite, 1 Guests share
Tariff: B&B (full) Double $80-$105, Single $65-$80,

Children welcome by arrangement, Dinner by arrangement, Not suitable for campervans, Credit cards (VISA/MC/AMEX), Reduced tariff for longer stays.
NZ B&B Vouchers accepted $20 surcharge
Nearest Town: Christchurch 10km

Enjoy a village atmosphere with great little restaurants, late night music at the Wunderbar and yet be within fifteen minutes from the centre of Christchurch! Lyttelton is a fun place to be. Our Victorian villa overlooks the harbour. In summer we often dine outdoors as the sun sets in the west. Spectacular! We enjoy meeting interesting people and have very happy memories of our many guests. Jonathan is a former member of Parliament, who is actively involved in community organisations, and enjoys lively conversation and strenuous exercise. I am an Interior Designer and Real Estate Consultant, and enjoy choral singing and playing the viola. We have travelled extensively, have three married children, including a German daughter-in-law, several grandchildren, and still feel young. Dougal a labrador and Liszt the cat live here. Accommodation: Studio: En suite, twin beds, feather duvets, kitchenette, private balcony, breakfast served in studio, or in the dining room. Garaging for car. House: Historic, comfortable, double attic bedrooms with guest bathroom downstairs. Commode and bathrobes.
Home Page: http://n.z.com/webnz/bbnz/ randolph.htm.

Christchurch - Fendalton
Homestay
Address: 'Fendalton House",
50 Clifford Avenue, Fendalton, Christchurch 1.
Name: Pam Rattray
Telephone: (03) 355 4298
(Please let ring at least 10 times)
Fax: (03) 355 0959
Email: fendhouse@xtra.co.nz
Beds: 1 Superking/Twin,1 King, 1 Queen, 1 Single (3 bedrooms)
Bathroom: 3 Ensuite
Tariff: B&B (special) Double $120-$130, Single $110-$120, Credit Cards.
Nearest Town: Driving, Airport 10 minutes, City Centre 5 minutes

Enjoy warm relaxed hospitality staying with us right in the middle of one of Christchurch's most beautiful suburbs with large trees and lovely gardens. Being central it's a pleasant walk into town through Hagley Park or Mona Vale. You can sit under the grape vine in the big conservatory that warms the whole house or wander down past the swimming pool to feed the wild ducks in the clear stream at the bottom of the garden. Eat your large home cooked breakfast (may include waffles with berry sauce, pancakes etc.) in the sunny dining room which has a small New Zealand art collection. Each room has large beds, an ensuite bathroom, colour TV and tea making facilities. The spa (jacuzzi) is usually hot but it's worth ringing 24 hrs in advance if you are really keen. Laundry facilities available. Major credit cards accepted. We are a non-smoking household with a small friendly cat.
Home Page: http://nz.com/webnz/bbnz/fendalt.htm

Christchurch - Lincoln
Country Homestay
Address: 'Menteith', Springs Road,
R.D.6, Christchurch 8021
Name: Fay & Stephen Graham
Telephone: (03) 325 2395 **Fax**: (03) 325 2395
Beds: 1 King/Twin, 1 Queen (3 bedrooms)
Bathroom: 1 Ensuite, 1 Private
Tariff: B&B (full) Double with ensuite $90, Double $85, Single $60, Children negotiable, Dinner $30, 10% discount 2 or more nights if booked directly with hosts. Credit cards: Visa/Mastercard
NZ B&B Vouchers accepted Surcharge ensuite-$15, double-$10
Nearest Town: Christchurch City, Airport very direct, 15 mins

Menteith, a 10 acre farmlet is nestled among mature trees with spectacular mountain views and country tranquillity, all within easy city, airport and Railway Station access. Relax in our warm indoor swimming/spa conservatory or explore the developing garden. Guest rooms offer tea/coffee making with cookies, electric blankets, heating, hairdryer, clock radios and cosy firm beds. We share our non-smoking home with 2 friendly cats, offering warm hospitality and home grown produce. Cooked breakfast - the choice and time is flexible. Delightful reasonable priced local restaurants are within 5 minutes drive or dinner is available here by arrangement. Lincoln University and golf course 3km away. An enjoyable day can be spent at Akaroa, 1 1/2 hours away. After many years involvement with tourism, our retirement interests are Rotary, genealogy, wine-making, skiing, tramping and golf. Fay is a keen spinner – you're welcome to try your hand!
Directions: *On the left, 9km along Springs Road from SH1 at Wigram.*

Christchurch City
Homestay/Bed & Breakfast
Address: 'Riverview Lodge' 361 Cambridge Terrace, Christchurch
Name: Ernst & Sabine
Telephone: (03) 365 2860 **Fax**: (03) 365 2845
Email: riverview.lodge@xtra.co.nz
Beds: 1 King/Queen, 2 Double, 1 Single (3 bedrooms)
Bathroom: 2 Ensuite, 1 Private
Tariff: B&B (special) Double $135-$160, Single $75-$120, Children neg.
Credit cards.
Nearest Town: 10 min walk into city.

Listed in FODOR'S as "pick of the B&B accommodation in Christchurch".
If you like quality accommodation in a relaxed and quiet atmosphere, still just minutes walking away from the centre of an exciting city: this is the place to stay.
Our house is a restored Edwardian residence that reflects the grace and style of the period with some fine carved Kauri and Rimu features.
It is ideally situated on the banks of the Avon River in a tranquil setting surrounded by an old English garden with mature trees.
Guest rooms are elegant, combining modern facilities with colonial furnishings. All rooms have ensuite/private facilities, colour TV and heating, balconies provide a superb river view.
Tea and coffee making facilities are available at all times. Breakfast is a house speciality with a wide choice of cooked and continental fare.
Kayaks, bicycles and golfclubs are available for guests to use.
As experienced travellers and tour operators we'll be happy to provide you with all the information that will make your stay in Christchurch and New Zealand unforgettable. German, Spanish, Dutch, French is spoken. For cancellations 48 hrs prior to arrival we charge the full amount of one night.
Directions: *RIVERVIEW LODGE is located on the corner of Cambridge Terrace and Churchill Street.*
Home Page: http://nz.com/heritageinns/riverviewlodge

Christchurch - Merivale
Bed & Breakfast Inn

VILLA VICTORIA

Address: 'Villa Victoria', The Lane,
27 Holly Road, Christchurch 1
Name: Kate McNeill
Telephone: (03) 355 7977 **Fax**: (03) 355 7977
Mobile: 025-397 376
Beds: 2 Double, 1 Single (3 bedrooms)
Bathroom: 3 Ensuite
Tariff: B&B (full) Double $140, Single $90, Credit cards (VISA/BC/MC).
Nearest Town: Christchurch. 5 minutes from City. 20 minutes walk

A warm welcome awaits you at "Villa Victoria".
Built from native kauri this 95 year old villa has been authentically restored by its owner Kate and reflects all the elegance and charm of a world gone by. Furnishings are appropriate to the late Victorian / Edwardian era with lace curtains / bedspreads, brass / iron beds, antiques and collectables. This tranquil haven has been designed to be a home away from home - it is small and intimate. Each bedroom is completely private with its own ensuite. Delectable breakfasts are speciality served in the formal dining room or during summer on the verandah overlooking the picturesque private garden. "Villa Victoria" is ideally situated within walking distance for all city activities, excellent restaurants, boutique shopping. Complimentary NZ wine / cheese or a port / coffee after dining.
Please phone for reservations and directions.
No smoking. Off-street parking.
Not suitable for children.
Home Page: http://nz.com/heritageinns/villa victoria

Members of
**The New Zealand Association
Farm & Home Host Inc.**
maintain the highest standards &
are always delighted to welcome
guests into their homes.

Christchurch - Tai Tapu
Farmstay (Orchard)
Address: 'Pear Drop Inn', Akaroa Road,
Highway 75, R.D. 2, Christchurch
Name: Brenda
Telephone: (03) 329 6778
Fax: (03) 329 6661
Mobile: (025) 399 498
Beds: 1 Queen, 4 Single,
Cot available (3 bedrooms)

Bathroom: 2 Ensuite, 1 Private, 1 Family share
Tariff: B&B (full) Double $80, Single $50, Children under 12 half price,
Dinner $25, Campervans welcome, Credit Cards.
NZ B&B Vouchers accepted $20 Surcharge
Nearest Town: Christchurch 10 mins drive on Highway 75

Your stay will be enjoyable - Superbly located - convenient for city and country activities. Home away from home, nestled in a large attractive garden. A comfortable country home. We desire to please and welcome visitors. Rooms have electric blankets, heaters and jugs. Showers are hot! You'll enjoy chatting in the kitchen while we cook! Our speciality is delicious home cooking with the organic fruit and vegetables grown here. Relax in the living rooms, spa pool, gazebo, TV room, or kitchen while meals are prepared, or use the BBQ. Organise your weekend retreat, or theme here - do something different! Art, gardens, walks, golf, skiing, horse trekking, wine trails etc. Let us help! Craft spinning is a hobby. Optional Art lessons and sketching - tailor made to suit you. Tuition in English as a second language given by arrangement. We open during holidays. Terminal pick-ups arranged. Si c'est bon (A little French spoken).
Home Page: http://nz.com/webnz/bbnz/pear.htm

Christchurch - Redcliffs
Homestay
Address: "Redcliffs on Sea",
125 Main Rd., Redcliffs, Chch 8
Name: Cynthia & Lyndsey Ebert
Telephone: (03) 384 9792 **Fax**: (03) 384 9703
Beds: 1 Double, 1 Single (1 bedroom). 1 Twin (1 bedroom)
Bathroom: 1 Ensuite, 1 Family share
Tariff: B&B (continental) $50 pp. NZ B&B Vouchers accepted $25 surcharge
Nearest Town: Christchurch 8kms

Relax and enjoy our comfortable home by the sea. Situated approximately 15 minutes from the city centre, our home is "absolute waterfront" on the Christchurch Estuary, with magnificent views of the sea, birds and boating. What more could you wish for? Nearby is the Sumner beach, Christchurch Gondola, and lovely walkways with hills and beaches to explore.
We are non-smoking and our guest facilities include a sunny double and single bed bedroom with ensuite, plus a twin bedroom with family share bathroom. Guests are welcome to enjoy the tranquil garden and seaside surroundings. Kayaks are available for exploring the estuary.
Local restaurants offer a wide choice of cuisine. A generous continental breakfast is included in the tariff, laundry facilities and off street parking are available. We have no pets or children. Please phone (03) 384-9792 or fax (03) 384-9703 before calling.

587

Christchurch - Richmond

Homestay, Bed & Breakfast
Address: 'Willow Lodge', 71 River Road, Richmond, Christchurch 1

Willow Lodge

Name: Grania McKenzie
Telephone: (03) 389 9395 **Fax**: (03) 381 5395
Beds: 1 King, 1 Queen,
3 Single (2 bedrooms incl. 2 room family suite)
Bathroom: 1 Ensuite, 1 Private
Tariff: B&B (full) Double $95-$120, Single $70, Childrenby arrangement.
Credit cards. Longer stays welcome, good discounts.
NZ B&B Vouchers accepted $30 surcharge/double
Nearest Town: 20 mins walk - central city, Lancaster Park.

THE SETTING is wonderful. "Willow Lodge" overlooks the Aron River in a peaceful location, with large trees. You can walk along the river to the central city - Cathedral Square, Arts centre, Hagley Park, good food and shopping. THE HOUSE retains plenty of original 1920's character - leadlight windows and lovely rimu doors and robes. THE GUEST ROOMS are spacious with ensuite or private bathroom and river and tree views, 1920/30's furniture and china combine with contemporary art and books. THE BREAKFAST is fresh and generous, organic breads, fresh fruit and cereals, B+E, good teas and coffee. OUR AIM is to provide fine quality accommodation in a friendly homestyle atmosphere. Extensive local knowledge of the South Island and the essential Christchurch. We have 2 elderly Labradors - downstairs and / or outside only. LASTLY! Guest phone, fax, TV's, mountain bikes, tea and coffee, local laundry.
Home Page: http://www.lynxmedia.co.nz/Canterbury/accom/willow
Directions: *Booking recommended. Shuttle service from Railway / Airport or phone for directions.*

Christchurch - New Brighton

Guest House
Address: 97 Lonsdale St New Brighton, Christchurch 8007
Name: The Pier Lodge
Telephone: (03) 388 3388 **Fax**: (03) 388 3387
Beds: 1 King, 1 Double, 1 Queen ensuite (Bridal), 4 Single (5 Bedrooms)
Bathroom: 3 Guests share, 1 Ensuite
Tariff: B&B (continental) Bridal Suite $80, Double $60, Single $40,
Children negotiable. Credit cards (Visa/MC/Diners/Eftpos).
NZ B&B Vouchers accepted $15 surcharge Bridal Suite
Nearest Town: New Brighton is suburb of Christchurch. 10 min drive to Christchurch city centre.

The Pier Lodge is a guest house with a difference, keeping in mind your expectations of comfort, warmth and friendly atmosphere.
This renovated building is steeped in history as it was previously a convent used by the sisters "Our Lady of the Mission". Experience breakfast in a centrally-heated chapel; this beautiful room is unique in design with arched amber glass windows and polished floors made from native 'Rimu' timber.
A new kitchen has been created for your use only and you have the choice of two heated lounges. Guests laundry. Off street parking. Bus stop 4 doors from Lodge. Surfing beach, Bungy Rocket, Golf Course, eating places and township all close walk from lodge. 10 speed and mountain bikes for hire.
Your host Rob, has a courtesy van to collect you when you arrive in Christchurch. Hear the sound of surf when you first wake up.

Christchurch - Cashmere

Homestay
Address: 12A Hackthorne Road,
Cashmere, Christchurch 2
Name: Janet Milne
Telephone: (03) 337 1423
Beds: 1 Kingsize + 1 Single (in same room),
2 Singles (3 bedrooms)
Bathroom: 1 Ensuite, 1 Guests share, 1 Hostess share
Tariff: B&B (continental) Independent Suite: $45 per person, Shared facilities:
$40 per person, Dinner $25, Children under 12 years half price.
NZ B&B Vouchers accepted
Nearest Town: Christchurch - approx. 10 minutes

My two storeyed home is situated in a quiet back section on the Cashmere Hills. The lower storey is an independent suite comprising a shower, handbasin, lavatory, kingsize bed, two bunks, television set, telephone, wardrobe, heater, table and chairs. The swimming pool is only a few feet away from the front doors. Guests may be accommodated in the lower storey and be independent or be upstairs sharing facilities. I invite non-smokers only. I am a Registered General and Obstetrics Nurse, English Language Teacher, and a university student studying for a degree in linguistics. If you speak Spanish so will I; if you revel in musical interludes my grand piano loves attention, and if you enjoy travelling to distant shores we do have mutual interests!

Christchurch City

Bed & Breakfast
Address: "Home-Lea", 195 Bealey Ave,
Christchurch
Name: Sylvia & Merv Smith
Telephone: (03) 379 9977
Fax: (03) 379 9977
Beds: 2 Queen, 1 Double,
6 Single (5 bedrooms)
Bathroom: 2 Private, 1 Guests share

Tariff: B&B (continental) Double $80-$95, Single $50, Credit cards (VISA/MC).
NZ B&B Vouchers accepted $10 surcharge 1 Nov - 31 March
Nearest Town: 10 minutes walk to city centre

Friendly warm hospitality is offered to guests in our charming character home built in 1904. We are very easy to find and close to the City Centre, Good Restaurants, Botanical Gardens, Museum, Casino and all Tourist attractions.
Bedrooms sleep 1-4 people, are elegantly furnished for comfort and have electric blankets on all beds.
Relax in the cosy Lounge with fire in the winter or the picturesque quiet garden. Complimentary Tea, Coffee and Home Baking available at any time.
We offer a special continental breakfast served in the Dining Room overlooking the garden. Off-street parking for guests.
For guests comfort no smoking is allowed indoors.
We look forward to meeting you and will endeavour to make your stay an enjoyable and memorable one. Inspection welcome.
Home Page: http://nz.com/webnz/bbnz/homelea.htm

Christchurch - Avonhead

Homestay
Address: 67 Toorak Avenue,
Avonhead, Christchurch 4
Name: Fleur Lodge (Beverley & Harry)
Telephone: (03) 342 5473
Beds: 1 Double, 2 Single (2 bedrooms)
Bathroom: 1 Guests share, 1 Family share
Tariff: B&B (full) Double $80, Single $60, Dinner $25.
NZ B&B Vouchers accepted $12 Surcharge
Nearest Town: Christchurch 8km

In a quiet residential street, our home attracts the warm rays of the days sun, with a cosy log burner for added warmth. An attractive visual setting has been created from our passion for gardening which we mix with travel, lawn bowls and membership of several clubs. Guest bedrooms offer bright, comfortable firm beds complete with electric blankets while the adjacent guest bathroom houses a luxurious spa-bath. Tea, coffee and homemade cookies always available and as we enjoy good food, we invite you to sample our three course dinner using local grown produce - prior notice advisable. A delightful selection of breakfast dishes are available together with freshly made muffins - special requests catered for. Our home is a smoke free zone. A handy location to airport (4km) city centre (9km), well served by regular buses, or with free pickup for sightseeing trips. A warm welcome awaits you at Fleur Lodge. We share our home with two burmese cats.

Christchurch - Avonhead

Homestay
Address: 101A Yaldhurst Road,
Avonhead, Christchurch 4
Name: "Yaldhurst Homestay"
Peter & Penny Davies
Telephone: (03) 348 9977
Fax: (03) 348 9585
Mobile: (025) 320 146
Email: p.p.davies@clear.net.nz
Beds: 2 Double, 2 Single (2 Bedrooms)
Bathroom: 2 Ensuite
Tariff: B&B (full) Double $85, Single $65, Children $15 each.
Credit cards accepted. NZ B&B Vouchers accepted $20 surcharge
Nearest Town: Christchurch

A warm Kiwi welcome awaits you when you arrive at our family home. We are in our early forties. We enjoy meeting people and are happy to assist with your travel plans. Our hobbies include gardening, crafts, golf, fishing, tennis and tramping. Our accommodation offers two spacious bedrooms, firm comfortable beds, each room having a double and single bed, ensuite bathroom, television, iron, ironing board, hairdryer, heater and electric blankets. There is a separate guest lounge with fridge and tea/coffee making facilities. Restaurants close by. Laundry services available.
Directions: *We are situated on the main road west (Highway 73), halfway between the airport and the city (6 km each way) and 2 mins from Highway 1. We live on a quiet rear section with off street parking (please drive in). City buses leave outside the gate.*

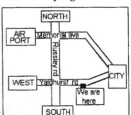

590

Christchurch - Sumner
Homestay
Address: Panorama Road,
Clifton Hill
Name: Jo & Derek
Telephone: (03) 326 5755
Fax: (03) 326 5701
Email: PANORAMAhomestay@xtra.co.nz
Beds: 1 Double
Bathroom: 1 Private
Tariff: B&B (continental) Double $85, Single $55, Dinner by arrangement.
Nearest Town: Christchurch 20 mins drive to city centre.

There are two of us to welcome you - one working and one retired. We are keen on sport, the outdoors, gardening and music and have both lived and worked overseas.
The house is quiet, warm, and has a relaxed atmosphere. Our three decks and terraced garden make the most of all day sun and breathtaking views. The guest bedroom and lounge have views over the ocean, the estuary, the city and the plains to the Southern Alps. The comfortable guest lounge has TV and stereo. The property is not suitable for young children. You are welcome to smoke but please do so outdoors.
We are about 20 minutes drive east of the city centre, 10 minutes from the Gondola and Ferrymead Historic Park, and 3 minutes from Sumner Village and beach. You can take a quiet scenic country walk on the Port Hills within minutes of the house.

Christchurch - Ilam
Homestay
Address: 7 Westmont St, Ilam,
Christchurch 8004
Name: Anne & Tony Fogarty
Telephone: (03) 358 2762
Fax: (03) 358 2767 **Mobile**: N/A
Email: Tony.fogarty@xtra.co.nz
Beds: 4 Single (2 Bedrooms)
Bathroom: 1 Guests share
Tariff: B&B (continental) Double $70, Single $40,
Credit Cards. NZ B&B Vouchers accepted
Nearest Town: Christchurch 7 kms

Our home is in the beautiful suburb of Ilam, ideally situated close to Christchurch Airport (7 mins by car) the Railway Station (10 mins) and the central city area (10 mins). Adjacent to the city bus route, we are very accessible to Christchurch's many attractions.
During our travels in Europe we have used the Bed & Breakfast system and appreciate the need for a comfortable bed and a good breakfast.
We look forward to sharing our New Zealand hospitality as well as our local knowledge. We would be happy to collect visitors from the Airport or Railway, for a small additional charge. We serve dinner by arrangement (extra charge).
As parents of four adult children, all of whom have attended nearby Canterbury University, we enjoy a broad understanding of people. We are interested in sport, travel, politics, gardening and happy to chat about almost anything!! We look forward to helping make your stay in Christchurch a special time.

Christchurch - Southshore

Homestay
Address: 71A Rockinghorse Road, Southshore
Name: Jan & Graham Pluck
Telephone: (03) 388 4067
Beds: 1 Queen, 2 Single (2 Bedrooms)
Bathroom: 1 Ensuite, 1 Family share
Tariff: B&B (full) Double $80, Single $50, Dinner $25pp.
NZ B&B Vouchers accepted $10 surcharge
Nearest Town: Christchurch centre 20 mins drive

Share with us an environment unique to Christchurch - Southshore.
Only 20 minutes from the city, Southshore is situated between the ocean and the estuary of the Avon River. This seaside enclave offers walkways to enjoy the open water views of the estuary and its varied bird-life, or miles of sandy beach for strolling or swimming.
Our house is situated down a private driveway with access to the beach.
A large double room with ensuite and a smaller twin room are available to guests. Both rooms are warm and welcoming and overlook the dunes wilderness.
We are in our fifties and together enjoy antiques, gardening and music. Jan is a keen embroiderer and Graham a member of the Vintage Car Club. Vintage car tours of city and the South Island arranged.
We are non-smokers.
Directions: *Please phone for reservations and directions. City and Airport pick up if required.*

St Albans, Christchurch

Homestay
Address: 'Hadleigh',
6 Eversleigh Street, Christchurch 1
Name: Betty & David Purdue
Telephone: (03) 355 7174
Fax: (03) 355 7174   **Mobile**: (025) 385 101
Beds: 2 Queen, 1 Single (1 bedroom & 1 suite)
Bathroom: 2 Ensuite
Tariff: B&B (special) Double $160, Single $140. Credit cards (VISA/MC). NZ B&B Vouchers accepted $84 Surcharge
Nearest Town: Christchurch centre

Fifteen minutes walk from Cathedral Square you will find 'Hadleigh' a unique arts and craft style home built for a wealthy merchant in 1904; and classified by the Historic Places Trust. Surrounded by trees and a romantic garden, Hadleigh has been our family home for twentyfive years; and is sometimes open for concerts; art exhibitions; and garden and historic home tours. We welcome you to enjoy the ambience of a gracious age with polished native timbers, leadlight windows and antique furniture throughout.
Each elegant bedroom has electric blankets and heaters; television and tea and coffee facilities.
Available for guests' use are the drawing, breakfast and billiard rooms; kitchenette and laundry facilities.
Our generous breakfast may include freshly squeezed juice, fresh fruit, choice of cereals and yoghurts, home made breads; and a traditional cooked breakfast. We have family pets. No smoking indoors.
Advance bookings are strongly recommended. Tariff valid until 30 Sept 1999
Directions: *Phone for directions.*
Home Page: http://nz.com/webnz/bbnz/hadleigh.htm

Christchurch - Taitapu
Farmstay+Self-contained Accom.
Address: "Ballymoney",
Wardstay Road, R D 2, Christchurch
Name: Merrilies & Peter Rebbeck
Telephone: (03) 329 6706 **Fax**: (03) 329 6709
Mobile: (021) 468 378
Email: rebbeckpandm@hotmail.com
Beds: 2 Double, 3 Single (3 Bedrooms)
Bathroom: 1 Ensuite, 1 Guest share or Private.
Tariff: B&B (special) Double $80/$100, Single $60,
Children under 12 half price, Dinner $25, Campervans welcome.
Credit cards. NZ B&B Vouchers accepted $20 surcharge
Nearest Town: Christchurch 20km, Lincoln and Taitapu 5km

"Ballymoney" is situated on a quiet road. The character farmhouse, surrounded by a two acre rambling garden. Guest accommodation includes a self-contained flat with a double and single bed and ensuite bathroom overlooking the spa and separated from the house by a courtyard. In the house is a large twin room opening onto a private veranda. Also a small room with a double bed. All rooms have heating, tea and coffee making facilities, hairdryers, TV and lots of extras. Relax in spacious surroundings, enjoy Irish-Kiwi hospitality and gourmet meals including our home-grown vegetables, fruit, meat, and free range eggs. Masses of animals include horses, a donkey, cattle, sheep, pigs, hens and friendly dogs and cats. The large pond hosts many ducks, geese, guinea fowl, peacocks, pheasants etc. Play croquet, boules or ride the bicycles.

Twenty four hour full farmstay includes three meals, a farm tour feeding the animals and horse riding.

Directions: *Please phone.*

Christchurch City
Guest House
Address: 56 Armagh Street, Christchurch
Name: The Grange
Telephone: (03) 366 2850 **Fax**: (03) 374 2470
Mobile: (021) 366 608
Email: info@the grange.co.nz
Beds: 2 King/Twin, 2 Queen, 2 Double,
1 Single (7 Bedrooms)
Bathroom: 5 Ensuite, 1 Guests share
Tariff: B&B (full) Double $99, Single $85.
NZ B&B Vouchers accepted $25 Surcharge from 1st of Nov to 30th of April.
Nearest Town: We are in Christchurch centre

At The Grange Guesthouse you will enjoy your visit in this tastefully renovated Victorian mansion with wood panelling and a magnificent wooden feature staircase, you can relax in the gracious guest lounge or in the tranquil garden. The Grange Guesthouse is situated within walking distance to most of Christchurch's favourite spots including; Cathedral Square, the Arts Centre, Art Gallery and Museum also the Botanic Gardens, Hagley Park and Mona Vale. During your stay at The Grange you will be treated to superior accommodation, complimentary tea and coffee, off-street parking, laundry service and sightseeing tours and onward travel can be arranged.

If you wish to stay indoors there is Sky TV including CNN News and the movie channel. Non-smoking is encouraged. Banks, shops, restaurants, night clubs and the Art Centre are all easy walking distance.

Paul and Marie Simpson are a mother and son team whose hospitality will ensure your stay is a pleasurable and pleasant one.

593

TURRET HOUSE

Christchurch City Central
Bed & Breakfast
Address: Turret House
Céad Mile Fáilte
435 Durham Street North, Christchurch
Name: Justine & Paddy Dougherty
Telephone: (03) 365 3900/0800 488 773 (0800 4 Turret)
Fax: (03) 365 5601 **Mobile**: (021) 220 5001
Email: turretb.bchch@xtra.co.nz
Beds: 1 King, 5 Queen, 1 Twin, 1 Single (7 bedrooms)
Bathroom: 7 Ensuite
Tariff: B&B (continental) Double $85-$110, Single $65.
Major Credit cards accepted. NZ B&B Vouchers accepted $20 surcharge
Nearest Town: Christchurch centre 10 mins walk

'Céad Mile Fáilte'
(One hundred thousand welcomes)
Turret House is a gracious superior Bed & Breakfast accommodation located in downtown Christchurch. It is within easy walking distance of Cathedral Square, the Botanical Gardens, Museum, Art Gallery, the Arts Centre and Hagley Park 18 hole golf course. Also Casino, new Convention Centre, Town Hall.
Built around 1900 this historic residence is one of only three in the area protected by the New Zealand Historic Places Trust. It has been restored to capture the original character and charm. Situated within the grounds is one of Christchurch's best examples of our native kauri tree. Attractively decorated bedrooms with heaters and electric blankets combine comfort and old world elegance, with private bathrooms, some with bath and shower, all offering a totally relaxed and comfortable environment. Tea, coffee and biscuits available 24 hrs. Cots and highchairs are also available. Family room sleeps 4.
If you're looking for a place to stay where the accommodation is superior and the atmosphere friendly - experience Turret House.
Directions: *Just 15 minutes from Christchurch Airport. Situated on the corner of Bealey Ave and Durham Street. (Off-street parking).*

Ilam, Christchurch

Homestay
Address: Waimairi Lodge, 58 Waimairi Road,
Illam, Christchurch
Name: Gaynor & Stewart Rutherford
Telephone: (03) 343 2269
Fax: (03) 343 2269
Mobile: (025) 358 707
Email: Christchurch
Beds: 4 Double, 2 Single (6 bedrooms)
Bathroom: 2 Ensuites, 2 Guests share
Tariff: B&B ($5 extra full or continental) Ensuite Double $75-$95, Double $60, Single $55, Children negotiable, Dinner (2 course) $25, Credit cards (no American Express). NZ B&B Vouchers accepted
Nearest Town: Christchurch City. (Approximately 6km to centre of Christchurch)

Nestled amongst established trees and shrubs we believe our garden setting to be well worth your visit. In 1998 we won the Dolph Trophy in the Canterbury Horticultural Society garden competition.

Situated close to University in Illam 10 minutes from Airport and only 2 blocks from large malls and restaurants. A drive through Hagley Park will take you into the heart of the city. Taxi and bus stops only minutes away, however if available we can certainly show you highlights such as the lights of Christchurch from the Port Hills at dusk. We have 6 bedrooms, 3 large Double with lounge chairs, colour TV and ensuites.

Christchurch is a beautiful city and we pride ourselves to be part of it. To be able to pass on some of its wonderful attributes to our visitors is our pleasure.

A Kiwi roast dinner can be arranged and a complimentary continental breakfast is included. We assure you of a very warm welcome and a most enjoyable stay.

CANTERBURY

Christchurch - Avonhead

Homestay
Address: Avonhead, Christchurch 4
Name: Sally's Homestay
Telephone: (03) 342 8172 **Fax**: (03) 342 8905
Beds: 3 Single (2 bedrooms)
Bathroom: 1 Family share
Tariff: B&B (continental) Double $60, Single $40, Dinner $20.
NZ B&B Vouchers accepted
Nearest Town: Christchurch 10 minutes drive.

Please come and share my attractive comfortable home. The very best in New Zealand hospitality awaits you. A twin bedroom and a single are available for guests. I also have a second living room in which you may may entertain your friends, or you may join me in my family room.

Situated 2km from Christchurch International Airport, also 1km from the Riccarton Racecourse and easy access to the North South and West Highways.

Bus stop two houses away, 10 minutes to Christchurch city centre, and handy to restaurants.

I belong to numerous organisations and really enjoy people and assure you of a warm welcome. On arrival I will serve you delicious home baked scones or bran muffins on my terrace or in one of my two sunny living rooms.

Directions: *Please phone. I am always home before 9.30am, if not home a message on my answerphone will get a prompt reply.*

Christchurch - Avonhead

Bed & Breakfast
Address: 302 Russley Rd., Christchurch
Name: "Russley 302"
Telephone: (03) 358 6543 **Fax**: (03) 358 6553
Mobile: (025) 730 822
Email: carpsrussley302@clear.net.nz
Beds: 1 Queen, 3 Single (3 bedrooms)
Bathroom: 1 Ensuite, 1 Private, 1 Family share
Tariff: B&B (full) Double $95, Single $50-$65,
Credit Cards (Visa/Mastercard)
NZ B&B Vouchers accepted $25 surcharge
Nearest Town: Christchurch City 15 minutes.

A warm welcome awaits you at "Russley 302" home of Sally and Brian Carpenter. We have recently retired from sheep farming and now live on 10 acres and farm a flock of black / coloured sheep. The wool from these sheep form the basis of Sally's involvement in the handcraft industry. Brian's interests include Rotary and sport.

We are situated 2 minutes from Christchurch International Airport, an ideal first or last night stay. Our modern home offers electric blankets, hair dryers, refrigerators, tea / coffee, laundry and fax facilities.

We have enjoyed many years of farm hosting and invite you to share this experience with us.

Directions: *Refer to map.*

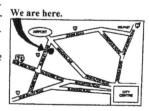

We are here.

596

Christchurch Inner City
Bed & Breakfast Hotel
Address: 63 Armagh Street, Christchurch
Name: Croydon House Bed & Breakfast Hotel
Telephone: (03) 366 5111 or 0800-CROYDON (276 9366)
Fax: (03) 377 6110
Email: b&bcroydonhouse@xtra.co.nz
Beds: 12 Bedrooms
Bathroom: 6 Guests share, 2 Private
Tariff: B&B (full) Share facilities: Single $65, Double/Twin $90.
Private facilities: Single $85, Double $110. Credit Cards (MC/VISA)
Nearest Town: Christchurch City

Croydon House is an attractive, small, personal Hotel. The colonial style house is located in the quiet historic part of Christchurch on the Hagley Park side.
The Establishment offers ample space for our Guests to unwind and relax in their own or each others company and all rooms are tastefully furnished, combining the elegance and comforts of the Character House. The Toilet and Shower facilities are very conveniently located to every room, to guarantee a pleasant stay for all our guests. The Garden Rooms have ensuite toilet and shower. Our Breakfast begins with a delicious Buffet incl. Orange Juice, Cereals, Fresh Fruit and Yoghurt followed by a full English Breakfast. Complimentary tea and coffee is available at any time.
Enjoy our unique, well looked after garden, you might run into one of our Garden Gnomes. Explore the sights of our Garden City by foot. Walk in only five minutes to Cathedral Square, Convention Centre, Casino, Botanic Gardens, Arts Centre, Town Hall and Restaurants.To Readers of this Book we offer a complimentary Ride on the Scenic Vintage Tram a great way to see the Historic Inner City.
For more information, view our webpage on the Internet.
Your hosts Nita and Siegfried Herbst.
Home Page: www.croydon.co.nz

597

Christchurch City - St Martins
Self catering Apartment/Homestay
Address: 'Locarno Gardens', 25 Locarno Street, St Martins, Christchurch 8002
Name: Aileen & David Davies
Telephone: (03) 332 9987 **Fax**: (03) 332 9687 **Mobile**: (025) 399 747
Beds: 1 King, 1 Queen, 1 Single (2 bedrooms)
Bathroom: 2 Private
Tariff: Villa B&B (continental) Double $85-$95, Single $65-$85, Children under 12 negotiable; Self-catering Apartment $90-$100, (Breakfast optional extra). NZ B&B Vouchers accepted $25 surcharge in Homestead.
Nearest Town: 5 minutes drive from Cathedral Square, Christchurch City Centre

Aileen and David invite you to relax in their fine 70 year old character slate roofed villa surrounded by mature trees (Birdlife, fantails etc), and established gardens. Located in a quiet, pleasant street, shops are conveniently near, and popular tourist attractions such as the Gondola, Lyttelton Harbour and Lancaster Park are just a short drive away. Two spacious bedrooms in the home offer tea and coffee making facilities and a television in each room.

For a totally private self-catering stay, they suggest the stand-alone APARTMENT. Queen bed, plus rollaway, television, microwave, fridge / freezer and private telephone are provided. Cot available.

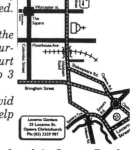

The friendly smoke-free atmosphere allows guests to relax in the picturesque garden courtyard by the goldfish pond, take alluring river walks or, if you feel like a game, there is a tennis court close by. Ample off-street parking is provided. Bus stop 3 minutes walk. Laundry facilities available.

Aileen's knowledge of restaurants is extensive, while David enjoys diving and deer hunting. It will be their pleasure to help with travel and entertainment plans.

Directions: *Locarno Street is opposite St Marks Anglican church in Opawa Road. Taxi from city-centre approx $8.00.*

598

Hambledon circa 1856

Christchurch City Central
Bed & Breakfast Inn
Address: 'Hambledon',
103 Bealey Avenue, Christchurch
Name: Jo & Calvin Floyd
Telephone: (03) 379 0723 **Fax**: (03) 379 0758
Email: hambledon@clear.net.nz
Beds: 5 King/Queen, 1 Double, 5 Single (6 bedrooms incl. 2 2-bedroom suites)
Bathroom: 6 Ensuite
Tariff: B&B (special, full) Double $135-$185, Single $105-$145. Gatehouse in the Garden: 4 double/twin ensuite rooms, lounge, dining room and full kitchen: $290 sole occupancy (includes breakfast).
Nearest Town: Christchurch City Central

Jo and Calvin welcome you to Hambledon, a gracious Historic Mansion built as a home for the prominent city father George Gould. Once again guests can enjoy the warmth and ambience of a grand family home. Relax in one of six charming character rooms or suites that offer privacy, the elegance of antique furnishings, crisp linen, flowers, comfort and convenience with ensuite bathrooms. Start the day with a wonderful breakfast in the magnificent dining room with its Lancaster Sideboard and NZ Art. Later read the paper and relax in the elegant guest lounge with its oriental rugs, in the conservatory, or on the wisteria clad verandahs. Enjoy the tranquil cottage gardens with the box hedges, brick paths, hollyhocks and roses, or stroll to restaurants, Hagley park or Cathedral Square. Ample off street parking and a guest laundry. For reasons of safety and the health of others we ask you not to smoke indoors. It will be our pleasure to ensure your stay at Hambledon is memorable.
Home Page: http://nz.com/webnz/bbnz/hambldn.htm

Christchurch -Halswell

Guest House
Address: Halswell Old Vicarage,
335 Halswell Road, Christchurch 3
Name: Rosemary & Tom
Telephone: (03) 322 6282 **Fax**: (03) 322 6582
Email: mcconnel@voyager.co.nz
Beds: 2 Queen, 1 Single (3 bedrooms)
Bathroom: 2 Private
Tariff: B&B (continental) Double $90, Single $50.
NZ B&B Vouchers accepted $20 surcharge
Nearest Town: Christchurch 6 Kms

We offer a comfortable home in a rural setting just 10 minutes drive from central Christchurch on Highway 75 to Akaroa. Originally St. Mary's Vicarage the house was built 100 years ago and stands in a garden of almost an acre. We have 2 friendly sheep, a small dog and cat. Guest rooms have new beds, duvets and electric blankets. There is a guest lounge with television. Breakfast is served in the sunny conservatory. There are many places nearby for those interested in walking, gardening, pottery, flowers or vineyards. Across the road is a shopping centre including family restaurant and bar. It is a 5 minute drive to the racecourses at Addington or Riccarton and another few minutes to central Christchurch. Our interests include computers and the Internet, gardening, company and conversation. You will be welcome whether you become part of the household or prefer privacy and independence. Please phone ahead.

Sumner, Christchurch

Homestay
Address: 'Villa Alexandra', Clifton Hill
Name: Wendy & Bob
Telephone: (03) 326 6291
Fax: (03) 326 6096
Beds: 1 Queen, 1 Double, 1 Twin (3 bedrooms)
Bathroom: 1 Ensuite, 2 Private
Tariff: B&B (full) Double/Twin $75, Single $60. Dinner $25. The Loft Apartment $95 for two adults (queen & single bed, private facilities and separate entrance). NZ B&B Vouchers accepted $20 surcharge for Loft apartment.
Nearest Town: Christchurch 12km.

Enjoy the warmest hospitality in our spacious turn of the century villa overlooking Sumner Bay. Our home retains the graciousness of a by-gone era while offering all the comforts of modern living. In cold weather enjoy the open fires, hot baths and cosiness of our farmhouse-style kitchen where all meals are cooked in the coal-range.
On sunny days, relaxing on the verandah or in our enchanting turret is a delight. Spectacular sea views extend from Sumner beach to the Kaikoura mountains.
Good food is a speciality, with home grown vegetables and our own free range eggs. Our interests are food, wine, music, gardening, tramping and travel. We have 3 children, all grown some flown; 2 cats and 4 hens. We are 20 minutes from the city centre; 5 minutes from Sumner beach and close to many attractions. Off-street parking; laundry facilities available.
Please phone for directions.

Christchurch - Merivale

Homestay
Address: 'Elm Tree House', 236 Papanui Rd,
Merivale, Christchurch
Name: Karen & Allan Scott
Telephone: (03) 355 9731 **Fax**: (03) 355 9753
Mobile: 025-794 016
Email: elmtreeb.b@clear.net.nz
Beds: 4 Queen, 4 Single (4 bedrooms)
Bathroom: 3 Ensuite, 1 Private
Tariff: B&B (full/continental) Double $115-$145,
Single $90-$115, Dinner $40,
Children over 12 years only. Triple and family room available $145-$165.
Credit Cards (VISA/MC/American Express/Bartercard).
Special offers apply for May, June, July.
NZ B&B Vouchers accepted $45 Surcharge April-October. 2 Vouchers Nov-March
Nearest Town: City Centre 5 minutes drive

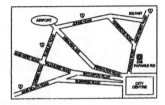

'Elm Tree House' is a spacious Historic listed home situated in the heart of Merivale, an area known for its fine homes, restaurants and boutique shops and mall.
Comfort and style is the theme of this gracious home built in 1920, with carefully chosen Queen beds for a peaceful nights sleep complimented by our large guest lounge and dining room with its Wurlitzer Jukebox, or relax by the solar heated pool in our garden setting.
Just 10 minutes by car to the airport and Trans Alpine Rail Station, or a 20 minute stroll takes you to the city centre's many attractions from beautiful Hagley Park and gardens, the Arts Centre and Gallery to punting on the Avon or trying your luck at the Casino.
Start each day with the breakfast of your choice and then sample the fine restaurants close by or enjoy an evening dinner with us, by prior arrangement please.
Karen and Allan, daughters Martina and Courtney and Summer our cat wish you a happy and enjoyable stay in our beautiful city.
Close to St Georges Hospital, laundry service, smoking in the garden please. Our home is fitted with a full sprinkler and smoke alarm fire system.
Home Page: http://www.friars.co.nz/hosts/elmtree.html

Christchurch - Avonhead

Homestay
Address: 14 Cataluna Place,
Avonhead, Christchurch
Name: "Crossroads"
Telephone: (03) 342 8849 **Fax**: (03) 342 8055
Beds: 2 Queen, 1 Single (2 bedrooms)
Bathroom: 1 Ensuite, 1 Private
Tariff: B&B (special) Double with ensuite $80, Double $75, Single $50,
Children negotiable, Dinner $20. Credit cards accepted.
NZ B&B Vouchers accepted $10 surcharge
Winter and long term rates negotiable.
Nearest Town: Christchurch city centre 15 mins

R
CROSS
A
D
S

Warm hospitality and superb breakfast menu are our speciality. Home made bread, yoghurt, jams; omelettes, pancakes, traditional English cooked plus cereals and fruit ensure a great start to your day. Situated in a quiet residential area 1km from West Coast roundabout, 300 metres from North/South highway and five minutes from Airport (call and we'll collect) make our new, one level home really accessible. City bus route close by. Comfortable, well appointed rooms with electric blankets and woolrests.

Alan, a chartered accountant with special interest in Dairy Industry, computers, reading, sports and video work. Lorraine enjoys church counselling, tutoring, writing, cooking and gardening. Our six children have left home so travellers are treated as extended family with washing and ironing offered.

A free outdoor Spa is available in pleasant garden surroundings. Smoking in outdoor areas. Special care and attention given to those with disabilities and senior citizens. Grandma cat in residence.

Members of
**The New Zealand Association
Farm & Home Host Inc.**
maintain the highest standards &
are always delighted to welcome
guests into their homes.

Christchurch - Halswell
Homestay+Self-contained Accom.

Address: "Overton", 241 Kennedys Bush Road,
Christchurch 3
Name: Judi & Joe
Telephone: (03) 322 8326 **Fax**: (03) 322 8350
Beds: 1 Queen, 4 Single (3 bedrooms)
Bathroom: 1 Private, 1 Family share
Tariff: "Garden Lodge": B&B (full) Double $80 (min of 2 persons Extra person
$30), Children $15. Self-Catering: Double $70 (min. of 2 persons), Extra person
$20 Home: B&B (full) Twin or Single $35 per person. Dinnerfrom $20. Credit
cards Visa/Mastercard/Bankcard NZ B&B Vouchers accepted $12 Surcharge
Nearest Town: Christchurch City, Airport 20 mins.

Best of all worlds ....
*Only 20 mins from Christchurch Cathedral Square, our 1/2 acre landscaped garden on the
Port Hills overlooks the rural setting of the Canterbury Plains to the Southern Alps.Tranquil,
cosy and convenient!Choose the completely self-contained "Garden Lodge" with one double
bedroom and one twin, toilet, shower, TV and cooking facilities, or, share the very comfortable
home with a New Zealand family experienced in tourist requirements.Fibre Arts, gardening
and walking Cass (our friendly Golden Retriever) are some of Judi's many interests in which
guests are welcome to participate. Judi is happy to provide New Zealand cuisine featuring
homegrown and local produce.Joe enjoys sharing his love of angling at local rivers and lakes
(although admittedly, not always successful!). He is also a keen debater and gardener with
an interest in history.Smoking acceptable outdoors.*
Directions: *Please phone anytime.*
Home Page: http://www.canterbury pages.co.nz/bnb/overton.html

---

Christchurch - Bishopdale
Bed & Breakfast
Address: 251 Harewood road,
Bishopdale, Christchurch.
Please phone or fax after 4 pm.
Name: The Home From Homee"
Telephone: (03) 359 2426 **Fax**: (03) 359 2416
Mobile: 025-222 3104
Beds: 2 Twin, 3 Single (3 bedrooms)

Bathroom: 1 Guests share
Tariff: B&B (full) Double $70, Single $40, School children half price,
Dinner by arrangement. Campervans parking only.
Credit Cards. NZ B&B Vouchers accepted
Nearest Town: Christchurch

*A warm, friendly welcome awaits all travellers at the "Home from Home", where we
speak French, German and Japanese.*
*We offer warm comfortable beds, with tea / coffee making facilities in each bedroom,
and a hearty English breakfast to send you on your way. You are welcome to use the
washing machine and the iron and, although we have two excellent restaurants just
across the road, feel free to bring back a take-away and eat it here.*
*Should you spend a few days with us, we'll be delighted to help you with sightseeing
arrangements. The bus stop is right across the road, and buses run frequently to the
city, which is only fifteen minutes away, while the airport, and the Antarctic Centre are
only 5 minutes away.*
*We have a friendly bearded collie and have been adopted by a timid stray cat, and we
all look forward to meeting you.*

603

Christchurch - Sumner Beach

Bed & Breakfast Guest House
Address: 'Cave Rock Guest House',
16 Esplanade, Sumner,
Christchurch 8
Name: Gayle & Norm Eade
Telephone: (03) 326 6844/326 5600
Fax: (03) 326 5600 **Mobile**: (025) 360 212
Email: eade@chch.planet.org.nz
Beds: 2 Double (2 bedrooms)
Bathroom: 2 Ensuite
Tariff: B&B (continental self-serve) Double $75-$90, Credit Cards.
Nearest Town: Christchurch City - 15 minutes

The Cave Rock Guest House is Christchurch's only seafront accommodation, directly opposite Sumner's famous "Cave Rock". Your hosts Gayle and Norm Eade have been in the hospitality industry for 10 years and enjoy meeting people from overseas and within NZ. Our large double rooms have lovely seaviews from every window. Both rooms have ensuites and colour TV, and can sleep up to 4 people. Full kitchen facilities are available. Cooked breakfast available if required.

Sumner Village is the ideal location being 5 minutes walking distance to top restaurants and cafe/bars, shops and movie theatre. Scenic hill walks offer magnificent views over the city and mountains to Kaikoura.

Christchurch city is only 15 minutes from Sumner and the Gondola only 5 mins away. Buses to the city run every half hour.

We have an ancient cat and Dalmatian dog. We look forward to welcoming you to Sumner.

Christchurch - Mt Pleasant

Homestay
Address: 2 Plains View
Name: Peter & Robyn
Telephone: (03) 384 5558
Beds: 1 Queen, 1 Double,
1 Single (3 bedrooms)
Bathroom: 1 Guests share, 2 Toilets
Tariff: B&B (continental)
Double $75, Single $40, Children negotiable.
NZ B&B Vouchers accepted Accepted all year - $10 surcharge Oct-April
Nearest Town: Christchurch 10-15 min drive

Enjoy our warm hospitality in the comfort of our modern home, spacious and sunny with wonderful views of the city and Southern Alps.

Close by is Sumner beach, Ferrymead Historical Park, Mt Cavendish, Gondola and a variety of restaurants.

There are three guest bedrooms, one queen, one double, one single, and a separate guests bathrooms.

We are in our 40's with a 9 year old daughter, our travels have taken us throughout New Zealand and we would be happy to share our experiences with you.

We provide laundry facilities, complimentary tea and coffee, we are a non smoking household. Please phone for directions.

Christchurch - Fendalton
Homestay
Address: 23A Jeffrey's Road,
Fendalton, Christchurch 5
Name: Mary & Gerald
Telephone: (03) 351 7330 **Fax**: (03) 351 8967
Beds: 3 Single (2 bedrooms)
Bathroom: 1 Private, 1 Family share
Tariff: B&B (full) Double $100, Single $60, Dinner $25pp,
Credit Cards. NZ B&B Vouchers accepted $30 Surcharge.
Nearest Town: Christchurch, 10 mins drive to city centre

Our spacious Colonial property is situated in a very private, tranquil garden setting.
We are midway between the Airport and City centre, 10 minutes from either by car.
A large sunny twin bedroom is available with private bathroom for guests plus one
single room.
Mary embroiders and sculpts when time permits. We both enjoy gardening, music,
good food, books, travel, and meeting people. Our elderly house minder is a little
Dachshund dog.
A fine breakfast is served in a charming dining room, dinner with some advance notice.
You are welcome to smoke but please do so outdoors. Off street parking.
Please phone for reservations and directions.

Christchurch - Merivale
Homestay
Address: 'Aldeburgh', 12 Holly Road,
Christchurch 1
Name: Sue and Eric Jackson
Telephone: (03) 355 2557 **Fax**: (03) 355 2537
Mobile: (025) 327 515
Beds: 1 King, 1 Queen, 1 Single (2 bedrooms)
Bathroom: 1 Ensuite, 1 Private
Tariff: B&B (full) Large Suite $120, Double $100, Single $70, Children $25,
Credit Cards (VISA/MC).
NZ B&B Vouchers accepted $45 surcharge for Aldeburgh Suite, $30 Holly Room.
Nearest Town: Christchurch City Centre (3 minutes by car)

A warm welcome awaits you at Aldeburgh (Circa 1880), a gracious gentleman's
residence, set in a private old world garden, within walking distance of the city's main
attractions. Enjoy the ambience of a bygone era, surrounded by antiques, arts and
collectables. Relax in the sun on the beautiful verandah or treat yourself to a
professional remedial massage. The spacious Aldeburgh Suite features a super king or
twin beds and has a dressing room and ensuite. The Holly room has delightful
leadlight windows and a private outlook. An additional bed can be made available
in either room. Other amenities include the Billiard Room, Sky TV, tea / coffee
facilities, fax, electric blankets, pure wool underlays and hair dryers. Our generous
breakfast may include pure orange juice, fruit, cereals, homemade bread and pre-
serves, or traditional cooked English. Laundry facilities and secure off street parking.
Inspection welcome. Bookings recommended.
Complimentary pick up available

Christchurch City

Guest House
Address: "Armagh Lodge",
257 Armagh St., Christchurch
Name: Armagh Lodge
Telephone: (03) 366 0744 **Fax**: (03) 374 6359
 Mobile: 025-317 026
Beds: 6 Double, 11 Single (10 bedrooms)
Bathroom: 3 Ensuite, 3 Guests share

Tariff: B&B (full) Double $75, Single $50, Children half price, free in parents
room, Dinner $10. Credit Cards. NZ B&B Vouchers accepted
Nearest Town: 5-10 mins walk to central city.

*Armagh Lodge is a charming Edwardian Villa with the original ornate plaster
ceilings and lead light windows. It is spacious, warm and comfortable with a large
garden area. Situated in the inner city residential area, it has the advantages of a short
(5-10 min) walk to shops, restaurants etc. with none of the bustle and noise of the city
at the end of the day. We have off-street parking or the number 11 bus will drop you
at the gate.*
*The large lounge has a TV, and coffee and tea is available 24 hours, or sit in the
conservatory and watch the garden grow or the cats trying to catch the birds.*
In the morning a generous full breakfast will be served. No smoking indoors please.

Christchurch Central

Bed & Breakfast
Address: The Worcester of Christchurch,
No. 15 Worcester Boulevard,
Central Christchurch
Name: Maree Ritchie & Tony Taylor
Telephone: (03) 365 0936
Freephone: 0800 365 015 **Fax**: (03) 364 6299
Email: the.worcester@clear.net.nz
Beds: 1 Super King/Twin, 2 Queen (3 bedrooms)
Bathroom: 3 Ensuite

The Worcester of Christchurch

Tariff: B&B (full) Double $180-$240, Credit Cards (VISA/BC/AMEX/DINERS).
Nearest Town: 5 minutes walk to Cathedral Square, Christchurch

*The Worcester of Christchurch is a beautifully preserved colonial mansion built in 1893 for
the Chief Constable of Lyttelton decorated in classic Victorian style with antiques and art.
Uniquely situated in Worcester Boulevard, just a walk across the road to the Arts Centre,
Botanic Gardens, Museum, wine bars and cafes, and a five minute walk to Cathedral Square
and central city shopping. The Worcester Suite features super king antique bed, dressing room
and ensuite, Rolleston and Gloucester Rooms are queen size with ensuites. All rooms have Sky
television, direct dial telephones, electric blankets, irons, ironing boards, hair dryers. A full
breakfast is served in the elegant dining room. Maree also has her fine art business at
Worcester, where guests can experience the rich history of New Zealand art, while enjoying the
warm hospitality and unique surroundings of the Worcester. Off street parking court. We have
a small black poodle "Joe".* **Home Page**: http://www.intermart.co.nz/worcester.
Directions: *Follow Hagley Park into Park Terrace and Rolleston Avenue, turn into Worcester
Boulevard opposite Museum.*

Christchurch - West Melton
Farmstay
Address: Hoskyns Road
Name: Yvonne & Robert Overton
Telephone: (03) 347 8330
Fax: (03) 347 8330
Mobile: (025) 311 234
Beds: 1 Queen, 2 Single
Bathroom: 1 Guests share
Tariff: B&B (full) Double $75, Single $45, Dinner by arrangement.
Nearest Town: Christchurch city 30 kms.

We have a 50 hectare property where we farm sheep, and are situated between State Highway 1 and State Highway 73, 15 minutes from Christchurch Airport, close to all the city amenities, but with a quiet rural setting with magnificent views of the mountains. (2 hours to the skifields.) Many day trips can be taken from our home - why not make it your base. We have enjoyed entertaining folk from many parts of the world and look forward to meeting and caring for many more. We have a cat.
Ours is a relaxed and warm atmosphere where guests can socialise with us, or alternatively rest in their own rooms after making a cuppa in their own mini-kitchen. If you choose to have dinner with us it will be real farmhouse fare. Fresh home grown meat and vegetables. We would love to help you make your holiday a memorable one. Smoke free home.

Christchurch - Mt Pleasant
Homestay
Address: "Hornbrook', Summit Road,
Mt Pleasant, Christchurch 8
Name: Julie & Jim Staddon
Telephone: (03) 384 0020 or
Freephone (0508) 467 627
Fax: (03) 384 0020
Mobile: (025) 398 541
Email: hornbrook@xtra.co.nz
Beds: 1 King, 1 Queen, 2 Single (3 bedrooms)
Bathroom: 1 Ensuite, 1 private or share.
Tariff: B&B (full) Double $130-$170, Single $70-$120, Dinner $30.
Credit Cards. NZ B&B Vouchers accepted $40 surcharge
Nearest Town: 12km to City Centre of Christchurch

Why Hornbrook? .... Elevation! Hornbrook's hillside farm setting immediately relaxes one, whilst the extraordinary view of sea, sky, mountains, city and plains, lifts the spirit. On Mt Pleasant, highest of the Port Hills of Christchurch, this 85 year old home offers exceptional comfort. The unique location has panoramic views, many hill walks, and access to the seaside village of Sumner, Lyttelton Harbour, Banks Peninsula, and Christchurch City. Both double bedrooms have private bathrooms. Three living areas provide comfort, entertainment and relaxation with open fires, books, magazines, television, music, and heated outdoor spa. The grand dining room has the finest view in Christchurch. Your Australian host Julie has a passion for cooking. Enjoy her homemade breads and muffins, old-style Swiss muesli, fresh fruit and juices, farm eggs and smoked local bacon. A New Zealander, Jim's passion, and profession is flying. Your hosts have a cat called bubbles and particularly enjoy travel and meeting people.
Home Page: web:hllp://www.nettravel.co.nz
Directions: *Please telephone.*

607

Christchurch - Avondale
Bed & Breakfast
Address: Hulverstone Lodge,
18 Hulverstone Drive,
Avondale, Christchurch
Name: Ian & Diane Ross
Telephone: (03) 388 6505
Fax: (03) 388 6025
Mobile: (025) 433 830
Email: hulverstone@caverock.net.nz
Beds: 1 Queen, 2 King or twin, 1 Single (4 bedrooms)
Bathroom: 1 Ensuite, 1 Private, 1 Guests share
Tariff: B&B (full) Double $80-$110, Single $60-$80,
Credit Cards welcome (VISA/MC). NZ B&B Vouchers accepted $0-$40 surcharge
Nearest Town: Christchurch. 15 mins from city centre

Hulverstone Lodge

Overlooking the Avon River Hulverstone Lodge is a comfortable, modern, Tudor-style home. Watch the sun rise over the river, look across to the Port Hills or catch glimpses of the Southern Alps. Delightful walks pass the door, and there are many recreational facilities nearby. Both the Queen Elizabeth II Park Sport and Leisure complex and New Brighton, with its unique new pier, sandy Pacific Ocean beach and shopping malls, are within walking distance.
Buses passing close by provide a quick, comfortable ride to the city and back. Just off the Ring Road, the Lodge has easy access to all parts of Christchurch, the airport and railway station, as well as main routes north and south, yet it offers a tranquil riverside haven. We, and our cat, look forward to sharing it with you.
We will provide complimentary pick-up from and transport to the airport, railway station and inter-city bus terminal on request.

Christchurch - Springston
Country Homestay
Address: "The Croft",Goulds Road,
Springston, Christchurch 4 RD.
Name: John & Jeannie Campbell
Telephone: (03) 329 5748
Fax: (03) 329 5741 **Mobile**: (025) 245 6748
Beds: 2 Double, 2 Single (2 bedrooms)
Bathroom: 2 Ensuite
Tariff: B&B (full) Double $90, Single $50,
Children under 12 half price, Dinner $20.
Credit cardsNZ B&B Vouchers accepted $20 surcharge
Nearest Town: Lincoln (10km) S, Christchurch (30km) SW

"The Croft" is a 1996 replica of a 19th century Scottish farmhouse complete with oil fired coal range and traditional kitchen and all modern comforts, situated 30 mins south-west of Christchurch and airport, only a few minutes from Main South Road and the Trans-Alpine Rail connection. A little over one hour by car has you in the early French settlement of Akaroa also from the nearby Summit Road you may see the finest views of Canterbury and the Plains. We have travelled extensively both home and abroad. Our farming interest now consists of summer hay-making and autumn grazing, having retired from farming close-by we still have farming contacts. We have a keen interest in building, decorating and gardening. We have two married daughters and two grand-children. City and airport pick-up can be arranged.

Christchurch - Harewood

B&B/Homestay
Address: 411 Sawyers Arms Road, Harewood.
Name: Fairleigh Garden Guest House
Telephone: (03) 359 3538 or 359 2411
Freephone 0800 611411 **Fax**: (03) 359 3548 **Mobile**: (025) 224 3746
Beds: 2 Queen, 2 Super Single (3 bedrooms)
Bathroom: 2 Ensuite, 1 Private (1 wheelchair access)
Tariff: B&B (special/full) Double $135, Single $80, Dinner $25 pp. Credit Cards
(Visa/Diners/American Express/Bankcard)
Nearest Town: Christchurch city 12 mins. Airport 4 mins.

A warm welcome awaits you at Fairleigh Garden Guest House. Our home and garden are so often referred to as "CHRISTCHURCH'S BEST KEPT SECRET". There is a wonderful atmosphere of complete relaxation.Our country style cedar-wood house has New Zealand Native Heart Rimu throughout with quality furnishings and native timber antique dressers. Each well dressed bedroom has luxury bedding, TV, telephone, door keys, hair dryer, electric blanket, warm woollen underlay, heater, modern heated bathrooms, fresh flowers and lovely garden views.Relax in our comfortable lounge and conservatories and enjoy listening to music, playing the piano, reading books, playing chess - or perhaps planning your holiday. We are very happy to help you with any queries you may have.Delectable breakfast of fresh fruits, juice, yoghurt, cereals, home-made bread and preserves, plus a variety of freshly cooked breakfast options.Splendid lunches, delicious dinners and NZ BBQ's are available by arrangement. The best of New Zealand fish and tender Canterbury lamb are a speciality and popular choices. We are happy to cater for guests requiring a special diet. Tea, coffee, juice and fresh baking is available for you at any time.The spacious and tranquil garden has many interesting areas to explore and rest a while - Rose covered arches, gazebo, lily pond, many deciduous trees, bulbs, iris, herbs and vegetables.Enjoy croquet and petanque on the lawn surrounded by colourful perennials, meet our loveable cat - Zambie. Discover Allan's vintage tractors that have worked the New Zealand farmlands in years gone by or Valerie's hobbies room amidst the garden. Explore the surrounding farmlands on foot or take a ride on our bicycles.
COME AND ENJOY GENUINE NEW ZEALAND HOSPITALITY AT ITS BEST - YOU WILL NEVER FORGET THIS WONDERFUL EXPERIENCE.
Complimentary supper - Ample off street parking - Free laundry facilities - Smoking outdoors only - Only 4 minutes from the airport - Free transfers to and from the Christchurch airport. Quotes:
"The delightful smell of home cooked breakfast, warm comfortable rooms, beautiful gardens and friendly hosts is all so wonderful. Christchurch is a lovely city and Fairleigh Garden Guest House is so well located in peaceful garden surroundings" - Cheng Siew Lin. Kuala Lumpur, Malaysia.
"Lovely people, beautiful gardens and excellent service and accommodation. Well done" - G Caverley, Australia
"Magical setting for our wonderful wedding day" - R&W Crampton, Marton, NZ.
"Fairleigh Garden Guest House is clearly rated 5 STAR PLUS" - John Smith, Warrant Officer, Royal Australian Air Force.
Directions: *800 metres off major bypass - Johns Road.*

Christchurch - Huntsbury Hill

Homestay
Address: Huntsbury House, 16 Huntsbury Avenue,
Huntsbury Hill, Christchurch 2
Name: Anthea & Paul
Telephone: (03) 332 1020 **Fax**: (03) 337 0666
Mobile: (025) 353 880
Email: huntbnb@voyager.co.nz
Beds: 1 King, 3 Single (2 bedrooms)
Bathroom: 2 Ensuite
Tariff: B&B (full) Double $90-$100, Single $60-$70,
Credit Cards (VISA/MC/BC). NZ B&B Vouchers accepted $20-$25 surcharge
Nearest Town: City centre 5 minutes drive

Welcome to our spacious, elegantly restored, 1920's style Port Hills home with magnificent city and mountain views - a great starting point for Banks Peninsula travels and city exploration. City centre, (Jade Stadium at) Lancaster Park, Casino and Gondola 5-10 minutes drive away, airport 20 mins, walking tracks and excellent restaurants close by. Off-street parking available. Bus stop at gate. Downstairs accommodation offers large rooms with tea / coffee facilities. Relax in the lounge with TV and fire, in the pool, romantic garden or BBQ area. Delicious breakfasts which include homemade preserves, yoghurt, muesli and cooked selection are served in our dining room with a view or by the pool. Laundry facilities available. We have a wide range of interests and enjoy listening to travellers' tales. Most of our children have left home though our cat is still with us. We would love to meet you and help plan your stay in our delightful city. Smoking outdoors please.
Home Page: http://www.voyager.co.nz/~huntbnb

Christchurch - Tai Tapu

Vineyard/Farmstay
Address: RD 2, Cossars Road,
Tai Tapu, Christchurch
Telephone: (03) 329 6160
Fax: (03) 329 6168
Mobile: (025) 364 041
Email: drewer.g.canvin@xtra.co.nz
Beds: 1 Queen, 1 Single (2 bedrooms)
Bathroom: 1 Ensuite with Queen, 1 Family share
Tariff: B&B (full) Double $110, Single $80, Dinner $35 pp incl. wines & nibbles,
Packed lunch available, Longer stays (3 nights+) negotiable.
Nearest Town: Christchurch 20 minutes

If you enjoy fine wines and food then Drewerys Vineyard is the place to come and relax. Our Mediterranean style home is nestled in a large rural garden setting surrounded by our vineyards and includes two ponds that attract native birds and wildlife.
We have two friendly dogs, a cat and a teenage son (also friendly). Anette and Graeme have travelled extensively, Anette having lived in Europe for three years. She also speaks fluent Dutch. Our hobbies include gardening, classic cars, fishing, interior design and fine living. Maybe just laze by the pool in the peace and tranquillity of the countryside or enjoy Croquet and Boules on the lawn. There is a picturesque golf course and trout fishing at our gate or perhaps a short stroll down to the local country tavern. Wake up to the call of the bellbird and the smells of a delectable country breakfast. Complimentary "drinks and nibbles at five". While you are with us "our home is your home" and we promise you a most memorable stay.
Directions: *Please phone. Pick-up available from the airport.*

Christchurch - Cashmere

Homestay
Address: 91B Hackthorne Road,
Cashmere, Christchurch
Name: Sara & Vic Newman
Telephone: (03) 332 6613
Fax: (03) 332 6613
Beds: 1 Double, 2 Single (2 bedrooms)
Bathroom: 1 Private, 1 Family share
Tariff: B&B (full) Double $100, Single $60,
Dinner by arrangement $35pp.
NZ B&B Vouchers accepted $20 surcharge
Nearest Town: Christchurch 10 minutes from centre

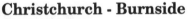

We offer a spacious warm comfortable modern home with panoramic views of the city, plains and Southern Alps, 10 minutes from the city centre and 20 minutes from the airport. We are a non smoking family and have a very small friendly dog. We are close to the walking trails over the Port Hills and to Lyttleton Harbour and have excellent restaurants close by. Now retired from professional life we have time to follow our interests in art, music and theatre and time to help you make the most of your visit to Christchurch.

Christchurch - Burnside

Bed & Breakfast
Address: 31 O'Connor Place, Burnside,
Christchurch 8005
Name: Elaine & Neil Roberts
Telephone: (03) 358 7671
Email: elaine.neil.roberts@xtra.co.nz
Beds: 4 Single (2 bedrooms)
Bathroom: 1 Guests share
Tariff: B&B (continental) Double $70, Single $45. NZ B&B Vouchers accepted
Nearest Town: Christchurch centre, 15 minutes drive

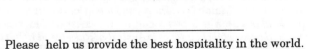

Elaine and Neil welcome you to their comfortable modern home situated in a quiet street 5 minutes from Christchurch Airport. Our home is close to the Antarctic Centre, Russley Golf Course and hotel restaurants.
We are near Memorial Avenue with frequent buses and an easy 15 minute drive to the city centre. A generous continental breakfast is included in the tariff. Tea and coffee are available at all times. Guests are welcome to relax in the garden or in the living room with books or television. We are a non-smoking family with one friendly cat. Our interests include golf, gardening, local history, bush walks and reading.
We enjoy having guests and look forward to meeting you.
Directions: *Please phone (03) 358 7671 for reservations and directions.*

Please help us provide the best hospitality in the world.
Fill in a comment form for every place you stay.

Christchurch - Richmond

TRELAWNEY HOUSE

Bed & Breakfast
Address: "Trelawney Bed & Breakfast",
138 Stanmore Rd, Richmond, Christchurch 1
Name: Pat & John Wray
Telephone: (03) 389 0206
Fax: (03) 389 0295
Mobile: (025) 220 2546
Email: jwray@xtra.co.nz
Beds: 2 Double, 5 Single (4 bedrooms)
Bathroom: 1 Guests share

BED & BREAKFAST

Tariff: B&B (full) Double $70, Single $40,
Credit Cards. NZ B&B Vouchers accepted
Nearest Town: 20 minutes walk to Cathedral Square, Christchurch

We invite you to stay with us in our lovely renovated colonial villa, built in 1908, and surrounded by trees. A leisurely 20 minute walk to the heart of Christchurch and one minute from the beautiful Avon River. We want you to enjoy a relaxing, warm and quiet stay on your holiday. All our guests' bedrooms have heaters and electric blankets. A hearty full cooked breakfast is served to start you off for the day. Our cosy dining room has tea / coffee making facilities, radio and TV. Unwind in our lovely garden at the rear of the villa. Non-smoking is encouraged. There is plenty of off-street parking. Banks, shops and restaurants are just around the corner. We have an extensive knowledge of the South Island and all that it has to offer. Assisting you in planning your itinerary would be a pleasure. We want to make your stay in Christchurch 'one to remember". We have a small dog and a cat.

Christchurch - Heathcote Valley

Homestay
Address: Bloomfield House,
146 Bridle Path Road, Heathcote Valley,
Christchurch 2
Name: Jean and William Cumming
Telephone: (03) 384 9217 **Fax**: (03) 384 9267
Email: cumming_bloomfield@clear.net.nz
Beds: 2 King/Twin (2 bedrooms)
Bathroom: 1 Guests share (spa bath and shower),
2 separate toilets with hand basins.
Tariff: B&B (continental. Full on request) Double $130 (sole use of bathroom $180), Single $90, Dinner $30 pp, Visa/Bankcard/Mastercard.
Nearest Town: Christchurch (13mins drive)

You may have seen Bloomfield House and Garden on TV or in a Gardening magazine. Bloomfield House is nestled in historic Heathcote Valley, a unique rural corner of the city surrounded by the distinctive Port Hills.Experience peace and tranquillity in beautiful surroundings only 13 minutes drive from the centre of Christchurch.Our interesting modern home was architecturally designed and the garden was designed by William. William teaches in a Design Degree programme, he is a practising artist, represented in major New Zealand collections and has exhibited in Australia, Japan, USA and New Zealand.Jean is a piano and voice teacher and experienced choral director having had successful choir tours to Australia, Russia and USA.Our interests include garden design, art collection, travel, cooking, mountain trekking, music, antiques and reading.There are many activities within easy reach, some within walking distance, the Gondola & restaurant, Lytttleton Harbour, Ferrymead Historic Park, horse riding, wind surfing, Port Hills walks and beautiful beaches.

Christchurch - Cashmere

Homestay
Address: 3 Lucknow Place, Cashmere 2, Christchurch
Name: 'Burford Manor' Kathleen & David Burford
Telephone: (03) 337 1905 **Fax**: (03) 337 1916
Email: burfords@xtra.co.nz
Beds: 2 Queen, 2 Single (3 bedrooms)
Bathroom: 1 Ensuite, 2 Private
Tariff: B&B (full) Double $100, Single $70, 10% discount for 2 or more nights
(only by direct booking & cash payment). Credit Cards (M/C & Visa).
NZ B&B Vouchers accepted Surcharge $30
Nearest Town: Christchurch (5 mins drive)

Our nine year old home is the ultimate in luxury, built in Halswell Quarry Stone, it incorporates the charm of yesteryear plus all the conveniences of a modern home, spacious and warm with private and ensuite bathrooms. Five minutes drive from city centre and conveniently located to excellent public transport. Prize-winning cottage garden. Million dollar views of rural Canterbury and the Southern Alps. Easy flat access and parking. Home-made patchwork quilts abound in each room. Quiet and peaceful. Your hosts David and Kathleen have three adult children and are an informal couple who love meeting people. We have travelled extensively in New Zealand and overseas and are happy to offer assistance with travel plans. Third generation Cantabrians our local knowledge and contacts are an asset to guests particular interests. Our hobbies include Rotary, travel, tramping, skiing, gardening, stamp collecting, embroidery and patchwork. Breakfast - the choice and time is flexible - try our home-made bread. Guests are welcome to share in all the facilities of our home. No smoking in the house. Tim, our friendly cat also offers a special welcome.
Directions: *Please telephone anytime. The map may be of assistance.*
Homepage: http://nz.com/webnz/bbnz/burford.htm

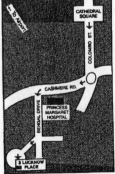

Members of
**The New Zealand Association
Farm & Home Host Inc.**
maintain the highest standards &
are always delighted to welcome
guests into their homes.

Christchurch - Merivale
Homestay
Address: 121 Winchester Street,
Christchurch
Name: Villa 121
Telephone: 03 355 8128
Fax: 03 355 8126
Beds: 1 King, 1 Queen,
2 Single (3 bedrooms)
Bathroom: 1 Guests share, 1 Family share.
Tariff: B&B (full) Double $95, Single $65,
Dinner $20, Children half price.
NZ B&B Vouchers and Credit Cards accepted
Nearest Town: Christchurch - 4 km

*We are well travelled, fun loving and really enjoy meeting people. We provide a
relaxing atmosphere and look forward to making your stay happy and memorable.
"Villa 121" is a tastefully and stylishly restored villa set in a lovely old world garden.
Delicious continental and / or cooked breakfast is available at a time to suit you, and
complimentary tea / coffee and home-baking is available at any time.*
*Your hosts are Trish (school teacher), Barry (consultant surveyor) and Melanie (4th
year Fine Arts student). We are very keen sports people, especially tennis, golf and
skiing and happy to help you organise your sporting activities. The closest golf course
and tennis courts are only 3 minutes away.*
*Relax in the sun on the wisteria and vine clad verandah in summer or enjoy the open
fire in winter.*

Christchurch - Dallington

Homestay + Self Contained Accommodation
Address: Killarney, 27 Dallington Terrace,
Dallington, Christchurch
Name: Russell and Lynne Haigh
Telephone: (03) 381 7449
Fax: (03) 381 7449
Beds: 1 Double, 1 Single (2 bedrooms)
Bathroom: 1 Ensuite, 2 Family share
Tariff: B&B (full) Double $80, Single $50
NZ B&B Vouchers accepted $10 surcharge
Nearest Town: Chirstchurch City Centre: 6 minutes

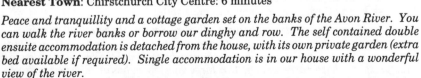

Peace and tranquillity and a cottage garden set on the banks of the Avon River. You can walk the river banks or borrow our dinghy and row. The self contained double ensuite accommodation is detached from the house, with its own private garden (extra bed available if required). Single accommodation is in our house with a wonderful view of the river.

We are only 6 minutes by car to the City Centre, and also close to The Palms Shopping Mall, golf courses and beaches. Buses 11 and 29 stop nearby.

Tea, coffee and home baking are always available, and Russell's breakfasts are great. You can join us for dinner if you wish ($15 max. pp) but please give us warning.

Directions: *Phone for directions. We will collect you from the airport, train or bus station if required. Both of us, as well as our cats and bearded collie Mac, look forward to meeting you.*

New Brighton Christchurch

Bed and Breakfast Homestay
Address: "Christchurch Pier B&B Homestay",
533 Pages Road, New Brighton, Christchurch
Name: Joyce and Des Lavender
Telephone: (03) 388 2190 **Fax**: (03) 388 0431
Beds: 3 Queen, 6 Single (6 bedrooms)
Bathroom: 3 Ensuite, 1 Guests share

Tariff: B&B (special/full) Double $88-$98, single $56. Children dollar by age.
Credit Cards NZ B&B Vouchers accepted $12 surcharge
Nearest Town: Christchurch City Centre 10 mins drive

We look forward to sharing our home sited in a sunny garden setting with you. Our seaside suburb has much to offer the busy traveller, relax for a while and smell the flowers or take a leisurely 10 minute stroll to the ocean, walk on the pier, visit our interestingly different village mall or even experience the excitement of a bunji rocket ride. Public transport at the gate provides a quick trip into the city centre for you to enjoy all the city has to offer. We endeavour to provide for our guests the ingredients for a happy comfortable stay with us, so help your self to the tea and coffee provided, relax in the guests lounge or in our spacious sheltered garden where you might meet our small friendly Aussie Terrier "Dusty".

Our generous breakfast includes a selection of cereals, yoghurt, fresh and cooked fruit, orange or tomato juice, bread, pastries and traditional English breakfast.

Off street parking available.

Courtesy pick up available

Smoking outside only

Christchurch City
Homestay
Address: 23 Eversleigh Street,
St Albans, Christchurch 1
Name: Karen and John Law
Telephone: (03) 365 6779
Fax: (03) 352 5617
Email: kjlaw@xtra.co.nz
Beds: 1 Queen (1 bedroom)
Bathroom: 1 Private

Tariff: B&B (continental) Double $70, Single $45, dinner by arrangement.
Children by arrangement - cot available.   NZ B&B Vouchers accepted
Nearest Town: Christchurch Centre 15 mins walk

"Eversleigh", just 15 minutes walk from Cathedral Square, the botanical gardens, the arts centre and gallery, is a large, two storey home built around the turn of the century. Surrounded by a beautiful garden containing huge trees, the house stands on a tranquil three quarter acre section. Our large guest room has an adjacent sunroom, queen size bed with electric blanket, and there is a bathroom for your exclusive use. We are a young couple who love meeting people and look forward to welcoming you into our home. Among our interests are travel, cooking, dining out, theatre and competitive badminton. We are non-smokers but you are welcome to smoke outdoors. Dinner is available on request (at extra cost) or we could guide your choice of one of Christchurch's many restaurants. Tourist information is available and we would be happy to pick you up from the airport. We enjoy having guests and look forward to meeting you.
Directions: *Please phone.*

Springston, Christchurch
Country Bed & Breakfast
Address: "Hamilton House", Curries Road,
Springston RD 4,Christchurch
Name: Glenn and Jill Travis
Telephone: (03) 329 5188 **Fax**: (03) 329 5189
Mobile: (025) 226 3589
Email: hamilton.house@xtra.co.nz
Beds: 1 King, 1 Queen, 2 Single (3 bedrooms)
Bathroom: 2 Ensuite, 1 Private

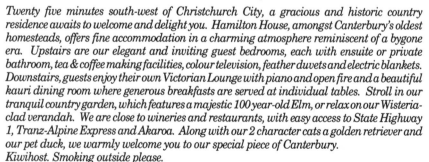

circa 1890

Tariff: B&B (full) Double $100-$120, Single $70-$90,
Dinner by arrangement, Children by arrangement.
Visa/Mastercard. NZ B&B Vouchers accepted $30 surcharge
Nearest Town: Lincoln 5 mins, City 25 mins, Airport 20 mins.

Twenty five minutes south-west of Christchurch City, a gracious and historic country residence awaits to welcome and delight you. Hamilton House, amongst Canterbury's oldest homesteads, offers fine accommodation in a charming atmosphere reminiscent of a bygone era. Upstairs are our elegant and inviting guest bedrooms, each with ensuite or private bathroom, tea & coffee making facilities, colour television, feather duvets and electric blankets. Downstairs, guests enjoy their own Victorian Lounge with piano and open fire and a beautiful kauri dining room where generous breakfasts are served at individual tables. Stroll in our tranquil country garden, which features a majestic 100 year-old Elm, or relax on our Wisteria-clad verandah. We are close to wineries and restaurants, with easy access to State Highway 1, Tranz-Alpine Express and Akaroa. Along with our 2 character cats a golden retriever and our pet duck, we warmly welcome you to our special piece of Canterbury. Kiwihost. Smoking outside please.
Directions: *Please phone.*

Christchurch - Cashmere Heights

Homestay
Address: Cashmere Heights B&B, 6 Allom Lane, Cashmere Heights, Christchurch 2.
Name: Karen and Barry Newman
Telephone: (03) 332 1778 **Fax**: (03) 332 9399 **Mobile**: (025) 241 0911
Email: rover@iconz.co.nz
Beds: 3 Super King, 6 Single (3 bedrooms)
Bathroom: 1 Guests Share
Tariff: B&B (Special/Full/Continental) Double $150-$165, Single $90.
Dinner by arrangement. Not suitable for children. Major credit cards accepted.
Nearest Town: Christchurch City approx 10 minutes

Cashmere Heights - where a warm friendly welcome awaits you in a home where you can relax in comfort and quiet elegance. This is our near new home on two levels in an exclusive suburb of Christchurch. Nestled high on the Port Hills amongst other high quality homes and 220 metres above sea level, Cashmere Heights captures the "Million dollar views" with 180 degrees unobstructed panorama from the Pacific Ocean, across the city and the Canterbury Plains to the playground of the South Island, the Southern Alps.

Our guest accommodation is located on a separate level of our home thereby ensuring total privacy and relaxation. All bedrooms are large and individually decorated in bold bright colours to enhance our desire to create and maintain a relaxing holiday and homely environment. All bedrooms are located to ensure all take advantage of the views. We have a separate guest lounge which is large and offers tea / coffee facilities, home theatre entertainment system, reading area, computer station, phone and fax. Adjoining this lounge is a sun deck with outdoor furniture, barbecue and a spa pool. A leisurely breakfast may be selected from the wide choices available and may be taken in the cafe style eatery, or weather permitting, al fresco on the sun deck or on the garden patio.

We are only 400 metres from the Historic "Sign of the Takahe Restaurant" and there are several other good restaurants close by. Also close by are numerous scenic walking trails.

We are aged in our early forties and have travelled extensively. We enjoy meeting people and welcoming guests into our home.

Our home is a non smoking home, which we share with our cat. You may also wish to take advantage of our Tour service, Rover Tours N.Z, which specialise in luxury customised tours. These are personally guided tours for a maximum of four persons anywhere in the South Island.

Directions: *Please phone.*
Home Page: http://nz-holiday.co.nz/cashmere

Christchurch - Lyttelton
Guest House
Address: Dalcroy House, 16 Godley Quay, Lyttelton.
Name: Shonagh O'Hagan
Telephone: (03) 328 8577
Beds: 3 Bedrooms - 1 King (or 2 singles) & 2 Queen.
Bathroom: 1 Guests share.
Tariff: B&B Double $90,Single $65, Breakfast caters to all tastes,
Dinner by arrangement - additional charge, Children welcome.
Nearest Town: Christchurch 9 kms, 15 mins & Akaroa 80 kms, 1 1/4 hours.

PARKING AND ACCESS: Good on street parking and access
COURTESY CAR: Check availability
DALCROY HOUSE: 1859 Established
1860-80 Boarding and Day School for boys
1880-86 Private Boarding House for Gentlemen & Families
1886-1928 Rental Property for Sea Captains
1928-42 Private Home
1960-67 Boarding House
1967-92 Private Home
1992-Guest House
SHONAGH O'HAGAN Your hostess CV:

- Cook
- Nurse
- Educator
- Health Manager
- Mother

Have a comfortable night's sleep in pleasant surroundings with a clear view of Lyttelton Port and Harbour, only five minutes' walk from the centre of Lyttelton.
Shonagh and her young son will ensure your stay is comfortable and memorable.

Banks Peninsula - Cass Bay-Lyttelton
Homestay & Self-contained Townhouse
Address: 'Harbour View Homestay',
3 Harbour View Tce., Cass Bay, Lyttelton
Name: Susi & Hank Boots
Telephone: (03) 328 7250 **Fax**: (03) 328 7251
Mobile: (025) 226 2633
Email: harbourview.homestay@clear.net.nz
Beds: 1 King, 1 Queen, 3 Single (3 bedrooms)
Bathroom: 1 Guests share, 1 Family share
Tariff: B&B (full) Double $90, Single $55-$60, 10% discount from 3 nights, 15% from 1 week (discounts only with direct booking). Self-contained facilities $100 double, $25 for each further person/bed. Discount applies as above. Dinner by arrangement $30pp. Credit cards (Visa/Mastercard) welcome. NZ B&B Vouchers accepted $30 surcharge
Nearest Town: Christchurch Centre 12km, Lyttelton 3km

Cass Bay, nestled in the Porthills, is only a short drive away from Christchurch and offers easy access to all city amenities. The beautiful and tranquil area around the harbour has walking tracks, nature reserves, several swimming beaches, a golf course, horse track facilities and the harbour provides for sailing and steam-boat trips. Harbour View Homestay is also an ideal retreat for small think-tanks. Our home incorporates warmth and luxury with comfort, has a relaxed atmosphere, an open fireplace, a lovely garden setting with a solar-heated swimming pool and breathtaking views. Separate lounge area also available. Our beds are very comfortable and extra long. The fully tiled bathrooms have a massage-shower which everybody loves. Gymnasium free to use. Sauna available at small cost.For guests' comfort no smoking indoors please. Wir sprechen Deutsch und Schweizerdeutsch. Nous parlons Français en spreken Nederlands.

618

Banks Peninsula - Diamond Harbour

Homestay
Address: 'Otamahua', Athol Place,
Church Bay, R.D. 1, Lyttelton
Name: Alison Gibbs
Telephone: (03) 329 4728
Mobile: (025) 288 8294
Email: a.gibbs@ext.canterbury.ac.nz
Beds: 1 Queen, 2 Single (2 bedrooms)
Bathroom: 2 Ensuite
Tariff: B&B (full) Double $90,
Single $50, Dinner $25,
Credit cards (VISA/MC).
NZ B&B Vouchers accepted $15 Surcharge
Nearest Town: Christchurch approx 40 minutes

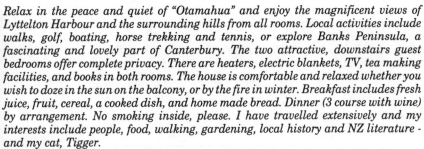

Relax in the peace and quiet of "Otamahua" and enjoy the magnificent views of Lyttelton Harbour and the surrounding hills from all rooms. Local activities include walks, golf, boating, horse trekking and tennis, or explore Banks Peninsula, a fascinating and lovely part of Canterbury. The two attractive, downstairs guest bedrooms offer complete privacy. There are heaters, electric blankets, TV, tea making facilities, and books in both rooms. The house is comfortable and relaxed whether you wish to doze in the sun on the balcony, or by the fire in winter. Breakfast includes fresh juice, fruit, cereal, a cooked dish, and home made bread. Dinner (3 course with wine) by arrangement. No smoking inside, please. I have travelled extensively and my interests include people, food, walking, gardening, local history and NZ literature - and my cat, Tigger.
Directions: *Church Bay is close to Diamond Harbour, but phone for directions – or to be collected.*
Home Page: http://nz.com/webnz/bbnz/otamahua.htm

Banks Peninsula - Governor's Bay

Homestay
Address: 'Orchard House', Governor's Bay
Name: Neil & Judy
Telephone: (03) 329 9622
Beds: 1 Double (1 bedroom)
Bathroom: 1 Ensuite
Tariff: B&B (continental)
Double $85, Single $60.
NZ B&B Vouchers accepted $15 surcharge
Nearest Town: Christchurch 13km,
Lyttelton 8km

Governor's Bay is one of the many scenic bays surrounding Lyttelton Harbour, and is only a short drive over the Port Hills from Christchurch.
Our hillside home is situated to take full advantage of the spectacular views over the bay. The area is noted for its beautiful gardens and walking tracks, and is ideally situated for exploring Banks Peninsula. A wide range of cuisine is offered by local restaurants.
Our separate guest wing has a large sunny bedroom with ensuite and French doors which open to a private balcony. The room has a TV and tea / coffee making facilities. We have two daughters, one still living at home, and Suzy the cat. We are a non-smoking home. We look forward to meeting you.
Directions: *Please phone.*

Banks Peninsula - Teddington, Lyttelton Harbour

Country Homestay
Address: Bergli B&B, RD 1, Lyttelton
Name: Rowena and Max Dorfliger
Telephone: (03) 329 9118 **Fax**: (03) 329 9118
Beds: 2 Queen, 2 Single (2 bedrooms)
Bathroom: 1 Family Share
Tariff: B&B (full) Twin/Double $70, Single $45,
Dinner $25, Children half price. NZ B&B Vouchers accepted
Nearest Town: Lyttelton (20 minutes), Christchurch (35 minutes)

Lyttelton harbour and the Port Hills create a dynamic panorama, superb for sunsets and star-gazing. Our 100 acre farm on the sunny slopes of Mt Herbert is near a comprehensive net of walking tracks, boating, swimming and golf course.
Our smoke-free home has two guest rooms with a double and single bed in each. We can arrange to collect you from the international airport, etc.
We are both self-employed (woodworker and shadow puppeteer) and able to take time out for a day sail on our yacht or a guided Peninsula tour. We have a wealth of stories from experiences of living 27 years in Japan (Rowena) and around the world sailing and mountain climbing by Max who is a German speaking Swiss.
Whether relaxing on the veranda at Max's hand-crafted table and benches or sipping wine in the spa bath, we are sure you will take away good memories of your visit. We have one cat.
Directions: *2km after Weatsheaf sign on RH side.*
Home Page: htto://www.es.co.nz/~macgill/bergli.htm

Banks Peninsula - Diamond Harbour

Bed and Breakfast
Address: Kai-o-ruru Bed & Breakfast,
32 James Drive, Church Bay,
Diamond Harbour, RD1.
Name: Robin and Philip Manger
Telephone: 03 329 4788 **Fax**: 03 329 4788
Beds: 2 Single (1 bedroom)
Bathroom: 1 Ensuite
Tariff: B&B (special) Double $80, Single $50, Dinner $25.
Nearest Town: Christchurch approximately 40 minutes

Church Bay is the ideal base for those wishing to explore Banks Peninsula.
In our separate, ensuite unit, you will wake up to bellbirds and a view across the harbour to Quail Island. The room is cosy, has electric blankets, TV, books, games and a tea / coffee tray with home-made biscuits. Our timber house commands marvellous views; our coastal garden is there for you to explore or sit in, or if you're energetic, a scramble down the bank will take you to a fascinating volcanic shore.
We are a non-smoking household and have an unobtrusive cat. Philip and I are travelled, retired teachers with wide interests who enjoy meeting people and making them welcome to our wonderful area.
languages: German, Dutch (some Spanish and Italian).
Directions: *Will meet ferry. Call us.*

Lavaud House

Akaroa

Homestay B&B
Address: 'Lavaud House', 83 Rue Lavaud, Akaroa
Name: Francis & Frances Gallagher
Telephone: (03) 304 7121 **Fax**: (03) 304 7121
Beds: 2 Queen, 1 King, 1 Twin (4 bedrooms)
Bathroom: 2 Ensuite, 1 Guests share
Tariff: B&B (continental) Double $80-$100, Single $60.
Credit cards (Visa/MC). NZ B&B Vouchers accepted $20 surcharge
Nearest Town: Christchurch 80 kms

Our historic French designed 2 storied home overlooks the main beach and harbour and is within 2 mins walk of restaurants, galleries and shops.
All rooms have fresh flowers, heaters and harbour or rural views plus television and electric blankets.
The ensuite bedroom upstairs has a king sized bed and harbour views.
The ensuite room downstairs has a queen sized bed and a woodland view with a glimpse of the harbour. Both twin and queen rooms upstairs have rural views.
The sunny guest sitting room has books, television, piano, and superb harbour outlook.
Enjoy our lovely antique furniture. Full continental breakfast is served in the dining room around our old dining table.
Tea and coffee are available.
Spend time in our large and colourful garden, enjoy the birds and harbour views.
Retired farmers, well travelled, we enjoy meeting people.
You will love this area as much as we do. Plan to stay awhile.
Directions: *Centrally situated in the main street, opposite the war memorial.*

Barrys Bay, Akaroa
Homestay/Farmstay
Address: Oihitu Estate, Barrys Bay, Akaroa
Name: Lynette & Ross Curry
Telephone: (03) 304 5804 **Fax**: (03) 304 5804
Beds: 2 Queen (2 bedrooms)
Bathroom: 2 Ensuite
Tariff: B&B (Special) Double $100, Single $70, Dinner $22.50,
Children negotiable. Credit cards (Visa/MC). Laundry no charge.
NZ B&B Vouchers accepted $30 surcharge
Nearest Town: Akaroa 12 km, Christchurch 60km

We are fortunate to live in one of the larger historic homes in the county, built in the 1860's, set amid the rolling hills of Banks Peninsula with views of the Akaroa Harbour. Our children Kirsten (6) and Matthew (4) are fourth generation on this 315 acre dairy farm which also runs deer, pigs and many pets.

We have converted two of the larger rooms to accommodate you in comfort, each with ensuite bathroom, a firm queensized bed, central heating and furnished in antiques of the period. You will receive traditional farm fare from the wood stove. Smoke cured bacon, eggs fresh from our own hens, and toast cooked on the embers topped with a selection of home-made jams, also fruit preserved from our orchard. Enjoy fresh bread and muffins still warm from baking. Coffee percolated on the stove and a selection of teas for many different tastes, for breakfast.

Tea, coffee and fresh home baking are offered upon your arrival and are always available by request. It is a pleasure for us to share our evening meal of a farm style roast with home grown vegetables, preceded by drinks and nibbles. However, we do appreciate sufficient notice to be able to serve a dinner of quality.

We have both travelled and try to offer our guests facilities such as the use of our laundry, spacious bedrooms and privacy that we value as travellers. We enjoy meeting and socialising with people whether it be relaxing in front of the open fire, on the large verandah or strolling though the informal gardens.

Directions: *Our front entrance is conveniently situated on the Akaroa Highway with our sign "Oihitu Estate" behind a white picket fence on the harbours edge. The homestead is set well off the road.*

Okains Bay, Akaroa

Farmstay
Address: 'Kawatea', Okains Bay, Banks Peninsula.
Name: Judy & Kerry Thacker
Telephone: (03) 304 8621 **Fax**: (03) 304 8621
Beds: 2 Queen, 1 Double, 2 Single (3 bedrooms)
Bathroom: 1 Ensuite, 1 Guest Bathroom.
Tariff: B&B (special) Double $90-$100, Single $55, Children negotiable.
Dinner $25.   NZ B&B Vouchers accepted $20 Surcharge.
Nearest Town: Akaroa 20km.

'Kawatea' is a large historic homestead set in spacious gardens in one of the beautiful Bays of Banks Peninsula.
The elegant rooms feature extensive use of native timbers and stained glass and have been refurbished with your comfort and warmth in mind. It is large enough to provide privacy but sufficiently informal to enable guests to feel at home.
Join us for summer barbecues on the expansive verandah, or enjoy seafood from the Bay, washed down with New Zealand wine, a delicious interlude. Sheep and beef are run on the 1400 acre hill country farm. Linger over breakfasts including speciality teas, freshly ground coffee, home-made bread, preserves and omelettes, served in the conservatory, or by the cosy kitchen fire in winter. Guests can be involved in farm activities, which may include moving stock, lambing, calving or shearing. There are also pet sheep which enjoy being fed and an aviary. The farm is bounded by 5km of scenic coastline, with interesting walks, panoramic views and a seal colony.
Explore or swim at one of Okains Bay's secluded sandy beaches, play tennis, golf, kayak or horse ride.
You may choose to relax in the garden with a book or listen to music from our varied collection.
'Kawatea' is conveniently situated to provide a base for visiting nearby attractions including a Maori and Colonial Museum, winery, cheese factory, and the township of Akaroa, noted for its French settlement, craft shops, harbour cruises and Hector Dolphins.
The family have farmed in Okains Bay for 150 years, so we have a wide knowledge of local history.
We look forward to sharing our special place with you.
Directions: *Take Highway 75 from Christchurch. Follow the signposts to top of Okains Bay. We are 6km down hill on the right hand side.*

Akaroa
Farmstay
Address: Paua Bay
Postal: c/- 113 Beach Road, Akaroa
Name: Murray & Sue Johns
Telephone: (03) 304 8511
Fax: (03) 304 8511
Beds: 1 Double, 1 Twin (2 bedrooms)
Bathroom: Guests share
Tariff: B&B (full) Double $70,
Single $40, Dinner $20.
NZ B&B Vouchers accepted Accepted all year round,same day restrictions Nov to March.
Nearest Town: Akaroa 15 kms

We are a family of four, William and Kate are teenagers. We have a sheep, cattle and deer farm of 900 acres at Paua Bay, surrounded by coast-line with valleys of native bush and streams. Those interested in taking a stroll can enjoy the unique scenery including seal and penguin colonies which are a 30 minute walk from the house. You would be most welcome to participate in any farm activity that occurs during your stay. Qualified riding instruction available. Our cosy colonial home is nestled against native bush surrounded by a large cottage garden including a swimming pool and spectacular views over the Pacific. The farm is a twenty minute drive from picturesque Akaroa, a French-style harbour village. You can be sure of a warm welcome here. **Directions**: *Please phone. Evening if possible.*

Akaroa
Homestay B & B
Address: 'Lavender Hill',
1 Lighthouse Road,
Akaroa, Banks Peninsula
Name: Erica & Allister Stewart
Telephone: (03) 304 7082
Email: allister.erica.stewart@xtra.co.nz
Beds: 1 Double, 2 Single (2 bedrooms)
Bathroom: 1 Guests share
Tariff: B&B (special) Double $80, Single $60.
Nearest Town: Christchurch 80km

Our home has wonderful views of harbour, hills and village. Opposite is the Garden of Tane, a lovely bush reserve with bellbirds and native pigeons and winding paths down to the historic lighthouse and waterfront. Only ten minutes walk to a selection of excellent restaurants and cafes.
Cruises on the harbour, historic homes and gardens, galleries and quiet walking tracks make Akaroa a unique place to explore. We will be happy to help you plan an enjoyable holiday. Erica, an artist works in stained glass and clay.
Bathroom and separate toilet are shared only by the two guests' bedrooms which have electric blankets and woollen underlays. The bedrooms have views to the garden. We appreciate you not smoking indoors.
Directions: *Turn left at the Akaroa Bakery. Continue to the top of Rue Jolie. Follow Onuku Road, past the Hospital, to next left, Lighthouse Road. Tea and scones on arrival.*

Akaroa
Bed & Breakfast
Address: 113 Rue Jolie, Akaroa, Banks Peninsula
Name: "La Belle Villa"
Telephone: (03) 304 7084
Fax: (03) 304 7084
Beds: 1 King, 2 Queen, 1 Twin (4 bedrooms)
Bathroom: 1 Ensuite, 2 Private, 1 Guest share
Tariff: B&B (special) Double $85/$100, Single $60.
Nearest Town: Christchurch approx. 80km

CANTERBURY

A warm welcome awaits you. Relax in the comfort of a bygone era, and appreciate the antiques in our picturesque historic villa. Built in the 1870's for a prominent business man it became one of the 1st doctor's surgeries in Akaroa and is now established on approx. 1/2 acre of beautiful, mature grounds, surrounded by rolling hills and lush scenery. Enjoy the indoor/outdoor living, large private swimming pool and gently trickling stream. We offer warm, spacious bedrooms, large guest lounge, fabulous fires in winter, breakfast 'Al Fresco' in the summer if you choose with the birds and trees. We offer to make your stay with us special. It will be a pleasure to book you on to any cruises, fishing trips, swim with the dolphins, horse treks etc that you may require. Being centrally situated, restaurants, cafes, and wine bars are all walking distance. So too, you will find, are the majority of galleries, shops and excursions available in New Zealand's most charming, quaint and quintessential French township.

Takamatua, Akaroa

Farmstay
Address: Takamatua Valley Road.
Postal: PO Box 4, Akaroa
Name: Hanne & Paul Lelievre
Telephone: (03) 304 7255 (beforee 8.30 am or after 6 pm)
Fax: (03) 304 7255
Beds: 1 Double, 1 Single (1 bedroom)
Bathroom: 1 Ensuite
Tariff: B&B (full) Double $80, Single $45, Children negotiable. Dinner optional $20 pp. Campervans welcome. NZ B&B Vouchers accepted plus $15 surcharge
Nearest Town: Akaroa 5km

Your hosts farm 800 acres running deer, sheep and cattle. The farm incorporates typical Inner Harbour easy hill country and Eastern bay coastline.
Our home, possessing a native bush outlook, is situated approximately 1.5km up the picturesque Takamatua Valley.
Only 5km from the lovely French village of Akaroa, you are in easy reach of all that Akaroa offers and only 20 minutes drive from the spectacular beaches, bays and walks of Banks Peninsula.
For those with a love of animals, we have a number of pets, whilst anyone interested in horses, can receive riding instruction upon request as an optional extra.
Hanne is of Danish origin and speaks that language fluently, whilst we have both lived and worked in Australia for more than 10 years.
We offer spacious yet cosy accommodation, in a sheltered position, and invite you to enjoy our home cured bacon and homemade bread, along with some good old fashioned country hospitality.

Akaroa Harbour

Farmstay
Address: 'Bossu', Wainui, Akaroa R.D.2,
Banks Peninsula
Name: Rana & Garry Simes
Telephone: (03) 304 8421 **Fax**: (03) 304 8421
Beds: 5 Single (3 bedrooms)
Bathroom: 1 Private, 1 Guests share
Tariff: B&B (full) Double $100, Single $55, Dinner $20
Nearest Town: Akaroa 20km

"Bossu" farm is situated on the edge of Akaroa Harbour with magnificent panoramic views to the picturesque French village of Akaroa. We are in our 50's with three adult children. We live in a modern sunny homestead and farm 100 acres of forestry, sheep, a small vineyard and cattle. It is situated on 2km of coastline nestled amongst bush, planted trees and shrubs in a garden including a well used grass tennis court. We have a power boat and can offer fishing and the viewing of hector dolphins, penguins and nesting sea birds. Enjoy our fresh fish and homegrown lamb vegetables with a selection of pre-dinner drinks and wine. Breakfast includes homegrown bacon and marmalade. Rana and Garry have travelled extensively and interests include bridge, spinning, golf and tramping. We look forward to your visit and offer you a very warm welcome.
Directions: *"Bossu" accommodation sign is on State Highway 75 at the commencement of Barrys Bay. Follow coastal road to Wainui 8km. Farm is located through Wainui first property on seaward side.*

Akaroa

Self-contained Accommodation
Address: Mill Cottage, Rue Grehan, Akaroa
Name: Joan & John Galt
Telephone: (03) 304 8007
Beds: 1 Double, 2 Single (3 bedrooms)
Bathroom: 1 Private
Tariff: B&B (continental) Double $110, Each extra person $40, Single $70.
Nearest Town: Christchurch 80km

Enjoy the unique experience of staying in a fully restored, listed historic pioneer cottage, in a tranquil rural setting. Wake to the dawn chorus, the sound of the nearby stream, and a generous breakfast hamper on your doorstep. Wander around the secluded two acre garden, relax on the wide verandah, or explore the attractions of the picturesque township of Akaroa, with its enchanting streets and waterfront cafes.
In restoring the cottage, care has been taken to retain as much as possible of its original form and character, while providing all essential amenities for guest comfort. The privacy of the cottage, and its historical charm, provide an ideal atmosphere for those seeking a romantic setting for a special holiday break. The cottage is exclusively yours during your stay.
Season: 1 September to 31 May.
Directions: *One kilometre up Rue Grehan.*
(We ask our guests to refrain from smoking)

Akaroa - Banks Peninsula

Homestay+B&B
Address: Bells Road, Takamatua, R.D. 1, Akaroa
Name: David & Sue Thurston
Telephone: (03) 304 7499
Beds: 3 Queen, 2 Bedrooms, 1 Semi-detached barn loft room.
Bathroom: 1 Private, 2 Ensuite
Tariff: B&B (continental) Double $100-$130, Single $90, Children welcome, Campervans.
Nearest Town: Akaroa 4km

This is New Zealand at its best.
A picturesque and easy 1 1/2 hour drive from Christchurch brings you to this spacious colonial home set amongst century old walnut trees, bounded by creeks and bush teeming with birdlife. Enjoy the tranquil garden with its roses, croquet lawn and swimming pool or the seaside resort of Akaroa is 5 mins away. Guest rooms are situated in a separate wing with rooms opening onto the verandah and are centrally heated by radiators from a wood-burning range, complemented by two open fires.
David is a nationally recognised furniture maker and the house features many fine examples of his work and his studio is open for viewing.
The family have many farm animals including tame eels, pet rabbits, sheep and ponies.
Sumptuous breakfast includes fresh fruit from the orchard, farm eggs, croissants, home-made preserves and freshly ground coffee.

CANTERBURY

Takamatua, Akaroa

Bed & Breakfast   1770
Address: "The Barn", Akaroa Main Road (Highway 75),
Takamatua (Akaroa)
Name: Jeanine & Theo Bakker
Telephone: (03) 304 7277
Fax: (03) 304 7277
Mobile: (021) 662 584
Beds: 1 King, 1 Queen, 2 Single (4 bedrooms)
Bathroom: 1 Ensuite, 1 Guests share
Tariff: B&B (full) Double Ensuite $100, Double $90, Single $60, 10% discount
from 3 nights, Campervans welcome $25, Credit Cards (VISA/MC) welcome.

Nearest Town: Akaroa 3km

*The "Barn" is a rustic home surrounded by 3 acres of beautiful gardens, an orchard,
tennis court and stream boundary offering peace and tranquillity. We are less than five
minutes away from Takamatua's peaceful bay which is a good fishing spot with many
opportunities to launch a boat. Akaroa is close by; thus, if you want to visit a beautiful
and historical township, it offers art galleries, interesting shops, licensed restaurants,
the pier, a swimming beach, sailing trips, swimming with the dolphins or just
watching them. It's a trampers paradise with several tracks to choose from.*
*Jeanine is a bubbly and outgoing personality, speaks five languages, worked and
travelled internationally as a general nurse and enjoys caring for people. She loves
tennis, skiing and surfing.*
*Theo will make your stay at "The Barn" exceptional; good contact with people is one
of his hobbies. He plays the guitar, is a professional sailor, speaks two languages and
loves travelling.*

Akaroa

B & B + Self-contained Cottage
Address: "Blythcliffe", 37 Rue Balguerie,
Akaroa 8161
Name: Rosealie & Jan Shuttleworth
Telephone: (03) 304 7003
Freephone: 0800 393 877**Fax**: (03) 304 7003
Email: blythcliffe@xtra.co.nz
Beds: 2 Queen, (2 bedrooms)
Bathroom: 1 Ensuite, 1 Private
Tariff: B&B (continental) Double $100, Single $75. Cottage: $125.
0Credit Cards (Visa/MC)
Nearest Town: Christchurch 84km

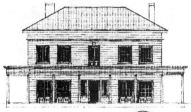

Saunter 200 metres from the town centre to Blythcliffe our historic home (circa 1857) set against a hillside of native bush with a chattering stream dividing the bush from the semi formal garden, croquet lawn and petanque terrain.Jan, Rose and Garfield the moggy, (the three grown up kids have transplanted themselves to other places), warmly welcome our guests to share the history of this unique piece of NZ family heritage.Upstairs we have two double bedrooms each with its own bathroom as well as a modern self contained, intimate cottage for two at the bottom of the garden.Play billiards on our full sized table, tinkle the ivories in the parlour or breakfast in our cosy country kitchen or outdoors, (in the pavilion or the cloister), during the summer.Jan supplements the family income with his woodturning.Smoke free zone in the house.
Home Page: nz-holiday/akaroa/blythcliffe>
Directions: *200 metres up Rue Balguerie on the left. Please phone.*

Akaroa

Self Contained Accommodation, B&B and Country Cottages
Address: 'Loch Hill' Country Cottages Motel,
Main Highway, Akaroa
Name: Donna and David Kingan
Telephone: 03-304 7195
Fax: 03-304 7195
Beds: 6 King/Queen, 1 Double,
4 Single (9 bedrooms)
Bathroom: 4 Ensuite, 2 Private, 1 Spa
Tariff: B&B (choice of special, full or continental) Double $90, Single $60, Children negotiable. Self contained cottages: Double $90-$140, each extra person $18. Credit Cards: Visa/Mastercard NZ B&B Vouchers accepted
Nearest Town: Akaroa 1 km, Christchurch 81 km

"Loch Hill" our thirty-five acre property, is set in a rural situation overlooking Akaroa Harbour.Our large, new stone cottages, nestled in the surrounding native bush, provide luxury accommodation for those who appreciate privacy, attractive park and garden setting, magnificent views and tranquillity.Whether your are staying in our self-catering, secluded one bedroom bush cottages, our 2 or 3 bedroom luxury self-contained cottages, or B&B studio unit with antique decor, we would like to extend the hospitality of "Loch Hill". Here you will find a warm welcome, cottages with their own individual design and character, large rooms, some air-conditioned, and country theme furnishings.Your hosts David and Donna Kingan, are well-travelled, semi retired business people. Interests include gardening, vintage and classic vehicles and antiques.Our cluster of private, tastefully appointed cottage motels, on the outskirts of the historic village of Akaroa, with its early French history, are ideal for the perfect holiday retreat, or the smaller business conference, or wedding group.
Directions: *On Akaroa Main State Highway 75, well signposted, on the right. One km north of Akaroa.*

CANTERBURY

Akaroa Harbour

Country Retreat + Llama Farm
Address: "Kahikatea", Wainui, RD 2, Akaroa, Banks Peninsula
Name: Jane & Joe Yates
Telephone: (03) 304 7400 **Fax**: (03) 304 7400
Email: kallamaty.jane@netaccess.co.nz
Beds: 2 Queen (2 bedrooms). Single party bookings only.
Bathroom: 1 Private
Tariff: B&B (full) Double $145, Single $100, Dinner $35pp,
Credit Cards (VISA/MC).
Nearest Town: Akaroa - 22km along spectacular harbour drive

High on the slopes of Banks Peninsula overlooking Wainui Valley and the impossibly blue Akaroa Harbour lies "Kahikatea", our beautiful colonial homestead and the home of Lands End Llamas. Featured in both US (Sept '92) and NZ (June '98) editions of House & Garden Magazine, our historic 1860's cottage has been faithfully renovated and more than doubled in size. French doors in every room lead to large verandas, English flower gardens, and dazzling views. The house has been meticulously designed with cathedral ceilings, native Rimu wood furniture and staircases, English and American antiques, and art collected from our worldwide travels. A central heating system has been installed for year-round comfort.

Our guests' luxurious two-storey accommodation includes a beautifully furnished living room with library, television and VCR. The second floor bedroom has a queen bed, a sunny balcony where breakfast can be enjoyed overlooking the llama paddocks, and views of the mountains and the sparkling South Pacific. Delicious home-cooked meals are served with NZ wines or we can suggest excellent restaurants in nearby Akaroa.

Treks with our gentle llamas (for an additional charge) can be arranged leaving directly from the barn and covering diverse terrain, including sheep-filled paddocks and kanuka forests. Or you can enjoy the privacy of our 15 acres including large gardens, a duck pond and a rushing stream bordered by lush native bush. Our menagerie includes pet lambs, miniature horses, 3 cats and a dog. We can help organise other activities for you such as golf, tennis, sea kayaking, fishing, or a swim with the dolphins.

Guests have called Kahikatea "truly breathtaking", "heaven on earth", and "the prettiest spot in NZ". Come experience the magic and leave knowing why our llamas hum so contentedly.

Directions: *Please phone. Advance bookings are necessary.*
Home Page: http://www.friars.co.nz/hosts/kahikatea.html

LANDS END
LLAMAS

Robinsons Bay, Akaroa

Homestay
Address: 'La Rue', Highway 75,
Robinsons Bay. Postal: RD1 Akaroa
Name: Fran and Peter Anderson
Telephone: 03-304 7657
Beds: 1 Double, 1 Twin.
Bathroom: 1 Private

Tariff: B&B (full) Double $90, Single $50, Dinner $30, Children negotiable.
Credit Cards Visa Mastercard. NZ B&B Vouchers accepted $20 surcharge
Nearest Town: Akaroa (7 mins)

Our home stands on the water's edge in Robinsons Bay, offering stunning views of harbour and hills. Location and space are our main advantages - we are just 7 minutes from Akaroa, an ideal starting point for exploring the outer bays and scenic reserves. Our two amiable Labradors will help you explore the large garden, and a pleasant stroll to the nearby wharf will acquaint you with the large variety of birdlife.

As our only guests, you will enjoy our amenities which include a cosy bedroom, private bathroom, and a huge lounge with log burner, dining table, piano, sound system and TV. A second twin bedroom is suitable for 1 or 2 more members of your group.

Peter is a master chef with 30 plus years experience. He guarantees a superb, hearty breakfast and, if required, a memorable dining experience at night. A warm welcome and comfortable stay is assured.

Sheffield

Homestay
Address: 'Pine House',
Waddington & Waimakariri Gorge Roads Corner,
Waddington, Sheffield
Name: Debra & Graeme Short
Telephone: (03) 318 3762
Beds: 2 Double, 3 Single (4 bedrooms)
Bathroom: 1 Guests share

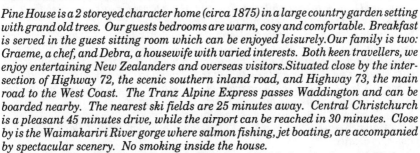

Tariff: B&B (full) Double $90, Single $50, Dinner $25.
NZ B&B Vouchers accepted $20 surcharge
Nearest Town: Darfield 12km east.

Pine House is a 2 storeyed character home (circa 1875) in a large country garden setting with grand old trees. Our guests bedrooms are warm, cosy and comfortable. Breakfast is served in the guest sitting room which can be enjoyed leisurely. Our family is two: Graeme, a chef, and Debra, a housewife with varied interests. Both keen travellers, we enjoy entertaining New Zealanders and overseas visitors. Situated close by the intersection of Highway 72, the scenic southern inland road, and Highway 73, the main road to the West Coast. The Tranz Alpine Express passes Waddington and can be boarded nearby. The nearest ski fields are 25 minutes away. Central Christchurch is a pleasant 45 minutes drive, while the airport can be reached in 30 minutes. Close by is the Waimakariri River gorge where salmon fishing, jet boating, are accompanied by spectacular scenery. No smoking inside the house.

Directions: *Pine House is on Highway 72, just north of the intersection with Highway 73 to the West Coast, and 12km west of Darfield.*

Castle Hill Village

Homestay
Address: 11 Torlesse Place, Castle Hill Village
(Rural Bag 55037), Christchurch
Name: The Burn
Telephone: (03) 318 7559 **Fax**: (03) 318 7558
Beds: 3 Double, 2 Single (4 bedrooms)
Bathroom: 1 Guests share, 1 Family share
Tariff: B&B (continental) Double $90, Single $50,
Dinner $25, Children half price.
Nearest Town: Springfield (33 km)

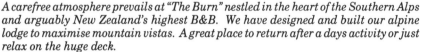

A carefree atmosphere prevails at "The Burn" nestled in the heart of the Southern Alps and arguably New Zealand's highest B&B. We have designed and built our alpine lodge to maximise mountain vistas. A great place to return after a days activity or just relax on the huge deck.

There are a host of outdoor sports on hand e.g. hiking, mountain biking, tennis, rock climbing, caving, children's playground, alpine golf, ski touring, ski / snowboarding (7 areas), High Country fly fishing, salmon fishing (5 lakes and rivers).

Professional guiding for fishing and alpine sports available in house. POA.

Your hosts are active friendly informative and well travelled. As we are often out enjoying the great outdoors we recommend advanced bookings so we can be on hand to meet you. This is preferred but not essential.

A home cooked evening meal is available by arrangement if required.

No smoking indoors please.

Directions: *State Hway 73, 33 km West of Springfield.*

Rakaia Gorge: Windwhistle

Self-contained Accommodation
Address: 'Birchview', Darfield RD2, Canterbury
Name: Tom & Jenny McElrea
Telephone: (03) 318 6813 **Fax**: (03) 318 6813
Beds: 1 Double, 4 Single (3 bedrooms)
Bathroom: 1 Private
Tariff: B&B (full) $45 per person, Children half price, Dinner $30 with wine.
Nearest Town: Methven 23km, Darfield 30km

Do you need a place to stay while you ski Mt Hutt or ski Porter Heights or Mt Cheeseman or Broken River or Craigieburn or for the foolhardy Mt Olympus?

Do you need a place to stay while you fish the Rakaia River for salmon or fish for trout in Lake Coleridge or Lake Selfe or Lake Georgia or Lake Lyndon?

Do you need a base while golfing the Hororata, Methven or Terrace Downs golf courses. Or alternatively just a place to rest up during your travels?

Our self-contained chalet is only 80 kilometres from Christchurch on the inland scenic route heading south West and is situated in the middle of our sheep cattle and deer property. Ideal first stop when arriving in Canterbury. There is also a fascinating canyon to explore for those who want to stretch their legs.

Guests do enjoy having their own self contained privacy.

Directions: *We are 23km northwest of Methven or 30km west of Darfield. Please phone for details.*

Mt Hutt, Rakaia Gorge, Methven
Farmstay
Address: 'Tyrone Deer Farm', Mt Hutt Station Rd, No.12 R.D., Rakaia, Mid Canterbury
Name: Pam & Roger Callaghan
Telephone: (03) 302 8096 **Fax**: (03) 302 8099
Beds: 2 Double, 2 Single (3 bedrooms) (max 5 people)
Bathroom: 2 Ensuites, 1 Private
Tariff: B&B (full) Double $90, Single $60, Children by arrangement, Dinner $25pp. NZ B&B Vouchers accepted Surcharge $20.
Nearest Town: Methven 8km

"Tyrone" Deer Farm is centrally situated in the Methven, Mt Hutt, Rakaia Gorge area. One hour from Christchurch international airport and in the centre of the South Island, which makes it an ideal place to stop over when either going south to Queenstown etc or north to Picton / Nelson, we are handy to Highway 73 which goes to Arthur's Pass and the West Coast.

The farm consists of 300 acres running deer, cattle and a few sheep. Our home is situated on the farm to take advantage of the mountain views (Mt Hutt) this forms the back drop for the deer grazing a few metres away.

As our family have left home we now have 3 spare bedrooms which we like to share with guests. There are electric blankets on the beds, heaters in the rooms, open fire in the lounge with Sky tv, tea and coffee making facilities, guest fridge and swimming pool. Come and meet Guz our pet deer, her daughter $$ and kitten called 10.30.

Dinner is a 3 course evening meal with pre dinner drinks and New Zealand wine.

For the visitor the surrounding area provides adventures and sporting activities ie skiing (Mt Hutt), Heliskiing (remote ranges), Jet Boating (Rakaia River), Ballooning, Tramping, Horse-riding, Guides are available for Hunting (Tahr, Chamois, Red Deer etc) also Trout and Salmon fishing (seasonal). Golf at Methven one of New Zealand's best 18 hole country courses, numerous walks: scenic, bush, garden or alpine.

Directions: *8 km from Methven on the alternativer Rakaia Gorge Route, 10 km from Rakaia Gorge Bridges. Please refer to map.*

633

Mt Hutt, Methven
Farmstay+Self-contained Accom.
Address: Hart Rd, HW 72, Methven
Postal: 'Glenview', R.D. 12, Rakaia
Name: Andrew & Karen Hart
Telephone: (03) 302 8620 **Fax**: (03) 302 8650
Mobile: (025) 335 136
Email: ahart@voyager.co.nz
Beds: 1 Queen, 1 Double, 3 Single + Cot (3 bedrooms)
Bathroom: 1 Ensuite, 1 Private, 1 Family share
Tariff: B&B (continental - full on request) Double $80, Single $45, Children half price, under 2 meals only, Dinner $25, Campervan power point available.
NZ B&B Vouchers accepted $10 surcharge
Nearest Town: Methven 10km

Our family invites you to sample their warm hospitality and come and join us on our large sheep and beef farm (1200 acres/480 hectares) at the top of the Canterbury Plains.

Our spacious, modern farmhouse at 1500ft/450m above sea level; is built to enjoy views of our animals grazing on the farm, to see more than 50 miles/80km out across the plains to Christchurch, or to look directly up into Mt Hutt Skifield and along the Southern Alps. Our farm is situated on the Inland Scenic highway 72 between Christchurch and southern destinations.

You are welcome to relax and enjoy the beautiful scenery, or take the opportunity to experience a large, working sheep and beef farm. Let Andrew take you for a tour. Go and observe the farming activities. There is always something to see and do on a working farm.There are many optional activities for you to experience. A choice of walks, horse riding, skiing, salmon and trout fishing, jet boating, golfing, parachuting and ballooning are all within 10 minutes drive.

Enjoy the comfort of our spacious guest areas. Family accommodation consists of 2 bedrooms sleeping 2-5. Also available is a self-contained unit (double) situated in a garden next to the house. Both areas have separate access, good heating, comfortable beds with electric blankets, and private facilities.

Meals are good quality NZ fare, and wine is included at dinner.

Come and enjoy our warm, relaxed hospitality. Andrew enjoys computing. Karen teaches and is a Marriage Celebrant. Jonathan (15) loves farming, and Renee (12) loves animals. Hartley (small, white fluffy dog) loves meeting people.

Our home is your home away from home.

Directions: *Christchurch or Timaru - 1 hour. Geraldine, Ashburton - 30 mins. Rakaia Gorge, Methven - 10 mins. Hart Road with our Farmhouse Accommodation signs, is on Highway 72 between Pudding Hill and the Mt Hutt Skifield Road.*

Mt Hutt - Methven

Farmstay-Country House
Address: 'Green Gables Deer Farm', S/Highway 77,
Waimarama Road, Methven
Postal: R.D.12, Rakaia
Name: Roger & Colleen Mehrtens
Telephone: (03) 302 8308;
Reservation Freephone 0800 466093 **Fax**: (03) 302 8309
Email: greengables@salmonsafari.co.nz
Beds: 3 Super King/Twin (3 Bedrooms)
Bathroom: 2 Ensuite, 1 Private with bath
Tariff: B&B (full) Double $95-$110, Single $70, Children $35, Dinner $30,
Credit cards.
Nearest Town: Methven - Mt Hutt Village 4km

*You are warmly welcomed to share a taste of tranquil country living on our deer farm
situated between the internationally recognised Mt Hutt Ski Area and the popular Mt
Hutt-Methven Village Ski resort, 1 hour south west of Christchurch Airport.*
*Hand feed "Lucy" our pet deer and friends Jacob, our pet sheep, meet Max our Golden
Labrador and Henry our marmalade cat. Enjoy viewing our Royal Danish white deer
and visit a herd of Alpaca.*
*Our guest wing is comfortably appointed with super king beds, ensuites, electric
blankets, wool underlays, hair dryers. French doors lead from all rooms to decking
and provide private access with superb views of magnificent Mt Hutt.*
*Complimentary pre dinner drinks and wine with dinner by arrangement or nearby
restaurants can be recommended.*
*Complimentary tea and coffee .
*Comfortable lounge with open fire and Sky TV.
*Breakfast served to suit YOUR schedule.
*Assistance with holiday plans.
**Wide range of interesting professionally run activities
nearby. *Salmon and trout fishing - guides available.*
*Skiing Mt Hutt - transport at gate.
*Closest B&B to ski area.
*Black Diamond safaris.
*Golf - 18 hole.
*Horse riding, Jet Boating.
*Scenic bush walks.
*Hot air ballooning.

Methven - Mt Hutt Village

Farmstay
Address: Methven Chertsey Road, Methven,
Postal: 12 RD, Rakaia.
Name: Pagey's Farmstay -
Gene and Shirley Pagey
Telephone: (03) 302 1713
Fax: (03) 302 1714
Beds: 1 Queen, 1 Double, 2 Single (3 bedrooms)
Bathroom: 1 Guests share
Tariff: B&B (full) Double $80, Single $50, Children under 12 half price,
Dinner $25,
Nearest Town: Methven 6km, Christchurch 1 hour, Ashburton 35km

*If you want great hospitality, mountain views experience the peace and tranquillity of
a NZ Romney Sheep Stud Farm of 400 acres close to Mt Hutt, then welcome to the
Pagey's. Our very spacious home set amidst old trees and rose garden has high
ceilings, beautiful carpet and large well equipped bedrooms each with woollen
underlays, electric blankets, quality pillows and feather and down duvets.*

*Treat your palate to some good old fashioned cooking made up of home grown meat and
veges and a pot full of conversation. You are welcome to participate in the feeding out
of sheep, cattle and horses and watch the dogs working or relax in the house with Sky
TV. Within minutes of the farm you could be skiing, jet boating, horse riding,
ballooning, bush walking, lawn bowling or golfing on our magnificent 18 hole country
course. Courtesy van if required to Methven.*

Directions: *From Methven town centre. Turn at the Medical Centre down Methven
Chertsey Road 6km on left.*

Mt Hutt - Methven

Homestay
Address: Airdrie House,
134 Forest Drive, Methven
Name: Margaret and Norman Riddle
Telephone: (03) 302 8827 **Fax**: (03) 302 8802
Beds: 2 Queen, 2 Single (3 bedrooms)
Bathroom: 1 Ensuite, 1 Guests share
Tariff: B&B (full) Double $98, $90. Single $55.
Credit Cards accepted. NZ B&B Vouchers accepted Oct-June only, $15 surcharge.
Nearest Town: Ashburton 34 km.

*We are a retired couple who moved to Methven and live in a warm and comfortable
home with wonderful views of the mountains. We have heaters, electric blankets and
TV in each room. A lovely upstairs sitting area where the sun pours in in winter. Tea /
coffee facilities available.*

*Methven is the base for the Mt Hutt ski field and is one hour from Christchurch. There
is a very good golf course available, trout and salmon fishing, jet boating, horse
trekking and tramping. Methven is also on the interesting route travelling from
Christchurch or further north to Geraldine, Fairlie, Tekapo, Mt Cook or further south
to Queenstown and Wanaka. We have drying and storage facilities available. Being
non smokers we appreciate you not smoking indoors.*

We have one cat and a small dog. We look forward to welcoming you.

Rakaia

Guest House
Address: 'St Ita's Guesthouse'
Barrhill/Methven Rd, Rakaia
Name: Ken & Miriam Cutforth
Telephone: (03) 302 7546 **Fax**: (03) 302-7546
Beds: 2 Double, 4 Single(3 Bedrooms
 2 Double +1 Twin bedroom with ensuites)
Bathroom: 3 Ensuite
Tariff: B&B (full) Double $90, Single $60, School Children $30, Dinner $25,
Hamper lunch $10. Tariff includes complimentary morning or afternoon teas.
Credit Cards. NZ B&B Vouchers accepted $12 surcharge
Nearest Town: Rakaia 2 minutes walking distance

A warm welcome is assured at St Ita's. Built in 1912, this former Convent is full of charm. The spacious home is set in more than an acre of grounds and is located on the western fringe of Rakaia township opposite the Domain.
Rakaia is 50 kilometres south of Christchurch, with its river famous for salmon fishing. Jetboating, horse trekking, golf and visiting the local pubs are popular pastimes in Rakaia. Within 30 minutes you can be at Mt Hutt Skifield, on the Transalpine Railway or a Scenic Walkway. St Ita's meals are based on local produce - fresh vegetables and fruit (mainly from our garden); lamb, beef, venison or salmon. Espresso coffee or tea is complimentary to wash down home baking. Cooked or continental breakfasts are served. Many guests choose St Ita's for its tranquillity - relax in front of an open fire with our cat and golden retriever; watch Sky Television; play tennis or pool.

Ashburton

Homestay
Address: 1 Sudbury Street, Ashburton
Name: Pat & Dave Weir
Telephone: (03) 308 3534
Beds: 1 Double, 2 Single (2 bedrooms)
Bathroom: 1 Family share
Tariff: B&B (full) Double $60, Single $30, Dinner $15,
Children under 13 half price. NZ B&B Vouchers accepted
Nearest Town: Ashburton is apprx 80 km south of Christchurch

We are 10-15 minutes walk from town, our comfortable home is situated in a quiet street and we have the added enjoyment of looking out onto a rural scene. The guest accommodation is comfortable. Your hosts are nearing retirement and have a variety of interests. We welcome the opportunity to meet and greet visitors and wish to make your stay a happy one. We do request visitors not to smoke in our home.
Vegetarian or additional meals to bed and breakfast available on request. We are a few minutes walk away from Ashburton River Walkway and Riding for Disabled grounds. Laundry facilities are available to guests.

Continental breakfast consists of fruit, cereal, toast, tea/coffee,
Full breakfast is the same with a cooked course,
Special breakfast has something special.

Ashburton

Farmstay

Address: 'Carradale Farm' Ferriman's Road, Lagmhor, No 8 R.D., Ashburton
Name: Jim & Karen McIntyre
Telephone: (03) 308 6577
Fax: (03) 308 6548
Mobile: (025) 338 044
Beds: 4 Single (2 bedrooms)
Bathroom: 1 Private, 1 Family share
Tariff: B&B (full,continental) Double $80, Single $50, Dinner $25, Children under 12 half price, Campervans & caravan power point $25. Spa pool. Credit Cards. NZ B&B Vouchers accepted
Nearest Town: Ashburton - 8 km West of Ashburton; 1 hour Christchurch International Airport.

Our homestead which captures the sun in all rooms is cosy and inviting. It is situated in a sheltered garden where you can enjoy peace, tranquility and fresh country air or indulge in a game of tennis.Both guest rooms have comfortable twin beds, electric blankets, reading lamps and tea making facilities. Breakfast may be served either in dining room or conservatory. Laundry and ironing facilities available.We offer home grown meat and vegetables.We have a 225 hectare irrigated sheep and cattle farm. You may like to join in farm activities or be taken for a farm tour; sheep shearing demonstration available (in season).Our 3 adult children have left home. As we have both travelled extensively we would like to offer hospitality to fellow travellers. Our hobbies include meeting people, travel, reading, photography, gardening, sewing, cake decorating, rugby, cricket, Jim belongs to Masonic Lodge and Karen is involved in Community Affairs.
Directions: *Turn off State Highway 1 and cross the railway line at Tinwald Tavern, heading west onto Lagmhor Road driving past Tinwald Golf Course. The road then becomes Frasers Road. Travel 6 km to 5 crossroads. Make a left turn onto Ferriman's Road. Our home is the only house on the right side of the road.*

Ealing/Ashburton

Farmstay

Address: 'Riverview', Ealing, No 3 R.D., Ashburton
Name: Valmai & Ken McKenzie
Telephone: (03) 303 7040 **Fax**: (03) 303 7008
Mobile: (021) 214-1936
Beds: 1 Double, 2 Single (2 bedrooms)
Bathroom: 1 Guests share
Tariff: B&B (full) Double $80, Single $40, Dinner $25, Children half price. Campervans welcome, Credit Cards. NZ B&B Vouchers accepted
Nearest Town: Ashburton - 32km, Christchurch Airport 1.5 hours

Visitors are welcome to stay at our small mixed farm where we specialise in hand rearing calves, with some sheep, dogs, a cat.Surrounded by many types of farms, we can offer visitors much to see - Ken is sometimes available for sightseeing and introduce keen fishermen to favourite fishing holes. Our farm is situated on the banks of the Rangitata River, world-wide noted for salmon fishing.Our house is behind a big hedge, in attractive sheltered surroundings, only 400 m off SH1, halfway between Ashburton and Timaru, near turn off SH79 to Mt Cook.Valmai's interests include handfelting, CWI, gardening, cooking, while Ken's include fishing and Lions. We invite you to enjoy a 3 course evening meal, including wine, and hospitality of a high standard, in our warm, comfortable home.
Directions: *Travel 32 k south from Ashburton. At Ealing, turn left onto Ealing Road. House 1st on right. Letter box named.*

Ashburton
Homestay B&B
Address: 'Weatherly House', 359 West St,
(S.H.1) Ashburton
Name: Helen Thomson
Telephone: (03) 308 9949
Beds: 1 Double, 2 Single (2 bedrooms)
Bathroom: 1 Guest share
Tariff: B&B (continental) Double $65, Single $35, Children by negotiation,
Dinner $15, Full breakfast extra, Campervans welcome (No power).
Credit cards. NZ B&B Vouchers accepted
Nearest Town: Ashburton (In town)

Weatherly House is a charming turn of the century villa set in an attractive and private garden and with off-street parking. There is an inviting spa pool which is very relaxing after a long day travelling or on the slopes, and Weatherly House is particularly suitable for the not so able as there is ramp access and hand rails on the toilet and shower

We are situated about 5 minutes walk from Ashford's Craft Village and from the lovely Ashburton Domain. A 15 minutes walk will take you to the town centre or the hospital. Christchurch and Timaru are both 1 hours drive away and mid-Canterbury has much to offer the travellers.

Your comfort is our aim, a courtesy car is available, hot drinks and home made goodies available at any time. Dinner is by arrangement and there is a cosy open fire in the colder weather.

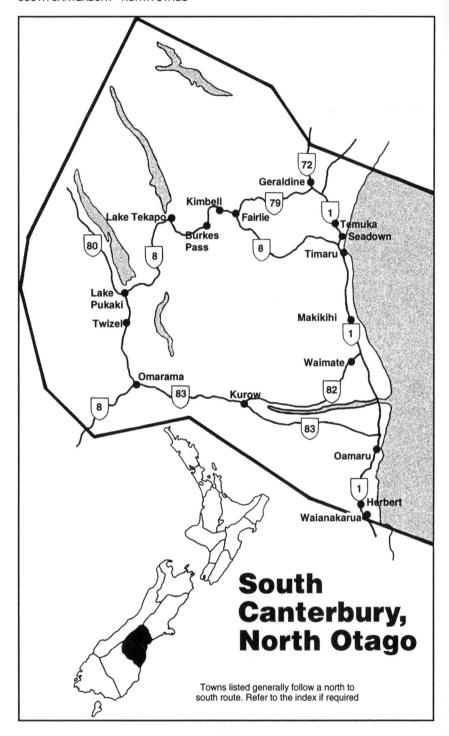

South Canterbury, North Otago

Towns listed generally follow a north to south route. Refer to the index if required

Geraldine
Guest Lodge
Address: 'The Crossing', Woodbury Rd,
R.D.21, Geraldine
Name: 'The Crossing'.
Telephone: (03) 693 9689 **Fax**: (03) 693 9789
Email: srelax@xtra.co.nz
Beds: 1 Queen, 3 Double, 2 Single (4 bedrooms)
Bathroom: 2 Ensuite, 2 Guests share
Tariff: B&B; Double $96-$147, Single $80-$117, extra person $20;
Full Breakfast included in overnight price. Dinner by arrangement.
Credit Cards Visa and Mastercard.
Nearest Town: Geraldine, 4 kms from 'The Crossing'.

The Crossing

"The Crossing" is a beautifully restored old English style manor house built in 1908. Situated on 37 peaceful acres near the base of the Four Peaks Range and bordered by the Upper Waihi River. The spacious lounges have open fires and ample leather seating. A shaded verandah overlooks the lovely gardens, where you can relax and read, or enjoy a leisurely game of croquet or petanque.

Enjoy a three course meal in our fully licensed restaurant. Local attractions include fishing for salmon or trout, white water rafting, nature treks, in Peel Forest, golfing, and ski fields nearby. We are located on the main route between Christchurch and Queenstown or Mount Cook. The Crossing is smoke free. Not suitable for children under 12. Member Heritage Inns.

Home Page: http://nzcom.co.nz/HeritageInns/TheCrossing/index/html
Directions: *Signposted on SH72/79 approx. 1km north of Geraldine. Turn into Woodbury Road, then 1km on right hand side.*

Geraldine
Farmstay + Backpackers Plus
Address: 90 Main North Road,
Geraldine, South Canterbury
Name: Raukapuka Roost - Hilary Muir Slater
Telephone: 0064 (03) 693 7665
Fax: 0064 (03) 693-7661
Beds: 1 Double, 1 Single sunroom (2 bedrooms)
Bathroom: 1 Guests Share (with bath)
Tariff: B&B (continental) Double $80, Single $40, Children under 14 yrs $10, Babies no charge. NZ B&B Vouchers accepted $10 surcharge
Nearest Town: Geraldine - on SH72/79 main north entrance to Geraldine on east side of road. Green 'Geraldine' township sign is outside the property. Sign at gate.

Clean, quiet, tidy, unique cottage in a sheltered, sunny rural setting. Breakfast in the porch and garden surrounds; 2kms from Geraldine and 10 minute easy walk to town. A short drive to Waihi Gorge (picnicking and swimming) and pleasant 10 minute drive to Peel Forest (native trees and walks). A home away from home, where Drysdale sheep and farmyard animals are available to watch or feed. "Buttercup", a Ewe will eat from your hand! and 'Puppit' a friendly working sheepdog will greet you. Relax outdoors and enjoy the musical notes of the NZ Bellbird.

2.25 hour drive to Mt Cook. 1.5 hour drive to Christchurch airport. Keen interests - organic food, community and golf.

Join us for a 'cuppa', a chat or a juice - you will be most welcome.

Geraldine

Bed & Breakfast
Address: 'Oak Grove', 26 Main North Road, Geraldine
Name: John & Ngaire Davis
Telephone: (03) 693 9830 **Fax**: (03) 693 9830
Beds: 3 Queen, 2 Single (4 bedrooms)
Bathroom: 1 Ensuite, 1 Guests share
Tariff: B&B (full) Double $90-$125, Single $45. Dinner $25pp.
Credit Cards: Visa/Mastercard. NZ B&B Vouchers accepted $20 surcharge
Nearest Town: Geraldine. We are 1 1/2 km north of Geraldine on S.H. 79.

"Oak Grove," our lovingly restored 1907 home, is nestled amongst 5 acres of hundred year old English trees. The setting, the food, the warm hospitality, make this a special "B&B", with all the expected comforts a superior home provides. Light airy bedrooms have the luxury of crisp white linen, fluffy towels and firm beds. Our honeymoon suite is perfect for that romantic weekend. Scrumptious breakfasts are served in the country-style breakfast room, warmed by the adjacent coal range. French doors open to a lovely garden courtyard. Dinner, a splendid three-course, silver service meal, changes with the seasons, and is served in the intimate dining room, where antiques and open fireplace complete the scene. Take time to visit John's fascinating workshop, where he hand makes gold and silver jewellery and wooden toys. We are smokefree.
Directions: *1 1/2 hours from Christchurch on S.H. 79, main route to Mt. Cook and Queenstown.*

Geraldine, South Canterbury

Bed & Breakast
Address: 20 Cox St, Geraldine 8751
Name: Hislop House
Telephone: (03) 693 8890
Fax: (03) 693 8890
Beds: 1 Queen, 3 Single (2 bedrooms)
Bathroom: 2 Ensuite
Tariff: B&B (full) Double $70, Single $40,
Children under 12 half price,
Dinner $20 by arrangement. Credit cards (VISA/MC).
NZ B&B Vouchers accepted
Nearest Town: Geraldine, 200 metres to Main Street

Hislop House - 20 Cox St, Geraldine Ph/Fax (03) 693-8890
A warm friendly welcome awaits you at Hislop House, which is a 1900's character home situated across from the Domain.
Each bedroom has an ensuite bathroom and electric blankets and heaters, and a TV in rooms. Enjoy supper with your hosts, and a nourishing fruit and cereal, and cooked bacon and eggs etc awaits you in the morning.
Jan enjoys gardening and meeting people and has travelled extensively overseas.
Hislop House is smoke-free and is situated very clsoe to the town amenities, including fine restaurants.
Directions: *200 metres from GeraldineMain Street on SH 79 to Fairlie – Mt Cook Queenstown*

Geraldine

Farmstay
Address: "Camberdown", State Highway 79, Geraldine
Name: Colin & Susan Sinclair
Telephone: (03) 697 4849 **Fax**: (03) 697 4849
Beds: 1 Queen, 2 Single (2 bedrooms)
Bathroom: 2 Guests share
Tariff: B&B (full) Double $90, Single $60, Children half price, Dinner $25pp, Credit Cards. NZ B&B Vouchers accepted Surcharge $20.
Nearest Town: Geraldine 22km and Fairlie 24km - We're halfway between the two.

Camberdown Homestead is situated on State Highway 79 between Geraldine and Fairlie, only two hours from Christchurch. The 430 acre farm is situated in lush green rolling country with mountain views. Bird life abounds in small areas of native bush. Relax on our sunny verandah with our cat or enjoy taking part in daily running of our sheep and cattle farm.

Nearby are wineries, golf courses, skifields, trout and salmon fishing and bush walking. Susan enjoys patchwork, needlework and runs a flock of coloured sheep. Where possible we offer our guests home grown fruit and vegetables. Home made bread, jam, preserves are part of our delicious meals. Non-smoking household.

Geraldine

Farmstay
Address: "The Woolshed",
211 Main North Road,
Geraldine
Name: Sue and Colin Matthews
Telephone: 03-693 9394
Fax: 03-693 9394
Email: Colin&Sue.Matthews@xtra.co.nz
Beds: 1 Queen, 2 Single (2 bedrooms)
Bathroom: 1 Guests share
Tariff: B&B (full/continental) Double $75, Single $40, Dinner $20, Children under 12 half price. NZ B&B Vouchers accepted
Nearest Town: Geraldine 2km.

Our small farm is in a lovely setting with river boundary, expansive views of Mt Peel and Four Peaks and handily located on the main State Highway. Our main emphasis is black and coloured sheep of special interest to spinners and weavers, and we also operate a worm breeding farm. We keep the usual array of domestic farm animals. A wool, art and craft gallery is situated on the farm. We run a clean and relaxed home. Guests have a separate bathroom and the choice of a separate lounge (with TV) or may share our lounge. We have computer facilities with Internet access, and fax. Sue is interested in horticulture (herbs, flowers and organically grown vegetables), art (painting sculpture and photography), and plays tennis. Colin plays squash and is interested in computing and writing. Both enjoy travel and have worked overseas. Both are non smokers. Guests are welcome to join in farm activities.

Temuka

Homestay B&B
Address: "Ashfield", 71 Cass Street,
Temuka
Name: Ann & Martin Bosman
Telephone: (03) 615 6157
Fax: (03) 615 9062
Beds: 2 King/Queen, 1 Double,
2 Single (4 bedrooms)
Bathroom: 1 Guests share
Tariff: B&B (special) Double $88, Single $50, Children $15,
Credit Cards (VISA/MC).
Nearest Town: Timaru 10 minutes, Christchurch 90 minutes

"Ashfield" is set on 4 acres of woodlands, situated inside the Temuka boundary. We are only a 10 minutes walk from the shops and restaurants. Our house was built around 1883 and features marble fireplaces and spectacular gilt mirrors. A warm welcome awaits you. Join us for a drink in the evening or maybe you would like to challenge Martin to a game of snooker on the full size table in the summer house. Two of our bedrooms open up to a balcony with beautiful views of the mountains in the distance. Several skifields are within one to one and a half hour drive. Lake Tekapo is one hour away. If salmon fishing is your thing then this is the place to come to. So come and join us and our 2 dogs and 2 cats for a wonderful stay in a lovely setting.

Timaru

Rural Homestay
Address: 'Mountain View',
Talbots Road,
Kingsdown, No 1 R.D., Timaru
Name: Mary & Graeme Bell
Telephone: (03) 688 1070
Fax: (03) 688 1069
Beds: 1 Double, 4 Single (3 bedrooms)
Bathroom: 2 Private, 1 Family share
Tariff: B&B (full) Double $70, Single $45, Children under 12 half price;
Dinner $20; Campervans $6 per person with power. Credit cards accepted.
NZ B&B Vouchers accepted
Nearest Town: Timaru 3kms from Southern boundary.

'Mountain View' is a farmlet on Talbots Road 200 metres from State Highway 1, just 3 kms from the southern boundary of Timaru. Blue and white Bed & Breakfast signs are on State Highway 1 north and south of the turn off into Talbots Road. Your hosts offer warm Kiwi hospitality and are semi-retired farmers who have hosted on their farm for 10 years. We still have a few deer and sheep. Our home is situated in a tranquil sheltered garden overlooking farmland and a wonderful view of the mountains. Electric blankets on all beds, two private bathrooms for guests and laundry facilities available. Breakfast of your choice is served at your requested time and an evening meal is available with prior notice. Our interests include gardening, spinning and engineering. Nearby fishing, golf courses, swimming both at beach and heated swimming pool and a walk on the sea coast to the lighthouse. Day trips can be comfortably taken to Mt Cook, Hydro Lakes and Ski Fields.

Timaru

Homestay
Address: 16 Selwyn Street, Timaru
Name: Margaret & Nevis Jones
Telephone: (03) 688 1400
Beds: 1 Double, 3 Single (3 bedrooms)
Bathroom: 1 Guests share
Tariff: B&B (full) Double $70, Single $40,
Children half price. NZ B&B Vouchers accepted
Nearest Town: Timaru

Our home is a spacious, comfortable, two-storeyed brick house with a grass tennis court in use from October until March. Situated in central Timaru – 5 minutes walk from the beach and 15 minutes from town, our home is set back from the road in a private garden surrounded by trees. We have travelled and worked overseas with our four children three and a half years of our married life, and share an enjoyment of meeting people from other countries and feel we have an appreciation of what it is like to be a visitor in a foreign country. Our main interests centre around music and the theatre in which we are both actively involved. We also play tennis and golf. We enjoy making use of the many walks and opportunities to get into the mountains which are so accessible from Timaru.
Directions: *Please phone.*

Seadown, Timaru

Farmstay
Address: Seadown, R.D.3, Timaru
Name: Margaret & Ross Paterson
Telephone: (03) 688 2468 **Fax**: (03) 688 2468
Beds: 1 Double, 4 Single (3 bedrooms)
Bathroom: 1 Guests share, 1 Family share
Tariff: B&B (full/continental) Double $70, Single $45, Children half price,
under 5 years no charge for meals.; Dinner $20; Credit Cards.
NZ B&B Vouchers accepted
Nearest Town: Approx 15km Timaru and 9km Temuka)

We are a mixed cropping farm situated in South Canterbury between Timaru and Temuka, east of State Highway 1. We grow grass-seed, clover, grain crops and freezing peas and also have 600 sheep. Our home is an older type home which has been modernised. Electric blankets on all guests' beds. Laundry facilities are available. A swimming pool can be enjoyed in the warmer weather. Your hostess is interested in spinning, gardening and breadmaking. You are welcome to have your meals with us. Day trips can be comfortably taken to Mount Cook, Hydro Lakes and skifields. Fishing and golf course a few minutes away; also a walk to the sea coast. A warm welcome awaits overseas and New Zealand visitors alike.
Directions: *From north approximately 5 km from Temuka to Dominion Road on left. Turn right if travelling from Timaru approx 11 km. To the end of Dominion Road – turn right then left onto Beach Road, till you come to Hides Road on left – first house on left on Hides Road.*

SOUTH CANT
NORTH OTAGO

Relax – Don't try to drive too far in one day.

645

Timaru

Homestay
Address: 264 Pages Rd, Timaru
Name: Carol Angland & Ross Carrick
Telephone: (03) 686 0323(h) or 688 4628(w)
Fax: (03) 686 0272

Beds: 1 Queen, 1 Double, 2 Single (2 bedrooms)
Bathroom: 1 Ensuite, 1 Private
Tariff: B&B (full) Double $85, Single $60, Dinner $25, Children half price,
Under 5 no charge, Credit cards.   NZ B&B Vouchers accepted $20 surcharge
Nearest Town: Centre Timaru 4km

Our spacious, sunny, comfortable home set on 1 acre in Timaru city, looks out over farmland to the mountains. The extensive garden features established trees, 100 roses and a tennis court. You can also relax on the sheltered terrace or play petanque or croquet.

The queen bedroom has an adjoining sunroom/childrens room. A cot and high chair are available. Laundry facilities.

Dinner by arrangement. Breakfasts are tempting, healthy and generous. Many extras. Smoke-free home.

We enjoy an informal lifestyle; theatre, literature, food, travel, sport and our grown-up family of five, three grandchildren and Harry-our (outdoors only) Labrador puppy. To find us - from Christchurch (150km north) turn right at Washdyke at the Mobil Truck stop and road sign to Gleniti and Pages Road. From Dunedin (230km south) left at Otipua Rd, left at Wai-iti Rd, right at Morgans Rd and left into Pages Rd.

Timaru

Garden Homestay
Address: Ethridge Gardens,
10 Sealy Street, Timaru
Name: Nan & Wynne Raymond
Telephone: (03) 684 4910 **Fax**: (03) 684 4910
Beds: 1 Queen, 3 Single (3 bedrooms)
Bathroom: 1 Private, 1 Guests share, Spa bath by arrangement
Tariff: B&B (full) Double $120, Single $90, Dinner (3 course with wine) $40pp,
Casual meals also provided $20-$30, Lunch $15pp. Laundry service available.
Credit cards
Nearest Town: Timaru centre 2km

Ethridge Gardens is a beautiful two storey red brick house built in 1911. High brick walls divide the romantic English-style garden into several garden rooms. Iron gates and rose-covered archways lead through to exciting vistas, each one differing in style, colour and design.

To stay here is to enjoy the very best in hospitality. Guests are welcome to relax in a spacious sitting room that opens out onto the terrace and garden with heated swimming pool. Tea, coffee, fruit and fresh flowers in the bedrooms. T.V in the main bedroom. A three course dinner with wine, flowers and candlelight can be served in the formal dining room, or enjoy alfresco in the gazebo during summer and a casual meal beside the fire in winter. Delicious breakfasts range from traditional to European. Good licensed restaurants nearby and transport can be easily arranged.

Wynne is presently Mayor of Timaru District and Nan is a renowned New Zealand gardener.

Directions: Please phone

646

Timaru

Homestay
Address: Please phone
Name: Dorothy & Ron White
Telephone: (03) 688 5856
Beds: 4 Single (2 bedrooms)
Bathroom: 1 Private (we only take one party at a time)
Tariff: B&B (continental) Double $70, Single $50, Children half price,
Dinner $25pp.
Nearest Town: Timaru

We are recently retired from farming and live in a comfortable two storeyed home situated in a quiet street in central Timaru - 5 minutes walk to the town centre and Caroline Bay. The guest bedroom has two single beds with electric blankets and own bathroom. There is also a smaller bedroom with two single beds, more suitable for children. Laundry facilities are available.

We are licensed to transport passengers, so can, if required, meet guests anywhere in the South Island. Day trips and longer guided tours can be undertaken on request. Timaru is central to the many attractions of South Canterbury.

These services are at a separate cost.

We both have many interests including golf, gardening and floral art and look forward to meeting and offering our hospitality to people who prefer homestays.

Directions: *Please phone. At least 24 hours notice is advisable to avoid disappointment.*

Timaru

Rural Self-contained Accommodation
Address: Otipua, No. 2 R.D., Timaru
Name: Lorraine & Wayne Calvert
Telephone: (03) 686 4874 **Fax**: (03) 686 4874
Beds: 1 Queen (1 bedroom)
Bathroom: 1 Ensuite

"Beaconsfield Lodge"

Tariff: B&B (continental) Double $80, Single $65, Dinner $20pp. Credit cards.
Nearest Town: Timaru 8km

We welcome visitors to our home with surrounding flower garden and lawns. We offer you a self-contained private detached unit with bed, living area and ensuite. A comfortable queen size bed with wool underlay and electric blanket, TV, microwave, refrigerator, toaster and tea making facilities. A continental breakfast is placed in your unit to enjoy at your leisure. An evening meal is available with prior notice.

Our property is used for market gardening. Lorraine's interests include flower gardening, sewing and children's smocking. Wayne enjoys corresponding with overseas pen-friends. We both enjoy meeting people and travel.

We are within easy travelling to Christchurch, Dunedin, Mt Cook and Queenstown. Non-smoking self contained accommodation. Garaging available.

Directions: *Take first turn right on Southern boundary of Timaru, Beaconsfield Road. We are situated 8km from the main highway approx. 10 minutes from Timaru. We are on the right hand side of road (cross roads on top of hill). Name on mail box. Vegetable sign at gate. Please phone in advance if possible.*

There are some good tips for easier travel on page 7

Timaru
Farmstay/B&B
Address: 'Benacre', Otaio,
No 1 RD, Timaru
Name: Peter and Jo Johnstone
Telephone: (03) 612 6719
Fax: (03) 612 6716
Beds: 1 King, 1 Double, 1 Single (2 bedrooms)
Bathroom: 1 Private
Tariff: B&B (full) Double $90, Single $70. Children at reduced rates.
NZ B&B Vouchers and Credit Cards accepted.
Nearest Town: Timaru 30 kms, 15km from Waimate

Peter and Jo Johnstone's beef and sheep farm, 'Benacre', is only a 25 minute drive from Timaru and 15 minutes from Waimate in South Canterbury, with an uninterrupted view to the foothills. The friendly, outgoing family (three children at boarding school) welcomes visitors from home and abroad. Private accommodation attached to the homestead sleeps five - electric blankets; tea and coffee making facilities; laundry service available; dinner and/or packed lunches by arrangement. Close to golf courses, ski fields and salmon and trout fishing. Peter is happy to guide and to take out his jet boat.
We have a friendly beagle dog.
Directions: Please Phone.

Makikihi - Waimate
Farmstay
Address: 'Alford Farm', Lower Hook Road,
Waimate R.D.8
Name: June & Ken McAuley
Telephone: (03) 689 5778 **Fax**: (03) 689 5779
Beds: 1 Double, 2 Single (2 bedrooms)
Bathroom: 1 Family share

Tariff: B&B (Continental) Double $65, Single $40, Dinner $20,
Campervans $10 pp. Credit cards. NZ B&B Vouchers accepted
Nearest Town: Makikihi 6km, Timaru 35km, Oamaru 50km

Welcome to 'Alford Farm' Conveniently situated approximately halfway between Christchurch and Dunedin, 2km from SH1.
Your hosts offer warm Kiwi hospitality, comfortable beds with electric blankets, delicious meals and relaxed atmosphere in smoke free home.
Our modern home is situated in a peaceful/sheltered garden with a variety of roses, trees, and birds with views of farm and hills.
If time permits enjoy a farm tour and see our farm dog performing. No household pets. We raise deer and cattle and run a few sheep at times. Visitors are welcome to view or join farm activities.
Our interests are American Square Dancing, gardening and farm related activities.
Our family have flown the nest.
We look forward to your company.
Happy to meet bus at corner.
Directions: *4km south of Makikihi turn inland into Lower Hook Road. "Alford Farm" is 2nd on right (2km).*

Waimate

Farmstay B&B
Address: "The Hills", Hodges Road, RD 7,
Waimate, South Canterbury
Name: Daphne and Fred
Telephone: (03) 689 8747
Email: mortthehills@xtra.co.nz
Beds: 1 Queen, 1 Double, 1 Single (3 bedrooms)
Bathroom: 1 Family share + 1 private.
Tariff: B&B (full/continental) Queen $65, Double $55, Single $35,
Dinner $20, Children $15. Credit cards accepted. NZ B&B Vouchers accepted
Nearest Town: Waimate 2 minutes. Timaru 46 km, Oamaru 46 km

A warm welcome awaits the tired traveler to our renovated character homestead tucked away on the foothills overlooking Waimate on 31 acres.
Whether you want to participate in the feeding of the farm animals or just lay back and listen to Freds tales of Goldmining on the West Coast your Hosts will ensure your stay is a memorable one . With comfortable beds, electric blankets, excellent home cooked meals, tea, coffee availalbe anytime you will enjoy the relaxed atmosphere in a mature garden setting. We share our surrounding with Bellbirds, Calves, Lambs, Ostriches, Emus and old farm dog. We also have a Cattery on the property.
Local activities include, golf, fishing, walks, country club and lakes 1 hour drive.
E-mail, Laundry facilities available. Smoking allowed (not in bedrooms). Can meet bus (Waimate).
Its worth the 8km drive off S.H.1.
Directions: *Halfway between Timaru and Oamaru go 8km Inland to Waimate, down Queen Street, past gardens, through ford, right into Hodges Road, first left.*

Fairlie

Farmstay/Homestay
Address: 'Fontmell', Nixons Road,
No 17 R.D. Fairlie
Name: Anne & Norman McConnell
Telephone: (03) 685 8379
Fax: (03) 685 8379
Beds: 2 Double, 4 Single (3 bedrooms)
Bathroom: 1 Guests share
Tariff: B&B (full) Double $70-$90,
Single $45, Children $25, Dinner $20.
NZ B&B Vouchers accepted
Nearest Town: Fairlie 3km

Our farm consists of 270 acres producing fat lambs, cattle and deer, with numerous other animals and bird life. The house is situated in a large English style garden with many large mature trees in tranquil setting.
In the area are two skifields, golf courses, walkways and scenic drives. Informative farm tours available.
Directions: *Travel 1 km from town centre, along Tekapo highway, then turn left into Nixon's Road when two more kilometers will bring you to the "Fontmell" entrance.*

Please help us provide the best hospitality in the world.
Fill in a comment form for every place you stay.

Fairlie

B&B on lifestyle block
Address: "Braelea", S. Hwy 79, Fairlie,
Sth Canterbury
Name: Les & Sandra Riddle
Telephone: (03) 685 8366 **Fax**: (03) 685 8943
Mobile: (025) 222 8650
Beds: 2 King (or 4 Single) (2 bedrooms)
Bathroom: 2 Private
Tariff: B&B (full) Double $80, Dinner by arrangement, Campervans welcome,
Credit Cards. NZ B&B Vouchers accepted
Nearest Town: Fairlie 3km.

Welcome to the Mackenzie Country. Our new home is situated 2 hours south of Christchurch and 4 hours north of Queenstown, on the main highway. We are on a 50 acre lifestyle block with sheep and hens, and are developing a wallaby area. Our resident puss is called Snoopy. We are 5 minutes east of Fairlie township, where there are diverse eating facilities, golf, squash, indoor swimming and beauty parlour. Our views to the mountains are spectacular. You may like to enjoy the privacy of your own guest lounge with its tea making facilities or join us in the family area. We are both employed part-time in the service industry so are committed to helping others. We enjoy home cooking and are happy to provide snacks. Our 2 older teenage children may be at home in the school holidays. We enjoy our countryside and are happy to help you do the same by providing a short sightseeing tour and providing information about hunting, fishing, flying, walking, hiking and tramping.

Kimbell, Fairlie

Country Homestay
Address: Rivendell Lodge, Stanton Rd,
Kimbell, RD 17, Fairlie
Name: Joan & Kevin
Telephone: (03) 685 8833 **Fax**: (03) 685 8825
Mobile: (025) 819 189
Email: Rivendell.lodge@xtra.co.nz
Beds: 1Queen, 1 Double, 3 Single (3 Bedrooms)
Bathroom: 2 Private, Spa bath available
Tariff: B&B (full) Double $90, Single $50, Children negotiable, Dinner $25pp,
Campervans welcome, Credit Cards (VISA/MC/Bankcard).
NZ B&B Vouchers accepted $20 surcharge
Nearest Town: Fairlie 8km, Tekapo 33km, skifield 5km, Lake Opuha 12 kms.

"They stayed long in Rivendell and found it hard to leave. The house was perfect whether you liked sleep, or work, or storytelling, or singing, or just sitting and thinking best, or a pleasant mixture of all them all. Everyone grew refreshed and strong in a few days there. Merely to be there was a cure for weariness, fear and sadness." – Tolkien
Joan is a writer who shares a passion for mountains with Kevin, a keen hunter and fisherman. Our home is set in a large garden complete with stream and two cats. Discover peaceful Kimbell on the Christchurch-Queenstown road, close to Mt Dobson skifield. Book two nights and come fishing, hunting, play golf (clubs available), ski, or try our easy alpine experience.
Complimentary beverages and homebaking on arrival.
Rivendell Lodge is 100 metres up Stanton Rd at Kimbell on SH 8.

Kimbell, Fairlie

Homestay/Farmstay
Address: "Poplar Downs", Mount Cook Road,
Kimbell, RD 17, Fairlie
Name: Shirley & Robin Sinclair
Telephone: (03) 685 8170 **Fax**: (03) 685 8210
Email: bigred@es.co.nz
Beds: 1 King (or 2 Single), 1 Double (2 bedrooms)
Bathroom: 1 Ensuite, 1 Private
Tariff: B&B (full) Double $90, Single $60, Children negotiable, Dinner $25,
Credit Cards (VISA/MC/BC).
NZ B&B Vouchers accepted $20 surcharge
Nearest Town: Fairlie 7km, Tekapo 30km, Skifield 6km

Our homestead is an elegant early 1900's villa tastefully restored with the comfort of modern amenities. Heated rooms open onto the verandah overlooking the garden to the mountains. Take a stroll over our farmland and take in some splendid views of the surrounding basin and mountains, explore the turn of the century Loafing Barn used then to house a large team of Clydesdales, or just wander around our spacious garden where there are numerous quiet spots to sit and relax and admire the many and varied birdlife. We have the usual menagerie of farm animals including pet lambs, hens, mares and foals, sheepdog and cocker spaniel as well as the household moggy.
Kimbell is a quiet rural village with beautiful trees and fresh clear air. Locally there is skiing, golf, fishing and tramping. Maori rock drawing, craft and art outlets, a colonial museum and excellent eateries from licensed to fast foods.
Directions: *On State Highway 8 from Fairlie to Mt Cook (7km). Sign at gate. Our home is smoke free with children most welcome.*

Burkes Pass

Bed & Breakfast/Homestay
Address: Dobson Lodge, Burkes Pass,
RD17 Mackenzie Country
Name: Keith & Margaret Walter
Telephone: (03) 685 8316
Fax: (03) 685 8316

Beds: 2 Queen, 1 Double, 2 Single (3 bedrooms)
Bathroom: 2 Ensuite, 1 Family share
Tariff: B&B (continental) Double $75-$120, Single $60,
Children negotiable. Dinner by arrangement $20pp. Winter rates apply.
Credit Cards. NZ B&B Vouchers accepted $25 surcharge
Nearest Town: Lake Tekapo or Fairlie - Approx 19km to Fairlie, 23km from
Tekapo

Come and share with us our unique stone homestead with exceptional character set in 15 acres. We are nestled in a picturesque valley, with views of Mount Dobson and close to Lake Tekapo. We are on the main tourist route between Christchurch, Queenstown and Te Anau, which makes us an ideal halfway stop. The entrance to Mount Dobson ski-field road is approximately 5 minutes away. Only one kilometre from the settlement of Burkes Pass, with a Swiss restaurant, miniature railway and craft gallery. Our house is something special, built from glacier stones, exterior walls 700 mm thick with cedar shingled roof, and large stone open fireplace. A welcoming aroma of rough sawn timber from the ceiling pervades the whole home. You will not forget your stay with us. We have a daughter aged 13. Our interests include photography, crafts, travel and animals. We have one cat, a friendly collie and pet sheep. No smoking indoors. **Directions**: *Watch for Dobson Lodge east of Burkes Pass village.*

651

Lake Tekapo

Homestay Lodge
Address: Lake Tekapo Lodge,
24 Aorangi Crescent, Lake Tekapo
Name: Lake Tekapo Lodge, John & Lynda
Telephone: (03) 680 6566/0800 525 383 Lake Tekapo
Fax: (03) 680 6599 **Mobile**: (025) 332 597
Email: lake.tekapo.lodge@xtra.co.nz
Beds: 2 King Zippers, 2 Single (3 Bedrooms)
Bathroom: 3 ensuite, (1 with wheelchair access, 1 with spa bath).
Tariff: B&B (full) Double $160, Single $100, Dinner $25 pp.
Credit Cards accepted.
Nearest Town: Lake Tekapo - Fairlie 30 minutes by car/bus.

Lake Tekapo Lodge - purpose built bed and breakfast lodge in the village of Lake Tekapo, across road from restaurants, shops, post shop. Two minutes walk to church of Good Shepherd, lake edge. Beautiful views of mountains and lake from lodge where John and Lynda welcome you.

Our adobe earth block home has antique entrance doors, guest dining and entrance clad in earth block with open fire. Separate lounge with gas fire, piano, books, chess set, tea / coffee making facilities, star watch window. Guest laundry.

Fishing / hunting guides available. Golf, skiing, horse riding, walking, mountain biking, scenic flights over lakes, mountains (including Mount Cook), glaciers. All available from Lake Tekapo Lodge (built 1998).

We have enjoyed home hosting since 1983. We hope you will come and spend some time with us in the beautiful area of Lake Tekapo as you travel from Christchurch to Queenstown on SH 8.

Lake Tekapo

Self-contained Farmstay
Address: 'Holbrook', State Highway 8
between Burkes Pass & Lake Tekapo.
12km east of Tekapo.
Name: Lesley & Alister France
Telephone: (03) 685 8535 **Fax**: (03) 685 8534
Mobile: (025) 387 974
Email: lesley@holbrook.co.nz
Beds: 1 Queen, 6 Single (3 bedrooms)
Bathroom: 1 Private
Tariff: (Accommodation only) Double & Single $80 plus $10 per extra person.
Breakfast: Continental $8 pp, Full $12 pp.
NZ B&B Vouchers accepted $25 Surcharge
Nearest Town: Lake Tekapo 12 kms

Holbrook is part of a high county sheep station of 14,000 hectares (35,000 acres) situated on the main tourist route (State Highway 8) between Burkes Pass and Lake Tekapo. Our cottage is close to our homestead, is fully self contained and is warm, spacious and comfortable. We provide electric blankets, feather duvets, wood for the log fire, telephone, TV, automatic washing machine and everything necessary to make your stay with us an enjoyable experience. You will be most welcome to explore our property and view any activities that are going on during your visit. Our area is well known for its many outdoor pursuits including fishing, tramping, shooting and snow skiing. We look forward to sharing our way of life with you over breakfast in the homestead and if you make a prior arrangement with us, we would be happy to prepare and share an evening meal with you.
Home Page: http://www.kiwi-nz.com/

Lake Tekapo
Bed & Breakfast
Address: 'Creel House', 36 Murray Place,
Lake Tekapo
Name: Grant & Rosemary Brown
Telephone: (03) 680 6516 **Fax**: (03) 680 6659
Email: creelhouse.l.tek@xtra.co.nz
Beds: 2 Queen, 3 Single (3 bedrooms)
Bathroom: 2 Private, 1 Ensuite

Tariff: B&B (continental) Double/Twin $125, Single $70. Off season rate $90
double/twin May - September. Credit cards (Visa/MC/BC).
NZ B&B Vouchers accepted $35 surcharge Oct-Apr, $30 May-Sept
Nearest Town: Fairlie 35 mins, Twizel 45 mins, Mt Cook 75 mins

*Our home built by Grant is three storeyed with expansive balconies and panoramic
views of the Southern Alps, Mt John, Lake Tekapo and surrounding mountains. We
have two primary school girls and we live on the ground floor, our living quarters thus
separate from our guests accommodation. All rooms are spacious and comfortable,
with guest lounge and separate guest entrance. A native garden adds an attractive
feature.*
*Grant is a fishing guide (trout / salmon) inquiries welcome. Lake Tekapo is an ideal
place to stay for those day trips to Mt Cook, for fishing, or to rest and relax along your
journey and enjoy the local walks and views of our turquoise blue lake, scenic drives
or a Scenic Flight. Restaurants in township. No smoking indoors.*
  Directions: *From SH 8 turn at Greig Street, 100ms east from bridge, follow road
round to top of hill and turn right. 200ms on left, signposted.*

Lake Tekapo
Bed & Breakfast

Freda du Faur House
LAKE TEKAPO

Address: 'Freda Du Faur House',
1 Esther Hope St, Lake Tekapo
Name: Dawn and Barry Clark
Telephone: (03) 680 6513
Beds: 1 Queen, 1 Double, 2 Single (3 bedrooms)
Bathroom: 1 Guest share
Tariff: B&B (Continental), Full extra $8, Double $85, Single $60, Children 1/2
price under 14. Credit Cards accepted, Full breakfast extra $8.
NZ B&B Vouchers accepted $25 surcharge
Nearest Town: Timaru

*Experience tranquillity and a touch of mountain magic at Lake Tekapo. You can be
sure of a warm and friendly welcome. Our comfortable home has lovely mountain and
lake views. Guests admire the rimu panelling, heart timber furniture and attractive
decor that blends with the Mackenzie Country. Guest bedrooms, bathroom and
separate toilet are in a private wing - all the rooms overlooking the garden with two
opening onto the terrace. Relax with tea / coffee on the patio surrounded by roses or
enjoy the ever changing panorama from the lounge. Guests are most welcome to swim
in our private pool. Several walkways are nearby and Mount Cook is just over an hours
scenic drive away. (Smoke-free).We have views of nearest ski field from our bay
windows. ur cat "Missy" welcomes all our guests. Open all day.*
Directions: *From SH8 turn into Lakeview Heights and follow the green B&B sign
into Barbara Hay Street. At the end of this street turn right to see the Freda Du Faur
sign.*

Lake Tekapo

B&B/Homestay
Address: "Charford House", 14 Murray Place,
Lakeview Heights, Lake Tekapo.
Name: Lorraine & Winston Swan
Telephone: (03) 680 6888 **Fax**: (03) 680 6888
Beds: 1 Queen, 1 Double, 3 Single (3 bedrooms)
Bathroom: 1 Private, 1 Guests share.
Tariff: B&B (continental) Queen $95, Double $85, Twin $85, Single $60,
Children 8 & over. Credit Cards (VISA/MC). Off season rates June to August.
NZ B&B Vouchers accepted $25 surcharge.
Nearest Town: Fairlie 40 km E, Twizel 56 km W

Charford House is a modern two storeyed home built by Cowan's Hill Walkway with panoramic views of the "Church of the Good Shepherd", Lake and Mountains. The ground floor bedrooms have a separate entrance leading on to a patio with glorious views. The upstairs Queen / family room has a private bathroom, TV and tea making facilities. Charford house with its flower gardens has a feeling of space and peace, ideal for relaxation. Enjoy tea or coffee on arrival with friendly hosts Winston and Lorraine who enjoy meeting people and like to make visitors welcome. We are a smoke free environment and look forward to sharing Tiger and Smudge our 2 cats and home with you. Park your car on site and walk to the village and shops.
Directions: *Turn from SH8, 100 m east of bridge into Lakeview Heights, follow road up hill, turn first right into Scott Street, then left into Murray Place, signposted on right side of street.*

Lake Pukaki

Homestay
Address: 'Rhoborough Downs', Lake Pukaki, P.B. Fairlie
Name: Roberta Preston
Telephone: (03) 435 0509 **Fax**: (03) 435 0509
Beds: 1 Double, 3 Single (3 bedrooms)
Bathroom: 1 Family share (guests have first option)
Tariff: B&B (full) Double $80, Single $50, Dinner $25pp
Nearest Town: Twizel 10 minute drive

A wonderful quiet place to stop a night or two approximately halfway between Christchurch and Queenstown.
It is a 40 minute drive to Mt Cook National Park and Ohau State forest.
The 18,000 acre property has been in our family since 1919 where merino sheep graze the high mountains to 6000 feet. We also have a cat and a dog.
Glorious mountain views from the homestead set in quiet, tranquil surroundings. Roberta is a Kiwi Host. Dinner can be served by prior arrangement.
Twizel is 10 minutes away has a bank, doctor, hairdresser, shops etc, golf tennis, squash facilities and several restaurants. Smoking not permitted in lounge or bedrooms.
Directions: *Please phone a day before or preferably earlier as bookings are necessary.*

Relax – Don't try to drive too far in one day.

Lake Pukaki / Mount Cook

Farmstay
Address: 'Tasman Downs Station',
Lake Tekapo
Name: Linda, Bruce & Ian Hayman
Telephone: (03) 680 6841 **Fax**: (03) 680 6851
Beds: 1 Double, 2 Single (2 bedrooms)
Bathroom: 1 Private, 1 Family share
Tariff: B&B (full) Double $90, Single $60, Dinner $25.
Nearest Town: Lake Tekapo 27kms.

"A place of unsurpassed beauty" Perfectly located on the shores of Lake Pukaki, behind which are magnificent views of Mount Cook and the Southern Alps. Our modern, local stone home, blends in with the natural surrounds. We have a 9-hole mini golf course, and peaceful surrounds to relax in. Your host, who is an ex RAF Pilot, and whose family have farmed this property since 1914, has rich pioneering, and surprisingly wide experiences. This high-country farm runs mainly cattle with crops grown for self-sufficiency. Informative farm tours are available by arrangement. This is your great opportunity to experience true New Zealand farm life, with friendly hosts.

Twizel/Mt Cook

Homestay
Address: "Aoraki Lodge",
32 Mackenzie Drive, Twizel
Name: Kerry & Steve Carey
Telephone: (03) 435 0300
Fax: (03) 435 0305
Email: aorakilodge@xtra.co.nz
Beds: 1 Queen, 1 Double,
2 Single (3 bedrooms)
Bathroom: 2 Ensuite, 1 Family share
Tariff: B&B (full) Double $85-$120, Single $65, Dinner $25,
Credit Card (VISA). NZ B&B Vouchers accepted $20 surcharge
Nearest Town: Twizel - 2 min walk to Twizel Village

Haere Mai Ki Aoraki (Welcome to Mt Cook / Mackenzie Country).
If you prefer a casual relaxed atmosphere with friendly genuine "Kiwi" hosts then Aoraki Lodge is the place for you.
Kerry is of Maori descent and would love to share with you her knowledge of Maori culture and history. Steve is a trout fishing guide and can offer helpful advice and information on local attractions and activities.
Aoraki Lodge does not have a set of rules. We are flexible and there to make your stay as enjoyable as possible. Breakfast (all homemade goodies) is at whatever time you choose, and there are free drinks and snacks for guests. Dinner is available with prior notice also there is a variety of excellent restaurants in the area.
Kerry and Steve are also happy to advise regarding travel plans and arrangements.
Directions: *Turn left Twizel Service Station, travel 200 metres, look for Aoraki Lodge sign on your left.*

Please help us provide the best hospitality in the world.
Fill in a comment form for every place you stay.

Twizel/Mount Cook - Aoraki

Homestay
Address: "Wedgwood Homestay"
17 Northwest Arch, PO Box 1, Twizel.
Name: Carolyn and Greg
Telephone: (03) 435 0451
Fax: (03) 435 0451
Email: info@mtcook.org.nz
Beds: 2 Queen, 1 Single (2 bedrooms)
Bathroom: 2 Ensuite
Tariff: B&B (special) Double $90, Single $60, Children half price.
Off Season rates. Dinner $30. Credit Cards accepted.
NZ B&B Vouchers accepted $20 surcharge
Nearest Town: Twizel, 10 minute walk to town centre.

Your enchantment with Mackenzie Country begins at Wedgwood Homestay. Our new colonial home offers you privacy and comfort nestled in the foothills of the magnificent Southern Alps. Your bedroom (with full ensuite) offers views of the ever-changing Alps and our famous "Nor'West Arch" cloud formations. Relax in a peaceful home amongst whispering trees and golden tussock grasses and enjoy our hospitality. We are 50km from the wondrous Mount Cook World Heritage Park and conveniently located halfway between Christchurch and Queenstown. From your safe and secure place at Wedgwood Homestay, you can enjoy everything Mackenzie Country offers from flyfishing, hunting, and skiing to horse treks, walks and boating. Finish with some stargazing from our porch. With daughter Grace and our golden Labrador, we look forward to hearing about your holiday thrills in the high country. Smokefree.

Home Page: http://mtcook.org.nz
Directions: *From SH8 (North of Twizel at bridge), turn onto GlenLyon Road, then 2km to NorthWest Arch on left, then 1km to Wedgwood Homestey on left.*

Omarama/Lindis Pass

Farmstay+Self-contained Accom.
Address: Dunstan Downs, Omarama
Name: Tim & Geva Innes
Telephone: (03) 438 9862 **Fax**: (03) 438 9517
Mobile: (025) 353 211
Beds: 1 Queen, 5 Single (3 bedrooms)
Bathroom: 1 Ensuite, 1 Guests share, 1 Family share
Tariff: B&B (full) Double $90, Single $45, Budget $12 Single, Children 1/2 price,
Dinner $35 wine served, Campervans $25, Credit Cards.
NZ B&B Vouchers accepted Surcharge $15
Nearest Town: Omarama: Dunstan Downs is 17 km west of Omarama on State
Highway 8.

Dunstan Downs is a Merino sheep, cattle and deer station in the heart of the South Island high country. We have two adult children seldom home. Our home is full of country warmth and you are welcome to join us for dinner (wine served) or bed and breakfast. The Ahuriri River is at our back door, fishing guides can be arranged. The Ahuriri Valley and surrounding mountains and valleys are an adventure playground: tramping, mountain biking, kayaking (bring your own), and of course farming activities, or maybe just lazing around soaking up the peace and tranquillity. If you would like to fend for youselves we have Budget Accommodation available: self-contained: - 9 singles and 1 double in 5 rooms with kitchen and bathroom/laundry facilities.

Omarama

Country Homestay
Address: 'The Briars', Ahuriri Heights,
Omarama, SH8
Name: Marylou & Don Blue
Telephone: (03) 438 9615 **Fax**: (03) 438 9655
Beds: 4 Single (2 bedrooms)
Bathroom: 1 Guests share
Tariff: B&B (continental) Double $70, Single $40.
NZ B&B Vouchers accepted
Nearest Town: 2km north of Omarama on State Highway 8

A perfect mountain location to overnight in the Mount Cook area.
"The Briars", a comfortable drive to Mt Cook, is approximately halfway between Christchurch and Queenstown. This quality homestay is also on the main turn off to Dunedin.
Marylou and Don graciously welcome guests to their charming hilltop home created with lovely antiques, paintings, embroideries and impressive porcelain collection. Beautiful formal country gardens blend into the countryside.
The attractive guests quarters are on a separate level where the bedrooms have electric blankets and heaters. Tea making facilities available.
Return from your evening meal, at one of Omarama's quality restaurants, in time to share supper with your congenial hosts. Next morning enjoy an elegantly served breakfast while viewing unsurpassed panoramic mountain landscapes.
The Blues have retired from farming and now enjoy gardening and tramping. They suggest you visit the 'Clay Cliffs'. Phone or just arrive.

Omarama

Farmstay
Address: 'Omarama Station',
Omarama, North Otago
Name: Beth & Dick Wardell
Telephone: (03) 438 9821 **Fax**: (03) 438 9822
Beds: 1 Queen, 4 Single (3 bedrooms)
Bathroom: 1 Ensuite, 1 Guest share
Tariff: B&B (full) Double $90, Single $55, Dinner $25.
NZ B&B Vouchers accepted with $15 surcharge.
Nearest Town: Omarama 1km

Experience a stay on a busy high country sheep station. Omarama Station is a merino sheep and beef cattle property adjacent to the Omarama township. The 100 year old homestead is nestled in a small valley in a tranquil parklike setting of willows, poplars and a fast flowing stream (good fly fishing), pleasant walking environs, an interesting historical perspective to the high country as this was the original station in the area. Swimming pool and a pleasant garden.
An opportunity to experience day to day farming activities.
We have travelled extensively overseas and enjoy meeting and entertaining our guests.
Dinner by arrangement.
Please phone in advance.

One of the differences between staying at a hotel and a B&B
is that you don't hug the hotel staff when you leave.

Omarama
Rural Homestay.

GLENBURN PARK
FLY FISHING and ACCOMMODATION

Address: "Glenburn Park", SH 83, Lake Benmore, Omarama
Name: Alan & Marie Campbell
Telephone: (03) 438 9624 **Fax**: (03) 438 9624
Email: glenburn.park@xtra.co.nz
Beds: 1 Queen, 2 Single (2 bedrooms) **Bathroom**: 1 Guests share
Tariff: B&B (full) Double $70, Single $40, Dinner $25, Campervans $10 per person, Self-contained Accom. from $15 per person, Credit Cards (VISA/MC).
Nearest Town: Omarama 7km

Glenburn is a "retired" high country sheep station now specializing in friendly rural accommodation. In addition to the homestead, with its open fires and sleep-maker mattresses, there is also the choice of 3 tourist flats, an ensuite cabin and special campervan facilities with private ablutions. We are situated at the head of Lake Benmore, home to swans, geese, ducks etc and only 1/2 hours walk to the world renown Ahuriri River giving us a brilliant fishing location. Try your hand at tying your own trout fly or cast to a cruising brown trout only 50 metres from the homestead. Your host is a registered member of the NZ Professional Fishing Guides Association. Fishing tackle is available including personally tied flies. Other activities include hill or lakeshore walks, and the French game of petanque. Our interests also include gardening, boating and golf. Fluent French spoken. Bookings essential. No smoking please.
Home Page: http://www.griffler.co.nz/glenburn
Directions: *7km east of Omarama on SH83. We will be happy to collect you if you are travelling by bus.*

Kurow – Oamaru
Farmstay+Self-contained Accom.
Address: 'Glenmac', 7K R.D., Oamaru
Name: Kaye & Keith Dennison
Telephone: (03) 436 0200 **Fax**: (03) 436 0202
Mobile: 025 222 1119
Email: glenmac@xtra.co.nz
Beds: 1 Queen, 1 Double, 4 Single (4 bedrooms)

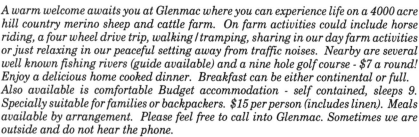

Bathroom: 1 Family share
Tariff: B&B (continental), (full) $5 extra, Double $60, Single $30, Children under 13 half price, Dinner $20, Campervans $20 (up to 4 people).
Credit cards. NZ B&B Vouchers accepted
Nearest Town: Oamaru 60 km East, Kurow 13 km West

A warm welcome awaits you at Glenmac where you can experience life on a 4000 acre hill country merino sheep and cattle farm. On farm activities could include horse riding, a four wheel drive trip, walking / tramping, sharing in our day farm activities or just relaxing in our peaceful setting away from traffic noises. Nearby are several well known fishing rivers (guide available) and a nine hole golf course - $7 a round! Enjoy a delicious home cooked dinner. Breakfast can be either continental or full.
Also available is comfortable Budget accommodation - self contained, sleeps 9. Specially suitable for families or backpackers. $15 per person (includes linen). Meals available by arrangement. Please feel free to call into Glenmac. Sometimes we are outside and do not hear the phone.
Directions: *We are 5km off Highway 83 which is a direct link to and from Mt Cook. Situated at end of Gards Road which is 4th road on right after Kurow or 4th road on left after Duntroon.*
Home Page: http://www.nzcentrepoint.co.nz/glenmac/

Oamaru

Homestay
Address: 'Wallfield',
126 Reservoir Road, Omaru
Name: Pat and Bill Bews
Telephone: (03) 437 0368
Beds: 1 Queen, 2 single (2 bedrooms)
Bathroom: 1 Guests share
Tariff: B&B (continental) Double $60, Single $35, Dinner $20.
NZ B&B Vouchers accepted
Nearest Town: 5 minutes to Oamaru.

*Our modern home is situated high above the North end of Oamaru with superb views
to the east and the mountains in the west. We have four children, all happily married,
and an ever increasing number of grand children. We have been home hosting for the
last seven years and although recently retired from farming, still enjoy the buzz of
meeting new friends. Our interests include gardening and tramping.*

Oamaru

Rural Homestay
Address: 'Tara', Springhill Road,
3. O.R.D. Oamaru
Name: Marianne Smith
Telephone: (03) 434 8187
Fax: (03) 434 8187
Beds: 2 Single (1 Bedroom)
Bathroom: 1 Private
Tariff: B&B (full) Double $75, Single $50, Dinner $25 by arrangement.
Credit Cards
Nearest Town: Oamaru - 8 minutes away

*Want to be pampered? "Tara" is the place for you. Enjoy the comfort and luxuries of
our character Oamaru stone home. "Tara" boasts all day sun and the privacy to soak
up the country atmosphere. Nestled amongst six acres of roses, mature trees and rural
farmland, "Tara" is the perfect place to unwind. Our livestock include Alpacas,
coloured sheep, and donkeys. We also have a Burmese cat and a Lassie collie. My
husband Baxter and I will ensure your visit is an enjoyable experience.*
Directions: *Turn off SH1 at Oamaru southern boundary drive to Weston. Turn left
at supermarket into Weston Ngapara Road. Take first left into Kia Ora Road. Second
left is Springhill Road, Tara 50 yds up Springhill Road on right.*

Continental breakfast consists of fruit, cereal, toast, tea/coffee,
Full breakfast is the same with a cooked course,
Special breakfast has something special.

Oamaru

Homestay
Address: 11 Stour St,
South Hill, Oamaru
Name: Jenny & Gerald
Telephone: (03) 434 9628
Beds: 1 Double, 2 Single (2 bedrooms)
Bathroom: 1 Private, 1 Family share
Tariff: B&B (continental) Double $90,
Single $65. Dinner $25pp.
NZ B&B Vouchers accepted $10 surcharge
Nearest Town: Oamaru

We have a charming, two storey, character home surrounded by gardens and easily located in a quiet street near the main highway. Our guest bedrooms are attractive and well appointed. Tea or coffee is available on arrival. Dinner - by arrangement if required - is a leisurely meal with New Zealand wine, preceded by drinks beside the fire. We are a middle-aged couple who have travelled, and enjoy meeting people, especially visitors to New Zealand . We share our home with one rather timid family cat.

Oamaru has many fine, stone, Victorian buildings and we are involved with the Historic Precinct and the Victorian Town at Work Programme. Our many interests include gardening and the vintage car club. Time permitting, you might enjoy one of Oamaru's many lovely walks, the attractive public gardens, or a visit to our art gallery, museum or penguin colony. A warm welcome awaits you. Non smokers preferred.
Directions: *Please phone first if possible. Use front gate - not driveway please.*

Oamaru

Homestay
Address: Glen Foulis, 39 Middle Ridge Road,
Waianakarua Postal: O.R.D. 9, Oamaru 8921
Name: John & Margaret Munro
Telephone: (03) 439 5559
Fax: (03) 439 5220
Mobile: (021) 940 777
Email: hjm@clear.net.nz
Beds: 1 King, 4 Single (2 bedrooms).
Bathroom: 1 Guests share, 1 Family share.
Tariff: B&B (full) Double $80, Single $50, Children half price, Dinner $25,
Children $25. Campervans $25 up to 4 people.
Credit Cards. NZ B&B Vouchers accepted.
Nearest Town: 20 mins south Oamaru, 1 hour north Dunedin

Glen Foulis, a modern, well heated home accented by efficient open fireplaces, elegantly styled with Oamaru Stone, surrounded by acres of green lawns, tall beech, birch, weeping willows, eucalyptuses. Beautiful vistas, up to the huge Herbert Forest, over bushy glades, looking down a unique river valley. Two wisteria and rose-clad terraces catch the sun and view. The song of native birds, only metres away. If you plan more than one night here, we can show you the hidden treasures of North Otago from our tough but comfortable 4 wheel drive. Margaret enjoys cooking with enough notice and a 5 star restaurant is minutes away in a picturesque, restored Mill House by the river. We both enjoy working at Energy related businesses here. Our two outdoor, well-trained Golden Retrievers are always very friendly, as is our matching ginger pussycat. Larger parties welcome, together with GlenDendron on the opposite hill.
Directions: *Please phone for directions.*

Oamaru

Homestay
Address: Innwoodleigh, 39 Forth Street, Oamaru, North Otago
Name: Howard & Vennessa
Telephone: (03) 437 0829 **Fax**: (03) 437 0829
Beds: 1 Double, 2 Single (2 bedrooms)
Bathroom: 1 Private
Tariff: B&B (continental) $55 pp, Full breakfast extra cost.
Nearest Town: In Oamaru township - in Borough

A unique private family Pole House nestled into the side of a hill with panoramic views of the town and ocean. Allow yourself the luxury of star gazing at night and a spectacular sun rise in the morning on your own exclusive private level that accommodates up to 4 people.

Catering for Honeymooners - Business Executives - Independent Free Travellers - Special memorable occasions - Healing Space - Time Out.

Your friendly outgoing hosts Howard and Vennessa specialise in - Aromatherapy Oil baths and Deep Sea Fishing on our own boat the 'Dolphin'. Local interests available by arrangement are: High Country Shooting trips, Historic Gold Mining Tours / Panning, Jetboat trips Waitaki River, Penguin Viewing, Whitestone Buildings, Whitestone Quarry, Moeraki Boulders.

(N)

Meadowbank Dairy

(W) **39 Forth Street**

Park

Thames Highway
(main route SHW 1)
between house
numbers 322a - 324

(S)

Herbert - Oamaru
Farmstay
Address: Herbert, 12.O.R.D. Oamaru
Name: Dorothy & Duncan McKenzie
Telephone: (03) 439 5614
Fax: (03) 4395814
Beds: 1 Double, 3 Single (3 bedrooms)
Bathroom: 1 Guests share

Tariff: B&B (full) Double $70, Single $40, Dinner $25, light meal $15.
Children half price. Credit cards. NZ B&B Vouchers accepted
Nearest Town: Oamaru 20km north of Herbert Township

We are a semi-retired couple living on a small sheep and cattle farm set in a beautiful area of rolling downland between SH 1 and the Pacific Ocean.
We have been involved in home hosting for the past 18 years and enjoy meeting guests from all parts of the world.
Our large retirement house set in one acre of garden was built with home hosting in mind. We are close to rivers, beaches and bush walks with the Moeraki Boulders the chief local attraction. Both yellow-eyed and little blue penguins may be seen at Moeraki or Oamaru. Oamaru, our nearest shopping centre, is famous for its early white stone buildings. The Oamaru stone quarries may be visited.
Evening meal by arrangement; cooked breakfast.
Directions: *Please phone.*

Waianakarua-Oamaru
Farmstay
Address: "Glen Dendron",
284 Breakneck Road, Waianakarua
Name: Anne & John Mackay
Telephone: (03) 439 5288 **Fax**: (03) 439 5288
Mobile: 021-615 287
Email: anne.john.mackay@xtra.co.nz
Beds: 1 Queen, 4 Single (3 bedrooms). Larger groups catered for in combination with 'Glen Foulis'
Bathroom: 2 Guests share
Tariff: B&B (full) Double $80, Single $50, Children $25, Dinner $25. Credit cards. NZ B&B Vouchers accepted
Nearest Town: 30km south of Oamaru, 95km north of Dunedin.

Our recently completed home neighbouring the Herbert Forest, has purpose built accommodation for homestay comfort with sunny, warm, stylish facilities and panoramic views of our developing garden, the Waianakarua river and the sea. Enjoy our riverside walks, native bush and waterfalls. Awaken to the sound of bellbirds, wood pigeons and swallows. Recently retired from a large West Otago property to this small sheep farm, we can share our knowledge of farming and forestry. Enthusiastic gardeners, also involved in farm forestry advising, landscaping and nursery production. Anne is national president of NZ Floral Art Society. We enjoy reading and overseas travel. Nearby attractions include Moeraki boulders, penguins, seals, forest walks and beaches. Access to a private family golf course possible.
Arrange to join us for dinner. Allow time to enjoy this tranquil area with caring hosts - we don't mind short notice!
Directions: *3km off Highway One. Phone for directions.*

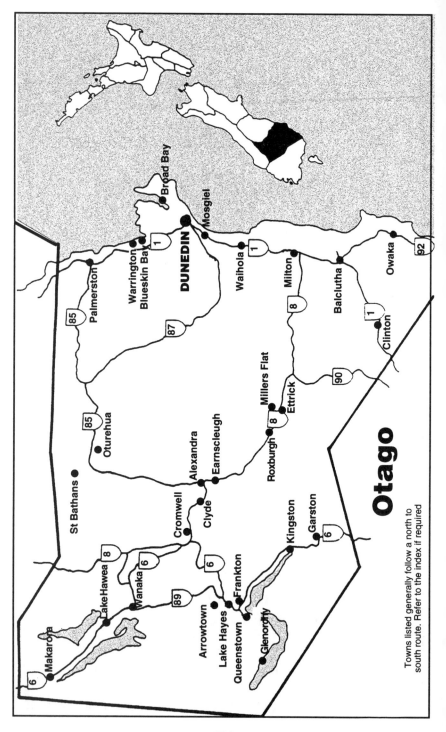

Otago

Towns listed generally follow a north to south route. Refer to the index if required

Makarora

Homestay+Self-contained Accomm
Address: Makarora, via Wanaka
(State Highway 6)
Name: Larrivee Homestay
Telephone: (03) 443 9177
Beds: Homestay: 1 Double (ensuite).
Second bedroom
(2 singles) available if needed. Cottage: 1 Double, 2 Single (2 bedrooms)
Bathroom: Homestay: ensuite (guests share if second bedroom is used).
Cottage: private
Tariff: B&B (full) Homestay: $100 Couple, $70 Single. Cottage $80 for 2 people, $20 each
extra adult. Children under 12 half price. Breakfast and dinner available at Homestay
next door. NZ B&B Vouchers accepted $30 surcharge for homestay. $10 surcharge for
cottage
Nearest Town: Wanaka 65km

*Nestled in native bush, my home is secluded. Only a short walk down the drive are a Mt
Aspiring National Park Information Centre and a tearooms / shop where jet boating and
scenic flights are available. A ten minute walk takes you to the Makarora River and some of
the best trout fishing in the country. Two walks in the National Park begin out my back door
with others nearby. Originally from the United States, I have lived in Makarora for over twenty
years. My home, which I share with Rufus the cat, is a unique, two storied octagon built mostly
with local and recycled materials. The upper storey contains the open living area with
mountain and bush views out every window making it a bird watcher's delight. The guest
rooms are on the ground floor and share their own bathroom. The self-contained stone and
cedar cottage is quaint and comfortable. Come and enjoy Makarora's relaxed, casual
atmosphere and spectacular scenery.*
Directions: *Last house on a private drive next to the National Park Information Centre.
Please telephone in advance, if possible.*

Lake Hawea

Homestay
Address: 4 Bodkin Street,
Lake Hawea, Otago 2RD Wanaka
Name: Lyall Campbell
Telephone: (03) 443 1343 **Mobile**: (025) 224 9192
Beds: 1 Double, 2 Single (2 bedrooms)
Bathroom: 1 Ensuite, 1 Family share
Tariff: B&B (continental) Double $70, Single $38, Children under 12 half price.
Nearest Town: Wanaka 15km

*I am a retired teacher actively involved in craft dyeing of silks. My other interests are
tramping, skiing and spinning. I have frequently entertained overseas visitors and
always enjoy the chance to meet new people. My three-storied A frame is set in an
extensive sheltered compound with many specimen trees. One guest room opens onto
a balcony with a mountain view; the other room has a mountain view and an ensuite.
Access to both via a circular staircase. Over the fence are tennis courts, a bowling green
and a children's playground. I have a cat and a small dog.*
*Lake Hawea - two minutes walk - is popular for boating, fishing and swimming.
Wanaka - ten minutes drive - offers good food, shopping and adventure activities.
Three skifields are within easy reach.*
Non-smokers preferred.
Directions: *Turn off the Wanaka - Haast road at Hawea Dam. Drive up past the hotel
to the store and you will see 'the A-frame through the Archway'.*

OTAGO

Lake Hawea

HILLKIRK **HOUSE**

Homestay
Address: 33 Noema Terrace,
Lake Hawea, Central Otago
Name: Mike & Doreen Allen at Hillkirk House
Telephone: (03) 443 1655 **Fax**: (03) 443 1655
Beds: 1 King, 4 Single (2 bedrooms)
Bathroom: 1 Ensuite, 1 Family share
Tariff: B&B (full) Ensuite $85, Double $80, Single $50, Children under 12yrs half price, Dinner by arrangement $25. NZ B&B Vouchers accepted Surcharge: Dble $15, ensuite $20
Nearest Town: Wanaka 15km

We are a congenial retired English couple, well travelled and actively involved in outdoor pursuits, who enjoy sharing our home and lifestyle. Our main interests are fly fishing, tramping and skiing, but the immediate area offers most outdoor sports imaginable. We happily share our local knowledge and contacts to help guests maximise this potential. Strategically located at the eastern foot of Haast Pass, within easy reach of Mt. Aspiring National Park and local ski fields, our comfortable modern Ridgecrest home offers impressive mountain views. A pleasant sundeck overlooks secluded garden. Lakeshore, 5 minutes stroll. Doreen boasts,"last all day breakfasts" - fresh fruit and percolated coffee - with dinner and lunch by arrangement, using home produce. 'All inclusive' stays negotiated to individual requirements. Mike regularly hosts famous overseas anglers. Quality hire gear, books, videos and fly tying facilities 'in house'. One twin (or king) with ensuite. Second bathroom, separate toilet and shower.
Directions: *Over Hawea Dam up past hotel, on past store, first right, first left, sign on right before bend.*

Lake Hawea

Self-contained Accommodation
Address: 37 Noema Terrace,
Lake Hawea, Central Otago
Name: Marjorie Goodger & Sheila McCaughan
Telephone: (03) 443 7056 **Fax**: (03) 443 1807
Email: marge@xtra.co.nz
Beds: 1 Double, 1 Single
(1 bedroom/sofa sleeper in lounge)
Bathroom: Private
Tariff: Unit $85, (Continental Breakfast included), Dinner available.
Visa/Mastercard. NZ B&B Vouchers accepted $20 surcharge
Nearest Town: Wanaka 15km

This new, spacious character, self-contained Alpine Chalet is situated at Lake Hawea - central to the scenic lakes area of Otago. It is 10 minutes drive to Wanaka and 1 hour to Queenstown.
Our one bedroom building is exceptionally well appointed and includes a stereo, dishwasher, microwave, television, video and an efficient log fire for winter visitors. In the lounge is an additional double-bed sofa sleeper. Within 5 minutes walk is a shop, tearooms, post office and hotel with 7 day restaurant.
Lake Hawea is an excellent fishing lake and has year round attractions including scenic walks and horse trekking. Four ski fields - Treble Cone, Cardrona, Coronet Peak and the Remarkables easily accessible.
Close by Wanaka has a range of restaurants, shops and water activities. Scenic flights available from Wanaka Airport, a 15 minute drive.

Wanaka
Homestay
Address: Rippon Lea B&B,
15 Norman Terrace, Wanaka
Name: Sue & Dick Williman
Telephone: (03) 443 9333,
Freephone 0800 169 674
Fax: (03) 443 9343
Email: williman@voyager.co.nz

Beds: 1 Queen, 3 Single (3 bedrooms)
Bathroom: 1 Private, 1 Family share
Tariff: B&B (special) Double $75, Single $40, Children $20.
NZ B&B Vouchers accepted
Nearest Town: Wanaka 2km

Our family home includes a warm visitors flat with twin and queen bedrooms, living room with colour TV, dinette with tea making facilities. It is particularly suitable for families. Our lavish continental breakfast, served for you to eat at your leisure, has been a point of commendation by many guests. Our home is less than 100m from Lake Wanaka. There is easy access to it and to pleasant lakeside walks through the trees of Wanaka Station Park. We have travelled extensively overseas ourselves and take a special delight in welcoming overseas visitors as well as New Zealanders. Wanaka is a holiday centre with appeal to those who like scenic grandeur. We look forward to advising you on the many fine summer and winter activities. Laundry facilities and garage space available. We request visitors not smoke in our home. Single travellers welcome.

Directions: *From the town centre follow west around the lake towards Glendhu Bay. Take the second on the right (Sargood Drive) into Rippon Lea. Norman Terrace is the first road on the right. Follow around the dog leg, ours is a back section on the left.*

Home Page: http://www.voyager.co.nz/~williman/

Wanaka
Homestay
Address: 75 Tenby Street, Wanaka
Name: Betty & Bill Miller
Telephone: (03) 443 7369
Fax: (03) 443 7800

Beds: 1 Double, 2 Single (2 bedrooms)
Bathroom: 1 Private, 1 Family share (Spa Bath)
Tariff: B&B (continental) Double $100, Single $50, Twin $80
NZ B&B Vouchers accepted $30 surcharge Double, $10 Twin
Nearest Town: Wanaka

Our spacious apartment for guests is on the ground floor of our modern 2-level home in Wanaka, close to the town centre, churches, bowling green and Wanaka's beautiful golf course. The apartment has a private entrance, lounge with TV, tea / coffee making facilities in a small kitchen which is also equipped with fridge, crockery and cutlery. You have double bedroom, bathroom and toilet.

Guests in our twin room share hosts' bathroom and toilet.

We are both retired, have travelled extensively and are interested in meeting visitors from both N.Z. and overseas. We can advise about things to do and see around Wanaka including walks, drives, trout fishing, lake cruises and scenic flights and are happy to help our guests organise their leisure time.

As an ex fighter pilot Bill is involved with the NZ Fighter Pilots' Museum, Wanaka. Smoke free. Please phone.

Wanaka

Homestay
Address: Lake Wanaka Homestay,
85 Warren St, Wanaka
Name: Peter & Gailie Cooke
Telephone: 03 443 7995, Freephone 0800 443799
Fax: (03) 443 7945
Beds: 1 Double, 2 Single (2 bedrooms)
Bathroom: 1 Guests share, 1 Family share
Tariff: B&B (full) Double $80, Single $45, Dinner by arrangement,
Children negotiable. NZ B&B Vouchers accepted $10 surcharge
Nearest Town: Wanaka, Centre of town.

Relax with us in our warm comfortable home ideally situated in the centre of Wanaka
with magnificent views of Lake and surrounding mountains.
Wanaka has an excellent choice of restaurants and shops all within 5 minutes walk
of our home.
We both enjoy skiing; golf; boating and outdoor activities. Peter who is in Real Estate
is a keen fly fisherman - happy to show guests his favourite fishing spots.
Guests are welcome to tea or coffee at anytime and enjoy a homemade muffin or biscuit
from 'Cookie' Jar. Our comfortable beds all have electric blankets.
We have met so many wonderful people over the years - we assure you of a warm
welcome. We are happy to meet public transport.
Directions: *Turn left Lakefront into Helwick St., 4 blocks right into Warren St., 2nd*
block 4th house on right opposite school. FOR RESERVATIONS FREEPHONE 0800
443799

Wanaka

Homestay
Address: Aspiring Images,
26 Norman Tce, Wanaka
Name: Betty & George Russell
Telephone: (03) 443 8358
Fax: (03) 443 8327
Email: grussell@xtra.co.nz
Beds: 1 Double,3 Single (3 bedrooms)
Bathroom: 1 Ensuite, 1 Private/Guests share.
Tariff: B&B (full) Double $80 - $95, Single $45 - $60, Children under 12 $20.
Dinner by arrangement $25, Credit cards. NZ B&B Vouchers accepted $10
Surcharge
Nearest Town: In Wanaka township.

Wanaka's scenic splendour and choice of activities should not be missed. There is
variety and contrast here; scenery grand or intimate, fishing in lake or river, walks
challenging or restful, mountain light ever-changing.
Our architect designed home, peacefully located by Wanaka Station Park, has views
over the park, Lake Wanaka (a minute's walk away) and to the mountains. Warm,
restful guest bedrooms enjoy views, sunny sheltered patios, and top quality bedding.
We enjoy skiing, sailing, golf, singing around the piano, sharing information on New
Zealand, and discussing Rotary, travel, geography, history, photography, sport,
literature and music.
Much spectacular scenery is off the beaten track - two good mountain bikes are
available free; we also offer guest discounts on George's Four Wheel Drive sightseeing /
photography tours, and on transport to skiing, fishing and tramping locations.
We fell in love with Wanaka years ago. Come and let us show you why.

Wanaka
Stone Cottage
Address: 'Queensberry Inn',
Wanaka Rd, No 3 R.D. Cromwell
Name: Bev & David Belsham
Telephone: (03) 445 0599
Fax: (03) 445 0014
Beds: 1 Double (1 bedroom)
Bathroom: 1 Ensuite
Tariff: B&B (full) Double $140.
Nearest Town: Wanaka 25 km

"Queensberry Inn" is a restored stone cottage circa 1860 which was originally the grooms quarters and tack room to the Inn. It is now fully heated, old style furnished with tea and coffee making facilities.
"Queensberry Inn" was an earlier travellers rest for gold miners, and others at the turn of the century. It is situated on a 5 acre property consisting of the farm buildings and amidst trees, gardens and lawn; and in excess of 400 white roses.
Ideal for honeymooners it is peaceful and relaxing. Also handy to Lakes Wanaka, Dunstan and Hawea which are renowned for their fishing.
Bev and David come from a farming background and Bev enjoys crafts and gardening. Family pet - cat called Lucy.
Directions: *Midway between Wanaka and Cromwell on State Highway 6. 15 minutes to Wanaka.*

Wanaka
Country Stay
Address: 'Wanaka Sky Lodge',
Orchard Road
Name: Claudia & Ron McAulay
Telephone: (03) 443 9349
Fax: (03) 443 9349
Email: wanaka-sky-lodge@xtra.co.nz
Beds: 3 Queen (3 bedrooms)
Bathroom: 3 Private
Tariff: B&B Double $110,
Credit Cards. Neg. 3 days or more.
NZ B&B Vouchers accepted to bring it to our charge.
Nearest Town: Wanaka (Queenstown: 1 hour)

'Welcome' to our farm home. Expansive view of farmland and mountains provide a tranquil setting on 90 acres. Guests are invited to relax in a rural environment yet to be within 3km from Wanaka's township with many tourist and recreational activities - skiing - heli-skiing - fishing - tramping - scenic flight, not to mention the number of cafes and restaurants. Accommodation is spacious and comfortable with own ensuites, large living areas with open fire. Coffee and tea always available. Ron is an airline pilot, hobbies being light aircraft and gliding which is operated of our property. Claudia is a keen gardener and cook, enjoys anything creative along with looking after or should say running after their two sons 13 and 16 years of age. Dutch is spoken. Home away from home!

Wanaka

Homestay Bed & Breakfast
Address: 'The Cedars',
7 Riverbank Road, Wanaka
Name: Brian & Jessie Anderson
Telephone: (03) 443 7933
Fax: (03) 443 7633
Beds: 2 Double, 1 Single (2 Bedrooms)
Bathroom: 1 Private, 1 Family share
Tariff: B&B (full) Double $100, Single $60, Children $25, Credit cards.
NZ B&B Vouchers accepted $20 surcharge. No vouchers Jan, Feb and March.
Nearest Town: Wanaka 2 km

We welcome you to our spacious home with breathtaking mountain views from every window. We are only two minutes from our tranquil, beautiful town and lake. There are many restaurants to choose from and a great choice of activities to help you enjoy your stay. We can guide you with fishing, boating, golfing, warbirds museum, tramping, 3 ski fields, scenic flights etc.

Our property is 12 acres, planted in many varieties of attractive trees and if you care to look over the garden wall, "Moses" and "Zachariah" (two adorable donkeys) will come and talk to you - especially if you have an apple or carrot to offer! We have tea and coffee facilities, spa bath, TV in your bedroom, laundry (at a small cost) and a delicious breakfast to last you all day. And of course "Edgar" our large cat will help you remember our friendly hospitality. Prior bookings are preferred.

Wanaka

Homestay
Address: 'Tirohanga',
102 Lismore Street, Wanaka
Name: Ken & Noeleen McDiarmid
Telephone: (03) 443 8302
Fax: (03) 443 8702
Mobile: (025) 314 066
Beds: 1 King, 2 Single (2 bedrooms)
Bathroom: 2 Ensuites
Tariff: B&B (continental) Double $90, Single $55, Dinner $25.
NZ B&B Vouchers accepted $20 surcharge
Nearest Town: Wanaka 400 metres

Without exception our guests acclaim our panoramic view to be the best in Wanaka. This glorious and grand stand action scene from lounge and bedrooms would equal any spectacular mountain vista in New Zealand. Our modern home overlooks the lake and boat harbour, being very central, five minutes walk to Post Office, garages, shops, restaurants, schools and heated swimming pool. We have one double unit and one twin room both with separate ensuites. Ken and Noeleen are semi-retired business people who have travelled widely and enjoy golf, the outdoors, boating, fishing, music and entertaining. It is their wish to help and advise with any requests in order to make your stay a happy and exciting one. We have plenty of on-site parking and we have no animals.

Directions: *Turn up Little Street opposite Post Office, first turn left and continue along Lismore Street to 102, Green letter box opposite pine tree.*

Wanaka

Homestay B&B,
Self Contained Unit.
Address: "Gold Ridge",
191 Anderson Road,
Wanaka (Box 6)
Name: Diana & Dan Pinckney
Telephone: (03) 443 1253
Fax: (03) 443 1254
Mobile: 025 354 847
Beds: 1 Queen, 2 Single
(2 bedrooms/unit)
Bathroom: 1 Private
Tariff: B&B (continental) Double $75,
Single $45, Dinner $25, Children $20.
NZ B&B Vouchers accepted
Nearest Town: Wanaka
(2 1/2km to 191 Anderson Road)

Our new comfortable spacious home with 10 acres of land is situated on the outskirts of Wanaka. Expansive views of farmland and mountains together with large cottage gardens, trees, lawns and tennis court. Very private and tranquil setting. Some of our many interests include cooking, gardening, flyfishing, boating, forestry, real estate, our children and grandchildren. We enjoy having our guests for dinner and helping them plan their stay. The cottage style unit is spacious, sunny with breathtaking views, log burner, bathroom, TV and microwave. We are very flexible and enjoy the company of guests.
Directions: *On entering Wanaka, 1st right passed the "Maze", Anderson Road. Travel to T section, turn right 600 metres on left, 191 Anderson Road.*

Wanaka

Farmstay+Self-contained Accom.
Address: Maxwell Road, Mt Barker,
R.D. Wanaka
Name: 'Willow Cottage'
Kate & Roy Summers
Telephone: (03) 443 8856
Fax: (03) 443 8856
Beds: 1 Double, 3 Single (3 bedrooms)
Bathroom: 1 Private
Tariff: B&B (full) Double $135 (complete cottage) + $40 extra person, Dinner $35.
Nearest Town: Wanaka

Less than 5 minutes drive from Wanaka is our charming 120 year old cob and stone cottage complete with its own old fashioned garden.
Step back in time and relax in the peace and tranquillity of our historic cottage with its stunning mountain views. The completely self contained character filled cottage is furnished with antique furniture and collectibles but has all mod cons including a washing machine and dryer.
Join Kate and Roy for breakfast at the homestead or enjoy breakfast at leisure from fresh ingredients provided in the cottage pantry.
We offer guests original charm and furnishing, great home cooked breakfasts, fresh flowers, lovely old-fashioned linen, a huge old bath for that luxurious soak and friendly warm hospitality. The historically listed cottage is exclusively yours during your stay. Nearby an original 1890 Stone Stables houses an Antique and Gift Gallery.
Home Page: http//nz.com/heritage inns/willow cottage

671

Wanaka

Homestay
Address: 'Becklee',
28 Upton Street, Wanaka
Name: John & Yvonne Gale
Telephone: (03) 443 8908
Freephone: 0800 207 099.
Fax: (03) 443 8908
Beds: 1 Queen, 2 Single (2 bedrooms)
Bathroom: 1 Ensuite, 1 Private
Tariff: B&B (full) Double $90 Single $50.
NZ B&B Vouchers accepted $20 Surcharge
Nearest Town: In Wanaka township.

We invite you to share with us the comfort of our new and spacious home nestling in the mature trees at the end of a quiet cul-de-sac right in the centre of Wanaka township. Enjoy the privacy of our loft, with ensuite, queen size bed, TV, tea making, moutain views. Or choose between a spacious queen or twin room with private facilities and garden access. Leave your transport behind as a short stroll takes you to shops, restaurants, golf course and the lake. In the winter, enjoy a large open fire, ski drying facilities. Ski transport can be arranged to pick you up from the door. We have a good knowledge of the many activities offered in the area including fishing, walking, skiing, climbing, rafting, boating. We look forward to entertaining you in our home.FOR RESERVATIONS FREEPHONE 0800 207 099.
Directions: *Entering into Wanaka on State Highway 8, turn left at Caltex service station, turn 3rd left - Helwick Street, turn 1st left - Upton Street, we are at the end.*

Wanaka

Country Home
Address: 'Champagne Heights',
P.O. Box 41, Wanaka
Name: John & Karen Hallum
Telephone: (03) 443 8280
Fax: (03) 443 8281
Mobile: (025) 366 589
Beds: 1 Double, 3 Single (2 bedrooms)
Bathroom: 2 Private

Tariff: B&B (continental) Double $90, Single $50, Children under 12 half price
Credit cards. NZ B&B Vouchers accepted $20 Surcharge
Nearest Town: Wanaka 3 Kms

Are you looking for amazing Lake and Mountain Views, Warm Luxury accommodation, Peace and Quiet? Welcome to "Champagne Heights".
Our large modern home, set on 10 acres is situated just 3km from Wanaka township, on the road to Mt Aspiring National Park and Treble Cone skifield.
Join our family of four (ex farmers), along with our pet sheep, cows and pony, for an interesting "typical Kiwi" country home stay.
Guest bedrooms are warm and spacious, with private bathrooms, each with magnificent lake and mountain views and opening out onto balconies. Our hobbies and interests include sports, wine tasting and over the last few years home hosting.
Wanaka has much to offer visitors, skiing, tramping, jet boating, fishing, golf and great restaurants. Our family welcomes you to your "Home away from home".
Laundry available.
Directions: *Please phone.*

Wanaka

Homestay
Address: 95 McDougall St, Wanaka
Name: Harper's
Telephone: (03) 443 8894
Fax: (03) 443 8834
Email: harpers@xtra.co.nz
Beds: 5 Single (3 bedrooms)
Bathroom: 1 Guests share
Tariff: B&B (special) Double $80, Single $45.
Credit cards accepted. NZ B&B Vouchers accepted Surcharge $15
Nearest Town: Wanaka 1 Km

'Harpers' is a homestay where friendliness, comfort and visitors need are a priority. Your hosts, Jo and Ian have travelled and lived in various parts of the world. We have been home hosting for several years and gain a lot of pleasure from sharing our home and garden.. Ian is: * a semi-retired builder who purpose built our house for home hosting. Jo is: * a retired schoolteacher and more recently retired office worker. Wanaka is a resort township and is noted for: *a wide variety of very good restaurants, *adventure activity, *fishing the local rivers and lake. *a top class scenic golf course, *walks around the lake and tramps into the Mt Aspiring National Park. *A Fighter Pilots museum of World War 2 planes. *flights to Milford Sound, Mt Cook and Mt Aspiring, *3 top class skifields, which can be easily accessed. We cater for skiers in the winter. Our black cat Bo completes the household. We are a smokefree home.
Directions: *Drive along the lake to the Queenstown / Cardrona turn off. Drive up this road - Highway 89 - for 4 blocks and look for our sign just past the 3 tall Redwood trees.*
Home Page: www.nzhomestay.co.nz

Wanaka

Country Stay
Address: Main Road, SH 6,
Luggate, RD3, Cromwell
Name: Tilburg Lodge - Van Riel
Telephone: (03) 443 7923 **Fax**: (03) 443 7953
Beds: 2 Double, 2 Twin (4 bedrooms)
Bathroom: 1 Guests share, 1 Family share
Tariff: B&B (continental) Double $100, Single $50, Children $40,
Dinner by arrangement $15. American express.
NZ B&B Vouchers accepted with surcharge
Nearest Town: Wanaka 10 minutes

Welcome. Enjoy a complimentary wine or ale when you arrive in our spacious home which is surrounded by 5 acres of flower gardens and natural landscape, and overlooks unsurpassed views of snowcapped mountains and pastures. Barbeque breakfasts and meals under the shade of giant walnut and oak trees are a summer features. Our home is filled with wood work, curiosities and herbal pot-pourris which are among our many interests. We are also musicians and often enjoy entertaining our guests with many styles of music. Our lodge is situated on SH6 of

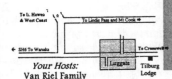

Your Hosts:
Van Riel Family

Luggate, a junction to Mount Cook, Queenstown, Wanaka, the West Coast and 30 minutes from 3 skifields.
Tea and coffee facilities, smoking area, friendly cat and dog. Dutch spoken.
Lodge located 500 metres Cromwell side of Tavern in Luggate.
Home Page: http://nzfpm.dcc.govt.nz/nzfpm/nzfpm.htm

Wanaka

Self-contained Accommodation
Address: The Stone Cottage, Dublin Bay,
2 R.D. Wanaka
Name: Belinda Wilson
Telephone: (03) 443 1878 **Fax**: (03) 443 1276
Beds: 1 King, 2 Double, 2 Single (2 bedrooms)
Bathroom: 2 Private
Tariff: B&B (full) Double $140-$160, Single $120, Children under 12 half price.
Dinner from $35. Credit cards (VISA/MC).
Nearest Town: 10km from Wanaka

Nearly fifty years ago, a spectacular garden was created at Dublin Bay on the tranquil shores of Lake Wanaka. Its beauty still blooms today against a backdrop of the majestic Southern Alps.

Elegantly decorated with family treasures. The Stone Cottage offers two self-contained loft apartments with breathtaking views over Lake Wanaka to snow clad Alps beyond. Featuring your own bathroom, bedroom, kitchen, living room and private entrance.

Enjoy breakfast at leisure, made from fresh ingredients from your well stocked fully equipped kitchen. A home cooked dinner with wine by the open fire or a gourmet picnic hamper by arrangement.

Walk along the sandy beach just 4 minutes from the Stone Cottage or wander in the enchanting garden. Guests can enjoy trout fishing, nature walks, golf, boating, horse riding, wine tasting and ski fields nearby.

Only 10 minutes from Wanaka, this is the perfect retreat for those who value privacy and the unique beauty of this area.

Relax in the magic atmosphere at the Stone Cottage and awake to the dawn bird chorus of native bellbirds and fantails.

Wanaka

Rural Homestay
Address: Halliday Lane, Wanaka
Name: "Stonehaven"
Dennis & Deirdre
Telephone: (03) 443 9516
Fax: (03) 443 9513
Beds: 2 Double, 2 Single (2 bedrooms)
Bathroom: 1 Private, 1 En suite.
Tariff: B&B (full) Double $80, Single $50, Children negotiated according to requirements, Dinner $25. NZ B&B Vouchers accepted $10 Surcharge
Nearest Town: Wanaka 4km away

Our home is set in a largely undeveloped two acres about five minutes drive from Wanaka. All beds have electric blankets and tea and coffee is freely available. We have extensive views of the mountains surrounding Wanaka. We have an adjacent ten acres planted as an arboretum. The accent is on Autumn colour and the collection includes about 150 Genus. The best represented are Rowans (nationally significant collection), Maples, Pines and crab-apples. Deirdre is a children's nurse and we have the appropriate toys and furniture including trampoline. Children welcome. Child care by arrangement. Dennis is interested in the region, conservation and trees / gardening. Dennis is familiar with Mt Aspiring National Park. Guided trips by arrangement. Organic fruit both in season and preserved. We have twin 9 year old girls, a small dog and three cats. Laundry facilities available. No smoking inside please. Please phone for directions.

Hawea/Wanaka

Historic Farmstay
Address: "Fork Farm",
R.D.2, Wanaka
Name: Lizzie Carruthers & Phill Hunt
Telephone: (03) 443 1055
Fax: (03) 443 1170
Mobile: (025) 223 0398
Email: forkfarm@xtra.co.nz

Beds: 1 Queen, 1 Double, 2 Single (3 bedrooms)
Bathroom: 1 Private
Tariff: B&B (continental) Double $140, Single $100, Single party bookings only. Full breakfast by arrangement. Credit cards.
Nearest Town: Hawea 4km, Wanaka 9km

Welcome to Fork Farm which is situated in the picturesque Maungawera Valley between Lakes Hawea and Wanaka. Both Lakes are easily seen from the farm along with impressive views of the Southern Alps foothills and surrounding landscape.
A historic Scottish style homestead designed by Basil Hooper forms the hub of a 470 hectare sheep and deer farm. The homestead is built of solid stone with interior wood work being recycled from gold dredges abandoned after the Cardrona gold rush. The large gardens are ideal for relaxing in with swimming pool, bar-b-que, tennis court and many shady trees to help enjoy the summer months. Open fires, two cats and warm hospitality keep out the winter chills.
We are actively involved in the farm and along with our six working dogs welcome guests to experience any of the seasonal operations that they wish.
Having extensively travelled ourselves we regard a comfortable bed and a warm welcome highly and look forward to meeting you.

OTAGO

675

Wanaka

Lodge
Address: Cameron Creek Lodge,
State Highway 6, Wanaka
Name: Grant & Angie Longman
Telephone: (03) 443 8784
Fax: (03) 443 1262
Beds: 2 Queen, 2 Single (3 bedrooms)
Bathroom: 1 Ensuite, 1 Guests share
Tariff: B&B (full) Double $95-$110,
Single $55, Children half price,
Dinner from $25, Credit Cards (VISA/MC).
Nearest Town: Wanaka 3km

Welcome, when you are looking for that special holiday in a relaxed atmosphere Cameron Creek Lodge has it all; Angie and I have had extensive involvement in the hospitality trade and are now channelling our talents into the Lodge.

The Lodge is built from 60 tons of natural rock and native timber milled from the surrounding 20 acre property. Rooms are centrally heated and situated with mountain vistas which can be viewed from the sweeping verandahs.

The hub of the Lodge is based around the warm hearth of the living area; and the domain of Angie's culinary delights - the kitchen; Angie creates superb meals using fresh New Zealand fare and home grown produce.

Horses and mountain bikes are available to explore the stunning surrounding terrain or hitch up Cedric the donkey to a cart for a more humorous alternative; we also have two cats, Bubble and Squeek.

Directions: *Phone or fax us today.*

Wanaka

Homestay
Address: "The Croft", 3 Oakwood Place,
Meadowstone Drive, Wanaka
(PO Box 264, Wanaka)
Name: Margaret and Gerald Scaife
Telephone: (03) 443 9272
Fax: (03)443 9270
Beds: 1 Queen, 2 Single (2 bedrooms)
Bathroom: 1 Guests share
Tariff: B&B (continental) Double $90, Single $60.
Cooked breakfast by arrangement. Credit cards.
NZ B&B Vouchers accepted $15 surcharge.
Nearest Town: Wanaka 2km

We welcome visitors to our new, comfortable, fully landscaped home. It has 2 private guests bedrooms, guest bathroom with spa bath, shower and separate toilet. Our house has alpine mountain views and is about 1 km from the lake.

We are both local born and bred and were local high country sheep and cattle farmers for many years. We sold this to be nearer the town and became moteliers on the outskirts of the township for 16 years and have recently sold these to retire.

We have travelled to Europe, the Pacific and Australia over the years. We are also KiwiHosts and believe we are well qualified to become Home Hosts. We prefer to keep our home smoke free.

Directions: *To find us proceed along the lakefront about 1km until you come to the Meadowstone stone wall on your left. Proceed up the road to the second cul-de-sac on your right. We are the 2nd house on your left on entry into the cul-de-sac.*

Wanaka
B&B, Homestay, Self-contained Apartment
Address: Temasek House,
7 Huchan Lane, Wanaka
Name: David & Poh Choo Turner
Telephone: (03) 443 1288
Fax: (03) 443 1288
Mobile: (025) 277 9594
Beds: 1 Queen, 1 Double, 1 Single (3 bedrooms)
Bathroom: 1 Ensuite, 1 Guests share
Tariff: B&B (continental) Double $80-$90, Single $55, Children under 12 half price. Credit cards. NZ B&B Vouchers accepted $5 surcharge
Nearest Town: Wanaka.

Our separate upper floor guest area offers panoramic views of the nearby mountains and lake. It also houses an extensive literature collection, TV and stereo (if required), coffee and tea making facilities, washing machine and dryer (small additional charge). Temasek House is a non-smoking home and has ample parking accessed from a private driveway. Heaters and electric blankets are provided in all rooms. Our home, including the name of the house, strongly reflects our travels and particularly our lengthy spell in SE Asia. We are still active and run and exercise regularly - or at least as much as a young family permits. We welcome children (toys, cot and high chair available). Ours will undoubtedly try to entertain you - but when it gets too much, we can lock them away with the cat. Everybody loves Wanaka - but we will provide that special touch to make your stay truly memorable.
Directions: *Take the Mt. Aspiring Road out of Wanaka and turn right into Sargood Drive, Rippon Lea (opp Edgewater sign). First left into Huchan Lane and we are to be found down the driveway between the 2nd and 3rd houses on the left.*

Wanaka
Homestay
Address: 56 Manuka Crescent,
Wanaka
Name: "Hunts Homestay"
Bill & Ruth Hunt
Telephone: (03) 443 1053
Fax: (03) 443 1355
Beds: 1 Double, 2 Single (2 bedrooms)
Bathroom: 1 Guests share
Tariff: B&B (continental) Double $80, Single $50, Children half price, Dinner $25 by arrangement. Credit Cards.
Nearest Town: Wanaka: 15m walk, 5 min car to centre.

We would like to welcome you to our new home in Wanaka. After retiring from our farm near Wanaka in 1995 we built our house overlooking the mountains and lake on a half acre section. Our interests are gardening, golf, travel and meeting people. Having lived in the Wanaka Districts virtually all our lives we have an extensive knowledge of the area and its attractions. Bill is a volunteer at the Wanaka Visitor Centre and a Kiwi Host and so keeps informed of the local tourist ventures and conditions. For those interested farm visits can be arranged.
We will welcome you with a cup of tea or coffee in our smoke-free home and settle you into our spacious ground floor accommodation.
Directions: *Follow Beacon Point Road, turn right into Manuka Cres. We are opposite the motels.*

Wanaka

Self Contained Accommodation
Address: 76 Golf Course Road, Wanaka
Name: Johanna and Wolfram Gessler
Telephone: (03) 443 1255
Fax: (03) 443 1255
Email: olive@xtra.co.nz
Beds: 1 Queen, 1 Double, 1 Single (2 bedrooms)
Bathroom: 1 Guests share
Tariff: B&B (full) Double $65, Single $40, Children $10 each.
Dinner in our restaurant 15% discount. NZ B&B Vouchers accepted
Nearest Town: Wanaka walking distance from town.

We invite you to stay with us in a rural setting above Wanaka (walking distance from town) with awesome views onto lake and mountains; the Golf Course is just across the road. The unit is a fully self-contained cottage: two bedrooms, bathroom, kitchenette, living-dining.
Originally from Germany we have lived in Italy, France and West Africa and found Wanaka the place to be. As a family of seven, a friendly Newfoundland dog, and two cats, we are now well settled here and would enjoy having you as our guests.
Wolfram is running a Tuscan style Restaurant on our property with in and outdoor dining, where you can enjoy the beauty and grandeur of Lake Wanaka and the mountains, while having a good Italian meal (for our B&B Guests 15% discount on lunch and dinner). Share our solar heated swimming pool with us in summer.
Directions: *Please use the common entrance with the Restaurant to the House which is 150 meters back from the road.*

Wanaka

B&B Homestay
Address: "Whispering Pines"
1 Kings Drive, Wanaka
Name: Robyn
Telephone: (03) 443 1448
Fax: (03) 443 1458
Mobile: (025) 776 959
Email: Whisper@voyager.co.nz
Beds: 2 Queen (2 bedrooms)

Bathroom: 1Ensuite with spa pool, 1 Family share.
Tariff: B&B (full) Double $110 - $140, single $95 - $135. Dinner if requested.
Visa, Mastercard
Nearest Town: Wanaka is walking distance.

Welcome to Wonderful Wanaka and also to "Whispering Pines' where comfort and luxury are the keynote.
Imagine the wind in the pines, the roaring of the log fire, conviviality and great hospitality; your warm bed waiting at the end of the day, or, relaxing in your own private spa pool under stunning star-filled skies after a great day's skiing, fishing, playing golf or enjoying any of the many other activities available.
It's all yours at "Whispering Pines".
Not only that. But imagine starting the day with a delicious, hearty cooked breakfast. Just sit at the table and be waited on while you enjoy the panoramic mountain and lake vista. Just be sure you've got somewhere nice to go to after "Whispering Pines" otherwise you'll never leave.
Home Page: nzholiday.com/whisper

Wanaka

Lodge/Homestay
Address: "Anubis Lodge",
264 Beacon Point Road, Wanaka
Name: Michele and Bob Mercer
Telephone: 03-443 7807
Fax: 03-443 7803
Mobile: 025-221 7387

Beds: 1 King which becomes 2 Single, 2 Queen, (3 bedrooms)
Bathroom: 3 Ensuites, 1 Private
Tariff: B&B (full) Double $100-$120, Single $80.
NZ B&B Vouchers accepted $20 surcharge
Nearest Town: Wanaka 2.8km

Recently completed our Oamaru Stone home is purpose built for Bed and Breakfast accommodation, with every consideration given to privacy and comfort for our visitors. Rooms are large and have their own dressing rooms and ensuite bathrooms. Beds are luxuriously fitted with quality linen, feather duvets and electric blankets. Native timber accents the decor throughout with touches of fresh flowers, Italian art, Belgium rugs, Scottish leather and English linens. The views are unobscured to lake and mountains, looking directly Northwest onto Treble Cone Ski field. a two minute walk brings you to the lake edge for fishing, swimming or secluded relaxation. The house is centrally heated plus two fireplaces.
Breakfast is varied and generous, special requests or dietary requirements need only be advised.
"Anubis" is an Egyptian name inspired by our two Pharoah Hound dogs, who you may choose to meet or not depending on your preference.

Wanaka

Homestay
Address: Mt Aspiring Road
Wanaka
Name: Glens of Roy
Telephone: (03) 443 7392
Fax: (03) 443 7848

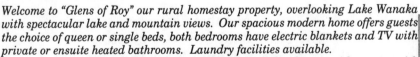

Beds: 1 Queen, 2 Single (2 bedrooms)
Bathroom: 1 Ensuite, 1 Private
Tariff: B&B (full) Double $95, Single $70. Credit cards accepted.
Nearest Town: Wanaka 4 km

Welcome to "Glens of Roy" our rural homestay property, overlooking Lake Wanaka with spectacular lake and mountain views. Our spacious modern home offers guests the choice of queen or single beds, both bedrooms have electric blankets and TV with private or ensuite heated bathrooms. Laundry facilities available.
Living and dining areas with native timber and stone fireplace provides guests with a homely comfortable stay.
Situated on Mt Aspiring - Glendhu Bay Road "Glens of Roy" is within close proximity to three major of skifields, Mt Aspiring National Park - a world heritage area and world famous brown trout fishing at Lake Wanaka's Paddock Bay, yet only five minutes drive from Wanaka's shops and restaurants.
We, our (outdoor) character dog George and cat Brian, look forward to meeting you.
Directions: *Travel West along Mt Aspiring - Glendhu Bay Road, 4 km from State Highway 89, Glens of Roy is on the left.*

Wanaka

Homestay
Address: 19 Bill's Way, Ribbon Lea, Wanaka
Name: Lake Wanaka Home Hosting
Telephone: (03) 443 9060
Fax: (03) 443 1626
Mobile: (025) 228 9160
Beds: 1 King, 1 Double, 2 Single (3 bedrooms)
Bathroom: 2 Private
Tariff: B&B (Special/full/continental) King $100, Double $80, Single $50.
NZ B&B Vouchers accepted $15 surcharge for Double, $20 surcharge for King
Dinner available. Children welcome.
Nearest Town: Wanaka 2 1/2km to post office.

We welcome visitors to Wanaka and enjoy sharing our natural surroundings with others. We have a large peaceful home where our guests can experience not only the austerity of the lake and mountains around them, but also experience the ambience of Wanaka itself.

The picturesque walk around the lake to Wanaka town is 20 to 30 minutes is well worth while.

Our guests room with a super king size bed has a joining lounge with tea and coffee making facilities, TV, a sofa that will convert into a bed, private bathroom. Our double room has private bathroom also.

Our home has smoke alarms, central heating and all beds have electric blankets. Good laundry facilities. We have no children living at home, and no pets. Our interests are sport, gardening, boating, farming and good cuisine. We wish your stay in Wanaka will be a very happy one.

Directions: *Please ring for directions (025) 228 9160 or 443 9060*

Cromwell
Orchard Stay
Address: 'Cottage Gardens', 3 Alpha St,
cnr. State Highway 8B.
Name: Jill & Colin McColl
Telephone: (03) 445 0628 **Fax**: (03) 445 0628
Email: eco@xtra.co.nz
Beds: 4 Single (3 bedrooms)
Bathroom: 1 Ensuite, 2 Family share
Tariff: B&B (continental) Double $70, Single $40/$50, Dinner $20,
Credit Cards. NZ B&B Vouchers accepted
Nearest Town: Cromwell, 1km to town centre

Welcome to our home and Apricot orchard overlooking Lake Dunstan, only 40 mins to Queenstown and Wanaka.
The historic goldmining town of Cromwell is an easy 5 hr drive from Christchurch viewing Southern Lakes, Alps and Mount Cook. An ideal stop over whether travelling to Queenstown, Te Anau, Dunedin or the West Coast.
We enjoy quiet evenings by the fire in winter or on the verandahs in summer with our guests. Our large purpose built double guest room has ensuite, TV, fridge, tea making facilities, private entrance and verandah.
Attractions and activities include golfing, fishing, tramping, goldpanning, visits to vineyards and four ski fields (one hour drive).
Colin is a member of Lions International and we both enjoy gardening, our golden Retriever Bradley and meeting people.
Come and enjoy Central Otago - the Centre of Attractions and Summer Fruit Bowl of New Zealand. Our home is smoke free. One house cat. We prefer no children.

Cromwell
Bed & Breakfast
Address: Quartz Reef Creek,
Northburn,
State Highway 8, Cromwell
Name: June Boulton
Telephone: (03) 445 0404
Beds: 1Queen, 2 Singles (2 bedroom)
Bathroom: 1 Ensuite, 1 Private
Tariff: B&B (continental) Double $90, Single $50.
NZ B&B Vouchers accepted $20 surcharge
Nearest Town: Cromwell 4km

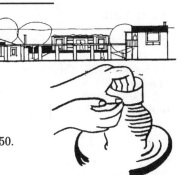

You are invited to stay at my home - an architecturally designed house situated near the lake edge with panoramic views of lake and mountains. There is a boat ramp within 200 metres and fishing spots virtually on the doorstep. Popular ski fields at Wanaka, Queenstown and Cardrona are within easy reach, or enjoy a game of golf, or explore the local gold mining areas.
Your sunny room has total privacy with its own entrance and deck. For your convenience there are tea making facilities, fridge, microwave and TV. Another room with twin beds has a private bathroom. I enjoy making pottery in my studio and supply craft galleries. Guests are welcome to view and purchase - ask for a demonstration if interested.
I possess a friendly black cat called Tom (should be Tomasina!).
Directions: *3.5 km north of Cromwell Bridge, SH 8, 1st house on lake front.*

Cromwell

Farmstay
Address: Swann Road, Lowburn
RD 2, Cromwell
Name: Claire & Jack Davis
Telephone: 0800 205 104 or 03 445 1291
Fax: (03) 445 1291
Email: hiburn@xtra.co.nz
Beds: 1 Double, 2 Single (2 bedrooms)
Bathroom: 1 Guests share

Tariff: B&B (full), Double $80, Children half price, Dinner $15 per person. NZ
B&B Vouchers accepted
Nearest Town: Cromwell 10km

*Situated at Cromwell the centre of beautiful Central Otago halfway between Wanaka
and Queenstown. Farming 400 hectares with merino sheep and deer. Guests are
welcome to join in farming activities and farm tour always included with working
sheep dogs a speciality. We encourage guests to come for dinner and enjoy time to chat
over a meal. Morning and afternoon teas complimentary home produce used as much
as possible.*

*Our joint interests include curling, sports, gardening, sheep dog competitions,
handcrafts.*

*Local attractions: gold mining history, fruit growing area, lakes, rivers and moun-
tains, fishing and walking, 4 ski fields nearby.*

*Come and relax in our beautiful and peaceful surroundings. Use us as a base to visit
the area. Children welcome. We treat our guests as friends.*

Please phone for reservations and directions - evening or meal times.

Cromwell

Homestay
Address: "The Poplars", K-Arni Cove,
No. 3 RD, Cromwell
Name: Judy & Bill Thornbury
Telephone: (03) 445 1107
Fax: (03) 445 3062
Mobile: (025) 311 415
Beds: 1 Queen, 2 Single (2 bedrooms)
Bathroom: 1 Guests share, separate toilet
Tariff: B&B (full) Double $90, Single $50, Children half price, Dinner $20,
Campervans facilities available.
NZ B&B Vouchers accepted $20 surcharge
Nearest Town: Cromwell 6km

*Welcome to "The Poplars" our new spacious home on the edge of Lake Dunstan situated
on the 45th parallel, 6 kilometres from Cromwell. We have recently shifted from a sheep
and deer farm in Southland along with our friendly cat "Ollie". Our interests include
Lions, golf, fishing, boating, gardening and crafts. Our sunny bedrooms have lake
views and attached open balconies, fridge, tea and coffee making facilities available
at all times. Guests share our spacious living areas with TV's and make free use of our
spa room and laundry. Attractions include golf course, orchards, fishing, boating,
walks, 4 skifields within easy reach and the Historic Quartz Reef Chinese gold
diggings - a 15 minute walk from our home. We welcome you to have an evening meal
with us or just bed and breakfast . No smoking inside please.*

Directions: *5km from Cromwell Bridge on Tarras / Omarama Highway 8. Sign at
gate.*

Cromwell

Homestay/Countrystay
Address: "Glenhaven" Gardens,
Ripponvale Road, Cromwell
Name: Lorna & Edwin Udy
Telephone: (03) 445 0768 **Fax**: (03) 445 0768
Mobile: (025) 397 460
Beds: 1 King, 2 Single (2 bedrooms)
Bathroom: 2 Ensuite
Tariff: B&B (full) King $85, Twin $75. Credit cards
NZ B&B Vouchers accepted $10 surcharge
Nearest Town: Cromwell 5km, Queenstown 55km

Welcome to our home set in a 5 acre garden just off Highway 6, only 5 km on the Queenstown side of Cromwell.

We can show you Central Otago at its best, with old gold workings, fruit orchards all around us, vineyards and wineries to visit, four skifields within 50 minutes.

Our large home has been built with guests in mind, to be as private as you wish or join in with us.

We have lived in Cromwell for 25 years, 10 years managing a Motel, Edwin's trade is building and Lorna's is nursing. We both love gardening and we own a Garden Centre Business.

Our cosy lounge is set up with an awesome home theatre system, there are 2 cats and pet birds, (our children have left home). Cromwell has a great golf course, great fishing, and if all this is to strenuous for you just sit back on our patio with a cup of tea, coffee or a glass of Central Otago wine and admire the gardens. "Glenhaven" is a smoke free zone.

Arrowtown

Homestay / Bed & Breakfast
Address: 20 Wiltshire St, Arrowtown, Central Otago
Name: Cynthia Balfour
Telephone: (03) 442 1326
Beds: 1 Double, 2 Single (2 bedrooms)
Bathroom: 1 Guests share
Tariff: B&B (special) Double $90, Single $80, Children half price.
NZ B&B Vouchers accepted Surcharge $20
Nearest Town: 19km Queenstown

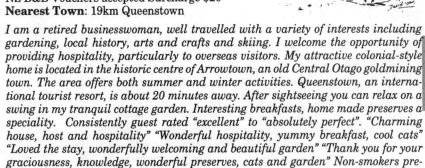

I am a retired businesswoman, well travelled with a variety of interests including gardening, local history, arts and crafts and skiing. I welcome the opportunity of providing hospitality, particularly to overseas visitors. My attractive colonial-style home is located in the historic centre of Arrowtown, an old Central Otago goldmining town. The area offers both summer and winter activities. Queenstown, an international tourist resort, is about 20 minutes away. After sightseeing you can relax on a swing in my tranquil cottage garden. Interesting breakfasts, home made preserves a speciality. Consistently guest rated "excellent" to "absolutely perfect". "Charming house, host and hospitality" "Wonderful hospitality, yummy breakfast, cool cats" "Loved the stay, wonderfully welcoming and beautiful garden" "Thank you for your graciousness, knowledge, wonderful preserves, cats and garden" Non-smokers preferred, reservations ahead please. Two house cats.

Arrowtown

Homestay/Self-contained Accomm
Address: Butel Road, Arrowtown
Name: Barry & Ann Bain
Telephone: (03) 442 1252 **Fax**: (03) 442 1252
Mobile: 025 274 3360
Beds: 1 Queen, 4 Single (2 bedrooms)
Bathroom: 1 Ensuite, 1 Private
Tariff: B&B (full, continental) Double $80-$90, Single negotiable, Children negotiable. Credit cards accepted. NZ B&B Vouchers accepted $10 surcharge
Nearest Town: Arrowtown 1 km to town centre. Queenstown 19km

We are retired business couple who have travelled extensively. Our interests include local history, music, gardening, pottery and patchwork. We welcome our guests to a spacious, sunny, self-contained upstairs suite, complete with kitchen. Plenty of space for children, who will love to play with our friendly black Cocker spaniel.

With no passing traffic to disturb the stillness, your private balcony commands 360 degree views of the mountains and overlooks our large landscaped garden and orchard, grazing sheep and the famous Millbrook Country Club. Their nearby restaurants are open to all visitors and as members, we can offer reduced green-fees. Extra continental breakfast with freshly baked bread and Ann's shortbread, jams and preserves is provided in your suite; or alternatively join us in the house for a full breakfast.

Complimentary laundry, road bikes, gold mining gear, BBQ etc. Our courtesy car is a former Archibishop's rare 1924 Austin drophead coupe.

Arrowtown

Homestay
Address: 'Rowan Cottage' 9 Thomson St, Arrowtown, Central Otago
Name: Elizabeth & Michael Bushell
Telephone: (03) 442 0443
Beds: 1 Double, 2 Single (2 bedrooms)
Bathroom: 1 Guests share
Tariff: B&B (full) Double $75, Single $50. Dinner $25pp.
NZ B&B Vouchers accepted $10 surcharge
Nearest Town: Arrowtown. Queenstown 19km

Rowan Cottage is situated in a quiet tree lined street with mountain views. We are 10 minutes walk to the town and 20 minutes drive to Queenstown.

We have a lovely cottage garden to relax in and have coffee, tea and homemade goodies. We are well travelled and can advise you on things to see and do in our beautiful part of the country. You will be assured of a friendly and comfortable stay.

"Comments" - Thanks so much for your wonderful hospitality, wonderful breakfasts and such helpfulness in organising our acitivities. We felt so welcome in your relaxed atmosphere. Wish we could have sat in your gorgeous garden for a few days but your country beckons us to see more of its beauty.

Private bathroom is for your use exclusively,
Guests share means you may be sharing with other guests,
Family share means you will be sharing with the family.

Arrowtown

Homestay
Address: 25 Caernarvon St,
Arrowtown
Name: Liz & Steve Daniel
Telephone: (03) 442 1227
Freephone 0800 186 844
Email: daniels@es.co.nz
Beds: 2 Queen (2 bedrooms)
Bathroom: 1 Ensuite, 1 Family share
Tariff: B&B (continental) Double with Ensuite $80; Double $70; Single $50;
Children negotiable. Special rates May - September, and consecutive nights.
Nearest Town: Arrowtown 3 mins walk, Queenstown 19km

Liz and Steve welcome you to our traditional stone built home. It is spacious and comfortable with a sheltered garden, sun baskers patio, two lounges and open log fire. The ensuite bedroom is very private with TV, and tea making facilities. The other room has French windows to the tree-lined garden. Three minutes walk to tranquil Arrowtown's main street with its shops, museum, post-office and restaurants. Our sunny sheltered climate here and proximity to Queenstown's activities give you the best of both worlds. With extensive knowledge of the hospitality trade our other interests, after our two school-age sons, are our cat, travelling, food and wine, reading, golfing, skiing, fishing, boating, local places and activities. Dine at one of Arrowtown's cafes or restaurants, try busy Queenstown just 20 minutes away, Millbrook County Clubs 3 restaurants, golf course, gymnasium and pool just 5 minutes drive. Laundry facilities available. Smoking outside only.

Arrowtown

Homestay
Address: 18 Stafford St, Arrowtown
Name: Anne & Arthur Gormack
Telephone: (03) 442 1747
Freephone: 0800 184990 **Fax**: (03) 442 1787
Beds: 1 King, 2 Single (2 bedrooms)
Bathroom: 2 Private
Tariff: B&B (continental) Double $90.00, Single $45.00.
NZ B&B Vouchers accepted $20 Surcharge
Nearest Town: Arrowtown - Queenstown 19km

Our spacious home, overlooking Millbrook Country Club and the Wakatipu Basin, offers spectacular views from every window. Although only 5 minutes walk from the town centre, our outlook is totally rural. We have a warm and comfortable home with plenty of space inside and out. Guest rooms have TV, reading lights, electric blankets and heaters. There is also a gym room with exercise equipment for your use. During the Summer, join us for a glass of wine beside our heated swimming pool. During the Winter you can curl up in front of the fire and read our many books on local history, or have a friendly chat. Bread, preserves, muesli and jam all homemade.

Continental breakfast consists of fruit, cereal, toast, tea/coffee,
Full breakfast is the same with a cooked course,
Special breakfast has something special.

Arrowtown - Gibbston Valley
Homestay+Self-contained Accom.
Address: Coal Pit Road, Gibbston,
R.D. 1, Queenstown
Name: Claire & Alan Perry
Telephone: (03) 442 5339
Fax: (03) 442 5339
Beds: 1 Queen, 2 Single (2 bedrooms)
Bathroom: 1 Private, 1 Guests share
Tariff: B&B (continental) Double $85,
Single $50, Children over ten $15.
Dinner by arrangement.
Nearest Town: Arrowtown 15km

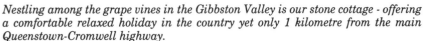

Nestling among the grape vines in the Gibbston Valley is our stone cottage - offering a comfortable relaxed holiday in the country yet only 1 kilometre from the main Queenstown-Cromwell highway.

The cottage is part of Coal Pit - vineyard and has been restored from an historic stable; well over 100 years old. Trees from the era make up the garden of the homestead and cottage. Guests can be self contained or share meals with their hosts.

The area offers beautiful Central Otago scenery and being in the Gibbston area gives easy access to the two local wineries, and is only 10 minutes to Arrowtown with its golf course, historic buildings and many restaurants.

Coronet Peak and the Remarkables ski-fields are within half an hour drive, as is Queenstown and all its subsequent activities.

Two twin rooms are available in the homestead with guest bathroom.
Directions: *Please phone.*

Members of
**The New Zealand Association
Farm & Home Host Inc.**
maintain the highest standards &
are always delighted to welcome
guests into their homes.

Arrowtown

B&B+Self-contained Accom.
Address: 43 Bedford St,
Arrowtown
Name: POLLY-ANNA COTTAGE'
Telephone: (03) 442 1347
Fax: (03) 442 1347
Beds: 1 Double, 2 Single (2 bedrooms)
Bathroom: 1 Ensuite, 1 Guest share
Tariff: B&B (continental) Double $80, Single $50.
Dinner by arrangement $25 pp. Credit Cards.
NZ B&B Vouchers accepted surcharge $10
Nearest Town: Queenstown

Daphne and Bill are retired business couple who have restored and renovated a quaint 100 year old cottage from the gold rush days. We recommend a restful and informative stay in historic Arrowtown, and offer our warm hospitality and completely private ensuite facility. Arrowtown is an area of great beauty and serenity the town is 15 mins from Queenstown with superb views and excellent tourist attractions. Features are 18 hole golf course, a superb lakes district museum, shops and restaurants. Three major ski fields are within easy reach. We are 5 mins from Millbrook International Golf Resort. We welcome the opportunity to share our hospitality with overseas and Kiwi visitors. Try Daph's delights, home preserves and fudge. Comments we have received include; "The highlight of our trip", "Came 2 days, stayed 6", "Wonderful experience", "Graciously warm people we shall return", "Thanks for the memory I feel so at home". Why not share historic Arrowtown with us. Can inform on all local attractions.
Directions: *"Polly Anna" sign at front gate on Main Road into Arrowtown*

Arrowtown

Homestay
Address: 13 Stafford Street,
Arrowtown
Name: Wiki & Norman Smith
Telephone: (03) 442 1092
Fax: (03) 442 1092
Email: norman@queenstown.co.nz
Beds: 1 Queen, 2 Single (2 bedrooms)
Bathroom: 1 Guests share
Tariff: B&B (continental) Double $75,
Single $50, Dinner on request $20.

Nearest Town: Arrowtown (5 mins walk), Queenstown 19km, Frankton Airport 12km.

Arrowtown is one of NZ's most famous old goldmining towns and as a living historic town (pop 1440) remains a popular holiday destination for locals as well as overseas visitors because it has - charm and tranquillity, with many interesting walks in and around the township - goldpanning in the Arrow River - restored Chinese village - Autumn colours - all the adventure attractions of Queenstown (20 mins away) or the more sedate life of golfing - Wine Trails - Art Trails - Historic Tours etc.
After 23 years in meat Industry management and 4 years as Moteliers in Arrowtown we have now retired to our architecturally designed home and garden. We have travelled widely and we are keen trampers, and enjoy gardening, golf, computing and helping other people to enjoy the beauty and tranquillity of our historic area. Off street parking is provided and we also have a cat. We look forward to meeting you. Please phone or fax for a booking.

687

Arrowtown - Queenstown

Farmstay Bed & Breakfast
Address: 'Golden Hills', Highway 6,
Highway 6, 1 RD, Queenstown
Name: Patricia Sew Hoy
Telephone: (03) 442 1427 **Fax**: (03) 4421 427
Beds: 2 Queen, 1 Double, 3 Single (4 bedrooms)
Bathroom: 3 Ensuite, 1 Private
Tariff: B&B (continental) Double $85-$95, Single $55.
Travellers cheques accepted. NZ B&B Vouchers accepted $15 surcharge.
Nearest Town: Arrowtown 4km, Queenstown 18km

Golden Hills is a distinctive, superior home with four large bedrooms, each with their own bathroom. Set in 30 acres, private, quiet, with beautiful mountain views, the home has all the extras one would expect from warm country hospitality in a charming spacious sunfilled house.

Surrounded by a 3 acres award winning garden with private terraces, barbecue, garden walks and ponds, it nestles back from, and is easy to find, on Highway 6. Arrowtown 4 kms away with dining, shops, walks, golf etc. Queenstown is 18 km away. One cheerful Labrador dog in residence assures a great welcome to escort you on a Garden Tour, so please call in to inspect, I am always here, it is too lovely to be anywhere else.

Home Page: www-southern lights.co.nz\qtnz\golden hills\index.htm.
Directions: *FROM NORTH: Keep on Highway 6, travel 300 metres past Arrowtown turnoff, stonewall entrance & sign on left. Turn in.*
FROM SOUTH: Reach Frankton turn right onto Highway 6, travel 11 km, stonewall entrance on right. Turn down drive - welcome!

Arrowtown/Queenstown
Guest House
Address: "Willowbrook", Malaghan Road, RD 1, Queenstown
Name: Roy & Tamaki Llewellyn
Telephone: (03) 442 1773 **Fax**: (03) 442 1773 **Mobile**: (025) 516 739
Email: wbrook@queenstown.co.nz
Beds: 1 King, 1 Queen, 4 Single (3 bedrooms), (cot available)
Bathroom: 2 Ensuite, 1 Private
Tariff: B&B (continental) Double $95-$105, Single $65-$75,
Credit Cards (VISA/AMEX/MC).
Nearest Town: Arrowtown 5 mins, Queenstown 15 mins.

Our little corner of paradise lies at the foot of Coronet Peak in the heart of the beautiful Wakatipu Basin. Behind us to the south are the Remarkables; to the east is Cardrona skifield; to the west, Queenstown, and from our front deck, the peaceful scene of hangliders and parapentes gently drifting downwards.

Our home is an old farmhouse, built in 1914 and now listed as a 'protected feature', which we have renovated and added to. Don't worry, the high ceilings, open fireplaces, T & G floors and wood panelling all remain. A couple of things they didn't have back in 1914 such as central heating and Sky TV, we've taken the liberty of adding. Guests' rooms all contain a bed (or beds) more comfortable than you would find in most hotels and are ensuite or have a private bathroom. The spacious lounge with its open fires and 'help-yourself' tea and coffee, is yours to enjoy, as is a large (usually sun-drenched) patio with BBQ. Adjoining the patio is a spa pool where you can luxuriate while gazing up at Coronet Peak.

Skiers will be in their element here. Coronet Peak is a mere 30 minute drive from our front door, the Remarkables 45 minutes and Cardrona 1 hour. Queenstown is only 15 minutes away and offers a dazzling array of shops, restaurants and nightlife not to mention a range of activities that will quench any adrenalin thirst, appeal to all ages and suit every budget. The quaint gold mining settlement of Arrowtown is just 4km up the road while for golfers, the greens of prestigious Millbrook Resort can be reached in 3 (minutes!)

I'm a Brit and my wife, Tamaki, is Japanese. We have both travelled extensively (including 13 years living in Tokyo) before deciding NZ was the most beautiful country we had seen. We have a young daughter, Jodie, and a nutcase dog. Please call if you can't find us - otherwise feel free to just 'arrive.'

Home Page: www.nz.com/Queenstown/Willowbrook

Directions: *We are on Malaghan Road (the 'back' road between Queenstown and Arrowtown). From Queenstown, take Gorge road out through Arthurs Point, make no turns and after about 15 minutes look for our sign on your right. From the north, turn right at Lake Hayes, go 5km and turn left into Malaghan Road. Millbrook Resort is on your left and we are 3km further along the road, also on the left.*

OTAGO

Arrowtown-Queenstown
Homestay, Bed & Breakfast
Address: Lake Hayes, No 1 RD, Queenstown
Name: Noelene and Ron Horrell.
"The Turret"
Telephone: (03) 442 1107
Fax: (03) 442 1160
Beds: 2 Queen, 1 Single
Bathroom: 1 Ensuite, 1 Guests share
Tariff: B&B (continental) Double $100-$120,
Single $55.
Visa/Mastercard
Nearest Town: Arrowtown 6 km. Queenstown 12 km.

Overlooking beautiful Lake Hayes. Behind a rose covered hedge. Be King and Queen of your own Castle. Enjoy luxury accommodation, with good old fashioned hospitality - at THE TURRET BED & BREAKFAST.
Take time to smell the flowers in our award winning garden. Cross swords on the pool table in the Games room, or put a log on the fire, and relax in our romantic little sitting room. Retreat to the upstairs turret and watch the sunset behind Coronet Peak. Wake to the aroma of home-made bread.
Heaven doesn't come much better than this!
Ron, Noelene and Burt the Cat. Enjoy guests, garden, sport and travel Close to cafes and restaurants, art galleries and museum (historic Arrowtown), wineries and golf (3 courses and Millbrook), jetboats and ski fields.

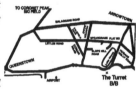

Queenstown
Homestay
Address: 'Colston House' 2 Boyes Crescent, Frankton, Queenstown
Name: Lois & Ivan Lindsay
Telephone: (03) 442 3162
Beds: 1 King, 1 Twin, 1 Single, all with hand basins.
Bathroom: 1 Private, 1 Guests share
Tariff: B&B (full) Double $80, Single $50, Children $25,
Dinner by arrangement $25. NZ B&B Vouchers accepted $10 surcharge
Nearest Town: Frankton 1 km, Queenstown 6 km

Our home, which is in a sunny situation overlooking Lake Wakatipu, has guest rooms with handbasins, electric blankets, bedside lamps, and heaters. Guests have exclusive use of bathroom with separate toilet, laundry facilities, and a sunny conservatory overlooking flower gardens. We are retired sheep and grain farmers with a family of six all married. We have been hosting tourists for a number of years and offer warm and friendly hospitality, taking a special pride in our meals which we share with our guests. (wine is served with dinners). Full cooked breakfast and tea or coffee on arrival if required. Shopping Centre, airport, coach-stop, golf, tennis, walking tracks, jet-boating, and bungy jumping coach all within 1 km of our home. Guests going to Milford or Doubtful Sound by coach picked up and returned to our gate at night. Bookings arranged for all tours. Personal transport provided from coaches, airport, and to and from Queenstown.
Directions: *Turn into McBride Street at Mobil service station, Frankton. Proceed to where road forks and our home "Colston House", with archway over drive will be seen.*

690

Queenstown
Homestay and Health Retreat
Address: Bush Creek Health Retreat, Bowen Street, Queenstown
Name: Ileen Mutch
Telephone: (03) 442 7260 **Fax**: (03) 442 7250
Beds: 1 Queen, 4 Single (4 bedrooms)
Bathroom: 2 Guests share
Tariff: B&B (per night) Double $100, Single $50, Children half price. (2 nights minimum) NZ B&B Vouchers accepted $10 surcharge
Nearest Town: Queenstown 1 km

- *3 acres of natural paradise only 10 minutes walk to the centre of town.*
- *One of the longest established Health Retreats in New Zealand.*
- *Nutritious organically grown and prepared food and pure natural spring water.*
- *Ileen Mutch, owner / operator, is an international recognised natural healing practitioner. One of the longest practising in this part of the globe.*
- *Bush Creek Health Retreat, is pet free and Illeen's family has left the nest.*
- *Deep Tissue Massage Therapy available.*
- *Revitalise your energies in harmony with the renowned old world garden, songs of native birds and the cascading waterfall.*
- *Rooms fully appointed with all the extras that provide the ultimate in comfort.*
- *Join the list of travellers that return again and again for their rejuvenating stay.*
- *Exceptional value.*
- *Bush Creek Health Retreat is signposted and easy to find, just follow the road to Coronet Ski Peak from Queenstown.*

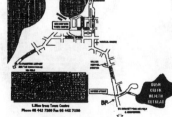

Queenstown
Country Guest Lodge &SC Accom.
Address: 'Trelawn Place', Arthurs Point,
Queenstown Postal: Box 117,Queenstown
Name: Nery Howard & Michael Clark
Telephone: (03) 442 9160 **Fax**: (03) 442 9160
Email: qvc@xtra.co.nz
Beds: 1 Twin, 2 Queen, 1 King (4 bedrooms)
Bathroom: 4 Ensuite
Tariff: B&B (full) Double $135-$165,
Single $110 (from October 1), Credit cards.
Nearest Town: Queenstown 4 km

Sited dramatically above the shotover river with gardens and lawns sweeping to the cliff edge, Trelawn Place is a superior country lodge only 4 km from busy Queenstown. Four comfortably appointed ensuite rooms furnished with country chintz and antiques. Guest sitting room with open fire, well stocked library, outdoor Jacuzzi / spa, shady vine covered verandas.

Generous cooked breakfast features home made and grown produce. If you are missing your pets, a cat and friendly corgis will make you feel at home. 48 hour cancellation policy.

FLY FISHING GUIDE. Michael, an Orvis Endorsed guide is available for trout fishing trips in the area. We can also help with bookings for all other local activities.

SELF CONTAINED COTTAGE. with its own fireside and roses framing the door, the 2 bedroom stone cottage is a honeymoon hideaway.

Home Page: http://nz.com/web nz/bbnz/trelawn.htm
Directions: *Take HW 6A into Queenstown, right at 2nd roundabout into Gorge Road, travel 4 km towards Arthurs Point. Trelawn Place sign posted beside gate on right.*

Trelawn Place
Bed & Breakfast

Queenstown
Homestay
Address: 'The Stable', 17 Brisbane Street, Queenstown
Name: Isobel & Gordon McIntyre
Telephone: (03) 442 9251 **Fax**: (03) 442 8293
Email: gimac@queenstown.co.nz
Beds: 1 Double, 1 King or Twin, 1 Single (3 bedrooms)
Bathroom: 1 Ensuite, 1 Private, 1 Guests share
Tariff: B&B (full) Double $120-$140, Single $60-$85,
Dinner $35 by prior arrangement, Credit cards.
Nearest Town: Queenstown town centre 3 minutes walk

A 125 year old stone stable, converted for guest accommodation, and listed by the New Zealand Historic Places Trust, shares a private courtyard with our home. The "Garden Room" and "Lake Room" are in the house, all providing convenience and comfort with fantastic lake and mountain views. Our home is in a quiet cul-de-sac and set in a garden abundant with rhododendrons and native birds. It is less than 100 metres from the beach where a small boat and canoe are available for guests' use. The famous Kelvin Heights Golf Course is close and tennis courts, bowling greens and ice skating rink are in the adjacent park. All tourist facilities, shops and restaurants are within easy walking distance, less than 5 minutes stroll on well lit footpaths.

All rooms are well heated with views of garden, lake or mountains. Tea and coffee making facilities are available at all times. Guests share our spacious living areas and make free use of our library and laundry.

A courtesy car is available to and from the bus depots. We can advise about and are booking agents for all sightseeing tours. Do allow an extra day or two for all the activities in the Queenstown region.

When it is convenient for us, and by prior arrangement, guests will enjoy 3 course dinners served with New Zealand wines. The choice includes lamb, venison, fresh fish and chicken. Breakfast is often served in the courtyard. No smoking indoors.

Your hosts, with a farming background, have bred Welsh ponies and now enjoy weaving, cooking, sailing, gardening and outdoors. We enjoy meeting people and have travelled extensively overseas.

Directions: *Follow State Highway 6a (Frankton Road) to where it veers right at the Millenium Hotel. Continue straight ahead. Brisbane Street ("no exit") is 2nd on left. Phone if necessary.*

Queenstown
Guest House
Address: Melbourne Guest House,
35 Melbourne St., Queenstown
Name: Ann and Allister Cowan
Telephone: (03) 442 8431
Fax: (03) 442 7466
Email: melbourne@xtra.co.nz
Beds: 33 Rooms
Bathroom: Private & Guests share
Tariff: B&B (full) Double/Twin $78, Single $49.50
Private Facility Double/Twin $128,
Single $106. NZ B&B Vouchers accepted
Nearest Town: Queenstown 300 m

The Melbourne Guest House has long been one of Queenstown's most popular Bed & Breakfasts. It is situated on Melbourne St in a quiet location set amongst beautiful rose gardens and only 3 minutes walk to the town centre. facilities are a spa pool, continental buffet and full menu breakfast available in the dining room. Rooms are available with basin but share bathroom or for those who prefer a touch of luxury and elegance, their own bathroom. Full kitchen facilities and family rooms are available for those who may wish to cook their own meals. Telephone and in house video available in all facility rooms. All sightseeing, ski buses or airport shuttle transport pick up at the gate. We know your stay with us will be enjoyable so we look forward to your arrival.
Home Page: http//nz.com/QueenstownMelbourneMotorLodge

Queenstown
Homestay
Address: 'Remarkable View',
22 Brecon Street, Queenstown
Name: Shirley Jackson
Telephone: (03) 442 9542
Beds: 1 Double, 2 Single (2 bedrooms)
Bathroom: 1 Family share
Tariff: B&B (full) Double $70,
Single $40, School age children half price.
Dinner $20.
Nearest Town: Queenstown - 3 minute stroll to Mall

Our home overlooks the town centre and has a fantastic view of the surrounding area, especially the rugged mountain range - "The Remarkables". Although so close to the centre of a very popular tourist resort we can offer a comfortable and peaceful stay. We offer 2 guest rooms, one with 2 single beds, the other with a double bed. All have electric blankets, warm bedding and are very comfortable. Bathroom facilities shared with hosts. Smokers welcome. If you don't agree not for you.
Breakfast either continental or cooked - your choice. We offer a nourishing 3 course dinner with wine. Being a tourist town, Queenstown has seven day shopping and many fine restaurants catering for most tastes. Plenty to do both summer and winter. "Sooty Cat" will be aloof or friendly as you like it.
Directions: *Look for the hill with the gondola's, find the street that takes you there. We are the black house, 2nd on the left.*

Queenstown
Self-contained Accommodation
Address: 'Braemar House',
56 Panorama Terrace, Queenstown
Name: Ann & Duncan Wilson
Telephone: (03) 442 7385
Fax: (03) 442 4385
Beds: 1 Double, 1 Single
+ 2 divans in lounge (1 bedroom)
Bathroom: 1 Private
Tariff: B&B (continental - plus) Double $85,
Single $60, Children half price, (enquire other options when booking).
Nearest Town: Queenstown 1.5km from town centre

The apartment on the middle floor of our home is self-contained and private if guests want it that way, but our personal hospitality is always available.

"Braemar House", is situated on a steep hill section but with easy access from roadways, provides magnificent panoramic views of lake and mountains, and as guests will realise, our interest include gardening with many varieties of native trees and plants. Other activities which could interest visitors are tramping (hill walking), skiing, golf, photography and local history.

For travellers with their own transport, we have off-street parking, but a courtesy car is available for others. Transport and Guiding services are also available to out-of-town locations.

We have travelled extensively at home and overseas, and believe we fully understand the requirements of visitors to Queenstown.

Directions: *Turn up Suburb St off Frankton Rd, then first right into Panorama Tce.*

Queenstown
Homestay
Address: 8 Sunset Lane,
Larchwood Heights, Queenstown
Name: Robin & Alwyn Rice
Telephone: (03) 442 6567
Beds: 1 Double, 2 Single (2 bedrooms)
Bathroom: 1 Guests share
Tariff: B&B (full) Double $90, Single $60
Nearest Town: Queenstown 1.5km from town centre

After spending 30 years in business in Invercargill, we moved to Queenstown and built our home in a quiet cul-de-sac with panoramic views of Lake Wakatipu and the surrounding mountains.

Our guest rooms are spacious and comfortable, with electric blankets, TV and private bathroom, as we take just one couple, or a party travelling together.

You can enjoy the magnificent scenery from the deck overlooking the lake, or relax in our private and sunny garden.

We have travelled extensively in new Zealand and overseas, and our interests include gardening, golf and skiing.

Directions: *Travelling along Frankton Road towards Queenstown, turn right into Hensman Road, 2nd road on left is Sunset Lane, we are last house on left, or phone if necessary.*

OTAGO

Queenstown
Homestay /Self-contained Accom
Address: 'Birchall House',118 Panorama Terrace,
Larchwood Heights, Queenstown
Name: Joan & John Blomfield
Telephone: (03) 442 9985 allow at least 10 rings.
Fax: (03) 442 9980 **Mobile**: by call diversion.
Beds: 1 Double, 2 Single (2 bedrooms)
Bathroom: 1 Private
Tariff: B&B (continental) Double $95, Single $70 (other options available).
NZ B&B Vouchers accepted $20 surcharge

We welcome you to our new home in Queenstown which is within walking distance of town centre, and from where we enjoy magnificent 200 degree views of Lake Wakatipu and surrounding mountains. Our guest accommodation, is completely self-contained, has the same views, separate entrance, is private, spacious, smoke free and centrally heated. Electric blankets on all beds. A continental or full breakfast is available and guests are very welcome to share our table. Before moving to Queenstown, we farmed sheep, cattle and deer in Western Southland where we were also active members of the Western Southland Farm Hosting Group. On a recent visit to U.K. and Europe we enjoyed the B&B experience immensely and feel confident we can make your stay a pleasant one. Our interests include most sports but golf in particular, together with gardening and handcrafts (embroidery, patchwork etc.). Off-street parking is available and courtesy transport to / from terminals is provided. Bookings can be arranged for all tours.
Directions: *From Frankton Road, turn up Suburb Street, then first right into Panorama Terrace. Access via Sunset Lane.*
Home Page: http://nz.com/Queenstown/Birchall.House

Queenstown
Homestay and Garden Room
Address: Grant Road, 1 R.D., Queenstown
Name: Pat & Ron Collins
Telephone: (03) 442 3801
Beds: 2 Queen, 2 Single (2 bedrooms)
Bathroom: 1 Ensuite, 1 Guests share
Tariff: B&B (full) Double $75, Single $50.
Garden Room $85.
Credit cards. NZ B&B Vouchers accepted
Nearest Town: Queenstown 10 mins

Pat & Ron offer warm relaxed Kiwi hospitality in a rural environment with lovely mountain views. Our new sunny home with separate guest wing is surrounded by lovely gardens. Bathroom with bath and shower. Rooms with Woolrests, electric blankets, heaters. Laundry facilities no charge. Ron works in the tourist industry and Pat plays golf, gardens and walks Sam, our outside Golden Labrador. BJ the cat prefers to lie in the sun. Having travelled extensively it's fun to swap travellers tales. "Home away from home"
GARDEN ROOM: New warm bedsit. 1 Queen with ensuite, TV, Regrigerator, Microwave, BBQ, breakfast hamper provided or join us at our table.
Looking forward to meeting you.
Directions: *1 km before Frankton on SH 6. Name on mailbox. Go down Grants Road, house through farm gate on left.*

Queenstown
Homestay
Address: 8B Birse Street, Frankton, Queenstown
Name: Shirley & Pat Paulin
Telephone: (03) 442 3387
Beds: 1 Double, 2 Singles (2 bedrooms)
Bathroom: 1 guests share
Tariff: B&B (full) Double $90, Single $50, Children $25, Dinner $25 per person. NZ B&B Vouchers accepted $10 surcharge
Nearest Town: Queenstown 6km

Welcome to "Paulin Place" where you are assured of superior hospitality. Coffee, tea and a gourmet surprise await you on arrival.
Our home is situated in sunny Frankton, 6km from the centre of Queenstown in a picturesque garden with views of Lake Wakatipu and the Remarkable Mountains. Courtesy transport provided if required.
Pat grew up in the district, so is conversant with history of the Wakatipu Basin. Our interests are gardening, walking, fishing, gold mining, reading, cooking, embroidery (free tuition, and an opportunity to learn new techniques), wine making, entertaining and meeting people.
Explore the secret wonders of our district by outings arranged with you hosts.
Directions: *Please phone for reservations and directions.*

Queenstown
Homestay/B&B
Address: BJ's Place, 36 Lochy Rd, Fernhill, Queenstown
Name: Berit & John Brown
Telephone: (03) 442 8348 **Fax**: (03) 442 8348
Beds: 1 Double, 3 Single (2 bedrooms)
Bathroom: 1 Guests share
Tariff: B&B (continental) Double $95, Single $50, Children under 12 half price, Dinner $30. Credit cards. NZ B&B Vouchers accepted $20 surcharge
Nearest Town: Queenstown 5 min

Welcome to BJ's Place where you are assured of warm and friendly hospitality - A home away from home - with peaceful and relaxed atmosphere in our new modern and spacious home overlooking Lake Wakatipu - Cecil Peak and the Remarkables.
We are an informal semi-retired couple of English / Norwegian origin with 3 children spread around the country and we love meeting people from all walks of life.
Our 2 guestrooms on the lower floor are warm, private and spacious 1 room with a double and a single bed the other with 2 single beds and guests share bathroom facilities.
Continental breakfast with fresh fruit, homemade muesli, yoghurt etc or cooked if you prefer with plenty of brewed coffee or tea.
Make Queenstown your destination which offers a wealth of activities for all ages all the year round.
We are "smokefree".
Directions: *Please phone for direction.*

697

Queenstown
B & B
Address: 15 Adelaide Street, Queenstown
Name: Adelaide Guesthouse - A "Home Away From Home"
Telephone: (03) 442 6207 (Int. 0064-3-442 6297)
Fax: (03) 442-6207 **Mobile**: (025) 220 7696
Beds: 2 King, 2 Double, 2 Twin, 4 Single (6 bedrooms)
Bathroom: 1 Ensuite, 3 Guests share
Tariff: B&B (continental) King with ensuite $110, Single $47.50-$59.50, Twin/Double/King $69.50-$95.00. Creditc cards Visa/Mastercard. NZ B&B Vouchers accepted surcharge may apply.
Nearest Town: 5 min. easy walk to Queenstown centre.

Adelaide Bed & Breakfast is perfectly situated in a quiet peaceful neighbourhood 50 metres from the shores of beautiful Lake Wakatipu, and yet a short scenic walk from central Queenstown.
The sundecks and spacious lounge, and most of our rooms enjoy breathtaking views of the 'Remarkables Mountain Range' and Lake Wakatipu.
Our rooms are heated and beds have duvets, electric blankets etc.
We enjoy hosting and like to ensure your stay in Queenstown is a memorable one.
In summer relax on the sundecks and enjoy the long twilight evenings and colourful sunsets.
In winter an open fire or woodburner warms the lounge which has panoramic views. Queenstown boasts a wide range of restaurants and is central to the skifields.
Sightseeing information and bookings for rafting, jetboating, Milford and Doubtful Sounds excursions etc are our pleasure. Laundry facilities available. Courtesy coach from airport and bus terminals.
Directions: *Follow SH 6 (Frankton Road) turn left at the Millennium Hotel into Adelaide Street.*

"NUMBER TWELVE"

Queenstown

Bed & Breakfast, Self-contained
Address: 'Number Twelve', 12 Brisbane St, Queenstown
Name: Barbara & Murray Hercus
Telephone: (03) 442 9511 **Fax**: (03) 442-9755
Email: hercusbb@queenstown.co.nz
Beds: 1 Studio King or Twin, 1 Room King or Twin (2 Bedrooms)
Bathroom: 1 Ensuite, 1 Private
Tariff: B&B (continental) Double $100, Single $60, Dinner by arrangement $35.
Credit Cards: Visa/Mastercard. NZ B&B Vouchers accepted $20 surcharge per night
Nearest Town: We are only a 3 minute walk to town centre,

We would like you to come and share our quiet convenient home situated in a no exit street. Our home has lake and mountain views. A warm, centrally heated home, all bedrooms have TV and tea / coffee making facilities. Laundry facilities available. We have a solar heated swimming pool (Nov - March), this plus sundeck and BBQ for your use. While we serve a continental breakfast, a cooked breakfast can be provided at a small additional charge. There are several walking routes to the town centre - a short one through the Botanical gardens or via the Lake shore if you would like a longer stroll. Once settled with us you will seldom need to use your car.

We have both travelled extensively, our interests include classical / choral music. Barbara had a nursing / social work career, Murray a retired chartered accountant. Our Burmese cat will join us in welcoming you to our home. We will be happy to assist you when planning your local activities.

Directions: *Highway 6A into Queenstown becomes Frankton Road. Do not veer right into Stanley Street at the Millenium Hotel corner, carry on straight ahead. Brisbane Street is the second street on your left, a sharp left turn and we are on the left side. Our sign is "Number Twelve".*

Queenstown
Guest House
Address: 27 Lomond Crescent,
P O Box 851, Queenstown
Name: 'Scallywags' Guest House
Telephone: (03) 442 7083
Fax: (03) 442 5885
Beds: 3 Double, 3 Twin (6 bedrooms)
Bathroom: 2 Guests share
Tariff: (Bed only-breakfast available on request)

Double $50, Twin $25pp, Children under 5 years free.
Nearest Town: Queenstown 700 metres

A unique New Zealand home for you to share. We are a "B&B with no B". However, bring your own food and use the excellent kitchen and great bbq area. Tea, coffee and milk is complimentary. Linen, towels, duvets and electric blankets are on all beds. Share bathroom facilities.

Famously Fantastic views - 180 degrees panorama - sunrise to sunset - lake mountains, valleys.

The ambience is casual and informal. Emjoy world class conversation. The house is situated adjacent to a bush reserve with native birdlife and song abundant. A peaceful haven just 10 minutes pleasant walk to village centre.

Please don't just view from the road. You are invited to come up and inspect the rooms and views etc.

Resident host/owner offers: personal service, visitor information, local knowledge, free pick-up, smoke free. Reservations recommended.

Service   Ambience   Value

Queenstown
Guest Units B&B
Address: 'Highview', 17 Wakatipu Heights, Queenstown
Name: Ann & Mike Walther
Telephone: (03) 442 9414
Fax: (03) 442 9414
Mobile: (021) 702 705
Beds: 2 Queen, 2 Single (3 bedrooms)
Bathroom: 3 Ensuite
Tariff: B&B (continental) Double $55pp, Single $76, Share Triple $42pp.
NZ B&B Vouchers accepted Surcharge $39
Nearest Town: Town centre 10 minutes walk or $5 taxi.

Imagine! Floor to ceiling glass with unobstructed panoramic lake and mountain views. The sound of birds. The convenience of your ensuite bathroom. Safe parking, walk to Queenstowns shops including fifty restaurants. Be uplifted for a jet boat safari, Milford, Doubtful Sounds or enjoy the view, alpine air and peaceful environment.

Welcome to our home, 100 metres above Lake Wakatipu on the side of Queenstown Hill. Ann, a nurse and Mike, a local government officer home hosted for five years prior to building these especially designed, warm private guests units. Each with separate entrance, ensuite bathroom, TV and tea/coffee facilities. Steps to the units which are secluded among rhododendrons and conifers allow spectacular views of Lake Wakatipu, golf course, yacht club and Remarkable Mountains.

Sumptuous breakfast included.

Directions: *Turn up Suburb Street off Frankton Road. Then first right into Panorama Terrace, second left into Wakatipu Heights.*
"A warm welcome awaits you"

Queenstown

Bed & Breakfast
Address: 'Brecman Lodge', 15 Man Street
Name: Pat & Kevin MacDonell
Telephone: (03) 442 8908 **Fax**: (03) 442 8904
Beds: 1 Double, 5 Single (3 Bedrooms)
Bathroom: 1 Guests share, 1 Family share
Tariff: B&B (continental) Double $85, Single $60. Credit Cards. NZ B&B
Vouchers accepted $15 surcharge
Nearest Town: Queenstown, 2 minutes walk from the centre of town

Brecman Lodge is homestyle NZ hospitality at its best. Brecman Lodge is situated on the corner of Brecon and Man Streets, opposite the top of the Brecon Street steps, just above Queenstown's town centre.

Brecman Lodge is friendly, warm and comfortable with single, twin and family accommodation. Upstairs is a bathroom and two bedrooms; one room has a double bed and the other has two single beds. Downstairs consists of guest lounge, bedroom with two single beds and a guest share bathroom. The warm comfortable guest lounge has a television and a wonderful view of the Queenstown's township, Lake Wakatipu, Walter Peak and The Remarkables. A continental breakfast is served in the lounge. From Brecman Lodge guests have easy walking access to the town centre, Lake Wakatipu and the Gondola. Queenstown's centre has a wide range of quality tourist shops, many restaurants and sporting and adventure opportunities all year round. There is ample and easy off street parking.

Do come and stay I'm sure you'll love it.

Queenstown

Homestay
Address: 'Terrace View' 8 MacKinnon Terrace,
Sunshine Bay, Queenstown
Name: Marjorie & Eddie Hutton
Telephone: (03) 442 6751 **Fax**: (03) 442 6787
Beds: 1 King, 1 Twin, 1 Single, (3 bedrooms)
Bathroom: 1 Private, 1 Guests share, Separate toilet
Tariff: B&B (full) Double $85-$90, Single $50, (other options available). Credit
cards (Visa/MC) NZ B&B Vouchers accepted $10 surcharge
Nearest Town: Queenstown 3km town centre

*Warm friendly hospitality is assured at "Terrace View". Our home is situated in
terraced gardens with mountain and lake views. Before moving to Queenstown we
farmed sheep and cattle in Southland. Our main interests now are gardening,
walking, fishing, meeting and making friends of people here in NZ and from around
the world. Guest rooms open onto patio and garden. Underfloor heating and electric
blankets on all beds. Log fire heated lounge and TV room, laundry. Complimentary
tea / coffee available at all times. Guests are invited to join us for supper in the evening.
Breakfast of your choice is served at your requested time. It is wise to book but not
essential.*
Directions: *5 minutes drive from Queenstown. Turn left into MacKinnon Terrace (No
exit) off Fernhill Road (3rd turn left past Fernhill Food centre) or phone for directions.
Courtesy transport to and from Airport and coaches.*

Queenstown

Homestay
Address: 4 Panorama Tce,
Queenstown
Name: Elsie & Pat Monaghan
Telephone: (03) 442 8690
Fax: (03) 442 8620
Mobile: 025-2231 880
Beds: 1 Queen (1 bedroom)
Bathroom: 1 Ensuite
Tariff: B&B (full) Double $90, Single $70.
NZ B&B Vouchers accepted $20 surcharge
Nearest Town: Queenstown 5 minute walk

*Our house is situated close to town with panoramic views of the mountains and Lake
Wakatipu. Off-street parking. Our spacious guest room is private with a separate
entrance and garden patio. It has a table for letter writing, heater, radio, television,
fridge, and tea, coffee and biscuits supplied; Queen bed with electric blanket and you
have your own bathroom, shower and toilet. Breakfast at the time that suits you.
Queenstown has an excellent variety of restaurants. Our interests include sport, music,
pottery, gardening, travelling and meeting people. We will enjoy your company but
respect your privacy. We can meet you at the airport or bus depot if required.*
Directions: *Turn right up Suburb St. off Frankton Road which is the main road into
Queenstown. The first right into Panorama Tce to No.4.*

Relax – Don't try to drive too far in one day.

Queenstown Central
A Small Boutique Hotel

Queenstown House
NEW ZEALAND

Address: 69 Hallenstein St, Queenstown
Name: Queenstown House
Telephone: (03) 442 9043 **Fax**: (03) 442-8755
Mobile: (025) 324 146
Beds: 8 King (8 bedrooms)
Bathroom: 8 Ensuite
Tariff: B&B (special) Double $165-$185, Single $145-$165.
Dinner by arrangement. Credit cards (VISA/BC/MC/AMEX).
NZ B&B Vouchers accepted 2 vouchers required
Nearest Town: Queenstown - 300 metres

In 1994 Louise Kiely transformed one of Queenstown's oldest guest houses into what is now firmly established as the "best small B&B Hotel" in town. The 8 rooms all have private bathrooms, king size beds, crisp white linen, European duvets and plenty of plump pillows. Each room is individually decorated and has a "Town and Country" elegance. The elevated position allows every room magnificent lake and mountain views. Off-street parking is available with the town centre only 300 metres away. Breakfast is included and is served in our private lake view dining room. It is hearty and wholesome, using the best local seasonal foods served with aromatic freshly brewed coffee. A selection of beverages are available all day long in the guests' kitchenette. Dinner is on request. Between 6.00 and 7.00pm each evening complimentary New Zealand wine and cheese is served in the cosy fireside sitting room or in the fragrant courtyard, depending on the season. Television, hairdryers and heating are in all rooms. Laundry, valet service and baggage storage is available. Louise and her staff know the surrounding area very well and will be happy to assist with booking the many excursions offered. We are "smoke free". A cancellation fee will apply - 25% if made within thirty days of arrival. Full tariff is payable if cancellation is made within 24 hours of arrival date.

Queenstown
Self-contained Accommodation
Address: "Anna's Cottage",
67 Thompson Street,
Queenstown
Name: Myrna & Ken Sangster
Telephone: (03) 442 8994 or 442 8881
Beds: 1 Queen,
1 divan double in living room (1 bedroom)
Bathroom: 1 Private
Tariff: Double $85, Single $50, $15 extra per person
Breakfast available on request $10 extra.
Nearest Town: Queenstown 5minute walk.

Enjoy the peaceful garden setting and mountain views at Anna's Cottage. Full kitchen facilities and living room combined. Tastefully decorated throughout the bedroom is furnished with Sheridan linen. Only a few mins from the centre of Queenstown. Private drive and parking at cottage.
Airport transfers by arrangement.

There are some good tips for easier travel on page 7

OTAGO

Queenstown
B&B
Address: "Turner Lodge",
Cnr Turner St. & Gorge Rd, Queenstown
Name: Hazel Seeto
Telephone: (03) 442 9432
Fax: (03) 442 9409
Beds: 1 Double,
2 Single (2 bedrooms)
Bathroom: 2 Ensuites.
Tariff: B&B (full) Double $100,
Single $65, Credit Cards (VISA/BC/MC).
Nearest Town: Queenstown 3 min walk

I offer friendly hospitality in a warm, comfortable home. It is 3 minutes walk to central Queenstown - you don't have to climb any hills but there is still a lovely view. On-site parking and laundry facilities are available. Each room has its own TV and tea / coffee making facilities. The double room has an ensuite with bath, shower box, vanity and toilet.
I serve a full menu breakfast which is available from 6-9am.
I am happy to help you organise your activities and make local reservations for you. Seasonal Rates available.

Queenstown
B&B
Address: Box 243, Queenstown
Name: Sierra Vista Bed & Breakfast'
Telephone: (03) 442 8301
Fax: (03) 442 8301
Mobile: (025) 383 983
Beds: 2 Queen, (2 bedrooms)
Bathroom: 2 Ensuite
Tariff: B&B (full) Double $100.
Nearest Town: 5 minute lakeside walk to Queenstown centre.

Sierra Vista has sensational lake and mountain views from a sunny elevated site. Your host, Leon Udy is a well travelled New Zealander with a lifetime experience in hospitality - travel guide, ski lodge operator, restaurateur .... Your welcome will be total and comprehensive activity assistance is offered. Airport transfers without charge by arrangement. Please use the mobile phone number above for reservation and for check-in arrangements.
Sierra Vista is smoke free.

One of the differences between staying at a hotel and a B&B
is that you don't hug the hotel staff when you leave.

Queenstown
B&B+Self-contained Accom.
Address: 10 Wakatipu Heights,
Queenstown
Name: Ruth & Owen Campbell
Telephone: (03) 442 9190
Fax: (03) 442 4404
Beds: 1 Queen, 1 Double, 3 Single (3 bedrooms)
Bathroom: 1 Private, 1 Guests share
Tariff: B&B (continental) Double $100-$120, Single $60-$70. Generous family rates.
Credit Cards. NZ B&B Vouchers accepted $20 surcharge on self contained units.
Nearest Town: Queenstown - 10 minutes walk

As we have 2 girls at school, children are welcome in our home. Our level section has covered, off street parking and playground. We can also provide child care. Tea, coffee and herbal teas are complimentary. Our tranquil home with one cat is in a quiet garden setting and has outstanding views over Lake Wakatipu and Queenstown. Owen and I have a good knowledge of the area. Our fully self contained 2 bedroom cottage garden unit with BBQ, laundry etc has proven immensely popular with guests - especially those with children! This allows you complete privacy or to mix with us as you wish. A super king or twin bedroom with private bathroom is in the house. There are no stairs as all guest facilities are on ground level. Enjoy a generous continental breakfast including fresh baked bread and real coffee at your leisure. Cooked breakfast $5 per person extra. Guest pick-up is available. We request no smoking inside please. Guests say "Excellent value for money".

Queenstown
Boutique Hotel

Chalet Queenstown
Bed & Breakfast

Address: 1 Dublin St,
Queenstown
Name: Chalet Queenstownn"
Telephone: (03) 442 7117
or (03) 441 8821
Fax: (03) 442 7508
Mobile: (025) 330 834
Beds: 6 King/Queen, 14 Single (6 bedrooms)
Bathroom: 6 Ensuite
Tariff: B&B (continental) Single Standard $145,
Double Standard $165,
Single Superior $165,Double Superior $185. Family $225.
NZ B&B Vouchers accepted 1 May-30 September
Nearest Town: Queenstown - 500m to town centre

Chalet Queenstown has been selected by "Superior Inns of NZ" for its commitment to providing quality accommodation, hearty breakfasts and gracious hospitality for the discerning traveller.
Chalet Queenstown offers 6 rooms, all with private ensuite, and decorated in a town & country elegance , plenty of pillows, feather duvets and fresh flowers to create a feeling of luxury. The elevated position gives each room magnificent lake and mountain views. Enjoy at your leisure a delicious cooked breakfast also home-made cereals, fresh seasonal fruits, croissants, muffins, yoghurt, home-made preserves, juice and freshly brewed tea or coffee. Complimentary drinks are available in the lounge, or courtyard garden from 6/7pm each evening.
We are situated in a very sunny and peaceful location only 400 yards easy walk to the town centre.

705

Fernhill, Queenstown
B&B+Self-contained Suite
Address: 107 Wynyard Crescent,
Fernhill, Queenstown
Name: "Haus Helga"
(Ed & Helga Coolman)
Telephone: (03) 442 6077
Fax: (03) 442 4957
Email: haushelga@xtra.co.nz
Beds: 2 King/Queen, 1 Double, 2 Single (3 bedrooms)
Bathroom: 3 Ensuite, 1 with Spa Tub, all with hair dryers
Tariff: B&B (special) Rooms $119 to $219. Credit Cards
(MC/Visa/BC) NZ B&B Vouchers accepted $30 Surcharge
Nearest Town: Queenstown 3km, 5 minutes

Haus Helga

Haus Helga overlooks Lake Wakatipu and the Remarkables Mountains and provides the "best view in all of New Zealand!" Our luxurious home has extra large tastefully furnished guest rooms, each with a private deck or terrace. The self-contained suite includes a large kitchen, dining, living room. We offer a lounge with TV and a games room with an octagon bumper pool table for our guests enjoyment. We can provide honeymoon specials, family plans, tour bookings and courtesy transport. We are now in our third year of operation and we feel truly fortunate to have made so many great new friends, our wonderful guests. They have been so kind in their comments: "Without a doubt, the Ritz-Carlton of B&B's." "Best bed, best views, wonderful hospitality." "I won't forget your great breakfast, Helga." "Perfect hosts, perfect breakfast, perfect accommodation." Helga speaks fluent German and some Japanese. We are smoke-free inside.
Directions: *Please call for reservations and directions.*
Home Page: http://nz.com/webnz/bbnz/helga.htm

Queenstown
Homestay
Address: "Windsor Heights"
5 Windsor Place, Queenstown
Name: Diane & Bill Forsyth
Telephone: (03) 442 5949
and 0800 27 16 17
Fax: (03) 441 8989
Email: bill&diane@xtra.co.nz
Beds: 2 Queen, 1 Single (3 bedrooms)
Bathroom: 1 Guests share, 1 ensuite.
Tariff: B&B (full) Double $95/$110, Single $70.
Children under 12 half price.
Credit Cards (VISA/MC).
Nearest Town: Queenstown - 10 minutes walk to town centre

Our new home sits high above the township of Queenstown, offering what can only be described as breathtaking views of mountains and lake. The sheltered courtyard provides a wonderful relaxed outdoor living style, complete with gas barbecue and large spa pool. On warm summer evenings, this area is a real favourite, before moving to the lounge and watching fabulous sunsets across the lake. A patio breakfast overlooking a clear blue lake surrounded by spectacular mountains, is an experience not easily forgotten. If walking is your pleasure, we have the Queenstown Hill track virtually on our back doorstep. Courtesy car is available to meet guests, and we will gladly help arrange your Queenstown itinerary. Ours is a non-smoking environment.
Home Page: http://www.powerup.com.au/~forsyth/billdi/index.htm

706

Queenstown
Guest House
Address: 10 Isle St., Queenstown
Name: The Dairy Guesthouse"
Telephone: (03) 442 5164
Freephone: 0800 333 393
Fax: (03) 442 5164
Mobile: (025) 990 840
Email: TheDairy@xtra.co.nz
Beds: 4 Queen, 6 Single, 3 King (7 bedrooms)
Bathroom: 7 Ensuite
Tariff: B&B (full) Double/Twin $140-$180, Single $140,
Dinner by request. Credit Cards.
Nearest Town: Queenstown (2 minute walk)

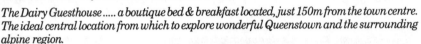

The Dairy Guesthouse ..... a boutique bed & breakfast located, just 150m from the town centre. The ideal central location from which to explore wonderful Queenstown and the surrounding alpine region.

This very special place....has six private rooms all with en-suite, lounge room with a cosy fire, ski storage and off street parking. A relaxing retreat. The Dairy.... once a 1930's general store, now lovingly restored offers the intimate appeal of a traditional setting, where a full breakfast served each morning ensures a great start to the day.

The Dairy Guesthouse....surrounded by views of the stunning Remarkables mountain range, Coronet Peak and tranquil Queenstown Bay. Conveniently situated below the Skyline Gondola, on the corner of Brecon and Isle Streets.

Reservations are recommended. Your hosts Brian and Sarah welcome you.
Home Page: Please e-mail us for website

Queenstown
Guest Lodge+S.C. Accommodation
Address: "Camelot Lodge"
24 McMillan Rd.,
Arthurs Point, Queenstown
Name: George & Liz McLeod
Telephone: (03) 442 5299
Fax: (03) 442 5299
Mobile: (025) 313 293
Beds: 1 Queen, 3 Single (3 bedrooms)
Bathroom: 2 Ensuite, 1 Guests share

Tariff: B&B (continental) Double $85, Double ensuite $95, Single $60, Also 3 Bedroom Self-contained Apartment from $100 a night all inclusive (sleeps 6). Ring for further details. Credit Cards (VISA/MC). NZ B&B Vouchers accepted $20 surcharge.
Nearest Town: Queenstown 4km

A warm welcome awaits you at Camelot Lodge, situated at historic Arthurs Point, with splendid rural views over the Shotover River towards Coronet Peak. Down some steps, our lovely home is spacious and sunny, with attractive guest rooms. The large lounge opens onto generous sundecks: a perfect spot to relax. A three bedroom fully self-contained holiday apartment is also available - sleeps six. We have lived and worked extensively overseas and have been involved with tourism / hospitality for 10 years. We also have a detailed knowledge of this region. Camelot Lodge is a short drive from Queenstown, and 2km from the Coronet Peak ski area turnoff. In winter George works as a professional ski instructor. Summers in this rural setting are delightful. Activities include golf, walking, riding and jet boating / rafting on the famous Shotover River. Complimentary tea / coffee available. No smoking indoors please. We look forward to making your stay with us memorable.
Directions: *Please ring for directions.*

707

Queenstown
Bed & Breakfast
Address: 3 Hobart Street
Queenstown
Name: Jenny James and Ed Askew
Telephone: (03) 442 5214
Fax: (03) 442 5214
Mobile: (025) 966 679
Beds: 1 King, 1 Queen,
2 Single (2 Bedrooms)
Bathroom: Guest Share
Tariff: B&B (full) Double $110, Single $60
Nearest Town: Queenstown

Ed and Jenny invite you to stay in their lovingly restored 70 year old villa, situated in a quiet street less than 500 metres to town. Stroll into town along the lakes edge or through the Queenstown Gardens. Our home is comfortably furnished with a hint of old world charm. Two stylishly appointed double bedrooms share a magnificent large bathroom with shower and bath. There is a separate toilet. Relax in an elegant private guest lounge with complimentary tea, coffee and port. We have a keen interest in all outdoor activities, Ed from a strong yachting background, having been involved in both Americas Cup and Whitbread around The World yacht race, with many a tale to tell. Enjoy a leisurely breakfast with the best of seasonal fruit breads and cereals, or a cooked breakfast if you prefer.
Television and video available in guest lounge.
We are smoke free.

Queenstown
Self-contained Accommodation
Address: LARCHWOOD HOUSE
6 Sunset Lane,
Larchwood Heights, Queenstown
Name: Roy & Gudrun Somerville
Telephone: (03) 442 7446
Fax: (03) 442 7446
Email: roy.somerville@xtra.co.nz
Beds: 1 King, 2 Single (2 bedrooms)
Bathroom: 2 Ensuite
Tariff: Roomrate $150, Credit Cards (VISA/MC).
NZ B&B Vouchers accepted $20 surcharge May & June.
Nearest Town: Queenstown - walking distance

Beautifully located self catering accommodation within walking distance of Queenstown. Larchwood House offers a very high standard of comfortable self catering accommodation. An extensive open plan living and dining area with fully equipped kitchen on the upper floor. Downstairs there are two independent double bedrooms each with its own ensuite bathroom and toilet.
Facilities include underfloor heating, full laundry and drying room for outdoor equipment. All linen is available.
The house is set in its own gardens and all rooms enjoy panoramic views of the lake and mountains. Car parking is provided.
We are just minutes from the airport and the centre of Queenstown.
Access from Frankton is via Hensman Road or from Queenstown via Suburb Street and Panorama Terrace. Breakfast provisions will be provided with advance bookings.
Home Page: http://nz.com/Queenstown/Larchwood

Queenstown
Bed & Breakfast
Address: PO Box 623, Atley Road,
Arthurs Point, Queenstown
Name: Kerry and Graeme Hastie,
Hollyhock Inn
Telephone: (03) 441 8037
Fax: (03) 441 8058
Email: hollyhock@queenstown.co.nz
Beds: 3 Queen, 2 Single (3 bedrooms)
Bathroom: 3 Ensuite
Tariff: B&B (special) Double $185, Single $155,
Not suitable for children, Credit Cards.
Nearest Town: Queenstown 6km

Hollyhock Inn is set in one acre of landscaped gardens on the bank of the Shotover River. Whilst we are only 5 minutes drive (6km) from Queenstown the atmosphere is alpine rural with unobstructed mountain vistas, views of Coronet Peak and the famous Shotover River. The three purpose built guest rooms offer complete comfort. All are large and elegantly decorated with ensuites and private balconies Although the atmosphere is alpine rurual within walking distance there are restaurants, the Shotover Jet, riding stables and the Coronet Peak Ski Field turn-off. Graeme and I enjoy meeting travellers and will happily advise you on visitors information and arrange any sightseeing bookings. We have laundry facilities available and are a smoke free environment. We have one pet cat. Forward bookings are essential.
Home Page: http://www.sp.net.nz/holly.htm.

Queenstown
Historic Cottage, B&B or Self Contained
Address: "Pear Tree Cottage", Rapid #51,
Mountain View Rd, Dalefield, Queenstown
Name: Terry & Erina McLean
Telephone: (03) 442 9340 **Fax**: (03) 442 9349
Email: info@peartree.co.nz
Mobile: (025) 370 935
Beds: 1 Queen, 1 Double, 1 Single (2 bedrooms)
Bathroom: 1 Guests share
Tariff: B&B (special/full) Double $125, Single $95, Dinner from $45,
Children negotiable. Credit Cards (A/X,M/C/VISA)
NZ B&B Vouchers accepted by negotiation
Nearest Town: Queenstown 12 mins

Halfway between Queenstown and Arrowtown, directly below Coronet Peak ski field, our cosy historic cottage (circa 1870's) was virtually derelict, now lovingly restored and crammed with rural memorabilia. Country kitchen, central heating and huge open fire. The natural textures and rustic feeling just fold around you. Outside is secluded and sheltered with jacuzzi and petanque. Hanging baskets, sweeping lawn, mature trees and Tess our golden retriever, complete this romantic hideaway. We will cook you a sumptuous meal & join you or leave you to a romantic evening alone, alternatively you may take control of the beautiful farmhouse kitchen. Guests can have exclusive use of the cottage, single party booking, rates on application. Total privacy or we will pamper you as much or as little as you desire. Let us pick you up, take you skiing, arrange fishing, Milford tours and all activities. We are at your beck and call. Crisp linen-goosedown duvets-perfect peace-privacy-comfort-guests never want to leave! No smoking indoors. Exclusive occupancy rates on application.
Home Page: http://nz.com/Queenstown/Peartree

FERRY HOTEL GUEST HOUSE Circa 1872

Queenstown
Guest House
Address: Ferry Hotel Guest House, Spence Road,
Lower Shotover, Queenstown
Name: Ferry Hotel Guest House
Telephone: (03) 442 2194 **Fax**: (03) 442 2190
Email: ferry@clear.net.nz
Beds: 2 Double, 2 Single (3 bedrooms)
Bathroom: 1 Ensuite, 1 Guests share + extra toilet
Tariff: B&B (continental-full on request) Double with ensuite $135, Double $110,
Twin $110, Single $100, Children under 13 half price, No smoking indoors
(verandah is good for smokers), No dogs.
NZ B&B Vouchers accepted by negotiation only.
Nearest Town: 11km from Queenstown & Arrowtown on SH6, 6km from airport.

This popular Queenstown landmark is fast becoming a tourist attraction in its own right, with many people stopping daily to photograph this delightful and unique old building.

First built in 1862, burnt down and rebuilt in 1872, and then relocated in 1915, its history is fascinating, why not see for yourself. Historic photos line the walls and interesting memorabilia is scattered everywhere.

"Old World Elegance" aptly describes the charming interior of this Historic Hotel. The Guest House has a lounge with an enormous wood burning fire, a character country kitchen that granny would have been proud of, three inviting bedrooms, two bathrooms and an additional toilet with vanity basin. Tea, coffee, milo and biscuits are all complimentary to guests. Laundry facilities available. All bedrooms are decked out with Bathrobes and Slippers, fresh flowers, tissues and drinking water, and are individually heated, and all beds have electric blankets, wool underlays and duvets; this together with the quiet location ensures you of a good nights sleep.

We are 10 minutes drive from Queenstown and Arrowtown and centrally located between Coronet and Remarkable ski fields.

Your hosts are Kevin, Glenys and daughter Clare. We have chosen Queenstown as our new home after spending 20 years in Perth, Western Australia. We have brought with us our lovable English Springer spaniel named Chester who most guests adore. Our accommodation is completely separate to the guest house giving guests the freedom of their own space when desired. We have beautiful cottage gardens which incorporate two outdoor eating areas and a portable barbecue is available for all to gather around during those long summer evenings. Our hobbies are gardening, fly fishing, fly tying, (Kevin is president of the Wakitipu Angling Club) tramping and getting to know this beautiful part of the world better. We look forward to meeting new people all the time and can assist with all tour and travel arrangements, including bookings. Airport just 5 minutes away free pick up on request. Phone, fax and email facilities available.
Home Page: http://www.ferry.co.nz
Directions: *Reservations and directions, please phone (03) 442 2194, fax (03) 442 2190 or Email: ferry@clear.net.nz* 710

Queenstown
Self Contained Accommodation/B&B
Address: 13 Panorama Terrace, Queenstown.
Name: Maree Dawson
Telephone: 03-442 9444
Beds: 1 Queen, 3 Single (2 bedrooms)
Bathroom: 1 Guests share
Tariff: B&B (continental) Double $110, Single $55. (+ $10 pp. one night only)
Dinner $25 per person.
Nearest Town: Queenstown, 8 min. walking - also on Bus route.

Our home in Panorama Terrace is in the dress circle, with fantastic views of Lake Wakatipu and the mountains. We are keen gardeners and have a private sunny courtyard garden for relaxing and outdoor living. Off street parking is provided.
All beds have duvets, electric blankets and reading lamps. Guests may have a private den with TV, VCR or share family living areas. Tea and coffee making facilities are available.
Our interests include overseas travel, education, local history, pottery, embroidery, music, golf and gardening. Help given with organising sight seeing and travel.
Directions: *Turn up Suburb Street, off Frankton Road (State Highway 6), then right into Panorama Terrace.*

Queenstown
Homestay
Address: 226 Moke Lake Road,
Queenstown, Central Otago
Name: Ray and Sandra Drayton
Telephone: 03-442 5389
Fax: (03) 442 5389
Beds: 1 Double, 2 Single (2 bedrooms)
Bathroom: 1 Guests share
Tariff: B&B (full) Double $90, Single $50,
Dinner (optional) $30 pp.
Not suitable for children. No credit cards.

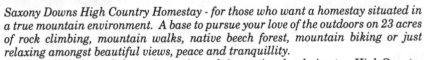

Nearest Town: Queenstown 10 kms. (15 minutes drive) off Glenorchy Road.

Saxony Downs High Country Homestay - for those who want a homestay situated in a true mountain environment. A base to pursue your love of the outdoors on 23 acres of rock climbing, mountain walks, native beech forest, mountain biking or just relaxing amongst beautiful views, peace and tranquillity.
Comfortable lodge style home in a unique alpine setting, bordering two High Country sheep stations.
*Magnificent views of lake and mountains.
*Walking-mountain bike tracks through wildlife reserve start from the property.
*Trout fishing on three alpine lakes near homestead.
*Personal guided walks available with your host or feel free to explore any number of tracks starting from the property.
*Mountain bikes and fishing gear available for guests' use.
*Bed and Breakfast - dinner optional.
*Ray and Sandra assure guests of a comfortable relaxing stay and a quality alpine experience.
We are smoke free and our season runs from September to May.

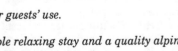

Queenstown
Boutique Bed & Breakfast
Address: 11 Arrowtown-
Lake Hayes Road,
RD. 1 Queenstown, Central Otago
Name: Villa Sorgenfrei
Telephone: (03) 442 1128
Fax: (03) 442 1239

Beds: 1 King/Twin (ensuite), 1 Queen (2 bedrooms)
Bathroom: 1 Ensuite, 1 Private
Tariff: B&B (full) Double $155, Single $120. Limited suitability for children.
Credit Cards accepted.
Nearest Town: Arrowtown 5 minutes. Queenstown 15 minutes

Villa Sorgenfrei means worryfree - that's what holidays should be, so make the most of it. Our enticing stacked stone house is easily found - fifteen minutes from Queenstown, five minutes from Arrowtown, by one of the most photographed lakes in New Zealand. Lake Hayes - an ideal centre point for all activities offered in this area.

Wake in a sunny spacious bedroom before breakfasting at leisure with fresh coffee and all the goodies. Pleasures abound right here or just there at the lake.

We could explain more about us, but the kind comments in our visitors' book are hard to beat. "Thanks for spoiling us and sharing your beautiful home". "We had an absolutely marvellous time - the type of place I feel we should have bought a gift. How lucky we have been". "Bless you both, what lucky people we are to have found you". "Hey don't push your luck - just phone or fax!"

Directions: *Take SH 6 for 15 minutes from Queenstown. Turn off onto the Arrowtown Lake Hayes Road - We are the first on the left - beside our sign.*

Kingston/Garston
High Country Station Experience.
Address: "Mataura Valley Station",
Cainard Rd., PO Box 2, Garston, 9660, Southland
Name: Robyn & David Parker
Telephone: (03) 248 8552 **Fax**: (03) 248 8552
Email: matauravalleystation@nzhomestay.co.nz
Beds: 1 King, 1 Double, 4 Single (4 bedrooms)
Bathroom: 1 Ensuite, 2 Guests share
Tariff: B&B (full) Double $100-$110, Single $50-$60, Dinner $20, Children under
12 meals half price. Credit Cards. NZ B&B Vouchers accepted $10 Surcharge
Nearest Town: Kingston 20km, Garston 17km, Queenstown 50km

Welcome to our 19,000 acre sheep and cattle station overlooking the Mataura river, famous for brown trout fishing. Comfortable modern home with glorious views and sunny site. Experience Alpine tranquillity 10 km from the Queenstown-Te Anau highway. Enjoy farm activities, go fishing, mountain biking, take a walk, or soak up the view. Enjoy skylarks, paradise ducks, water birds, hawks and New Zealand falcons. Farm-style meals with vegetables fresh from David's organic garden. Only an hours scenic drive from Queenstown. We have 10,000 sheep, 250 cattle, 6 sheep dogs and 2 cats. Fishing guides arranged with advance notice. A great base for travel to Fiordland or Queenstown. Aerial trips by arrangement. Complimentary mini-tour of farm, 4-wheel drive mountain tours, 1/2 day (extra cost). Adult family involved in travel, shearing, white-water rafting, studying and teaching outdoor skills. We aim to make your stay a special memory. We look forward to meeting you. Pre-arrival notification please.

Garston

Homestay
Address: 17 Blackmore Road, Garston.
Name: Bev and Matt Menlove
Telephone: (03) 248 8516
Beds: 1 Double,
2 Single (1 Bedroom)
Bathroom: 1 Ensuite
Tariff: B&B (continental) Double $70,
Single $40, Dinner $20.
NZ B&B Vouchers accepted
Nearest Town: Lumsden 30 km,
Queenstown 50 km

We are organic gardeners and our other interests include lawn bowls, sailing, gliding and alternative energy.
Garston is New Zealand's most inland village with the Mataura River (famous for its fly fishing) flowing through the valley, surrounded by the Hector Range and the Eyre Mountains. A fishing guide is available with advance notice.
For day trips, Garston is central to Queenstown, Te Anau, Milford Sound or Invercargill. We look forward to meeting you.
Directions: *Please phone for directions.*

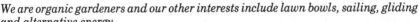

St Bathans Village

Self-contained Accommodation
Address: "The School Teachers (1879)
Cottage", St Bathans, R.D. Oturehua,
Central Otago 9071
Name: Lorraine and Tristan
Telephone: (03) 447 3624
or (03) 473 6400 or (03) 482 2219
Beds: 2 Queen, (2 double bedrooms), one
fold-down double settee.
Bathroom: 1 Private
Tariff: Self contained: B&B (continental) Self contained: Double $95 per day,
minimum stay two days. Self Contained Double $80 per day for 3 days and over.
Children under 12 free. Discounts negotiable for extra people or stays over a
week.NZ B&B Vouchers accepted $20 Surcharge
Nearest Town: Alexandra 30 minutes, Ranfurly 20 minutes.

This delightful, 100 year old stone cottage (1879), is nestled in the tranquil, historic, gold-mining village of St Bathans, at the foot of Mt St Bathans, Central Otago's highest mountain. Amidst spectacular, tussock covered high country. It is a place where nature holds sway and time is forgotten. Wrapped in snow in winter, gold leafed in autumn, fresh green and lush with wild-flowers in spring, and in summer, swimming in the Blue Lake with its magnificent sculptured cliffs. St Bathans has many heritage buildings, beautiful walks, horse riding, trout fishing, mountain biking and hunting. The cottage provides peace, privacy and comfort. Enjoy a cosy log fire, fresh flowers, and generous breakfast provisions. All modern conveniences are provided for self catering, you can provide your own meals or dine at the historic Vulcan Hotel (1882). Within easy driving distance of Queenstown, Wanaka, the Lakes District, historic Naseby, Clyde, Alexandra and Cromwell.
Directions: *Turn off Highway 85, 90 minutes from Queenstown, Wanaka, 2 hours from Dunedin.*

713

Clyde

Homestay
Address: 6 Drivers Rest, Clyde
Name: Evelyn & Hugh Smith
Telephone: (03) 449 2419
Beds: 1 Double, 2 Single (2 Bedrooms)
Bathroom: 1 Family share
Tariff: B&B (continental) Double $65, Single $35,
Children half price, Dinner $15pp, NZ B&B Vouchers accepted
Nearest Town: Clyde (Alexandra) 10km.

Your hosts Evelyn and Hugh, semi-retired, family all married.
We have travelled overseas many times enjoy meeting people.
Warm welcome awaits you in our spacious new home, electric blankets on all beds,
laundry facilities available.
Clyde's historic gold mining town with many old stone buildings fishing in new Lake
Dunstan.
We're walking distance to Hydro Dam (Clyde Dam), Historic Engine Museum, Olivers
Restaurant, golf club, bowling club. One hour drive to Queenstown, Wanaka, skifields
in winter.
Directions: *Clydes 2nd turn of into Hazziet Street. 4th street on left Whitby Street,*
turn left into Drivers Rest, first on right.

Alexandra

Homestay
Address: 6 Rapuke Street, Alexandra
Name: Marion & John Clarke
Telephone: (03) 448 7885
Beds: 1 Double, 2 Single (2 bedrooms)
Bathroom: 1 Guests share
Tariff: B&B (full) Double $60, Single $35, Children half price, Dinner $18.
NZ B&B Vouchers accepted
Nearest Town: Alexandra

We are retired sheep and cropping farmers who are enjoying the unique beauty of
Central Otago and wish to share our home with guests. Our home is modern sunny and
warm and in a very peaceful cul-de-sac. All bedrooms have electric blankets, bedside
lamps and easy access to guest bathroom. Laundry facilities available. Alexandra has
the distinction of being the driest town in New Zealand and noted for its fruit growing
and vineyards. With its unique scenery and close proximity to Lake Dunstan it offers
fine fishing as do the rivers close by. We are only 1 hours drive from Queenstown,
Wanaka and ski fields. Restaurants are within walking distance. We do not have pets.
Directions: *From monument in town continue out Tarbert Street, turn right at*
Rawhiti Street, then right into Rapuke Street.

Continental breakfast consists of fruit, cereal, toast, tea/coffee,
Full breakfast is the same with a cooked course,
Special breakfast has something special.

714

Earnscleugh - Alexandra
Orchard Stay
Address: 'Iversen', 47 Blackman Road,
Earnscleugh, Alexandra
Name: Robyn & Roger Marshall
Telephone: (03) 449 2520 **Fax**: (03) 449 2519
Mobile: (025) 384 348
Beds: 2 Queen (2 bedrooms)
Bathroom: 1 Guests share
Tariff: B&B (continental) Double $80, Single $45, Dinner $25.
NZ B&B Vouchers accepted $10 surcharge
Nearest Town: Alexandra 6km, Clyde 8km

Our detached guest accommodation offers you privacy and comfort and combined with a warm welcome into our home, you can share with us, the peaceful and relaxing location of our orchard setting. Around the festive season you can enjoy our cherry harvest. Take in our garden setting, swim in the pool, walk the adjoining hills, or just relax. Rooms have tea making facilities, heating, electric blankets, TV and radio. Golfing, fishing, ice-skating, vineyards, craft galleries, and museums all within 10 minutes drive. Experience the grandeur and contrasts of the Central Otago landscape by staying an extra night and joining us on a 4WD trip into the mountains, an orchard tour, or a wine trail. (Indicate interest at time of booking - extra cost)
Directions: *From Alexandra or Clyde, travel on Earnscleugh Road, turn into Blackman Road, look for our sign on left. Advance bookings preferred.*

Alexandra
Vineyard Homestay/Bed & Breakfast
Address: Hawkdun Rise Vineyard,
Letts Gully Road, Alexandra RD3
Name: Judy & Roy Faris
Telephone: (03) 448 7782
Fax: (03) 448 7752
Mobile: (025) 337 072
Email: rfaris@clear.net.nz
Beds: 2 Queen, 1 Double (3 bedrooms)
Bathroom: 2 Ensuite, 1 Guests share
Tariff: B&B (special) Double $115, Single $85, Dinner by arrangement.
Credit cards.
Nearest Town: Alexandra 6 Kms(approx)

Less than five minutes from Alexandra our spacious new home is set in a small developing vineyard and commands expansive views of the Dunstan, Hawkdun and Old Man Ranges. We have designed our home to provide a semi-detached guest accommodation wing with verandahs and deck.
We are a professional couple with grown family and have travelled widely. We share our home with Tess, a small springer spaniel and Rodger, a Burmese cat, all non smokers. Laundry, tea and coffee making facilities are available.
Complimentary wines and cheeses served early evening.
You can enjoy the privacy, views, a spa and our small underground cellar.
We are able to arrange wine trails, lake fishing and 4WD trips.
If you are looking for privacy, tranquillity accompanied by first class accommodation along with the space to be as sociable as you please - you have found us.
Directions: *Please phone or fax.*

Alexandra

Country Homestay
Address: "Ardshiel",
Letts Gully, Alexandra
Name: Ian & Joan Stewart
Telephone: (03) 448 9136 **Fax**: (03) 448 9136
Mobile: (025) 732 973
Beds: 1 King, 1 Double, 2 Single (2 bedrooms)
Bathroom: 1 Ensuite, 1 Guests share
Tariff: B&B (full) Double $105, Single $75, Dinnerby arrangement, Credit Cards.
Nearest Town: Alexandra 3km

Nestled in a peaceful sheltered valley, our country homestead offers superior accommodation only minutes from Alexandra.

A new Cape Cod design house, spacious rooms, an air of elegance, luxurious suite for guests, ensuite, formal dining room, spacious lounge and outdoor spa for total relaxation.

Rest, enjoy the crystal clear air and absorb the tranquil atmosphere. Stroll amongst the mature trees and gardens of the old established house site.

Meander through the fruit trees, up the thyme covered hill for breathtaking views of Central Otago, or simply put your feet up and relax in our sun drenched private courtyard.

We provide a full travel service including guided tours, historic goldfield excursions, ski trips (in season), golf days, pick up and delivery to airports or other tourist destinations. Sample the superb local cuisine, bookings can be arranged at several excellent local restaurants or enjoy a beautiful meal in our own dining room. We enjoy the company of our little dog Ollie.

Alexandra/Clyde

Country Homestay
Address: 'The Willows',
3 Young Lane, 1 RD, Alexandra
Name: Daine and Allen Hansen
Telephone: (03) 449 2231
Fax: (03) 449 2231
Beds: 1 Double, 3 Single (3 bedrooms)
Bathroom: 1 Guests share, 1 Family share
Tariff: B&B (continental) Double $70, Single $40,
Dinner $20 (by arrangement), Children half price.
Nearest Town: 3 km south of Clyde off SH8

Diane and Allen are semi retired Southlanders, who would warmly welcome you to our centrally heated home. We are situated on 10 acres of land (private setting) with some orchard, a few sheep (some black), a friendly foxy ("Emma") and a cat ("Duck"). Pets would be most welcome. We have a very attractive garden and a swimming pool, for your relaxation.

The area is well known for its extremes, hot dry summers and cool winters.

We are only 5 minutes drive from Lake Dunstan and an hours drive from both Wanaka and Queenstown ski fields.

The area caters well for walks, fishing, golf, bowls, winery tours, skiing and ice skating, and for the more energetic, running. Transport can be provided by arrangement.

We have no children living at home.

Roxburgh - Dumbarton

Country Inn
Address: 4760 Roxburgh-Ettrick Road,
SH8, No. 2 R.D., Roxburgh
Name: The Seed Farm
Telephone: (03) 446 6824
Fax: (03) 446 6024
Beds: 3 Queen, 2 Single (4 bedrooms)
Bathroom: 4 Ensuite
Tariff: B&B (continental) Double/Twin $90,
Dinner a la carte, All credit cards.
Nearest Town: Roxburgh 9km

The Seed Farm is one of the oldest properties in the Teviot Valley constructed in 1869 of local schist, it comprises a two storeyed cottage and separate stables set amidst two acres of cottage gardens. The buildings all carry Historic Places Trust 2 classification reflecting their historic significance to the district.

The stables have been refurbished and offer 4 bedrooms (with ensuites), central heating, TV and tea making facilities.

The ground floor of the cottage was converted to a restaurant in 1990 and offer an eclectic menu in an olde world ambience.

The Teviot Valley is the centre of NZ's cherry and apricot growing region and the property is bounded by apple orchards and farms. The Clutha River is minutes away offering salmon and trout fishing in season. Queenstown / Wanaka area 1 1/2 hours drive.

A warm country style welcome awaits you at the Seed Farm.

Millers Flat

Self-contained Accommodation
Address: Millers Flat, R.D.2,
Roxburgh, Central Otago
Name: Sheena & Wallace Boag
Telephone: (03) 446 6872
Beds: 2 Single (1 bedroom)
plus double bed settee (upstairs)
Bathroom: 1 Ensuite
Tariff: B&B (continental) Double $65,
Single $40. Children $20,
Dinner $20.Credit Cards.
NZ B&B Vouchers accepted
Nearest Town: Roxburgh 16 km

An easy 2-hour drive from Dunedin, Wanaka, Queenstown and Invercargill, Millers Flat is an ideal place to break your journey. Originally a goldmining settlement, Millers Flat is an attractive village in farming and fruitgrowing country. It has a strong sense of community and is well equipped with facilities - swimming pool, tennis courts, bowling green, easy access to fishing, walking tracks, gardens to visit, and the well known community-owned general store "Faigan's".

We live on 10 acres in a 110 year-old house of rammed-earth construction (one of the building methods used in the early days of Central Otago settlement) and our guest accommodation is a detached 2-storey building of more recent vintage, an interesting composition of space and light, formerly Wallace's architectural studio.

Directions: *Turn off SH8 at Millers Flat, then left through the village for 1 km. Turn off to Lake Onslow for 100m. Phone ahead if possible.*

Ettrick, Roxburgh
Farmstay/Self-contained Accom.
Address: 'Clearburn Station', Dalmuir Rd, No 2 R.D., Roxburgh
Name: Ian & Margaret Lambeth
Telephone: (03) 446 6712 **Fax**: (03) 446 6774
Beds: 2 Single + Bed Settee (1 bedroom)
Bathroom: 1 Ensuite
Tariff: B&B (continental) Double $70, Single $50, Dinner $20.
NZ B&B Vouchers accepted
Nearest Town: Roxburgh 10km

Clearburn Station is a 7000 acre property with a Homestead Block and Hill Country Run stocked with Merino sheep and Cattle. The property is operated as a family partnership with son John and his wife Linda and children living in the main homestead while we, Ian and Margaret, have a smaller house.
Guest accommodation is a detached unit containing twin beds with ensuite and a bed settee in the large lounge. Electric blankets, heaters, tea making facilities, fridge and TV provided. Laundry facilities available.
Guests are very welcome to join in the farm activities occurring on the day which vary from high country mustering to work on the Home Block, or simply feed the hens, pigs and pony. Visits to local places of interest can be arranged - restaurants, golf course and fishing are within 5 mins drive.
Directions: *Please phone. We are 1 3/4 hour drive from Dunedin and only 300 metres from the main road.*

Palmerston
Homestay
Address: Shag Valley Station,
3 RD Palmerston, Otago
Name: Louise & Alf Bell
Telephone: (03) 465 0821
Fax: (03) 465 0821
Email: Bell.ShagValley@xtra.co.nz
Beds: 2 Twin (2 bedrooms)

Both rooms with electric blankets and heaters.
Bathroom: 1 Ensuite, 1 Private
Tariff: B&B (continental) Double $140, Single $80, Children under 12 half price; Dinner $30pp (wine). Museum & Garden only (Non stay $5pp by arrangement)
Nearest Town: Palmerston 25km

Welcome to Shag Valley Station. The Station was taken up by our family in 1864. Six generations later we are still here so it must be worth while staying! Many of the farm buildings date back to around that period. The Homestead, part of which dates back to 1868, is set in 10 acres of garden and trees. The Garden was planned by Baron Von Mueller in the 1880s who was responsible for laying out the Melbourne Botanical Gardens. We are fortunate that having been in the family for so long, we have a great collection of early life of that time including a scientific laboratory the equipment from which we have retained and have in our museum on the property. As my Grandfather was a Scientist as well as a Farmer. We suggest you allow yourself plenty of time to explore Shag Valley get to know us, and relax. 2 Burmese cats.
Directions: *Please phone. 25km from Palmerston on Highway 85 on the road to Central Otago or 45km from Ranfurly if heading East.*

Palmerston

Homestay (Historic Homestead)
Address: "Centrewood Historic Homestead",
Bobby's Head Road,
Goodwood, Palmerston, Otago
Name: Jane & David Loten
Telephone: (03) 465 1977
Fax: (03) 465 1977
Email: centrewood@xtra.co.nz
Beds: 1 Queen, 1 Double, 1 Single (2 bedrooms)
Bathroom: 1 Guest share or private
Tariff: B&B (special) Double $120, Single $100,
Dinner $30 (includes wine). Single party booking optional extra. Credit cards
Nearest Town: Palmerston (SH 1) 5 minutes, Dunedin 40 minutes.

Experience the peace and charm of yesteryear in our large colonial homestead, rambling gardens and park-like grounds. Our spacious and private guest wing comprising 2 bedrooms, bathroom and living room, has its own entrance and verandah overlooking the croquet lawn. The extensive living room has a billiard table, desk, piano, TV, tea / coffee facilities and refrigerator. Breakfast in our large country kitchen includes home-made bread, croissants, fruit and yoghurt. Scrumptious afternoon tea is served on the verandah, and dinner in the dining room. Adjacent is a penguin reserve and sandy beach with a spectacular cliff top walk allowing easy viewing of seals and penguins and seabirds. On-site attractions include tennis, croquet, native bush walks, bird life and tame farm animals. As Lord Ernest Rutherford's great grand daughter, Jane has set up a corner of Rutherford memorabilia. Nearby are the Moeraki Boulders, Macraes Goldmine and Dunedin City. No Smoking please.
Directions: *Take SH 1 to Palmerston. Turn East at Warrens Garage into Goodwood Rd. After 10 mins turn left into Bobby's Head Road. Centrewood Homestead is 1 km on the right.*

Warrington

Country Home Accommodation
Address: 'Sunny Hill Farm',
367 Coast Road, Warrington, Otago
Name: Angela & Maurice Corish
Telephone: (03) 482 2631
Beds: 2 Queen (2 bedrooms)
Bathroom: 2 Ensuite
Tariff: B&B (full) Double $80, Dinner $25pp.
NZ B&B Vouchers accepted $15 surcharge
Nearest Town: 18km north of Dunedin, off SH1

We live in a 100 year old farmhouse, nestled in a rambling wild garden and orchard. The 25 acre farmlet, with sheep, goats, 2 kune pigs, 1 cat and Jess the sheep dog are worth a visit after breakfast. Enjoy a leisurely cooked breakfast accompanied by freshly brewed coffee and homemade bread, in our large comfortable farmhouse kitchen with wood-burning stove. Your chef host serves innovative, delicious food using fresh organically home grown and local produce. We offer two double rooms, one upstairs with panoramic views of sea and farmland. The other is in detached accommodation, with a private sunny patio fringed with aromatic herbs. Our interests are in country life, antiques, old houses, books, tramping and biking. New Zealand's tallest tree is close by. Warrington beach, Blueskin Bay and the Silverpeaks offer superb walks. World famous Otago Peninsular (albatross, yellow-eyed penguins, seals) is close to Dunedin, which is 25 minutes from Warrington. A large games cupboard. No smoking and no pets please.

Blueskin Bay, Dunedin

Homestay
Address: 'Ngeratua Farm',
Kilpatrick Road, Waitati
Name: Adrienne & Stuart Heal
Telephone: (03) 482 1152 **Fax**: (03) 482 1153
Email: heals@es.co.nz
Beds: 1 Double, 2 Single (1 bedroom)
Bathroom: 1 Private
Tariff: B&B (full) Double $90, Single $60, Children half price. Dinner $35pp.
Credit cards (VISA/MC). NZ B&B Vouchers accepted $10 Surcharge.
Nearest Town: Dunedin, 18km south

Situated 15 minutes north of Dunedin at Blueskin Bay is our lifestyle farm overlooking the Bay and Pacific Ocean. On our property we graze sheep and cattle and are developing an expanding garden, including a commercial flower venture.

Our home offers a large guest room with a double bed and two singles, lounge suite, TV and private bathroom and toilet. Guests are encouraged to join the family for an evening meal where we enjoy quality local food and wines. Breakfast on our sunny deck is a relaxing way to start the day.

Our home, a non smoking environment, is shared with our pet cat, Whisky.

We are located near many bush and hill walks, Dunedin's unique wildlife and architecture, or you may simply enjoy a walk on our property, which is less than one kilometre off State Highway 1. We offer a peaceful environment, minutes from the city.
Directions: *Please phone for details and reservations.*

Broad Bay-Otago Peninsula, Dunedin

Homestay+Self-contained Accom.
Address: 'Chy-an-Dowr' 687 Portobello Road, Broad Bay, Dunedin
Name: Herman & Susan Van Velthoven
Telephone: (03) 478 0306 **Fax**: (03) 478 0306
Mobile: 025 270 5533 **Email**: hermanvv@xtra.co.nz
Beds: 1 Queen, 2 Single (2 bedrooms)
SC Cottage: 1 Queen, 1 Bed settee (1 Bedroom)
Bathroom: 1 Guests share. SC Cottage: 1 Private
Tariff: B&B (full) Double $90.
Self-contained cottage $95, extra person in cottage $20.
Credit cards. NZ B&B Vouchers accepted - Surcharge $20
Nearest Town: Dunedin 16km

Our lovely home, on scenic Otago Peninsula halfway between Dunedin and the Albatross Colony, has beautiful views, all day sun and is situated directly opposite a small beach. The guestrooms are upstairs; comfortable bedrooms with electric blankets, heating, bathrobes and hairdryer. A sunroom with extensive harbour views, Tea / coffee making facilities, TV. The upstairs bathroom is shared by guests. "Sleepy Hollow", our luxury, private self-contained cottage is situated in Portobello on a quiet country road with rural outlook, a five minute drive from our house. Full breakfast included in the cottage. The Otago Peninsula has many walkways, and is well known for its Albatross Colony, Yellow-eyed Penguins, seals and Larnach Castle. Also a good restaurant, for which forward bookings are advisable. In 1981 we emigrated from Holland. We have an adult daughter and son living at home, also two cats. Our accomodation is smoke-free. Welcome to our home.
Directions: *Follow signs Peninsula. Follow Portobello Road along the harbour until you come to Broad Bay, we are on the corner Portobello Road and Clearwater Street in Broad Bay.*
Home Page: http://www.visit-dunedin.co.nz

Otago Peninsula, Dunedin

Homestay
Address: 'Captains Cottage',
422 Portobello Road,R.D.2. Dunedin
Name: Christine & Robert Brown
Telephone: (03) 476 1431
Fax: (03) 476 1431
Mobile: (021) 352 734
Beds: 1 Double, 2 Single (2 bedrooms)
Bathroom: 1 Guests share, 1 Private
Tariff: B&B (continental) Double $95
or with private bathroom $135, Single $60, Dinner $25.
Nearest Town: Dunedin 9km

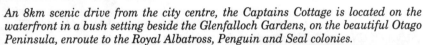

An 8km scenic drive from the city centre, the Captains Cottage is located on the waterfront in a bush setting beside the Glenfalloch Gardens, on the beautiful Otago Peninsula, enroute to the Royal Albatross, Penguin and Seal colonies.
Robert is a specialist wildlife cameraman for the BBC and TVNZ who loves to share his interest in wildlife with visitors. Christine has travelled widely and with her wealth of local knowledge and contacts can help you organise an interesting stay.
We have our own sport fishing boat and can take you fishing or explore the unique bird and marine life found in the area.
So if you enjoy great food and hospitality; BBQ's, boating, lying in the sun, relaxing beside the log fire or having a drink as the sun sets on the deck of our boat shed, then let us share our interesting home with you. Our two dogs are Penny and Socrates.

Broad Bay – Otago Peninsula, Dunedin

Self-contained Accommodation
Address: 'The Cottage',
748 Portobello Road, Broad Bay, Dunedin
Name: Lesley, Janet and Leonie
Telephone: (03) 478 0073 **Mobile**: (025) 381 291
Beds: 1 Double (1 bedroom)
Bathroom: 1 Ensuite

Tariff: B&B (special) Double $95 (weekly rate: $570).
NZ B&B Vouchers accepted $25 surcharge for B&B..
Nearest Town: Dunedin - 18km from city centre

Our self-contained cottage, built at the turn of the century as a fisherman's retreat, is right on the Otago Harbour. A picket fence encloses a mature native bush garden. Wonderful vignettes of the harbour are enjoyed from the privacy of the verandah and garden. Full of old-world charm, this cosy cottage with original matai floors reflects the nostalgia of a bygone era (No TV!), whilst fresh linen, a comfortable bed and modern conveniences ensure a relaxing stay.
Our generous hamper breakfasts are a speciality. Evening meals may be self-catered or taken at one of the fine Peninsula restaurants.
Enjoy the freedom to come and go as you please whilst exploring the many Peninsula attractions.
Kayaks and bicycles maybe hired for active days whilst books and games are available for leisurely evenings. Local friendly golf course nearby.
Here is a travellers' oasis that will be difficult to leave.

OTAGO

Portobello Village - Otago Peninsula, Dunedin

Homestay
Address: Peninsula Homestay B&B,
4 Allans Beach Road, Portobello Village,
Otago Peninsula, Dunedin.
Name: Rachel and Mike Kerr
Telephone: (03) 478 0909
Fax: (03) 478 0909
Beds: 2 Queen (2 bedrooms)
Bathroom: 2 Ensuite
Tariff: B&B (continental) double $95, Single $85, Extra person $20.
Credit Cards: Visa/Mastercard.
Nearest Town: Dunedin, city centre 25 mins.

Our lovely home is an historic villa set among an 1/2 acre of beautiful gardens with sea views and rural outlook. We have two LUXURIOUS BEDROOMS EACH WITH A PRIVATE ENSUITE, TV, electric blankets, heating and hairdryers.
We are situated in the heart of Portobello Village, overlooking Lathum Bay, opposite the 1908 Cafe, Otago Peninsula's famous restaurant.
Portobello is most central to all the attractions on the Otago Peninsula. The Albatross, Seal and Penguin colonies, Larnach Castle and a variety of scenic walks, drives and harbour cruises are all close by.
Rachel's family are descendants of the 1st European Settlers in 1838 and have farmed on the Otago Peninsula for 5 generations. Farm tours available upon request.
Mike and Rachel enjoy gardening, rugby, tennis and golf and look forward to sharing their home with you.
A WARM WELCOME AWAITS YOU AT PENINSULA HOMESTAY B&B

Otago Peninsula, Dunedin

Bed & Breakfast
Address: The Mission, Mission Cove,
Company Bay, Otago Peninsula
Name: Pat & Phillipa Cummings
Telephone: (03) 476 1321
Fax: (03) 476 1028
Mobile: (025) 751 782
Email: cummings@deepsouth.co.nz
Beds: 1 Twin, 1 Double, 4 Single (6 bedrooms) **Bathroom**: 3 Guests share
Tariff: B&B (continental) Double $85, Single $45, (Downstairs $35).
Nearest Town: Dunedin 12 Kms

Situated on the picturesque Otago Peninsula, our place is a recently refurbished ex-nurses home (19 bedrooms originally), built in 1948. We have a very pleasant double bedroom and a twin room upstairs with 2 guest bathroom facilities. Downstairs include 4 single rooms and self-contained. We have a large garden and landscaped area which includes a stream, "summer house", expansive patio area and courtyard with established trees, breathtaking harbour views and a chapel with stained glass windows. We are 15 minutes from the centre of Dunedin and about the same from the Royal Albatross Colony, world famous penguins, seals and only 3km from Larnach Castle and Glenfalloch Gardens. A warm welcome is guaranteed from Pat, Phillipa, Daniel (14 year old son), Grace (Weimeraner) and Ruby (Poodle) our "very well mannered people-friendly dogs".
Directions: *Travelling from Dunedin go 1.1km past Macandrew Bay Store on Portobello Road, turn right into Mission Cove at Company Bay, go straight to the top of the drive. Reservations recommended. Smoke free.*
Home Page: http://www.visit-dunedin.co.nz

Dunedin

Homestay
Address: Magnolia House,
18 Grendon Street, Maori Hill, Dunedin
Name: Joan & George Sutherland
Telephone: (03) 467 5999 **Fax**: (03) 467 5999
Beds: 1 Queen, 1 Double, 2 Single (3 bedrooms)
Bathroom: 2 Guests share
Tariff: B&B (full) Double $80, Single $55. Special full menu of cooked and
continental foods.
Nearest Town: Dunedin city centre 2 km

*We live in a superior suburb on half an acre of land, one third of which is native bush
with wood pigeons, tuis, bellbirds and fantails. The rest is in lawn and attractive
gardens.*
*Our 1910 house is spacious with a large dining room and drawing room, and a more
intimate sitting room.*
*The Queen room has its own large balcony looking out on lawns and bush. The guest
rooms are airy and have antiques. Guests' bathrooms with showers. There is central
heating and piano.*
*Two nights in Dunedin is a must. We are very close to Otago Golf Club and can supply
clubs and bag. Also nearby is Olveston stately home and Moana Olympic-size
swimming pool. The Otago peninsula is a wonderful day's sightseeing.*
*We have two cats, a courtesy car, bus nearby and no smoking. Not suitable children.
Prefer non-smokers.*
Directions: *Please phone*

Dunedin

Homestay
Address: 'Harbourside Bed & Breakfast', 6 Kiwi Street, St Leonards, Dunedin
Name: Shirley & Don Parsons
Telephone: (03) 471 0690 **Fax**: (03) 471 0063
Beds: 2 Double, 3 Single (2 bedrooms)
Bathroom: 1 Guests share
Tariff: B&B (full) Double $75, Single $45, Children 4-12yrs $10, Under 4 free
share room; Dinner $20pp. 10% discount 2 or more nights, Credit Cards.
NZ B&B Vouchers accepted
Nearest Town: Dunedin - 7 km to City Centre

*We live in a quiet suburb 10 minutes from the city centre. Our home overlooks the lovely
Otago Harbour and is within easy reach of many of the local attractions - Larnach
Castle, Olveston, the Albatross colony and Disappear-ing Gun, Portobello Aquarium,
Harbour Cruises and Taieri Gorge Excursion Train, also Yellow-eyed penguins.
Dunedin is a lovely city situated at the head of the Otago harbour with many
interesting and historic stone buildings to view. There are also many lovely bush walks
within easy reach of the city. We have two rooms available, one with a double and
single bed and one with a double and bunks and cot available. Children very welcome
and we have a generous amount of living space for you to relax..*
Directions: *Driving into City on the one-way system watch for Port Chalmers
Highway 88 sign, follow Anzac Avenue onto Ravensbourne Road. Continue down the
Harbourside approximately 5 km to St Leonards. Turn left at the church opposite the
boatshed into Pukeko Street then left into Kaka Road then straight ahead to Kiwi
Street, turn left. Courtesy car available. See you soon.*

723

Dunedin
Bed and Breakfast
Address: Deacons Court,
342 High Street, Dunedin
Name: Karen & Dene MacKenzie
Telephone: (03) 477 9053
Fax: (03) 477 9058
Mobile: (025) 518 664
Email: Deacons@es.co.nz
Beds: 3 Double, 3 Single (3 bedrooms)
Bathroom: 2 Ensuite, 1 Private
Tariff: B&B (full) Double $110-$120,
Single $70, Credit Cards.

New tariff commences 1 October 1998. NZ B&B Vouchers accepted $30 surcharge
Nearest Town: Dunedin 1 Km from centre city

Enjoy that special feeling of being a guest in our comfortable private Victorian home which is surrounded by trees and a sheltered rose garden. Guests can relax in one of our three spacious bedrooms, the sunny conservatory or the cosy guest lounge. We are 1 km to the city centre, the Dunedin art gallery, the visitors centre, the Octagon, and a wide choice of restaurants. our Rose Room has a stunning view across the city to the harbour and the sea while our Garden Room overlooks the rose garden. Our generous breakfast may include fruit juice, fresh fruit, choice of cereals and yoghurt, home-made muffins and a traditional cooked breakfast. Complimentary tea, coffee and home baking on arrival. We have a wide knowledge of Dunedin attractions and can help you with your sightseeing. Family groups welcome. We cater for non smokers and have two children and a cat.

Dunedin
Homestay
Address: Pine Heights Retreat,
431 Pine Hill Road, Dunedin
Name: Eli & Lindsay Imlay
Telephone: (03) 473 9558
Fax: (03) 473 0247
Beds: 1 Queen, 2 Single (2 bedrooms)
Bathroom: 1 Guests share
Tariff: B&B (full) Double $85, Twin $80,
Single $50, Children (under 12) 1/2 price,
Dinner $25, Credit cards.
NZ B&B Vouchers accepted Surcharge $10
Nearest Town: Dunedin (4.5 kms to centre)

Relax in the comfort of our cozy home with tranquil rural setting where native birds are frequent visitors. Enjoy our sheltered patio and cottage garden which we love. Absorb the peacefulness of our surroundings - views shared by all living and bedroom areas. It's like living in the country yet only a few minutes by car from the city centre. Public transport nearby, courtesy car available and ample off-street parking. We will do our utmost to make your stay memorable. Flexible mealtimes allow time for sightseeing in our lovely city. We enjoy meeting people and welcome you to share our home and informal lifestyle. Eli, who has lived in Dunedin for over 30 years is Norwegian, and offers a unique blend of Scandinavian and New Zealand hospitality. Continental or full breakfast with wide choice including fresh homemade bread and waffles. Our dinners including wine, followed by Norwegian style coffee are speciality. Children most welcome.
Directions: *Please phone, preferably before 9.00am or after 5.00pm*

Dunedin Central

Bed & Breakfast
Address: 'Castlewood'
240 York Place, Dunedin
Name: Peter & Donna Mitchell
Telephone: (03) 477 0526
Fax: (03) 4770526

Email: Relax@castlewood.co.nz
Beds: 2 Queen, 1 Double, 1 twin or1 Single (4 bedrooms)
Bathroom: 1 ensuite, 2 Guests share
Tariff: B&B (Continental) Single $65, Twin $85, Double $95-$120. Visa &
Mastercard Credit Cards welcome. NZ B&B Vouchers accepted $25 Surcharge
Nearest Town: Only 800 metres walking distance to Dunedin's city centre.

Relax at Castlewood and experience the old world charm of our graciously restored Tudor residence. Set on a rise above Dunedin, Castlewood offers expansive views and all day sun yet is only 800 metres, (10 minutes walk) from the best restaurants, live theatre, cafes, shops and attractions such as Olveston, and the Dunedin Art Gallery. Both Peter and Donna are Dunedin born and know New Zealand intimately. They provide useful and friendly advice on local attractions and having travelled internationally, appreciate the requirements of discerning travellers. Peter is a well known artist and his water-colour paintings are displayed throughout Castlewood. "For warm hospitality in a beautiful home, the comfiest bed, and best breakfast muffins in NZ(!!) Look no further than Castlewood." Dr Jonathan Williams (U.K.)"A beautiful house, lovely city, and most friendly hosts," Michaela, Germany. "Wonderful and cosy, lovely outlook and brilliant artwork," Steve Amos, Australia.
Home Page: www.castlewood.co.nz
Directions: *From the top of the Octagon proceed up Stuart Street, turning left into Cargill Street, then left again into Arthur Street. At the next traffic lights Castlewood can be seen diagonally opposite.*

Dunedin City

Guest House
Address: 3 Peel St, Mornington, Dunedin
Name: 'Glenfield House' (Cal & Wendy)
Telephone: (03) 453 5923
Fax: (03) 453 5984
Beds: 2 Queen,
2 Double (4 bedrooms)
Bathroom: 2 Ensuite,
1 Guests share
Tariff: B&B (special) Double $185, $140, $130,
Single $135, $95, Dinner $30. Credit cards welcome.
Nearest Town: Dunedin City

Glenfield is our restored Victorian residence situated on the edge of the town belt 2 km from the centre city. All of our rooms have heating, electric blankets, feather and down duvets, television, tea and plunger coffee. Our facilities include an original billiard room with 3/4 size table, a congenial lounge with fire, laundry and off-street parking. At the top of our range we offer a special queen room with ensuite and adjoining sun room - a suite of rooms where you may dine if you prefer and have your own access to the verandah to enjoy the harbour views and Dunedin's night lights. With notice, a sumptuous 3 course meal, prepared from Otago produce, will be served in the guest dining room. If you are staying more than one night and have a craving for some particular food just let us know. We thank you for not smoking.

725

Dunedin Central
Heritage Inn
Address: 'Barnett Lodge',
34 Alva Street, Dunedin
Name: Margi & Paul Harris
Telephone: (03) 477 9413
Fax: (03) 477 3114
Mobile: (025) 320 350
Email: Polaris@earthlight.co.nz
Beds: 2 King or Twin with Ensuite, 1 Queen,
plus Single with private bathroom
Bathroom: 2 Ensuite, 1 Private
Tariff: B&B (full) Double $195, Single $165,
All Credit Cards welcome.
Nearest Town: Dunedin central

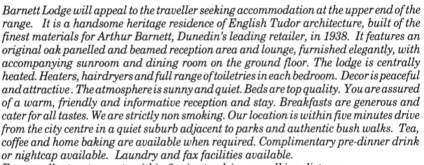

Barnett Lodge will appeal to the traveller seeking accommodation at the upper end of the range. It is a handsome heritage residence of English Tudor architecture, built of the finest materials for Arthur Barnett, Dunedin's leading retailer, in 1938. It features an original oak panelled and beamed reception area and lounge, furnished elegantly, with accompanying sunroom and dining room on the ground floor. The lodge is centrally heated. Heaters, hairdryers and full range of toiletries in each bedroom. Decor is peaceful and attractive. The atmosphere is sunny and quiet. Beds are top quality. You are assured of a warm, friendly and informative reception and stay. Breakfasts are generous and cater for all tastes. We are strictly non smoking. Our location is within five minutes drive from the city centre in a quiet suburb adjacent to parks and authentic bush walks. Tea, coffee and home baking are available when required. Complimentary pre-dinner drink or nightcap available. Laundry and fax facilities available.
Four excellent restaurants within 2 minutes drive or walking distance.

Warrington, Dunedin
Self Contained Villa
Address: Please phone
Name: Margaret & Paul Harris
Telephone: (03) 477 9413
Fax: (03) 477 3114
Mobile: 025 320 350
Email: Polarise@earthlight.co.nz
Beds: (3 bedrooms)
Bathroom: 2 Private
Tariff: B&B (S.C or full) $150 per night plus $10 per person.
Nearest Town: Dunedin 20 minutes

Montrose: Barnett Lodge seaside heritage
Montrose is a seaside villa with a sweeping view over Warrington Beach. It was built following WW1 using original kauri timber salvaged from the historic 1880 military barracks on nearby Taiaroa Head. Located 20 minutes from the centre of Dunedin. 3 large bedrooms. Beautifully restored bathroom. Two toilets. Panelled lounge with logburner. Restored kauri floors. Large sunny verandah. Tennis court. Double garage. Large garden. Self catering or fully serviced including cooked breakfast.

⚓ Albatross Inn

Dunedin City
Bed & Breakfast/Private Hotel
Address: 'Albatross Inn', 770 George St, Dunedin
Name: Kerry Kirkland & Nigel Brook
Telephone: (03) 477 2727: Reservations Freephone: 0800 441441
Fax: (03) 477 2108
Email: albatross.inn@xtra.co.nz
Beds: 1 King, 4 Queen, 3 Double, 5 Single (8 bedrooms)
Bathroom: 8 Ensuite
Tariff: B&B (continental) Double $85-$125, Single $65-$85, Children $15 (under 5 years free), Extra adult in room $20. Credit cards. Winter and long stay rates available.
Nearest Town: Dunedin Central.

Welcome to Dunedin! Our family, Nigel, Kerry, Zoe (7), Joanna (5) invite you to stay with us at Albatross Inn. Our Edwardian House is superbly located close to University, gardens, museum and centre city.

Our beautifully decorated bedrooms have ensuite bathrooms, telephone, TV, radio, tea / coffee, warm duvets and electric blankets on modern beds. Extra firm beds available for those with back problems. Very quiet rooms at rear of house.

Several rooms have own kitchenette / cooking facilities and fridge.

Enjoy breakfast in your room or in front of our open fire. We serve freshly baked bread, fresh fruit salad, muffins, yoghurt, juices, cereals, choice of teas, fresh brewed coffee.

We are both Dunedin born and have an intimate knowledge of the city and its surrounds. We offer our guests a warm welcome and can recommend great things to do and see and excellent places to eat, laundry service, non smoking, cot and highchair.

Quotes from 1998 Visitors Book:
- *The convenience of your location is wonderful. You can walk everywhere! Combined with a gorgeous house: Such friendly hosts to make an unbeatable combination. Best B&B in NZ!*
  Joe & Cathy Wallace, Georgia, USA.
- *This is everything a B&B ought to be...our only regret is leaving.... Thank you Kerry and Nigel for organising 3 wonderful days and making our stay so special!*
  Diana and William McDowell, England.

Homepage: www.albatross.inn.co.nz

Dunedin

Homestay
Address: 'Harbour Lookout', 3 Taupo St, Ravensbourne, Dunedin
Name: Ron & Maire (Moya) Graham
Telephone: (03) 471 0582
Beds: 2 Single (1 Bedroom)
Bathroom: 1 Family share
Tariff: B&B Double $60, Single $35,
Children under 12 half price, Dinner $18, NZ B&B Vouchers accepted
Nearest Town: Dunedin 3K

Welcome to Dunedin, Edinburgh of the South. We are a retired couple who can assure you of a warm welcome to our comfortable home in Ravensbourne, only 3km from Dunedin's Railway Station and therefore close to all wonderful attractions Dunedin has to offer. To find us follow Port Chalmers Highway 88, along Anzac Ave, continue into Ravensbourne Road, along the harbour side until you reach Adderley Terrace which turns uphill behind Harbour View Hotel. On entering first bend be alert for signpost on your right for Taupo St and Lane, drive in turn right downhill and into our drive with ample off street parking. Your twin bedroom with private toilet adjacent is on this level. No carrying luggage upstairs, however our bathroom and living areas are upstairs and here you can relax with a cuppa and enjoy the wonderful view. Our interests are golf, bowls and gardening. We look forward to meeting you.

Dunedin

Homestay
Address: 'Kincaple',
215 Highgate, Roslyn, Dunedin
Name: Del Cox
Telephone: (03) 477 4384
Fax: (03) 477 4380
Beds: 1 Double, 3 Single (3 bedrooms)
Bathroom: 1 Guests share, 1 Family share
Tariff: B&B (full) Double $80, Single $55.
$5 surcharge for cooked breakfast
Nearest Town: Dunedin city centre 2km

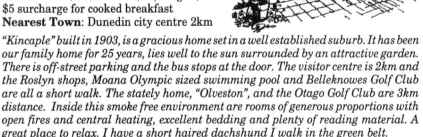

"Kincaple" built in 1903, is a gracious home set in a well established suburb. It has been our family home for 25 years, lies well to the sun surrounded by an attractive garden. There is off-street parking and the bus stops at the door. The visitor centre is 2km and the Roslyn shops, Moana Olympic sized swimming pool and Belleknowes Golf Club are all a short walk. The stately home, "Olveston", and the Otago Golf Club are 3km distance. Inside this smoke free environment are rooms of generous proportions with open fires and central heating, excellent bedding and plenty of reading material. A great place to relax. I have a short haired dachshund I walk in the green belt.
FOR RESERVATIONS FREEPHONE: 0800 - 269 384 / PIN 4774
Directions: *Please phone*

Please help us provide the best hospitality in the world.
Fill in a comment form for every place you stay.

Dunedin City

Homestay
Address: 'Brownville Lodge',
49 Brownville Cres.,
Maori Hill, Dunedin
Name: Gaynor & Neville Dippie
Telephone: (03) 467 5841 (home)
or (03) 477 8773 (work)
Fax: (03) 467-5841
Beds: 3 Queen, 1 Double,
3 Single (5 bedrooms)
Bathroom: 2 Private,
Tariff: B&B (special) Double $110, Single $90, Children $20.
Credit cards Visa/Mastercard. NZ B&B Vouchers accepted.
Nearest Town: Dunedin City

A warm welcome awaits the discerning traveller at our modern home which is a few minutes by car from the city centre. Facing the northern hills, the house is warm and spacious. Bedrooms are private, on a separate level, and furnishings and bedding are of a superior quality. We are non smokers who enjoy gardening and travel, and look forward to welcoming guests from other places to our city. Laundry available. Choice of breakfasts. Booking in time after 6 pm or by arrangement.

Dunedin

Homestay
Address: Gowrie House,
7 Gowry Place, Roslyn, Dunedin
Name: Vivienne & Rod Nye
Telephone: (03) 477 2103
Fax: (03) 471 9169
Beds: 1 Double, 2 Single (2 bedrooms)
Bathroom: 1 Guests share, 1 Family share
Tariff: B&B (full) Double $80, Single $50,
NZ B&B Vouchers accepted
Nearest Town: Dunedin

"Gowrie House" is in a quiet suburb, on a sunny west-facing site, with lovely rural views. We are only 20 minutes walk from the city close to bus routes. A courtesy car is provided, within the city.
Our garden has a cosy cottage atmosphere with all available space occupied by perennial and biennial flowers - regularly picked for rooms. The guests' bedrooms are warm and sunny. The bathroom is handily placed across the hall, and shared with one quiet family member. All beds have electric blankets. The double room has access to the patio and cottage garden where one can enjoy the floral fragrances. Otago Peninsula is easily accessible, as are bush walks and historic buildings. We will happily provide information about popular attractions.
Only Daniel, the youngest of our 3 children, remains at home. No smoking please.
Directions: *Please phone.*

Relax – Don't try to drive too far in one day.

Caversham, Dunedin
Bed & Breakfast Inn
Address: 15 Lisburn Ave,
Caversham, Dunedin
Name: Karolyn & Allan Forbes
Telephone: (03) 455 8888
Fax: (03) 455 6788
Mobile: (025) 224 6419
Beds: 3 Queen (3 bedrooms)
Bathroom: 1 Ensuite, 2 Private

Tariff: B&B (full) Double $165/$175, Single $125, Credit Cards.
Nearest Town: Dunedin 5km to centre

Lisburn House (c. 1865)
Bed & Breakfast Inn
Relax in the grandeur of yesteryear.
The 12 roomed, two storeyed building has a category 1 classification from the Historic Places Trust, guests at 'Lisburn House' can relax confident that there every need will be catered for and revel in the luxury of there surroundings. Strolling among delphiniums and roses in the English style garden. Enjoying a complimentary port and cheese board by the drawing room fire, sleeping in the fine linen and lace of a queen sized four-poster bed and waking to the sweet smell of flowers.
Downstairs in the dining room there's a light or cooked breakfast; fresh squeezed orange juice, muffins, croissants, fruit platter, scrambled eggs with smoked salmon, mushrooms with blue cheese sauce. Selection of teas and freshly ground coffee. All served on fine china. Karolyn and Allan extend a warm welcome to all enquiries and guests.
Homepage:*http://nz.com/Heritage Inns/Lisburn House.*

Dunedin
Homestay
Address: 20 Belmont Lane,
Musselburgh, Dunedin
Name: Jane, Charlotte
& Jamie Hamilton-Kerr
Telephone: (03) 455 4496
Beds: 1 Double, 1 Single
(2 bedrooms)
Bathroom: 1 Private
Tariff: B&B (continental) Double $85, Single $65,
Children half price,
Dinner $27. NZ B&B Vouchers accepted $16.50 surcharge
Nearest Town: Dunedin

Welcome - we are situated in a quiet garden lane, surrounded by mature trees, flowers and sweeping lawns.
Our house is tastefully decorated, spacious and warm; your comfort is assured. Relax in the secluded surroundings of a fragrant garden. The upstairs area is all yours with a private bathroom. Complimentary tea and coffee are available.
I serve a delicious continental breakfast, with a wide selection, including home made muesli, fruit, yoghurt and freshly ground coffee. We are a non-smoking household.
Our home sports two great children, aged fifteen and thirteen, a fat cat, and a chinchilla. We are five minutes drive from the main beaches, at the beginning of the scenic peninsula and there is a direct ten minute route to the city centre. Come and enjoy a fun stay with us.

St Clair, Dunedin
A Boutique Lodge
Address: Averleigh Cottage,
7 Coughtrey Street, St Clair, Dunedin
Name: Joanne McKellar
Telephone: (03) 455 8829 **Fax**: (03) 455 6380
Mobile: (021) 631 725
Email: joanne@averleigh.co.nz

Beds: 1 Queen (with ensuite), 1 Twin (guest bathroom) (2 bedrooms)
Bathroom: 1 Ensuite, 1 Private
Tariff: B&B (special) Room rate $135-$185, Credit Cards accepted Visa/
Mastercard/Bankcard/American Ezpress/Diners.
Nearest Town: Dunedin 5 kms

- *Welcome to Averleigh Cottage, a classic Edwardian 1910 villa*
- *For sophisticated, discerning travellers who appreciate a class act*
- *St Clair beach 2 min walk, 10 min drive from City Centre*
- *Restaurant at St Clair beach* • *"Tarlton Room" (Queen) with ensuite*
- *"Watson Room" (King / Twin) with Victorian open fire, guest bathroom with antique bath* • *Gourmet continental breakfast included*
- *Two elegant sitting rooms plus formal dining room, all with open fires*
- *Central heating* • *Morning Room leads to the courtyard rose gardens*
- *Garden rooms include roses, lavenders, rhododendrons, natives*
- *Garden house with outdoor spa. Petanque, croquet*
- *Brunch, picnic hampers, dinners, private guided tours - by arrangement*
- *Finbar & Brodie (curly coated retrievers)* • *Reservations essential*
- *Call Joanne for more information.*

Home Page: http://www.averleigh.co.nz

Roslyn, Dunedin
Homestay
Address: 33 Littlebourne Road,
Roslyn, Dunedin
Name: Eileen & Wallie Waudby
Telephone: (03) 477 4963
Fax: (03) 477 4965
Mobile: (025) 228 7840
Beds: 1 Double, 2 Single (2 bedrooms)
Bathroom: 1 Guests share
Tariff: B&B (full) Double $85, Single $50.
Nearest Town: Dunedin City Centre 1 km away.

Eileen and Wallie would like to welcome visitors to Dunedin to their smoke free home situated in a quiet street just off Stuart Street and opposite Roberts Park. We have travelled extensively ourselves and understand how visitors feel when they arrive in a new town. Our home is in short walking distance to Dunedin's stately home "Olveston", the Moana Swimming Complex and just over a kilometre to the town centre. The guest bedrooms situated on the top floor for privacy and quietness are warm and sunny and as a back up all beds have an electric blanket. Tea and coffee making facilities. You are sure of a warm welcome and comfortable stay at No.33.

OTAGO

Dunedin

Bed and Breakfast
Address: Nisbet Cottage,
6a Elliffe Place, Shiel Hill, Dunedin
Name: Hildegard & Ralf Lübcke
Telephone: (03) 454 5169 or 454 5590
Fax: (03) 454 5369
Email: wingsok@es.co.nz
Beds: 2 Queen, 2 Single (3 bedrooms)
Bathroom: 3 Ensuite
Tariff: B&B (special) Double $95-$110, Single $75. Credit Cards Visa/MC. Prices valid until 15th October 1999. NZ B&B Vouchers accepted $25-$30 surcharge
Nearest Town: Dunedins city centre 7km.

A warm welcome to Nisbet Cottage! We offer character accommodation in a peaceful and quiet environment. Situated near the high road to Otago Peninsula yet close to the city, Nisbet Cottage is the perfect base for your trips to Dunedin and its wildlife. Enjoy panoramic views from the large sun deck or relax in front of the open fireplace in the guest lounge, and meet Basil our cat. Restaurant and bus stop nearby.

Ralf works at Dunedin Hospital, Hildegard operates "Wings of Kotuku" nature tours. We can assist in planning your holiday and are happy to arrange necessary bookings. For a taste of real nature join our Sunrise Penguin Walk - a truly magic wildlife adventure!

Home Page: http://homepages.ihug.co.nz/~wingsok
Directions: *Turn from Highway 1 into Andersons Bay Road, continue into Musselburgh Rise and Silverton Street, turn left into Highcliff Road, proceed 700m, turn left into Every Street, 1st right Albion Street, 1st left Elliffe Place.*

Members of
**The New Zealand Association
Farm & Home Host Inc.**
maintain the highest standards &
are always delighted to welcome
guests into their homes.

732

Dunedin

Homestay
Address: 117 Easther Crescent,
Kew, Dunedin
Name: Bill & Jenny Smith
Telephone: (03) 455 5731
Beds: 1 King, 2 Single (2 bedrooms)
Bathroom: 1 Guests share
Tariff: B&B (full) Double $80, Twin $75, Single $55,
Dinner $25pp by prior arrangement.
NZ B&B Vouchers accepted $15 surcharge
Nearest Town: Dunedin 3km

Enjoy the relaxed atmosphere of our "Smokefree" Spanish style home with panoramic views over St Clair and St Kilda beaches, the Otago Harbour Basin and the hill suburbs of Dunedin City. The focal point of the House is a centrally situated "Atrium" with fernery, fish pond with fountain and a spa pool for your relaxation. We share our home with a pearly pied cockatiel named Sam. We have travelled extensively and enjoy meeting people from all walks of life. Dunedin has many architecturally significant buildings, an internationally recognised art gallery and museum. Other local attractions include the Otago Peninsula wildlife, Albatross Colony and Larnachs Castle. Sporting facilities within easy reach include golf (hire clubs available), bowls and tennis. The Carisbrook International Rugby / Cricket Ground is within easy walking distance. The house is situated down a quite private drive with off street parking. A warm friendly welcome awaits you.

Dunedin

Homestay Bed & Breakfast
Address: Dalmore Lodge
9 Falkirk Street,
Dalmore, Dunedin
Name: Loraine & Mike
Telephone: (03) 473 6513
Fax: (03) 473 6512
Beds: 1 Queen, 1 Twin,
1 Single (3 bedrooms)

Bathroom: 1 Guests share + extra shower/toilet downstairs
Tariff: B&B (continental) Queen/Twin $80, Single $50, Dinner N/A, Children under 12 $25, Children under 5 free. Credit Cards accepted.
NZ B&B Vouchers accepted $10 surcharge
Nearest Town: Dunedin 3.2 kms to city centre.

Come and enjoy the peaceful setting of Dalmore Lodge whilst at the same time being close to all the amenities and attractions the city of Dunedin has to offer. Our colonial home offers views of the harbour, Pacific Ocean, city lights, Botanical Gardens, hills and rural areas.
The balcony leads out onto a sheltered garden where you can relax, read a book or just enjoy watching the native birds along with our cat Teagan.
A three minute drive or a 20 minute walk can take you into the main business and shopping area. Public transport is available at the end of the driveway. We will meet you to / from airport, train, bus by prior arrangement at an extra minimal cost.
There is ample off street parking. Guests please no smoking indoors. We look forward to your visit.
Directions: *Please phone / fax for reservations / directions before 8.30am or after 5pm.*

East Taieri, Dunedin

Homestay
Address: 19 Main South Road (SH 1),
East Taieri, Dunedin
Name: Dorothy and Wyn Chirnside
Telephone: (03) 489 5790
Fax: (03) 489 1410
Email: chirnsides@xtra.co.nz
Beds: 2 Single (1 bedroom)
Bathroom: 1 Private
Tariff: B&B (full) Twin $80, Dinner $30 pp, Children half price.
Credit Cards accepted. NZ B&B Vouchers accepted $12 surcharge
Nearest Town: Mosgiel 2 kms

We invite you to share with us our near new spacious home, situated on over 1 acre of developing grounds and having a restful rural outlook over the Taieri Plains.
Our home is located on State Highway One between Dunedin Airport and Dunedin City, with each being approximately 15 minutes away by car.
Our home, a non smoking environment, is shared with our family cat.
The generously sized twin bedroom is located adjacent to the bathroom which has both a bath and shower, hairdryer etc. Both beds have electric blankets.
Guests are most welcome to relax with the family in the evenings for friendship and conversation.

Dunedin

Homestay
Address: 'Harbour Homestay',
19 Finch Street, Burkes, Dunedin
Name: Jill and Warwick Graham
Telephone: 03-471 0027
Beds: 1 Double, 1 Twin (2 bedrooms)
Bathroom: Handbasin in double room, shower in spa room across hall. 1 Ensuite.
Tariff: B&B (continental) Double $60, Single $35.
Children under 12 years half price.
Nearest Town: Dunedin (8 mins) 4.6kms.

We live in a quiet suburb 8 minutes from the city centre. Welcome to our interesting home overlooking the beautiful Dunedin harbour.
Our guest room has a comfortable bed with electric blanket, and we also have a full size spa available for your use at no extra charge.
our interests are boating, rugby, crafts, gardening and meeting people. Our cats mainly live outside but are very people friendly.
Directions:*Follow Port Chalmers Highway 88 along Anzac Avenue into Ravensbourne Road. Continue down the harbour side about 4.6 kms. Turn left at the 'Burkes' sign into Finch Street. Continue to top of hill, we are the last house on the left.*

Private bathroom is for your use exclusively,
Guests share means you may be sharing with other guests,
Family share means you will be sharing with the family.

Dunedin
Homestay
Address: 65 Every Street, Dunedin
Name: Alloway
Telephone: (03) 454 5384
Fax: (03) 454 5364
Mobile: (025) 229 5081
Email: alloway@xtra.co.nz
Beds: 1 Queen, 1 Single,
1 Double, 1 Single (2 bedrooms)
Bathroom: 1 Guests share

Tariff: B&B (continental) Double $90 and $120, Single $85, Dinner not available.
Not suitable for children.   NZ B&B Vouchers accepted $20 surcharge
Nearest Town: Dunedin 4.5km

*We are situated on the gateway to the Otago Peninsula, which features wildlife,
Walking Tracks, Taiaroa Head Albatross Colony, Disappearing Gun, Seal Colonies,
Yellow Eyed Penguins, Glenfalloch Gardens, and much more.*
*We are seven minutes to town centre. Our home is a modern interpretation of a
traditional Scottish house, and set in 1 acre of gardens and lawns, with indoor/
outdoor living. Awaken to the sound of abundant bird life in a quiet and secure
neighbourhood. We serve delicious healthy breakfasts.*
*One luxury bedroom complete with one queen and one single bed, plus one luxury
bedroom with one double and one single bed. Both rooms have tea-making facilities,
TV, heaters, electric blankets. Separate facilities with modern guest bathroom.*
*Relax far from the madding crowd. Businessmen welcome. All non smoking, no pets
and not suitable for young children.*
Home Page: www.bnb.co.nz

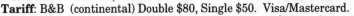

Dunedin
Bed & Breakfast
Address: 52 Tennyson Street, Dunedin
Name: Hulmes Court
Telephone: (03) 477 5319
Fax: (03) 477 5310 **Mobile**: (025) 351 075
Email: normwood@earthlight.co.nz
Beds: 3 Queen, 2 single (5 bedrooms)
Bathroom: 1 Ensuite, 2 Guests share

Tariff: B&B (continental) Double $80, Single $50. Visa/Mastercard.
NZ B&B Vouchers accepted $12 surcharge for Double, $39 surcharge for Ensuite.
Nearest Town: Dunedin (in fact right in the heart)

*Hulmes Court is a beautiful 1860's Victorian mansion, an architectural treasure situated
right in the heart of Dunedin. Just 2-3 minutes walk to restaurants, theatres, information
centre, Octagon, Art Gallery, and more. There is plenty of off-street parking in our grounds
of trees and gardens, providing tranquillity from the hustle and bustle so near by. Your host
Norman Wood and his staff are frequent travellers around New Zealand and the world. We
will provide you with warm, friendly and informative stay in our beautiful city. Hulmes Court
provides guests with a continental breakfast, free tea and coffee making facilities, use of our
kitchen, complimentary laundry, mountain bikes, email and internet, phone and fax (free for
local calls).*
Directions: *Drive up Stuart Street from the Octagon, over the Moray Place intersection, then
left into Smith Street, then veer to the left, this is Tennyson Street, and Hulmes Court.*
Home Page: http://www.earthlight.co.nz/business/hulmes/

Dunedin-Mosgiel

Homestay
Address: 14 Mure Street, Mosgiel
Name: Lois and Lance Woodfield
Telephone: (03) 489 8236
Email: l.l.woodfield@clear.net.nz
Beds: 1 Queen, 2 Single (2 bedrooms)
Bathroom: 1 Guests share
Tariff: B&B (full) Double $60-$80, Single $40.
Credit Cards accepted. NZ B&B Vouchers accepted
Nearest Town: Mosgiel (14kms South of Dunedin - 15 minutes drive)

Welcome to "The Old Vicarage", our English-style cottage home, set in a fragrant garden. Originally built by a dentist in the 1920's, it later served as the local vicarage for 46 years, before passing into the hands of various private owners, all of whom made sympathetic restorations and improvements. The outstanding feature is the exquisitely balanced garden with many varieties of rhododendrons, perennials, spring bulbs, and over 70 roses, all laid out in garden 'rooms'. The two upstairs guest rooms and bathroom enjoy a commanding view of the archery lawn and rock garden below, while warm Oregon panelling and unique leadlight windows throughout enhance the atmosphere.

Situated in Mosgiel, close to the Airport on the beautiful Taieri Plains, the property is just 15 minutes drive from central Dunedin. We are a retired Christian couple who have travelled extensively, have a collector's library and enjoy gardening, architecture, tramping, theology and history.

Waihola

Homestay/Self-contained Accomm
Address: Sandown Street,
Waihola, South Otago
Name: Lillian & Trevor Robinson
Telephone: (03) 417 8218
Mobile: (025) 545 935
Beds: 1 Double, 2 Single(2 bedrooms)
Bathroom: 1 Ensuite, 1 Family share
Tariff: B&B (full) Double $60, Single $40,
Dinner by arrangement $20.
NZ B&B Vouchers accepted
Nearest Town: 40 km south of Dunedin, 15 min to Dunedin Airport

We have a very comfortable home which is situated in a quiet street with views of mountains, Lake and township.
Our double bedroom has ensuite, tea making facilities, fridge, TV and heater. All beds have electric blankets.
Lake Waihola is very popular for boating, fishing and swimming. There is a bowling green and a golf course within 10 minutes drive.
We enjoy meeting people and ensure you a very pleasant stay.
Dinner by arrangement.
Directions: *Please phone night before where possible.*

Waihola

Lakeside Cottage Homestay
Address: 'Ivy Cottage', 7 SH 1,
Waihola, Otago 9055
Name: Bryan & Robin Leckie
Telephone: (03) 417 8946 **Fax**: 03 4178966
Beds: 1 Double, 2 Single (2 bedrooms)
Bathroom: 1 Private, 1 Family share
Tariff: B&B (full) Double $65, Single $40, Children under 12 $20,
Dinner $25 per person. Credit cards (MC/BC/VISA).
NZ B&B Vouchers accepted
Nearest Town: 40 km South of Dunedin on SH 1 (30 minutes) 15km from
Dunedin Airport.

"Ivy Cottage" has unique views of Lake Waihola, farm lands and forests.
Our double guest accommodation is detached from "Ivy Cottage" in an eye-catching
building affectionately known as "The Shed" with own bathroom, tea making facilities,
TV and heater. In "Ivy Cottage" we offer 2 single beds with share facilities. All beds have
electric blankets. We are retired restaurateurs, and continue our interests in food and
wines. Other interests include, power boating, sailing, fishing, bird watching, golf,
bowls, travelling, gardening, crafts, bridge, and keeping in touch with our extended
family. Lake Waihola and the waterways are well known for their birdlife and fishing.
The waterways extend to the Sinclair Wetlands, a wildlife reserve, Waipori Lake and the
Taieri River down to the sea at Taieri Mouth. We have a friendly Golden Retriever "Bud".
We enjoy hosting people and sharing the warmth of "Ivy Cottage".
Directions: *Please phone. Transport can be arranged from the Airport & Bus / Train*
terminals.

Milton

Farmstay
Address: 'Rhebrisk', Coal Gully Road,
Glenledi, Milton
Name: Alan & Glenise Weir
Telephone: (03) 417 4031
Fax: (03) 417 4031
Beds: 1 Double, 4 Single (3 Bedrooms)
Bathroom: 1 Guests share
Tariff: B&B (full) Double $60, Single $35,
Children half price, Dinner $20, Campervans $25. NZ B&B Vouchers accepted
Nearest Town: Milton 10 minutes

We live on a sheep and cattle farm in the Glenledi district 12km east of Milton.
Our modern home overlooks the Pacific Ocean, Tokomairiro River Estuary and
holiday settlement.
Well situated 1 hour drive from Dunedin, and on the main route to Southland, Catlins
or Fiordland and Lakes District.
Ideal stopover when travelling from Christchurch to Milford, Queenstown etc.
Our family are all married so we enjoy entertaining guests from all over the world.
Dinner by arrangement and 'spa' on request.
Close to fishing and golf.
No smoking in the house please.
For guest arriving by train or bus we are happy to meet you in Milton.
Directions: *Please phone.*

Balclutha

Farmstay+Self-contained Accom.
Address: 'Balcairn', Blackburn Road,
Hillend No.2 R.D, Balclutha
Name: Ken & Helen Spittle
Telephone: (03) 418 1385
Fax: (03) 418 4385
Beds: 1 Double, 2 Single (2 bedrooms)
Bathroom: 1 Guests share
Tariff: B&B (continental) Double $80,
Single $40, Children under 14yrs half price.
Dinner by arrangement $25pp. Campervans $5 per head.
NZ B&B Vouchers accepted
Nearest Town: Balclutha 22km, Milton 25km

Join our family at "Balcairn" a 500 acre sheep, beef and deer working farm for a relaxed friendly farmstay.
We are located not far from State Highway 1 and 8, just one hour south of Dunedin - an ideal stopover for guests travelling through the beautiful Catlins Scenic Reserve with its wonderful wildlife. Te Anau is 2 1/2 hours drive and Queenstown a 3 hour drive through lovely Central Otago.
Our home is a modern spacious two storey house with fully self contained guest accommodation all downstairs. All beds have electric blankets and full cooking and laundry facilities are available. We welcome our guests to join in any farm activities that they wish. Fishing, Deer-stalking, Golf and Tennis can be arranged with prior notice. Children most welcome. Guests arriving by bus or train can be met at Balclutha or Milton, or by plane at Dunedin Airport, 60km.
No smoking in our home please.
Directions: *Please phone*

Clinton - South Otago

Farmstay
Address: 'Wairuna Bush', Rural Delivery Clinton,
South Otago. Situated on Main South Highway 1
Name: LAR & KF Carruthers
Telephone: (03) 415 7222 If no reply ring after 5pm.
Beds: 1 King/Queen, 1 Double, 2 Single (3 bedrooms)
Bathroom: 1 Guests share
Tariff: B&B (full) Double $60, Single $40, Dinner $20.
Nearest Town: South/Gore, North/Balclutha both 1/2 hour drive on SH1.

KATHLEEN and ROY CARRUTHERS welcome you to their warm spacious home, set on 60 acres of farmland surrounded by native Podocarp Bush.
Unwind from your travel in peace and tranquillity.
Listen to Bellbirds, fantails and wood pigeons.
Follow newly formed walkways through 5 acres of native flora.
See Kahikatea, Matai, Miro and Totara trees (some being over 500 years old).
If you wish, Roy will be happy to introduce you to their farm dogs and thoroughbred horses, sheep, cows and calves.
Or take you for a game of bowls. There is a very challenging 9 hole golf course in Clinton and some extremely good fishing spots close by, or you can just laze around.
Please phone or book in advance.

Nuggets - The Catlins
Homestay+Self-contained beachfront.
Address: Nugget Lodge,
Nugget Road, RD1, Balclutha
Name: Noel & Kath Widdowson
Telephone: (03) 412 8783 **Fax**: (03) 412 8784
Beds: Two self contained private units with panoramic sea views. Both units
have a separate bedroom with a double bed plus sleeping for 2 in living area.
Bathroom: Ensuite each.
Tariff: Units $70 double, dinner $30 each. Breakfast $10 each or dine at the
Lumber Jack cafe, Owaka. Credit Cards (VISA/MC/BC).
Nearest Town: Balclutha, Owaka 24km

*Our large comfortable home is situated on the edge of the Nuggets Wildlife Reserve and
historic lighthouse, Home for Fur Seals, Hooker Sea-lions, Yellow Eyed Penguins,
large flocks of sea birds and in spring and early summer Elephant Seals and Leopard
Seals.*
*Sleep to the roar of the sea as we are right on the waters edge, awake to spectacular
views and sunrises. We offer warm hospitality and good food from our organic and
herb garden. Full cooking facilities, TV, fridge, Microwave, Central Heating in both
units. Kath as the Department of Conservations Wildlife Honorary Ranger spends
part of her day in the reserve guiding the public, educating and in seeing to the
protection of the wildlife. As our guests you are welcome to join her. Kath is also a keen
walker and photographer. Noel is employed in valuation and farm finance. All our
children are away from home. Our cat and dog respect the privacy of guests.*
We are the only accommodation at the Nuggets.
Directions: *20 minutes from Balclutha, 20 minutes from Owaka. Please phone.*

Owaka – The Catlins
Farmstay+Self-Contained Cottage (Papatowai Beach)
Address: 'Greenwood', Purakaunui Falls Road,
Owaka, South Otago
Name: Alan & Helen-May Burgess
Telephone: (03) 415 8259 (if no reply, phone after 6pm).
Fax: (03) 415 8259 **Mobile**: (025) 384 538
Beds: 1 Queen, 3 Single (3 bedrooms)
Bathroom: 1 Ensuite, 1 Private, 1 Family Share
Tariff: B&B (full/continental) Double $65, Single $45, Children half price, Dinner
$23, Lunch if required; Campervans $25; Self contained house at Papatowai beach
(sleeps 8) $60 per night (4 persons), $10 each extra person.
NZ B&B Vouchers accepted
Nearest Town: Owaka 14 km

*We welcome you to our 1900 acre farm in the heart of the Catlins, where our homestead
is situated within walking distance from the beautiful Purakaunui Falls. Our home,
which is set in a large garden, offers warm, comfortable accommodation for up to five
persons. The main guest bedroom which has an ensuite, walks through to a furnished
day-room and this opens to the outdoors. Other guest rooms are serviced with a private
bathroom. We enjoy providing a three course dinner and dining with our guests in the
evenings. Alan enjoys taking people around our sheep, cattle and deer farm. The district
features the yellow-eyed penguin and many beautiful, scenic drives and walking tracks
through native bush and beaches. Trout and sea fishing may also be enjoyed.*
Directions: *Take Highway 92 (Southern Scenic route) to Owaka from Balclutha or
Invercargill. From Owaka follow the signposts to Purakaunui Falls for 14 km. Our
name and farm name is on the gate entrance (just before you reach the falls).*

Owaka – The Catlins
Farmstay
Address: 'Tarara Downs', 857 Puaho Rd, R.D.2 Owaka
Name: Ida & John Burgess
Telephone: (03) 415 8293
Beds: 1 Double, 2 Single (2 bedrooms)
Bathroom: 1 Ensuite, 1 Family share
Tariff: B&B (full) Double $55, Single $35, Children half price; Dinner $15 (2 course), Campervans welcome.
NZ B&B Vouchers accepted
Nearest Town: Owaka 16 km

Our 2000-acre farm is situated in an area renowned for its bush and coastal scenery, within walking distance of the beautiful Purakaunui Falls. Our farm runs sheep, cattle and deer. As well as seeing normal farm activities, horse riding, bush walks and fishing trips are available in the district. We live in a comfortable New Zealand farmhouse with two cats, as our family have all left home, and enjoy eating our own produce and local delicacies. Children very welcome.
Directions: *Follow State Highway 92 to Owaka from Balclutha or Invercargill. Approximately 1 3 / 4 hours drive from Dunedin or Invercargill on a scenic road, follow signposts to Purakaunui Falls - we are the closest house to them.*

Owaka – The Catlins
Farmstay
Address: Glenomaru, No1 R.D., Balclutha
Name: Bruce & Kathryn Wilson
Telephone: (03) 415 8282
Fax: (03) 415 8282
Beds: 1 Double, 4 Single (3 bedrooms)
Bathroom: 2 Family share
Tariff: B&B (full) Double $60, Single $35, Children half price; Dinner $15; Campervans $25.   NZ B&B Vouchers accepted
Nearest Town: Balclutha 22 km, Owaka 11 km

We farm a 1500 acre property carrying sheep, cattle and deer.
Guests may be taken on a farm tour, which includes an inspection of a 130 year old home presently being preserved and water wheel. We have a friendly fox terrier called "Boon".
Fishing trips may be arranged. Golf equipment available, 9 hole golf course only ten minutes drive.
We are near Kaka Point, renowned for beach, lighthouse and viewing the yellow-eyed penguins and seals.
You may have family dinner with us or if preferred bed and breakfast.
Guests can be collected off public transport from Balclutha free of charge.
Directions: *Take Highway 92 from Balclutha towards Owaka, first turn right past sawmill. Matuanui Rd No Exit. From Owaka turn left beside Sawmill up gravel road Matuanui Road No Exit.*

Relax – Don't try to drive too far in one day.

Members of
The New Zealand Association
Farm & Home Host Inc.
maintain the highest standards &
are always delighted to welcome
guests into their homes.

Owaka – The Catlins
Homestay
Address: 'Kepplestone Park', Surat Bay Road, Newhaven, RD 1, Owaka
Name: Gay & Arch Maley
Telephone: (03) 415 8134 **Freephone**: 0800 105 134 **Fax**: (03) 415 8137
Beds: 1 Double, 4 Single (3 bedrooms) Separate guest unit, tea/coffee & TV
Bathroom: 2 Ensuite, 1 Family share
Tariff: B&B (special) Double $60/$85, Single $45, Dinner $25.
NZ B&B Vouchers accepted Surcharge $25 excess
Nearest Town: Owaka 6km

*Having taken early retirement we welcome guests to our home, situated one minute
from a beautiful beach, at the confluence of the Catlins and Owaka rivers. For the
enthusiasts, unpolluted beach, golf links, clubs available, Hooker seals basking on
beach, all within five minutes, or Amateur Radio (Gay ZL4JO.)*
*Having travelled extensively we understand the needs of fellow travellers and wish to
share with you our homely atmosphere and hospitality. Approximately 20 minutes
from Penguins and Purakaunui Falls.*
*We are both keen gardeners of our two acre property and organically grow our own
vegetables. Share an evening meal with us, served with a glass of wine. Choice of menu
with prior notice.*
*Bicycles for riding on the beach. Smoking negotiable (being ex smokers we understand
the needs of smokers!).*
Directions: *At north end of Owaka (at Royal Terrace St) follow signs to Newhaven,
at golf course, go "across" bridge, follow signs to Newhaven and Surat Bay. 3km from
bridge, first house on left on Surat Bay Road.*

Owaka – The Catlins

Farmstay+Self-contained Accom.
Address: 'Hillview' Hunt Rd, Katea, RD 2, Owaka, South Otago
Name: Kate & Bruce McLachlan
Telephone: (03) 415 8457 **Fax**: (03) 415 8650
Beds: Cottage;1 Queen, 4 Single (3 bedrooms) Homestead; 1 Queen 2 Twin (3 bedrooms)
Bathroom: Cottage; 1 Guests share. Homestead; 1 guests share
Tariff: B&B (continental) Homestead: Double $70, Single $40.
Cottage: Double $85. Dinner $20. NZ B&B Vouchers accepted - $10 Surcharge.
Nearest Town: Owaka 6km, Balclutha 27km

Our cosy farmstay cottage is adjacent to our homestead. It is fully self-contained with all modern appliances including microwave, TV and video. Telephone available.
Breakfast is provided in the privacy of the cottage and you are invited to dine with us in the evening by arrangement.
Our 450 acre sheep and cattle farm is also a haven for numerous unusual animals and pets. We have a large developing garden.
Bruce enjoys breeding and training working farm dogs and Kate's interests are gardening, handcrafts and children. She breeds black sheep and spins their natural wool. We both enjoy meeting people.
We are 5 mins from the golf course and 15 mins from Nugget Point where you may visit the lighthouse or view the yellow-eyed penguins and seals. Hooker sea lions are 10 minutes away at Cannibal Bay.
Phone bookings essential. Please phone after 4pm.
Directions: *27km from Balclutha, 5km north of Owaka. 1.5km from the main highway.Please phone ahead.*

Owaka - The Catlins

Guest House
Address: Catlins Retreat Guesthouse,
27 Main Road, Owaka, Catlins, South Otago
Name: Catlins Retreat Guesthouse
Telephone: (03) 415 8830
Beds: 3 Queen, 2 single (4 bedrooms)
Bathroom: 2 Guests share
Tariff: B&B (full/continental) Double $65,
single $40, School children half price,
Dinner $25 (3 course). NZ B&B Vouchers accepted
Nearest Town: Balclutha

Steve and Melanie, both early thirties and widely travelled, welcome you into their elegantly restored Rimu villa. All rooms are spacious and comfortable, warm with plenty of room to relax. We have no children and offer a relaxed informal home away from home. A cat may join our home shortly.
Ideally situated in the Catlins main town, within an easy stroll to the information centre and amenities. An excellent base to explore the Catlins wildlife, beaches and many walks. We will gladly give advice and directions to get the most out of your stay.
After an active day collapse in our hot spa, relax in the garden, enjoy a scrumptious home cooked meal or wander to local restaurants.
To find us we are on the Southern Scenic Route, 1 1/2 hours south of Dunedin and 2 1/2 hours north of Invercargill. You can't miss our blue picket fence and signs in Owaka.

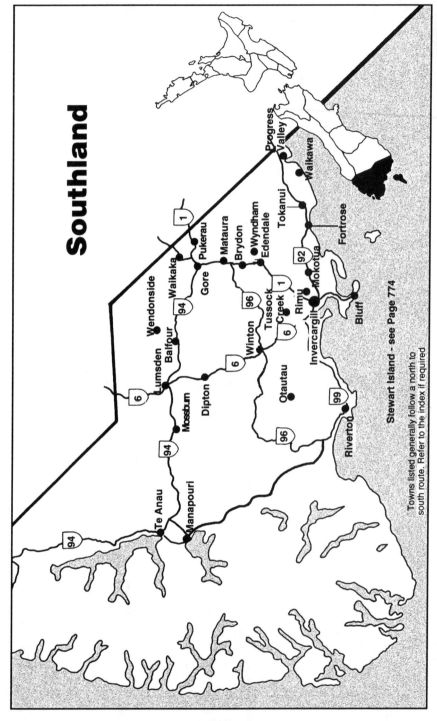

Southland

Towns listed generally follow a north to
south route. Refer to the index if required

Stewart Island - see Page 774

Te Anau

Farmstay
Address: Sinclair Road, R.D.1, Te Anau
Name: Dave & Teresa Hughes
Telephone: (03) 249 7581 **Fax**: (03) 249 7589
Mobile: (025) 344 016
Beds: 2 Single (1 bedroom)
Bathroom: 1 Ensuite
Tariff: B&B (continental) Double $70, Single $50.
NZ B&B Vouchers accepted May to October
Nearest Town: Te Anau 5 km

A warm welcome to travellers visiting Fiordland. We live on a deer farm, 5 minutes drive from Te Anau township, just 1 kilometre off the Milford Highway.
David, besides farming, works in the Deer Industry, while I teach at the local Primary School. We have three children; all are away from home now. Our pets, 2 dogs and a cat, enjoy meeting our visitors as well.
Your accommodation, which has magnificent views of Lake Te Anau and the Kepler and Murchison mountains, is a self-contained bed-sittingroom with ensuite, TV, tea / coffee making facilities and private entrance. We can assist with information and reservations to ensure your stay in Fiordland is memorable.
We request guests do not smoke in our home.
Directions: *Continue through Te Anau on road to Milford Sound for 5 km to Sinclair Road, turn right. We are the second house on the left - our name is on the letterbox.*

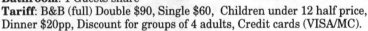

Te Anau

Farmstay
Address: 'Tapua' RD 2, Te Anau
Name: Dorothy & Donald Cromb
Telephone: (03) 249 5805
Fax: (03) 249 5805
Beds: 4 Single (2 bedrooms)
Bathroom: 1 Guests share
Tariff: B&B (full) Double $90, Single $60, Children under 12 half price, Dinner $20pp, Discount for groups of 4 adults, Credit cards (VISA/MC).
NZ B&B Vouchers accepted $10 surcharge
Nearest Town: Te Anau - 15 minutes, Manapouri 15 minutes.

You are surrounded by "Million Dollar" views while enjoying the comfort of our modern large family home. Electric blankets on all beds - heaters in bedrooms. Enjoy traditional Farm Style Meals, Homemade Preserves and Jams.
We are situated in a very handy position close to the main road, only 15 minutes from Te Anau or Manapouri making an excellent base for your sightseeing trips to magnificent Milford and Doubtful Sounds. We recommend a two night stay so that you can enjoy a relaxing trip to the Sounds, as well as a look over our 279 Hectare (700 acres) farm which carries 3000 sheep and 100 cattle. Some of New Zealand's best fishing rivers within a few minutes drive as are the finest walking tracks in the world, golf courses etc. We are happy helping plan your day trips. We have 2 cats.
Personal attention and service assured. Smoke Free home.
Directions: *Please phone.*
Homepage: http://www.fiordland.org.nz/html/tapua.html

Te Anau

Homestay + Self-contained Acco
Address: 13 Fergus Square, Te Anau
Name: Rob & Nancy Marshall
Telephone: (03) 249 8241
Fax: (03) 249-7397
Mobile: (025) 226 1820

Beds: 2 King, 2 Single (3 bedrooms)
Bathroom: 1 Ensuite, 1 Guests share
Tariff: B&B (full/continental) Double $80-$90 s.c., Single $50 Dinner $35, Credit cards. No smoking. NZ B&B Vouchers accepted $10 surcharge
Nearest Town: Te Anau 5 minutes walk

Rob, Nancy & Misty, our Sealpoint Burmese cat, welcome you to our quiet and tranquil home facing a park and only 5 minutes walk from the town and lake.

We are a couple retired from farming and are grandparents who enjoy meeting people from all walks of life. Rob is a member of the Lions Club and involved in community affairs.

Our modern home has two bedrooms, one king and one twin share facilities, a self-contained suite, sheltered courtyards and gardens. All rooms have tea making facilities and meals are served in the main dining room.

Most excursion tours, including Milford and Doubtful Sounds, can be booked from our home and guests are picked up at the door.

Off-street parking is available and baggage can be securely stored for those walking the tracks.

Directions: *Follow Lakeside Drive past town centre turn right into Matai Street then left into Fergus Square. RESERVATIONS: Please ring or fax.*

Te Anau

Farmstay
Address: Perenuka Farm,
R.D. 1, Te Anau
Name: Margaret & Les Simpson
Telephone: (03) 249 7841
Fax: (03) 249 7841
Beds: 2 Queen (2 bedrooms)
Bathroom: 2 Ensuite
Tariff: B&B (continental) Double $85. Commission extra for Agency Bookings.
Nearest Town: Te Anau 5km

Our 750 acre sheep and cattle farm is 5 km North of Te Anau, on the highway to Milford Sound. Our smokefree home and accommodation is situated well back from the road, on a terrace with panoramic views of the lake and surrounding mountains from all rooms. Spacious guest rooms are private, individual buildings in a garden setting. We enjoy guests joining us for breakfast and evenings of friendship and conversation. Each unit has high quality furnishings, fridge, tea / coffee making, electric blankets, heating, hair dryer, and full sized ensuite bathroom.

We both enjoy the outdoor opportunities of this region, so feel we can offer impartial information on the areas attractions. We also have a small flock of very friendly pet sheep.

Directions: *Follow Milford Sound Highway 5km north of Te Anau. Turn right into Sinclair Road, and immediately right into our driveway. Second house up the drive.*
Home Page: http://nz.com/webnz/bbnz/perenuka.htm.
www.fiordland.org.nz/html/perenuka.html

Te Anau
Guest House
Address: 'Matai Lodge', 42 Mokonui Street, Te Anau
Name: Richard Bevan
Telephone: (03) 249 7360 **Fax**: (03) 249 7360
Beds: 1 Queen, 2 Double, 9 Single (3 Twin, 1 Triple) (7 bedrooms)
Bathroom: 2 Guests share
Tariff: B&B (full) Double/Twin $76, Single $55, Triple $102,
Credit cards. NZ B&B Vouchers accepted
Nearest Town: Te Anau

The Matai Lodge is ideally located in a quiet residential area just 2 minutes walk from the lake and 5 minutes walk from the town centre. It offers clean, friendly, "homestyle" accommodation in a smoke-free environment. Full (and substantial) breakfasts are served in the dining / lounge area with tea and coffee always available, whilst there is also a separate TV lounge. All rooms are on the ground floor, have hot and cold vanity units, electric blankets and heaters. Te Anau is the hub of Fiordland, a World Heritage National Park. Among the main attractions of the area are Milford Sound, Doubtful Sound and Te Ana-au glowworm caves. World famous walking tracks including the Milford, Kepler, Routeburn and Hollyford all start close to the town. All excursion trips can be booked at the lodge, with bus pick-up at the gate. Off-street parking is available, with vehicles and baggage stored for guests walking the tracks.

Te Anau
Country Homestay
Address: 'The Farmyard', Charles Nairn Rd,
R.D.1, Te Anau 9681 -
Name: Ray & Helen Willett
Telephone: (03) 249 7833
Fax: (03) 249 7830 **Mobile**: (025) 289 0939
Beds: 1 Double, 1 Single (1 bedroom)
Bathroom: 1 Ensuite

Tariff: B&B (continental) Double $88 ($80 if booking direct), Single $55.
Nearest Town: Te Anau 3km.

Our home is on a 12 acre 'Hobby' farm 3km from Te Anau with spectacular views of mountains and bush. We have lived in Fiordland for many years, and invite you to share our knowledge and enthusiasm of the region with us.
We are ideally situated for excursions to Milford and Doubtful Sounds. As we both drive visitors to Milford, and for many years worked on the Milford Track, we are able to offer the very best advice for your Milford experience.
Our accommodation is a detached, self-contained cottage (microwave, fridge, etc) with privacy assured.
If possible, please phone before 8 am or after 5.30 pm, but we are often available during the day. Our pets - donkey, pony, Kune Kune pig, terriers (2), goats, sheep, will all be delighted to meet you.
Come and enjoy your stay with us. Welcome to Te Anau-Fiordland.

Private bathroom is for your use exclusively,
Guests share means you may be sharing with other guests,
Family share means you will be sharing with the family.

Te Anau

Homestay
Address: 'House of Wood',
44 Moana Crescent, Te Anau
Name: Elaine & Trevor Lett
Telephone: (03) 249 8404
Fax: (03) 249 7676 **Mobile**: 025-220 4356
Beds: 1 Queen, 1 Double, 2 Single (3 Bedrooms)
Bathroom: 1 Ensuite, 1 Guests share

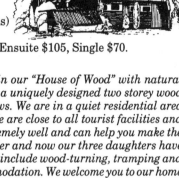

Tariff: B&B (continental) Double $90, Queen Ensuite $105, Single $70.
Nearest Town: Te Anau 3 minutes walk.

Welcome to Te Anau. We invite you to join us in our "House of Wood" with natural timber throughout interior. "House of Wood" is a uniquely designed two storey wood house with outside balconies and beautiful views. We are in a quiet residential area with the town centre just a short walk away. We are close to all tourist facilities and Lake. We know the Otago / Southland area extremely well and can help you make the most of your time in this area. Trevor is a builder and now our three daughters have left home we have more time for interests which include wood-turning, tramping and biking. We offer smokefree friendly Kiwi accommodation. We welcome you to our home and advise early bookings for our peak period November-March. Please phone for directions.

Te Anau

Bed & Breakfast
Address: 2 Lake Front Drive,
Te Anau
Name: 'The Cats Whiskers'
Hosts: Irene & Terry
Telephone: (03) 249 8112
Fax: (03) 249 8112
Beds: 1 King, 2 Queen, 4 Single (3 bedrooms)
Bathroom: 3 Ensuite
Tariff: B&B (full) Double $110, Single $65, Children half price.
Credit cards. Off Season rates.
Nearest Town: Te Anau 10 minute walk to centre.

Our home is situated on Te Anau lakefront opposite the Dept of Conservation Park Headquarters. We provide guests with comfort and outside access to all 3 rooms. Two bedrooms have 1 Queen and 1 Single. One large bedroom has 1 King and 2 Single and extra single can be added to the room, ie families. All have TV and tea making facilities. We are happy to provide a courtesy car to any of the variety of restaurants for dinner or as most of these are close by enjoy a walk along the lovely lakefront. We have a good car park and cars and luggage may be left while walking any of our famous tracks. We can book you any of the daily excursions to the famous Milford and Doubtful Sounds trips.
Directions: *To Lakefront Drive turn left off Highway 94 where signposted on edge of town. 1st house on right.*
Home Page: http://nz.com/webnz/bbnz/catwh.htm

Relax – Don't try to drive too far in one day.

Te Anau

Homestay
Address: Scott Homestay
57 Mokonui Street, Te Anau
Name: Jean & Bill Scott
Telephone: (03) 249 7875
Beds: 1 Double, 2 Single (2 Bedrooms)
Bathroom: 1 Guests share
Tariff: B&B (full) Double $70, Single $40, Children half price.
NZ B&B Vouchers accepted
Nearest Town: Te Anau

Our modern home is situated right in the town of Te Anau, with just 5 mins walk to the town centre, where there is a very good shopping area and an excellent range of good restaurants. The lake front is just around the corner, 3 mins, where there is a magnificent view of some of Fiordland's natural beauty. Te Anau is famous for its world-wide walks, the Milford Track, Routeburn and Kepler etc.

We are happy to help you organise day trips of your choice. We are retireed farmers and have been hosting overseas tourists for several years and enjoy meeting people from all over the world.

Our home is comfortable with central heating, and electric blankets on beds - guests have own bathroom.

We offer a choice of continental or cooked breakfast, and do our best to make your stay a happy one.

Our main interests are lawn bowls and gardening.

A homely welcome awaits you.

Te Anau

Guest House+Self-contained Acc
Address: "Shakespeare House",
10 Dusky Street, Te Anau
Name: Margaret & Jeff Henderson
Telephone: (03) 249 7349
Fax: (03) 249 7629
Mobile: (025) 392 225
Beds: 4 King, 3 Double, 4 Single (7 bedrooms)
Bathroom: 7 Ensuite
Tariff: B&B (full) Double $98-$112, Single $70-$80, Children phone for price, Credit Cards. (Off season rates). Self-contained: 1 Double, 3 Single (2 bedrooms), TV, lounge, galley kitchen, own bathroom.
Nearest Town: Te Anau, 10 minutes walk to centre.

Shakespeare House is a well established Bed and Breakfast where we keep a home atmosphere with personal service. We are situated in a quiet residential area yet are within walking distance of shops, lake, restaurants and attractions. All our rooms are ground floor and we have a choice of King, double or twin beds. Each room has private facilities, TV and tea / coffee making. Our self-contained two bedroom unit is popular for families. We also have a wheelchair unit. Our rooms open onto a large warm conservatory. Laundry facilities are available and non-smoking is preferred. Our tariff includes the choice of continental or a delicious cooked breakfast. A courtesy car is available. Off street parking. Baggage can be stored for guests walking tracks. A warm welcome awaits you from Margaret and Jeff and our cats Brothersoul and Sleepy.

Te Anau
Rural Homestay
Address: 'Eatons Coach House',
11 Charles Nairn Road, Te Anau
Name: Pam & Barry Eaton
Telephone: (03) 249 7078
Fax: (03) 249 7078
Beds: 1 Double,
2 Single (2 bedrooms)
Bathroom: 2 Private
Tariff: B&B (full) $90, Single $70,
Credit cards (VISA/MC) accepted.
Nearest Town: Te Anau - 3km south off Manapouri Highway

Our farmlet is situated with breathtaking mountain views, and a scenic 18 hole golf course next door. Horses, sheep, hens, ducks and Bob the cat share our life. Choose our self-contained 'Rose Cottage' or in-house twin room. Barry has an intimate knowledge of Fiordland, having spent much of his life hunting and guiding within this unique area. Pam is a horse riding instructress. Lessons can be arranged. Safe storage for gear/cars. Te Anau, gateway to Fiordland, has much to offer: Tramping, fishing, boating, golf and lots more. Please discuss your plans with us as we can provide extensive and impartial information and bookings can be made for you. We look forward to meeting you and know you will enjoy Fiordland, The Real New Zealand. Phone us direct for personal service.

Te Anau
Farmstay
Address: The Wilderness, No 1 RD, Te Anau
Name: Phyllis & Wayne Burgess
Telephone: (03) 249 5833
Fax: (03) 249 5833
Beds: 1 Double,
2 Single (2 bedrooms)
Bathroom: Family share
Tariff: B&B (continental) Double $70,
Single $55, Children negotiable,
Dinner $25, Full breakfast $6 extra per person.
Nearest Town: 19km east of Te Anau State Highway 94

Phyllis and Wayne welcome you to their sunny and warm home situated in a quiet garden setting with mountain views. We are a middle aged couple. Wayne combines farming and operating a Balage Contracting business over the summer months, he enjoys hunting, boating, fishing and the outdoor life.
Phyliis interests are gardening and the outdoors also cooking, which include home grown lamb and beef and fresh vegetables from her garden, followed by home made desserts. Breakfasts are according to you needs and range from light to hearty with my bottled fruit and tasty homemade jams. We would be happy to assist you with your planning of day trips around the "Walking capital of the World" and see the splendour and ruggedness of the real New Zealand Fiordland.
Directions: *4km past the Key on State Highway 94, 19km east of Te Anau. Name of mailbox. A friendly and warm welcome awaits you.*

Te Anau

Countrystay
Address: Country Style B&B,
Sinclair Road, R.D.1, Te Anau 9681
Name: Kerri & Stephen James
Telephone: (03) 249 7252

Freephone: 0800 200 865 **Fax**: (03) 249 7672 **Mobile**: (025) 316 765
Email: CountrystyleBB@xtra.co.
Beds: 1 Double (1 bedroom) - may make up extra bed.
Bathroom: 1 Family share
Tariff: B&B (continental) Double $75, Single $65, Children $10, Dinner $25,
°Full breakfast $6 extra per person, Campervans $8pp, Credit Cards (VISA/MC).
NZ B&B Vouchers accepted Accepted April-November
Nearest Town: Te Anau 7km

A "Kiwi" welcome awaits you to our home which captures the sun or relax beside our cosy fire in winter.We are situated just off the Milford Sound highway in a garden setting, where you can enjoy peace, tranquillity and fresh country air. Surrounded by impressive sheep and deer farming views and mountains.Our daughters Shelly (11) and Katie (8) along with ourselves enjoy meeting our guests. We have farming backgrounds and enjoy the outdoors.Help feed our pet lambs from September - February and other farm pets throughout the year.Our guest bedroom is tastefully decorated with heating and electric blankets. Tea, coffee and herbal teas always available. Full laundry service.We provide our guests with a smokefree environment indoors.
Directions: *Continue through Te Anau towards Milford Sounds for 5 km to Sinclair Road, turn right. Travel 2 1/2 km. Our green mail box has our name and flowers painted on it.*

Te Anau

Rural Homestay
Address: William Stephen Road, Te Anau
Name: Kepler Cottage
Telephone: (03) 249 7185
Fax: (03) 249 7186
Mobile: (025) 314 076
Email: kepler@teanau.co.nz
Beds: 1 Ensuite, 1 private
Bathroom: 1 Guests share, 1 Family share
Tariff: B&B (full) Double with ensuite $90, Twin with ensuite $80, Single $60.
Single with ensuite $70 NZ B&B Vouchers accepted From 1 April to 1 December.
Nearest Town: 5km Te Anau

Jeff and Jan Ludemann welcome you to their small lifestyle property, situated on the edge of Fiordland and just five minutes drive from Te Anau. Jeff is an aircraft engineer and Jan works from home as a freelance journalist and marketing consultant. Our hobby farm carries deer and sheep and our family includes two dogs and "Floyd" the cat. We have both travelled widely and in return welcome International and New Zealand visitors to share the magic of Fiordland. We can advise on tours and sightseeing and make bookings where needed. Te Anau is a comfortable base for travellers visiting the world famous Milford or Doubtful Sounds, or for anyone planning to walk one of the many popular walking tracks in the area. There is an excellent golf course nearby and several trout laden rivers, and we have mountain bikes, golf clubs and fishing gear available for your use.
Home Page: http://www.fiordland.org.nz/html/kepcot.html
Directions: *Phone (03) 249-7185 for directions.*

Te Anau

Farmstay/S.C. Cottage
Address: 'The Key', 2 R.D., Te Anau
Name: John & Carolyn Klein
Telephone: (03) 249 5807 **Fax**: (03) 249 5807
Beds: 1 Queen, 3 Single (2 bedrooms) with adjoining bathroom
Bathroom: 1 Private
Tariff: B&B (continental) Double $75 plus $20 per extra person,
Single $55, Children negotiable. Dinner $20pp. Campervans negotiable.
Credit cards accepted. NZ B&B Vouchers accepted Winter rates; May-October
inclusive $65 double.
Nearest Town: The Key is 32km from Mossburn and 15 minutes out of Te Anau.

*We are a family with three children , Chris 17, Alistair 16 and Casey 11 years old and
we all enjoy meeting people. We share our home with 2 cats (Joe and Nipper) and Misty
the dog who loves to play fetch. We also have a pet lamb over the summer which you
are welcome to help bottle feed.*

*Carolyn is a keen gardener and a superb cook with local venison or fresh Fiordland
fish a favourite, she also offers a special "Lobster" menu during our rock lobster season
(Prices will vary on availability and size) - Nobody has ever left our place hungry! John
operates a contracting business in the local farming community. His interests include
"winter" squash and he is also an active member of our local Lions Club. His first love
though is hunting and fishing in Fiordland so he is well qualified to offer guided
fishing on our local rivers for brown and rainbow trout.*

*We are also available to arrange wilderness fishing or hiking trips whether they be
guided or not. We can supply the necessary gear and advice and plan any trips to suit
your budget and make them a memorable experience.*

*Our country property overlooks the scenic Mararoa River which is itself famous for its
trout fishing and only a 5 min walk away.*

*We live at "The Key" a small rural community on the main Queenstown - Te Anau
highway (15 min drive to Te Anau). Surrounded by sheep, beef and deer farms and
majestic mountains it makes an ideal base to explore Fiordland (Day trips to Milford
Sounds and Doubtful Sounds are a must) and get away from the hustle of town. For
your convenience we also operate a booking agency for any of the local tourist trips. We
also offer free of charge for anyone interested evening bike rides, bushwalks, fishing or
small game hunting for those wanting a "country experience".*

*Your accommodation is a warm, sunny 3 year old self-contained cottage with large
bedrooms and adjoining bathroom. The kitchen and lounge have everything you'll
need for a comfortable stay.*

*Your cottage has a beautiful country view and privacy if you prefer, or you are welcome
to join us at your leisure for some good old country hospitality - We'd love to see you!*

Te Anau
Farmstay, Gardens
Address: Lynwood Park, State Highway 94,
8km before Te Anau, on left,signposted
Name: Allan & Trina
Telephone: (03) 249 7990 **Fax**: (03) 249 7990
Email: lynwood.park@xtra.co.nz
Beds: 2 Queen, 3 Single (3 bedrooms)
Bathroom: 2 Ensuite
Tariff: B&B (continental) Double $80, Single $55, Children $20. Full breakfast
by prior arrangement $5 extra, Credit Cards (Visa M/C, Bankcard, American
Express, Diners) NZ B&B Vouchers accepted $10 surcharge
Nearest Town: Te Anau 8km.

*Lynwood Park is a developing 6 acre display garden set amidst a 450 acre sheep, cattle
and deer farm.Our new home was built to ensure maximum comfort and privacy for
guests with semi detached accommodation. Each guest has a private entrance and
tea / coffee making facilities. We both have a keen interest in horticulture, growing our
own plants for sale and inclusion in 6 acre of gardens. Having built our own home we
have a well equipped workshop that is now used to build garden furniture.*
*We offer the use of our barbecue, laundry facilities, guest fridge, kitchen and children's
playground which our children Zach and Daniella look forward to sharing with you.
Come and meet our friendly dog named Gunther. We are able to advise or arrange most
activities to make your holiday a memorable experience. Wheelchair access and
facilities.Come as guests - leave as friends.*
Directions: *Lynwood Park, State Highway 94, 8km before Te Anau, on left, 100
metres past Lynwood Homestead. Signposted.*

Te Anau
Rural Lifestyle/Self Contained Accommodation
Address: Te Anau Milford Sound Rd,
RD 1, Te Anau
Name: Jane and Ross McEwan
Telephone: 03-249 7393
Fax: 03-249 7393
Email: rossjane.mcewan@xtra.co.nz
Beds: 1 Queen, 1 Single (1 bedroom)
Bathroom: 1 Ensuite

THE COTTAGE

Tariff: B&B (continental) Double $85, Single $60, Children $20.
Nearest Town: Te Anau 3 km

*Just 3 km from the centre of Te Anau, on the Milford Sound Highway, our detached
guest cottage offers you privacy and comfort, combined with a warm welcome into our
home.*
*We look across our farmland to the mountains and lake. The cottage is new, warm and
comfortable, with both a Queen and a single bed, and TV. Use the kitchen with
microwave, fridge, hot plates, if you wish. We welcome you into our home for breakfast
or have it served in your cottage.*
*Our three teenage children are in Dunedin, at Boarding School during the school year.
Ross is a builder and I am a part-time teacher. We both enjoy the rural lifestyle and
gardening. We have a friendly Jack Russell dog and two cats, and a small flock of
sheep.*
Directions: *Follow Te Anau-Milford Sound Road 3 km north of Te Anau. Look for
2nd mail box on the left after the Upukerora Bridge - Rapid No 153.*

SOUTHLAND

Te Anau
Self-Contained B&B Guest House
Address: 186 Milford Road, Te Anau
Name: Cosy Kiwi
Telephone: (03) 249 7475
Freephone: 0800 249 700
Fax: (03) 249 8471
Email: cosykiwi@teanau.co.nz
Beds: 4 Queen, 9 Single
Bathroom: All ensuites

Tariff: B&B (special) Double $75-$95, Single $50-$60, Family room $110-$145.
Children negotiable. Credit Cards accepted.
NZ B&B Vouchers accepted from 1 May - 30 September (surcharge $12)
Nearest Town: Te Anau 3 min walk.

Virginia and Gerhard and our two children welcome you to our all NEW Bed & Breakfast House. (We both have worked in Hospitality for over 20 years, we can speak German). We are located on the main road towards Milford Sound, close to the police station, only 3 minutes walk to Town Centre, Shops, Restaurants and other amenities. All rooms come with ensuite, TV and new decor, double glazed windows for warmth and sound proofing. (Paraplegic room is available).We offer you off-street parking, safe storage, laundry, telephone, fax, dining room / lounge room with coffee making facilities, outdoor BBQ and an upstairs terrace with sun loungers overlooking our beautiful mountain ranges.All excursion trips can be booked with us, with bus pick-up at the gate.Our breakfast buffet will be served in our dining room with lots of home-made breads, jams, preserves, yoghurt and pancakes.
Directions: *Main Road to Milford Sound opposite school on right, just look for our sign 'COSY KIWI'. Inspection welcome. (Introductory offer receive a free gift).*

Te Anau
Farmstay, Self Contained Accommodation
Address: Rose n' Reel,
Ben Loch Lane, RD2, Te Anau.
Name: Lyn and Lex Lawrence
Telephone: (03) 249 7582
Fax: (03) 249 7582
Mobile: (025) 545 723
Beds: 1 Queen, 1 Double,
1 Single (3 bedrooms)
Bathroom: 1 Guests share, 1 private.

Tariff: B&B (full) Double $75, Single $45. Credit Cards accepted.
Nearest Town: Te Anau 3 kms

Genuine Kiwi hospitality in a magic setting. Our small deer farm is only 5 minutes from Te Anau and you will be able to hand feed our tame fallow deer. Two friendly cats and a farm dog complete the menagerie. Our fully self contained cabin has two rooms plus bathroom with 1 Queen and 1 single. Complete with cooking facilities, fridge, microwave and TV. Sit on the veranda and watch the deer with a lake and mountain back drop.
Our modern two storey smoke-free home is set in an extensive garden. Two downstairs guest bedrooms. Laundry available.
Lex is a keen fly fisherman and average golfer, while I love to garden.
Fiordland is a special area and we will do all we can to make your time here memorable. Leave your car and baggage in safety with us while walking tracks etc.
Directions: *Please phone.*

FIORDLAND LODGE
Self contained log cabin sleeps four
Guided Fishing, Hunting & Nature Walks
Magnificent Mountain Views

Your Hosts Ron & Robynne Peacock
Kakapo Road • RD2 Te Anau • Ph/Fax 0-3-249 7832

Te Anau

Self Contained Accommodation
Address: Kakapo Road, RD2, Te Anau
Name: Ron and Robynne Peacock
Telephone: (03) 249 7832 **Fax**: (03) 249 7832
Email: fiordlandguidesltd@xtra.co.nz
Beds: 1 Queen, 2 Single (2 bedrooms)
Bathroom: 1 Private
Tariff: B&B (continental) Double/Twin $120
(each extra person $20), Single $100.
Children $10. Visa/Mastercard.
NZ B&B Vouchers accepted $48 surcharge.
May 1 - September 30 no surcharge.
Nearest Town: Te Anau 4 kms.

LOCATION MAPS

Milford Sound
Queenstown
Te Anau
Dunedin
Invercargill

Lake
Te Anau
Te Anau
4 km
To Mossburn

FIORDLAND
LODGE

Fiordland Lodge is our specially designed log cabin which has been built in the traditional method with sun dried logs that have been hand peeled. The interior is completed with recycled New Zealand native timbers. The Lodge is situated on our 80 acre farm, just 5 minutes from the Te Anau township and looks across a large pond to rural farm land, with the mountains of Fiordland National Park beyond. The lodge is fully self-contained and fitted out with a queen sized bed downstairs and two single beds upstairs.

We can cater for one extra with a comfortable roller bed for upstairs.

The grounds are landscaped with barbeque area. Laundry facilities are available in our house. Other facilities include telephone , facsimile and email. You have all the privacy you need, but we enjoy meeting our quests and welcome you to share our hospitality. Transport can be arranged from Te Anau.

Ron is a liscensed professional guide. He specialises in Wilderness fly fishing, with access by fourwheel drive vehicle, boat, floatplane or helicopter. He supplies all the fishing equipment required plus tuition for the less experienced . Ron also provides nature guiding services for birdwatching, natural history and geology. Guided hunting is also available for all species of wild game animals. Two hour, half day, full day or longer trips are available.

Ron's expertise is unique. He was a National Park Ranger for 25 years, seventeen of those in Fiordland. His love and knowledge of the area is extensive.

Robynne works part-time at the local College. Her interests include hiking, reading, travelling and gardening.

Together we enjoy the outdoors, both in New Zealand, and overseas. We have three teenage children, two dogs, one cat, cows, calves, sheep and lambs. Please phone for directions.

Note that off-season rates for the cabin apply, May 1st - September 30th.

Te Anau/Manapouri

Farmstay+Self-contained Accom.
Address: Hillside / Manapouri Road, Te Anau
Name: Murray & Marie Christie
Telephone: (03) 249 6695
(If no reply, phone after 1pm)
Fax: (03) 249 6695
Beds: 1 Double, 2 Single (2 bedrooms)
Bathroom: 1 Private
Tariff: B&B (continental) Double $75, Single $50, Children negotiable,
Credit Cards (VISA/MC). Winter rates May - September.
NZ B&B Vouchers accepted accepted all year
Nearest Town: Manapouri

We invite you to spend time in beautiful Fiordland. Murray and I with our two children live on a sheep / cattle farm approx. 5 minutes from Manapouri and 10 minutes from Te Anau. We have a delightful, warm self-contained cottage exclusively yours, with all facilities. Your tranquil setting overlooks the Mararoa River and the rugged Takitimu Mountains. This gives you full privacy but you are welcome to join our family at your leisure.

Within walking distance the Mararoa River provides superb trout fishing. Murray, who knows the Southland and Stewart Island areas well is willing to share his experience and knowledge of hunting, fishing and tramping. Guided walks / hunting trips are available including lake / river fishing.

I enjoy gardening and have a wide selection of native plants and trees. I especially welcome travelling families.

We really look forward to meeting you; travel safely.

Manapouri/Te Anau

Farmstay
Address: 'Crown Lea', Gillespie Road,
1 R.D., Te Anau
Name: Florence & John Pine
Telephone: (03) 249 8598 **Fax**: (03) 249 8598
Mobile: (025) 227 8366
Beds: (3 bedrooms)

Bathroom: 2 Private
Tariff: B&B (full) Double $90, (continental) Double $80, Single $65, Dinner $25,
Campervans welcome. NZ B&B Vouchers accepted $15 Surcharge
Nearest Town: Manapouri 20 minutes, Te Anau 30 minutes

Our 900 acre sheep, cattle and deer farm offers you a farm tour at 6pm and the wonderful views of the whole Te Anau Basin, the beautiful Fiordland mountains and Lake Manapouri, can be seen from the farm and our home.

Two nights are more restful for the traveller, and we are an ideal base for day trips to Doubtful and Milford Sounds, Te Anau Glow-worm Caves, or hikes on the many walking tracks in "The Walking Capital of the World".

Our grown family of three have "flown the nest", but their pets - sheep, deer and cat extend their warm welcomes to guests!

We have enjoyed hosting and meeting overseas guests and have travelled ourselves to England, Wales, Scotland, Ireland, Europe and Canada.

We look forward to welcoming you to our home.
Homepage: http://www.fiorldland.org.nz/html/crownlea.html

Te Anau - Manapouri

Self-contained Farmstay
Address: No. 1 R.D., Te Anau
Name: Carol & Ray McConnell
Telephone: (03) 249 8553
Fax: (03) 249 8553
Email: ray.mcconnell@xtra.co.nz
Beds: 2 Double, 6 Single (3 bedrooms)
Bathroom: 2 Private
Tariff: B&B (continental) Double $70,
Single $10, Children $5.
Nearest Town: Manapouri 15 mins, Te Anau 25 mins

Our sheep and beef farm is situated at the base of the Takitumu Mountains with magnificent views. Your accommodation is a comfortable fully self contained spacious farmhouse. It has an attractive private setting and is an excellent base for families or groups to explore The Fiordland National Park.
Many visitors return to enjoy another happy holiday.
There are wonderful day trips to doubtful Sound or Milford Sound plus several good walks in Fiordland. The Mararoa - Warau Rivers are popular for fishing.
We look forward to meeting you.

Manapouri

Self-Contained Accommodation
Address: 1 Home Street, Manapouri
Name: Ruth & Lance
Telephone: (03) 249 6600 **Fax**: (03) 249 6600
Email: eco@xtra.co.nz
Beds: 2 Double, 2 Single (2 1/2 bedrooms)
Bathroom: 2 Ensuite
Tariff: B&B (continental) Double $70,
Single $50. Credit Cards.
NZ B&B Vouchers accepted $5 surcharge
Nearest Town: Manapouri

FIORDLAND
ECOLOGY HOLIDAYS

Lance and I live in a small town on the perimeter of Fiordland National Park, only 3 minutes walk from Lake Manapouri, and 15 minutes drive from Te Anau. We are the gateway to Doubtful Sound.Our home is a popular Bed & Breakfast stopover for birds as we are surrounded with mature trees. Wake up to the call of the bellbird or tui, and watch the birds feeding while you have breakfast. A warm, homely self-contained flat with an open fire will help make your stay comfortable. You have the option of total privacy or joining us.We both have a keen interest in underwater and natural history photography, sailing, diving and conservation. I was a Social Worker for 15 years, working mainly with teenagers and drug addicts. I now help Lance run our own business, Fiordland Ecology Holidays.Lance worked with the Department of Conservation for 12 years as skipper of a research vessel. He now skippers our 65ft charter / research yacht Breaksea Girl, which is based in Doubtful Sound. He works with scientists and film crews from all over the world, but our main clients are travellers.We also run 3, 5 and 10 day live aboard charters in Fiordland throughout the year. Why not join us on board for a few days and learn about our rainforest, be introduced to fur seals and play with dolphins? We feel it is a privilege to be able to share our knowledge and love of this part of the world. Having both travelled widely, we know how important it is to have somewhere that feels like home. We suggest at least a 3 to 4 day stay as there is so much to do off the beaten track, especially if you join us on one of our trips. If we can help plan your holiday, please write to us.We really look forward to meeting you and hope that where ever you come from your travels are safe and happy.
Home Page: www.fiordland.gen.nz.   757

Manapouri
Homestay
Address: 'The Cottage',
Waiau St, Manapouri
Name: Don & Joy MacDuff
Telephone: (03) 249 6838
Freephone: 0800 677 866 **Fax**: (03) 249 6839
Beds: 1 Queen, 1 Double, 1 Single (2 bedrooms)
Bathroom: 2 Ensuite

Tariff: B&B (continental) Double $75, Single $55, Dinner by arrangement.
Full Breakfast $5 extra pp. Laundry facilities available (small charge).
Credit Çards. NZ B&B Vouchers accepted by arrangement
Nearest Town: Te Anau 15 mins.

Charm tranquillity and a warm welcome is assured if you choose to stay with us in our lovely picturesque cottage, situated by the lower Waiau River in the Manapouri township. We are only a few minutes walk to where the boat departs for the power station and Doubtful Sound. Our home is surrounded by trees and we offer magnificent views of the mountains, river and lake. Our guestrooms are ensuite with tea and coffee making facilities. Each bedroom has French doors that open to an English cottage garden. Wander outside and listen to the birds, sit and enjoy the peace and quiet. An ideal stay is 3 nights to enjoy both Milford and Doubtful Sounds and the many walks in the area.
We are middle-aged and have enjoyed living in many parts of New Zealand, including the wilderness of Fiordland. We (Don, Joy, Rosie the Skye terrier and Kittie) look forward to meeting you and making our cozy cottage your home away from home.
Home Page: www.fiordland.org.nz.html/cottage.html

Lumsden - Dipton
Farmstay
Address: 'Bilberry Oak',
98 Boundary Road, Dipton
Name: John & Judy Buchanan
Telephone: (03) 248 5228 **Fax**: (03) 248 5228
Mobile: (025) 284 6006
Beds: 1 Double, 2 Single (2 bedrooms)
Bathroom: 1 Family share
Tariff: B&B (continental) Double $60, Single $40, Children half price,
Dinner $20 per person, Campervans welcome.
Credit cards. NZ B&B Vouchers accepted
Nearest Town: 24km south of Lumsden, Invercargill 65 km, Dipton 6 km.

Our farm is situated on one of the main roads from Invercargill through to the attractions of Te Anau, Milford Sound and Queenstown so is a convenient stopover point during your travels.
Our comfortable farmhouse is set in a large garden which includes a covered swimming pool. We welcome you to have dinner with us or just bed and breakfast, the choice is yours. We also offer the use of our laundry facilities.
John is always very willing to take folk about the property, explain about the New Zealand way of farming and if possible, let you see at close hand such activities as shearing. Ours is a sheep farm with cropping and a few cattle. We also have a Hampshire Sheep Stud, 2 cats and Rose, the Jack Russell.
We are interested in most sports and if you feel like a day's break from sightseeing, a game of golf or a few hours fishing on the Oreti River could be easily arranged.
Directions: *Please telephone first.*

Lumsden

Farmstay
Address: R.D. 4, Lumsden
Name: Annette & Bob Menlove
Telephone: (03) 248 7114
Fax: (03) 248 7114
Mobile: (025) 226 8426
Beds: 2 Double, 4 Single (4 bedrooms)
Bathroom: 2 Private, 1 Family share.
Tariff: B&B (full) Double $60,
Single $30, Dinner $20.
NZ B&B Vouchers accepted
Nearest Town: 9 km south of Lumsden, Invercargill 80 km

Josephville Gardens

We have a 480 hectare farm which runs sheep cattle and deer. Surrounding our comfortable warm home we have a large garden with a small nursery attached. The garden has a large selection of Rhododendrons, specimen trees, roses and perennials. The golf course is 3 kms away, golf clubs are available, a good fishing river nearby. We have hiked in our mountains a lot and can give advise on where and what to see. If you wish, a four wheel drive trip is available.
We live on State Highway 6 (Rapid sign 824), 9 kms south of Lumsden.

Lumsden

Farmstay
Address: Caroline Valley Road,
Dipton, Southland
Name: Mern & Nathlie McLean
Telephone: (03) 248 5268
Fax: (03) 248 5268
Beds: 5 Single (3 bedrooms)
Bathroom: 2 Family share
Tariff: B&B (continental) Double $65,
Single $40, Dinner $20,
Credit Cards. NZ B&B Vouchers accepted
Nearest Town: 13km south of Lumsden, Invercargill 67km

Our home is 13km south of Lumsden on State Highway 6, the second house on Caroline Valley Road.
Our central location means travellers have just over an hours drive to Te Anau and Queenstown, with only 50 mins to Gore and Invercargill.
We farm sheep and stud beef cattle, giving you an opportunity to experience a typical working New Zealand farm.
Our area provides good bush walking, trout fishing and golf.
We offer friendly hospitality and enjoy meeting people.
If previously arranged an evening dinner will be available.
We look forward to your visit. Please phone first.

Relax – Don't try to drive too far in one day.

Balfour

Farmstay
Address: 'Hillcrest', 206 Old Balfour Road,
No. 1 R.D., Balfour
Name: Ritchie & Liz Clark
Telephone: (03) 201 6165 **Fax**: (03) 201 6165
Email: clarkr/@esi.co.nz

Beds: 1 Double, (2 single, studio unit) 2 bedrooms.
(Fold-up bed + cot available for children)
Bathroom: 1 Private, 1 Family share
Tariff: B&B (full) Double $80, Single $40, Children half price; Dinner $20p.p.;
Campervans $20. NZ B&B Vouchers accepted
Nearest Town: Balfour 3 km, Lumsden 16 km, Gore 40 km

We welcome you to join us on our 650 acre sheep and deer farm. We have three school-age children and our interests include handcrafts, gardening, tennis, photography, fishing and our two cats. Enjoy a relaxing dinner with fine food, wine and conversation. Breakfast is served with fresh baked bread, homemade yoghurt, muesli, jams and preserves.Relax in our garden and enjoy the farm and mountain views or a game of tennis on our asphalt court. We are close to the Mataura, Waikaia and Oreti rivers which are great for trout fishing. A fishing guide can be arranged on request. A complimentary farm tour is included. Our farm is situated 3km from Balfour which is a popular stopover, being on the main tourist route from the lakes to Dunedin via Gore. (S.H.94) Smoke free home.

Directions: *When arriving at Balfour crossroads, take the road to Waikaia, then the first turn to the left Old Balfour Road and travel 2.5km, we are on the right. Please phone, fax.*

Wendonside

Farmstay
Address: 'Ardlamont Farm',
110 Wendonside Church Road North,
Wendonside, No.7 R.D., Gore
Name: Lindsay & Dale Wright
Telephone: (03) 202 7774
Fax: (03) 202 7774
Email: ardlamont@xtra.co.nz
Beds: 1 Double, 2 Single (2 bedrooms)
Bathroom: 1 Private
Tariff: B&B (full) Double $80, Single $40, Children half price. Dinner $25.
Nearest Town: Riversdale 15 km, Balfour 12 km

Come and experience 'Ardlamont', a 4th generation 1200 acre sheep and beef farm which offers panoramic views of Northern Southland.
Gourmet meals are a speciality and will be served with fine New Zealand wines. Our farmstyle breakfasts are another treat - the aroma of freshly baked bread to greet you in the morning.Take a tour of the farm, then return to the comforts of our large recently renovated 90 year old homestead.Having travelled widely and experienced this kind of hospitality in other countries we enjoy welcoming visitors into our home. We have 3 school-age children and welcome family groups.We have a wide range of interests including sport, the arts, Toastmasters, music and restoring our house to its former glory.Two of New Zealands best trout fishing rivers only five minutes away.
We are 15 minutes off S.H.94 - (Queenstown - Dunedin route) and well worth the detour.
Directions: *Please phone or write.*

Waikaka

Farmstay
Address: Blackhills, R.D.3 Gore, Southland
Name: Blackhills Farmstay - Dorothy & Tom Affleck
Telephone: (03) 207 2865
Fax: (03) 207 2865
Beds: 1 Queen, 2 Single (2 bedrooms)
Bathroom: 1 Family share, 1 Guest share
Tariff: B&B (full) Double $60, Single $40, Children under 13 half price;
Dinner $20. NZ B&B Vouchers accepted
Nearest Town: Waikaka township 8km, Gore 30km.

*Our sixty-year-old home, renovated to give generous comfortable living area, is
situated on our 360 ha intensive sheep farm on a ridge above Waikaka River. You may
have dinner with us or if you prefer only bed and breakfast. A farm tour is available
and as our family becomes more independent we like to share time with guests. Venture
off the main road and enjoy warm hospitality, superb views and the refreshment of a
quiet rural visit.*
Directions: *Turn off State Highway 1 just north of Gore, onto State Highway 90. Turn
left at Waikaka Valley corner, marked by church and windmill, follow signposts to
Waikaka until T corner (approx 10 km). At T corner turn left, then first right onto
gravel Nicolson Road. Proceed 4 km veering right at each intersection. We live on
Robertson Road, the last kilometre a steep hill - 20 minutes from State Highway 1.*

Waikaka Valley, Gore

Farmstay
Address: 'Glenellen',
Waikaka Valley,
No 5 R.D., Gore
Name: Brigette & Donald Morrison
Telephone: (03) 207 1857
Fax: (03) 207 1857
Email: rosedale@esi.co.nz
Beds: 1 Double, 3 Single (2 bedrooms)
Bathroom: 1 Private, 1 Family share
Tariff: B&B (full) Double $75, Single $45, Dinner $25.
NZ B&B Vouchers accepted
Nearest Town: 10 km northeast of Gore on SH90

*Welcome to "Glenellen" and to Waikaka Valley, a small traditional rural community,
10 km from Gore. We are a young family on a 1,500 acres mixed farm of sheep and
arable with our two boys representing the sixth generation on the property. We also
maintain a Romney Stud amidst this setting of beautiful green rolling countryside. We
are both well travelled and enjoy our sport and outdoor activities. There is fishing on
the farm and most other amenities are available locally. Our spacious home secluded
by mature gardens offers a warm and relaxed stay and our labrador and spaniel
provide a hearty welcome. Verandahs and sunny lounge and open fires accommodate
all seasons. You may have dinner with us and enjoy the best of New Zealand cuisine,
or if you prefer just bed and breakfast. There is a good range of restaurants in Gore.
We prefer no smoking in the dining room and bedrooms.*
Directions: *Please phone*

SOUTHLAND

Pukerau, Gore

Country Homestay
Address: State Highway 1, Pukerau
Name: Dawn & David Connor
Telephone: (03) 205 3896
Fax: (03) 208 1989
Email: ewen@esi.co.nz
Beds: 1 Double, 2 Single (2 bedrooms)
Bathroom: 1 Private, 1 Guests share
Tariff: B&B (full) Double $70, Single $45,
Dinner $25, Credit Cards. NZ B&B Vouchers accepted
Nearest Town: Gore 12km

We welcome you to our warm and comfortable home. We have a small private garden with mature trees and shrubs and have a lovely rural outlook. We have two acres where we run a few pet South Suffolk sheep. Growing a variety of Orchids is our main interest and we enjoy sharing these beautiful flowers with others. We are just minutes away from several rivers including the Mataura which is well known for brown trout fishing. All beds have electric blankets. Laundry facilities available. We welcome you to have an evening meal with us, or if you prefer, only Bed and Breakfast, cooked or continental. We are 12km east of Gore on State Highway 1. We prefer guests not to smoke in our home.
Directions: *Please phone for directions and bookings.*

Gore

Farmstay
Address: 'Dellmount',
Woolwich Street, Gore, Southland
Name: Brian & Noelene Ross
Telephone: (03) 208 1771
Beds: 1 Double, 2 Single (2 bedrooms)
Bathroom: 1 Private, 1 family share

Tariff: B&B (full) Double $70, Single $45, Children half price, Dinner $20pp (by prior arrangement). Campervans facilities available. NZ B&B Vouchers accepted
Nearest Town: Gore 2km

A warm Kiwi welcome awaits you at "Dellmount". We are situated approximately 2km from the town centre, on the banks of the Mataura River, which is famous for brown trout fishing. We have a small farm of 50 acres, where we run our Arabian Horse Stud, plus sheep and cattle also a few hens, two cats and two dogs. Our modern home is warm and comfortable with spacious lounge and dining areas. Being handy to the local golf course, shops and bush walks, we will provide you with a comfortable base from which to explore the delights of the area or a pleasant peaceful overnight haven on your travels. A home cooked meal using local produce is available by prior arrangement if required or just Bed & Breakfast. We, Brian and Noelene, would enjoy meeting and sharing our home with you.

There are some good tips for easier travel on page 7

Gore

Homestay
Address: 584 Reaby Road, 7 RD Gore
Name: Irwin's Farmstay
Telephone: (03) 208 6260
Beds: 1 Queen, 4 Single (3 bedrooms)
Bathroom: 1 Guests share, plus 1 extra toilet
Tariff: B&B (full) Double $70, Single $40, Children half price, Dinner $25 pp.
Nearest Town: Gore (10 minutes)

Sandy and Tricia are semi retired having left two sons farming where we did eight years of farmstays. Sandy goes back to lend a hand when necessary. We have 43 acres with native bush covered hills nearby, run sheep and have two sheep dogs and are in the process of building a completely new garden, come and share our joys and frustrations.

Gore is 10 minutes away and we are on the road to Dolamore Park (another 5 minutes) where there are several walks and a playground. Many trout fishing rivers are an easy drive away. We enjoy meeting people having done some overseas travel and other interests include sport, reading, gardening and knitting. Beds have electric blankets, laundry facilities, cot and highchair available. No smoking indoors please. We have a geriatric cat that may get company. Please phone for directions.

Mataura

Farmstay
Address: 291 Glendhu Road,
No. 4 R.D., Gore
Name: 'Kowhai Place'
Telephone: (03) 203 8774
Fax: (03) 203 8774
Beds: 1 Queen, 6 Single (4 bedrooms)
Bathroom: 1 Guests share, 1 Private
Tariff: B&B (full) Double $70, Single $40, Children half price, Dinner $20pp.
NZ B&B Vouchers accepted
Nearest Town: Mataura 3 kms

John and Helen have a mixed farm of cattle, sheep, deer, goats. We farm at the bottom of the South Island, and have been told, several times by overseas visitors - this area is the most beautiful in the world. We live 5 minutes from one of the best brown trout fishing rivers in the world. Five minutes to a beautiful 9 hole golf course. Drive one hour south and you are at the seaside. One and a half hours to beautiful lakes district, and ski fields.

We both play golf, enjoy gardening and working on our farm.

15 minutes south of Gore at 291 Glendhu Road. Turning off State Highway 1 opposite the Freezing Works at Mataura. 3 minutes from Mataura. 30 minutes from Invercargill. A warm welcome and a farm style, cooked meal, if orderd in advance, awaits you on arrival.

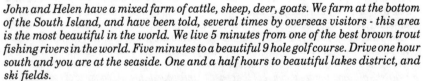

Wyndham

Farmstay
Address: Mimihau, No 2 R.D,
Wyndham, Southland
Name: Smith's Farmstay,
Beverly & Doug Smith
Telephone: (03) 206 4840 **Fax**: (03) 206 4840
Email: smith'sfarmstaynzhomestay.co.nz
Beds: 4 Single, 1 Queen (3 bedrooms)
Bathroom: Guests share, two separate toilets
Tariff: B&B (full) Double $80, Single $45, Children negotiable, Dinner $25.
Credit Cards: Visa/Mastercard. NZ B&B Vouchers accepted All year.
Nearest Town: Wyndham 5km, Edendale 10km

You are assured of a warm welcome to our 44 year old home and 172 hectare sheep farm. We are situated on the hills 5km from Wyndham giving a panoramic view of the Southland Plains and the mountains beyond.The Mataura, Mimihau and Wyndham Rivers, renowned for brown trout, are just a short 5km drive away. Doug is a keen and experienced fisherman will only be too happy to share his knowledge of these rivers with you.Beverly, a qualified nurse, enjoys cooking, floral art, gardening and knitting. We have two friendly cats.You will enjoy comfortable and homely surroundings and genuine home cooking including preserved fruits, jams, home grown meat and vegetables. Special diets available. Your are welcome to join us for an evening meal, if required. Please ring the night before.We enjoy meeting people and both are of friendly disposition with a sense of humour. We enjoy travel and have three adult sons. Tours of lovely gardens offered. Long stayers most welcome: - Please book in advance, to avoid disappointment. We are members of New Zealand Association of Farm & Home Hosts.
Directions: *5km from Wyndham on the Mokoreta Road. Sign at gate.*

Progress Valley, South East Catlins

Farmstay
Address: 'Catlins Farmstay' 174 Progress Valley Road,
Progress Valley, R.D. 1, Tokanui
Name: June & Murray Stratford
Telephone: (03) 246 8843 **Fax**: (03) 246 8844
Beds: 2 Double, 2 Single (3 bedrooms)
Bathroom: 1 Ensuite, 1 Guests share, 1 Family share
Tariff: B&B (full) Double $80-$90, Single $50, Children half price, Dinner $25,
Campervans welcome. Credit Cards. NZ B&B Vouchers accepted $10 surcharge
Nearest Town: Invercargill 80 km, Dunedin 170 km

Welcome to our place in the Catlins situated 6 km from Waikawa and close to the Petrified Forest at Curio Bay and Hectors Dolphins.Our home is centrally heated, plus open fire in lounge and is set in large garden with tennis court. The farm is 1000 acres and runs 3000 sheep, 50 cattle including Dexters and 500 deer along with one eye dog and two huntaways. Our family is grown up and interests include meeting people, music, cooking, gardening and most sports including rugby. Guests are most welcome to join in farm and community activities or walk the hilltops for great views of the coast. Our favourite menus consists of local seafood for entree, followed by home grown meat and fresh veges from the organic garden, followed by home-made desserts. Breakfasts are according to your needs and range from light to hearty with my bottled fruit and home-made jams and jellies hard to resist.
Directions: *From Invercargill follow scenic route and 22 km past Tokanui take right turn to Progress Valley. We are first house on right. Alternative coastal route Invercargill via Curio Bay, 6 kms north Waikawa turn right into Manse Road, we are 2nd house on the right. From Dunedin go to Balclutha on to scenic route through Owaka and Catlins Forest until sign post to Progress Valley. Turn left, we are first house on right.*

Tokanui
Farmstay
Address: 'Egilshay', R.D.1, Tokanui
Name: Jean & John McWilliam
Telephone: (03) 246 8703
Fax: (03) 246 8551
Email: jeanmcw@xtra.co.nz
Beds: 1 Double, 3 Single (2 bedrooms)
Bathroom: 1 Guests share
Tariff: B&B (full) Double $70,
Single $40, Dinner $25, Children half price,
Campervans welcome. Credit Cards. NZ B&B Vouchers accepted
Nearest Town: Invercargill, 60 km, Dunedin 165 km

Welcome to our home, which is a 640 acre sheep and cattle property on the "Southern Scenic Route" - the Gateway to the Catlins. We have a modern home in attractive surroundings with sunny bedrooms, comfortable beds and electric blankets. Guests have own bathroom and toilet.Come and see our unique Porpoise Bay with its friendly Hectors' dolphins, and Curio Bay on the rugged south coast of New Zealand. Trout fishing, golf course, bowling green and tennis courts are all nearby. Deep sea trips available. You are welcome to inspect the many seasonal activities on the farm.
Join us for dinner, which features our own homegrown produce. Continental and cooked breakfast available.Our interests include cooking, gardening, woolcrafts and service clubs. Come and enjoy our warm Southern Southland hospitality in a relaxed, rural setting. Our home is a smokefree zone.
Directions: *Easy to find. Southern Scenic Route Highway 92, 6km east of Tokanui Rapid No 583*

Waikawa
Farmstay
Address: 595 Yorke Road, Progress Valley,
No. 1 RD Tokanui, Southland.
Name: Bruce & Alison Yorke
Telephone: (03) 246 8833
Fax: (03) 246 8833
Beds: 1 Double, 2 Single (2 bedrooms)
Bathroom: 1 Guests share,
1 family share
Tariff: B&B (full) Double $80,
Single $50, Dinner $25.
 NZ B&B Vouchers accepted
Nearest Town: Invercargill 85km, Dunedin 175km

A warm welcome awaits you at Bay Farm, your hosts are Bruce and Alison Yorke. Bay Farm is a tranquil retreat situated in native bush overlooking Waikawa Harbour South Catlins. (It is one of Catlins best kept secrets.) We farm sheep and cattle on 1200 acres. Dinner with us includes fresh home grown produce.
Opportunities exist for farm tours, fishing, walks on a private beach and sailing. Non-smokers preferred.
Our interests include tramping, sailing, horticulture and meeting people.
Directions: *From Invercargill take Southern Scenic Route 70km, turn right at Progress Valley turn right into Yorke Road. We are 6km in Yorke Road. From Dunedin take Southern Scenic Route, turn left at Progress Valley, turn right into Yorke Road. Bay Farm 6km.*

Fortrose Gateway to the Catlins

Farmstay
Address: 'Greenbush' 298 Fortrose - Otara Road,
No. 5 R.D., Invercargill
Name: "Greenbush Farmstay"
Ann & Donald McKenzie
Telephone: (03) 246 9506 **Fax**: (03) 246 9506
Beds: 1 Double, 2 Single (2 bedrooms)
Bathroom: 1 Guests share
Tariff: B&B (full) Double $80, Single $40, Children negotiable, Dinner $25.
NZ B&B Vouchers accepted $10 surcharge
Nearest Town: Invercargill 50km

*Our farm is on the 'Southern Scenic Coastal Route' where we farm sheep and cattle.
The property is boundaried by Foveaux Strait where you can stroll on a wild beach.
We are the forth generation at 'Greenbush'. Our home is nestled in a well established
garden where you can wake up to birdsong, enjoy our quiet surroundings and our two
friendly cats.*

*A golf course is nearby at Fortrose, Waipapa Lighthouse - scene of the worst maritime
disaster is nearby and sealions can sometimes be seen basking on the beach.*

Curio Bay - the petrified forest is only half an hour away.

*You are welcome to join us for an evening meal or just Bed and Breakfast. Please ring
the night before if possible to avoid disappointment. Non smokers preferred.*

Directions: *Approximately 4 km from Fortrose Garage. 298 on the Fortrose-Otara
Road.*

Invercargill on Southern Scenic

Farmstay/Self-contained Cottage
Address: 'Fernlea', Mokotua, No 1 R.D., Invercargill
Name: Anne & Brian Perkins
Telephone: (03) 239 5432 or (03) 239 5412
Fax: 03 239-5432 **Mobile**: (025) 313 432
Email: fernlea.farmstay.htm
Beds: Self-contained Cottage - 1 Double + Double divan in lounge (1 bedroom)
Bathroom: 1 Private
Tariff: B&B (full) Double $90 one night, $160 for two nights. Extra persons $20,
Children negotiable, Dinner $25, Breakfast foods provided - self-catering.
NZ B&B Vouchers accepted $15 surcharge
Nearest Town: Invercargill 15km

*Anne's cottage nestles tranquilly in its own olde world garden, lovingly restored as a romantic
hideaway, close to the beautiful unspoilt area of the Catlins and Mataura fishing river; it holds
particular attraction for those wishing to get away from it all. The cottage is completely self
contained with colour TV, electric blankets, microwave in fully equipped kitchen, shower,
toilet, and cosy pot belly stove. Our family farm milks 160 pedigree Holstein Friesian cows and
we are happy to take folk around the farm. Our extensive gardens surround a large in-ground
swimming pool and barbecue area which guests are welcome to use. Dinner with us, including
home grown produce is available by prior arrangement. Cityrail and airport pick-ups can be
arranged.*

Home Page: wwwnzcountry.co.nz/fernlea
Directions: *From Invercargill follow SH92 to Mokotua Garage (15km) turn left, 4th house
on right is Fernlea. From Dunedin on SH1 - 17km from Invercargill - turn left at
WOODLANDS BP garage, over railway line turn sharp right to Rimu Church (6km), veer left
for 2.4k and at Mokotua sign turn right and Fernlea is on left.*

Winton - Invercargill

Farmstay
Address: 'Tudor Park', Ryal Bush,
RD 6, Invercargill
Name: Joyce & John Robins
Telephone: (03) 221 7150
Fax: (03) 221 7150
Mobile: (025) 310 031
Beds: 2 King/Queen, 1 Double,
2 Single (3 bedrooms)
Bathroom: 2 Private
Tariff: B&B (continental) Double $70, Single $35, Dinner $20.
Credit Cards. NZ B&B Vouchers accepted
Nearest Town: Winton 12km, Invercargill 14km

If you are garden lovers or travellers looking for a warm comfortable place to stay that is close to all amenities but peaceful with good food, comfortable beds (electric blankets), your own bathroom and always a warm welcome.
Tudor Park is for you.
We enjoy sharing our large garden with others. As well as gardening our interests include a Simmental Beef Cattle Stud, showing cattle, horse racing, and breeding, art and we have travelled overseas.
Directions: *Please phone preferably after 5pm before 8am or at meal times.*

Rimu, Invercargill

Homestay/Farmstay
Address: Rimu, No. 1 R.D., Invercargill
Name: Margaret & Alan Thomson
Telephone: (03) 230 4798
Beds: 4 Single (2 bedrooms)
Bathroom: 1 Guests share
Tariff: B&B (special/full/continental)
Double $70,
Single $40, Children $12, Dinner $20 NZ B&B Vouchers accepted
Nearest Town: Invercargill - approx 13 kms.

We welcome you to our comfortable and sunny home, surrounded by colourful gardens, and the farm beyond. We are semi retired and enjoy meeting people, we graze cattle and sheep, and both play golf - several courses are nearby. The beautiful city of Invercargill is 13 km away - interesting museum, housing the pre-historic live Tuatara Lizard, historic buildings and parks. The choice of trips by sea or air easily arranged to wonderful Stewart Island. We are just off the Southern Scenic highway. You may have dinner with us and share an evening of relaxation and friendship. We provide the breakfast of your choice - stay as many nights as you wish - a "welcome" is always assured. Member of NZAFHH.
Directions: *From Invercargill travel approximately 7 km towards Dunedin - turn right at Clapham Road (towards large green building with red roof) - turn left - then right over railway line. Travel straight ahead for 4 km AJ Thomson on mail box - rural number 375.*

Please help us provide the best hospitality in the world.
Fill in a comment form for every place you stay.

SOUTHLAND

Tussock Creek, Invercargill
Farmstay
Address: Sherwood Farm, Channel Road, Tussock Creek, No.1 R.D., Winton
Name: Pat & Derek Turnbull
Telephone: (03) 221 7270 **Fax**: (03) 221 7270
Email: Iere@southnet.co.nz
Beds: 4 Single (2 bedrooms)
Bathroom: 1 Guests share
Tariff: B&B (full) Double $70, Single $35. Dinner $20; Campervans $25.
NZ B&B Vouchers accepted
Nearest Town: Invercargill

If you are looking for an interesting stay in a spacious residence in a peaceful setting then this is it. Native birds are usually present in the garden and the adjacent reserve. We have a grown up family of six (including triplets) and farm 600 acres of river flat with sheep and cattle. Our interests include veteran athletics, tramping, gardening, C.W.I., and genealogy. We have travelled extensively. Derek is a current world record holder in veteran running. We are suitable for a base as all Southern tourist attractions are within easy daily reach. Having 400 acres on Stewart Island helps us to arrange connections and accommodation over there.
Directions: *On Highway 6, coming from Invercargill, turn right into Wilsons Crossing Road 18.5km from the Information Centre, Ingill or turn left 12km from the centre of Winton. Proceed east for 9.3km on bitumen.- and 2.2km on gravel on Channel Road, passing the radio mast, cross the Makarewa River and our gateway is by the bridge. Follow the arrows up drive. Please phone first.*

Winton
Self Contained Accommodation
Address: 710 Riverside Road,
Centre Bush (near Winton)
Name: Nethershiel Farm Cottage
Telephone: (03) 236 0791
Fax: (03) 236 0101
Mobile: (025) 340 598

Beds: 2 Queen, 2 Single plus bunks
Bathroom: 1 Private
Tariff: B&B (continental) Double $75, Single $50, Children under 12 years of age $25. Credit Cards accepted NZ B&B Vouchers accepted
Nearest Town: Winton (10 mins)

Enjoy your own comfortable fully equipped three bedroom house plus separate bunkhouse for energetic children. It is set in its own historical garden on a sheep and flower farm, in the heart of Southland. Flowers are packed from October to June and you can lend a hand. There is a tennis court on the property and a trout river two minutes away at the bottom of the farm. Excellent 18 hole golf is 10 minutes away and only $10 per round! (Choices of six other hole courses as well).
Winton is 10 minutes south and has super markets, banks, three pubs, two take-aways and a delightful cafe. The cottage is central to all Southern region activities including Stewart Island, Catlin's, Borland, Lake Hauroko, the Southern Lakes and coastal drives. It's a good area to settle into for a few days and meet the friendly locals.
Home Page: www.nz.country

Mossburn

Farmstay
Address: No. 1 R.D, Otautau
Name: Joyce & Murray Turner
Telephone: (03) 225 7602
Fax: (03) 225 7602
Email: murray-turner@clear.net.nz
Beds: 1 Double, 4 Single (3 bedrooms)
Bathroom: 1 Guests share
Tariff: B&B (full) Double $70, Single $40, Children under 12 half price,
Dinner $25. NZ B&B Vouchers accepted accepted March to October.
Nearest Town: Mossburn 25 km, Otautau 40 km

Our modern home is on 301 hectares situated approximately halfway between
Invercargill and Te Anau which can be reached in an hour.
We enjoy meeting people and will provide good quality accommodation and farm fresh
food in a welcoming and friendly atmosphere.
We winter 3000 sheep and 200 beef cattle.You are welcome to join in on farm activities
if you wish, come for a tour of the farm or just relax. Swimming pool is available in
summer.Murray is a keen fly fisherman and will enjoy taking you to the Aparima River
which is adjacent to the property.Joyce is a keen gardener and is currently Area
Representative for the International Agriculture Exchange Association.
You are welcome to join us for an evening meal or bed and breakfast at your discretion.
(No pets please)
Directions: *Please write, phone or fax. At least 24 hours notice is advised to avoid*
possible disappointment.

Riverton

Farmstay
Address: 124 Otaitai Bush, No.3 R.D., Riverton
Name: Ian & Elaine Stuart
Telephone: (03) 234 8460 **Fax**: (03) 234 8460
Beds: 2 Single (1 bedroom)
Bathroom: 1 Private
Tariff: B&B (full) Double $65, Single $35, Dinner $15;
Campervans $10 (2 person). Credit cards. NZ B&B Vouchers accepted
Nearest Town: 5 km from Riverton on Southern Scenic Route, Highway 99
40km from Invercargill.

Our 350 acre sheep farm is situated on the Southern Scenic Route 5km from Riverton.
Our sunny and well heated house is surrounded by flower and vegetable gardens. The
guest room has twin beds with electric blankets. Guest bathroom facilities. View of
Foveaux Strait and Stewart Island from lounge window. You may share dinner with
us or if you prefer just bed and breakfast.
Riverton is one of the oldest settlements in NZ, a fishing port with safe swimming
beaches. A game of golf or squash can be arranged.
We enjoy sharing our home and farm with visitors and a friendly stay assured.
Directions: *Please phone.*

One of the differences between staying at a hotel and a B&B
is that you don't hug the hotel staff when you leave.

Tuatapere
Farmstay
Address: Papatotara Coast Road, Bluecliffs Beach,
RD 1, PO Box 23, Tuatapere.
Name: "Rarakau", Sheryll and Thomas Bowen
Telephone: (03) 225 8192 **Fax**: (03) 225 8192
Beds: 1 Double, 1 Single (1 bedroom). Cot available
Bathroom: 1 Family share, extra shower
Tariff: B&B (continental) Double $60, Single $30, Children $10. Full breakfast
and Dinner by arrangement. Credit Cards accepted. Campervans negotiable.
Nearest Town: Invercargill 100 km, Tuatapere township 20km, Te Anau 120km.

*Come and experience the magnificent South Coast, while staying on a 3000 acre farm
with the South Coast Tracks and Fiordland at our backdoorstep. We offer you bush,
beach, mountains, rivers, and a friendly welcome to our comfortable home. Our farm
and location are ideally suited for many outdoor activities, such as walking, hunting,
fishing, and relaxing! We can arrange bookings for activities such as Jet boat and
Helicopter rides. Through the Department of Conservation, we offer vehicle parking
for people walking the Tracks (e.g. Port Craig and Hump Ridge).*

*We have 2 young active children, a friendly dog, cat, pet lamb, horses, deer, cattle and
sheep. Our guest room is semi detached for privacy, but we do enjoy guests joining in
family and farm activities. We are novice B&B's, but are keen hosts who enjoy
entertaining. Children welcome. No smoking inside please. Please phone ahead for
bookings and directions.*

Invercargill
Country stay + Self-Contained Acco
Address: 352 Lorne–Dacre Road, 6 R.D.,
Lorneville, Invercargill
Name: Bill & Pauline Schuck
Telephone: (03) 235 8031 **Fax**: (03) 235 8031
Email: lorneville@kiwi-camps.co.nz.
Beds: 2 Double, 3 Single, 1 child's cot (3 bedrooms)
Bathroom: 1 Guests share
Tariff: B&B (special) Double $70, Single $45; Dinner $25; Children under 13 half
price; Campervans $8.50 per person. Self-contained tourist flat + cabins, from $15
per person. NZ B&B Vouchers accepted $3 Surcharge
Nearest Town: Invercargill 12 km

*We are situated 3 km from the main highway to Queenstown and Te Anau.We are a family
who have moved out of town to enjoy the "good life" on a 17-acre farmlet. We have sheep, hens,
cat, dog. Our home has had extensive renovations so that we can provide the most comfortable
accommodation possible. All beds have Sleep Well mattresses, electric blankets and sheepskin
overlays. You have a private bathroom if requested.You may wish to spend time with us
helping with chores or perhaps you want to sit and relax to take time out from your busy
itinerary.You may have a family dinner with us or if you prefer only bed and breakfast. All
meals are prepared from farm fresh produce and our vegetables come from our own organic
garden. I enjoy cooking and can promise you a delightful meal.If you are travelling by bus or
plane we are happy to meet you.*
Directions: *Travel north on State Highway 6 from Invercargill city for 8 km. Turn right at
Lorneville garage on to State Highway 98 (Lorne-Dacre Road), proceed for 3.5 km.*

Invercargill

Bed and Breakfast Hotel
Address: 240 Spey Street,
Invercargill
Name: Montecillo Lodge
Telephone: (03) 218 2503
Fax: (03) 218 2506
Beds: 2 Queen,
3 Double, 6 Single (6 bedrooms)
Bathroom: 6 Ensuites, 6 Guests Share
Tariff: B&B (full) Double $96, Single $76;
Dinner $25, Children $12. Most credit cards accepted.
NZ B&B Vouchers accepted $25 Surcharge
Nearest Town: Invercargill - C.B.D

Our Bed & Breakfast Hotel is in a quiet street and close to the centre of town. The main building is almost 100 years old. Bedrooms have ensuite facilities, telephone, tea and coffee, and central heating troughout. We provide a full cooked breakfast up to 9 am, served in the dining room. Marian cooks a three course dinner for our guests during the week, served at 6 pm - please request early. You can walk to the city centre, museum, parks and golf course in ten minutes. We can arrange trips to Stewart Island, and make a free call to your next B&B. We recommend a two night stay to at least find out about Invercargill, Bluff and Stewart Island. Your Host: Marian and Harry Keil

Invercargill

Bed & Breakfast
Address: 22 Taiepa Road, Otatara,
No 9 R.D., Invercargill
Name: The Oak Door'
Telephone: (03) 213 0633 **Fax**: (03) 213 0633
Beds: 1 Double, 1 Queen, 2 Single (3 Bedrooms)
Bathroom: Two Bathrooms
Tariff: B&B (full) $60 per room (includes breakfast), Children welcome, Fax,
Laundry facilities extra. NZ B&B Vouchers accepted
Nearest Town: Invercargill 5 minutes from city centre 2 minutes from airport

THE OAK DOOR takes its name from the front door, which welcomes our guests. A two storey home, built by the present owner, is situated in the scenic native bush and country setting of Otatara, just three minutes from downtown Invercargill, and two minutes from the airport. Our location offers guests the opportunity to visit Invercargill, the world's most southern city, population 57,000, and the gateway to New Zealand's Fiordland, the Catlins and Stewart Island. The tranquil homestyle atmosphere is the courtesy of your hosts, Bill and Lisa. Both have travelled throughout New Zealand and overseas. Lisa a Canadian, has lived in Holland and the USA as well as Canada. Note: No smoking No pets Thank you
Directions: *At Clyde and Tweed St, Take Tweed West at the roundabout, pass the airport, take the first left (Marama Ave South) take the first right (Taiepa Road) enter at the second driveway on the right "The Oak Door" Please call ahead to avoid disappointment.*

Invercargill
Bed & Breakfast
Address: 'Aarden House',
193 North Road, Invercargill
Name: Aarden House
Telephone: (03) 215 8825
Fax: (03) 215 8826
Beds: 1 Queen, 3 Single (2 bedrooms)
Bathroom: 1 Guest share
Tariff: B&B (full) Double $65-75, Single $40-$50.
NZ B&B Vouchers accepted $5 Surcharge
Nearest Town: invercargill centre 5 mins drive

Being retired farmers we enjoy meeting people and wish to make your stay as pleasant and comfortable as possible. Our home is five min's drive from the centre of Invercargill on the main highway (to / from) Queenstown or Te Anau. Bus stops to City Centre close by. Good fishing rivers handy.
There are seven town or country golf courses within 30 mins of Aarden House.
Visits to Stewart Island can be arranged, Catlins Information available.
Aarden House has a comfortable lounge with open fire, tea coffee and TV facilities plus an adjoining conservatory for your use. All beds have electric blankets. Off street parking.
Our house is a non smoking zone. We look forward to having you visit us.
Dorothy & Raymond

Invercargill
Farmstay
Address: 154 Oteramika Road,
R.D. 1, Invercargill
Name: The Grove Deer Farm
Telephone: (03) 216 6492
Fax: (03) 216 6492
Beds: 1 Double, 4 Single (3 bedrooms)
Bathroom: 1 Guests share, 1 Family share
Tariff: B&B (continental or full) Double $60, Single $40.
Nearest Town: Invercargill 1 Km

Alex and Eileen Henderson hosts.
Bed and Breakfast accommodation on deer farm. Unique quiet rural setting only 1 kilometre from city boundary. Homestyle atmosphere and welcome. See farmed deer and sheep, guests welcome to tours of the farm.
We are the gateway to Fiordland-Chaslands and major tramping tracks of NZ. Halfway stopover on the Southern scenic route, Invercargill-Dunedin or Invercargill-Te Anau. Air or sea trips to Stewart Island or tour the Aluminium Smelter.
Southland is one of the great pastoral farming areas and we offer tours of sheep and cattle farms (a charge for this). Famous trout fishing rivers within easy reach.
Alex is a vintage car and farm machinery enthusiast and can arrange good viewing.
Directions: *Find Tweed Street - travel east and cross Rockdale Road - we are then 1 kilometre on right. Look for "The Grove" sign.*

Invercargill
Farmstay/Self Contained Accommodation

Address: Long Acres Farmstay,
Waimatua No. 11 RD, Invercargill
Name: Helen and Graeme Spain
Telephone: (03) 216 4470
Fax: (03) 216 4470
Mobile: (025) 228 1308
Beds: 2 Double, 3 Single (4 bedrooms)
Bathroom: 1 Private, 1Family Share
Tariff: B&B (full) Double $80, Single $40,
Children half price, Dinner $25. Campervans welcome.
NZ B&B Vouchers accepted $12 surcharge
Nearest Town: Invercargill 10 kms on SH92

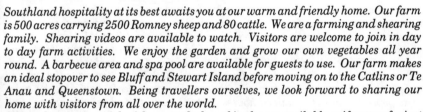

Southland hospitality at its best awaits you at our warm and friendly home. Our farm is 500 acres carrying 2500 Romney sheep and 80 cattle. We are a farming and shearing family. Shearing videos are available to watch. Visitors are welcome to join in day to day farm activities. We enjoy the garden and grow our own vegetables all year round. A barbecue area and spa pool are available for guests to use. Our farm makes an ideal stopover to see Bluff and Stewart Island before moving on to the Catlins or Te Anau and Queenstown. Being travellers ourselves, we look forward to sharing our home with visitors from all over the world.
Stay as long as you wish. A home cooked meal is always available or if you prefer just B&B. A welcome is assured.
Directions: *Please phone for directions and bookings.*

Waianiwa - Invercargill
Country Homestay

Address: Annfield Flowers,
126 Argyle - Otahuti Road, Waianiwa,
RD 4, Invercargill
Name: Mike and Margaret Cockeram
Telephone: (03) 235 2690
Fax: (03) 235 2745
Email: annfield@clear.net.nz
Beds: King/King twin (1 bedroom)
Bathroom: 1 Ensuite
Tariff: B&B (full or continental) Double $70, Dinner $25. :
Visa/Mastercard. NZ B&B Vouchers accepted
Nearest Town: Invercargill 18 km, Riverton 22 km.

Annfield, originally built in 1866, has around 17 acres of ground, of which five acres are being converted to the commercial growing of flowers, mainly gentians and lilacs. The rest is still in pasture with coloured and white sheep and also Dexter cross cattle. The house has recently been renovated, from foundations to roof, with the old character being kept and the convenience of modern facilities added. The garden is still being developed.There are a couple of dogs and cats around but they have only limited access to the house. The children have been away from home for some years.
There is good trout fishing - in season - an easy distance away and we can arrange for a guide if you let us know in advance. We are just over 1 km from the Southern Scenic Route.
No smoking please.
We look forward to welcoming you to our home.
Directions: *Please phone, as it depends where you are coming from.*

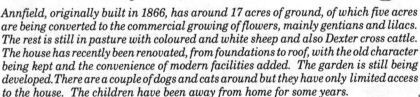

Stewart Island

Homestay+Self-contained Accom.
Address: 'Thorfinn Charters', PO Box 43,
Halfmoon Bay, Stewart Island
Name: Bruce + BJ
Telephone: (03) 219 1210
Fax: (03) 219 1210
Email: thorfinn@southnet.co.nz
Beds: 2 Double, 1 Single (2 bedrooms)
Bathroom: 1 Ensuite, 1 Family share
Tariff: B&B (full) Double $90, Single $55, Dinner up to $25. Credit cards (
VISA/MC). Self-contained: $90 per night/2 people + $15 additional people, Family
& Weekly Rates available. NZ B&B Vouchers accepted $15 surcharge
Nearest Town: Invercargill

Situated on a sheltered peninsula and only 50 metres from a beautiful beach, our home commands a magnificent sea view. Formerly a hill country farmer, now as charter boat operator, we enjoy meeting people with a love of the outdoors.As Department of Conservation Concessionaires we specialise in photographing / viewing birds and marine wildlife, bush walks and scenic / historic cruises.Our home is modern, comfortable and centrally heated with two double rooms. Both have attached bathroom and toilet, one private, and one family share. Evening meals available by prior arrangement.Two self-contained houses share the setting and provide privacy and independence. They have double and twin bedrooms, well equipped kitchens, bathroom / toilets, lounge / dining rooms, conservatory and central heating. A sleepout is also available. A courtesy transfer on arrival. We shall enjoy showing you Stewart Island's magnificent scenery, wildlife, and interesting history.

Stewart Island

B&B+Self-contained Accom.
Address: "Goomes" B&B, PO Box 36,
Halfmoon Bay, Stewart Island
Name: Jeanette & Peter Goomes
Telephone: (03) 219 1057/217 6585
Fax: (03) 219 1057
Beds: 1 Double, 3 Single (3 bedrooms)
Bathroom: 1 Guests share, 1 Family share
Tariff: B&B (special) Double $120, Single $65.
Self Contained $95/night/2 people + $18 additional person. Credit Cards.
Nearest Town: Oban 5 minute walk

Our modern home is only five minutes walk from the township, quiet and private on a bush clad point with magnificent views of Halfmoon Bay and the islands beyond. You can relax in the comfort of our lounge and watch the boats coming and going and observe the ever changing moods of the sea. There are many native birds including tuis, bellbirds and kakas only metres from the windows.
We are a fifth generation Stewart Island family. Peter and I have travelled extensively in New Zealand and overseas and know how travellers appreciate relaxing in a homely atmosphere. Breakfast can include home-made bread and jams, home grown stewed fruits, and if you wish something cooked as well.

Our self-contained holiday houses have been completely refurbished and have a similar setting and outlook to our B&B. We have a three star Qualmark grading. our courtesy car will meet you.

PLEASE HELP US
TO KEEP OUR STANDARDS HIGH

To help maintain the high reputation of *The NZ Bed & Breakfast Book* we ask for your comments about your stay. It will help us if you return all comment forms in one envelope.

Name of Host ....

Address ....

It was (please circle one):
Absolutely Perfect, Excellent, Good, Adequate, Not Satisfactory.

Do you have any comments which could help your host, on such things as breakfast, meals, beds, cleanliness, hospitality, value for money?

Complete this section. It will be detached before we send your comments to the host.

YOUR NAME ....

YOUR ADDRESS ....

....

Please mail this form to Pelican Publishing Company, Inc., P.O. Box 3110, Gretna, LA 70054-3110, USA

FOLD HERE. FASTEN LIP ON FRONT WITH CLEAR TAPE.

PLEASE FASTEN SIDES WITH CLEAR TAPE.

CUT

PLEASE FASTEN SIDES WITH CLEAR TAPE.

FOLD HERE

RE: 10th edition NZB&B

Place first-class postage here

CUT

NEW ZEALAND B&B
Pelican Publishing Company
1000 Burmaster Street
P.O. Box 3110
Gretna, Louisiana 70054

Index

782